ANTHROPOLOGY AND
THE HUMAN EXPERIENCE

Fifth Edition

ANTHROPOLOGY AND THE HUMAN EXPERIENCE

E. Adamson Hoebel
Regents Professor Emeritus
of Anthropology
University of Minnesota

Thomas Weaver
Professor of Anthropology
University of Arizona

McGraw-Hill Book Company

New York St. Louis San Francisco Auckland Bogotá Düsseldorf
Johannesburg London Madrid Mexico Montreal New Delhi
Panama Paris São Paulo Singapore Sydney Tokyo Toronto

This book was set in Souvenir Light by Black Dot, Inc.
The editors were Janis M. Yates and David Dunham;
the designer was Jo Jones;
the production supervisor was Dennis J. Conroy.
The photo editor was Hildegard Kron.
The drawings were done by Russ Peterson.
Von Hoffmann Press, Inc., was printer and binder.

Cover photograph by Allen C. Reed: Full Moon Arch, Mystery Valley, Monument Valley, Arizona.

ANTHROPOLOGY AND THE HUMAN EXPERIENCE

1 2 3 4 5 6 7 8 9 0 V H V H 7 8 3 2 1 0 9

Library of Congress Cataloging in Publication Data

Hoebel, Edward Adamson, date
Anthropology and the human experience.

Fourth ed. published in 1972 under title: Anthropology, the study of man.
Bibliography: p.
Includes index.
1. Anthropology. I. Weaver, Thomas, joint author. II. Title.
GN24.H64 1979 301.2 78-13108
ISBN 0-07-029140-3

To Irene and Dora

CONTENTS

PREFACE

This fifth edition of *Anthropology and the Human Experience* is the first to become the product of joint authorship. We have combined our knowledge to provide a broader and more contemporary approach to the study of anthropology.

We view anthropology as a basic field of study which accepts the human being as the product of about four million years of evolution as a hominid who lives in organized social groups in accordance with biologically *and* culturally determined modes of behavior. We accept that human culture, like the human organism, has evolved from simpler beginnings. We see the major tasks of anthropology as centered on the following: (1) to discover and explain the biological course of development of the human species, using the resources of prehistoric archaeology, paleontology, primatology, genetics, and physical anthropology; (2) to unfold the wide diversity of recent and contemporary social systems through ethnographic field study of all types of human societies, wherever they are found; (3) to develop scientifically based methods and theories, from the interplay of biology, ecology, cultural anthropology, and linguistics, in order to explain why, and how, specific kinds of societies and institutions develop, survive, function, and change.

This large enterprise requires a unified four-field approach. Therefore, equal treatment is given, where possible, to a coverage of physical anthropology, archaeology, cultural and social anthropology, and linguistics. Anthropology is here presented as a unified whole within the covers of a single, integrated book, which is, nonetheless, so designed that it can be used in separate courses in prehistory or cultural and social anthropology.

A number of key qualities distinguish this text.

Objectivity and Sensitivity Modern anthropology sees each cultural system as a complex way of life undergoing continuous change in adaptation to special environmental and biosocial challenges. It emphasizes data gathering in as scientifically objective and as humanistically sensitive ways as possible. This text shares with students and their teachers a sense of appreciation and respect for others' values and ways of life, however different they may be from what one is used to. An integrated concern with scientific precision and analysis, enriched with sensitivity to all peoples and their ways, is evident throughout the book. It embraces both the natural science and humanistic modes of learning and understanding.

Fact and Theory Great care has been expended to provide enough interesting descriptive and factual materials to give substance and reality to the patterns of behavior described. Anthropology has long since ceased to be the "study of strange customs and strange peoples." Nonetheless, its facts are inherently fascinating and should not be slighted in favor of generalized description. This book strives to achieve the best possible balance between theory and facts.

Facts alone are not enough. A good introduction to anthropology must balance valid fact with sound interpretation and significant cross-cultural generalization. A wide range of ethnographic studies and theory has been carefully reviewed and evaluated. Our effort has been to present a reasoned discussion incorporating ideas which have been tested and supported by highly qualified researchers and scholars.

This book builds on an evolutionary, ecological, functional-structural theoretical framework with illuminating case studies for each major topical area in each subfield. In order to enhance the feel for societies as whole units, we have confined the case study materials, for the most part, to those derived from seven to ten distinctive societies. These have been selected for their cogency as intensively researched societies which represent different ecological and geographic areas of the world and varying levels of cultural complexity.

Descriptive data are enhanced with a program of photographs paralleling the text. Extensive illustrations are provided for the most frequently referred to societies: Eskimo, Navajo, Pueblo, Cheyenne, Crow, Nuer, Bushmen, Trobriand Islanders, and other selected groups from the Northwest Coast of North America, New Guinea, and Africa. Numerous charts and tables compress worldwide cross-cultural data into easily understood packages.

In-text Learning Aids In addition to photographs and line drawings, there are a number of special features to assist the student: (1) *A chapter outline* on the opening page of each chapter delineates the subject content. (2) *Section* and *subsection headings* throughout each chapter identify the building blocks with which the chapter is constructed. (3) *Learning Goals* are stated at the beginning of each chapter to alert the student to the major facts and ideas to be assimilated from the chapter. (4) A concise *Summary* wraps up each chapter. (5) *Full documentation* with *footnote references* provide both the teacher and student with ready access to the authoritative sources for additional learning. (6) A critically annotated list of *Selected Readings* for general exploration is provided at the end of each chapter. (7) All references are brought together in a comprehensive *Bibliography* at the end of the book. (8) In addition, all anthropological and other technical terms are carefully explained in the text when they are first introduced and are also made readily accessible for reference and review in an inclusive *Glossary* of over six hundred terms. (9) Four *maps* outline major culture areas around the world and give the locations of the tribal groups referred to in the text. (10) An especially refined *Index* aids in locating subjects and authors.

Readability The text of the previous (fourth) edition has been tightly edited and extensively rewritten to clarify concepts and to improve readability. Although 12 to 15 percent of *new* material has been added in this revision, the overall size of the text has been reduced by about 20 percent. Our goal has been to present the reader with lucid, concise, and interesting writing.

Contemporary Coverage This revision is updated with a new chapter on applied anthropology. The entire section on physical anthropology has been thoroughly revised to include the latest information on the recent fossil finds in East Africa, new dimensions in primate studies, blood precipitates and human evolution, and a revision of race concepts. Several new sections emphasize cultural ecology, culture as an adaptive mechanism, the "new archaeology," and give a fuller treatment of how archaeology and physical anthropology developed. New theoretical inputs on social class, race, role and social status, Kuhn's paradigms, Émile Durkheim, genetic findings, and linguistics may be found throughout the book.

Instructor's Manual An *Instructor's Manual* contains comments on the use of the text in courses of different lengths and emphases, including annotated audiovisual aids, lecture and discussion topics, research projects, overview sections, and objectives for each chapter unit. Approximately 1200 examination test items (multiple-choice, true-false, and essay) are divided into Forms A and B according to part divisions of the text so that an instructor may use Form A in one term, Form B in the next term, or in an individualized course. Test items in Form B that also appear in Form A are asterisked. Answer keys contain both the correct answer and the text page number on which the answer may be found.

Acknowledgments We salute those numerous colleagues who gave us the benefit of their ideas and who responded to the publisher's request for expert evaluation and criticism of the manuscript in its evolving phases. This book is a better one as a result of their generous efforts.

The high quality of the bookmaker's art which is evident in this volume deserves our sincere expression of appreciation. Janis M. Yates, senior editor, David Dunham, development editor, Jo Jones, designer, Dennis Conroy, production supervisor, as well as others too numerous to name, have completed the complex and difficult task of transforming raw manuscript, photos, and charts into a book we are proud of, and their efforts have been marked by outstanding skill and patience.

Our warm thanks to all!

E. Adamson Hoebel

Thomas Weaver

PART ONE

Introduction

1
What Is Anthropology?

CHAPTER OUTLINE

LEARNING GOALS

Define anthropology.

Discuss what anthropology can teach us.

Specify the attributes that make anthropology a distinct science.

Identify the subdivisions of anthropology.

Enumerate the ways in which anthropology is related to the other social sciences.

Anthropology is the study of humanity in all places and at all times. Other disciplines, such as philosophy, history, sociology, and psychology, have also claimed to study humanity in its broadest aspect. Anthropology, however, is the only field which provides humanistic, scientific, biological, historical, psychological, and sociological views of the subject.

The primary purpose of this book is to summarize the information and theories provided by anthropology from this broad perspective on the human experience.

In this chapter we will discuss general anthropology by presenting some of the questions its workers ask and answer, by discussing its major interests, by relating it to neighboring fields, and by describing how the subject may be useful.

Anthropology produces a different image in the eyes of each of its beholders. The most common response is to identify an anthropologist as someone having something to do with bones and stones. The excavation of the skeletal or architectural remains representing ancient cultures is usually done by persons called *archaeologists*. Thus, the most common understanding of anthropology is that it is archaeology, which is only one of its subfields and does not represent the range of interests and topics of the full field.

Archaeology, however, is a dramatic subject and certainly one which fires the public imagination quickly. Who is not amazed at the excavation of tombs under the pyramids of Egypt, and at the means taken by the pharaohs to hide their riches? Who is not excited by the thought of the adventure of digging for unknown treasures in far-off places? Many people know of the decoding of the Rosetta stone, which allowed Egyptologists to decipher the languages of the ancient Egyptians, or of the glamour of Schliemann, the retired merchant, who used the stories of *The Iliad* and *The Odyssey* to discover the ancient city of Troy.

Archaeology shares with other subfields of anthropology the adventure, the sense of discovery, and the attempt to get behind the ordinary, to dig deep into history, to understand the extraordinary in the commonplace and the commonplace in the extraordinary.

Anthropology is, thus, a type of intellectual tourism in that it allows people to view the customs of others and to find them sometimes like their own and sometimes very different. It provides an escape from the ordinary, the familiar, and the common. One can travel far, vicariously, by reading the accounts of early travelers and anthropologists and letting the odd names of places visited roll off of one's tongue as if familiar. Anthropology provides information to enlighten friends, to entertain them, to astound them, to leave them agape at the wonderful ways of the world.

Do some people go naked all the time? Is sex permitted before marriage in some places? Do some people eat grasshoppers and snakes? Are other people capable of physical or mental feats that we cannot perform? Do some societies allow or encourage multiple spouses?

Answers to these questions sometimes come as a by-product of the inquiries of anthropologists in the field.

Anthropology also deals with the questions each generation of people ask about self-identity: "Who am I? Where do I come from? Who can I be?"

Are all these people from other places related to me? How does what they do affect me? Are these customs or actions advantageous to me? Is one group smarter than another group? Are any people "closer" to our primate ancestors than I am? Why do people speak different languages? Did the American Indians really walk all the way from Asia to the tip of South America? Why?

Are people really "naked apes," as a noted zoologist suggests?[1] What sets them apart from the rest of the animal world? The use of tools? The development of language? Their penchant

[1]D. Morris, *The Naked Ape.*

FIGURE 1.1
L. S. B. Leakey, discoverer of many fossil remains of human ancestors, at work in the field, Olduvai Gorge, Tanzania. (Des Bartlett/Photo Researchers, Inc.)

for religion? Or is it curiosity about themselves?

Is the family necessary? Are there "better," that is, happier, ways for contemporary people to rear children than in a nuclear family? Is there a better way for people to use our environment and natural resources? Is it wise to promote more efficient agriculture, better health, sanitation, advanced technology, family planning, higher education where they have not existed.

Is there some basic aggressive instinct, "territorial imperative," or other deep-seated factor that makes the achievement of a peaceful world society totally unfeasible? Is violence ubiquitous? Is war inevitable? As people colonize new worlds in space, are there any rules or values from the millions of years of human experience that should go with them?

Anthropologists have learned a little about what the earliest human beings looked like and even something about their creations. Will the future see radical changes in the human physique? In brainpower? Or are people now biologically "complete," having gone as far as they can go, evolutionally speaking?

Anthropologists have taken these and similar questions seriously enough to spend over one hundred years in difficult places trying to find answers. Anthropology, then, helps to explore the limits of human experience.

An improved understanding of ourselves may enhance our ultimate capabilities to direct our futures with improved knowledge. Thus anthropology, like any other reasoned study, not only satisfies the human intellect; it can serve larger ends as well. By knowing about previous human experiences, we can more effectively understand our problems and how to cope with them.

In addition, by writing and talking about other places and times, anthropologists hold up a mirror for people to see reflections of themselves in all their varieties, to see themselves in others, to see that those things which appear different in other contexts are really similar to those which run through their own lives. In this sense, anthropology provides a demythologizing view of the self as a cultural being. It is not enough to learn how to operate in one's own culture and society, how to manipulate the symbols of one's own destiny. One must also place tradition in historical perspective and in the context of the possible activities and values of all humanity. Anthropology gains this historical and universal perspective through cross-cultural analysis.

THE USES OF ANTHROPOLOGY

The relevance of anthropology to the broad quest for deeper knowledge about human nature and behavior may be seen in the rapid growth of anthropology as an academic discipline. Until World War II, only a handful of universities and colleges had anthropology departments, and a small number of others offered a course or two. In 1970 there were more than 200 departments giving anthropology degrees and by 1975 there were 315. Courses dealing with anthropology are increasingly being offered in junior colleges, adult education programs, high schools, and grade schools.

Further, both the methods and the concepts of anthropology have had a noticeable impact on the natural and physical sciences, social sciences, businesses, and government. Such terms as "culture," "cultural relativity," "comparative method," and "culture shock" are no longer the special property of anthropologists. It is perhaps not widely known that Ruth Benedict's wartime study of Japanese culture unquestionably influenced, with beneficial results, the policy of United States relations with Japan at the end of World War II.[2] Better known is the Peace Corps emphasis on educating its volunteers in the cultures of the peoples they seek to aid. With the emergence of developing countries in Asia and Africa, lawyers, political scientists, and economists have become actively interested in the indigenous cultures of these parts of the world. Programs for technical assistance, economic development, agriculture, and even missionary activities can be successful only insofar as they relate meaningfully to the cultures of the peoples involved. Planners, administrators, and business people dealing with new nations give increasing attention to this premise.

The expansion of public health programs to all parts of the world has had similar effect in stimulating close cooperation between anthropology and medicine. Anthropology is now widely accepted as indispensable to the training of public health professionals and has been recognized by the United States National Institutes of Health as a basic, medically related science. To change a society's methods of food production, its eating habits, its sanitation practices, and the size of its ideal family are not projects to be undertaken lightly, even for such lofty goals as increased longevity, better health, and less physical suffering. Such changes are not easily accomplished; anthropology can explain why.

Although anthropology can be useful in the attempt to solve life's problems, its basic goal is to explore and describe the nature of human beings as evolving, culture-bearing creatures, living in organized societies—each different and yet similar in many ways.

---

[2]R. F. Benedict, *The Chrysanthemum and the Sword.*

THE DISTINCTIVE QUALITIES OF ANTHROPOLOGY

People are part of nature—of the universe with all its phenomena. Anthropology (Gr. *anthropos*, "man," and *logia*, "study"), when followed in accordance with the principles and methods of science, is a natural science.

A discussion in anthropology for many years concerned whether anthropology is science or art. Certainly "art" is part of any endeavor; artist and scientist alike must possess technical dexterity and creativity. The data produced by anthropology, however, must also be verifiable. They must be more than a single person's impressions. Scientists, unlike artists, must produce the same observations under similar circumstances. Malinowski, a leading anthropologist, addressed the issue when he cautioned the student to distinguish which results derive from observation, which derive from the person giving information, and which are the result of psychological insight.[3]

The requirements for adequate data in anthropology include the assurance of *validity*, *representativeness*, *replicability*, and *generality*. To assure validity, the anthropologist verifies the statements of one informant against other sources of information and assesses the probability that the statements given are correct. Representativeness is accomplished by interviewing a sufficient number of people to account for all social and cultural variation in their community or group. Replicability means that another worker using the same research techniques in similar circumstances can produce the same results. Generality refers to establishing the applicability of a generalization from a single study to other units of the larger group of which it is part. As anthropological knowledge has grown, its practitioners have become more aware that what they once thought of as single, isolated, closed societies are in fact part of larger systems with great cultural variability.

But anthropology involves a good deal more than just a scientific study, for humans are also culture-producing animals. Therefore, anthropology is the *science of humans and culture*. As such it is a major social and behavioral science, and more, for in its efforts to sense and communicate the total lifeways of specific peoples, it is also a *humanistic discipline*.

Anthropology is the study of human behavior in all places and at all times. Anthropologists study people wherever they find them—in arctic snows or desert wastes; in temperate prairies and woodlands; and in verdant jungles. They search out human remains in prehistoric sites, and they carry on field studies in villages and urban settings. Anthropology is concerned with both fossil and living peoples. In the words of Clyde Kluckhohn, it "holds up a great mirror to man and lets him look at himself in his infinite variety."[4] For many years anthropologists were busy gathering the worldwide inventory of human social and cultural invention—filling in the image that would be reflected in the mirror. That task is now nearly done. There are few remaining societies to be discovered and reported on, although many problems wait to be solved. New research techniques and theories, often leading to the reevaluation of prior findings, and the constantly changing cultural scene mean that anthropological work will survive as long as our species survives.

Now the frontiers of anthropology have shifted from survey reports to in-depth analyses, to questions of human evolution, motivation, social structure, and function, and to the study of cities.

The Concept of Holism

Anthropology sets as its first goal the study of humanity as a whole. Political science studies government; economics studies the production

[3]B. Malinowski, *Argonauts of the Western Pacific*.

[4]C. Kluckhohn, *Mirror for Man*, p. 11.

FIGURE 1.2
Fieldwork is the anthropologist's laboratory. Karl Heider in the field with the Dani of West Irian, Indonesia. (Film Study Center, Harvard University.)

and distribution of goods; neurophysiology, the nervous system; architecture, housing and building; musicology, music; and sociology, society. But none of these, nor any other discipline, such as geography or history, professes to research all manifestations of the human being and of human activity in a unified way.

The human being is a culture-creating and culture-bearing animal. As evolving creatures, hominids (see pages 280–283) reached a level of development of the nervous system that enabled them to invent many new ways of behaving which were not in their genetic codes. This became manifest some two million or more years ago. Since that time all human behavior has been simultaneously biological *and* cultural.

A fundamental proposition of anthropology is that no part can be fully or accurately understood apart from the whole. Conversely, the whole cannot be accurately perceived without specialized knowledge of the parts. To understand any aspect of human sexual behavior, for example, one must examine it in terms of genetics, physiology, climatic features, the value system, and the technical, economic, kinship, religious, and political structures of each human society.

This notion of holism is based on the expectation that each patterned element or system is dependent upon and linked to some other elements within a specified time, situation, and locality. The anthropologist finds that change within one system may have repercussions in other systems. For example, changes in a group's economic system may have effects in religious roles, family organization, political behavior, or other parts of the culture. The basis of this postulate is that every culture constitutes an organized whole in which apparently strange and disparate elements are linked and dependent within the total culture.

The Concept of Culture

A second distinguishing feature of anthropology is its development of the concept of culture and the importance of this concept in anthropological thought. *Culture is the integrated system of learned behavior patterns which are characteristic of the members of a society.* (See Chapter 16 for a detailed discussion of culture.)

Every separate society has a distinctive culture. The consequent effect is that the behaviors of the members of one society are in some respects significantly different from the behaviors of the members of other societies. Anthropology has demonstrated that the distinctive behavior of different societies is mainly the product of cultural experience rather than of genetic inheritance.

However, research in the past fifteen years by anthropologists has shown that differences in behavior are not solely related to cultural learning. For example, a population living in a malarious area with a high frequency of sickle-cell anemia—and thus also a protective gene against malaria—exhibits a behavior pattern different from that of one lacking the protective gene (discussed on pages 53–57). The physical environment also has a clear effect on the material culture and institutions of any group of people. Therefore, while cultural heritage is of major inportance, human biological variability interacts with the environment to produce the behavior characteristic of any society.

The Use of the Comparative Method

A third hallmark of anthropology is its deep-rooted and long-standing commitment to the use of the *comparative* method. Anthropologists refuse to accept any generalization about human nature that emerges from their own social experiences only or even from two or three other societies, especially if these are a part of the same cultural tradition in which they have been brought up. If one is to talk about human nature, one needs to know the whole range of human biology, human behavior, and human social forms. To acquire this knowledge, the physical anthropologist studies and compares the widest possible range of human populations, ancient and modern, to determine their common and unique biological qualities. The cultural anthropologist, the archaeologist, and the linguist study and compare the widest possible range of human societies in all parts of the world, to determine and relate the common and the unique social and cultural features of language and behavior. They are interested in making comparative generalizations to find out what is similar and what is different among cultures and to see whether they can discover any common threads that will allow them to understand why humans behave the way they do and how they got that way.

The importance of comparative cross-cultural testing for another behavioral science has been stated by an eminent psychologist.

> *. . . [A]nthropological evidence has been, and can continue to be, of invaluable service as a crucible in which to put to more rigorous test psychology's tentative theories, enabling one to edit them and select among alternatives in ways which laboratory experiments and correlational studies within our own culture might never make possible.*[5]

The Community as Equivalent to the Experimental Laboratory

A fourth distinctive feature of anthropology is its long-standing emphasis upon fieldwork for obtaining data and testing hypotheses. A scientist, such as a chemist, confronted with a problem, works out an experiment designed to test the validity of the resultant hypothesis. The method of laboratory experimentation is to manipulate and thereby control the quantity and action of certain known factors in order to determine how

[5]D. T. Campbell, "The Mutual Methodological Relevance of Anthropology and Psychology," in F. L. K. Hsu (ed.), *Psychological Anthropology*, p. 334.

FIGURE 1.3
Margaret Mead in the field with Balinese villagers, Indonesia. (Ken Heyman.)

they influence one another or an unknown *x* factor. This fundamental tool of the physical sciences is ordinarily not available to the social sciences, which must to a great extent be limited to the observation of existing situations rather than of those which may be experimentally designed. Anthropologists, however, have found a highly useful substitute in the combination of field studies with the comparative method. Faced with a problem, the anthropologist seeks a society or a series of societies that already contain the combination of factors necessary for testing the theory or hypothesis in question. The anthroplogist may search for the data in existing field reports or may plan a field expedition to study an appropriate society.

Margaret Mead's Study in Samoa Margaret Mead's famous study of adolescence in Samoa is a classic example of this procedure. In the United States during the 1920s, the storms and stresses of adolescence were generally accepted as natural parts of the process of growing up. This view had the scientific imprint of the work of the psychologist G. Stanley Hall.[6] Dr. Mead entertained an alternative hypothesis that the emotional disturbance suffered by adolescents in American and Western European society is a psychological reaction to specific stresses built into American and European cultures. If a society could be found in which these stress conditions were absent (and in which no hidden variables were present that could also produce the emotional upset), that society should reveal an absence of adolescent disturbance and the presence of an easy transition from childhood to adult life. Such a conclusion, then, would point to the cultural determination of adolescent behavior. Familiar with the ethnographies of the South Seas (Polynesia), Mead believed that the culture and social organization of Samoa, which

[6]G. S. Hall, *Adolescence*.

was also reasonably accessible, probably would provide the requisite "controlled" conditions. She therefore chose Samoa as her first "laboratory." Her field observations, reported in *Coming of Age in Samoa* in 1928, supported the prediction and invalidated Hall's theory.

THE SUBDIVISIONS OF ANTHROPOLOGY

Anthropology is so diversified that, in order to achieve precision, its practitioners must specialize. The two major aspects of the subject are biological and cultural; the main subdivisions are therefore physical, or biological, anthropology and cultural anthropology. It is sufficient to know for the moment that the subfields under cultural anthropology are archaeology, ethnology, and linguistics. Most anthropology departments in the United States require a basic understanding of each of the fields before specialization in one. Another way of noting the relationships between the four subfields is to compare the higher degrees awarded in anthropology in 1975. Of the total of 413 doctorates, 60 percent were awarded in ethnology, 23 percent in archaeology, 14 percent in physical anthropology, and 3 percent in linguistics.

Physical Anthropology

Human beings are first biological organisms and only secondarily social animals. The study of the human organism through physical anthropology is therefore basic to understanding human behavior. The aim of physical anthropology is to develop knowledge concerning the biological, physical, and genetic characteristics of human populations, ancient and modern. It is only through the study of living or recently deceased people that physical anthropologists can learn about the structure, growth, and physiology of the human body in detail. They have developed and borrowed instruments and special techniques for precisely measuring innumerable ratios of body size, dental patterns, hair form and color, skin color, blood pressure, blood groups, basal metabolism, and so forth. Because physical anthropologists customarily deal with measurements which are statistically processed, they are commonly the most practiced statisticians among anthropologists. Their field is also close to genetics, physiology, anatomy, and zoology.

Human evolution is also the special concern of physical anthropology. Evolutionary theory proposes to answer two questions: "What happened?" and "How did it happen?" The first is answered largely through the comparative study of fossils, including those of the monkeys, apes, and humans, known as *paleontology* (Gr. *palaios*, "old," and *onta*, "living things," and *logia*, "study"). The answer to the query "How?" is derived largely from human genetics and the study of biological adaptation to environment.

A "new" physical anthropology has developed since World War II. Its major feature is a shift of emphasis from measurement and classification of human types toward a concern with the influence of genetics on variation in human populations. Experimental and field studies are carried out on adaptation to climatic extremes. Physical anthropologists have also, since 1960, become interested in field studies of primate behavior (especially of baboons, chimpanzees, macaques, and gorillas) in an effort to obtain insight into protohuman social behavior as an aspect of evolution (see pages 92–94).

Cultural Anthropology

The branch of anthropology that deals with learned behavior in human societies is known as *cultural anthropology*. It, in turn, has many subdivisions, of which *archaeology*, *ethnology*, and *linguistics* are the most prominent.

Archaeology Archaeology (Gr. *archaios*, "ancient," and *logia*, "study") has the same goals as the other subdivisions of cultural

FIGURE 1.4
Richard Leakey and Bernard Ngeneo at work in the field near Lake Turkana, Kenya. They are examining the newly discovered remains of a humanoid skull which is estimated to be more than two million years old. (National Geographic.)

FIGURE 1.5
Biruté Galdikas has observed wild orangutans in Indonesia so intimately that some of them are willing to travel in a canoe with her. (Rod Brindamour/National Geographic Society.)

anthropology—to understand and describe the ways of living of people. The major difference is that the archaeologist mostly focuses on prehistoric peoples—that is, groups who lived before the invention or introduction of written language. The archaeologist uses all material remains for reconstructing extinct cultures: settlement patterns, art objects, pollen, geologic and geographic features, coprolites (feces), potsherds, arrowheads, clay figurines, and tools. These remains are dated by techniques involving radioactive elements, magnetic reversals, geological strata, the presence of extinct animals, and tree rings in the wood and charcoal specimens encountered.

The field archaeologist has meticulous and refined techniques of excavation.[7] In the larger intellectual task of giving meaning to what is found, however, archaeologists are no different from other anthropologists concerned with cultural history and developmental processes. A student of prehistory must understand cultures and cultural processes to breathe life and meaning into the dead bones and silent stones of the long-lost past.

Previously mentioned was the post-World War II development of a "new" physical anthropology. In the early 1960s there also occurred a "new" archaeology. It was not completely divorced from past achievements in that field, but it did begin a rather dramatic shift away from an almost exclusive concern with description and chronology. The new emphasis in archaeology centered on (1) a cultural evolutionary point of view, (2) adoption of a general systems theory approach, and (3) a heavy dependence on deductive or logico-deductive reasoning. An evolutionary position gives priority to technology and economy as determinative factors with resulting changes in the social and ideational element of culture. Adoption of a systems theory has placed heavy emphasis on understanding ecological and environmental factors and their interrelations with local and regional populations. Finally, utilizing deductive reasoning, ethnography, ethnohistory, and computers, the "new" archaeologist formulates and tests hypotheses about the past.[8]

In recent years, archaeologists have also become interested in modern literate societies and in research on urban renewal and environmental impact areas. Research has entailed a concomitant move toward working with scientists from such fields as history, computer technology, statistics, and cultural geography. This has continued a long trend of cooperation with such natural sciences as botany, geology, and zoology; interdisciplinary work is not new. But, the concern for modern, historic, complex society and the need for working with documentary history and the quantification of findings have added a new corps of collaborators. Historic society provides an excellent body of data for testing and developing social and archaeological models.

Ethnography The foundation of cultural anthropology is ethnography (Gr. *ethnos*, "race," "peoples," and *graphein*, "to write"). Literally, the word "ethnography" means to write about peoples. As we use the term, it refers to the descriptive study of human societies. Early ethnographies were almost wholly products of the reports of explorers, missionaries, traders, and soldiers. It was only toward the end of the nineteenth century that trained observers entered the field to study human societies directly. Now, most ethnographic work is done by trained anthropologists who have carefully learned techniques calling for objective and penetrating observation and interviewing, empathic rapport,

[7]See B. M. Fagan, *Introductory Readings in Archaeology*, and F. Hole and R. F. Heizer, *An Introduction to Prehistoric Archaeology*.

[8]See M. P. Leone (ed.), *Contemporary Archaeology: A Guide to Theory and Contributions*, and G. R. Willey and J. A. Sabloff, *A History of American Archaeology*.

and accurate reporting. Modern cultural anthropologists are expected to undertake ethnographic fieldwork to become fully qualified anthropologists.

All ethnographic monographs have an implicit theoretical framework, but they do not deal explicitly with theoretical problems. They are descriptive reports of data and are little concerned with comparison, hypothesis, or theory. Ethnographies provide the building blocks for cultural anthropology, but it is necessary to look elsewhere for the grand design.

Ethnology Ethnology (Gr. *ethnos*, "race," "peoples," and *logia*, "study") differs from ethnography in that as a science it seeks interrelationships between peoples and their environments, between human beings as organisms and their cultures, between different cultures, and between the differing aspects of cultures. As a science, ethnology derives explanations that go beyond description, emphasizing analysis and comparison. Since each culture is clearly a changing continuum through time, ethnology is concerned with the historical background of

(a)

(b)

FIGURE 1.6

(a) E. Adamson Hoebel at work with Seedeater Shoshone informant and interpreter, Raphael Lavatta, left, and Charles Engatura, right, in field study of Shoshone tribal law. Bannock Creek, Idaho, 1934. (Photo by F. Gore Hoebel.) (b) Thomas Weaver presenting a report to the Pima-Maricopa, Sacaton, Arizona, 1971. At left is John E. Crow, political scientist member of the research team. At center is Tribal Governor Alexander Lewis, Jr., and behind Weaver is Lt. Governor Don Antone. (Photo by B. Alan Kite.)

cultures. When its concern is with general principles of cultural development, it expresses itself as *cultural evolutionism.*

Ethnology includes specialists who focus on kinship and family life, economic activities, law and government, religion; material culture and technology; language, the arts, folklore and mythology—almost any major aspect of human cultural manifestation.

Social Anthropology Ethnologists who concentrate on social relations, such as family and kinship, age groups, political organization, law and economic activities—in short, what is called *social structure*—prefer to be called *social anthropologists.*

How can we explain the different terminology used so far? It is a matter of changing emphasis, topics, and goals within the discipline. The oldest term is "ethnographer," which refers to one who describes different cultures and societies. The term "ethnologist" was at one time reserved for those interested in cross-cultural comparison and in specific topics such as religion, economics, mythology, warfare, and kinship. In a sense, however, all ethnologists were also ethnographers.

As time passed, more attention was paid to the work and findings of British anthropologists, who were making important contributions under the direction of Radcliffe-Brown and Malinowski. Although they shared with the Americans the concept of culture, they were not concerned with culture history or with an interrelated four-fields approach. They established a separate subdivision of anthropology under the rubric *social anthropology*, which they also at times called *comparative sociology*. As the work of the British social anthropologists became better known in the United States through Radcliffe-Brown's visit in Chicago in the early 1930s, his students and those who studied under them began to call themselves "social anthropologists."

At the present, few anthropologists are interested in pure description; the field is more problem-oriented and comparative, so the term "ethnographer" has somewhat fallen into disuse. "Ethnologist" and "cultural anthropologist" are terms which refer to people interested in human behavior in its holistic and historical sense, and "social anthropology" refers to a more restricted field which includes those mainly interested in kinship and social organization. Now, however, the three terms are used interchangeably in the United States.

Linguistics Linguistics is the science of language. Many linguists look upon their discipline as a completely autonomous science, and there is a growing trend in American universities to establish independent departments of linguistics. However, languages are aspects of cultures, intimately interacting with all the other manifestations of culture, and are therefore best understood in the cultural context. In the United States, all the larger departments of anthropology include linguistic analysis as a part of their programs.

Anthropologists, once they had begun to base their studies on objective fieldwork, were forced to learn many primitive languages from scratch. A universal system of phonetic writing had to be developed so that records could be kept of what native informants were saying. This soon led to a realization that some societies organize speech in accordance with grammatical principles very different from those which govern the Indo-European languages. Some anthropologists, fascinated by their new discoveries, began to concentrate their efforts on recording and analyzing preliterate languages, and linguistics, as a specialized branch of anthropology, developed in a way that revolutionized all language study.

Today, the anthropological linguist describes disappearing languages, establishes linguistic universals, studies language change and nonverbal communication, and is interested in the further development of historical linguistics. The anthropological linguist is also concerned with interrelations between the language of a people and other aspects of their culture, such as social status, ethnicity, learning language and socialization, speech communities, and the various other social implications of language. Sociolinguists, of whom many are anthropologists, are involved in the study of dialects and special languages spoken by minority groups and generally with the way in which social and cultural variables influence the development and use of language.[9] (See Chapter 33.) Psycholinguistics, which brings together the theory and information of psychology and linguistics to study the processes underlying the acquisition and use of language, has much to offer in relating its findings to anthropological data on socialization and education.

Topical Specialties of Cultural Anthropology Every major aspect of human endeavor is cultivated as a special subfield of anthropological study. The adaptation of people to the total environment is the concern of the *ethnoecologist.*

Material culture is the province of the specialist in technology. There are fields of dance, *ethnomusicology,* art, religion, family and kinship, political anthropology, economic anthropology, and legal anthropology. Symbolic anthropology tries to fathom the social meaning and cultural functions indirectly expressed in myth, art, and ritual.

There are also medical anthropologists interpreting non-Western systems of medical thought and practice, and *ethnobotanists* who specialize in the study of herbalism and vegetable stuffs. Teachers and anthropologists have joined in the subspecialty of *educational anthropology* to study problems endemic to educational subcultures. *Urban anthropologists* bring the unique attributes of anthropology to the study of subcultures in contemporary cities. *Applied anthropologists* work as advisors to governments, industries, and human relations organizations. Practically every chapter in this book is an expression of the thought and findings of a special subfield of anthropology.

Area Specialization Finally, all anthropologists specialize by geographic area. One can be a North American archaeologist or cultural anthropologist, or a South American, African, Oceanian, South or East Asian, or Near East specialist, as the case may be.

Anthropologists are expected to know about peoples in all parts of the world but to concentrate fieldwork in one or two selected areas.

THE RELATION OF ANTHROPOLOGY TO THE SOCIAL SCIENCES

Anthropology is usually organized as a social science in American universities, although it is more than that. Nonetheless, the bulk of anthropological work is focused upon culture and, within culture, upon social organization. Let us more closely compare anthropology with history, sociology, psychology, and other outside disciplines.

Before this can be done, however, the problem of subfield and discipline as a referent must be clarified. One must take care in making statements about the relationship of a particular outside field to anthropology. What kind of anthropology is referred to in this context? Is reference made to the general field of anthropology, which encompasses the biological as well as the cultural (ethnology, social anthropology, linguistics, archaeology), or is reference made only to one of the subfields? It is true that archaeology, for example, is part of general anthropology

[9] S. S. and J. C. Baratz, "Early Childhood Intervention: The Social Science Base of Institutional Racism" (*Harvard Educational Review,* vol. 40, no. 1), reprinted in T. Weaver (ed.), *To See Ourselves: Anthropology and Modern Social Issues.*

and as such shares in the data and theoretical structure which the general field shares with an outside discipline such as sociology. Each anthropological subfield, however, has unique relationships and working arrangements with different outside fields. In this sense, the ethnologist and social anthropologist have more in common with the sociologist, the archaeologist with the physicist, the physical anthropologist with the geneticist, and the linguist with the philologist, than does any of the other subfields with each of the outside disciplines cited. What follows is a discussion of the relationships that exist between outside disciplines and the general field of anthropology, or occasionally between outside disciplines and the subfield of social and cultural anthropology.

History

A balanced view of the relation of anthropology to history holds that a comparison of directly observable contemporary societies places anthropology on a firmer scientific footing in terms of verifiable results. Yet it is scientifically important to study the processes of the growth and change of cultures. Culture and society are not momentary things. They come out of the past, exist in the present, and continue into the future. What they *are* is the product of what they *have been.*

Historians are social scientists when they derive general laws of social change or explain specific events by noting repeated regularities through time. They are philosophers of history if they explain what took place at particular times in terms of a scheme of interpretation. Or, if the historians' interests are only the pursuit of special knowledge of particular events, they are neither social scientists nor philosophers; they are simply collectors of facts.

In science, as opposed to history, a fact is not itself of central interest. The object of science is to examine a multitude of facts to produce valid, general propositions. The anthropologist's ways of organizing knowledge, the data base, and research techniques are different from those of the historian. The "field" for the historian is the library. The working unit is a document. For the anthropologist, the "field" is more often a remote tribal group, a central-city population, or an archaeological site. The working unit is the person and a people. A student of contemporary Africa puts it succinctly: "Africa has two kinds of history: the conventional kind to be studied through European accounts of exploration, settlement, and colonial rule, and an unconventional kind to be studied through anthropological accounts of indigenous economic and social organization."[10]

Sociology

Sociology and social and cultural anthropology are the closest kin among the social sciences. This is why they are frequently found in the same department in American universities. Their similarity is in their interest in social organization and behavior. In many respects the basic theoretical approaches are indistinguishable. But their specific interests and the research techniques of each may be very different. Sociologists do not usually receive the biological, archaeological, and linguistic training that is so important to anthropologists. Anthropologists work as participant-observers in small societies. Their emphasis is on people-in-culture. Sociologists usually work with samples of more limited aspects of a larger society; hence their heavy emphasis on statistical data and procedures. The questionnaire and census reports are likely to be the sociologist's major factual resource. Also, American sociology devotes much attention to social problems and social work: delinquency, crime, poverty, mental illness, and broken homes. Anthropology has only lately turned its

[10]G. Dalton, "Traditional Production in Primitive African Economies" (*The Quarterly Journal of Economics,* August 1962), p. 378.

attention to social problems with the development of applied and urban anthropology.

Psychology

Anthropology and psychology are both concerned with behavior. However, anthropology is interested primarily in groups and the cultural patterning of behavior, whereas psychology is more concerned with the behavior of the individual and with the response to specific stimuli. Psychologists are much more oriented to laboratory experiments, tests, and the statistical expression of their findings. The behavioral situations studied by experimental psychologists tend to be simplified, controlled experiments designed to eliminate extraneous variables. Anthropologists try to relate the simple but verified findings of psychology to the complexities of real-life situations, where their findings are less rigorously verified.

While contemporary social psychologists also incline strongly toward laboratory experimentation, clinical psychologists and psychoanalysts treat persons in the context of their total social settings. The probing of psychoanalysis into hidden psychic processes has engendered a number of insightful concepts that have proved useful to anthropologists in the interpretation of cultural systems and personalities. Similarly, contemporary family psychotherapy draws on anthropology for the analysis of family processes. The field of culture and personality (see Chapter 19) was one of the most active and productive areas of anthropology in the decades of 1930 to 1960.

Learning theory as developed in psychology is of great importance to anthropology; culture is acquired only through learning. Psychology probes the processes of how the human animal learns. Anthropology, in turn, teaches us what is learned and how it is taught and describes the rewards and punishments provided by each society for proper learning or failure to learn. Anthropology offers psychology a wider factual base against which to test its theories and assumptions. This is recognized by a psychologist in these terms:

Implicitly, the laboratory psychologist still assumes that his college sophomores provide an adequate base for a general psychology of man. . . . For social psychology these tendencies have been very substantively curbed through confrontation with the anthropological literature. Continued confrontation, however, will be required to prevent relapse.[11]

Law, Political Science, Economics, and Public Health

Law is an exceedingly important shaper of cultures, since it is explicitly devoted to discouraging certain forms of behavior while supporting others. Because legal anthropology places so much emphasis on the functions of law in total social systems, it has proved particularly fruitful in illuminating by comparison the foundations of our own law system.

Only since World War II and the consequent emergence of independent, developing countries in Asia and Africa have economics and political science in the United States become actively interested in the indigenous cultures of these parts of the world. But now the economics and government of these areas have taken on extreme importance.

The expansion of public health programs to all parts of the world has had similar effect in stimulating close cooperation between anthropology and the practice of medicine.

So far, we have compared the neighboring social disciplines with only one subfield—social and cultural anthropology. The purpose of the comparison has been to discuss the anthropological perspective by comparing and contrasting the field of anthropology with other disciplines. Linguistics, archaeology, and physical anthropology, in the same way, can be fruitfully com-

[11] D. T. Campbell, op. cit., p. 334.

pared with other behavioral and physical disciplines in their findings, research interests, and methodologies. Linguistics, for example, shares its findings and topical interests with such fields as modern language studies, psychology, sociology, psychiatry, speech, classical studies, mathematics, systems analyses, and the computer sciences. Physical anthropology and archaeology also share the techniques of mathematics, systems analyses, and the computer sciences, and in addition share topical interests with geography, climatology, geology, astronomy, palynology, zoology, geochronology, physics, chemistry, and others in their research and dating techniques.

It should be clear by now that anthropology in many of its aspects participates vitally in the dynamic complex of the social sciences.

SUMMARY

Depending on the methods utilized and the goals sought, anthropology may be a biological science, a social science, or a humanity. Because people are part of nature, anthropology is a natural science with two major subdivisions: physical, or biological, anthropology and cultural anthropology. Physical anthropology is concerned with the evolutionary development and biological characteristics of human populations. Cultural anthropology is concerned with the customs and ways of living of human societies. When approached with the methods of science, cultural anthropology is a social and behavioral science. When cultures are studied with emphasis upon the feeling expressed in their art, literature, and beliefs, anthropology takes on the quality of the humanities.

Anthropology studies humanity as a whole; first, as a biocultural phenomenon in which culture is viewed as a means of continuing adaptation to the total environment; second, with the basic functional proposition that all parts of a culture are interrelated and that no part may be understood except as a component of a whole.

Culture is the integrated system of learned behavior patterns which are characteristic of the members of a human society.

Anthropology has always been devoted to comparative methods. It searches out all types of societies, in all times and places. It formulates generalizations about human behavior based on the discovery of regularities found in all cultures and discovers the range of variation in human cultural systems. Anthropologists refuse to make generalizations based on experience with one society only.

Anthropology uses fieldwork in communities as its equivalent to work in the experimental laboratory. When there is a special problem to be solved, the anthropologist seeks a society with the desired combination of variables.

Archaeology is the subfield of anthropology which reconstructs and dates past cultures. A "new" archaeology utilizes deductive reasoning, ethnography, ethnohistory, and computers to formulate and test hypotheses about past societies. This has gone hand in hand with a new interest in cultural ecology, systems theory, and cultural evolution.

Cultural anthropology has numerous subspecialties and alternate labels. Chief among them are ethnography, ethnology, social anthropology, and linguistics. Ethnography is the descriptive recording of the lifeway of a particular people, as a result of field study. Ethnology is the comparative analytical science of cultures in time (historical) and space (ecological). Social anthropology concentrates on the organization of social groups, such as kinship, and political and economic structures. Anthropological linguistics identifies the characteristics of all languages. In addition, there are almost as many topical and areal interests of cultural anthropology as there are manifestations of culture: art, dance, folklore, botany, technology, politics, economics, law, medicine, religion, education, and child training.

Anthropology overlaps all the social sciences and many of the biological sciences and thus is intimately related to each of them. Anthropology retains, however, a unique identity by virtue of a holistic orientation and its special theories and methods.

SELECTED READINGS

Beattie, J., *Understanding an African Kingdom: Bunyoro* (1965). A straightforward, short account of the technique and methods used in the field study of a given society.

Casagrande, J. B. (ed.). *In the Company of Man* (1960). Twenty distinguished anthropologists offer a profile of the key informant central to his or her anthropological fieldwork.

Hammel, E. A., and W. A. Simmons (eds.), *Man Makes Sense* (1970). A reader in cultural anthropology in which part I, "The Personality of Anthropology," provides an extended introduction to the nature of anthropology.

Henry, J., *Culture against Man* (1964). The author combines the technique of the participant-observer with the use of anthropological theory to shed new light on American family life, schooling, mental illness, and treatment of the aged.

Leone, M. P. (ed.), *Contemporary Archaeology: A Guide to Theory and Contributions* (1972). The best collection of essays representing assessments and contributions in recent "new" archaeology.

2
How Anthropology Grew

CHAPTER OUTLINE

LEARNING GOALS

Trace the earliest beginnings of anthropology.

Identify the contributions of William Robertson to anthropology.

Learn about nineteenth-century evolutionism.

Understand Franz Boas's rejection of cultural evolutionism in America.

Discuss the rise of functionalism and structuralism.

Specify the three forms of recent evolutionary studies.

Discuss the rise of cross-cultural studies in anthropology.

The seeds of anthropology were planted during the Renaissance in Europe; then followed a long period of germination during the fifteen and sixteenth centuries. The roots were formed during the seventeenth and eighteenth centuries, as the age of discovery resulted in growing curiosity about the meaning of the many strange societies that explorers and travelers were encountering. Then, during the first half of the nineteenth century, something different from philosophies of history began to take shape, until, between 1860 and 1871, anthropology emerged full-flowered as an eagerly cultivated field.

By the turn of the twentieth century, great anthropological collections had been gathered in the major museums of natural history, chairs of anthropology were being established in various universities, and anthropological societies were flourishing in England, in Europe, and in the United States. Systematic fieldwork in ethnology and archaeology was well under way. Professional journals devoted to anthropology were firmly established. The nineteenth-century evolutionary theories of Tylor, Morgan, Frazer, and others were being challenged as the young science showed signs of maturing in methods and thought.

The years between 1900 and 1925 marked the period of Boasian historical reconstructionism in the United States and of diffusion theory and research in Germany and Austria. In France, this was the period when the foundations of functionalism and social structure were being laid by Émile Durkheim and his associates. During these decades, ethnographic fieldwork techniques were perfected and modern anthropology reached its first phase of maturity.

From 1930 to 1940, functionalism as developed by Malinowski and Radcliffe-Brown dominated the scene in both Britain and the United States. The Boasian movement in the United States was transformed by the infusion of psychological interests. The following years brought a veritable explosion of anthropology around the world, not only in terms of professional developments but also in the areas of university response, public interest, and practical applications of anthropological findings.

This chapter traces the main outlines of the course of this growth and development.

A FRAMEWORK FOR ANALYZING THE HISTORY OF ANTHROPOLOGY

In 1962 Thomas S. Kuhn proposed a model for analyzing and explaining the progress of thought in any field. Kuhn suggested that a paradigm or scheme of explanation is developed by a group of scientists to explain a phenomenon. The paradigm involves an approach to a subject or field, which includes a series of concepts, hypotheses, theories, research techniques, and values which dictate how a subject should be investigated and how the data should be analyzed and interpreted. This paradigm predominates as more and more writers and investigators apply and modify it. Soon, however, possibly as a result of working out the logic in the original paradigm, or because of its inability to explain some cases, an alternate paradigm or scheme is proposed. The new paradigm, if successful, predominates as the explanatory device.[1]

We can thus view the evolutionary theories of Tylor, Maine, and Frazer as a paradigm for explaining the existence and development of different cultures. In this same sense, the work of Boas in the United States, of Malinowski and Radcliffe-Brown in England, and of Schmidt in Germany were reactive formations of new paradigms to account for the inadequacies of the evolutionary paradigm. In more recent times the culture and personality models of Benedict and

[1]T. S. Kuhn, "The Structure of Scientific Revolutions" (*International Encyclopedia of Unified Science*, 2d ed., vol. 2, no. 2, 1970).

FIGURE 2.1
Franz Boas (1858-1942), the founder of modern American anthropology. (Photo courtesy of E. Adamson Hoebel)

FIGURE 2.2
Major J. W. Powell (1834-1882) with a Paiute Indian. Powell carried out anthropological fieldwork in the Grand Canyon area from 1871 to 1875. In 1869 he led a party of explorers down the Green and Colorado Rivers through the Grand Canyon in rowboats. In 1879, he became the first director of the Bureau of American Ethnology. (Photo by J. K. Hillers, Smithsonian Institution National Anthropological Archives, Bureau of American Ethnology Collection.)

Mead, the structuralism of Lévi-Strauss, cultural ecology, and ethnoscience have been attempts, sometimes unsuccessful, to create new paradigms to replace perceived shortcomings in the older explanations of cultural phenomena.

ANTHROPOLOGY IN CLASSICAL THOUGHT

Anthropology is one branch of knowledge that does not claim to have its origin among the Greeks. The Greeks, to be sure, were much interested in social organization, especially in political structure, but their thought was more concerned with ideal systems, rather than in studying living social and cultural systems or in comparing how societies actually dealt with human problems. Herodotus (484–425? B.C.) is sometimes credited with being the father of anthropology because of his comments on customs of peoples other than the Greeks in the fifth century B.C., but his observations were neither systematic nor firsthand.

Tacitus (ca. A.D. 55–120), a Roman historian living five hundred years after Herodotus, wrote a tract on the origin and locality of the Germans that is much referred to as an early ethnography and as a rare, early source of some anthropological significance.

Herodotus and Tacitus notwithstanding, there was no body of literature and no systematic discourse comparing various societies. There is little basis for a claim that anthropology had its origins in classical antiquity.

ANTHROPOLOGY IN THE AGE OF REASON

The Renaissance did not give birth to anthropology per se, but it did establish a comparative point of view. Renaissance work, however, focused on past rather than on contemporary societies.[2]

[2]J. H. Rowe, "The Renaissance Foundations of Anthropology" (*American Anthropologist*, vol. 67, 1965), p. 12.

The opportunity for studying contemporary peoples came with the European discovery of America and the subsequent exploratory voyages. For many decades, the journals of explorers and the accounts of the conquistadores—such as Bernal Diaz del Castillo, who left vivid pictures of Mexico and the Aztecs as he saw them in 1519, and Cook and Bougainville, who in the eighteenth century wrote many descriptions of the peoples of the Pacific—provided fragmentary and episodic accounts of diverse cultures. Such bits of information did not constitute anthropology, but they did stir discussion. The *Jesuit Relations*, a vast body of reports from the Jesuit priests working in North and South America from 1610 to 1791, contains much of ethnographic interest in its seventy-three published volumes. This, too, was not yet anthropology.

The first systematic anthropology was done by two Catholic missionaries, the first a Spanish Franciscan, Sahagun, who worked in Mexico between 1529 and 1549, and the second a French Jesuit, Lafitau, who worked at the mission of Sault Saint Louis among the Iroquois and the Hurons of western New York.

Sahagun's General History of Things in New Spain

Tenochtitlán, the capital of the Aztecs, was conquered in 1521. Fray Bernardino de Sahagun arrived eight years later to aid in the religious conversion of the Indians of Mexico. Before long he was engaged in a full-fledged ethnographic effort to record the beliefs and customs of the Aztecs in a systematic manner. He trained young Aztecs of the nobility—those who would have become priests under the old order—to write their native tongue, Nahuatl, in Spanish script. He traveled about questioning informants, who provided answers accompanied by hieroglyphic paintings in the old Aztec manner. With the glyphs as the framework, he questioned his "research assistants," who carefully wrote the answers in their native language, recording a true "inside view" of Aztec culture.

The *Florentine Codex*, as the text is called, covers a diverse range of subjects. Parallel to the Nahuatl text, Sahagun added his own loose, running Spanish translation and commentary. Sahagun's work contains no reflective analysis of Aztec society. As a matter of fact, the good priest, who undoubtedly had his eye on the Inquisition, would not have dared make a dispassionate analysis of Aztec usage. For the record, he declared: "My tears fall like hailstones as I think on the multitude of lies by which people here in New Spain were led into error."[3] It was, he said, the work of Satan.

In the century following Sahagun, many Spanish chroniclers wrote on the customs and government of the conquered Indian nations. Some of these were official "intelligence" reports, and some were the products of personal scholarship. Of all, the four-volume *Historia del Nuevo Mundo*, written between 1650 and 1660 by the Jesuit Bernabé Cobo, is both clear and accurate in content and scientific in its approach.[4] Ethnography was gaining definite substance, but it was still far from becoming a reliable and orderly discipline.

Lafitau's Comparative Ethnology

Father Joseph François Lafitau wrote almost a century later in a different religious and cultural climate. His work is a continuation of Renaissance classical interests. The very title of his book indicates this; published in Paris in 1724, it was called *Customs of the American Savages, Compared with Customs of Early Times*. Just as Greece and Rome represented an earlier stage of civilization than eighteenth-century Europe, so too, he reasoned, the cultures of the Hurons and the Iroquois represent an even earlier condition of humanity. Evolutionary theory was taking shape.

Lafitau gave clear expression to three principles that have since become basic in anthropology: (1) contemporary nonliterate cultures throw light on ancient cultures, and vice versa; (2) possible historic relations between cultures cannot be speculatively established but are determinable only on the basis of careful content analysis that demonstrates significant similarity of specific traits; and (3) alien cultures must be evaluated on the basis of the total conditions under which they operate, not in terms of European standards (the principle of cultural relativity).[5]

Robertson's Evolutionary Ethnology

The first modern, systematic anthropological theorist is the Scottish historian William Robertson (1721–1793). Robertson's *History of America*, first published in 1777, is not a good ethnography of the American Indians, but it advanced a rational and sophisticated anthropological theory and methodology. He is the first modern formulator of cultural evolutionism and cultural determinism in systematic terms.

Three Stages of Evolution In common with the thought of the Enlightenment, Robertson accepted the comparative evolution of human society as his primary model. In the organization of his material, Robertson used three stages of evolutionary typology: savagery, barbarism, and civilization, in ascendant order. Savages do not have writing, metals, or domesticated animals, he noted; thus he treated most of the New World tribes under the rubric of savagery.[6]

[3] A. J. O. Anderson and C. E. Dibble, *Florentine Codex: General History of the Things of New Spain*, part II, p. 46.

[4] J. H. Rowe, "Inca Culture at the Time of the Spanish Conquest," in J. H. Steward (ed.), *Handbook of South American Indians*, vol. 2, p. 194.

[5] See W. N. Fenton, "J. F. Lafitau (1681–1746), Precursor of Scientific Anthropology" (*Southwestern Journal of Anthropology*, vol. 25, 1969), pp. 173–187.

[6] W. Robertson, *The History of America*, vol. 2, p. 176.

FIGURE 2.3
Frank H. Cushing (1857-1900), Bureau of American Ethnology, was one of the earliest anthropological field workers to practice participant-observation. In 1880, Cushing was adopted into a Zuni clan and became head priest of the Bow Society. (Photo by John K. Hillers, Smithsonian Institution National Anthropological Archives, Bureau of American Ethnology Collection.)

Robertson clearly articulated the priority of subsistence technology over other aspects of culture, which modern evolutionists and ecologists are apt to treat as an idea originating with Morgan, Tylor, Marx, and White. Nor was his long-range view of human development derived from speculative philosophy. Robertson explicitly recognized the significance of prehistoric stone artifacts a half century before Boucher de Perthes rocked Europe with his discoveries (see page 26). He gave temporal priority to stone cultures over bronze and iron cultures three-quarters of a century before European prehistorians worked out the sequence in detail.[7]

Parallelism Robertson also established the principle of parallelism for use in evolutionary theory:

The character and occupations of the hunter in America must be little different from those of an Asiatic, who depends for subsistence on the chase. A tribe of savages on the banks of the Danube must nearly resemble one upon the plain washed by the Mississippi. Instead then of presuming from this similarity, that there is any affinity between them, we should only conclude, that the disposition and manners of men are formed by their situation, and arise from the state of society in which they live.[8]

In addition, with perfect logical induction, Robertson suggested from known zoological and ethnographic facts that the Bering Strait had been used to cross from the Old World to the New and that the American Indians had come from Asia by way of Siberia.

Cultural Determinism In explaining behavioral differences among different peoples, Robertson discarded racism, which was the common explanation of cultural differences during his time, as it often is today. His statement of enculturation expresses the fundamental postulates of cultural determinism in modern personality and culture theory:

[7]Ibid., vol. 1, pp. 309–311.
[8]Ibid., vol. 1, pp. 249–250.

A human being as he comes originally from the hand of nature, is everywhere the same. At his first appearance in the state of infancy, whether it be among the rudest savages, or in the most civilized nations, we can discern no quality which marks any distinction or superiority. The capacity of improvement seems to be the same and the talents he may afterwards acquire, as well as the virtues he may be rendered capable of exercising, depend, in a great measure, upon the state of society in which he is placed. To this state his mind naturally accommodates itself, and from it receives discipline and culture.[9]

Finally, he contrasted the world views, personalities, and social institutions of the Aztecs and the Incas in terms of their distinctive "national character,"[10] the very words reintroduced into American anthropology after World War II in the work of Benedict, Mead, and other personality and culture specialists as applied to modern nations.

One can say that cultural anthropology began with William Robertson.

Developments in Archaeology

Although Robertson's ideas on the three stages of cultural evolution were sound in logic, the direct evidence was not to come until appropriate methods and techniques were developed in archaeology and prehistory.

Prehistory ended and history began when writing was invented. Daniel Wilson was probably the first person to use the term "prehistory" in this sense, in his *Archaeology and Prehistoric Annals of Scotland* (1851). Archaeologists are primarily interested in prehistoric social activity, and archaeology as a distinct discipline has a history of little more than one hundred years, although people have been fascinated for centuries with the remains of ancient peoples and civilizations.

[9]Ibid., vol. 1, pp. 368–369.
[10]Ibid., vol. 2, pp. 206–227.

In the Old World, the Danes are credited for the earliest systematic development of archaeology. The principle of superposition, that lower strata in an undisturbed context are older than the overlying strata, was first proposed by Nicolaus Steno (1638–1686), a Danish physician. However, systematic digging did not take place until 1806, when R. Nyerup directed the excavation of shell middens in Denmark. Based on detailed examinations of the artifacts recovered from these sites, C. J. Thomsen in 1836 established the three-ages system in which first stone, then bronze, and finally iron was used in making tools. This sequence was later confirmed by J. J. A. Worsaae in the 1850s, and it indicated that prehistoric peoples in Denmark, as well as in the rest of Europe, went through several stages of cultural evolution with respect to technology. This was a major intellectual achievement.

While the Danes were making great strides in archaeology, other Europeans were showing that life had been on the earth for vast periods of time, and that humans and other animals had inhabited the earth long before the 4004 B.C. date proclaimed by Archbishop Ussher in 1650.

Jacques Boucher de Perthes (1788–1868), often called the father of paleolithic archaeology, found some Middle Pleistocene hand axes near Abbeville in northern France in 1838. His belief that they were made by very ancient people was not accepted until 1859, a monumental year.

Developments in Physical Anthropology

Physical anthropology developed as a discipline throughout the eighteenth century. Edward Tyson (1650–1708) made the first detailed comparative study of primate anatomy. He and William Cowper dissected a young chimpanzee and accurately noted a close resemblance to human anatomy. Tyson published the results in 1699. Somewhat later the Comte de Buffon (1707–1788) wrote rather extensively on matters of human evolution in his forty-four volumes of *Histoire Naturelle.* Jean Baptiste de Lamarck (1744–1829) believed that organismic evolution must have occurred, but the evolutionary mechanism he proposed, the inheritance of acquired characteristics, proved to be incorrect. J. F. Blumenbach (1752–1840), a contemporary of Buffon and Lamarck, is considered by many to be the father of physical anthropology. He was a German physician and comparative human anatomist who wrote extensively on human variation in the skeleton, dentition, hair, and skin. In *De generis humani varietate nativa* (1775), he developed a descriptive racial classification based on physical characteristics and geographic origin. James C. Prichard (1786–1848) was another distinguished, early physical anthropologist; his major works were *Researches into the Physical History of Mankind* (1813) and the *Natural History of Man* (1843).

NINETEENTH-CENTURY EVOLUTIONISTS

Charles R. Darwin's *Origin of Species* (1859) is not a work in anthropology, but it should be clear from the discussion to follow that it has had a profound influence on anthropology. It established humanity's natural place in the biological world and confirmed the proposition that humans evolved from a primitive antiquity. The *Origin of Species* established the continuity of all life and demonstrated how natural selection working upon inheritable variations results in adaptive modifications in life forms, which in turn lead through speciation to radiating evolution. Although Darwin reserved his exploration of human evolution for a second book, *Descent of Man* (1871), the *Origin of Species* made it clear that humans are the product of biological evolution just as technology, the arts, and society are the products of cultural evolution. Even Robertson had been content to accept the literal truth of the biblical story of Genesis, but after Darwin this would never be true again of any anthropologist of major stature. He made it possible for prehistoric studies and zoological analysis to parallel the development of cultural anthropology.

It is amply clear that Darwin *did not* supply the idea for cultural evolution and that he cannot be credited with starting the great anthropological outburst of the decade that followed the *Origin of Species.* Bastian, Morgan, Maine, and Tylor were well along with their works when Darwin's epoch-making study appeared. Morgan and Tylor were clearly building on Robertson (although neither appears to have so acknowledged), and even Darwin attributed his inspirational stimulus to Thomas Malthus (1766–1834), who cited Robertson extensively in the second edition of his *Essay on the Principle of Population* (1803). Darwin's stimulus quickened the movement to work out in detail just how human societies did evolve. But more important for anthropology was the establishment by Darwin of humanity as a subject within the natural sciences. It was this fact which gave anthropology such a strong place in the developing museums of natural history and which turned cultural anthropology from a loose philosophy of history into an empirical science.

Physical Anthropology and the Fossil Evidence In the middle and late nineteenth century the development of modern evolutionary theory and concepts in paleoanthropology burgeoned. Charles Darwin (1809–1882) and Alfred Russel Wallace (1823–1913) propagated an ideological revolution which filtered into all the biological and social sciences—an ideological revolution based on the demonstration of organic evolution through the mechanism of natural selection. Not until Darwin's *Origin of Species* (1859) had substantial evidence been mustered to support a plausible theory to account for the origin and diversity of animal life. Thomas Henry Huxley (1825–1895), a friend and staunch supporter, tirelessly defended Darwin's work. In

1863 Huxley published *Man's Place in Nature*, in which he clearly and objectively demonstrated our close physical similarities and close ancestral relationship with the other primates, especially the apes.

The fossil evidence that was to lend support to the theory of evolution came to worldwide attention in 1857. This was the Neandertal remains found near Düsseldorf, Germany, the year before. Drs. Schaaffhausen and Broca correctly assessed the skull and other bones as representing an early human being. In 1891 Eugene Dubois discovered in Java a fossilized *Homo erectus* skullcap which verified the old age of the Neandertal find and suggested that still older humans once existed.

Archaeological Contributions The work of Charles Lyell (1797–1875), a geologist and lifelong friend of Darwin, was instrumental in demonstrating the antiquity of humans by establishing that vast periods of time were necessary to form the earth's crust. Lyell set forth the principle of "uniformitarianism" in his *Principles of Geology* (1830–1833), which held that geological processes were the same in the past as they are today. In the *Antiquity of Man* (1863) Lyell used geological, archaeological, and linguistic evidence to prove that tools and extinct animals were contemporaneous and were tens of thousands of years old.

By the latter part of the nineteenth century, more careful archaeological techniques were being developed and more thorough data gathering was taking place. Heinrich Schliemann, the first person to excavate a tell (a mound of ancient cultural deposits), utilized the principles of stratigraphy. He wanted to find Homer's Troy, and from 1869 to 1889 he excavated a site in western Turkey (Hissarlik) which proved fruitful. Importantly, Schliemann excavated in order to solve a problem, rather than to recover works of art, an activity which predominated in previous archaeological work.

From 1880 to 1900 General A. H. Pitt-Rivers thoroughly excavated prehistoric and historic sites and stressed the importance of stratigraphical observation and the recording of positions in which artifacts were found. Flinders Petrie followed Pitt-Rivers's lead. In his research in Egypt and Palestine, Petrie was known for meticulous work during excavation and for the collection and description of everything found. His *Methods and Aims of Archaeology* (1904) marked the beginnings of modern archaeology.

While the Danes were conducting rather sophisticated excavations and Lyell was demonstrating that a very long geological past existed, and while Darwin was instigating a scientific revolution, people in the New World were barely embarking on a rudimentary archaeology. In 1784 Thomas Jefferson excavated an Indian shell mound in Virginia and carefully recorded his findings, fully recognizing the significance of stratigraphic relationships. However, his truly innovative work, published in *Notes on the State of Virginia* (1801), failed to attract attention. From 1841 to 1843 John L. Stephens and Frederick Catherwood traveled extensively throughout the Maya area in Central America, Chiapas, and Yucatan and described and illustrated their archaeological discoveries. Somewhat later E. G. Squier and E. H. Davis surveyed and excavated mounds in the Ohio and Mississippi Valleys.

Lewis Henry Morgan: *Ancient Society* Lewis Henry Morgan (1818–1881) and E. B. Tylor are the preeminent figures of nineteenth-century cultural evolutionism. Of the two, Morgan made the broader contributions. As a young lawyer in upstate New York, he converted his literary society into the New Confederation of the Iroquois at the inspiration of his Iroquois friend Ely Parker, later a general in the Union Army, Commissioner of Indian Affairs under President Grant, and a Grand Sachem of the League of the Iroquois. An amateur naturalist who had published a classic ethological study, *The American Beaver,* Morgan became an ethnographer and ultimately produced an enduring professional monograph on the Iroquois in 1851.[11] He sent comprehensive questionnaires on kinship around the world to get the comparative data which he presented in his monumental *Systems of Consanguinity and Affinity of the Human Family* (1871), thus starting anthropologists on the study of kinship systems and social structure. In the meantime, he made a small fortune in railroad building and iron mining, which allowed him to become a full-time ethnologist and successful defender of Iroquois land rights.[12]

Lineal Evolutionary Theory Morgan expanded his explanation of classificatory kinship systems as survivals of earlier stages of social organization into a full-fledged evolutionary account entitled *Ancient Society, or Researches in the Lines of Human Progress from Savagery through Barbarism to Civilization* (1877).

The essence of lineal evolution as summed up by Morgan is as follows: (1) Culture evolves in successive stages, which are (2) essentially the same in all parts of the world, from which (3) it is to be inferred that the order of the stages is inevitable and their content limited because (4) mental processes are universally similar among all peoples (that is, there is a psychic unity among all peoples).[13]

Morgan elaborated Robertson's three stages of savagery, barbarism, and civilization by dividing savagery and barbarism into three substages each (lower, middle, and upper). He then identified specific technological traits as diagnostic of each successive era as follows:

1. *Lower savagery* represents the transitional state from ape to human, before fire and speech were used. No populations representing this stage have survived.
2. *Middle savagery* is marked by the development of speech, control of fire, and hunting and fishing subsistence. The Australian aborigines are cited as contemporary representatives of this stage.
3. *Upper savagery* is distinguished by the invention and use of the bow and arrow and, in Morgan's scheme, is represented by the Polynesians.
4. *Lower barbarism* is characterized by the invention and use of pottery and is exemplified by the Iroquois.
5. *Middle barbarism* is marked by the domestication of plants and animals in the Old World and by irrigation and adobe-brick architecture in the New World; the Pueblo Indians and the high cultures of Mexico and Peru represent this stage.
6. *Upper barbarism* begins with the use of iron for tools and weapons, as in Homeric Greece.
7. *Civilization* is achieved with the invention of writing. It is divided into ancient and modern substages.[14]

The Evolution of Kinship Morgan's greatest effort was to reconstruct the evolution of kinship systems. In so doing, he seized upon the most fundamental aspect of nonliterate social organization. Morgan and others began with the proposition that nonhuman animals are promiscuous and therefore the earliest transitional protohumans must have been promiscuous. Highly civilized societies (that is, European) are monogamous and narrowly restrict mating by means of the incest taboo; therefore, since evolution proceeds through gradual modifications, mating went through a series of successive steps during which the range of individuals with whom one

[11] *The League of the Ho-dé-no-sau-nee or Iroquois.*

[12] See B. J. Stern, *Lewis Henry Morgan: Social Evolutionist*; and H.R. Hays, *From Ape to Angel: An Informal History of Social Anthropology,* chaps. 2 and 5.

[13] L. H. Morgan, *Ancient Society,* pp. 17–18.

[14] Ibid., pp. 12–13.

FIGURE 2.4
Lewis Henry Morgan (1818-1881), American social anthropologist and founder of kinship studies. Morgan wrote important works on the Iroquois, comparative kinship, and the evolution of social systems. (Smithsonian Institution National Anthropological Archives.)

might mate or whom one might marry was always narrowing. The evolution of mating is from promiscuity to monogamy.

Criticism of Morgan's Theory Morgan was on solid ground in accepting the archaeological sequence of hunting and gathering followed by domestication of plants and animals, of preceramic followed by ceramic, of bow and arrow preceding iron, and of writing coming late in culture history.

Reconstructing the evolution of social organization is a very different matter from tracing general developments in material culture, however, and this was Morgan's sole concern. Cultural evolutionists such as Morgan are forced into *inferential reconstructions* of culture patterns and social structures that are to be associated with each evolutionary stage. Their major tool is the weak instrument of analogic inference, and if they try to produce very specific results, it is easy to demolish the product. It is extremely difficult to give detailed substance to a theory of general evolution. Morgan built his system on the concurrent evolution of subsistence technology, kinship, property, and government. Of these, only the first leaves significant archaeological evidence, and our discussions in Part 3 will indicate the limits of what is known even today. Lafitau established the principle that contemporary primitive societies can throw light on prehistoric societies, but "throwing light on" is something less than establishing valid sequential details of evolution of nonmaterial culture.[15]

Evolution in Marxist Theory A political philosopher, Karl Marx (1818–1883) was inspired by Morgan's evolutionary thesis. He found the key to history, according to his close companion, Friedrich Engels, in the study of the American Indian. After Marx's death, Engels wrote a book based on Marx's notes and ideas, bearing the title *The Origin of the Family, Private Property, and the State in the Light of the Researches of Lewis H. Morgan.* Marx and Engels used Morgan's scheme of lineal evolution as the framework upon which to build an account of the linkage between private property, the monogamous "patriarchal" family, and the state as the institutions that are responsible for the exploitation of workers and the degradation of women. It is this work which established Morgan and cultural evolutionism as official theoretical dogma in Marxist thinking and which largely characterizes Soviet ethnology to this day.[16]

[15]See R. H. Lowie, *The History of Ethnological Theory,* pp. 54–67; and "Lewis Henry Morgan in Historical Perspective," in *Essays in Anthropology in Honor of Alfred Louis Kroeber,* pp. 169–181, for a fuller critique of Morgan's work.

[16]See M. Harris, *The Rise of Anthropological Theory,* pp. 246–249.

Henry Maine: From Status to Contract

Sir Henry S. Maine (1822–1888) was a highly specialized legal historian and cultural evolutionist who confined his theoretical writings to the evolution of law. He used no data from any extant society. His comparative sources were almost entirely limited to Greece and Rome, although he did draw on his knowledge of the village community in India. Maine's value to anthropology does not lie in his specific series of evolutionary stages in law; this has long since been disproved.[17]

Maine established the theoretical use of *ideal types* of societies and institutions as *polar opposites* for comparative analysis in social science. In *Ancient Law* (1861), he formulated the contrast in terms of ancient (primitive) societies in which social relations were dominated by *status*, as opposed to "progressive" (modern) societies in which social relations are predominantly determined by *contract*. Status means that a person's kinship identity predetermines his or her legal position. Contract means that legal positions arise from free agreement among individuals. The contrast is between obligations and identities which are *family*-centered and those which are *individual*-centered.

Maine not only drew out the details of the contrasts but also tried to link the two poles in an evolutionary model, as Morgan had done. He inserted the dimension of time and phrased it in a famous formula: ". . . the movement of the progressive societies has hitherto been a movement *from Status to Contract*."[18] Maine also contrasted the dominance of private law in primitive societies with that of criminal law in civilized societies. We should note that many sociological theories have been built on foundations laid by Maine: Tönnies's "gemeinschaft" (community) versus "gesellschaft" (society), Durkheim's "mechanical" and "organic" solidarity, and Redfield's "folk-urban" continuum. There is little question that Maine not only formulated ideas of lasting value for anthropology, sociology, and law but first fashioned some of the basic tools of the modern social scientist.

[17]See R. Redfield, "Maine's *Ancient Law* in the Light of Primitive Societies" (*Western Political Quarterly*, vol. 3, 1950), pp. 574–589.

[18]H. S. Maine, *Ancient Law*, p. 165.

E. B. Tylor and J. G. Frazer: The Evolution of Religion

Morgan dismissed religion as a subject of evolutionary study. He wrote:

> *The growth of religious ideas is environed with such intrinsic difficulties that it may never receive a perfectly satisfactory exposition. Religion deals so largely with the imaginative and emotional nature, and consequently with such uncertain elements of knowledge, that all primitive religions are grotesque and to some extent unintelligible.*[19]

Morgan has been proved right to doubt the first point: no valid general evolutionary sequence can be established for religious forms. He was wrong on the second point, for all religions can be understood if the principle of cultural relativity is grasped and the basic postulates are perceived upon which religions are built, as our later discussions (Chapters 31 through 32) should demonstrate.

Morgan notwithstanding, Sir Edward Burnett Tylor (1832–1917), who has been called the "father of anthropology in all its British developments,"[20] had already published his great work[21] from which the anthropological concept of culture is derived, and which is almost wholly devoted to the evolutionary development of religion in culture. Sir James Frazer (1854–

[19]Morgan, op. cit., p. 5.

[20]G. W. Stocking, Jr., "Tylor, Edward Burnett" (*International Encyclopedia of the Social Sciences*, vol. 16, 1968), p. 175. The entire article, beginning on page 170, is well worth reading.

[21]E. B. Tylor, *Primitive Culture: Researches into the Development of Mythology, Philosophy, Religion, Language, Art and Custom*.

FIGURE 2.5
Sir Edward Burnett Tylor (1832-1917), outstanding English evolutionary anthropologist of the nineteenth century.

1941) followed with his monumental twelve-volume classic on magic and religion.[22] The outlines of Tylor's theory of the evolution of religion from the invention of animism and the soul concept, through ghost and ancestor worship, nature worship, and on to polytheism and monotheism will be presented in Chapter 31 and are consequently passed over here.

Frazer attempted to trace the origins of magic and religion. The path he outlined was somewhat different from that of Tylor. Frazer identified both religion and magic as means of controlling natural forces, but he assumed that early peoples first invented magic, turning to religious belief only after experience demonstrated the fallibility of magic. Frazer's theory was wholly psychological, and he used the device of thinking as he believed early humans must have thought. (Max Gluckman tells us that Radcliffe-Brown called this the "if-I-were-a-horse" method of evolutionary reconstruction, the method of the farmer whose horse has strayed from the barnyard. Before starting on an aimless search, he scratches his head, chews on a bit of straw, and asks, "Now if I were a horse, where would *I* go?"[23])

The evolutionary theory of *The Golden Bough* is an intellectualist dream without a wisp of reality, and yet the book is a treasury of ethnographic and classical learning, a compendium of strange doings and fanciful beliefs, both primitive and classical, written in elegant English. It deserves to be read for generations to come, but not for its method or theory.

TWENTIETH-CENTURY DEVELOPMENTS

At the turn of the century anthropologists became dissatisfied with the lack of empirical basis for the schemes of the cultural evolutionists. This was to be the century of scientific thinking, and science is as impatient with meta-anthropology as it is with metaphysics. The reaction came first in the work of Franz Boas (1858–1942) and his followers.

Franz Boas: Historical Reconstruction

The great achievement of the Boasian reaction was the replacement of speculative evolutionism by empirical anthropology, and it initiated the effort to develop reliable and objective methods of observation and recording in ethnography,

[22]J. G. Frazer, *The Golden Bough: A Study in Magic and Religion.*

[23]M. Gluckman, *Politics, Law, and Ritual in Tribal Society,* p. 2.

physical anthropology, archaeology, and linguistics. It was Boas who reintroduced Sahagun's practice of recording the statements of informants in their own languages. To make this possible, he devised a system of phonetic recording and set the pattern for American graduate programs in anthropology that require intensive linguistic training. He also laid the foundation for all American Indian language studies and for the present techniques of teaching foreign languages (emphasizing use of vernacular conversation rather than memorization of word lists and grammatical rules). He insisted on detailed reporting of ethnographic observations derived from field research. He developed statistical techniques for handling growth and development data in physical anthropology.

In addition, through his considerable ability as administrator and entrepreneur, Boas helped establish the scientific study of Meso-American archaeology, trained the leaders of modern Mexican anthropology, helped establish the sequence of cultures in the central valley of Mexico, and founded an internationally sponsored school of anthropology in Mexico City.[24]

Boas was born a year before the *Origin of Species* was published. He was trained in physics and mathematics, but his interest was the study of human beings. Boas's aim in the period from 1890 to 1930 was to convert anthropology from the deductive speculations of the evolutionists to the inductive exactitude of natural science. This he did with marked success. We do not say that he made a science of anthropology, but he converted anthropologists in the United States to a scientific orientation in tackling the problems of anthropology.

Controlled Comparison and Areal Anaylsis Boas maintained that universal laws of culture could be found, but he insisted that they be extracted from painstakingly gathered facts. He abhorred premature generalization—which in his time meant almost all generalization. Boas introduced the methods of both *controlled comparison* and *areal analysis* of the development of cultural forms through the distribution of traits within a culture area.

The development and application of these combined methods were presented by Boas in 1916, when his study of Tsimshian mythology was published.[25] Tsimshian myths were classified and analyzed by motifs. The components of each myth throughout the Northwest Coast were also analyzed and plotted. From these data, the steps in the development and elaboration of the myths were reconstructed and the lines of diffusion of the components were depicted. The specific evolution of myths within the Northwest Coast environment was thus worked out with exactitude. What is more, Boas took special pains to show how myths that have intercontinental distribution were changed by the Kwakiutl Indians to reflect Kwakiutl culture. He did not talk in terms of evolutionary adaptation or of myth as symbolism, but he demonstrated how specific cultural forms were adapted to the total environment—physical, cultural, and social.

The Aims of Boasian Methodology Boas's major objection to evolutionist methodology, to be more emphatically reiterated by Malinowski and Radcliffe-Brown, was that it treated traits out of context and disregarded cultures as meaningful wholes.

Myth, art, material culture, ceremonial and social organization—all were to be studied in depth, in context, within a culture area; distributions were to be plotted to determine which manifestations of a trait were universal within the area, which were special, and where the cultures of greatest complexity lay. *Then* one could say

[24]R. Parmenter, "Glimpses of a Friendship," in J. Helm (ed.), *Pioneers of American Anthropology*, pp. 83–148.

[25]F. Boas, *Tsimshian Mythology*.

something about the developmental (historical) cultural processes for that area and the conditions it represented. When this had been done for a number of areas, it would be time to compare results to see whether higher levels of generalization with empirical validity were possible.

Boas's associates and followers in the first quarter of this century expanded his research. From the anthropological division of the American Museum of Natural History in New York, Clark Wissler (1870–1947) sent out expeditions to round out the ethnographic data on Plains Indian military clubs and the sun dance. Robert H. Lowie (1883–1957) analyzed the data on military societies, while Leslie Spier (1893–1961) did the same for the sun dance.[26]

The Boasian method is usually treated as though it were concerned solely with the reconstruction of historical fragments of cultures. The concern was not with chronology so much as with the dynamics of cultural process.[27]

To sum up in Boas's own words:

> *In short then, the method which we try to develop is based on a study of dynamic changes in society that may be observed at the present time. We refrain from the attempt to solve the fundamental problem of the general development of civilization until we have been able to unravel the processes that are going on under our eyes.*
>
> . . . [I]*f we look for laws, the laws relate to the effects of physiological, psychological, and social conditions, not to sequences of cultural achievement.*[28]

With Boas, anthropology became firmly grounded in empiricism. Nonliterate cultures were fast disappearing. The job was to get in the field and make objective studies before time ran out. As carefully obtained information was analyzed, the errors in the current evolutionary schemes began to pile up.

As the recognized errors increased, so did the Boasian rejection of nineteenth-century evolutionism. In some extreme instances, the enthusiasm for the empiricism that Boas insisted upon was converted into a scorn of all theory. In 1939 Kluckhohn reported the state of American anthropologists to be such that "to suggest something is 'theoretical' is to suggest that it is slightly indecent."[29]

R. H. Lowie's great work, *Primitive Society*, published in 1920, seemed to put an end to Morgan. By 1925, English, American, German, and French anthropologists had turned away from any interest in the evolution of culture. In England and France, anthropologists were absorbed in functional analysis of living cultures. Evolutionism was dead and buried—so it seemed.

Diffusionism

In Germany and Austria, an anthropological theory of diffusion of cultures on a broad scale (*Kulturkreislehre*) developed as a second alternative to evolutionary anthropology. This theory held that intensive development of culture occurs only in a few select centers, from which it spreads outward through borrowing. Under the leadership of Father Wilhelm Schmidt (1868–1954), this theory flourished for several decades (from 1910 to 1940), but it had little influence on the general development of anthropological method; it disappeared with World War II—at least, for the time being.[30] Discussion of the

---

[26]R. H. Lowie, *Plains Indian Age Societies: Historical Summary* (American Museum of Natural History, Anthropological Papers, vol. 11, 1916), pp. 877–984; and L. Spier, *The Sun Dance of the Plains Indian* (American Museum of Natural History, Anthropological Papers, vol. 16, part 1, 1921).

[27]J. W. Bennett, "The Development of Ethnological Theories as Illustrated by Studies of the Plains Indian Sun Dance" (*American Anthropologist*, vol. 46, 1944), pp. 162–181.

[28]F. Boas, "The Methods of Ethnology" (*American Anthropologist*, vol. 22, 1920), pp. 316 and 328.

[29]C. Kluckhohn, "The Place of Theory in Anthropological Science" (*The Philosophy of Science*, vol. 6, 1939), p. 333.

[30]See C. Kluckhohn, "Some Reflections on the Method and Theory of the Kulturkreislehre" (*American Anthropologist*, vol. 38, 1936), pp. 157–196.

Kulturkreislehre (culture complex theory) will be waived, as will be that of the British diffusionist writers G. Elliot Smith and W. J. Perry, who set forth highly speculative diffusionist schemes.

Functionalism and Social Structure

In England, the major reaction to evolutionism came in the form of a total rejection of culture history as a subject for anthropological study. In its stead, Bronislaw Malinowski (1884–1942) and A. R. Radcliffe-Brown (1888–1955) built a new approach to anthropology which emphasized cultures as social systems. Negatively, they took the position that, at worst, historical and cultural evolutionary studies are a futility: there are few verifiable facts to work with, and hence there are no chronological data other than archaeological data for a science of anthropology to use. At best, they argued, historical reconstruction is a waste of anthropological time—much richer results may be harvested by focusing on living societies.[31]

Durkheim's Basic Contribution The forerunner of functionalists Malinowski and Radcliffe-Brown, and the intellectual ancestor of later British social anthropologists, was the French social scientist Émile Durkheim (1858–1971). Durkheim and Boas were contemporaries, and each gave a new direction to anthropology at the turn of the century. Boas's influence was more direct during the first third of this century; Durkheim's was longer delayed, but since 1930 his influence has grown progressively.

Like Boas, Durkheim emphasized the importance of rigorous method and empiricism in building a scientific base for the understanding of society. Unlike Boas, he did not participate in, or contribute to, the development of ethnographic field studies. Nonetheless, he welcomed anthropological contributions to his highly influential journal, *Année sociologique* (1898 to 1914). His one avowedly anthropological book, *The Elementary Forms of the Religious Life*, was less successful than his analysis of social interdependence in his *Division of Labor* and his development of the idea of collective identity, particularly in his study *Suicide*.

The question of what holds a society together was of primary importance to Durkheim. He took as a variable the division of labor and tried to correlate its variations with other social phenomena. As polar opposites, he contrasted what he called "mechanical solidarity" with "organic solidarity."

Mechanical solidarity was considered to be characteristic of small, homogeneous societies—namely, the simpler tribes and peasant groups. Such societies were characterized by moral and social homogeneity, with differences due to heredity. The purpose of law was individual repression and reinforcement of the moral conscience of the group. There was unanimity of public opinion, and justice was meted out in the public meetings of its members. Property was communal, and religion consisted of beliefs in impersonal forces. Local and tribal patriotism prevailed.

Organic solidarity was characterized by an increase in individuality and a decrease in tradition. Heredity became less important for the transmission of property and office. Social control was less rigid; law and justice had the goal of restitution of property instead of punishment, since offenses were considered to be against individuals rather than against society. The division of labor by different statuses and roles led to a new kind of unity, or social solidarity: people came to need each other, so society continued to function as an entity in spite of increased individuality. Political functions became specialized, and property became private. In terms of religion there was a transition to polytheism and mono-

[31]Radcliffe-Brown's *The Andaman Islanders* and Malinowski's *Argonauts of the Western Pacific*, both published in 1922, opened the era of functional anthropology.

theism; politically, local ties and patriotism gave way to nationalism and internationalism.

The function of a social institution, or usage, Durkheim held, is the relation between it and the needs of the society as a whole. The concept of "functional prerequisites for societal maintenance" derives from Durkeim's notion of needs of the social organism. The idea of social function was developed in differing ways by Malinowski, Radcliffe-Brown, and their followers.

Malinowski's Theory and Method Malinowski's great contribution was the standard he set for ethnological field research. A citizen of Polish Austria, he was interned at the outbreak of World War I while attending a meeting of the British Association for the Advancement of Science in Australia. He was permitted to spend the duration of the war among the nearby Trobriand Islanders. Although he was trained as a mathematician in Poland, people and anthropology were his natural passion. He was the first anthropologist to insist that what people *do* (no matter how seemingly trivial or irrelevant) is what must fill the ethnographer's notebook. What *they say they do* is important to record, but it must not be taken as fully representing their culture.

Beyond observing and reporting, Malinowski's credo was that the total body of data must fit together and make sense. Every aspect of culture is functionally significant in its context.

Malinowski's theory and method dealt with *function* as the organizing principle operating on three levels: (1) the effect of a custom or institution on other customs or institutions within the culture, (2) the goal-achievement effects of a practice as goals are defined by the members of a society, and (3) the part played by a custom or institution in promoting social cohesion (solidarity) and the continuance of a way of life in a given environment. Whether an anthropologist correctly identifies the functions of culture traits and institutions is a subtle problem of validation. There is no foolproof methodology in functionalism, but it is frequently possible to demonstrate the interacting effects of the various aspects of the culture. Societies became living, pulsating, dynamic entities under the Malinowskian method of fieldwork and analysis. The superb quality of field studies done by Malinowski-trained students in England and the United States is testimony to the marked advance made in anthropological methods under his stimulus.

FIGURE 2.6
Émile Durkheim (1858-1917), French forerunner of functionalism and structuralism in anthropology.

Radcliffe-Brown and Structuralism Radcliffe-Brown's organic analogy of functionalism is presented on page 287. Radcliffe-Brown and subsequent British social anthropologists moved from functionalism to a concern with social structure, which has been the chief focus of British—and a number of North American—

social anthropologists since 1940. Functionalism became an implicit, but not a primary, aspect of almost all British, French, and North American cultural anthropology.

Social structure is the network of ways in which individuals and groups within a population are related to each other in their ongoing activities. It is the system of statuses (or social positions) held by individuals, and the roles (or ways of behaving) that are formally expected of the status holders.[32] In British social anthropology, however, the focus is not on the whole gamut of social relations but on the structure of corporate groups—lineages, clans, work groups, age classes, and territorial organizations—which have an enduring existence within a society. The concern is, for the most part, with economic, political, religious, and ritual activities.

Social structure rests on and utilizes a technological base; it also reflects and is sustained by an ideological and symbolic system of knowledge and beliefs. In the chapters to follow, we deal with each of these aspects of culture in turn.

French Social Structuralism British and American social structural studies focus on in-depth field research in specific societies. Their aims and methods are those of natural science—a movement *from* specific, empirical research *toward* general classification of types of societies and the formulation of cultural laws of social organization.

A contrasting approach by the French anthropologist Claude Lévi-Strauss begins with theoretically conceived images (models) of societies which can then be compared to discover the deep-lying rules which govern the actual forms that societies take. British social structuralism is largely inductive-deductive: it moves from specific observation to the use of general laws. French social structuralism is more deductive-inductive. It emphasizes the general principles which govern the overall organization of societies regardless of the specific forms they may take.

Since Lévi-Strauss's structuralism has excited considerable interest among anthropologists, it will be explored later in this text (see Chapter 21).

Culture and Personality Research

The development of general theory in the study of the interaction of culture upon personality development and the feedback effect of personality types upon cultural institutions will be covered in Chapter 19. Historically, it is interesting to note that while the linguist Edward Sapir provided much stimulus to the psychoanalytic interest in the *individual* in nonliterate societies, it was Benedict and Mead who gave culture and personality studies the impetus that made them the major interest of American cultural anthropologists from 1930 to 1950.

The great excitement created in the 1930s by relating personality psychology to the problems of anthropology has now calmed down, but culture and personality research will continue to yield useful applications, both in psychotherapy and in economic development programs.

Cross-cultural Correlational Methods

A major research resource for anthropology was created when G. P. Murdock initiated the Yale Cross-cultural Survey in 1937. The survey was designed as a classified repository of ethnographic fact. The data were indexed in such a way that anyone could find what had been reported on almost any feature of culture by selecting cards bearing the index key for the subject. The cultures included in the survey represented all the geographic areas of the world and all forms of society. The value of the Yale Cross-cultural Survey was such that it was subsequently made an interuniversity project in the form of the Human Relations Area Files.

By their very nature, the files invite statistical

[32] See Chap. 17.

testing of anthropological hypotheses. It is usually easy to determine whether certain types of culture traits are present or absent in a given culture. If this determination is made with reference to all cultures, the relative frequency of the trait can be quickly determined. This makes possible the substitution of a more exact expression of frequency than "rarely," "commonly," or "usually," which have so long been characteristic of anthropological generalizations.

Cultural anthropologists for years had to rely on the memory of ethnographic fact for the formulation of tentative hypotheses. When a hypothesis was put forward, other anthropologists would try to think of contradictory cases. If there were not too many serious exceptions, the hypothesis would be accepted for the time being. This is the *method of disproof by the crucial instance,* still the favorite methodological test of most anthropologists. Obviously, it has its weaknesses. How many facts from how many cultures can even the best-read ethnologist remember?

In any science, relationships count for more than mere frequencies, and this is where statistical coefficients of correlations may be helpful.

FIGURE 2.7
George Peter Murdock (1897-), developed the method of comparative cross-cultural research by using sophisticated statistical techniques.

Murdock's Statistical Study In 1941, Murdock built up a checklist of significant facts on family, kinship, kin and local groups, and sexual behavior. The data from eighty-five societies in the Human Relations Area Files were registered as indicating presence (+) or absence (−) of a given trait. Similar data lists were made for additional societies not included in the files. By counting each occurrence or absence of a trait as a positive or negative unit, Murdock was able to produce quantified four-cell tables for a large number of paired traits, on the basis of which coefficients of correlation could be calculated.

In his epoch-making book *Social Structure*, published in 1949, Murdock ran statistical tests of correlations on twenty-six theorems derived from a postulate identifying the factors which govern the grouping of kin under a single relationship term (see Chapter 24). The results were mostly positive and statistically significant.

Since then, Murdock and others have refined and improved the method, which has several inherent difficulties. The first is the representativeness of the sample. What, for instance, is a discrete culture suitable for counting as a unit? If two historically related groups show the same trait, does it count as one occurrence—or two? This is important when one is attempting to discover the causal significance of an indicated relation between two traits. Should the sample be drawn from a universe of societies, each of which has an equal chance of being included? Or should the universe be presorted into cultural clusters (some of which will include a number of related groups) so that the sample will include a representative selection of clusters, by cultural type and geographic distribution?

These thorny problems (and others) have not been wholly solved. But, moving in that direction, Murdock first tested the statistical reliability of the sample used in his book on social structure. The statistical results differed sufficiently in each test so that he judged it necessary to select a larger sample that would represent culture types and areas. The product is the *World Ethnographic Sample* of 585 cultures coded according to subsistence, types of community, kinship organization, marriage, kinship terminologies, residence, social classes, and political integration.[33] The *Sample* differs from the *Human Relations Area Files* not only in the number of societies covered but in the nature of its data as well.

Murdock's *Ethnographic Atlas* Murdock finally decided that sampling presents such difficulties that cross-cultural analysis should be based on a total universe of human societies. The formulation of the universe has been undertaken in his *Ethnographic Atlas*, first published in twenty-one installments in the journal *Ethnology*, between 1962 and 1967, and finally in book form (1967). The *Atlas* purports to be not a sample but the "known cultural universe" of all the world during the past 500 years. It is based on 863 societies which are reduced to 412 cultural clusters to provide independent (nonoverlapping) cultural types coded like the cultures in the *World Ethnographic Sample*.

[33]G. P. Murdock, "World Ethnographic Sample" (*American Anthropologist*, vol. 59, 1957), pp. 664–687; also available in the Bobbs-Merrill Reprint Series in the Social Sciences, No. A-166.

Cultural Evolution

Although social evolution as a method and theory seemed to have been dead and buried by 1920 (outside Marxism), it now has a new vitality. The data derived from archaeological research around the world demonstrate that cultures have evolved (changed in form).

If the record goes back far enough, it shows the simple material technology of hunters and gatherers, who had no metals, no domesticated plants or animals, no weaving, no pottery, no writing, no permanent house structures, and no public buildings. Because of limited technology and food-getting techniques, such societies are limited both in numbers of people and in the complexity of social institutions. In later archaeological levels appear domesticated plants and animals, permanent housing, weaving and pottery, and settlement patterns indicating an increase in population. People are classed as incipient agriculturalists if their culture contains domesticated plants and animals and settled villages or homesteads, but no writing, cities, or monumental ceremonial centers. The highest archaeological levels reveal all this and a good deal more. They yield the remains of societies whose cultures include agriculture and cities; diversified craft specialties, including metallurgy; monumental, ceremonial, and governmental structures; writing; and innumerable additional items.

Most of the span of human experience occurred before the invention of writing. The archaeological record testifies to an orderly pattern of cultural development within the prehistoric era (that is, before the time of written records). By inference, patterns of social culture must also show some regularities of development. The task of studies in cultural evolution is to determine the content of such patterns, if possible.

The pendulum of Boasian antievolutionism had completed the swing of its arc by 1945, and three kinds of neoevolutionism emerged.

Specific Evolution A refinement of the idea of cultural evolution was introduced in 1960 by Marshall Sahlins, who calls it *specific evolution*, "the historic development of particular cultural forms . . . phylogenetic transformation through adaptation."[34] In specific evolution, the concern is with the sequence of changes in the cultural history of particular societies; for example, what actually happened in the development of American culture between 1776 and now? In what specific senses were these modifications responses to the potentialities of the North American continent? Or how, specifically, were Pueblo Indian cultures changing and modifying between A.D. 1200 and today? This is more than history, for specific evolution is concerned with more than a chronicle of events; it wants to know how the *cultures* changed. It is really cultural history or Boasian *historical reconstruction* under a new name in a theoretical framework more congenial to thinking in evolutionary terms.

Multilineal Evolution As developed by Julian Steward, multilineal evolution searches for parallels in specific evolution. It does not attempt, at least in its present stage, to develop a comprehensive set of evolutionary principles to cover the growth of culture from earliest prehistoric times to the present. Rather, it deliberately narrows its focus to parallel developments in limited aspects of the cultures of specific societies. It tries to determine whether identifiable sequences of change occur in the same order in independent cultures. When such apparently similar sequences are identified, it then determines whether like causes have produced them.

Multilineal evolution is a methodology based on the assumption that significant regularities in cultural change occur, and it is concerned with the determination of cultural laws. It is inevitably concerned also with historical reconstruction, but it does not expect that historical data can be classified in universal stages.[35]

Multilineal evolutionary studies aim to examine whole cultures in detail to see what specific social forms do in fact take shape on different levels, that is, degrees of complexity, of social integration. It expects great diversity in detail but assumes the probability of limited generalizations with respect to directions of evolutionary change.

General Evolution General evolution differs from multilineal evolution mainly in the level of its formulations. It attempts to establish evolutionary trends for culture in toto rather than for limited cultures of comparable types, as does multilineal evolution. Its formulations are consequently much broader in scope. They are of the type that V. Gordon Childe, Leslie White, Robert Redfield, Elman Service, and Darcy Ribeiro, among others, have formulated with respect to the great changes in culture that accompany the development from Paleolithic to Neolithic to Metal Age technological bases.[36] General evolution does not assume that every culture develops exactly comparable details in cultural patterns. But it does hold that broad-scale trends in the succession of cultural forms are demonstrable.

To study the general evolution of culture is to examine the courses along which human societies have arrived at distinct patterns of behavior.

Archaeological Achievements

Substantive achievements in archaeology were attained after the beginning of the twentieth century through research conducted in the central Andes and on the Peruvian coast by Max Uhle, a German archaeologist who was influ-

[34]M. Sahlins, "Evolution: Specific and General," in M. D. Sahlins and E. R. Service (eds.), *Evolution and Culture*, p. 43.

[35]J. H. Steward, "Evolution and Process," in A. L. Kroeber (ed.), *Anthropology Today*, p. 318.

[36]Or as indicated for legal evolution in "The Trend of the Law," in E. A. Hoebel, *The Law of Primitive Man*, chap. 12; see also L. Pospisil, *Anthropology of Law*, chap. 5.

enced by Petrie. He constructed a chronological sequence of the Peruvian area based on the stylistic seriation of pottery (1892–1912).

As Uhle was working in Peru, A. V. Kidder was making important contributions to the archaeology of the southwestern United States (1915). He was the first archaeologist in the Southwest to use the stratigraphic method on a large scale. Kidder's digging techniques and thorough data gathering were unparalleled. He also developed hypotheses regarding the social significance of ancient pottery, thereby using the scientific method for the treatment of archaeological data.

The antiquity of human beings in the New World was finally established when projectile points were found in association with Pleistocene fauna at Folsom, New Mexico, in 1927. Comparable findings were subsequently made in Colorado, Texas, and Arizona.

Many more and varied achievements were and have been made in New and Old World archaeology. We have presented some of the more notable developments which set the groundwork for archaeology as a distinct, yet integral, subfield of anthropology.

Progress in Physical Anthropology

By the turn of the century Franz Weidenreich (1873–1948) had foreshadowed many modern concepts of human evolution and later recapitulated these in *Apes, Giants, and Man* (1946).

By virtue of the australopithecine finds in South Africa during the early 1920s and 1930s and the understanding of their evolutionary significance through the efforts of Drs. Raymond Dart and Robert Broom (1866–1951), criticism about human evolution was stilled.

Franz Boas made numerous contributions to the development of physical anthropology, the most notable of which was his demonstration of human plasticity. Variations in head form among 17,821 American immigrants (Italians, Czechs, and Jews) and their American-born children were measured, and the results appeared in a 1912 article, "Changes in the Bodily Form of Descendants of Immigrants." The cranial morphology of the immigrant parents significantly differed from that of their offspring. Although head form was considered to be stable and had therefore been used in racial typology, Boas showed that physical change can occur without hereditary change. This helped to establish the notion that genes transmit characteristics which are dependent on the environment for their expression. Racial groupings could no longer be conceived of as immutable biological entities.

Aleš Hrdlička (1869–1943), who founded the American Association of Physical Anthropologists, and E. A. Hooton elaborated on Boas's approach in their research. They were interested in the normal variation *within* a population with respect to its origins and biological adaptations. Hrdlička studied variability in skeletal remains with regard to race, sex, and age. The typological studies and preoccupation with nonadaptive racial characteristics which prevailed through the nineteenth century were becoming insignificant to physical anthropologists.

Gregor Mendel (1822–1884) published his laws of inheritance in 1866, but they were not widely noted until 1900 and their full implications for evolutionary theory were not grasped until the 1930s and 1940s. They finally resulted in the "new synthesis" in physical anthropology and the development of population genetics.

The historical development of the various subfields of anthropology cannot be fully explored within the confines of this chapter. Further discussion is reserved for appropriate sections in the remainder of this book.

SUMMARY

Anthropology as an identifiable subject is a child of the Age of Reason, when thinkers of the Enlightenment began to form an evolutionary philosophy of history to account for the peoples revealed by the voyages of discovery. Sahagun's account of the Aztecs, coming early in the sixteenth century, is the first systematic ethnography of a non-European people. Early in the eighteenth century, Lafitau published the first comparative ethnology—a study of American Indian cultures compared with those of Greece and Rome. Robertson's *History of America* formulated a number of basic principles of evolutionary anthropology and laid the foundation for the birth of anthropology as a full-fledged field.

Nineteenth-century evolutionism is best characterized in the work of Morgan, who attempted to correlate successive steps in the limitation of sexual relations from promiscuity to monogamy with stages of technological evolution. Kinship systems, social organization, and ownership of property were also inferred in progressive steps related to forms of marriage. The resulting scheme collapsed when twentieth-century anthropologists proved that there is no evolutionary sequence in types of kinship systems.

Tylor and Frazer formulated analogous evolutionary sequences for spirit beings, from animism to monotheism (Tylor), and for magic, religion, and scientific thought (Frazer). Maine treated the evolution of law as a progressive shift from nonliterate status-dominated cultures to civilized cultures, which he characterized as basing personal relations on individual contract. The two types of society resulting from such cultures were treated as polar opposites.

In the twentieth century, the American rejection of cultural evolutionism was initiated by Boas, who emphasized the gathering of empirical data in the field and trait analysis of specific institutions within a culture area as a means of limited historical reconstruction.

In England, Malinowski and Radcliffe-Brown rejected all historical goals for anthropology. Instead, they substituted the study of whole cultures as integrated systems. Field studies should overlook nothing in the way of behavior or attitudes because every custom and act is functionally significant. The object of research is to discover the functions as a means of learning how societies hold together and achieve their purposes. Radcliffe-Brown moved from a concern with function to an emphasis on social structure, the organization of interpersonal relations within a social system. Structural theory and research have been characteristic of British social anthropology since 1940 and are also a major feature of contemporary French and North American cultural anthropology.

Cross-cultural studies have been gaining a steadily increasing foothold in North American anthropology since the establishment of the Human Relations Area Files and Murdock's use of coefficients of correlation to test a number of long-standing anthropological hypotheses.

Interest in social and cultural evolution has revived in recent decades. Modern evolutionary studies take three major forms: (1) *specific evolution*, or the continuing modification of particular societies as they adapt to changing conditions; (2) *multilineal evolution*, or the study of parallel developments in societies at comparable levels of cultural development and environmental circumstance; and (3) *general evolution*, the delineation at a higher level of abstraction of the development of human cultures and societies.

SELECTED READINGS

Daniel, G. *The Origins and Growth of Archaeology* (1967). A collection of quotations from writers on the origins and growth of archaeology, together with a running commentary.

Hallowell, A. I., "The Beginnings of Anthropology in America," in F. de Laguna (ed.), *Selected Papers from the American Anthropologist: 1888–1920* (1960), pp. 1–103. A comprehensive account of the events which led to the establishment of anthropology as a science in the United States.

Heine-Geldern, R., "One Hundred Years of Ethnological Theory in the

German-speaking Countries: Some Milestones" (*Current Anthropology*, vol. 5, 1964), pp. 407–429. Should be read to round out the history, which, as we have given it, concentrates on developments in English-speaking countries.

Helm, J. (ed.), *Pioneers of American Anthropology* (1966). Interesting biographical accounts of some nineteenth-century anthropologists at their work.

Kardiner, A., and E. Preble, *They Studied Man* (1961). Essays on Darwin, Herbert Spencer, Tylor, Frazer, Durkheim, Boas, Malinowski, Kroeber, Benedict, and Freud.

Langness, L. L., *The Study of Culture* (1974). A thorough history of anthropology, covering recent changes in the field.

Lowie, R. H., *The History of Ethnological Theory* (1937). To fill in on the English and Austrian diffusionist schools.

Murra, J. V. (ed.), *American Anthropology: The Early Years* (1976). Papers on early history of American anthropology. Easy and interesting reading, with fascinating personal accounts.

Stocking, W. G., Jr., *Race, Culture, and Evolution* (1968). Exceedingly thoughtful and well-researched anthropological history.

Willey, G. R., and J. A. Sabloff, *A History of American Archaeology* (1974). This history divides the subject into periods and provides interesting narrative.

PART TWO

Human Evolution

3
Genetics and Evolution

CHAPTER OUTLINE

LEARNING GOALS

Enumerate the four main divisions of physical anthropology.

Explain the difference between mitosis and meiosis.

Identify the laws of Mendelian inheritance.

Discuss genotype and phenotype.

Specify the factors that upset genetic equilibrium.

In the first chapter we described some of the differences among the subdisciplines of anthropology. We will focus on the results and methods of physical anthropology in the next several chapters.

Physical anthropology shares with other subdisciplines of the general field the goal of understanding human behavior in all places and at all times. Because more is known about living peoples, cultural and social anthropology has provided much of the data and many of the concepts that constitute the core which is central to the four fields. The concepts of culture, cultural relativity, holism, functionalism, social structure, socialization, role and status, adaptation, and many others are part of this core of shared understanding among the four subdisciplines. These are used directly by the subdisciplines or indirectly—when, for example, the archaeologist and the physical anthropologist try to understand the "living" context of excavated materials. The study of the social life of nonhuman primates, for another example, is accomplished with human society as a referrent.

All this, of course, is not to say that the other three subdisciplines are completely dependent on cultural and social anthropology, or that they do not have subject matter, research techniques, and interests that are different and independent from the core of mutual understanding described. They have such wide-ranging interests that some persons often wonder why the four subfields continue to stay or work together.

We can only highlight the main aspects of the important and captivating work of physical anthropology. The suggested readings at the end of each chapter provide additional information for the enterprising reader. For the moment, however, it is important to identify the range of topics and results.

Physical anthropology studies the biological foundations of human variation, human life, and culture. It makes anthropology a unique field in that it is one of the few disciplines in the behavioral sciences with a branch concerned with humans as biological organisms. Significant advances have been made in physical anthropology because it integrates perspectives, techniques, and data from anthropology with such fields as biology, genetics, cytology, and comparative anatomy.

The subject matter of physical anthropology can be broadly grouped into four topics: primatology, the study of nonhuman primate behavior; primate evolution, including interests in comparative physiology, comparative anatomy, and genetics; human variation and race, which includes such subjects as genetics, human adaptation to different environments, and the relation of race and intelligence; and human palaeontology, more commonly identified as the study of human fossil remains.

Primatology has become increasingly important as a field of study for physical anthropologists in recent years because the study of free-ranging and confined monkeys and apes has contributed new knowledge to understanding human and nonhuman primate behavior and its role in adaptation to different physical environments. Primate evolution combines the study of biological evolution with theories about the development of the capacity for culture. The modern study of human variation has taken the field away from a primary concern with skin color, head form, and stature as indicators for classifying human groups. Now there is more interest in blood proteins and immunological factors, because their genetic transmission is better understood than the more visible and more complexly inherited characteristics. In its study of human paleontology, physical anthropology shares tools and techniques with archaeology.

With the tools of archaeology to uncover the fossil evidence, the techniques of physics and botany to prove the antiquity of the fossils, and the science of genetics to reveal how evolution takes place, we have a firmer hold on the reality of the past than was the case fifty years ago.

In this chapter, we shall discuss the mechanics of biological evolution and reserve discussion of the fossil evidence for later.

GENETIC PRINCIPLES

How do new genera and species come into being? If it is through the process of evolution, how does it happen? Only when this is understood can we begin to answer the more specific questions concerning human origins: "How did the primates develop from simpler mammals?" "How did humans derive from the primates?" "How are the many types of fossil and living primates related to one another?"

Some answers have been found in the biochemistry of the gene, the microbiology of cellular reproduction, the Mendelian laws of inheritance, and Darwin's principles of natural selection. Although anthropology is not primarily concerned with the biochemical nature of the genetic code, it is very much concerned with the macrolevel effects of Mendelian inheritance and natural selection—problems of population genetics. For this reason, a summary review of the more relevant genetic principles will be given here.[1]

Cellular Reproduction

Up until 180 years ago, the idea of spontaneous generation of life was commonplace. By the middle of the nineteenth century, however, the microscopic study of living organisms had demonstrated that all organisms are communities of cells and that every cell is reproduced from other cells.

Mitosis The mature human body is made up of trillions of cells, organized in an integrated system. Every cell is the product of repeated reproduction of a single pair of sex cells (*gametes*). The fusion of a male gamete, or sperm, with a female gamete, or ovum, produces a *zygote*, or fertilized egg. At this point the zygote contains the basic genetic materials that will largely determine the nature of the molecular structure of its subsequent cell development. The organism itself grows by multiplication of additional cells through cell division, or fission. In multiple-celled organisms, each cell has a center (nucleus) and each nucleus contains genetic materials in a substance called *chromatin* (so called because it becomes visible when colored with dyes added to the cell). The cell division that occurs is known as *mitosis* (Gr. *mitos*, "thread") because it is characterized at one stage by the formation of threads out of the chromatin. The threads in turn break up into microscopically visible bodies of distinctive shapes, which are known as *chromosomes* (colorable bodies). Human cells contain forty-six chromosomes in twenty-three pairs. In mitosis, chromosomes split longitudinally into two separate halves, which then migrate to opposite poles in the cell, whereupon the cell itself divides into two new cells, each of which contains identical chromosomal complements of twenty-three pairs. By means of mitosis, each chromosome produces an exact replica of itself that is repeated in all the trillions of cells that subsequently mature to form the organism—except for the sex cells. Gametes go through a special process of self-reproduction called *meiosis* (Gr. *meioun*, "to make smaller").

Meiosis The *diploid* state occurs when there is the normal chromosome complement of paired chromosomes characteristic of all but sex cells. Fertilization joins two gametes, which, if the sex cells were diploid, would double the chromosome count every generation. To prevent this from happening, sex cells have a special process of self-reproduction, in which a gamete receives only one of the chromosomes out of each pair.

[1]Those who retain a good mastery of basic biology may overlook the rest of this chapter. For those who wish more detailed and authoritative background material, the following are recommended: I. M. Lerner and W. J. Libby, *Heredity, Evolution, and Society*; and R. C. King, *Genetics*.

Human gametes have only twenty-three chromosomes. Whether it is the chromosomes inherited from the father or those inherited from the mother which go into any given gamete is apparently a matter of chance. As a result, there is variation among the offspring of any mating pair.

Genes in Heredity

Chromosomes are exceedingly gross units of hereditary reproduction, for they are constituted of an undetermined number of smaller units, called *genes*. Genes in turn are known to be constituted of combinations of deoxyribonucleic acid (the now-famous DNA) and ribonucleic acid (RNA). Variations in the molecular structure of DNA constitute the hereditary determinants in genes. The DNA code, or molecular structure, sets the pattern for subsequent molecular synthesis in cell formation.[2]

A gene is thought of as that minimum part of a chromosome (1) which functions to control the synthesis of a *polypeptide* (the basic structure of a protein) in a cell; (2) which, when its own molecular structure changes (mutates), alters just one trait of a cell; or (3) which can separate from its own chromosome and transfer, or "cross over," to the other chromosome in the pair in a reproductive cell. In other words, a gene is a unitary segment of the continuous molecular chain that constitutes a chromosome. The genetic constitution of an organism consists of the products of the genes that an organism inherits. The traits that can be detected as characteristic of an organism develop, under the direction of genes, according to the DNA code in the genes interacting with the total cellular environment of the organism and the external environment that impinges on the organism. More briefly, organic traits are the product of the interaction of genetic activity with the environment.

[2]Actually, a gene is a theoretical construct designed to explain the process of heredity. New, and successively smaller, units have been proposed to explain the mechanisms of heredity. A good explanation is found in J. Buettner-Janusch, *Physical Anthropology: A Perspective*.

The Laws of Mendelian Inheritance

The Austrian monk Gregor Mendel (1822–1884), breeding peas in the garden of an Augustinian monastery, knew little of the cellular mechanisms outlined above, but he discovered laws for the inheritance of traits that hold for all living things. He noted that when two pure lines of unlike peas (for example, with smooth versus wrinkled surfaces) were crossed, all the offspring were smooth. But when the hybrid offspring were mated with one another, smoothness and wrinkledness showed up as distinct traits in a proportion of 3 to 1. Furthermore, in all subsequent hybridizations, the characteristics of smoothness and roundness were inherited independently and recombined in all possible ways (see Figure 3.1). Mendel also showed this to be true of other traits, such as color.

In explaining his observations, Mendel reasoned that the sperm and the egg each contain "factors" that control the development of traits. These are now called "genes." Further, he reasoned, each plant must get at least one factor from each parent plant. Therefore, there must be two factors for each trait in the offspring. But only one factor can be passed on when the offspring mate, so there must be a reduction of the two factors to one in the sperm and egg. How it was done, he did not know, but he predicted meiosis as a process. He further noted that the redistribution of factors among the offspring was entirely random and also that differences in the effects of the factors influenced specific traits. For example, the factor for smooth skin is dominant over that for wrinkled skin when the two are combined in the cells of an offspring. Because the hereditary factors transmitted through reproductive cells are separable units and are inherited as such, Mendel's first law of inheritance is called the *law of segregation*. Phrased in modern terms, in which "gene" is

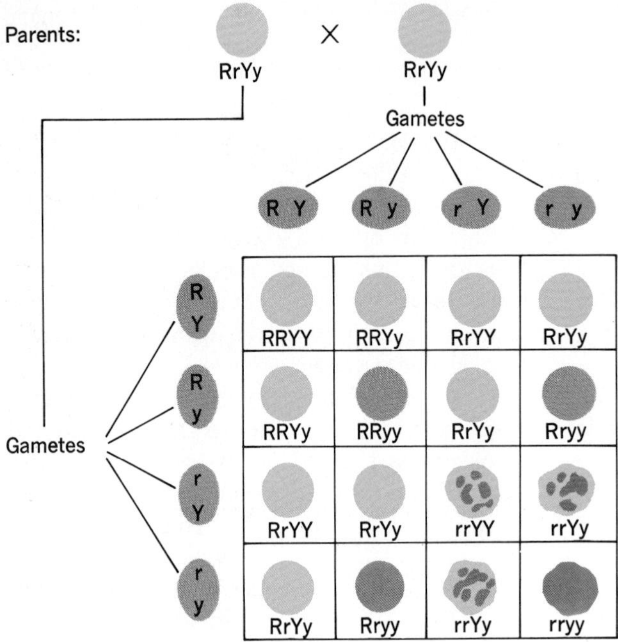

FIGURE 3.1
Independent assortment and recombination of genes. In this model, each parental gamete contains a heterozygous combination of dominant and recessive genes for smooth (R) and wrinkled (r) shape and for yellow (Y) and green (y) color. In meiosis, the genes are segregated, independently assorted, and recombined, as indicated in the block diagram. (P. B. Weisz, *Elements of Biology.* Copyright 1965 by McGraw-Hill Book Company.)

synonymous with "factor," it states: "Genes do not blend, but behave as independent units. They pass intact from one generation to the next, where they may or may not produce visible traits, depending on their dominance characteristics. And genes segregate at random, thereby producing predictable ratios of traits in the offspring."[3]

Mendel's second law specifies that inherited gene pairs for a given trait are not influenced by the inheritance of, or the failure to inherit, any other specific genes *located on other chromosomes.* The genetic controllers of traits are independently assorted among offspring and are expressed independently of the location of other genes on other chromosomes. This is known as the *law of independent assortment.* It explains how each individual, except an identical twin, may receive a unique *total* combination of inherited traits. In humans, the possible number of gene combinations for any twenty-three hypothetical traits that are controlled by genes located on different chromosome pairs is 2^{23}, or more than 8 million different gamete combinations. In fertilization, the fusion of two such gametes gives the mathematical possibility of 8,000,000 × 8,000,000, more than 64 trillion gene combinations. Since many more than twenty-three different traits are controlled by genes located on different chromosome pairs, the number of possible total trait combinations is astronomical.

The third law of Mendelian inheritance was discovered not by Mendel but by T. H. Morgan (1866–1945), early in the present century. It is the *law of lineal order of genes*; the genes for specific traits are located in regular sequences along a chromosome, and they are linked together by chemical bonds, so that they are all normally inherited as a chromosome group. When chromosomes match up in the zygote, they ordinarily bond in parallel strands. Some-

[3] P. B. Weisz, *The Science of Biology* (2d ed.).

times, however, they twist across each other, and a segment of each chromosome may become detached at the point of crossing-over (Figure 3.2). Each detached segment "joins" the chromosome of its opposite number, and a switch of chromosome segments is effected. The genetic code of each particular chromosome in the pair is thus altered. Although genes are independently assorted in inheritance, their relative positions on the chromosomes are important, for genes influence one another's effects in the development of traits. Crossing-over, by changing the proximity of specific genes, can alter their combined effects, thus producing yet another source of variation.

Genotypes and Phenotypes

Each individual receives two matching genes of each type, one from each parent. The separate genes that match or pair with each other at the same chromosome locus are *alleles* (Gr. *allelon*, "of one another"). The total complement of genes transmitted to a zygote makes up its *genotype* (Gr. *gen*, "to reproduce", and *typos*, "type"), or the genetic constitution of a given organism. When the pair of alleles for a given trait in an organism is the same (that is, both dominant or both recessive genes), the condition is called *homozygous* (Gr. *homos*, "like", and *zygotos*, "yoked"). The trait then directly manifests its genetic base. When the pair of alleles for a given trait in an organism is unlike (one dominant and one recessive gene), the condition is *heterozygous* (Gr. *heteros*, "unlike", and *zygotos.*)

The appearance of an organism is known as the *phenotype* (Gr. *phainein*, "to reveal", and *typos*). Because recessive genes are masked in heterozygous genotypes, their presence is not directly revealed in the phenotype and can be determined only by their known occurrence among the ancestors or descendants of a particular organism. This has certain evolutionary consequences of importance that are noted in the discussion of genetic drift on pages 57 and 58.

Mutations

The genetic variations occurring among individuals in the transmission of traits from one generation to another, discussed above under Mendelian Inheritance, all operate as a *sexual recombination of genes.* Additional variations also occur as a result of internal changes in the molecular structure of genes themselves (*point* mutations) and in changes of whole chromosomes (*chromosomal* mutations). When the DNA code is altered, changes occur in the control of the gene over cell growth, and thus the phenotypic expression in an individual is changed. Gene mutations which are sufficiently stable are heritable. *Mutagens*, factors which cause mutations, include radiation (for instance, x-ray and ultraviolet), temperature, and possibly certain drugs and chemicals.

The average frequency of point mutations is

FIGURE 3.2
Crossing-over as a form of genetic variation. Genes that are far apart in locus on their chromosomes are more apt accidentally to cross over and become "misplaced" than genes that are close together. (P. B. Weisz, *Elements of Biology.* Copyright 1965 by McGraw-Hill Book Company.)

estimated as possibly 1 in 100,000 genes. But because a single human gamete may contain some ten thousand genes, it is possible that one gamete in ten contains a spontaneous mutation.[4] An investigation showed that among 94,075 births in a Copenhagen hospital, ten chondrodystrophic dwarfs were born, only two of which had a dwarf parent. From this evidence the rate of point mutation was determined to be forty-three genes per million.[5] A gene mutation that is lethal in its effect may cause the early death of the organism, as is sometimes the case with the mutation that produces hemophilia. The individual then has no chance to reproduce, and the mutant gene is not passed on through heredity. Such mutations have no significant evolutionary consequences unless they are linked to other genes that are consequently lost because of the lethal mutation.

If the mutant gene is recessive, there will be no visible trait effect in the generation in which the mutation occurs. Its effects will show up in homozygous genotypes in later generations, in very low frequencies. If, on the other hand, the mutation is dominant, it may establish its phenotypic effects immediately. These same effects will be inherited by a majority of the organism's offspring.

Mendelian Populations and Gene Pools

A Mendelian population is a localized grouping of members of a given species who interbreed and occasionally breed with members of other populations. All the genes possessed by all the members of the population constitute its *gene pool.* The gene pool is therefore the reservoir of genetic materials available for the genotypic inheritance of the next generation. Because of the reproductive process of meiosis, the tendency is for the organisms of a particular species to convey the gene pool relatively unchanged to succeeding generations.

The Hardy-Weinberg law, the cornerstone of evolutionary theory, states that if mating within a population is random, if mutations do not occur, and if the population is not just large, but infinite in size, the frequencies of genes in a gene pool will remain constant from generation to generation; a condition of genetic equilibrium will be maintained, and there will be no evolution. Such stability preserves the species and works against evolution. *Evolution means changes in the gene frequencies of populations.* These changes in gene frequencies are reflected in subsequent generations of individuals in the populations. But what lends direction to the change?

EVOLUTIONARY PROCESSES

Variation, Natural Selection, and Adaptation

The factors that upset genetic equilibrium are (1) mutation, (2) natural selection, (3) population mixture, and (4) genetic drift. The first two are the most important as evolutionary processes. Charles Darwin (1809–1882) and Alfred Wallace (1823–1913) first systematically explained species origin in terms of developmental sequences. Darwin, in particular, demonstrated that inheritable variations are *differentially* affected by the environment in which a population lives. Some individuals carrying new genes survive and have offspring, the new genes are added to the gene pool, and the characteristics of the population are changed. If, however, the individuals carrying new genes fail to reproduce because of the effects of the new genes, the new variation does not alter the gene pool. If the individuals who possess the new genes and their resulting traits reproduce with greater relative frequency than those who do not have them, the frequency of the new genes in the population will be increased, and evolution has occurred.

---

[4] King, op.cit., p. 201.

[5] Lerner and Libby, op.cit., p. 287.

Natural selection is the operation of environmental factors upon genetically based phenotypic variations that results in *differential reproduction.* Those variant individuals which reproduce most are the individuals best adapted to the environment; from generation to generation, they contribute a progressively larger proportion of descendants in the population. Eventually their genes may become preponderant in the population, and the population gene pool will be altered.

In the evolutionary context, the important questions to be asked about a mutation are whether its survival value is negative (and possibly lethal) or positive (adaptive) and, in either case, to what degree. However, in the case of protein evolution, mutations may be neutral, with neither a negative nor a positive effect. *Population genetics* is the study through which gene frequencies and the *survival quotients*, or *reproductive potential*, of different genes in specific environments are mathematically determined. Such quotients are indicators of rates of evolutionary change. A mutation has to have both high selective advantage and dominance to change the gene pool of a population very rapidly in a stable environment.

The Effect of Population Mixture

Interbreeding between two populations with differing gene pools results in new combinations of genes in succeeding generations. Although we have been talking as though each gene were responsible for a single trait, genes actually work in concert to influence the development of many phenotypic traits. The new phenotypes can become characteristic of the population either because of continued *hybridization* or because the hybrids have a higher survival and reproductive quotient than the nonhybrids. Eventually a new Mendelian population may result, as has been the case in recent centuries with the Afro-American and the so-called South African Colored populations.

The Selective Effect of Environmental Changes

Environments as well as genes are subject to change. Any environmental change may alter the selective effect of the populations inhabiting such an altered environment. Environmental variation is therefore just as important to evolution as genetic change. Any change in plant or animal life is itself an environmental change affecting everything else in the environment. Thus, every evolutionary change has a feedback effect that produces environmental changes for other organisms. Hence, evolution has been cumulative from one geologic era to the next.

Adaptive Effects of Sickle-cell Anemia Whether or not a given mutation has a selective disadvantage depends upon the specific environment with which the population has to contend. An example that has excited much interest among geneticists and anthropologists is the discovery of a mutant recessive gene that causes a blood disorder known as *sickle-cell anemia*, so named because the defective red blood cell is sickle-shaped and unable adequately to supply oxygen to body cells (see Figure 3.3). The homozygous genotype is believed to be 100 percent lethal, and homozygotes for this gene usually die in childhood. Few live beyond 30 years of age. However, in its heterozygous state, in which a person receives a normal gene from one parent and the mutant gene from the other, the genotype is not lethal. Heterozygous children do not die because of their single sickle-cell gene.

The factor which has intrigued modern scientists is that the heterozygotes have a special resistance to malaria. In the malaria zones of the Old World tropics, thousands of normal, nonsicklers are seriously impaired by, and eventually die from, malaria. This disease is caused by various parasites that are carried by Anopheles mosquitoes. The mosquito bite injects the parasite into the human bloodstream. The red blood

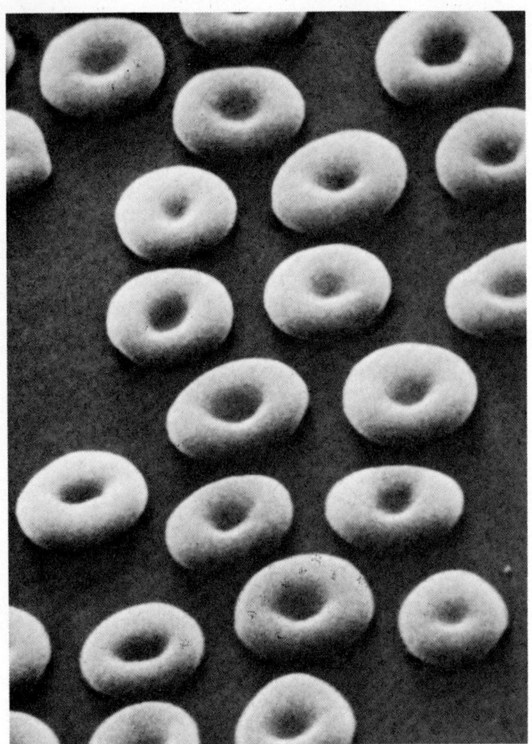

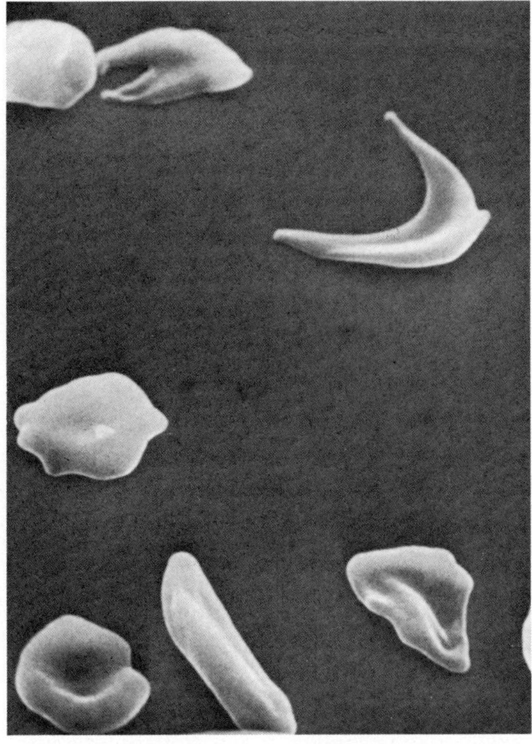

FIGURE 3.3
Human red blood cells as shown by scanning electron microscopy. Left: normal cells. Right: cells from a sickle-cell anemia patient. Magnification is 3000 times natural size. (Dr. Marion I. Barnhart, Wayne State University, Detroit, Mich.)

cells (hemoglobin) become infected, and the normal hemoglobic functions are impaired (see Figure 3.4). Racking chills alternating with burning fever, combined with the weakness of anemia, result in the condition called malaria. However, the red blood cells of persons who have inherited the sickle-cell gene are evidently not as receptive to the malaria-producing parasite. It is thought that this organism becomes fixed on the surface of the cell, starves for want of oxygen, and is then destroyed by antibodies. Thus, heterozygotes with one sickle-cell gene have malaria symptoms, but they have the symptoms in a milder form which leads to a lower mortality. They are better adapted to malaria-infested tropical lowlands than those who do not carry the gene at all.

In a malarial environment, it is thus advantageous for the population to have the sickle-cell trait in the gene pool, even though it means that every child born a homozygote is doomed to an early death.

In tropical West Africa, one-fifth to two-fifths of the indigenous populations carry the sickle-cell trait. In the United States, where it is estimated that approximately 30 percent of the Afro-American gene pool is derived from European ancestry through black-white matings, the sickle-cell gene is carried by about 9 percent of the Afro-American population (see Figure 3.5). Al-

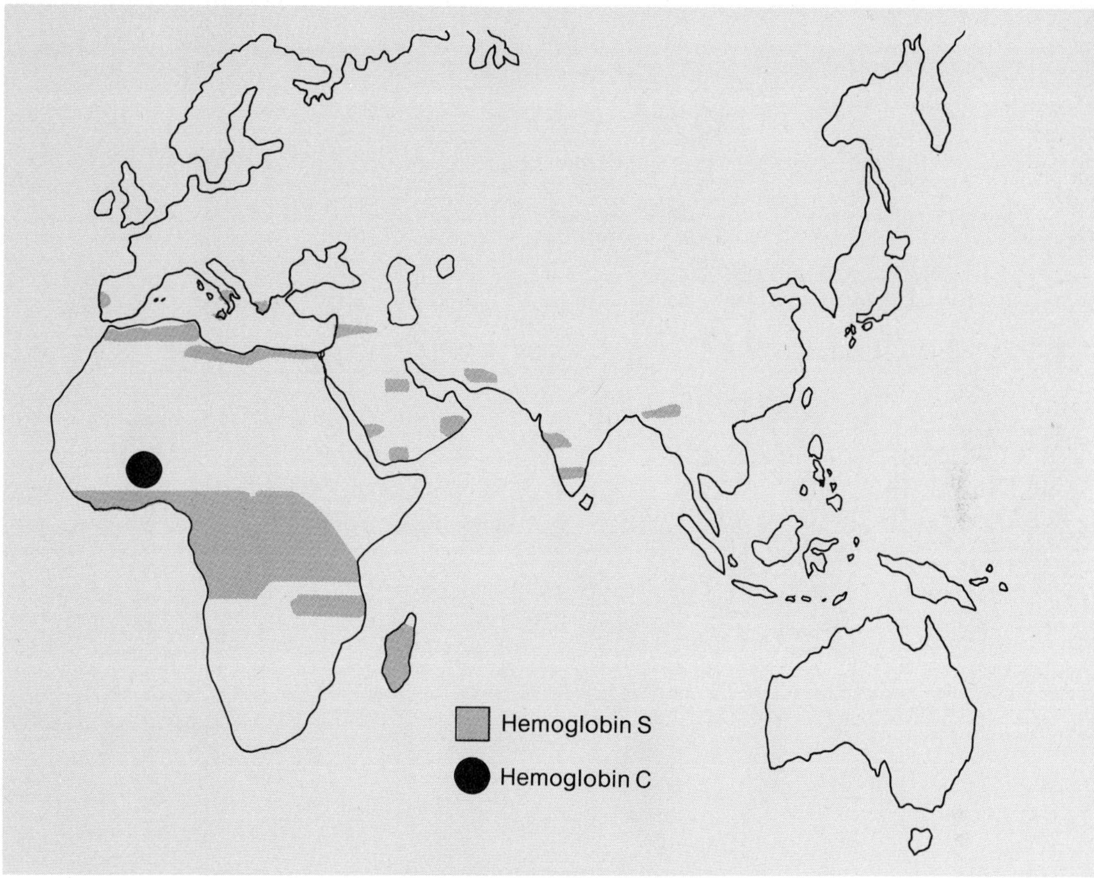

FIGURE 3.4
The distribution of hemoglobins S and C. (S) hemoglobin occurs frequently among individuals in areas where falciparum malaria is endemic (compare with following figure). The heterozygous condition provides resistance to malaria. (C) hemoglobin is frequent in heterozygous form in some populations of West Africa. This hemoglobin also produces a severe anemia if homozygous. (Redrawn from Arno G. Motulsky, 1960; taken from Lasker, 1976, p. 98.)

though malaria ravaged populations of the South Atlantic coastal area of the United States in the eighteenth and nineteenth centuries, mosquito eradication eliminated it by 1910. There is no longer a survival advantage for sickle-cell carriers among blacks living in the United States. Yet, at the beginning of 1970, the sickle-cell gene meant premature death for the 300,000 sickle-cell homozygotes then living among the country's 22 million blacks. Now, however, there is hope. Medical research at the University of Michigan (announced early in 1971) indicates that small daily doses of urea, the main ingredient of urine, will check the disease. Intravenous injections suppress the crisis symptoms in advanced cases within a few hours. However, urea

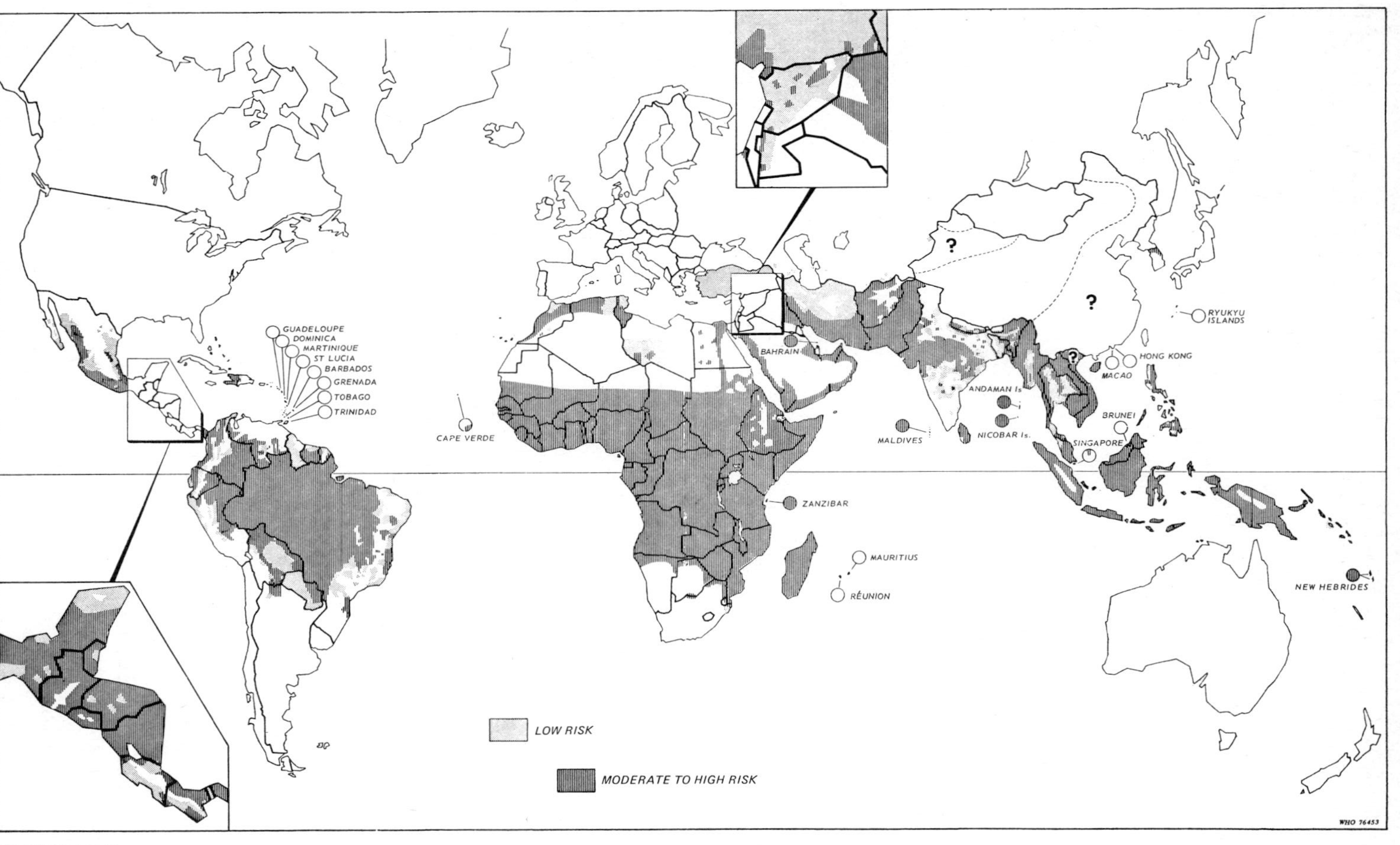

FIGURE 3.5
The distribution of falciparum malaria. (Redrawn from Arno G. Motulsky, 1960; taken from Lasker, 1976, p. 98.)

does not influence the inheritance of the sickle-cell trait.

Malaria eradication modifies the environment in such a way that there is no longer an advantage in the sickle-cell mutant; hence, the mutant has a very low frequency in long-time nonmalarial zones as compared with zones where the disease is still rampant.[6]

The presence of malaria works selectively to increase the recessive sickle-cell gene in a population. Therefore, evolution in the direction of sickle-cell anemia as a trait has been maintained among populations that live in malarial zones. But now a new dimension has been added to upset the biocultural environment. Homozygotes for sickle-celling will not necessarily die (if the suppressive treatment for its effects holds up to its promise). Many more will live to pass on the sickle-cell allele. Whether the percentage of such genes in the local gene pools will then increase or decrease will depend on other variables, such as the presence or absence of malaria.

Genetic Drift

It is also possible for an isolated population to experience a change in its original genetic composition without the effect of mutation or natural selection, through *genetic drift.*

Genetic drift may operate when a small group of people (or any other organisms) migrates to a new territory and subsequently loses contact with the ancestral group. If the gene frequency for a given trait is only 15 percent for the original population, it could happen that by chance no more than 5 percent of the migrants carry the gene. In the gene pool of the emigrant population, the frequency of this gene is automatically reduced by two-thirds. The gene pools of the original and the new societies are different by that much. Furthermore, in the absence of intermating, mutation, and changes in factors of natural selection, the change would remain constant indefinitely. Now suppose that in the course of time, a handful of descendants of the emigrants move on to new territories. There is only a 5 percent frequency of the gene in the total pool of their parent population. By chance, it is possible that none of them will carry the gene. In that event, the gene would drop out of the population entirely. The new population would be absolutely different from its ancestors in the phenotypic trait to which the gene in question contributed. This type of genetic drift, called the *founder principle*, involves chance fluctuations in gene frequencies and is evolutionarily very significant.

A *population bottleneck*, in which a population, because of war, or other reasons, is greatly reduced in size, can cause a type of genetic drift similar to the founder principle. The surviving group will probably not have the same gene frequencies that the original population had.

Drift may also move in two or more directions simultaneously. Figure 3.6 is a simplified model

FIGURE 3.6
Hypothetical genetic drift in a series of subdividing populations, with two genes represented as x and y. The genetic character of two populations with a common ancestry may change without mutations solely by operation of the laws of probability in the distribution of genes.

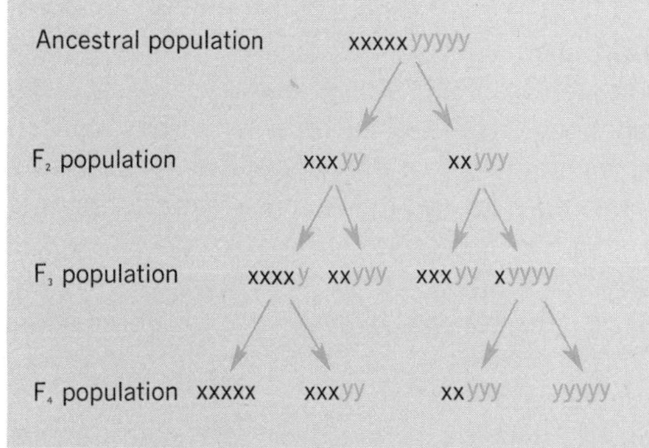

[6]See A. C. Allison, "Aspects of Polymorphism in Man" (*Cold Spring Harbor Symposium in Quantitative Biology*, vol. 20, 1955), pp. 239–255.

of how this may take place. Let us assume equal frequencies of two alleles, *x* and *y*. In the model, each *x* and each *y* represents a gene frequency of 10 percent in the total gene pool of the original population. Therefore, we begin with five *x*'s and five *y*'s. Assume that the population divides equally and that half the people move away. It is hypothesized that one population contains three *x*'s and two *y*'s, and the other population two *x*'s and three *y*'s. Now, let us follow the three-*x*, two-*y* population. It inbreeds; then half of its children migrate. The chances are one in five that the migrating group will carry away a ratio of four *x*'s to one *y*, leaving the home F_3 generation with two *x*'s to three *y*'s. The migrants inbreed; then half their children carry on the tradition of moving on. The chances are one in five that the migrating group will carry away a ratio of five *x*'s to zero *y*'s, leaving the home F_4 generation with a ratio of three *x*'s to two *y*'s.

The third generation of isolating migrant (F_4) has lost all *y* genes. In the character that *y* determines, it has nothing in common with its ancestors. On the two-*x* to three-*y* side of the F_2 generation (the right of the model), similar splitting and isolating migrations can produce a population totally devoid of *x*. From the original equally heterogeneous ancestral population have come several new populations with varying proportions of *x* and *y*, one that is pure *x*, and another that is pure *y*. The ancestral group has spawned three genetically different populations, and each one exhibits different *x* and *y* gene frequencies. All this has occurred without any changes in the original gene structures but through the roll of the genetic dice when group fission occurs and the resulting groups inbreed.

Speciation

A *species* consists of one or more populations whose members are capable of interbreeding. Simultaneously, either they are incapable of interbreeding with members of other populations or they do not habitually do so. Genetically, species members exchange genes through reproduction. Nonspecies members do not.

Speciation occurs when two or more groups from an original population become isolated from one another and, in adaptation to their separate environments, go through genetic modifications such that they no longer can exchange genes. The result is *differential evolution* through *adaptive radiation*. Most new species are formed in this manner. In limited conditions, however, such as on a small island, a species may change through time without producing additional species. A new species simply replaces the original through straight-line change. Such species are known as *allochronic species* (or *paleospecies*).

In the evolution of the hominoids, the lines leading to the human species, gorilla, chimpanzee, orangutan, siamang, and gibbon were simultaneously radiating from a common ancestral species in the Oligocene epoch about 34 to 25 million years ago.

Genetics and Linguistics

Speciation is the way two groups acquire separate biological status. It is a biological, as opposed to a cultural, evolutionary process, and the question has been raised whether the processes correspond. A study has been conducted by linguists and geneticists to compare linguistic (cultural) and biological differences among the Yanomamö Indians of South America. Although they reside in 150 or more villages in a relatively small area measuring 500 by 300 kilometers, the Yanomamö have developed distinguishable genetic and linguistic characteristics. The researchers found that the linguistic divergence of the seven language areas corresponded significantly with the pattern of genetic microdifferentiation which they discovered. Time-depth studies also indicated that the Yanomamö dialects have been diverging for about one thousand years and that the languages had diverged at least one thousand years earlier than that.[7]

Extinction

The fossil record is replete with the eloquent testimony of species that had their day and survive no longer. Extinction is the outcome of failure to adapt to environmental change, whether the change occurred in other organisms, climate, or geology.

Evolution has diversified the forms of life from its beginnings in the Paleozoic era. New forms have generally become more complex and more varied. The primates represent the most complex of all living orders. By virtue of our nervous system, humans are the most complex creatures of all. We are the product of the interacting forces that have just been summarized.

SUMMARY

The evolution of life has consisted of the continuous development of greater complexities and varieties of living organisms. Evolution is the result of genetic variation and adaptation to specific environments through natural selection. The continuity of life is maintained by cellular reproduction involving mitosis, which is the process by which the original cell is duplicated. In bisexual reproduction, however, gametes, through meiosis, receive only half the usual number of chromosomes, so that when male and female gametes join, the fertilized egg, or zygote, will have the normal complement of chromosomes. Which chromosome goes into which gamete is a matter of chance. Thus all individuals have unique genotypes, and variation occurs. Genes are the units of DNA molecules that are the basis of specific traits. They have a standard alignment along the chromosome body. But in the formation of new chromosome pairs, parts of chromosomes may be realigned through crossing-over. When this happens, more variation results.

In addition to variation produced by gene recombination in bisexual reproduction (Mendelian variation), gametic variation is produced by mutation, population mixture, and genetic drift.

Evolution occurs whenever natural selection acts upon genetically based phenotypic variation to produce differential reproduction, that is, when organisms possessing certain genes reproduce more frequently than other organisms in the population. A Mendelian population is a localized group of species members who interbreed (exchange genes). Enduring changes in the gene pool of a population caused by natural selection produce adaptation to the environment on the part of the population. When one or more groups from an original population become isolated and adapt to different environments to the point where they can no longer interbreed, speciation has occurred. Evolution has then produced two new organic species. This is the process of adaptive radiation, through which branching, leading to different living forms, has taken place.

[7]R. S. Spielman, E. C. Migliazza, and J. V. Neel, "Regional Linguistic and Genetic Differences among Yanomamö Indians" (*Science*, vol. 184, no. 4137, May 10, 1974), pp. 637–644; also see E. Giles, "Culture and Genetics" (*Bulletins of the American Anthropological Association*, vol. 3, no. 3, part 2, September 1970), pp. 87–98.

SELECTED READINGS

Cavalli-Sforza, L. L., "The Genetics of Human Populations" (*Scientific American*, vol. 231, September 1974), pp. 81–89. An excellent article which relates genetics to physical anthropology.

Lerner, I. M., and W. J. Libby, *Heredity, Evolution, and Society* (1976). Explains the mechanics and products of evolution and heredity and their meaning in human thought and affairs.

Stern, C., *Principles of Human Genetics* (1973). The third edition of an important and clearly written textbook in genetics.

4 Human Variation

CHAPTER OUTLINE

LEARNING GOALS

Define a species.

Discuss the two approaches for describing human variation.

Specify how variation in adaptation to different geographical environment is manifested.

Discuss the use of clinal studies.

Explain the concept of geographical races.

Determine the relative importance of racial differences.

Assess the relationship between race, cultural history, and intelligence.

All the living members of the hominid family form one genus and one species, *Homo sapiens* (see Chapter 5, pages 79–81, for the biological classification of humans). Within this species there are no two individuals (except for identical twins) who are exactly alike in genetic makeup. Beyond the variability of a local group, anyone can observe different clusters of physical traits in different populations. When such populations differ in the incidences of alleles of some genes, they are commonly referred to as human races, varieties, or subspecies.[1] For a discussion of alleles, see Chapter 3, page 51.)

REASONS FOR STUDYING HUMAN VARIABILITY

Anthropologists study human variability and the geographic distribution of human genetic traits for several reasons. First, since visible human variation seems to be central to many of the world's social and political problems, it is desirable to separate the biological aspects of human variation from the cultural ones. Second, by identifying the biological variations of human populations, anthropologists and human biologists hope to understand the population processes which differentiate individuals and groups from one another.

In Chapter 3 the mechanisms which produce genetic variability were summarized as the foundation of organic structure and evolution. We are now interested in what it is that produces differences within *Homo sapiens sapiens.*

CLOSED AND OPEN GENETIC SYSTEMS: SPECIES AND SUBSPECIES

In Chapter 3 a Mendelian population was defined as a localized grouping of members of a species who interbreed and who occasionally breed with members of other populations within the species. A species was defined as one or more populations whose members are capable of interbreeding and are incapable of breeding with members of other species or do not habitu-

[1] I. M. Lerner and W. J. Libby, *Heredity, Evolution, and Society*, p. 315.

FIGURE 4.1
The kinds of human variation are readily apparent at the United Nations General Assembly. (Courtesy of the United Nations.)

ally do so. Thus, a species is characterized by (1) common inheritance among the members, (2) capacity of the genes to spread throughout the group, and (3) inhibition of gene flow to other groups.[2] Each species is, therefore, genetically isolated from other species. It is a *closed genetic system*. Members of the species *Homo sapiens* are incapable of breeding with any other animal.

Within a species, however, populations are found which possess gene pools in which certain genes occur in frequencies different from the frequencies of those in other populations. These populations may be distinguished as subspecies. They have differing gene pools. However, the members of the populations can interbreed and exchange genes. They constitute *open genetic systems*.

Within a species, gene pools can be altered by genetic inputs from other populations; genetic changes that are not the result of population mixture or mutations can also take place through genetic drift.

If the changes within a gene pool of a population accumulate to the point where breeding can no longer take place with other populations, then the two populations have become separate species. There is no evidence that any such genetically isolated subgroups of *Homo sapiens* have existed, at least since Middle Pleistocene times, and that is why we can say there is only one human species, *Homo sapiens*.

The classification of human beings has caused problems for anthropologists and geneticists because the gene pool of the species is an open one. There have been two approaches to describing human variation: the racial approach and the clinal approach. In the racial (or typological) approach, human groups are classified by observable physical traits of unknown or complex inheritance, such as skin color, eye color, eyelid form, hair color, hair form, stature, body form, facial bone structure, and so on. An attempt is then made to assign geographic boundaries for each group, and each group is assigned an "ideal" set of physical characteristics.

[2]Ibid., pp. 19–20.

Although many racial classifications have been proposed over the past 200 years, anthropologists are aware that the differences between populations included in those classifications are less than the differences within them.

Opinions on the number of races range from three major branches to over 200. Dobzhansky indicates that the more studies are conducted on human populations, the less clear-cut the races seem. The problem is better stated in his words:

> *The difficulty is fundamental. Biological species are genetically closed systems; races are genetically open ones. Species do not interbreed and do not exchange genes, or do so rarely; they are reproductively ioslated. The gene pools of the species man, chimpanzee, gorilla, and orang are quite separate; gene interchanges do not occur between these species. . . .*
>
> *Not so with races. Mankind, the human species, has been a single evolutionary unit, at least since the mid-Pleistocene epoch (Ice Age). It continues to be a single unit, all segregations and apartheids notwithstanding.*[3]

The clinal approach to the classification of human groups involves determining the geographic distribution or gradients of single-trait variants without regard to any defined population. This approach is based on the view that "the study of single genes is probably more useful for reconstructing a common ancestry than the study of superficial traits or of bone shape and size, which are probably the effects of many genes and are subject to short-term environmental effects."[4]

In the clinal approach, individuals are tested

[3]T. Dobzhansky, "Race Equality," in R. H. Osborne, *The Biological and Social Meaning of Race*, pp. 15–16.

[4]L. L. Cavalli-Sforza, "The Genetics of Human Populations," p. 89.

for a variety of physical traits, including those of known genetic inheritance, such as blood groups and hemoglobin structure. Each local population is then characterized by the frequency of the trait or allele. Clinal maps can then be drawn, showing variation in frequencies of each trait among various populations.

NATURAL SELECTION AND CLINAL DISTRIBUTION

Natural selection is only one process by which the composition of gene pools may be altered. It is, however, the major process by which populations achieve more efficient adaptation to specific environments. Some genes in a Mendelian population are either selected for, greatly reduced in frequency, or eliminated altogether. Naturally selected genetic traits may not coincide in distribution with geographically localized populations. For example, although sickle-cell anemia (pages 53–57) has the highest gene frequency in the African and Afro-American populations, it also occurs in other populations living within 15 to 30 degrees on either side of the equator. The frequency distribution of sickle-cell genes is clearly related to the prevalence of malaria and cuts across a number of geographic groupings.

Variation in Adaptation to Geographical Environment

There are a number of visible human traits which have variable distribution and which are believed to be linked to adaptive functions through natural selection. They include pigmentation, body size, and relative prominence of protruding body parts. These relations are generalized in Gloger's, Bergmann's, and Allen's rules.

1. *Gloger's rule.* Mammals and birds which inhabit warm and humid regions have more melanin pigmentation than those of the same species found in cooler and drier regions; arid regions are characterized by populations with an accumulation of yellow and reddish-brown pigmentation.
2. *Bergmann's rule.* The smaller-sized representatives of a species are found in the warmer parts of the area, the larger-sized specimens in the cooler districts.
3. *Allen's rule.* Protruding body parts, such as tails, ears, and bills, are relatively shorter in the cooler parts of the range of the species than in the warmer parts.[5]

Gloger's Rule and Human Skin Color

Do tropic dwellers in fact have more melanin pigment than people who inhabit colder and drier climates?

Most human beings have relatively light-colored skin, which, if not covered by clothing, tans in strong light as a response to natural ultraviolet radiation. Those exposed constantly to sunlight become quite dark the year round. Those who live in middle latitudes go through an annual cycle of skin coloring, tanning in the summer and bleaching in the winter. In order to ascertain the standard (unmodified) skin color of a person, skin-color tests must be taken near the armpit.

Dark skin color results from high melanin content. It is fairly constant and subject to little or no seasonal variation. The original geographic distribution of this genetic trait is along the tropic regions of the Old World within 10 to 20 degrees of the equator (Figure 4.2).

Of several hypotheses which have been advanced to provide functional explanations for variation in skin color among human populations, the one that applies the physiological effects of vitamin D is the most impressive.

Vitamin D is necessary to the absorption of calcium from the human intestine. Calcium is necessary to bone development and mainte-

[5]C. S. Coon, "Climate and Race," in H. Shapley (ed.), *Climatic Change*, p. 14.

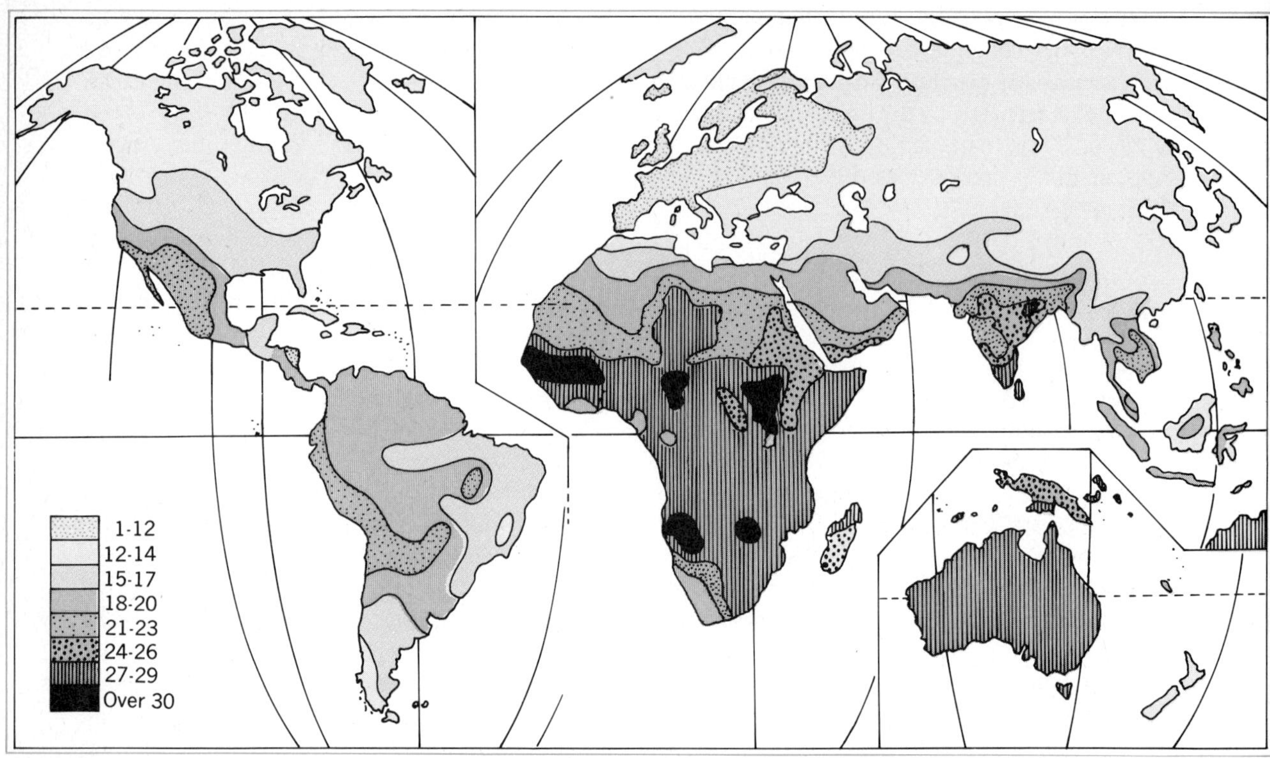

FIGURE 4.2
Worldwide distribution of intensity of pigmentation (color) of skin, according to Biasutti. 1–12 represents the lightest skinned peoples and over 30 the darkest skinned peoples. This distribution of human skin color disregards European and African population movements into the New World and the Pacific after 1400 A.D. (Adapted from Coon, *The Living Races of Man*, with permission of Alfred Knopf.)

nance. Vitamin D deficiency results in soft bones and rickety bodies. Most diets do not provide enough of the vitamin to maintain calcium absorption at an adequate level. Prior to the practice of vitamin D enrichment of foods, the only way to overcome a dietary insufficiency of this vitamin was its manufacture by the human body, stimulated by absorption of ultraviolet rays from sunlight. However, too much vitamin D (hypervitaminosis D) causes calcification of soft tissues and contributes to skin cancer. Skin cancer should have no effect on natural selection, however, since it usually occurs after the reproductive period is ended. Calcification of the soft tissues could eliminate those people who are overreactive to ultraviolet radiation, and they could be selected out of populations living in areas of intensive sunshine. It is hypothesized that in equatorial latitudes dark skin prevents hypervitaminosis D by screening out unnecessary amounts of ultraviolet light so that overdosing with internally produced vitamin D is prevented.[6]

[6]Lerner and Libby, op. cit., p. 328.

In the nonforested regions of the tropics, the adaptive usefulness of black or near-black skin under the high and constant equatorial sun is clear. However, some of the equatorial region in which the black peoples live is rain forest and has been so in the past, at least in postglacial times. Much larger areas of the world are open parkland, desert, and water. It is here that the adaptation of black skin occurred. In the Americas, the more open areas of the western equatorial region have a heavy, permanent cloud cover. This, and the relatively short inhabitation of these regions, should account for the absence of dark pigment in the aboriginal New World.

At the opposite extreme of the color spectrum is the skin which sunburns but does not tan. This characteristic is confined to a very small minority of the world population located in the cloudy areas of northwestern Europe. For these people, the conditions of natural selection were reversed. Those who did not get enough ultraviolet rays because of dark skin color became undercalcified, suffered from rickets, and did not survive to pass on their genetic heritage. Northland populations thus became progressively less pigmented as those with lower melanin production survived at a higher ratio.

This explanation for the evolution of differently pigmented populations is very interesting and suggestive, but it has not been proved. Also, the present distribution of skin color is as much the result of historical events as of differential selection.

Bergmann's Rule and Human Body Size Bergmann's rule for warm-blooded animals states that the smaller the skin area relative to total body volume, the lower the loss of body heat, and vice versa. Tall, lean persons have more skin area relative to body volume than do short, stocky people. A short and stocky Eskimo physique conserves body heat, while the long, lanky physique of the Nilotic Negro (Figure 4.3) helps to dissipate it. Bergmann's rule applies with moderate consistency to human beings. Heavier populations are concentrated in the north, while slighter ones are found in equatorial regions.

Allen's Rule and Human Bodily Extremities The shape of the protruding parts of the body facilitates or inhibits heat loss. Populations in hot climates have longer extremities. Desert Negroes as well as desert Caucasoids have long limbs and slim torsos. The forehead and hands are the concentrated sweat areas. A long, narrow head and long hands allow greater heat dissipation, which is especially important for the brain. Heat control in the hands and feet is more than a matter of sweating, however. The capillary system in the hands acts like the thermostat at the head of the engine block in a water-cooled automobile, which controls the flow of water to the radiator according to temperature. In high temperatures, arterial blood returning to the heart flows through the close-to-the-surface veins on the back of the hand. When the temperature drops below a critical threshold, vasoconstriction shuts down blood flow to the surface arteries, while vasodilation opens it to the deeper-lying ones. Thus internal heat, carried in the blood, is conserved.

Other Adaptations The cranial features of Mongoloid populations are all thought to be adaptations to the extreme cold: round heads; flat cheekbones; small, flat noses; heavy layers of subcutaneous fat; and fatty double eyelids, which produce an internal epicanthic fold, or almond-shaped eye (see Figure 4.4). Theoretically, these adaptations took place among the Northeast Asian populations during the Upper Pleistocene. They are, of course, characteristic of Eskimos and many North Asian local populations.

Thus, some human variability has been tentatively associated with the effects of selective adaptation in relation to the differing environ-

FIGURE 4.3
The long-limbed Batutsi of Burundi (right), with their lean torsos, exemplify bodily adaptation to hot climates. This body shape produces the largest heat-dissipating skin area relative to total body volume. On the other hand, the short-limbed arctic Mongoloids, such as the Chukchi female (left), with their large, heavy torsos, exemplify bodily adaptation to cold climates. This body shape produces the smallest skin area relative to body volume. Surface radiation is minimal and body heat is more effectively preserved. (Right, United Nations; left, courtesy of the American Museum of Natural History.)

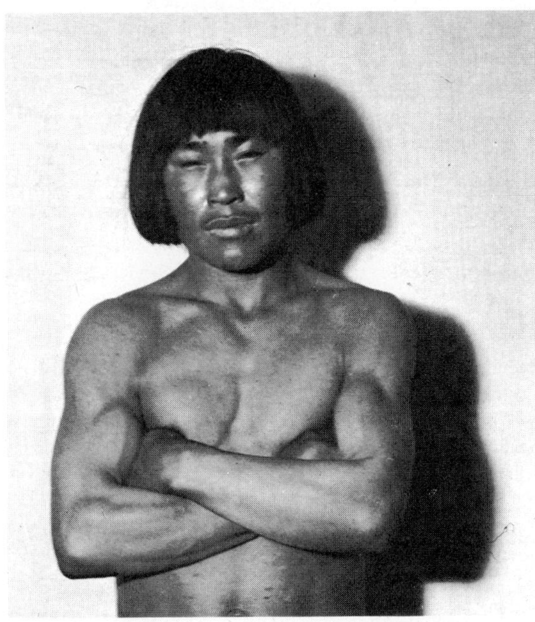

FIGURE 4.4
Adaptation to extreme cold climate in the arctic Mongoloid face. A Greenland Eskimo with heavy subcutaneous fat covering the cheeks, the flat nose, and heavy double eyelids. (Courtesy of the American Museum of Natural History.)

ments of various populations.[7] Experimental observations have thus far been too limited, and research techniques too underdeveloped, to account for all geographic distributions of human variations in terms of naturally selected traits. Further, some naturally selective forces are not necessarily limited to one, or even a few, restricted geographical locations.

In summary, one of the mechanisms which produces variation in gene frequencies among populations *is* the process of natural selection. This process can produce geographically patterned variation, if the selective factors occur in geographic patterns. But at the same time, some population variations which are due to environmentally selective factors may not coincide with geographic differences between, or within, continents.

Clinal Studies, the Nonrace Theory, and Selective Trait Patterning

As we have seen, in *clinal studies* individual traits are analyzed and the geographic distribution of their variants is mapped. Figure 4.2 offers an example of this method. It shows the worldwide distribution of intensity of skin color. The lines, which are called *clines*, are smoothed curves connecting geographic locations from which similar degrees of skin color have been reported. In conception, it is similar to a conventional weather map with isobars which run through weather stations reporting similar barometric readings. There are two related purposes to a clinal approach.

Clinal distributions of several traits can be mapped together to determine coincidental geographical distributions of their variants. Such clustering might be the product of geographically related forces of natural selection acting in unison on the variants of several traits. So far, analysts, such as the physical anthropologist Frank Livingstone, find no such coincidental clusterings and feel that this demonstrates the lack of significant correlation between geographically distributed populations and naturally selected traits. *The logical extension of this point of view would be that biologically there are no races of humankind.* Rather, it would hold that humanity constitutes one large, intraspecific gene pool.[8]

The implications of separating the consideration of naturally selective trait patterning (revealed in the correlation of clines to environments) from the identification of geographically located Mendelian populations must then be

[7]See P. T. Baker, "The Biological Adaptation of Man to Hot Deserts," in T. W. McKern (ed.), *Readings in Physical Anthropology*, pp. 174–185; R. W. Newman, "Human Adaptation to Heat," in A. Damon (ed.), *Physiological Anthropology*, pp. 80–92.

[8]F. B. Livingstone, "On the Non-existence of Human Races" (*Current Anthropology*, vol. 3, 1962), p. 297; and C. L. Brace, "On the Race Concept" (*Current Anthropology*, vol. 5, 1964), pp. 313–314.

understood as a product of two processes which cause trait patterns. First, naturally selected traits can produce geographical patterning in human variation. Second, nonrandom breeding patterns of Mendelian populations can produce genetic drift (pages 57–58) in the patterning of human variation. It is important to perceive the two patterning processes separately. For this reason geographic racial classifications must be viewed as analytic tools to isolate and describe *general* patterns of population variations. Also, clinal studies isolate and describe *single* trait patterns of human population variation. Combinations of the two kinds of studies can aid in analyzing the processes which produce and pattern variation. Racial classification is not a scientific end product but rather a tool for analysis. Such analysis, it is hoped, will lead to a better

FIGURE 4.5
The European, Asiatic, and African races dominate the world scene in the twentieth century both in numbers and in geography. European immigration has swamped the original American population except in Middle America and central South America. Immigration, has had a similar effect in Australia. Asiatics have expanded into the once-glaciated areas of their continent and southeast into Indonesia. Asiatic migration into the southwest Pacific has severely reduced the Pygmy peoples. The southward migration of Africans in Africa has reduced the Pygmies and Bushmen to small, barely surviving remnants. Africans, brought as slaves, are found in southeast North America and northwest South America. (Adapted from W. W. Howells, "The Distribution of Man," in W. S. Laughlin and R. H. Osborne (eds.), *Human Variation and Origins*.)

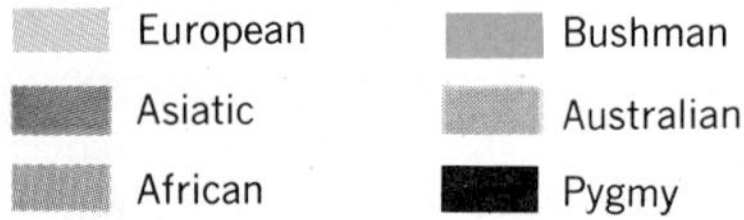

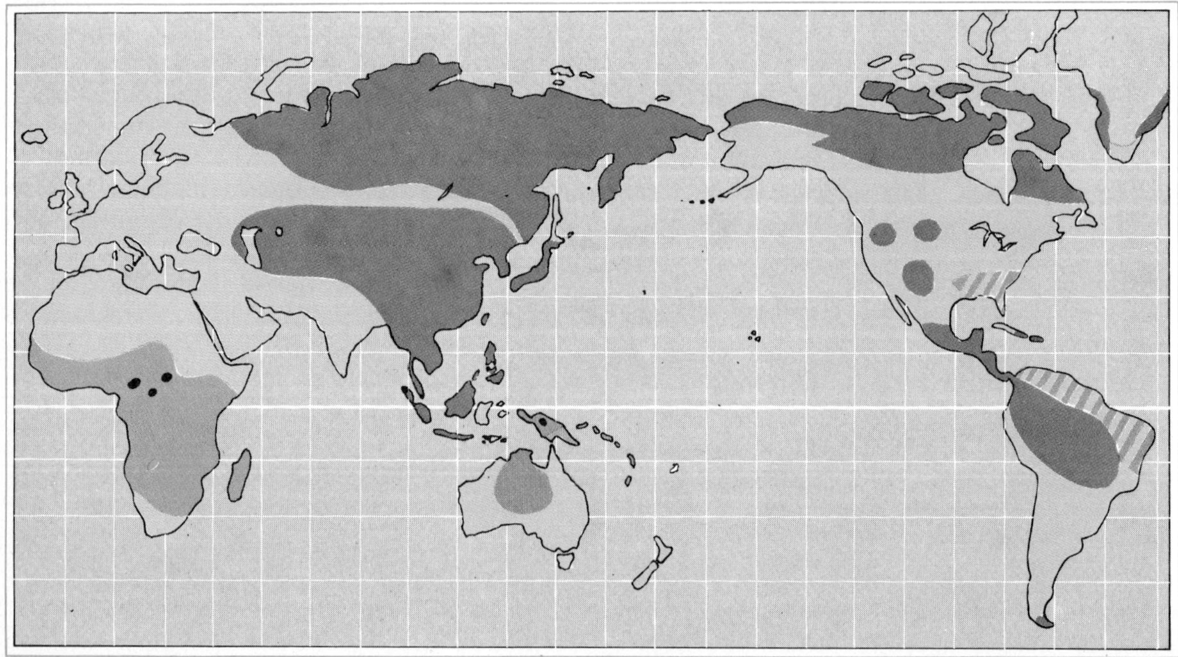

understanding of human variation and how it arose.

GEOGRAPHIC RACES

The kind of population commonly meant when people talk about race is an aggregation of people who have inhabited in the past, and who still inhabit to a great extent, a given continent or a large section of a continent. The effect of geographic barriers on prehistoric populations can be seen in Figure 4.5. Such populations tend to be sufficiently isolated from the inhabitants of other continents so that they share more common ancestors among themselves than they share with other populations on other continents.

Local Races

Within a continent, there may be barriers to easy intermixture of the continental population. Thus, the people of the North Baltic area breed among themselves to a much greater extent than they do with the people of the Mediterranean belt of southern Europe. They can be distinguished as subpopulations, localized over broad areas *within* a continent or island chain. This produces a lower-level classification of races, such as the Nordic, Alpine, and Mediterranean within the European. Some physical anthropologists would push the analysis further and distinguish even more narrowly defined local races in the Balkan area, for example, where an unusual cranial shape, called "sugarloaf," and certain other physical features are common, thus identifying a so-called Armenoid race. The Basques of the Pyrenees are another example of a local race. There is no agreement on just how many local races one could identify in the world. Garn and Coon suggest that the number might be about thirty.[9]

[9] S. M. Garn and C. S. Coon, "On the Number of Races of Mankind" (*American Anthropologist*, vol. 57, 1955), pp. 996–1001. Also S. M. Garn, *Human Races*, chap. 2.

The Relative Importance of Racial Differences

Lewontin has analyzed the distribution of variability among and within major human races. Nine blood groups and eight serum proteins and red-blood-cell enzymes were used in this analysis. Each population studied was given equal importance, in spite of varying sizes, so that any measure of human diversity would not be decreased.

How to classify races posed problems for Lewontin. Although most people argue that different races of humans exist, racial boundary lines must be arbitrary. For instance, no one can objectively provide a dividing line "in the continuum from South American Indians through Polynesians, Micronesians, Melanesians to Papuans."[10] Lewontin's racial classification was based on genetic divergence, and it included seven major races, each with subpopulations. The results of this study are enlightening: genetic traits such as blood groups provide less bias in studying human variation; physical appearance varies greatly from one population to another; and, genetic variability is actually greater within "races" than between them.

Although this classification is useful for distinguishing the more obvious populations in the world, Lewontin still has reservations. He states: "Human racial classification is of no social value and is positively destructive of social and human relations. Since such racial classification is now seen to be of virtually no genetic or taxonomic significance either, no justification can be offered for its continuance."[11]

Blood Groups and Other Simple Genetic Traits

Almost everyone is familiar with the existence of the O, A, B, and AB blood types. The blood-

[10] R. C. Lewontin, "The Apportionment of Human Diversity," in T. Dobzhansky, M. K. Hecht, and W. C. Steere (eds.), *Evolutionary Biology*, p. 385.

[11] Ibid., p. 397.

clotting agents were the first to be isolated (antigen A and antigen B). Type O blood is immune to the effect of both antigens; hence it can ordinarily be used in transfusions to any other person (O-type persons are universal donors). Type A can be transfused to types A and AB, but not to type B. Type B can be transfused to types B and AB, but not to type A.

Soon after blood types were discovered, it was noticed that the ABO allele frequencies vary among human populations. It was observed that most European populations show from 50 to 79 percent O, 20 to 39 percent A, and 1 to 14 percent B. In sharp contrast, some American Indian tribes revealed almost all O, little A, and virtually no B. For example, the Navajo exhibit around 83 percent O, almost 17 percent A, and just 0.4 percent B. The Mato Grosso Indians of Brazil show 100 percent O allele! Compared with the allele frequencies of Europeans, here is surely a clear-cut population difference. Among Asians, the allele frequencies show roughly from 50 to 70 percent O, 15 to 25 percent A, and 15 to 25 percent B. Local populations within the larger geographic populations just mentioned vary in O, A, and B distributions to some extent, but the major differences follow the trend indicated.[12]

The advantage of blood types as genetic criteria of subspecies is that they are discrete traits. A type is either present or absent in a

[12]J. Underwood, *Biocultural Interactions and Human Variation*, pp. 3–4; Harrison G. A., et al., *Human Biology*, pp. 255–257; F. E. Johnston, *Microevolution of Human Populations*, pp. 36–47.

FIGURE 4.6
The frequencies of the genes A, B, and O, of the ABO blood-group system, are shown in (a), (b), and (c), respectively. (Redrawn from Mourant, Kopec, and Sobczak, *The Distribution of Human Blood Groups* (2d ed.), 1976.

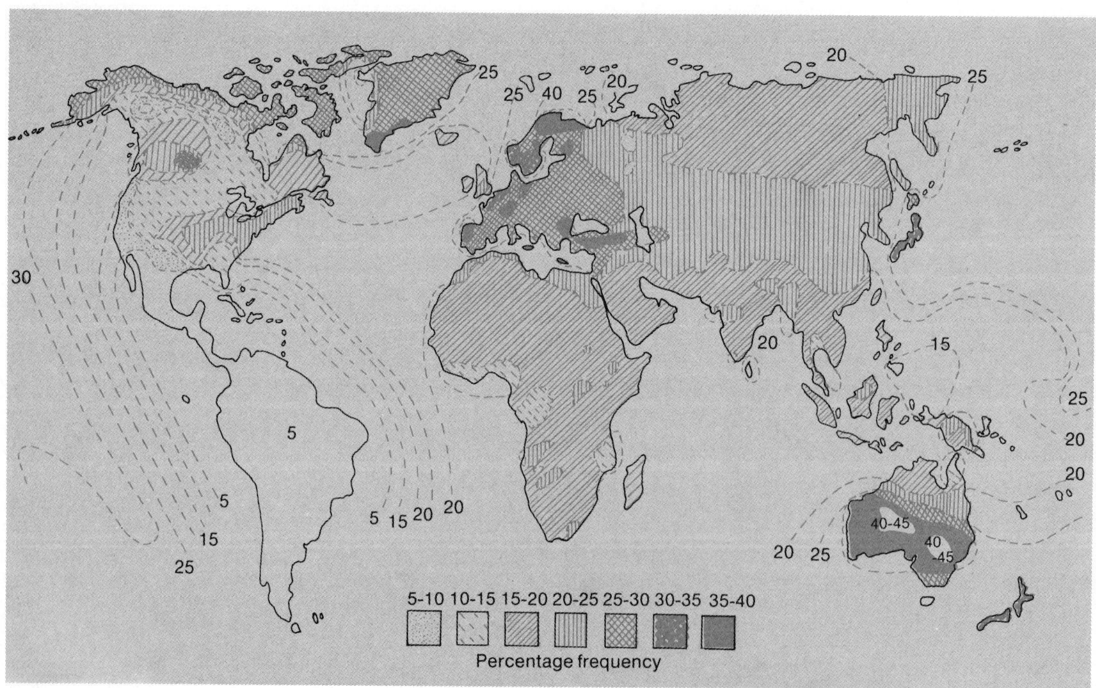

(a)

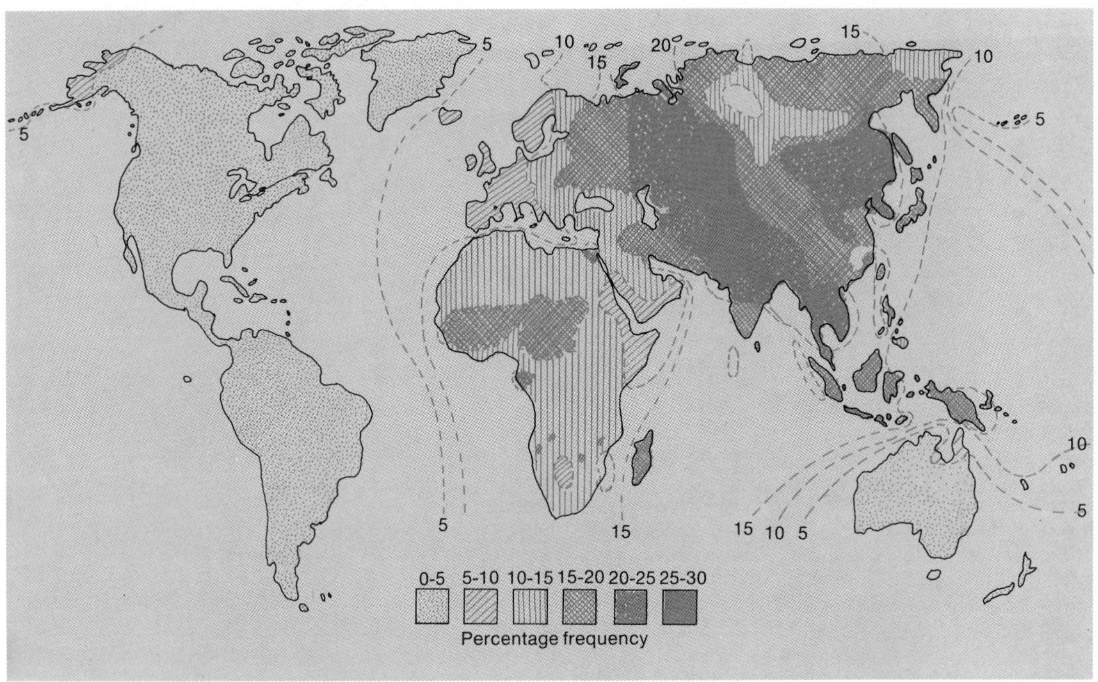
0-5 5-10 10-15 15-20 20-25 25-30
Percentage frequency

(b)

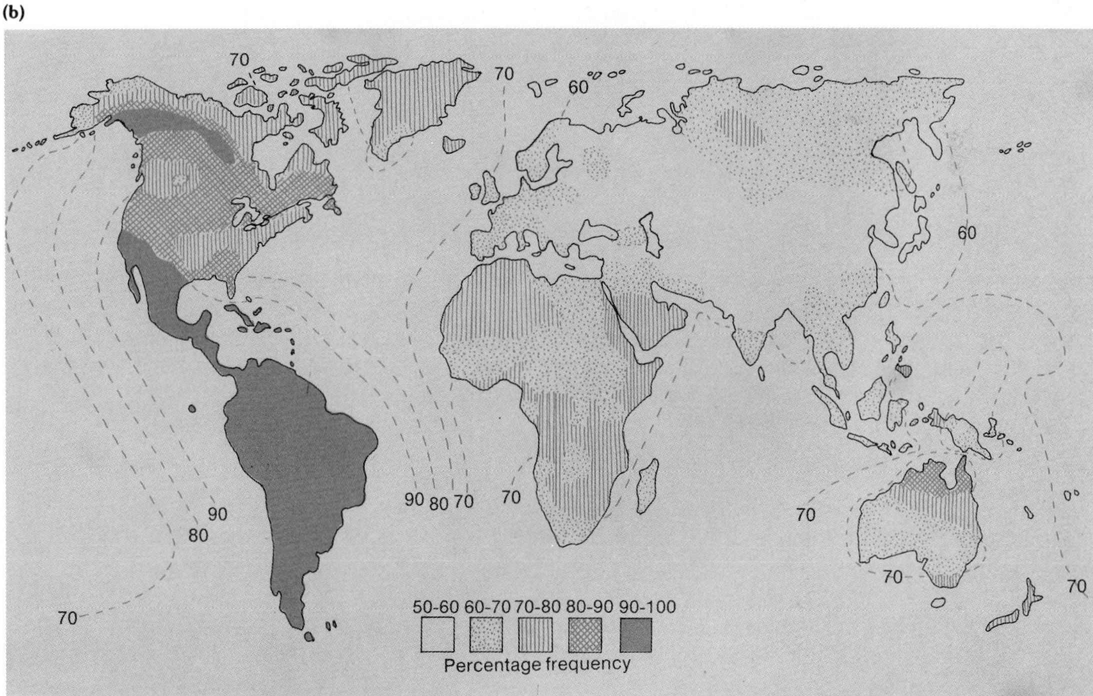
50-60 60-70 70-80 80-90 90-100
Percentage frequency

(c)

person. It is neither ambiguous, as is "olive skin," nor continuously variable, as is stature. Therefore, the gene distribution in the population for a number of blood types can be precisely calculated.

There may be some selective advantage of the ABO blood group alleles. It has been shown, for example, that the *anopheles* mosquito, which transmits malaria and other destructive diseases in parts of Africa, prefers to take blood from persons of O type. This would give persons of A and B types a selective advantage in that they would be bitten less often and therefore receive immunity reactions rather than the lethal disease.[13]

In addition to the classic blood types, numerous other blood systems have been discovered. These include the M and N types and the Rh negative and positive, as well as several

[13]C. S. Wood, "Preferential Feeding of *Anopheles gambiae* Mosquitoes on Human Subjects of Blood Group O: A Relationship between the ABO Polymorphism and Malaria Vectors" (*Human Biology*, vol. 46, 1974), pp. 385–404.

TABLE 4.1
Distribution of Major Blood-group Systems

Blood-group system (alleles in parentheses)	**Description of phenotype frequencies**
A, B, O (including A_1 and A_2)	O most common group; over 50% of individuals in most populations are of this type. B nearly absent in aboriginal America and Australia, and progressively more common in Europe (15%), Africa, India, and Asia (up to 40%). A_2 practically limited to Europe.
MNS, U (or S^u)	American Indians almost exclusively M. N most common in Australia and the Pacific. MS and NS absent in Australia. U-negative rare and apparently limited to Africa.
Rh (CDe, Cde, cDE, etc.)	Rh-negative individuals (rh) rare or absent in most of the world, but approximately 15% of Europeans are Rh-negative. Of the Rh-positive alleles (R_1, R_2, etc.), the R_0 form is found primarily in Africa (up to 70%).
Duffy (Fy^a, Fy^b, Fy)	Most Australians and Polynesians and 90–99% of Asians are Duffy-positive (Fy^a), 90% of Indics, 85–90% of most American Indians, 65% of populations of England and America, and 27% of Afro-Americans. Fy^a very low in Africa, but the gene Fy extremely common (>80%).
Diego (Di^a, Di^b)	Diego-positive (Di^a) individuals limited to Amerindians (2–20%) and Asians. Di^a absent in Europe, Africa, Australia, Micronesia, and Polynesia and in Eskimos.
Kidd (Jk^a, Jk^b)	Kidd-positive (Jk^a) most common in West Africa and Afro-Americans (>90%), North American Indians (70–90%), and Europeans (approximately 70%) and least common in Chinese (50–55%).

SOURCE: Based on S. M. Garn, *Human Races*, p. 47.

subtypes—the Lewis, Lutheran, Kell, Duffy, Kidd, and others. The distribution of the major blood-group systems, by geographical race, is shown in Table 4.1.

The A antigens fall into two subtypes, A_1 and A_2. It is significant that the A occurring in American Indians, Asiatics, Pacific Islanders, and Australoids is all A_1.

Rh-negative genes occur in about 15 percent of Europeans. They are absent among the Asians, Australians, Pacific Islanders, and American Indians. The Mongoloid affinity of the American Indian has apparently been confirmed.

Beyond blood groupings, not much progress has thus far been made in isolating easily identifiable genes for studying human variability. However, an interesting gene is the one that determines the ability to perceive a bitter taste in phenylthiocarbamide (PTC).

The allele for tasting ability (T) is inherited as a Mendelian dominant over the nontasting allele (t). In the United States, 70 percent of the population are tasters, and 30 percent are nontasters. In terms of gene frequency, this means that 55 percent of the United States population carry the t gene.[14] Within a sample of Navajo Indians, the proportion of nontasters is only 2 percent. The frequency of the t allele in this Navajo population is 0.02, or 14 percent. This is a significant difference. Although few populations have been tested for T, t, the indications are "that the results for the tasting gene parallel in general what has already been observed for the Rh negative and A_2 genes, that is, that European populations tend to differ rather strikingly from Mongoloid populations. In both cases there is insufficient information about the Africans."[15]

[14]The frequency of a recessive gene in the gene pool is equal to the square root of the genotypes for the recessive gene in the population: $\sqrt{0.30} = 0.55$.

[15]*See* W. C. Boyd, *Genetics and the Races of Man*, p. 281; F. S. Hulse, *The Human Species*, chap. 11, provides a comprehensive summary of blood-type distributions as of 1971, including a number of useful maps.

Apparently, the ability to taste PTC has some adaptive significance. PTC has a similar chemical structure to the substance which causes nodular goiter (a disease of the thyroid), and persons with this disease have a significantly high incidence of PTC nontasting ability. Also, tasters contract fewer cavities in their childhood dentition than do nontasters.

RACE AND INTELLIGENCE

In 1777, when the American Colonies were struggling to win their war of independence, William Robertson wrote:

> *A human being . . . is everywhere the same. At his first appearance in the state of infancy, whether it be among the rudest savages, or in the most civilized nations, we can discern no quality which marks any distinction or superiority. The capacity of improvement seems to be the same and the talents he may afterwards acquire, as well as the virtues he may be rendered capable of exercising, depend, in a great measure, upon the state of society in which he is placed. To this state his mind naturally accommodates itself, and from it receives discipline and culture.*[16]

Time has not altered, nor the doctrines of racism impaired, the clarity of this simple truth.

In this century, there have been numerous efforts, beginning with the first intelligence tests administered to American soldiers during World War I, to ascertain whether there are significant differences in the behavioral potentials of different races. After many years of ingenious psychological measurements, the evidence is largely inconclusive.

What the link is between heredity and intelligence is still not completely known. However, it is known that intelligence is developed on some genetic base. The hereditary basis of intelligence is said to be *polygenic*, that is, it is influenced by

[16]W. Robertson, *The History of America*, vol. 1, pp. 368–369.

more than one gene; how many or which ones are not known.

The work done in race and intelligence so far demonstrates a number of points: (1) So-called intelligence tests measure inherited skill plus cultural experience. No test has yet been developed that can eliminate the cultural factor, and differential ratings of various groups in intelligence tests must be critically evaluated. (2) Aptitude tests reveal group differentials in visual, motor, and vocal skills, but these are subject to cultural influences. (3) Many skills of intelligence and aptitude change when the cultural environment changes. (4) Enriched or stimulating educational environments can have substantial effects on the ability of young children, but it is not clear yet whether the results are lasting. (5) Large-scale social change (such as massive educational programs) can cause large changes in average performance on intelligence tests. (6) Severe malnutrition has adverse effects on brain and cognitive development, but such severe malnourishment is uncommon in the United States. Moderate malnourishment appears not to have such severe adverse effects on cognitive development. (7) Average differences in the intelligence scores of members of different ethnic groups in the United States probably reflect cultural biases in the tests, differences in environmental conditions, and genetic differences among the groups. (8) The relative weight given to these three factors (number 7 above) depends upon the social and political biases of the interpreter, and a rather wide range of interpretation is possible on the basis of available evidence. (9) It seems clear that differences among individuals within ethnic and socioeconomic groups are greater than the differences between such groups. (10) Finally, considering the broad overlap in scores between groups and the fact that the distribution of differences is greater within groups than between groups, it is unjust and incorrect (based on available facts) to label members of one group as being inferior to members of another group.[17]

Race and Culture History

It is the judgment of anthropologists that all people are equally capable of cultural development and that culture operates independently of racial ancestry. How, then, it is often asked, can it be that some are culturally "more advanced" than others? Is it not true that the highest modern civilizations have been developed by the European whites?

Three principles must be grasped in formulating the answers to these questions: (1) Although all cultures are fundamentally similar in their nuclear cores, the range of cultural variability in human societies is truly remarkable. Limits to the range of culture are imposed by the physical nature of human beings. Cultural variation results from processes of culture growth, not from genetic inheritance. (2) The behavior and cultural ingenuity of different peoples are so variable that the racial factor is of little importance. (3) The same people may exhibit astounding cultural energy at one period of their history and be almost wholly devoid of it at another. Peoples who have been quiescent for centuries suddenly burst into a veritable fury of cultural development without any determinable change in racial composition. The Japanese are the most spectacular example in modern times.

It is easy for North Europeans and their descendants to forget how late they came to the forefront of civilization and cultural development. The centers of cultural invention did not shift to northern Europe until the Renaissance, only 500 years ago. During the Dark Ages, the Maya Indians of Central America showed greater cultural accomplishments than the European whites.

[17]For the most unbiased review by qualified scholars, see J. C. Loehlin, G. Lindzey, and J. N. Spuhler, *Race Differences in Intelligence*. The summary presented here is based largely on this work.

The history of the Uto-Aztecans is also pertinent. The Aztecs, Comanches, and Shoshones speak similar languages indicative of a common historical background. They are genetically similar, and 700 years ago they were hunters and gatherers with a simple technology, living in the western deserts of North America. Historical events radically altered their cultural development.

The Aztecs wandered southward until they settled in what is now Central Mexico among several long-established high cultures. In 1325, they founded Tenochtitlán (the present Mexico City), and 175 years later they were overlords of the land: maize growers, road builders, astronomers, artists, and possessors of a city with public buildings of cut stone so magnificent that Cortez cried out that in all Andalusia there was nothing to compare with the glory of this city.

The Comanches wandered into the southwestern plains at a somewhat later date. There they acquired Spanish horses and guns and came into contact with the warlike tradition of the Plains tribes. They became nomadic raiders and violent fighters.

The Shoshones, who retained the attitudes and culture once shared with the Comanches, obtained neither guns nor horses. They were regularly attacked by the Blackfeet, who had guns and horses, so they hid out in the desert—peaceable, because they dared not make war with the better equipped Blackfeet.

What causes cultural spurts is a complex and difficult question that must be analyzed in terms of cultural process. Outstanding among the multitude of factors is cross-fertilization of cultures, the stimulation of new ideas and new ways of coping with the environment. Isolated peoples always stagnate, whether they are Asian, African, or European. But the bent of the culture is important too—a backward-looking, ancestor-worshipping culture is not usually amenable to change and further development. The physical environment is also influential. All these can be active factors. But since it cannot be shown that people differ in the possession of mental capacities, because the performance of different groups within a single population varies so markedly through time, it becomes evident that race per se is of small moment in cultural achievement.

The UNESCO Statement on Race

In conclusion, we can do no better than cite from the *Statement on Race*, formulated in 1950 by an expert panel of physical anthropologists and geneticists convened by the United Nations Educational, Scientific, and Cultural Organization. It reads as follows:

> *We have thought it worth while to set out in a formal manner what is at present scientifically established concerning individual and group differences.*
>
> ***a.*** *In matters of race, the only characteristics which anthropologists have so far been able to use effectively as a basis for classification are physical (anatomical and physiological).*
>
> ***b.*** *Available scientific knowledge provides no basis for believing that the groups of mankind differ in their innate capacity for intellectual and emotional development.*
>
> ***c.*** *Some biological differences between human beings within a single race may be as great as or greater than the same biological differences between races.*
>
> ***d.*** *Vast social changes have occurred that have not been connected in any way with changes in racial type. Historical and sociological studies thus support the view that genetic differences are of little significance in determining the social and cultural differences between different groups of men.*
>
> ***e.*** *There is no evidence that race mixture produces disadvantageous results from a biological point of view. The social results of race mixture, whether for good or ill, can generally be traced to social factors.*[18]

[18]For the entire statement, see H. L. Shapiro, "Revised Version of UNESCO Statement on Race" (*American Journal of Physical Anthropology*, vol. 10, 1952), pp. 363–368.

SUMMARY

All humanity constitutes a single species. Species are closed genetic systems in that while all normal members of the species population are capable of interbreeding, they cannot interbreed outside the species. Within the species there may be Mendelian populations, which are localized groupings of species members who interbreed and occasionally breed with members of other populations. They represent open genetic systems.

There are two lines of approach to the study of variation in human traits. The oldest and most commonly known is to classify geographically localized populations according to observable physical traits. This results in the identification of races. The other method is to determine the geographic gradients of genetic traits according to clines. A cline is a line on a map connecting similar values of a measured trait—such as intensity of skin color (degree of pigmentation).

Natural selection is the major process by which populations genetically adapt to specific environments. Gloger's rule states that in mammals and birds, pigmentation is more intense in warm and humid regions and lessens as one moves toward the poles. Bergmann's rule states that the warmer the climate, the smaller the members of a species are in physical size, compared to those which live in cooler regions. Allen's rule states that protruding body parts are relatively shorter in the cooler areas of a species' range than in the warmer ones. These rules appear, in general, to apply to human beings.

However, some contemporary physical anthropologists hold that clinal mapping of several genetic traits does not show coincidental distribution variations. If this is indeed true, then it would follow that there are biologically no human races. The idea of race would exist as a cultural concept and a biological chimera.

Nonetheless, some physical anthropologists believe that populations may be identified as geographic and local races. Such classifications are somewhat arbitrary in that boundary delimitations between groups are difficult to place clearly and unequivocally.

The relative frequency and, in some cases, the total absence of genes for the several known blood types (for example, most American Indian groups are almost entirely O, with little A, and virtually no B) indicate that there *are* genetically different populations within *Homo sapiens*, even though the influence of natural selection in the distribution of most blood-group types is not yet known.

Finally, there is no scientifically demonstrated relationship between race and intelligence. Culture history demonstrates that the capacity to develop culture is independent of race and is the product of a number of convergent factors, such as cross-cultural stimulation and environment.

SELECTED READINGS

Downs, J. F., and H. K. Bleibtreu (eds.), *Human Variation: Readings in Physical Anthropology* (1971). An interesting and comprehensive collection representing all aspects of the subject.

Hulse, F. S., *The Human Species* (rev. ed., 1971). A good general summary with reasonable detail. Particularly useful for its summary of blood-type distributions among the populations of the world.

Johnston, F. E., *Microevolution of Human Populations* (1973). Offers a thorough discussion of the mechanics of human biology and race.

Loehlin, J. C., G. Lindzey, and J. N. Spuhler, *Race Differences in Intelligence* (1975). Presents an unbiased review of recent issues which have caused great and heated discussion.

5
The Living Primates

CHAPTER OUTLINE

LEARNING GOALS

Specify the problems inherent in classification.

Define the Linnean system of biological classification.

Discuss the characteristics of primates.

Explain what living primates are.

Determine if primate behavior can be viewed as an antecedent of culture.

An interest in humanity has led the anthropologist to study apes and monkeys, both as fossils and as living social groups. For although it is true that if you want to learn about humanity you should study human beings, it is also true that additional insights may be gained through knowledge of near relatives and ancestors. Consequently, anthropologists study primates and fossils to understand our biological background, seeking the prehuman roots of social and physical existence. In this chapter we discuss primate classification and primate behavior as they relate to problems of biological and cultural evolution. As we proceed in this chapter and later ones, many questions about classification arise. Hence, an understanding of classification is necessary.

PROBLEMS IN CLASSIFICATION

It is important to understand that a system of classification is merely *a tool created to organize knowledge.* The study of classification, called *taxonomy* (Gr. *taxis*, "arrangement," and *nomia*, "distribution"), is based upon a set of principles that define the criteria by which the phenomena in question are to be ordered.

Criteria in Classification

The criteria are (or should be) actual attributes of the phenomena. The ordering is (or should be) done according to a rational master scheme, or theory, of relationships between the classes. Similarities of structure, function, development, and evolutionary history all enter into the classification of organisms. *Structure* refers to bodily form, or *morphology; function*, to the manner in which an organ works in maintaining the organism as a whole; *development*, to the sequences in the growth process, or life history, of the organism; and *evolutionary history*, to the sequences of development of the type.

Ideally, there should be no ambiguity in the classificatory criteria according to which an object is put into one category or another. In fact, too often there exists ambiguity, confusion, contradiction, and lack of agreement. What are seen as attributes of the subjects to be classified are influenced by one's preconceptions and one's tools and techniques.

Classifications as Mental Constructs

Fossils of which there are few specimens do not offer a sufficient number of clear-cut diagnostic features for comparison and classification. A leading physical anthropologist warns us:

> *How do we decide at what taxonomic level to make the divisions we are discussing? Strange as it may seem to students and others who believe there are no ambiguous answers in science, or ought not to be, this decision is largely a matter of opinion formed from admittedly fragmentary materials. Some people prefer to emphasize distinctions, others continuities.*[1]

Thus when a very ancient and fragmentary fossil of a new type of hominoid is first discovered, the cries go up in paleontology: "It's an ape!" "It's a man!" "It's an ape-man!" The battle lines are drawn, and the war of words begins. The result has been dubbed the "chaos of anthropological nomenclature" by George Gaylord Simpson, who wryly but cogently observes:

> . . . [*T*]*he significance of differences between any two specimens has almost invariably come to be enormously exaggerated by one authority or another in this field. Here the fault is not so much a lack of taxonomic grammar as lack of taxonomic common sense or experience. Many fossil hominids have been described and named by workers with no other experience in taxonomy. They have inevitably lacked the sense of balance and the interpretive skill of zoologists who have worked extensively on larger groups of animals. It must, however, be sadly noted that even broadly equipped zoologists often seem to lose their judgment if they work on hominids. Here factors of prestige, of personal involvement, of emo-*

[1] J. Buettner-Janusch, *Origins of Man*, p. 164.

tional investment rarely fail to affect the fully human scientist, although they hardly trouble the workers on, say, angleworms or dung beetles.[2]

Many hominid fossils have been discovered or first identified by amateurs for whom the urge to convince the world that they have found a new ancestor is well-nigh irresistible. Each stakes a claim by posting a new genus, or at least a new species, label on the creature. Others counter with what they consider to be more suitable labels. And so a single find may receive a variety of Latin sobriquets, and a number of different finds which should properly be grouped within a single classification are put into separate pigeonholes with different names.

The famous Java fossil (see pages 130–134) is an example of what has too often taken place. The discoverer, Eugene Dubois, named the fossil *Pithecanthropus erectus:* genus, *ape-man;* species, *upright.* Three decades later, a leading American evolutionist, Henry Fairfield Osborn, argued that the specimen was not an ape at all, but that it belonged to an ancient fossil hominid who had not evolved far enough to be classed as *Homo;* therefore, he proposed to call the find *Paleoanthropus trinilensis:* genus, *ancient man;* species, *of Trinil* (the locality of discovery). Today, the consensus of European and American specialists is to designate the type as *Homo erectus erectus:* genus, *human;* species, *upright;* variety, *upright.*

If, therefore, inconsistency and contradiction occur among the names and classification systems used in this text and among the nomenclatures of other authors, there is nothing to do except to understand the provisional nature of all classifications.

However, science struggles continually to supplant disorder with order, unreason with reason, and dogma with objectively sustained theory. In this process, zoologists have arrived at a logical international formulation of rules and methods for making scientific classifications.[3] In 1962, an international symposium was convened under the auspices of the Wenner-Gren Foundation for Anthropological Research. It was not the aim of the symposium to formulate a code of primate classification, but much debris was nonetheless cleared away. The detailed results are to be found in the volume edited by S. L. Washburn, *Classification and Human Evolution.* New knowledge and experience have warranted some changes since this work.[4]

THE LINNEAN SYSTEM OF BIOLOGICAL CLASSIFICATION

It is entirely possible to classify living organisms without reference to evolutionary development, as did Carl von Linné (1707–1778), the great Swedish naturalist who devised the basic system of classification in use today. The Linnean system was synchronic: it treated all forms on a single time plane. Today, however, biologists use classification to imply common ancestry as well as physical resemblances. Two separate ideas are involved in this statement. The first rests upon the zoological proposition that two or more animal forms showing a large number of significant similarities in form and function must be more or less closely related. The second proposition is that close relationship means common ancestry. Further, the greater the detailed similarity in form and function, the more recently they shared that ancestry.

The Linnean system as now used not only groups organisms according to similarities but also implies a good deal about evolutionary relations between living forms in terms of com-

[2]G. G. Simpson, "The Meaning of Taxonomic Statements," in S. L. Washburn (ed.), *Classification and Human Evolution*, pp. 6–7. By permission of the Wenner-Gren Foundation for Anthropological Research, New York.

[3]N. R. Stoll et al., *International Code of Zoological Nomenclature*, and G. G. Simpson, *Principles of Animal Taxonomy.*

[4]"Symposium: Recent Developments in Hominoid Evolution, 1973" (*Yearbook of Physical Anthropology*, vol. 17, 1974).

mon ancestors and closeness of collateral relationships. In the system now in use, the category levels are ranked in descending order as follows:

kingdom
phylum
class
group
order
family
genus
species
variety

Intermediary categories are frequently established by use of the prefixes "super-," "sub-," and "infra-." For example,

superfamily subfamily
family infrafamily

The Taxonomy of Humans

It is not difficult to identify humans as to kingdom, phylum, and class. Each primate is clearly a member of the animal *kingdom* and not of the plant kingdom (see Figure 5.1). Because of a spinal cord and nervous system, humans belong to the *phylum* of chordates. The human spinal column of bony segments and the associated skeletal structure put us in the *subphylum* of vertebrates. The practice of nourishing the young by the female mammary glands gives us membership in the *class* of mammals. Because the unborn young are developed in the maternal womb, we are members in the *subclass* of

FIGURE 5.1
A classification of living primates. (Buettner-Janusch, 1973.)

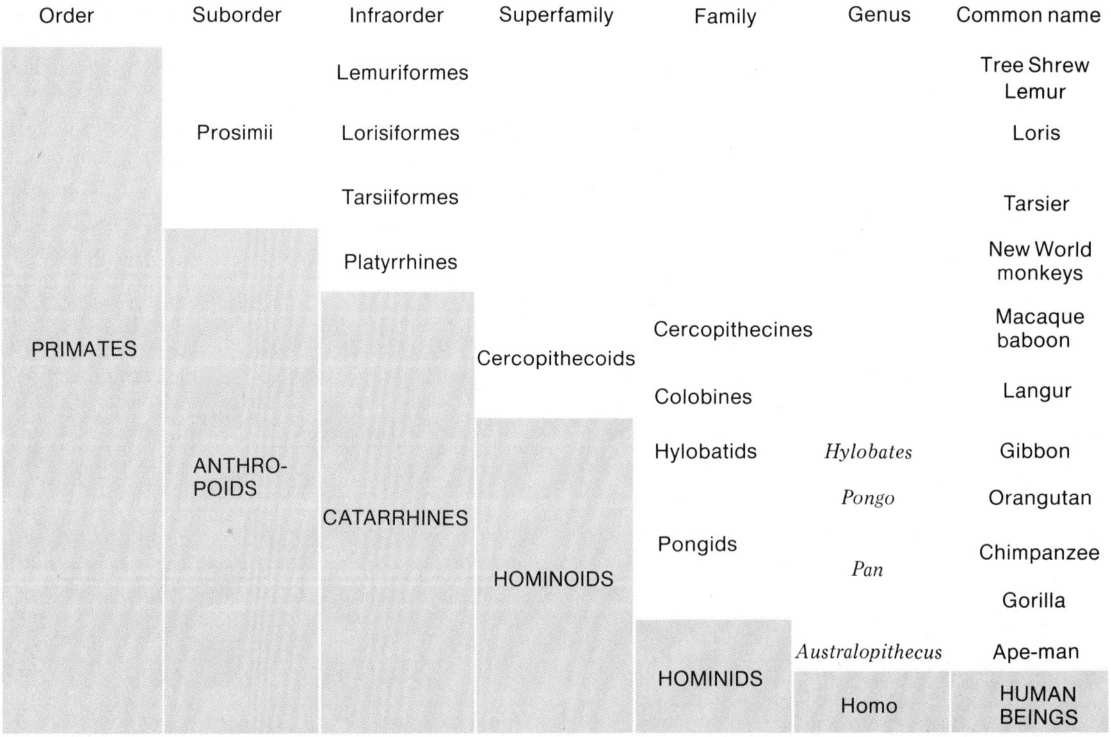

Order	Suborder	Infraorder	Superfamily	Family	Genus	Common name
PRIMATES	Prosimii	Lemuriformes				Tree Shrew Lemur
		Lorisiformes				Loris
		Tarsiiformes				Tarsier
	ANTHROPOIDS	Platyrrhines				New World monkeys
		CATARRHINES	Cercopithecoids	Cercopithecines		Macaque baboon
				Colobines		Langur
			HOMINOIDS	Hylobatids	*Hylobates*	Gibbon
				Pongids	*Pongo*	Orangutan
					Pan	Chimpanzee
						Gorilla
				HOMINIDS	*Australopithecus*	Ape-man
					Homo	HUMAN BEINGS

eutherians, within which we are identified as belonging to the *infraclass* of placentals, since the fetus is nourished directly from the bloodstream of the mother through the placenta.

Within the *order* of primates, taxonomists identify two *suborders*: (1) the anthropoids, which include all apes, monkeys, and human beings, and (2) the prosimians, which include tarsiers, lemurs, lorises, and tree shrews—the most primitive in development of the primates.

Within the suborder of anthropoids there are two *infraorders*: (1) the catarrhines (Gr. *kata*, "downward," and *rhis*, *rhinos*, "nose"), the Old World anthropoids, whose nostrils are usually narrow and closely spaced, and (2) the platyrrhines (Gr. *platys*, "broad," and *rhis*, *rhinos*, "nose"), the New World monkeys, whose nostrils are usually flat and widely spaced. A human is clearly a catarrhine. The catarrhines in turn subdivide into two *superfamilies*: (1) the hominoids, which include humans and apes, and (2) the cercopithecoids (Gr. *kerkos*, "tailed," and *pithekos*, "ape"), which include baboons, macaques, vervets, and langurs.

The hominoids group into three *families*: (1) the hominids, humans; (2) the pongids, great apes; and (3) the hylobatids, within which fall gibbons and siamangs. There are two living *genera* of pongids: (1) *Pan* and (2) *Pongo*. *Pan* is made up of at least two *species*: (1) chimpanzees and (2) gorillas. *Pongo* exists today only in the form of the orangutan, in Sumatra and Borneo. The hominid family today has but one surviving *genus*, *Homo*. It also produced one other identified *genus*, *Australopithecus*, probably ancestral to *Homo*. And finally, there is but one surviving *species* of human being, *sapiens*, and but one surviving *variety*, also called *sapiens*. For humans, then, the taxonomic identity is:

kingdom—animal
phylum—chordate
subphylum—vertebrate
class—mammal
subclass—eutheria
infraclass—placental
order—primate
suborder—anthropoid
infraorder—catarrhine
superfamily—hominoid
family—hominid
genus—homo
species—sapiens
variety—sapiens

One may say (and be quite correct) that a human is a hominid, hominoid, catarrhine, anthropoid, primate, placental, eutherian, mammalian, vertebrate, chordate animal.

THE CHARACTERISTICS OF PRIMATES

We must now backtrack a little and ask: "When is a mammal a primate, or what is distinctive about primates within the mammalian class and placental group?"

There is no absolute answer, for as Le Gros Clark has put it: "It is peculiarly difficult to give a satisfying definition of the Primates, since there is no single distinguishing feature which characterizes all the members of the group."[5]

The differences between primates and other mammals are relative; they exist mainly in degree rather than in kind. Among the primates, the major morphological differences are those which are associated with tree life; among the hominids, they are those which result from adaptations leading to upright posture and intensified manipulation (see Figures 5.2 and 5.3). In major respects they are:

1. Brain: Increasing size and complexity as one goes from prosimians to monkeys to apes to human beings.
2. Eyes: Located well forward on the skull, rather than back and toward the sides. The back

[5]W. E. Le Gros Clark, *History of the Primates*, p. 28.

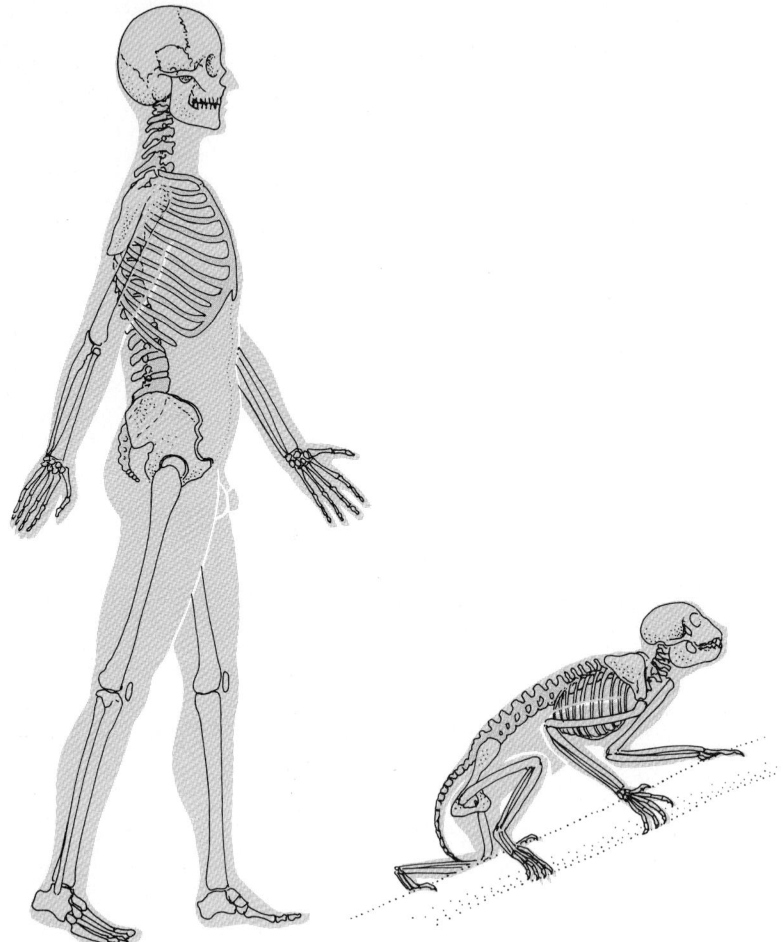

FIGURE 5.2
Skeletal modifications in the shift from pronograde (horizontal) to orthograde (vertical) posture. The spine gets a double curve; the rib cage broadens, rather than forming an underslung basket; the pelvis broadens and becomes rounded; and the skull balances above the vertebral column.

of the eye socket is closed and encircled with a bony ridge, whereas in other mammals it is open at the sides and rear. Vision is stereoscopic and very acute.

3. Face: Snout and jaws are reduced in size. Olfactory sense is also reduced.

4. Hands: (*a*) Hands are prehensile. The five-toed characteristic of primitive mammals is retained. (*b*) Claws have become flat nails on the top of the digits in most primates.
(*c*) Digits have soft, tactile pads on their undertips, richly provided with sensory nerves. Primates can feel and manipulate.

5. Feet: Retain five flexible toes, which makes extensive grasping possible, while the big toe is often prehensile. In hominids the foot is more stable and acts as a weight-bearing structure.

6. Reproductive traits: (*a*) Among adults there tends to be a continuous association of the sexes rather than association only during well-defined rutting seasons. (*b*) The female normally bears only one offspring at a time instead of a litter. (*c*) Generally, the female has only two mammary glands. (*d*) Postnatal development is relatively much more prolonged.

The human, as the most highly developed

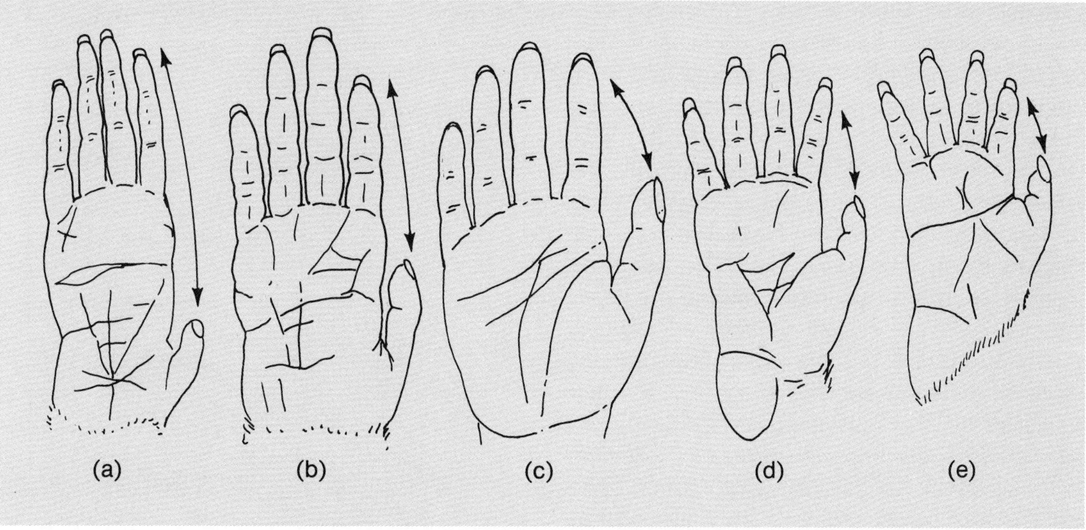

FIGURE 5.3
The fronts of primate hands, showing relation of thumbs to fingers in the retention of prehensility. (a) orangutan, *Pongo pygmaeus*; (b) chimpanzee, *Pan troglodytes*; (c) human, *Homo*; (d) baboon, *Papio*; (e) Gelada baboon, *Theropithecus*. (Biruta Akerbergs.)

primate, possesses many of the above characteristics in their most clearly distinguishable forms. This means that we have the largest and most complex brain, eyes set fully forward in completely enclosed sockets with the back walls of the orbits fully formed, the smallest jaw relative to the braincase, the most reduced snout, and the most upright posture of all primates.

Biochemical Evidence

Less visible similarities and distinctions among the primates have been identified as the result of increasingly refined laboratory techniques for blood and genetic analysis. The main results follow.

Immunology and Blood Precipitates

Refinements in serology, the study of blood, provide additional dimensions to the identification of the human as a primate. Antiserums are produced by injecting foreign substances into the bloodstream of a host animal, which produces antibodies specific to the alien substance. The clear part of the blood, the serum, is extracted to be used as an antiserum for the specific. If dog blood is injected into a host, the resulting serum is specific for dog. When this antidog serum is mixed with dog blood, it produces a white precipitate. Weaker precipitation occurs when antidog serum is mixed with the blood of any canine, but no precipitate occurs if it is mixed with noncanine blood. *Only the blood of closely similar animals reacts to the serum of a member of its order.* Thus, antihuman-specific serum produces a white precipitate when mixed with ape blood and a weaker precipitate when mixed with the blood of monkeys, but no precipitate when mixed with nonprimate bloods. Even more specifically, the hemoglobin and fibrino peptide molecules of chimpanzees and human beings are indistinguishable.

Serum Protein Patterns Current work is greatly refining the serologic proof of human relationships to other animals. By means of a process of electrophoresis, the proteins of various blood serums may be separated into from nineteen to twenty-five components showing characteristic shapes and patterns. In this process, a serum is inserted into a gel, which is placed between a positive and a negative electrode; an electric current flows between the electrodes and through the gel. The positively charged serum proteins move toward the negative pole, and the negatively charged proteins move toward the positive pole. The proteins move at differing speeds, according to their molecular weights and charges. A filter placed before each pole traps the proteins, collecting them according to their rates of motion. The similarities of serum protein shapes among humans and the other primates are shown in Figure 5.4. Inspection reveals that the patterns of the human being, gorilla, and chimpanzee are very much alike, while those of the gibbon and the orangutan are different. Thus, serum protein analysis reaffirms that humans are more closely related to the gorilla and chimpanzee than to the orangutan or gibbon. The serum patterns of other animals are found to be very unlike those of the hominoids. The cellular structure of blood protein thus confirms the more gross anatomical identification of humans with the primates.[6]

Chromosome Patterns Chromosomes, the structures on which genes are found, vary in number and in gross form among different plants

[6]M. C. King and A. C. Wilson, "Evolution at Two Levels in Humans and Chimpanzees" (*Science*, vol. 188, April 11, 1975), pp. 107–116.

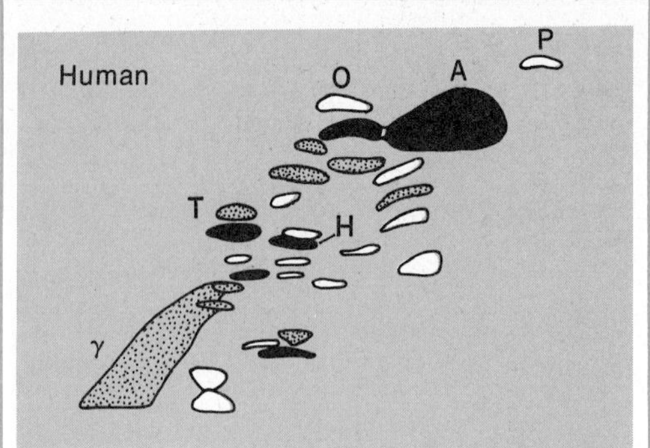

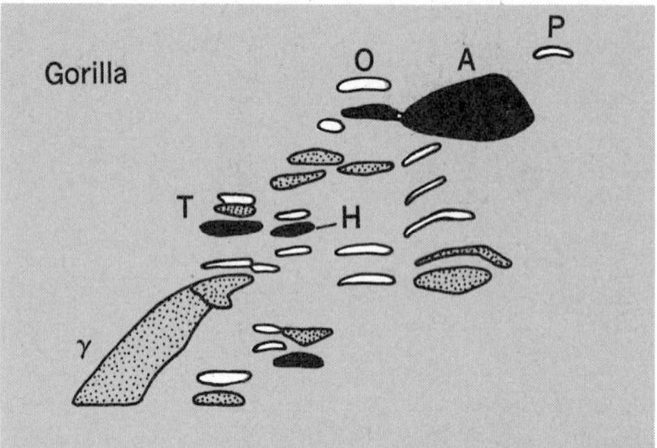

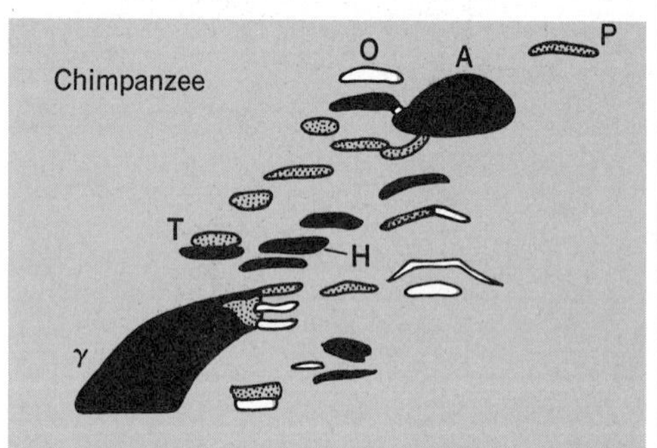

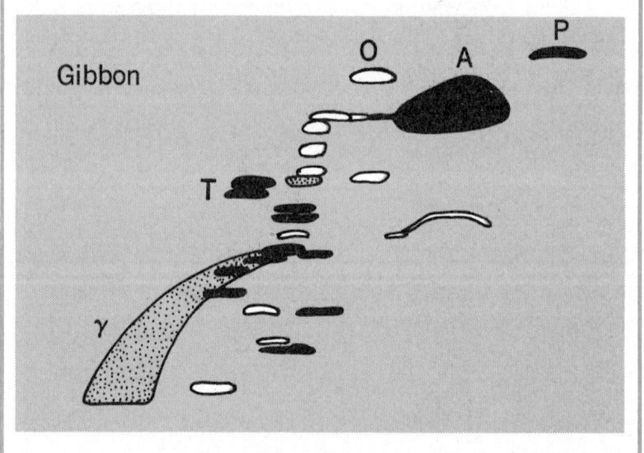

FIGURE 5.4
The close similarity of shapes of the proteins found in the blood serum of humans and in that of the great apes is one type of evidence of their close evolutionary origins. (After M. Goodman, in S. L. Washburn (ed.), *Classification and Human Evolution*, Aldine Publishing Co. Copyright 1963 by the Wenner-Gren Foundation for Anthropological Research, Inc.)

and animals. The chromosome forms of humans and apes show close similarities, although the African chimpanzee and gorilla are more similar to humans than are the Asiatic orangutan and gibbon. All are much more similar to one another than they are to any other animal chromosome forms.

Such similarities detail a close relationship among the primates as a whole and between humans and great apes in particular.

Ontogenetic Development: Baer's Rule

At various stages of human embryonic development, structures such as the notochord (the primitive backbone), gill arches, and gill grooves are present. They represent important features of certain early evolutionary forms that are not present in the fully developed human being. In broader terms, the human embryo passes through successive stages roughly similar to an undifferentiated cell mass, a coelenterate, a worm, and a generalized fish with the foundation of gill arches in its neck region. Finally, it takes on mammalian qualities and is ultimately born a human child.

As first formulated by K. E. von Baer (1792–1876), these facts were expressed in the following proposition, called "Baer's rule": *The younger the embryos of different animals, the more alike they are; the older the embryos, the more distinctive they become.* Ernest von Haekel (1834–1919) subsequently reformulated Baer's rule into a "biogenic law," which states that the embryonic development of each individual is a compressed recapitulation of certain major features of the development of the species. This is the origin of the commonly stated principle, "ontogeny recapitulates phylogeny," or "each individual climbs its own family tree."

Overstatement of the theory by uncritical early evolutionists brought it into disrepute among some biologists. But the theory has some validity, as is made clear by Dobzhansky: "Yet making allowances for overstatements and exaggerations, it remains true that many features of human ontogeny make no sense at all except on the assumption that they are retentions of the developmental patterns of remote ancestors."[7] More important for the question of taxonomy is the accepted fact that the successive stages of embryonic morphology of humans, apes, and monkeys are very similar until quite late in fetal development, when they begin to diverge significantly. In other words, the prenatal morphological similarity of humans, apes, and monkeys reinforces their grouping in common categories.

THE LIVING PRIMATES

Phylogenetically, we should not think of contemporary apes and monkeys as our ancestors. Instead, we should view them as related but modern animals differently adapted to different ecological situations. Apes and monkeys have similarities to humans because we had a common ancestor. Since that time apes, monkeys, and people have developed separately, each adapting to different environments with specialized structures and behavior.

Our ancestors can be known only from the fossils of earlier Cenozoic times. Consideration of our fossil progenitors is reserved for a subsequent chapter. We shall first take a brief look at the living primates to broaden our understanding of the order[8] (see Figure 5.5).

Prosimians: The Tree Shrew, the Tarsiformes, the Lemuriformes, and the Lorisiformes

A few shy species of surviving genera of the oldest of primate types survive in out-of-the-way

---

[7]Dobzhansky, *Mankind Evolving: The Evolution of the Human Species*, p. 165.

[8]M. Cartmill, "Rethinking Primate Origins" (*Science*, vol. 184, no. 4135, April 26, 1974), pp. 436–443.

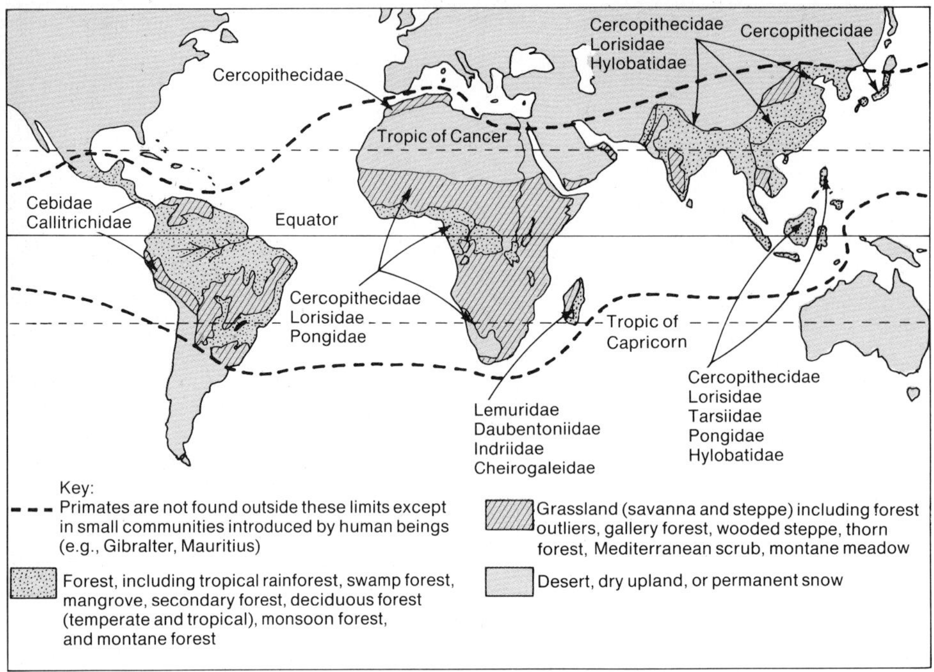

FIGURE 5.5
The distribution of primates. Each major habitat has its own distinctive primate fauna. (After J. R. Napier and P. H. Napier, 1967.)

(a)

FIGURE 5.6
Living prosimians are the most primitive of all primates and the most similar to our earliest primate ancestors. (a) (facing page) Tree shrew, *Tupaia glis*; (b) Ring-tailed lemur, *Lemur catta*; (c) Slender loris, *Loris tardigradus*; (d) Tarsier, *Tarsius spectrum*. [(a) San Diego Zoo Photo; (b) F. D. Schmidt, San Diego Zoo Photo; (c) Des and Jen Bartlett/Bruce Coleman Ltd.; (d) Lilo Hess/Three Lions.]

(b)

(c)

(d)

places in the tropical belt of the Old World (Figures 5.6a, 5.6b, 5.6c, 5.6d). Tree shrews are rather widely distributed throughout South and Southeast Asia. The Tarsiformes are located in north-central Indonesia (Borneo, Celebes, and the Philippines). Lemuriformes survive only in Madagascar. The Lorisiformes are found in Africa south of the Sahara and in parts of Asia (especially India, Burma, Ceylon, and Southeast Asia).

The Tree Shrew The tree shrew is classified by some authorities as a primate and by others as an insectivore. Yet with its generalized incisor teeth, which are not of the gnawing type developed by rodents, great mobility of fingers and toes, relatively larger brain, and greater acuity of vision, it is—if an insectivore—an insectivore that shows notable primate propensities. Indeed, in a number of details of skeletal and muscular construction, it shows specific lemuroid leanings. All in all, in the judgment of Simpson: "The living tree shrews . . . are either very unprogressive primates or equally unprogressive descendants of the immediate ancestors of the primates"[9] (see Figure 5.6a).

The Tarsier The tarsier, so named because of the extreme development of the tarsal bones in its foot, exhibits many of the general features of early primates, and in spite of its specializations, it could be very close to the original ancestral type. It is smaller than the lemur, with a small nose and large goggly eyes—the better to see at night—and a free upper lip like that of monkeys and humans, a lip that can be curled. It has full flexion of the neck, which can be swiveled in a complete half circle. These are all traits that point in the direction taken by the higher primates.

The evolutionary adaptation of the tarsier is for life in the trees. Figure 5.2 shows a similar skeleton. It has developed round, platterlike toetips and fingertips with increased friction surfaces for clamping onto boughs (see Figure 5.9). Like other primates it does not dig with sharp claws to climb and move about. Safe hand-and-foot contact is made much more quickly without claws, even though it may seem that squirrels and birds do all right in this respect. Its most remarkable specialization, however, is the elongation of its tarsals. This provides extra-effective leverage for sudden, propulsive jumping, while at the same time the toes at the end of the foot retain prehensility for grasping.

The Lemur The lemur looks rather like a little raccoon, except for its fingered hands and feet. A long snout, with wet, doglike nostrils, is more generalized mammalian in character than it is primate, as are the large, movable ears and split upper lip. But the lemur's brain, prehensile "hands," and flexible limbs distinguish it as a primate. It is a timid little animal which spends the greater part of its life in the trees and is active mostly at night. In evolutionary morphology, the lemur occupies an approximate midpoint between insectivores and monkeys. The tree shrew, the tarsier, and the lemur are contemporary, specialized animals similar to the early Paleocene primates.

The Loris and the Galago Within the family Lorisidae are found slow climbers and creepers (lorises and pottos) and fast hoppers (galagos). These primates are all arboreal, nocturnal, and omnivorous. They have an adaptation of the eye which concentrates minimal amounts of available light for effective night vision. The Lorisiformes are found in groups, but these do not appear to be very well structured socially.

The Anthropoids: Monkeys, Apes, and Human Beings

The other suborder of living primates, Anthropoidea, includes two infraorders, (1) Platyrrhini, with only one superfamily, the Ceboidea, New World monkeys, and (2) Catarrhini, with two

[9] G. G. Simpson, *The Meaning of Evolution*, p. 80.

superfamilies, the Cercopithecoidea, Old World monkeys, and the Hominoidea, apes and human beings.

The Ceboidea The ceboids are found only in the New World and are widely distributed from southern Mexico to northern Argentina. They are notable mainly for their flat faces and long, frequently prehensile tails (Figure 5.7). All are arboreal, and most are diurnal and live in social groups. Because they lead away from the main line of human evolution, we will not discuss them further.

The Cercopithecoidea The Old World Catarrhini divide into two superfamilies: the hominoids, which include humans and the great apes, and the cercopithecoids, which include the macaques, langurs, baboons, and other monkeys of Asia and Africa. They are adapted to both arboreal and terrestrial niches, walk quadrupedally, and lack the prehensile tail.

Of these the macaques are probably the most familiar, for they have by far the widest distribution and are very common zoo, research, and pet monkeys. They are found from Japan through China, Southeast Asia, India and west-

FIGURE 5.7
A comparison of the nose shapes of (a) New World (Platyrrhine) and (b) Old World (Catarrhine) monkeys. (After S. Eimerl and I. Devore, 1972; taken from Poirier, *In Search of Ourselves*, 1977.)

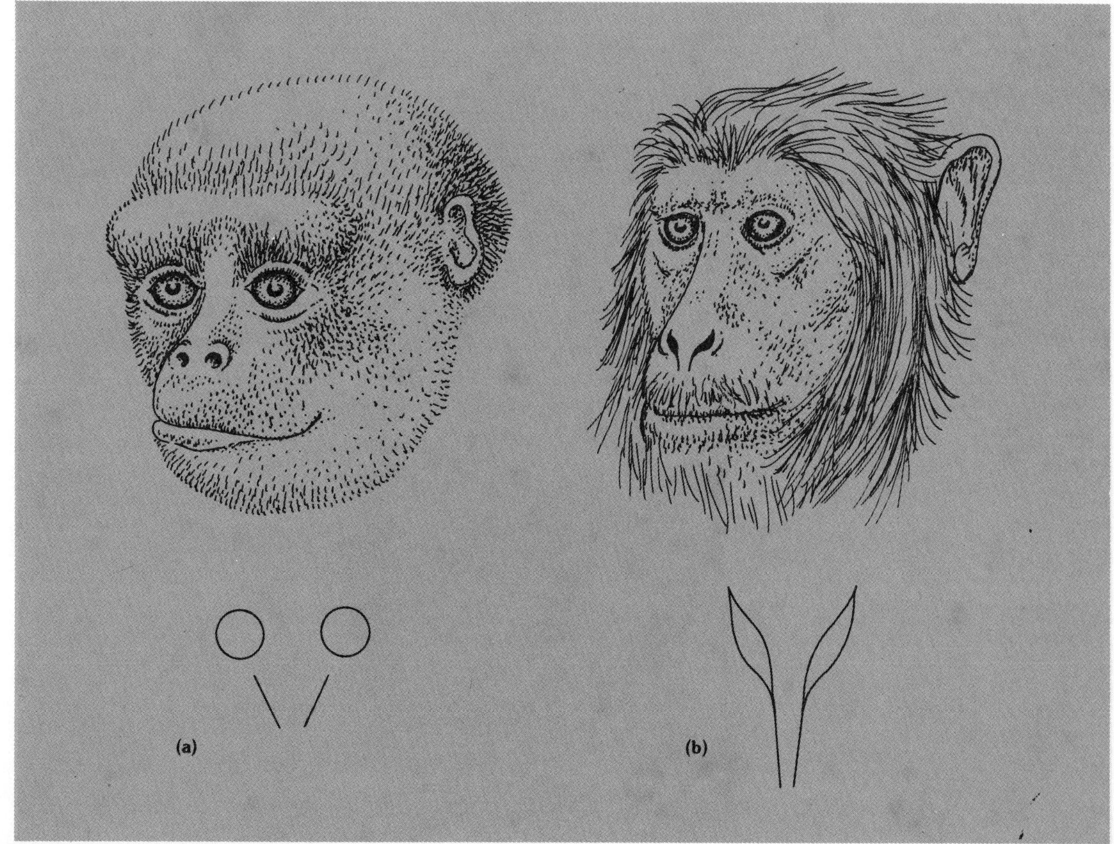

ern North Africa, to Gibraltar. Over fifty species and hundreds of varieties of macaques are alive today, and there is no point in trying to describe them in general terms.

Langurs are Asiatic monkeys, confined in their distribution to Tibet, India, and Ceylon and eastward to Java. Their territory overlaps that of the macaques, but it is more restricted, probably because of their specialized adaptation to eating leaves.

The baboons and mandrills are ground dwellers who have adapted to living in open country rather than forests. They have large muzzles, quadrupedal gait, and moderate-sized tails.

(a)

(b)

FIGURE 5.8
(a) An adult female and male orangutan; (b) a brachiating gibbon. [(a) San Diego Zoo Photo; (b) A. W. Ambler of National Audubon Society.]

The Hominoidea: Pongids, Hylobatids, and Hominids

The living pongids consist of the African gorilla and chimpanzee and the Indonesian orangutan. The Malayan gibbon and siamang are classed separately as hylobatids.

Almost all the distinctive features of the gorillas and chimpanzees are related to their adaptation for semierect posture, quadrupedal knuckle walking, and occasional bipedalism for locomotion. In knuckle walking, the gorillas and chimpanzees support themselves on the middle segment of the backs of the third and fourth fingers of their hands and on their feet. They use this method of locomotion on the ground and in the trees. Gorillas lift and lower themselves by their arms through the trees in the search for fruit and to build nightly nesting areas (they nest in trees about 50 percent of the time). Chimpanzees sometimes brachiate, sometimes move bipedally, and sometimes knuckle walk in the trees and on the ground.

The Asiatic apes, the orangutan, the siamang, and gibbon, are highly adapted to arboreal existence in Southeast Asia (Figure 5.8b). The orangutan does not knuckle-walk but instead walks quadrupedally on the side of its fists or with open palms facing down (palmigrade). When in the trees (where they spend most of their time), orangs sometimes brachiate.

Many skeletal and muscular adjustments have accompanied this change from the climbing and leaping of the prosimians to the arboreal quadrupedalism of the great apes. The ape's feet are less mobile and considerably less prehensile (Figure 5.9). The leg bones are much stouter and the femur has a more pronounced dorsal ridge for anchoring the flexing muscles that run to the thigh and pelvis. The ilia in the pelvis are flared out, and the whole hip structure is shorter and wider. The spine is more massive and rigid, with fewer vertebrae. The shoulders are broader, the chest is more like a barrel and less like the prow of a ship, and the breastbone is shorter.

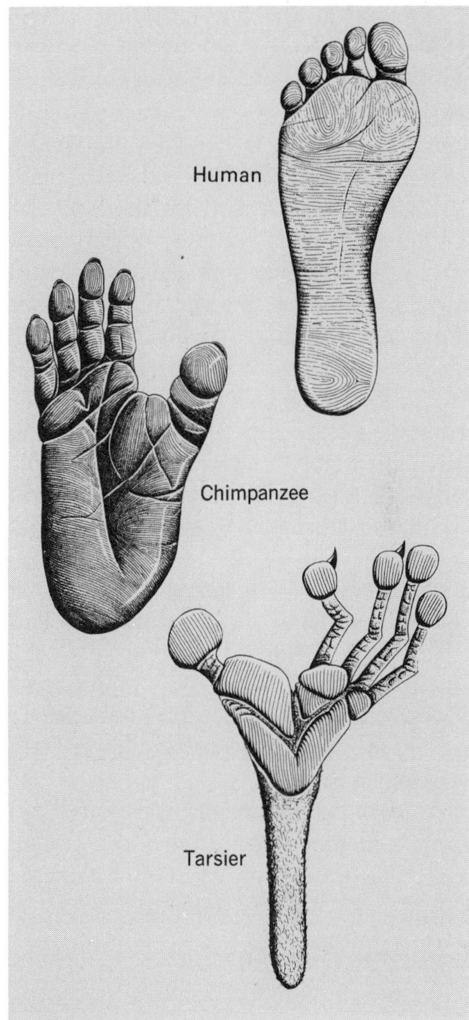

FIGURE 5.9
The undersides of primate feet, showing strengthening of big toe, reduction of grasping powers, and solidification of the foot as a walking and standing base in humans. (J. Biegert, in S. L. Washburn (ed.), *Classification and Human Evolution*, Aldine Publishing Co. Copyright 1963 by the Wenner-Gren Foundation for Anthropological Research, Inc. Courtesy of the author.)

The forelimbs of the apes are enormously elongated and strengthened relative to the length of the body, for they bear most of the weight in brachiation. Apes and humans have no external tail except the coccyx, the vestigial tailbone.

In the skull, the occipital condyles, the hinges on which the skull articulates with the spine, have moved from a position far back on the occipital bone forward to an intermediary position. The related foramen magnum, or great opening, through which the spinal cord passes from the cranium as an appendage of the brain, has also moved forward, perhaps as a function of the reduction of the face.

In adult male apes, especially heavy chewing and neck musculature is attached to remarkable bony ridges that form sharp crests along the top of the skull (sagittal crest) and across the occiput (nuchal crest).

The apes have cusp patterns for the upper and lower molar teeth similar to those of humans. The canine teeth of the apes are very different from humans, however, for the apes possess conical, daggerlike canines projecting well beyond the surface level of the lower teeth and overlapping them.

The brains of the apes, while inferior to those of humans in mental capacity and development, are greatly superior to those of all other animals.

PRIMATE BEHAVIOR

Before 1958, very little was known about the behavior of chimpanzees and gorillas in their natural habitats. Now, however, the daily lives of wild chimpanzees and gorillas have been painstakingly scrutinized by trained observers.[10] Figure 5.10 shows their behavior in some typical situations. However, we still know little about the behavior of gibbons, siamangs, and orangutans.

Research done in their natural habitat shows the great apes to be timid and nonaggressive. It took Goodall fourteen months of almost daily, quiet contact before the chimpanzees of the Gombe Stream Reserve on Lake Tanganyika would accept her presence without becoming disturbed and fleeing.[11] Gorillas became used to the presence of a peaceful investigator in the vicinity more readily, however. African apes have apparently survived by keeping out of harm's way. Populations are small (twenty to sixty chimpanzees and two to thirty gorillas), divided into subgroups among which individuals readily transfer their membership. Among gorillas, each primary group focuses about a large, adult male gorilla, who is clearly the leader. Male gorillas are dominant over females, and dominance hierarchies exist within the sexes; yet chimpanzees and gorillas are remarkably tolerant in personal relations, and there is little fighting to establish or maintain dominance. Accession to authority, mildly exercised, seems to be readily accepted.

The infant-mother dependency-protective relation is close and attentive for three years. Adults of both genera, but particularly gorillas, give one "the impression of having an independent and self-dependent temperament, appearing stoic, aloof, and reserved in their affective behavior."[12] They are social creatures, but they are not sociable. Social organization is minimal and loose, and yet very cohesive in that individuals rarely tend to get very far apart. Communication within the proximate group is accomplished more by means of bodily and facial gesture than by sounds. On the other hand, subgroups that are out of sight of one another regularly indicate their locations by calls.

Goodall emphasized the tool-using and toolmaking propensities among the chimpanzees under her observation. Wild chimpanzees prepare stems which they insert in termite holes until they are covered with insects, which they

[10]See I. DeVore (ed.), *Primate Behavior: Field Studies of Monkeys and Apes*, for generalized comparative accounts of the studies and their results.

[11]Ibid., p. 428.

[12]G. B. Schaller, "The Behavior of the Mountain Gorilla," in ibid., pp. 345–346.

(a)

(b)

(c)

(d)

FIGURE 5.10

African apes, the chimpanzee and gorilla, are semiadapted to ground dwelling and more closely related to humans. (a) Chimpanzees in upright and quadrupedal postures engaged in a tiff over possession of the infant, which is clinging to its mother's back in the normal carrying position. (b) Chimpanzee females and juveniles engaged in grooming and establishing mutual feelings of close interdependence. (c) A chimpanzee hunting for termites. (d) The forest gorilla normally moves about on all fours. (a, b) Copyright 1969, Dr. H. Albrecht, Bruce Coleman, Inc. (c) Baron Hugo van Lawick, National Geographic Society. (d) Reprinted from *The Year of the Gorilla* by permission of the author, George B. Schaller. Copyright 1964 by the University of Chicago.

then bite off (Figure 5.10c). A chimpanzee in the Omaha, Nebraska, zoo was reported in 1968 as having learned to pick the lock on his cage with a piece of wire which he kept hidden. Captive chimpanzees will occasionally throw sticks and stones, with poor aim, at "enemies." The apes manifest learning capacities in circuses and in the laboratories of experimental psychologists (see page 283) that appear more extensive than those observed under natural circumstances.

Gorillas are vegetarian, and six to eight hours a day are required to collect enough plants and fruit to sustain their large bodies. Chimpanzees have been observed eating honey, eggs, insects, caterpillars, grubs, and plant foods. The deliberate hunting of small animals for food by chimpanzees has been clearly documented. Hunting is a male cooperative venture, and the consumption of the product involves a series of structured behaviors. There is also increasing evidence of predatory behavior among baboons, but without the elaborate sharing behavior of chimpanzees.[13]

Antecedents of Culture

It is impossible for an outside observer to *know* what takes place in the mind of a chimpanzee, but Kortlandt may not be overimaginative when he observes:

> *The chimpanzees were unceasingly alert and curious. They seized every opportunity to bring variety into their lives, taking different paths down the hill on different occasions and continually changing their gait and their mode of locomotion. They were fascinated by everything new and unusual. They carefully examined all the objects I laid in their path and even collected some of them. Once I saw a chimpanzee gaze at a particularly beautiful sunset for a full 15 minutes, watching the changing colors until it became so dark that he had to retire to the forest without stopping to pick a papaw for his evening meal.*
>
> *Another respect in which the animals resembled human beings was in their doubting and uncertain nature. They appeared to ponder such problems as whether to turn to the left or the right, or whether or not a papaw tasted good. Often, just like laboratory chimpanzees puzzling over a difficult problem in an intelligence test, the chimpanzees I observed scratched themselves elaborately while making these decisions.*[14]

Four socially significant traits of apes and monkeys of fundamental importance for human beings are: (1) multigenerational group sociability and year-round association of the sexes; (2) prolonged infant dependency and protection of the females and their young by the males; (3) incipient tool using and food sharing (especially among chimpanzees); and (4) communication and rudimentary conceptualization, but without the capacity for speech.[15] These traits provided the basic behavioral elements for the first human societies and "culture."

Building upon such a base, the hominids ultimately achieved (1) a transition to hunting large game animals and meat eating; (2) upright posture and regular reliance upon toolmaking and tool using; (3) family grouping with local bands; (4) outgroup mating (consciousness of incest sensitivities); and (5) speech. The first two of these hominid traits we derive from the fossil record. The last three are inferred from our knowledge of human societies and comparisons with living primates.

SUMMARY

Classification is a way of simplifying the world of experience. Scientific classification is the process

[13]G. Teleki, "The Omnivorous Chimpanzee" (*Scientific American*, vol. 228, January 1973), pp. 32–42; S. C. Strum, "Primate Predation: Interim Report on the Development of a Tradition in a Troop of Olive Baboons" (*Science*, vol. 187, February 28, 1975), pp. 755–757.

[14]A. Kortlandt, "Chimpanzees in the Wild" (*Scientific American*, vol. 206, May 1962), pp. 128–134.

[15]See, especially, J. Van Lawick-Goodall, "A Preliminary Report on Expressive Movements and Communication in the Gombe Stream Chimpanzees," in P. C. Jay (ed.), *Primates*, pp. 313–374.

of identifying common characteristics in a number of differing phenomena and of grouping them in categories. It is the search for the like among the unlike. Classifications are always arbitrary constructions of the human mind in that the taxonomist decides which traits are sufficiently alike and significant to be included among the attributes of a class. A good taxonomy must be empirically sound; that is, the traits that it uses for classification must be genuine characteristics of the subjects to be classified and not imputed by the prejudices of the observer. Nevertheless, there is always subjective judgment in every assignment of a specimen to a given category within a system of classification. Using such criteria, and on the basis of biological and behavioral features, we classify living human beings among the primates as anthropoid, hominoid, and hominid.

Primates are mammals possessing highly complex brains, stereoscopic and color vision, a sense of smell and a snout that have been reduced in acuity and size, prehensile hands (with nails and fleshy pads), and feet with a big toe. They have two mammary glands, usually one offspring at a time (normally there are no litters), and a long period of postnatal development.

In addition to such gross morphological and functional characteristics, which are shared by the prosimians, monkeys, apes, and humans, a number of similarities among primates are revealed through advanced techniques in scientific laboratories. These include similarities in immunological reactions, serum protein patterns, chromosome patterns, and ontogenetic development.

The living primates are represented by the prosimians (the tree shrews, the tarsiers, the lemurs, and the lorises) and by monkeys, apes, and humans. The prosimians, which are the most primitive in form, are quadrupedal tree dwellers of small size. Monkeys exist in hundreds of varieties and more than fifty species. They too are mostly arboreal forest dwellers and are quadrupedal, although the members of some genera, such as baboons and mandrills, are terrestrial. The apes are limited to only two families: (1) the pongids, which include the chimpanzee and gorilla (*Pan*), the orangutan (*Pongo*); and (2) the hylobatids, which include the gibbon (*Hylobates*) and siamang (*Symphalangus*). These large, tailless creatures are forest dwellers, but the African chimpanzee and gorilla spend more time on the ground than in trees, and they can walk in a semiupright position. When moving about, they knuckle-walk or walk bipedally and lift by the arms.

All nonhuman living primates subsist on leaves, shoots, berries, and possibly insects. Chimpanzees occasionally kill and eat the meat of young monkeys and antelopes, but the human is the only modern primate who is a habitual meat eater and hunter of large game.

SELECTED READINGS

DeVore, I. (ed.), *Primate Behavior: Field Studies of Monkeys and Apes* (1965). A very useful summary of field studies of primate behavior written by people who have done the original research.

Jay, P. C. (ed.), *Primates: Studies in Adaptation and Variability* (1968). A representative collection of studies in primate behavior.

Jolly, A., *The Evolution of Primate Behavior* (1972). One of the best recent treatments of primate behavior.

Kummer, H., *Primate Societies: Group Techniques of Ecological Adaptations* (1971). Presents the study of primates from an ecological point of view.

Lancaster, J. B., *Primate Behavior and the Emergence of Human Culture* (1975). A brief, readable discussion of primate behavior as it relates to understanding human behavior.

Rowell, T., *The Social Behaviour of Monkeys* (1972). A balanced view of the study of monkeys available in an inexpensive paperback edition.

PART THREE

Human and Cultural Development

6
The Study of Fossil Primates

CHAPTER OUTLINE

LEARNING GOALS

Determine if the concept of the "missing link" is valid.

Identify the methods of dating prehistoric remains.

Specify the geologic eras and periods that are relevant to primate evolution.

Discuss the early Eocene and Oligocene primates.

Learn about the *Dryopithecus* and *Gigantopithecus* fossils of the Miocene.

Review the Pliocene hominid *Ramapithecus*.

Remains of ancient organisms are occasionally preserved in earth layers of different ages. Such remains are known as *fossils*. They may be reconstituted shells or skeletons permeated with mineral materials from the surrounding deposits or transformed by pressure and heat. Or they may be imprinted molds left by the original organism. They may also be preserved specimens found in tar pits, logs, permafrost layers (permanently frozen earth), or glacial ice. The fossil record, as it has been fitted together, adds time depth to the biological picture. It frequently yields the ancestral types from which living organisms could have been derived. It provides the *diachronic* proof, or proof through time, of common ancestry by placing the solid evidence of gradual divergence from the earlier types before our eyes.

THE MISSING LINK

That humans and other living primates have so many traits in common provides evidence of a common ancestry. However, this must not be taken to mean that the numerous kinds of monkeys, apes, and humans have *one* common ancestor. The primates have enjoyed some seventy million years of evolutionary development as a distinctive order. During that span, hundreds of primate genera and species have existed. It is therefore wrong to speak of any of these forms as *the* missing link, as though there were just one ancestral form. Any discovered fossil constitutes only one of the many possible phenotypic representatives of the genetic variation which must have been present in successive ancestral gene pools. Many of these phenotypes are still missing from the fossil record, but enough have been found to show the lines of development of the primates. Any discussion of fossils as missing links must be done in the context of gene pool variation and phenotype (see Chapter 3 for a discussion of these concepts).

All living higher primates have some common heritage, but because the apes have certain traits today does not necessarily mean that human early ancestors also had them. Apes, too, have evolved and changed during the past several million years, and they have developed their own distinctive specializations, such as knuckle-walking adaptations in the hands and wrists. At no time, then, did humans pass through an evolutionary stage which exhibited all the characteristics now displayed by the living apes or living monkeys.

ARCHAEOLOGY AND PHYSICAL ANTHROPOLOGY

It is possible that in studying the subject of fossils as excavated objects for the first time, one could become confused about the different efforts of archaeology and physical anthropology. The description of the principal activities of these two fields was provided in the first chapter. The main distinction is that archaeology is primarily concerned with the cultural activities of prehistoric humans and physical anthropology is more concerned with the physiological, anatomical, and genetic aspects of humans, both present and past. It is in their concern with the human past that physical anthropology and archaeology share research techniques and dating methods. The two fields actually overlap when culture becomes perceptible in the fossil record. It is for this reason that prehistoric culture and fossils are considered together in this section. Additionally, both archaeologists and physical anthropologists are trained in general anthropology and contribute to the understanding of human behavior in its environmental context. The rest of this chapter will review dating techniques, geologic time, and early nonhuman primates.

DATING PREHISTORIC REMAINS

Concern with evolutionary sequences makes it necessary to know which forms of life came after which. For this purpose, the *relative dating* of materials is sufficient. Often, however, it is not possible to link a deposit in one part of the world directly with another elsewhere so as to be able to say with certainty which is older. This, then, may seriously inhibit the establishment of evolutionary sequences. In such instances, *absolute dating* is a great help. In absolute dating, the most exact years, integrated with our modern calendar, may be established. When such dates are available, relative ages are then readily determinable.

Physiochemical Dating

Early in this century, physicists demonstrated that radioactive isotopes gradually decay into nonradioactive elements. Rates of decay were expressed in years of half-life. A *half-life* is the span of time necessary for 50 percent of a given amount of a radioactive isotope to change to a nonradioactive element. Table 6.1 shows the half-lives and residual products of six radioactive minerals. In 1907, it was hypothesized that if the ratio of residual to radioactive elements could be assessed, the age of the original material could be determined. For example, if the number of atoms of uranium 238 in a rock is equal to the number of lead 206 atoms, it means that one-half of the original uranium 238 has converted to lead 206; a half-life of uranium 238 has elapsed, and the rock is 4.5 billion years old (assuming no contamination or other upsetting factors). Recent derivations indicate a probable age of 4.5 to 6 billion years for the earth, and more than 6 billion years for our portion of the universe. In paleontology, potassium 40-argon 40 (K^{40}-A^{40}) readings are potentially important, since under optimum conditions they can fix dates between 100,000 and 2,000,000 years.[1]

TABLE 6.1
Radioactive Isotopes and Their Decay Products, with Half-lives

Radioactive element	Nonradioactive decay product	Half-life (million years)
Carbon 14	Nitrogen	.00573
Uranium 235	Lead 207, helium	710
Potassium 40	Calcium 40, argon 40	1,330
Uranium 238	Lead 206, helium	4,500
Thorium 232	Lead 208, helium	13,900
Rubidium 87	Strontium 87	50,000

Carbon 14 Dating

Immediately after World War II, a new possibility for dating archaeological materials was conceived by the nuclear physicist W. F. Libby. The method is based on the same principle of disintegration of radioactive elements, but it is usable with organic materials: wood, bone (provided it is not too fossilized), seeds, and other plants and animals, all of which contain carbon. It also works with the charcoal from prehistoric campfires.

Carbon 14 (C^{14}) is formed in the stratosphere when neutrons freed by cosmic rays bombard atmospheric nitrogen. The nitrogen becomes transmuted to radioactive C^{14}. Atmospheric movements are assumed to mix C^{14} evenly throughout the earth's air. Plants absorb C^{14} from the air; animals absorb it from the plants they eat. When a plant or an animal dies, the absorption of C^{14} ceases, and its disintegration begins. The half-life of C^{14} is now calculated at 5730 $\pm$ 40 years.[2] The number of radioactive emissions per minute, as measured by specially devised counters, indicates the amount of C^{14} still residual in a specimen. From this, its age may be calculated. Carbon 14 dating presents a number of technical problems, and its readings need to be used with care. It is also reliable only up to 30,000 years ago although with recent improvements in technique usable readings up to 70,000 years may be possible.[3]

[1]H. Brown, "The Age of the Solar System" (*Scientific American*, April 1957. S. A. Reprint 102); A. Knopf, "Measuring Geologic Time" (*The Scientific Monthly*, November, 1957), pp. 225–236. And see especially F. Hole and R. F. Heizer, *An Introduction to Prehistoric Archaeology*, 3rd ed.

[2]Libby's original figure was 5568 years.

[3]See Hole and Heizer, op. cit., for other less commonly used physicochemical methods.

Dendrochronology

Dendrochronology (Gr. *dendron*, "tree," *khronos*, "time," and *logy* "study of"), or tree-ring dating, exploits the fact that trees grow faster in wet years than in dry years, provided their roots are not waterlogged. This shows better in the annual growth rings of some types of trees, especially pine. Growth rings of comparable thickness belonging to trees that grew in the same area are matched to provide a master key (see Figure 6.1). This method of absolute dating is precise, but applicable only in certain environments. So far, keys going back 1500 years in the American Southwest and 4000 years in Nevada have been worked out. Efforts are being made to apply the method to Turkey and other semiarid regions.

Relative Dating Techniques

Paleontology, the study of past life through the fossil remains of animals, adds another dimension to chronological analysis. Woolly mammoths are Ice Age mammals and their fossils do not occur in deposits laid down in warm Mesozoic times. Consequently, the mere presence of such fossils in a deposit indicates that the stratum is almost certainly post-Mesozoic. In favorable instances, the total assemblage of fossil plants and animals may indicate rather clearly whether it is a Lower, Middle, or Upper Pleistocene deposit.

Under favorable circumstances it is possible to reconstruct general climatic conditions for a given time and place by analyzing the pollen content of the soil. For example, birch grows under cold, wet conditions, while beech requires a much milder climate. It is also known that late, postglacial conditions were cold and wet. The presence of a large quantity of birch pollen, combined with an absence of beech (along with varying ratios of other selected plants) in a soil sample, suggests that the soil dates from a time when the climate was cold and wet, such as the Late Pleistocene.

Palynology, or *pollen analysis*, is particularly

FIGURE 6.1

The basic technique of dendrochronology. Matched annual rings in overlapping segments, beginning with one of known age, fix the date at which each beam was cut. (Modified from J. D. Jennings, *Prehistory of North America*, 2nd edition. Copyright 1974 by McGraw-Hill Book Company.)

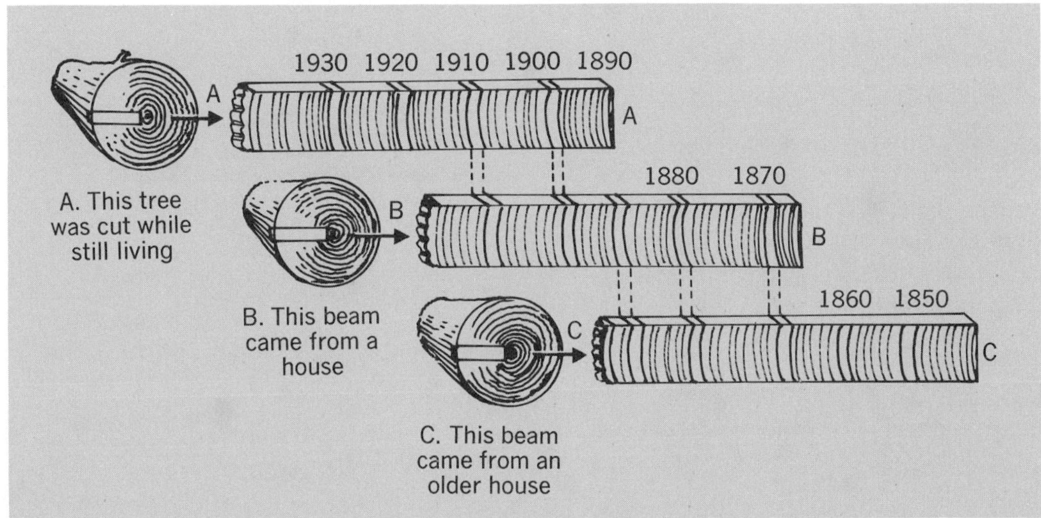

useful for specifying local climatic and environmental conditions at sites dating from the end of the Pleistocene on. There are several conditions which must be met before a pollen analysis can be applied. They include environmental conditions at the area favorable for the preservation of pollen; past environmental conditions that resulted in general, areawide vegetational changes rather than local, specialized changes; and finally, the establishment of a standardized pollen sequence near the area in a naturally deposited context such as a lake or swamp. The analyst must have a comprehensive knowledge of the ecology of the area. The researcher must also distinguish one magnified grain of pollen from another and count the number of grains of each type of plant in a standard sample.

Coprolitic Analysis

Akin to pollen analysis, although not a dating technique, is the analysis of human and animal fecal matter preserved in dry caves. Fecal remains contain the undigested remnants of prehistoric meals: seeds, plant fibers, animal hair, and bits of shells of nuts and molluscs. Not only do such remnants shed light on the diet of humans and animals, but they also reveal something of the plant and animal life of the period in which the diners lived. This in turn provides clues to climatic conditions. Because the materials are largely organic, they are suitable for C^{14} dating.[4]

Taken separately, or in combination as circumstances permit, such techniques as just presented make prehistoric dating more accurate. As additional experience leads to greater precision and reliability, the replacement of inference with direct facts will be achieved.

GEOLOGY AND THE ANTIQUITY OF THE PRIMATES

Stratigraphy is the analysis of geological deposits in terms of discernible layers. Time sequences are inferred from the relative positions of the strata, for the underlying strata are older than those overlying them—barring serious disturbances of the earth. In any local site, the relative ages of major geological strata are ordinarily clear. But in no single locality is one likely to find the entire sequence of major strata for all geologic periods. The master key is produced by matching overlapping sequences, after which the relative position of an isolated geological stratum can be determined by matching it to the corresponding stratum in the key. Stratigraphy thus makes it possible to tell the relative ages of geologic formations and of the fossils and archaeological materials contained within them.

Geologic time began with the laying down of the first sediments 4 to 6 billion years ago, and extends to the present. Major blocks of geologic time are called *eras.* Eras are brought to a close by drastic changes in earth conditions. The three geologic eras and their dominant life forms are indicated in Table 6.2. Minor changes in earth conditions, called *disturbances*, produce the subdivisions of eras, called *epochs* and *periods.*

The evolution of the primates occurred entirely within the final geologic era, the *Cenozoic.* Within this era are seven epochs: the *Paleocene*,

TABLE 6.2
Beginning Dates and Dominant Life Forms Developed in Each Geologic Era

Geologic era	Beginning date (before present)	Dominant life forms
Cenozoic	70,000,000	Humans Primates Mammals
Mesozoic	230,000,000	First mammals Birds Dinosaurs
Paleozoic	6,000,000,000	Land plants Reptiles Fish Trilobites Oldest dated algae

[4]R. F. Heizer and L. K. Napton, "Biological and Cultural Evidence from Human Coprolites" (*Science*, vol. 165, 1969), pp. 563–568.

TABLE 6.3
Dates and Newest Life Forms Developed in Each Epoch of the Cenozoic Era

Epochs	Beginning date (before present)	Newest life form
Recent	15,000	
Pleistocene	2 to 5,000,000	*Homo sapiens* *Homo erectus* Australopithecines
Pliocene	13,000,000	*Ramapithecus*
Miocene	25,000,000	Apes (*Dryopithecus*)
Oligocene	35,000,000	Monkeys, early apes (*Aegyptopithecus*)
Eocene	60,000,000	Small mammals, including first primates
Paleocene	70,000,000	Placental mammals

the *Eocene*, the *Oligocene*, the *Miocene*, the *Pliocene*, the *Pleistocene*, and *Recent* (see Table 6.3). The Miocene, Pliocene, and Pleistocene epochs are of critical importance for the immediate antecedents of human beings, and the Pleistocene is the period in which the hominids evolved.

FOSSIL PRIMATES FROM THE EOCENE TO THE PLIOCENE

The opening epochs of the Cenozoic era were long, moist, and warm. The Eocene, lasting from about 60 million until about 35 million years ago, was a time of extensive forests that provided a rich habitat for myriads of small, tree-dwelling primates, who had evolved from the insect-eating, long-snouted, sharp-eared, ground-dwelling mammals of the order Insectivora.

Eocene Prosimia

The prosimians ("before simians") were the earliest primates. Today fifty or sixty fossil genera of prosimians have been found in the Northern Hemisphere of the Old and New Worlds. Initially, the adaptive success of the prosimians was remarkable in the development of grasping digits for running on branches and of stereoscopic vision for judging distances. Then, during the Oligocene, environmental changes were such that in North America and Europe they disappeared. However, the prosimians did successfully maintain themselves in Central and South America, where subsequent evolution produced the New World monkeys but no hominoids. In South Asia and Africa, the prosimians carried through the critical Late Eocene and Oligocene periods to provide the ancestral stock for the anthropoids. It is presumed that tree living gave a selective advantage to those primates who possessed stereoscopic vision and larger brains.

The Oligocene Catarrhines

We have no Oligocene fossil primates from Europe. In Egypt, however, the story is very different. Two jaw fragments and a few other bones, collected at Fayum at the beginning of this century, represent two Oligocene fossil genera, *Parapithecus* and *Propliopithecus*. *Parapithecus* is a possible ancestor to the New and Old World monkeys. *Propliopithecus* has been evaluated as a generalized hominoid. This would make it a representative of the Oligocene ancestral pool from which humans and apes evolved.

A very important recent Fayum find is *Aegyptopithecus zeuxis*, estimated to be 28 to 30 million years old. The fossils represent a small, monkeylike skull with pongidlike dentition. The skeletal material suggests that it was an arboreal quadruped with a tail, which has been interpreted as representing the earliest known probable antecedent to all the later hominoid forms.[5]

[5]E. L. Simons, "The Earliest Apes" (*Scientific American*, vol. 217, 1967), pp. 28–35; W. E. Le Gros Clark, *History of the Primates*, pp. 55–58; D. Pilbeam, *The Ascent of Man*, pp. 29–32, 42–48.

The Miocene and Pliocene Hominoids

The Miocene was a period of environmental conditions once again highly favorable to the arboreal primates. The climate was mild, generally moist, and wetter than today. Rain forests covered much of Asia, Africa, and Europe in the lower altitudes. Higher plateaus were richly grassed and sprinkled with open tree areas; they were pleasantly cool. Over wide spaces, the country was verdant and rich in vegetable foodstuffs. The cercopithecines were on hand, and the stage was set for the great primate evolutionary outburst that would produce the immediate hominoid precursors of modern apes and humans.

The result, in the Miocene, was the wide dispersal of the genus *Dryopithecus*, from which derive the members of the genus *Pongo* (orangutans) and of the genus *Pan* (chimpanzee and gorilla). Another Miocene fossil ape, now classified as a dryopithecine, was originally called *Proconsul*. *Pliopithecus* is another important Miocene fossil hominoid genus, probably ancestral to the gibbon and siamang.

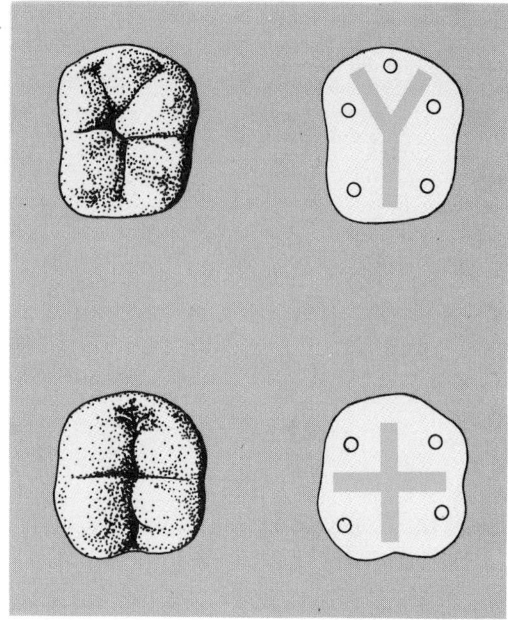

FIGURE 6.2
Lower second molar of an adult *Dryopithecus*, showing the *Dryopithecus* Y-pattern formed by the fifth cusp (above). The equivalent tooth of modern humans, showing the pattern formed by the four-cusp structure (below). (Adapted from M. H. Day, *Guide to Fossil Man*. World Publishing Company.)

Dryopithecus The first dryopithecine fossil fragment was described by the French paleontologist Edward Lartet in 1856, three years before Darwin's *Origin of Species*. For many decades the one significant feature of the dryopithecine family was its dentition, notably the much-talked-about "*Dryopithecus* Y-pattern" of the molars. The molar teeth of Old World monkeys and baboons, when looked at from above, have four peaks, or cusps. The deep valleys between them are in the form of a plus sign. The molars of humans and apes, on the other hand, usually have an additional fifth cusp, although this cusp has disappeared from some molars in modern humans. The extra valleys made by the presence of the fifth cusp form a Y between cusps 3, 4, and 5 (Figure 6.2).

Dryopithecines may be ancestral to some later hominoids, extinct and living. Innumerable dryopithecine teeth and skeletal fragments have been found in Europe, Africa, and Asia, but unfortunately no complete skeletons.

Dryopithecine Variability In Kenya, Africa (mostly on Rusinga Island, near the eastern shore of Lake Victoria), L. S. B. Leakey, who devoted his life to the discovery and interpretation of prehistoric primates, found several species of Miocene fossil apes. Dates on two *Dryopithecus* fossils, announced in 1970, are 18 and 19.7 ± .5 million years by the K^{40}-A^{40} technique.

The nearly five hundred individuals discovered come in three distinguishable types, which are identified as separable species: *Dryopithecus africanus* (a small, chimpanzee-size type), *Dry-*

opithecus nyanzae, and *Dryopithecus major* (who could match a gorilla for size).

Dryopithecus africanus is the best preserved and therefore the best known. It is small-brained when compared with humans, but it had already achieved a cranial capacity that put it between the range of the gibbon and the chimpanzee (100 to 400 cubic centimeters) (Figure 6.3). Its teeth are pongid. Its limbs, hands, and feet are considered to be those of a creature which could either brachiate in the trees or get about on the ground on all fours. It probably did both, but the fact that it could do either shows that the gorilla-chimpanzee pattern of life was already being established by these Miocene apes, who were beginning to exploit the ground as a possible habitat.[6] But more important in the Miocene stage of evolution is the apparent fact that the African *Dryopithecus* got about in the trees by swinging from the branches rather than by running along them, as all earlier primates had done. This is a primate adaptation that accompanies increasing body size in the direction of the hominoids. It, in turn, leads to adaptive radiation that selects for full mobility of the shoulder joint.

[6]For details, see W. E. Le Gros Clark and L. S. B. Leakey, *The Miocene Hominidae of East Africa* (British Museum Fossil Mammals of Africa, no. 1).

Gigantopithecus An expedition working in Pliocene deposits in India added a fourth jaw to three found in China and further confirmed the actual existence of a giant ape long known only from teeth found among so-called dragon bones in a Hong Kong drugstore in the 1930s. The large, humanlike teeth had been variously interpreted as those of a giant ape or a hominid ancestor to *Homo erectus* (see pages 130–145). The discovery in India dates from at least 5 million years ago. The interpretation of the material now suggests that *Gigantopithecus* was

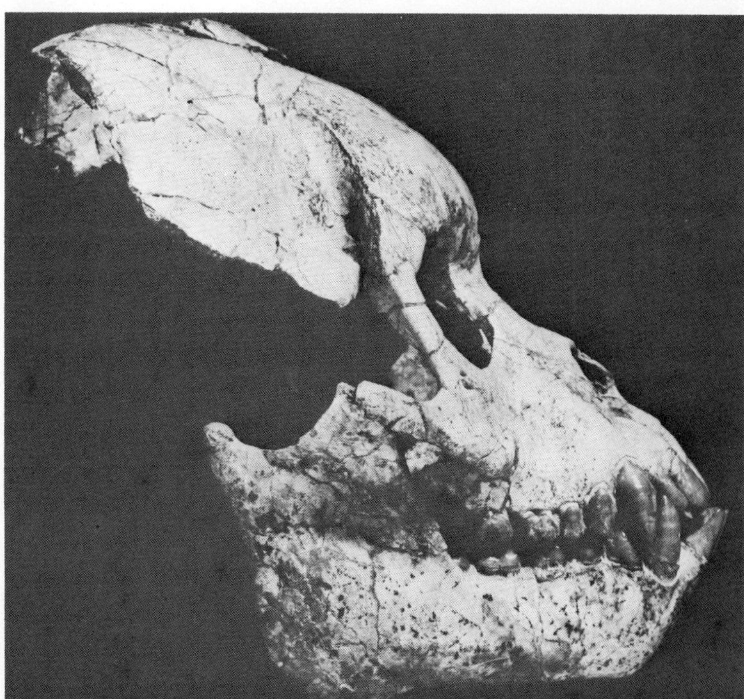

FIGURE 6.3
A side view of the skull of *Dryopithecus africanus* from Rusinga Island, Kenya. (The Trustees of the British Museum (Natural History).)

a massive ape who was probably descended from *Dryopithecus indicus.* The wear on the teeth of *Gigantopithecus* indicates that it probably lived in an open, woodland and grassland environment where it developed a specialized mode of feeding called "graminivorous"—meaning the eating of small, tough grass seeds and stems and rhizomes which require a great amount of grinding. This grinding of plant products is the trait which explains the wear pattern on the teeth. *Gigantopithecus* is distinguished as the largest known primate. However, its size did not guarantee its survival, and it was apparently extinct by early Pleistocene times.

The Pliocene Hominids

During the mid-1930s, a combined Yale–Cambridge University expedition carried out intensive explorations in the famous fossil beds of the Siwalik Hills along the northern border of India and West Pakistan. Among the finds were remains of great potential significance, named *Ramapithecus*[7] (see Figure 6.4).

The dental complex of *Ramapithecus* has been analyzed to suggest that it represents dietary changes leading away from the arboreal, quadrupedal, fruit-eating adaptation of *Dryopithecus* in the direction of a bipedal, terrestrial, seed-and-small-object-eating adaptation. Such a terrestrial adaptation would have been in response to environmental changes during the Miocene that were reducing the forests and expanding the grasslands. The dryopithecines who took to the ground developed the reduced canine, incisor patterns, and increased molar sizes which we recognize as characteristic of the hominids and first see in *Ramapithecus.* In short, the first adaptation which differentiated the hominid line from that of the hominoids (dryopithecines) was a ground-dwelling, seed-and-small-object-eating adaptation that led to frontal dental reduction and bipedalism.[8]

Although there is some debate, the conclusion to be drawn is that *Ramapithecus* had developed dental features that point strongly in the direction of human beings. If additional finds show a skull with an adequately protohuman cranium and a pelvis indicating at least partially upright posture, we may conclude that *Ramapithecus* was an early human ancestor distinct from the pongids.

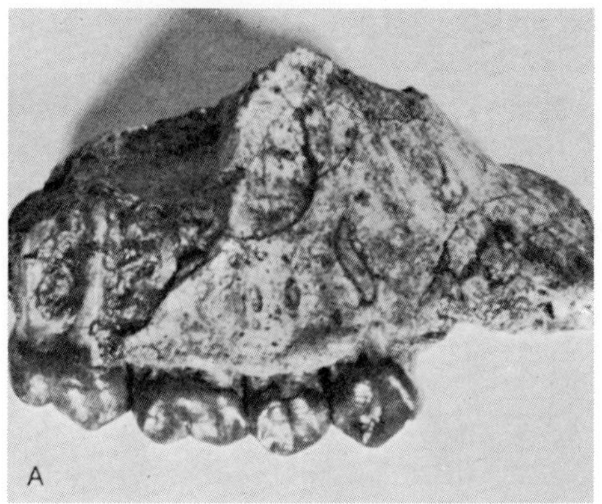

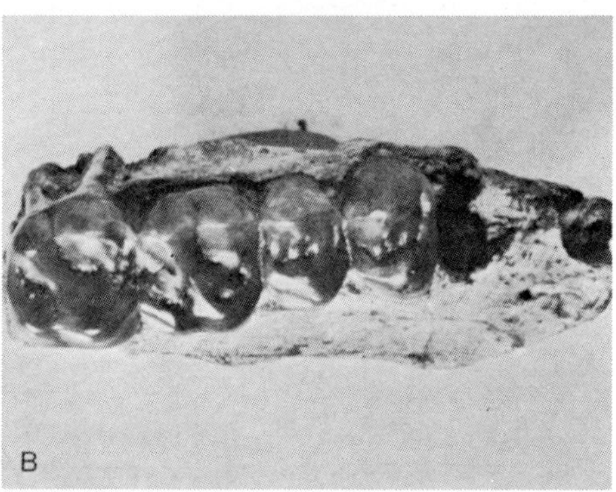

FIGURE 6.4
An upper jaw (maxillary) fragment of *Ramapithecus punjabicus*, (a) side view and (b) occlusal view. (E. L. Simons, 1972.)

[7]Rama is a legendary Hindu culture hero. Closely related dryopithecine types discovered in the Siwalik beds and named by G. E. Lewis were *Sivapithecus, Bramapithecus, Sugrivapithecus,* and *Paleosimia.* Siva and Brama are highly revered Hindu gods. Sugri is a monkey god. Taxonomically, these names are neutral. Culturally, they are in questionable taste.

[8]C. J. Jolly, "The Seed-Eaters: A New Model of Hominid Differentiation Based on a Baboon Analogy" (*Man*, vol. 5, 1970), pp. 5–26.

TABLE 6.4
A Summary of various early fossil primates

Name	Location	Time	Materials discovered
Parapithecus	Fayum	Oligocene	Lower jaw; although other fragments have been discovered, they are not described. (Before 1960, misinterpretations were common due to the absence of the middle portion of the jawbone, which went unrecognized until then. Probably the earliest Old World monkey.)
Apidium	Fayum	Oligocene	Originally a few fragments, additional material, including some juveniles, discovered recently; perhaps a close relative of *Parapithecus*
Propliopithecus	Fayum, Kenya	Oligocene	Lower jaw and teeth; small form that may be ancestral to apes
Aegyptopithecus	Fayum	Oligocene	Five partial lower jaws and an almost complete skull
Oligopithecus	Fayum	Oligocene	Left mandibular half
Aeolopithecus	Fayum	Oligocene	Mandible
Limnopithecus	East Africa	Miocene	Represented by fragmentary remains, including limb bones; perhaps more correctly included with *Pliopithecus*
Pliopithecus	Europe	Miocene to Pliocene	Several discoveries assigned to this genus including an almost complete skull; in the gibbon phylogeny
"Proconsul"	East Africa	Miocene	Considerable remains, including limb bones, a skeleton of a hand, and an almost complete skull; an African member of the *Dryopithecus* group
Dryopithecus	Europe, Asia, Africa	Miocene to Pliocene	Known mostly from a large inventory of jaws and teeth
Mesopithecus	Europe, East Africa	Miocene to Pliocene	Abundant remains particularly from Greece
"Sugrivapithecus," "Bramapithecus," "Sivapithecus," "Paleosimia"	Africa, Europe Asia (mostly India)	Miocene to Pliocene	Several fragmentary upper and lower jaws and isolated teeth, propably all of these should be included with *Ramapithecus*
Kenyapithecus	Africa	Miocene to Pliocene	Upper jaw fragments with one lower tooth; possibly an African variety of *Ramapithecus*
Oreopithecus	Europe	Miocene to Pliocene	Abundance of remains including an almost complete skeleton
Ramapithecus	Originally from India; now believed to have had wide distribution over the Old World	Miocene to Pliocene	Originally, one fragment of an upper jaw; a few other jaws and teeth have been assigned to this genus
Gigantopithecus	India, China	Pliocene, Pleistocene	Very large teeth and jaws; probably of an ape now extinct

SOURCE: Adapted from F. Poirier, *Fossil Evidence* (1977).

Africa has turned up a close cousin of *Ramapithecus* in the discovery by Leakey, in 1961, of a fragment of upper right maxilla containing a couple of molars and premolars. A canine tooth was found separately. This specimen has been dated at 14 million years by K^{40}-A^{40} analysis and falls within the Early Pliocene range. So far as presently reported, there is nothing to distinguish it as a genus separate from *Ramapithecus*. It is referred to as *Ramapithecus wickeri*.[9] Other similar discoveries have been made in Hungary, Spain, and the Near East.

THE PLEISTOCENE EPOCH

The Pleistocene was an unstable epoch of fluctuating cold and moderate warmth.

During spans of extreme cold, snow that falls in high altitudes or in high latitudes of the Northern Hemisphere does not melt off in the short, cool summers. It accumulates year by year, packed by its own weight, until it is metamorphosed into ice. Although ice is a solid, it has a low viscosity which allows it to flow downgrade, scouring mountain valleys and spreading outward from the massive ice cap over vast areas. The locking of water in the ice, during *glaciations* (advances of ice sheets), lowers sea levels around the world by several hundred feet. The great glacial weight upon the continents and the lightened weight of the water in the ocean basins cause continental subsidence and changing of land contours. Temperate and tropical zones outside the frigid glacial areas shift and change, forcing extensive migration and new adaptations by plant and animal life. The unstable Pleistocene was thus a time that tested and stimulated the adaptive capabilities of humankind.

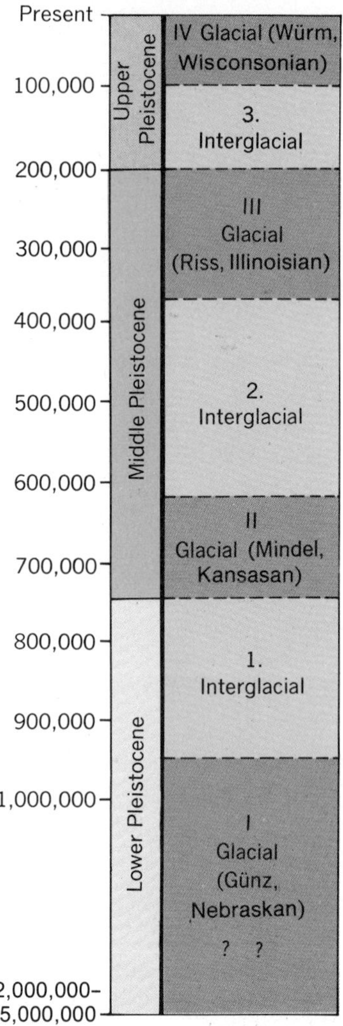

FIGURE 6.5
The Pleistocene time scale, with European and North American nomenclature for major glacial phases. The prolonged second interglacial is sometimes called the Great Interglacial.

The long heaps of debris left at the points where glacial advances ceased (called *morains*), outwash deposits, and river terraces all correlate with specific glaciations. Changes in flora and fauna also correlate with glacial and interglacial phases. The major climatic cycles within the

[9] Leakey, whose dedicated enthusiasm led him to the discovery of more important human precursors than any scientist of his day, also tended to give each of his new finds at least a new species status, if not that of a new genus, too. In this case, he did both. Hence, he called his specimen *Kenyanthropus wickeri*, after Kenya and Mr. Fred Wicker, on whose farm the fossil was found. See L. S. B. Leakey, "A New Lower Pliocene Fossil Primate from Kenya" (*Annals and Magazine of Natural History*, vol. 14, 1961), pp. 689–696; B. G. Campbell, "Conceptual Progress in Physical Anthropology: Fossil Man" (*Annual Review of Anthropology*, vol. 1, 1972), pp. 30–32.

Pleistocene produced four primary advances of the ice sheets or glaciations. In Europe, these are named after Alpine valleys, while in North America they are called after the states in which their effects are most prominent.[10] For our purposes, it is sufficient to refer to them by numbers, using roman numerals for glaciations and arabic numerals for interglacials (Figure 6.5).

Recent research on the Pleistocene epoch is based primarily upon the analysis of microorganisms and molluscs found in the cores of ocean-bed drillings. This research has revealed a prolonged cool period preceding the first actual glaciations. There is no firm evidence as yet, however, that there was anything like the Alpine glacial advances before the Günz glaciation. There is general agreement that a million or more years of cold climate should be attributed to the beginning of the Pleistocene epoch. This phase of the Pleistocene is known as the *Villafranchian*—the time in which the first modern genera of animals appear.

The whole span of the Pleistocene covers from 2 to 5 million years. Fossil primates of the Late Pliocene and the Pleistocene will be discussed in the following chapters.

SUMMARY

Studies in biology, paleontology, geography, and anthropology overwhelmingly demonstrate that the earth and all its living forms have been undergoing continuous evolution.

The antiquity of human antecedents is established through stratigraphy and geochronology based upon the rates of distintegration of radioactive elements, pollen analysis, tree-ring counts, and chemical content of fossil materials. The ancestry of all primates goes back to some Late Mesozoic insectivore from which the prosimians of the Eocene period of the Cenozoic era were derived. The prosimians radiated over both hemispheres, but under Oligocene conditions most types become extinct. Modern prosimians are represented by tree shrews, lemurs, lorises, and tarsiers, among others. In late Oligocene times, anthropoid precursors evolved in Africa (and probably Asia) and are known in part from the fossils of *Propliopithecus* and *Parapithecus*.

Cercopithecoids and ceboids evolved separately in the Old and New Worlds after the Oligocene, and New World monkeys have only a remote relationship to humans. Old World monkeys are more closely related to humans, but they are not ancestral. In Miocene times, the hominoid *Dryopithecus* became widely dispersed throughout the Old World. *Ramapithecus*, as a probable representative of our Pliocene precursors, is apparently sufficiently human in dentition to indicate that hominid ancestors were already distinguished from the pongids in Miocene times. A gap of approximately seven to eleven million years exists between *Ramapithecus* and the first humanlike creatures in the Late Pliocene or Early Pleistocene.

[10]Günz, Mindel, Riss, and Würm, in Europe; Nebraskan, Kansan, Illinoisan, and Wisconsonian, on the North American continent.

SELECTED READINGS

Buettner-Janusch, J., *Physical Anthropology: A Perspective* (1973). A detailed, modern, summary of all aspects of physical anthropology including fossil primates.

Hole, F., and R. F. Heizer, *An Introduction to Prehistoric Archaeology* (1973). A guide to archaeological methods for the nonprofessional; excellent sections on stratigraphy, dating.

Le Gros Clark, W. E., *History of the Primates* (1966). A well written, easy to read account of primate evolution available in paperback.

Pilbeam, D., *The Ascent of Man* (1972). For a more detailed and comprehensive presentation of human antecedents.

Poirier, F. E., *Fossil Evidence: The Human Evolutionary Journey* (1977). An excellent modern introduction to the subject.

Simons, E. L., *Primate Evolution* (1972). The best summary by the acknowledged authority on pre-australopithecine fossils.

Woodall, J. N., *An Introduction to Modern Archeology* (1972). A short discussion of advances in archaeology. Clear treatment of the subject.

7 The Australopithecines

CHAPTER OUTLINE

LEARNING GOALS

Discuss the discovery and distribution of *Australopithecus*.

Identify Australopithecines from East Africa and Asia.

Identify the chief characteristics of *Australopithecus africanus*.

Explain how the characteristics of *Australopithecus africanus* differ from those of *Australopithecus boisei*.

Discuss the fossil evidence of *Australopithecus robustus*.

Determine the main features of the Oldowan culture.

Where does *habilis* fit?

The moist and moderate Miocene provided the seedbed for the growth of the prehuman hominoids. The Pliocene tested their survival capacities to the utmost, for it was a time of climatic catastrophe for all Africa. The Miocene rains had all but stopped, and for more than ten million years an incredible desert, which very likely linked the Sahara of the north and the Kalahari of the south, smothered the vast continent in searing heat and choking sand and dust.

In the high hills flanking the southern shoulders of the Himalayas of India, and perhaps on the flanks of the high equatorial mountains of Africa, there was, however, sufficient moisture to sustain the grasses, shrubs, and trees necessary for a primate environment. Thus the protohominids survived until the resumption of rains and snowstorms in the Pleistocene, when in Africa verdure again returned to the lowlands and water filled the lakes and streams.

The significant effect of the Pliocene climate on primate evolution would seem to have been the shrinkage, and even disappearance, of the Miocene forests, and the expansion of grasslands, with a resultant premium placed upon genetic adaptability to terrestrial living. Those primates which could come down from the trees and move from grove to grove in search of food and security would have had the best chance to survive and perpetuate their kinds. What happened in the Pliocene can be inferred only, for the 7- to 11-million-year gap between *Ramapithecus* and the next higher fossil primate remains unknown for the time being.

By the end of the Pliocene, however, an early form of hominid had definitely evolved (see Figure 7.1). Remains of this hominid have been found in Late Pliocene and Early Pleistocene deposits in Africa and probably Indonesia. These are the australopithecines and related hominids.

DISCOVERY AND DISTRIBUTION

The discovery and final acceptance of *Australopithecus* as a hominid and probable human ancestor were important markers in human history. Before these events it was believed that the creature which would ultimately be acceptable as a contributor to the human ancestral genetic pool would have a more gallant appearance and demeanor. The child's skull presented by Raymond Dart in 1925 as a likely candidate was too ape-looking. If a child could have such a small brain and such a protruding jaw, what would it look like as an adult? Certainly a Shakespeare must come from better parentage!

Even scientists were not ready to accept the australopithecines as believable human ancestors. Perhaps this was one reason they were gullible enough to accept the Piltdown remains as evidence of a more logical progenitor. Someone had combined the skull of a hominid with a simian jaw, filed and tinted the canines (Figure 7.2) to the right shape and color, and convinced the world, including some of the best physical anthropologists, that it indeed was a proper and ancient fossil. By 1955, however, newly devised tests proved the Piltdown "fossil" a hoax by demonstrating that the skull and jaw showed different amounts of fluorine, not only between skull and jaw but between skull and jaw *and* the other fragments of bone recovered from the same place.[1] The decks were now cleared for the acceptance of the discoveries of early humans in South and East Africa.

The South African Australopithecines

In 1925, Raymond A. Dart, professor of anatomy at the University of Witwatersrand, Johannesburg, South Africa, reported the find in the previous year of a nearly perfect juvenile primate skull in quarries near Taung, South Africa. Its association with numerous extinct Pleistocene fossils made its antiquity apparent. The specimen was approximately 6 years old at death, as indicated by its teeth. Its face, as well as the

[1] J. S. Weiner, *The Piltdown Forgery*, tells a fascinating story of scientific detective work.

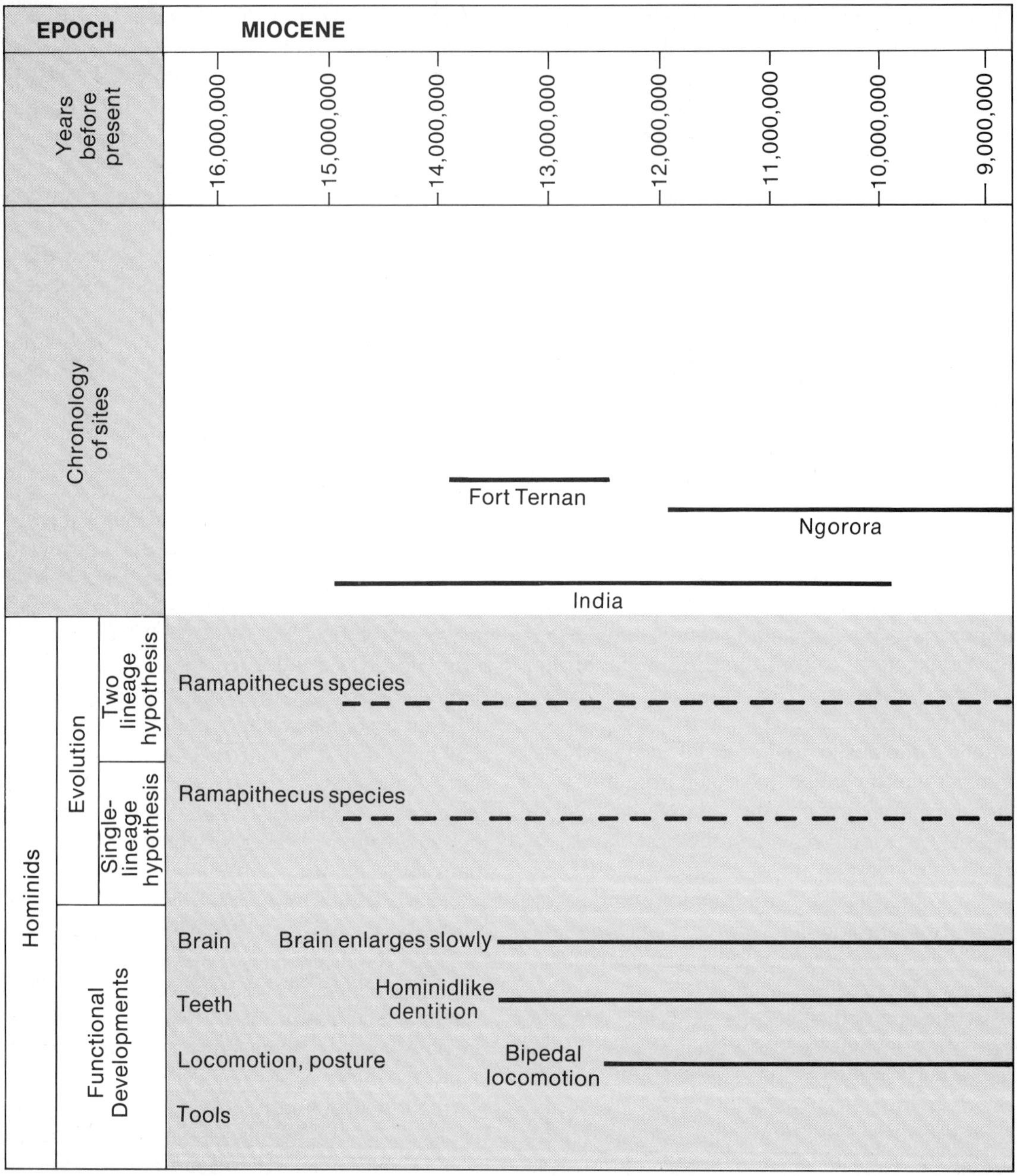

EPOCH			MIOCENE
Years before present			16,000,000 · 15,000,000 · 14,000,000 · 13,000,000 · 12,000,000 · 11,000,000 · 10,000,000 · 9,000,000
Chronology of sites			Fort Ternan; Ngorora; India
Hominids	Evolution	Two lineage hypothesis	Ramapithecus species
		Single-lineage hypothesis	Ramapithecus species
	Functional Developments	Brain	Brain enlarges slowly
		Teeth	Hominidlike dentition
		Locomotion, posture	Bipedal locomotion
		Tools	

FIGURE 7.1
Chronology of fossil-bearing sites and functional developments of hominids of the Miocene, Pliocene, and Pleistocene epochs. (Buettner-Janusch, 1973.)

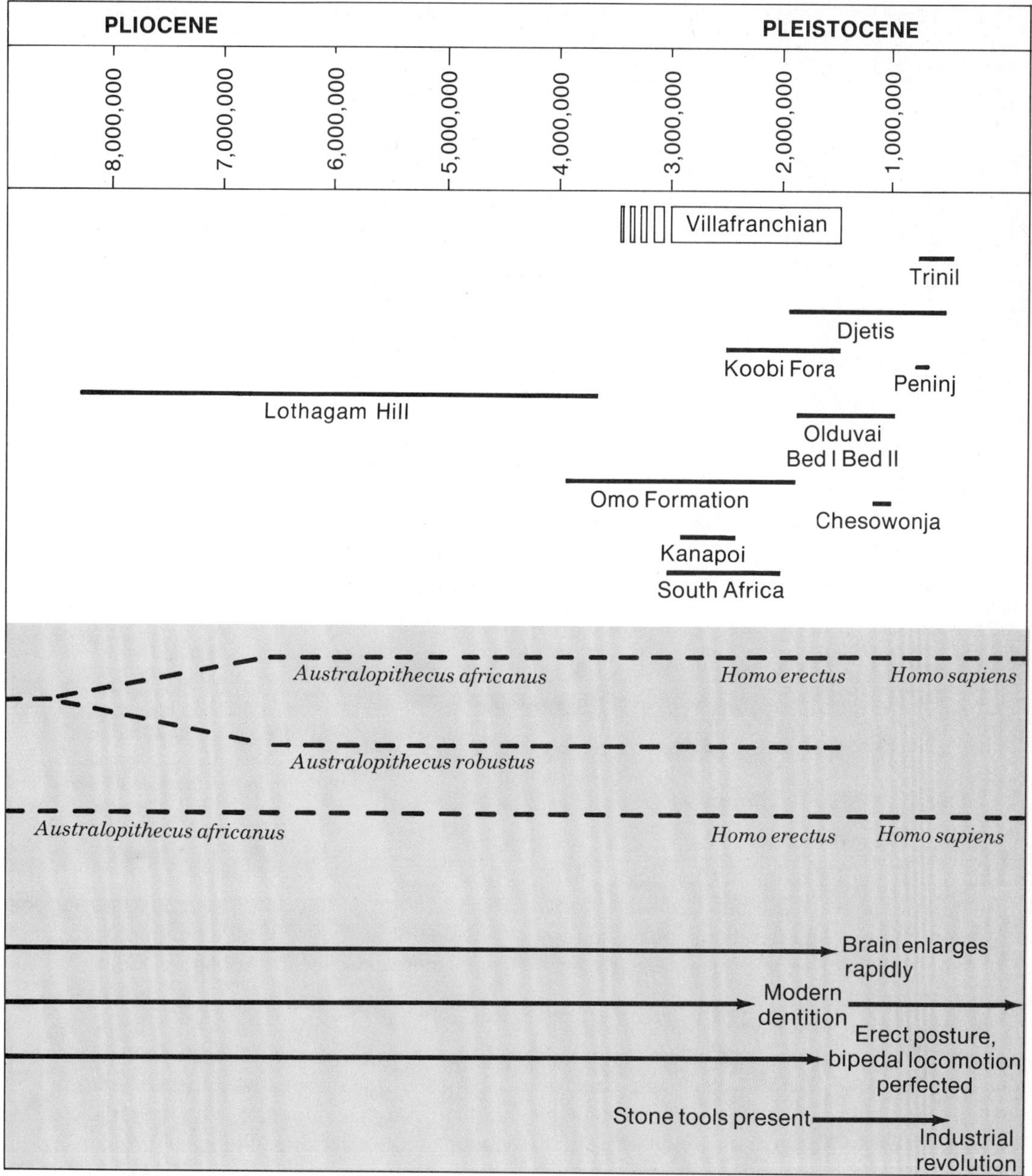
PLIOCENE
PLEISTOCENE
8,000,000
7,000,000
6,000,000
5,000,000
4,000,000
3,000,000
2,000,000
1,000,000
Villafranchian
Trinil
Djetis
Koobi Fora
Peninj
Lothagam Hill
Olduvai
Bed I Bed II
Omo Formation
Chesowonja
Kanapoi
South Africa
Australopithecus africanus
Homo erectus
Homo sapiens
Australopithecus robustus
Australopithecus africanus
Homo erectus
Homo sapiens
Brain enlarges rapidly
Modern dentition
Erect posture, bipedal locomotion perfected
Stone tools present
Industrial revolution

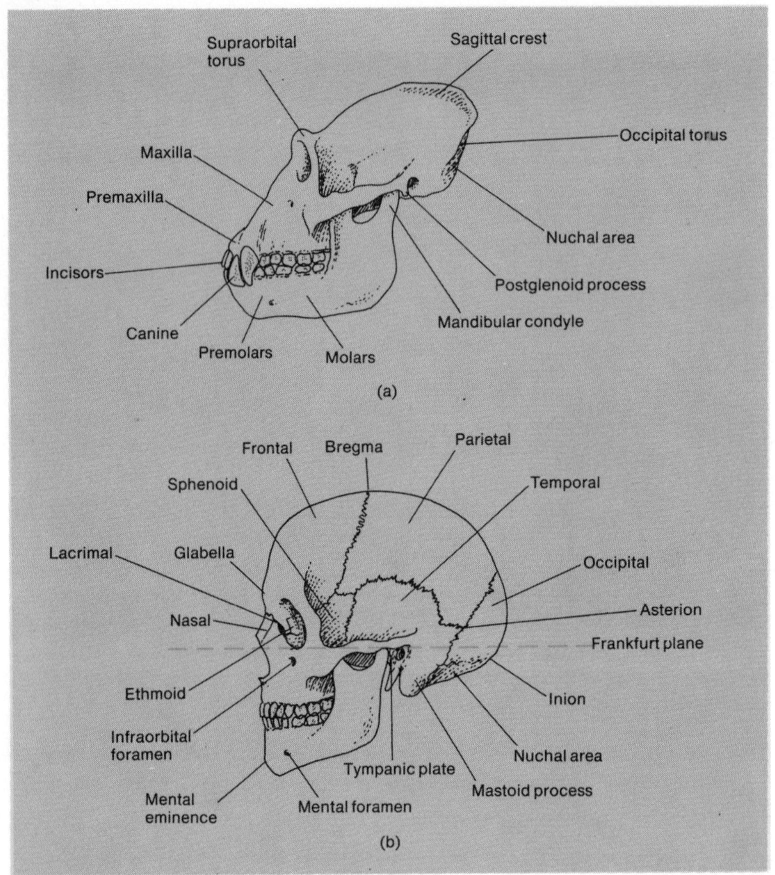

FIGURE 7.2
The skull of a male gorilla (a) and of modern *Homo sapiens* (b) to illustrate various anatomical landmarks to which the text refers. (From W. E. LeGros Clark, 1964.)

frontal region of the cranium, was intact. The larger part of the braincase had been dislodged and lost in the mining operations, but a perfect fossil endocranial cast of the brain itself was attached to the face.

The anatomical character of the first known *Australopithecus* as a type was difficult to determine with certainty because diagnostic characteristics are somewhat indefinite in the young; much surer comparisons can be made with adult skeletons. After 1936 other *Australopithecus* fossils were found at Sterkfontein, Makapansgat, Swartkrans, and Kromdraai—all in southern Africa—and the validity of the first Taung specimen as representative of a new genus was thoroughly established (see Figure 7.3). By 1972 nearly 1000 australopithecine teeth had been recovered from the South African sites, and the remains of at least 135 different individuals are represented. Collecting continues today.

The East Africa Australopithecines

If our knowledge of the australopithecines was opened by the discoveries in South Africa, it has been given new dimensions by the rapidly accumulating discoveries at Olduvai, Tanzania, in the Koobi Fora area east of Lake Rudolf, in Kenya, and in the Omo Basin of Ethiopia, north of Lake Rudolf.[2]

[2]The President of Kenya renamed Lake Rudolf in 1976. It is now Lake Turkana.

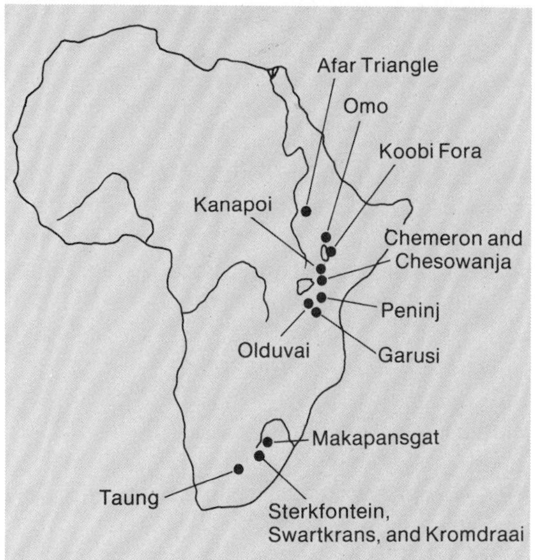

FIGURE 7.3
The distribution of Lower Pleistocene sites from East and South Africa. (After P. Tobias, 1972; taken from Poirier, *In Search of Ourselves*, 1977.)

Olduvai Gorge has been called "the Grand Canyon of human evolution." It is not so awe-inspiring to see, but it is stupendous in its yield of human fossil and prehuman historic cultures, extending throughout Pleistocene times. The gorge is cut from west to east into the west wall of the Great Rift Valley. It is now a dry canyon in wild country, lying midway between Lake Victoria and fabled Mt. Kilimanjaro, 150 miles by air southwest of Nairobi. The weathering faces of the canyon continually expose the buried fossils and artifacts.

The stratigraphy of Olduvai presents five major strata, or beds. Bed I contains Lower Pleistocene fossil fauna such as the modern elephant, the one-toed horse, the cow, and a number of Pliocene survivors such as three-toed horses, mastodons, and antlered giraffes. The upper strata of Bed 1 indicate a time of interpluvial dryness and subdesert. The K^{40}-A^{40} (potassium 40–argon 40) dates indicate an age of 1.85 million years for the lower sections of Bed I, and 1.75 million years for the upper portions. Upper Bed II represents a mid-Pleistocene pluvial in Africa. Bed III represents a time of violent erosion, indicating sporadic runoff of heavy occasional rains in a generally dry country. Bed IV is another layer of lake deposits, with fish, crocodiles, and hippopotamuses. It represents a Late Pleistocene pluvial phase, possibly equivalent to the fourth glacial. The idea of Bed V has now been abandoned as a distinct feature, being replaced by named stratigraphic units. Figure 8.7 (page 140) shows a cross section of the Olduvai beds.

In 1960, L. S. B. and Mary Leakey discovered in Bed I fragments of a child consisting of three pieces of the cranium, parts of the mandible with all teeth, an upper molar tooth, and a set of hand bones. On the same floor, crudely chipped stone tools of quartz rocks were also discovered. This is the famous Oldowan pebble (or chopper) culture, which extends into Bed II and which is also found elsewhere in Africa.

Australopithecines in Asia

No australopithecines have been found in Europe, and considering how intensively the prehistory of Europe has been explored, it is not very likely that any ever will be.

It is otherwise in Asia. Two fragments of lower jaws were found in 1941 and 1952 in Lower Pleistocene beds in Java at Sangiran. They are large and thick. In size and other characteristics the teeth are australopithecine. G. H. R. von Koenigswald, who made the first discovery, considered it to be a human type and named it *Meganthropus* (Gr. *mega*, "large," and *anthropos*, "man") *paleojavanicus* (Gr. *paleo*, "ancient," and *Java*). The consensus, however, is that these Java individuals are australopithecines.

AUSTRALOPITHECUS: AFRICANUS, ROBUSTUS, AND BOISEI

Although the several discoverers of the various australopithecine fossils at first enthusiastically named four or five different genera, in addition to a couple of species, there is now some consensus for one genus and three species, *Australopithecus africanus, Australopithecus robustus*, and *Australopithecus boisei*.[3]

The fossils from Sterkfontein, Makapansgat, and Taung are classified as *Australopithecus africanus* and described as gracile because they are small and "delicately" built. The robust forms from Kromdraai and Swartkrans are classified as *Australopithecus robustus*. Other differences between the two forms are in tooth size and shape, in cranial capacity and shape, and in limb and body structure (postcranial anatomy). Brace and Jerison maintained, separately, in 1963 that the two fossils were simply variants of the same creature. The robust differed from the gracile form only in that it had the brain and limb size and cranial adjustments which would be expected with a larger creature of the same species. Further, Brace maintained that the gracile was the female and the robust the male of the species, a view which Mary Leakey feels deserves serious consideration.[4] A year before the statements by Brace and Jerison, Robinson had emphasized the differences between the two types by placing the gracile form in the genus *Homo* and the robust form in a separate genus, *Paranthropus*.[5]

The lessons to be learned from the classifications described above are two. First, there are different people toiling in the fossil fields and each has an opinion. Second, as new discoveries are made and as research, dating, and analytical tools are invented or perfected, the taxonomic position of a fossil may change. As Campbell and others have stated, a taxonomy is a kind of hypothesis; hypotheses are made to be tested, and supported or disproved.[6]

Australopithecus lived from Late Pliocene to Middle Pleistocene times (5,500,000 to 700,000 years ago). Clearly, it represents a branch of some ramapithecine ancestral stock which had probed the open areas between the forests for a living in Miocene times. The skull structure of each species is shown in Figure 7.4. *Australopithecus* had made the critical evolutionary adaptation of bipedalism. It had fully freed its hands for tool using.

Morphology of the Cranium: *Africanus*

The skulls of *Australopithecus africanus* present a generally hominid quality, with small braincases and protruding, chinless jaws (Figure 7.4). The brains assume moderate proportions, varying from about 400 cubic centimeters to a maximum of 530 cubic centimeters. Gorilla brains run from around 300 cubic centimeters to a recorded maximum of 752 cubic centimeters, while the chimpanzee-orangutan range is 290 to 475 cubic centimeters. The average brain of *Australopithecus africanus* was thus larger than that of the average chimpanzee but similar to that of a gorilla. Relative to body size, however, the brain of *Australopithecus africanus* is distinctly larger than that of the massive gorilla and somewhat larger than those of the chimpanzee

[3]D. Pilbeam and S. J. Gould, "Size and Scaling in Human Evolution" (*Science*, vol. 186, 1974), pp. 892–901; B. Campbell, "A New Taxonomy of Fossil Man" (*Yearbook of Physical Anthropology*, vol. 17, 1973), pp. 194–201; P. V. Tobias, "New Developments in Hominid Paleontology in South and East Africa" (*Annual Review of Anthropology*, vol. 2, 1973), pp. 311–334 [a slightly updated version of this item appears in G. L. Isaac and E. R. McCown (eds.), *Human Origins*]; B. G. Campbell, "Conceptual Progress in Physical Anthropology: Fossil Man" (*Annual Review of Anthropology*, vol. 1, 1972), pp. 27–54.

[4]H. J. Jerison, "Interpreting the Evolution of the Brain" (*Human Biology*, vol. 35, 1963), pp. 263–91; C. L. Brace, "Review of *Evolution und Hominisation*" (*American Journal of Physical Anthropology*, vol. 21, 1963), pp. 87–91.

[5]J. T. Robinson, *Early Hominid Posture and Locomotion*; for a more detailed comparison of the anatomies of *Australopithecus africanus* and *Australopithecus robustus*, see J. T. Robinson, "The Origins and Adaptive Radiation of the Australopithecines," in G. Kurth (ed.), *Evolution und Hominisation*, pp. 120–140.

[6]B. Campbell, "A New Taxonomy of Fossil Man," op. cit., pp. 194–201.

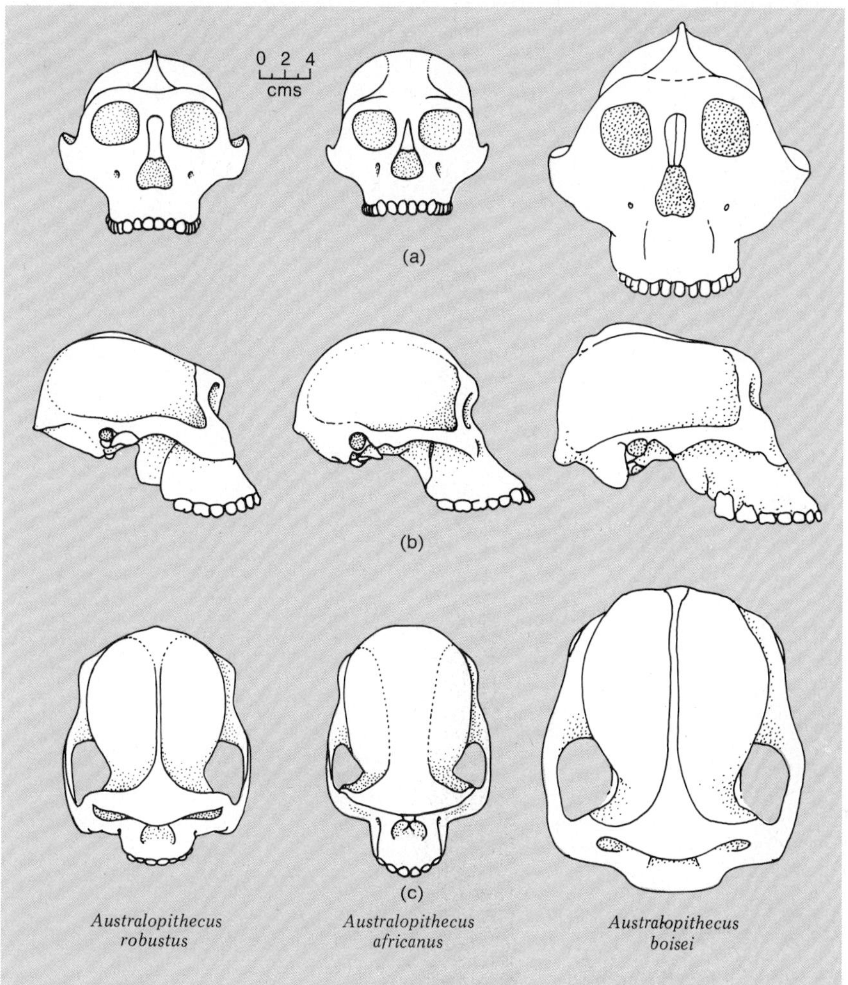

FIGURE 7.4
Frontal (a), lateral (b), and superior (c) views of *Australopithecus africanus* (1), *A. robustus* (2), and *A. boisei* (3), contrasting facial and cranial structures. *A. boisei* shows the largest grinding dentition, muscular attachments, and bony buttresses. (After Tobias, 1967.)

and orangutan. Figure 7.5 shows various cranial capacities in contrast.

Halloway has recently examined available endocasts of primate fossils and concludes that the size of australopithecine brains is slightly smaller than originally thought and essentially human in neurological organization. He explains that this creature's brain had the same proportional relation to the size of its body that the modern human's brain does to its body.[7]

It is well established that no correlation exists

[7]R. L. Halloway, "The Casts of Fossil Hominid Brains" (*Scientific American*, vol. 231, July 1974), p. 112.

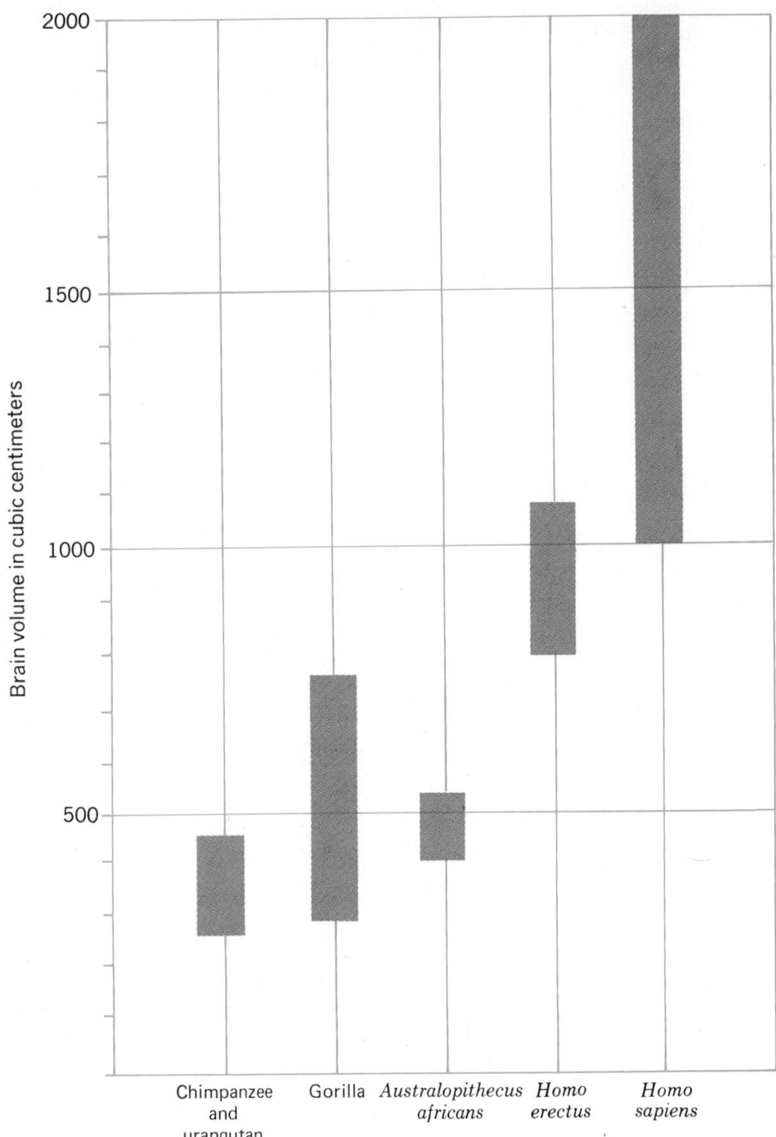

FIGURE 7.5
The ranges of cranial capacities of the great apes, *Australopithecus africanus*, *Homo erectus*, and *Homo sapiens*.

between brain size and mental ability within the human species except in pathological cases of microcephaly and macrocephaly. It will be seen that the higher fossil hominids all have relatively large brains; in the case of humans, the minimal size (except for microcephalics) is 1000 cubic centimeters, whereas the largest nonpathological brains run to 2000 cubic centimeters. The human mean is 1361 cubic centimeters for males and 50 cubic centimeters less for females. Males have larger brains because their bodies are generally bulkier. This size difference between male and female of the species is called *sexual dimorphism.*

We hasten to point out, however, that an assumption made too easily in the past has been that a simple relationship exists between brain size and the evolution of cognitive powers. There are several reasons why this is wrong. There is no evidence for a direct correlation between size of the brain and development of cognitive skills. There are no features observable in the brain or a cast of the brain which would rule out toolmaking for even the smallest brained hominid ancestors or for the many living, tool-using vertebrates. Further, there is no area of the brain or minimal amount of brain which can be associated with a toolmaking area. The brain appears to work as a total unit, with things going on simultaneously in different areas in an interconnected manner, and with parts of the brain "taking over for" other parts which have been damaged or incapacitated. The amount of convolutedness (how much the brain surface is "wrinkled") is also not a good indication for the level of organization of the brain. As Jerison points out:

> *The bottlenose dolphin's brain is much more convoluted than the human brain, just as the human brain is more convoluted than the chimpanzee brain. A horse brain is more convoluted than a monkey brain. Comparisons with respect to convolutedness should be made among brains of approximately equal size rather than within a phylogenetic series of brains of increasing size. In such comparisons one recognizes that convolutedness is no better a criterion for level of organization than is absolute size. In the evolution of the primate brain to the hominid grade, new convolutions had to be added simply because the brain was enlarged.*[8]

The skull of *Australopithecus africanus* presents a high, fairly rounded cranial vault when compared with that of the gorilla. The next feature that excites interest is the low position of the occipital ridge for the attachment of neck muscles. This phenomenon is distinctly hominid rather than apelike. The mammalian skull hinges on the atlas (the first cervical vertebra) by means of two bulbous knobs, the occipital condyles. In quadrupeds these are located on the vertical rear wall of the skull. In apes they are at the back of the skull but moved forward and oriented on a slanting plane. In *Homo sapiens* they are well under the skull, beneath the auditory meatus, and horizontally oriented. The position of the occipital condyles of *Australopithecus africanus* approximates their position in humans and is therefore hominid rather than pongid in quality. The position of the occipital condyles is functionally related to the orientation of the foramen magnum. It follows that in this feature, too, the australopithecines are hominid.

All these traits together indicate that in spite of the apparent general primitiveness of the cranial appearance of *Australopithecus africanus* and the relative puniness of its brain, the structure of the cranium exhibits generalized hominid features and predicates upright posture.

The dental features of *Australopithecus africanus* also link the creature to *Homo sapiens*. The alveolar arch is rounded and short instead of being narrow and deep as is the ape's. The canine teeth are much reduced in size and do not flare out or project beyond the cutting edges of the incisors and premolars, as do the tusklike canines of the pongids. The incisors and premolars (the cutting teeth) are relatively larger than the molars (the grinding teeth) when compared to those of the vegetarian apes. This is very much a humanlike feature. In details of cusp form and root structure of the teeth, *africanus* points toward humans. More than this, the immature fossils of *Australopithecus africanus* indicate a tendency toward early replacement of the deciduous teeth by the permanent dentition—a trait which is characteristic of the hominids. This development is a function of the growth period relative to the total lifespan.

---

[8]H. J. Jerison, "Fossil Evidence of the Evolution of the Human Brain" (*Annual Review of Anthropology*, vol. 4, 1975), p. 35.

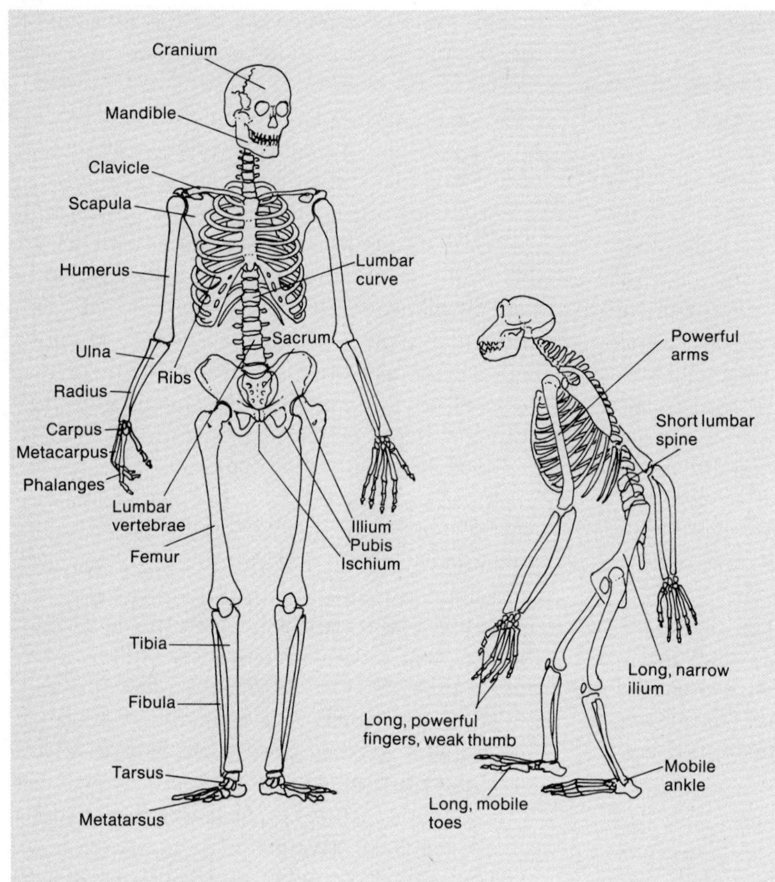

FIGURE 7.6
Comparison of *Homo sapiens* and *Pan troglodytes* to illustrate various bones to which the text refers. (Biruta Akerbergs.)

The Pelvis and Upright Posture: *Africanus*

On the evidence from the skulls of *Australopithecus africanus* and their teeth alone, we are probably confronted with an upright, ground-living creature who was less ape than human, in spite of its small brain. But then, it takes more than just brains to walk upright. It requires a proper skeletal and muscular structure to do so with even moderate efficiency (see Figure 7.6).

Among the earliest hominoids, it was the chest-shoulder-forearm complex that first underwent marked modification through adaptation to brachiation. Then, as the ancestors of the hominids took habitually to the ground, the next great segment to be generally modified was the pelvic-lower-limb complex. Modification of the jaw-face-cranial complex (particularly the great enlargement of the brain) came later in the phylogeny of human precursors.[9] It is now held that the complex of features related to upright posture is the most important morphological characteristic of the hominid line and the prelimi-

[9] S. L. Washburn, "The New Physical Anthropology" (*Transactions of the New York Academy of Sciences*, vol. 13, 1951), pp. 298–304; also "Tools and Human Evolution" (*Scientific American*, vol. 203, 1960), pp. 62–75. See also W. E. Le G. Clark, *The Fossil Evidence for Human Evolution*, pp. 11, 13–14, 123.

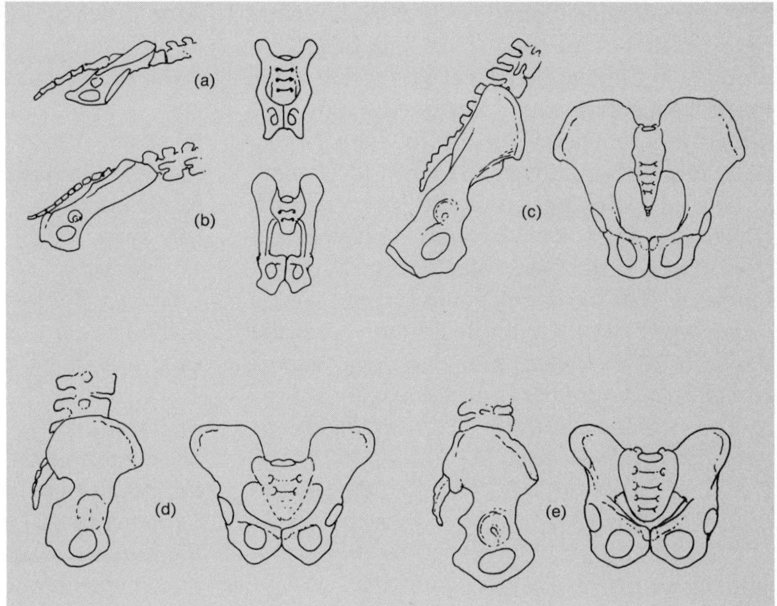

FIGURE 7.7
Side and front views of the pelvis of (a) lemur, (b) macaque, (c) gorilla, (d) Australopithecus, and (e) *Homo sapiens*. (McKern and McKern, 1974.)

nary condition for the later mental development that came to characterize the genus *Homo.*

What of the pelvis and legs of the australopithecines? With additional finds, there now exists sufficient evidence to state the following conclusions about the australopithecine adaptive modifications of the pelvic configuration that make it functionally effective for upright posture and walking (see Figure 7.7).

1. The extension of the lateral attachment of the gluteal musculature of the buttock in a broadening of the ilium. This produces an adequate balancing effect for the upper portions of the body, which rest on the sacrum.
2. The downward swing of the iliac crest in the sacral area. This places the point of attachment of the gluteus maximus behind (instead of at the side of) the hip, improving the effectiveness of its extensor function in erect walking.
3. The shift of the sacrum (on which the spinal column now rests) upward and closer to the hip socket (acetabulum). This improves stability in transmission of the weight of the trunk to the hip joint and also provides a basinlike support for the internal organs which now rest in the abdominal-pelvic basin.
4. The new ruggedness of the anterior iliac spine. This provides a first rooting for the ligament (the iliofemoral) that extends to the femur to provide countertension to the gluteus maximus in erect standing.
5. The shortening of the distance between the ischial tuberosity and the acetabulum. This brings the anchorage of the upper end of the hamstring muscles into a position behind the hip joint rather than under it, a further aid in the maintenance of upright posture.[10]

In addition to the pelvic and leg-bone materi-

[10]Le Gros Clark, op. cit., pp. 151–152. For a good summary discussion of the associated musculature, see J. Buettner-Janusch, *Origins of Man: Physical Anthropology*, pp. 138–141.

als, the australopithecine finds include many fossilized bones of the hands and feet. One group from Olduvai Gorge includes twelve of the major bones of a single foot so perfectly preserved that the details of the foot are readily reconstructable. Although this fossil foot is smaller than an adult human foot, the first metatarsal, which is the key bone to the arch, is hominid and the big toe is structured and positioned like a human's. That is, it is *big*, points forward, and is not splayed out. It is the lever that bears the thrust of the forward stride as each step is completed and the next one started.

The skeletal structure of *Australopithecus africanus* reveals a small, 50- to 90-pound individual who stood from 4 to 4½ feet tall and ran on its hind legs.

Australopithecus robustus

A creature first discovered by Robert Broom at Kromdraai in 1938 and called *Paranthropus* (Gr. *para*, "near," and *anthropos*, "man") is today recognized as *Australopithecus robustus*. It is bigger, bulkier, more muscular, and, above all, has larger molar teeth than *Australopithecus africanus*.

The cranial bones of *robustus* are thick and the braincase itself is not larger than that of *africanus*. Instead of the rounded forehead of *africanus*, however, *robustus* has a sloping forehead, which leads back to a sagittal medial crest like a gorilla's (Figures 7.2 and 7.4). This makes it clear that it was heavy-jawed, for the sagittal crest anchors the thick muscles that work the jaws. The lower jaw is indeed made of massive bone. Concomitantly, the nasal area of the face is flat.

Robustus's teeth also fit the same picture. The chewing and grinding teeth (premolars and molars) are very large, larger than human teeth and those of *africanus*. Its incisors are smaller than those of *africanus*, however. Its immense molars have enamel 3 millimeters thick, three times as thick as those of *africanus* and humans. They are worn down and pitted, as if from chewing gritty food.[11]

Finally, *robustus* has added a unique sixth cusp to its molars. It is rare among hominids, but invariable with *robustus*. It may turn out to be an important diagnostic feature for linking it to fossils elsewhere, whatever its functional significance was for the living creature.

The pelvic remains are similar to those of *africanus*, but larger. The long bones indicate a much heavier body size (100 to 150 pounds, as against 50 to 90 pounds for *africanus*).[12]

Australopithecus boisei

More information is available on the gracile and robust forms of the australopithecines than on the other fossils. In 1959 L. S. B. Leakey found the remains of another australopithecine with a robust cranium, which he first called *Zinjanthropus boisei*, in Bed I at Olduvai. Mary Leakey had discovered two milk teeth in Bed II in 1954. Since then other remains have been found in East Africa, at Lake Natron and Olduvai in Tanzania, east of Lake Turkana in Kenya, and at Omo in Ethiopia.

The level of the cranium from Olduvai is dated as 1.75 million years old. Fossils of *Australopithecus boisei* from Omo deposits date from 3.7 to 1.85 million years ago. The richest source of the remains of this creature are found east of Lake Turkana. The material found there dates from 2.5 to 1.5 million years ago and by 1972 included parts of sixteen individuals. The most recent evidence for this fossil has been reported from northern Kenya and is about 1.1 million years old.[13]

---

[11] J. T. Robinson, "The Dentition of the Australopithecinae" (*Transvaal Museum Memoirs*, no. 9, 1956), p. 149.

[12] J. T. Robinson, "The Origins and Adaptive Radiation of the Australopithecines," in G. Kurth (ed.), *Evolution und Hominisation*, pp. 120–140.

[13] J. Carney, A. Hill, J. A. Miller, and A. Walker, "Late Australopithecine from Baringo District, Kenya" (*Nature*, vol. 230, 1971), pp. 509–514.

There appears to be little difference between *Australopithecus boisei* and the other australopithecines in postcranial anatomy. However, its enormous cheek teeth in a massively buttressed face, small brain, low vaulted skull, and massive browridges clearly set it off from *africanus* and *robustus*. The information published so far provides evidence of sexual dimorphism, immense face and jaws, evidence of a very powerful masticatory apparatus, a braincase with sagittal crest, wide zygomatic bones, and very large molars and premolars, about $1^1/_2$ times the size of those of *Australopithecus robustus*. This suggests a heavy dependence on a diet which demanded prolonged grinding and chewing. The endocranial capacity of the brain is estimated at 530 cubic centimeters, significantly larger than *africanus* but the same as *robustus*.

It can be said that *africanus* and *robustus* are more like each other than are *robustus* and *boisei*. Thus, the differences between *boisei* and the other australopithecines are related to those adjustments which must be made in the skull to accommodate an increase in cheek-tooth size. Tobias would agree with this, stating that the australopithecines are "variations on a theme."[14] Pilbeam and Gould, after reexamination of the fossil evidence, conclude that "the three australopithecines are, in a number of features, scaled variants of the 'same' animal."[15] *Australopithecus boisei*, like the other australopithecines, occupied a special open-country niche, coming later than *africanus*, possibly its descendant.

LIFE AND CULTURE OF *AUSTRALOPITHECUS*

It is not enough to know from the skeleton that *Australopithecus africanus* had risen to the potential of early humanity. One wants immediately to ask, "Did it use or make tools? Is there evidence that it had a culture?"

Australopithecus africanus, the gracile form, continued the adaptation by *Ramapithecus* in Miocene times of eating seeds and small food items.[16] The adaptive change added by *Australopithecus africanus* was a taste for meat along with vegetables, which seems to have been a critical factor in early human history, for it is associated with tool production and use. *Africanus* entered upon the exploitation of tools and weapons as extensions of the arm and so started our ancestors on the road to cultural adaptation. Henceforth, all hominid evolution is simultaneously biological and cultural. "Human evolution," to repeat Dobzhansky's dictum, "can be understood only as a product of interaction of these two developments."[17]

The social consequences of the new dietary adaptation of *africanus* held tremendous implications for the future evolution of hominid temperament and relationships. Although present-day foraging monkeys and apes move about their territories in groups, each individual is independent in feeding itself. The operation is collectively organized largely in terms of mutual protection against outside aggressors. With their unweaned infants clinging tightly to their furry bodies, females forage exactly as do the males, who feed only themselves.

Hominid hunters and foragers must, however, act differently. Their hands have been freed to fashion and use tools and weapons, and hunting has elicited a further bisexual differentiation in food getting. The role of females in hunting is limited. The mother (with her young) gathers and shares seeds and vegetables near a home base. The active male brings home his kills to share with members of the band or home

[14]P. V. Tobias, *Olduvai Gorge*, vol. 2.

[15]Pilbeam and Gould, op. cit., p. 900.

[16]C. J. Jolly, "The Seed-Eaters: A New Model of Hominid Differentiation Based on a Baboon Analogy" (*Man*, vol. 5, 1970), pp. 19–22.

[17]T. Dobzhansky, "Evolution: Organic and Superorganic" (*The Rockefeller Institute Review*, vol. 1, no. 2, 1963), p. 1.

base.[18] The freeing of the female's hands for tool using has been accompanied by the prolongation of infant dependency, which is related to the protracted postnatal growth of the increasingly complex brain. At the same time, the human species was losing its body hair. There was nothing for human babies to cling to as the mother moved from place to place. In the transitional stages of cultural development, the mother had to carry her young in her arms. Later cultural adaptations have provided net, woven, and fur slings, or even more specialized cradleboards, but still women do not actively hunt.[19]

The Oldowan Culture

The commonest implement at Olduvai was shaped from a river-worn pebble or nodule of quartz or quartzite. The tool took the form of a crude chopper, "varying in size from about the dimensions of a Ping-Pong ball to that of a croquet ball." The irregular and jagged cutting edge was formed by removing flakes in two directions on one side of the stone core.[20] The pebble tool was probably an all-purpose instrument that was used in cutting, digging, and chopping activities.

The most important feature of the tools is that they are intentionally constructed (Figure 7.8). There is a plan and a purpose, an idea and its execution, in these simple worked stones. If one definition of a human is *a primate who is capable of the manufacture of definite tools*, then there were indeed humanlike creatures at Olduvai when Bed I was being deposited.

In addition to the chopper and pounding tools, smaller tools for scraping and cutting have been recovered in association with animal and hominid fossil remains from living floors at Oldu-

[18]J. D. Clark, "African Origins of Man the Toolmaker," in G. L. Isaac and E. R. McCown (eds.), *Human Origins: Louis Leakey and the East African Evidence*, pp. 25–26.

[19]W. C. Mackey, "The Adult Male-Child Bond: An Example of Convergent Evolution" (*Journal of Anthropological Research*, vol. 32, Spring 1976), p. 66.

[20]L. S. B. Leakey, *Olduvai Gorge*, p. 34.

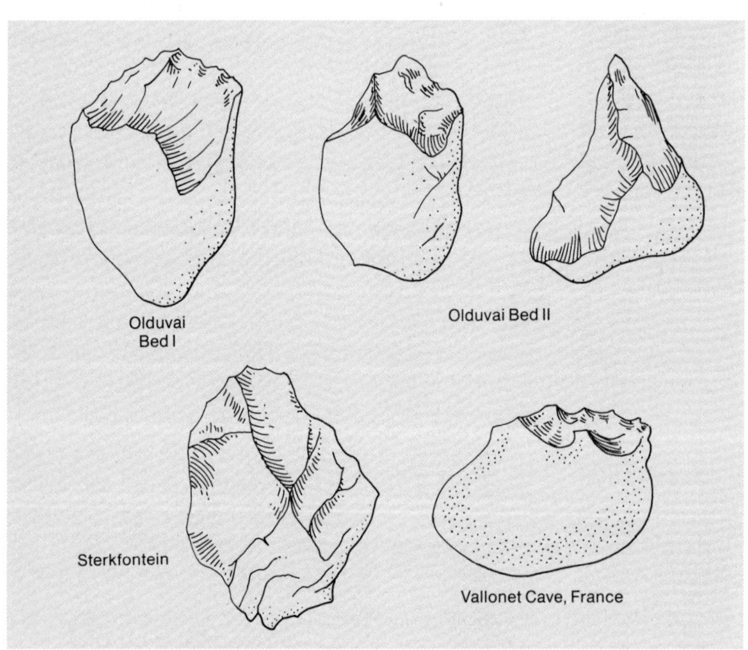

FIGURE 7.8
Various kinds of chopping tools. (Bordes, 1968.)

vai. There were no living floors found in the South African australopithecine sites. An artificial circle of stones found low in Olduvai Bed I seems to suggest the erection of some type of windbreak. According to Mary Leakey the Oldowan culture continues in Upper Bed II and is found in association with hand ax industries. She believes that this evidence indicates the existence of two distinct cultural traditions and that the Acheulean hand ax culture was brought in from elsewhere.

At first the makers of Oldowan tools were thought to be the australopithecines, because no other creature able to make these tools appeared to be present. Now there are a half dozen fossils identified as *habilis* found in various South and East African sites. Authorities are still debating whether to recognize it as a distinct species. Mary Leakey has presented evidence that *habilis* was responsible for the Oldowan assemblage of tools; six instances of *habilis* are found in direct association with these ancient tools.[21] This fossil hominid is described in the next section.

Olduvai Gorge, however, is not the earliest incidence of Oldowan tools. In 1970 an expedition under the leadership of Richard Leakey found Oldowan tools in deposits east of Lake Turkana dating from approximately 2.6 million years ago. Campbell reports a personal communication he received from Howell that tools with an associated date of approximately 3 million years have been found in the Omo Basin of Ethiopia, north of Lake Turkana.[22] This pushes the origin of tools back more than 1 million years before their earliest dated occurrence at Olduvai.

[21]M. D. Leakey, "Preliminary Survey of the Cultural Material from Beds I and II, Olduvai Gorge, Tanzania," in W. W. Bishop and J. D. Clark (eds.), *Background to Evolution in Africa*, p. 417.

[22]R. E. F. Leakey, "Fauna and Artifacts from a New Plio-Pleistocene Locality near Lake Rudolf in Kenya" (*Nature*, vol. 226, 1970), p. 223; B. G. Campbell, "Conceptual Progress in Physical Anthropology: Fossil Man," op. cit., p. 41; J. T. Robinson and R. J. Mason, "Occurrence of Stone Artifacts with *Australopithecus* at Sterkfontein" (*Nature*, vol. 180, 1957), pp. 521–524.

Other Tools

Prehistoric cultures, especially those of Pleistocene hunters, may be reconstructed in only their thinnest outlines. So much rests on inference from limited facts that enthusiastic opinion and intellectual prejudice frequently run far beyond the reasonable limits of the evidence. This leads to a surprising amount of argument over the tool habits of the australopithecines.[23]

Raymond Dart has maintained that *africanus* was a slayer of baboons and other game, used a thighbone of an antelope as a bony bludgeon, and may, somewhat like Samson, even have used half of the lower jaw of an antelope.[24]

Africanus's environment was that of the moderately well-watered savanna, with scattered shrubs and trees among lush grasses. It was prime grazing country and well stocked with game. *Australopithecus africanus* was not a tree dweller, but ran on the ground; its teeth, like those of *Homo sapiens*, were those of an omnivore.

Africanus may have started to eat meat when scavenging for carrion in competition with vultures and hyenas, and undoubtedly continued to do so. *Africanus* seems also to have been a wily predator, but most of its diet, like that of modern hunters, probably consisted of vegetable matter.

Dart argues that these South African australopithecines used weapons in a patterned way—not *stone* tools, to be sure, but clubs of bone. How else could one account for the numerous crushed baboon skulls in the caves in which

[23]The conflict is well summarized by D. L. Wolberg, "The Hypothesized Osteodontokeratic Culture of the Australopithecinae: A Look at the Evidence and the Opinions" (*Current Anthropology*, vol. 11, 1970), pp. 23–38.

[24]See R. A. Dart, "The Predatory Implemental Technique of Australopithecus" (*American Journal of Physical Anthropology*, vol. 7, 1949), pp. 1–16; "The Predatory Transition from Ape to Man" (*International Anthropological and Linguistic Review*, vol. 1, 1953). The argument for *Australopithecus africanus* as killer is given in great detail and with no little vehemence by Robert Ardrey in his *African Genesis*, especially chaps. 7, 9, and 10. Per contra, see S. L. Washburn, "Australopithecines: The Hunters or the Hunted?" (*American Anthropologist*, vol. 59, 1957), pp. 612–614.

Australopithecus africanus is found? Out of one collection of fifty-two *Parapapio* skulls, forty-eight, or 92 percent, had fractured crania. Most of the fractures are on the left frontal region of the baboon skulls, and many bear the imprint of a dual point of impact. Using the reasoning of an expert in forensic medicine testifying on a case of presumptive criminal homicide, Professor Dart argued that the circumstantial evidence shows death by frontal attack with a double-knobbed crusher wielded by a right-handed killer.

A count of the more than a million fossil bones taken from the *Australopithecus* breccia of the cave of Makapansgat shows that 11.2 percent are thighbones of antelope. This is far above the normal proportion of thighbones in ordinary collections of fossilized antelope skeletal material, and of these thighbones, 90 percent are pieces from the knee end (the joint that has double-knobbed condyles). This end most readily serves as a club. Halves of antelope jaws with their sharp molar teeth are also found in numbers out of proportion to reasonable expectancy.

Many feel that Dart overstated the case for the use of bone tools and weapons by these creatures. Recent evidence is contradictory. On one hand, the use of wood and other handy artifacts as tools and weapons by nonhuman primates would seem to make Dart's point more believable. However, there is also strong evidence that predators can create the bone conditions and accumulation used by Dart for his thesis.

HOMO HABILIS

In addition to a gracile juvenile, remains of several other individuals of a similar type have been found by the Leakeys in Olduvai Bed I. Most paleontologists and prehistorians at first accepted the Bed I group tentatively as a local population of *Australopithecus africanus*, but Leakey and his two associate physical anthropologists, P. V. Tobias and J. Napier, claimed membership in the genus *Homo* for the little Olduvai Bed I hominids, on the following grounds: (1) Their estimated cranial capacity of 649 to 724 cubic centimeters gives a mean of 80 cubic centimeters more than the largest known capacity of the australopithecines. (In 1974, Halloway reestimated these measurements as 590, 650, and 687 cubic centimeters for three specimens from Olduvai.) (2) Their small teeth and cranial contours give a "total pattern more markedly hominized than that of *Australopithecus*." (3) They may have produced the Oldowan tools.[25] Leakey and his associates therefore named this hominid *Homo habilis* (L. *habilis*, "apt," "skillful").

It appears that a form of australopithecine akin to *africanus* lived at Olduvai in the Pleistocene, at least 1.5 million and possibly 1.8 million years ago. It almost certainly made the simple Oldowan stone tools and an occasional bone tool; for food it ate a variety of bits of small game and tortoises—and, of course, vegetables.

The species is now well represented with finds from East Africa—from Olduvai (15 individuals from Beds I and II), East Turkana, Omo, and a few other places. *Homo habilis*, or *Australopithecus habilis* as some prefer to call it, is gracile like *Australopithecus africanus* but has smaller cheek teeth, larger anterior teeth, and a larger brain. The position of the foramen magnum and the postcranial skeleton indicate that *habilis* is more like *Homo erectus* than the other South and East African fossils. The analysis of cranial and postcranial materials available on *habilis* indicates that it was a small biped, perhaps no more than 4 to 4½ feet tall, with arm and chest girths which may have been slightly more robust than those of modern humans.

Whether to assign this fossil to *Homo* or to *Australopithecus* is still being widely debated.

[25] P. V. Tobias, "Early Man in East Africa" (*Science*, vol. 149, 1965), p. 27. See also S. Tax (ed.), "The Origin of Man" (*Current Anthropology*, vol. 6, no. 4, 1965), pp. 342–438.

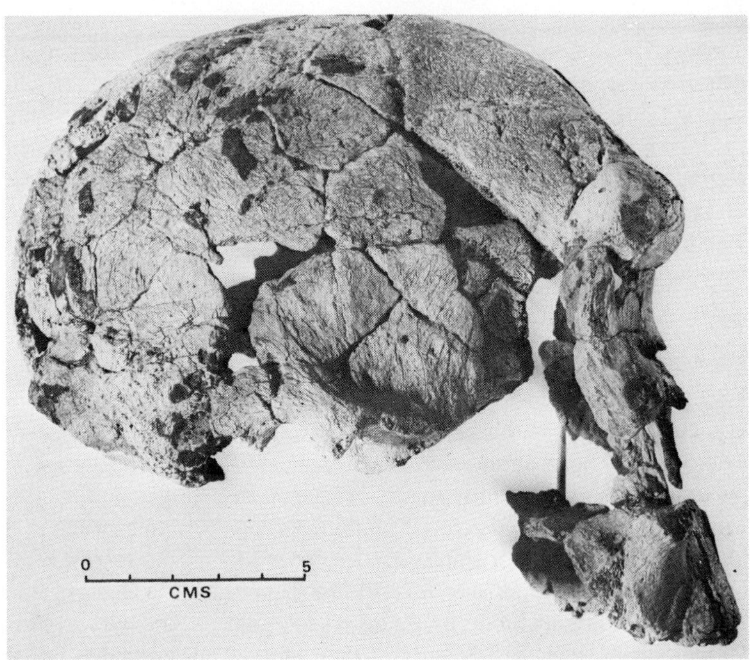

FIGURE 7.9
Assembled KNM-ER 1470 skull from East Rudolf, East Africa. (National Museum of Kenya.)

The discussion befits the seriousness of the problem of assigning a transitional form to one genus which may have been evolving from another. Campbell, among others, refers to it as *habilis* and leaves the genus open. For the reasons stated above, we will use the terms interchangeably until the matter has been adequately settled.

Homo habilis at Olduvai, East Turkana, and Omo spans an accepted radiometrically determined time period of between 3.5 and 1.5 million years ago. Three fragments, a temporal bone at Chemeron, a humerus at Kanapoi, and a piece of mandible at Lothagam, have been dated from 5.5 (Lothagam) to 1.5 (Chemeron) million years ago. The number of finds for this fossil exceeded fifty in 1972. Whether or not it is ultimately granted separate specific designation, it is apparent that the form was contemporaneous with the three australopithecine fossils of South and East Africa.

Richard Leakey, following in the footsteps of his remarkable parents, after a series of expeditions into the region east of Lake Turkana in Kenya, in 1972 recovered an amazing new fossil skull. The skull is known as KNM-ER 1470 and was estimated at 2.9 million years old (see Figure 7.9). The surprising aspect of the specimen is that its brain is considerably larger than any of the australopithecine or *habilis* brains. Halloway examined an endocranial cast of the skull and verified that the relatively large brain is essentially human in neurological organization. Halloway feels that this pushes the history of hominid brain evolution back in time to the boundary between the Pliocene and Pleistocene epochs.[26]

KNM-ER 1470 has been tentatively assigned to *Homo habilis* and is believed to be a large-brained (775 to 800 cubic centimeters) early hominid that was contemporaneous with the australopithecines. The cranial capacity of this

[26]R. L. Halloway, op. cit., p. 110.

find is above the habiline range and is in the lower part of the *Homo erectus* range. The disturbing aspect of this fossil was that its brain seemed too large for its early geologic age. Redating of the tuff (a type of rock) in the formation which yielded the fossil shows an age of 1.6 to 1.8 million years. This pushes KNM-ER 1470 more comfortably toward the *Homo erectus* arena.[27]

SUMMARY

The australopithecines of South and East Africa are the first upright, bipedal hominid fossil primates. There are three recognized species—*Australopithecus africanus*, *Australopithecus robustus*, and *Australopithecus boisei*. Morphologically, *africanus* is rather small (50 to 90 pounds) and agile. Its cranium is smooth and broad, with a rounded frontal contour, and it housed a brain varying from 400 to 530 cubic centimeters—about the size of an ape's, but smaller than the minimum for *Homo sapiens*. Its dentition consists of canines and molars that are relatively much reduced in size, combined with enlarged incisors and premolars. It had evolved from normal primate vegetarianism to become omnivorous and a predatory hunter, who in South Africa may have used bone clubs and at Olduvai produced a stone-tool industry (the Oldowan). Whether it was an australopithecine or *habilis* who made and used the tools at Olduvai, is not entirely clear from the evidence available. From the use of such tools, we infer that it had a genuine culture.

Australopithecus robustus grew to almost double the size of *africanus*. Its heavy jaw housed massive masticatory molars, which were worn down by chewing gritty roots and vegetables. Its forehead was low and recessive, running back to a strong sagittal crest.

At Olduvai Gorge, Tanzania, a number of other interesting fossils have thus far been found. Those in Bed I are associated with an Oldowan lithic industry; the inhabitants were unquestionably toolmakers and probably meat-eating hunters. Except for the *robustus* specimen of Bed I, the others are small, with a brain size that is estimated by Tobias to run up to 725 cubic centimeters. With Leakey and Napier, Tobias takes the position that these forms should be classed as *Homo habilis* on the basis of their purported toolmaking dexterity. Others believe they fit into the *Australopithecus africanus* range of variability.

The australopithecines of Africa had the essential attributes of human beings—upright posture, a large brain and tools with which to hunt, fight, and butcher. They were already humanlike and they had given evolution a new direction.

[27]G. Curtis, T. Drake, R. Cerling, and T. Hampel, "Age of KBS/tuff in Koobi Fora Formation, East Rudolf, Kenya" (*Nature*, vol. 258, 1975), p. 395.

SELECTED READINGS

The following are suggested in addition to those recommended at the end of the previous chapter:

Brace, C. L., *The Stages of Human Evolution* (1967). A book which is easy to read and which presents a concise overview.

Isaac, G. L., and E. R. McCown (eds.), *Human Origins: Louis Leakey and the East Africa Evidence* (1976). An excellent collection of articles by many of the experts in the field. Nice reviews; some articles are reprinted.

McKern, S. S., and T. W. McKern, *Living Prehistory: An Introduction to Physical Anthropology and Archaeology* (1974). An interesting review of the two fields. Highly recommended.

Pilbeam, D., *The Ascent of Man* (1972). One of the best and most detailed accounts of the stages of human evolution, including discussions of the various fossils involved. Authoritative. Good bibliography.

Washburn, S. L., and R. Moore, *Ape into Man: A Study of Human Evolution* (1974). A popular and readable account, with interesting examples.

8
Homo Erectus

CHAPTER OUTLINE

LEARNING GOALS

Identify the morphological characteristics and culture of *Homo erectus erectus.*

Examine the morphology and culture of *Homo erectus pekinensis.*

Review the culture of *Homo erectus* in other places.

Discuss the Acheulean tradition at Olduvai Gorge.

Evaluate the fossil evidence for *Homo erectus* in Africa, Europe, and Hungary.

The first *Homo erectus* fossil was discovered in 1891 in Java. *Homo erectus* (L. *erectus*, "upright") stands midway between the australopithecines and *Homo sapiens* in the sequential order of hominid development (see Table 8.1). The dominant view among human paleontologists is that *Homo erectus* evolved out of the *Australopithecus africanus* gene pool. It should be kept in mind that the australopithecines were sparsely dispersed over Africa, the Near East, and South Asia, and that not all populations would necessarily be evolving at the same rate. Some could have changed to bring forth one or more hominid features of *Homo*, while yet other populations produced other new features. Still other populations might, at the same time, have changed little genetically, or not at all.

Eventually, however, under generally similar environmental conditions, the new surviving genes would tend to spread. For a long while australopithecine populations that had become noticeably *Homo*-like would exist simultaneously (but in different areas) with those which remained australopithecine. Thus, fossil remains of *Homo erectus* and *Australopithecus* are found in geological deposits of the same geological age. In Java and Africa, fossil australopithecines and the earliest representatives of the genus *Homo* are both found in late Lower Pleistocene or early Middle Pleistocene beds. By the end of the Middle Pleistocene the *australopithecines* had become extinct and were replaced by *Homo erectus*.

HOMO ERECTUS ERECTUS

When first discovered in Java, the original fossil seemed to be as much ape as human in the opinion of its discoverer, the Netherlander Eugene Dubois. Hence, it was named *Pithecanthropus erectus* (Gr. *pithecos*, "ape," and *anthropos*, "man"; L. *erectus*, "upright") or

TABLE 8.1
A Classification of the Hominidae*

Date of taxon boundary in millions of years B.P.	Europe	N. Africa	E. Africa	S. Africa	W. Asia	E. Asia	Species	Genus
Present								
	Living Subspecies of Homo sapiens						sapiens	Homo
0.05								
	neandertalensis		*rhodesiensis*		*palestinus*	*soloensis*		
0.3								
	heidelbergensis	*mauritanicus*				*pekinensis*	*erectus*	
0.8								
			leakeyi			*erectus*		
1.3								
			robustus				*africanus*	*Australopithecus*
2.0								
			africanus					
6.0								
					punjabicus			*Ramapithecus*
12.0								
			wickeri					

*This table includes all recognized hominid taxa down to subspecies except for the lineage which is classified as *Australopithecus boisei*.
SOURCE: B. Campbell, "A New Taxonomy of Fossil Man" (*Yearbook of Physical Anthropology*, vol. 17, 1973), p. 197.

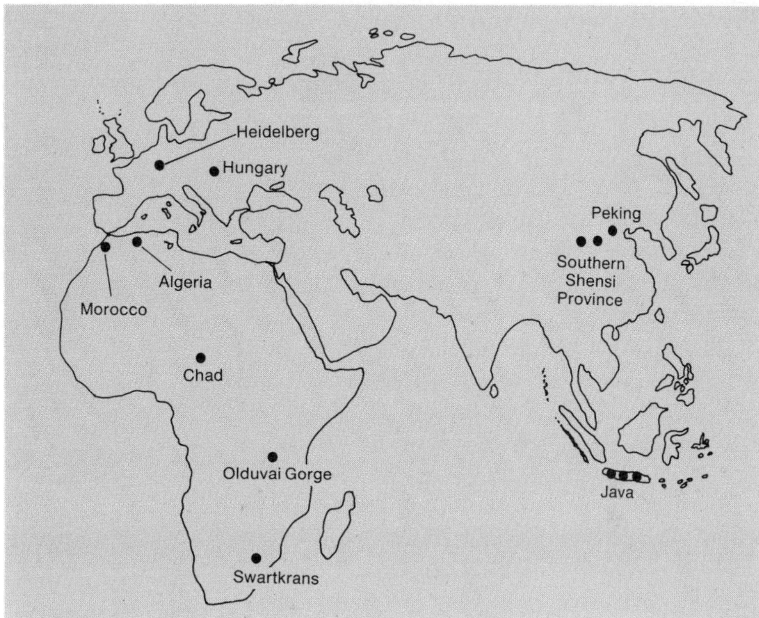

FIGURE 8.1
Locations where *Homo erectus* specimens have been found. (Lasker, 1973.)

"ape-man who stands erect." By 1930, some specialists were convinced that the type was human, albeit not yet *Homo*. Not until 1960 were the majority of physical anthropologists willing to classify the fossils within the human family as *Homo erectus*.

The discovery of the first *Homo erectus* was made in sandstone and conglomerate deposits in the valley of the Solo River near Trinil in Central Java (see Figure 8.1). Dubois first recovered a fossilized and very primitive calvarium of a hominid along with some teeth. A year later, he found a fossilized femur at the same level, some 15 yards away. For at least two decades, skeptics expressed doubt that the femur and calvarium belonged to the same individual and that a being with so primitive a skull could walk bipedally. By 1920, however, the association of the leg bone and skull was generally accepted.

In the mid-1930s, G. H. R. von Koenigswald brought forth a rich harvest of new finds in Java, confirming the validity and expanding our knowledge of Dubois's original contribution. Between 1936 and 1941, when the Japanese invasion put a stop to von Koenigswald's work, six new representatives were found at Sangiran in close proximity to the old Trinil site. Von Koenigswald's assemblage of Java fossils includes a skull (the Modjokerto infant), two complete and two partial calvaria, an excellently preserved upper jaw and teeth, three fragmented lower jaws, and a number of miscellaneous teeth. New discoveries, including three calvaria, fragments of four others, a clavicle, a maxillary fragment and teeth, have been reported from the Trinil and lower levels. A potassium-argon date of more than 1.9 million years of age has been associated with a mandible in the lower (Djetis) level. Very little new information has been added by these finds.[1]

[1]B. G. Campbell, "Conceptual Progress in Physical Anthropology: Fossil Man" (*Annual Review of Anthropology*, vol. 1, 1972), pp. 48–49.

Early and Late *Homo erectus erectus*

Two distinct geological strata are identifiable at Sangiran, Java, where von Koenigswald first worked. The top layer is the same as that which yielded Dubois's Java find at Trinil. Hence, it is called the *Trinil bed*. The Trinil animal fossils and geology show it to have been laid down in a mid-Pleistocene pluvial period, probably equivalent to the second glacial, or about 1,000,000 to less than 600,000 years ago.

The lower stratum contains earlier types of fossil fauna identified as post-Villafranchian and therefore early Middle Pleistocene or, possibly, late Lower Pleistocene. Because they are older than the Trinil beds, these are probably first interglacial, or as old as 1 to 2 million years. These deposits are the *Djetis beds*.

This geological detail is important because two of the known Java skulls of *Homo erectus* come from the Trinil beds and two from the older Djetis bed at Sangiran. It establishes the long continuity of evolutionary development of *Homo erectus* in Southeast Asia.

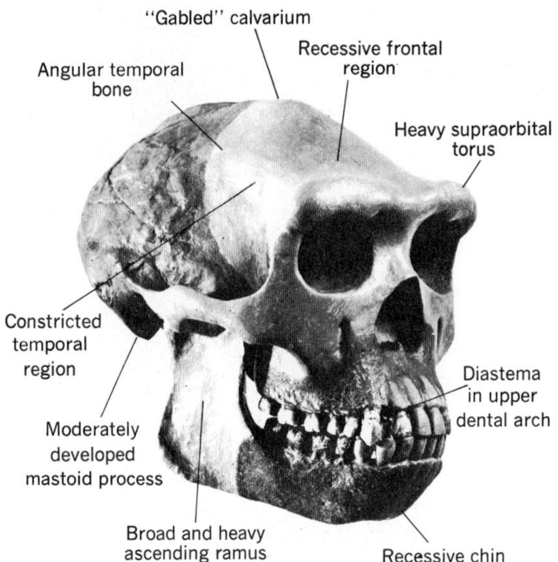

FIGURE 8.2
Restored skull of *Homo erectus erectus* (Java skull no. IV). The dark areas represent the original fossilized sections; the light areas are restorations. (Courtesy of the American Museum of Natural History.)

Morphology of *Homo erectus erectus*

On the basis of the abundant assemblage, it is now possible to be quite specific about the human qualities of *Homo erectus* in Java.

Cranial Characteristics The Java cranium (Figure 8.2) is quite unlike the craniums of the australopithecines. Instead of the relatively high and rounded cranial vault which characterizes *Australopithecus*, the Java specimen has a flat, receding forehead that slopes back from a massive browridge (supraorbital torus). The temporal regions behind the orbital area are very constricted and narrow, and the greatest breadth of the skull is far back toward the occiput and low down in the temporal area. Although there are no sagittal and occipital crests such as are found in the adult male chimpanzee and gorilla, the roof of the skull is markedly gabled, and the occipital region is angular. The mastoid process is only slightly developed, while the foramen magnum is far forward under the skull, much as it is in *Homo sapiens*, contemporary human beings. These indicate upright posture. The general robustness of the cranium suggests the necessity for a heavy neck and jowl musculature to support a powerful jaw.

The palate is huge and there is a strong facial prognathism (forward protrusion of the lower face) conforming to massive jaws with a recessive chin. At the same time, it does not show the slightest trace of a simian shelf (a bony buttress on the inside front of an ape's mandible). The teeth are intermediate in size between those of apes and *Homo sapiens*, but they are preponderantly hominid. Their pongid features are the presence of a slight canine-incisor diastema, or gap, in some but not all individuals, and the large size of the molar teeth relative to those in front of the dental arch.

Halloway made endocasts of five of the avail-

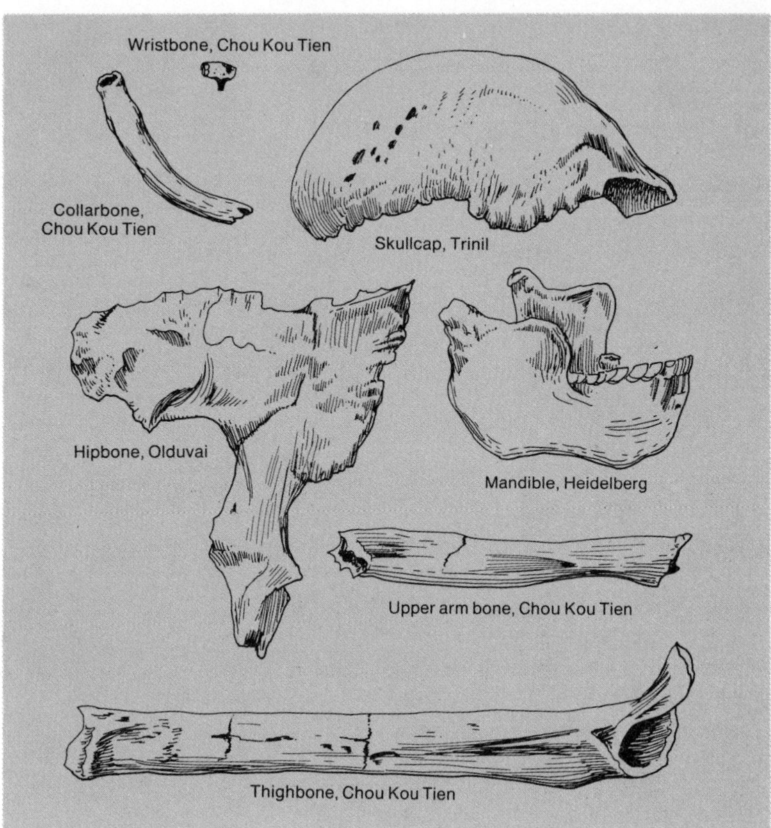

FIGURE 8.3
Various fossil bones of *Homo erectus.* (Adapted from White, 1973.)

able six specimens from Java and of the two from Olduvai in Africa. The largest cranial capacity is Olduvai hominid 9, with 1067 cubic centimeters, and the smallest is one from Java, with 815 cubic centimeters. The average, measured from endocasts, is 930 cubic centimeters.[2] This puts *Homo erectus* well above the apes and australopithecines but somewhat below the average for *Homo sapiens* (about 1350 cubic centimeters).

The Femur In all respects the femur is a human type of thighbone, one that goes with bipedal posture: it is long and slender and has a ridge (the linea aspera) running down the dorsal side for the anchorage of the hamstring muscles, which are so important in the upright position. Recent fluorine analysis confirms the contemporaneousness of all the femurs with the skull and with the extinct Pleistocene mammals that come from the same deposit. In addition, the later Peking finds conform to the same kind of skull-leg complex (see Figure 8.3).

Cultural Evidences

No stone or bone artifacts have as yet been recovered in direct association with the remains of *Homo erectus* in Java. However, a stone-flake industry, called *Patjitan*, is best known from the

[2]R. L. Halloway, "The Casts of Fossil Hominid Brain" (*Scientific American*, vol. 231, July 1974), pp. 113–115.

FIGURE 8.4
Patjitan chopper tools from the upper Trinil beds in Java. (Courtesy of the American Museum of Natural History.)

upper portions of the Trinil beds in other parts of Java (see Figure 8.4). The implements are crude, scrapers or chopping tools with beveled U-shaped edges such as those which characterize adzes. The Patjitan choppers are early representatives in Java of the great Eastern *chopper-tool tradition*, which extends through Java, Burma, India, and Pakistan to the Valley of the Indus and north through China and into Japan.[3] Pointed "pebble" tools similar to those of the Oldowan are also included in the inventory of the tradition. It is reasonable to infer that Java hominids were toolmakers. They have not left such direct evidence of their hunting prowess as has *africanus*. However, their later descendants in Java (*Homo sapiens soloensis*) and their close relatives in China (*Homo erectus pekinensis*) were great hunters and eaters of human brains (see pages 137–138).

[3]The Burmese form of the tradition is known as *Anyathian*; in Pakistan it is the *Soan*; in China it is the *Choukoutienian*.

HOMO ERECTUS PEKINENSIS

A more developed variety of *Homo erectus* has been found in profusion, not far from the capital of mainland China.

The great homesite of the first Peking finds, called Choukoutien, was originally a vast cavern with a lofty ceiling 100 feet above the floor and $1^2/_3$ times as long as a football field. During its prolonged use through a time of relatively stable climate, it became filled with bones, tools, and muck. During the long Middle Pleistocene it was a refuge as well as a refuse dump for *Homo erectus*. The approximate dates of the deposits range between 800,000 and 500,000 years ago.

Between 1924 and 1939, in the years preceding the Japanese invasion of China, fourteen different skulls, some facial bones, quantities of teeth, and eleven limb bones were recovered—the remains of forty or more individuals. The diggings also showed ample evidence of the use of fire and yielded a plentiful supply of simple stone tools and other evidence of cultural activities. The fossils were all lost in the Japanese invasion of December 1941.[4] Fortunately, Franz Weidenreich had sent excellent casts of the fossils to the United States before World War II, and his detailed reports make the total loss of the original fossils less of a catastrophe.

Once the war was over and the revolution which followed completed, the new Chinese government continued the fine tradition established by the old Chinese Geological Survey. Since 1949 there have been numerous additional discoveries of *Homo erectus* as well as of fossilized early *Homo sapiens* and some forms which appear to be transitional between *erectus* and *sapiens* in China.[5]

The evidence shows that the Peking humans had at least four characteristics that went beyond those of their south-country cousins in Java. They had distinctly larger cranial capacities. They had fire—which was one reason they could live in caves. They had better tools and weapons, and they seem to have had a penchant for eating other Peking people.

Morphology of *Homo erectus pekinensis*

Comparison of Figures 8.2 and 8.5 shows the superficially observable similarity and the singular differences between *Homo erectus erectus* and *Homo erectus pekinensis*.

[4]C. L. Brace and M. F. Ashley Montagu, *Man's Evolution*, pp. 175–179.

[5]K. C. Chang, "New Evidence on Fossil Man in China" (*Science*, vol. 136, 1962), pp. 749–760.

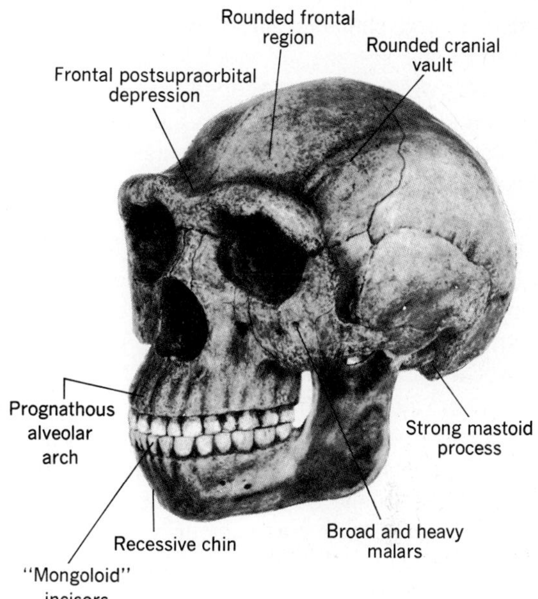

FIGURE 8.5
Skull of *Homo erectus pekinensis*. (Courtesy of the American Museum of Natural History.)

Cranial Characteristics There is the similar heavy supraorbital torus, the recessive forehead, the constricted frontal region, the angular occiput, the protruding face, and the massive jaw with a receding chin. In *pekinensis*, however, there is no diastema (gap) of the upper dental arch. The most significant difference is in the size and contour of the calvarium. There is a marked expansion of the brain itself, and the braincase has enlarged and rounded out to accommodate it. The cranial capacity of the Peking *Homo erectus* not only overlaps but also attains volumes well above that of the Java fossils. The Peking cranial vaults run from 850 to 1300 cubic centimeters, with a mean of about 1075 cubic centimeters. The Chinese fossils thus have a much larger cranial capacity than those of the living apes and *Australopithecus*.

The relative geographic isolation of the Peking population is reflected in a number of osteological characteristics. The first is possession of the so-called Mongoloid shovel-shaped incisor, which is scoop-shaped on the posterior surface, with a ridge across the back of the cutting edge and down the sides. The Java remains lack this characteristic, but it has survived as a diagnostic feature of modern members of Mongoloid peoples, including many American Indians. All the grinding teeth (molars and premolars) have enlarged pulp cavities extending downward into fused roots, a condition known as *taurodontism* (Gr. *tauros*, "bull," and *dontos*, "tooth"). This feature is not exclusively distinctive of *pekinensis*, however. European Neandertals have it, as do many American Indians, Eskimos, and South African Bushmen. The Peking canine teeth are large but, as is true of the rest of the teeth, they are definitely human.

Two other features of the mouth are notably distinctive of *pekinensis*. One is the mandibular torus, a heavy bony ridge inside the lower jaw from the canine to the first molar on each side. It is a common characteristic of subarctic peoples; more than half the Eskimo population has it, and prehistoric Japanese, Chinese, and Scandinavians, among others, reveal the trait in proportions running from one-fifth to two-thirds of their populations. In all likelihood, these peoples were heavy skin chewers, as Eskimos are known to be; skin chewing is a technique that keeps wet boots and clothing from becoming unwearably stiff when they dry. The heavy, deep, but polished wear characteristic of all adult Peking teeth, may indicate the cultural pattern of heavy chewing of soft but tough materials.

The other mandibular feature is the presence of multiple foramina mentalia, the openings in the lower jawbone beneath the first and second premolars, through which pass the nerves and blood vessels serving the muscles and other tissues of the chin and lower cheeks. Most human beings have only one foramen on each side of the jaw—not so *pekinensis*. In the seven recovered mandibles, all have from two to five such openings. Among all the hundreds of known fossil humans, none but *Homo erectus pekinensis* and the human fossils of Ternifine, Algeria, and of Heidelberg, Germany, have more than one. This could have been a special adaptation to the hearty use of chewing muscles, particularly for distribution of the facial blood with less crowding of the major veins and arteries.

Bodily Characteristics The body and limb bones of *pekinensis* have a few distinctive features of the kind which would characterize a localized population. Yet, taken as a whole, the skeleton is indistinguishable from that of *Homo sapiens* today. Just as the australopithecines developed upright posture and other bodily changes far in advance of their cranial development, so *Homo erectus* achieved the modern level of bodily development while it still had a moderately primitive skull, teeth, and face. The evolution of the postcranial (below the skull) human anatomy was thus completed 500,000 years ago. *All subsequent morphological evolution, except for minor variations, has been concentrated in the brain and head.*

The Culture of *Homo erectus pekinensis*

There is no way of knowing whether the Peking population habitually made the Choukoutien caves their home base or whether they just periodically visited them. That they camped in the caves again and again is clear. Deliberately broken and split bones of animals are found by the thousands throughout the deposits; ashes and scorched bones give testimony of the first-known human hearths. The quantities of worked choppers show the continuation of the australopithecine tool tradition.

The people of Peking dined mostly on venison. Two-thirds of the animal bones are those of two species of the fallow deer. Other game that graced their menus included sheep, antelope, roebuck, small horses, and camels. But *Homo erectus pekinensis* was clearly a more wily and ferocious hunter than this inventory alone would indicate. Making up another sizable part of their garbage are the bones of elephants, rhinoceroses, bison, and water buffalo—creatures which would not have invaded the caves themselves. The Peking hunters could have killed these huge beasts by means of fire drives, stampeding them over cliffs before deliberately set grass fires or lines of men, women, and children waving flaming brands. They might also have trapped them individually in pitfalls, or, like the Congo Pygmy, they might even have brought down the great elephant by hiding near the game trails and leaping up under the belly of the lumbering beast, thrusting with a fire-hardened wooden spear, and dodging to safety behind sheltering rocks or trees. Or they might have collected the carcasses of the big game which had stumbled to their death through disease or old age.

Lithic Industry The chopper tools of the Peking artisans did not reach the level of technical excellence attained by *Homo erectus* at the same time in Africa and Europe, where the Chellean-Acheulean tradition was common. The Peking, or Choukoutien, industry, as described by Kenneth Oakley,

> *. . . consists principally of roughly broken pieces of quartz, with a few crudely flaked pebbles of greenstone, quartzite and cherty rocks . . . [O]nly a small percentage of the pieces are recognizable as tools, but these include chopper-like cores and flakes trimmed as points and scrapers. The industry proved to be practically uniform throughout the thickness of the . . . deposits.*[6]

It is as though the cultural adaptation of the Peking human stabilized as an adjustment to an unchanging environment—there was little impulse to improve the stone-tool industry. Another possibility, of course, is that they may have concentrated on wooden tools. More probably, however, in terms of what we know of the dynamics of culture growth, the stability of the long interglacial environment, and their relative geographic isolation from what was going on among other peoples, shielded them from changing selective pressures and isolated them from new ideas generated elsewhere.

Cannibalism Lastly, there is the matter of cannibalism. Cannibalism is of three kinds, classified according to the dominant motivation.

The first is *ritualistic* and *incorporative*. It involves the idea that the special qualities of the victim are contained in the body, which the feaster may incorporate by eating. In some cultures, the transference may be made without ingestion. Head-hunting, such as in Melanesia or among the Ifugao of the Philippines, is practiced to secure the head, which contains the "soul stuff"; this is incorporated in the souls of the slayers through ritual transference.

The second form of cannibalism may be called *gustatory*. People eat people because they like the taste. This practice had a sporadic but widely scattered distribution in recent times. It was common in Oceania and parts of Africa, especially among Congo societies. In both places, prisoners were penned and fattened for the feast, like the hand-stuffed geese of France. Gustatory cannibalism occurred also in parts of Central and South America.

The third form of cannibalism is *survival cannibalism*. It is a final recourse of starving people. Eskimos practiced it without pleasure. In the words of a King William Island Eskimo speaking to Knud Rasmussen:

> *Many people have eaten human flesh, but never from any desire for it, only to save their lives, and that after so much suffering that in many cases they were not*

[6]K. P. Oakley, *Man the Tool-Maker*, p. 113.

sensible of what they did . . . But we who have endured such things ourselves, we do not judge others who have acted in this way, though we may find it hard, when fed and contented ourselves, to understand how they could do such things. But then again how can one who is in good health and well fed expect to understand the madness of starvation? We only know that every one of us has the same desire to live.[7]

In 1847, a wagon train of emigrants from Illinois, the famous Donner party, became snowbound at the foot of the Sierra Mountains in Nevada. As starvation took its toll, a few rose to heights of heroism in snowshoeing across the mountains to bring aid from California; others turned to eat their own dead.[8]

There is no way of knowing what kind of cannibalism *Homo erectus* indulged in, but that members of the species ate human brains and the marrow of human bones seems quite likely. The recovered bones of *Homo erectus* in the Choukoutien caverns were found scattered helter-skelter throughout the deposits, just as were most of the animal bones; both kinds of bones are fractured and split. These are not river-terrace deposits, in which the bones could have been scattered by running water. The bodies of humans and animals had been dismembered, and the bones seemingly smashed and tossed aside by those who crouched and cooked about the campfires.

More significant, in all five of the skulls the foramen magnum at the base of the braincase had been artificially enlarged to the size of a fist. The operation was the same as the one performed on a number of skulls of late Middle Pleistocene *Homo sapiens* (see page 158).[9]

[7]K. Rasmussen, *Across Arctic America*, pp. 223–224.

[8]Grippingly described by G. R. Stewart in *Ordeal by Hunger.*

[9]As late as 1900, five Winnebago Indians in Wisconsin, seeking to prove their manhood and to obtain supernatural war power, went on the warpath by train to kill a Potowatamie Indian, whose heart they cut out, cooked, and ate. See P. Radin (ed.), *Crashing Thunder: The Autobiography of an American Indian*, chap. 22.

THE CULTURE OF *HOMO ERECTUS* IN OTHER PLACES

Homo erectus was found throughout much of the Eastern Hemisphere in Middle Pleistocene times (about 700,000 to 200,000 years ago). Fossil remains have been found in North and East Africa, southwestern Europe, and Southeast and East Asia. These people were probably nomadic and were pushed to the outer limits of the available land areas of the Eurasiatic heartland. Northern Europe and Asia were evidently climatically too intemperate for most of these warmth-loving creatures. With greater adaptability than the australopithecines, they extended the range of occupation somewhat further north than had any earlier hominids. In living habits, *Homo erectus* continued the first thrust of *Australopithecus's* biocultural innovations: fully upright walking, specialized toolmaking, and hunting. To these were added the controlled use of fire.

Tools of the Middle Pleistocene Hunters

In the West, in North Africa,[10] and as far east as the Indus Valley in Pakistan, the basic tool tradition of *Homo erectus* is known as the *Acheulean*, after the original site at St. Acheul, in France. The Acheulean is a stone-tool tradition focused on the hand ax or *coup de poing*, in the terminology established by French archaeologists in the last century. Although the hand ax is the dominant artifact of the Acheulean, varieties of flake tools such as scrapers and knives were also important parts of *Homo erectus's* tool kit.

Hand Ax The hand ax was made from an oblong nodule of flint. Such nodules have a smooth, irregular surface more or less like the skin of a russet potato. This is the *patina.* When flint has been freshly dug, it fractures quite easily.

[10]J. D. Clark, *The Prehistory of Africa*, p. 78.

Using a round rock, 2 or 3 inches in diameter, as a hammerstone, the flint knapper strikes sharp blows around the outer surface of the flint nodule, turning it over and over, removing flakes from both sides. The core could be held in the hand or rested on the worker's knee or on a log. More flakes were removed from one end of the nodule than from the other. The result is an almond- or pear-shaped tool with a broad butt end which fits comfortably into the fist. Projecting below the grip is the pointed working edge of the tool. As a weapon, it could crush skulls. As a tool, it served for hacking limbs from trees, butchering large game, and cracking bones for marrow. In view of the tens of thousands of Middle Paleolithic hand axes recovered in the past 150 years, it must have been that no early man or woman was ever without one.

The perfection of the skills of flint working as applied to the hand ax continued steadily from its earliest manifestations during the crude Abbevillian and Chellean phases of the Acheulean tradition in second glacial and early second interglacial times. By the time of the third glacial advance, control of a hammerstone percussion technique had been much improved. In addition, the introduction of a method of using bars of hardwood or antlers with which to deliver sharp blows for the removal of thinner and smaller flakes resulted in beautifully shaped and finished hand axes of the Upper Acheulean types (Figure 8.6).

FIGURE 8.6
Acheulean hand axes. (Specimens on right, courtesy of the American Museum of Natural History; on left, Museum of Anthropology, University of Minnesota. Photo by Don Breneman.)

The evolution of technological skills of tool production, extending from the Chellean through the Acheulean, spanned 500,000 years and more than 20,000 generations. Early humans could pattern and retain the mental blueprint of learned behavior. They could communicate and transmit the slowly won mastery of new achievements to other members of the group and from group to group, so that the tool traditions became part of an intercontinental cultural pool. But the rate of technical growth and diffusion over half a million years was slow. Compare, in contrast, the technical and social innovations which have been added to the human cultural inventory since James Watt first invented the steam engine eight generations ago.

Flake Tools The Acheulean inventory included, in addition to the hand ax, nicely retouched and especially shaped stone flakes for cutting, planing, and scraping the flesh off hides to be made into leather, and awls to punch holes for sewing.

A few rare finds of ends of sharpened wood

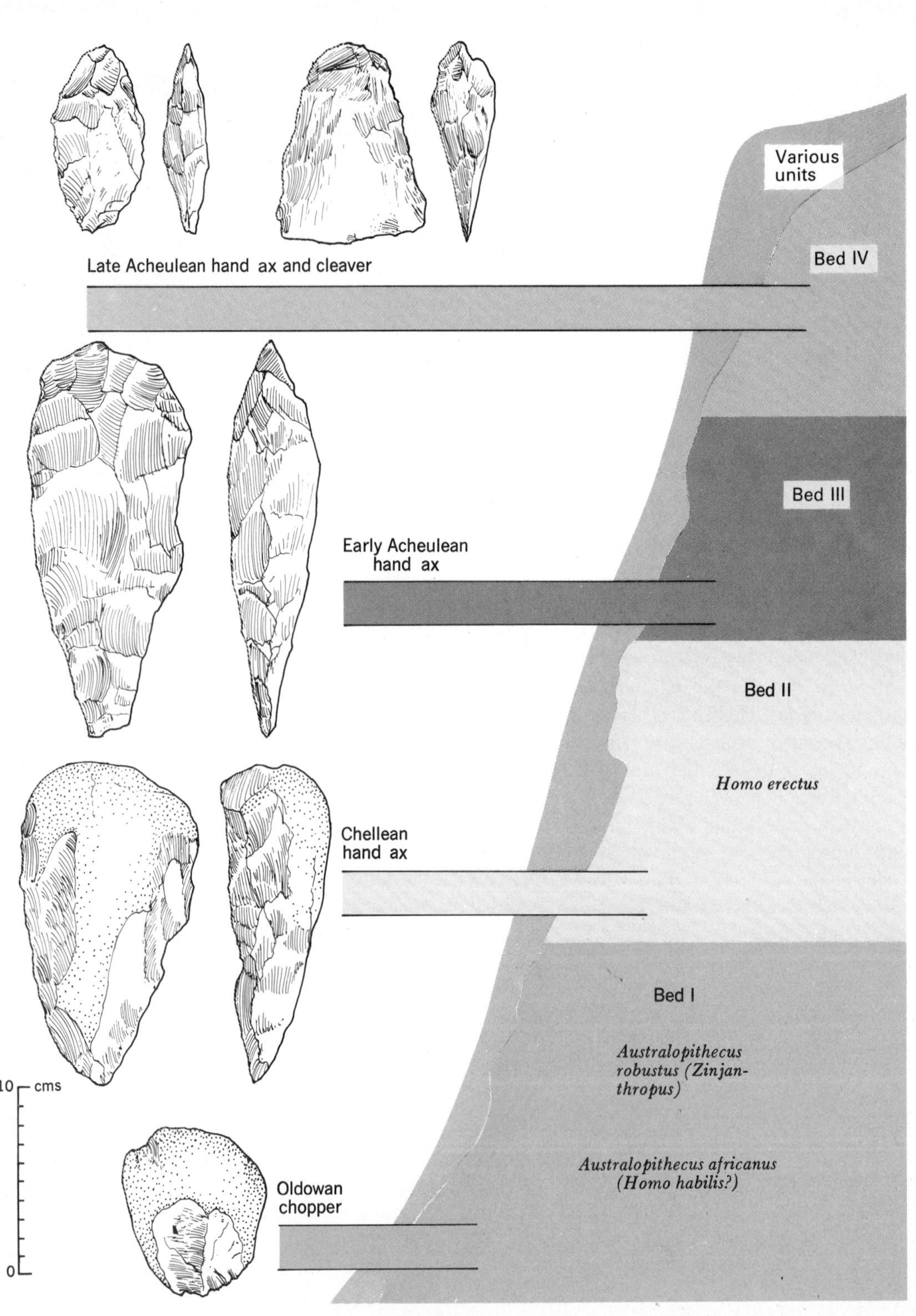

Various units
Bed IV
Late Acheulean hand ax and cleaver
Bed III
Early Acheulean hand ax
Bed II
Homo erectus
Chellean hand ax
Bed I
Australopithecus robustus (Zinjanthropus)
10 cms
Australopithecus africanus (Homo habilis?)
Oldowan chopper
0

staffs indicate that *Homo erectus* possessed spears for hunting and fighting, and digging sticks (dibbles) for root, grub, and rodent gathering.

The Acheulean Tradition at Olduvai Gorge

The relationship of the hand ax traditions to the Oldowan pebble-tool tradition of the australopithecines is neatly exhibited at Olduvai (Figure 8.7). In 1960, Leakey found a *Homo erectus* skull and numbers of Chellean (Early Acheulean) artifacts in the middle of Bed II at a level which yielded a K^{40}-A^{40} date of 500,000 years, although this date is now considered unreliable and the real age may be close to 1,000,000 years. At the very bottom of Bed II, half the artifacts are "indistinguishable from the types found in Bed I, and in appearance characteristic of the Oldowan culture."[11] However, the other half of the artifacts represent a distinct evolutionary advance over the types of tools found in Bed I and are hand axes of the Chellean I type.

At a second level, 10 to 15 feet above the base of Bed II, the hand axes have taken on a specialized quality: the butt ends are thick and massive and usually with a marked flattening on the lower face. Still within Bed II and 20 feet higher are found "large thick hand axes more or less triangular but sometimes roughly oval in outline when viewed from above. The lower face is remarkably flat . . . due to careful flaking which usually extends over the whole inferior face."[12]

[11]L. S. B. Leakey, *Olduvai Gorge*, p. 34.
[12]Ibid.

FIGURE 8.7
Sequence of lithic industries represented by Oldowan pebble-tool chopper and Acheulean hand axes at Olduvai Gorge, Kenya, correlated to geologic strata and fossil remains of hominids. (Tools after L. S. B. Leakey, *Olduvai Gorge, I*, Cambridge University Press.)

At Olduvai Gorge most of the technological evolution of the hand ax is revealed in firm stratigraphic sequence. Yet, this is by no means the full story of the Acheulean traditions in Africa; rich Middle Pleistocene sites with deep stratigraphy covering tens of thousands of years have been exposed all over Africa except for heavy rain-forest areas of the Congo basin.[13] A majority of the African Acheulean industries, however, represent highly developed forms of the tradition.

Of the ecological setting of *Homo erectus* bands, Grahame Clark writes:

> *. . . Acheulean man lived like his forebears of Bed I at Olduvai on alluvial flats surrounding a lake. The banks of the lake itself seem to have been avoided, possibly on account of mosquitoes or in order to avoid disturbing game. The locations chosen for actual occupation were commonly sandy patches along the courses of seasonal runnels; these would have been free of vegetation and no doubt water could have been secured from them by scooping into the bed . . . The areas of occupation . . . suggest that they were limited by some form of shelter or possibly even by a thorn brush hedge.*[14]

The Use of Fire

The Late Acheulean people of Africa also controlled fire, but it is at the open site of Torralba, in Spain, that we learn of the first use of fire in hunting. Although no fossil remnants of humans have been found in the extensive excavations undertaken by F. Clark Howell in 1961, many Acheulean tools attest their presence in the area 300,000 years ago (see Figure 8.8).

The end of the Lower Pleistocene was a time of marked climatic variability in this region. The valley served as a passageway for herds of the great (and now extinct) straight-tusked elephant,

[13]See F. Bordes, *The Old Stone Age*, pp. 64–76, for a handy summary of the African sites. For more technical treatment, see S. Cole, *The Prehistory of East Africa*.
[14]G. Clark, *The Stone Age Hunters*, pp. 36–37.

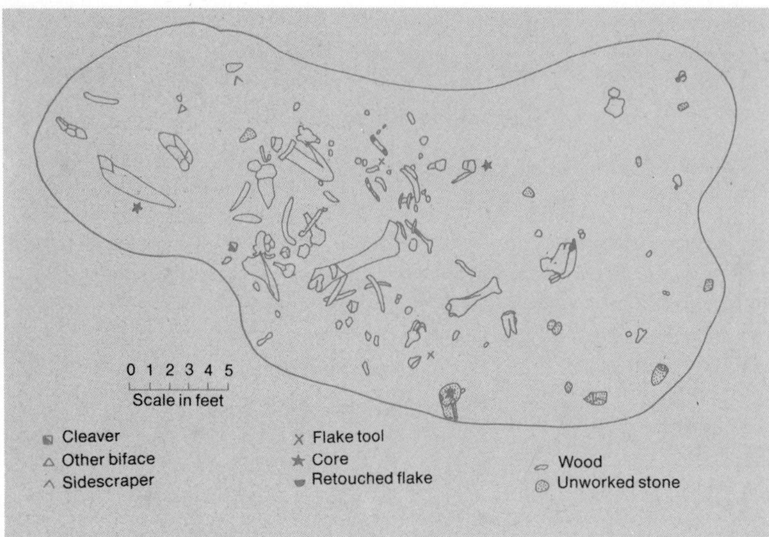

FIGURE 8.8
Living floor at Torralba. (Redrawn from Pfeiffer, 1972.)

deer, aurochs, horses, and many lesser beasts. There they were killed by people armed with Acheulean weapons. The use of fire is attested to by charred pieces of wood and charcoal throughout and around the kill sites. The sites themselves, as soil and pollen analyses indicate, were bottomland bogs into which the herds were stampeded, possibly by setting fire to the dry, late summer grasses. The racing flames would then drive the animals deep into the muck from which there was no escape. Armed with heavy hand axes and wooden spears, *Homo erectus* could then move in for the kill—after the beasts had worn themselves out in fruitless struggles against the sucking embrace of the deadly swamp[15] (see Figure 8.9). The vast numbers of scattered skeletons, well preserved (but few complete), suggest that they were butchered on the spot, with such parts as could be carried away to the campsites stripped and hacked off. The skeletal bulk remained where the beast had died.

One can imagine the gluttonous gorging that followed such a kill. Even if *Homo erectus* had learned how to sun-dry or smoke meat for preservation, there were no means for transportation of food stores beyond what could be carried. These people were migratory hunters, living from hand to mouth and day to day. Like Eskimos who, after a big whale kill, eat as much as 10 pounds of meat each at one sitting, so the Torralba hunters may have similarly indulged themselves a half million years ago.

Consumption of game in such quantities also meant that humans had learned the rudiments of cookery. Knowledge of the art of outdoor barbecuing is surely among the most ancient marks of being human. Our long ancestry of primate vegetarianism did not equip us with the digestive system to handle large amounts of uncooked meat. Cooking effects the chemical and physical transformations necessary to start the digestive process.

It may be too much to attribute the success of *Homo erectus* to a mastery of fire, but there is

[15]For a comparative study of the use of fire drives and their ecological consequences, see O. C. Stewart, "Fire as the First Great Force Employed by Man," in W. L. Thomas (ed.), *Man's Role in Changing the Face of the Earth*, pp. 115–133.

FIGURE 8.9
The close of an elephant hunt. Except that they possess iron-headed, rather than flint-pointed, spears and that the environment is semitropical rather than glacial, these Mandari hunters of the eastern Sudan, Africa, could be reenacting a Paleolithic mammoth hunt. (From P. Molloy, *The Cry of the Fish Eagle*, Michael Joseph, Ltd.)

good reason to believe that this was a key factor in their ecological adaptation.

HOMO ERECTUS IN AFRICA

Recent finds in Algeria and at Olduvai Gorge in Africa add new dimensions to the picture of Middle Pleistocene human accomplishments. At Ternifine, Algeria, during the second glacial, there was a watering hole where humans and animals congregated for their dawn and evening drinking. The humans waylaid antelope, zebras, and giraffes; they feasted on elephants, rhinoceroses, giant baboons, and hogs; and they contested with the saber-toothed tiger. In 1954 and 1955, at the site of this ancient watering hole, C. Arambourg found three human jaws in good condition and part of a human skull among the animal bones. The human materials are too fragmentary to give definitive results, but the expert view is that the heavy jaws and the teeth have much in common with those of Peking finds, while at the same time exhibiting some similarities to features of *Australopithecus robustus*. As is so common with the discoverers of new fossils, Arambourg was convinced that he had a new genus. He named it *Atlanthropus mauritanicus*, while at the same time indicating that it was closely related to the Peking and Java hominids. The contemporary consensus is that "together with other Middle Pleistocene N. African fossils,[16] they may represent a variety of the species *Homo erectus* which can reasonably be associated as a single subspecies."[17] This species, named *Homo erectus mauritanicus*, is the Western counterpart of *Homo erectus pekinensis*.

[16]That is, the 1953 discovery in the quarry of Sidi Abd er-Rahman at Casablanca; the Smugglers' Cave discovery in 1935 at Temara, Morocco; and the Rabat skull of 1933.

[17]B. Campbell, "Quantitative Taxonomy and Human Evolution," in S. L. Washburn (ed.), *Classification and Human Evolution*, p. 66.

In 1960, in the middle of Bed II at Olduvai Gorge, at a level which yields many stone tools and a date of from 500,000 to 1,000,000 years ago, Leakey found a fossil skull that shows "certain superficial characters such as a very large brow ridge and relatively low vault, which recall the Pithecanthropicines."[18] Although Leakey preferred not to think of the new find from Bed II as *Homo erectus,* most anthropologists do. It is presumed to be an East African ancestor of *Homo erectus mauritanicus* and the Olduvai successor to the australopithecines. It has now been named *Homo erectus leakeyi* in honor of L. S. B. Leakey.[19]

HOMO ERECTUS IN EUROPE

The variety of human discovered in 1907 in first interglacial sands at Mauer, near Heidelberg, Germany, deserves mention. It is represented by a massive lower jaw with a perfectly preserved set of teeth more similar in size and character to those of *Homo sapiens* than those of other *Homo erectus* specimens. The jaw itself bespeaks *Homo erectus;* the teeth hint at evolution beyond that level. Without facial or cranial bones, there is no way of knowing whether this is a local European variant of *Homo erectus erectus* or whether it might have come from a population which had already crossed the *Homo sapiens* threshold in first interglacial times.

In 1965, a fossilized human occipital bone plus several teeth were found in association with living floors, hearths, stone artifacts, and Pleistocene mammalian remains in a stratified site at Vertesszöllös, in northern Hungary. The deposits date from the second glacial period. That the people were hunters is evidenced by the remains of rodents, deer, wild cattle, rhinoceroses, and several carnivores. In addition to the hearths, the cultural remains include the kind of chopper tools that are found at Choukoutien in association with *Homo erectus pekinensis.* Nor are they unlike some of the choppers found in certain of the industries in the Oldowan tradition of East Africa.

Although the teeth are similar to those of the Asiatic forms of *Homo erectus* (hence, the provisional classification with *Homo erectus*), the rounded character and other details of the occipital bone suggest affinities with the later European *Homo sapiens steinheimensis,* the early form of *Homo sapiens* found in second interglacial deposits in Europe. It could be that the Vertesszöllös find is a *Homo erectus* in transition to *Homo sapiens.* Time will tell.

SUMMARY

With *Homo erectus* the evolutionary development of upright posture, enlargement of the brain, and basic technology had reached levels unequivocally acknowledged as human. This phase of early humanity was achieved more or less simultaneously in Africa, Europe, and Asia during early Middle Pleistocene times.

Homo erectus is represented by fossil materials from Java, Olduvai Gorge, possibly Heidelberg, Germany, and other sites. Java humans are found in two distinct strata (the Djetis and Trinil beds) of the late Lower Pleistocene and early Middle Pleistocene age. They had a maximal cranial capacity just short of the minimum for *Homo sapiens,* while the largest exceeds that of the australopithecine skulls. The skull is angular, with a recessive forehead behind heavy browridges. The jaw is massive, but the teeth are hominid. The structure of the femur is the same as that of contemporary humans.

No cultural remains have been found in the same deposits with the Java fossils, but the presence of chopper tools in the Trinil beds of Patjitan in Java implies the continuation of the

[18] L. S. B. Leakey, "East African Fossil Hominoidea and the Classification within This Superfamily," in Washburn, op. cit., p. 43.
[19] B. G. Campbell, "Conceptual Progress in Physical Anthropology: Fossil Man," op. cit., pp. 48–49.

pebble-chopper tradition begun by the australopithecines.

In Africa and in Europe, *Homo erectus* developed stone-tool traditions distinguished by the hand ax but also containing a number of specialized varieties of flake tools for cutting and scraping. *Homo erectus* had become a big-game hunter. The site at Torralba in Spain, shows that fire was used in animal drives and in cooking.

The evolution of the Chellean-Acheulean hand ax tradition is clearly depicted at Olduvai Gorge.

While Western *Homo erectus* was building the hand ax tradition, *Homo erectus pekinensis*, who evidently indulged in cannibalism, diversified the Patjitan chopper-tool tradition into that of Choukoutien.

SELECTED READINGS

Bordes, F., *The Old Stone Age* (1968), pp. 51–97. General summary of the Abbevillian and Acheulean traditions in Europe and Africa, compared to Lower Paleolithic Industries in Asia.

Clark, J. D., *The Prehistory of Africa* (1970). Contains a thorough coverage of *Homo erectus* in Africa.

Cole, S., *The Prehistory of East Africa* (rev. ed., 1963), chap. 5, "The Hand-Ax Makers." Covers a number of manifestations of the Chellean in Africa, with an interesting account of the fabulous site of Olorgesaile.

Lasker, G. W., *Physical Anthropology* (1973). A good general coverage of fossil human physical and cultural remains.

Pilbeam, D., *The Ascent of Man* (1972). An authoritative, detailed exposition on early fossil humans, their culture and environments.

9
Early *Homo sapiens*

CHAPTER OUTLINE

LEARNING GOALS

Trace the development from *Homo erectus* to *Homo sapiens*, using evidence from Steinheim, Swanscombe, and Fontechevade.

Examine the Middle Paleolithic Acheulean tradition.

Identify the characteristics of the Clactonian flake tool complex.

Discuss the morphology of *Homo sapiens neandertalensis* and its relation to modern humans.

Review the Mousterian culture of *Homo sapiens*.

Nearly two million years elapsed from the time pebble tools were first used to the threshold of the Upper Paleolithic Age. The process had been started by the australopithecines, or perhaps *habilis*, and was consolidated in Africa, Asia, and southern Europe by *Homo erectus*. In the Middle Paleolithic, it was carried forward by *Homo sapiens*.

As in earlier times, hunting and gathering were still the source of human sustenance, but the techniques were slowly changing. By the middle of the long second interglacial period, human mental development had expanded to the point where, for the first time, present-day paleontologists are willing to classify the fossil remains as those of *Homo sapiens* (L. *sapiens*, "intelligent"). In this group are the Steinheim, Swanscombe, and Fontechevade forms of early *Homo sapiens*. They were the forerunners of the Neandertal people and the later *Homo sapiens*, who would introduce the advanced hunting cultures of the Upper Paleolithic.

HOMO SAPIENS STEINHEIMENSIS

The Steinheim fossil fragments were discovered in southwestern Germany, not far from Stuttgart, in the summer of 1933 (see Figure 9.1). They came from second interglacial gravels containing extinct Pleistocene fauna such as mammoths, rhinoceroses, and bison. The skull and face are well preserved, although twisted and compressed by the pressure of the overlying gravels or possibly by a crushing blow. Nonetheless, they are in sufficiently good condition to allow for clear identification of their features. The forehead is moderately recessive behind marked supraorbital ridges. The occipital region is less angular and more rounded than that of *Homo erectus*; it has a very slight occipital torus, and the mastoids are small but sharp. The cranial capacity of 1150 cubic centimeters is at the lower end of the range for modern human beings. The face is relatively small, and the overall dental configuration is human. It is the skull of a *Homo sapiens* who antedated the Neandertalers and

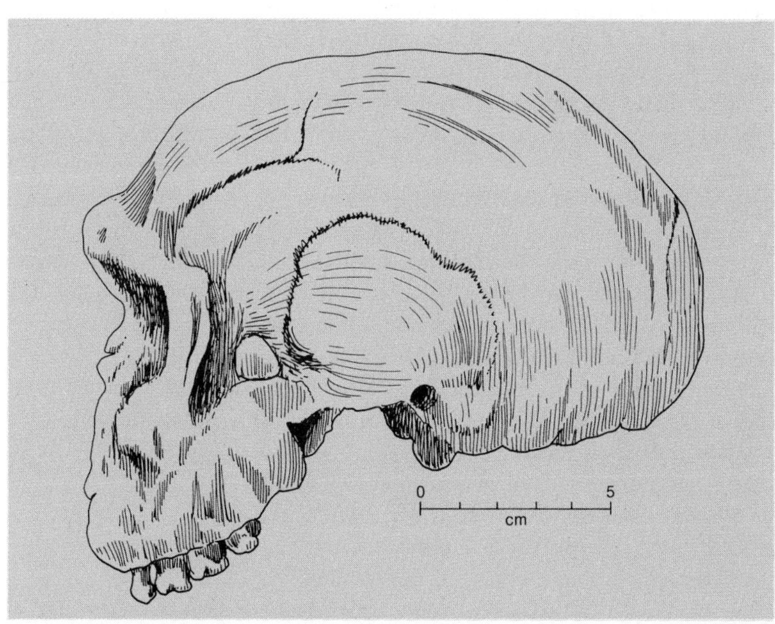

FIGURE 9.1
The Steinheim skull. (Brace, Nelson, and Korn, 1971.)

modern forms of *Homo sapiens* by 250,000 or more years.

The Swanscombe Skull

No artifacts have been found at Steinheim, but at Swanscombe the situation is very different. The Swanscombe fossil comes from a second interglacial terrace of the Thames River. These terraces yielded the first-known Lower Paleolithic hand ax, a beautiful Acheulean specimen found at Gray's Inn Lane, London, in 1680. The usual early, interglacial boreal forest fossil fauna (including elephant, rhinoceros, bison, and horse) abound to demonstrate that the terrace gravels were laid down in second interglacial times.

Samples of the hunters of these beasts, who roughed out the hand axes with which they were killed and knocked off the stone flakes with which they were butchered, were found in 1935 and 1936 by Alvan T. Marston. He first found a human occipital bone embedded in the face of the gravel workings 24 feet beneath the ground surface. Nine months later, after the gravel had been worked back 8 yards, the left parietal of the same skull was found at the same level. And again, in 1955, the right parietal of the same individual was discovered about 50 feet from the first fragment. Fluorine analysis proved the bones to be as old as those of the extinct associated Pleistocene mammals.

Because the muscular markings are light in comparison to the size and thickness of the skull, it is inferred that the individual was a female. Within the thick-boned cranium was housed a brain of approximately 1325 cubic centimeters, just about the modern female average. Even more significant is the modern complexity of cortical convolutions shown on the endocranial cast. The foramen magnum is located well under and forward on the cranium. The Swanscombe woman was upright and human-brained. Although we have no evidence concerning her face, teeth, or bodily structure, she is certainly a member of the genus *Homo;* and, indeed, Morant concluded after detailed study, there is nothing about the fragments that would justify excluding her from the species *sapiens*. By the same token, Weiner and Campbell have shown through multivariant statistical analysis that she does not qualify as a member of the variety *sapiens* (namely: *Homo sapiens sapiens*), to which contemporary modern human beings belong.[1] She is a representative of *Homo sapiens steinheimensis.*

The Fontechevade Specimens

The portions of two skulls found at Fontechevade in southeastern France in 1947 are also classified as *Homo sapiens steinheimensis*. Associated with a Late Clactonian industry called *Tayacian*, and separated from an overlying Mousterian level by a seal of limestone, these skulls are clearly interglacial, possibly second interglacial rather than third. The Fontechevade cranial capacity, 1460 to 1470 cubic centimeters, is slightly larger than the modern average. The skull is long, broad, and low.[2]

The inference to be drawn from these large-brained Middle Pleistocene fossils is that human evolution had achieved its present plateau in Europe and Africa by second interglacial times, with the exception, perhaps, of some changes in the brain which accompanied the full development of language at a later point in time. Populations of *Homo erectus* were still present, but sufficient genetic modifications were widespread, so that many individuals were clearly showing *Homo sapiens* characteristics. Keeping in mind the principles of genetic variation, natural selection, and adaptive radiation (Chapter 3), it is reasonable to hold that there would be just a few

[1] G. M. Morant, "The Form of the Swanscombe Skull" (*Journal of the Royal Anthropological Institute*, vol. 68, 1938), pp. 67–97; J. S. Weiner and B. G. Campbell, "The Taxonomic Status of the Swanscombe Skull," in C. D. Ovey (ed.), *The Swanscombe Skull—A Survey of Research on a Pleistocene Site* (1965).

[2] H. V. Vallois, "The Fontechevade Fossil Men" (*American Journal of Physical Anthropology*, vol. 7, no. 3, 1949), p. 352.

manifestations of sapienization at first among predominantly *erectus* populations. Gradually, as the selective advantages of *sapiens* traits began to take effect, higher percentages of genes of the *sapiens* type would be established, until at last they characterized whole populations. This was fully achieved by the time of the third interglacial but was well under way in second interglacial times.

Homo erectus had completed the skeletal adaptation to upright posture. After the achievement of full human cranial capacity by *Homo sapiens steinheimensis,* the major changes are in the face and dentition.[3] Human facial and dental adaptations that occur with *Homo sapiens* appear to be closely related to improved skills as a hunter, toolmaker, and user of fire, and ultimately to drastic changes in dietary habits. The possible mechanics of these changes are discussed after a consideration of the cultural developments.

MIDDLE PALEOLITHIC CULTURES

The Acheulean Tradition

The Steinheim people did not develop the Acheulean hand ax industry that is found in such profusion in the Thames second interglacial terraces. This development occurred in East Africa. When the Steinheim people followed the retreating glaciation into Western Europe, they brought knowledge of the hand ax and flake-tool techniques.

At Olduvai, the evolution of the hand ax had continued through Bed III (third pluvial) and into Bed IV. In these later deposits, the hand axes were produced by a more controlled flaking technique than was used earlier. Instead of striking directly on the core with a hammerstone to remove flakes, the toolmakers struck the core with the round edge of a stick, bone, or horn. The force of such a blow is diffused and results in removing thinner flakes. This is called the *cylinder-hammer technique.*

The invention of the cylinder-hammer technique made possible the manufacture of thin, symmetrically refined hand axes of the Acheulean type such as the samples shown in Figure 8.6 (page 139).

The maker of a hand ax also produces quantities of flakes in the process, and a workshop floor near a good source of raw materials will be littered with thousands of unused chips and flakes. It would be a simple and obvious matter to use appropriately shaped flakes for cutting meat and scraping wood and hides.

The Levalloisian Flake-tool Tradition

The special technique of producing a highly serviceable flake tool, known as Levalloisian (after the type site at Levallois, France), appeared in Western Europe during the second interglacial period, and at Olduvai, in East Africa, in Bed III. The pattern and technique for producing Levalloisian flakes are sufficiently important to require special attention. Levalloisian flakes are not simply by-products of hand ax production. They are the primary object of the flintworker's task. The procedure is called the *striking-platform-tortoise-core technique.* It involves the following steps, which are illustrated in Figure 9.2.

1. An oval-shaped flint nodule is flaked around its edge to remove irregularities and to give it symmetry.
2. A series of blows is directed along the edge toward the middle so that the surface of the nodule resembles the surface of a tortoise shell.
3. A striking platform is next prepared by removing a flake from one end, roughly at a right angle to the long axis of the nodule. This flat plane forms a striking platform.
4. A large flake is removed with one clean blow delivered obliquely to the striking platform. The flake comes off in a single piece which is

[3]See C. L. Brace and M. F. Montagu, *Man's Evolution,* pp. 255–264.

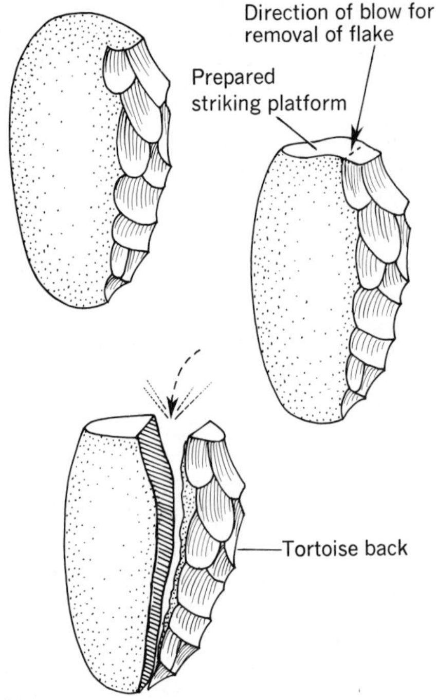

FIGURE 9.2
The manufacture of a Levalloisian flake. After the surface is shaped and a striking platform is prepared, the flake is removed with a single blow. Edges may be resharpened after use. Such a tool, which is ready for immediate use without further preparation, was probably used as a skinning knife or skin scraper.

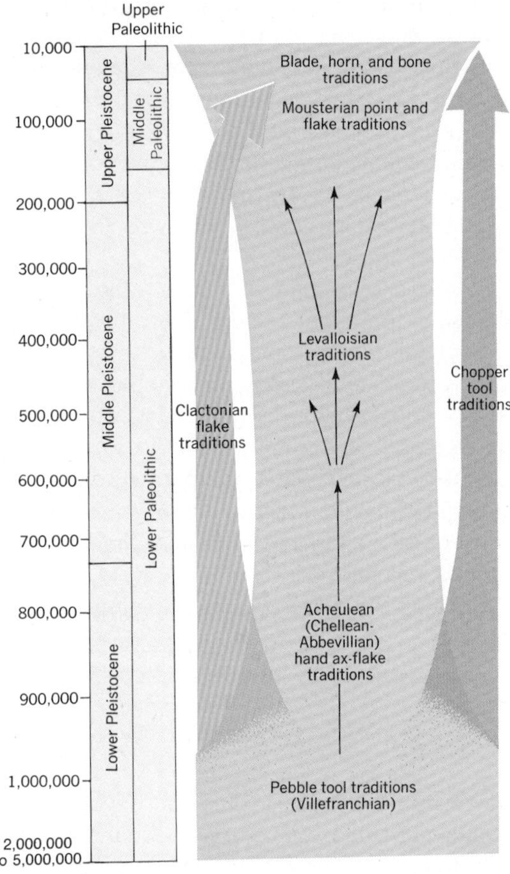

FIGURE 9.3
Developmental relationships of the major tool traditions of the Paleolithic Age in the Old World. All the Paleolithic complexes began in the Villefranchian pebble-tool tradition. The Acheulean (Chellean-Abbevillian) hand ax–flake tradition and the Clactonian developed separately and fused in the Mousterian traditions. The Asiatic chopper-tool traditions remained separate.

tortoise-shell-shaped on the backside and smooth on the front.

5. The cutting edges are resharpened by the removal of small flakes from the outer edges, by firm application of pressure against the edge with a bone or antler.

In southern Europe, Africa, and the Near East, the Levalloisian method of producing flakes was joined to the Acheulean hand ax tradition. Hence, in that part of the world, during the times of *Homo sapiens steinheimensis,* it resulted in the Acheulean-Levalloisian tool complex (see Figure 9.3).

The Clactonian Flake-tool Complex

Although the hand ax complexes clearly dominated in Africa, Western Europe, the Near East, and Southwest Asia, the chopper and flake-tool complexes of Asia spread in a broad band along the northern edges of the Chellean-Acheulean territory (see Figure 9.8). In France, there are strata dating from the Middle Pleistocene which yield Clactonian flake-tool assemblages in which there are no hand axes.[4]

The Clactonian complex is named after the English resort of Clacton-on-the-Sea, where it was first discovered early in this century. The most spectacular diagnostic tool of the complex is the so-called Clactonian flake. This is a large flake which consistently shows an oblique 130-degree angle from the striking facet to the bulb of the removed face. Clactonian flakes are prepared by steps similar to those in the Levalloisian technique, except that the tortoise-back effect is not produced and the flakes often have broad chopper edges. Such chopping tools are functionally equivalent to the Acheulean hand ax.

The Clactonian complex also includes tools for performing other tasks; these are shown in Figure 9.4. The endscraper is not too different from the Upper Paleolithic tool produced by *Homo sapiens sapiens*, shown in Figure 10.4a (page 171). It was probably used as a bone and woodworking gouge. The so-called denticulate tool has a saw-tooth cutting edge usable on meat or softwoods. The sidescraper could have served as a knife, but its primary use could have been for scraping down the fleshy sides of hides to be used as clothing and for utensils. No such hides have been found, but people living in the subarctic climate of glacial times very likely wrapped themselves in fur robes and slept under fur coverings. The nicest of Clactonian specialties is the all-purpose tool called the "bill hook." It is a combination sidescraper, spokeshave, knife, and drilling tool—the original Boy Scout knife. The spokeshave would have been well adapted for shaping the wooden spear point which has survived over 500,000 years in the Pleistocene deposits at Clacton.

FIGURE 9.4
Clactonian flake tools. The classic Clactonian chopper flakes are at the bottom. Characteristic special flakes are shown above. (Museum of Anthropology, University of Minnesota. Photo by Don Breneman.)

Seasonal Migrations and Housing

In the last chapter, we discussed the use of fire by *Homo erectus* at Torralba in Spain. Although the people who used these sites were probably *Homo erectus*, they could have been *Homo sapiens*. Both species lived in Europe during the Middle Pleistocene and they shared essentially similar Acheulean hand ax traditions.

The seasonal seaside Mediterranean homesite, Terra Amata, is discussed within the context of this chapter (rather than the preceding one) simply because it falls within the larger ecological zone which produced the Steinheim and Fontechevade fossil representatives of *Homo sapiens*. On the other hand, the only possible *Homo erectus* fossil from the same zone is the Heidel-

[4]F. Bordes, *The Old Stone Age*, p. 92.

berg specimen. It comes from first interglacial deposits and is hence too early in time to be linked to the site. Torralba and the nearby Ambrona site are contemporary with the Terra Amata site, but they are on the other side of the Pyrenees in a different eco-area.

We know that Middle Paleolithic humans were big-game hunters who regularly used fire. Some lived in caves, but others roved the forests, tundra, and open plains, and built houses. They were not palaces, but when we realize that a third of a million years ago springtime migrants built 50-foot-long gabled houses on the shores of the Mediterranean, we cannot but be impressed. This knowledge comes as the result of a great discovery made in 1965 in Nice, France.[5]

Nice, a fashionable resort city with a fine harbor, can claim the oldest remains of housing known. The discovery came as a result of bulldozing for a new construction site on an ancient sand beach that lies well above the present mean level of the Mediterranean. The beach was formed at the end of the second glaciation, as determined by the fauna, flora, and tool assemblages uncovered. When fossils and hand axes were exposed in numbers, construction work was temporarily halted and a crash archaeological salvage program launched. Three hundred workers, mostly volunteers, went to work under professional scientific supervision. Because of their efforts, the site, now known as Terra Amata, yielded 35,000 archaeological objects, but more important, twenty-one house sites.

Postholes in the compacted sands show the oval outlines of the houses. Circles of boulders lay in place around the postholes. A line of large postholes down the center of the elongated floor marks the location of the uprights which supported the ridgepole. Each house faced the sea, where the southern sun shone through the doorway. Inside the doorway, where ventilation would be best, lay a small, scooped-out hearth. And on the northwest side of each hearth was a loose wall of stones to shield the fire from the drafts that blew along the floor. The floor on the east side of each dwelling shows a clear area surrounded by myriad flint chips. Here squatted the master toolmaker of the household, preparing and repairing the hand axes and flake tools for the hunters and food processors.

Two Early Acheulean cultural traditions were represented by the people who frequented the spot. The more primitive is seen in a pebble-tool assemblage consisting of choppers and a small number of rock scrapers and projectile points (evidently intended to be hafted on spears). The producers of these Oldowan-like tool kits built their housing closest to the nearby shore of the Pleistocene sea.

The second tradition is associated with the living floors which were located higher up from the ocean on the prehistoric sand dunes. The assemblages here combine Early Acheulean hand axes with Clactonian choppers and a few worked bones.

Because no human skeletal remains were discovered, it is not possible to say anything about the identity of the early populations at Terra Amata. Nor can one tell whether they were contemporary or not, although the similarity in their house forms would seem to so indicate.

Coprolitic analysis (see page 102) of human feces found in the same sand strata, but always outside the floors, show that these people only visited Terra Amata for brief periods in the spring. Their main homes were elsewhere, as yet undiscovered. We know this because the coprolites contain undigested pollen such as is shed by plants in the late springtime. It could be that these early nomadic hunters came down to the warm coast mainly to eat their fill of fresh greens after a long winter of heavy meat protein and carbohydrate diet. While on the coast, they also dined on fish and shellfish. Yet this alone could not have been their reason for the seasonal visits

[5]H. de Lumley, "A Paleolithic Camp at Nice" (*Scientific American*, vol. 220, 1969), pp. 42–50.

to the coast, because seafood is available the year around, and the coprolites indicate the migrants stayed only as long as the spring plants were fresh.

It is clear, however, that these people were not simple vegetarians. Fossil remains of elephant, rhinoceros, stag, ibex, ox, and wild boar show that the house builders were true Paleolithic big-game hunters, who yearned for a little variety in their diets.

HOMO SAPIENS NEANDERTALENSIS

The first Neandertal skull was found on Gibraltar in 1848. It was viewed as an interesting specimen, but its significance struck no responsive chord until a second fossil, after which the Neandertal subspecies is named, was found. This second fossil was found in a cave in the Neander Valley near Düsseldorf, Germany, in 1856, three years before the publication of Darwin's *Origin of Species*. The discovery was made just in time to take its place in the excited debates over human evolution which enlivened the latter half of the nineteenth century. The evolutionists hailed the find as an example of an intermediary, submodern human fossil. The conservatives sourly held that the fossil was nothing but the remains of a pathological freak, probably a peasant. It was even suggested that it might have been the remains of a "stupid" Roman legionnaire who crawled into the cave for twenty winks and liked it so much that he stayed. However, the discovery of two more skulls of the same genre at Spy, Belgium, in 1887 put an end to such scurrilous reflections on the character of the man of Neander Valley.

Immediately after the turn of the century, Neandertal men, women, and children began to rise from their graves in profusion—from France and Spain to the Crimea, and later from Palestine and North Africa, until there was no doubt that the Neandertal people had been very important figures who lived in widely dispersed areas (see Figure 9.5).

Morphology of *Homo sapiens neandertalensis*

Keeping in mind the wide range of variability, we can list the more generalized skeletal features of the Neandertals:

1. Long, low, wide, large cranium (1300 to 1600 cubic centimeters)
2. Cranial base acutely oriented upward with tilted foramen magnum (Figure 9.7)
3. Bun-shaped or angular occipital profile
4. Large facial area
5. Semicircular supraorbital ridges fused above the nose with the temporal regions
6. Convex curvature of the upper jaws, fusing directly with the cheekbones without forming a suborbital depression (canine fossa)
7. Short, massive spinal column
8. Long, vertical dorsal spines on the cervical vertebrae
9. Limited forward curvature of the cervical and lumbar areas of the spine
10. Heavy, short upper arm (humerus) with a massive head
11. Pronounced curvature of the radius (bow bone in the forearm)
12. Short forearm relative to upper arm
13. Broad, flattened ilia in the pelvis
14. Highly curved thighbone of massive structure
15. Short shinbone
16. Very short leg in proportion to thigh

In appearance the Neandertals were short, massive-chested, powerfully armed, large-bodied, beetle-browed, broad-nosed, and large-headed. This body build is particularly characteristic of the Western European Neandertals. Applying Bergman's rule (pages 63, 65), we might surmise that the stocky, powerful Neandertal physique was an adaptation to extremely cold climatic conditions.

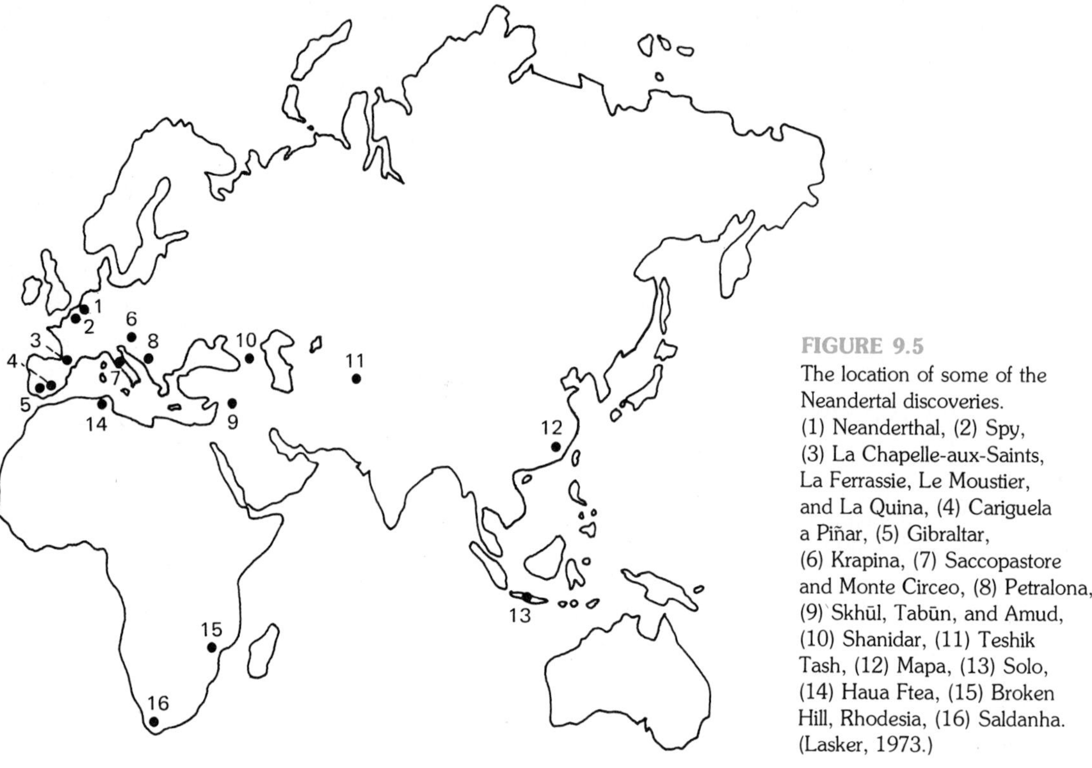

FIGURE 9.5
The location of some of the Neandertal discoveries. (1) Neanderthal, (2) Spy, (3) La Chapelle-aux-Saints, La Ferrassie, Le Moustier, and La Quina, (4) Cariguela a Piñar, (5) Gibraltar, (6) Krapina, (7) Saccopastore and Monte Circeo, (8) Petralona, (9) Skhūl, Tabūn, and Amud, (10) Shanidar, (11) Teshik Tash, (12) Mapa, (13) Solo, (14) Haua Ftea, (15) Broken Hill, Rhodesia, (16) Saldanha. (Lasker, 1973.)

Neandertal and Modern Humans

For nearly a hundred years an incredible amount of confusion was engendered by the "Neandertal problem." The problem is: What is the evolutionary (phylogenetic) relation of Neandertal to modern humans?

For half a century (about 1890 to 1935), the dominant theme was that the Neandertal people were a distinct species of the genus *Homo* and that this species evolved directly from the *Homo erectus* forms of Asia (see Figure 9.6). It produced the Mousterian culture of the Middle Paleolithic Age. Meanwhile, somewhere, somehow, in Asia Minor or North Africa, the species *sapiens* evolved and developed the basic Upper Paleolithic culture (Châtelperronian), moved into Europe during the middle of the fourth glaciation, and proceeded to exterminate the Neandertals in the span of a few millennia. Finally, it was held that because "Neandertal" traits are so rare in skeletons of the late Upper Paleolithic and thereafter, species differences must have made interbreeding impossible. This is the "theory of hominid catastrophism."[6]

One thing is certain. The Classic Neandertal type disappeared from the scene around 40,000 years ago.

In the 1930s, two events set in motion a

[6]See C. L. Brace, "The Fate of the 'Classic' Neanderthals: A Consideration of Hominid Catastrophism" (*Current Anthropology*, vol. 5, no. 1, 1964), pp. 3–46.

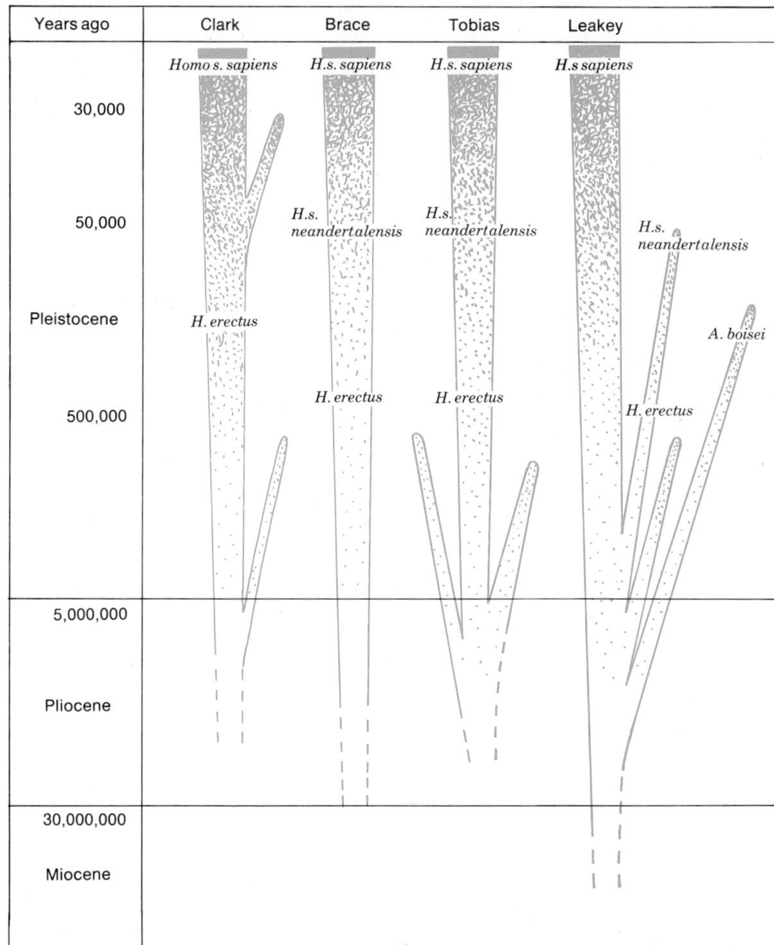

FIGURE 9.6
Alternate interpretations of the fossil evidence for human evolution advanced by J. D. Clark, C. L. Brace, P. V. Tobias, and L. S. B. Leakey. (McKern and McKern, 1974.)

reevaluation of the whole question of the historical relation of the Neandertals to modern human beings.

The discovery of the Swanscombe and Steinheim fossils showed the existence of a type of person in Europe in second interglacial times with "little indication of specifically Neanderthal morphology."[7] Mid-Pleistocene humans in Europe and North Africa are not Neandertal prototypes in a narrow sense. Next, the characteristics of a number of fossil individuals discovered in Palestinian caves by Dorothy Garrod were published. On Mt. Carmel, near the Sea of Galilee, two sites yielded Early and Middle Mousterian cultural inventories in association with many human skeletal remains.

The remarkable aspect of the Mt. Carmel population is its variability. From the lower levels of the Tabūn Cave came an adult female similar to the Swanscombe-Steinheim variety of *Homo sapiens*. In the upper levels of the cave were genuine *Homo sapiens sapiens* and others with

[7]F. C. Howell, "The Evolutionary Significance of Variation and Varieties of 'Neanderthal' Man" (*The Quarterly Review of Biology*, vol. 32, no. 4, 1957), p. 334.

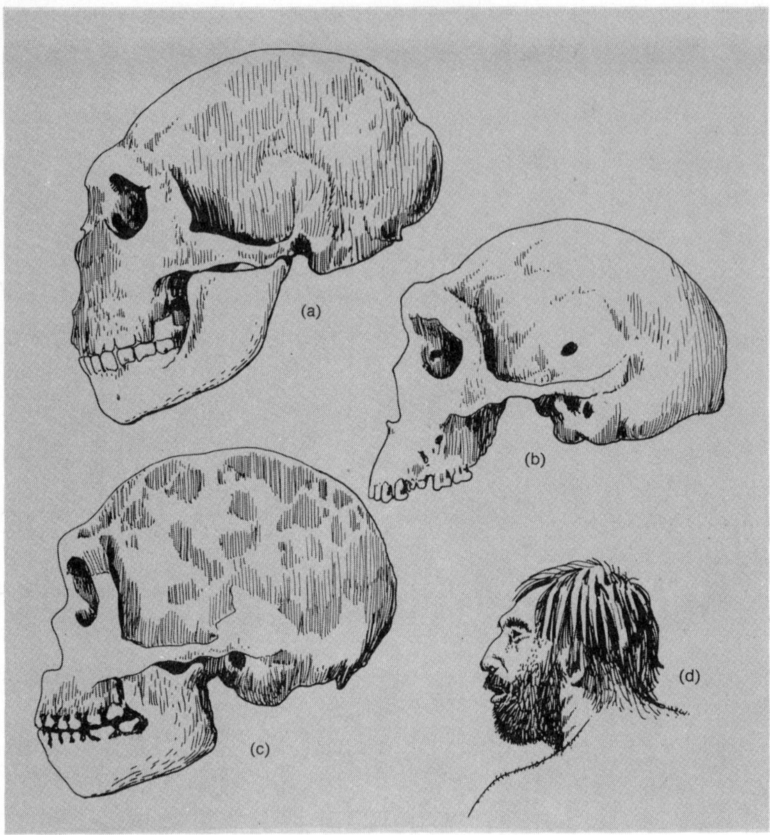

FIGURE 9.7
Homo sapiens neandertalensis. (a) Skull from Monte Circeo, Italy. (b) "Rhodesian man" from South Africa. (c) Tabūn skull from Mt. Carmel, Israel. (d) Hypothetical reconstruction of classic Neandertal from Monte Circeo. (Adapted from Howell, 1965.)

mixed Neandertal and *Homo sapiens sapiens* traits. At Skhūl, a rock shelter not far from Tabūn, a Mousterian burial plot yielded remains of ten persons with features varying from Neandertaloid to distinctly modern *sapiens* (see Figure 9.7). These fossils are of the early last pluvial in the Near East, contemporary to the Neandertals of the first part of the fourth glacial epoch in Europe. In the light of the then-prevailing theory, the discovery of primitive *Homo sapiens* types, of fossils with mixed Neandertal-modern *Homo sapiens* traits, and of fossils that were similar to the Cro-Magnon type of *Homo sapiens sapiens* (Figure 9.8b) was extremely surprising.

Theodore McCown and Sir Arthur Keith proposed at the time that a basic Neandertal population was evolving into modern humans.[8] They examined and rejected an alternative hypothesis that the Mt. Carmel population represented the hybridization of a population of Neandertals with a population of *Homo sapiens sapiens,* both having originated separately elsewhere (the place being left undetermined). The possibility that evolutionary divergence and polymorphism were occurring simultaneously seems to have been ignored. At any rate, it was held that both modern types and Neandertals were present in the Holy Land 45,000 years ago.

In 1957, excavations by Ralph Solecki in

[8]T. D. McCown and A. Keith, *The Stone Age of Mt. Carmel,* vol. II (1939).

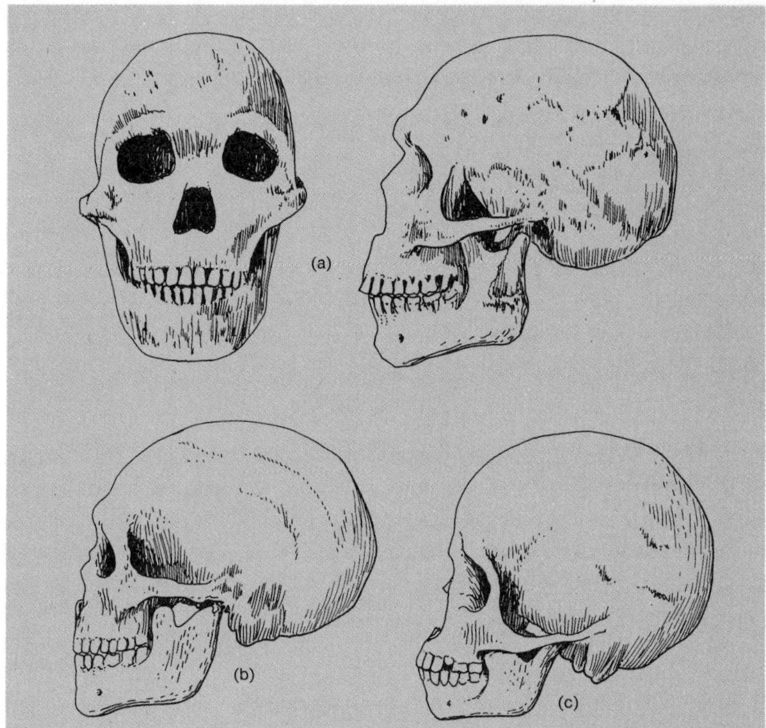

FIGURE 9.8
Homo sapiens sapiens. (a) A front and side view of the Skhūl V skull, a late Pleistocene *Homo sapiens sapiens* from Mt. Carmel which shows Neandertaloid traits. (b and c) Skulls from Combe-Capelle, France, and Grimaldi, Italy. (Drawn from photographs in Hulse, 1971.)

Shanidar Cave in Iraq showed that what had happened in Palestine was no fluke. Seven rather complete skeletons were found, along with a rich Mousterian tool assemblage. The famous first skeleton of Shanidar is that of a smashed 40-year-old male upon whom the roof had literally caved in 44,000 years ago, according to carbon 14 dating. All the Shanidar individuals looked like "modernized Neandertals."

More recent finds in Central and Eastern Europe, including the remains of as many as eighteen individuals in a single site, confirm the implications of the Near Eastern finds.[9] It is now clearly established that there is a wide range of variability in the cranial and postcranial (trunk) features of Middle Pleistocene Neandertals. Traits characteristic of the Classic Neandertal of Western Europe appear alongside traits held to be characteristic of *Homo sapiens sapiens,* both in individual fossil specimens and within fossil populations from single sites. *Homo sapiens sapiens* fossils from the same areas overlap the Neandertal fossils in time, and they also show great variability, including features characteristic of the much earlier *Homo sapiens steinheimensis.*

Put into contemporary perspective, the "problem" of the Neandertal people does not disappear. It takes on different and broader dimensions. Originally it had a narrow and misleading focus, because the type was for so long known only in the highly specialized form found in Western Europe—the so-called Classic Nean-

[9]J. Jelínek, "Neanderthal Man and *Homo sapiens* in Central and Eastern Europe" (*Current Anthropology,* vol. 10, no. 5, 1969), pp. 475–503.

dertal. In this form the diagnostic physical traits of the Neandertal skull appear in their most pronounced manifestations (see Figure 9.7a). Yet it is now recognized that West European Neandertals drew for their ancestry on the same generalized *Homo sapiens* gene pool as did those of Africa and the lands to the east. Human evolution, from 400,000 to 30,000 years ago, was going through a fairly volatile phase of adaptation under widely varying ecological conditions—both in space and through time. Mousterian hunters were wanderers who mixed genes from local population to local population throughout the whole Euro-Afro-Asiatic heartland. The West European bands, however, seem, under conditions of extreme glaciation, to have been more isolated than most and to have shared in the greater gene pool of *Homo sapiens* to a lesser degree. Hence, they intensified their genetic changes away from the more generalized characteristics that were developing among other *Homo sapiens* populations. They are recognized as a distinct variety of *Homo sapiens* but not as a species in their own right.

Homo sapiens soloensis and *Homo sapiens rhodesianensis*

The first of these two special varieties of *Homo sapiens* was found in the Ngandong beds, which overlie the Trinil and Djetis beds in Java. Eleven fragmentary skulls and two tibia (shinbones) of the Solo humans were found 6 miles from Trinil, on the Solo River, in 1931 and 1932. The geological matrix places the fossils in the Upper Pleistocene.

Each skull had been subjected to postmortem butchery. In all but one instance, the face had been hacked off entirely, and no lower jaws were found. In all but one skull, the foramen magnum had been enlarged. Apparently, the Solo people were practicing cannibalism. The skulls all lay bottom up and carefully placed. And they were in such good condition that the absence of teeth or other body parts, except for the two shinbones, indicates they had been carried in their butchered condition to the river bank. For a feast, or as ritual sacrifices? Who can say?

Viewed superficially, the Solo find is a Neandertal-like *Homo sapiens.* The skulls are thick-boned. The browridges are heavy but do not form a massive, continuous shelf. The range of the Solo cranial capacities is from 1035 to 1255 cubic centimeters with an average of about 1100 cubic centimeters. This places the type in the lower ranges of *Homo sapiens.*[10]

The Rhodesian fossil represents another Upper Pleistocene variety of *Homo sapiens.* Like *soloensis,* it has heavy Neandertaloid browridges, discontinuous over the nose; a recessive, low-domed calvarium with a strong occipital ridge and angular roof; weak mastoids; and a cranial capacity of 1280 cubic centimeters. The lower face projects to a prognathous upper alveolar arch, a feature that indicates possible ancestry to later African populations.

THE MOUSTERIAN CULTURE OF *HOMO SAPIENS NEANDERTALENSIS*

The basic subsistence of Neandertal *Homo sapiens* was not appreciably different from that of the pre-Mousterian big-game hunters of the Steinheim type. The Neandertal timespan ran from the very end of the third interglacial through the first half of the fourth glacial, when it came to an abrupt end. The Mousterian complex existed from approximately 100,000 to around 35,000 years ago.

The Mousterian Complex

The distribution of tool assemblages of the Mousterian complex is vast—Europe, Africa, and all South and East Asia (see Figure 9.9). But variety in the local assemblages is also consid-

[10]B. Campbell, "Quantitative Taxonomy and Human Evolution," in S. L. Washburn (ed.), *Classification and Human Evolution,* p. 66.

FIGURE 9.9
Distribution of Mousterian and other derived cultures. (Adapted from Brace and Montagu, 1965.)

erable. In the main, it may be said that the Mousterian stone technology continued the trend which had been slowly developing through the Lower and Middle Paleolithic. However, a definite shift occurs from the production and use of hand axes to more and more emphasis on varieties of flakes (see Figure 9.10). Thus, in what Bordes calls *Mousterian of Acheulean Tradition*, the frequency of hand axes in early (so-called type A) sites varies from 8 to 40 percent of the lithic assemblages, with the mode falling between 10 to 15 percent. These hand axes are diminutive when compared to their Acheulean antecedents. In later levels (type B), hand axes are found less frequently (less than 8 percent) and are usually small and crudely made.

In the *Typical Mousterian*, hand axes have all but disappeared, while points (probably meant to be attached to spears) are common and well made. Levallois flaking continues in this tradition, as well as in the two additional Mousterian traditions which Bordes identifies for Europe.

In Africa, Typical Mousterian assemblages are found in Egypt and along the Mediterranean coast. South of the Sahara, an Acheulean derivative called *Sangoan* extends from Kenya to southern Rhodesia. Here, hand axes continue, with the addition of a special adaptation in the form of large biface picks, plus large flint gravers or planing tools. It is thought that these were special woodworking tools developed by forest-dwelling peoples. In South Africa, heart-shaped hand axes give way over time to increasing

FIGURE 9.10
Representative Mousterian tools. Top row (left to right): Typical Mousterian convex sidescraper, Levallois point, and sidescraper. Second row: Levallois point, Quina-type sidescraper, and discoidal scraper. Third row: Mousterian of Acheulean tradition endscraper, and denticulate flake. Bottom: Mousterian of Acheulean tradition hand ax, point with thinned butt, and denticulated concave scraper. (Museum of Anthropology, University of Minnesota. Photo by Don Breneman.)

numbers of flake tools in the local manifestations of the Mousterian complex.[11]

Bone-tool Inventory

The Neandertal people made extensive use of bone implements. It has always seemed reasonable to suppose that early human beings surely made as much use of wood and bone for tools and weapons as they did of stone. Rare fragments of worked wood are proof of wood use, but the loss of most pieces through decay gives little idea of what the relative importance of wooden artifacts may have been. The situation with respect to bone is different. Bone fossilizes better than wood and many more fragments have been preserved. In 1959, an English archaeologist, James Kitching, analyzed an osteodontokeratic (bone, tooth, and horn) assemblage from Mousterian deposits in the English site known as Pin Hole Cave. Only seventy-three Mousterian stone tools were found, but there were hundreds of used bone flakes. Except for the teeth of rabbits, which the Pin Hole Neandertals extracted to use as sharp punches, the skeletons of small animals were not used as sources of bone artifacts. Large animals were treated differently. Carcasses of reindeer, bison, bears, hyenas, and wolves were dragged into the cave. Horses, woolly rhinoceroses, and giant deer were usually butchered where killed and only selected bony parts were taken home. These parts were commonly antlers, teeth, and jaws—all serviceable as tools.

Half-jaws of carnivores, with their projecting canines, were used as ripping tools. Antlers, shoulder blades, and jawbones of reindeer and leg bones of rhinoceroses were used as splitting wedges and hammers. Split and trimmed ribs of reindeer and bison and spirally broken splints of leg bones served as knives. Shoulder blades of rhinoceroses and reindeer were trimmed and used as spades for digging. Rounded bone flakes from large leg bones, the hip blades (ilia) of rhinoceroses and the shoulder blades of reindeer, bison, and horses were all used as skinning tools. Other bones were put to use as hide scrapers. A really nice adaptation was the use of the large hip socket of the rhinoceros as a pounding bowl or mortar. And for pestles with which to grind and pound, what could be better

[11]For a comprehensive, more detailed, but not too technical, comparison of the major manifestations in the Old World, the best treatment is F. Bordes, *The Old Stone Age*, pp. 98–146.

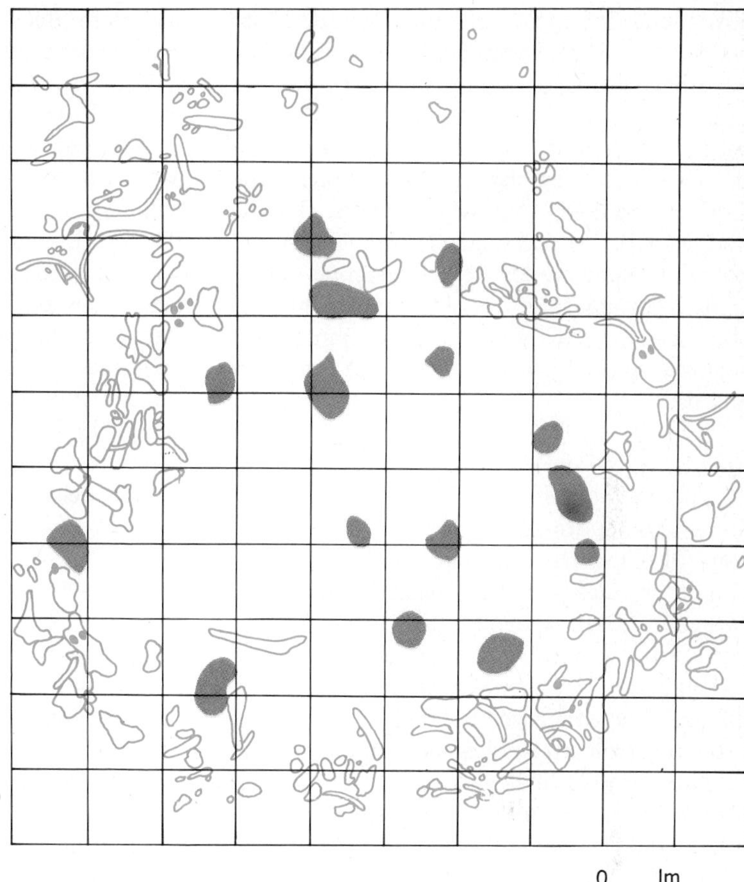

FIGURE 9.11
Ground plan of site of Mousterian dwelling on the open plains of western Russia at Molodova. The small dark dots represent mammoth teeth, and the outlined objects represent bones; the larger dark areas are hearths within the original hut and indicate repeated occupation. (After F. Bordes, *The Old Stone Age*, p. 143.)

than the foot bones of the rhinoceros? The braincase of the reindeer made a cup or scoop, as did the hip socket of the rhinoceros. Kitching also thinks that the hollow humerus (armbone) of the rhinoceros, with the marrow removed, served as a prepottery tankard.[12] The hardware of a Neandertal household was plentiful.

Housing

Most known Mousterian homesites have been found in caves, probably because preservation is better there than in open sites. In the more extreme fluctuations of cold in the fourth glaciation, caves must have appealed to the Neandertal people as shelters. Overhanging rock cliffs also provided good homes, especially those which formed rock shelters on the north side of a river valley. The noonday sun provided welcome reflected solar heat which continued to radiate into the cold night. Yet neither the pre-Neandertal *Homo sapiens* nor the Neandertal people were exclusively cave dwellers.

One example of Mousterian open-plains housing comes from Molodova, in western Russia. A ring of huge mammoth bones, lying close together, surrounds a floor 18 feet in diameter (Figure 9.11). Within the floor are the remains of fifteen hearths. This Mousterian home was prob-

[12]J. W. Kitching, *Bone, Tooth and Horn Tools of "Paleolithic Man."*

ably made of supple tree trunks inserted into hollow tubes of mammoth leg bones, which have been found buried upright in the ground. Animal skins would have covered the frame. The piles of bones around the circle may have served as weights to keep the skins tight against the ground and keep out wintry blasts. To the northwest is an accumulation of mammoth bones, presumably left from butchering operations. The large number of hearths within the floor space could indicate that the inhabitants were seasonal migrants who returned from time to time.

Ritual and Death

Of the prerequisites for the maintenance of human society (discussed more in Chapter 16, page 293), the most uniquely human is a definition of "the meaning of life" which maintains the motivation to survive and engage in the activities necessary to survival. Two expressions of human feeling by the Neandertalers stand out: burial of the dead and a ritualized bear cult. A good many fossil skeletons of Neandertals have been found carefully bedded in shallow pits and accompanied by flint tools and occasional bones. One Neandertal was buried in Shanidar Cave, Iraq, on a bed of pine boughs and flowers, according to the pollen concentrated in the earth surrounding the skeleton. Whatever this might lead us to infer about belief in immortality and a continued spiritual existence apart from the body, it does show concern for the individual as a person. Even newborn infants were buried in a planned pattern in the cavern of La Ferrassie in France.

The evidence of a bear cult among different groups of Neandertals is ample. Bear burials have been discovered in the cavern of Regourdon, in southern France, confirming the importance of the bear-skull cache from the Dragon's Lair in Switzerland, where a stone-lined pit held a collection of bear skulls. The hole was closed with a large stone slab. The Swiss site also yielded a bear skull without a lower jaw but with the right thighbone of another bear pushed between the cheekbone and the braincase. This device was found placed upon two shinbones from still two other bears.

Variations in cults are so vast that it would be foolhardy to try to reconstruct the Neandertal cult. However, the possibilities may be sensed in the Bear Dance, and its accompanying mythology, as it is still performed every spring among the Ute Indians of Colorado and Utah. It commemorates the emergence of the bear from its long hibernation and its confrontation by a legendary Indian who learned the dance from a bear. When the Utes perform the bear's dance, they are sure that the friendship of the bear for human beings is secured and hunting therefore is made safer.[13]

SUMMARY

By the second interglacial period evolutionary processes had modified the skeletal traits and mental capacity of *Homo erectus* into those of early *Homo sapiens* and modern human beings. The Middle Pleistocene forms of *Homo sapiens* are represented by the fossils from Steinheim, Swanscombe, Fontechevade, and other sites.

The culture of early *Homo sapiens* continued the big-game subsistence patterns of *Homo erectus*. Likewise, the technology in Europe and Africa showed no developmental break. The production of hand axes was refined by the invention of the cylinder-hammer technique and pressure retouching. Increasing variety in the flake tool kit was achieved through invention of the Levallois flaking technique and the spread of the Clactonian tradition. All were fused in varying degrees by different populations as local manifestations of the Acheulean complex.

The great new development, on the basis of

[13] J. H. Steward, "A Uintah Ute Bear Dance, March 1931" (*American Anthropologist*, vol. 34, 1932), p. 265. See also A. I. Hallowell, "Bear Ceremonialism in the Northern Hemisphere" (*American Anthropologist*, vol. 28, 1926), pp. 1–175.

present evidence, was housing sufficiently large to shelter a small composite band. Such bands were probably the basis of social life.

The evolution of humans and culture continued through the rest of the Middle Pleistocene, into the fourth glacial epoch. The product was *Homo sapiens neandertalensis* and the Mousterian cultural complex.

When compared to the earlier Steinheim type of *Homo sapiens*, Neandertals first appeared to be a regression, except for their very large cranial capacities. Later discoveries at Mt. Carmel (in Israel), at Shanidar Cave (in Iraq), and elsewhere have demonstrated that the rugged Classic Neandertals are a specialized variation within a broad range of *Homo sapiens* including, at the other extreme, noticeably modern individuals.

The Mousterian tool complex, which is intimately associated with the Neandertal people, is found in many combinations throughout the ice-free parts of Europe, the Near East, Africa, and Asia. In general, it is characterized by a decline in frequency of the hand ax. At the same time, specialized varieties of flake tools increased. Research at Pin Hole Cave in England also shows the importance of bone for tools in Mousterian times.

Although most known Mousterian sites exist in caves and rock shelters, work in Czechoslovakia, Hungary, and South Russia shows that the Neandertal people had also adapted to life in the open. At Molodova in the Ukraine, mammoth bone tent-rings outline the floors of Neandertal homesites. Human burials and bear-skull interments give hints of a growing concern with personality and symbolic representation of belief and "meaning in life" through ritual expression.

SELECTED READINGS

Bordes, F., *The Old Stone Age* (1968). Chapters 8, 9, and 10 are highly recommended for more (and lucid) detail on the specifics of the several varieties of the Mousterian complex.

Brose, D. S., and M. H. Wolpoff, "Early Upper Paleolithic Man and Late Middle Paleolithic Tools" (*American Anthropologist*, vol. 73, no. 5, 1971), pp. 1156–1194. An authoritative, detailed, although technical review of the whole problem.

Howell, F. C., and the Editors of Time-Life Books, *Early Man* (1968). The primary author is an outstanding authority; the text is informative and reliable. Color photos of artifacts are excellent; numerous sketches, helpful; and paintings of imaginatively reconstructed scenes of prehistoric activities add life to the story.

Solecki, R. S., *Shanidar: The First Flower People* (1971). An interesting account of excavations of Neandertal remains, with good reviews in the introductory and concluding chapters.

10
Homo sapiens sapiens

CHAPTER OUTLINE

LEARNING GOALS

Trace the orgins of *Homo sapiens sapiens.*

Explain the morphological characteristics of *Homo sapiens sapiens.*

Examine the Upper Paleolithic cultures of Europe.

Discuss the development of Paleolithic art.

Discuss the development of the Paleolithic Age in Africa and Asia.

Review the diffusion of *Homo sapiens sapiens* to the New World.

Identify the major Paleolithic traditions in the New World.

The era of the Neandertal people ended approximately thirty-five thousand years ago. Modern people took over the scene midway through the fourth glacial period. Thereafter only one genus, one species, and one subspecies, *Homo sapiens sapiens*, remained on the scene to continue the story of humankind. Biological evolution has continued to operate, although change has, since the beginning of the Upper Paleolithic, been mostly cultural innovation, and genetic modification has been less evident in gross morphology.

THE ORIGIN OF MODERN PEOPLE

It is unlikely that modern human beings originated in any one precise location. There was no Garden of Eden, except in an allegorical sense. Aleš Hrdlička, of the Smithsonian Institution, argued that modern people evolved directly from the Neandertals. This same thesis has been revived by C. L. Brace and analyzed by Brose and Wolpoff.[1] They found that in no instance is modern *Homo sapiens* found contemporary with or before the Neandertals, as would have to be the case if the former had evolved elsewhere and then replaced the Neandertals. Furthermore the morphological evidence indicates that there is a continuity between *all* Neandertals and modern human beings. Apparently the uniqueness of the Neandertal people from an anatomic point of view has been exaggerated to exclude them from the ancestry of modern peoples. Whatever differences existed were adaptations to local climatic conditions later rendered unnecessary by the invention of clothing, better housing, and better tools. The Neandertals evolved into modern *Homo sapiens* about 35,000 to 40,000 years ago in the Near East (see Figure 10.1).

Modern humans represent a continuing evolution of Pleistocene peoples. Geographic isolation and differential natural selection were sufficient to produce different populations, but there was apparently enough genetic intermixture so that *Homo sapiens sapiens* was developing in Africa, Asia Minor, and the outer edges of Asia more or less simultaneously.

European and American writers have, in the past, been prone to think of early *Homo sapiens sapiens* in the image of the Cro-Magnon person (see Figure 10.2). The first fossil remains of the Cro-Magnon variety of *Homo sapiens sapiens* were discovered in a grotto behind the present Hotel des Cro Magnons, in Les Eyzies, France, in 1868. These remains looked so modern, and so little was then known about human prehistory, that the mayor of Les Eyzies had them reburied in the local cemetery! Later they were disinterred for scientific study. Because Cro-Magnon people lived in Europe, produced excellent art a good 20,000 years ago, were large-brained, high-domed, upright, and so much more obviously like northwestern Europeans in appearance and capabilities than *Homo sapiens neandertalensis*, it was easy for European scholars to accept them as ancestors.

However, the Cro-Magnon fossil group is but one manifestation of *Homo sapiens sapiens*. It is not the only type that lived in the Late Pleistocene and produced Upper Paleolithic culture, nor is it the earliest (Figure 10.3). There are also the local varieties of Late Pleistocene *Homo sapiens sapiens*, found as fossils at Grimaldi, Combe Capelle, and Chancelade, in France, and at Brno and Predmost, in Czechoslovakia. In southern Africa, there is the Boskop type. In Southeast Asia, there is the Wadjak predecessor of later Australoids and the 40,000-year-old fossil skull from Niah Cave in Borneo. And in China, the human fossil of the Upper Cave at Choukoutien is also *Homo sapiens sapiens*, as are a number of other more recently discovered Chinese specimens. These finds by no means exhaust the list.

[1] C. L. Brace, *The Stages of Human Evolution*, pp. 83–106; D. S. Brose and M. H. Wolpoff, "Early Upper Paleolithic Man and Late Middle Paleolithic Tools" (*American Anthropologist*, vol. 73, no. 5, 1971), pp. 1156–1194.

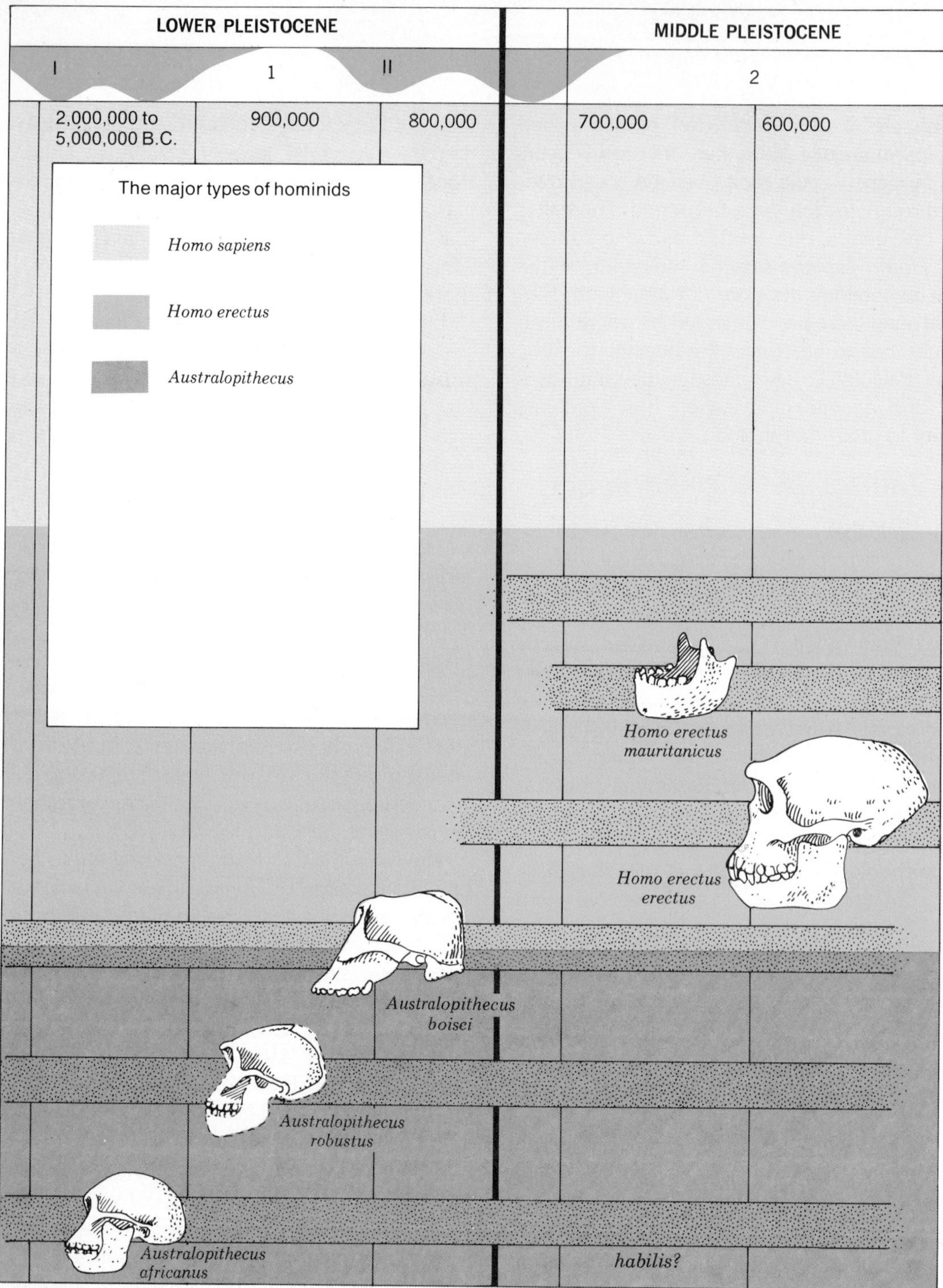

FIGURE 10.1
The known types of hominids. *Homo sapiens steinheimensis* existed 150,000 to 200,000 years ago. *Homo sapiens neandertalensis* should be dated around 100,000 to 35,000 years ago. *Homo sapiens sapiens* should be dated from 35,000

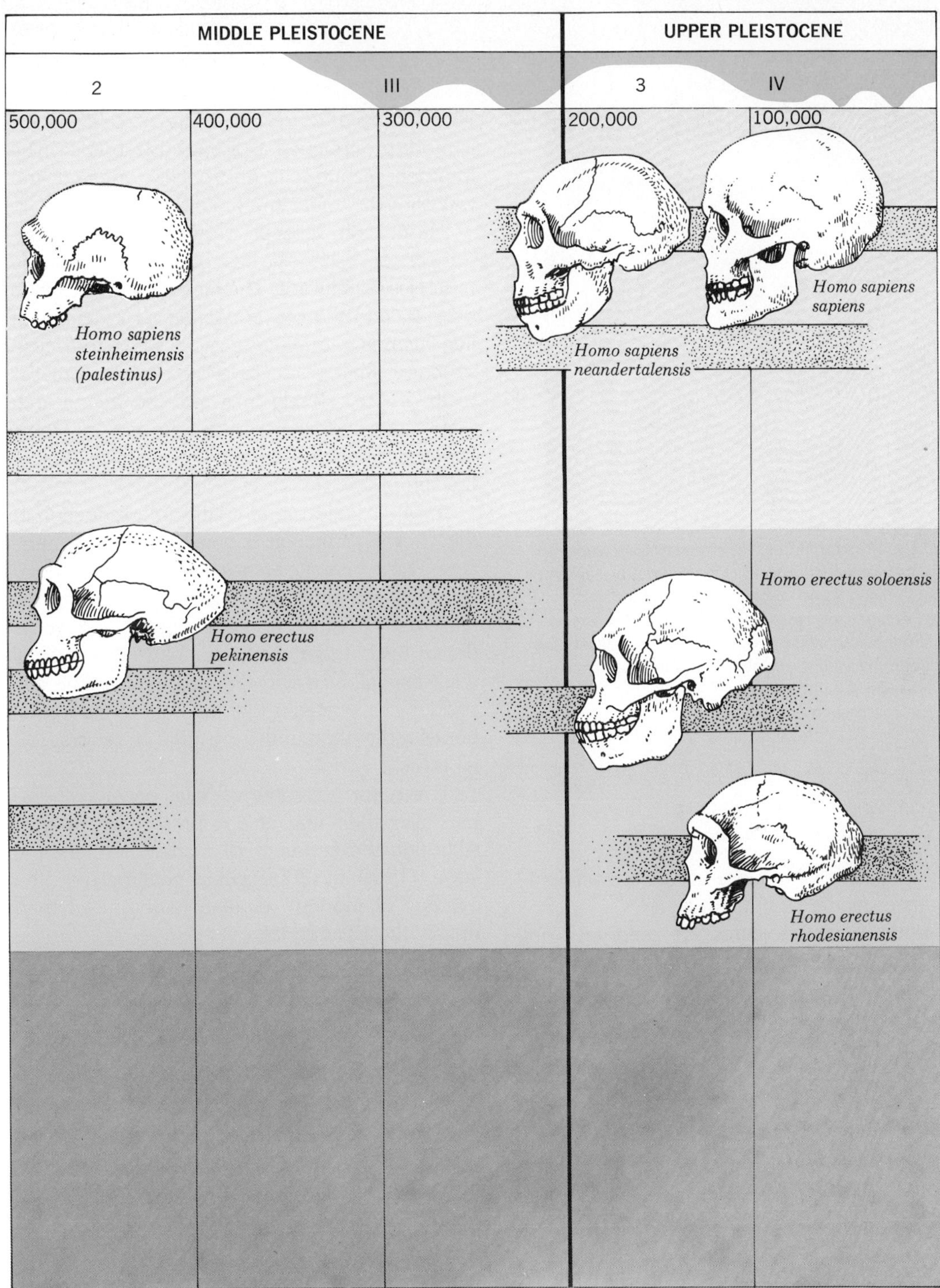

years to the present. The relationship among these hominids is difficult to depict accurately because of space limitations. (Skull drawings adapted from S. L. Washburn, "Tools and Human Evolution," *Scientific American,* with permission of publisher.)

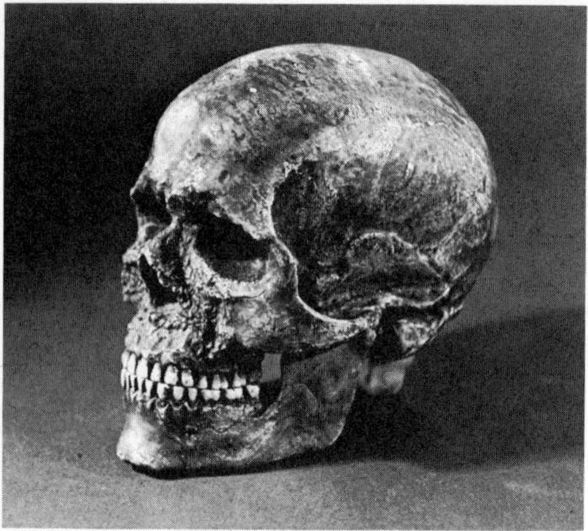

FIGURE 10.2
Skull of Cro-Magnon, a Late Pleistocene *Homo sapiens sapiens*. Its thoroughly modern characteristics are evident in its smooth-contoured cranium with high forehead, rounded occiput, and large volume. Also to be observed are its strong nasal bridge, prominent malars (cheekbones), and generally recessive face above a strong, jutting chin. (Cast, Museum of Anthropology, University of Minnesota. Photo by Don Breneman.)

THE MORPHOLOGY OF *HOMO SAPIENS SAPIENS*

What, in generalized terms, are the morphological traits of modern human beings?

Various skeletal features are different from those of their Neandertal predecessors. The long bones of the legs lose their curvature and become more slender and less robust. The iliac wings of the pelvis become more smoothly rounded and tilted more toward the rear. The radius in the forearm is less bowed, and the humerus is relatively longer and generally more delicate. The scapula (shoulder blade) broadens out at the top and is less elongated.

The modifications of major significance leading to *Homo sapiens sapiens*, however, are found in the skull. Modern people exhibit a globular braincase and a marked reduction of the face and lower jaw (see Figure 10.2). The supraorbital ridges virtually disappear; the occipital torus becomes residual. The mastoid process is more pronounced as a muscular anchor. The foramen magnum is horizontally oriented and well forward under the braincase.

Mastication, except in the special circumstances of Eskimos, has become functionally much less significant. The molars are persistently smaller, and the old *Dryopithecus* Y-pattern of five cusps is frequently replaced with a four-cusp structure that produces a + pattern. Smaller teeth are set closely in a reduced dental arch embracing a smaller palate. The jaw in *Homo sapiens sapiens* is reinforced by the thickening of the symphysis.

Another feature that relates to a reduction of the chewing function is smaller temporal muscles. The zygomatic arches bridging the temporal bones of the face are reduced and the face is narrowed, Eskimos excepted. The whole face is drawn back under the frontal part of the cranial vault as well as being reduced in size. The eye sockets are located under the bulb of the frontal bones rather than under the ridge of a supraorbital torus.

The stature of some varieties becomes notably taller than that of any premodern people. Although the brains of all modern humans are large (1000 to 2000 cubic centimeters), the average of modern populations is smaller than that of the Neandertals.

UPPER PALEOLITHIC CULTURES

The Upper Paleolithic lasted from 35,000 to 9500 B.C., when the first great cultural revolution of human history began—the domestication of animals and plants. The hand ax almost wholly disappeared, but flake and blade tools traceable to earlier forms abounded. In the latter phases of the Upper Paleolithic, as reindeer became relatively more numerous than the rhinoceros and elephant, harpoons carved from antlers became the chief weapon. This was a refinement of what had existed for several hundred thousand years—the stone-pointed spear.

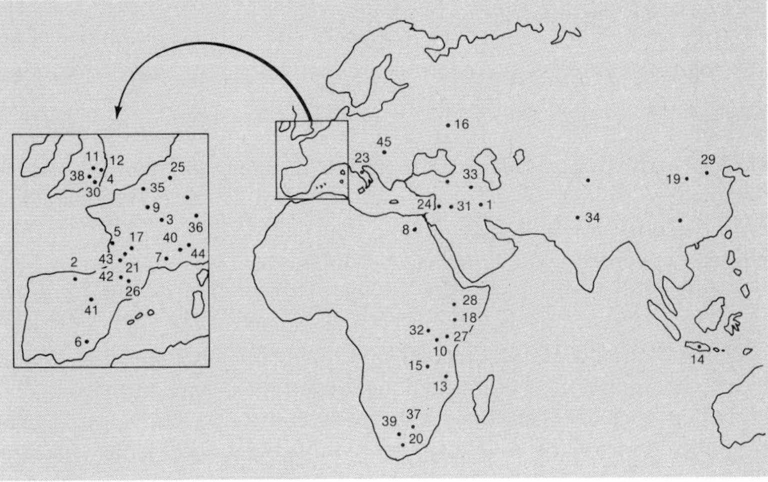

Dating of site:
I 60 million to 4 million B.P.
II 4 million to 1 million B.P.
III 1 million 200,000 B.P.
IV after 200,000 B.P.

Articles found:
A art
B bones of primates
F fire
L living floors
T tools

Key to sites on map
1 Ali Kosh IV, L, T
2 Altamira IV, A, T
3 Arcy IV, B, F, L, T
4 Clacton-on-Sea III, F, L, T
5 Combe Grenal IV, B, F, T
6 Cueva de Ambrosio IV, B, F, T
7 Escale cave III, B, F, L, T
8 Fayum depression I, B
9 Fontainebleau IV, A, F, L, T
10 Fort Ternan I, B
11 High Lodge IV, T
12 Hoxne IV, T
13 Isimila IV, F, L, T
14 Java site III, B
15 Kalambo Falls IV, B, F, L, T
16 Kostenki IV, A, B, F, L, T
17 La Chapelle-aux-Saints IV, B, T
18 Lake Turkana site II, B, T
19 Lantian site III, B
20 Makapan II, B
21 Mas D'Azil IV, A, T
22 Mauer site III, B
23 Monte Circeo IV, B, T
24 Mt. Carmel IV, B, F, T
25 Neanderthal IV, B
26 Niaux IV, A, T
27 Olduvai Gorge II, B, L, T
28 Omo II, B, T
29 Chou Kou Tien III, B, F, T
30 Piltdown (discredited)
31 Qafzeh IV, B, F, T
32 Rusinga Island I, B
33 Shanidar cave IV, B, F, L, T
34 Siwalik Hills I, B
35 St. Acheul III, T
36 Steinheim IV, B
37 Sterkfontein II, B, T
38 Swanscombe IV, B, T
39 Taung II, B
40 Terra Amata IV, F, L, T
41 Torralba-Ambrona III, B, F, L, T
42 Tuc d'Audobert IV, A, T
43 "Valley of Caves" IV
44 Vallonet cave III, B, T
45 Vérteszöllös III, B, F, L, T

FIGURE 10.3
Major prehistoric sites in Europe, Africa, and Asia. (Poirier, *In Search of Ourselves*, 1977.)

The spear thrower (called *atlatl* after the Aztec name for the tool) was introduced in the Upper Paleolithic. It was indeed something new, but again it was hardly revolutionary, for all it really accomplished was to extend the arm as a lever. Efficiency and force were thus increased.

The late Paleolithic hunters brought the Stone Age hunting tradition to a climax. To an improved material technology was added an imaginative intellectual culture. Sympathetic magic enhanced a faith in the likelihood of success and survival. Out of this was generated a remarkable cave art of multicolored wall paintings and low-relief murals, plus etchings and engravings on bone, and very "modernistic" sculpture. The forms of the art and its implications will be discussed later in this chapter.

Upper Paleolithic Traditions in Europe

It is now well understood that the relative frequencies of different types of flake and other tools vary from site to site among prehistoric populations. They also vary through time. Since it would be impossible to discuss all variations, for purposes of orientation only the major general traditions of the Upper Paleolithic of the Dordogne sequence will be discussed. The *Dordogne sequence* is the record of archaeological sites and their cultural sequence in southwestern France.

The early Upper Paleolithic consists of the Châtelperronian (also called Lower Périgordian), Aurignacian, and Gravettian (also called Upper Périgordian) traditions. A brief interlude, the Solutrean, constituted the middle Upper Paleolithic. It was followed by the Magdalenian tradition of the late Upper Paleolithic. Keeping in mind that none of these traditions began or ended in a given year, the sequence and the probable duration of each are given in Table 10.1.

The Châtelperronian Tradition: 32,000 to 29,500 B.C. The first Upper Paleolithic tradition is not richly represented among archaeological assemblages, and there is a question as to whether it evolved in France or developed in Southwest Asia, from where it diffused westward. The Châtelperronian does not show the specialization that marks the succeeding Upper Paleolithic cultures. Nor does it include the elongated flake blade that is the hallmark of the Upper Paleolithic. The distinctive Châtelperronian blade has a curved cutting edge. The back edge, on which finger pressure would be applied in use, is blunted with fine transverse chipping (see Figure 10.4). Simple, pointed bone tools were also produced, but there was none of the art that became so important in the Gravettian and Magdalenian.

TABLE 10.1
Upper Paleolithic Cultures and Their Durations

Tradition	Radiocarbon dates
	B.C.
Magdalenian	15,000–9,500
Solutrean	19,000–17,500
Gravettian (Upper Périgordian)	26,500–20,500
Aurignacian	33,000–28,500
Châtelperronian (Lower Périgordian)	32,000–29,500

SOURCE: After Grahame Clark, World Prehistory, p. 66.

The Aurignacian Tradition: 33,000 to 28,500 B.C. Unlike the sparsely distributed Châtelperronian industry, Aurignacian industries are numerous. Their distribution, which ranges from France, where the tradition appears quite suddenly, through Hungary to the caves of Israel, Iraq, and Afghanistan, strongly suggests a point of origin in Southwest Asia. The occurrence of a hybrid Mousterian-Aurignacian tradition, known as the Szeletian, in Hungary, Slovakia, and Moravia, suggests the possible fusion of an indigenous Middle Paleolithic and a migrating Upper Paleolithic population from the southeast.

In Europe, as in the Near East, Aurignacians were usually rock shelter and cave dwellers. They had fire and were avid hunters and skin dressers. Their tool kit was characterized by elongated, parallel-sided flakes which were triangular in cross section and retouched to give steep, rounded working ends (Figure 10.4a and b). Also included were tools known as *gravers,* or *burins*—elongated blades with one end coming to a sharp-pointed chisel edge. These tools were used for working wood, bone, ivory, antler, and soft stone. Burins are the implement of the carver. They also could have served as leather punches or awls for sewing skin clothing and hide tent covers, although fine, highly polished bone awls were also present. Humpbacked "nosed scrapers" were produced from small cores. Finally, the makers of the Aurignacian assemblages produced bone "javelin heads" having fine, sharp, piercing points and cleft bases for fixing the bone heads into wooden shafts (Figure 10.5).

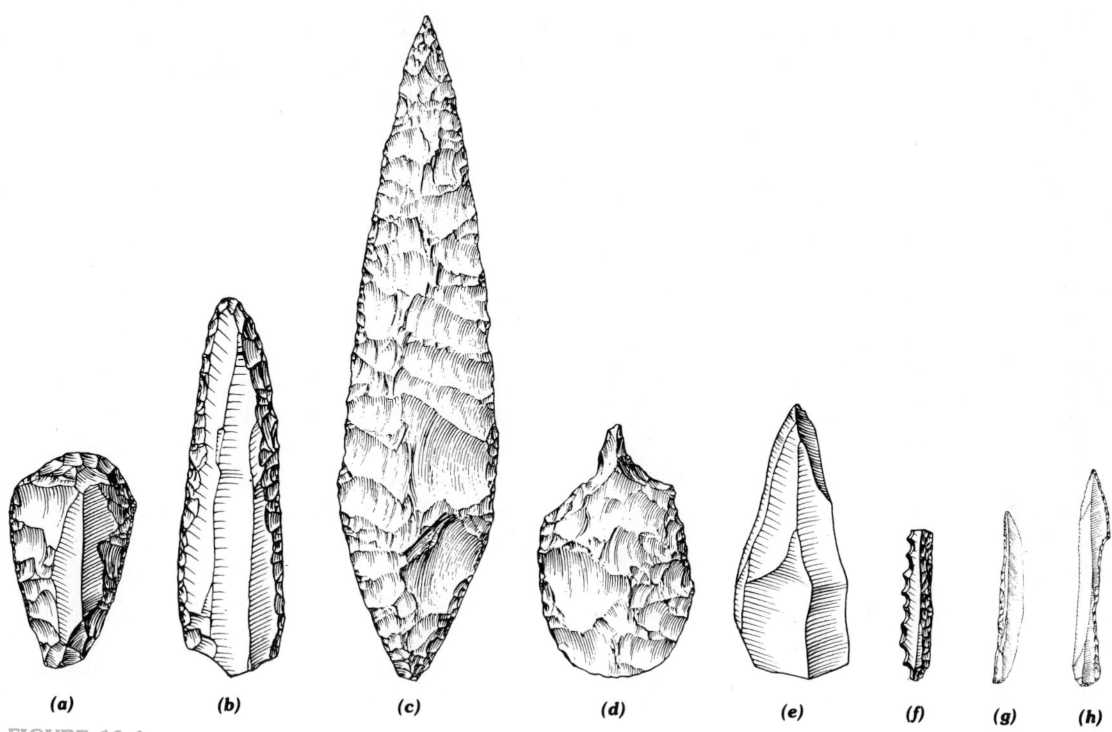

FIGURE 10.4
Upper Paleolithic stone tools. (a) Aurignacian scraper; (b) Aurignacian blade; (c) Solutrean laurel-leaf point; (d) solutrean borer-endscraper; (e) Gravettian burin; (f) Gravettian denticulated backed blade; (g) Magdalenian backed blade; (h) Magdalenian shouldered point. (SOURCE: Stein and Rowe, 1974.)

The Gravettian Tradition: 26,500 to 20,500 B.C. The Gravettian tradition flourished during a brief warming of the frigid climate of the fourth glaciation. In East Europe, the interstadial climate softened sufficiently to permit the creators of the Gravettian cultures to live in skin tents or oval huts on the loess plains of Hungary and South Russia. Although Gravettian blades have some features in common with the Châtelperronian (and for this reason French archaeologists hold that the one is an outgrowth of the other, both together constituting what they call the Périgordian), the gap in time between the end of the Châtelperronian and the onset of the Gravettian makes it unlikely that the Gravettian tradition was an outgrowth of the Châtelperronian.

Gravettian flintworkers produced delicate, slim blades with dull back edges which are so refined that they are often likened to pen-knife blades (Figure 10.4e and f). Burins were produced in large variety, and Mousterian-like triangular points appear, with the added feature of biface retouching (that is, the removal of flakes from both faces of the artifact). A further innovation can be seen in points worked down to a tang at the base, probably for hafting a handle to the blade.

FIGURE 10.5
Evolution of the Upper Paleolithic harpoon. At the left are two Aurignacian plain bone harpoon heads, one with cleft base. On the right are a single-row barbed harpoon of Early Magdalenian, followed by the more developed double-rowed barbed harpoon with swallowtail base. (Museum of Anthropology, University of Minnesota. Photo by Don Breneman.)

Gravettians not only relied on flintworking but applied their flint carving tools to ivory, bone, and antlers to make awls and lance heads, spatulas, scoops, and shovels. They also produced decorated pins and bracelets of ivory, plus beads and pendants of clay, bone, iron, and stone to be worn about the neck by both men and women. These decorative objects were incised with rows of dots and parallel lines in complex geometric designs. The Gravettians were truly skilled artisans. More than that, they were artists who modeled small animals in clay and carved excellent stylized human (mostly female) figurines in ivory and baked clay. They planted the seeds of artistic creativity that were to flower so gloriously in the Magdalenian of France between 15,000 and 9,500 B.C. The Gravettians added to the practice of burying the dead the extra flourish of arraying the bodies in full clothing and personal ornaments and sprinkling red ochre over them.

The Solutrean Tradition: 19,000 to 17,500 B.C. Immediately overlying the Gravettian strata in some parts of France is a distinctive culture named Solutrean. Its main feature is the biface laurel-leaf point, which in its most developed form is the apogee of the flintworker's technique (Figure 10.4c). Solutrean workers also produced excellent barbed and tanged arrowheads, delicately worked over both surfaces (like the laurel-leaf points) by means of carefully controlled pressure flaking. They also made bone and ivory pendants, beads, bracelets, and long-bone pins. For the first time, "eyes" were put in awls; the needle was invented 20,000 years ago! Although some examples of sculpture and paintings have been found in Solutrean deposits, it appears that the Solutrean had little interest in representative art. Nevertheless, Solutreans were true artists in flintworking. They gave form, rhythm, and symmetry to their products beyond the needs of simple utility.

The distribution of true Solutrean sites is limited to France west of the Rhone River. Bordes suggests that the Solutrean might be a belated Mousterian extension in which flint working was carried to its climax for the prehistoric Old World.[2] The Solutrean correlates in time with a very cold phase of the fourth glacial. It seems to be an aberrant Upper Paleolithic culture that intrudes as a brief, alien interlude in the Gravettian-Magdalenian sequence. In its interaction with the Gravettian, it may have provided a kind of stimulus—a challenge that gave impetus to the Gravettian trends which flowered in the rich exuberance of the Magdalenian.

[2]F. Bordes, *The Old Stone Age*, p. 158.

The Magdalenian Tradition: 15,000 to 9500 B.C. The Magdalenian tradition elaborates the boneworking propensities of the Gravettians, producing an intriguing series of barbed bone harpoons. In the Lower Magdalenian, harpoons were fashioned with a single row of barbs carved along one side. In the Upper Magdalenian, the barbs were fashioned to alternate along both sides, and a "swallowtail" base was developed to facilitate hafting into a wooden shaft (Figure 10.5). Magdalenians also invented the spear thrower, or *atlatl*, mentioned earlier.

Flintworking went into an abrupt decline. Biface points were replaced by the staghorn harpoon. Aurignacian-type tortoise-backed scrapers, or push planes, also disappeared. Scrapers became rare, perhaps replaced by bone fleshers. Crude knives, made mostly of splinters of flint rather than of blades, became the dominant tool of the day. Except for the *atlatl* and harpoon, the Magdalenians had but minor interest in technology. Their interest had shifted to a new form of environmental control—magical art.

Paleolithic Art Painting, engraving, sculpture, and modeling were familiar expressions, and the Upper Paleolithic artisans (except the Solutreans) were skilled in all these fields. Their art began in experimental crudeness and developed steadily to the sure technique of masters. It offers a rich field for the study of developmental processes in art because the sequences in improvement are clearly discernible.

Although they represent different techniques, engraving and painting were closely integrated by the Gravettian-Magdalenian artists. They developed hand in hand to produce closely similar forms of expression. The incised lines of an engraving were always painted in. Sometimes a wall surface was given a paint wash, after which the engraving was incised. The effect was to contrast the engraving on the painted background.

Early Gravettian engravings and paintings were no more than crude, stiff outlines. Later Gravettian pictures became more accurate representations, and in the Lower and Middle Magdalenian, skill in composition, contour, and the use of polychrome were achieved.

Sculpture does not show such a progressive trend, since most examples reveal reasonably good technique. Mural sculpture was wall engraving developed to produce medallion types of low and high relief. The best work, however, was done in sculpturing in the round on bone, antler, and ivory, and in shaping such articles as dagger grips and spear throwers in animal and bird forms. The most famous example of plastic modeling is a family group of a bison bull, cow, and calf from the cavern of Tuc d'Audubert.

Much light is shed on the beliefs and mentality of Upper Paleolithic people by the art they produced. There have been argumentative exchanges between functional-minded anthropologists and those who insist that art be evaluated as an end in itself. Aesthetes have held that it manifests the essential artistic and creative genius of its makers. Anthropologists have insisted on a magico-religious explanation of the art, for they see the cultural functions of art as more significant than the aesthetic aspects.

Upper Paleolithic art had the latent function of maintaining the population by serving as a magical aid in hunting and procreation. But besides being a means to these ends, it was also an end in itself. Upper Paleolithic artists produced not merely images, but beautiful images. They not only strove to produce magically efficacious representations of their desires but also developed artistic skill for its intrinsic pleasure. Their sculpture deserves to be called "the Paleolithic Greek," and because of their painting, it is not hyperbole to call the cavern of Lascaux "the Sistine Chapel of the Ice Age."

It is likely, however, that magical purposes never left the artist's mind. This is especially evident in the case of mural art, which is rarely found where it may easily be seen. The Upper Paleolithic artist did not adorn the walls of a home or the entrance of a cavern. On the contrary, the works of art are found deep in the earth's bowels, in the dark, mysterious caverns where the artist worked by the fitful smoky flare of a stone lamp. Animals were drawn there: the woolly mammoth, bison, reindeer, wild cow, bear, woolly rhinoceros, horse, and ibex—most of them now long since extinct in Europe. Again and again the artist painted red gashes dripping with blood. Projectile points are often shown piercing the flesh, and in some instances streams of red blood are painted flowing from nostrils and mouth. Diagrammatic scenes of what appear to be log-covered pits into which mammoths are falling have been found in such sites as the cavern of Font-de-Gaume. All these expressions of realism are possibly acts of wish fulfillment through compulsive, mimetic magic (see also pages 554–555).

The psychology and the act must have been not unlike that of Navajo Indian sand painting today. The sand paintings are highly stylized, but together with their accompanying image-filled chants, their effect in curing or crop growing is compulsive. There is firm faith that the act guarantees the result. An even more apt analogy is spelled out in the autobiography of a Winnebago Indian, written in the first decade of this century. Crashing Thunder tells of a holy hill in Wisconsin in which there was a cave wherein lived twenty spirits:

My father had control of them and when he wished to bless a man he would take his bow and arrows and, holding them in his hands, lead the man around the hill and into the lodge (i.e., into the hill). There he would look for a stone pillar, and upon it, . . . he drew the pictures of a number of different animals. My father possessed only one arrow, but that one was a holy one. Then dancing around the stone pillar and singing some songs, he finished by breathing upon the pillar. Finally he walked around and shot at it and . . . it had turned into a deer with large horns which fell dead at his feet. . . . My father was a very famous hunter. . . .[3]

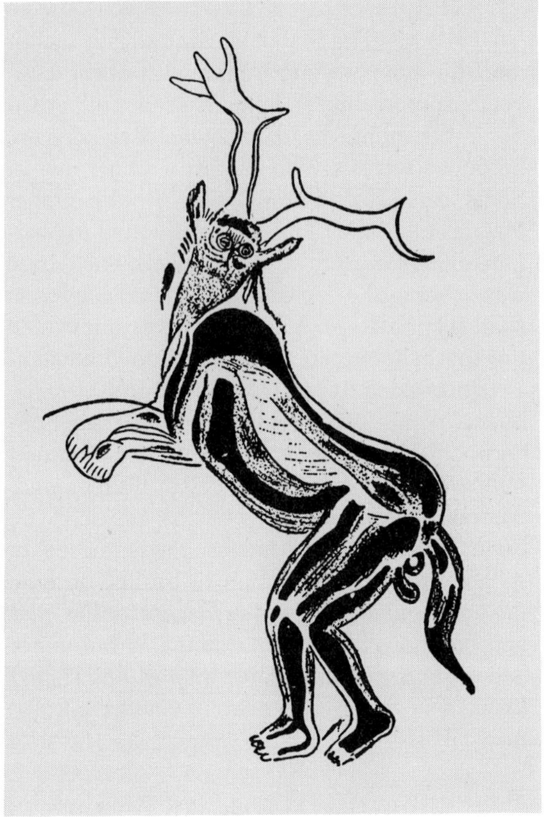

FIGURE 10.6
An Upper Paleolithic masked deer dancer, commonly known as The Sorcerer. A male-animal fertility figure, 29½ inches high, painted over engraved outline, and located high on the wall of the most inaccessible recess of the Caverne les Trois Freres, Ariege, France. (After the tracing and restoration by H. Breuil.)

Rarely did Upper Paleolithic artists portray themselves. Sometimes, however, cave paintings present anthropomorphic figures such as the famous "Sorcerer of Les Trois Frères," in France, shown in Figure 10.6. The Sorcerer was

[3] P. Radin (ed.). *Crashing Thunder*, pp. 27–28.

FIGURE 10.7
An antelope dancer, New Mexico. Modern water color by Ow-u-Te-wa. (Courtesy of the School of American Indian Art, Santa Fe, New Mexico.)

probably a medicine man endowed with deer-hunting power. He wears a wolf's tail and a deerhead mask and is prancing in a ritual dance similar to the Deer Dance performed by Pueblo Indians today (Figure 10.7).

Some magic may be wholly beneficent. This is particularly true of fertility magic. The Gravettians were especially fond of statuettes of pregnant women of whom the Venus of Willendorf (Figure 10.8) is the most famous. The parts of her torso which swell with pregnancy are given lavish exaggeration and virtually every line is a segment of a perfect circle: the apotheosis of the feminine curve. The face, arms, legs, and feet are ignored. The detail of her coiffure and that of the Venus of Brassempouy (Figure 10.9) show that the hairdo had its social significance 20,000 years ago.

Whether the charming statuettes, which stand only 2 to 6 inches high, were talismans to be carried by the woman who wished for a child, or whether they were worshipped by men and

FIGURE 10.8
The Venus of Willendorf. A Gravettian goddess of fertility. She represents the idealization of a reproducing mother. (Courtesy of the American Museum of Natural History.)

FIGURE 10.9
The Venus of Brassempouy, a stylistically "modern" fragment from Upper Paleolithic times. The hairstyle is quite different from that of the Venus of Willendorf. (Courtesy of the Musée des Antiquités Nationales.)

women alike as mother-goddess idols, cannot be known. It seems possible that they represent a cult of this goddess, for in the Mesolithic and Neolithic Ages to follow, there is no question of the importance of worship of the mother goddess in the Near East.

The Upper Paleolithic art of Europe and North Africa was a vividly representational art—an art of flesh, blood, and hope—a functional art which aided in survival, an art which was eagerly used by a hunting people in a glacial age as a symbolic expression of their major interests.

The Upper Paleolithic Age in Africa and Asia

The distribution of the Upper Paleolithic tradition reveals that it must have been an efficient environmental adjustment. Aurignacian complexes are found throughout the Near East, in the Crimea, and into Siberia, where they are associated with remains of semisubterranean houses (Figure 10.10). Eastward, these complexes extend into India to the boundary of the old Acheulean and East Asian chopper- and flake-tool complex. Aurignacian and Gravettian traditions also occur in East Africa and the Mediterranean coastal areas as the Capsian tradition.

In Africa, the Middle Paleolithic Acheulean traditions went through a number of local developments, but a general Upper Paleolithic complex, called the *Sangoan*, spread over East Africa and the Congo basin. Related local traditions of South Africa and the Cape regions are known as *Fauresmith* and *Stillbay*, respectively. As a forest tradition, the Sangoan could not do away with the hand ax, as the Upper Paleolithic traditions of Europe did. Thus, in the Sangoan, the hand ax of the preceding Acheulean tradition was elongated to take on the form of a pick, or broadened along the cutting edge and narrowed at the butt to become very similar in form to a modern steel ax. The more generalized hand ax evolved into two specialized artifacts in the Sangoan. The Sangoan equivalent of the Mousterian point consists of elongated biface lance heads that are analogous to Solutrean blades far to the north. The Sangoan also included tanged and shouldered points resembling those found in the Solutrean tradition. In other words, the Upper Paleolithic traditions of most of Africa evolved in much the same directions as those of Europe and Asia Minor, while at the same time developing certain distinctions.[4]

[4]For details, consult S. Cole, *The Prehistory of East Africa*, pp. 183–199, or J. D. Clark, *The Prehistory of Africa*.

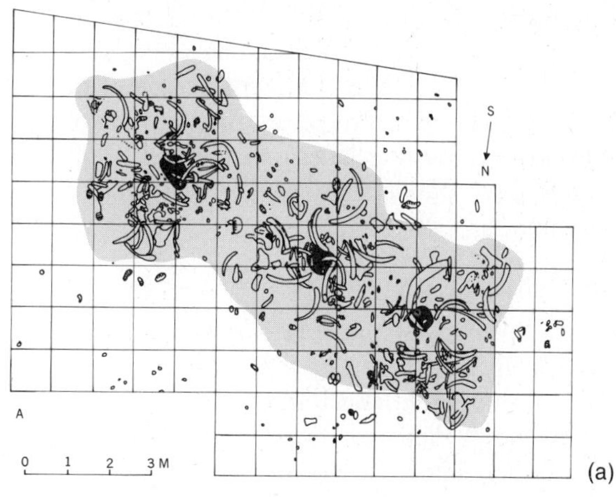

FIGURE 10.10
(a) Ground plan of an Upper Paleolithic (Pushkari I) joint family homesite on the open Russian plains. The three hearths down the middle of the long tent could have been the foci for individual families within the joint family establishment. The debris consists mostly of mammoth tusks, teeth, and bones. (From A. Mongait, *Archaeology of the USSR*, p. 79.) (b) An ethnographic reconstruction of the dwelling. (By V. D. Zaporozhaskaya, in Mongait, ibid., p. 80.)

We have little knowledge of the Upper Paleolithic in India or Malaysia. However, an Upper Paleolithic industry has been identified in the upper cave at Choukoutien. Stone tools are scarce, consisting of sidescrapers, choppers, and various flakes. An eyed bone needle and several ornamental objects, including a pierced pebble and pierced seashells, have been recovered. The needle and ornamental objects, in spite of the archaic stone industry, clearly attest to an Upper Paleolithic stage. In Japan the Upper Paleolithic is represented by various blades, burins, and flake tools.[5]

[5]Bordes, op. cit. pp. 200–202, 210–211.

During the time of low sea levels, when Siberians were first crossing into North America, people from South Asia were pushing down into what is now the Indonesian archipelago and into Australia. They may have needed rafts in places, but they reached Australia before 33,000 B.C..[6] The absence of big game and good flaking stone reduced their technology to crude choppers and flakes, with reliance on wood spears, dibbles, and simple utensils. A way of life developed which remained little changed for millennia after

[6]J. P. White, "New Guinea: The First Phase in Oceanic Settlement," in R. C. Green and M. Kelly (eds.), *Studies in Oceanic Culture History*, vol. 2, pp. 45–52.

the rising postglacial seas cut off the prehistoric Australians from Asia. Another interesting discovery is an isolated human population with archaic cranial features suggesting the survival of *Homo erectus* in Australia as recently as 10,000 to 9000 years ago alongside a *Homo sapiens* population.[7]

THE NEW WORLD PALEOLITHIC

Toward the end of the fourth glacial period, people from Asia followed the big-game trails eastward across the land bridge connecting Siberia to North America. Even today, the gap across Bering Strait is such that it is possible, if foolhardy, to get from Siberia to Alaska by leaping from one ice floe to another. It was done in the 1920s by a former whaling captain who wanted to prove the point. But at times in the Late Pleistocene the Bering Strait was a broad plain of rich grassland over 1000 miles wide. The sea level was lowered because of water locked in the continental glaciers and the land between the continents was raised by the weight of billions of tons of ice on the continental land masses.

J. M. Campbell, writing in 1963, states that the ice-free corridor through which wandering hunters could have passed most easily was available between 20,000 and 18,000 years ago. J. D. Jennings, writing in 1974, accepts as most probable the thesis that 18,000 to 10,000 years ago "would seem to bracket man's entry into the New World . . . with some certainty."[8] Although not accepted by all authorities, some recent redating of human fossils in California has yielded dates of up to 50,000 years ago.[9] It is not possible to specify the first peopling of the New World with fine detail, but that the first arrivals came some time between 30,000 and 10,000 years ago is highly probable.

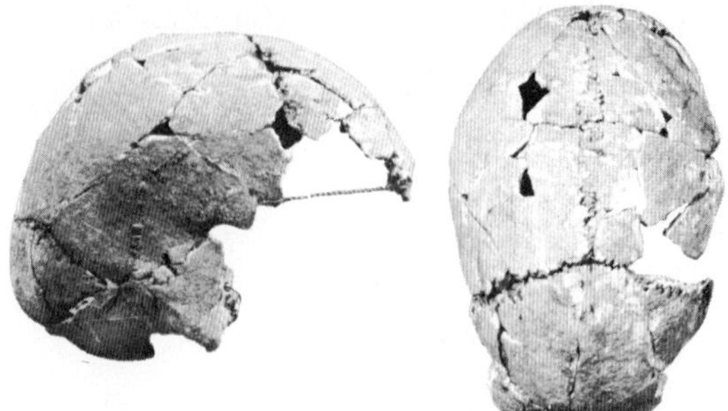

FIGURE 10.11
The oldest authenticated American. The Midland skull viewed from the right and above. In cranial capacity and structure, it is in every respect a *Homo sapiens sapiens.* (Courtesy of the Museum of New Mexico.)

Early People in the Americas

Nearly a score of fossil hominid skeletons of the Late Pleistocene age have been found in North and South America. None is claimed to be older than the fourth glaciation and only two were reported with sufficient care that their geological setting is beyond doubt. The one sure find is from Midland, Texas, discovered in 1954. The skull, which was crushed and fragmented by overlying deposits, is sufficiently complete to allow for reconstruction of the cranium. It, along with the body bones, indicates a true *Homo sapiens sapiens*, as can be readily seen in the photo in Figure 10.11. The stratigraphy, radiocarbon and fluorine analyses, plus comparative evidence, indicate a probable date of 18,000 B.C., and a minimal date of 10,000 B.C., for the specimen. Associated animal fossils include Pleistocene horses, bison, and antelope. Miscellaneous flint chips, scrapers, and knives from the same level as the skull suggest that the Midland woman (for the features of the fossil are female) died at a lakeside or streamside campsite.

[7]A. G. Thorne and P. G. Macumber, "Discoveries of Late Pleistocene Man at Kow Swamp, Australia" (*Nature*, vol. 238, 1972), pp. 316–319.

[8]J. D. Jennings, *Prehistory of North America*, 2d ed., p. 52.

[9]J. L. Bada, R. A. Schroeder, and G. F. Carter, "New Evidence for the Antiquity of Man in North America Deduced from Aspartic Acid Racemization" (*Science*, vol. 184, May 17, 1974), pp. 791–793.

Other possible American ancient human fossils, such as that of Tepexpan from Mexico and the Brown's Valley and Pelican Rapids fossils from Minnesota, are sufficiently similar to the Midland fossil to indicate that the latter is a typical specimen.[10] Late Pleistocene people in northeastern Asia and in North America were not very different physically from the later American Indians.[11]

The Chopper-Tool Complex in America

Many enthusiastic searchers for early humans in North America have recovered thousands of chopper tools and scrapers from sand blowouts and exposed high beaches and terraces in desert areas of the western United States where glacial lakes and rivers once lapped. On the basis of these artifacts, it is held by some that the earliest migrants brought the Asiatic chopper tradition with them. The trouble is that *all* the chopper implements have been surface finds. There is no stratigraphic identification for any of them. Their true age is, therefore, wholly a matter of guesswork and an expression of faith. In dry country, light soils and sand are blown away by strong winds; as the sand blows out from under small stones they gradually settle lower and lower until at last they rest on a resistant soil base. Water action from cloudbursts can have the same effect. The stones covering a desert floor, the so-called desert pavement, may originally have been scattered throughout the whole thickness of a once-overlying layer representing thousands of years' difference in time. Now they all lie together and there is no way of telling which is the older.[12] Tough-minded archaeologists insist that until such a day as a chopper assemblage is found in situ (as it was originally deposited) in a stratigraphic setting indubitably ascribable to the earlier phases of the fourth (Wisconsin) glacial epoch, the chopper-tool phase remains problematic.

The Lithic—or "Big-Game Projectile"—Traditions

After 15,000 B.C. it is a different story. Since 1925, a number of sites yielding the fossil skeletons of mammoths and bison in direct association with skillfully made projectile points have been found in the Plains, while assemblages of similar projectiles without the fauna have been found all the way to the east coast.

The Llano Tradition: 9500 to 7500 B.C. The earliest of these lithic traditions is labeled the *Llano*, after the Llano Estacado, or Staked Plains, of Texas and New Mexico. This was a time of cool, moist climate in the North American heartland beyond the reaches of the ice sheets. Here there were vast expanses of grass and lightly forested parklands. Lakes and marshes, the products of rain and glacial runoff supported herds of mammoths, great-horned bison, elk, giant beaver, antelope, horses, wolves, and many smaller mammals. There is no direct evidence of fire drives such as were employed at Torralba in Acheulean times. The Llano people used fire for roasting their kills, however, as indicated by a concentrated charcoal-bearing hearth area.

The hallmark of the Llano industries is the channeled or fluted projectile point known as the Clovis point (see Figure 10.12, top). The fine flaking and elongated shapes of the Clovis point and all subsequent points of the Big-Game

[10] H. de Terra, J. Romero, and T. D. Stewart, *Early Man in Mexico* (1949); A. R. V. Arellano, "Some New Aspects of the Tepexpan Case" (*Bulletin of the Texas Archaeological and Paleontological Society*, vol. 22, 1951), pp. 217–225; on the Minnesota girl (Pelican Rapids), see E. A. Hooton, *Up from the Ape* (1947), pp. 405–407 and 648.

[11] T. D. Stewart, "A Physical Anthropologist's View of the Peopling of the New World" (*Southwestern Journal of Anthropology*, vol. 16, no. 3, 1960), p. 269.

[12] Cf. F. W. Sharrock, "Prehistoric Occupation Patterns in Southwestern Wyoming and Cultural Relations with the Great Basin and Plains Cultural Areas" (*University of Utah Anthropological Papers*, no. 77, 1966).

Clovis fluted points
Llano tradition

Folsom fluted points
Folsom tradition

Sandia points
Folsom tradition

Cody knife
Eden point
Plano tradition

tradition are reminiscent of Solutrean techniques. The highly skilled flint-flaking capability of the big-game hunters has little in common with the crude chopper tools made earlier. Although no specialized flake tools have been found, the Llano industry includes scrapers, knives, burins, and choppers.

The Folsom Tradition: 9000 to 7000 B.C. While the Folsom industry is not the oldest in North America, it was the first to be discovered (1920 to 1927) and the most famous. In the original site at Folsom, New Mexico, twenty-three bison had been slaughtered and nineteen of the deeply fluted Folsom points left in the flesh between the ribs of some of them. At another Folsom site near Fort Collins, Colorado, the fossil bones of a hundred or so of the same species *(Bison antiquus)* of giant longhorn bison lay in a heap where the animals had been stampeded over a river bank. A dozen and a half points of the Plainview variation of the Folsom type (Figure 10.12) were found among the fossil bones. The Folsom people focused on longhorned bison (the mammoth had become extinct) and rounded out their meat diet with camels and occasional elephants, all Pleistocene mammals that have been extinct since the last glacial retreat.

The Plano Tradition: 8000 to 5000 B.C. The Paleolithic Big-Game traditions of the western High Plains ended with the final disappearance of the Pleistocene fauna. Over the final millennia many local variations of the projectile-point hunting complex were developed, but the

FIGURE 10.12
Artifacts from the Big-Game, or Lithic, traditions of the Late Upper Pleistocene epoch in North America. A high skill in flintworking is revealed in the Clovis (Llano) and Folsom fluted points shown in the top row. Quite different but truly beautiful expressions of the artisan's skill are the Cody knife and Eden point of the Plano tradition shown in the bottom row. (Museum of Anthropology, University of Minnesota. Photo by Don Breneman.)

way of life remained essentially what it had been 10,000 years earlier. The material inventory was limited. The special, localized varieties of Plano points and knives are too numerous to summarize here; Jennings' *Prehistory of North America* provides a clear treatment for those who are interested in more detail.

In Plano times, the big game was replaced by smaller varieties, changing from the mammoth elephant and giant longhorn bison to the modern bison and antelope. The ecology was becoming modern—drier and temperate, with shorter grasses on the plains and fewer lakes, bogs, and marshes.

The time was at hand for the culture of the foragers to take over, providing the base for the next stage of cultural evolution: that based upon the *domestication* of plants and animals. This is the subject of the next chapter.

After 5000 B.C., hunters persisted in and around the Plains of North America, the marginal savannas of Africa, in some forests of the major continents and the arctic wastes of Eurasia and North America—but the Big-Game Stone Age way of human life, beginning in the Middle Pleistocene about a million years ago in Europe and Africa, played itself out at long last on the plains of northern Mexico and the United States.

SUMMARY

Homo sapiens sapiens, modern people, emerged during the third interglacial and were fully established in Africa, Asia Minor, and South Asia by the beginning of the fourth glaciation. In Europe during the fourth glacial interstadial, they succeeded the Neandertals.

Homo sapiens sapiens quickly developed inventories of specialized flake and horn or bone artifacts all over the northern half of the Western Hemisphere, replacing the hand ax tradition. In Africa, refined and specialized axes were developed in the Upper Paleolithic Sangoan.

In Asia, east of India, the chopper-tool and flake complex continued unmodified as long as the ancient Paleolithic hunting traditions survived. The Chinese had an Upper Paleolithic modification with bone needles and pierced ornamental objects.

It is reasonable to infer that the Upper Paleolithic societies had fully developed cultures comparable to those of any recent societies of skilled hunters such as the Bushmen, Eskimos, or nomadic Plains Indian tribes. They had fully developed religion and magic, family and kinship systems, government and law, folklore and mythology, and dance, painting, and sculpture. Although they are thought of as cave dwellers, they also built semisubterranean houses.

Wherever they went, *Homo sapiens* populations took fire and fire making. The remains of their art and the burial of their dead give evidence of an imaginative intellect.

They quickly spread out to inhabit the entire world, peopling the South Pacific and the Americas. They were ready to move beyond direct dependence on wild plants and animals as hunters and gatherers. They were ready to domesticate plants and animals and to revolutionize life as farmers and founders of towns and cities.

SELECTED READINGS

Bordes, F., *The Old Stone Age* (1968), pp. 147–241. Excellent brief account of the Upper Paleolithic stone industries. Many helpful line drawings of typical artifacts.

Braidwood, R. J., *Prehistoric Man* (8th ed., 1975). Easy-to-read; well-written summary; excellent illustrations.

Jennings, J. D., *Prehistory of North America* (1974), pp. 47–125. The best comprehensive introduction to the question of Upper Pleistocene cultures and peoples of the New World.

Klein, R. G., *Ice-Age Hunters of the Ukraine* (1973). A critique and summary of the subject, written for the undergraduate or layperson; concise, well written, a useful source for the scholar.

Patterson, T. C., *America's Past: A New World Archaeology* (1973). An excellent summary of the field in paperback. Good illustrations.

11 The Beginnings of Urbanism

CHAPTER OUTLINE

LEARNING GOALS

- Explain the shift from intensive foraging to incipient agriculture
- Describe the Natufians as an example of intensive foragers.
- Discuss the Mesolithic in Northern Europe.
- Identify the Mesolithic in North America.
- Trace the rise of the Neolithic.
- Describe early Neolithic farming communities in the Near East.
- Learn about the origins of domesticated plants and animals.
- Compare the Neolithic manifestations in Asia and the New World.
- Discuss the rise of urbanism as exemplified by Mesopotamian cultures.
- Identify the characteristics of early civilizations.

Big-game hunting continued in some parts of the Old World in the Late Pleistocene, as it did in the Plano complexes east of the Rockies in North America, but the disappearance of many of the great Pleistocene mammals forced most peoples to change their living habits. As early as 15,000 B.C. in some areas they began to settle down in more or less permanent locations and to develop intensive foraging as a form of adaptation necessary to exploit a varied environment (see Figure 11.1).

Intensive foraging led to the domestication of plants and animals and to the establishment of settled farming communities. In the early phases (circa 8300 to 6000 B.C. in the Near East), these developments produced a pre-pottery period of incipient agriculture. As the complex was expanded and refined, it became the *Neolithic Era of Developed Agriculture* (6000 to 4200 B.C. in the Near East). After this, ceremonial and market centers became towns and cities. Bronze tools and weapons were produced. Writing evolved from pictographic notations (see pages 602–604), while specialized artisans made quantities of diverse goods. Priests and kings organized religion and government. The urban revolution was under way, the world of people was being transformed, and the first civilizations were taking shape (3800 to 2800 B.C. in the Near East).

INTENSIVE FORAGING AND INCIPIENT AGRICULTURE

In Africa, Europe, Asia Minor, and Asia, the lithic hallmark of Mesolithic technology is the microblade (Figure 11.2). Microblades are minute to small flakes of more or less geometric form that were set in a row in a piece of wood or bone to give a durable cutting edge to harpoons, swords, and above all, sickles.

Equally important to the complex were milling stones for grinding seeds. They were either the mortar-and-pestle type or the hollow-slab-and-rubbing-stone. In America, this latter combination is called by the Mexican and Spanish names *metate* and *mano* (Figure 11.3).

Mesolithic populations, like their Paleolithic predecessors, were still hunters and food gatherers, but they lived by stalking and trapping deer, wild boars, and smaller animals while relying heavily upon wild seeds, berries, nuts, and roots, and in special cases, upon fish, shellfish, and water birds. Their subsistence base was much more diversified than that of the Paleolithic big-game hunters. It was a mode of life more conducive to experimentation and elaboration of culture. The result was wide local and regional diversity leading to a degree of cultural and social change far beyond any previously experienced in human history. For this reason, it is not feasible in this study to follow in detail all manifestations of the Mesolithic around the world.

The Natufian Tradition: 10,000 to 8000 B.C.

The late Mesolithic and early pre-Neolithic of the Near East is best known through the Natufian complex of Palestine (Israel and Jordan of today), even though earlier assemblages of Mesolithic traditions exist in the Zagros Mountains, east of the Tigris River in Iran. The Natufian lithic assemblage contains flints of which 80 percent are microliths. The rest are familiar survivors from the Upper Paleolithic—backed blades, awls, scrapers, and picks. Sculpture in stone, bone awls, needles, and harpoon heads are particularly reminiscent of the Solutrean and Magdalenian work of an earlier age. So also is the inset blade "machete" with an animal-head hilt. Other stone artifacts include metates, basalt pestles, hammerstones, and net sinkers. Bone fishhooks are also numerous. A distinctive sheen on many microliths results from the abrasive effect of the silicate in stems of grass. The Natufian also displays various ornamental and artistic objects, including beads, pendants, bracelets, and figurines.

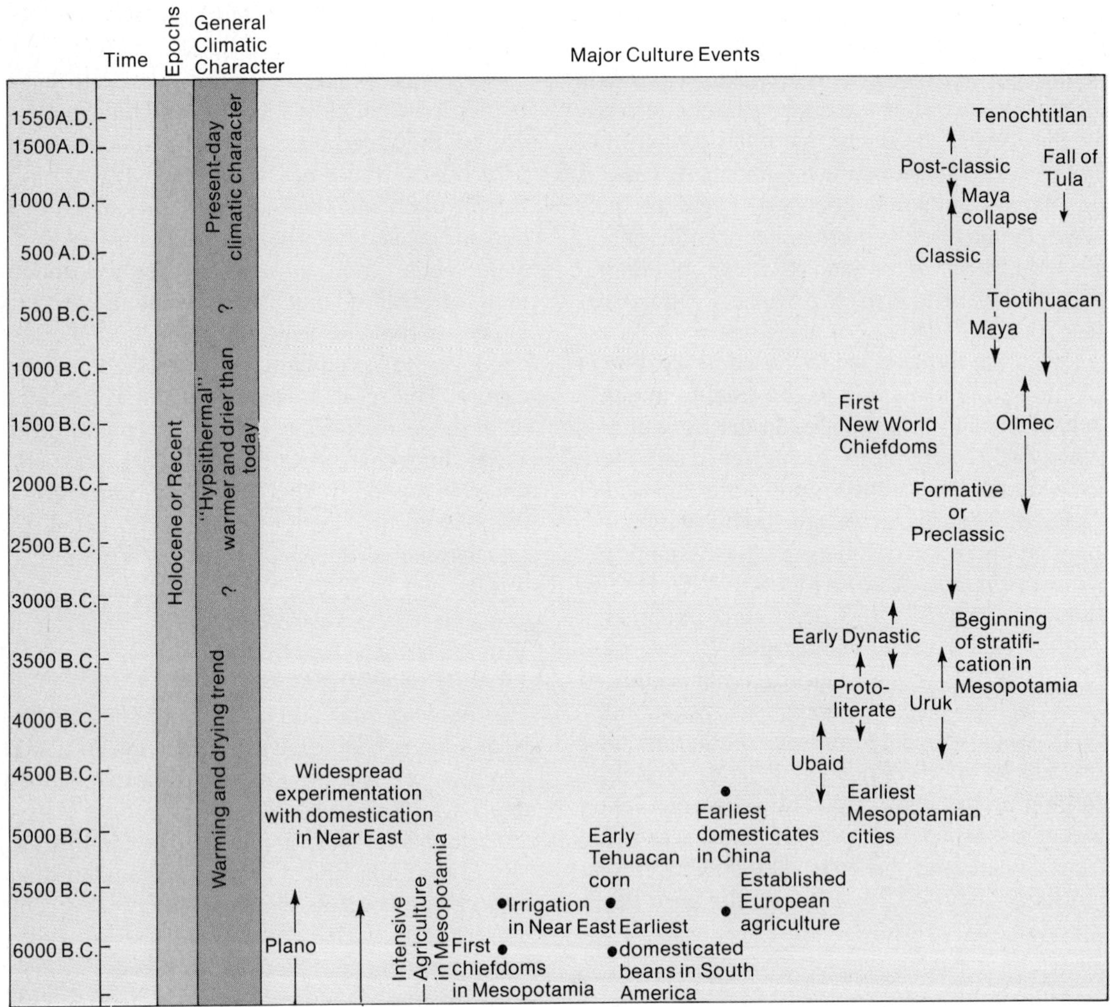

FIGURE 11.1
Time chart of human evolution. (Adapted from Jolly and Plog, 1976.)

Although the Natufians of Palestine lived in caves and rock shelters, they were also village dwellers, constructing settlements of round, stone-walled pit dwellings. At Eynam, a stratified Natufian site in Israel, three early Natufian villages, one above the other, have been excavated. Each contained roughly fifty dwellings compacted into a tight little hamlet covering about 2 acres. The circular floors of the houses were dug several feet into the ground. Then a

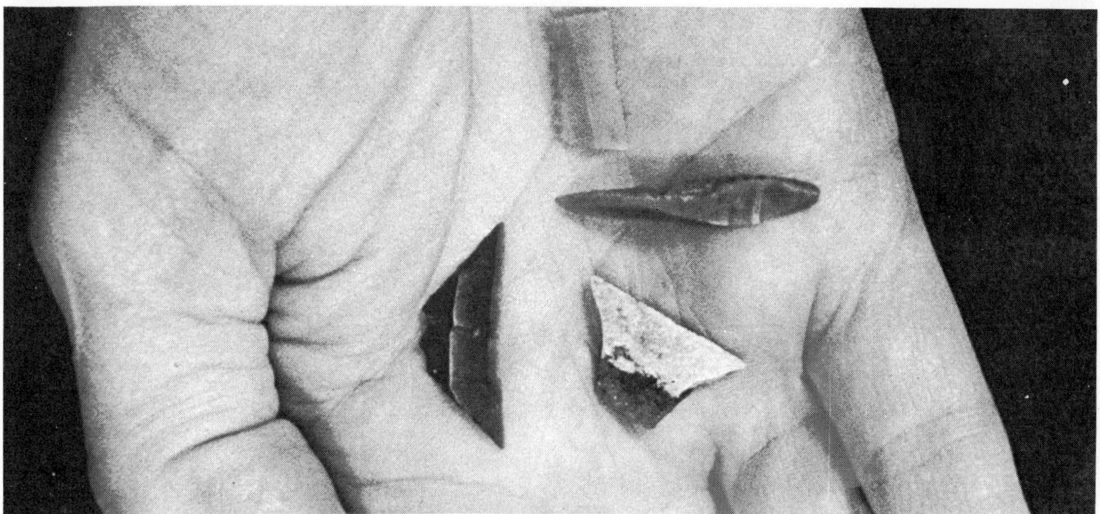

FIGURE 11.2
Microlithic blades from the European Mesolithic. A minuscule punch and three geometric cutting blades. (Museum of Anthropology, University of Minnesota. Photo by Don Breneman.)

FIGURE 11.3
This Navajo woman is grinding corn on a metate with a mano; widely used for grinding grains in many parts of the world. (Josef Muench/Pictorial Photography.)

plastered stone wall around the pit raised the solid interior room walls another 3 feet. Over this wall a perishable reed or mat dome probably completed the shelter, which could be up to 21 feet in diameter. The ground between the houses was pocked with clay-lined storage pits, or caches, indicative of seasonal surpluses of seeds held for later use. Some pits were reused for burials, and in some instances burials were beneath the floors of the houses (Figure 11.4).

The technique of sinking the floor of the house into the ground before raising the superstructure above is adapted to the conditions of temperate climates with cold winters. The semisubterranean house has two advantages: (1) It is easier to keep warm, and (2) it provides more space without raising high side walls.[1]

Inasmuch as no actual foodstuffs have as yet been found in the storage pits at Eynam, one cannot say with certainty that the Natufians had domesticated plants. They clearly foraged inten-

[1]See p. 239, for a discussion of modern pit dwellings and their ethnographic distribution.

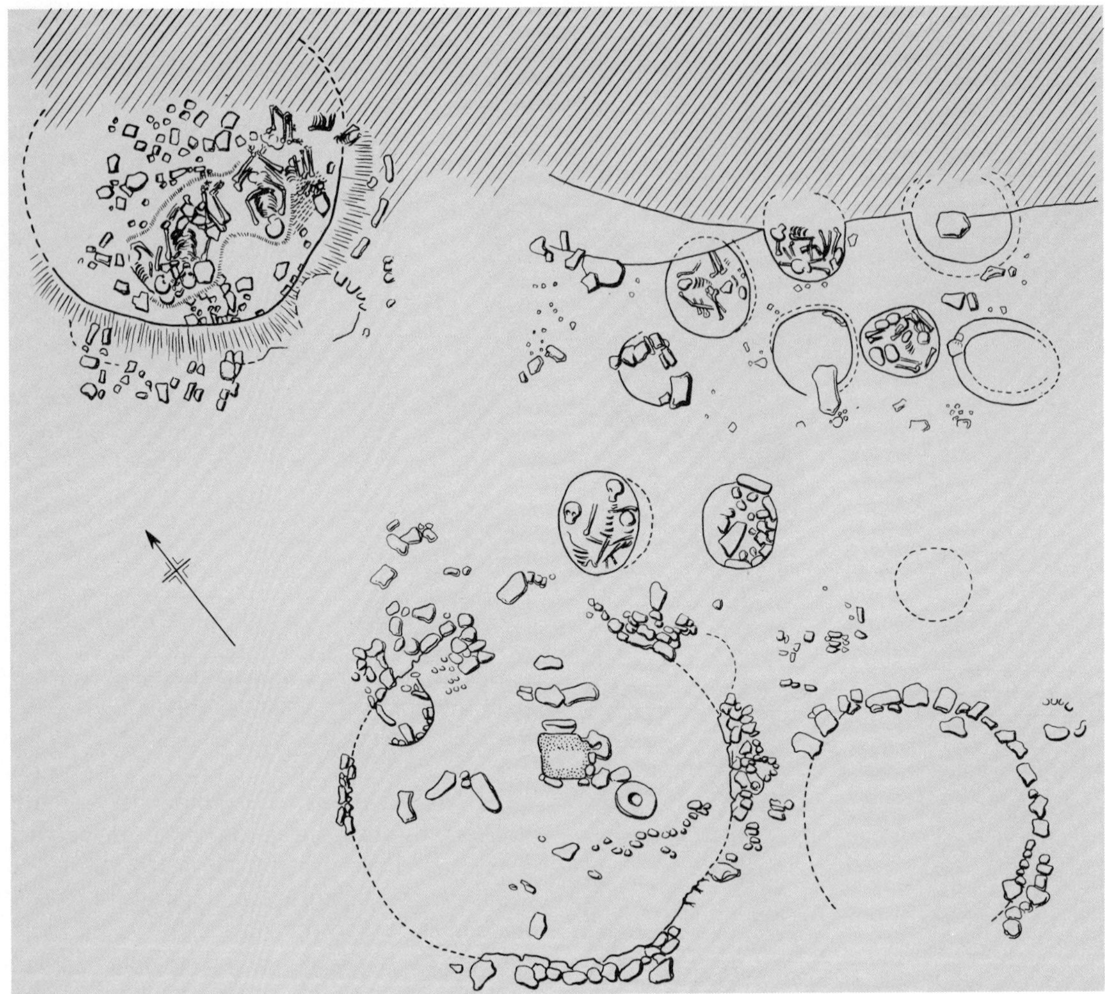

FIGURE 11.4
Ground plan of a part of Eynam with circular houses and storage pits for cereals, some of which have been reused as graves. (From Mellaart, *Earliest Civilizations of the Near East*; drawn by Gillion Jones after Perrot. Reproduced by permission of Thames and Hudson, London.)

sively for seeds and other wild plant edibles. In addition to the storage pits, the numerous sickle-blade microliths and the bone sickles in which they were set attest to harvesting techniques which have gone well beyond the less efficient method of beating the ripened seeds into a pouch or basket with a flat stick or woven fan. The presence of Natufian assemblages of manos and metates, as well as mortars and pestles, is suggestive of a diet in which stone-ground meal was cooked for porridge and gruel, possibly flavored with bits of fish or meat. Pottery was not used, but solid stone bowls and carved drinking mugs (beakers) ground out of basalt are found in numbers.

Quantities of bone fishhooks and notched

stone sinkers, plus the presence of shells of fresh-water snails and mussels, testify to the exploitation of lakes and streams. The bones of wolf, boar, fox, hyena, cattle, deer, gazelle, rabbit, rodents, birds, sheep, goats, bear, leopard, and horse in Natufian sites give continuing evidence of the importance of hunting in the Mesolithic and early pre-Neolithic.

The Khartoum Tradition in Africa

The Mesolithic complex took many forms in varying local situations as it diffused south, east, north, and west. Four thousand years after the Natufian, it was well established along the upper reaches of the Nile in the form of the Early Khartoum.

These people were food collectors, living in large settlements along the Nile. Their stone technology was a Mesolithic variant, and they are distinguished by having pottery. The introduction of pottery here, as in a number of other places, precedes the domestication of plants and animals.

Marginal Mesolithic Adaptations in Northern Europe

When the microlithic tradition became established north and west of the Near East, it included special adaptations to the forest environments which had replaced the glaciers. Mesolithic microlith traditions became established along the river deltas and lake shores of North Europe around 5000 B.C. The small flakes were set in harpoons or were used as arrowheads, rather than as sickle teeth, for these people harvested berries rather than grasses. They were people of the forests and did not have mortars, pestles, or sickles to suggest the exploitation of cereal grains (Figure 11.5).[2]

A more characteristic tool is the straightedged ax. The axhead was shaped by symmetrically chipping a flint nodule and partially smoothing the surfaces with an abrasive polishing stone to give it a well-ground cutting edge. Later, similar axheads were ground wholly from small unflakable igneous rocks. The finished stone axhead was then glued into a socket formed of the soft antler horn of a stag. This, in turn, was hafted into a wooden or antler handle.

Barbed bone or antler-headed spears were used as in Upper Paleolithic times, but the really new hunting invention was the bow and arrow. No longer was it necessary to rely on the *atlatl* for projectile force. Maglemosian (Great Bog) bows, of which original elmwood specimens have been found, are simple, so-called self-bows, which means that they are unreinforced slats of wood without reflex curves.

The presence of skeletons of domesticated dogs is a possible indication of the intensive nature of the hunting of these people. The human being and the dog may already have entered into a mutual-aid relationship as a hunting team. Dugout canoes hewn from solid logs were another adaptive device. They made it possible to penetrate the swamps for hunting and to communicate between one shore settlement and another.

The European northerners were making no contribution to the agricultural revolution by domesticating new plants. Nonetheless, they were working out a settled pattern of adaptation to the woodland habitat.

The Mesolithic of India and China apparently developed independently of the Near Eastern tradition.[3]

The Mesolithic in North America

While late Upper Paleolithic big-game hunters were still searching out their prey in Europe and parts of Asia, seed-gathering foragers were at work in North America laying the foundations for their horticultural revolution. New World archaeologists lump the many local manifestations of

[2]H. T. Waterbolk, "The Lower Rhine Basin," in R. J. Braidwood and G. R. Willey (eds.), *Courses Toward Urban Life*, p. 233.

[3]K.-c. Chang, "The Beginnings of Agriculture in the Far East" (*Antiquity*, vol. 44, 1970), pp. 175–185.

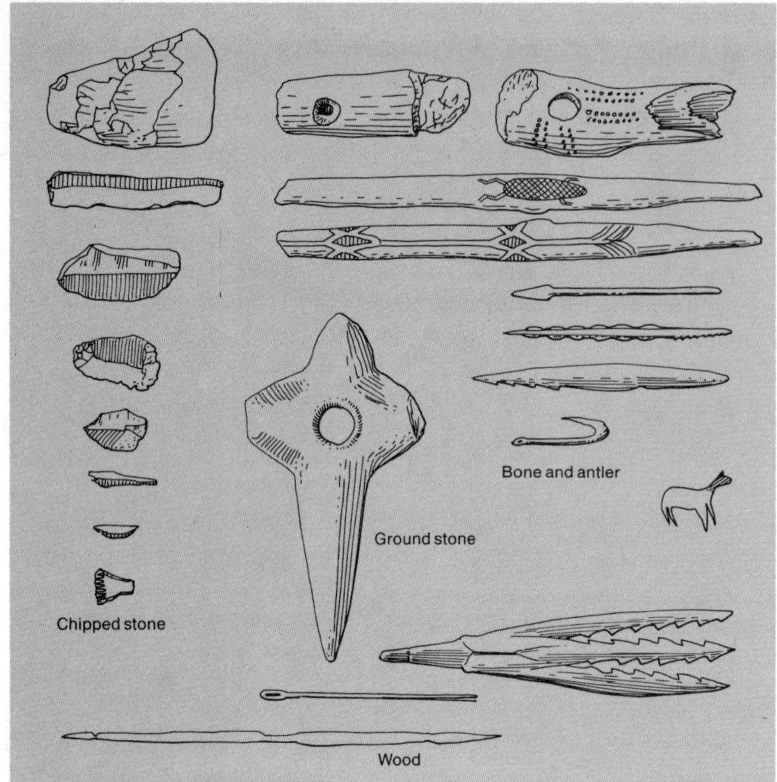

FIGURE 11.5
Maglemosian artifacts. In the left column (top), a chipped and partially polished flint axhead. Below it are flaked flint knives and microliths. On the right (top) are perforated staghorn sockets for flint axheads. Below them are a variety of bone harpoons, a fishhook, and needle. (Braidwood, 1967.)

the foraging pattern of existence under the rubric *Archaic.*

The Western Archaic, found in the Great Basin (Utah and Nevada), the Southwest (New Mexico and Arizona), and the Pacific Coast regions, is well known from a number of cave sites. Its earliest manifestations are dated from around 10,000 B.C. It continued with very little change right into the nineteenth century in the living cultures of the Shoshonean-speaking Indians of the Great Basin. The Western Archaic was a many-sided exploitation of a predominantly desert environment.

The Eastern Archaic was a complex exploitation of the more luxurious environment of the woodlands east of the Mississippi. The big-game hunters of the Lithic stage still existed between the Rockies and the woodlands at this time. The Eastern Archaic did not get underway until around 6000 B.C. in the Middle West, although on the Atlantic Coast it was well differentiated from the Lithic of a thousand to fifteen hundred years earlier (7500 to 7000 B.C.). The focus of the Eastern Archaic subsistence techniques is identified as "forest efficiency," a skillful combination of woodland hunting of deer, smaller animals, and migratory birds, and the harvesting of nuts, berries, wild seeds, and roots.

The Desert Tradition: 9000 B.C. to A.D. 1850 Jennings, who defined the Desert tradition early in the 1950s, summarizes it as follows:

. . . cave and overhang locations for settlement, bark or grass beds, seasonal gathering, intensive exploitation of resources, small-seed harvesting and special cooking techniques, basketry (twined predominant), netting and matting, fur cloth, tumpline, sandals (moccasins rare), atlatl, pointed hardwood dart shafts, varied (relatively small) projectile points, preferential use of glassy textured stone, flat milling stone and mano, a high percentage of crude scraper and chopper tools, digging stick, firedrill and hearth, bunt points, wooden clubs, horn–shaft wrenches, tubular pipes, use of olivella and other shells, vegetable quids.[4]

[4]J. D. Jennings, "The Desert West," in J. D. Jennings and E. Norbeck (eds.), *Prehistoric Men in the New World*, pp. 154–155.

The presence of deer-hoof rattles and medicine bags is evidence of shamanism (see pages 558–561). Most significant, however, is the use of shoulder-blade grass cutters as the analogue of the Old World microlith sickle. The presence of grinding stones in all sites further confirms the fundamental importance of seed harvesting. Hunting of small animals rounded out the subsistence diet. In Utah and Nevada (the Great Basin), climatic variations did not seriously alter the ecology, which remained consistently marginal desert around the fluctuating lake shores. Population has always been sparse and meager in this area, which is incapable of supporting grasses outside the limited edges of

FIGURE 11.6
Desert Culture foragers. Southern Paiute seed gatherers on the Kaibab Plateau, north of the Grand Canyon, in 1873. The women (left) wear basketry hats and carry baskets on their backs, while they hold seed-catching baskets in their hands. The girls (right) carry basketry water bottles sealed with pitch pine and slung across the forehead with tumplines. (National Anthropological Archives.)

fresh-water basins and high mountain valleys. Hence, the Desert culture remained virtually unchanged from 9000 B.C. to A.D. 1850 and did not contribute appreciably to the development of agriculture in the Western Hemisphere.

In the nineteenth century, the Gosiute, Paiute, Bannock, and Shoshone Indians were living in comparable groups of 50 to 200 people. Each local group was known by the name of the food which it foraged most intensively (Figure 11.6). Thus, the band which occupied the Snake River Desert of southern Idaho called itself the Seed Eaters. Other Shoshone bands are the Root Eaters, Pine Nut Eaters, Groundhog Eaters, Rabbit Eaters, Mountain Sheep Eaters, Fish Eaters, and the Salmon Eaters.

The Mid-Continental Archaic Traditions: 6000 B.C. to A.D. 1850 The archaeology of the Eastern Archaic stage is much too complex for us to consider more than the characteristic features of one manifestation.[5]

We select Indian Knoll, a hunting and shellfish-gathering site in western Kentucky. Here, from around 4000 B.C. to the time of the birth of Christ, forest foragers returned again and again. Their debris of shells, bones, tools, burials, and dirt built a compacted 2-acre mound 8 feet in thickness.

The absence of permanent dwelling structures is notable. Numerous charred hickory, walnut, and acorn shells around the fireplaces testify to the gathering proclivities of these Archaic people. Ninety percent of the thousands of animal bones are of deer. The rest are those of small, modern nonmigratory forest mammals such as raccoon and opossum.

Flaked projectile points by the hundreds also continued from the Lithic tradition. *Atlatl* weights and ends show that the bow had not yet been introduced. Bone fishhooks reveal that the foragers of Indian Knoll took not only shellfish from the river. Ground stone pestles and metates indicate the milling of seeds, nuts, and probably of dried deer meat to produce *pemmican*, or jerky, for winter use.[6]

Splintered bone awls and chipped flint drills, knives, and scrapers speak of hide dressing, clothing, and skin shelters. Shell beads, pins, rings, and gorgets provided personal jewelry. Of the numerous burials in the living mound, somewhat more than half the bodies were found in round pits, flexed on their sides or backs in the fetal position. Prone burials were not put in graves, but were laid out on the ground, painted red, and mounded with earth.

Other Archaic sites yield fragments of coiled baskets, used to collect and store seeds, berries, and roots. Nets for trapping fish, rabbits, and birds were woven—and sandals to protect the feet. Weaving and netting (see pages 248, 250) are technological achievements added in the Mesolithic era of intensive foraging.

The foraging complex of the New World developed independently of that of the Old World. The situation seems to have been one of parallel development. Small bands of people were settled in favorable locales near good sources of water and were squeezing the land for all it was worth in terms of fully exploiting plants, fish, and small game.

THE EARLY NEOLITHIC

The domestication of both plants and animals was a gradual process that took place in a number of different parts of the world along independent lines. Domestication consists merely in controlled cultivation and husbandry. A

[5]Readers who are interested in a very useful overall summary by subregions should refer to J. D. Jennings, *Prehistory of North America*, pp. 127–189, or G. R. Willey, *An Introduction to American Archaeology*, vol. 1.

[6]Later American Indians, especially on the Plains, hung thin slabs of meat on racks to sun-dry (see Figure 12.4, p. 218). The dried meat was then pounded to shreds which were mixed with berry pulp and formed into cakes. The cakes were stored in transportable rawhide envelopes (*parfleches*). The pemmican could conveniently be added to boiled nut or seed meal for a basic soup or gruel.

domesticated plant is one that is useful and is cultivated. The first steps in plant cultivation were probably taken in the process of weed elimination (a weed is any plant that is held to be undesirable). A patch of wild plants was tended and weeded. Kwakiutl Indians, for example, cared for wild-clover patches which were the property of specific families who dug them for pieces of roots. The main roots, however, were never taken out.[7]

Real domestication began, however, when seeds, roots, or shoots were deliberately planted and stored from one season to the next for planting. Not only did this call for foresightedness and self-restraint, but it also required dry storage to prevent mildew and rot and to ensure security from rats and mice (a good reason for domesticating cats). There was also the very difficult task of preparing the soil and selecting those plants which would yield the largest or the most easily harvested and processed seeds. The idea of plant domestication quickly caught on and spread over all continents and the isles of the Pacific in a matter of 8000 years.

Lightly forested upland grass areas may strike the reader as strange places for the origins of primitive gardening, but new evidence does not support the old theory that gardening first began in irrigation oases of the arid river valleys of the Old and New Worlds. Irrigation comes later, and it is where the grasses grew naturally but not too densely that the process of plant domestication began. Primitive wild wheat and barley grow in a natural state at elevations of 2000 to 4300 feet above sea level in the Anatolian highlands of modern Turkey and on the hilly flanks of the Fertile Crescent, which swings from the Nile along the eastern edge of the Mediterranean and down the Tigris and Euphrates Rivers (see Figure 11.7). In Mexico, at the site of the earliest known manifestation of plant domestication (see pages 198–200), pollen analysis indicates a semidry climate supporting mesquite and grassland.

[7]E. S. Curtis, *The Kwakiutl*, p. 43.

Jericho

During the 1950s, Jericho and Jarmo were two sites of intense interest and excitement. Jericho is actually the biblical city that rested on top of Tell es-Sultan (*tell* is the Arabic equivalent of the Turkish *hüyük*, which refers to a mound built up by generations of village or town life on a given spot).

Underneath the 70 feet of debris and dirt, the English expeditions, directed by Kathleen Kenyon, uncovered an early Neolithic town, where an ancient spring created an oasis. On the bedrock are the clay-paved floors of Natufian huts whose burned posts yielded a carbon 14 date of 7800 B.C. ± 210 years.

In later levels, the huts had been superseded by semisubterranean houses with stone foundations and adobe brick walls surmounted by domed wattle-and-daub roofs. Walls and floors were mud-plastered for cleanliness and coolness. The later town covered 10 acres, with an estimated population of two to three thousand, and was surrounded by a stone wall 6 feet thick and 12 feet high, with a 30-foot tower at one point (and possibly at others not yet excavated). The oasis, an attraction for marauders, was heavily defended. The village, or a section of it, was burned out, and its charcoal has been given a carbon 14 date of 6850 B.C. ± 210 years.

Although actual grain from Jericho was not reported as present before about 6000 B.C., serrated sickle blades and a specialized wedge-shaped metate attest to its use as food. Beautifully modeled reproductions were made of heads of the deceased and were buried in clusters. Yet in spite of their skill in ceramic sculpture, the Jerichoans made no pottery.

Jarmo

Jarmo, a small village-farming community of some 200 inhabitants located in northeastern

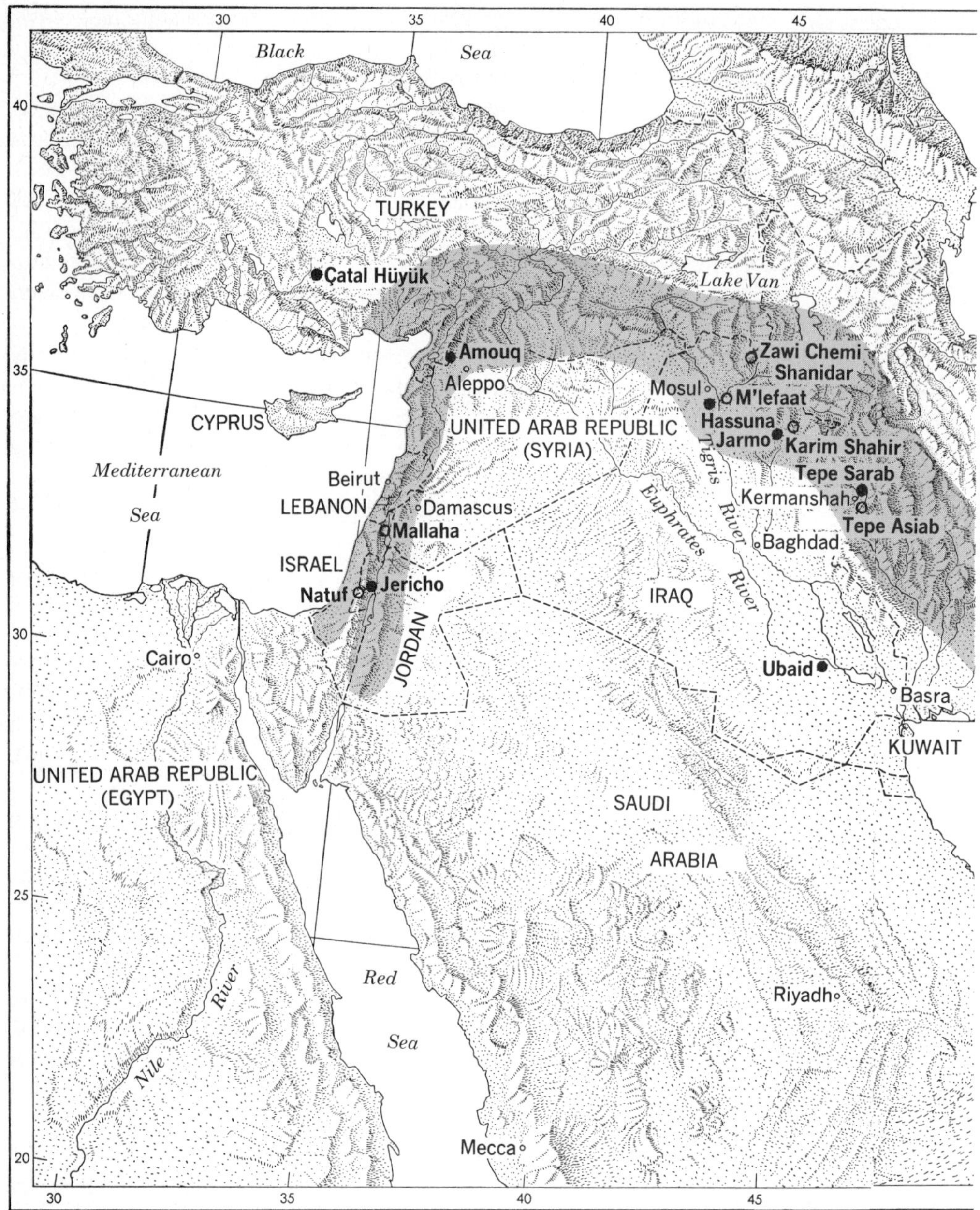

FIGURE 11.7
Early agriculture communities of the Near East. The major known sites in Anatolia and the Fertile Crescent. (Adapted from R. J. Braidwood, "The Agricultural Revolution," *Scientific American*.)

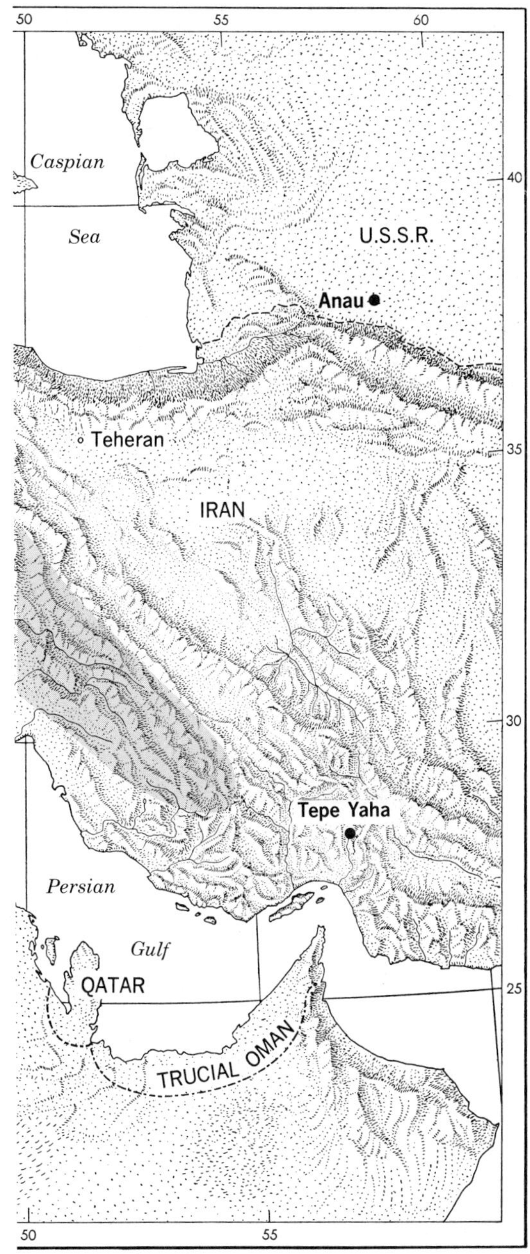

Iraq, is dated at 6750 B.C. ± 700 years. Braidwood, its excavator, enlisted the able collaboration of expert geologists and biologists in his study of the total cultural and ecological setting of Jarmo at the time when domesticated wheat and barley had just been established in this area. Jarmo is one of dozens of Early Neolithic village sites showing the pattern of incipient agriculture in the countryside of Iraq (see Figure 11.7).

Braidwood and Howe give a summary of Jarmo's revelations:

1. *It does yield positive traces of a village-farming community way of life; several-roomed rectangular houses within villages of some degree of permanence; the remains of at least domesticated wheat, barley, probably the dog and the goat, and possibly even the sheep, with the pig appearing in the upper levels; the conventional artifactual traits of the "neolithic," with pottery appearing before the phase is completed. . . . [A]rtifacts are querns and rubbing stones, mortars and pestles, flint sickle blades with sheen, occasional subfloor storage pits, a peculiar form of oven, possibly for the parching of grain, a few large celts (hoes?), and an occasional large pierced stone ball (digging stick weight?). Overwhelmingly, however, it is the demonstrated presence of the plant and animal domesticates and the apparent year-round permanence of a village of perhaps twenty-five well-built houses that make Jarmo impressive. . . . It should remain clear, however, that a very significant portion of the Jarmo subsistence pattern still depended upon collected foods.*
2. *Jarmo does indicate firm traces of longer-range trade, especially evidenced by the great bulk of obsidian (closest natural flow near Lake Van in Anatolia) in its chipped-stone category.*[8]

Çatal Hüyük

Ever since excavations were begun at Çatal Hüyük in southern Turkey in 1961, under the direction of James Mellaart, the picture of Neolithic culture has been undergoing rapid change. The first four years of work were sufficient to establish that barley, wheat, lentils, and peas

[8]R. J. Braidwood and B. Howe, "Southwestern Area beyond the Lands of the Mediterranean Littoral," in Braidwood and Willey (eds.), op. cit., p. 138. (By permission from the Wenner-Gren Foundation for Anthropological Research, New York.)

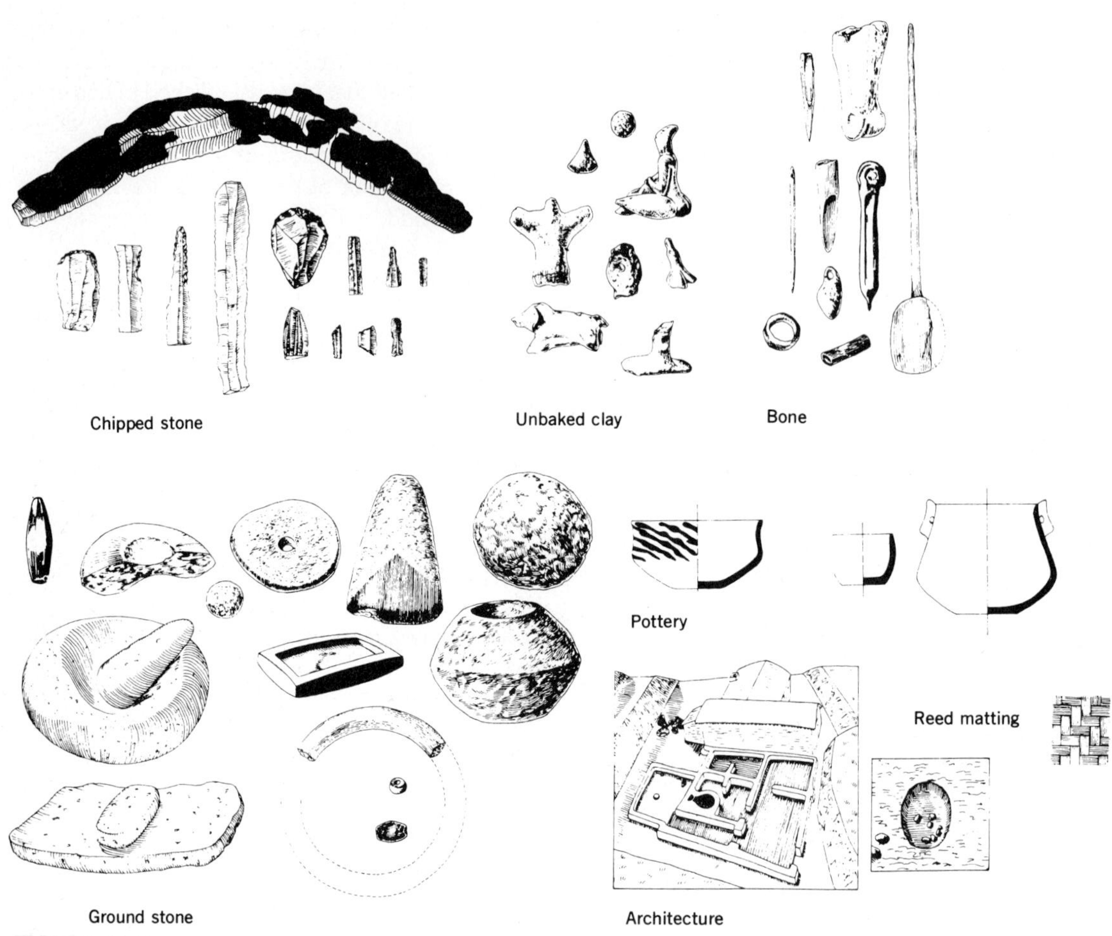

FIGURE 11.8
Neolithic artifacts from Jarmo, Iraq. (From Stein and Rowe, 1974. Originally from Braidwood, *Prehistoric Men*, 1967.)

were thoroughly domesticated and were producing surplus yields in Anatolia by about 6400 B.C. Sheep were domesticated and sheared for wool, which was woven into fine cloth. Cattle were domesticated by about 5800 B.C. An amazingly rich inventory of specialized handicrafts included beautifully worked wooden bowls and boxes; baskets; obsidian and flint daggers, spearheads, lance heads, arrowheads, knives, scrapers, awls, and sickle blades; jewelry of bone, shell, and copper; obsidian mirrors; and bone awls, punches, knives, ladles, spoons, clay bowls, spatulas, bodkins, belt hooks, toggles, and pins. This was a creative and well-off people.

The town was a solid community of adjoining rooms like those of the Indian Pueblos of the southwestern United States. Like the Pueblos, the rooms had to be entered through an entrance in the roof, which also served as a smoke vent for the hearth and oven on the floor beneath. The doorless and windowless walls of mud brick made a defensive citadel of the community house.

Numerous shrines are scattered throughout

the complex, with full-sized clay cattle heads protruding from the walls, some with statuettes of a fertile mother goddess (Figure 11.9), as well as of a bearded consort god seated on a bull. Layer after layer of religious murals, painted on the walls and then plastered over to make way for the next painting, attest to a vital and highly developed cult and religious-belief system, much concerned with the mystery of life and death. Life-associated scenes, done in symbolic red paint, are on the west walls of the shrine rooms. Death scenes created in black paint are on the east side (Figure 11.10).

Mellaart expressed puzzlement after the conclusion of the 1963 dig that no workshops had been exposed among the 200 rooms excavated.[9] It could well be that the town was a ceremonial and administrative center for farmsteads and cottage industries dispersed about the countryside—a regional community.

Mellaart's view that the city's wealth depended on its control of a well-organized trade carries conviction. The heart of the trade appears to have been the obsidian that came from the volcanoes some fifty miles away—obsidian that found its way to Jericho and Jarmo and to Cyprus in the Mediterranean. It would seem that the people of the town were too specialized in trade, politics, and religion to have spent much time in farming. They hunted for sport and for game food; bones of wild animals are profuse in the refuse dumps, and wall paintings depict hunts containing hundreds of human and animal figures.

The town at Çatal was burned out and rebuilt a number of times between its Early Neolithic founding circa 6500 B.C. and its final abandonment in the Hittite period circa 1900 B.C.

One cannot avoid being impressed, on the basis of what is known from the excavations at Çatal Hüyük, Jericho, and Jarmo, at how rapidly the transition from Paleolithic hunting bands to regionally organized communities occurred. Comparisons of the three sites indicate the rapid establishment of village and town settlements based upon an incipient agricultural foundation, with specialization centers sustained by trade and some serving as regional markets. Such comparisons also indicate that the domestication of plants probably occurred first in Anatolia rather than on the hilly flanks of the Fertile Crescent (see Figure 11.7), as had been previously thought.

FIGURE 11.9
A mother goddess from Çatal Hüyük giving birth while seated on a "divine" throne of two felines. (From Mellaart, *Earliest Civilizations of the Near East*, with permission of Thames and Hudson, London.)

[9]J. Mellaart, "A Neolithic City in Turkey" (*Scientific American*, vol. 210, no. 4, 1964), p. 99.

FIGURE 11.10
A mortuary ceremony at Çatal Hüyük performed by priestesses of the vulture cult. The large bull-heads, wall paintings, room shape, and human remains are just as excavated. The vulture priestesses are artistic reconstructions. (From Mellaart, *Earliest Civilizations of the Near East*, with permission of Thames and Hudson, London.)

The Domestication of Wheat and Barley

It is now well accepted that wild einkorn *(Triticum boeoticum)* is the sole ancestor of domestic einkorn wheat *(Triticum monococcum)*. The wild form is found over a broad region extending from Greece to Afghanistan. Another domestic plant, emmer wheat *(Triticum dicoccum)*, is derived from wild emmer wheat *(Triticum dicoccoides)*, and the distribution of the wild variant is thought to be the same as for wild einkorn. The first domestic wheat of both varieties is reported from the eastern part of this area at Ali Kosh (7000 B.C.) and Jarmo (6750 B.C.). The significance of the wide distribution of the wild wheats in large fields was emphasized when a botanist, J. Harlan, demonstrated that a family could collect enough wheat in three weeks to fill the family's needs for a full year.

The wild form of two-row barley (*Hordeum spontaneum*) is present in quantity at Jarmo. Six-row barley, a less primitive form, occurs further south and also at Çatal Hüyük. Barley is usually found associated with wheat throughout the Old World Neolithic. Wheat, however, is the foundation crop and "staff of life" for all the Near East and European village–farming communities. Carbonized field peas, lentils, and vetchling at Çatal and Jarmo reveal that these early horticulturalists also had the ingredients for basic vegetable soup, and the remains of their pottery show that they had the vessels in which to cook it.

The Domestication of Animals

A domestic animal is one which breeds in captivity and is kept for economic purposes. Present evidence suggests that the domestication of animals may have occurred in the Near East as early as 12,000 years ago. The first direct evidence (sheep) is from Zawi Chemi Shanidar in Iraq, dated 11,000 years ago. Further east from Zawi Chemi Shanidar is the first indication of the domesticated goat at Ganj Dareh (7500 B.C.) and Ali Kosh (7000 B.C.). Cattle appear at Çatal Hüyük at about 6400 B.C., but the pig was evidently not domesticated until the end of the seventh millenium. Certainly by that time the record shows that animal husbandry had become diversified and spread throughout the Near East.[10] There is also evidence that cattle and pigs may have been domesticated first in Europe, which appears to have been an important center of domestication comparable to the Near East.[11]

Dogs had already been domesticated elsewhere during the Mesolithic, but there is no certain evidence that they were at Jarmo, although pottery models of doglike figures with upturned tails occur. Changes in the shape of the horns of goats at Jarmo in more recent levels show that these animals were domestically bred, and the fact that goat skeletons make up 80 percent of all those found at Jarmo tells us that these people were no longer dependent upon hunting. Immature male goats were evidently slaughtered for eating, while only a few were kept to mature as breeding studs. Females were allowed to mature for breeding and possibly for milking.

[10]D. Perkins, Jr., and P. Daly, "The Beginning of Food Production in the Near East," in R. Stigler (ed.), *The Old World: Early Man to the Development of Agriculture*, pp. 71–97.

[11]R. Protsch and R. Berger, "Earliest Radiocarbon Dates for Domesticated Animals" (*Science*, vol. 179, no. 4070, Jan. 19, 1973), pp. 235–239.

Early Neolithic Manifestations in East and Southeast Asia

The dim outlines of the Neolithic in the Far East become evident only as new archaeological findings are reported. The discovery of pottery with carbon 14 dating of 8000 B.C. from the Jomon culture of Japan indicates an early start on some of the material aspects of post-Pleistocene development in that part of the world. But even more important is the discovery in Thailand in 1967 and 1968 of nuts, oil seeds, spices, water chestnuts, cucumbers, beans, and peas in strata dating (C^{14}) from 10,000 to 6000 B.C. This may indicate that Asians had made the transition from hunting to gardening before the Near Easterners.[12]

Kwan-chih Chang provides the following summary of emergent gardening in southeast Asia:

1. *Most of [the] earliest cultivators of tropical and subtropical southeast Asia inhabited estuarial plains and low terraces and engaged for subsistence mainly in fishing. . . . These fishermen led a settled, stable life and were familiar with . . . the nature and uses of many plants. Utilization of select plants gradually gave way to their control and cultivation as a perhaps minor but essential means of subsistence.*
2. *Wild and initially-domesticated plants in the fishing-hunting cultures of southeast Asia were probably first used mainly for containers (e.g. bamboo trunks and bottle gourds) or for cordage for use in fishing (nets, fishlines, and canoe-caulking material); or were herbs with various uses, or poisons. . . .*
3. *Under these circumstances the first wild but utilized plants that became the cultigens in southeast Asia probably included bamboos, the bottle gourd, fruit*

[12]See K.-c. Chang, op. cit., pp. 175–182, and W. G. Solheim, II, "Reworking Southeast Asian Prehistory" (*Paideuma*, vol. 15, 1969), pp. 125–139.

FIGURE 11.11
Reconstruction of a Neolithic house in the village site of Pan P'o, China. (Treistman, 1972.)

trees, some aquatic plants, and such roots and tubers as the taro and the yam. . . .

4. *The initially-cultivated crops probably played a minor role in the total subsistence system of the inhabitants, supplementing a diet derived mainly from fish, wild animals, and shell-fish. Food cultivation was at first probably a small-scale undertaking. . . . Only small peripheral forest clearings were necessary, and no tool more elaborate than a digging stick was used.*[13]

Well over 1000 Neolithic sites have been excavated in the northern region of China. Rice was domesticated in southern China and the Indus Valley by 5000 B.C. Farming villages in the Honan Province date back to around 2000 B.C., and their beautiful pottery designs of vegetation, flowers, and leaves seem to reflect a dependence on agricultural life. Digging implements and sickles have been recovered. Pigs, goats, cattle, and various millets were domesticated. These Chinese villagers were superb artists as well as artisans. They left behind rings of polished stone and mother-of-pearl, pendants of turquoise and shell, bone hairpins and combs, and pottery-bead necklaces.[14]

[13] K.-c. Chang, op. cit., p. 180.

[14] J. M. Treistman, *The Prehistory of China: An Archeological Exploration* (1972), pp. 51–71.

Parallel Developments in the New World

While the hill people of the Near East were taming wheat and barley, and subsequently chick-peas, beans, lentils, rye, flax, and various vegetables, the American Indians of the highlands of southern Mexico were engaged in the same process at almost the same time.

The question was where to look for the antecedents of the New World domesticate, since prior to 1950 no wild corn had been discovered. The picture suddenly changed, however, when the pollen of wild corn was unexpectedly discovered in borings of 80,000-year-old soil taken from the prehistoric lake bottoms where Mexico City now stands. This demonstrated that corn was present before humans arrived.

The oldest known corn at the time had been uncovered in Bat Cave, New Mexico, in 1948, with a carbon 14 date of from 2000 to 3000 B.C. The Bat Cave corn was primitive when compared with the corn being grown when the Spaniards first arrived, but it was far from being wild corn and was not the earliest domesticated corn.

Ten years later, R. S. MacNeish began a dedicated and systematic search for the origins of domesticated corn in the Guatemalan and

Honduran highlands and the hill country of Chiapas in southeastern Mexico. In 1960, the thirty-ninth cave tested, in Puebla, Mexico, produced minuscule corncobs, bearing kernels that were best studied under a magnifying glass. Their carbon 14 date goes back to 5000 B.C. This was not cultivated corn, but the Mesolithic foragers of Mexico were definitely harvesting the parent of modern corn 7000 years ago.

The culture sequence in the valley of Tehuacán in Puebla sketches the outline of incipient agriculture in the New World (Figure 11.12). The sequence is as follows.

From 6700 to 5000 B.C., foragers had domesticated squashes and avocados. They also collected wild beans, chili, and amaranth, but they had no corn.

Between 5000 and 3500 B.C., corn was domesticated, as were amaranth, jack bean, common bean, chili, black and white zapotes, maschata squash, and the waterbottle gourd. These foods appear to have constituted only about one-tenth of the population's total diet. For the rest, they hunted and trapped small game.

By 3400 B.C., settlements of pit houses (see page 239) had replaced caves and rock shelters. The farming village was established in America, and one-third of the food of the inhabitants was made up of garden produce.

Eleven hundred years later (2300 B.C.), a number of varieties of hybridized corn and pumpkins had been bred, and the first pottery was made. Irrigation agriculture began later, at about 700 B.C. By A.D. 700, true cities, under dynastic Mixtec rulers, were flourishing in the valley of Tehuacán, and 85 percent of all food was agricultural in origin.

This is the sequence for only one valley in Mexico.[15] Nonetheless, the essential story is there. Squashes, beans, and maize were domes-

[15]R. S. MacNeish, "The Origins of New World Civilization" (*Scientific American*, vol. 211, no. 5, 1964), pp. 29–37.

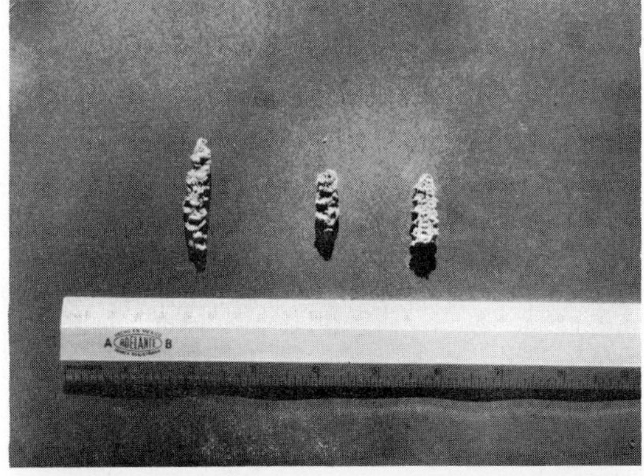

FIGURE 11.12
Stages in the evolution of corn in the valley of Tehuacán, Mexico. Wild corn (top), first discovered in 1960, dates from circa 5000 B.C. Successive improvement of breeds through domestication and crossbreeding is revealed in (middle) early hybrid corn, circa 3500 B.C., and (bottom) early modern corn, circa 1500 B.C. (Courtesy of R. S. MacNeish.)

ticated, in that order—and all between 7000 and 5000 B.C. They became the "triumvirate that forms the basis of much of American Indian agriculture."[16] They provided the nutritional source for the energy that went into building the civilizations of the Olmecs, Toltecs, Aztecs, and other groups.

In South America, the domesticated potato became the staple for Andean peoples, while in the Amazonian rain forests, techniques for growing and processing manioc were developed to meet special environmental conditions (see page 223), much as the Southeast Asians developed rice in place of wheat and barley as a special agricultural adaptation to the physical environment.

New World cultures did not use domesticated animals extensively until the Spanish introduced horses, sheep, and cattle. Andean peoples domesticated the llama and alpaca—whose wild ancestors were native American camels—and the guanaco and vicuña. The llama was bred and used mainly as a beast of burden and the alpaca for its wool. Guinea pigs were domesticated for food in the Andes. The earliest known American domesticated dog was unearthed at Jaguar Cave, Idaho, and is dated at approximately 8400 B.C.

The independent domestication of cotton in the semitropical parts of Asia and the Americas produced a new source of fiber for weaving. Cotton was substituted for the flax that was domesticated earlier in the Near East as a source of thread in addition to the fleece of goats and sheep.

THE ERA OF DEVELOPED AGRICULTURE

By the end of the Neolithic, people depended mainly on gardening and domesticated animals for food and sustenance. Communal life focused in the village or town, which may have been moved periodically as fields became exhausted. Except for pastoralists and marginal hunters, the nomadic way of life was gone.

Domesticated Plants and Animals

Wheat and barley, plus the goat, sheep, and dog, as already indicated, had been domesticated by the end of the period of incipient agriculture. During the Era of Developed Agriculture, the remaining basic cereals (rye, flax, and millet) were added to the list of domesticated plants of Asia Minor, western Asia, Africa, and Europe. Flannery suggests that the combinations of the twenty or so foods available to these early farmers probably left them better nourished than today's Iranian villager, for example.[17]

In Southeast Asia, the cultivation of rice was developed as the staple food source for Neolithic societies located in the rain forests, where wheat and barley will not grow. Yams and taro were also added.

Although wild horses were of much interest to Upper Paleolithic artists, no horses were domesticated in Mesolithic times. Taming a wild horse is no gentle operation and the first known domestication of the horse occurred in the Upper Yenisei basin, Siberia, circa 3500 B.C.

Other domesticates of the Neolithic Old World are the water buffalo and yak, elephant, camel, ass and mule, cat, ferret, mongoose, rabbit, and dormouse.

Artifacts

In contrast to Paleolithic hand axes, Neolithic adzes and axes were generally hafted. Wooden drills and wet sand were used to drill holes through stone axheads into which the handle could be fitted (Figure 11.5). War clubs and maces became differentiated from industrial axes.

[16] G. F. Carter, "Origins of American Indian Agriculture" (*American Anthropologist*, vol. 48, 1946), p. 1. There is evidence, however, that the Maya relied heavily on the nut of the ramon tree as a basic food source.

[17] K. V. Flannery, "Origins and Ecological Effects of Early Domestication in Iran and the Near East," in P. J. Ucko and G. W. Dimbleby (eds.), *The Domestication and Exploitation of Plants and Animals*, pp. 73–100.

A prevalence of flint arrowheads throughout all Neolithic deposits, except for those of the Lower Neolithic in the Balkans and parts of the Near East, attests to the wide use of the bow and arrow for both hunting and war. In the area where the bow was little used, baked-clay sling pellets show that the weapon with which David felled Goliath was not just a Hebraic device, by any means. Daggers of flint and bone, as well as the familiar scrapers and blade sickles, continue well into the Bronze Age.

Perhaps most significant of all is the development of pottery, which fits in with the making of gruel, so important to the diet of Neolithic people. Early Neolithic pottery is usually plain and undecorated, and the forms are simple and clean-lined. Although plain ware continued to be used for kitchen purposes, painted and decorated pots were usually developed quite rapidly. The possibilities for distinctive variations led to numerous local types.

The Urban Revolution

More important than pottery or artifacts were the new gardening techniques developed in the Neolithic in the great river valleys of Mesopotamia (the Euphrates and Tigris), Egypt (the Nile), and western Pakistan (the Indus). In the fertile floodwater lowlands, it was possible to carry on intensive gardening to the extent that continuous settlements could develop along the Nile and full cities could emerge in Mesopotamia and Pakistan. The development of towns into cities changed the whole scheme of life for more and more of humanity. Civilization means "city making." Where civilization took over, food collectors and cultivators moved into towns or remained on the land as satellite peasant villagers and supplied food for the townspeople. Of the first towns and cities, the essential characteristics described by Henri Frankfort are worth noting:

To understand the importance of the city as a factor in the shaping of society, one must not think of it as a mere conglomeration of people. . . . The city sets its citizens apart from the other inhabitants of the land. It determines their relations with the outside world. It produces an intensified self-consciousness in its burghers, to whom the collective achievements are a source of pride.[18]

The Urban Culture of Mesopotamia: Al Ubaid and the Sumerian Civilization The early events in the Tigris-Euphrates Valley serve as a good model of the process of urbanization.

The Ubaid Period The alluvial delta of southern Iraq offered neither timber nor stone, but it was rich in soil and water. Al Ubaid, an early village located on a low rise of land near the Euphrates, was settled around 4000 B.C. by highlanders who brought a subsistence economy of developed agriculture into the river bottoms. They had microlithic sickles and a new type of sickle made of hard fired clay. They made simple wattle-and-daub-walled huts with palm-stalk frames. They also made Quonset-type huts of reed bundles set vertically and arched to meet along the center top, a type of construction that survives in the Euphrates delta to this day. But elsewhere more impressive Ubaid towns were constructed of adobe bricks, such as those used at Çatal Hüyük, thirteen hundred years earlier.

Forecasting a most important feature of the early civilizations were the sizable temple structures of the Ubaid towns. Monumental public works of a religious nature were the most visually prominent feature (Figure 11.3).

The Sumerian Protoliterate Period As the name of this period indicates, it is marked by the appearance of the earliest form of writing. Clay tablets bear signs and pictograms incised with reeds (Figure 11.14). The predynastic texts have not yet been deciphered, but the contents of those of the early dynasties shed a flood of light on the role of the temple priests as organizers of work and society. The tablets list wages paid and goods received and often include lists

[18]H. Frankfort, *The Birth of Civilization in the Near East*, p. 48.

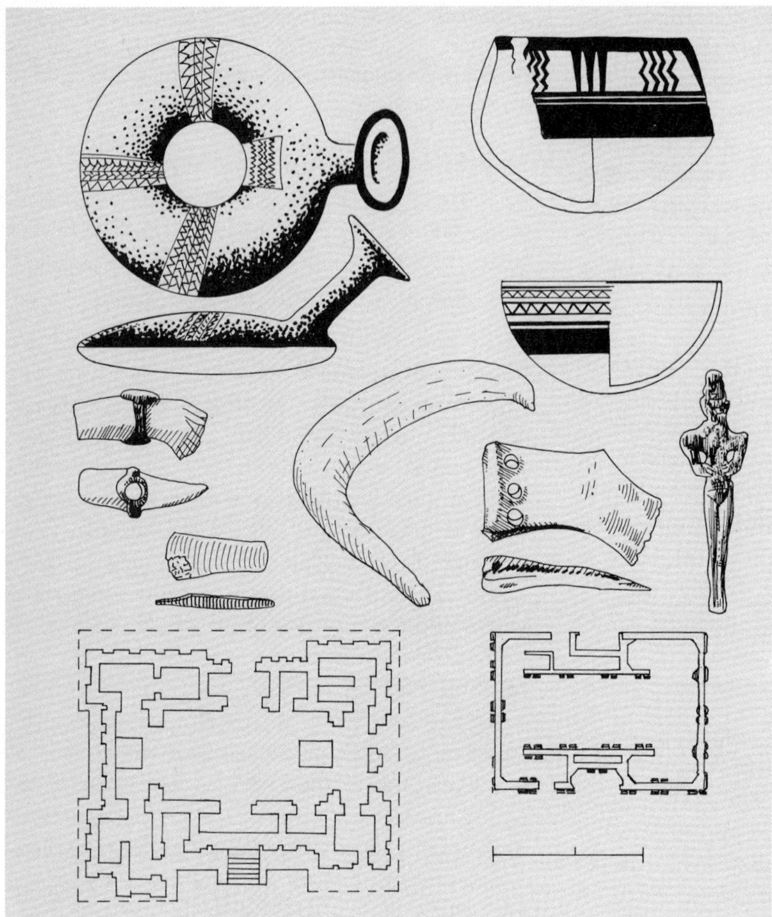

FIGURE 11.13
Selected items of Ubaid material culture. At the top are decorated pottery vessels. Center, a baked clay sickle. Bottom, the floor plans of large buildings. (Braidwood, 1967.)

of names. Religion was obviously of extreme importance, as attested by the very large temples constructed on artificial mounds (Figure 11.15).

Pottery had for some time been turned on a wheel and produced commercially in quantity for daily use. Copper and silver bowls and dishes were now wrought for ceremonial use or display. Statues were carved and used in association with the temples.

The Sumerian Early Dynastic Period: Full Civilization (3200 to 2800 B.C.) Technologically, the most significant development is the harnessing of the ass and oxen to solid-wheeled chariots and to plows and carts. Agricultural efficiency was reaching a peak, while trade and wars were spreading. Each citizen, whether artisan, fisher, or soldier, was, in the early phases of development, also a part-time farmer. As the culture expanded, some soldiers, governmental officers, priests, and traders became full-time specialists.

The city was the political unit in relations with the outside world. In the protoliterate phase, it had governed itself in matters of war and intercity relations through a democratic town council. Matters of boundary conflicts, safe conduct, and

FIGURE 11.14
Stages in the development of cuneiform writing. Visual symbols impressed in clay gave the first permanence to the spoken word. (Courtesy of the University Museum, Philadelphia.)

irrigation were its main concerns. Internal organization of town activities focused on the temples. Each city "belonged" to a god, and every citizen belonged to a temple district and served the temple god. Allotments of land, work assignments, and raw materials were designated by the head priest-administrator of the temple district. Each worker had to deliver a specified amount of produce; anything beyond this was the worker's own. Some goods went to maintain the priests, and much was redistributed among the producing populace. Thus, the division of labor and the economic exchange necessary to effective civilization were achieved—in this case without an internal market system. A fair part of the Sumerian cities' output was exported in exchange for precious stones, metals, and incense.

FIGURE 11.15
Monte Alban, early Mesoamerican ceremonial center, located near Oaxaca, Mexico. (George Holton/Photo Researchers.)

In Sumer, in the early dynasties, the system of exaction of labor was not overly exploitative. People were in effect taxed by not being allowed to keep all they produced. But through highly organized effort, they received or retained a good deal more than they could have produced alone or than their Mesolithic progenitors had been able to enjoy. The people were induced to accept an elaborate theology of catastrophism and beneficence. Floods and pestilence were common disasters. Anxieties born of human insecurity and intellectual concern with cause and effect had elaborated the supernatural element for the explanation and relief of tensions. Gods properly served could benefit rather than punish, the Sumerians believed, and they apparently served willingly.

Characteristics of Early Civilization

In this account, Sumer serves as a prototype of the process of the urbanization that followed the food revolution. It exemplifies the ten characteristics of early civilization specified by Childe[19]:

1. The great enlargement of an organized population means a much wider level of social integration than had occurred in any prehistoric society of gatherers and hunters.
2. Social means for the collection of the "surplus" production of farmers and artisans are devised to produce a central accumulation of goods for "managed" use.
3. Specialization of production among workers is instituted, along with systems of redistribution and exchange of goods.
4. Specialization and exchange are expanded beyond the city in the development of far-reaching trade.
5. Monumental public works in the form of temples, palaces, storehouses, and irrigation systems are constructed and maintained through the centrally organized use of available time not devoted to food production or basic manufactures.
6. Highly developed art forms give expression to symbolic identification and provide aesthetic enjoyment.
7. The art of writing is developed to facilitate the process of organization and management. It is later expanded to other uses, especially theological and protoscientific.
8. Arithmetic, geometry, and astronomy are developed as scientific techniques.
9. A well-structured political organization comes about in which membership based on residence replaces group membership based on kinship.
10. A privileged ruling class of religious, political, and military functionaries organizes and directs the whole system.

All this, as we have described it for the first thousand years of Sumer's evolution (Ubaid through the early dynasties), took place in what Julian Steward identifies as a regular phase of civilizational development in early times, and labels *the era of regional development and florescence.*[20]

SUMMARY

The end of the fourth glaciation brought a new type of adaptive response from *Homo sapiens sapiens*. They shifted from predominant reliance on hunting of big game to intensive exploitation of the vegetative and small-game and fish potentials of the local environment, developing thereby a Mesolithic era of intensive foraging. In the Mediterranean, the Natufian tradition exem-

[19]V. G. Childe, "The Urban Revolution" (*Town Planning Review*, vol. 21, no. 1, 1950), pp. 3–17.

[20]J. H. Steward, *Theory of Culture Change*, p. 195. The details of the specific regional development of other Mediterranean civilizations, plus those of the Indus Valley, China and Southeast Asia, Mexico, Middle America, and the Andes, become at this point too complex for the scope of this book. Hence, Sumer is allowed to stand as the prototype. However, see the list of selected readings at the end of this chapter for further leads.

plifies early experimentation with the domestication of grains. In Africa, it is the Khartoum, and in North Europe, where a forest environment prevailed, it is the Maglemosian, which are examples of the Mesolithic. In North America, a specialized form of the Mesolithic existed from 10,000 B.C. to A.D. 1850 in the Desert culture west of the Rocky Mountains. The mano and metate are the hallmarks of the era (except in the Maglemosian of the North European forests). Woven fibers were introduced for baskets and nets.

The Mesolithic era of intensive foraging evolved very quickly within a few thousand years into the Neolithic Era of Agriculture, which rested upon hoe cultivation of newly domesticated plants and the transformation of wild animals into household domestics.

Old World domestication led to the development of a number of starchy cereals, of which wheat and barley were first and basic. In the New World, the focus was on maize, squashes, and beans. The dog was domesticated in both hemispheres, but the Old World provided more domesticable animals, such as cattle, sheep, the goat, pig, cat, and horse; and hence, pastoralism emerged as an important secondary environmental adjustment there.

Over a span of several millennia, the small, settled farming village gave way to towns as political and religious centers, staffed by priests and chiefs along with their subordinates. Specialization in crafts contributed to the development of the towns as market centers. As efficiency of production increased, cities emerged in many parts of the Mediterranean, South Asia, and China. Complex social structures on a broad level of integration produced a new order of living. Writing was invented, and the replacement of a world of nonliterate, hunting and gathering people by the historic world of simple gardeners and urban handicrafters, organized and managed by a literate elite of priests and military leaders, was under way. Civilization was born and humankind was caught up in the first great cultural transformation since australopithecine times.

SELECTED READINGS

Braidwood, R. J., *Prehistoric Men* (1975). Comprehensive overview written in popular style by one of the pioneers in the field.

Braidwood, R. J., and G. R. Willey (eds.), *Courses toward Urban Life* (1963). Contains many excellent papers covering the manifestation of the eras of Intensive Foraging and Incipient Agriculture in all parts of the world.

Flannery, K. V., "The Ecology of Early Food Production in Mesopotamia" (*Science*, vol. 147, no. 3663, 1965), pp. 1247–1256. Collates data and new theory in a useful synthesis.

Hamblin, D. J., *The First Cities* (1973). A Time-Life book written by a professional journalist in a popular, yet authoritative, contribution. Nicely illustrated and very readable.

Jennings, J. D., *Prehistory of North America* (1974). Highly recommended for its treatment of the Late Paleolithic big-game hunters, the Archaic foragers, and the formative stage as manifest in Mexico and the United States.

Lamberg-Karlovsky, C. C. and J. A. Sabloff (eds.), *The Rise and Fall of Civilizations* (1974). The collection of readings is valuable and covers the subject excellently. Contains some classic articles.

Leonard, J. N., *The First Farmers* (1973). A Time-Life book, written for the general public, well illustrated.

Mellaart, J., *The Neolithic of the Near East* (1975). A comprehensive review by a person who has had firsthand experience. Somewhat technical, but worthwhile.

Stigler, R. (ed.), *The Old World: Early Man to the Development of Agriculture* (1974). Five chapters on the subject written by experts in each area. Easy to read, yet covers the field in an authoritative manner. Contains bibliographic essays at the end of each chapter.

PART FOUR

Cultural Ecology

12
Environment and Subsistence

CHAPTER OUTLINE

LEARNING GOALS

Define ecology and human ecology.

Discuss environmental determinism as an explanation of subsistence practices.

Discuss the evolution and distribution of subsistence techniques.

Identify hunting practices and techniques.

Describe intensive foraging as a life-style.

Review incipient agricultural techniques.

Trace the origin and development of plow culture.

Explain the difference between pastoralism and transhumance and discuss the main characteristics of each.

The subsistence resources available to a people depend upon three factors: natural environment, population, and culture. People who subsist by gathering roots, berries, seeds, and insects are for the most part directly dependent upon what the natural environment offers. People who have acquired the techniques of planting, cultivating, and harvesting crops, or of the husbandry of animals, and who have mastered methods of cooking or otherwise changing the substance of natural products to make them useful or more desirable as foods, are less directly dependent upon the physical environment. For many years, anthropologists have focused on the study of relationships among culture, modes of subsistence, and environment.

ECOLOGY

Ecology is the study of the reciprocal relations between organisms and their environments. What does a specific environment offer in mineral resources, water, air temperatures, surface features, and plant and animal life? How well- or ill-adapted is the organism to the environment in which it finds itself? In other words, what are its relations to the environment in ingesting air, water, and minerals (foodstuffs), and what is its effectiveness in converting them into life-maintaining energy (the metabolic process)? What are its spatial arrangements relative to the characteristics of the environment and to all other living things which impinge upon it, directly or indirectly? With whom does it cooperate for mutual aid (symbiosis)? With whom and with what must it contend for survival?

Organic evolution, we know, has produced many highly specific plant and animal adaptations to particular ecological niches. Even *Homo sapiens*, as we have seen in previous chapters, shows intraspecies adaptations to intense environmental selective pressures. These are manifest in body form, skin color, the presence or absence of sickle-cell genes, specific blood types, and varieties of diseases—to name only a few examples. Increasingly, however, as human beings progressed through time, they interposed culture as an intermediary adaptive mechanism in their linkage to the environment.

Human ecology is concerned with the ways in which people relate to their surroundings and the effects their activities have on the natural and social environments. The concepts of ecology and human ecology constitute a new paradigm in anthropology. Because it leads to an evaluation of functionalism and holism and because it has led to more cooperation with other disciplines, especially in the biological sciences, ecology promises to help explain human behavior better than ever before.[1]

Environmental Determinism

Culture can modify environment and environment imposes limits on cultures. For example, the natural environment does not absolutely determine the housing of a people, but it does define its possibilities. Igloos are not built on deserts; nor are thatched-palm pile dwellings found in the arctic. The same is true of basic subsistence techniques. The natural environment limits but does not wholly determine the nature of the foodstuffs a human population can enjoy. The complexity and efficiency of the technology of each culture are of tremendous significance. In a stable adjustment to the limits of marginal desert living, the prehistoric food foragers of the Desert culture in the Great Basin of North America eked out a meager but surviving existence for 11,000 years. In that limiting environment, technology and social organization, as well as all other aspects of their culture, remained simple and underdeveloped. Yet prehistoric Pueblo Indians, equipped with domesti-

[1]For reviews of ecology in biology and anthropology, see P. J. Richerson, "Ecology and Human Ecology: A Comparison of Theories in the Biological and Social Sciences" (*American Ethnologist*, vol. 4, no. 1, 1977), pp. 1–26. Also see other articles in the same special issue on human ecology.

cated plants and sophisticated gardening techniques, were able to establish themselves in some parts of the Great Basin.[2] Given a sufficiently developed technology, deserts can be made to bloom, hothouses can be maintained in the arctic, and ice cream can be frozen on a Pacific isle.

The Navajo and Pueblo Indians

The cultural ecology of the Navajo and Pueblo Indians aptly illustrates the significance of total cultural focus in a people's use of their environment. These tribes share the same part of the southwestern desert in New Mexico and Arizona. They have been neighbors ever since the Navajos arrived from the north some 500 years ago. Both tribes practice gardening and pastoralism, and yet their utilization of the environment and their social systems are very different. The Pueblo Indians of today live in compact masonry villages housing 100 to 1500 people (see pages 239–242). They garden with intensive proficiency and exhibit more interest in religious and ceremonial control of weather and crop fertility than they do in the mechanics of gardening. Dominance of the group over the individual is tight and relentless. The political system is that of a totalitarian theocracy.

The Navajos, on the other hand, live in widely dispersed hogans (semisubterranean earth lodges; see pages 239–240), and their main interest is in sheep. They also garden, but in a minor way. They do virtually nothing about weather control or crop fertility. Their interests in the supernatural rest in the maintenance of personal health. Until recent times, they had no centralized government, or even chiefs. Their social system is loose and highly atomistic. Navajos and Pueblos, in personality, life styles, and social organization, are as unlike as night and day, despite a similar physical environment.

[2]A. L. Kroeber, in *Cultural and Natural Areas of Native North America*, provides an excellent and detailed analysis of the geographic areas of North America and the varieties of aboriginal cultures found in each of them.

SUBSISTENCE TECHNIQUES: THE EVOLUTIONARY PERSPECTIVE

In Part 2, as we followed the evolutionary development of human beings and culture, we saw how the australopithecines and early humans lived by hunting and gathering for several million years throughout the Ice Age. Then, shortly after the end of the Pleistocene, when *Homo sapiens sapiens* was fully established, people quickly shifted to intensive foraging as a new way of life in the Mesolithic Era. Out of the new preoccupation with domesticated plants and animals, the Neolithic Era of Incipient Agriculture quickly followed. The urban revolution was generated and social organization was transformed from simple to complex. In the following Bronze and Iron Ages, draft animals were linked to the newly developed plow, and intensive agriculture supplanted incipient agriculture.

In areas not readily adaptable to gardening, some peoples intensified their reliance upon domesticated animals as a source of food energy, thus inventing pastoralism (animal husbandry) as a way of life. As a subsistence base, pastoralism is neither earlier nor later than incipient agriculture in evolutionary emergence.

Each successive food-producing system has, in the main, increased the food energy available per capita in inverse ratio to the amount of work and energy expended in producing it. This means that increasing surpluses of energy are made available for other social uses. Whether these surpluses will be utilized, and how, will depend upon the values and goals which come to characterize a people's culture. But, in general, more complex subsistence technologies result in increased levels of social complexity and heterogeneous integration, and in the diversity of specialized functions, functionaries, and organization. The subsistence techniques on which the simpler societies rely were first developed in prehistoric times. Their relative lack of complexity and internal differentiation are related to the size of the population supportable by existing subsistence resources.

The levels of subsistence techniques arranged in the order of increasing complexity of cultural integration can be listed as follows:

1. Hunting and gathering
2. Intensive foraging
3. Incipient agriculture (gardening/hoe culture) and pastoralism
4. Intensive agriculture (plow culture)

DISTRIBUTION OF SUBSISTENCE TECHNOLOGIES

In 10,000 B.C. all human populations were hunters and/or gatherers.

By 7000 B.C. intensive foraging prevailed in North Africa, Asia Minor, and South Asia, in the Old World, and in the Desert and Archaic cultures of the New World.

By 3000 B.C. civilizations based upon incipient agriculture were well under way in the Mediterranean and the South and East Asiatic belts of the Old World, and in Nuclear America (the area of high cultures which extended from northern Mexico to the southern Andes).

In A.D. 1500, when Columbus had opened the world to European exploration, Murdock estimates, perhaps only 15 percent of the earth's surface was still occupied by hunters and gatherers.[3] There were no hunting and gathering *or* foraging peoples left in Europe or the Mediterranean areas. On the edges of Greenland, Eskimos clung to a precarious hunting existence. The Lapps had become intensive reindeer pastoralists. Across the north of Siberia, the Yukaghir, Samoyed, and Tungus continued as hunters who also herded reindeer.

Africa was given over wholly to pastoralists and food-growing peoples, except for the Bushmen (Figure 12.1), Congo Pygmies, and a few other scattered groups. All Indonesians, except for a few small groups, were gardeners or agriculturalists.

Agriculture in the Old World attained a continuous distribution from Europe, around the Mediterranean and well into Africa, and across India and South Asia.

In North America, although hunting and gathering predominated, all the prairie and eastern woodland groups south of the Great Lakes and the St. Lawrence River raised some maize, beans, and squashes. The Indians of the Southwest were intensive gardeners and growers of maize.

Even in the Great Plains, settled villagers gardened in the river bottoms, and there were few hunting groups on the far reaches of the Plains. Hunting and foraging were characteristic of California, the Great Basin desert, the woodlands of Canada, and the arctic wastes inhabited by the Eskimos. Texas and northern Mexico were still mostly exploited by food foragers, but most of Central and South America was given over to horticulture.

Throughout the Pacific the islanders were gardeners and fishers, except for natives in Australia and Tasmania and small enclaves of Pygmies. Only in Australia did hunting and gathering survive as the dominant form of food getting. However idyllic the "natural existence" of the life of the hunter and gatherer may seem to the city-bound romantic, most human beings have readily abandoned it for more reliable food sources whenever the cultural and environmental opportunity has been offered.

By the nineteenth century, Neolithic and Iron Age gardening and agricultural techniques had so diffused around the world that, of 863 selected cultures, only 26 percent were "heavily de-

[3]G. P. Murdock, "The Current Status of the World's Hunting and Gathering Peoples," in R. B. Lee and I. DeVore (eds.), *Man the Hunter*, p. 13.

FIGURE 12.1
San (African Bushman) hunters cooperate to bring down a large gembok with poison arrows, eventually to kill it with a spear or knife. (Shostak/Anthro-photo.)

pendent" on hunting, fishing, and gathering as a combined subsistence base.[4] In contrast, nearly 72 percent were gardeners or agriculturalists who used these modes of production for 25 percent or more of their subsistence. Even more important, two-thirds of all the cultures of the world had become dependent on horticulture or agriculture for more than half their subsistence requirements. We emphasize this because Americans are apt to be misled by their image of American Indians as representative of non-European peoples in the world at large. Nine out of ten North American cultures were still those of hunters and gatherers, while this was true of seven out of ten South American cultures.

Animal husbandry definitely shows up as a secondary, rather than a primary, food source. A mere 2 percent of the 863 cultures were pastoral to the degree that they relied on herds of domesticated animals for three-fourths or more of their food. All but one of these cultures were concentrated in the Mediterranean and Asiatic areas. On the other hand, virtually every African culture included the care and use of some domesticated animals for food. In Oceania, the care of domestic pigs and water buffalo (in Indonesia) was ancillary to fishing or gardening in more than three-fourths of the subsistence economies. In the New World, in post-Spanish times, horses came to be herded by a quarter of the North American tribes but by very few in the continent to the south.

None of the categories of subsistence tech-

[4]E. Bourguignon and L. Greenbaum, *Diversity and Homogeneity*, tables 1 to 9, pp. 23–31.

niques, it must be emphasized, is absolutely exclusive. All food economies are mixed, to a greater or lesser degree. Gardeners still hunt and fish. Pastoralists raid or exchange meat for flour. Even an atomic, industrialized society such as ours includes agriculture, pastoralism, fishing, and hunting within its activities.

HUNTING

Human beings are omnivorous. This more than any other single trait distinguishes them from their predominantly vegetarian hominoid relatives. Meat eating may have appeared first among the australopithecines. Yet hunters always rely to some extent upon berries, nuts, and roots to round out their diet. The Cheyenne Indians, for example, were great meat eaters, like other nomadic Plains Indian tribes. Nonetheless, some sixteen varieties of wild fruit, a dozen or more kinds of vegetable stalks and buds, plus eight to ten varieties of roots, were regularly included in their diet.

Hunting Tools

In almost all hunting situations, human beings rely upon some device to assist in bringing down their quarry. Thus they use clubs, spears, darts, arrows, deadfalls, pitfalls, snares, nets, weirs, hooks, axes, knives, and poisons. They enlist the aid of dogs, or mount horses, or camels. They may fashion boats to carry them. Whatever device they use, their hunting techniques are those of assult (shooting, spearing, clubbing, axing, stabbing), trapping and snaring, the pitfall, and poisoning (Figure 12.1).

Paleolithic people had clubs, spears, and hand axes. While there is no direct evidence that they utilized traps and snares or pitfalls, it is likely that they had invented simple devices of this order. We know that fire drives were used in Middle Pleistocene times, half a million years ago (pages 141–142).

Because it is so efficient a weapon, the bow, invented in late Paleolithic or early Mesolithic times, had attained almost worldwide distribution by the seventeenth century. The skill of most hunters in tracking and stalking game to bring it within bowshot is well known. Bushmen artists have depicted disguised archers stalking the unwary ostrich. Western Indians wore antelope skins to approach that fleet and shy beast. To down eagles on the wing, Cheyennes hid camouflaged in a pit from which they slowly rotated a stick with a bit of cloth on the end. This aroused the curiosity of the king of birds, who warily soared lower and lower until the patient hunter could spring from the blind for a shot. They also lured the eagle to land on a pit blind, where it could be seized by the legs.

In the jungles of Malaysia and South America and in the woodlands of the southeastern United States, the blowgun with darts, sometimes poison-tipped, is often preferred for the hunting of small game and birds. The blowgun is a hollowed-out tube of bamboo or wood (sometimes 8 or 10 feet long), used exactly like a beanshooter. The heavy jungle growth inhibits any long-distance shooting, and in such a setting darts are often more effective than arrows.

Communal Hunts

Most subsistence hunting involves sustained, organized group effort by bands of men, although it may engage the participation of all able-bodied women and children as well. Among Plains Indians individual hunting of bison and antelope was permitted during the fall and winter seasons, when game was hard to find and people were widely scattered in small camps. In the late spring and summer, however, the bands came together for the great tribal ceremonies, such as the sun dance. Then they moved en masse to seek out the huge herds of buffalo. Scouts went ahead, and the whole line of march was policed by the members of a military society. When a herd was discovered, all the hunters approached in a line from down wind, with the soldiers keeping them in order. At last, upon signal from the hunt chief they would ride out to surround the herd in a circle. If the circle was successfully closed, the bison could be run down and shot from the right side by a bowman shooting to the left from across the neck of his rushing steed.

The Ritual of the Hunt

The hunting of large animals is not usually a matter of technique pure and simple. Ritual and magic are evoked to reinforce the hunter, because of anxiety for personal safety and fear of failure. Much of the cave art left by the Cro-Magnons is eloquent, if mute, evidence of this (pages 173–176).

The Cheyenne Antelope Hunt Although the secular, soldier-policed hunt sufficed for the buffalo surround on the plains, the skittish antelope required different methods. For killing it a magic technique was used.[5] A shaman who had received power from antelopes in vision experiences directed the hunt. Guns and bows and arrows were forbidden; only clubs could be used, indicating great antiquity for this type of hunt. After an all-night ceremony to activate his power, the shaman led the people to the open prairie. Two highly esteemed virgins were given sacred wands. They then set outward in the direction of the antelope along each arm of a V path. The shaman used his power to draw the antelope into the V. After a while, two young men on fast horses rode forth on the paths of the virgins. As they overtook the girls, they received the antelope wands, like relay runners. Behind the leaders a line of hunters on their fastest horses followed along the routes to post themselves at intervals on the sides of the V.

As soon as the horsemen were on their way, the women and children formed a circle at the point of the V, with the shaman in the center. After several miles, the lead riders reached the herd; they crisscrossed behind it and rode back outside the lines of hunters. Other riders drove the antelope down the V and into the waiting circle of women and children. While the shaman directed the movements of the animals caught within the circle, the women and children waved blankets and branches to keep them from breaking through. As panic and exhaustion immobilized the befuddled creatures, the hunters moved in with clubs to kill them. One such hunt, observed by the frontier trader George Bent in 1858, produced a kill of over 600 antelope.[6]

The Alaskan Eskimo Whale Cult Whaling among the Eskimos and certain Northwest Coast Indians is assuredly one of the bravest and most technically skillful hunting-by-assault accomplishments of any people. However, in order to reinforce their hunting skills, to give social recognition to the outstanding hunter, and in consequence of their belief in the spirit nature of whales, the Alaskans made of whale hunting not only a hunt activity but also a cult of magical and religious observances.

Lantis's analysis of the Alaskan Whale Cult[7] has revealed it as a complex of technological, economic, sociopolitical, magico-religious elaborations. Whale hunting, in addition to the actual chase, which involves skilled use of boats, paddles, harpoons, lines, and floats to locate, trail, attack, destroy, and land the great sea monster (Figure 12.2), is worked into a web of behavior and beliefs that includes the following chief elements:

1. The headman of a whaling crew is a headman of the local group. Whaling leadership is integrated with social leadership.
2. Distribution of the parts of the whale is

[5]The magic surround was widespread throughout the Plains, the Great Basin, and the Southwest of North America. See R. Underhill, *Ceremonial Patterns in the Greater Southwest*, pp. 28–34.

[6]G. B. Grinnell, *The Cheyenne Indians*, vol. 1, p. 288.

[7]M. Lantis, "The Alaskan Whale Cult and Its Affinities" (*American Anthropologist*, vol. 40, 1938), pp. 438–464.

(a)

(b)

FIGURE 12.2
An Eskimo whale hunt at Point Hope, Alaska. (a) The hand-hurled harpoon has a detachable head which embeds in the whale. A line from the harpoon head is fixed to a seal-bladder float. (b) The flukes of a harpooned whale show above the water as the creature sounds for the depths. The float marks the whale's position. (c) The exhausted prey is dispatched with spear thrusts. The highly maneuverable skin *umiak* is used for this hazardous operation. (Courtesy of the American Museum of Natural History.)

(c)

regulated by customary usage, and the boat owner, harpooner, and others hold special rights.
3. Initiation into the Whale Cult is through a long, arduous period of instruction in which the young whaler learns the rituals and songs and seeks a vision.
4. Special amulets to ensure good luck are used in the whale hunt and are hidden away in a secret cave between seasons. Knowledge of such caves and of the use of the amulet is passed from father to son.
5. Whaling songs are sung. They are private property (see pages 274–275).
6. The season of whaling is a special ceremonial and taboo season. The whalers are isolated from the main village. They are unclean, must sleep in the open, and (in northern Alaska) must not eat raw meat.
7. Whalers must be sexually continent before and during whaling activities.
8. All those left in the village during the actual hunt must neither sleep nor work.
9. The wife of the chief whaler must remain quietly at home without eating, "in order to draw the whale to her."
10. Corpses or parts of the bodies of deceased whalers are used in ceremonial preparation for the hunt or are carried in the whale boat.
11. All gear must be repaired and cleansed before the onset of the whaling season; otherwise the whale will be offended.
12. When the whale is hauled ashore, it is given a symbolic drink of water by the whaler's wife.
13. As the whale is cut up, certain parts of its body are ceremonially handled, and very special rituals are performed to return the whale's spirit to the sea unangered. It is given food, and no disturbing noises are permitted.
14. The length of the ritual period following a whale killing is the same as for a human death (three to five days).

This is only a brief sketch of the Whale Cult complex, but it indicates how much more there is to hunting than tracking and killing.

INTENSIVE FORAGING: THE SHOSHONES OF THE GREAT BASIN

Foraging differs from gathering in the greater dependence upon wild seeds, fruits, and roots. Instead of using wild plant life to supplement a predominantly meat diet, the forager relies upon hunting to supplement a predominantly vegetarian diet (Figure 12.3). To illustrate the subsistence techniques of a group of hunters and foragers, we take the Great Basin Shoshones as our exemplars.

The Shoshoneans (speakers of Shoshone, a linguistic family within the Uto-Aztecan stock) lived in small local groups thinly distributed throughout the Great Basin. We have already noted them as carriers of the Desert tradition of North American Mesolithic foragers (pages 189–191). Each band was named for the food with which it was most intimately associated.

Bands were bilateral in kinship reckoning and very loosely organized. There were no chiefs, but each had a headman. The headman knew the ecology of the area, directed camp movements to where the ripened seeds and roots were to be found at appropriate times. Every morning he ritually warned his people not to waste food and not to forget that hard times and food shortages were surely ahead.

Julian Steward lists over 100 species of seeds, roots, and nuts known to have been eaten by the Shoshones.[8] Roots were extracted with a simple, pointed digging stick, or dibble. Seeds were collected with a fanlike beater used to knock the grass seeds into a woven basket. Of all the delectable seeds offered by the desert, those of the sunflower were the most prized. Roasted lightly and ground on a stone metate, they were reduced to an oily paste which tasted, according to the Shoshones, "just like peanut butter." Pine nuts also played a great part in the economy of the various Shoshones.

[8] J. H. Steward, *Basin Plateau Aboriginal Socio-political Groups* (Bureau of American Ethnology Bulletin 120, 1938), pp. 21–32.

FIGURE 12.3
San Bushman food-foraging women returning to camp with a harvest of mongongo nuts. (Shostak/Anthro-photo.)

Not only was the environment exploited for roots, berries, and nuts, but insects were looked upon as an epicurean delight. Regular communal grasshopper drives were organized. A sizable pit, 3 or 4 feet deep and 30 to 40 feet across, was laboriously prepared. Then men, women, and children formed a large circle and converged slowly on the pit as they drove the grasshoppers before them with brush beaters. A good drive netted countless grasshoppers, which could then be roasted.

Ants were a more favored delicacy because of their pungent flavor when properly prepared. In March, when the ants had left the larva stage but were not yet up and around, a woman would scoop up an entire ant nest in her large, scallop-shaped winnowing basket. With dextrous and wonderful manipulation, she shook the basket so that the ants gathered in its heel, while the sand and dirt bounced off the outer edge. When only ants remained, she scooped up hot coals with the basket. Rapidly jouncing them in the air, she kept the coals and ants turning together and the basket from burning up. When at last the ants were properly toasted, her motions were deftly altered; the ashes bounced off the edge of the basket, while the ants once again foregathered in its heel. They were then dumped upon a grinding stone, rolled out, and reduced to a delectable paste—from the Shoshone point of view.

Small rodents were trapped by means of

FIGURE 12.4
Crow Indian women sun-drying finely sliced meat for jerky. (Courtesy of the Museum of the American Indian, Heye Foundation.)

simple deadfalls. Rabbit hunting took the form of a great communal hunt under the direction of a hunt chief. Nets were set up, and beaters drove the quarry into the waiting meshes. Soft robes were plaited from thin strips of rabbit fur for winter use. Antelope were occasionally hunted in much the same way, but with the addition of magical lures and antelope disguises worn by the hunters. A fence of brush supplanted the nets of the rabbit hunt.

Deer, mountain sheep, and mountain goats were sometimes pursued alone by the most energetic hunters. A hunter with much endurance would chase a deer or sheep for two whole days until exhaustion of the quarry made it possible to get close enough for a shot.

Fear of starvation constantly haunted the Shoshones. Like the Eskimos, they sometimes took a desperate last resort in cannibalism. But cannibals were feared and hated, and occasionally lynched.[9]

It would be an error to conclude from the above remarks that the Shoshones were devoid of all fastidiousness. They will not eat dogs or coyotes, for Coyote is a supernatural culture hero—a lovable rapscallion who figures in many a myth. He is the younger brother of Wolf, whom some Shoshones look upon as the Supreme Deity.[10] To kill a coyote or its cousin the dog is unthinkable; to eat them, impossible. Modern Shoshones, in 1934, were even loath to eat the surplus Navajo sheep sent them by the government. Skinned sheep look too much like flayed dogs.

Bands of food gatherers are necessarily seminomadic. Tacit agreement allocates to each group its landed property, unless the equilibrium is upset by war or migration. A given band tends to move around within its own familiar territory because (1) people secure food and water more efficiently if they know the land; (2) all human groups practice some storage of food (Figure

[9]E. A. Hoebel, *The Political Organization and Law-ways of the Comanche Indians* (American Anthropological Association Memoir 54, Contributions from the Laboratory of Anthropology, 4, 1940), p. 141.

[10]R. H. Lowie, *The Northern Shoshone* (American Museum of Natural History, Anthropological Papers, vol. 11, part 2, 1909), pp. 233ff.

12.4); (3) they may also practice conservation and control of food resources. In addition, their movements are hindered to a certain extent by possession of material goods.[11]

INCIPIENT AGRICULTURE: HOE CULTIVATION OR GARDENING

Rainfall and the seasons control the basic patterns of primitive agriculture. There are four major crop complexes. Two are basically adapted to dry uplands and seasonal variation in climate; two are adapted to tropical rain forests. One of each type is found in the Old World and the New.

The Old World upland-seasonal complex is the old Neolithic one of Asia Minor centered on wheat, barley, flax, rye, and millet. These crops are fall-sown, make a large part of their growth of stalk and leaf in cool weather, and mature during the long summer days of warmest weather. These climatic adaptations made easy the diffusion of such plants into northwestern Europe. In the European lands, there was still the same condition of a cool, moist starting period, although the start was shifted to spring; maturity still took place during the long days of midsummer.[12] Old World cereals are sown broadcast. New World plants are individually planted in hills. Threshing may still be a primitive process among certain peoples.

The Old World wetland complex centers around rice cultivation or the growing of such tubers as yams or taro. The New World dryland-seasonal plants are the maize-beans-squash complex (Figure 12.5) and, in the Andean region, the potato. The New World tropical-wetland complex centers on the cultivation of manioc.

[11]J. H. Steward, "The Economic and Social Basis of Primitive Bands," in *Essays in Anthropology in Honor of Alfred Louis Kroeber*, p. 332.

[12]C. Sauer, "American Agricultural Origins," in *Essays in Anthropology in Honor of Alfred Louis Kroeber*, p. 285.

Forest Horticulture

Lightly forested highlands may strike the reader as strange places for the origins of gardening. Clearing forests is hard work, and it would seem at first that open country would be more suitable. However, two factors militate against horticultural origins in open lands. Deserts are deficient in water, even if the soil is workable. Grasslands are impenetrable to planting by peoples who do not have heavy plows. Even our own pioneers avoided the heavily sodded prairies, until special sod-breaking plows were developed (which was not so long ago). Although the best grain-producing lands in the world are the American and Russian prairies, they have become so only under modern conditions.

Clearing the forest for planting requires energetic labor. For people who are not rushed for time, it can be effectively done with simple tools and the *slash-and-burn method*. Each tree is killed by cutting a ring through the bark. The dead trees may then be burned out or left standing. The weedless floor of the virginal forest is a light rich humus, and the gardeners simply plant around the dead stumps. The land is abandoned after two or three years to allow the regeneration of forest cover to prevent extensive leaching and to replenish the soil.

Dryland-Seasonal Complex

Dry-Rice Cultivation in the Old World

As practiced by the Siang Dyaks of central Borneo, whose methods are typical, dry-rice cultivation involves selecting a sloping plot for clearing and planting. If it is a new plot, the trees on the lower side of the slope are cut partially through. Large key trees at the top of the plot are then felled so as to smash down the lower trees. All are trimmed, left to dry, and, after several weeks, burned. In all this the cultivator is usually helped by neighbors, who are helped in turn.

Planting is done by poking holes in the ground with a pointed stick, after which a couple

FIGURE 12.5
Hopi Indian floodwater irrigation garden plots (foreground and left center) at the modern village of Moenkopi, translated "Running Water," in the Arizona desert. (Photo by Joseph Muench.)

of grains of rice are dropped in. Weeding is done occasionally. A new field is cleared every two or three years because of soil depletion by crops and the leaching effect of heavy rainfall.[13]

Maize Cultivation among the Maya

High cultures that support large populations may not enjoy a margin of safety. The *milpa* system, as it is known among the Mayas, was (and still is)[14] basically similar to the system described above. In J. E. Thompson's account in *The Civilization of the Mayas*, we read that:

Land suitable for agriculture was prepared by burning off trees and undergrowth. After the first rains, the sower, with a bag of seed and a sharp-pointed stick, crossed and recrossed the field, making a hole with his stick in the ground at every pace, and throwing a few grains of maize into the pit. . . . At the end of the season the field was abandoned, and next year the Maya farmer marked out a new piece of land to be cleared and sown. In the course of time and with the large increase of population . . . the Mayas must have been driven farther and farther afield in search of virgin soil. The exhausted soils nearer home must have been resown after shorter and shorter periods of recuperation. In time the yield . . . would have fallen below the level of consumption, and, faced with evacuation or starvation, the people chose the former.[15]

In this we have one of the theories to account for the decline and abandonment of the great cen-

[13]J. H. Provinse, "Cooperative Ricefield Cultivation among the Siang Dyaks of Central Borneo" (*American Anthropologist*, vol. 39, 1937), pp. 77–102.

[14]See R. Redfield, *The Folk Culture of Yucatan*, pp. 115ff.

[15]Field Museum of Natural History, Anthropology Leaflet 25, 4th ed., 1942, p. 15.

ters of the Old Empire of the Mayas (A.D. 320 to 890). Morley has advanced the theory that intensive slash-and-burn gardening by the ancient Mayas resulted in the invasion of grasses that converted the tropical forest of southern Yucatán to tough sod savanna. With their primitive dibbles, they were unable to pierce the sod, he thinks, and so by the natural consequences of their own efforts, were driven from their cities.[16]

Another explanation suggests the introduction of outside aggressive forces. Maya cities were not urban centers of population concentration. They were religious and court centers supported by small farms more or less evenly distributed for miles around, not clustered like European peasants' homes beneath the walls of citadels. Such a pattern requires a pacifistic society. It is quite possible that the upset of the delicate social balance by the introduction of war forced the abandonment of Mayan centers in southern Yucatán around A.D. 900.[17]

Tropical-Wetland Complex

Yam Cultivation in the Old World In the tropical rain forests of Africa, Melanesia, and New Guinea, the yam is the staff of life. Clearings in the rain forest provide growing space for the yams and other root crops (Figure 12.6). Giant yams can grow to 20 pounds. In both Africa and Melanesia, yam growing, processing, and eating evoke intense feelings and provide a focal point for numerous magico-religious rites.

For no people has this been more explicitly

[16] S. G. Morley, *The Ancient Maya*, pp. 71–72.

[17] J. E. S. Thompson, "A Survey of the Northern Maya Area" (*American Antiquity*, vol. 2, 1945), pp. 2–24. The whole problem of the possible causes of the decline of the Mayan society of the Old Empire is being subjected to restudy by prehistorians and ecologists.

FIGURE 12.6
Incipient agriculturalists. Melanesian women of the New Hebrides Islands in the South Pacific peel and prepare taro roots for cooking. (Kal Muller/Woodfin Camp and Associates.)

FIGURE 12.7
Ifugao handmade irrigated rice terraces in Northern Luzon, Philippines (1955). The mountain village of Datad is in the grove of trees in the lower right-hand corner. (Courtesy of Fred Eggan.)

and meticulously documented than for the Trobriand Islanders by Malinowski in his classic study, *Coral Gardens and Their Magic.* A few observations are quoted to convey the meaning of gardening in this one people's lives:

A considerable amount of energy is spent on purely aesthetic effects, to make the garden look clean, showy and dainty [*page 80*].

As to the varieties of yam, taro and taytu, they have literally hundreds of names for each of them [*page 76*].

It may be said that among the forces and beliefs which bear upon and regulate gardening, magic is the most important, apart, of course, from the practical work [*page 62*].

Garden magic . . . is in the Trobriands a public and official service. It is performed by the garden magician . . . for the benefit of the community [*ibid*].

To each village community this magic . . . is a very precious possession and a symbol of its social integrity as well as of its standing in the tribal hierarchy [*page 68*].

Food is displayed on all occasions—at death and at dancing, at marriage and at mourning feasts [*page 82*].

Accumulated food is to them a good thing—its absence is not only something to be dreaded, but something to be ashamed of [*Ibid*].[18]

The richness of practice and belief, of which these statements are but the driest essence, is truly an expression of the human capacity to invest mundane survival activities with meaning and purpose.

Wet-Rice Cultivation in the Old World

Wet-rice irrigation was probably developed in India some 3000 or more years ago, from where it spread into China, Southeast Asia, and western Indonesia.

Wet-rice culture requires extensive water control and irrigation systems (Figure 12.7), which

[18]B. Malinowski, *Coral Gardens and Their Magic* (vol. 1, 1935).

sustain and require heavy population density. These societies are confined to specific localities because of the work required to build and maintain the systems. Some of the most populous areas of the world are those of wet-rice-growing societies in the Orient.[19]

Manioc Cultivation in the New World

Manioc, also called cassava, is a New World plant whose tuberous roots are rich in carbohydrates. It is the source of tapioca. The use of manioc as a basic foodstuff by Amazonian Indians reveals a genuine ingenuity. The domesticated forms with large yields contain poisonous prussic acid. This necessitates a leaching process of some complexity before the manioc tubers can be converted to edible cassava. The roots, after being dug, must be sliced and fermented to free some of the poisons. Next they are pulped on hand graters and then wrung dry of liquids. The dried pulp must then be ground to a flour or meal and heated to free the remaining volatile poisons.

The Kuikuru of central Brazil grow eleven varieties of manioc, all of which are poisonous. Yet manioc makes up 80 or 85 percent of their diet.[20] The heavy rain forest is opened for gardens exactly as we have described. Before 1900, stone axes and the jaws of the piranha were used to girdle the trees. Now trade axes, machetes, and brush hooks are used. Plants are allowed to grow for one and one-half years to get a maximum starch output, although they could be harvested in half a year. Men do the gardening and have to put in only two hours at agricultural labor and an hour and a half at fishing, daily. The remaining ten to twelve waking hours are spent in dancing, wrestling, relaxing, or other informal means of recreation. They could grow much more food as surplus with the available time and land. But the jungle has not favored extensive trade, so no more is raised than is required to eat well.

INTENSIVE AGRICULTURE: PLOW CULTIVATION

The development of plow cultivation combined the two basic inventions of the Neolithic—domestication of plants and domestication of animals—into a synthesized productive unit. The hand hoe was enlarged and changed from a hacking tool to a scarifier dragged through the earth by one or two harnessed draft animals. The most common animals used were oxen in the West and water buffalo in the East; horses, camels, and people have done field service too. Plow culture enhanced the limited energy input of the hoe wielder with the greater energy input of the grain- and grass-eating draft animal.

The oldest extant evidence of the plow goes back to Mesopotamian cylinder seals and Egyptian paintings, both from the fourth millennium B.C.—a good 3000 years after the first development of horticulture in the Old World. After 3000 B.C. the plow is known in Cyprus, Greece, and India. Fifteen hundred years later, plows were in use in Bronze Age northwestern Europe. At the other end of Eurasia, China did not receive the plow until 300 B.C.

No native cultures of Africa south of the Sahara were, until modern times, based upon plow agriculture, even though 82 of 116 (71 percent) African societies in Murdock's *World Ethnographic Sample* were horticultural. In contrast, 49 of 78 (63 percent) Mediterranean societies included in that sample practiced plow agriculture.

In Asia, 54 of 85 (64 percent) societies in Murdock's sample used the plow and a mere 5 were still gardeners.

---

[19]The economic organization of irrigation societies is too complex to summarize here. An excellent overview is presented in T. E. Downing and M. Gibson (eds.), *Irrigation's Impact on Society* (Anthropological Papers of the University of Arizona, no. 25, 1974).

[20]R. L. Carneiro, "Slash and Burn Cultivation among the Kuikuru and Its Implications for Cultural Development in the Amazon Basin," in *The Evolution of Horticultural Systems in Native South America: Causes and Consequences—A Symposium* (Anthropologica Supplement No. 2, Caracas, 1961), pp. 47–67.

The spread of plow agriculture in 5000 years is phenomenal testimony to its efficiency, especially when combined with fertilizing.

PASTORALISM

Pastoralism, the term applied to cultures whose major subsistence centers around the herding and husbandry of domesticated animals, is an adjustment to specific ecological factors. Historically, this occurred in the Neolithic Age, at the same time that incipient agriculture was developing in regions more suitable to the raising of crops.

Pastoralism is preeminently an Asian-African economic complex. In Africa it covers the whole Sahara, where it centers on the camel and the horse, as it also does in eastern Arabia. In the northern Sudan and most of East Africa, it combines with hoe culture, and in the extreme south, the Hottentots and Hereros live on their cattle. The great Asian steppes, from the east shores of the Caspian to the boundaries of China and from the Himalayas to the arctic wastes, support such eminently pastoral peoples as the Kazaks, Tartars, Altai, Kalmucks, and Mongols with their herds of horses, sheep, and cattle.

It should be mentioned that the possession of animals is not the exclusive prerogative of pastoralists; all gardeners keep some domesticated animals—pigs, goats, chickens, and dogs being the most common. Such animals may or may not be eaten. Domesticated animals also may be kept as pets, for emotional reasons, or as objects of religious sacrifice as often as for food.

Hambly notes that goats are present everywhere, but neglected in Africa; they are neither milked nor used extensively as a meat supply.[21] What Hambly failed to note is that in their omnivorousness, goats are good garbage disposers. So are pigs and dogs, a fact that has led Ashley Montagu to suggest this as the original reason for the domestication of dogs in Neolithic times.[22]

The known practical uses to which domestic animals can be put are (1) consumption of their meat, blood, or eggs; (2) use of their hides; (3) use of their hair or wool for weaving or felting; (4) milking and dairying; (5) load carrying or pulling; and (6) riding.[23] To these should be added (7) the use of their dried dung for household fuel and (8) their value as media of exchange and reciprocity.

Yet most societies ignore or fail to take advantage of one or several of these uses. In East Africa south of Abyssinia, the art of riding was totally unknown to the native people. In Africa beef is eaten only occasionally. In some societies women may toil under heavy loads, but cattle must not be burdened or set to pulling loads. So, although the cult of the cow is the dominant theme of most East African cultures, the use of this animal falls far short of its potentialities, and in India religious taboos severely limit its utility as a food product.

Of course, we, in our use of horses, reverse the situation. We ride them, make them haul burdens, and pet them. But we neither milk nor eat them. The mayor of New York City in 1943 insisted that the eating of horse flesh is "immoral and uncivilized," and because of such lofty, if ethnocentric, principles he forbade the sale of horsemeat as a wartime measure to relieve an acute meat shortage.

Lactase Deficiency

The failure of most pastoralists to make maximum use of their animals has baffled many observers and scientists. The rejection of most dairy products by both the Chinese and the East Africans has presented one such puzzle. It has long been known that Chinese pastoralists do

[21]W. D. Hambly, *Source Book for African Anthropology* (Field Museum of Natural History, Anthropological Series, vol. 26, part 2, 1937), p. 596.

[22]M. F. A. Montagu, "On the Origin of the Domestication of the Dog" (*Science*, vol. 96, 1942), pp. 111–112.

[23]C. D. Forde, *Habitat, Economy, and Society*, p. 401.

not milk their cattle, nor do they eat cheese or other dairy products (although they are not averse to beef as food). Similarly, most East Africans drink little sweet milk, although they draw cattle blood to drink and make a cult of sour milk. For all their familiarity with sour milk, few Africans have developed the art of cheese making, and butter is less often eaten than used in dressing the hair or applied as a cosmetic for lending the body a glossy sheen.

Until 1966, the Chinese aversion to all dairy products, and that of Africans to sweet milk, seemed to be a deep-seated cultural fixation. Medical research now suggests that it has a genetic base. Lactase, an enzyme produced in the small intestine, is necessary to the digestion of milk sugar, or lactose. Medical studies indicate that most adult Chinese, Asiatics, and American Indians, and 70 percent of Afro-Americans and West African Negroes, are unable to digest milk. Most, but not all, whites have no difficulty. The symptoms of lactase deficiency are abdominal bloating, cramps, and diarrhea after drinking more than a glass of milk. By implication, European populations have developed genes for lactase production. Most Asians and Africans have not. It appears that, except for infants, not everybody needs milk. Not everybody can stand it. After all, the possibility for human access to dairy products is not more than 8000 years old.[24]

Pastoralism in Africa and the New World

It is well known that in India the cow is considered sacred, but in East Africa it is the heart and core of life. "First, last, and always the role of cattle in Karamojong life is to transform the energy stored in the grasses, herbs, and shrubs of the tribal area into a form easily available to the people."[25] The cattle do not represent wealth; they *are* wealth. (Figure 12.8). As Elizabeth Marshall Thomas has written of the pastoral Dodoth of East Africa, among whom the women are millet growers:

> *For the Dodoth, cattle are the warp of life. They are the only wealth, the foundation of economic and social stability, the origin of all human ties. . . . Cows give milk. This is drunk daily, and churned into butter, and curdled with cow's urine into a salty cheese. Oxen give their blood. . . . People drink the blood raw . . . , or they cook it with green millet flour into a delicate delicious pudding, as airy as a souffle. Cowhides make sleeping mats and clothing. Cow dung makes flooring. Fresh cow urine, in its sterile stream, washes dirty hands or cleans utensils or softens leather or curdles milk for clabber or speeds the making of ghee. The first morsel a baby eats in his life is a drop of butter. From then on, he will be involved with cattle; every day and night of his life his nostrils will be filled with their sweet odor, his ears with their vibrant voices; and when he dies, if he dies at home, his body may be wrapped in the hide of one of his oxen and buried in the soft earth of their pen.*[26]

This passage conveys a small touch of the significance of cattle for African pastoralists, but the intensity of emotion felt for cattle cannot be fully appreciated by an outsider.

In the New World, only the Navajos became pastoralists—and then only in modern times with sheep acquired from the Spanish. In the southern Plains, such tribes as the Comanche became herders, but not pastoralists, in the mid-nineteenth century. Their horse herds numbered in the thousands, but horses were eaten only occasionally, were never milked, and were used mostly for riding in war and hunting. As mount-

[24] S.-S. Huang and T. M. Bayless, "Milk and Lactose Intolerance in Healthy Orientals" (*Science*, vol. 160, 1966), pp. 83–84; G. G. Harrison, "Primary Adult Lactase Deficiency: A Problem in Anthropological Genetics" (*American Anthropologist*, vol. 77, no. 4, 1975), pp. 812–835.

[25] R. and N. Dyson-Hudson, "Subsistence Herding in Uganda" (*Scientific American*, vol. 220, 1969), p. 78.

[26] E. M. Thomas, "The Herdsmen" (*The New Yorker*, May 1, 1965), p. 52. (By permission from *The New Yorker* and Alfred A. Knopf, Inc., New York.)

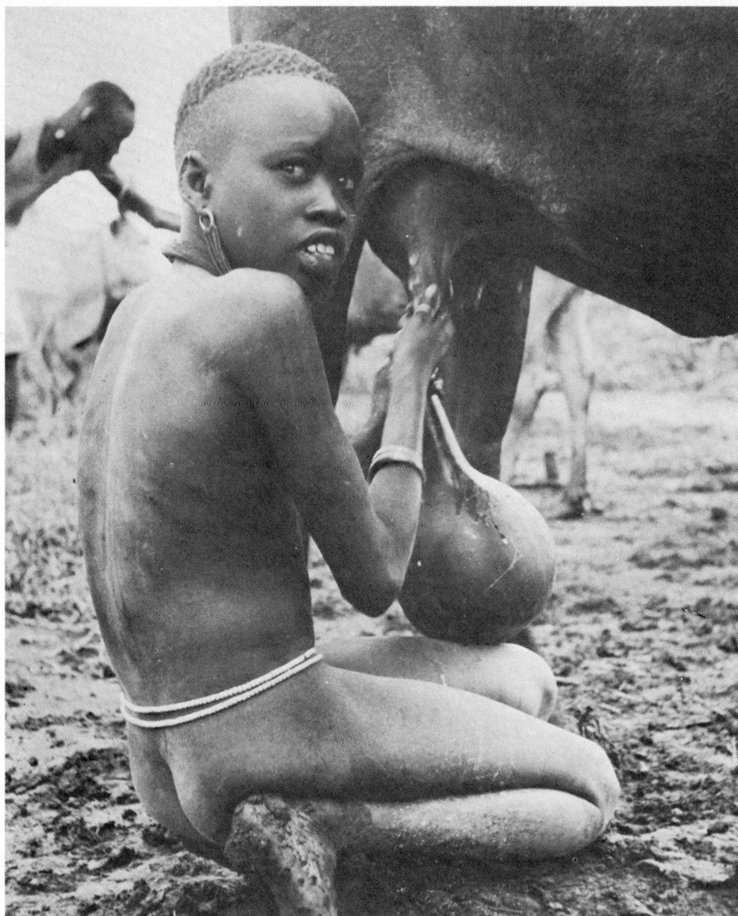

FIGURE 12.8
A Nuer pastoralist drawing milk into a gourd milk bottle. The small udder of the cow indicates that Nuer cattle are not bred for high milk production. (Courtesy of Pitt Rivers Museum, University of Oxford.)

ed cavalry, the Comanches overwhelmed the sedentary horticultural Apaches of the South Plains and drove them out of Texas. Horses were also useful in trade and as prestige tokens akin to the war bonnet. A man identified so completely with his favorite horse that the killing of such an animal was treated as murder. It required a revenge killing of the horse killer, even as a man would avenge the death of his brother.

Transhumance

Transhumance is an essential activity of pastoralism. Herders seasonally drive the sheep, goats, reindeer, and cattle to upland summer ranges for grazing and return to their permanent lowland villages in winter.

The Jie of northeastern Uganda are an excellent example of this mode of subsistence. In Gulliver's[27] summary statement:

The life of the Jie is based on a mixed economy: but although agriculture provides the bulk of the staple food—sorghum for porridge—the Jie themselves give major importance to the care and value of their

[27]P. H. Gulliver, "The Jie of Uganda," in J. L. Gibbs, Jr. (ed.), *The Peoples of Africa*. Copyright © 1965 by Holt, Rinehart and Winston, Inc. Used by permission.

livestock, particularly cattle. . . . [L]ivestock have . . . a notable aesthetic value, and they are essential to the rich complex of rituals that would be thought ineffective without the slaughter of oxen [page 159].

Permanent settlement is limited to a small area. . . . Here in fixed homesteads [see Figure 13.9, page 239] *arranged in stable communities live some four fifths of the population—women, children, and most of the men. . . . The bulk of the herds are kept in separate mobile camps in the pasture lands and are tended by youths and young men subsisting directly off the livestock [pages 161–162].*

The pastoral cycle is briefly as follows: by . . . the middle of the rainy season the stock camps are all located in the eastern region, where . . . new grass has grown sufficiently and surface water collects in pools and stream beds. . . . Dairy herds are at their largest in the homesteads. . . . As the dry season sets in, both grass and water quickly become exhausted and camps must shift westward. There is an irregular migration of the camps, for it is entirely the responsibility of each herd owner to determine the timing and direction of movement as he assesses the situation. At first in the western region water supplies are sufficient to allow a widespread scatter of camps, but as the time of the last rains recedes, surface water dries up and camps are compelled to converge on . . . the half-dozen permanent watering places for the remainder of the season. . . . With the onset of the next rainy season it again becomes possible for camps to scatter through the western region as fresh grass and water are available [page 162].

Pig Culture in Melanesia

Throughout the southwest Pacific the raising of pigs on a share-crop basis is a focus of prestige in most societies. Gardening provides the yams that are the staple food, but pigs are wealth, and a "big man" is the one who can put a "call" on hundreds of pigs for slaughter and distribution when he wishes to dedicate a new men's meeting house, settle a dispute, or appease his ancestors. When pigs are slaughtered, cooked, and distributed among the guests, it may be that only a minute portion is actually eaten. The slabs of pork may pass through a number of hands, like worn currency, in payment of debts or as gifts, imposing new obligations on others, until at last, in rancid decay, their usefulness is over.[28]

SUMMARY

An elemental feature of every culture is a complex of techniques for production, consumption, and distribution of food. The physiological need for the replacement of used-up energy in the body imposes a biologic imperative on every society to organize its culture so that minimal food requirements are met. Otherwise, the society and its culture will not survive. The adjustment of a culture to the physical environment in which it operates is therefore of prime importance. Consequently, the culture areas of the world are, in large measure, also food-getting or subsistence areas.

Environments limit but do not determine the content of cultures. Thus cultures as diverse as those of the Pueblo Indians and the Navajos, each influenced by a separate historical background of culture, exist side by side in the same geographic area, sharing a similar physical environment.

The prehistoric evolution of subsistence techniques resulted in four primary levels of food getting. They are: (1) hunting and gathering, (2) intensive foraging, (3) incipient agriculture (gardening/hoe culture) and pastoralism, and (4) intensive agriculture (plow culture). By the nineteenth century, only a small minority of the world's societies were still based on hunting and foraging. Half had evolved to gardening; a few were pastoralists; and approximately a fifth had achieved plow culture, which provides the foundation for urban civilizations.

Thus, the vast majority of recent nonliterates shared in the great Neolithic complex of gardening. Pastoralism represents a specialized adjustment to physical environments that are not

[28]See Chap. 26, *Economic Organization*, pp. 455–456, for a more detailed description of the pig-exchange networks.

suitable for gardening by people who possess only simple horticultural techniques, or it may be joined to gardening in a mixed economy.

Forest gardening involves temporary clearing of woodlands by means of the slash-and-burn techniques. Few forest gardeners fertilize their plots; hence, gardens are allowed to return to the forest after a few years as new plots are opened up.

Plow agriculture (prior to the modern overseas expansion by Europeans) was confined to Asia Minor, North Africa, Europe, and South and East Asia. Although 80 percent of human societies had not acquired plow agriculture before the modern era, most of the world's population was concentrated in the north temperate belt of Eurasia in which subsistence by intensive agriculture was concentrated.

The only domesticated animal brought from the Eastern Hemisphere into the Western in pre-European times was the dog. Because the specific plants cultivated by American Indians were (with the possible exception of cotton) entirely indigenous to the Western Hemisphere, and because the techniques of cultivation used in the New World were quite unlike those established in the Old World, we infer that New World horticulture developed independently.

Pastoralism, as a dominant mode of subsistence, is an alternative ecological adjustment to dry or semiarid grassland environments.

SELECTED READINGS

Barth, F., *Nomads of South Persia* (1961). Near East pastoralism, based on sheep, described and analyzed by an outstanding social anthropologist.

de Schlippe, P., *Shifting Cultivation in Africa: The Zande System of Agriculture* (1956). A study based on anthropology and agronomy, with very enlightening results.

Ekvall, R. B., *Fields on the Hoof* (1968). A case study of the pastoral complex of the nomads of Tibet, who have adopted yak culture (with subsidiary animals) to the maintenance of human society at altitudes of 16,000 feet.

Forde, C. D., *Habitat, Economy, and Society* (1937). Contains condensed descriptions of the subsistence activities of a number of tribes and the relation of their social structures to such activities.

Klima, G. J., *The Barabaig: East African Cattle Herders* (1970). A case study of a pastoral tribe.

Little, M. A., and G. E. B. Morren, Jr., *Ecology, Energetics, and Human Variability* (1976). A brief review of recent developments in the field.

Nelson, R. K., *Hunters of the Northern Ice* (1969). A systematic study of traditional and modern techniques of hunting on sea ice and of the life of the Eskimos of the Arctic coasts of Alaska.

Netting, R. M., *Hill Farmers of Nigeria* (1968). An ecological-social anthropological study (1960 to 1962) of a contemporary intensive-gardening society in Northern Nigeria, West Africa.

Steward, J. H., *Basin-Plateau Aboriginal Socio-political Groups* (1938). The ecology and livelihood of the peoples of the Great Basin desert.

Vayda, A. P. (ed.), *Environment and Cultural Behavior* (1969). A collection of good quality, containing reprints of some classic articles.

13 Housing Adaptations

CHAPTER OUTLINE

LEARNING GOALS

Identify the relationship between ecology and settlement patterns.

Identify the relationship between subsistence and choice of housing.

Explain how social organization influences house types.

Trace the evolution of Pueblo housing from pit houses to communal apartments.

Technological adaptations in housing depend upon the adjustments required by the local climate, the materials available, and the kind of subsistence economy and social organization of the society.

CULTURAL VALUES

A strange conservatism marks the entire development of housing. Human societies have not concentrated interest or attention to the elaboration of housing as they have to myth making, religion, art, song, and dance.

The state of technology, the skill with which people have learned to build structures, may be a key factor in the kind and quality of the homes found in a given society, but examination fails to reveal a satisfactory correlation. For example, the majority of New Guineans live in simple thatched huts, but the Sepik River men's clubhouses are imposing, highly decorated structures with great gabled roofs rising sometimes to heights of more than 100 feet. As Herskovits points out, the term "dwelling" is by no means synonymous with shelter or building. "The magnificent Central American structures, or those of . . . Malaysia were not dwellings at all. They symbolized the power of the ruler, the splendor with which the gods were worshipped."[1] It is clear that a similar dichotomy between building skills applied to monuments, cathedrals, and commercial skyscrapers, and building skills applied to peoples' *homes* has chronically existed among literate and nonliterate societies.

Only in the last century have people turned their architectural attention to developing comforts and convenience in their homes.

ECOLOGY AND SETTLEMENT PATTERN

The impact of the environment on a culture can often be perceived through an inspection of where and how the members of a social group locate, arrange, and shelter themselves. *The spatial arrangement of the subgroups of a society in relation to each other, to their environmental resources, and to other societies is called the settlement pattern.* No single factor ever determines where and how a given group of people will settle. In the previous chapter it was made clear that one variable affecting the location of a society is the food resources available and the skills people have to make use of them. Experience is another important settlement factor. The complexity of food-getting procedures and the general area of habitation of a society depend in part on its previous adaptations, developmental changes, cultural contacts, migrations, and locations. Another factor in determining settlement is the relations between societies sharing a geographical area.

Anthropologists have found it useful to classify societies by their general settlement patterns based on the relative permanence of residence and the comparative symmetry and spacing of the territorial arrangement.[2] Five types of settlement patterns have been identified in the six geographic areas (see Figure 13.1).[3] Nomadic societies constitute 7 percent of a world sample; *seminomadic or semisedentary communities* constitute 24 percent of the sample; and *compact, impermanent villages shifting locations every few years* form 2 percent of the sample. In contrast, societies more permanently located in the pattern *of scattered neighborhoods* total 20 percent of the sample, while those groups having *compact, permanent towns or villages, or complex towns with outlying settlements,* form nearly half (47 percent) of the sample.

An important factor determining the relative

[1]M. J. Herskovits, *Cultural Anthropology*, p. 131.

[2]R. K. Beardsley, P. Holder, A. D. Krieger, B. J. Meggers, J. B. Rinaldo, and P. Kutsche, "Functional and Evolutionary Implications of Community Patterning," in *Seminars in Archaeology: 1955* (Memoirs of the Society for American Archaeology, no. 11, 1956); and G. P. Murdock, *Ethnographic Atlas*, column 30.

[3]E. Bourguignon and L. Greenbaum, *Diversity and Homogeneity*, p. 40.

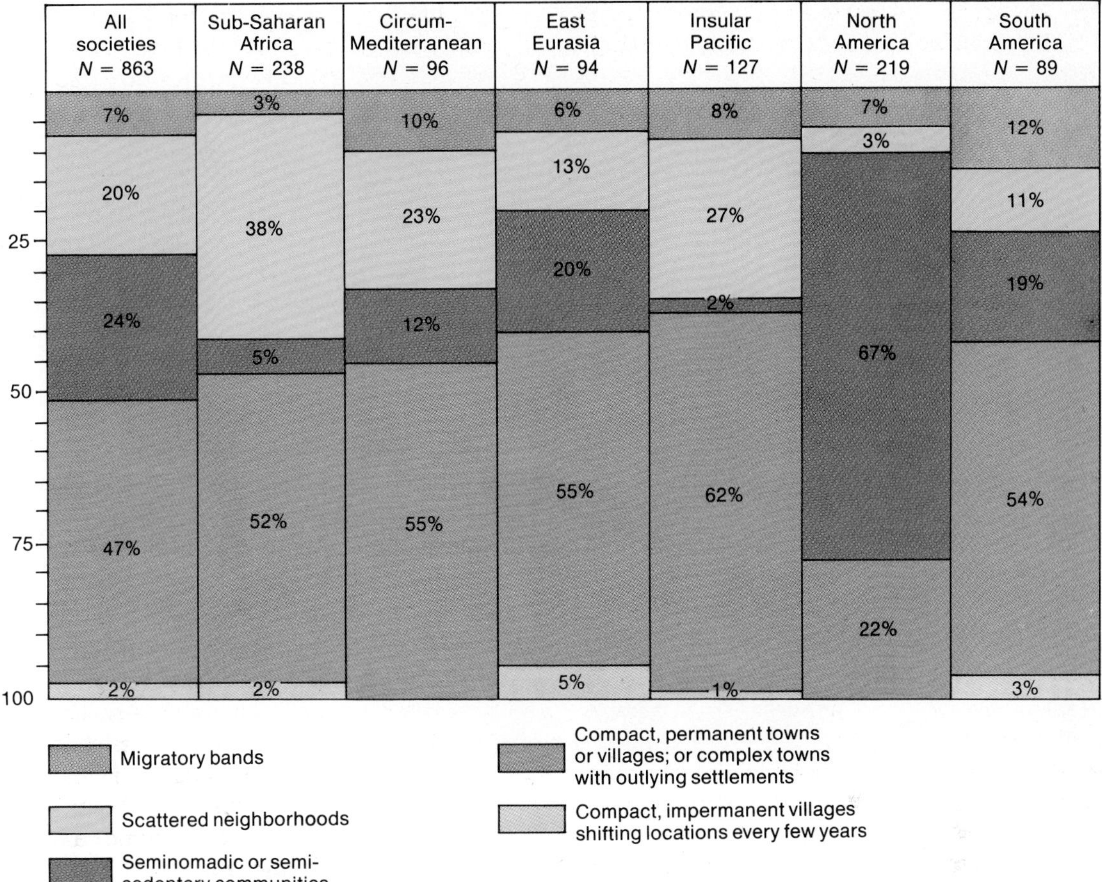

FIGURE 13.1
Relative frequency of settlement patterns according to geographic area. (Data adapted from E. Bourguignon and L. Greenbaum, *Diversity and Homogeneity*, table 17, p. 39.)

permanence in a society's settlement pattern is its food-getting activity. Practices such as hunting and gathering and intensive foraging often require the social group to move frequently from location to location, seeking out plants when they are ready for harvest and animals in their natural habitat. Similarly, pastoralism may require mobility of settlements so that herders can move their animals as they seek plentiful grazing areas. In contrast, agricultural practices demand that people reside in one location while the land is prepared and planted and the crops weeded, watered, and harvested. Many semisedentary societies are those which practice hoe or garden agriculture in one location for several years until soil fertility is exhausted. Then, these societies must seek out virgin lands for new planting or return to lands which have been lying fallow.

The internal arrangements within settlements are influenced by many variables, especially such factors of social organization as kinship groupings, class and caste differences, and varying roles in the division of labor. The relative compactness of a settlement may be determined by defensive needs, land hunger, population size, or topography.

FIGURE 13.2
A tropical rain forest rectangular, walled, and thatched gable-roofed pile dwelling in northern Luzon, the Philippines. (United Nations.)

ENVIRONMENT AND HOUSING

Housing materials used depend partly on availability, climate, and cultural norms.

Taking the world as a whole, the most readily available building materials are wood and vegetable fiber. Poles have formed the framework for houses since Lower Paleolithic times. In the arctic where wood is scarce, however, the ribs of whales served prehistoric peoples in the construction of their summer houses.

Forest peoples, contending with frequent rain, roof their houses with thatch or slabs of bark. Thatch is also effective in providing numerous pockets of dead air to serve as insulation against the heat of the sun. In the rain forests of Southeast Asia, the Pacific, and South America, the raising of the house floor on stilts (the pile dwelling) provides dryness and improved circulation of air for better health and comfort (Figure 13.2). In the coastal areas of the Melanesian Islands, pile dwellings are commonly built over the waters of lagoons (Figure 13.3).

Heavy mud or baked-clay roofs and walls provide maximum heat insulation from the searing temperatures of the desert.

Stone houses were built only by Mayas, Aztecs, Incas, and other groups in Central and South America; Pueblo Indians in the North American Southwest; and the early predecessors of Mediterranean civilization.

SUBSISTENCE AND HOUSING

If environment influences the choice and availability of materials suitable for housing, the food-

FIGURE 13.3
After World War II, the village of Peri, Manus Island, New Guinea, went "modern." Pile houses built over the water along the shore were abandoned in favor of relocated pile houses on the mainland, erected along a street and village square. Peri is the village made famous by Margaret Mead in *Growing up in New Guinea* (1930) and *New Lives for Old* (1953). (Photo by E. A. Hoebel, 1967.)

FIGURE 13.4
A century ago (1871–1875), when visited by Major John W. Powell, the Paiute Indians along the Arizona–Utah border were living in simple brush windscreens and subsisting as hunters and gatherers. (Photo by J. K. Hillers, Smithsonian Institution Anthropological Archives, Bureau of American Ethnology Collection.)

getting activities of peoples constitute a second important factor. Nomads and hunters on the move have housing needs different from those of settled farmers (Figure 13.6).

Marginal Foragers: The Windscreen

The shelter of foragers is usually the simple windscreen. Such dwellings are little more than temporary nests (Figure 13.4). Murdock describes the usual Tasmanian shelter as "a simple windbreak, constructed of interlaced boughs or strips of bark in the form of a crescent and open on the leeward side."[4] This is the exact counterpart of the Shoshones' windbreak previously used in summer wanderings. For more permanent settlements, beehive-shaped grass houses,

[4]G. P. Murdock, *Our Primitive Contemporaries*, p. 5.

FIGURE 13.5
In the Kalahari Desert of South Africa, Bushman hunters and gatherers live in windscreens similar to those of the Paiutes of the Great Basin Desert in southern Utah and northern Arizona. The family's entire collection of household goods (grinding stones, pots, gourds, cord, quiver and arrows, spear, digging stick, and cloth) are set out for display. Note the absence of beds, stools, and benches. (L. K. Marshall/Peabody Harvard Smithsonian Expedition.)

called *wickiup*, were constructed by the Shoshones.

All such people wandered in search of food. None had domesticated animals capable of carrying house materials from campsite to campsite. Therefore, they built no more than was minimally necessary, something that could be abandoned with little loss of labor expended (Figure 13.5).

Hunters and Pastoralists: The Tent

Hunters who have dogs or horses, such as the Plains Indians, and hunters whose food supply is sufficiently adequate that they need move only seasonally, rely on the tent as a dwelling (Figure 13.6a). The same is true of nomadic pastoralists. Although modern technology makes rectangular, roofed tents feasible, the tents of hunters and pastoralists were either dome- or cone-shaped: the floor plan was round or elliptical. The tent is indeed a "structurally brilliant invention . . . light in weight, composed of small members and easily errected, dismantled . . . [which] if we judge it by the modern structural criterion of 'the most work from the least material' (like all tension structures), ranks as a very advanced form of construction."[5] Compared with other structures, the tent offers maximum resistance to strong winds, exposes the least surface area against wind, heat, and cold, and requires the least structural support for the volume of enclosed space. And it is portable.

[5]J. M. Fitch and D. P. Branch, "Primitive Architecture and Climate" (*Scientific American*, vol. 207, 1960), p. 136.

Gardeners and Agriculturalists: Fixed Dwellings

Oblong, gabled structures greatly increase the internal volume of usable living space and produce a tighter roof and stronger walls. A great deal of additional work is required to build this type of structure, and the work will not be expended unless the house is going to stay in place for some time. People with cultivated fields are those most likely to be stable in their residence; therefore, it is not surprising to find more permanent houses associated with agricultural economies.

SOCIAL ORGANIZATION AND DOMICILE

In recent years, there has been some concern expressed about the physical isolation of the American family in its private home or apartment unit and how this affects relations between children, their aunts and uncles, and their lonely elderly grandparents (see pages 430–432). Yet, the intimate and subtle relations between house forms and the functional manifestations of individual, familial, and kinship behavior and the more general aspects of social and economic institutions have been neglected until recently in both anthropological and sociological literature.

a

b

c

FIGURE 13.6

Eskimos adapt their housing to the seasonal variations of the climate. (a) The seminomadic hunters of Cape Nome, Alaska, build portable skin tents for summer dwellings. (Courtesy of the Museum of the American Indian, Heye Foundation.) (b) The more sedentary Eskimos of the interior of Alaska build permanent semisubterranean sodhouses. The background mountains are the Brooks Range. (Steve McCutcheon/Alaska Pictorial Service.) (c) Coastal Eskimos build snow-block igloos when halted on trips by winter storms or when relocating a winter hunting village. Today, of course, many Eskimos live in villages, modern towns, and cities. (Steve McCutcheon/Alaska Pictorial Service.)

Family Attitudes and Living Patterns

It is difficult to make valid general statements about the many nuances of the relation between household structure, attitudes, and living patterns. Malinowski, however, provided a good capsule summary in the following terms:

> *The isolated homestead distant from all others makes for a strongly knit, self-contained, economically as well as morally independent family. Self-contained houses collected into village communities allow of a much closer texture in derived kinship and greater extent of local cooperation. Houses compounded into joint households, especially when they are united under one owner, are the necessary basis of a joint family. . . . Large communal houses where only a separate hearth or partition distinguishes the various component families make for a yet more closely knit system of kinship. Finally, the existence of special clubhouses, where the men, the bachelors or the unmarried girls of a community sleep, eat or cook together, is obviously correlated to the general structure of a community when kinship is complicated by age grades, secret societies and other male or female associations and is usually also correlated to the presence or absence of sexual laxity.*[6]

Separation of Men and Women

In some parts of the world, sexual segregation requires individual houses for each woman, her unmarried daughters, and her prepubescent sons. The adult males, however, live together in clubhouses.

The Enga Among the Enga-speaking peoples of the Central Highlands of New Guinea, the men's house is a meeting and sleeping center. It holds no ritual activities. By the time a boy is 6 years old, he is expected to have left his mother's house to live in a men's house of his own patrilineage. A demographic survey done in the 1950s found that 309 men and boys lived in 57 men's houses. Associated with these were 155 women's houses for 235 women and 266 girls (under 15 years of age) and little boys—plus 9 men who "were elderly or poor, and their behavior was thought to be eccentric."[7] Linked to this separateness is a pervading belief among the men that women are dangerous to their powers and that their polluting effect must be reduced through minimal contact.

Joint-family Households

The Jivaro Indians In contrast to the pattern just described for the Enga, the Jivaros of eastern Ecuador practice sexual segregation within a communal joint-family household.[8] The unit of Jivaro social organization is the patrilineal family group, perhaps with several conjugal units, living under a single roof. The typical Jivaro house is about 75 feet long and 40 feet wide, with parallel sides and rounded ends. The walls are made of 10-foot laths of palm or bamboo lashed vertically to the frame. The roof is thatched. At each end of the house is a door, one reserved for men only and the other for women. In like way, one-half of the interior is for men, and the other half for women. Each man has his private sleeping platform against the wall on his side; each woman has her platform on the women's side.

The Iroquois Longhouse In the longhouse of the Iroquois we find an internal organization more typical of joint-family households. The structure of an Iroquois longhouse was something like that of a Quonset hut. A roof consisting of slabs of dried bark was laid on vertical walls. The house could be enlarged or shortened merely by adding or removing sections at either end. Doors were at the ends, with an open passage down the entire house, which

---

[6]B. Malinowski, "Culture" (*Encyclopaedia of the Social Sciences*, vol. 4, 1931), p. 632.

[7]M. J. Meggitt, "Male-Female Relationships in the Highlands of Australian New Guinea" (*American Anthropologist*, vol. 66, no. 4, part 2; Special Publication, 1964), p. 207.

[8]M. W. Stirling, *Historical and Ethnographical Materials on the Jivaro Indians* (Bureau of American Ethnology Bulletin 117, 1938), p. 38.

in one instance was 110 yards long—more than the length of a football field (Figure 13.7). Down the center of the passage were evenly spaced fireplaces (Figure 13.8). As had been observed by Lafitau:

Along the fires there extends on each side a platform of twelve to thirteen feet in length by five or six in width and nearly as high. These platforms, shut in on all sides except that towards the fire, serve as beds and as chairs to sit down upon; on the bark which forms the floor of the platform they spread rush mats and furs. . . .

The base of the platform, on which they sleep, is elevated at most one foot from the ground . . . to avoid the dampness, and it is not greater, on the other hand, to avoid the inconvenience of the smoke which is insupportable in the cabins when standing erect, or even a little raised.

The bark which covers the platforms above and which forms the ceiling of the bed, serves them as a closet and larder, where they place . . . their dishes and all the little utensils of their household. Between the platforms are placed large chests of bark . . . five or six feet high, where they put the corn when shelled. . . .[9]

[9]Translation from the French by M. L. LeBrun in L. H. Morgan (H. B. Lloyd's ed.), *League of the Ho-dé-no-sau-nee or Iroquois*, vol. 2, appendix B, pp. 290–291.

FIGURE 13.7
The Iroquois longhouse at the height of its development was longer than an American football field. The stakes, set by archaeologists, mark the location of postholes. The small roundhouse in the excavated square at the right probably housed a sublineage. A second longhouse was located behind the roundhouse. (Courtesy of J. A. Tuck.)

FIGURE 13.8
The ground plan of a "five fire" Iroquois longhouse according to Lafitau's description, from L. H. Morgan's *League of the Ho-dé-no-sau-nee or Iroquois*.

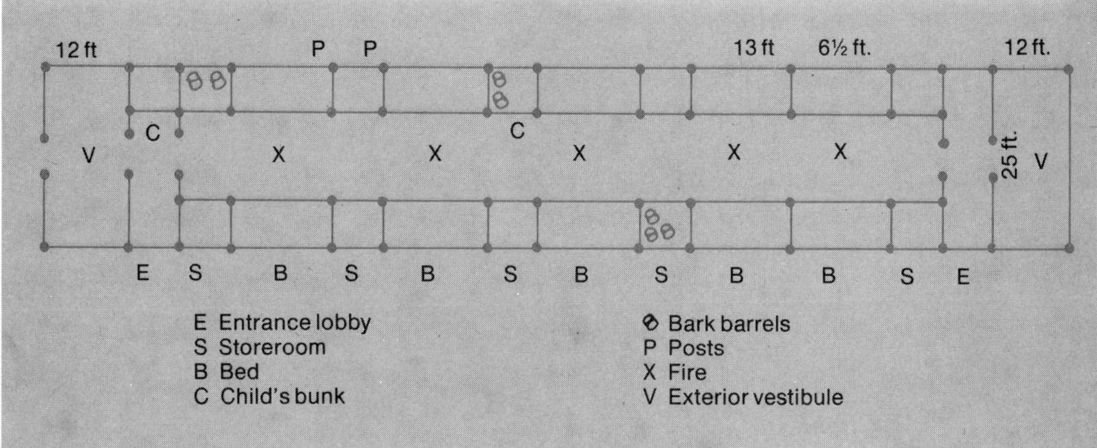

Each longhouse "belonged" to a lineage of related women (a matrilineage) headed by an influential older woman. The household included her daughters and their husbands and children. It usually also included her sisters and their families, as well as the families of her married granddaughters. The longhouse bore the name and insignia of its dominant matrilineal family (except in the case of the Seneca tribe). Married men were supposed to move into the longhouse of the wife, but the son of an influential mother married to a girl from a family of less prestige might choose to stay in his mother's home. And since the Iroquois were given to adoption of captive enemies as replacements for dead relatives, there were always some of these in the household.

The women could throw their husbands out at any time. For the dispossessed divorcé, there was nothing to do but pick up his gear and leave. He had no legal claim on children or home.

Segregation within the longhouse was by conjugal families. Each woman had her cubicle, which was shared by her husband and children. Eating was partly a joint-family, partly a separate-family, affair. Each conjugal family shared a cooking fire with the occupants of the opposite compartment.

An Iroquois village consisted of several longhouses within a protective palisade. A number of villages together made up a tribe. The six original Iroquois tribes made up the Iroquois nation.

As the cultural environment of the Iroquois changed under the impact of white colonization of their country, the longhouse organization began to break down, giving way to log houses of smaller dimensions, until by 1800, the longhouse as a dwelling form disappeared.[10]

[10]W. N. Fenton, "Locality as a Basic Factor in the Development of Iroquois Social Structure," *Symposium on Local Diversity in Iroquois Culture* (Bureau of American Ethnology Bulletin 149, 1951), pp. 35–54.

The Compound Homestead of African Pastoralists

The joint households described above are those of gardeners who live in wooded areas where long timbers are available and where the main problem is protection of human, not animal, life. African pastoralists have a different form of the joint-family homestead. In their ecological setting, materials for large buildings are rare, and a major need is to protect both people and stock from raiders. The homestead of the Jie, whose seasonal cycle was described in a previous chapter, may be taken as typical (Figure 13.9).

A Jie homestead ordinarily contains the families of from six to eight men, all descendants of one grandfather. The social base of the household is therefore the patrilineage (see pages 413–414). Families are polygynous (multiple wives) (see pages 399–401). All the wives, their children, and the married sons with their wives and children live within the compound—thirty to forty people. The compound is a palisaded pole brush fence in which the only openings are small apertures 3 feet square. Anyone entering must crawl on hands and knees, presenting the head for a death blow in case the person is not welcome.

Ringing the inner side of the wall is a series of fenced yards—one for each married woman. Here she has a small thatched hut with no windows, which is used only for sleeping in rainy weather. Otherwise, sleeping, cooking, and eating are done in the open yard, although some wives build a kitchen hut with open sides. Every woman's yard also contains a small house for young cattle, and this is used as a kitchen if there is no regular one. Each yard also has at least two large plastered baskets on stilts for storage of grain. The yard of each wife is her own domain. Although the yards of co-wives are adjacent to each other, no door leads directly from one to another. It is necessary to go out into the cattle pens to achieve passage to any other yard. The

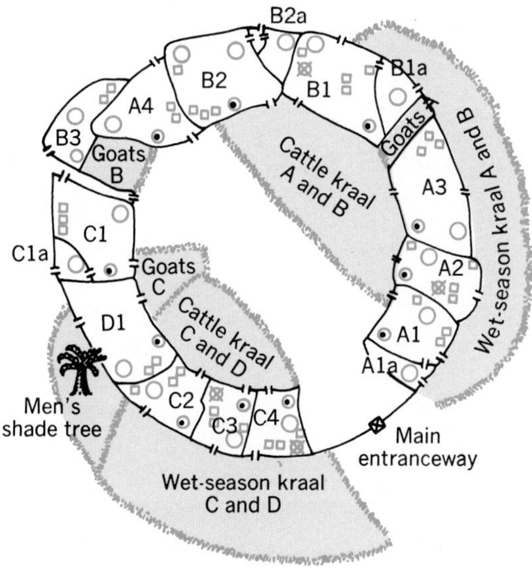

FIGURE 13.9
The ground plan of a Jie household. The yards lettered A belong to the wives of one man; the Bs are the yards of the wives of a brother; and the Cs, the yards of yet another brother, and so forth. The entire homestead is physically and socially a tight unit, discrete among all the other homesteads of a tribe. (From *The Family Herds* by P. H. Gulliver, Routledge & Kegan Paul, Ltd., London, 1955. By permission.)

cattle and goat pens (kraals) take up about half the interior courtyard of the homestead. Here the livestock are herded at night, except in the rainy season, when they are kept in outside kraals.

The unity of the lineage is clearly symbolized and reinforced by the nature of the homestead.[11]

[11]For more detail, see P. H. Gulliver, *The Family Herds.*

Pueblos: From Pit House to Communal Appartment House

From the pit house to the great five-storied apartment buildings of the Pueblos of the Southwest United States is a great distance to travel in the span of a millennium. The Anasazi, of which the contemporary living Pueblos are descendants, lived in the high plateaus of the Southwest. In their earliest known phases (about 2,000 years ago), these people lived in pit houses.

Sinking the floor of the house into the ground before raising the superstructure is a technique adapted to cold winters. The semisubterranean house has two advantages: (1) it is easier to keep warm, and (2) it can be made roomy without raising high side walls.

The pit house was in frequent use in Late Pleistocene Siberia and survived into the present century among the sedentary fishing cultures of that land. Its archaeological distribution and details of structure indicate clearly that the pit house was carried into western North America by early migrants from the Asian mainland.[12]

The Anasazi Tradition The evolution of the Anasazi begins with the Basket Maker period (A.D. 100 to 500). Basket Maker houses were constructed of inclined posts, poles, and twigs laid horizontally to form a dome around and above a saucerlike pit 10 to 20 feet in diameter. The frame was plastered over with mud. Individual houses were built in small groups, either within shallow caves or in the open.

In the succeeding Modified Basket Maker period (A.D. 500 to 700), pit houses still prevailed. They consisted of a framework of four or five uprights supporting a flat roof. Entrance was

[12]See W. Jochelson, "Past and Present Subterranean Dwellings of the Tribes of North Eastern Asia and North Western America" (*Proceedings of the Fifteenth International Congress of Americanists*, 1907).

FIGURE 13.10
The Hopi pueblo of Walpi was built atop a steep-sided mesa, or table rock. All supplies had to be carried up steep and well-protected trails. A graded highway now provides access to Walpi, but physically the pueblo is little changed from what it was many centuries ago. (Roland Reed, 1913/Kramer Gallery.)

gained either through the smoke hole over the fire pit or through a projecting passageway on the south side of the house. A low ridge of mud separated the south from the north half of the house.

Two lines of architectural development emerged in this period. In addition to the pit house described above, there was a long, flat-roofed structure of poles and mud that contained two rows of contiguous rooms. Some of these buildings were in the shape of crescents.

In the period of the Modified Basket Maker, the pit houses were used for ceremonial and dwelling purposes. The multiroomed surface houses were apparently used mostly for storage. Later, in the Pueblo periods, the pit house evolved into the underground ceremonial chamber, or *kiva*. The aboveground storage rooms became the multiple-apartment houses for which the Pueblo Indians are justly famous. The climax was reached between A.D. 1000 and 1300 in the Pueblo III period. To this period belong the large settlements in rock shelters, including Cliff Palace in Mesa Verde National Park. Of the open sites of this period, Pueblo Bonito in Chaco Canyon, New Mexico, is the

FIGURE 13.11

Taos Pueblo in northeastern New Mexico is a classic, multistoried compact stone and adobe-plastered sedentary village. Except for the addition of doors and windows, it remains much as it was when first visited by Coronado, the Spanish explorer, in 1540. The tribe allows no electricity or piped water within the pueblo, although these utilities are available to pueblo members who live just outside the old village. (Joseph Muench.)

best known. These buildings contained hundreds of rooms built of coursed masonry walls rising often to four stories. The modern pueblos are smaller versions of the Great Period (Figures 13.10 and 13.11).

The Configuration of Pueblo Culture

There is a close nexus between the communal houses of the Pueblos and the general configuration of Pueblo culture. The pueblos of the Great Period were defensive citadels as well as domiciles. The outer ground-level walls of the open-site pueblos were blank surfaces with no doors or windows. To enter a house, one had to climb to the roof and go down the smoke hole, as in the pit house. To the hostile outer world the pueblo turned its back. It faced inward upon the court, in which the dances of rich ceremonialism occurred. The great building formed a compact, architecturally integrated, in-turned whole (Figure 13.11). The members of the pueblo were forced to live in the closest intimacy with one another; not just the members of one household, each of which had its own apartment of one or several rooms, but all families, all clans, were piled together in a great heap. The cooperative emphasis of Pueblo life was thus reflected in its housing.

We agree with the conclusion of Steward in speaking of the Basket Maker and Pueblo I cultures: "It is difficult to reconcile the division of the early villages into small house clusters with any other social unit than the unilateral lineage or band."[13] Steward and Titiev[14] both suggest that a movement of consolidation of independent clans or bands in Pueblo II times resulted in the building of communal houses. "The formerly separated small groups are amalgamated, but do not lose their social and ceremonial integrity."[15]

The crowded intimacy of Pueblo living produced factionalism, excessive touchiness, quarreling, backbiting, and fear of witchcraft—centrifugal forces which led again and again to the breakup of pueblos and the establishment of new settlements. Well-integrated religio-ceremonial structures have to a great degree counteracted the tendency toward breakup in Pueblo society. However, the hundreds of ruined pueblos which make the Southwest an archaeologist's paradise are rich testimony to the long Pueblo struggle to adjust their house forms to changing social organization.

SUMMARY

The settlement pattern of a group of people depends on the food resources available, the skills the people have to make use of the resources, previous adaptations, developmental changes, cultural contacts, and other factors. The five types of settlement patterns range from those of nomadic societies to those of groups having compact, permanent towns or villages or complex towns with outlying settlements.

Housing is variable in structure, depending upon local climate and materials, the subsistence economy, and the social organization of the society.

Nomadic peoples, hunters and gatherers, ordinarily construct simple, temporary shelters. Nomadic pastoralists produce technologically more elaborate structures. The ground plans of the homes of wanderers are usually round, for this type of layout produces the largest volume of living space for the least expended effort. Domed houses and tents are capable of withstanding more wind pressure for the amount of material used than any other form of structure.

Gardeners and agriculturalists construct more permanent dwellings. With a subsistence based on cultivated fields, these people are most likely to be stable in their residence and thus willing to expend the work required to build more permanent homes.

Dwelling patterns are intimately related to social structure as well as to physical environment. Sexual segregation in New Guinea results in separate small houses for males and females. In societies built around the joint-family or localized lineage, such as the Iroquois, a single housing unit may serve as a common dwelling. Such joint-family houses found in many cultures, both prehistoric and contemporary, exemplify the close interrelationship between social and architectural forms.

[13]J. H. Steward, "Ecological Aspects of Southwestern Society" (*Anthropos*, vol. 32, 1937), p. 99.

[14]M. Titiev, *Old Oraibi* (Papers of the Peabody Museum of American Archaeology and Ethnology, Harvard University, vol. 22, no. 1, 1944), pp. 96–99.

[15]Steward, op. cit., p. 96.

SELECTED READINGS

Fortes, M., *The Web of Kinship among the Tallensi* (1949), chap. 3, "The Homestead and the Joint Family." A model study of the functional interrelation of home and family.

Loeb, E. M., and J. O. M. Broek, "Social Organization and the Long House in Southeast Asia" (*American Anthropologist*, vol. 49, 1947), pp. 414–425. A useful analysis of the relation between lineage and homestead.

Murdock, G. P., *Our Primitive Contemporaries* (1934). Sections in each chapter devoted to the ethnography of a tribe describe a variety of house types.

Rapoport, A., *House Form and Culture* (1969). Written by an architect–city planner who utilizes information from various disciplines.

14 Technological Adaptations

CHAPTER OUTLINE

LEARNING GOALS

Identify the types of materials used for tools and handicrafts.

Review the varieties of containers fashioned by humans.

Identify the uses of fabrics.

Discuss the different kinds of clothing and ornaments worn by people and how these are related to environmental factors.

We have seen in Chapters 12 and 13 that the requirements of making a living, together with the limitations imposed by the environment, dictate the type of subsistence and housing enjoyed by a society. In the same manner we saw how available materials and knowledge of their use played a large part in these matters.

We now turn to tools, handicrafts, clothing, and ornaments as manifestations of other cultural adaptations to the environment. We will see how subsistence, environment, available materials, and cultural know-how influence form and function here, too.

TOOLS AND HANDICRAFTS

Tools are devices for transforming, transmitting, or storing energy. In this they are similar to domesticated plants and animals. The energy theory of culture (pages 634–636) holds that the cultural and social complexity of a people is directly related to the energy-utilization capacities created by their technology. Thus far, we have given attention to the larger food-getting and subsistence activities of human beings: hunting-fishing-gathering, foraging, gardening, pastoralism, and intensive agriculture. We have studied them as systems. We have not, however, except in a few cases, explicitly discussed the artifacts which make the operation of these systems possible.

We have seen the development of garden tools from simple digging stick to hoe to plow (to tractor and combine). As subsistence methods became more efficient, resulting food surpluses required containers for storage, cooking equipment, utensils for eating, transport for trading.

Herskovits has pointed out that the machine, a contrivance by which energy is converted from one form to another, is known to nonliterate peoples, and cites wedges, levers, rollers, bellows, looms, and drills as examples of simple machines which maximize strength or produce more energy.[1]

> *Even peoples whose equipment is of the simplest, who have no machines such as these, employ mechanical principles that are quite complex. The boomerang of the Australian, the heavy knobkerrie of the South African Bantu, the spear-thrower—all show a shrewd utilization of physical forces that give the individual added flexibility and power in using his physical capacities. The use of the principle of the spring in the manufacture of the compound bow is another instance of this. Even the simpler type of bow, made of one piece of wood, recognizes and allows for the elasticity of wood, while the bow-string compounds the same principle, and the feathered arrow insures better aim.*[2]

Certainly, in examining material culture, one is struck by the ingenuity and resourcefulness of the toolmakers. It is an observable fact that many modern hand tools vary little from ancient models except in materials and method of production; the basic principles, and often the design, are identical.

Materials

Before the recent invention of plastics, the materials from which instruments could be made were limited mostly to stone, bone, horn, shell, wood, hide, animal and vegetable fibers, gold, copper, tin, bronze, and iron.

Stone Almost all preliterate peoples were dependent upon stone as the material for making cutting and scraping implements. The greater part of human existence in Europe occurred in the Stone Age. In North and South America, while the peoples of high culture knew metallurgy, it is proper to say that all the Indians were "Neolithic people" as were all the Oceanic peoples of the Pacific, although it must be remembered that on coral islands rocks other

[1]M. J. Herskovits, *Cultural Anthropology*, pp. 119–120.
[2]Ibid., pp. 120–121.

FIGURE 14.1
!Kung Bushmen (Africa) prepare a deadlly hunting poison from natural vegetable and insect products. The technologist carefully smears it on the arrow shaft, enabling the hunter to bring down large game, such as the giraffe, which his arrows would otherwise only slightly wound. The bowl in which the paste is mixed is made from the kneecap of a giraffe. (Irven DeVore.)

than flint had to be used. Africa south of the Sudan was given over to tribes with lithic technologies, while many of the Sudanese people were well advanced in ironworking and bronze casting.

The most fundamental classification of stone implements is the one that draws a distinction between chipped and abraded (polished) artifacts.

Flint, chert, and chalcedony are preferred materials because of their fracture qualities. By percussion delivered by means of a hammerstone, which is a round or oval igneous or metamorphic rock, a fresh nodule of flint yields flakes from its surface. Since the outer edge of the flake is almost always thin and sharp, flakes may be used as crude cutting or scraping tools with no further preparation. The residual core of the nodule is also suitable for use as a crude ax.

The addition of pressure flaking permits skilled workers possessing high-quality flint to manufacture specialized flint artifacts. In pressure flaking the force is applied on the nodule to remove flakes with a piece of antler or other bone rather than with a hammerstone or cylinder.

The basic flake implements of almost all nonliterate people are scrapers, points, and awls. Scrapers are used mostly in the preparation of skins or in the shaping of wooden shafts for weapons and tools. Points are used as penetrating heads for various kinds of projectiles: darts, arrows, spears (Figure 14.1), or as knife blades. Cores may also be worked into scrapers and points, but generally they are shaped to form hand axes or celts.

Abrasion is used to shape rocks that fracture poorly. The outer surface of an intended artifact may be worn into shape by being rubbed on sandstone or with a piece of sandstone held in the hand, and sawed in two by using thin slabs of sandstone or by pouring wet sand under a piece of wood that is rubbed back and forth.

The simplest form of hafting is to bind a strip of sapling around the stone. Elaborations of this technique, using cord or rawhide, occur in all parts of the world. An advantageous improvement is to groove the axhead by grinding or pecking in order to give a firmer setting to the head. The process of drilling a hole in a stone hammerhead is actually the most advanced technique for hafting purposes.

Bone, Shell, and Horn Unworked shells make serviceable if not durable scrapers and saucers. Caribbean Indians rubbed heavy seashells into polished celts. The long bones of birds and animals, splintered and polished to a smooth point, have always found favor as perforators and awls, and the earliest needles were made of slivers of bone. Fishhooks made of bone occur almost everywhere. Harpoon heads of bone, antler, or ivory were characteristic of the Magdalenians and Eskimos alike (Figure 10.5, page 172).

One of the most interesting bone implements is the garden hoe produced by Indians in the eastern Plains area from the shoulder blade of the bison. The scoop-shaped scapula was lashed at right angles to a wooden handle and used exactly as we use a hoe today.

Wood It seems certain that Paleolithic peoples relied as much upon wood as upon stone for artifacts. This statement, however, is based on inference from recent nonliterate cultures rather than direct archaeological evidence. Eskimos use relatively less than most peoples, for the simple reason that trees do not grow in the arctic. Northwest Coast Indians, endowed as they were with excellent workable cedar, used wood to manufacture plank houses, totem poles, adze handles, canoes, paddles, clubs, bows, arrows, helmets and slat armor, bowls, dishes, spoons, boxes, rattles, batons, and masks in a profusion of carved and painted varieties.

With stone-bladed adzes as weapons and as woodworking tools, the Oceanic peoples of the South Pacific shaped wood into canoes as they made the ocean and its far-scattered islands their own.

Because of the importance of the controlled use of fire in cultural development, it may be well to underline the universal use of the wood drill.

By setting the drill in a wood socket and pouring dry tinder about it, it is possible to generate enough heat by friction to start a fire. Hand-rotation, strap, bow, and pump methods are all used. In Indonesia the fire saw, a variant form, is preferred. In this method, a piece of split bamboo is sawed so rapidly that the dust ignites.

The ability to drill through solid stone has been evident since Neolithic times. The drills are simple wooden rods or tubes rotated between the hands or by mechanical means. Wet sand does the actual cutting. Although rotation between the hands was unquestionably the earliest drill technique, it is probable that Neolithic peoples hit upon the bow drill, since they had the bow and arrow. The trick of the bow drill, as every Boy Scout who has passed his fire-by-friction test knows, is to wind the bowstring once around the drill, hold the top of the drill in a hand socket, and then saw back and forth with the bow like a cello player. The Eskimo takes a bite on the socket instead of a handgrip (Figure 14.2). The strap drill works on the principle of the bow drill, except that there is no bow. The ends of the working thong are simply held in the hands and drawn back and forth. A clever refinement is the pump drill. By first winding up the string on the drill shaft and then pushing the crossbar down, a spin is imparted to the drill. The momentum given to it by the stone or pottery flywheel automatically rewinds the string. Another downward push keeps it spinning.

Metals Metallurgy is scarcely a simple craft, for it requires a highly developed technological knowledge. Yet preliterate people did acquire metalworking skill. This was probably true of the Europeans, as well as of the peoples of the Mediterranean and Asia, during the prehistoric Bronze and Iron Ages, of many Africans, the Peruvian Indians, and Indonesian peoples.

The beating out of gold nuggets or chunks of

FIGURE 14.2
The ancient bowdrill is still preferred by many Eskimo craftsmen for drilling in bone and ivory. The drill is held firmly in the mouth and rotated by sawing back and forth with the bow. (Steve McCutcheon/Alaska Pictorial Service.)

pure copper does not constitute metallurgy. Indians in the copper-rich regions of Lake Superior made tubular arrowheads and spearheads of beaten native copper. Eskimos fashioned a few rare tools out of the iron residue of meteorites found on the frozen surface of the ground. But no North American Indian knew how to smelt metal.

The Mexicans, who knew how to melt gold nuggets with the aid of blowpipes, came close to the secret of smelting ores. The Peruvians smelted copper and tin, which were mined from hills looked upon as sacred shrines. Inca metalworking processes included smelting, alloying (bronze), casting, hammering, repoussé, incrustation, inlay, soldering, riveting, and cloisonné.

The Africans concentrated upon the more prosaic tools of the blacksmith's forge. From iron smelted in little clay blast furnaces with hand bellows, they shaped such utilitarian tools as knives, adzes, axes, and hoes; even the most mundane tools may be shaped with artistic love when they are to be endowed with symbolic value. Bronze casting in West Africa reached a peak of artistic perfection in the work of the Bina at Benin that has made the Benin masks precious collectors' items. The Benin method of casting is the "lost-wax" technique, or cire perdue, in which a model is first made of wax and then covered with clay. The wax is then melted

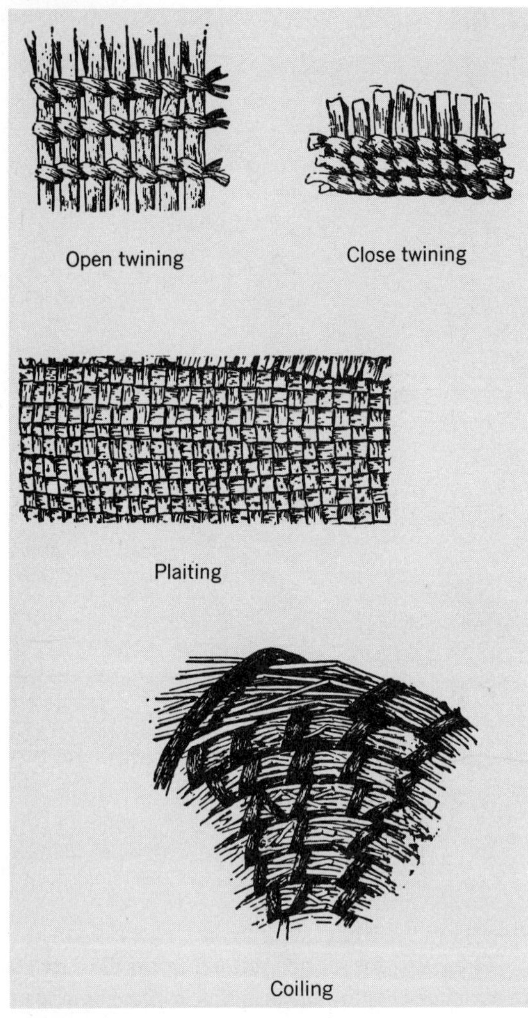

FIGURE 14.3
Basketry techniques. (After C. Wissler, *The American Indian.*)

out when the molten metal is poured into the mold. When the clay molds are broken, the casting is freed.

Containers

All human beings use containers. Skin pouches or bags may serve to meet this need. Containers may also be made of wood or clay. But of all these possibilities, baskets, which are made of interwoven reeds, grass, or shredded bark (bast), have by far the widest distribution.

Bags and Baskets Direct archaeological evidence yields basketry remains from the Neolithic sites of Europe and the Archaic Desert culture of the United States. In the American Southwest, elaborate basketry skill gave the name Basket Maker to the potteryless pre-Pueblo inhabitants of the area.

The simplest basketry container (made by the marginal food collectors, the Fuegians and other southern South Americans, the Australians, and Bushmen) is a loose, open-weave bag such as that used to package onions and oranges in the United States.

Bags of genuine netting are not so much woven as worked out in crochet patterns. *Knotless netting*, as this technique is called, occurs throughout a large part of the Western Hemisphere and in Oceania and Australia.[3]

A basket differs from a bag in that it is at least semirigid, if not actually stiff. It is built upon its own frame, or its foundation is formed as it is made (Figure 14.4). The body is produced by the interlocking of long strips or threads of fibrous materials such as dried reeds, grasses, split cane, or shredded bark. Basketry materials can be found in all environments. Several of the basketmaking techniques, including plaiting, twining, and coiling, are illustrated in Figure 14.3.

Twined and coiled baskets are used to hold not only dry stuffs but also water when they are closely woven and sealed with clay or pitch. The Shoshone Indians made their drinking-water baskets slightly permeable, like Western water bags. Enough liquid seeps through to keep the water cool by evaporation, and a gentle flavoring

[3]D. S. Davidson, "Knotless Netting in America and Oceania" (*American Anthropologist*, vol. 37, 1935), pp. 117–134.

FIGURE 14.4
A contemporary Navajo Indian woman fries bread in American-made metal pans, which are substitutes for pottery, but serves it in a traditional basket. (Ray Manley.)

from the pine gum used as the sealing agent makes a delectable drink.

In North America there is a close association between tightly twined and coiled basketry and stone boiling as a method of cookery. Preheated stones are grasped with wooden tongs and held in the basketful of water. The heat of the stones brings the water to a boil. In the Plains area, a pouch of skin suspended on four stakes was used in the same way.

Pottery Conversely, where pottery is well developed, basketry is not used for cooking purposes. Once the techniques are known, pottery is quicker and easier to make than baskets.[4] More than that, it is more efficient for cooking purposes, since it may be put directly over the fire.

The first pottery was not invented until Mesolithic times. The earliest migrants to North America left Asia before the technique of pottery making had spread to Siberia. There are no

[4]The reader interested in the details of basketry should consult O. T. Mason, *Aboriginal American Basketry* (United States National Museum, Annual Report, 1904), pp. 171–548. For a discussion and analysis of ethnological problems in basketry, see G. Weltfish, "Prehistoric North American Basketry Techniques and Modern Distributions," (*American Anthropologist*, vol. 32, 1930), pp. 454–495.

shards (pottery fragments) associated with the earliest prehistoric finds in North America. Not until the Modified Basket Maker period (A.D. 500 to 700) did the people of the Anasazi culture, who were later to become such skilled potters, start to make ceramic vessels.

In Central America and the Andean region, archaic pottery making began earlier. It is most likely that pottery was invented in this area, from where it spread out to other parts of the New World.

In general the distribution of primitive pottery follows the distribution of gardening and agriculture. Food gatherers and hunters either are too far removed from the centers of pottery invention to have received the art by diffusion, or, because of their nomadic life, have rejected clay pots as too burdensome.

Fabrics

Weaving is an outgrowth of netting and basketry. Its product is textile fabric. It differs from basketry in that the strands are so pliable and fine that they must be worked on a loom,[5] which is a device for holding the warp threads taut.[6] Such strands are string or thread made of animal or vegetable fibers.

Twine The manufacture of twine is universal. In the simplest method, fibers are simply rolled between the palms or between the thigh and the hand. Spindles were independently developed in Egypt and much later in Central and South America. The simple spindle is a long, narrow stick with a stone or pottery collar near one end which serves as a balance wheel and keeps the thread from running off. A rough string of fiber wound several times about the spindle and held taut with the left hand is tightly twisted and simultaneously wound around the spindle, which is spun by hand. Several spinnings are needed to produce an even thread.

Weaving In spite of the fact that cord or thread making is universal, weaving is not. Although an ancient art in the Mediterranean area, India, Indonesia, and prehistoric Europe, it did not extend deeply into the tropical forests of Africa (although it is practiced in the Sudan). It was a lost art in most of Polynesia, where its absence was adequately met by bark cloth (as it was in the African Congo). In Melanesia and the Micronesian Caroline Islands, a limited amount of weaving was done, but here, too, the preference was for bark cloth.

In the Americas, the Andean region around A.D. 1200 became the center for some of the finest and most complicated handwoven fabrics the world has ever known. The direction of the textile industry became one of the most important interests of the Inca government, which levied taxes, fines, and tribute in cloth.

Archaeological stratigraphy gives a clear sequence for the development of looms in the Andean area. The belt loom was the earliest (Mochica culture, A.D. 600 to 700). It was followed by a horizontal frame loom supported on stakes, which is still preferred by Aymara Indians. Finally, it was followed by a vertical four-pole frame loom built against the wall.

From the Inca center, true loom weaving is distributed north and south along the Andean cordillera, and up through Central America and Mexico into the Southwest. Native American cotton is the chief material used from the Southwest down through South America.[7]

Suspended-warp weaving is done without a true loom. It calls for finger weaving without the aid of a heddle. Chilkat blankets from the North-

[5]Knitting and crocheting are special forms of close netting, not weaving.

[6]The *warp* is the group of parallel-lying foundation threads over and through which the *weft*, or *woof*, is woven at right angles.

[7]See L. M. O'Neale, "Weaving," in J. H. Steward (ed.), *Handbook of South American Indians*, vol. 5, *The Comparative Ethnology of South American Indians*, pp. 97–138.

west Coast are the most famous product of this kind of weaving. The warp of shredded cedar bark is suspended free-hanging from a horizontal pole supported on two uprights. The weaving is done from top to bottom, as the weaver works the woolen weft in and out with the fingers.[8]

Felting Weaving and spinning are two ways to interlock fibrous materials to form a compact cloth covering; felting, in which animal wools are matted together by wetting, beating, forming in sheets, compressing, and drying, is another. Of course, felting is possible only where woolly animals provide a source of materials.

Bark Cloth In such tropical areas as Indonesia, Oceania, Central Africa, and Central and South America, bark fibers are used in the same manner as wool. The principle underlying the manufacture of felt and bark cloth is the same: a sheet of material is produced by matting fibers so tightly that they adhere permanently. However, geographical distribution and analysis of its cultural context make it clear that bark-cloth manufacture was independently invented.

The fibrous inner bark of a suitable tree, such as the paper mulberry (which is cultivated for this purpose in Polynesia), is stripped, scraped, and beaten out with a grooved wooden mallet or paddle on a wood anvil. It may or may not be soaked in water as a part of the preparatory process. Where it is, there is no limit to the size of the cloth that can be made, since one piece may readily and effectively be "felted" into another.

CLOTHING AND ORNAMENTS

In all times and climes, people undertake what they believe are improvements upon their bodily appearance. The time and effort that have gone into making clothing and painting, pricking, scarring, puncturing, and otherwise mutilating and deforming the human body for aesthetic and prestige reasons are beyond calculation.

People living in frigid climes build shelters and fire with which to warm themselves. They also utilize animal hides and blankets as a substitute for their deficiencies (Figure 14.5).

The invention of clothing for insulation was not the only culturally adaptive alternative. In the mountains of New Guinea even today, a thick coating of pig grease serves to hold in body heat during the chill, dank night and foggy morning hours. Prehistoric peoples could have done the same. And this may well have provided one foundation for overall body paint, the grease forming a natural medium for pulverized dry pigments, such as red ocher, which was all the Tasmanians commonly wore.

Protection against the elements, however, is but one of the factors which underlie the impulse toward clothing, and in view of the fact that clothing is often ill-adapted to a specific environment, it may not be the primary motivation. A sense of modesty or shame, the need for visible distinctions between classes and social groups, and a desire for display and adornment all come into play. There is considerable uniformity of dress (or undress) and style within each society, but almost universally there are distinctions between the costumes of men and women, children and adults, leaders, kings, chiefs, and commoners.[9]

The Undressed Person

People who wear little or no clothing do not contradict what has just been said. They wear G-strings, sport nose, ear, or lip plugs, bear tattoos or scarifications, paint the face, curl the hair or cut it off, blacken the teeth or knock them out or file them to a point. Thus, the Central

[8] See C. Amsden, "The Loom and Its Prototypes" (*American Anthropologist*, vol. 34, 1932), pp. 216–235.

[9] L. Spier, "Inventions and Human Society," in H. L. Shapiro (ed.), *Man, Culture, and Society*, p. 228.

FIGURE 14.5
Piegan Blackfoot family wrapped in blankets makes its way through a snowstorm, an armed warrior in front, followed by the head of the family leading his wife, whose horse drags the travois on which rides their child. (Roland Reed, 1912/Kramer Gallery.)

Australians, for example, seem never to have hit upon the idea of wearing animal skins for clothing. For the men, armbands of twisted fur and a conspicuous pubic tassel suspended from a belt of human hair sufficed. A woman was "dressed" if she had a string of beads around her neck.

People who dwell in the tropical rain forests get along with a minimum of clothing. Generally, however, the men wear some sort of pubic covering, a suspensory or supporter (Figure 14.6). An alternative is a small apron of leather, grass, or cloth worn in front, or fore and aft, or between the legs and about the waist. Such a garment is frequently worn by women as well as men.

Modesty Modesty is a habit, not an instinct. The discomfiture that is felt when one's sense of modesty is disturbed is a diffused, neurophysiological upset of the nervous and organic system, triggered by a situation that contrasts sharply with the usual and standard state of affairs. Apprehension of dire consequences contributes fear and anxiety to color the feelings of immod-

FIGURE 14.6
Adapting to the climate of a mountainous tropical rain forest, the Ifugao warrior wears little but a woven loincloth, cap, and an auxiliary blanket. (Benny Araw-Panamin.)

esty. As late as 1936, for example, old-timers among Comanche males felt acutely uncomfortable and indecent if they thoughtlessly went out without a G-string, even though fully clothed in pants and shirt.

Robes When warmth is needed, something more must be added. Shoshones wove rabbit-skin robes, as did the early prehistoric Basket Makers. African Bushmen provided themselves with skin cloaks. The Yahgan of Tierra del Fuego wore a small sealskin, sea-otter, or fox cape as the sole protection against a nasty subantarctic climate—except for a small pubic covering worn by women.

In North America, the artistically woven Chilkat blankets of the Northwest Coast Indians, made in four colors of dyed goat's wool and cedar-bark thread, were totemically elegant versions of everyday robes woven of cedar bark only.

In the Plains, the buffalo-hide robe was also a form of cape, later to be replaced by the trader's blanket, which is to this day the symbol of the conservative Indian, the "blanket Indian," who clings to the old ways (Figure 14.5).

Tailoring

Tailoring means that by cutting and sewing, clothing may be made to fit the human frame. In

FIGURE 14.7
The tailored skin clothing of the Eskimo hunter makes life in the Arctic humanly possible. The fur of the skins is worn on the inside for maximum insulation and preservation of body heat. Not only is the clothing a highly efficient form of adaptation, but its pleasing decoration expresses a strong aesthetic value and artistic technique. (Courtesy of the American Museum of Natural History.)

temperate and arctic climates, it is functionally advantageous to have tailored clothes. The insulating efficiency of clothing is greatly enhanced by the closed, tubular effect of the garment, which gives little room for the play of chilly breezes upon the body. In the tropical rain forest or torrid desert, the very advantages of tailored clothing become its disadvantages.

Tailored clothing was made originally among the arctic and subarctic peoples of Siberia and North America and the ancient Chinese. Real tailoring is done by the Eskimos and Indians of the Canadian woods. Coats are fitted with genuine sleeves and necks. Eskimo garments with the fur turned in and the outer skin dyed and decorated are not only functional but also aesthetic (Figure 14.7).

The westward diffusion of tailoring from China or Siberia did not occur until a number of centuries after the European conquests of Caesar. When tailored clothing became the symbol of the European conqueror, human creatures in all parts of the world enclosed their bodies in suits and dresses.

Footgear

Among nonliterate peoples, footgear is more common than headgear. The status functions of headgear can be served readily enough by hairdos. The protective function of hats is notably less important than the protective function of shoes. Here again, the physical environment is an important factor in influencing the adoption of an element of material culture.

The problem of fabricating a foot covering that will stand up under the wet rot of the tropical jungle is practically unsolvable. Even the best contemporary efforts, with all the resources of science, are still not very satisfactory. Jungle inhabitants prefer to go barefoot. An unshod foot dries more quickly and comfortably than one encased in a soaking and muddy moccasin.

Even more important is the simple fact that it is easier to walk barefoot on mud-slick trails, especially on hills and mountains. Flexed toes in the mud can get a grip which corrugated soles or cleats cannot—the latter clog up and encase the feet in a gooey ball.

Yet, however calloused the soles of unshod feet may become, cuts can be seriously crippling through opening the system to parasitic diseases and leprosy. Consequently, if the climate does not discourage it, most peoples have provided themselves with sandals, moccasins, shoes, or boots.

FIGURE 14.8
Leather making. A Bushman hunter pegs out a hide on the ground to stretch it for tanning. (Anthro-Photo.)

Sandals In reasonably mild, not too wet, temperate parts of the world such as the Mediterranean area and into South Asia, the sandal finds most widespread use. In its simplest form, it is a piece of leather roughly fitted to the sole and held firm by thongs passing over the foot.

Sandals with woven fiber soles were very popular with prehistoric Southwestern and Great Basin Indians. Wissler noted, "In eastern North America moccasins were discarded when walking in the rain, in wet grass, or upon moist ground."[10] This was also true of the Incas with their rawhide-soled sandals, which would become soft and squishy when wet, and then hard and out of shape when dried (Figure 14.8).

[10]C. Wissler, *The American Indian* (3d ed.), p. 65.

Moccasins and Boots Another simple footgear is a piece of hide folded about the foot. When tailored, it becomes a moccasin of the type made famous by the North American Indians. Further development of this form produced the boot. The so-called arctic boot, which extends well above the knee, is an adjunct of true tailoring. People who have to plod around in snow and cold find high tops more comfortable. However, we have learned in anthropology not to expect that necessity mothers invention or emulation. The Indians of the Canadian woodlands, who made tailored clothing and were confronted with heavy snows, made moccasins instead of boots, in spite of the fact that the more

FIGURE 14.9
A coiled headring enables the Ifugao women of northern Luzon, the Philippines, to carry basket trays with ease. Tattooing embellishes her arms. (United Nations.)

northerly of these Indians were in contact with boot-wearing Eskimos.

Hairdo and Headgear

We do not know when the earliest prehistoric men and women first began to play with the cranial hair, but archaeological evidence from the Upper Paleolithic in Europe demonstrates that people laid great emphasis upon the female hairdo. In the Gravettian statuette of the Venus of Willendorf (Figure 10.8, page 175), no facial features were carved by the artist, but the pattern of the hairstyle is meticulously incised.

Add to this the fact that all recent peoples, whatever their culture, give attention to the dressing of hair, and we may thus conclude that it is a universal trait in human culture.

Hairstyles and Social Status The trimming and arrangement of the hair are not merely matters of decoration and ornamentation; in culture after culture, it also serves to symbolize one's social position. The most basic status represented in the treatment of the hair is that of sex. Males and females within any society usually fix the hair differently.

Hairstyles also indicate age status. Omaha Indian boys had their heads shaved close, with isolated tufts of hair left here and there. Men either wore their full head of hair lying loose or shaved it off except for a continuous roach along the sagittal line. Among the Omahas, the shaved heads of the boys indicated more than just age status, for the patterns of the remaining tufts were different for each clan. "The cutting of the hair was done, it was said, in order to impress on the mind of a child, as in an object lesson, the gentes [patrilineal clan] to which a playmate belonged."[11]

Headgear It is probably safe to say that only in the coldest regions do we find headgear related to climate. The fur-lined parka of the Eskimo is so well adapted to frigid temperatures that it has long been copied by other contemporary dwellers in cold winter areas. The Eskimos of East Greenland developed gorgeous caps made of foxskin with visors of embroidered sealskin—works of elegance which went far beyond purely utilitarian requirements. Along with eyeshades attached to the parka, some Eskimo tribes developed snow goggles made of wood with a narrow open slit to protect hunters from snow blindness.

Aside from the frigid zones where covering is an absolute necessity, head covering is more a matter of pure beautification, status identification, or ceremonialism than of comfort. Almost every material available is employed in the construction of the highly decorative creations with which men and women have adorned their heads: feathers, furs, reeds, grasses, leather, hair, teeth, shells, insect wings, bones, seeds, beads, fibers, metals, flowers, tusks, and more. Seldom is only one material used. A rattan basketry crown may be embellished with animal teeth, bone hairpins, and feathers (Figure 14.9). Masks for special occasions may be a complementary and necessary part of the hat.

Feathers are among the most widely distributed head decorations; their use ranges from a single feather stuck in the hair or headband to the elaborate Plains Indian war bonnet, an intricate construction of hide, beads, fur, horns, and eagle feathers which may trail from the crown of the head to the heels of the wearer.

In most societies, the type of headgear and/or hair dressing provides instant social identification. The chief, king, priest, shaman, or other leader is usually literally "topped off" by some symbol of headship. As nonliterate societies became acquainted with European fashions, the hat of the foreigner was often the most envied article of apparel, and the chief frequently abandoned the traditional "crown" for the visitor's top hat.

In all the foregoing discussions, certain parallels with contemporary civilizations will immediately come to mind. Specialized roles, particularly those denoting authority, often call for specialized garb: the doctor's white coat, the police officer's cap and badge, the priest's vestments.

Ornaments and Ornamentation

Jewelry and cosmetics are purely decorative "luxuries." Yet to obtain them, Americans spend well over 5 billion dollars annually; in nonliterate societies men and women not only expend vast amounts of energy and time but undergo agony, torture, and discomfort to achieve the gratification of proper grooming.

Cosmetics Lotions, pastes, powders, pigments and perfumes to alter the texture, color, feel, and smell of the external surfaces of the human body are universal cultural responses to the basic human need for favorable response. They are designed to heighten the stimulus intensity of the physical presence of one person upon the touch, smell, sight, and perhaps taste of others. Those others are usually members of the opposite sex, but not exclusively so.

Rouge is the most common cosmetic, perhaps because red ocher (iron oxide) occurs in many places and is readily obtained. It is interesting to speculate on the relationship between the popularity of rouge and the fact that red is the primary color with the longest wavelength perceptible to the human eye and the color with

[11]A. C. Fletcher and F. LaFlesche, *The Omaha Tribe* (Bureau of American Ethnology, Annual Report 27, 1911), p. 198.

the greatest natural stimulus value. When mixed with grease, it may be harmlessly applied to the human body. Yellow, black, blue, and white are the other favored colors.

Body painting is for the most part limited to special occasions, usually ritual and ceremonial. These events are out of the ordinary, and painting changes the individual from an ordinary person to one of distinction. War paint is usually linked to magical potency and serves less to frighten the enemy than to bolster the faint heart of its wearer.

Tattooing The trouble with paint and cosmetics is that the application is not lasting. The solution hit upon by many peoples is tattooing. A tattoo is made by puncturing the skin with needles carrying an indelible dye—usually carbon black. In North America, light tattooing is found among the Eskimos, continuing down the West Coast and into South America. The two high centers of the art, however, were Polynesia and Japan. Curiously, the status associations of tattooing in Polynesia and the civilized world are just reversed. Among Americans, soldiers and sailors in the lower ranks, longshoremen, unskilled laborers, and Hell's Angels are usually the persons who get tattooed. Among people of higher status, it is considered déclassé. But within the lower classes it serves as a symbol of masculinity and toughness. In Polynesia, the higher the social status, the fuller the tattooing. It extended over face, body, and limbs, and in some overenthusiastic cases, even to the tongue. The process was long drawn out and painful, but socially rewarding.

Scarification Tattooing posed a problem for the Africans and Australians. No white dye for tattooing was ever discovered by them. The solution hit upon in Africa and Australia was to incise the skin instead of puncturing it. Then ashes, grit, or other irritants were rubbed into the wounds, encouraging scar tissue to form, so that a series of raised lumps remained in a permanent visible pattern.

In Central Australia cicatrization, or *scarification*, as the process is called, is a part of the adolescent initiatory rites for boys. The patterns are simply parallel rows of lines on the chest and back. So important are they as symbols of manhood that individuals voluntarily repeat the operations in later life to keep their scars large and fresh.

Traditional German corps (fraternity) students and university men gave great kudos to dueling scars, which reputedly had much sex appeal. A wound that did not fester and leave a glaring scar was a dead loss. So important were the duel-born scarifications that persons who had no such scars were known to slash themselves with razors and rub salt in the wounds to create the impression that these, too, were the scars of honor.

Decorative Deformations and Mutilations Piercing of the nasal septum, the lips, or the ears, so that sundry bones, feathers, or shell, wood, or metal ornaments may be shoved through them, is found everywhere. The invention of the screw and spring clip has only recently obviated the need for ear piercing among women, who find the external earlobe a convenient appendage from which to dangle pretty baubles.

Incas, in South America, and Bagandas, among others in Africa, gradually extended the earlobes to receive thin disks as much as 6 to 8 inches in diameter. Inca nobility wore disks of gold. Separation of the cervical vertebrae and extension of the neck in ringed brass collars by Burmese women is another familiar distortion.

Cranial deformation was much esteemed as a mark of beauty by various Northwest American Indian tribes and also by the Incas and other Andean peoples, who bound a flat board against the frontal region of the head of a baby in the cradleboard in order to produce a recessed forehead and a high, peaked occipital. Binding with cloth to produce long heads was also practiced.

Circumcision, subincision, and clitoridectomy are not so much mutilations for ornamentation as they are mystical and status operations. The one is the removal of the foreskin of the penis; the second, a slitting of the skin and urethra along the length of the male sex organ; while the third is the surgical excision of the clitoris. Among the Central Australians, the first two operations symbolize masculinity in a male-dominated and ideologically masculine society; like scarification, they are performed without anesthesia and with flint knives on adolescent boys as a part of initiation into manhood. About half of the sub-Saharan African tribes also circumcise at adolescence, and for similar reasons. Circumcision is an absolutely required status mark of the Islamic male and orthodox Jew.[12]

Filing or knocking out of incisor teeth occurs in scattered distribution from Australia up through Melanesia and Indonesia, and over into Africa.

As this dicussion has shown, what is lost physically is gained socially, and perhaps psychologically. The need that is met is elemental. The fashion and jewelry industries, the cosmetic manufacturers and purveyors, and the beauticians may rest secure that their services have an assured future.

SUMMARY

Tools are artifactual extensions or substitutes for human limbs and other features of the body. With tools, human beings adapt their activities to a more efficient exploitation of their environment.

Stone tools are as old as humanity. Bone implements date from the Old Stone Age and are found in all parts of the world. Pottery and weaving represent high arts not developed until Neolithic times, but they subsequently spread virtually everywhere. Felting and the production of bark cloth are interesting specialized methods of producing fabrics used as body covering.

We can say that an age of handicrafts began in the Paleolithic Age and lasted until the industrial revolution in Europe. For most of humanity that age is dying only now. Although handicrafts have served humanity well for a million years, they do not greatly increase the human energy output. They require a heavy output of time and effort for a relatively small return in food or other consumable goods. Handicrafts survive as specialized arts in advanced civilizations, and handicraft technology reveals remarkable ingenuity, technical skill, and a high aesthetic quality.

Few, if any, peoples appear content with their bodies "as is." Body painting and jewelry found in burial sites dating as far back as the Upper Paleolithic attest to the antiquity of the practice of bodily decoration. The factors underlying this tendency are multiple. Protection from the weather is one clear motivation; however, except in arctic and desert zones where adequate covering is necessary for survival, the clothing of nonliterate peoples may be ill suited to the environment. Where insulation against cold is vital, people have fur or hide robes. A heavy body coating of grease is another means of conserving warmth. Bark, grass, woven reeds, and wool, depending upon which materials are available in the environment, are also used to make protective capes or robes. Tailored, or tubular, fitted clothing is a fairly recent Chinese or Siberian invention which diffused to northern American Indians without reaching the tropics of Middle and South America.

The sense of modesty, or shame, is postulated as another reason for clothing and bodily ornamentation. All societies have clear norms as to what constitutes proper dress, and all peoples seem to feel modesty. In many societies naked-

[12]See pp. 359–361 for a discussion of cicatrization, circumcision, and clitoridectomy as important symbols of status transition through initiatory rites.

ness is customary for one or both sexes, but propriety demands a particular headdress, lip plug, or piece of jewelry. Modesty is clearly a habit rather than an instinct.

Sexual enhancement, the display of wealth, and identification between social groups are other factors which assume significance as one examines patterns of clothing, jewelry, hairstyles, or body decoration. All attributes of dress are seemingly invested with deep emotional gratification, quite apart from utility or comfort.

Footgear is generally more utilitarian than other aspects of dress. Tropical people usually go barefoot. The sandal is worn in temperate and desert areas. The moccasin may have been the first form of self-shodding. When tailored (fitted), it becomes the American Indian type of moccasin, and when the sides of the moccasin are extended up the leg in the form of a tube, it becomes the arctic boot.

The artificial hairdo is a universal human cultural attribute as old as the Upper Paleolithic. Different patterns of hair arrangement and hat styles signal tribal, clan, band, sex, and age identification. However, while hairdos are ubiquitous among human beings, headgear tends to be limited to persons of higher rank, and in many cultures no form of headgear is found.

Body painting is usually symbolic, whereas tattooing and scarification may combine symbolism with status identification. Bodily mutilation in the form of filing and knocking out front teeth, piercing the nose, ears, and lips for the insertion of ornaments, chopping off segments of fingers, and artificially deforming the cranium are all sporadically distributed about the globe. Circumcision is especially a Mediterranean and North African feature. With subincision and clitoridectomy, it also appears in sub-Saharan Africa and Oceania.

SELECTED READINGS

Amsden, C. E., *Navaho Weaving* (1949). From sheep to blankets in all their varieties among the Navahos.

Bunzel, R., *The Pueblo Potter* (1929). A comprehensive analysis of an important handicraft complex.

Lechtman, H., and R. Merrill (eds.), *Material Culture: Styles, Organization, and Dynamics of Technology* (1977). Reports of a conference, with interesting papers representing current trends and views.

Mason, O. T., *Aboriginal American Basketry* (1904). A complete survey of American Indian basketry.

Roach, M. E., and J. B. Eicher, *Dress, Adornment, and the Social* [illegible] (1965). A rich collection of writings [illegible] the sociocultural significance of bo[illegible] adornment.

Spier, R. F. G., *From the Hand of Man* (1970). A simply stated overview of the gamut of primitive tools.

15
Property Ownership

CHAPTER OUTLINE

LEARNING GOALS

Define property.

Describe property as a social creation.

Discuss land as property.

List the different types of land tenure.

Identify property rights in consumables.

Identify property rights in artifacts.

Explain rights to nonmaterial property.

From the anthropological point of view, the concept of property embraces a far larger inventory of possessions than the twentieth-century person is likely to realize. The land upon which the social group is located and from which it draws its sustenance, the beasts that rove upon it wild, the animals that graze upon it tame, the trees and crops, the houses people erect, the clothes they wear, the songs they sing, the dances they dance, the charms they incant, these and many more are objects of property.

THE NATURE OF PROPERTY

People may relate to property in various ways: individually (to personal property), by groups (to joint property), or by the society at large (to communal property). Property may be fixed and immovable (real estate), or it may be movable (chattel). It may be material and concrete, or it may be an idea or a way of acting (incorporeal). It may be transferable by gift, barter, sale, inheritance, or confiscation, or it may be inalienable. It may or may not be protected by law. It may be reinforced by ritual or protected by magic. Or it may be sustained as customary usage, sanctioned without the aid of either law or the supernatural. Many people habitually think of property only as a thing or as things. Yet the thing itself is but one aspect of property, for the essential nature of property is found in its qualities as a social institution. Property lends formal expression to social structure. It specifies and allocates access not only to concrete necessities such as land and food supplies, but to items of symbolic value such as a feathered headdress, house decoration, and honorific titles.

Property: A Social Creation

Property in its full sense is *a web of social relations with respect to the utilization of some object (material or nonmaterial) in which a person or group is tacitly or explicitly recognized to hold quasiexclusive and limiting rights of use and disposition.*

As an illustration, a stone conveniently shaped for use as an axhead lies unnoticed and unused for years on the surface of the ground. It is not property. A wandering tribesman finds it, takes it, and uses it as a hand ax. If the custom is such that other group members recognize the finder's special *rights* in possessing that rock and that all others have a *duty* to desist from using or taking it, then it is an object of property. The stone has not changed. It is the special and peculiar set of social relations which has transformed the rock into an object of property. Thus, we have two irreducible aspects of property: (1) the object, and (2) the web of social relations that establishes a limiting relationship between persons and the object.

This limiting relationship is often referred to by lawyers and economists as an *exclusive right of use.* It is exclusive insofar as it excludes nonowners from legitimate use without the express or tacit approval of the owner. However, the right is rarely, if ever, so absolutely exclusive that the owner may utilize the object in any way whim may dictate. Rights of use are always limited to some extent by the demands of society. The point of emphasis is that an object does not become property until the members of the society agree to bestow the property attribute upon it by regulating behavior in a self-limiting manner. This is done because social experience has led to the conclusion that social benefits are derived from granting "exclusive" rights to individuals and groups with respect to certain classes of objects that they have created or acquired. By the same token, people always limit the extent of that exclusiveness in accordance with their conception of the needs of social good. Thus it is that as social concepts change from time to time, the specific content of property concepts undergoes alterations. The form and content of property notions are not the expression of immutable instinct or of any imagined laws of nature.

FIGURE 15.1
A Yurok canoe owner and family. (Peabody Museum, Harvard University.)

Property in the United States today is not what it was in the mid-nineteenth century, nor what it will be at the dawn of the twenty-first.

Yurok Canoe Ownership As an example of the way in which property is constituted, we may briefly cite canoe ownership among the Yuroks of California—a highly individualistic people (Figure 15.1). A Yurok boat owner nominally possesses his canoe as private property. It is his. He has a series of demand-rights against all other persons not to molest or damage his boat. He has the privilege-right to use it upon the public waters. Yet he is also subject to a series of well-recognized duties which limit his exclusive prerogatives. For one thing, he is obligated to ferry any traveler over the river when called upon to do so. Failure to perform this duty gives the traveler a demand-right for legal damages equal to one dentalium shell.[1] On the other hand, if the owner suffers injury because of the service he has to render, the traveler is subject to damages. Thus, when one canoeman's house burned down while he was in midstream, his passenger had to pay for it.

Property and Law

Finally, we should take note of the relation of

[1]A narrow, tubelike seashell, harvested by the Nootka tribe, traded and used as shell money among other tribes of the Northwest Coast of North America. See P. Drucker, *Cultures of the North Pacific Coast*, pp. 151–152, 177–178.

property to law. In the modern world, it is a fact that a vast proportion of the law of the state is devoted to the definition of the relationships between owners of property. Much of the activity of our courts and police is concerned with maintaining and enforcing these relationships.

But to state that property rights "exist only because government recognizes and protects them"[2] is an expression of an amazingly myopic point of view. Property rights are tacitly and explicitly recognized and upheld by all forms of social sanction, legal and nonlegal alike. And in the case of primitive society, the recognition and support of property institutions are in fact more frequently nonlegal than legal. Even when legal in nature, primitive property law falls predominantly within the area of private law, which operates independently of the formal governmental machinery.

LAND AS PROPERTY

All societies are territorially based,[3] and most sustenance is drawn from the soil, either directly or indirectly. Land is therefore the most important kind of property.

Land Tenure among Food Gatherers and Hunters

Most human societies claim property rights in land as communities. Such seminomadic peoples as the Australians, African Bushmen, the Veddas of Ceylon, and the Tasmanians recognize clearly discernible natural boundaries as marking off local group territories. Each resents uninvited or surreptitious incursions—usually reacting with recourse to regulated combat or war for the purpose of redress or retaliation. Recognition of true communal property right is seen in the Australian practice whereby one band sends an emissary to ask permission to collect certain foods on the lands of the second community. It is up to the band elders to consider and grant or reject the request.

In addition to the obvious economic reasons for exclusiveness in the use of their land, some Australian tribes have a vital, mystic relation to the land. The land is tied up with their ancestors; they cannot migrate from it because that would break an immutable tie to the ancestors, and neither do they wish to have strangers poking around their sacred territory.

Special Sharing of Resources Although Shoshone Indians of the Great Basin identified local groups with specific home territories, they freely moved into each other's domains under certain conditions.

Steward has given an admirable explanation of the situation in terms of ecological factors. The uncertainty and variability of the pine-nut and wild-seed crops are so great that territories exploited by different groups shifted widely from year to year. When there were good crops in any locality, they ripened and fell to the ground so quickly that the people who lived in the area could not gather them all. When a good harvest was promised, they therefore spread the news so that people whose crops had failed could come to share their harvests.[4]

Among the Eskimos, land is not considered property in any sense, nor is local sovereignty applied to territory. All may hunt where they please; the idea of restricting the pursuit of food is repugnant to all Eskimos (except for some groups in western Alaska, who were influenced

[2]R. M. MacIver, "Government and Property" (*Journal of Legal and Political Sociology*, vol. 4, 1946), p. 5. For an opposite point of view refer to A. I. Hallowell, "The Nature and Function of Property as a Social Institution" (*Journal of Legal and Political Sociology*, vol. 1, 1943), pp. 115–138, especially pp. 130ff. Above all, every student should read the article by W. H. Hamilton and I. Till, "Property" (*Encyclopaedia of the Social Sciences*, vol. 12, 1934), pp. 528–538.

[3]One notable, possibly the only, exception to this is the case of the Orang Laut, the Malayan sea gypsies of the Java and Flores Seas. These tribes are autonomous units, living a roving existence entirely in boats.

[4]J. H. Steward, *Basin-Plateau Aboriginal Socio-political Groups* (Bureau of American Ethnology Bulletin 120, 1938), p. 254.

by the property-minded Indians of the Northwest Coast).

Eskimo interest is in game per se. Land is ignored and not conceptualized as property, in spite of the fact that each local group is identified by the territory in which it lives.

Such exceptions as these indicate that territorial exclusiveness is by no means universal. However, it is correct to say that the vast majority of food-gathering and hunting tribes hold their land in common.

Land as Joint or Individual Property

On the other hand, a few hunting peoples have developed practices of joint, and even individual, ownership of hunting and fishing areas. Notable among these are certain Indians of California and the Northwest Coast.

The Kwakiutls of British Columbia partitioned coastal areas of water as private property for fishing purposes. All intruders were driven off. In a similar vein, the California Yuroks exhibited a partial private proprietary right to ocean areas. Kroeber told of a Yurok family that "owned" a portion of the sea off the beach extending about four miles in either direction from their house site. Other people could fish there, but they had to surrender the flippers of all sea lions taken within the area.[5]

Land Tenure among Pastoralists

Among pastoral herders, there is a notorious carelessness about land. The Comanches, for instance, who were horse herders and hunters of game, had no concept of land ownership. "Land was a matter of unconcern for them, being held neither individually, jointly nor communally."[6] Buffalo herds could be found anywhere, and pasturage for their horses was unlimited.

Even among people whose grazing resources are limited, the tendency is to treat the pasturage as public domain. Notable exceptions have, nevertheless, been reported for the Tungus reindeer herders of Siberia and the Kazaks (or Kirghiz, as the Russians call them to avoid confusion with the Cossacks) of Central Asia east of the Caspian Sea.

The Tungus treat the pastures as the common property of a group of cooperating and intermarrying clans, from which they exclude other groups and their herds by force, if necessary. In some instances, a territory is divided among clans as such. In recent times, individual families have utilized customary grazing grounds somewhat exclusively and irrespective of clan ties.[7]

Kazak practices are even more distinctive. These excellent herders subsist on large flocks of sheep and a few goats and camels. As is so often the case in the economy of pastoralists, they vary their life and social organization according to the seasons. It is their custom to summer in the lowlands, where they graze their herds at will in the tribal territory. In April, each household sneaks out of the winter village in an attempt to get to good pasturage before the others. In midsummer, drought so parches the land that constant movement from one grass spot to another is necessary. The families and clans do not lay claim to any piece of the country at this season, for the richness of the herbage varies greatly from year to year. Winter camps are fixed settlements conveniently located near a well-protected pasturage amid the trees in a deep river valley. Each lineage or family group has its winter grazing sites marked with natural boundaries or rock piles and stakes.

Land Tenure among Gardeners

Since full-fledged gardeners and farmers are

[5]A. L. Kroeber, lecture, "Seminar in Psychological Approaches to Culture" (University of California, Spring, 1941). An interesting legal case arising from failure to surrender the flippers is analyzed in E. A. Hoebel, *The Law of Primitive Man*, pp. 54–55.

[6]E. A. Hoebel, *The Political Organization and Law-ways of the Comanche Indians* (American Anthropological Association Memoir 54; Contributions from the Laboratory of Anthropology, 4, 1940), p. 118.

[7]C. D. Forde, *Habitat, Economy, and Society*, p. 361.

intimately bound to the soil, it is hardly surprising that they show greater interest in it.

For the most part, gardeners work their lands individually, by lineages or by clans, and occasionally by clubs, but the ultimate title to the land commonly rests in the community. This makes it necessary to draw a clear distinction between ownership and *rights of use*. The basic principles of land ownership and use in Indonesia clearly exemplify the distinction.

Land Tenure in Indonesia In Indonesia, among the indigenous rice growers, we find the relationship between communal ownership and individual holding clearly delineated. In the autonomous villages of the independent tribes, all land belongs to the village, which is made up of a core of related clanspeople. The solidarity of the group is strong and mystically symbolized in the possession of a common temple and sacred relics. The village ancestors are buried in the soil, which contributes to the group's feeling of sacred intimacy with its land. Members of the community may reclaim and cultivate from the unused communal land as much ground as they can handle, provided they first inform their leader, obtain consent, and make a ritual sacrifice. Then they are entitled to cultivate that land as long as they work it and keep it clear. Among some Indonesians, however, if a farmer neglects to prepare the field at the start of any season, the farmer may be confronted by someone else who wants to take it up. Then the farmer must set to work or let the field go. Generally, however, if one abandons a field, one retains rights of use until the jungle has reclaimed it. Then it reverts wholly to the community domain. If someone has built dikes, it may be that that person's hold remains unimpeded until all traces of the dikes have disappeared.

One may borrow goods or money on such lands as one holds by pledging the land as security. But one may never "sell" the land, nor can a creditor ever obtain a complete foreclosure. There is no possibility of alienation. Land belongs forever to the community.

Outsiders may acquire use of land from the community domain by arranging for payments to the local headman. The contract is in theory for one year only and must be renewed annually. The importance of the concept of inalienability of land to the survival of native life was recognized by the Dutch in the last century when they forbade the selling of Indonesian land to nonnatives and limited the duration of leaseholds by Europeans and other aliens.

Among the inhabitants of a village, the rights of use are inheritable within the family line, but if a line dies out, the land reverts directly to the community domain for redistribution by the leader.[8]

The rule that a person must work lands recently acquired from the public domain in order to retain title is a general and basic one among gardeners the world over. It effectively guards against one of humanity's besetting social evils—land hoarding by a wealthy few and the closing of the doors of opportunity to the land-hungry.

Pueblo Indian Land Tenure Land-use principles similar to those in Indonesia are found widely in gardening societies. This can be seen from Titiev's comment on the Hopi pueblo of Oraibi in Arizona:

The village chief is the theoretical owner of all his town's lands; these lands are divided among the clans residing in his pueblo; and each individual farms a specified portion of his clan's holdings. In addition, there is a large piece of unassigned land, part of which may be used by any villager with his chief's consent. Under such a system land is never bartered or sold, and only rarely exchanged. Ownership is restricted to the privilege of use, but this right is so carefully recognized that if a man decides to allow some of his

[8]B. ter Haar, *Adat Law in Indonesia*, pp. 81–127.

fields to lie fallow, no other farmer may use them without the specific permission of the owner.[9]

Grazing land for sheep, goats, cattle, and horses is communally shared. The Hopi practice is characteristic of all the pueblos of New Mexico and Arizona (Figures 15.2a and 15.2b).

The rights of use in pueblo land are, however, contingent upon the fulfillment of obligatory duties toward the maintenance of the well-being of the pueblo as a whole. These duties are many, including participation in ceremonial dances. For failure to fulfill these duties the members of a Sia Pueblo family, who had been converted to the Pentecostal faith, were exiled from the pueblo and their rights of use in the land, which had been inherited by the family for generations, were revoked. They received no compensation for their houses, for these were made of the earth and stone belonging to Utset, the Mother Creator, and through her assigned to the pueblo forever.[10]

Land Tenure in African Tribal States

In a different type of political development, as seen in a number of nineteenth-century West African tribal states such as the Ashanti of Ghana, all land "belonged" to the paramount chief, or king. He assigned it to various chiefs; they allocated it to clans, whose headmen assigned individual plots to each gardener. In return, the landworking populace owed fealty to the chiefs and above all to the king. They had to do public work, pay taxes, and perform military service. As long as they were loyal and faithful in their duties and as long as they were not involved in serious crime, they could not be ousted from their lands. The privilege of use passed down through the family. However, one could not transfer or sell one's plot outside the family without approval of clan elders. Often the family would pawn or sell a member into slavery in order to avoid alienation of its hold on the land. Since the services which are called for from landholders are general public duties, they are actually services to the king only in theory. The kingship serves as the symbol of community unity, and landed property is phrased in terms to fit the ideal.

The symbolic and emotional overtones of the relation of people to their lands are nicely expressed in the words of Max Gluckman:

The secular value of the earth lies in the way it provides for the private interests of individuals and groups within the larger society. They make their living off particular gardens, pastures, and fishing-pools; they build their homes, make their fires, and eat their meals on their own plots of ground; they beget and rear their children on the earth. Their ancestors are buried in the earth. Men and groups dispute over particular pieces of earth to serve these varied ends. But men live, work, dance, breed, die, on the earth in the company of other men. They obtain their rights to earth by virtue of membership of groups, and they can only maintain themselves by virtue of this membership. To live on the earth they require friendship with other men over a certain area. The earth, undivided, as the basis of society, thus comes to symbolize not individual prosperity, fertility, and good fortune; but the general prosperity, fertility, and good fortune on which individual life depends. Rain does not fall on one plot, but on an area; locust swarms and blights and famine and epidemics bring communal disaster, and not individual disaster alone. With this general prosperity are associated peace and the recognition of a moral order over a range of land. In West Africa men worship the Earth, and in this worship groups who are otherwise in hostile relations annually unite in celebration.[11]

Principles of Land Tenure among Nonliterate Peoples

Gardeners assign rights of use to individuals or families. In some instances, title is vested in the clan, but usually ultimate ownership is vested in

[9]M. Titiev, *Old Oraibi* (Papers of the Peabody Museum of American Archaeology and Ethnology, Harvard University, vol. 22, no. 1, 1944), p. 181.

[10]The case is described in full in E. A. Hoebel, "Keresan Pueblo Law," in L. Nader (ed.), *Law in Culture and Society*, pp. 112–116.

[11]M. Gluckman, *Custom and Conflict in Africa*, pp. 16–17.

(a)

(b)

FIGURE 15.2
Among Pueblo Indians, all land belongs to the tribe, but rights of use to particular plots are passed within clans to specific families for many generations. (a) Here a group of related women are preparing water-conserving waffle grids for planting. (The Bettman Archive.) (b) Zuni family plots are carefully walled off in separate units. (Museum of the American Indian, Heye Foundation.)

the community. In parts of Africa, communal ownership is transformed into a type of feudal monarchy, where the king symbolizes community entity. Unused land is public domain from which enterprising individuals may carve their plots, with or without official approval, depending on tribal practice.

On the whole, nonliterate peoples overwhelmingly treat their land resources as a communal asset. Pastoralists, for the most part, hold land communally because the necessity to rove makes individual ownership impractical. In the case of hunters and gatherers, there is also little impulse to private ownership of land, since so far as the hunters are concerned, most animals are free-ranging, and it is more advantageous to rove at will when on the chase. When the habits of prized animals made it feasible, such peoples as the Algonkians and Northwest Coast Indians were quite ready to abandon communal land for vested rights. Primeval societies were not "by nature" communistic. They responded to ecological and economic factors which usually made communal land ownership the most feasible means of allocating access to basic food resources.

Theories which assume "primitive communism" as the first step in social evolution thus have some foundation, as far as use of the land resources goes. But, it must be remembered that communism as a political ideology refers to communal ownership of property, *and* the means for production and subsistence, *plus* a classless society.

Some of those who uphold the institutions of private property point to the widespread ownership of communal property by nonliterate people as proof of the "advanced" quality of private-property institutions. Communism, they hold, is representative of a primitive state, and the spread of modern Communism is a reversion to a condition of savagery.

With equal lack of balance, many Marxists see the land communism of nonliterate peoples as proof that communism is the "natural" and therefore the proper and manifest condition for all human society.

The anthropologist notes that the real estate practices of nonliterate peoples cannot be a justification for any particular economic or political forms in modern civilization. These varying property practices merely demonstrate that people adjust their social institutions to the special needs of subsistence and the natural resources available.

PROPERTY RIGHTS IN CONSUMABLES

Food is undoubtedly one of the most basic property interests of omnivorous *Homo sapiens*. Land may seem important, but that is largely because it is the chief original source of the food supply. We have already seen that some foodstuffs are free goods in some societies. But elsewhere access to food is limited. The sense of the necessity of mutual aid and the interdependence of people struggles eternally with the self-assertive urges of barebones survival and selfish gratification. Property rights in food are the formal crystallization of each society's struggle to regulate food distribution and use.

Property Rights in Game

While the general principle of collective ownership of free-running game and unharvested plants holds good, we find that in most instances the expenditure of work in reducing the game and plants into consumable food stocks converts them into private property. All peoples recognize private ownership of food. Yet inasmuch as private ownership never entails absolute exclusiveness, and since among hunters and gatherers food is derived from communally owned resources, the communal claim upon privately owned foodstuffs is important (Figure 15.3).

Among the Comanches, anyone coming upon a hunter who had just made a kill could

(a)

(b)

FIGURE 15.3
(a) The members of an Eskimo whaling crew divide the carcass for distribution among themselves and all members of their community, according to customary portocol. (b) Women and children come to receive their families' shares. (Steve McCutcheon/Alaskan Pictorial Service.)

claim the choicest quarter of the animal merely by placing a hand upon it. If four different people happened on the unfortunate hunter, they took everything except the hide. This, custom decreed, the hunter could retain by hanging onto the tail of the beast. Any hunter returning to camp with game was obliged to share the spoils with all who came to the hunter's lodge.[12] To frustrate this social lien on the products of their individual efforts, some families camped alone during hard times.

After the communal antelope hunts of the Plains Indians, the meat was equally divided among all participating families. However, in communal bison hunts, after the acquisition of horses, all Plains tribes allowed each man whose marked arrow had killed a bison to keep the meat. But even so, the old and infirm who could not hunt and the wives of luckless hunters received shares from those who had made a kill, and it was the usual thing to teach a boy to give away all his first kill of any large game animal.

Food Sharing Sharing of food, even though the food is privately owned, is the basic virtue of almost all American Indian tribes and of most hunting societies of the world. But the psychological and social response to private beneficence results in an order of social prestige ranking different from that which is produced by common ownership.[13]

Successful hunters reap prestige from their beneficence as public providers. In return for food, which does not come easily, they are accorded leadership positions among their people. They are motivated to extend themselves as hunters not only that they may eat but also that they may enjoy the pleasures of socially recognized achievement. There is real survival value for a marginal subsistence society in this arrangement. Additionally, the importance of kinship and reciprocity in the distribution of foods must not be overlooked.

Outright pooling of food occurs less commonly among the hunting and collecting peoples than among gardeners. In the South Pacific, it is associated with prestige competition between local groups and tribes. Great quantities of produce are offered to the chief to be used in feasting rival tribes. The chief's storehouses among the Maori, for example, were the people's storehouses, for the people identified his needs as their needs. They were regularly fed from the great storehouses, but above all, their great concern was that the chief should be able to entertain visitors munificently. Should he fail in this, their outraged pride would make them ashamed before the world. Eating was to the Maori the supreme pleasure, and only by the joint efforts of all could it reach the great heights they so cherished.

Communal pooling of certain foods is also characteristic of American Pueblo Indians. Annual rabbit hunts are held in the fall, and all men are required to participate as a religious duty. The dried rabbits are offered to the head priest-chief of the pueblo, who stores them in his house to be used in ceremonial meals and to be doled out to the hungry families of the pueblo.

Individual Property Rights In Game At the opposite extreme, certain Algonkian hunters of North America, such as the Ojibwa, demonstrate the ideological lengths to which rugged individualism in food procured from wild game can go. Says Landes:

The game and fish that a man catches in the winter are his private property. When he returns with them to his lodge . . . he decides what to do with them. . . . It is never said that he gives game to his wife for her use in making food and clothing for the family; but they phrase it that a man gives game to his wife and therefore the game belongs to her to do with as she pleases. . . . The wife now employs "her" property in

[12]E. A. Hoebel, *The Political Organization and Law-ways of the Comanche Indians*, p. 119.

[13]R. H. Lowie, *Primitive Society*, pp. 207–210.

the manufacture of food and clothing. She gives the finished product to her husband, immature children, and herself. When these gifts have been given, they become the property of the recipients.[14]

Among many hunting tribes, animals having a fixed abode, such as a hibernating bear, a bee, or an eagle, are often seized upon as objects of private ownership, even where all other claims to animals are communal. A Sia Indian publicly announced the location of bee trees which he had discovered—not to invite others to find the way to the delicacy, but to warn them off. Eagle nests were privately owned among all the Pueblo Indians, so that eagles born in the nest belonged to the owner of it. A Pueblo hunter who found a bear's den marked it, and the bear was his to take in the spring.

Property Rights in Garden Produce

Ownership of foodstuffs produced by gardening is generally vested in individuals or family households, but the lines are not drawn with universal consistency. Since most garden plots are worked under individual rights of use or outright ownership, and since most of the expended effort is individual effort, harvests are commonly individually owned. Polynesian practices in contravention of this usage have already been noted, however. Among the Keresan-speaking Pueblos, just as rabbit hunts are communal duties, so are the planting and cultivating of the cacique's, or chief's garden. The harvest is stored in the cacique's house for communal use.

Matrilateral practices in the Trobriand Islands require that a man raise his crops on his sister's behalf. Since his sister's household is not his own household, in effect he has to transfer the yams from his own garden to the storehouses of her husband. His storehouses in turn are filled at least in part by his wife's brother. What one produces does not necessarily remain one's own property.

Property Rights in Livestock

Livestock are privately owned (Figures 15.4a and 15.4b). The one great known exception occurred in that remarkable precursor of the totalitarian socialist state, the Inca empire. Among the Incas, private citizens could own up to ten llamas, but the vast majority of the beasts were state property. The wool collected from the state herds was stored in government warehouses, to be distributed annually in equal allotments to each family head.[15]

Grazing land among migratory pastoralists does not lend itself economically to subdivision. Hence, as has been noted, it is usually communally held and used. But livestock comes in individual units to which individuals may readily attach themselves. Undoubtedly, there is a deep emotional impulse underlying this tendency. Domestication begins in a symbiotic relationship between human and animal which is fundamentally personal. It is most clearly seen in the affectionate relation between people and dogs, the first of the domesticated beasts. It runs through all herders to some degree. Nuer men, having nothing more pressing to do, spend hours in sensuous contemplation of their cattle.[16]

"Some men," said Post Oak Jim, of the Comanche herders of 1850, "loved their horses more than their wives." Favorite horses among most Plains Indians were treated almost as family members. Among the Solomon Islanders, the New Guinea highlanders, and other Melanesians, pigs are the chief objects of value.

In the history of humankind, the domestication of animals has been a great stimulus to the development of private-property institutions. Thus the *World Ethnographic Sample* shows wealth to be a significant factor in the social differentiation of freemen only among pastoralists.[17]

[14]R. Landes, "The Ojibwa of Canada," in M. Mead (ed.), *Cooperation and Competition among Primitive Peoples*, pp. 90–91.

[15]J. H. Rowe, "Inca Culture at the Time of the Spanish Conquest," in J. H. Steward (ed.), *Handbook of South American Indians*, vol. 2, pp. 219, 267.

[16]E. E. Evans-Pritchard, *The Nuer*, pp. 16–50.

[17]A. D. Coult and R. W. Habenstein, *Cross Tabulations of Murdock's Ethnographic Sample*, p. 518.

FIGURE 15.4

(a) Karamojong cattle are part of the village scene in Kenya, East Africa. (Pitt Rivers Museum, University of Oxford.) (b) The cattle are individually owned, and pastoralists place their brands on each animal. (*Natural History*/Rada and Neville Dyson-Hudson.)

PROPERTY RIGHTS IN ARTIFACTS

Weapons and implements for personal use are ordinarily owned by their creator or by their user. Women ordinarily own the pottery they have modeled. A man owns the spear or ax he has shaped. There is to some extent an identity between artisan and the creation, as though it were an extension of the artisan's personality. Most of humanity has recognized this identity and respected it by establishing protection in the form of personal-property institutions.

Joint and mixed ownership of artifacts is also common. Thus, among the Trobriand Islanders, each canoe is nominally "owned" by one man; yet others, who make up its crew, have proprietary rights in the use of the vessel.

All these men, who as a rule belong to the same sub-clan, are bound to each other . . . by mutual obligations; when the whole community go out fishing, the owner cannot refuse his canoe. He must go out himself or let someone else do it instead. The crew are equally under an obligation to him . . . each man must fill his place and stand by his task. Each man also receives his fair share in the distribution of the catch as an equivalent of his service. Thus the ownership and use of the canoe consist of a series of definite obligations and duties uniting a group of people into a working team.[18]

NONMATERIAL PROPERTY

It no longer surprises anthropologists that nonmaterial objects are considered property in nonliterate society.[19] It never would have surprised us if our grandparent's generation and its predecessors had not been so smugly self-assured that "uncivilized" people were of childlike mentality and that Europeans alone were capable of mental abstraction.

However, to understand better the nature of incorporeal (nonmaterial) property, consider the case of a Plains Indian visionary who fasted and sought supernatural power. A bear appeared to him in a dream; it spoke and taught him four new songs, and it also instructed him in the preparation of a rawhide shield to be painted with a bear symbol and other devices. The bear indicated that this shield would provide immunity in battle if the four songs were sung before an engagement. The visionary made a shield as instructed; he sang the songs; his comrades heard the words; and he deliberately exposed himself to the missiles of the enemy, coming through unscathed. The value of the shield and the songs was publicly demonstrated. The shield, as Lowie states, is clearly personal property.

But the shield as such, in the culture of the Plains Indians, was of little value. What was of value were the shield *and* the songs, and the mystic power which the two engendered together. The complex of shield, song, and power was transferred as a gift to son, nephew, brother, or friend. (In at least one Comanche case, recorded by Hoebel, the transfer had to be followed by the recipient's having a vision before the mystic power would become operative, and this may frequently have been the case among other tribes.) Or this same complex could be sold. In either case, the recipient could use the complex if the rights had been properly transferred. The consequence of unauthorized use of the shield and songs was that the usurper would most certainly be killed by enemy missiles because of the punitive action of the supernatural power.

Certainly we have here a sufficiently large aggregate of rights denoted by ownership so that we may properly speak of them as nonmaterial property. Thus, we find again and again that magic rites and charms, songs, dances, and names are the property of persons and groups of persons. Myths and legends may belong to lineages, as among the Indians of the Northwest

---

[18]B. Malinowski, *Crime and Custom in Savage Society*, p. 18.

[19]See R. H. Lowie, "Incorporeal Property in Primitive Society" (*Yale Law Journal*, vol. 37, 1928), p. 551; and *Primitive Society*, pp. 235–243. See also E. A. Hoebel, *The Law of Primitive Man*, pp. 60–63.

Coast. These are objects of property in exactly the same sense as are our copyrights and patents.

SUMMARY

Property is not a thing, but a network of social relations governing the conduct of people with respect to the use and disposition of things. Each member of a society has a social position in relation to the property object. These positions are associated with customary ways of behaving (roles), which determine each person's rights to use the object, on the one hand, or which forbid or limit its use, on the other.

If any object can be used by anybody or everybody, it is not "property" but a free good. If it is thought by the members of a society to be equally accessible (even though only in theory) to all the members of that society, it is *communal property*. If the statuses (or social positions) of the members of a group, such as a family, lineage, or association, are predominantly similar in relation to the use of an object, it is *joint property*. If the position of an individual in relation to the object is such that the individual alone has priority in its use and disposition, it is *private property*. Property relations, however, are so complex that such labels must be used with great restraint, for any given manifestation of property may be compounded of qualities of all three orders. Property can properly be analyzed only in terms of the detailed norms of behavior that exist in each culture.

Land is the most basic form of property. Among most nonliterate peoples, the ultimate title to land is vested in the tribe, although a few hunters, like the Eskimos, have no concept of land as property.

Pastoral people, in particular, tend not to establish property claims in land, although they have highly refined individual or lineage property rights in their herds. Gardening tribes vest rights of use in family lines, which in turn assign the land to individuals, or else village leaders assign plots periodically, acting on behalf of the tribal chief, who symbolically is the owner for all the tribe.

Food is usually private property, but its use and distribution may require sharing through exchange, tribute to a chief, or hospitality. Tools, weapons, clothing, and ornaments are generally private property.

Romantic notions that all nonliterate societies are marked by the free sharing of all necessities are dispelled by an examination of the ethnographic facts. Ownership as defined by various groups is remarkably complex, often rigidly structured, and sometimes bewilderingly varied. Nonliterate societies frequently extend the concept of ownership to intangibles (ideas, songs, rituals, arts) as well as to concrete objects.

SELECTED READINGS

Gluckman, M., *The Ideas in Barotse Jurisprudence* (1965), chaps. 3, 4, and 5. Presents and analyzes the concepts and uses of a South African tribe with respect to status and rights in land, immovable property, and chattels.

Goody, J., *Death, Property, and the Ancestors* (1962). Part III (pp. 273–327) is an excellent analysis of property. The entire book is a masterful study of mortuary ceremonies and property transmission and of their functional relation to social structure in two African tribes.

Hallowell, A. I., "The Nature and Function of Property as a Social Institution" (*Journal of Legal and Political Sociology*, vol. 1, 1943), pp. 115–138. The most thorough anthropological treatment of the subject available.

Herskovits, M. J., *Economic Anthropology* (1952), part IV, "Property." An extensive treatment of the subject.

PART FIVE

Culture, Society, and the Individual

16
Culture and Society

CHAPTER OUTLINE

LEARNING GOALS

Define culture and its characteristics.

Explain how humans have a culture-creating capacity.

Discuss culture as a symbolic system.

Specify the ways in which culture integrates a society.

Discuss functionalism and the components of culture.

Explain how culture is a construct or reality.

Describe the relationship of culture to society.

Describe culture as an adaptive mechanism.

In every country, town, city and rural place, the casual observer sees different hair and clothing styles, different foods, and unusual behavior. In some places people marry close relatives such as those we would call first cousins, or they are allowed to indulge in sexual experimentation before marriage. In other places boys are separated from girls and adults in special bachelor houses. In still other locales, people drink blood or eat roots and berries. People speak a wide array of languages and live in houses of different materials from our own. That there are different ways of life in the world is obvious to the curious bystander.

The anthropologist, who studies and reports these human differences, uses as a major guiding principle the concept of culture and the series of postulates, generalizations, and explanations which are linked to it. These variables are the subject of this chapter.

CULTURE DEFINED

The word "culture" is used in two different ways by anthropologists.[1] One group can be called *materialists* or *behaviorists*, since they view culture as observed behavior and material objects which help a people adjust to a particular social, political, or physical environment. The other group is referred to as the *mentalists* or *ideationists*, since they consider culture an abstraction, as a series of standards or rules *for* behavior and for making material objects. The view taken here is that both are right. They differ in referring to different parts of the social system.

The things that distinguish one group of people from another are readily apparent—differences in clothing, housing, language, behavior. The pencil I hold in my hand is a cultural attribute of my society. The book you are reading is a cultural attribute of your society. If we are reluctant to include these material trappings within what the materialists call "culture," then we must invent another word. But to say that pencils and books are characteristic traits of one group, whereas a stylus and scroll are characteristic of another group, is not sufficient.

Also one must consider that one of the major aspects of culture is the set of standards, rules, or norms in the minds of people which tell them how to behave, how to evaluate, and how to construct a stone ax or a skyscraper, and by which they know who is better than whom, who does what, how to love, when to love, and all other knowledge regarding proper and effective action in a particular society.

Culture is acquired from other people in the same society. People receive not only ideas and rules about culture but also houses, axes, money, social positions, grandmother's weaving loom, father's farm, older brother's favorite bow, and the skills required to make and operate all these things.

Culture, then, is the integrated system of learned behavior patterns which are shared by the members of a society. It also includes distinctive material objects, in addition to distinctive behavior, and both material goods and behavior are associated with a set of rules or standards which tell people how to make these things, and how and when to use them.

These are the essential components of the concept of culture. However, because of the extensive field over which it is applied, there is some variation among anthropologists on the use of the concept. Nevertheless, the following are the major points of agreement.[2]

First, culture refers to the *full range of behavior* in a group.

Second, all aspects of each group's culture are closely interwoven into a *pattern which is unique* for that group.

[1]W. Goodenough, *Culture, Language and Society*; R. Keesing, "Theories of Culture" (Annual Review of Anthropology, vol. 3, 1974), pp. 73–97.

[2]Y. A. Cohen, "The Conceptualization of Culture," in Y. A. Cohen (ed.), *Man in Adaptation: The Cultural Present* (1968), pp. 7–12.

Third, cultures *change* as a result of contact between human groups, interactions with the natural environment, and forces within a group (such as technological innovation) that create new challenges and problems (Figure 16.1).

Fourth, every culture is a set of *symbols* (people respond to cultural symbols rather than to objective reality).

Fifth, all *social* life takes place in *groups.*

Sixth, every culture has a *range of permissible behavior,* not a set of inflexible rules about how each activity must be conducted.

Seventh, every culture is *transmitted from generation to generation* by means of specific techniques and procedures.

THE CULTURE-CREATING CAPACITY

Culture is humanity's most important characteristic. Materially, it ranges from the crudest pebble tools of the earliest known humanlike creature of Africa to the interplanetary space vehicle launched to explore Mars. Each gradation and change added by different people over three or more million years is part of this great accomplishment. Culture is humanity's long invention in the sense that it has been cumulative.

How did the human animal acquire the capacity to create culture? The process has been a prolonged and unceasing response to environmental situations in which the biological processes of natural selection, working upon genetic variations in living organisms, have produced biological evolution. Two million or more years ago, humans had become sufficiently differentiated from other animals so that they represented a new form of life. A feature of this differentiation was the elaboration of the nervous system, the brain in particular, so that it was possible not only to see, smell, and act but also to symbolically represent a wide range of experience. Humans acquired the capacity to think, to speak, and to remember. They learned how to communicate experience through those symbolic representations we call "thoughts," expressed in gesture, word, dance, and art. Thinking began a process of self-organization, enabling people to "see" the universe not only in terms of immediate stimuli but also in terms of what was "remembered," not just through conditioned habit but also through word representations of past experience. Humans acquired the capacity to project past experience and to imagine what had not yet happened and what might never take place.

As a result of biological evolution, humans acquired the capacity to produce culture and in turn to become the product of these cultures. Culture, like life, began very simply. It has gradually grown and assumed a greater variety of forms in an unbroken continuity from previous forms.

The Noninstinctive Nature of Culture

Culture has been defined as the integrated system of learned behavior patterns shared by the members of a society and not the result of biological inheritance. It is the essence of the concept of culture that instincts, innate reflexes, and any other biologically predetermined forms of behavior are ruled out. Culture is therefore acquired behavior.

We must, however, avoid the impression that humans are completely unlike animals and that all nonhuman behavior is genetically coded and all human behavior is completely learned. Such activities of a new-born infant as sucking, swallowing, urinating, and crying are mostly reflexive, or precoded. So are adult reactions such as the contraction and dilation of the pupil. As Dobzhansky warns: "In higher animals and most of all in man instinctual behavior is intertwined with, overlaid by, and serves merely as a backdrop to learned behavior. Yet it would be rash to treat this backdrop as unimportant."[3]

[3] T. Dobzhansky, *Mankind Evolving*, pp. 204–205.

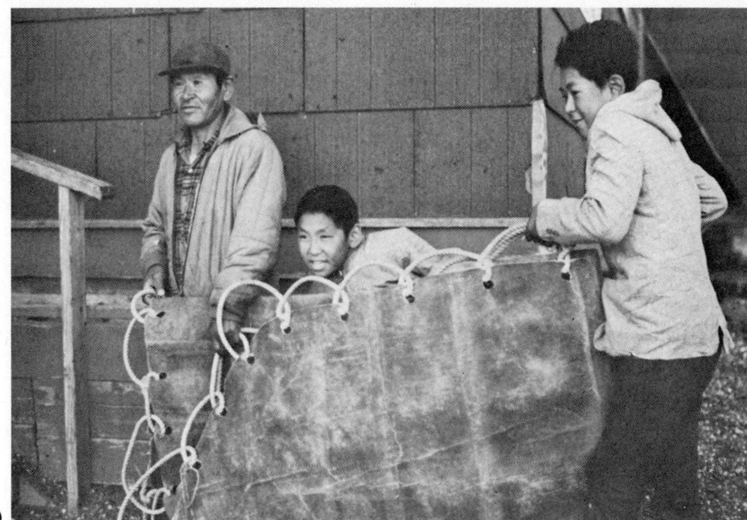

FIGURE 16.1
(a) Modern Eskimos at Kotzebue, Alaska, with a leather blanket for the blanket toss. The "blanket" works like a trampoline, except that the spring action is supplied by a ring of people holding the laced rope. (Herb and Dorothy McLaughlin.)

(a)

(b) Originally the Eskimo practice of tossing a keen-eyed hunter high into the air was a means of enabling him to see far out across the ice and snow in order better to spot game or leads of open water through the ice. Today, the "toss" serves as a sport and entertainment for tourists. Its use and function have altered, and probably its meaning as well. (Steve McCutcheon/Alaska Pictorial Service.)

(b)

In addition, almost all animal species are capable of learning from their social and physical surroundings. The main problem is how to separate those behaviors which are learned from those which are innate. For some time it was believed, for example, that birds could reproduce calls without contact with other members of their species, that is, that birdcalls were instinctual. However, in some bird species the male cannot reproduce the mating call unless it is exposed to a learning situation with an adult male bird at a certain point in its life.[4]

Learning is possible in most living animal species, but species vary in the proportion of total behavior which is learned. However, the greatest part of the human behavioral repertoire is derived from learning in a cultural framework.

Learned Behavior That cultural behavior is learned behavior may be demonstrated by answering the questions: "What would happen if a group of babies could be fed and protected without adult supervision, training, or contact? Would they manifest any of the special traits of behavior that were characteristic of their parents?"

Our answer cannot be based upon direct empirical observation; legend, mythology, and the testimony of honorable persons notwithstanding, wolves, jailers, or scientific experimenters have not set up such a situation under conditions of controlled observation that meet the elementary canons of science. But enough is known of infant physiology, learning, and psychology to justify an answer in unequivocal terms. Assuming the survival of the infants, they would eat, drink, defecate, urinate, and gurgle and cry. But what they would eat, when they would eat, and how they would eat would not be according to the tastes and palates of any group of humans we know. It is quite unlikely that they would cook their food. Presumably they would sooner or later stand on their legs, and even before adolescence they would experiment in mating without incest taboos or rules of courtship. They would communicate emotional states through gesture and sounds. But they would be devoid of language, utensils, fire, arts, religion, government, and all the other features of life that distinguish humans from other animals.

In spite of their shortcomings, however, these children would constitute an animal society. The question remains, however: Would they create culture?

Instinctive Behavior Many animals, insects, and birds in addition to humans have an organized social life. Ant society has a well-delineated division of labor among drones, workers, fighters, males, females, and queen. The organization of the colony, with living quarters and storage rooms for eggs, presents the picture of a well-ordered society. The ants interact in an integrated, sustained set of relationships. These relationships are preset in the genetic organization of the ants. So far as is known, little if any of their behavior is learned from adult ants. If eggs are hatched without any adult present, new ants are produced, which, when they attain maturity, apparently reenact every aspect of social life that has characterized their species for untold generations.

The behavior of other insects is also highly social and involves the communication of information within the society. Honeybees have been studied with great care and with fascinating results by von Frisch and others. A female "scout" bee finds sweet, pollen-bearing plants and returns immediately to the hive. A dance follows in which the scout moves along a straight line pointing toward the source. It circles back to the starting point, alternately to the left and right. The speed of the straight run indicates the approximate distance of the supply. The smell of the pollen indicates the potential honey content. The workers fall in behind the dancer, and when

[4] A. Alland, *Evolution and Human Behavior*, pp. 148–150.

they have received the message, they take off to the right spot, perhaps after "watching" the dance as many as six times.

This fascinating dance of the bees emphasizes the importance of communication in group living, but it does not represent cultural behavior.[5]

Protoculture among Apes and Monkeys

Some social animals other than humans display learned behavior. Monkeys and apes are capable of solving a number of problems posed by experimenters. Chimpanzees show considerable intelligence and inventiveness. What is more, they can learn from one another through imitation.

Thus, when one experimental ape accidentally jabbed the end of a pole into the ground and found that he could hoist himself skyward, other members of the colony were soon searching for sticks; pole vaulting became the rage. Another discovered that by scattering bread outside the bars of his cage, he could lure unwary yard chickens in close, while he lurked with a stick with which to jab them. Annoying the chickens then became the current sport of the group. The alarmed squawks of the hens provided rich simian diversion. When these tricks had spread among the group, they had for the time being all the qualities of customs. But, after a few days or weeks, each practice was discontinued.

However, semiwild Japanese monkeys clearly show that elemental discoveries are communicated within the group and become established. Direct observation of colonies of Japanese monkeys reveals, for example, that each troop has characteristic food prejudices.

According to the investigator: "The monkeys of the Minoo Ravine know how to remove the earth of the slope by scratching with their hands to get the roots of . . . [several species], while those of Takasakiyama entirely lack such knowledge."[6]

Food habits are established among unweaned infant monkeys who, sitting by their mother, pick up the food she drops. Without a mother's example, infants of the same species find it hard to learn to take any food but milk.[7]

New foods have been experimentally introduced to troops of semiwild monkeys by Japanese scientists. When candy was introduced, the 2- or 3-year-olds were the first to accept it. Once the mother had acquired a taste for candy, it was "handed down to her baby without exception." The adult males who supervised the young monkeys also soon learned to eat candy, but the young males who had little to do with juveniles learned last.

In another troop, eating wheat was introduced by an adult male. His example was followed by the "chief" of the troop and passed on to the "chief female," who in turn transmitted it to her offspring. Within four hours, wheat had been tried and accepted by the entire troop. However only half of another troop ever accepted the candy eating introduced by a juvenile.[8]

Incipient culture building is clearly within the province of nonhuman primates. Yet they evidently lack the capacity to express experience symbolically or to remember learned behavior long enough to continue to transmit it after a period of time.

SYMBOLISM AND CULTURE

Many behavior patterns that make up a culture may be learned directly, without reliance on symbolic content. This may be seen in the deaf child who masters simple manual skills without

[5]K. von Frisch, "Dialects in the Language of the Bees" (*Scientific American*, August 1962), p. 3; K. von Frisch, "Decoding the Language of the Bees" (*Science*, August 23, 1974), pp. 663–668; J. L. Gould, "Honey Bee Recruitment: The Dance-Language Controversy" (*Science*, August 29, 1975), pp. 685–693.

[6]S. Kawamura, "The Process of Sub-culture Propagation among Japanese Macaques," in C. H. Southwick (ed.), *Primate Social Behavior*, pp. 83–84.

[7]Ibid.

[8]Ibid., pp. 85–88.

FIGURE 16.2

Culture as symbolism is dramatically represented in a contemporary procession which is a part of the Otavalo Indian harvest ritual in Otavalo, Ecuador. The Otavalo, who were conquered by the Incas in late pre-Columbian times, reenact the arrival of the Inca emperor, escorted by "Chosen Women," his concubines. (Loren McIntyre/Woodfin Camp and Associates, Inc.)

the use of language and without the usual means of assimilating many complex ideas which other children get at an early age. Without skillful remedial education, congenitally deaf children rarely share thoughts, beliefs, or attitudes or acquire reasoning skills except on the crudest level. They will know only a little of their group's music, folktales and legends, star lore, or magic. They will be barred from more than elementary comprehension of kinship systems, law, politics, and rules of inheritance and trade. They may learn to paint through imitation but will know little of the meanings of the designs. All these manifestations of culture, and more, will be beyond them, because the infirmity denies them the one truly distinctive attribute of humans—language.

The clue to understanding the nature of language, that cultural product without which culture is limited, is to realize that language is the major device for *symbolizing.* A sound may be no more than a noise, a disturbance of the air. A sound may also be a *signal* that evokes a response, such as the whistle that calls a dog. On a higher level a sound may be a *symbol,* which is a signal or sign that stands for something. It has *meaning.* Languages are arbitrary systems of vocal symbolism, to which literate cultures have also added visual symbols: writing. Mythology and religion, with their ritual drama, exist as elaborated symbol systems, impressing and sustaining the cultural system of a people (Figure 16.2).

THE INTEGRATION OF CULTURE

A member of a society never exhibits *all* the behaviors present in that particular culture. Culture can be thought of as a group memory bank, in that no one person knows, can operate, or can explain the whole culture. Each person working through a particular role understands and works only a small part of the total repertoire. But, together, sufficient representatives of a society can demonstrate and explain the standards and rules about how to behave, how to evaluate, and how to do things in that society.

Predictability, Efficiency, and Selection

As each society builds its culture, it ignores or rejects many potential behavior patterns. This is partly because the majority of these potential patterns remained undiscovered by most of the isolated societies of the past and hence were not available for inclusion in their cultures. Yet even if they had been available, many of them would necessarily have been excluded. Social behavior must be predictable, and it must be efficient in the sense that members of the society are not forced by their culture to make an infinite number of choices.

The limitation of ways of behaving is not only a social necessity but also an individual necessity. Experimental psychology and psychiatry have demonstrated that habit formation and habitual rewarding of responses are necessary for good mental health.[9]

Behavior must be integrated to a high degree for the effective functioning of personality. Further, many behavior patterns are mutually contradictory and inherently incompatible. One cannot enjoy free sexual license and at the same time practice celibacy; no one has yet discovered how to eat cake and have it too. This principle applies to many other aspects of culture and is the basis of the *imperative of selection*, as summed up by Ruth Benedict:

> *The culture pattern of any civilization makes use of a certain segment of the great arc of potential human purposes and motivations. . . . The great arc along which all the possible human behaviours are distributed is far too immense and too full of contradictions for any one culture to utilize even any considerable portion of it. Selection is the first requirement.*[10]

Fundamental Cultural Postulates

The selection of the elements that make up a culture is never wholly random and haphazard. Selection is made with reference to a set of underlying assumptions, or postulates, about the nature of the external world and the nature of humanity. There are also underlying assumptions about whether things or acts are good or bad and whether they are effective.

For a brief example of what is meant consider the Trobriand Islanders who live in the South Pacific and who are organized in matrilineal clans. At the foundation of life is the following self-evident Trobriand proposition:

Pregnancy results from the entry by a spirit of a dead matrilineal clan ancestor into the body of a woman.

From this flow two corollaries: (1) the father is not genetically related to the child; and (2) a person belongs only to the clan of his or her mother. This is elemental Trobriand truth. Many Trobriand specifics of social life and feeling are understandable only in these terms. One exam-

[9]S. J. H. Masserman, *Principles of Dynamic Psychiatry*, pp. 126–129.

[10]R. F. Benedict, *Patterns of Culture*, p. 237.

ple is the belief that the male plays no part in procreation.

Cultural postulates are the reference points which color a people's view of things, giving them their orientation toward the world and toward one another.[11]

The basic assumptions of a culture are generally internally consistent, although there are usually some exceptions. If a society is to survive, the gears of its culture must mesh, even though they may growl and grind.

In selecting customs for day-to-day living, the society chooses those which accord with its thinking and predilections—ways that fit its basic postulates concerning the nature of things and what is desirable and what is not. If these ways are consistent with the basic postulates, and with one another, integration is achieved. The culture is then a harmonious working whole.

To recapitulate:

1. *Every culture represents a limited selection of behavior patterns from the total of human potentialities.*
2. *The selection tends to be made in accordance with certain postulates or dominant assumptions and values which are basic to the culture and which have survival or adaptive value.*
3. *It follows that every culture exemplifies a more or less complete and coherent pattern, structure, or system of actions and relationships.*

Some of the basic postulates of a culture may be explicitly stated by the people who hold them. Others are not explicitly stated, either because they are taken for granted or because the people are not accustomed to reflecting about their beliefs. The anthropologist, thoroughly familiar with the behavior of a society in all its aspects, may generalize as to the principles that underlie behavior,[12] like the linguist who analyzes a language and formulates the rules and principles of grammar. The speaker knows only that one form is right and another is not, without being able to verbalize the principles. The striking parallels between general cultural and linguistic processes are further discussed in Chapter 33.

Configurations of Culture

The significance of a culture lies less in its inventory of elements than in the manner of their integration. For this reason we have phrased the definition of culture in terms of an "integrated system of learned behavior."

Benedict, who introduced the configurational idea into modern anthropological thought, has written of culture: "The whole . . . is not merely the sum of all its parts, but the result of a unique arrangement and interrelation of the parts that has brought about a new entity."[13]

The configuration of a culture is the distinctive and characteristic form that derives from the special relationship of its parts to one another. It presumes internal integration in accordance with some basic and dominant principles or value systems underlying the whole scheme. Thus, Pueblo culture is characterized by collectivistic, ritual emphasis under priestly direction, while Plains Indian cultures emphasize self-realization through aggressive fighting against outsiders and hallucinatory vision experiences. (See pages 528–532.)

Cultural Relativity and Ethnocentrism

Each culture has general features in common with all others but is different from every other in

---

[11]For fuller exposition of several systems of fundamental cultural postulates, see Chapter 30, on culture and world view.

[12]A detailed description of how basic cultural postulates are expressed in Cheyenne culture may be found in E. A. Hoebel, *The Cheyennes: Indians of the Great Plains.* Other examples may be found in J. A. Hostetler, *The Amish* , and, for traditional China, in F. L. K. Hsu, *The Study of Literate Civilizations*, pp. 61–71.

[13]Benedict, op. cit., p. 47.

some respects. Anthropologists recognize this diversity through the *concept of cultural relativity.*

The concept of cultural relativity states that standards of right and wrong (values) and of usage and effectiveness (adaptive value) are relative to the given culture of which they are a part. In its most extreme form, cultural relativism holds that every custom is valid in terms of its own cultural setting. In practical terms, it means that anthropologists strive to suspend judgment, to understand what goes on from the point of view of the people being studied, that is, to achieve empathy, for the sake of humanistic perception and scientific accuracy. The anthropologist assumes the role of detached observer rather than of apologist, condemner, or converter. The field worker learns to laugh with people, not at them, and to put aside *ethnocentrism*—that is, the habit of uncritically judging other peoples' behavior according to the standards set in one's own culture.

HOLISM AND FUNCTIONALISM

Each culture is made up of a multitude of parts integrated into a total system with all parts having a special relationship to the whole. Each part has its specific *form* as, for example, a bow, a canoe, a pot, a marital arrangement, or a legal process. No form exists in a vacuum, however, or stands as an isolated unit. Each plays a part in contributing to a total lifeway. The way each part relates to others forms the *structure* of the culture. The contribution that each part makes to the maintenance or survival of the total cultural system is its *function.*

Thus the bow, whose form may be expressed in measurements and pictures, may function in meeting the needs of food getting and defense, as ritual symbolism in the religious and governmental systems, in fire making, and in musical activities. To understand all functions of the bow in any culture, it is necessary for the anthropologist to trace its relationships to every other related aspect of the culture. This must be done for each unit of culture, to see finally how all units work to maintain the total lifeway of the people being studied.

A custom may seem meaningless, or tantalizingly exotic, at first. Within its cultural setting, and in relation to those who practice it, and in terms of its functions within the system of which it is a part, the significance of the custom becomes scientifically meaningful. It is no longer an unusual custom, but a socially significant act with reference to the system of which it is a part (see Figure 16.3).

Functionalism emphasizes the dynamics within a culture. It is concerned with a good deal more than the mere description of habits and customs.

Radcliffe-Brown, who contributed a good deal to the understanding of functionalism, used a biological analogy to make its meaning clearer. In his words:

> *An animal organism is an agglomeration of cells and interstitial fluids arranged in relation to one another not as an aggregate but as an integrated whole . . . [I]t is a complexly integrated system of complex molecules . . . [T]he organism* is not *itself the structure; it is a collection of units (cells or molecules) arranged in a structure, i.e., in a set of relations; the organism* has *a structure. . . . The structure is thus to be defined as a set of relations between the entities. . . . As long as it lives the organism preserves a certain continuity of structure although it does not preserve the complete identity of its constituent parts. . . . Over a period its constituent cells do not remain the same. But the structural arrangement of the constituent units does remain similar. . . . [T]he life of an organism is conceived as the* functioning *of its structure. . . . [A] cell or an organ has an* activity *and that activity has a* function.[14]

[14]A. R. Radcliffe-Brown, "On the Concept of Function in Social Science" (*American Anthropologist*, vol. 37, 1935), pp. 394–395; reprinted in A. R. Radcliffe-Brown, *Structure and Function in Primitive Society*, pp. 178–187. See also B. Malinowski, "Culture" (*Encyclopaedia of the Social Sciences*, vol. 4, 1931), pp. 621–646.

FIGURE 16.3
Culture both symbolizes and defines technological and social acts. Among the Crow Indians of Montana, growing tobacco was traditionally a religiously controlled activity limited to the members of a sacred Tobacco Society. Crow culture had changed in many respects at the time this picture was taken (1915–1925). Buffalo hunting and intertribal wars were things of the past. The Crows had adopted wagons, umbrellas, and American-style clothing. Yet tobacco was still ceremonially planted, and singers drummed, sang ritual songs, and performed symbolic acts in accordance with the requirements of traditional Crow Indian culture. (Courtesy of Museum of the American Indian, Heye Foundation.)

The functions of each part are found in the contributions the part makes to the maintenance of the life process of the whole organism. So it is with culture. The functions of each custom and institution are found in the special contributions they make to the maintenance of the lifeway that is the total culture.

Malinowski emphasized that the interrelatedness of all parts of a culture means that the modification of any single part will inevitably produce secondary changes in other parts. Missionaries and the officials of governmental technical-aid-and-development programs have often overlooked this simple principle, with the result that their efforts have had many unforeseen and undesired consequences. But even with awareness it is exceedingly difficult to foresee the ultimate social consequences of any induced cultural change.

THE COMPONENTS OF CULTURE

Cultures include behavioral norms. Norms may be classified according to the scope of their applicability to the members of a society, namely, as *universals, alternatives,* and *specialties.*

Behavioral Norms and Patterning

Human behavior is organized and patterned. This means that it is ordinarily not random but repetitive and fairly consistent. For analytical reasons social scientists prefer to think in terms of *norms* rather than *custom*, for "custom" has too many popular meanings.

When possible, analyses of social behavior should be statistically based. Anthropological experience has shown, however, that it is not usually feasible to make rigorous statistical studies of behavior. Consequently, when anthropologists describe norms, they usually state what appears to be the modal (most common) behavior. Only in extremely rare cases do they make an actual count of all behavior over a given period of time to determine an arithmetically accurate distribution. Such precision may be ideally desirable but under the given situation either impossible or impractical. Sometimes it is not possible to observe all behavior, since a behavior may have died out or may be secret, or the field worker may not be present when the event occurs.

Universals, Alternatives, and Specialties

Norms that apply to every member of a society, such as the use of the fork in Western societies, are called *universals*.

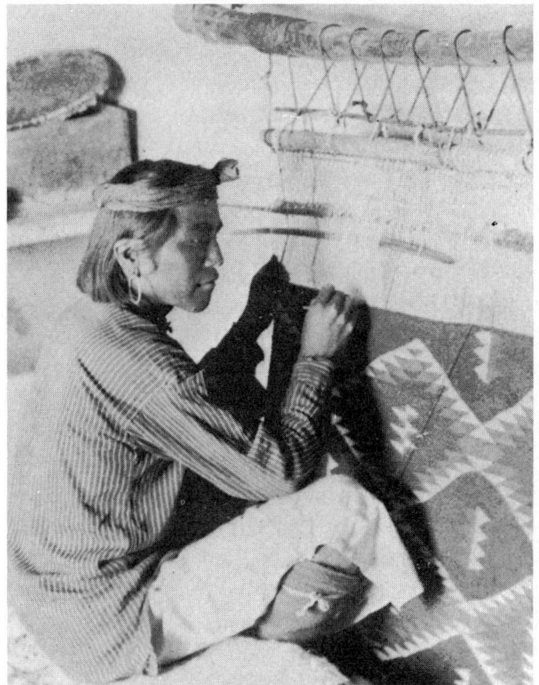

(a)

(b)

FIGURE 16.4
Culture defines sex roles and technology. (a) Among the Hopi and other Pueblo Indians, weaving is a male activity linked to ceremonial privileges. (Smithsonian Office of Anthropology, Bureau of American Ethnology Collection.) (b) Among the neighboring Navajos, however, even though they borrowed the technique of weaving from the Pueblo Indians, weaving, which has in modern times become commercially important to the Navajo, is exclusively women's work. Navajo women own and sheer their sheep, hand card, dye, and spin their own wool, as well as weave all the blankets and rugs. (Joseph Muench/Pictorial Photography.)

Although certain kinds of behavior may be required of everyone, most cultures allow some degree of choice for specific situations. These are known as *alternatives*. A Cheyenne warrior, for example, could make a personal choice of weapons between a bow and arrow, a spear, or a club.

Behaviors restricted to a particular subgroup, such as the common taboos of medicine men or the hairdos of married women, are *specialties*. The specialties of one group may be known to the other members of the society and yet not used by them, because they are not prescribed for their behavior (Figures 16.4a and 16.4b). Many American adult men know the Boy Scout salute, but they do not use it as a form of greeting after they have left scouting. In a complex society, however, most specialties remain unknown to most of the people. This may be because the specialties require unique aptitudes or a rigorous course of training, or it may be that the specialties are the secret knowledge of a few. The result is that no individual can ever acquire or manifest all the elements of a culture. It means also that no anthropologist, even the most assiduous, can record all aspects of even the simplest culture.[15]

This, then, provides one answer to the question, often asked: "How can one speak of American culture when there is such a difference between the culture of New Yorkers and that of Kentucky mountaineers?—between the Italians of Lower Manhattan and the Scandinavians of Minnesota?—between the Yankees of Vermont and the *Hispanos* of New Mexico?" The universals shared by Americans are the common binding and integrating elements of American culture and society. The specialties of the different regional groups and socioeconomic classes are internally differentiating elements which, when taken together, are referred to as "subcultures."

In any analysis of a society and its culture, it is essential, in the interests of clarity and accuracy, never to generalize from the norms of a subgroup to the society as a whole, unless it has been observed that the norms of the subgroup are also characteristic of the whole.

CULTURE AS CONSTRUCT OR REALITY

Do cultures really exist, or do they exist only in the imagination of the social scientist? To some extent the answer relies on the difference between observable behavior, the standards which guide it, and the anthropologist's description of what is seen and heard.

The Culture Construct

Cultures are constantly changing. Yet in anthropology we investigate a society on a field trip, after which we write a monograph describing its culture. In so doing, we fix those main lines of behavior that have been noted as though they were static. It is as though action recorded with a high-speed camera had been stopped to obtain an instantaneous picture. We get the main contours of the action frozen in what Linton called the *culture construct*.[16] It is a statement that includes descriptions of modal behavior, in which each mode represents what is actually a variable range of behavior produced by the members of a society.

The Real Culture

It should be realized, then, that what we deal with in anthropology is the *culture construct* rather than the *real culture*. The culture construct presents the real culture as accurately as scientific methodology permits.

The real culture is what all the members of a society do and think in all their activities in their

[15] The analytical concepts of universals, alternatives, and specialties were introduced into anthropology by Ralph Linton (1893–1953). See his *The Study of Man*, pp. 272–275.

[16] R. Linton, *The Cultural Background of Personality*, pp. 43–46.

total round of living. The real culture, however, is never sensed by anyone in its entirety. It can be only partially perceived as it is ordered and translated into understandable terms by the anthropologist, the philosopher, or the novelist. This is why such radically different accounts of the same society and culture are formulated by different reporters. Reality is never known raw, for it is always processed through one's previous experience and knowledge.

The Ideal Culture

Ideal culture consists of a people's verbally expressed standards for behavior, which may or may not be translated into behavior. Ideal norms are generally phrased in terms of group well-being, and they are often violated when individual self-interest induces another course of action or when hidden, or unstated values stimulate contradictory behavior.

An outstanding example of the clash between public and private interests is found in Malinowski's account of incest among the Trobriand Islanders:

> *[T]he natives show horror at the idea of violating the rules of exogamy and . . . they believe that sores, disease and even death might follow clan incest. . . . [But] from the point of view of the native libertine . . . the breach of exogamy . . . is indeed a specially interesting and spicy form of erotic experience. Most of my informants would not only admit but actually did boast about having committed this offense or that of adultery . . . ;and I have many concrete, well-attested cases on record.*[17]

The Trobriand native manages to get away with it, provided he keeps it from becoming a publicly recognized scandal, and if protective magical charms are used.

We need not discuss here the gaps that exist between our own ideals of democracy and practices that negate them. It is because of such ever-present gaps between thought and deed, between ideal and real, that the social scientist will not rely solely on one person's statement as valid evidence of actual behavior norms.

THE RELATION OF SOCIETY TO CULTURE

Society and culture are not one. A human society is made up of people; a culture is made up of the behavior of people, the rules which govern behavior, and cultural artifacts. We may say that a person belongs to a society, but it would be wrong to say that a person belongs to a culture; people manifest a culture.

Society Defined

Although a society is made up of people, it is more than just a human aggregation. It is a population or a group of individuals united by some common principle or principles.

A society occupies an identifiable space, for it is territorially localized even though its boundaries may not be clearly marked. Its members interact in a focused network of relationships. Even though they may have numerous contacts with the members of other societies, the majority of their activities occur with each other. Further, their relationships are far from random. They are patterned and ordered according to learned norms of conduct and belief which differ in some respects from those of other populations. In short, the patterns of relationships in a society are distinctive, culturally defined, and limited. Finally, the members of a society are affectively bonded by common symbolic representations. They speak a common language, even though there may be wide dialectic variations. They are emotionally stirred to a consciousness of kind by common life experiences, myths, rituals, and other symbolic identifiers: clothing, ornaments, and foods ("as American as apple pie"). The discovery of how fabulously intricate, imagina-

[17] B. Malinowski, *Crime and Custom in Savage Society*, pp. 79 and 84.

FIGURE 16.5
The technological culture of the Melanesians of Big Namba Island in the New Hebrides is well adapted to its tropical rain forest environment. It requires a tremendous input of human energy, however, as shown by this scene of a woman at work with a huge dibble breaking the cleared forest floor for taro planting. (Kal Muller/Woodfin Camp and Associates.)

tive, and effective the systems of symbolic representation can be in both modern and so-called primitive cultures continues to delight and interest even the best-informed anthropologists.

In sum, a human society is: (1) a spatially identifiable population, (2) interacting in a centrally focused network of relations, (3) which are culturally patterned and limited, (4) distinctive in some respects from other cultures, and (5) affectively bonded by common symbolic representations.

Culture as an Adaptive Mechanism

Culture, expressed as a set of variable rules and behaviors, helps people adjust to the physical and social environment in which they live. Using culture as an adaptive mechanism, succeeding generations of people continually adjust their behavior to changing circumstances. Cultural anthropologists and archaeologists, through their study of modern and ancient populations of diverse complexity, find that groups of people formulate ideas and ways for maximizing their use of the environment (Figure 16.5). As stated by Cohen:

> *Every culture is a special case of the adaptive process, of the complex ways in which people make effective use of their energy potentials. Thus culture must first be defined in terms of specific sources of energy and their social correlates.*

Every cutlure can be conceptualized as a strategy of adaptation, and each represents a unique social design for extracting energy from the habitat. Every energy system requires appropriate organization of social relations; no energy system can be effective in human society without groups that are designed for using it.[18]

Change in a culture requires a *decision-making process* and agreement in the group, or some part of the group, regarding implementation of change before adaptation can take place.

Because all productive activities in all societies at all levels of adaptation take place in groups, in an organized, systematic, and predictable manner, all of these activities rest on decisions that must be made about the allocation, use, and distribution of energy.

Similarly, decisions have to be made about who will engage in each of these activities (about how labor will be divided, allocated, and organized) and about the distribution of income (about the criteria according to which each person, family, and household will be awarded a share in the social product).[19]

Thus, decision making and implementation are central features of every adaptation. Culture changes because of changed environments, including the changes made by humans. Values, modes of cognition, and personality characteristics are all intrinsic aspects of the human environment.

Cultures develop by this constant process of adaptation to changing conditions as described above (Figure 16.5). At any one point in time a given culture provides a set of answers to the problems of individual and group living faced by the members of the society. One imperative of living is to keep alive, and all surviving biological forms are so built that a sufficient number of the species lives long enough to reproduce a succeeding generation. Living forms, therefore, have a built-in survival capacity relative to the environments experienced in the past. Cultures consist, on the one hand, of set ways of meeting the survival needs of individuals. Because of the prolonged dependency of the human infant, a stable societal and group relationship is a prerequisite to continuance of our species. Cultures provide individuals with ways to extract food and energy resources, make fire and tools, defend themselves, relate to other members of their society, cure illnesses, and assuage their feats and anxieties.

Societies, too, have their needs which must be met by each culture if the societies are to survive. These have been identified as the "functional prerequisites of societal survival and continuity." Bennett and Tumin, an anthropologist and a sociologist, identify six such prerequisites:

(1) To maintain the biologic functioning of the group members; (2) to reproduce new members for the group; (3) to socialize new members into functioning adults; (4) to produce and distribute goods and services necessary to life; (5) to maintain order within the group, and between itself and outsiders; and (6) to define the "meaning of life" and maintain the motivation to survive and engage in the activities necessary for survival.[20]

Every cultural system therefore includes ways of providing food, shelter, and health, of organizing sex relations, enculturating individuals, maintaining the economy, technology, trade, government, law, and defense, making war, and providing meaningful world and religious views. The cultural complexes that develop in relation to the basic interests of social living are called *institutions.* For example, those concerned with subsistence activities and the production and distribution of goods are called *economic institu-*

[18]Y. Cohen, op. cit., p. 42.
[19]Ibid., p. 47.

[20]J. W. Bennett and M. M. Tumin, *Social Life, Structure and Function*, pp. 45–59.

FIGURE 16.6
Ceremony and ritual always have at least some entertainment value for participants and spectators, alike, in addition to their functions of cultural symbolism. Contemporary Point Barrow, Alaska, Eskimos have here turned the dramatic dance of a mythological walrus hunt into a song and dance act for the secular entertainment of tourists. (Herb and Dorothy McLaughlin.)

tions; those concerned with sex, reproduction, and kinship are called *kinship institutions.*

It is not enough that a people *know how* to do things, however. It is also imperative that they find satisfaction in doing what they do (Figure 16.6). Human beings must *want* to eat, drink, and mate. Motivation on this level is so elementally physiological that societies have no great difficulty in eliciting such engagement from their members. The rewards of reproduction and enculturation of children are much less direct, however, and require adequate cultural provision. To work in order to procure enough food is an automatic animal response to food deprivation. But if people are to be induced to work to satisfy secondary and derived wants in terms of self-gratification and social duty, very special cultural rewards must exist. Each society must learn how to provide the rewards that keep its workers working.

Cultures vary in the usefulness of the institutional devices they provide for societal survival. Behaviors that are ineffective or less effective in meeting the demands of the functional prerequisites reduce the efficiency and survival capacity of the society. Although cultural relativity teaches us that each custom or usage is valid in terms of its own cultural context and therefore should not be judged morally good or bad, the fact remains that one norm or usage may be more effective in serving individual or societal ends. Thus, if the notion that sex is evil spreads to all the members of a society, resulting in celibacy, that society will soon be extinguished because the second prerequisite, that of reproduction of new members for the group, will not be met.

Finally, the most human of all functions of culture is to define the meaning of life and to maintain the motivation to keep going. The humanities search for the motivation for individual work—that which provides the commitment to life and society and helps to answer: "What is it all about?"

SUMMARY

Culture is essentially a human phenomenon. Other creatures are capable of some social behavior, but only humans create and utilize symbolic conceptualizations (the essence of culture) on a massive, systematic, and continuous scale.

A culture is not a thing, nor is it a precise entity. Nevertheless, it is conceived of as having an existence and as being distinctive. It is expressed in individual behavior and yet it transcends the individual, for culture existed before each individual's birth and continues after the individual's death. It consists not only of all the learned behavior manifested *by* the members of a society but also of rules or guides *for* the behavior of members of a society. Language and symbolism are major attributes of all cultures.

Anthropology demonstrates the vast range of behavior of which human beings have proved capable. Yet no society could exist if its members were to indulge in all these behaviors. Some are contradictory and incompatible. Aside from this, sheer diversity of possible actions would make behavior so unpredictable that social conditions would be chaotic. To organize people's activities, the establishment of standardized behavior is a social imperative. Thus cultures are selecting and limiting, and cultural norms are internally consistent and integrated.

The components of culture are identified as *universals, alternatives,* and *specialties.* The elements of a culture are functional in that each part tends to be related to the others in ways which contribute to the operation of the whole culture. The differing ways in which variant cultural elements are related to one another lend to each culture its configuration.

The formulation of a culture by the anthropologist is a *construct,* an abstraction from the *real culture,* which itself can be perceived only partially. The *ideal culture* is a people's formulation of the standards of behavior it believes should prevail.

Society and culture must not be confused. A society is people: a population which occupies an identifiable space. The relations of its members are culturally patterned and distinct from those of other societies, and its members are emotionally bonded by common linguistic and other symbolic representations. Culture consists of set solutions to problems; it is the major adaptive device used by humanity. If a society is to survive, its culture must satisfy certain functional prerequisites, involving decision-making processes and emphasizing effective environmentally adaptive strategies.

SELECTED READINGS

Cohen, Y. A. (ed.), *Man in Adaptation: The Cultural Present* (1968, 1974). A collection of readings with introductory materials which outline the various uses of the concept, culture, with special emphasis on its use in the adaptive sense.

Goodenough, W., *Culture, Language and Society* (1971). An excellent overview of the various recent uses of the culture concept.

Singer, M. "Culture: The Concept of Culture" (*International Encyclopedia of the Social Sciences*, vol. 3, 1968), pp. 527–543. Summarizes and compares the competing theories of culture and social structure in anthropology.

Spuhler, J. N. (ed.), *The Evolution of Man's Capacity for Culture* (1959). A symposium discussing factors relating to the development of the capacity to create and maintain culture.

17 Social Structure and Social Status

CHAPTER OUTLINE

LEARNING GOALS

Define social structure.

Explain the nature of status and role.

Understand the difference between ascribed and achieved status.

Discuss sexual statuses and roles.

Discuss age statuses and roles.

Identify the relationship among ability, prestige, and status.

Identify the connection among wealth, prestige, and status.

Relate social structure and change.

Describe kinship and marital statuses.

In the previous chapters we have been concerned with the concepts of culture and society, the evolution of society and culture, the subsistence base of society, technology and material culture, and the ownership of property. We now turn to the organization of society and to that part of anthropology which is known as *social anthropology,* the study of social structure and relationships.

SOCIAL STRUCTURE

By *social structure* we mean the patterned ways in which groups and individuals are organized and related to one another in society. The culture of every society lays out the major tasks to be performed, the job descriptions of personnel, and specific directions for carrying out the assigned tasks. The tasks to be performed constitute what Malinowski called the *charter of social institutions.* The job descriptions and the assignment of persons to carry them out may be called *social statuses.* The directives for accomplishing various tasks are called *roles.*

Social Institutions

An institution is a network of procedures centered upon certain focal interests. Economic institutions, for example, comprise the characteristic behaviors that focus upon the production, the allocation and distribution, and the use and consumption of goods and services. Economic institutions include behavioral networks of food production and the manufacture of artifacts; gift exchange, trade, sale, preemption, and inheritance; utilization, hoarding, and consumption; and ownership, possession, and rights of use—everything which focuses upon production and utilization of goods and services. Marital institutions focus upon organization of intersexual relations, particularly the stabilization of mating, the nurture and enculturation of the young, household economic activities, the establishment and maintenance of mutual aid between kinship groups, and the legalizing of inheritance. Religious institutions focus upon the conceptualization of the supernatural, the formulation of effective ritual for dealing with the supernatural, and symbolic representation of the social entirety. All institutions within a society overlap and interweave. That is why we have emphasized "focus upon" in stating the central interests or goals of given types of institutions. Institutions are far from being mutually exclusive.

The Charters of Institutions The charter of an institution consists of "statements" explaining why the institution exists and for what purpose. Myths, legends, beliefs, and judgments give sanctity and authority to the choices and commitments a society has made; they state why things are the way they are and why they must be that way. They also state why individuals must commit themselves to the goals as they are defined.

Institutional charters, social statuses, and social roles may or may not be explicitly spelled out. Most of them are not; they are implicit in customary action.

Symbolic art, music, ritual, and dance express and reinforce with emotional overtones the structural relationships between persons and groups which constitute the institutions.

All institutions have personnel. Institutions represent stability and order established by past experience; yet they exist only in the present action of persons. The people who act out the statuses of any institution constitute its personnel. Institutionally organized groups are recognized as *kinship groups* (family, extended family, ramage, lineage, clan, phratry, and moiety) or are recognized as *associations* (age sets, clubs and fraternities, cults, corporations, work groups, guilds, and the state).

The Nature of Status

From this point forward, this book will be largely concerned with the characteristic patterns of

FIGURE 17.1
New Guinea "Big Men" in their accoutrements of status and rank. (United Nations.)

statuses and roles in a number of institutional contexts, such as family, kinship, economics, associations, politics, law, and religion. First, a general overview of the manifestations of status and role should be useful.

The problem which comes from using a word such as "status" as a concept in anthropology is that it has wide common use and different meanings assigned by the general public. In the ordinary sense, "status" refers to a person or thing considered in relative standing to others of its class. With respect to things it implies a state or condition. It also refers to the legal standing or condition of a person, such as "the status of a minor." A "status symbol" is an object, manner of dress, activity, or condition which stands for the relative social standing or rank of a person (Figure 17.1). Other meanings attributed to "status" are wealth, prestige, and situation. These are all dictionary meanings, words used by the public in everyday discourse.

Behavioral scientists have tried to give a more precise meaning to the term "status," when used as a concept. They hold that an individual's status is a social position or identity which is related to other positions in a society and is determined by a cluster of binding rights and duties. Every person has a number of statuses simultaneously, which of course, are not acted out at the same time. For example, a man could have the simultaneous statuses of husband, father, son, professor, lecturer, president (of an association), cook, school board member, etc. Statuses can be classified as achieved or ascribed, and by such characteristics as age, sex, bodily traits, and specific social experiences and affiliations. Statuses can also be classified according to the institution in which they exist; thus there are kinship, religious, occupational, political, and other institutional statuses.

The Nature of Role

Role is the complex of customary behavior associated with a particular status. Every person is to some degree an actor, because life in society is a playing of roles associated with successive statuses. Behavior becomes "natural," free of posing, only when the person has mastered the role of each status and does not register awareness of its performance.

Because every person has multiple statuses, that person also manifests many different roles. A married professor behaves differently with the family (the husband and father, or wife and mother, roles) than in the classroom (the professor role). And the person who works as a volunteer in an association behaves quite differently in that role than when engaged in professional or household-oriented roles. At different times, therefore, different roles come to the fore. Several roles may be operating simultaneously, but their intensity is variable.

At times, various statuses and related roles may be held in abeyance or inactivated. A Pueblo Indian, while cultivating his fields, holds his dancing as a member of the Flint society in abeyance. A person's roles could be likened to a wardrobe, from which the costume suitable for each occasion is selected.

Ascribed and Achieved Status

The statuses that an individual holds are attained in various ways. They may be sought through competitive mastery of the behavior linked to the various statuses. Such statuses in the terminology suggested by Linton are called *achieved*.[1] Other statuses devolve upon the individual by

FIGURE 17.2
Decorative garb of the wives of Asari "Big Men" in the Western Highlands of New Guinea. Their varicolored headdresses are made of tropical birds. The crescent shells suspended from their necks are shimmering gold in color and represent great wealth—three months of hand scraping to get the thinness which produces the gold color. (E. A. Hoebel.)

virtue of innate biological characteristics such as sex, age, and by virtue of preexisting social affinities, such as the statuses of parents and kin and the involuntary associations into which the child is born. These statuses are *ascribed* to the individual by society.

It is important to note that achieved statuses are attained only by first mastering the roles. As Barton has observed of the Kalinga in northern Luzon: "Elevation to rank and power in the community is a gradual process of emergence in which power is attained before the rank is acknowledged by the people."[2] When the role is finally mastered, the status flows from this fact. A master hunter must first master hunting.

In the case of ascribed statuses, on the other hand, the status comes first, and the roles are mastered subsequently. It is even possible to inherit ascribed status without mastery of the roles. There are unkingly kings, ignoble nobles, unladylike ladies, and not-so-gentle gentlemen.

[1] R. Linton, *The Study of Man*, pp. 113–114.

[2] R. F. Barton, *The Kalinga*, p. 148.

Ascribed status distinctions based on age, sex, childbearing, and kinship are the universal foundations of human social structure.

Achieved status criteria that are ubiquitous to all societies are those based on technological skill or artisanship, supernaturalism, the marital state, fecundity, and political leadership.(Figure 17.2).

Ascribed statuses may include caste-determined occupations and such inherited conditions, states, or materials as supernaturalism, wealth, various religious and social perquisites and paraphernalia, and political position (such as that derived through royalty).

Achieved statuses may include those based upon skills in hunting, in games and dances, and in war (Figure 17.3), storytelling ability, possession or distribution of wealth, bodily mutilation, and membership in various specialized associations. (This list is not exhaustive.)

The functional importance of all these different statuses rests in the fact that they limit and influence the degree and direction of cultural participation and the manner and amount of interaction for individuals and groups. No person ever manifests all the behavior characteristics of a society because, for one reason, no one person ever embodies all the statuses existent in that society.

Societies that emphasize achievable status are marked by internal social mobility, social striving, and (on the whole) competitiveness and individualism. Emphasis is placed upon "fulfillment of self" and assertiveness. The social gain is ideally a greater ultimate efficiency because capable persons are not barred from effective performance in those capacities for which they have aptitudes. Conversely, caste and rigid class systems ascribe roles to people who may not be well suited to their performance, while at the same time they bar potential adepts.

On the other hand, the advantages to social systems that emphasize ascribed statuses lie in reduced strain and anxiety for the participating members of the society. Insecurity which derives from competition is presumably reduced.

FIGURE 17.3
Aztec painting depicting high-ranking warriors and nobles, known as Knights of the Sun. The distinctive shields and obsidian-bladed swords and the tufted hairdress tied with red cord and hanging feathers show that the fighter at the left has captured prisoners of war. The netted and tufted robe worn by the other is another insignia of bravery. (Diego Duran Series/University of Oklahoma Press.)

When persons in statuses of marked social disability begin to feel frustration, they begin to aspire to achievable statuses. The anxiety of those in the threatened ascribed positions becomes acute as they begin to lose authority. This subsequent strife marks relations between groups in many parts of the world today.

Status Hierarchy: Rank

Every society involves a certain amount of ranking. But, it should be noted, status and rank are not the same. "Status" is a neutral term, which refers only to position. "Rank" refers to hierarchical standing—higher or lower with reference to other statuses. The rank order of a society is its system of status gradations. A high ranking is one that carries prestige; that is, the attitudes associated with it are those of deference, reverence, submission, and subordination on the part of those of lower ranking. Prestige translated into action means power—the capacity to influence or direct the behavior of others.

The range embraced in a rank order will be wide or narrow depending upon the disparities in power structures formed by the culture. In simple democratic hunting and gathering societies, such as that of the Eskimos, the range is narrow. In complex, class-organized societies, such as that of the Aztecs, the range between slave and king was great (Figure 17.3).

SEXUAL STATUSES AND ROLES

Sex difference is a biological fact upon which social statuses are built. But what is biological and what is cultural in sex differences are not established with certainty for all types of activity. *Homo sapiens* is a bisexual animal in which the reproductive roles are biologically fixed. So long as babies are born of women, differential statuses of male and female will be recognized. The real social revolution will come when biogenetic techniques make possible the regular fertilization and incubation of the human ovum outside the womb.

But even this impressive possibility may be bypassed in favor of *cloning*. In this process a whole new organism will be grown from a single body cell of an already existing organism. The new individual will be an exact genetic replication of the genitor, for every normal body cell contains the genetic code for the entire organism within its nucleus. There will no longer be a biological need for males and females. Sex will be obsolete, and so, in all probability, will be status differences between men and women. Responsible biologists, such as J. B. S. Haldane and Lord Rothschild, see cloning as a reality in the near future.[3]

In the meantime, however, every society assigns different roles to males and females, as depicted in Table 17.1 (page 302) for the Lesu of Melanesia and as in the following example.

San Ildefonso Pueblo

In San Ildefonso there is a sharp line between men's work and women's work, and in the respective attitudes of the sexes towards their work. Men's work on the whole tends to be cooperative. The ditches are dug by the male community in the spring; . . . Among women, on the contrary, work has tended to become competitive; women seldom carry on any of their activities as a group. . . . Theoretically, at least, women play comparatively minor roles. San Ildefonso men do work which elsewhere is frequently the task of women. . . . Traditionally they hunt, dress the skins of the animals they kill, cut and sew moccasins . . . , weave baskets, and weave and create their own dance costumes. . . . Men till the fields and the gardens, plant and reap, cut and haul firewood. Within the village itself they build the houses, care for the kivas, and clean the plaza before fiestas and dances. . . . Women's work is "inside." They care for the household, grind the grain, cook, and tend their children. They make and fire the pottery, and if there is no man in the family who can decorate it, the women . . . decorate their own.[4]

Sexual Division of Work Roles

Although each society distinguishes men's from women's work, what is distinctly men's work in one society may be women's work in another. As examples we may note that the weaving of Navajo blankets is women's work, while among the neighboring Hopi, spinning and weaving are confined to men (Figure 16.4, page 289). Among the Maricopa Indians of southern Arizona, weaving was properly men's work. Women harvested and ginned the cotton, which was grown exclusively by the men, and both sexes spun the yarn.[5] In nineteenth-century America, boys were supposed to be able to swim, and girls were not; yet among the Yahgan of Tierra

[3]See G. R. Taylor, *The Biological Time Bomb*, pp. 22–30.

[4]W. Whitman, *The Pueblo Indians of San Ildefonso*, pp. 99–100.

[5]L. Spier, *Yuman Tribes of the Gila River*, p. 104.

TABLE 17.1
The Division of Labor in Lesu, Melanesia

Masculine	Feminine	Joint
Clearing ground for new garden and building garden fence Planting trees Getting sago	Planting taro and yams; weeding; gathering crops and carrying them home	
Fishing	Catching crabs on the reef	Catching the sea worm, *beta*
Hunting wild pig and phalanger	Feeding domestic pigs	
Cutting firewood; making the *liga;* bringing the leaves for cooking	Drawing water	
Preparing pigs, fish, and sago to be cooked Burying bananas in the sand	Preparing taro and yams to be cooked	
Housebuilding and repairing	Sweeping the house and keeping it in order	
Making of masks, canoes, *malanggans,* fishing-nets, spears, ornaments	Carrying heavy burdens with the exception of fish and pigs	Making baskets and mats. Taking care of children. Medicine and magic. Making "paint" for the hair

SOURCE: After H. Powdermaker.

del Fuego, women are the swimmers. Among the Pueblo Indians, most garden work is done by men; among the Iroquois, tilling was for women only.

Thus, anthropologists have learned to reject all generalizations such as that women are "naturally" housekeepers or that they are more "peaceful" or more "religious" than men. But anthropology has also established that throughout the world, certain activities are quite consistently assigned to men and others to women.

Distribution of Labor by Sex

In three-fourths of all societies, the tasks of food and fuel gathering, grinding seeds and grain, preparing foodstuffs for preservation, weaving, and manufacturing pottery, baskets, and mats are assigned to women. These are all jobs that, except for the gathering of foodstuffs, can be carried on in the immediate vicinity of the hearth and infant.

Hunting, on the other hand, is exclusively men's work in all societies covered in Murdock's *Ethnographic Atlas*, except in Thailand. Fishing is largely, but not exclusively, a male activity. Cattle herding in the Old World is almost exclusively limited to men, but no clear division of labor by sex is discernible with respect to other domesticated animals in other parts of the world.

Participation of men and women in gardening

and agriculture varies from region to region. Women predominate in sub-Saharan gardening in Africa. Around the Mediterranean, men carry on most plow agriculture. In Asia men and women gardeners work side by side, while in the South Seas, gardening responsibilities are held by women in one-third, by men in one-fifth, and by both sexes in nearly half of the societies.[6]

AGE STATUSES AND ROLES

From a gross biological point of view, life may be reduced to a simple formula: birth, maturity, reproduction, and death. However, even the biologist will acknowledge that at least a few other events of significance occur along the way.

Age statuses are recognized in all societies. The universal minimum includes at least three categories: child, adult, and old person, or, respectively, those not yet ready for full social participation, those who perform the major maintenance activities of the society, and those who are beyond the stage of active participation and responsibility. Generally, recognized age statuses are more numerous. Thus, the Comanches recognize five ages: baby, preadolescent, unmarried "brave" or girl, grown person, and old man or woman. Each age has its separate, specific name. Young children may be highly valued and desired, but they never have prestige merely by virtue of being infants. In the exceptional instances in which infants enjoy high status and prestige; it is always as a consequence of some special factor other than age, as with a princeling by birth or a twin with imputed supernatural qualities (as among the Dahomeans).[7]

Youths and persons of middle age rarely enjoy favored status by virtue of their age, as such, although possession of special skills and wealth may bring prestige status.

Adulthood means full participation in the responsibilities and privileges of the society. It means marriage and parenthood and political, religious, economic, and club life, all to be spelled out in detail in the remaining chapters.

The aged have almost always enjoyed statuses of respect, reverence, and privilege because of the attributes ascribed to being old.[8] It is not just being old that brings prestige; it is the accumulated wisdom and lore gained through experience.

In most societies, the oldsters hold important positions in politics and government, serve as magicians and priests in supernaturalism, and are owners of property. These are sources of power. Since such sources are more available to men than to women, old men usually have higher ranking than old women.[9] The positions of the aged are more secure in the settled horticultural tribes than among hunting and collecting peoples, especially those who live in the arctic and its fringes, where old people are unable to participate in primary productive activities to any extent.

The support of the aged is a luxury which many marginal societies are unable to sustain in times of stress. Senilicide was general among the Eskimos. Old people might be blocked up in a snow hut to be abandoned to cold and starvation, or they might be killed by more violent means when they themselves requested it.[10] However, of the seventy-one societies tabulated by Simmons, only two (both Eskimo) violently remove the aged; seven abandon or expose them to natural elements to hasten their deaths.[11] This does not mean that in these seven societies, all old people are destroyed when their powers wane. It depends upon individuals and circumstances.

Almost all observers remark that old people are respected in the tribes they have visited.

[6]E. Bourguignon and L. Greenbaum, *Diversity and Homogeneity*, p. 12.

[7]M. J. Herskovits, *Dahomey*, vol. 1, pp. 263, 270–272.

[8]L. Simmons, *The Role of the Aged in Primitive Society*, p. 79.

[9]Ibid., pp. 47–49.

[10]E. A. Hoebel, *The Law of Primitive Man*, pp. 76–79.

[11]Simmons, op. cit., table 6.

Only the Bushmen of South Africa and the Witotos of South America are said definitely to withhold respect from aged men. Eight of the seventy-one tribes studied by Simmons deny deference to old women.

In Australia, seniority reached its greatest significance—so much so that Australian social organization is dubbed *gerontocracy,* "the rule of elders." The preeminent domination of the Australian local group by grizzled old men gave birth and impetus to the nineteenth-century notion that the primeval condition was that of browbeaten youth frustrated by the hoary patriarch. Australia, however, represents a special elaboration of age status in a way not universally characteristic of the hunters and gatherers (in contrast are the African Bushmen and American Shoshones).

In stable societies, accumulated experience is valuable. Elders know more than youngsters, and what they know usually holds good. But in a rapidly changing culture, accumulated knowledge often becomes quickly shopworn. What was valid in the youth of the aged is no longer so. Wisdom based on outdated knowledge is of little use to those who clutch it as a source of prestige.

Changing Statuses: Transition Rites

Early in this century, Arnold van Gennep (1873–1957) published the classic work known in English as *The Rites of Passage.* He demonstrated that changes of status are frequently apprehended as crisis situations. In the transition from one basic status to another, as an individual moves through the developmental stages of life, the person must be detached from the previous status and incorporated into the new one. In the "in between" phase the transient is viewed with anxiety. The transient is leaving familiar roles and has not yet acquired new ones, a situation which is unpredictable, dangerous—a threat to everyone involved. Hence, in many societies the person is isolated and quarantined—sometimes even ritually "killed." At the climax of the transition rites the individual is then reborn (a neophyte) as a new and more mature person, schooled in new roles, ready to be reincorporated into community life.

To take an example from Western society, when old-time Army sergeants bullied and insulted rookies, they were not being merely sadistic, nor were they necessarily working off personal frustrations. Although sergeants may not be aware of any principles of functional anthropology, they do know that recruits have to be made over and put through a quick transition rite. A first act is the destruction of civilian ways and civilian thoughts.

Torture in the puberty rites of many societies approaches sheer cruelty. Yet beneath it can usually be found a functional rationalization. In Australia, circumcision and subincision, painful and dangerous surgical operations when crudely performed with stone knives (Figure 20.3), are but symbolic acts signifying the sexual and social completeness of the males in a type of society that rejects and culturally suppresses the significance of women.

In all cases, transition is the main theme—transition from the limited and undeveloped state of childhood to that of the adult endowed with the wisdom and privileges of a mature person. Thus, death and resurrection are recurrent themes of puberty rites: death means the destruction of the childhood personality, and resurrection means that the person is restored to the community in a new status with new roles. The boy who retires to the hidden initiatory school in the bush, secreted from the eyes of all females and preadolescent boys, is "dead." When he returns to the camp of the band, circumcised, subincised, and cicatrized, with a few teeth knocked out and with new knowledge of totemic mythology, he is a new man. Such an episode was depicted in the television serialization of Alex Haley's *Roots.*

In like manner, Gerlach and Hine, in their studies of contemporary movements of social change, such as the Black Power and the Pentecostal, note that one basic feature is, "*Personal commitment* generated by an act or experience which separates the convert in some significant way from the established order (or his previous place in it), identifies him with a new set of values, and commits him to changed patterns of behavior."[12] Transition rites are not things of the past or of places with strange names only.

Functions of Transition Rites

Crisis periods are times of critical uncertainty when the fate of the individual or the group seems to hang in the balance. At such times societies are not inclined to leave the outcome to chance or unbridled circumstance. Positive techniques of rational assistance are employed, along with magic and ritual ceremonialism, to frustrate destructive and disruptive supernatural powers or to invoke positive and helpful forces. Through ritual and ceremony, a bridge is thrown across the yawning chasms of fear and doubt that carries people over transitional states to a safe arrival and a firm footing in the new status awaiting them on the other side. Their very enactment also serves another purpose. For those who participate and those who watch, the scene and the ceremony provide reassurance that life and society shall be reborn through unending cycles of regeneration.

A succeeding chapter, on the life cycle, deals in more detail with the transition rites encountered in birth, puberty, marriage, and death.

ABILITY, PRESTIGE, AND STATUS

Skill in any valued function brings prestige to the expert. By and large, anthropological data support this supposition. Proficiency in a craft usually brings moderately high prestige among nonliterate people, but it tends to rank below skills in military prowess, supernaturalism, political leadership, and wealth manipulation. Polynesians gave the most conscious and organized recognition to proficiency in a craft. The *Tuhunga*, or "great adept," of the Tonga in Polynesia was highly revered whether a master of oratory, tribal lore, house building, or canoe manufacture.

At the other extreme, occupations linked to inferior castes in Africa, India, and Japan bring no kudos to their practitioners, no matter how skilled the artisan. A Masai blacksmith is doomed for life to subordination, for that is the value ascribed to the status of blacksmith. Among the Japanese, the *Eta* form a polluted caste of hereditary butchers, or in some instances fishers, whose pariah pollution is unmodified by the necessity of their work or their skill in performing it.[13]

WEALTH, PRESTIGE, AND STATUS

There are definite limits to the amount of goods that roving collectors of food are able to carry around with them. It is not possible for such people to accumulate wealth. The possession of wealth is not, for them, a significant determinant of prestige.

The giving away of food and goods is yet another matter, however. Food supplies are shared in almost all hunting societies. Prestige and leadership go to hunters who have food to dispense, hides to bestow, arrows to give, and (among Plains Indians) horses to lavish upon favored friends, wayfaring visitors, and indigent neighbors. Plains Indians recognized as families of good standing those whose tepees were well kept and decorated and whose industrious men and women kept their lodges well supplied with victuals, fine robes, and handsome clothes (Figure 17.4); but above all, they respected those who gave freely of what they possessed. This is what settlers on the Indian frontier could not

[12] L. P. Gerlach and V. H. Hine, *People, Power, Change*, p. xvii; see also pp. 110–158.

[13] E. Norbeck, *Takashima*, pp. 113–114.

FIGURE 17.4
A wealthy Piegan Blackfoot medicine man at home in his lavishly equipped skin tepee. The wall of the lodge is hung with skin robes for warmth. The triangular backrests face each other so that he may converse easily with guests. His pipe and tobacco bag lie on the floor in front of him. Behind him is his medicine bundle. His sacred war shield hangs on the wall at the right, and his feathered lance may be seen beneath his drum on the left-side backrest. (Roland Reed/Kramer Gallery.)

understand when silent Indians appeared at the cabin door expecting a "sharing" handout.

Reciprocal-exchange systems are not likely to generate wealth distinctions: they tend toward reciprocal equality in goods. Yet, the organization of wealth as carried out by the "Big Men" in Melanesia (pages 355–356) links economic and political activities in a status-ranking system. To rise through the various degrees of the all-important men's club of the Banks Islanders calls for the payment of heavy initiation fees. Only the richest can afford to purchase the higher degrees. Indeed, as Lowie has summarized the data:

[T]he aboriginal conception is not that of avariciously hoarding wealth but rather of displaying one's greatness by exhibiting contempt for property. So a man of the loftiest status in the club may still promote his renown by providing the lavish entertainment associated with certain festivals; nay, a suggestion of niggardliness on these occasions would go far to destroy his influence.[14]

[14] R. H. Lowie, *Primitive Society*, p. 277.

The Potlatch of the Northwest Coast Indians of North America

Among some tribes of the Northwest Coast, elaborate honorific ranking distinctions were ascribed through family and clan inheritance. At the same time, they had to be validated and kept up through display and manipulation of wealth in the most ostentatious manner possible (Figure 17.5). This was done in part by means of showy totem poles and the potlatch—an elaborate institution of feasting accompanied by the lavish distribution of presents by the host and his kinsmen to guests of another lineage or tribe (Figure 17.6). Its primary function was to serve as a demonstration of the family and individual statuses of the hosts. The guests were witnesses to the hosts' claims to certain statuses. Although accumulations of wealth were necessary for potlatching, it was not wealth that gave status; it was the legitimate possession of honorific prerogatives, which were linked with specific names and titles, and which were inheritable, but which could not be used until publicly assumed at a potlatch given for the purpose. To use a name not validated at a potlatch was a shameful presumption, and to address a person by a name he had inherited but not yet validated was an insult to his standing.[15]

Record of a Tsimshian potlatch that took place around 1930 illustrates the old principle with some modern touches. When Gusgai'in, chief of the Gitlan, died, his nephew announced

[15]H. Codere, *Fighting with Property: A Study of Kwakiutl Potlatching and Warfare*; P. Drucker and R. F. Heizer, *To Make My Name Good.*

(a)

FIGURE 17.5

A Chilkat Indian chieftain from the Northwest Coast displays symbols of his wealth and status. The symbolic animal, bird, and fish designs portrayed on his wooden helmet and woven blanket and leggings all represent mythologic and legendary achievements of his totemic ancestors. (American Museum of Natural History.)

(b)

FIGURE 17.6

Chieftains of high status from the Northwest Coast validate their claims to titles through the potlatch. (a) A potlatch display of food and blankets (in the trunks) ready for distribution to guests, around 1910. (b) A chief orates before the pile of Hudson Bay blankets which he is bestowing upon his rival. (American Museum of Natural History.)

that he would take up his uncle's name at some later date. Before this could be done, he and a Wolf clansman jammed their motorboat between the piles of a bridge. They were hung up when the tide flowed out. This would be enough to cause any good boatman chagrin, but when they were badgered with the remark, "We saw a Wolf hanging up under the bridge," the prestige of all Wolves was diminished.

A potlatch was necessary to rehabilitate their position, and so they undertook to give a traditional ceremony, the family Feast of the Early Snow, commemorating the exploit of the ancestral chief, Gusgai'in, whose name was now to be assumed by his descendant. This ancestor had passed beneath a glacier in his flight from enemy captors, so with poetic flavor the pièce de résistance of the banquet should be a native sherbet made of snow mixed with olachen grease, berries, and crabapples. In keeping with the times, however, ice cream was served instead at this potlatch. A heaping dish of ice cream, more than could be eaten, was placed before each person who had taunted the Wolves.

Gorging a guest and then making fun of him was a favorite form of ridicule and provided much amusement for the guests. . . . When the feast and hilarity were over, the chief arose and explained the mythological background of the feast. . . . He thanked the guests for coming and announced that, in so far as he was able, he would fill the position of his late uncle. Then La'is, the senior Wolf of the Gilustsa'u tribe, arose as the chief's spokesman and said that, as the chief had been publicly addressed as Gusgai'in, the latter was hereby acknowledging the name and assuming the position. . . . Spokesmen for each guest chief affirmed Gusgai'in's right to the name and welcomed the new chief as a brother. They also acknowledged that the bridge incident and other slurs would be forgotten. Much of tribal history was narrated during the speeches and many compliments were paid the host and his lineage. Gifts of food and handkerchiefs were then distributed among the guests. Dancing ended the potlatch.[16]

The potlatch serves to affirm the status of the host; and the protocol of seating, serving of food, and distribution of gifts affirms the ranking for the guests. Invariably the giving is in order of rank. The person with the highest rank is called upon first to receive an allotted share, and so on down the line. The position of each person with respect to every other is rigidly determined by the nature of the validated titular prerogatives held. The mere giving of a potlatch does not validate a person's claim. The real validation comes when that person is called forth to receive gifts as a guest at other potlatches. Only if one is called forward at the moment warranted by the position claimed is the claim validated.

KINSHIP AND MARITAL STATUSES

Marriage and kinship are universal and fundamental phenomena. Premarital, marital, and postmarital statuses are therefore ubiquitous and of such extreme importance in any society that kinship, marriage, and the family are subjects requiring special treatment in subsequent chapters (Chapters 21, 22, 23, and 24).

SOCIAL STRUCTURE AND CHANGE

A word of caution must be entered regarding the tendency to view the social system as unchanging. A contributing factor is the inflexibility of the language used to describe the social structure of a society. The fact is that systems change. Some remain constant and unchanged for long periods of time. Others change over a span of a single generation or even more rapidly. How does this change come about? Where does the change occur?

[16]V. E. Garfield, *Tsimshian Clan and Society* (University of Washington Publications in Anthropology, vol. 7, no. 3, 1939), pp. 205–206.

There are no simple answers to these questions. Since many factors contribute to change in a culture, there can be many answers to these questions. However, something can be said, although tentatively, about where changes occur. Roles can change, that is, the rules for behavior in a given status can change, so that the manner of conducting an office becomes different and so that holders of that office or position are expected to behave differently from what was expected previously. New statuses can be introduced because new needs have replaced old needs. The ranking, or prestige attributed to a status or status group, can change in time, so that a position is different and carries different expectations than previously. New statuses can be added because of new economies, new institutions, new social goals, or changes in other parts of the system, all of which may have concomitant reverberations in the social structure of the society.

Thus it can be said that the cultural system is unchanging only when viewed at a single point in time. When viewed over sufficient time, it is seen as an evolving, changing entity.

SUMMARY

The social structure of a society is the patterned way in which people are organized into groups and how they relate to each other. The concepts of status and role are fundamental to the understanding of all social systems. Statuses are specified positions within the social system. Roles are the characteristic ways of behaving that go with specific statuses. Social structure, thus, consists of sets of statuses and roles organized as institutions. Institutions are networks of behavior patterns focused upon specific goals and interests.

Statuses are attained (1) through achievement by mastering the linked behaviors, (2) through ascription, that is, the individual acquires a status through some biological characteristic such as sex or age, or (3) through some affinity, such as to the statuses of parents and kin, and the associations into which the child is born. Statuses can be ranked in a society; rank refers, in this instance, to hierarchical standing.

The use of status by behavioral scientists must be clearly distinguished from the ordinary use of the term. Status in the former sense is restricted to social position or identity. In common use it refers to rank and prestige, among several meanings. This latter use must be clearly distinguished from the scientific use of the term.

Age, sex, marital, and kinship statuses are fundamental and universal in human societies. At each stage of life, human beings make a social issue of transition crises. Each crisis marks a change in social status. Transition rites usually involve rituals of detachment, isolation, and reincorporation. They are practiced particularly at birth, adolescence, marriage, and death. Life is never drab for any group of people. Ritual and ceremony, anticipation and anxiety, and preparation and performance all color and lend zest to the act of living.

Finally, it must be reiterated that social systems continually change, and as they change so do the constituent roles, statuses, and institutions.

SELECTED READINGS

Banton, M., *Roles: An Introduction to the Study of Social Relations* (1965). The best review of the concept available, with ethnographic examples.

Drucker, P., and R. F. Heizer, *To Make My Name Good* (1967). A contemporary reexamination of the potlatch as practiced by the Kwakiutl Indians.

Gross, N., W. S. Mason, and A. W. McEachern, *Explorations in Role Analysis* (1958). Chapters 1 to 5 and 15 to 18 review the extensive literature from anthropology, sociology and psychology, and clarify many problems.

Kuper, H., *An African Aristocracy: Rank among the Swazi* (1947). Royalty and commoners in a South African tribe.

Mead, M., *Male and Female* (1949). An insightful and informative cross-cultural study of sexual roles in a changing world.

18

How Cultures Change

CHAPTER OUTLINE

LEARNING GOALS

Specify how invention and discovery can lead to culture change.

Define diffusion.

Discuss the diffusion of material and nonmaterial culture.

Explain the dynamics of diffusion.

Describe ideology and structure in cultural change.

Identify the role of the individual in culture change.

Understand the process of acculturation.

Discuss culture crises and enumerate some reactive movements.

All cultures change. Some have changed with great rapidity; others have remained relatively stable for hundreds and thousands of years. We have seen that the changes in Stone Age cultures from generation to generation were minuscule and that it took tens of thousands of years to develop even so simple a thing as a chipped-stone hand ax. Yet the culture of Japan changed from that of a feudal-peasant society to that of a front-rank industrial society in less than one hundred years.

The problem of differential rates of culture growth intrigues and puzzles layperson and scientist alike. One way to begin moving toward a solution to this problem is to examine the mechanisms or processes of culture change and growth.

Any culture changes and grows by acceptance of inventions devised by members of its own society or by acceptance of new ways invented elsewhere and brought to its members through diffusion.

INVENTION AND DISCOVERY

A discovery is the act of becoming aware of something which has been in existence but which has not been previously perceived. Vitamins and sunspots were discovered, not invented.

An invention is an alteration in, or a synthesis of, preexisting materials, conditions, or practices so as to produce a new form of material or action.

To illustrate the distinction between discovery and invention more fully, it might be noted that the first ninety-two elements, from hydrogen to uranium, were *discovered* by means of scientific perception. But the new transuranium elements, such as neptunium and plutonium, which have come into being since 1940, are truly *invented* elements. They did not exist in nature; they were produced as a result of the development of techniques for separating neutrons from their elemental nucleus and causing them to enter another elemental nucleus without producing fission. New combinations of protons, neutrons, and electrons were produced—hence, the new elements.

Homer Barnett, the anthropologist who has devoted more thinking and research to the problem of cultural innovation than any other in our time, uses the invention of manufactured gas as one example of this process:

Innumerable people have known that vapors emitted from crevices in certain parts of the earth are inflammable. About 1684, John Clayton verified reports of this phenomenon. . . . Conjecturing that there was a relationship between the gas, the earth's heat, and the coal deposits in nearby mines, he applied heat to coal placed in a retort . . . as a substitute for the earth. . . . Then, in a second step, he caught the released gas . . . in a bladder . . . instead of letting it escape into the atmosphere. . . . He punctured the bladder with a pin, brought a candle flame near the vent, and so produced the precursor of gas lights and burners.[1]

Clayton *discovered* that a volatile, flammable gas is locked in a solid state in coal; he *invented* an artificial technique for releasing and capturing it. In each act, however, there is a common element. Invention creates a new material combination by synthesizing a new idea from previously disconnected ideas. Discovery involves a perception of something that has been present but unnoticed. Until such time as someone performs the mental act of separating and isolating the unnoticed event from its natural context and then recombining it with other things in a new way, it has no recognized significance; it remains undiscovered.

Purposeful invention of this order is a rational process of imaginative substitutions and recombinations. It represents the most sophisticated level of cultural modification. Such a process is

[1]H. G. Barnett, "The Innovative Process" (*Kroeber Anthropological Society Papers*, no. 25, 1961), p. 32.

characteristic only of highly complex societies with a cultural bent toward dynamic change. Even here, however, relatively few societies include a great number of active, willful inventors.

Accidental Juxtaposition and Invention

In the nonliterate world, purposeful inventiveness is a rare occurrence. Conscious tinkering with the social structure or with material improvement is not usual. Most primitive inventions are nonvolitional. They result from what Greenman has called *accidental juxtaposition.*[2]

The operation of the principle of accidental juxtaposition on the pongid level may be illustrated in the activities of Sultan, one of Köhler's famous apes. Sultan was presented with a problem—how to get a banana. He was also presented with two hollow bamboo sticks, neither long enough in itself to reach the banana. They were so fashioned, however, that one could be snugly fitted within the other to make a stick long enough to meet the need. Sultan strained for a solution, but the best he could work out was to push one stick toward the banana with the other. This failed to capture the banana. At length, he gave up.

As he roamed around his cage looking for amusement, his attention was once more directed to the sticks. He picked them up and began to play with them in a casual manner and entirely without interest in the elusive banana. Suddenly he found himself holding the two sticks end to end. He pushed the one into the other. Lo, he had it! Accidental juxtaposition had resulted in a new set of relationships, a combination that constituted an invention. Immediately he went to the bars, used his tool, and pulled in the banana.[3]

We actually know very little of the precise steps by which most early inventions came into being. Long archaeological sequences such as those established for Old World and Southwest prehistory reveal only the external form of the gradual steps by which many artifacts have been developed over generations of time.

In the technical field the creation of a new type of artifact as a result of juxtaposition is a mental reaction to a stimulus in the environment. For the most part, "the progressive evolution of technical forms had to wait upon such accidental juxtapositions."[4]

Mere juxtaposition does not in itself automatically generate an invention. The current use, meaning, and function of particular artifacts or social forms may block acceptance of new forms, uses, meanings, and functions proposed by the new ideas. Resistance to new inventions is proverbial, and inventors are by no means always heroes.

Any new idea or new form must be created somewhere, sometime. Therefore it would be the height of foolishness to deny all inventiveness to preliterate people. Were they not inventive, cultures would never have changed. There would be none of the rich diversity in cultures which anthropology has discovered for us, nor would there have been any evolution of culture whatsoever through the ages. But the protracted span of the Old Stone Age—over two million years of hunting and gathering technology before the domestication of plants and animals—testifies to the rarity of innovation.

The vast majority of human societies can claim relatively few inventions. Abundant evidence proves that most accretions occur through borrowing, and this leads us to a consideration of diffusion.

DIFFUSION

If we find a particular trait or activity spread over a wide area and practiced by different societies,

---

[2]E. F. Greenman, "Material Culture and the Organism" (*American Anthropologist*, vol. 47, 1945), pp. 212ff.

[3]W. Köhler, *The Mentality of Apes*, pp. 130–133.

[4]Greenman, op. cit., p. 218.

FIGURE 18.1
Culture contact. An aboriginal elder, adorned for a traditional tribal ceremony, waits for a chance to cross the street in an Australian settlement on Melville Island, 1970. (W. Pedersen/Australian Information Service.)

there are several possible explanations. Each society may have invented the trait independently, or one or more groups may have invented it, after which it spread to the others by borrowing (Figure 18.1).

We can safely say that the first hypothesis is an impossibility. Historical observation establishes that all peoples have always borrowed. We know, for instance, that American Indians did not invent the domestication of the horse, nor the art of riding, nor halters, bits, reins, saddles, or any of the other accoutrements of riding. They were all adopted from the Spaniards, first by the tribes of the Southwest frontier, who passed them on to the north and east.[5]

The Diffusion of Material Culture

Material culture and technological processes are more readily borrowed than ideas and abstract concepts.

No one has expressed this better than the two missionaries to the Shipibo of the Upper Amazon, Fathers Girbal and Marques, who in 1792 wrote to their headquarters:

> *To reap it wholly and to bring to God all these heathens certain things are necessary, of which we are in need. . . . You will find added to our letter a note of these requisitions. . . . 400 axes, 600 cutlasses, 2000 straight knives, 1000 curved knives, 4 quintos of iron, 50 pounds of steel, 12 books of small fish-hooks, 8000 needles, one case of false pearls, 500 flints and steels, 4 gross of scissors, 2 gross of rings, 3000 brass crosses, 1000 varas of calico to cover the skin of those who are naked, an assortment of colours to paint our church, a . . . [Most I]mmaculate Virgin and some ornaments. We also want two skins of wine, both for the celebration of the holy sacrifice and to stop diarrhoea and bloody flux among the infidels.*[6]

Fathers Girbal and Marques sensed that if metal were first accepted, *then* these Stone Age gardeners might be ready to consider a new religion, the assumption being that a superior technology is the product of a more powerful mastery of the supernatural.

It does not take long to perceive the value of iron implements. Captain Cook, who was deified by the native Hawaiians in 1779, was later killed by them when he tried to recover one of his

[5]C. Wissler, "The Influence of the Horse in the Development of Plains Culture" (*American Anthropologist*, vol. 16, 1914), pp. 1–25; F. Haines, "Where Did the Plains Indians Get Their Horses?" (*American Anthropologist*, vol. 40, 1938), pp. 112–117, and "The Northward Spread of Horses among the Plains Indians" (*American Anthropologist*, vol. 40, 1938), pp. 429–437.

[6]Quoted in H. Hoffman, "Money, Ecology, and Acculturation among the Shipibo of Peru," in W. H. Goodenough (ed.), *Explorations in Cultural Anthropology*, p. 266.

ship's longboats which had been stolen so it could be stripped of its metal parts. It was thirty years later that Hawaiians decided to abandon their old ideational order and social system for the culture presented by the sailors; they realized that the material and ideational aspects of that culture went together, and they wanted both—plus the fact that certain members of the Hawaiian royal family found the taboo and social class system increasingly onerous and repugnant.[7]

The Diffusion of Nonmaterial Culture: Myths

Complex nonmaterial elements also spread through borrowing. In reconstructing histories of cultures, a number of similar practices are frequently found to have existed in two or more cultures. It is a canon of anthropological analysis that such similarities are the probable result of diffusion rather than of independent invention, especially if the group of traits has no inherent reason for existing as a complex.

Tylor was the first to formulate and apply this principle in a study of the diffusion of the ancient East Indian game of pachisi into prehistoric America, where it appeared among the Aztecs as *patolli* and in various other forms among other Indians.[8] Tylor established the historical relationship between the Asiatic and American forms of these games by "analysing such phenomena into constituent elements showing so little connection with one another that they may reasonably be treated as independent. The more numerous such elements, the more improbable the recurrence of the combination."[9]

This technique may be applied to any aspect of culture, but it is remarkably effective with myths because of the stability of myth complexes.[10] For our demonstration of the application of diffusion analysis by establishing internal congruity of traits, we shall use the "Tale of the Wandering Animals."

This story is familiar to all readers of Grimm's *Fairy Tales* as the "Musicians of Bremen." The old donkey, the worn-out hound, the abused cat, the rooster destined for the pot, and other rejected, decrepit animals all joined forces to go to the fair port of Bremen. Night closed in as they found themselves deep in the woods. Frightening a band of robbers out of a forest hut, they made themselves at home, each in a favorite spot—the cat on the hearth, the rooster in the rafters, the dog on the doorstep, the donkey on the dungheap. The robbers sent back a spy in the darkness. But when he lighted the fire, the cat flew in his face; the dog chewed his leg as he fled through the door; the donkey planted a kick; and the rooster crowed his doom. The weak and despised creatures frightened away the robbers, who are symbolic of those who normally rule and dominate, and the animals lived prosperously ever after in the snug little hut in the woods.

In Southeast Asia and Japan an ancient story is told, which is very similar, except it involves an egg, a scorpion, a needle, a piece of feces, and a rice mortar (or any hard, heavy object). They come together upon a journey, enter the house of an old woman during her absence, and, strategically placing themselves and using customary strengths appropriate to each, they drive her from her home upon her return.[11]

Here is the "Musicians of Bremen" all over again. Aarne justifiably concluded: "The concur-

[7]W. Davenport, "The 'Hawaiian Cultural Revolution': Some Political and Economic Considerations" (*American Anthropologist*, vol. 71, 1969), pp. 1–20.

[8]E. B. Tylor, "On the Game of Patolli in Ancient Mexico, and Its Probable Asiatic Origin" (*Journal of the Royal Anthropological Institute of Great Britain and Ireland*, vol. 8, 1879), pp. 116–129.

[9]E. B. Tylor, "American Lot Games as Evidence of Asiatic Intercourse before the Time of Columbus" (*Internationales Archiv fur Ethnographie*, vol. 9, supplement, 1896), p. 66. For a critical evaluation of Tylor's method, see C. J. Erasmus, "Patolli, Pachisi, and the Limitation of Possibilities" (*Southwestern Journal of Anthropology*, vol. 6, 1950), pp. 369–387.

[10]F. Boas, *Tsimshian Mythology* (Bureau of American Ethnology, Annual Report 31, 1916), pp. 393–558. This is the classic study of the reflection of a people's material culture and social organization in their mythology.

[11]A. Aarne, *Die Tiere auf der Wanderschaft* (Folklore Fellows Communications, no. 11, 1913), p. 100.

rences between the tales are so significant that . . . we must conclude that the stories stand in an interdependent relationship in their origin."[12]

A favored story of the Northwest Coast Indians of North America has now a familiar ring. It is "Raven's War on the South Wind."[13] Raven is the mythological culture hero of this area, and the South Wind often brings too much rain from the ocean.

The South Wind, so the story runs, was blowing so incessantly that all the creatures had to stay in their huts. They could not hunt, and they were hungry. The smoke blew back down their smoke vents and made their eyes sore. At last Raven proposed an attack on the Master of the South Wind. The war party made the journey but had trouble landing because the gale caused by the flatulence of the Master of the South Wind was so strong that they were nearly overcome.

But once ashore, Halibut and Flounder or Skate (all flat, slippery fish) arranged themselves according to Raven's orders just outside the South Wind's doorstep. Red Cod or the Wren went in and started a smudge. As the Master of the South Wind staggered from the house, he slipped on the fish and slithered down the beach, where the waiting animals tried to beat his brains out with clubs—which are as hard as a rice mortar or a donkey's hoof. The South Wind made a successful deal for his life—four days of good weather to alternate with four days of bad.[14]

Here, again, is a basic plot in which lowly objects or lowly animals overcome masters by combining their own little natural aptitudes. Its appeal as a vicarious release of suppressed resentments is clear. The ludicrousness of the event provides an elemental sort of gusty humor. The story is too good to keep. It has a broad appeal because it meets a common need. From Asia it spread westward into Europe and northeastward into the northwest corner of North America. This, however, is not the end of its history. In post-Columbian times, variants of the "Musicians of Bremen" form of the tale were brought to the eastern American Indians by early trappers, and on the Plains and in the Woodlands these variants were adapted into a charming story known as "Big Turtle's War Party."

Thus, by word of mouth, crossing language barrier after language barrier, the "Tale of the Wandering Animals" girdled the globe, penetrating North America from the west and from the east to meet itself along the rocky spine of the Western mountain area (Figure 18.2).

Dynamics of Diffusion

Diffusion is no simple, straight-line process in which an idea is put on wheels, figuratively speaking, and given a shove to send it around the world.

Every spreading idea, as it moves from one society to another, must face the test of its acceptability in the culture of the receivers; and if it is accepted, it is invariably reworked in form, use, meaning, or function. No people take an alien trait without altering it to some degree.

The Sun Dance The Plains Indian sun dance illustrates this clearly. The sun dance is a fairly complex ritual shared by a score of tribes in the western part of the Plains area. The ceremony is most elaborated among the Arapaho and Cheyenne. From these tribes, according to Spier's classic analysis, the complex spread to the other nomadic tribes.[15] The fundamental form of the dance is universal within the area of its distribution. Nevertheless, considerable variation in content occurs from tribe to tribe.

Selection often works in subtle ways that we cannot always determine later. Some of the

[12]Ibid., p. 162.

[13]Eleven versions are recorded in Boas, op. cit., pp. 79–81, 658–660.

[14]An analysis in full detail is given in E. A. Hoebel, "The Asiatic Origin of a Myth of the Northwest Coast" (*Journal of American Folklore*, vol. 54, 1941), pp. 1–12.

[15]L. Spier, *The Sun Dance of the Plains Indians* (American Museum of Natural History, Anthropological Papers, vol. 16, part 7, 1921).

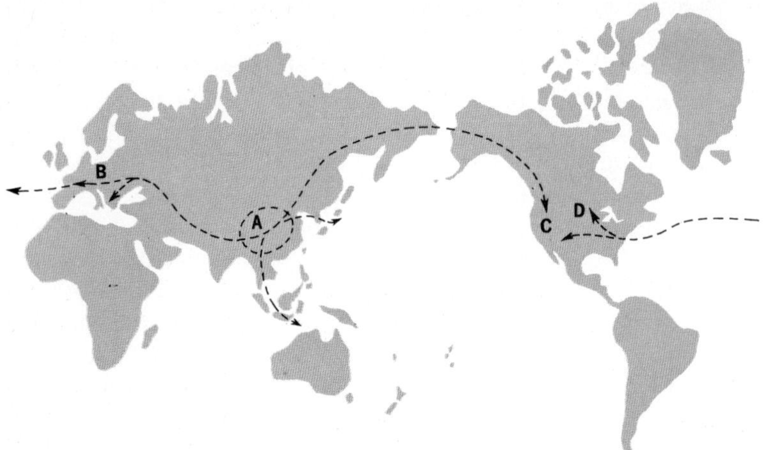

FIGURE 18.2
Diffusion of the Asiatic "Tale of the Wandering Animals." *A*, Asiatic center of origin; *B*, the "Musicians of Bremen" version; *C*, "Raven's War on the South Wind"; *D*, "Big Turtle's War Party."

more obvious determinants, however, may be quite clear. Thus, two features of the Arapaho sun dance are the use of medicine bundles and the special roles played by the military fraternity which sponsors the dance. Among the Wind River and Idaho Shoshones, neither of these occurs in connection with the dance. The reason is simply that the Shoshones have no military societies and no priesthood of bundle owners. As they adapted it, the sun dance became primarily a purification and curing ceremony, designed to bring general well-being to the entire tribe.

The Crows used the sun dance to generate war power against specific enemies. Revenge was the motif; a scalp, the object; a war party, the follow-up.

The Cheyenne sun dance was, and still is, a world-renewal ceremony. In the Cheyenne world view, the energy of the universe is being continuously used up and must be annually recharged mimetically through the ceremonies. Although the dance is pledged by one individual, the entire renewal effort is directed toward the welfare of all members of the tribe.

Thus, the function and meaning of the sun dance varied as it was worked into each culture. For the buffalo hunters in the mid-nineteenth century, its chief function was that of tribal integration. The scattered bands that eked out the winter separately were brought together in early summer for a grand socializing prior to the communal buffalo hunt. For individuals, the dance functioned to relieve anxiety. It also expressed a subconscious submissiveness to the supernatural through self-imposed hunger and thirsting and bloody immolation of the self to gratify the spirit forces. It functioned to make more probable the acquisition of power through visions by means of heightened social suggestion.

As the sun dances are performed today, they function mostly as reinforcers of social integrity in the face of all the surrounding forces of disintegration.

The selective effect of ideology, or meaning, on culture diffusion and reinterpretation may be seen if we compare the celebration of the Fourth of July by the Crows and Northern Cheyennes in the 1970s. On the Crow reservation, a large crowd gathers at a racetrack. The betting is as spirited as the horses ridden by Crow Indians in colorful jockey costumes. The shouting is loud. The fireworks are deafening. There is no sun dance.

At the Cheyenne reservation, a few miles away, an essentially traditional sun dance comes to its four-day climax. The dancers move through the ceremonial forms with somewhat weary dignity. The audience watches quietly. A neatly lettered sign reads: "Quiet. No Fireworks Allowed."

Why such a difference between the two Plains societies, whose acquaintance stretches back over many years and who still live side by side?

It is obvious that both groups are celebrating the Fourth of July and that as citizens of the United States they recognize this date as a symbol of American identity. The Cheyennes, with their age-old emphasis on world renewal and group solidarity, seem not so much to be celebrating the birth of the nation as seeking to revivify it through their tribal efforts. The basic meaning of the dance has changed little, although its form has worn a bit thin. The time of the dance has been changed from early June to July 4, signifying tribal integration into a new and larger society. School vacations and work schedules make this a convenient date.

The original function of the Crows' sun dance, to bring success in scalp hunting, has long vanished. The meaning of the dance was too specialized to permit adaptation to contemporary conditions. But gambling and horse racing, with their attendant noisy clamor, are ancient pastimes. It was natural for the Crows to seize on the festive aspect of July Fourth and to make of it a noisy carnival as they, too, proclaim their identity with the United States.

The Importance of Meaning This fundamental anthropological fact—that in cultural transference a trait or complex will be evaluated and rejected, or accepted and modified, in terms of the meaning it has for the receiving people—is one of the most difficult for professional agents of change to perceive and apply. This applies alike to teachers, Peace Corps volunteers, economic-development programmers, public health workers, and missionaries. When this principle is ignored, the consequent mischief worked is often monumental.

Over one hundred years ago, a wise and not too doctrinaire Episcopalian missionary demonstrated a full recognition of this aspect of intercultural transference. Sensing the likelihood of misinterpretation of the Christian rite of communion by the Tsimshian Indians he omitted the ritual from his services. Cannibalism among the Northwest Coast Indians, although quite different in meaning for the Indians, was too similar to communion in form and function. Not only in this but in other points as well did the missionary in question deliberately eliminate "many of the potential danger spots in Christian metaphysics for a native whose only basis for interpreting new belief was in terms of the old."[16]

Even with foresight, one cannot anticipate some consequences of interpretation of new phenomena in terms of old meanings. For example, the Dani people of the Balim Valley in West Irian (New Guinea) are active cannibals. American missionaries who entered the area in the 1950s discouraged the practice in their efforts to promote civilization and Christianization. As the Dani became familiar with eating canned goods, they quickly comprehended that a tin bearing a picture of beans on its label contained beans, that one picturing pears contained pears, and so forth. When one of the mission wives gave birth and cans of Gerber's baby food with pictures of healthy babies on the labels were flown in, the Danis's idea of the eating habits of the American missionaries need not be guessed.[17]

The consequences of negative meanings Traits that have positive meaning in one culture may be blocked in diffusion because their forms are associated with negatively colored uses, meanings, or functions in the existing cultures of potential receivers.

At a Northern Cheyenne peyote meeting, the senior author once became interested in a decorative staff used in the ritual. It seemed to be

---

[16]H. G. Barnett, "Applied Anthropology in 1860" (*Applied Anthropology*, vol. 1, 1942), p. 24.

[17]Personal communication from a member of the mission organization, 1962.

(a)

(b)

FIGURE 18.3
Cultural adaptation to change. (a) In 1960, Australian natives helped celebrate the Northern Territory Centennial at Alice Springs. The long wooden tube, called a *didjeridu*, is played to a rhythmic stick accompaniment. (Australian News and Information Bureau.) (b) Thirteen years later, in 1973, Mr. George Winunguj accompanied the Adelaide Wind Quintet with his *didjeridu* on a concert tour of the United States. (J. Fitzpatrick/Austrialian Information Service.)

carved with figures of bison quite similar to those of Franco-Cantabrian cave art. The thought was intriguing. Upon closer examination, however, the carved scenes proved to be of matadors and charging bulls. There was also the Mexican eagle sitting on a cactus, but the snake in its claws had been scraped out. Black Wolf, the peyote leader, explained that the staff had come from Mexico, and he pointed out that the eagle is good medicine. The matador confronting the bull suggested the vision-seeking Indian confronted by a bison. However, he said, "Those people down there worship snakes, but we don't. So we took the snakes out. We can't have any snakes in our ceremony." The Cheyennes, in point of fact, are not simply neutral with respect to snakes. In their mythology, the Horned Snake (or the Plumed Serpent) is a creature to be feared and avoided.

This example demonstrates that the preexisting biases of the members of a receiving society facilitate or block the accepting or borrowing of any new cultural elements. The compatibility of a new way with the basic postulates underlying the receiving culture is of vital importance. On the other hand, the acceptance of materials of apparently neutral significance but of demonstrated technical efficiency, such as iron or tractors, may ultimately lead to disruptions that were not anticipated. The successful development of lunar and interplanetary rockets, for example, obviously holds undreamed-of future cultural consequences. Yet we seem quite willing to take our chances.

The consequences of cultural indifference A thing or an idea may be seen or encountered and yet not be borrowed, adapted, or even desired. It meets no felt need of a people; or its usefulness is not perceived by them; it rings no bell. Their interest is in other things or ideas. Loren Eiseley astutely comments of the Maya, who were capable of inventing such an abstraction as the concept of the zero, plus a hieroglyphic symbol to represent it:

These men who could predict eclipses never learned to weigh or to use the wheel for transportation, though wheeled toys were in use among their neighbors. No better example could be utilized to reveal that a given society has just so much energy and interest at its disposal, and that its intellectual achievements will move in the path of its deepest motivations. The Mayan intellect centered upon a divine mathematics that controlled the human world, just as different cultures, including our own, have pursued reality in other shapes and guises.[18]

IDEOLOGY AND STRUCTURE IN CULTURAL CHANGE

We have been discussing the acceptability and rejection of innovations in terms of their compatibility to preexisting cultural standards (ideal norms). Usually, however, this is not a clear and simple matter. Every innovation begins with the act of somebody. Who that somebody is and how the new idea is introduced can make a great difference.

The Place of the Individual

Values are never absolutely consistent and tensions engendered by alternative choices are always present. In no phase of human life is this more evident than in the conflict between the urges of individual sexuality and the standardized channeling of sex in society.

To take a Cheyenne case in illustration: Cheyennes viewed the energy quotient of the universe as limited, and they extended this view to sexual relations. Unlike their neighbors the Comanches, they did not allow for sexual competition among the males. The Comanches frequently stole one another's wives; the Cheyennes did not. But then a wily Cheyenne who wanted another man's wife schemed to alter the Cheyenne pattern:

A war party was organizing. Walking Rabbit approached the leader with a question. "Is it true that you have declared we must all go afoot? If so, I would like to be able to lead a horse to pack my moccasins and possibles." The leader gave him an answer: . . . "I want no horses, that it may be easier for us to conceal our movements. However, you may bring one horse." Then Walking Rabbit asked for instructions concerning the location of the first and second

[18]L. Eiseley, "In the Beginning Was the Artifact" (*Saturday Review*, Dec. 7, 1963), p. 52.

nights' camps, for he would start late and overtake the party.
camps, for he would start late and overtake the party.

Walking Rabbit's sweetheart had been married only recently. . . . "My husband is not the man I thought he was," she told her former suitor. So Walking Rabbit took her to join the war party. . . .

When they saw this woman there, the warriors got excited. The party turned into the hills and stopped. The leader opened his pipe. The leader's pipe was always filled before they left the camp, but it was not smoked until the enemy was seen or their tracks reported. Now the leader spoke. "When we take a woman with us it is usually known in the camp. Here is a man who has sneaked off with another's wife. Now what is going to happen?" . . .

The decision was that he had to go back. "If you had told us you wanted her so badly, we might have waited for you to settle for her. Then we could have taken her the right way. If you really want to go to war with us, you will be able to overtake us. We are afoot."

Then three or four warriors spoke up, each promising Walking Rabbit a horse to send to the husband. Everyone gave one or two arrows to be sent as well.

In the meantime Walking Rabbit's father had fixed it up with the aggrieved husband. Since he and his wife were incompatible, he was willing to release her. When Walking Rabbit came in and told his father the story of the soldiers' action, the father said, "Just let that stand. The thing is fixed. When those fighters come back they may want to give to the girl's parents. You go back after your party." . . .

When Walking Rabbit did not go out, his closest relatives raised a big tipi. . . .

The warriors came charging in, shooting; they had taken many horses. The first coup-counters were in the van. Walking Rabbit's father had a right to harangue; he was a crier. "Don't go to your homes! Don't go to your own lodges! Come here to the lodge of Walking Rabbit, your friend!"

When they were all in this lodge the old man entered and told them his story. "I had this thing all settled before my son returned. You have sent arrows and promised horses. Now I have kept this girl here pending your return. I shall send her back to her parents with presents. I have waited to see what you are going to do."

The leader replied for his followers. "Yes, we will help you. We promised to help your son. When you send her back, we'll send presents with her." The men who had promised horses went out to get them. . . .

Sending her back with these presents was giving wedding gifts. Her relatives got them all. They gathered up their goods to send back. The war party was called together once more; to them this stuff was given. It was a great thing for the people to talk about. It was the first and last time a woman was sent home on enemy horses the day they came in.[19]

In this instance, which took place about 1820, an innovation was rejected and, with ceremony and gift giving, was made so memorable that the people could never forget it. What is more, the reinforced norm against wife stealing stuck: from then until the end of the raiding days (1878), there were no more attempts by lovers to travel with war parties. Walking Rabbit failed as an innovator. Cheyenne moral ideology was reaffirmed and reinforced.

Successful Innovation

On the other hand, a Kapauku schemer, who was wholly successful in abrogating the incest rules of his society, illustrates in fine detail some of the specific factors of motivation and action involved in cultural change.

The Kapauku are gardeners living in West Irian (New Guinea).[20] Awiitigaaj was a Big Man, a village headman, and a leader of a political confederacy that links a pair of lineages (groups formed by descent through a single parental line) and their several villages. Up to the year 1935, the penalty for incest within the lineage was death. Like Walking Rabbit, Awiitigaaj took a fancy to a forbidden woman and wanted to marry her. "I liked her; she was beautiful." So he ran off with her. "The infuriated relatives of the couple pursued the lovers, and the girl's

[19]K. N. Llewellyn and E. A. Hoebel, *The Cheyenne Way*, pp. 13–15.

[20]L. Pospisil, *Anthropology of Law*, pp. 214–232, and "Structural Change and Primitive Law: Consequences of a Papuan Legal Case," in L. Nader (ed.), *Law in Culture and Society*, pp. 208–229.

father, Ugataga, who was coheadman of the Ijaaj-Jamaina sublineage . . . ruled that both his daughter and her lover must be executed by arrow according to Kapauku customary law. His decision was upheld by the head of the Ijaaj-Pigome Confederacy."[21]

Awiitigaaj knew, however, that when the girl's father's anger had cooled, he would realize that the execution would deprive him of a very large progeny price and an important son-in-law—a serious conflict of public and private interests. So the couple hid out in the jungle, aided and abetted by Awiitigaaj's maternal kin, who were custom-bound to protect him regardless of his offense. The outraged father of the bride continued to put on public temper tantrums and speeches, but under pressure from neutral leaders gradually agreed to settle for a progeny-price payment. In so doing, he accepted the legitimacy of the marriage. Eventually, because the members of the girl's sublineage became impatient over delays in the payment of the progeny price, they attacked Awiitigaaj's lineage mates with sticks. In a countersuit the latter were freed of the need to pay any progeny price whatsoever, whereupon they too publicly agreed to the acceptability of the marriage. The precedent became a new alternative. By 1954, 22 percent of the marriages within the lineage were with previously forbidden lineage mates.

Neighboring lineages followed suit and a fundamental change in the postulates requiring sib-exogamy was clearly effected. A significant change in the social structure had been brought about by a skillful self-seeker who successfully manipulated a complex situation to achieve a change in ideology, kinship organization, and law. In 1954, nearly two-thirds of the adult members of the village originally involved reported that they approved of the change.

Stimulus Diffusion

Culture contact generates culture change. In the two case studies just cited, the Cheyenne had the Comanche example to provide the idea, and Awiitigaaj knew of the existence of lineage endogamy (marriage restricted to one's own lineage) in a neighboring population. In these instances the change process is one which is known in anthropology as *stimulus diffusion.*

Stimulus diffusion occurs when the general idea of a culture trait or complex is transferred from one society to another without a transmission of the actual detailed content. Stimulus diffusion as a process stands midway between invention and diffusion. Awareness of a need or an inventive possibility is stimulated by contact with an alien source. The stimulated people, who lack the trait, create an equivalent of it.

ACCULTURATION

Acculturation occurs when a society undergoes drastic culture change under the influence of a more dominant culture and society with which it has come in contact.[22] The acculturating society alters its culture in the direction of adjustment and (greater or lesser) conformity to cultural ideology and patterns of the dominant society. However, the acculturating society, although significantly modified in its lifeway, retains a discrete identity.

Acculturation is a special form of culture change. But it works both ways (Figure 18.3). European Americans, as they built up the culture of the United States, borrowed many traits from the American Indian: cultivation of maize, beans, and squash in hills; maple syrup and sugar production; snowshoes, toboggans, and canoes, to name only a few items. The government of the United States built an elaborate legal subculture to accommodate to the presence of the

[21]L. Pospisil, *Anthropology of Law*, p. 216.

[22]A standard definition of acculturation emphasizes "changes in the culture patterns of either or both groups"; R. Redfield, R. Linton, and M. J. Herskovits, "Outline for the Study of Acculturation" (*American Anthropologist*, vol. 38, 1936), p. 149.

many tribes within the federal legal system. There was indeed a good deal of culture change produced in response to the presence of American Indian societies on the continent. But few Americans were assimilating to the Indian way of life. On the other hand, many American Indians, over the decades, changed their cultures in the direction of Westernized modes of life.

Differential Acculturation: The Menomini Indians

Once again it must be emphasized that culture change occurs first in individual behavior. The change appears as a deviation from previous customary norms. It can be hailed with enthusiasm, be overlooked, be mildly disapproved and lightly sanctioned, or be rejected outright and heavily sanctioned. At any rate, it never takes place totally and instantaneously throughout any society.

The most effective demonstration to date of the point of differential acculturation is found in the study of the psychology of the Menomini Indians of Wisconsin. By using a schedule of sociocultural indices "for placing subjects on an acculturative continuum and defining explicit values associated with the native or American culture," plus autobiographies and intensive personal interviews, the investigators developed a fivefold classification by degree of acculturation.[23] In summary form, they are as follows:

A. *Native-oriented*—all members of the Medicine Lodge and/or Dream Dance group where the patterns of traditional culture survive to the greatest extent.
B. *Peyote Cult*—composed of participating members and constitutes a unique variation of culture conflict resolution with the transitional position.
C. *Transitional*—consisting of persons in cultural transition who have participated in native-oriented religious activities and Catholicism and Western culture during their lifetimes, but are at present not clearly identified with either group.
D. *Lower class acculturated*—persons who were born Catholic and maintain this identification, know little or nothing of native traditions, but who have acculturated to a laboring class standard.
E. *Elite acculturated*—composed of persons who participate regularly in Catholic services, are members of the prestigeful Catholic Mother's and Holy Name Societies, and, if male, occupy managerial or semiprofessional positions in the tribal lumber industry or agency.[24]

Figure 18.4 shows the relative positions of the Menomini groups on the continuum of acculturation from native to American, combined with degree of socioeconomic status *within* the larger, midwestern regional society of Wisconsin.

The most valuable and significant feature of the Spindler studies lies not so much in the explicit demonstration of differential acculturation in behavior but rather in the revelation of parallel differences in the deeper psychological adjustments of the different Menomini groups. This was achieved through use of Rorschach's inkblot tests, which show that

. . . [T]he native-oriented group operate with deep internal controls over aggression. The people are inward-oriented, not achievement-oriented; they lack overt emotional responsiveness but are sensitive to the nuances of interpersonal relations; they are fatalistic in orientation, and exhibit quiet endurance under stress or deprivation. . . . There is no marked evidence of anxiety or internal conflict, nor a free-flowing spontaneity.

The Peyotists . . . are highly committed to the ideology and ritual of Peyotism stressing rumination about one's self, sins, and salvation, attainment of power individually and through partaking of Peyote.

[23]G. D. Spindler, *Sociocultural and Psychological Processes in Menomini Acculturation* (University of California Publications in Culture and Society, vol. 5, 1955); L. Spindler and G. D. Spindler, "Male and Female Adaptations in Culture Change" (*American Anthropologist*, vol. 60, 1958), pp. 217–233.

[24]L. Spindler and G. D. Spindler, op. cit., pp. 218–219.

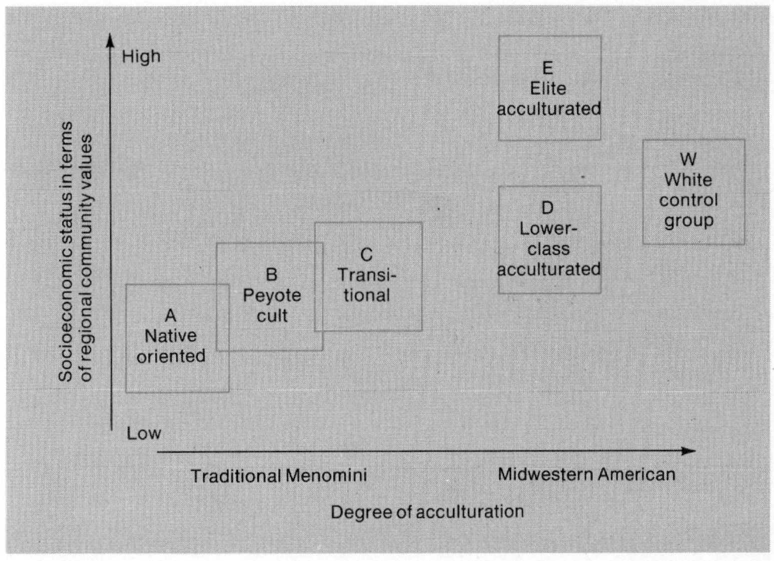

FIGURE 18.4
Differential acculturation and socioeconomic status of Menomini Indians in relation to the larger American (Wisconsin) regional society. (Adapted from G. D. Spindler.)

. . . There is significant relaxing of controls over emotions and overt expression of feelings, with public crying during testimonials and rituals and bids for collective expressions of sympathy. . . .

The . . . transitionals are characterized by very uneven adjustments. . . . Some are striving for . . . goals recognizable in the surrounding non-Indian community; others are withdrawn and mostly just vegetate; others go on destructive rampages, during or between drunks. Beating, murders, illegitimacy, dirt and disorder are a way of life for many in the latter group. The Menomini transitionals are like human populations everywhere who have lost their way; for them neither the goals of the traditional or the new culture are meaningful.

The acculturated, and particularly the elite, are radically different from any of the other groups. The roles they occupy demand punctuality, regular hours of concentrated work, orderly behavior and planning, pride in material possessions and economic status. The psychological data on them shows that they are emotionally open, but not disorganized. They utilize their emotional energy in the attainment of goals—personal success, material acquisition—approved of by middle-class persons in the surrounding communities. They are concerned about production and competition. They react to environmental pressures in a controlled but aggressive manner. They are also more anxious and tense than the native-oriented, but this anxiety is focused, rather than diffuse (as it is among the transitionals).

The acculturated Menomini deny their identity as Indians and specifically disclaim any relationship to "those Indians"—the members of the native-oriented group. Most of them do not speak their own language. The few who do rarely use it. Their homes and possessions are indistinguishable from those of Whites in nearby towns.

It is evident that the radical departure represented by the elite acculturated in the acculturative continuum of the Menomini occurs in both the manifest and psychological phases of adaptation. In order to "make the grade" on the terms of American middle-class culture the elite had to learn to stop being Menomini and learn how to be middle-class, achievement-oriented Americans.[25]

If the Spindlers' study were repeated today, it would probably include a sixth category—"elite acculturated militant." It would consist of edu-

[25]G. D. Spindler, "Psychocultural Adaptation," in E. Norbeck, D. Price-Williams, and W. M. McCord (eds.), *The Study of Personality,* pp. 329–330. (© Holt, Rinehart, and Winston, Inc. Quoted with permission.)

(a)

(b)

FIGURE 18.5
Modern technology transforms Eskimo culture. (a) Oil-heated houses replace igloos in Bethel, Alaska, while the car is left in outdoor winter storage in favor of the newly developed snowmobile on which the Eskimo woman drives her children on a shopping trip. (b) Staple American foods are purchased in a superette market. (Steve McCutcheon/Alaska Pictorial Service.)

cated Menomini with urban experience who have the object of reviving tribal identity and gaining tribal rights from the United States government and the state of Wisconsin.[26]

Finally, not only are the psychological characteristics of the male Menomini different in degree and kind of acculturation, but Menomini women show much less psychological change than do Menomini men. In their more traditional roles as wives and mothers, less is demanded of them in acculturative adustments. "They do not find the

[26]D. McNickle, *Native American Tribalism: Indian Survivals and Renewals.*

flux and conflict of rapid change as disturbing as do the males."[27]

To sum up: Some Menominis have acculturated so completely that they are assimilated within Midwestern white society—behaviorally and psychologically. Some are in marginal transition. Some have sought a new type of adjustment in a "reactive movement," the Peyote Cult, which is neither white nor old Menomini, and a small handful cling to a residual belief in what is left of old Menomini ways.

Can one say that all the Menomini Indians are acculturated? No. Can one say that most Menomini Indians are significantly acculturated? Yes. Can one say that all Menomini Indians have experienced significant culture change in the past 200 years? Most definitely. With variations in degree and form, it seems probable that a Menomini-like model holds good for all Eskimos and Indians who have survived in the Western Hemisphere and for peoples in other parts of the world.

Forced and Voluntary Change

Throughout human history, trade and alliance have provided the major pipelines for diffusion and cultural change. Traders bring new objects of material culture and news of people who have different lifeways. Traders are almost always welcomed (once the nature of their roles is perceived) and their technically superior or more easily acquired goods are quickly incorporated (Figure 18.5). This is as true of prehistoric and aboriginal traders as it is of the harbingers of civilization (see pages 459–462, on trade).

Intertribal alliances produce intermarriage and ceremonial visitations in which cultural forms may be copied or transferred. In the early 1930s, religious specialists from Taos Pueblo, for instance, were invited to Santa Ana Pueblo, in New Mexico, ritually to repair the roof of the mission church. In exchange, the Santa Anas taught them the songs and steps of a dance, giving them the right to perform it thereafter. Such culture change is obviously voluntary.

Slave taking, the forcible removal of individuals from their societies and their injection into an alien one, forces anguishing cultural readjustments. Conquest and political subjugation, with or without slavery, has even greater acculturative effects, for the conquered must accommodate to the rule and presence of the conquerors in their own territory.

Settlers, missionaries, educators, medical and technological specialists, and even tourists and travelers all play their roles. Nor are we speaking only of the European expansion and colonial imperialism of recent centuries. The Indonesian archipelago was Hinduized by conquering Indian princes and priests beginning in the tenth century and continuing until overthrown by Muslim converts in the fifteenth and sixteenth centuries. Centuries before (600 B.C.), Greek traders and settlers Hellenized the Upper Indus Valley, and later, Greek teacher-slaves gave much to the intellect of Rome; then Rome transformed the barbarian world of Europe. For some hundreds of years, Arab slavers, traders, and teachers have made a cultural mark on the Africans of the Sudan. Acculturation is the response to militantly dominant cultures and/or those which offer more effective adaptations to environments and answers to the mysteries of life.

CULTURE CRISIS AND REACTIVE MOVEMENTS

When value systems are too inconsistent with existing realities, a condition of cultural crisis may occur. Culture crisis may breed reactive movements. Such movements are the product of the gap between present circumstance and dreamed-of expectancy.

If the dominant aim of a movement is to raise up a depressed group which has long suffered in an inferior social standing and which has its own

[27] L. Spindler and G. D. Spindler, op. cit., p. 229.

special subcultural ideology, the movement is called *millenarism.* Prophetic Judaism and early Christianity are examples.

If the movement aims to reconstitute a destroyed but not forgotten way of life, it is called *nativistic* or *revivalistic.* The Plains Indians' ghost dance is an example.

If the movement seeks to speed up the acculturation process in order to share more quickly and fully in the supposed benefits of dominant cultures, it may be called *transitional.*

Finally, if the aim of the movement is directed primarily to the ideological system and the attendant social structure of a cultural system from within, the movement is called *revolutionary.*

Millenarism: Christianity

Although aspects of millenarism may be found in other parts of the world, it is particularly a Western phenomenon found in the Judaic, Christian, and Islamic cultural traditions. It is a form of religious utopianism based upon a firm conviction that the gap between the ideal in culture and the real in social life can be and will be closed.

The Latin term *millenium* literally means a period of a thousand years. According to the millenarian tradition, which is based on Jewish apocalyptic literature and the Revelations of St. John, Christ will appear in the guise of a warrior, vanquish the Devil, and hold him prisoner. He will then build the Kingdom of God and reign in person for a thousand years. Those saints who have remained steadfast and who have given their lives for their faith shall be raised from the dead and serve as His royal priesthood. At the end of this period, Satan will be let loose again for a short while and will finally be destroyed. The victory will be followed by the general resurrection of the dead, the last judgment, and final redemption.[28]

Through the centuries, millenial cults have risen and fallen, often with a messianic leader, often without. The means are always supernatural and mystic. The end is cultural perfection realized—at a stroke.

[28]Y. Talmon, "Millenarism" (*International Encyclopedia of the Social Sciences,* vol. 10, 1968), p. 349.

Nativistic Movements: The Ghost Dance

Wave after wave of crisis movements swept through the American Indian populations in the nineteenth century. Of these, the Ghost Dance Movement of 1890 is the most famous.

The last of the tribes had been subjugated by the United States, the buffalo were gone, measles, smallpox and cholera had decimated many tribal populations, most of their lands had been ceded and opened to white settlement, the religious powers on which their security rested had proved inadequate. Destructive catastrophe had overwhelmed virtually all the tribes.

In 1890 a Paiute prophet arose. Wovoka was his name. He had learned some Christian theology from the ranch family for whom he worked.

In a delirium of fever, he was lifted up to see God. Heaven was full of happy dead persons who would never grow old and who enjoyed pleasant work and games. Their idyllic life would be brought to all on earth in a grand reunion of dead and living, in a good life that would never end, God said, if living human beings would stop fighting, live in loving goodness, and dance the ceremony God gave to him. An earthquake or flood would wipe out the bad old earth in preparation for the new, but good people need not fear it.

At the news of the messiah, various tribes reacted variously. Since they would soon rejoin the dead, the Arapaho gave up shooting their horses and gashing their arms in mourning when someone died. To escape the flood, they should go to high mountains, leaving skeptics behind to turn to stone and the whites to be covered. On the new skin of the earth, game would once again abound. . . . The Shoshone said a deep four-day sleep would come over all believers, and they would awaken on the fifth to a new world. Kiowa thought the new earth would slide from the

FIGURE 18.6
On Tana Island, New Hebrides, the Messiah of the members of the cargo cult is a legendary American, John Frum, who like the American troops of World War II will provide them with all good things. Tannese followers drill like soldiers every February 15, John Frum Day. (Kal Muller/Woodfin Camp.)

west over the old one, bearing buffalo and elk upon it, and their sacred dance feathers would lift the faithful up onto the new world. Some Arapaho spoke of a wall of flame that would drive the whites back to their own country; sacred feathers would lift them over the fire and a twelve-day rain would subsequently extinguish it. The Walapai awaited a hurricane, the thunder of which would kill the whites and unbelievers. All these tribes believed the whites would be eliminated through supernatural means, and they bitterly blamed the warlike Sioux for later taking naturalistic means to this same end.[29]

A few Sioux, under Yellow Shirt, turned the Ghost Dance into an active resistance movement. They died at Wounded Knee.[30]

Transitional Movements: The Cargo Cult

In the South Seas, crisis cults first began in the 1870s and 1880s as nativistic movements, but by 1914 the emphasis shifted from overturning the white colonialists (so as to revert to "the good old days") to getting direct access to European goods. Proper ceremony would bring in the cargo ships loaded with canned food, tobacco, cloth, lamps, axes, knives, and rifles. These were all material objects which the whites did not make (so far as the Melanesians could observe). Nor did most of the whites in the South Pacific know *how* to make them. If you want these things, how do you get them? You order them! The ships and planes bring them. That is all there is to it, as any reasonable person can see.

"Ordering" is a form of ritual control over the remotely located, unseen beings who make the goods. Old aboriginal rituals are abandoned, masks destroyed or sold off to Europeans; fields may be abandoned, new ceremonies with new symbols introduced, marching drills abound (Figure 18.6). Wharfs are built to receive the ships and welcoming miniature airstrips are hacked out on jungle mountain ridgetops to receive cargo planes far from the ocean.

A central idea among New Guineans is that their own spirit ancestors actually produce all the material goods, which are intended for them and not for the Europeans. But the whites developed a magic (religion) to divert the goods to themselves. The new cargo cult religions will ritually rectify that.

World War II intensified the cargo cult move-

[29]W. LaBarre, *The Ghost Dance*, p. 230.
[30]J. Mooney, *The Ghost Dance Religion and Sioux Outbreak of 1890.*

ments in Melanesia. The thousands of American ships and planes which flooded the beaches and bases with seemingly inexhaustible supplies of goods, many carelessly tossed away or generously given to the Melanesians, confirmed the belief that all these things could be theirs—always—if only the proper compelling rituals could be invented.

Transition cults reach out to the new. They may appear to be irrational and unrealistic when viewed from the outside, but they have their own logic, in terms of the original world views and the limited knowledge of the total cultures with which the groups are confronted.[31]

Revolutionary Movements: Cultural

Max Gluckman has written with much insight on the social function of "rituals of rebellion" designed to "oust the incumbents of offices of power or influence without attempting to alter the nature of those offices or the claims of particular types of persons to be their incumbents."[32] In political revolution, attempts are made to seize the offices of power in order to change social structure, belief systems, and their symbolic representations. Political revolutions are usually turbulent, violent, and not long-lasting. A successful revolution soon moves to reestablish a stable, though changed, social structure; yet, "it has far-reaching political, social, and sometimes economic and cultural consequences."[33]

Cultural revolutions, on the other hand, extend over decades and centuries. They are the cumulative product of culture change that has moved technologies and societies in a given direction which can hardly be discerned while the change is going on. Looking back, however, evolutionary leaps can be seen to have occurred. In human culture history, we have seen that the first such revolutionary change was the development of Paleolithic culture, when human beings learned toolmaking, controlled the use of fire, and developed speech along with belief and symbolic systems. The second such revolutionary change was initiated in the Mesolithic Age when human beings gave up hunting and gathering for intensive foraging. It was intensified in the Neolithic urban revolution and the rise of civilization. It is just now being completed as the last of the globe's preliterate peoples are being brought within the cultural network of industrialization. But industrialization, as a phase of cultural evolution, is in the process of being replaced by new forms of culture expressive of the Atomic Space Age.

[31]For an overall view of cargo cults, see P. Worseley, *The Trumpet Shall Sound.*

[32]M. Gluckman, *Politics, Law, and Ritual in Tribal Society*, p. 137.

[33]W. Laqueur, "Revolution" (*International Encyclopaedia of the Social Sciences*, vol. 13, 1968), p. 505.

SUMMARY

Cultures grow and change by discovery, invention, and borrowing. A discovery is an act of becoming aware of something in existence but not previously perceived. In an invention, on the other hand, preexistent materials or ideas are rearranged to produce a new material or form of action. Nonvolitional inventions often result from accidental juxtaposition. Two things happen: somebody sees significance in the combination, and brings the two things together.

Most cultures grow by borrowing from other groups. The process is that of diffusion. Material culture diffuses much more rapidly than ideas and concepts. The utility of a steel ax when compared to one of stone is easier to sense than is belief in a particular spirit being, for example. Nonetheless, complex, nonmaterial elements, such as myths, ceremonies, and games, also spread through borrowing.

However, no people ever takes an alien trait without altering it. First, it must pass the test of acceptability in terms of a people's basic values. If it is accepted, it is invariably reworked in form, use, meaning, and function. Individuals as innovators may strongly influence how a given people evaluate a new possibility, as the Cheyenne and Kapauku cases illustrate. When a general idea is borrowed, but its specific form and other qualities are provided by the borrowers of the idea, the process is known as *stimulus diffusion.*

Acculturation occurs when a society undergoes drastic culture change under the influence of a dominant society. Within a society, acculturation proceeds at different rates, as illustrated by the Menomini.

Culture crisis occurs when traditional values cannot be realized. Culture crisis usually creates reactive movements. *Millenarism* is a movement based on the belief that a complete and perfect transformation of society will take place by the will of God and will last a thousand years, whereupon the forces of evil will be destroyed forever. *Nativistic movements*, such as the Ghost Dance, seek to reestablish an old way of life and to wipe out the forces which have altered or destroyed it. *Transitional movements*, such as the cargo cults of Melanesia, seek to establish a material or spiritual incorporation of new elements, derived from culture contact, within the context of old ideological patterns. Political *revolutionary movements* differ from rebellions in that the latter seek only to change officeholders without seriously altering institutions. Political revolutionary movements seize the offices of power in order to change social structure, belief systems, and their symbolic representations.

Cultural revolution tends to be drawn out over decades and centuries and has occurred on a grand scale but three times in human history: when human beings first learned toolmaking and developed speech and symbolic belief systems; when they domesticated plants and animals, and developed cities and civilization; and when human beings produced industrialization and entered the Atomic Space Age.

SELECTED READINGS

Barnett, H. G., *Innovation: The Basis of Cultural Change* (1953). The most intensive effort so far at systematic analysis of the processes of culture growth.

Bee, R. L., *Patterns and Processes: An Introduction to Anthropological Strategies for the Study of Sociocultural Change (1974).* A review of contributions to the study of change.

Goodenough, W. H., *Cooperation in Change: An Anthropological Approach to Community Development* (1963). Two-thirds of this excellent book is devoted to a conceptual analysis of cultural change. The rest is given over to practical problems in community development.

Hogbin, H. I., *Social Change* (1958). This book discusses change and acculturation in Africa and Melanesia with great acumen. A very worthwhile book.

Lurie, N. O., "Culture Change," in J. A. Clifton (ed.), *Introduction to Cultural Anthropology* (1968), pp. 275–303. A comprehensive review of theoretical contributions in change; provides principles of change and hypotheses about the consequences.

Nisbet, R. (ed.), *Social Change* (1972). Excellent representation of articles of the modern sociological view of social change; theoretical, comparative, and historical.

Walker, D. E., Jr. (ed.), *The Emergent Native Americans: A Reader in Culture Contact* (1972). A balanced selection of articles in theory, policy, technical and economic change, and other factors in culture change and acculturation of American Indians.

19 Personality and Culture

CHAPTER OUTLINE

LEARNING GOALS

Identify the determinants of personality.

Specify the cultural determinants of personality.

Explain the relationship between culture and personality.

Discuss the relationship between child training and personality.

Summarize the major theories of culture and personality.

Explain the Whiting-Child theory and correlational method.

Review other contributions to culture and personality studies.

Societies are made up of individuals, and cultures, while manifest through the behavior of individuals, set rules for behavior which exist before the individual is born and persist after the person's death. All cultures change through time, but they have an enduring continuity that supersedes the mortal span of the person. Culture, with roots in individual behavior, still, transcends the individual.

A personality is the integrated system of behaviors, learned and unlearned, that are characteristic of an individual. A culture is the integrated system of learned behavior patterns that are characteristic of the members of a society. The interrelations of the two have posed three problems for study by psychologists and anthropologists: (1) How does culture affect personality? (2) How does personality affect culture? (3) In what sense are individual personalities intermediary links in a chain of cause and effect between different parts of a culture?

The field of *psychological anthropology* has developed in the process of trying to answer these questions, although the term for the subject has not received unanimous acceptance. The reason for this lack of complete enthusiasm for the term is that it seems too narrow for the total subject matter it is intended to encompass and places too much emphasis on psychological features. For this reason some workers still prefer the older phrase, *culture and personality*, to incorporate the multiple interests of the topic. Later we will have an opportunity to consider some of these broad interests. For now it is sufficient to indicate that the field encompasses the study of all those aspects of culture which interact with the individual and with the resulting concept, personality.

DETERMINANTS OF PERSONALITY

A given personality is the product of many interacting factors, which may be classified under four main categories: (1) constitutional characteristics (the person's biology, neurophysiology, endocrine system, body type, etc.); (2) the individual's physical environment; (3) the person's culture; and (4) the unique biological-psychological-social experience or history of the individual. These components are fused in the creation of each personality.

Constitutional Characteristics

The most obvious, although not necessarily the most important, factors in the determination of personality are the physical and mental capacities with which the individual is endowed at birth. Included are such factors as body build, certain aspects of mental functioning, neurological makeup, presence or absence of deformities, and the like.

Morphological factors which can be readily seen as having a direct influence on personality are stature, weight, and physical appearance. We must keep in mind, however, that the social meaning of a physical characteristic is culturally determined. In Western culture, big men are expected to be dominant in interpersonal relations. Different cultures attach often widely differing meanings to such physical attributes as above-average size.

To illustrate this point, we may contrast American behavior with that of the Trobriand Islanders with respect to identification of a relative's physiognomy among offspring. In American society a newborn baby is carefully observed to see whether it looks like the mother or the father, or some other relative. Americans have an obsession for finding a resemblance to a relative. Maternal relatives project maternal identities upon the infant. Paternal relatives project their counterparts. If the physical traits are definitely identifiable with those of one line or the other, the stimulus value is quite marked, and behavior may be influenced.

Trobrianders, on the other hand, say that children do not and cannot resemble the mother or her relatives. To hint as much is offensive. Yet resemblance to the father is always assumed and affirmed, even though it is believed the father has nothing to do with procreation.[1]

Physical Environment

Anthropogeographers of the nineteenth century attempted to explain national character in terms of physical environment. Mountain dwellers are ruggedly individualistic, it was suggested. Enjoyers of temperate climates are creative and vigorous. Residents of the tropics are indolent and sexually precocious, and so on through a long list of stereotypes. Most early anthropogeographic work was so facile and superficial that it was tossed out by twentieth-century anthropologists. Nonetheless, the mineral content of diet can and does affect the endocrine system of whole populations. Whether a people must adapt to an arctic, desert, or rain-forest environment is a factor of significant influence. Differences in the altitudes at which people live and the characteristic barometric pressures to which they must adjust are not without personality effects. The work of Whiting, in seeking a causal relation between male initiation practices, multiple marriages, and climate, is a good example of taking the environment into account (see pages 341–344).

Cultural Determinants

Cultural determinants are the limits for normal behavior found within any society. Each person born into a society finds a system of behavior adapted to a particular environment. The individual, except in rare instances, will be influenced by culture more than influence it. The operation of these cultural determinants, together with the feedback effect of personality responses, constitutes the subject of most of this chapter.

Idiosyncratic Features

Every individual has a unique personal history. Not all aspects of the society's culture are open to all persons, and class differences mean differences in social opportunity and experience. Even more important, however, is that persons of identical class do not have the same experiences. A mother prefers one child over the other. One child burns a finger; another does not. One woman has an automobile accident; another does not. One infant falls in the river; another does not. No two persons ever have the same social experience, not even identical twins. From psychoanalysis we have learned how important the fortuity of personal history can be in shaping the direction of personality development.

Culture tends to standardize personalities by channeling the experience of all individuals into the same broad stream. But life is made up of such a rich variety of experience that absolute standardization can never be realized.

A Comprehensive Classification of Personality Determinants

Personality is therefore to be understood as a behavioral synthesis of an individual's physical (including neural and glandular) constitution, the physicochemical character of the environment, the internalization of the patterns of the culture, and the reactions to the individual's life history by people.

CHILD TRAINING AND PERSONALITY

"As the twig is bent, so grows the tree." A major factor in the development of the child as a person is the accumulation of innumerable pressures, most of them subtle, others not so subtle, that shape its images and feelings of the surrounding world (Figure 19.1). The child's growing perception of what that world will give and what it demands serve as a guide for adapting.

The world that awaits the child includes people who already have a multitude of cultural commitments concerning how to behave—people with culturally colored emotions, expectancies, and anxieties. It is a world of many physical things, some beneficial, even essential

[1] B. Malinowski, *The Father in Primitive Psychology*, pp. 87–92.

FIGURE 19.1
The Navajo infant, like the young of most tribes in the Southwest area of the United States, has traditionally been securely bound in a sun-shaded cradleboard. It makes for easy handling and closeness to the working mother, but provides little body contact. (Joseph Muench.)

to human existence; some inexorably destructive; some now one and then the other. Of all these the child must in time become knowledgeable.

Investigations of human adults show that much of their behavior consists of patterns derived from processes of conditioning in early childhood. Under ordinary circumstances the child's first experience, and its experience for some time thereafter, is in the conjugal-natal family (or nuclear family) of father, mother, and siblings. Margaret Mead, for one, has shown how this world differentially puts the imprint of its finger on the child:

The Arapesh [*of New Guinea*] *treat a baby as a soft, vulnerable, precious little object, to be protected, fed, cherished. . . . When the mother walks about she carries the child slung beneath her breast in a bark-cloth sling, or in a soft net bag in which the child still curls as he curled in the womb. Whenever it is willing to eat . . . it is fed, gently, interestedly.*

Among the neighboring Iatmul headhunters:

From birth the baby is handled as if it were a separate little entity capable of a will of its own. . . . As soon as the Iatmul child is a few weeks old, the mother no longer carries it everywhere . . . but instead places it some distance on a high bench, where it must cry lustily before it is fed. . . . [*T*]*he sense of the mouth is built up as an assertive, demanding organ, taking what it can from a world that is, however, not unduly unwilling to give it. The child learns an attitude towards the world; that if you fight hard enough, something which will treat you as strong as itself will yield—and that anger and self-assertion will be rewarded.*

And again:

The Mundugumor [*another New Guinea tribe*] *women actively dislike child-bearing, and they dislike children. Children are carried in harsh opaque baskets that scratch their skins, later, . . . high on their mother's shoulders, well away from the breast. Mothers*

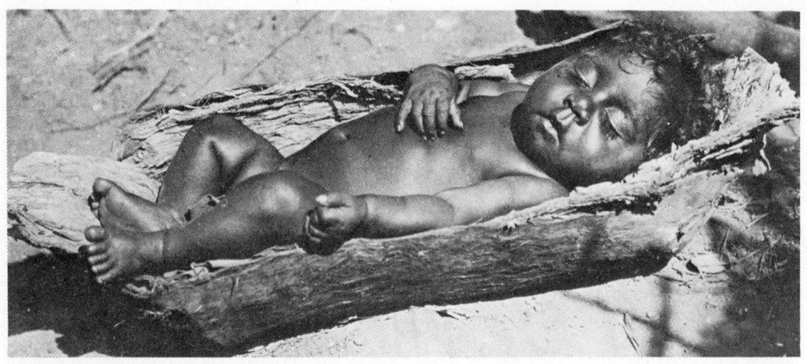

FIGURE 19.2
The native Australian infant is carried, unbound, in a dugout cradleboard. (Australian Information Service.)

their children standing up, pushing them away as soon as they are the least bit satisfied. . . . Here we find a character developing that stresses anger, eager avidity. In later life love-making is conducted like the first round of a prizefight, and biting and scratching are important parts of foreplay.[2]

Child training thus encompasses a good deal more than consciously directed education.

Enculturation and Socialization

The ways in which various needs may be satisifed are limited and standardized in every culture. No society permits its members to eat what, when, or how they please. No society permits its members to urinate and defecate whenever or wherever they wish. No society permits unlimited expression of sexuality; on the contrary, all societies exert considerable social control in this matter.

Each person must learn which responses lead to goal achievement and satisfaction. The individual must learn to inhibit impulses to act in prohibited ways and to habituate behavior to culturally acceptable ways.

The total process is called *enculturation*, which is defined as conscious or unconscious conditioning in the learning process whereby children and adults achieve competence in their culture. A well-adjusted personality is one that successfully gratifies personal urges within the allowable expectancies of the culture. In social psychology and sociology, the term of long-standing use that is synonymous with enculturation is *socialization*. Although the term "enculturation" is better suited to the notion of learning culture, the more popular word, "socialization," still persists in the anthropological literature.

Human life is lived in a state of continuous tension that may only be minimized, never permanently eliminated. The battle is unending between desires, opportunities, and the limitations imposed by a culture. Maturity in personality represents an acceptance of the terms within which life can be lived. When a growing child has adjusted its behavior to the patterns of its culture, when pertinent values, beliefs, and action have become *internalized* as a normal part of thinking and behavior, the child has become enculturated.

Formal and Informal Education

Education, as opposed to child training, implies the more formal efforts of adults to mold the personalities of the young, but among nonliterate peoples the gap is nowhere as great as it is in American society, for example. Nonliterate societies never make an issue over "education for life," as American schools do. In a tribal group, education *is* life. The parents do not work in a factory or an office the child never sees. The child is not shut up in a school away from the home for hours and days on end. In the camp or village, children are around while all the funda-

[2]M. Mead, *Male and Female*, pp. 65 and 68–70. By permission from William Morrow and Company, New York.

FIGURE 19.3
Older San Bushman boys, watched by little ones, imitate the trance behavior of a shaman possessed by a spirit. Play is preparation for adulthood. (Richard Lee/Anthro-Photo.)

mental activities of adult life take place. They play with bows and arrows until old enough to hunt. They can play around the older children who are watching the herds until they are ready to herd. They see and imitate the dancers until admitted to the dance (Figure 19.3). They listen to the tales of tribal lore and myth until they know them by heart. Most knowledge comes as a by-product of living with family members as natural, nonprofessional instructors and from play with older children.

Formal learning is usually limited to the more specialized aspects of religion and magic. But where tribal initiations are held, they almost invariably involve formal instruction in these affairs.

Hart has pointed out that in most tribal societies, the education of children before puberty is left to the informal ministrations of parents and other relatives. In many societies, however, boys (and sometimes girls) are taken to a "bush school" at puberty to be put through a severe course of discipline and training in knowledge covering the "value system of the culture, its myths, its religion, its philosophy, its justification for its own entity as a culture."[3] According to Hart: "The initiation schools are directed at imparting instruction that cannot be given in the home, under conditions as unlike home conditions as possible, by teachers who are the antithesis of the home teachers the boy has hitherto had."[4]

Initiation and Education among the Tswana An example of the scope of such initiation education, from the Tswana, is provided by Schapera:

All the eligible boys were initiated simultaneously in groups, kept secluded in one or more special "camps" . . . away from all the villages for three months or so. The details of the ceremony were kept a profound secret from women and all other non-initiates, who were forbidden under penalty of severe assault and even death to approach too near to the camp. At the camp the boys were first circumcised in order of tribal precedence. They were then systemati-

[3]See C. W. M. Hart, "Contrasts between Prepubertal and Postpubertal Education," in G. D. Spindler (ed.), *Education and Anthropology*, p. 141.
[4]Ibid., p. 140.

cally taught a number of secret formulae and songs, admonishing them to honour, obey, and support the Chief; to be ready to endure hardships and even death for the sake of the tribe; to be united as a regiment and help one another; to value cattle as the principal source of livelihood, and so herd them carefully; to attend the kgotla *regularly, as this was the place for men, and to look after its fire; to honour and ungrudgingly obey old people; and to abandon all boyish practices. Much of this instruction dealt also with the important topic of sex, the boys being taught the physiology of sex relations, the duty of procreation and other rules of conduct in married life, and the dangers of promiscuous intercourse with ritually "unclean" women. They were further taught tribal traditions and religious beliefs, and the tribal songs of war and self-glorification, and were made to participate in symbolic dances of many kinds. They were, moreover, subjected to starvation and blows, discomfort and actual torture, and rigorous and irksome taboos of many kinds, and were made to participate in strenuous hunting expeditions, all with the object of hardening them.*[5]

The rituals of priests, and often of shamans, are ordinarily taught on an apprenticeship basis, for these are frequently so complex and secret that they can be imparted only under isolated conditions which encourage the students' strict attention and rigorous study.

On the whole, it is safe to say that tribal children find their education less irksome than ours do. It demands less of them, and they can readily see the utility of what they learn because it is evident all about them in everyday living. They use their knowledge as they acquire it; they do not have to learn in a vacuum things that they will not have a chance to put to use for some years to come—or, perhaps, never.

THEORIES OF CULTURE AND PERSONALITY

The first anthropological studies on personality and culture were Malinowski's *Sex and Repression in Savage Society* and Mead's *Coming of Age in Samoa.* Malinowski tested Freud's theory of the Oedipus complex against the facts of Trobriand society. In the matrilineal system of the Trobriand Islanders, authority over children is exercised by the maternal uncle (mother's brother) rather than the father. Malinowski asked the question: "In this type of social setting does a boy have incestuous desires for his mother and 'hate' for his father as an authority figure and rival for the affections of the mother?" After analyzing Trobriand behavior and mythology, Malinowski concluded that the answer is "No." It is the uncle who is resented and the sister (particularly the clan sister) who is the object of intrafamilial sexual interest. Therefore, the basic principle of the Oedipus complex exists, but its manifestation alters with the culture.[6]

Mead's work in *Coming of Age in Samoa* was discussed in the first chapter as an example of the use of the comparative method in anthropology as a substitute for laboratory-controlled experimentation to test hypotheses. Mead's conclusion was that Samoan adolescents do not go through the period of psychological stress that characterizes American adolescence because Samoan culture is free of certain stress-producing features.

Neither Malinowski nor Mead expressed an explicit theory of culture and personality at that time (1926 and 1928, respectively). In 1934, however, Ruth Benedict published *Patterns of Culture*, which became the theoretical prototype for a number of studies. Subsequently, Abram Kardiner, a psychoanalyst, with the cooperation of Benedict, Cora DuBois, Ralph Linton, and other anthropologists, developed a "theory of basic personality structure" for handling questions of the effect of culture upon personality and vice versa. This, too, became the model for a number of studies. All these theories rest on intensive psychocultural analysis of one

[5]I. Schapera, *A Handbook of Tswana Law and Custom*, p. 106. By permission from Oxford University Press, London.

[6]B. Malinowski, *Sex and Repression in Savage Society*; also *The Father in Primitive Psychology.*

or a few tribes. In 1953 John Whiting published a broader theory of culture and personality, in which specific hypotheses are put to correlational tests that are statistically devised.

We will now consider each of these theories.

The Configuration of Culture and the Ideal Personality Type

Benedict's central thesis was that the ideological contours of a tribal culture are impressed upon individuals in terms of an ideal personality type. Each society has a more or less clear idea of what constitutes the kind of person an individual ought to be.

In Benedict's analysis, the precepts, maxims, rewards, and punishments are all directed toward molding all men and women in the image of the ideal. The person who approximates the ideal becomes the object of attention and admiration. The character of this ideal personality is equated with an abstracted tribal character structure (Figure 19.4).

In *Patterns of Culture*, Benedict tried to demonstrate the empirical validity of the theory through descriptions of what she called the "Dionysian configuration," represented by the Kwakiutl Indians of the Northwest Coast of North America, and the "Apollonian configuration," exemplified by the Zuni Indians of New Mexico.

Dionysian-Apollonian Configurations

The Dionysian and Apollonian concepts were phrased as follows:

The basic contrast between the Pueblos [of which the Zuni are one group] and the other cultures of North

(a)

(b)

(c)

FIGURE 19.4
Cultural patterning of behavior; New Zealand Maoris threatened enemies and thieves with far-out tongues and popeyed look. (a) The pattern is portrayed in the image of a protective spirit carved in the panel of a Maori food storehouse; (b) Maori war dancers live it; and (c) Maori small boys practice it. (American Museum of Natural History.)

FIGURE 19.5
Even before initiation into the secret rites of the kiva, the little San Ildefonso (New Mexico) Pueblo Indian girl is indoctrinated to the solemnity of public participation in the Corn Dance with her mother in celebration of the annual harvest and in honor of the village saint. (John Running.)

America is the contrast that is named and described by Nietzsche in his studies of Greek tragedy. He discusses two diametrically opposed ways of arriving at the values of existence. The Dionysian . . . seeks to attain . . . escape from the boundaries imposed upon him by his five senses, to break through into another order of experience. The desire of the Dionysian, in personal experience or in ritual, is to press through it toward a certain psychological state, to achieve excess. The closest analogy to the emotions he seeks is drunkenness, and he values the illuminations of frenzy. . . . The Apollonian distrusts all this, and has often little idea of the nature of such experiences. He finds means to outlaw them from his conscious life. . . . He keeps the middle of the road, stays within the known map, does not meddle with disruptive psychological states.[7]

The validity of Benedict's characterizations of Kwakiutl society and Pueblo society is open to serious challenge.[8] She drew configurations with the artistic license of a poet, rather than with the exactitude of a scientist. Nonetheless, her beautifully written exposition has exerted great influence on anthropology, education, and public thinking from 1934 to the present. It is the most popular book on anthropology written in the twentieth century.

Like culture, the ideal personality type is an abstraction. While it suffers from dangers of oversimplification, it nonetheless offers a useful approach. For example, when we speak of the "national character" of a people we are really speaking of a collective ideal personality type. The French national character is different from the British, and the British is in turn different from the German. Plains Indians' personalities are typically strikingly unlike those of Pueblo Indians.

Accurate analyses of national character can aid in understanding national conduct. The problem is to see that such characterizations are validated by adequate empirical data and critical checking.

Basic Personality Structure and Cultural Projection

Although the concept of basic personality structure developed by Kardiner originated in the concept of the ideal personality type, they are not identical concepts.[9] The concept of ideal

[7]R. F. Benedict, *Patterns of Culture*, pp. 78–79. By permission from Houghton Mifflin Company, New York.

[8]See V. Barnouw, *Culture and Personality*, pp. 93–112, for a discussion.

[9]A. Kardiner, *The Individual and His Society*, and A. Kardiner (ed.), *The Psychological Frontiers of Society*. A concise summary of the historical development of the concept may be found in Kardiner's article, "The Concept of Basic Personality Structure as an Operational Tool in the Social Sciences," in R. Linton (ed.), *The Science of Man in the World Crisis*, pp. 107–122.

personality type demonstrates the close interrelation between culture and personality, but it does not explain how the interrelationship arises.

Kardiner, a psychoanalyst, attempted to determine the effect of social institutions upon personality and of personality upon institutions. Kardiner and his associates and students proposed the following related hypotheses: (1) Certain culturally established techniques of child treatment, called *primary institutions*, shape the basic attitudes toward parents, and these attitudes exist throughout the life of the individual. (2) The pattern of attitudes and behavior formed by the standardized patterns of child treatment, which persist among adults, is the *basic personality structure* characteristic of that society. (3) Through projection, the basic personality structure is subsequently reflected in the development of other institutions such as religion, government, and mythology. Institutions derived as a result of projective systems are called *secondary institutions*.

The Kardinerian system attempts to establish two things: (1) the identification of the basic personality structure; and (2) the carry-over effect of basic personality patterns into some of the larger institutional structures of the society.[10] In other words, Kardiner is striving to show how one phase of culture shapes personality and how the resultant personality in turn shapes other phases of the culture.

The method in its present stage of development does not attempt to discover how the primary institutions, the child-care complexes, came into being. "The primary institution is treated as the taking-off point for the individual, not for the culture."[11] It assumes that various elemental aspects of culture, such as certain technologies (for example, basket making), may have no direct bearing on the basic personality structure. Further, it acknowledges that in many cultures certain institutions are independent of the projective system.

Alorese Culture and Basic Personality Structure It is quite impossible to illustrate the basic personality structure with reasonable adequacy here. Yet a skeletal sketch will portray the idea better than none at all. We have selected Alor for the purpose, since it is the only culture on which Kardiner has published psychodynamic analysis based upon adequate data.[12] All his analyses of other groups, Marquesan, Tanala, and Comanche, must be recognized as experimental probing; the conclusions must be treated as wholly provisional.

The Alorese, who live on the island of Timor in eastern Indonesia, are gardeners in a tropical forest. For women, the main cultural activity is gardening; for men, it is an endless round of wealth exchanges, the making and collecting of loans. Money, which in Alor consists of pigs, Javanese bronze vessels, and gongs, is lent out at interest with tight bonds of obligation of the debtor to his creditor. Marriage and death, among other occasions, call for extravagant consumption of pork and tremendous exchanges of bronze vessels and gongs. The heavy burdens of these occasions force the principals deep into debt.

Capitalism in Alor is primarily a vehicle for dominance over one's fellows. The internal tensions and hostilities of the Alorese household fail to gratify the security needs of the child. Alorese culture is integrated about the basic insecurity of the individual. Dominance through credit control is an attempt at compensatory adjustment.

In like manner, Alorese wars were only a means of getting even, a sort of irritable gesture expressed not in any art of warfare but in a series

[10]Note that Kardiner's secondary institutions are institutions in the ordinary sociological sense. However, his primary institutions are not institutions at all. This leads Kardiner in his later work to amend the concept of primary institution to read: "primary institution or related practices, whether institutionalized or not" (*The Psychological Frontiers of Society*, p. 25).

[11]Ibid.

[12]C. DuBois, *The People of Alor*.

of long-drawn-out feuds marked by cowardly assaults carried out by trickery and stealth. Women, as well as men, were victims.[13]

The Alorese child is wanted, but neglected. The mother works hard in her scattered fields. After the fourteenth day following birth, she has little time for her child. The father is away from home much of the time. The hunger pangs of the infant are irregularly and inconsistently met. The mother does not take the child to the fields with her; someone else around the house must tend it—the grandmother, an older child, or the father, if he is home. Several women may nurse the infant now and then. Hunger cravings are physiologically met, but no consistent image of any person upon whom the child can depend for relief of hunger tensions is developed. Premasticated food may be given by anyone who wants to stop the infant's incessant bawling, but rejection and spitting out of such food indicates that this does not relieve the emotional tensions of the child. Hunger is more than an empty stomach.

Although the child is not left alone and is usually lugged around half-sitting in a shawl, it is not fondled or caressed in the usual sense by parents. The mother, elder brother or sister, or whoever else is paying any attention to the infant masturbates it to calm it.

Early childhood illnesses are indifferently treated and are aggravated by rough handling and irritating medication. The child learns to walk without assistance or encouragement. Defecation and urination are not brought under coercive control.

When the time for weaning comes, the child is pushed away or slapped. Jealousy and rage are deliberately evoked by taking another child to the breast. The adults think this is very funny.

These are the main lines of the primary institutions. What is the basic personality structure?

[13]War among the Alorese was suppressed by the Dutch administration of the Netherlands Indies, now Indonesia.

As children the Alorese are shy and reserved—they do not expect favorable response, but they readily fly into tantrums and become vituperative. Because they cannot obtain their desires or rewards in a direct way, they steal and forage regularly. The child may reject its family by running away from home to live with some remote relative.

None of the childhood patterns builds toward emotional solidarity within the family. The ego development and social conscience of the adult are very weak. There is little self-confidence or sense of responsibility to others or to society. The adult male's relations to women are a projection of his almost complete defeat, as a child, in his relations to his mother. Husband-wife relations are bitter and nonintimate. Woman is the economic provider, and the male is dependent upon her. He cannot really dominate her. Compensation is found in the elaborate activity of loans and exchanges, the functions of which are essentially to gratify the psychological rather than the production-consumption needs of the economy.

Warfare and religious institutions in Alor bear quite clearly the imprint of the personality system. War was disorganized, fitful, and vengeful. Religion falls within the category of ancestor worship, but the ancestors are neither exalted nor revered. Their powers for good are not exaggerated, and the Alorese feel no desire to assuage them by suffering or renunciation in their names. Because there is no interest in, possibility of, or benefit to be derived from getting back in their good graces, there is no restitution by penance. One expects no more from the ancestral gods than one expects from parents.

Ancestors, however, want to be fed. The failure to feed the gods makes them angry just as failure to feed the child was the supreme frustration. Angry gods punish their descendants. With great reluctance and only under the duress of misfortune, the Alorese make sacrificial food offerings to the ancestral spirits.

Religious art is careless and slipshod. Gods are projected "fathers" and "mothers." With no idealization of parents in the culture, there is no idealization of the gods. Representative carvings of ancestral deities are carelessly made, perfunctorily used, and quickly discarded. The dead are projections of the powerful and insistent creditors who bedevil adult life. In short:

The basic personality in Alor is anxious, suspicious, mistrustful, lacking in confidence, with no interest in the outer world. There is no capacity to idealize the parental image or deity. The personality is devoid of enterprise, is filled with repressed hatred and free floating aggression over which constant vigilance must be exercised. The personality is devoid of high aspirations and has no basis for the internalization of discipline. Individuals so constituted must spend most of their energy protecting themselves against each other's hostility. Cooperation must be at a low level and a tenuous social cohesion can be achieved only by dominance-submission attitudes, not by affection and mutual trust.[14]

Alor is a society with an old culture. It has survived for quite some time. This means that it has made the necessary minimal adaptations necessary for survival. Yet, that it is a precarious adjustment cannot be doubted; the continuance of the society must hang on a very thin thread. One of its strengths has been that island isolation has protected it from too much external pressure.

The work in the field of culture and personality has progressed into new arenas, and since the time of Kardiner researchers have changed the theory and added new observations. However, as an object lesson in the interaction of culture and personality, the examples above are superb in highlighting the important features of the problem.

The Whiting-Child Theory and Correlational Method

Whiting, an anthropologist, and Child, a psychologist, have combined psychoanalytic theory, learning theory, and cross-cultural statistical techniques to produce a different and intriguing approach. Although many hypotheses derived from psychoanalytic thought are used, the emphasis of the approach is on hypothesis testing—something in which psychoanalysis has been weak.

Whiting and Child propose the following propositions:

1. Child training is universal: "In all societies the helpless infant . . . must be changed into a responsible adult obeying the rules of his society."[15]
2. Societies differ in their rules and in their methods of teaching conformity to the rules. These differences have differential personality effects.
3. Specific qualities of personality effects are projected on adult institutions and influence their content.

So far, this is no different from Kardiner's theory. Now behavioral theory comes in.

4. Adults reward responses that correspond to culturally established patterns of behavior. Positive reinforcement increases the frequency of the approved response. Responses that do not correspond to culturally established patterns of behavior may be punished. Negative reinforcement decreases the tendency to repeat the unapproved response.
5. The intensity of negative sanctions and the ages at which they occur contribute to socialization anxiety. Approved responses bring satisfaction. Because they are rewarded, each successful repetition intensifies the satisfaction potential of the behavior.
6. Excessive frustration or excessive gratification in socialization results in negative or positive fixation. Fixation means that events of a certain

[14]A. Kardiner (ed.), *The Psychological Frontiers of Society*, p. 170.

[15]J. W. M. Whiting and I. L. Child, *Child Training and Personality*, p. 63.

(a)

(b)

FIGURE 19.6

(a) Small boys of the Dani tribe in western New Guinea (West Irian) practice spear throwing in a game called "Kill-the-hoop." (b) As adults they face their enemies in serious battle. [Photo (a) by Samuel Putnam and (b) by Karl G. Heider. © 1968 by the Film Study Center, Peabody Museum, Harvard University, from *Gardens of War* by Robert Gardner and Karl G. Heider, Random House.]

kind have greater or lesser psychological importance for someone who has had the fixating experience than for someone who has not.

7. Illness is anxiety-producing. Explanations of illness are colored by the projection of fixations customarily established by child-training experience.

For example, oral fixations will produce such "causes" of illness as eating and drinking (especially "poisonous" foods), curses and other magical spells. Anal fixations will generate explanations of illness in terms of failure to hide one's feces or other personal waste.

A number of special hypotheses were refined for testing. The method consisted in giving numerical values on a scale of rating for degree of severity of socialization of oral, anal, sexual, dependent, and aggressive behaviors. This was done wherever possible for fifty selected societies. (Middle-class practices in Chicago, which represented the United States in the sample, rated very high in severity and low in indulgence in virtually every measure of early child training. North Americans, it seems, are severe with, and demanding of, their children.) Each society was also classed, if the data warranted, as *having* or *not having* oral, anal, sexual, dependent, or aggressive explanations for illness. Correlations were statistically derived between negative and positive fixations on the one hand and type of "disease theory" on the other.

The study established high correlations for the effect of severe, or negative, sanctions in producing illness projections. Positive fixations were not shown to be effective in influencing an adult theory of disease causation.

Other Correlates of Child-training Practices Modifications of the Whiting-Child theory and method have subsequently been made by Whiting and other investigators.

Games Roberts and Sutton-Smith studied the occurrence of types of games relative to child-training practices in a sample of fifty-six societies. Tribal societies possessing *games of strategy* (in which the outcome is the product of rational choice among several courses of action) are societies which emphasize and reward obedience, while punishing disobedience on the part of children. Such societies are relatively more complex in culture and social organization. Societies with a cultural emphasis on *games requiring physical performance skills* pay less attention to obedience in child training while rewarding achievement. Societies in which preadolescent children are shouldered with the responsibility of tending younger siblings show a cultural preference for *games of chance.*

Games provide models for cultural participation (Figures 19.6 and 19.7). Strategy games prepare one for finding the way in a complex cultural setting, as the associated child training conditions one to role conformity. Games of physical skill prepare one for individual initiative and extroverted activity and are linked to hunting types of societies. Games of chance take control of life out of the hands of the player, whose role is passive.

The studies also show that, across the board, "[T]here are consistent differences cross-culturally in the training of boys and girls. Boys, for example, are given higher achievement training, while girls are given more consistent obedience and responsibility training."[16]

Parental rejection and adult personality A cross-cultural study by Rohner indicates that parental rejection of children, as manifest in an absence of doing things to please the child, enjoying it, playing, singing, plus other failures to exhibit warmth and affection, generates children who are "anxious, hostile, insecure, and who devaluate their feelings of self-worth." Further, "adults who were rejected as children tend to devaluate their feelings of self-esteem and self-

[16] J. M. Roberts and B. Sutton-Smith, "Child Training and Game Involvement" (*Ethnology*, vol. 1, 1962), p. 176.

FIGURE 19.7
Navajo child play focuses on the domestic life of sedentary herders in the desert. The hogan (front center), brush corral, *ramada* (brush shelter, at left), and clay sheep imitate their actual family homestead quite realistically. (Joseph Muench.)

adequacy (low self-evaluation)...to be dependent, emotionally unresponsive and to evaluate the world negatively,...lacking in generosity."[17] Whether children are deprived of food, or fed generously, is not a major correlate of the type of personality syndrome indicated above.

Evaluation of the Whiting-Child Method This method stands or falls on the true randomness of the ethnographic sample and on the validity of the coding made by the evaluators of the descriptive ethnographic records. The evaluations are usually subjective and often rest on inadequate ethnographic data. Yet the judgments are processed as though they were "hard" quantitative units. Those who feel that a science must have numbers applaud the effort. Those who are skeptical of the value of the results are apt to think of it as "the method of putative precision." It does, however, produce a provocative new look at the materials.

[17]R. P. Rohner, "Parental Rejection, Food Deprivation, and Personality Development: Tests of Alternative Hypotheses" (*Ethnology*, vol. 9, 1970), p. 421.

OTHER CONTRIBUTIONS TO CULTURE AND PERSONALITY STUDIES

After serious criticisms were raised of the work of Benedict, Kardiner, and other early scholars, culture and personality studies lost popularity among anthropologists. However, a number of recent studies have continued to utilize psychological methods and to explore hypotheses which derive from the earlier studies.

Projective Testing

Projective testing consists of presenting a subject with a series of meaningless pictures or patterns. Statements about what is seen are used to assess the subject's psychological state. There were a series of attempts in the late 1940s and 1950s to study the relationship between culture and personality through the use of such projective tests as the Rorschach and the TAT (the Thematic Apperception Test). Even though problems were found in their application on a cross-cultural basis, they provided useful insights. Attempts continue to find new uses for these tests and to improve them. Edgerton has summarized the present state of the method as follows:

Even though projective techniques continue to be used in cross-cultural research, they no longer exercise the dominance over psychological anthropology that they once did. There are many reasons for their loss of popularity. Their dubious validity is but one, their expense to administer is another, and their association with theories of "depth" psychology is yet another. Still another, perhaps equally important reason, is that most of the projectives have been associated with the study of typical personality, and psychological anthropology is no longer centrally concerned with typical personality. Other interests, and thus other methods, have grown up alongside the projectives, and have begun to take over center stage.[18]

Anthropology and Education

A direct outgrowth of studies of comparative socialization is the study of the differences between formal and informal education, especially as anthropology has begun to study modern society, urban settings, and ethnic groups.

The continuity between formal and informal education seems to have been overestimated. The conclusion now is that the "school represents a specialized set of educational experiences which are discontinuous from those encountered in everyday life and that it requires and promotes ways of learning which often run counter to those nurtured in practical daily activities."[19] It has also been shown that the major differences in performance on Western-based tests and tasks is directly correlated with whether the child has attended and successfully participated in formal schooling rather than with differences in culture or inherited abilities.

Another interesting feature of this work, in addition to the conclusion that the setting and teacher have much to do with the success of learning, is the heavy emphasis which is placed on language, and especially on verbal skills in learning in the formal setting. In the informal situation the child learns from doing and seeing, by example, and by recognizing the connection between the lesson and the final activity or goal. In formal schooling, on the other hand, where the "linguistic forms carry the full burden of communication, the amount of information available to the learner is restricted."[20] It follows that success in the school process and in Western-judged and -graded tests is related to success in learning verbal skills and codes.

Another related area of research is that of Segall, Campbell, and Herskovits, in which they found that there is no difference in the perceptual abilities of different peoples. Differences lie in the linguistic terms used to describe differences perceived, as for example in color shading.[21]

Comparative Socialization Theories

The early work of Kardiner, Linton, Benedict, and others in comparative socialization was heavily influenced by psychoanalytic theories. More recent influence comes from child-development psychology. Piaget's work, especially, has had important implications for educational anthropologists and anthropological linguists.[22]

Piaget suggests that the child passes through stages of development, each characterized by the acquisition of new skills and abilities. Further, he states that all development proceeds in a natural trend from simple to complex. Each developmental aspect begins with ordinary experiences, and proceeds from experience of the physical to the social, and finally to the ideational world. The three major phases of development are the sensorimotor phase (roughly, ages 0 to 2); the period of preparation for conceptual

---

[18]R. B. Edgerton, "Method in Psychological Anthropology," in R. Naroll and R. Cohen (eds.), *A Handbook of Method in Cultural Anthropology*, pp. 341–342.

[19]S. Scribner and M. Cole, "Cognitive Consequences of Formal and Informal Education" (*Science*, vol. 182, no. 4112, 1973), p. 553.

[20]Ibid., p. 556.

[21]M. H. Segall, D. T. Campbell, and M. J. Herskovits, *The Influence of Culture on Visual Perception*.

[22]For excellent summaries of Piaget and other psychological contributions, see H. W. Maier, *Three Theories of Child Development*, and R. A. Thompson, *Psychology and Culture*.

thought (roughly, ages 2 to 11); and the phase of cognitive thought (roughly, ages 11 or 12 and up).[23] Another psychologist, Bruner, has advanced the work of Piaget by demonstrating a sensitivity to its cross-cultural application. The theories of Piaget and Bruner have influenced anthropologists working on education, socialization, and language learning in cultural situations.

Other Advances

Other work in the field of culture and personality is too extensive to review here. Sufficient reference is made in footnotes and suggested readings so that interested readers can explore these areas on their own. It is worthwhile, however, to mention a few other examples of the richness and variety of the field. Anthropologists have demonstrated a continuing interest in mental illnesses in various cultures and in how special social and physical environments influence these illnesses. For example, a number of mental conditions which have been attributed to specific ethnic groups now seem on further examination to result from nutritional or other environmental deprivation.[24]

Another research issue in personality and culture is the work on socialization for sex role. Draper summarizes trends in this work as follows:

It is likely that certain cultural constellations produce early and differential treatment of girls and boys. For example, societies having (a) a high degree of separation of men and women in space, work and leisure activities, (b) status inferiority of women relative to men, and (c) women's spheres of interest and influence limited to the domestic sphere may set into motion a characteristic set of socialization demands. Girls may be tapped by their mothers for work (obedience and responsibility training) more than boys and at earlier ages due to the fact that boys' eventual roles are presumed to require skills unrelated to routine domestic work. The earlier and more consistent responsibility training of girls may work directly or indirectly to keep them closer to home where their behavior is continuously, and perhaps more consistently, shaped and where they will do little exploring of the larger environment. Boys in such societies, like their adult counterparts, may gravitate increasingly to the periphery of the domestic setting where fewer demands are put on their time. Once boys are more removed from immediate adult supervision they come under less consistent discipline; as a result of fewer restrictions on their mobility they have more access to a wider range of environments which lie at greater distances from home base than those routinely traversed by girls. The suggestion here is that sexual differences in adult roles and spatial separation of the male and female spheres may predict the onset of strong socialization pressures and separation of ideal sex roles along the dimensions of self-reliance, activity, independence, passivity, and conformity.[25]

SUMMARY

The personality of the individual is analogous to the culture of a society in that it is a sum of integrated behavior. The bodily constitution, physical environment, culture, and unique personal experience, as reacted to by the individual, combine to produce the total personality.

Enculturation encompasses all the learning processes through which the individual internalizes the norms of the culture.

All cultures provide means for goal achievement. The growing individual must learn to adapt behavior to the expectancies of society and to its peculiarities. The person who fails in this is subjected to mental stress and may become neurotic or psychopathic.

Ruth Benedict showed how *ideal personality types* reflect differing configurations of culture. Abram Kardiner developed the concept of *basic*

[23]Maier, op. cit., pp. 75–143.

[24]This material has been admirably summarized by J. Kennedy, "Cultural Psychiatry," in J. J. Honigmann (ed.), *Handbook of Social and Cultural Anthropology*, pp. 1119–1198.

[25]P. Draper, "Comparative Studies of Socialization" (*Annual Review of Anthropology*, vol. 3, 1974), pp. 272–273.

personality structure, a modal personality syndrome developed in response to child-training practices. Secondary institutions are projections of basic personality structures.

A recent trend in anthropology has been to attempt to establish statistical correlations between formal aspects of culture and cultural features of child training and experience. Research has continued in this very important field and has included a reexamination of the uses of projective tests, new views on formal and informal education, and the utilization of the theories of child-development psychologists, such as Piaget and Bruner. In addition, anthropologists may contribute to the better understanding of mental illness through their cross-cultural contributions.

SELECTED READINGS

Aberle, D. F., *The Psychosocial Analysis of a Hopi Life History* (Comparative Psychology Monographs, serial no. 107, vol. 21, 1951). A systematic interpretation in terms of general personality and culture theory of the life history of a Hopi Indian, whose autobiography was edited by L. Simmons (see below).

Barnouw, V., *Culture and Personality* (1973). Useful as a general introduction to contributions in the field and the methods used.

Hsu, F. L. K. (ed.), *Psychological Anthropology* (1972). This book reviews several culture areas (Japan, Africa, North America, Oceania), and such special topics as national character studies, projective testing, mental illness, dreams, socialization and kinship.

Simmons, L. (ed.), *Sun Chief: The Autobiography of a Hopi Indian* (1942). Not only does this book give the inside view of what it means to grow up as a Hopi, but it also lays bare the severe personal conflicts caused by living under two incompatible cultures.

Wax, M. L., S. Diamond, and F. Gearing, *Anthropological Perspectives on Education* (1971). A thorough review of contributions to this aspect of the field. A must for those who want to understand the concepts and developments in this subfield.

Whiting, J. W. M., and I. L. Child, *Child Training and Personality* (1953). Spells out the theory, method, data, and results of their application of the correlational technique and use of cross-cultural data.

PART SIX

Life Cycles, Kinship, and Social Organization

20
Life Crises and Transition Rites

CHAPTER OUTLINE

LEARNING GOALS

Discuss the cultural relations that accompany conception.

Discuss the regulations that accompany childbirth.

Define the couvade.

Summarize the life crises of childhood.

Discuss the rituals and regulations of puberty.

Identify the relation of puberty rites to social identity.

Review the cultural practices that follow death.

Explain the functions of mortuary rites.

Birth, maturity, reproduction and death are the four basic and universal crises in the life cycle. Individuals who live long enough pass through each of these cycles. In no human culture are these critical periods wholly ignored. However, each culture focuses on these periods with varying degrees of intensity and anxiety.

CONCEPTION

The life cycle begins with conception. Yet many (literate and nonliterate) people do not have accurate knowledge of the nature of conception. This ignorance is not too surprising if we keep in mind that even modern people have acquired a knowledge of genetics only in the last hundred years.

However, most peoples recognize causal sequences with sufficient astuteness to be able to associate sexual intercourse with conception. Some peoples recognize that semen plays a part in the generation of life. Yet the naïve notion that the male plants a seed, which the female nurtures, is the closest they come to scientific reality.

Explicit notions of miraculous conception abound. In its most common form, the belief is expressed that a child is the reincarnation of an ancestral spirit who has slipped into the womb of the mother to be regenerated.[1] In Australia, this belief is raised to the level of a dogma so strong that the natives deny any relation between the sex act and conception other than to admit that the womb must first be opened so that ancestral spirits may enter.

The Physiology of Paternity

Earlier anthropologists took the Australian's denial of the physiology of paternity at face value. Modern anthropologists interpret this denial as functioning to sustain the exclusiveness of the social system.[2] Ancestor worship and totemism are important themes in Australian culture. The continuity of the totemic group is sustained by means of the doctrine of spiritual reincarnation. To give expression to physiological paternity would be a subversive undermining of the sacred institutions of Australian social life.

The matrilineal (see page 413) Trobriand Islanders say that the male plays no role in conception. Rather, the spirit of a dead clan ancestor enters the womb when the woman is wading in the lagoon. It grows and becomes a child. The nearby Dobu, who believe that semen is voided coconut milk, which, when it enters a woman, causes the blood within her womb to coagulate and form a fetus, say bluntly that the Trobriand Islanders lie. The point is a sore one. So many angry words have been exchanged over this moot issue in the past that nowadays when Dobuans and Trobriand Islanders meet, they tacitly avoid the subject. Dobu companions of Fortune, the anthropologist, scolded him for broaching the subject on a visit to the Trobriand Islands.[3]

The Dobu notion that babies are formed by the coagulation of blood is shared by many nonliterate peoples sporadically distributed about the globe. They reason from the observed fact of cessation of menstruation during gestation that the clotting of the blood to form the baby stops the regular flow.

Pregnancy

There are a number of externally observable biological alterations that occur in all women after conception. More notable among them are enlargement of the breasts and nipples, cessation of menstruation, abdominal enlargement, and nausea.

From the little that has been written on this

---

[1]See, for example, B. Malinowski, "Baloma: The Spirits of the Dead in the Trobriand Islands," in *Magic, Science and Religion and Other Essays*, pp. 125–227.

[2]See M. F. A. Montagu, *Coming into Being among the Australian Aborigines.*

[3]R. F. Fortune, *Sorcerers of Dobu*, pp. 238–239.

subject, most peoples seem to focus on one or two of the symptoms as signs of coming events, although they may note all of them. Cessation of menstruation is the one universally recognized sign. A fair percentage of societies even calculate the expected birth at ten lunar months after the last menstrual period.

Various Oceanic and African tribes make note of breast changes; the Arunta of Australia, the Pukapuka of Polynesia, and others are recorded as noting "morning sickness." Others have told field workers that a significant clue is diminution of appetite and a tendency to become lazy.[4]

Pregnancy is, in itself, a crisis condition. Most peoples view the gestation period as calling for a relief of related anxieties. Chief among these anxieties are fear that (1) the child will not develop ideally, (2) the woman will miscarry, and (3) the birth will be difficult. Pregnancy taboos and injunctions are supposed to correct the problem and bring freedom from these and other fears.

Thus Ray reports for the Sanpoil Indians of Washington that a childbearing woman and her husband could not eat trout, lest the child shake like that lively fish. They could not eat rabbit, lest the child get weak legs. They could not eat "fool hen," lest the child be a moron. More than this, the mother-to-be had to rise before sunrise, stay awake through the day, swim in cold water, walk and run, and ride horseback to strengthen her for the ordeal to come.[5]

It may reassure some contemporary mothers, and induce some husbands to more indulgent understanding, to know that strange food preferences in pregnancy are found in other societies. Ford notes, however, that there do not seem to be any universally common foods that are craved. The desire is for *variety*. What the basis of this desire may be we do not know.[6]

CHILDBIRTH

It is strange, perhaps, that most of the anxiety over the crisis of childbirth comes before, not during, the event. Magic, ritual, and taboo dominate the prenatal period; yet when the moment of birth is reached, the obstetrical problems are, in normal cases, handled with matter-of-fact effectiveness. For the most part, birth is strictly a woman's affair. However, a few tribes permit or require the husband to assist or to be present. Generally, however, the expectant mother retires into the house with one or two older female relatives or a midwife to assist her.

A widely accepted falsehood is that childbirth is easy for women among nonliterate peoples. It has even been maintained that just as domestication increases birth difficulties for animals, so increasing domestication through civilization makes birth progressively more difficult for women in complex societies. There is little evidence for this idea. On the contrary, there is much empirical evidence that women in all societies may suffer much agony and difficulty in childbirth.

Practically all peoples have special emergency medical practices for difficult birth. In cases of drawn-out labor, medicine men and women are hastily invoked. The Cheyennes sent for a medicine man who had derived power from the otter. Otters make a delightful sport of sliding down mudbanks. This is the way the baby should behave and an otter medicine man could bring it about—so they say.

The Couvade

A very unusual custom is the *couvade*. After the birth of the child, the mother gets up and goes about her affairs, while the father goes to bed, apparently to recover from the effects of child-

[4]C. S. Ford, *A Comparative Study of Human Reproduction* (Yale University Publications in Anthropology, no. 32, 1945), p. 44.

[5]V. F. Ray, *The Sanpoil and Nespelem* (University of Washington Publications in Anthropology, vol. 5, 1932), p. 124.

[6]Ford, op. cit., p. 48.

birth. During the period of confinement, he is subjected to many taboos. This may be variously interpreted as a demand for attention on the part of the male, as a symbolic assertion of the father's identification with the child, or as a form of magical assistance to the child. That it is the symbolic assertion of identification of father and child seems to be the likeliest possibility.

Not many cultures have the couvade in its classic form. The Caribs and various of their South American neighbors are the outstanding examples. The Ainus of Japan and the Chinese of Marco Polo's time should be included, as well as certain tribes of South India and the people dewlling in the northern mountains of the Iberian peninsula.

According to informants, the Seed Eater Shoshone also practiced the couvade in the old days.[7] When the expectant mother retired to her birth hut, the father went into a retirement hut made by his mother. There he stayed isolated for five days, until the umbilical cord dropped from the newborn babe. He observed all the taboos that normally applied to a menstruating woman. No meat or soup could be eaten, only cereals. On the day of birth, his mother came to him, and he rubbed himself with sage. If she said, "You have a boy," he took a long walk in the mountains—where the game abide—but he did not hunt. If she said, "You have a daughter," he walked down into the valleys, where the wild seeds grow. Thus he magically associated his child with its future occupation. When the five days were up he bathed; and when he killed his first game, he gave it away to the people.

Although found in its classic form in only a few societies, couvade symptoms, such as sympathetic pain, weight gain, and food preferences, are found among modern societies.

[7]E. A. Hoebel, *Shoshone Field Notes* (unpublished, 1934); also R. H. Lowie, *Notes on Shoshonean Ethnography* (American Museum of Natural History, Anthropological Papers, vol. 20, part 3, 1924), pp. 265–270.

Naming and Presentation of the Child

Birth does not necessarily complete the transition from fetus to member of the community. Many people feel that there must be a formal presentation to the people and the spirits, and that until this act is completed, mother and child must remain in isolation. The mother is contaminated by her blood and by the dangerous forces of the birth crisis. This is the putative rationalization. Practically, of course, it is also a good thing for the mother to rest.

Postnatal Isolation The Hopi child and mother, although visited by relatives on the day of birth, remain isolated for twenty days. On the twentieth day, mother, father, and child are bathed many times. Relatives of every clan give the infant at least one name associated with their clan. Then as the sun rises, the infant is carried out to be held before the Sun God, who is told all the names of the child.[8]

The Seed Eater Shoshone mother and child were isolated even longer—forty days. The birth hut was built by the woman's mother a long way from the camp. When the baby's umbilical cord dropped off after five days, the hut was moved closer to the camp. All menstrual taboos were observed, but, in addition, the maternal grandmother prepared each day a bed of grass over hot coals for the mother to lie upon. (Today a hot-water bottle is used.) Throughout the day, the mother worked busily at weaving and other small tasks. Few friends came to visit her. After six weeks, she and the child rejoined the village.

Naming Ceremonies The Omaha Indian child was touchingly introduced to the entire cosmos in a traditional ritual always performed by a priest of a given subclan. On the eighth day after birth, the priest was sent for. When he

[8]A fascinating autobiographical description of the entire birth ritual may be found in L. Simmons (ed.), *Sun Chief*, chap. 1.

arrived, he took his place at the door of the lodge in which the child was born. His right hand raised, palm up to the sky, he intoned a beautiful invocation in a loud, ringing voice for all to hear.[9]

Yet even this ritual did not make the child a real member of the tribe, for a baby did not complete its transition until it could walk. Then it went through a "turning of the child ritual," wherein it discarded its baby name and got new moccasins. Baby moccasins always had a hole cut in the sole so that if a messenger from the spirit world came to claim the infant, the child could answer, "I cannot go on a journey—my moccasins are worn out!" New moccasins without holes were an assurance that the child was prepared for the journey of life and that its journey would be a long one.

Presentation: Becoming a Tribal Member In Africa, the Ashanti entertained similar notions. The child was not ceremonially named and publicly presented until eight days had passed. Then it became a genuine human being. Should it die before that time, its corpse would be casually thrown on the garbage heap, for it was believed to have been the husk of a ghost child whose mother in the spirit world had pawned it off on a living mother for a short period while she went off on some jaunt. On returning from her undertaking, she recalled her little spirit baby.

Further to the south in Africa, a Swazi baby, until the third month of life, is described as a "thing." It has no name, it cannot be handled by the men, and if it dies, it may not be publicly mourned. It is recognized as being very weak and vulnerable (infant mortality is tragically high), and the parents perform various rituals to protect it against dangers emanating from animals, humans, and nature. In the third month, the infant is shown to the moon and symbolically introduced to nature. It is entered into the category of persons and is given a name, which may be sung to it in its first lullaby.[10]

Not all societies undertake a formal presentation, but most, including Western Christianity with its christenings and baptisms, seem to do so. Virtually all societies isolate mother and child for periods of time varying from a few days to several months.

Naming, incidentally, is a universal human practice. Shakespeare to the contrary, there is much in a name. It symbolizes the individual's personality and often indicates social status. The name is usually bestowed at the end of the seclusion period. If the name is ceremonially bestowed, this is usually done by a near relative; otherwise, the most common practice is for the mother to decide what her child is to be called. Names that are associated with good luck or great deeds tend generally to be preferred. Thus the Menomini discarded their original names if they were chronically sick, in the hope that a new name would bring about a healthier state of being.

Change of names or acquisition of additional ones often occurs in the course of the individual's lifespan in many societies, as new names are assumed to indicate new statuses.

CHILDHOOD

Producing, rearing, and educating children to take their roles in the life of the community are prime motivations in all societies. We have already seen in Chapter 19 (pages 232–234) that a wide variance exists in attitudes toward children. The popular myth that all nonliterate peoples treat their children gently, with a maximum of bodily contact and a tender indulgence of all behaviors, is, alas, only a myth. Some do, some

[9]A. C. Fletcher and F. LaFlesche, *The Omaha Tribe* (Bureau of American Ethnology, Annual Report 27, 1911), pp. 115–116.

[10]H. Kuper, *The Swazi*, p. 50.

don't. All are primarily concerned with the eventual readiness of their children to assume a proper place and responsibility in the social order. Grandparents and other relatives frequently assume major parenting responsibilities. In some parts of Polynesia adoption is frequent and casual, and parenting is diffused among older siblings and numerous members of the extended family.

It is probably safe to say that no other society is marked by the "child-centered family" as it is known in the contemporary United States. Elsewhere children are valued primarily as ptoential members of the kinship group. They spend their childhood learning these future roles. While not participants in most adult activities, they are free to watch much of what occurs. Imitative play is a major medium of all children's learning. In some societies boys are removed from their homes at about 6 years of age, and their education is more formally structured after the habits of men. In most instances, however, all children remain with their parents and with no particular sex segregation of siblings until puberty.

PUBERTY

The second crisis in the life cycle is adolescence or puberty. Puberty, like birth, is a basic alteration of the biological state of the individual. It is the time of maturation of the secondary sexual characteristics and the final growth to functional capacity of the sex organs.

In both boys and girls, puberty is not an abrupt transition, but an accelerated development extending from about the eleventh to the sixteenth year. Body hair does not sprout overnight on boys; the lengthening of the vocal cords, with embarrassing sound effects, is not instantaneous; and the relative broadening of the shoulders is a process of adolescent growth as much as the production of fully formed seminal fluid.

In the female, the majority of puberty changes, including emergence of body hair, broadening of the hips, increase of subcutaneous fatty tissue (especially on the hips and breasts), and development of the sex organs, all occur over a period of months. The onset of menstruation clearly signals the attainment of puberty for the female (Figure 20.1).

Adolescence, however, is a cultural thing, manifesting different features and lasting different lengths of time in different societies.

The Cultural Definition of Puberty

The transition from adolescence to adulthood is keyed by a biological phenomenon. For human beings it also represents a sociological transition. The first fact to note is that some cultures handle adolescence most casually.[11] The second is that societies vary in that some ritualize it for one sex only or for both, with most placing heaviest emphasis on rites for boys. The third factor is that puberty rites do not necessarily synchronize with biological pubescence. They occur when, sociologically, childhood is left behind and adulthood is entered.

Negatively, this principle is admirably demonstrated in the case of the Alorese in the East Indies. For boys, the attainment of adulthood is a long-drawn-out process calling for extensive economic enterprising. Because of this, and since there are no men's clubs and no secret societies, there are no rites of transition, no tribal initiation. Instead, "at about sixteen the boys begin to let their hair grow long. At this time they begin to acquire male dress ornaments: sword, shields, areca basket, wide belt, bow, combs, and head plumes. This is ridiculed by the women, who hoot the men, and scoff at this manifes-

[11]For example, in Samoa, "Adolescence represented no period of crisis or stress, but was instead an orderly development of slowly maturing interests and activities. The girls' minds were perplexed by no conflicts, troubled by no philosophical queries, beset by no remote ambitions." M. Mead, *Coming of Age in Samoa*, p. 157.

(a)

(b)

(c)

(d)

(e)

FIGURE 20.1
In the matrilineal society of the Navajos, the cultural focus at puberty is on the four-day transition rites for girls. (a) Each morning, the initiate must run to the four directions, and back to her hogan, to make her active and industrious as a married woman. (b) On the first day her father builds a fire on her behalf in a carefully made excavation. (c) Later, the fire is removed and the hot pit is lined with corn husks. Corn meal batter, which has been prepared by the girl and her mother, is poured into the pit oven by her female relatives. The batter is covered with more corn husks and hot coals. (d) At sunrise the next day, the ceremonial cake is removed, cut, placed in large pieces on a fine basketry dish, and distributed to relatives and guests by the girl. (e) Each visiting relative and guest loans the girl's mother a fine blanket. At sunrise of the fourth day (note the father's shadow on the eastward facing door of the hogan), she stretches face down on the piled-up blankets. A model woman, chosen by the mother, molds her entire body with a weaving batten to endow her for life with a good disposition, strength, beauty, and skill. The girl then tosses the blankets back to their owners, and she is now a woman. (Alan Reed Photo.)

tation of masculine vanity."[12] The boys also file their incisors and blacken their teeth.

Incision of the foreskin (supercision) was practiced by some oceanic societies (Figure 20.2). Among the Marquesan Islanders the operation was performed between the ages of 25 and 50. It had nothing whatsoever to do with puberty. And then again, among the Tongans, although boys were usually supercised between the ages of 12 and 16, it could be done as early as 6. Adolescence was not important, but the status symbol of manhood was. As Gifford has written, "any youth who declined to be operated upon would be forbidden to eat with the other members of the household, could not touch

[12]C. DuBois, "The Alorese," in A. Kardiner (ed.), *The Psychological Frontiers of Society*, p. 139.

(a)

(b)

FIGURE 20.2
Initiation for boys on Big Namba Island in the New Hebrides, southwest Pacific, requires an entire year of isolation in a "bush school." (a) When the initiates are 6 to 8 years of age, the ritual year begins with circumcision and separation. (b) The boys are tended by their mothers during the day, but may not return to the village until the rites of passage are completed. (Kal Muller/Woodfin Camp and Associates.)

another's food, and would be spurned by the girls."[13]

Among the warrior tribes of the Plains and eastern North America, there were no puberty rites per se. But at adolescence young men set out on vision quests to obtain the supernatural power that was believed so essential to a successful life. However, vision vigils were carried on by adults, too, so it cannot be said that any great emphasis was placed upon puberty by these people. In the same manner, they treated the adolescence of girls casually. Although all the tribes isolated the menstruating woman, nothing much was made of the first menses, except that the Cheyenne father proudly stood in the door of his tepee shouting the good news to the whole camp and celebrated his daughter's woman-

[13]E. W. Gifford, *Tongan Society* (Bernice P. Bishop Museum Bulletin 61, 1929), p. 187.

hood by a giveaway of a fine horse to some poor oldster.

But the Northern Shoshones and other peoples of the Columbian Plateau made a real crisis of the event for the girl. The pubescent Shoshone girl was isolated for the period of her flow, but she had to be very busy so that she would not become a lazy woman. "Whatever she does then lasts for life." She could eat no meat and could not scratch herself except with a special stick. At the end of her first isolation, she was brought new clothes by her mother—women's clothes.

In societies such as those of Africa and aboriginal Australia, where peoples place much emphasis on age grading (see Chapter 25), adolescence rites become genuine "tribal initiations." This is especially true where men's secret societies are of great importance, such as in many parts of eastern Melanesia.

Andaman Island Rites As an example of the more dramatic forms of puberty rites, we may cite an account of the Andaman Islanders. These pygmy people had no secret societies or other associations, but they did place great emphasis upon age status. To be accepted as an adult, each boy and girl had to go through specific ceremonies. Beginning early in childhood, both sexes were gradually scarred over their entire bodies with small incisions "to help them grow strong," but the culmination was reached at puberty.

At the first sign of her menses, the girl was wept over by her mother and other female relatives. Such weeping did not express sorrow but rather marked an occasion of importance. The lass then plunged into the ocean for a two-hour bath—an act of ritual cleansing—after which she was tastefully decorated with pandanus leaves and clay.

Thus covered with leaves the girl must sit in the hut allotted to her, with her legs doubled up beneath her and her arms folded . . . for three days. Early every morning she leaves the hut to bathe for an hour in the sea. At the end of the three days she resumes her life in the village. For a month following she must bathe in the sea every morning at dawn.[14]

When the friends and relatives of a boy decided that he was old enough to have the incisions made on his back, a dance was held throughout the night and the next morning.

The boy kneels down and bends forward until his elbows rest on the ground in front. One of the older men . . . makes a series of cuts on the boy's back. Each cut is horizontal, and they are arranged in three vertical rows, each row consisting of from 20 to 30 cuts. When the cutting is finished the boy sits up, with a fire at his back, until the bleeding stops. During the operation and a few hours following it the boy must remain silent.[15]

Immediately upon completion of the puberty rites, a number of food taboos were imposed upon both sexes. These were gradually removed in a series of formal ceremonies over a period of several years. Neither a boy nor a girl became a full-fledged adult until all the taboos had been removed.

Relation of Puberty Rites to Other Factors

Becoming a man or a woman means finding one's adult place in the social system. It means accepting ascribed statuses and winning those which may appropriately be achieved. Psychologically, it means internalization of a self-identity that is adequately related to the social system in which one must function. It means anchoring of the self primarily within a kinship or other group.

The Factor of Social Independence Cohen classifies two types of societies: (1) those which train for social independence, that is, those in which anchorage and identification are in the nuclear family, and (2) those in which

[14] A. R. Radcliffe-Brown, *The Andaman Islanders*, p. 93.
[15] Ibid., p. 95.

(a)

(b)

FIGURE 20.3
Puberty rites of Native Australians. (a) Initiates symbolically painted and lying prone upon their ceremonial sponsors undergo circumcision. (Fritz Gore, *Life* Magazine, © Time, Inc.) (b) Adults perform dances interpreting the origin myth of the tribal group. (C. Mountford/Australian Information Service.)

children are brought up for sociological interdependence, that is, anchorage of the individual in wider kinship groups such as lineages and clans (see Chapter 23). Statistical correlations based on data from sixty-five societies show that type 2 societies overwhelmingly (36 to 1) use initiation ceremonies as a part of the socialization process. Among the type 1 societies in Cohen's sample, the ratio is only ten with initiations to eighteen without.[16]

[16]Y. A. Cohen, *The Transition from Childhood to Adolescence,* p. 114.

Circumcision and Personal Identity In pre-Columbian times circumcision was exclusively an Old World practice of which the American Indians knew nothing. In the Old World, it has been predominantly a feature of the Mediterranean area—an expression of Semitic and Arabic cultural symbolism. Thus, 68 percent of the Mediterranean societies regularly practice circumcision or some other surgical modification of the male genitals. Among Africans south of the Sahara, slightly more than half (56 percent) of the societies circumcise or subincise their boys. In Asia, only a handful of peoples (17 percent) mutilate male genitals, while in Oceania (Figure 20.3) the proportion is somewhat higher (one-fourth).[17]

Whiting and his associates have engaged in an intensive search for the whys and wherefores of circumcision as a part of transition rites. They discovered that the circumcision of boys, particularly when it occurs as a part of initiation rites, is strongly associated with three other cultural phenomena: (1) the custom of having a mother and baby sleep together while the father sleeps separately; (2) the so-called postpartum taboo, a taboo of a year or longer on resumption of sexual relations between parents after the birth of a child; and (3) virilocal residence, in which a married couple resides with the husband's kin. The first two customs result in strong mother-son identification, and the third intensifies the ultimate claim of the father's kinship group to the boy's social allegiance or identification. Hence, the severe hazing at puberty serves to break the mother-son tie and to transfer the boy into the world of men.[18]

Female Puberty Rites In a representative ethnographic sample of sixty societies, Brown found that approximately one-half observed mandatory puberty rites for girls between the ages of 8 and 20. Cross-cultural correlations shed some light on which societies initiate girls and which do not. In sum, if girls bring their husbands to live with them in their mothers' homes (uxorilocal residence), the chances are greater that the culture will include female puberty rites. By implication, removal of a girl from her parental home to her husband's sufficiently signals the status change from unmarried to married. If the girl remains at home, a ceremonial "booster shot" is helpful in effecting the personal identity transfer from mother (and her family) to the husband (and his). Brown also found that most female initiation rites are not painful. The relatively few societies (30 percent of those which initiate girls, or 15 percent of the total sample) which do inflict pain, such as in clitoridectomy (surgical removal of the clitoris), tend to be societies in which little girls sleep after birth with their mothers to the exclusion of their fathers. Finally, the greater the woman's contribution to subsistence activities, the more likely her society will be to emphasize her passage from the child's to the woman's statuses and roles. What is important in life tends to be signalized.[19]

There are a number of ancillary functions tied up with puberty ceremonialism. Cicatrization and the filing or knocking out of front teeth serve as both decorative elements and status identifications and also as tests of the neophyte's ability to endure physical pain (Figure 20.4). Strict discipline imposed during the rites works to fix the authority of elders. The instruction in etiquette, mythology, and magic that usually accompanies puberty initiations embraces education and training in a practical sense and enhances loyalty to the institutions of the tribal society. Yet under and through it all is the basic fact of transition—a transition that is fundamen-

[17]E. Bourguignon and L. Greenbaum, *Diversity and Homogeneity*, table 35, p. 57.

[18]J. W. M. Whiting, R. Kluckhohn, and A. S. Anthony, "The Function of Male Initiation Ceremonies at Puberty," in E. E. Maccoby, T. M. Newcomb, and E. L. Hartley (eds), *Readings in Social Psychology*, pp. 359–370.

[19]J. Brown, "A Cross-Cultural Study of Female Initiation Rites" (*American Anthropologist*, vol. 65, 1963), pp. 837–853.

FIGURE 20.4
Transition rites for women of the Mbotogote tribe of the New Hebrides include five days of public dancing and pig sacrifices and the removal of the upper incisor teeth on the sixth day. A toothless girl or an adult woman enjoys high prestige. She is eligible to marry, and her ghost after death is as strong as that of a man's. (Kal Muller/Woodfin Camp Associates.)

tally biological but often elaborately cultural—the transition to maturity.

MATURITY

Adulthood means full participation in the responsibilities and privileges of society. It usually means marriage and parenthood, as well as economic, political, religious, and club life. As new statuses are acquired in each of these areas, transition rites are observed to note the new life phases and new behaviors. Maturity is what most of the remainder of this book is about as we spell out marriage and family, kinship, club life, economics, law, politics, religion, and art.

DEATH

For the individual, death is the last of the life crises. Every person lives with awareness of death, and every society has evolved some method for coping with it.[20] Death has no absolute finality for any society. All believe that something happens after death.

Yet all people well know that death marks the end of corporeal existence. Belief in the transition from the carnal to a wholly spiritual existence at death comes through faith and imagination, a projection of life from a tangible and material state to an ethereal illusory condition. Because the dead are almost always relegated to another state of being in human cosmogony, one societal task is that of assigning new relationships between the deceased and the survivors. The new status of the deceased (spirit) may be viewed as hostile or benign, and the new behavior of the living may range from excessive fear, with attempts to placate, to idolatrous worship.

The Neandertals of Middle Paleolithic times were the earliest human beings known to leave tangible evidence of concern over death. They deliberately buried their dead in carefully prepared graves and left the bodies accompanied by flowers and other funerary goods. All humans, since then, have consistently worked into their cultures some form of disposal of the corpse. A great variety of methods has been recorded. A partial listing by Kroeber includes: "burial, cremation, water burial, setting away in vaults or canoes or houses, scaffold burial, exposure or simple abandonment, cremation with eating or drinking of the ashes by the relatives, temporary inhumation with either reburial or preservation of the bones—not to mention previous mummification, dismemberment, and other related practices" (Figure 20.5).[21] As we have seen from archaeological evidence in former chapters, even burials were handled in a

[20] J. W. Riley, Jr., "Death and Bereavement" (*International Encyclopedia of the Social Sciences*, vol. 4, 1968), p. 19.
[21] A. L. Kroeber, *Anthropology* (2d ed.), p. 402.

FIGURE 20.5
A Plains Indian scaffold burial. The dead man's war spear, shield, and enemy scalps hang from the supporting poles. (Roland Reed, 1912/Kramer Gallery.)

wide variety of ways, with bodies stretched out, curled up, richly adorned, and undecorated. Regardless of how the deceased body is disposed of, it is accompanied by transitional funerary rites.

Death Rites

Death rituals have two foci. The first deals with the deceased, the separation of the spirit from the body, and the disposal of the corpse: the funeral. The second focuses on the bereavement of the survivors, the transfer of property rights and other statuses from the dead to the living, and the reincorporation of the bereaved into the ongoing community: mourning.

Cheyenne Death Practices To illustrate these facets of the social management of death, let us take a summary look at the nineteenth-century Cheyennes, nomadic hunters of the Plains:

For the Cheyenne there is no Hell or punishment of any sort in after-life; no Judgment or Damnation. Although Cheyennes sin when they commit murder . . . , murder is expiated in the here and now, and wrongdoing builds up no burden of guilt to be borne beyond the grave. For the Cheyenne there is no problem of salvation; goodness is to be sought . . . for its own sake and for the . . . approval of one's fellow man. When at last it shakes free of its corporeal abode, the Cheyenne soul wafts free and light up the Hanging Road to dwell thereafter in benign proximity to the Great Wise One and the long-lost loved ones. Only the souls of those who have committed suicide are barred from this peace.

In spite of the happy destination that awaits the dead, death is clearly a traumatic experience for the surviving relatives. Each individual is highly valued, for the population is small, and every loss is keenly felt. This is why revenge drives are so strong against enemies who kill Cheyennes.

The corpse of one who has died in camp is quickly disposed of, for people feel that its ghost will not start its journey to the Milky Way until the body has been removed to its final resting place . . . It is believed, further, that spirits like company on their journey and that some of them try to take the spirit of a living person with them, and hence, if the body is not disposed of with alacrity, someone may die. Children are especially susceptible to this danger.

. . . Relatives and close friends dress the body of the deceased in its finest clothing. They wrap it, extended full length with the arms at the sides, in a number of robes lashed round about with great lengths of ropes. The burial bundle is . . . placed

either in the crotch of a tree or upon a scaffold. Or it may be covered over with rocks on the ground. The owner's favorite horses are shot and left at the grave along with his weapons, or, in the case of a woman, her utensils. A man's shield and war bonnet are usually left to his son or best friend; a woman's flesher is left to her daughter. Everything else is given away, usually to nonrelatives who come to the survivor's lodge to mourn until everything has been disposed of, including the lodge.

. . . Female relatives, especially mothers and wives, cut off their long hair and gash their foreheads so that the blood flows. If the dead one has been killed by enemies, they slash their legs so that they become caked with dried blood; sometimes the blood is not washed off for many weeks. Widows who wish to make an extravagant display of their bereavement gash themselves fearfully and move off alone to live destitute in the brush. The isolation may last a full year, until relatives begin gradually to camp around her, slowly reincorporating her into kin and community life.[22]

In this description, the transitional isolation of the bereaved, with the ultimate aim of reincorporation into the living society, is made clear. The Cheyennes were a hunting society in which most statuses were achieved rather than ascribed, and a society with relatively few material possessions compared to more settled groups. There was, therefore, not much to pass on through inheritance.

Death Practices of the Siuai Conversely, in societies where social structure is more complex, we expect funeral rites and mourning to be more highly elaborated.[23] This holds true of such Melanesian peoples as the Solomon Islanders studied by Douglas Oliver, whose results we briefly summarize.

The horticulturalist Siuai of Bougainville are sharers of the Melanesian tradition of "Big Men," reciprocal pig exchange, and shell money. "The death of a child or young person occasions smaller funerals, and an infant's dying is usually a matter for near relatives alone. On the other hand, the death of a high-ranking leader gives rise to a more elaborate train of events and the funeral may be attended by hundreds of persons."[24]

If a leader dies in the prime of life, it is assumed a sorcerer had a hand in his death. At the moment of death, his nearest kin crowd around the corpse and wail loudly. The largest slit gong in the men's house to which he belonged is sounded to announce the death. The men withdraw to make plans, and more female relatives crowd into the house to carry on the crying.

After consulting with the widow, a son gives valuable shell money to his paternal uncle and mother's brother's son. An even larger amount of shell money is then distributed to other relatives and friends to pay for the pigs they must contribute to the funeral. Enough pigs are required to feed all who will attend from other villages. The "bigger" the man, the more villages to be invited. Relatives keep arriving throughout the day to join the wailing.

During the next day a funeral pyre is built and delegations continue to arrive between sunset and midnight. There is much ritualistic weeping.

Before dawn the corpse is prepared and placed on the pyre, which is then lighted. The bereaved members of the family cling close to the burning heap as long as they can stand the heat. By dawn, most visitors have drifted away. The widow and son gather up unburnt bits of bone, dispose of them, and purify their hands in a final act of separation.

The funeral is over, but the period of mourning goes on. For some days, no work is done by the kin. Little is eaten. No one washes, for this would remove the mourning clay. It used to be

[22]E. A. Hoebel, *The Cheyennes*, (2d ed.), pp. 92–93. It should be understood that most of these practices are no longer followed.

[23]This proposition has not, in fact, been subjected to extensive cross-cultural testing and no satisfactory general theory has been developed to account for the wide range of variation in form and intensity of death rites.

[24]D. L. Oliver, *A Solomon Island Society*, pp. 214–215.

(before Australian administration suppressed revenge expeditions) that an ally and his henchmen symbolically killed the sorcerer during this phase. After a week or two, the kin resume normal activity. Phase 1 of mourning is ended.

Phase 2 ends several weeks later when every relative who has received shell money brings in pigs. The pigs are butchered and strips of pork are carried to all the villages whose members had attended the funeral.

Seclusion and separation continue for months for the widow—and many widowers undertake this voluntarily, in honor of their wives—until some relative or friend presents a "bringing-out" gift of a pig or shell money. Thus, the last of the mourners is incorporated once again into normal social life.

Yet a form of symbolic exclusion, or separation, may linger for years in the gardens, forest, or parts of rivers which are "set-aside"—tabooed in memory of the deceased. For a child, it might be only a corner of a garden. Reincorporation of a "set-aside" area requires a feast and a formal release of the ghost of the dead from its guardianship of the space.

Functions of Mortuary Rites

As transition ceremonies, funeral rites serve five basic functions. (1) Participation in mortuary ceremonies, by habitual dramatization of the faith in immortality, prepares the living for the death that awaits them. (2) Funeral rites serve magically to assure the separation of the soul (or spirit) from its body, to guide the deceased through the supreme transition safely and properly. (3) The rites serve to readjust the emotional disturbances in the community resulting from the upset of affective habits in connection with the deceased. Death usually evokes grief. (4) Where feasting and property gifts are involved, mortuary rites facilitate the redistribution of wealth and statuses. (5) Finally, the rites lend color, richness, and depth to life through the drama of their performance. They are often somewhat theatrical and have a certain entertainment function.

SUMMARY

Birth, maturity, reproduction, and death—each is conceptualized and handled in cultural, as well as physiological terms. The degree of cultural intensity in dealing with these phases of life varies from culture to culture. Most human beings are haunted by anxieties during these changes. In response, they apprehend the transitional phases as life crises, developing specific ritual practices and correlative techniques for handling each situation.

All peoples have a theory of conception, although most such theories are not scientifically sound. A few, such as those of the Australian aborigines and Trobriand Islanders, deny the physiology of paternity altogether, attributing conception to spirit behavior. Many peoples attribute conception to the growth of a seed implanted by the male in the female, but a few believe the fetus is caused by coagulation of the female blood initiated by the sex act.

Once pregnancy is perceived, the woman (and probably her husband) is subject to a number of taboos designed to forestall abnormal development of the child, miscarriage, and difficult labor. The birth itself is usually handled in a routine manner, although postnatal isolation of the mother and child is common. In a few widely scattered parts of the world, the father simulates childbirth and postpartum recovery in a practice known as the couvade, evidently a form of symbolic identification of the father with the infant.

Merely being born is not sufficient. Formal rites of naming and presentation to the world complete the transition into society.

Adolescence produces the second crisis of the life cycle. Puberty rites mark the transition to adulthood in many cultures. Such rites appear to be associated with early (in life) mother-son identification and residence with the husband's family (virilocal); their function is to weaken "momism" and to effect a psychological identification with the world of man. Conversely, if upon marriage the newlyweds live with the bride's parents, there is a greater likelihood that the girl will go through puberty ceremonies than if the residence is virilocal. Girls are much less likely than boys to be mutilated or hazed in their rites.

Maturity marks full participation in the responsibilities and privileges of full social life. It generally means marriage and parenthood, and economic, political, religious, and club life in many different manifestations.

Most peoples believe in some form of life after death. Mortuary rites effect the transition of the dead from their carnal life to their spirit existence. They also reassign and effect the transfer of the statuses of the deceased with respect to social responsibilities and property. Thus, there is the funeral, which disposes of the corpse and separates spirit from body. Then there is bereavement, the placing of the kin in limbo, so to speak, and finally reincorporating them fully into the community with reconstructed relationships.

SELECTED READINGS

Cohen, Y. A., *The Transition from Childhood to Adolescence* (1964). Distinguishes prepubertal and postpubertal rites of separation of the child from its family and correlates each type with specific social orientations.

Erikson, E. H., "Life Cycle" (*International Encyclopedia of the Social Sciences* (vol. 9, 1968), pp. 286–292. A very compact and useful statement of the attributes of the major psychosocial crises in the individual developmental cycle.

Ford, C. S., *A Comparative Study of Human Reproduction* (Yale University Publications in Anthropology, no. 32, 1945). Summarizes nonliterate natal attitudes and birth practices.

Goody, J., *Death, Property and the Ancestors* (1962). The most comprehensive analysis available of death practices and their functional significance in a nonliterate culture.

21 Mating and Marriage

CHAPTER OUTLINE

LEARNING GOALS

Discuss cultural restrictions on permarital mating.

Discuss the prohibition of incest.

Summarize the explanations for the incest taboo.

Define exogamy and endogamy.

Describe levirate, sororate, and extended affinal marriages.

List the modes of marriage.

Explain what is meant by fictive marriage.

Describe divorce and the dissolution of marriage in different cultures.

There is no such thing as a promiscuous human society. All societies impose limitations on sexual activities. The amount of inhibition varies from culture to culture.

An examination of the cross-cultural record shows that American society imposes a greater degree of inhibition than is usual with other societies, although in recent times it appears to be moving away from this distinctive position. Murdock's survey of kinship institutions among 250 societies showed that "it seems likely that a general prohibition of sexual relations outside of marriage occurs in as many as five percent of the peoples of the earth."[1] From this it can be seen that the American position is highly atypical. Nevertheless, all societies impose limitations on sexual activity and attempt to regulate reproduction and mating.

MATING

Mating is *the pairing of individuals of opposite sex for the purpose of sexual relations.* It is preponderantly a psychophysical phenomenon but among human beings it is influenced by various culture patterns that control the forms of its expression. Mating is not to be confused with marriage; intimately related though the two may be, they are separable. As in the case of nonhuman animals, mating can occur on a purely biological plane, without benefit of marriage. Conversely, marriage can occur without mating.

Marriage is an institution regulated by culture. Marriage is the complex of social norms that define and control the relations of a cojoined pair to each other, their relatives, their offspring, and society at large. It includes all the institutional rights, duties, and privileges of the pair as husband and wife. It helps shape the form and activities of the group known as the family.

Premarital Mating

The majority of human societies accept premarital sexual experimentation. Of the 863 societies in Murdock's *Ethnographic Atlas*, 67 percent impose little restriction on premarital sexual behavior. The greatest proportion (75 percent) of permissive societies is found in the Pacific area, thus supporting the romantic image of the permissive Pacific brought back by nineteenth-century sailors. The most restrictive area of the world is the Circum-Mediterranean, the home of the Semites and Muslims, where only 41 percent of the societies tolerate premarital sexual behavior.[2]

The Trobriand Islanders exemplify, perhaps in a somewhat extreme fashion, one of the these patterns. In Malinowski's words: "Chastity is an unknown virtue . . . At an incredibly early age they become initiated into sexual life, and many of the innocent looking plays of childhood are not so innocuous. . . . [P]romiscuous free-love . . . gradually develops into more permanent attachments, one of which ends in marriage."[3]

In the absence of the severe guilt feelings that traditionally colored premarital sex activity among our youth, premarital activity may function in some societies to prepare young people for marriage. It can provide an intimate test of the compatibility of mating pairs before they actually enter into marriage, with all its social and economic responsibilities. This is Malinowski's principle of the *social function of premarital sexual activity.*[4]

This set of attitudes is well exemplified by the Kadara of the Nigerian plateau, a gardening and hunting people who practice infant betrothal. The young groom, after his fiancee is three or more years of age, labors in her father's gardens for a set number of days each year until, after ten years, he may claim his wife. Marriages, however, are expected to last only through the births of the first three offspring. These children belong to

[1] G. P. Murdock, *Social Structure*, p. 264.

[2] E. Bourguignon and L. Greenbaum, *Diversity and Homogeneity*, p. 54.

[3] B. Malinowski, *Argonauts of the Western Pacific*, p. 53.

[4] B. Malinowski, "Culture" (*Encyclopaedia of the Social Sciences*, vol. 4, 1931), p. 630.

the husband's kinship group. What is valued are the children *per se*, not the chastity of the bride. "It is fairly common," writes M. G. Smith, "for unmarried girls to be impregnated or to give birth to children by youths other than their betrothed. Offspring of such premarital pregnancies are members of the patrilineage of the girl's betrothed and are welcomed as proofs of the bride's fertility."[5]

Restrictions on Premarital Mating

At any rate, not much emphasis can be placed upon the *function of premarital experience* as a factor in mate selection in the vast number of societies in which the boy and girl have very little to say about whom they marry. Such societies are much more concerned with (1) the biological perpetuation of the group, (2) the perpetuation of the culture through proper nurture and training of the oncoming generation, and (3) furthering immediate special interests in prestige, property, and prerogatives of the kinship groups of the pair that is to be joined in marriage.

This last point is well illustrated in the practices of the Philippine Ifugaos, who permit free premarital sexual activity only for members of those classes in which there is not much at stake in property and prestige. Each night, adolescent boys of the lower and middle classes seek the congenial comfort of the house of a widow, which also serves as a dormitory for unmarried adolescent girls. Much experimentation in different dormitories ultimately leads to a permanent attachment that eventually blossoms into a fully accredited marriage, after numerous exchange gifts have been made and family rituals of marriage have been observed.

Upper-class Ifugaos, however, behave in quite a different manner. The society rests on a subsistence base of wet-rice culture in paddies that have been carved in rugged mountainsides (see Figure 12.7, page 222) through the prodigious efforts of generations of labor. Possession of rice fields is a precious heritage: a necessary means to wealth, prestige, and upper-class status—the cherished goal of the Ifugao. Because family status rests heavily on property, marriage is a useful instrument for augmenting the status of the next generation by combining the properties of two families. To have a scion find a compatible but propertyless bride in the damsels' dormitory is, for the upper-class Ifugao, an economic calamity. To avert such an eventuality, rich children of the Ifugaos are betrothed in infancy or before birth. Figure 23.1, page 410, shows such a contract marriage. A contract marriage is arranged by the parents, who guarantee the amount of land and other goods to be

FIGURE 21.1
Kana courtship. Waghi Valley, Central Highlands of New Guinea. (Laurence LeGuay.)

[5]M. G. Smith, "Secondary Marriage among Kadara and Kagoro," in P. Bohannan and J. Middleton (eds.), *Marriage, Family, and Residence*, p. 113.

conveyed to the bride and groom. Throughout childhood, the boy and girl take turns living in each other's parents' homes until they establish a home of their own on marriage, shortly after adolescence.[6]

The illustrations cited above indicate that economic factors can influence premarital sexual activity. Other factors must also be recognized. In the area of sex control, the power of religious belief cannot be overestimated. Inca maidens dedicated to serve the sun in the nunneries of Cuzco were required to remain virgins until they were married off to a worthy dignitary. Rome had her vestal virgins. And the military societies of the Cheyenne Indians each had four honorary virgins to perform ritual services in the society ceremonies. An active sexual life is often incompatible with religious specialization.

Shamans are generally devoted to this principle. Unless they are engaged in fertility rites to bring on a crop of babies or food, they almost universally submit to temporary celibacy when they are about to invoke their mystic powers. The belief is that the female physiology is charged with an evil and dangerous power. Contamination of a male's supernatural power is believed to result from sexual association.

When this attitude is exaggerated, it leads to the sexual asceticism of some of the Late Classical cults and early Christianity, an asceticism that survives in the celibacy of the Catholic clergy and the puritan distrust of sex embedded in our culture. Psychiatry and psychology adduce manifold instances of malfunctioning as a result of sex asceticism in our culture.

One or more of the considerations just mentioned have led a slight majority of contemporary nonliterate societies to inhibit premarital sexual activity. The Trobriand Island instance represents a minority situation. These societies impose a check on adolescent premarital sex experience not because they view such activity as inherently evil, but rather because economic and other social interests have priority over sex. However, *every society prohibits sexuality between brother and sister, and between parents and their children.*

THE PROHIBITION OF INCEST

Sometimes a confusion occurs between incest prohibition, which refers to restricting sexual relations with some or all relatives, and exogamy, which refers to restrictions as to whom one may marry. It follows, naturally, that if one cannot have sexual relations with certain persons, then certainly one cannot marry them. But the reverse is not necessarily true.

Incest taboos and exogamy are two different concepts with different social functions; they must be kept conceptually and analytically separate.

Incest taboos are found among all peoples. The universality of incest prohibition led to the common view that it is instinctive. Incest prohibition is not instinctive; rather, it is based on social, not biological principles.

Exceptions to the Incest Taboo

Let us observe how this works. *The taboo on the mating of brother and sister occurs everywhere, as does the taboo on mating between parent and child.* The exceptions that bar absolute universality are few. They include the famous cases of the royalty of Egypt, Hawaii, and the Incas. In these instances, marriage between brother and sister of royal lineage was required in the belief that the supreme royalty was divine and that marriage with mortals was a corruption of the divinity. Brother-sister marriage as a means of keeping property within the family was evidently not uncommon in Egypt during the period of Roman rule following the death of Cleopatra.[7]

[6]R. F. Barton, *Ifugao Law* (University of California Publications in American Archaeology and Ethnology, vol. 15, 1919), pp. 15–22.

[7]R. Middleton, "Brother-Sister and Father-Daughter Marriage in Ancient Greece" (*American Sociological Review*, vol. 27, 1962), pp. 603–611.

Another special exception to the brother-sister taboo exists among Balinese villagers, who assume that boy and girl twins have been intimate in their mother's womb. The penalties for incest are severe in Bali, but in the case of baby twins, temporary banishment of the parents and the "erring" twins, followed by a ceremony of purification and atonement, negates the sin. This makes it permissible for the mating in the womb to be completed as a true marriage in later life.[8]

Edmund Leach has reported a Southeast Asian example of marriage between brothers and sisters under certain circumstances. In calling attention to the Lakher, he writes:

They consider that the child of a properly married man is exclusively his and that his divorced wife has absolutely no rights in the child whatsoever. It follows that if a woman has a son and a daughter by two different husbands the children are deemed unrelated to one another. Therefore they may marry without restraint. In contrast, the son and daughter of one man by two different mothers stand in an incestuous relationship to one another.[9]

The Penalties for Incest

The punishments for the violation of the incest taboos vary greatly from one society to another, but a regional distribution of characteristic reactions is discernible. In Australia, most tribes punish incest with death. Plains Indians, on the other hand, did not consider incest either a crime or a sin. They simply looked upon it as impossible behavior, so inconceivable that only insane persons indulge in it. Yet the punishment was mild in the few rare cases recorded. A Dakota father of an incestuous brother and sister proclaimed, "Now I am the father of dogs!" Comanche informants cannot remember a single actual case of incest among their people, nor can they stretch their imaginations sufficiently to give a specific statement of what the public reaction would have been had such a case occurred, except to say that the people would have shunned them and called them crazy.

In ancient Bali, the punishment was symbolic and devastating. The hapless couple were adorned with yokes customarily worn by pigs. They were then made to crawl on all fours to drink from the swill trough of the hogs. After this humiliation, they were banished forever from the village, and their lands were confiscated. No other village would take them in for fear of ill luck and disaster. They were doomed to a fearsome existence alone in the jungle.[10]

Biological Explanations of the Incest Taboo

It was argued by earlier anthropologists[11] that primitive people were cognizant of genetic deterioration resulting from close inbreeding. They reasoned that humanity preserved its health by preventing close inbreeding through the establishment of incest prohibitions. This is the popular belief of most people in the United States. The fact is, however, that inbreeding does no more than intensify the traits that the inbreeding population possessed at the outset. Recessive traits have a better chance of being expressed where inbreeding is marked. Nevertheless, it is equally true that inbreeding intensifies the influence of dominant traits. The end result may be good or bad; it all depends on whether the traits are good or bad. Cleopatra, the last of the Ptolemies and the product of twelve generations of brother-sister marriages, was hardly a specimen of physical degeneration.

In the long run, however, modern population genetics holds that the effect of inbreeding in *Homo sapiens* is negative. This comes about because deleterious and lethal genes are many times more frequent in the offspring of closely

[8] J. Belo, "A Study of a Balinese Family" (*American Anthropologist*, vol. 38, 1936), p. 30.

[9] E. R. Leach, *Rethinking Anthropology*, p. 14.

[10] J. Belo, op. cit., p. 29.

[11] E. Westermarck, *The History of Human Marriage*, vol. 2, pp. 218–241; L. H. Morgan, *Ancient Society*, p. 424.

related parents. The closer the inbreeding, the greater the relative frequency of homozygous inheritance, hence the greater probability of the inheritance of destructive genes. The incest taboo, whatever its specific cultural content, inhibits close inbreeding. We can now feel certain, on sound scientific grounds, that its effects are genetically beneficial for humanity.

Westermarck's Instinct Theory Westermarck has stated that human beings raised in the same family circle have an instinctive aversion to sexual relations with each other. He held that the social rules prohibiting incest lend cultural expression to a biologically natural repugnance.[12] Most anthropologists of today have wholly rejected this hypothesis on the ground that there is too much evidence of an actual proclivity for sexual relations with those who are conveniently at hand; it is to suppress this tendency in favor of structural solidarity of the basic kinship groups that the strong anti-incest rules exist, they maintain.

Adopted Sister Marriages Nonetheless, support for Westermarck's position has recently been revived through a study of two forms of marriage among Chinese settlers in Taiwan. The prestigious form of marriage is called the "grand" or "major" marriage. It creates an alliance between two extended families, establishing important interfamily obligations, along with payment of dowry and progeny price (pages 380–383). Such marriages, which were common before 1930, were arranged by the elders, and the bride and groom did not see each other until their wedding day.

The "minor" marriage was also common (40 percent of all marriages from 1900 to 1925). This type, however, was "socially despised." In the "minor" marriage pattern, used only by disadvantaged families, poor parents adopted a baby girl to raise as a future wife for a son, thus obviating the need to pay out the progeny price for the bride if she were to come as a mature member of another kinship group. And by giving away their own baby daughters to other families, they also eliminated the raising of dowries for them when their time came to marry.[13] They seemed to think that the stigma of propertyless marriages could be reduced by effecting the betrothal through infant adoption years before the marriage would occur. How does this affect the Westermarck argument?

Professor Wolf proposes that if Westermarck's hypothesis is right, then couples who were raised together would find that sexual aversion persisted after marriage and would permanently mar their marital relations; they "should be less intimate and more prone to marital discord." With data that are unusually good, he shows that "minor" marriages resulted in 33 percent fewer children than did the "major" variety, along with a relative frequency of divorce and/or adultery of $4^1/_2$ to 1.[14] Wolf believes his data establish that there is "some aspect of childhood association sufficient to preclude or inhibit sexual desire" in the "minor" marriages.

But the question still remains: Are these facts the indices of lesser sexuality in "adopted sister-brother" marriages in Taiwan? Or do they indicate only that in the old Chinese society there was less at stake socially in the prestigeless and disdained "minor" marriages, and that there was less commitment to marriage when there was less to win or lose?

The Relation of Social Structure to the Incest Taboo

Although the incest taboo may well serve eugenic ends, there is much about the specific manifes-

[12] E. Westermarck, op. cit., p. 192.

[13] A. P. Wolf, "Adopt a Daughter-in-law, Marry a Sister: A Chinese Solution to the Problem of the Incest Taboo" (*American Anthropologist*, vol. 70, 1968), pp. 864–874.

[14] A. P. Wolf, "Childhood Association and Sexual Attraction: A Further Test of the Westermarck Hypothesis" (*American Anthropologist*, vol. 72, 1970), p. 506.

tation of the principle of incest prohibition that can be explained only in sociocultural terms. The fact is that although parent-child and sibling sex relations are almost universally prohibited, the incest taboo is often extended far beyond the membership of the nuclear family.

Marriage with known cousins is tabooed in two out of every three societies.[15] In a notable number of social systems, however, sex relations with cousins who fall outside a person's kinship group are allowed, and marriage with these particular cousins may even be socially encouraged or prescribed.

Cross-cultural anthropological research amply demonstrates that the degree of genealogical closeness is irrelevant to the application of the incest taboo. Rather, the specific identification of the individuals who are brought within the scope of the incest taboo is a function of the forms of kinship organization that prevail in a given society.

Kinship Terminology and the Incest Taboo Modes of addressing relatives reflect the structure of the kinship groups in any society (see Chapter 24). In standard American terminology, a sister is a girl born of the same parents as oneself. However, Catholics stretch the term to include nuns, and members of a sorority extend the term to include one another. When Indians of today make the distinction between "sister" and "Indian sister," they are trying to make clear that the Indian concept of "sister" is somewhat different from the standard American concept. If the speaker is a Seed Eater Shoshone from Idaho, the term "sister" in its native sense means not only "daughter of my own mother" but also all female cousins through both father and mother. Relationship terms may be taken quite literally; therefore, a girl called "sister" *is* a sister and must be treated as such in all respects. Sex relations and marriage with all "sisters" are therefore automatically tabooed.

This broadening of relationship categories has been aptly called *lumping*.[16] It is the usual characteristic of relationship systems that are identified as *classificatory*, that is, kinship systems which group relatives of different kinds under one term. In societies with a classificatory kinship system, many individuals are embraced within the incest prohibition by the simple fiat of a social system that dubs them "father," "mother," "brother," or "sister," when in biological fact they are not actually such. (See pages 425–431 for a more detailed discussion of this phenomenon.)

Types of Cousins Many societies lump all persons we call "cousins" in a single category. Other peoples make a distinction between two types of cousins. The first type of cousin anthropologists call *parallel-cousins*, because the parents through whom they are related are of the same sex. The other type of cousin we call *cross-cousins*, because the parents through whom they are related are of opposite sex (Figure 21.2). In any tribe in which cross-cousins are distinguished from parallel-cousins, cross-cousins are never reckoned as belonging to the same kinship group. To have sexual relations with a parallel-cousin who is a member of one's own clan *is* incest. However, to have sexual intercourse with a cross-cousin may be the accepted thing to do; marriage with one may be required.

Functional and Demographic Explanations of the Incest Taboo

There are two types of functional and demographic theories for explaining the incest taboo. One rests primarily on psychological principles and emphasizes the potentially disruptive effect of sexual competition within the kinship group. The fullest statement of this theory came from

[15] Bourguignon and Greenbaum, op. cit., p. 53.

[16] R. H. Lowie, "Kinship" (*Encyclopaedia of the Social Sciences*, vol. 3, 1931), pp. 568–572.

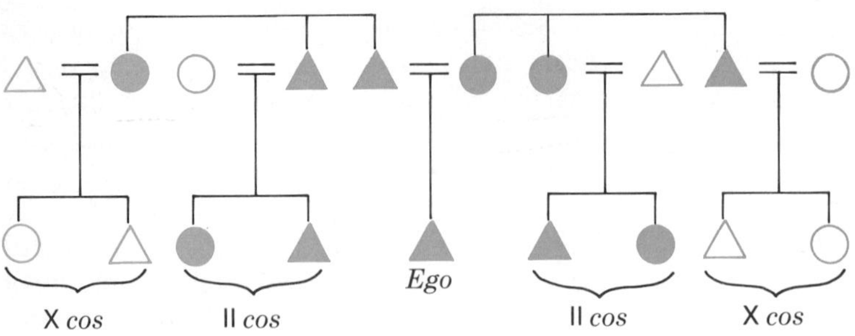

FIGURE 21.2
Genealogical separation of cross- and parallel-cousins. *Ego* refers to the individual from whose point of view the system is described. X *cos* = cross-cousin; II *cos* = parallel cousin.

Malinowski. The other emphasizes demography and improved nutrition.

The Psychological Theory Malinowski proposed that sexual affection is precluded by strongly conditioned parental and fraternal affection, based on intimate family associations, which occurs before the maturation of the sex drives. These are the affective emotions that cement the bonds of family and kin. The family is founded in part upon the sexual association of spouses, between whom the sex drive may have legitimate play. But sex is a dangerous element. In preadolescence, the sex drives are unmatured; they are not yet dangerous. On maturation, under unrestricted conditions, however, gratification of the sex drives would frequently be sought with those nearest at hand. This would naturally lead to mating between siblings, and between parents and offspring. The violent emotions engendered by sexual affection would disrupt the family unity built upon the earlier established affections.

Overt sexual rivalry within the functioning kinship group cannot be permitted. The solidarity of the foundation unit of society is protected against its disruptive effects through the universal incest prohibition.[17]

The Demographic Theory The demographic theory of the incest taboo argues simply that in the earliest hominid groups incestuous matings were unlikely or not possible because no sexual mates were available in the primary family.[18] Men in these early societies were forced to breed out of the family, and this pattern motivated the organization of kinship structures and rules based on outbreeding.

A basic premise of the demographic theory is that an explanation of the origin of the incest taboo might be different from an explanation of its persistence. The taboo's origin is hypothetically postulated from the demographic limits on mating among early hominid populations:

Life would have been short (a maximum expectation of say 35 years), and puberty late—say 15 or later. The infant mortality rate would have been high—at least 50 per cent. Man tends to produce infants singly rather than in litters, and hence there is spacing of births. This spacing can be increased by the death of a child, and by such population-control measures as infanticide, abortion and abstinence. . . . There is also a possibility that long suckling in relatively undernourished mothers inhibits ovulation. . . . All these factors would place severe limits on the possibilities of inbreeding. By the time a young boy reached puberty, his mother would probably be past breeding age or dead. . . . [A]lthough the chances would be better for brothers and sisters, they would still be slender. . . . A boy's elder sister would in all probability be 'taken' by the time he reached puberty, and he himself would be mated by the time his younger sister came of age. A

[17]B. Malinowski, "Culture" (*Encyclopaedia of the Social Sciences*, vol. 4, 1931), p. 630.

[18]M. K. Slater, "Ecological Factors in the Origin of Incest" (*American Anthropologist*, vol. 61 ,1959), pp. 1042–1059.

run of same-sex children in the family would of course increase the chances of outbreeding.

Thus, the theory claims, the earliest hominids were perhaps unable to commit incest very often even if they wanted to. In the simplest ecologies (and similar ones exist today) most of the people most of the time mate out, not because of the problem of inbreeding and competition, but in order to mate at all.[19]

According to Fox the persistence of the incest taboo has a different explanation. As culture evolved, the demographic conditions of hominid families changed with the increased production and improved food-getting adaptations. These changes allow the closer spacing of children, an earlier and longer period of sexual fertility, and a greater possibility for intrafamilial mating.

> . . . [*B*]*ecause since earliest times men have bred out, they have erected a whole lot of institutions at the kinship level that assume outbreeding—that are predicated on it. . .* [*A*]*s technological sophistication increased, life lengthened and infant mortality and all the other barriers to incest progressively disappeared. In many societies today, therefore, it would be quite possible for most people to commit incest if they wished, i.e., there would be a partner available. But it is in a sense too late. We have already built up our societies on the premise that people will breed out of the family, and we cannot easily reverse this. The improvements we have mentioned are, in evolutionary terms, very recent. So the taboo persists.*[20]

EXOGAMY

Exogamy (Gr. *ex*, "outside," and *gamos*, "marriage") is defined as *the social rule that requires individuals to marry outside of a culturally defined group of which they are members.* The conjugal-natal family, sometimes called the *nuclear family*, composed of parents and their children, is always exogamous, with the few exceptions already noted. Whether other kinship groups are exogamous varies with each society.

Simple Exogamy

When the prohibition against marrying kinspeople is applied to all known genetic relatives, exogamy is simple or undifferentiated. Two-thirds of the societies in the *Ethnographic Atlas* practice simple exogamy.[21] Generally speaking, simple exogamy occurs in societies in which kinship is organized bilaterally; that is, members receive identity through both parents. Hence, simple exogamy was highest in North America (83 percent), where 65 percent of the Indian tribes were bilaterally organized. It was (and still is) lowest in the Mediterranean area (34 percent), where only 31 percent of the societies are bilaterally organized.

Restricted Exogamy

In restricted exogamy, marriage is forbidden with certain kin, while at the same time it is preferred or required, as the case may be, with other relatives who are not culturally defined as relatives. These persons are almost always cross-cousins. This calls for marriage to a mother's brother's child or a father's sister's child (Figure 21.3) among first cousins, or to their equivalents if the preference applies to second or third cousins or beyond. Such cross-cousin marriages are *symmetrical*; that is, marriage is allowed with cross-cousins through either parent.

In the *Ethnographic Atlas*, 20 percent of the societies forbid marriage to parallel-cousins but make it permissible with *either* kind of cross-cousin (defined as *ambilateral cross-cousin marriage*). A mere 4 percent (32 out of 762) prescribe marriage of a male to a mother's brother's daughter (*matrilateral cross-cousin marriage*), and less than 1 percent (4 in 762) require

[19]R. Fox, *Kinship and Marriage*, pp. 66–67. By permission of Penguin Books Ltd.

[20]Ibid., p. 68.

[21]Bourguignon and Greenbaum, op. cit., pp. 51, 53.

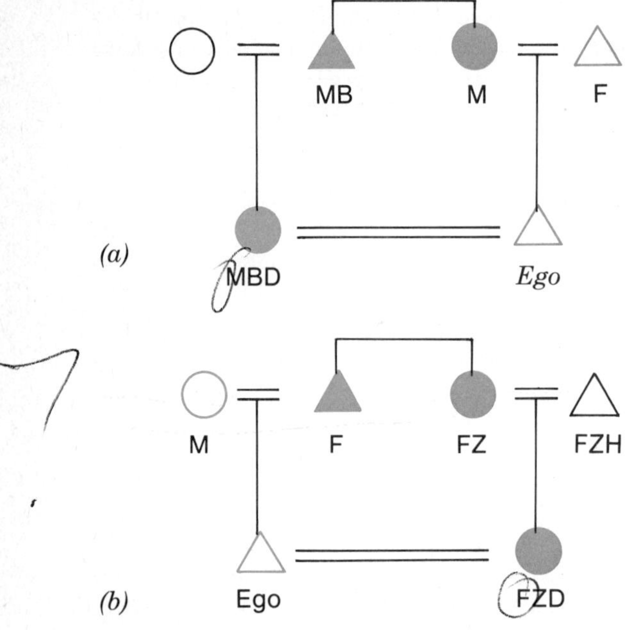

FIGURE 21.3
(a) Matrilateral cross-cousin marriage in a patrilineal society. A male ego marries his mother's brother's daughter, who does not belong to his patrilineage. (b) Patrilateral cross-cousin marriage in a matrilineal society. A male ego marries his father's sister's daughter, who does not belong to his matrilineage. (For a definition of matrilineage and patrilineage, see page 413.) Anthropological symbols for types of kin are as follows: *F*, father; *M*, mother; *B*, brother; *Z*, sister; *S*, son; *D*, daughter; *H*, husband; *W*, wife. Secondary relatives are indicated by combinations of these: e.g., *FB*, father's brother; *MZ*, mother's sister.

marriage to a father's sister's daughter (*patrilateral cross-cousin marriage*).[22] Such cross-cousin marriages are *asymmetrical*; that is, marriage is required with cross-cousins through one parent or the other, but not both.

Marriage Alliance Theory

Why should cousin marriage, especially cross-cousin marriage, be preferred? And why should more peoples prefer the symmetrical to the asymmetrical form of cross-cousin marriage? Why are matrilateral cross-cousins preferred as wives three times as often as patrilateral cross-cousins? The distinguished French anthropologist Claude Lévi-Strauss argues that cross-cousin marriage exists because it promotes social integration and group interdependence through exchange of women.[23]

The basic function of exchange and trade is to promote interdependence and social solidarity. Women, holds Lévi-Strauss, are the most highly valued scarce commodity because it is through them that children, the continuers of the group's survival, are born. Therefore, exchange of women is of prime importance in ordering interdependence. In symmetrical cross-cousin marriage, the exchange of women occurs in all directions; it may tie closely related groups more tightly to one another, but it is not a strong integrating principle. Lévi-Strauss demonstrates that matrilateral cross-cousin marriage in a society with matrilineal descent groups results in group A's giving its women to group B, which gives its women to group C, which gives its women to group A. The three groups, which constitute a society, are thus bound to one another in a closed circle.[24] This presupposes that matrilateral cross-cousin marriage is prescriptive, or is required, rather than merely preferential.

Lévi-Strauss's theory is built on the proposition that the needs of social solidarity produce asymmetrical cross-cousin marriage (a structural argument). However, the empirical fact that so few societies have incorporated matrilateral cousin marriage as a preferred form indicates that although the system logically leads to social solidarity, it obviously is not universally a necessary condition for societal maintenance. Most societies survive quite well without it.

[22]Ibid.

[23]C. Lévi-Strauss, *Les Structures Élémentaires de la Parenté (The Elementary Structures of Kinship)*.

[24]Of course there may be more than three kinship groups in the system.

ENDOGAMY

Endogamy (Gr. *endo*, "within," and *gamos*, "marriage") is the converse of exogamy. It is *the social rule that requires individuals to marry within a culturally defined group of which they are members.* Endogamy is much less common than exogamy. Unlike exogamy, which predominates in kinship groups organized on a bilateral basis, there is no particular type of kinship group in which the endogamous rule prevails. The discussion of incest prohibitions has shown, however, that because of the prevalence of exogamic rules, the application of endogamy to family or clan is most exceptional. Rules of exogamy and endogamy are contradictory and cannot apply simultaneously to the same social group.

The world's most famous system of endogamy is the caste organization of India, with its two thousand or so castes and subcastes, between which marriage was formally prohibited on the ground that contact with lower castes is ritually polluting for members of upper castes. The new constitution of India attempts to apply Mahatma Gandhi's principles of democratic equality and brotherhood through the legal abolition of castes and caste rules of endogamy, but, as with racial integration in the United States, India still has a long way to go to achieve Gandhi's ideal.[25]

Slightly less than 10 percent of the world's societies are organized in *demes*, or small village communities which are predominantly endogamous. The highest proportion of such units of community organization are found in the rainforest areas of South America. In North America, village endogamy is almost an absolute must among the Pueblo Indians.

The roots of endogamy everywhere are found in the desire to retain the exclusive and distinctive qualities of ingroups. Ingroups who hold that their values are too dear to leave open to competition raise the barricade of endogamy. Orthodox Hebrews may not marry Gentiles on pain of banishment from synagogue and family, followed by the performance of mourning rituals for the dead. Stumbling blocks are put in the path of marriage between Catholic and non-Catholic.

Parallel-Cousin Marriage

The marriage of a man to his father's brother's daughter is a unique exception to the usual rule of lineage and clan exogamy (lineage and clan are discussed on pages 413–416). It originated among the biblical Semites, who were patrilineal pastoralists; it became firmly fixed among the Arabic Muslims and the Muslims of India and Pakistan. As a preferential, and sometimes prescribed, form of marriage, it requires selection of a wife from within the kinship group. Thus in the King James version of the Old Testament (Num. 36:8–9), it is stated: "And every daughter that possesseth an inheritance in any tribe of the children of Israel, shall be wife unto one of the family of the tribe of her father [patrilineage], that the children of Israel may enjoy every man of the inheritance of his fathers."

And so it was that Jacob, when he followed the orders of Isaac, his father, that he not take a wife from among the daughters of Canaan, but rather marry a daughter of his mother's brother, was marrying within his own patrilineage. The fact that Leah and Rachel were cross-cousins (mother's brother's daughters) was irrelevant. The significant fact can be readily seen if Jacob's and his wives' ancestries are traced. Abraham is Jacob's father's father, through Isaac. Jacob's wives, Leah and Rachel, are direct patrilineal descendants of Terah through Nahor, Bethuel, and Laban (Figure 21.4). Jacob married his father's father's brother's son's son's daughters—all members of the same patrilineage derived from Terah (Gen. 12–30).

Among some Near Eastern peoples a man

---

[25] M. Gallanter, "Law and Caste in Modern India" (*Asian Survey*, 1963), pp. 544–559.

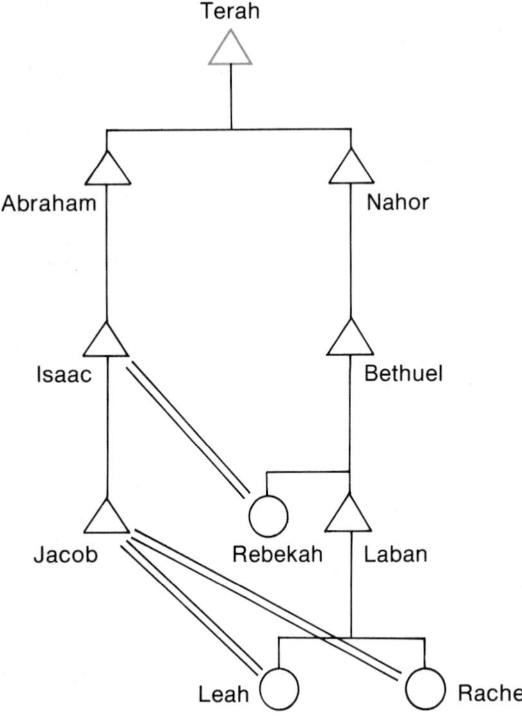

FIGURE 21.4
Patrilateral parallel-cousin marriage among the pastoral Hebrews of the Old Testament. The patrilineage of Terah, showing the prescribed marriage of Isaac to his patrilateral parallel-cousin Rebekah, and of their son Jacob to his parallel-cousins Leah and Rachel. (This diagram is limited to the male offspring through whom the line of descent devolved.)

has an absolute right to marry his father's brother's daughter; a girl must marry her father's brother's son unless he explicitly waives his right. For this waiver of his right, he can demand and receive a good payment. What is more, if a girl marries another man without her cousin's permission, he may kill her or her father (his uncle), if the uncle arranged her illegal marriage.

Parallel-cousin marriage is a consequence of low-level political organization among fighting, pastoral peoples, who in the absence of a centralized authority need all their manpower and herds to counter the assaults of competitive local lineages. By marrying within, they intensify the solidarity of the fighting male cadres.[26]

Where moderately adequate politico-economic institutions of a different type supplement the Arabic lineage structure, parallel-cousin marriage becomes functionally less significant and, in fact, much less frequent in occurrence.[27] Patai reports that modernized city Arabs, for whom the lineage increasingly loses it significance, are rapidly reducing the practice of cousin-right to a vestigial custom, as its functional reasons for existence dissolve.

AFFINAL, SUBSTITUTION, OR CONTINUATION MARRIAGE

Much more pervasive than the rules of endogamy are the rules of preferential marriage that bring about marriages between in-laws, hence called *affinal marriages.* To identify such marriages as affinal, as is the usual practice of American and English anthropologists, is to emphasize the form of the marriage. The Dutch anthropologists, who have given more weight to the functional aspects of such marriages, call them *substitution* or *continuation marriages,* for their function is to continue the relationship between the two kinship groups of the original marriage partners and to hold the children of the original marriage within the extended family.

The Levirate

Marriage of a woman to her brother-in-law, known as the *levirate* (L., *levir,* "brother-in-law"), is the most popular affinal marriage form. Under the simple levirate, the marriage occurs only after the death of the husband, when the widow is inherited by the dead man's brother. In

[26]R. F. Spencer, "The Arabian Matriarchate: An Old Controversy" (*Southwestern Journal of Anthropology*, vol. 8, 1952), pp. 481–490; R. F. Murphy and L. Kasdan, "The Structure of Parallel Cousin Marriage" (*American Anthropologist*, vol. 61, 1959), pp. 17–29.

[27]F. Barth, "Father's Brother's Daughter Marriage in Kurdistan" (*Southwestern Journal of Anthropology*, vol. 10, 1954), pp. 164–171.

the case of the *junior levirate*, only a younger brother may be the inheritor. This practice occurs in all parts of the world among peoples of diverse levels of cultural development. Australians made it a rule; the biblical Hebrews approved of it; and the Incas provided for the inheritance of all a man's secondary wives by his younger brother or his sons.

Whether the young man who finds himself with his brother's widow on his hands likes it or not depends partly on personalities but also on cultural determinants. The Comanche inheritor of a widow was apt to look on this inheritance as a right and a privilege, especially since the widow might not marry another man without that person's obtaining permission from the heir. And that required a consideration—a horse or two, or perhaps some blankets.

The woman had a claim on him as much as he had a claim on her. His family also had a voice, as in the case of a Shoshone Indian who in 1933 was forced to divorce the wife of his own choice in order to marry his dead brother's wife. His people wanted to keep the girl in the family, and the laws of Idaho do not permit a man to have two wives.

The purpose of the levirate is not hard to discern. It continues the link between the two kinship groups that was established through the original marriage. It is a manifestation of the intergroup character of marriage in that the defunct husband's kin have the privilege and right to prevent the widow from leaving their group. Her obligation is not only to the man she married but also to his relatives. Of equal importance, because the children usually follow the mother, they are not lost to the father's group. On the other hand, the claims of the widow's kinfolk upon the group of the defunct husband are maintained in the substitution of a brother. The situation is one of balanced reciprocity.

The Sororate

In the *sororate* a bereaved husband marries his deceased wife's sister. From the woman's angle, she marries her dead sister's husband.

The sororate is observed by virtually every tribe of North America outside of the Pueblo area and is widely distributed throughout the world.

The common mistake of confusing the sororate with *sororal polygyny* should be avoided. Under the true sororate, a man is married to only one sister at a time. Under sororal polygyny, he does not wait for the death of his wife to marry her younger sister; he marries her when she becomes of age.

Extended Affinal Marriages

In a few societies, if a sibling is not available within the immediate conjugal-natal (nuclear) family for substitution for a husband or wife and if there is not an available cousin who stands in the brother or sister category, a substitute from an older or younger generation may be taken. The results in such practices are (1) marriage of a man to his wife's brother's daughter, (2) marriage of a woman to her father's sister's husband, and (3) marriage of a woman to her husband's sister's son (see Figure 21.5). Wife's-brother's-daughter marriage is an extension of the sororate principle to another generation. Such extensions are limited to societies in which the unilineal principle of descent is strong, and each type of marriage is closely related to the kind of unilinealism that prevails.

Thus, in a patrilineal system, a girl automatically belongs to the same clan as her father's sister (her paternal aunt). She has the same clan identity as her aunt, and her individuality is submerged in this identity. She represents her unilineal group in the continuation of the marital alliance.

On the other hand, in a matrilineal system, a boy belongs to the same clan as his mother's brother (his maternal uncle), and his individuality is submerged in the identity of the maternal kinship group. He steps forward to represent his

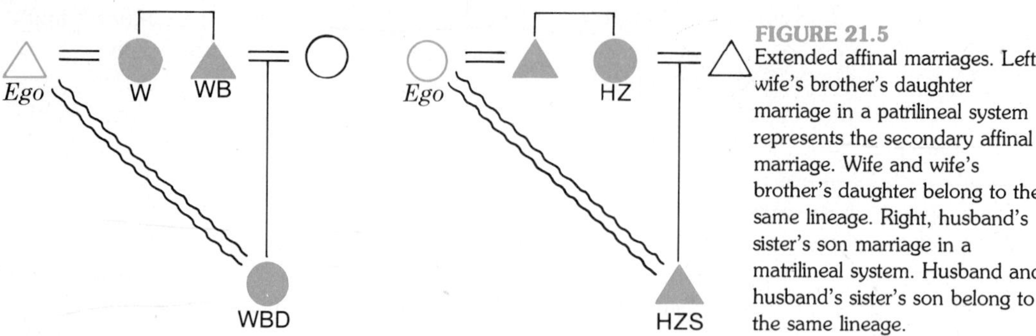

FIGURE 21.5 Extended affinal marriages. Left, wife's brother's daughter marriage in a patrilineal system represents the secondary affinal marriage. Wife and wife's brother's daughter belong to the same lineage. Right, husband's sister's son marriage in a matrilineal system. Husband and husband's sister's son belong to the same lineage.

unilineal group in the continuation of the marital alliance.

Marriage with extended affinal relatives is not common. But in a strong unilineal system inclined to generalize the principle of clan identity, such marriages follow logically enough.[28]

MODES OF MARRIAGE

We have thus far been concerned with the matter of whom one may or may not marry. The next question is: "How does a man get a wife, or a woman, a husband?" Very few societies leave it to individuals to decide for themselves. The North American practice of personal choice is most exceptional, although it represents an increasing trend in many parts of the world. Most marriages either are still arranged by the families concerned or involve family consent and participation. For this reason, to understand marriage at all, it is necessary to grasp this basic principle: *marriage constitutes an alliance between two kinship groups in which the couple concerned is merely the most conspicuous link.* Every man learns, sooner or later, that when he marries the "one and only," he marries not only her but all her relatives as well. Brides, of course, have the same experience.

Of the seven formalized modes of acquiring a wife, only two (marriage by capture and marriage by elopement) may not heavily involve the active participation of the kinship groups of the bride and groom. The seven modes are (1) by progeny price, or bridewealth; (2) by suitor service; (3) by gift exchange; (4) by capture; (5) by inheritance; (6) by elopement; and (7) by adoption.

Progeny Price

Among nonliterate peoples, the formal exchange of goods for the offspring a woman is expected to produce is the normal, or most usual, method of getting a wife. *Progeny price* was found to prevail in virtually all societies of Africa, where 214 of 238 (90 percent) of those listed in the *Ethnographic Atlas* practice it, usually in the form of payment of cattle. Taking the world as a whole, well over half (58 percent) of all societies expect progeny price to be paid to the bride's family by the groom's kin.

It must not be assumed that the payment of progeny price for a woman means that she is a degraded slave to be sold from the auction block of a marriage mart. An economic element necessarily colors the institution, for, after all, a family with five daughters and one son for whom a bride must be acquired is economically better off than the family with one daughter and five sons.

Nor does the occurrence of progeny price mean that the position of women in terms of

[28] L. A. White, "A Problem in Kinship Terminology" (*American Anthropologist*, vol. 41, 1939), pp. 569–570.

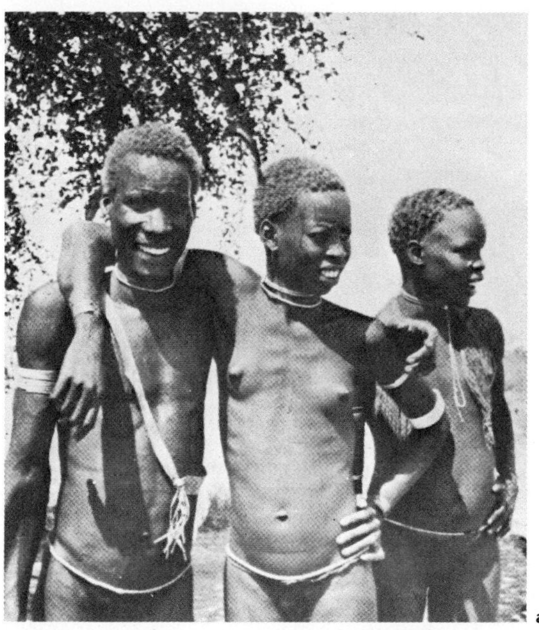

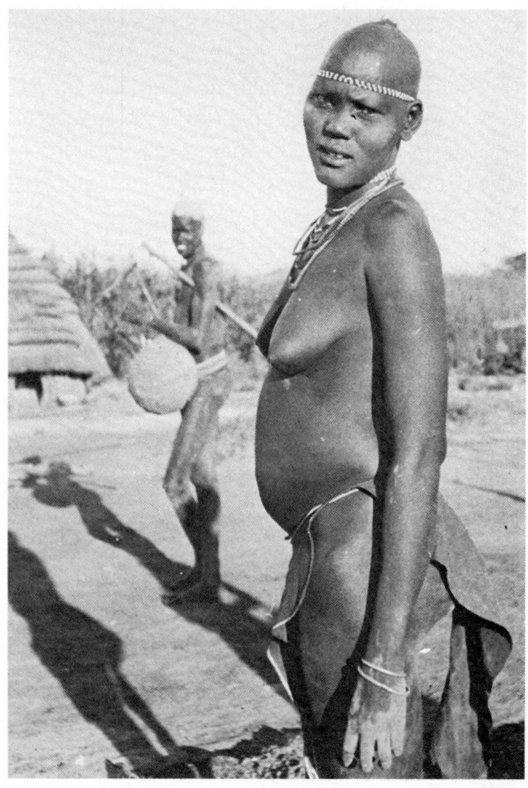

FIGURE 21.6
(a) Nuer sweethearts. The unmarried wear no pubic covering. (E. E. Evans-Pritchard. Pitt Rivers Museum, University of Oxford.) (b) The Nuer married woman wears a distinguishing leather apron and shaves her head. (Pitt Rivers Museum, University of Oxford.)

prestige, privilege, power, and labor is necessarily high or low. It does mean, however, that women as progenitors have value as members of the kinship group.

The social prestige of a married woman is directly influenced by the amount of the progeny price paid on her account. A twenty-cow wife in East Africa has a definite advantage in any argument with a woman on whose account only ten cows have been given.

Progeny price may be in part compensation for the loss of the girl by her kinship group, but it is much more an act of compensation to that group for its loss of a legal claim to the children that she will bear. Two facts make this clear. The transference of progeny price is closely correlated with patrilineal-descent systems and residence of the married couple with the groom's kinfolk (virilocality). Again referring to Murdock's comparative data, we learn that of 217 societies demanding progeny price, all but 18 are virilocal.[29]

That progeny price is in exchange for future value, so to speak, rather than *for* the bride may be seen more clearly in the fact that an implicit warranty of the fertility of the bride is part of the transaction. It is therefore a common expectancy among Africans that the bride's family must substitute a younger sister without charge if no issue is forthcoming from the first daughter. As an alternative, the progeny price must be refunded. This is often difficult, however, because the capital received in payment for the daughter

[29]A. D. Coult and R. W. Habenstein, *Cross Tabulations of Murdock's World Ethnographic Sample*, p. 378.

may already have been invested in the purchase of a wife for a son. Thus, it has been reported (for the Thonga, for instance) that the family may be required to surrender their son's wife to their son-in-law in lieu of their barren daughter. These same requirements hold if the married daughter deserts her husband.

Establishment of Jural Rights Linton's report on Madagascar shows to what extent progeny price is actually the establishment of a legally effective right to children. In the case of divorce, neither a refund of the cattle paid nor the substitution of another woman is socially permissible. The divorced wife may remarry, but only with her former husband's permission. This will be forthcoming upon agreement by the wife and her husband-to-be that the first children born to them (up the limit of three) will be relinquished to the first husband, who is the one who paid the progeny price to her family. The woman nurses and keeps the children until weaning, whereupon they are turned over to her first husband and become his legal heirs without the formality of adoption.[30] All this illustrates another basic principle to be referred to in more detail later on: *among nonliterate societies, jural fatherhood is generally of more significance than biological fatherhood.*

An interesting twist to progeny price as a means of obtaining offspring is found among the Dahomeans of West Africa. Here a married woman may arrange for a second wife for her husband as a means of providing him with children. These children call their sire's first wife "father" because she, after all, is the one who paid for them.[31] This may seem to be carrying the principle of sociological fatherhood a bit far, but who can deny that it is logical?

[30]R. Linton, "The Tanala" in A. Kardiner (ed.), *The Individual and Society.* For numerous like examples from Africa see M. D. W. Jeffreys, "Lobola Is Child-price" (*African Studies*, vol. 10, 1951), pp. 145–184.

[31]M. J. Herskovits, "A Note on 'Woman Marriage' in Dahomey" (*Africa*, vol. 10, 1937), pp. 335–341.

Social groups are often in opposition to one another, disputing, quarreling, even feuding and fighting. Intermarriage imposes a check on the disruptive tendencies of intergroup conflict. Progeny price involves a number of relatives in a network of economic obligations and expectancies. The distribution of marriage cattle among the Nuer, discussed in Chapter 26 "Economic Organization," is a concrete example of the broad network of persons involved. Figure 26.3 shows the range of relatives concerned with the progeny price (see page 456–457).

Suitor Service

A cheap, but not easy, way to obtain a wife and rights to her children is to work for them. Jacob put in seven years of labor to win the hand of Rachel, plus seven for Leah, who was not part of the agreement. Among the Siberian Chukchi, Koryak, and Yukaghir tribes, service for the bride is the regular practice; it seems to have replaced progeny price, which was the earlier form for acquisition of a wife.

A few societies in all parts of the world require service in the bride's household as the price the groom must pay (77 out of 565 cultures).[32] Many of these groups allow no alternative, but in others, suitor service is simply a substitute for payment of the progeny price.

Gift Exchange

In cultures in which descent is not exclusively vested in a particular line of kin (that is, bilateral descent), there is little likelihood of payment of progeny price. Equivalent exchanges of gifts between the families are an alternative possibility.

When gift exchanges are customarily equal, no one comes out ahead. This was the case with the Cheyenne. A boy who had set his heart on a particular girl talked it over with his family. If they saw the choice as a good one, after taking into consideration not only the qualities of the girl but

[32]Coult and Habenstein, op. cit., p. 424.

also the character of her family, they placed their nicest transferable possessions at the disposal of the young swain. These were carefully loaded on a fine horse. They then called upon a respected old woman to lead the horse to the tepee of the girl's elder brother. There she staked it out for all the camp to see, while she entered the lodge to press the suit of her protégé. The elder brother called in his cousins for a family conclave. If they decided that the proposal was acceptable, they unloaded the horse and distributed the gifts, the brother taking the horse. All then dispersed to their separate lodges to rustle up what each wished to offer as a return gift. Each was expected to bring back in the next day or two something equal in value to what had been received. In the meantime, the bride was made beautiful, and when all was ready, she was mounted on a good horse, the presents were loaded on another, and the old woman was called upon to lead the bride and the gift horse back to the groom's tepee. There she was received by all his family, and her accompanying gifts distributed among them in accordance with what they had given. So far as economic value goes, they were exactly where they were before.

Perhaps we can appreciate the social function of such activity better if we think about the elaborate North American gift exchanges at Christmas. The amount of energy, trouble, and effort that goes into acquiring and distributing suitable gifts is immense. As often as not, we end up with a collection of items we would just as soon do without. Nevertheless, in the exchange we reaffirm and bind anew the friendships and relationships we value or find desirable.

Capture

Novelists and romanticists formerly wrote of the cave man who beat his beloved into insensibility with a knobby club and then dragged her by her flowing hair to his lair, where she forthwith became his loving wife. When anthropology was young, serious consideration was given to this fantasy as the earliest method of getting a wife. Indeed, marriage by capture was the first premise underlying the theory of social evolution of the Scottish anthropologist J. F. McLennan more than a hundred years ago.[33] Suitors' trials and sham battles at marriage were thought to be symbolic survivals of the scuffles that accompanied the abduction of the feminine prize.

Mock capture is a real and not uncommon practice. When a young Bushman and his bride are to be married, the folk gather from all around to join in the wedding feast. In the midst of the meal, the groom seizes the bride. This is the signal for all her relatives to grab their dibbles and set to beating him. If he can keep his hold on the girl, he succeeds in his marriage. If he lets go under the hail of blows, he loses her.[34]

Of course, the hilarious horseplay that may climax our weddings and the escape of the bride and groom in a cloud of exhaust smoke (provided a spark plug has been removed) are cut of the same cloth. Modern anthropology provides a functional explanation: it is as a symbolic expression of latent and repressed hostilities of the two marrying families.

Real capture is a supplementary way of getting a wife. Its advantage is that it is cheap and adventuresome, if risky. On the other hand, its disadvantages, aside from risk, are heavy. Since marriage is an alliance between kinship groups, capturing a wife brings none of the advantages that are to be derived from such an alliance. There are no wife's relatives to back a man up or contribute their share of property. His children will not have the advantages and status that his wife's family might bestow, and if his sole wife is from an alien tribe, his children will not be raised in the pure tradition of his own culture. Often his captured wives are secondary additions to his household: his concubines and his wife's household drudges. Here, as elsewhere, the position of the captive woman may be closer to that of a slave than of a true wife.

---

[33] J. F. McLennan, *Primitive Marriage.*

[34] G. W. Stow, *The Native Races of South Africa*, p. 96.

Inheritance

Inheritance of widows through the operation of the levirate and filial inheritance is of course of extreme importance as a form of marriage. However, nothing further need be added here to what we have already said on this subject except to note that the Palvic and Bura tribes of northern Nigeria allow a man to inherit his grandfather's wives. Attention has already been called to the Inca practice of permitting a brother or a son to inherit the secondary wives of a dead man. Inheritance of the wives of his father, except for his uterine mother, is also known from the Caribs of South America and some African societies. Filial inheritance is obviously possible only where there is polygamous marriage. It also serves to keep the women in the family.

Elopement

Elopement is a safety valve. It is one of those saving cultural forms whose function is to provide an escape from restrictive custom. Marriage, as we have seen, is never left open to the untrammeled choice of the marrying individuals. There are incest and exogamic prohibitions; there are the limitations of preferential mating; and there are the personal prejudices of family members to be considered. On the other hand, there is love. Although many cultures do not lend much weight to love in marriage (indeed, many seem to ignore it entirely), the fact is that all persons have their amorous likes and aversions, too.

From the evidence, it would appear that elopements take place in every known society. When familial or social disapproval blocks a fervently desired marriage, or when a planned marriage with a distasteful partner is about to be forced on the unwilling one, elopement is a way out.

It is difficult to formulate a generalization concerning the status of elopement marriages. Among the Cheyennes, the elopement would ultimately be recognized as a marriage and be validated by gift exchanges only if the pair ran off before the girl had actually been engaged by her brother to another man. It was a different matter if the promise had already been made. In several Cheyenne cases, brothers committed suicide when their sisters eloped after they had been promised to someone else.[35]

Elopement resulted from overdeveloped marriage rules among the Kurnai tribe of Australia.[36] Broad rules of exogamy combined with narrow rules of localized mating (that is, the mate had to be taken from a specific band) to reduce the field of legitimate choice. Old men dominated the society and had the first choice of young girls. Matters were so carefully controlled that a boy could scarcely find a girl to marry. Most marriages of young couples were by elopement, and customarily medicine men were expected to help them escape. What then? The righteous citizenry (most of whom married in just this way) were terrible in their anger. A posse of vigilantes set forth to do social justice. The couple fled to a traditional place of asylum. If they were overtaken, they were cruelly wounded and could be killed. Once at the asylum, however, they were safe. They stayed there until a baby was born. Then they could return home to face a softer music, for they would merely be given a beating and then be accepted as legitimately married.

Adoption

In Indonesia and modern Japan, a man may obtain a wife by being adopted into her family.[37] It is a device by which a patrilineally organized family may maintain its line when there are no sons. By legal fiction, the son-in-law thus becomes a "son" in his wife's family, and his children belong to her family. A peculiar aspect of this device is that technically the groom's bride becomes his own "sister." It is necessary that the people close their eyes to this bit of logic, for

[35]K. N. Llewellyn and E. A. Hoebel, *The Cheyenne Way*, chap. 9.
[36]A. W. Howitt, *The Native Tribes of South-east Australia*, pp. 273ff.
[37]B. ter Haar, *Adat Law in Indonesia*, pp. 175–176; and J. F. Embree, *The Japanese Nation*, p. 162.

FIGURE 21.7
A Kwakiutl high-ranking bride (center) flanked by two paid dancing attendants. Her father is at the extreme left, while the groom's father stands at the right. (Edward Curtis/Bayard Gallery.)

that, of course, would be incest. Convenience masters logic, and the husband is a "son" of his father-in-law for purposes of reckoning descent. The adoption of a girl to become a son's wife in Taiwan has already been discussed (see page 312).

FICTIVE MARRIAGE

Forms of fictive marriage occur occasionally. Among them are the special practices of the Kwakiutl (Figure 21.7) and the Nuer. In the case of the Kwakiutl the inheritance of chiefly prerogatives passed from a titled man to his grandson through his son-in-law. It was not possible for the titles to pass to succeeding generations through the chief's sons directly. If there were no daughters, such inheritance could be blocked for lack of a son-in-law. Boas wrote:

In such a case a man who desires to acquire the use of the crest and the other privileges connected with the name performs a sham marriage with the son of the bearer of the name . . . In case the bearer of the name has no children at all, a sham marriage with a part of his body is performed, with his right or left side, a leg or an arm, and the privileges are conveyed in the same manner as in the case of a real marriage.[38]

The son-in-law acquired the titles and then begot children by a second (real) wife. These children were able to inherit from their jural grandfather.

So important is the maintenance of lineage inheritance that the Nuer often rely on what they call *ghost marriage* to give offspring to a male who has died without begetting heirs. In such an instance, one of his "brothers" (from a kinship line that is overstocked or less important) marries a woman on behalf of the dead man or, as they say, "to the name of his brother." The children that he begets take their place in the lineage as the offspring of their ghost father; they inherit accordingly.[39]

[38]F. Boas, *Social Organization and Secret Societies of the Kwakiutl Indians*, p. 359.

[39]Compare the ancient Hebrew practice spelled out in the Old Testament: "If brethen dwell together, and one of them die, and have no son, the wife of the dead shall not be married without [the lineage] unto a stranger: her husband's brother shall go in unto her, and take her to him as a wife, and perform the duty of a husband's brother unto her.

"And it shall be, that the first born which she beareth shall succeed in the name of his brother which is dead, that his name be not put out of Israel" (Deut. 25:5–6).

The Nuer also have a form of "wife marriage." A woman who is beyond childbearing age may sometimes use the cattle that belonged to her dead husband to set up a marriage between a man and woman in the name of her husband and herself. The children of such a marriage then belong to her deceased husband and herself, and they inherit accordingly.

In another Nuer variant, an old woman whose lineage is about to die out because she has no living paternal relatives may, if she has the requisite cattle for the progeny price, marry a woman to the name of a dead man of her lineage. Then she invites some unrelated male to have intercourse with the "ghost bride," thus legally establishing a line of heirs.

Pushing the use of fiction to its ultimate, the Nuer give a barren woman the status of a male. A marriage between a man and woman is arranged in which the *man* is the legal substitute for the barren woman in question. The children belong to her name, which means, because she is accorded the status of a male, that they take their patrilineal descent from her, so closing a link in the patrilineal lineage.[40]

The Kwakiutl case and several of the Nuer practices emphasize the importance of passing jural and property rights from one generation to another through offspring. In these situations, fictive marriage provides the necessary heirs, and the social and legal consequences of a regular marriage flow from it.

DIVORCE AND THE DISSOLUTION OF MARRIAGE

In spite of the desire of relatives to retain the marriage link, marriages can be brittle. Hobhouse, Wheeler, and Ginsberg found that of 271 societies only 4 percent forbid divorce; 24 percent allow it for specific causes; 72 percent permit it on the basis of mutual consent based on incompatibility or whim.[49]

Aside from the economic arrangements that may have to be untangled where a high progeny price was paid or a rich dowry given, divorce does not entail such difficulties among the nonliterate peoples as it does in Western society. The first reason rests in the fact that although religious ritual may enter into the marriage ceremonies, marriage is hardly a religious affair. In addition, the problem of the care and disposition of the children is more easily handled. Ordinarily, they go with the mother. If the mother does not remarry right away, it is easy for her and her brood to settle among her relatives, for the community is small and she has not been far from her kin at any time.

The prevalence of wife stealing is another important unsettling factor. In societies in which sexual competition among the men is a means of attaining social status, no home is truly safe. Eskimos may cooperate economically, but they engage in violent competition for women. To steal another's wife and get away with it proves the abductor a better man than the loser. The risk is great, however, because the husband, if half a man, will attempt to murder the absconder. A would-be wife taker often anticipates this by killing the husband first and marrying the widow afterward.

In the 1920s, Knud Rasmussen visited a village of Musk Ox Eskimos in Canada. He found that every adult male in the community had been involved in a murder centering on wife stealing.[42]

Until recently, anthropologists were of the opinion that men were allowed more leeway than women in the matter of divorce. However, a cross-cultural survey by Murdock invalidates this conclusion. Among forty selected cultures from all parts of the world, there was no substan-

[40]P. P. Howell, *A Manual of Nuer Law*, pp. 74–75.

[41]L. T. Hobhouse, G. C. Wheeler, and M. Ginsberg, *The Material Culture and Social Institutions of the Simpler Peoples*, p. 164.

[42]K. Rasmussen, *Across Arctic America*, p. 250.

(a)

(b)

FIGURE 21.8
In earlier times, the Hopi girl spent four consecutive days grinding corn in a kneeling position when she had her first menses. She observed special taboos and was the object of complex ritual activities. On the fifth day, (a) her mother carefully shaped and tied her hair to produce (b) the beautiful unmarried maiden's squash-blossom coiffure which she wore until marriage. Thereafter, she wore her hair in two wrapped ponytails over her shoulders. (A. C. Vroman, 1901/Southwest Museum.)

tial difference in the rights of men and women to terminate an unsatisfactory marriage.[43]

Matrilineal descent, plus residence in the locality of the wife's kinship group, strengthens the hand of the woman. Among the matrilineal Hopi (Figure 21.8) and Zuni, where women own the houses, a woman can divorce her husband simply by setting his gear outside the door. Any man who comes home and sees his pile of belongings outside the door knows just what it means. It is time to go home to mother.

The causes of divorce and the grounds for it may be two quite different things. Yet it may be illuminating to close this chapter with a listing of what the Ifugao of Luzon consider grounds for divorce:

1. A bad omen of the bile sac of the sacrificial animal at any one of the four feasts of the marriage ritual
2. A bad omen of the bile sac at any of the three principal rice feasts of either family during the first year after the completion of the marriage rituals
3. Barrenness
4. Death of several offspring
5. Permanent sexual disability
6. Unwillingness to perform the sexual act
7. Neglect in time of sickness; "failure to cherish"
8. Insulting language by an in-law

[43] G. P. Murdock, "Family Stability in Non-European Cultures" (*The Annals of the American Academy of Political and Social Sciences*, vol. 272, 1950), pp. 195–201.

9. Reduction of the area of fields agreed on in the marriage contract
10. Selling of a rice field for insufficient reason and without consent of the other spouse
11. Continued refusal of a father-in-law to deliver the fields called for in the marriage contract when the couple reaches a reasonable age
12. Incurring of unreasonable debts[44]

SUMMARY

Most societies are not concerned about premarital mating, but all societies limit sexual activities and define sexual and social obligations in marriage.

The prohibition of sexual relations between certain relatives is universal. It is known as the incest taboo. Except for a few special cases such as between divine royalty, brother-sister and parent-child incest is taboo everywhere.

Westermarck offered a specific explanation for incest prohibitions: children raised in a common household have an instinctive aversion to sexual intimacy with each other. Instinct theories have been rejected by twentieth-century anthropologists largely because they do not satisfactorily account for the variable extension of the incest taboo outside the immediate nuclear family. Modern population genetics has established that very close inbreeding in a species with slow reproduction rates results in the production and homozygous establishment of many more deleterious genes. Consequently, whatever the original cause for the introduction of the incest taboo, its genetic effects are positive.

An extension of the incest taboo occurs when all cousins are classified by the same terms as brother and sister. On the other hand, when kinship terminology distinguishes between parellel- and cross-cousins, sexual relations and marriage with parallel-cousins may be tabooed, while marriage to certain cross-cousins may be preferred or required.

Malinowski's theory of the incest taboo holds that sexual competition within the family and larger kinship units engenders emotional hostility which is disruptive to kinship solidarity. The taboo exists to prevent destructive disruption of the foundation units of any society. The alliance theory, which finds high favor among anthropologists today, holds that the incest taboo results in exogamy—marriage outside the group. Exogamy, in turn, produces reciprocal ties between kinship groups, enlarging their social and economic base.

Restricted exogamy forbids marriage to certain types of cousins, while permitting (or requiring) it with others. Matrilateral cross-cousin marriage, according to the theory of Lévi-Strauss, enhances social solidarity by relating the kinship groups in a closed circle linked in regular marital alliances of woman givers and woman receivers.

Endogamy works to preserve social inclusiveness by requiring marriage within a defined group. Castes, classes, and religious groups may practice endogamy. Parallel-cousin marriage as practiced by the biblical Hebrews and extended into modern times by the followers of Islam is the most notable manifestation of kinship endogamy.

Continuation marriages exist to maintain the alliance bond between two affinal groups of kinspeople. The levirate (marriage to a brother-in-law) and the sororate (marriage to a sister-in-law) are its major forms. Other varieties are marriage to a husband's sister's son, to a wife's brother's daughter, and filial inheritance.

In the acquisition of wives, over half of all societies require the transfer of valuables to the bride's family as progeny price. This compensates her family for the release of their claim to her children as heirs. In a few instances, suitor service may substitute for progeny price. Reciprocal gift exchange is found in a few bilateral societies.

[44] R. F. Barton, *Ifugao Law*, pp. 23–24.

Wife capture, fantasy notwithstanding, is a rare practice, although dramatized bride capture as a symbolic expression of affinal tensions does have its occurrence in a number of wedding rituals.

Finally, fictive marriages are sporadically entered into in order to provide continuity of inheritance for a family line or to make possible kinship alliances when a person of the proper sex status is not available.

Although there is almost always a strong emphasis on alliance continuity, virtually all societies allow for personal incompatibility and divorce.

SELECTED READINGS

Bohannan, P., and J. Middleton (eds.), *Marriage, Family, and Residence* (1968). A book of readings. Part 1, pages 1 to 46, consists of two very useful papers on the incest question.

Fox, R., *Kinship and Marriage* (1967). An excellent, clearly written account, with discussions of marriage, incest, and alliance theory.

Leach, E. R., *Claude Lévi-Strauss* (1974). A complete interpretation of Lévi-Strauss's theories and views by one of the leaders in the field.

22
The Family

CHAPTER OUTLINE

LEARNING GOALS

Enumerate the functions of the family.
Describe the conjugal-natal family.
Identify the different types of residence patterns.
Define polygyny and polyandry.
Describe the joint family.
Discuss the matrilateral group and its drawbacks.
Describe the function of communal life.

Marriage establishes the conjugal-natal family (sometimes called the nuclear family), a group consisting of spouses and their offspring. Marriage defines sets of statuses and related roles and expectancies governing the relations of the conjugal-natal group as spouses, parents, offspring, affines, and siblings. It defines and relates them to wider groups of kin and to nonkin. Marriage is the institution; the family is the group, or body of personnel, whose actions are designed to fulfill the aims of the institution.

FUNCTIONS OF THE FAMILY

The functions of the family may be grouped in four categories: (1) sexual, (2) reproductive, (3) economic, and (4) educational.[1] More explicitly, the functions of the family may be stated as follows: (1) The institutionalization and channeling of sexual outlets, thus establishing legal parents for children; each partner (spouse) acquires a "monopoly" in the sexuality of the other. (2) The nurture and enculturation of the young in an atmosphere of intimacy, preparing them to accept the statuses they will fill. (3) The organization of a complementary division of labor between spouses, allocating to each certain rights in the labor of the other and in such goods or property as they may acquire. (4) The linkage of each spouse and offspring within the wider network of kin: the establishment of relationships of descent and affinity. These functions are universally performed by the family as a social unit (Figure 22.1). Other social arrangments may also exist wherein these functions are performed, such as the matrilateral group (pages 404–406), in which the mother's brother takes on some of the functions normally performed by the father in the conjugal-natal family. Matrilateral groups are, however, relatively rare.

The family, in one form or another, is the primary unit of human culture and sociality. In the words of Marion Levy, Jr.:

> ***1.*** *There is no known case of a society lacking families as subsystems thereof.*
> ***2.*** *There is no known society in terms of which initial placement of individuals fails to be . . . overwhelmingly, if not exclusively, in family terms.*
> ***3.*** *There is no known society in terms of which not only initial but a substantial part of the basic learning—that is, the learning institutionally expected*

[1] M. J. Levy, Jr., and L. A. Fallers, "The Family: Some Comparative Considerations" (*American Anthropologist*, vol. 61, 1959), pp. 647–651.

FIGURE 22.1
Bushman family life focuses on the intimacy of the campfire. (Anthro-Photo.)

(a)

to be shared by all or virtually all the members of a given society—is not learned in a family context. . . .[2]

In many societies, the sex drive may be legitimately satisfied prior to marriage; in such cases, there would be no reason for the individual to take on the responsibilities of marriage if sex gratification alone were a function of the family.

The care of infants and children is the matter of overriding concern. The rather casual interest of some societies in the question of actual biological fatherhood has already been sufficiently discussed. But that some man or group of men must be tagged with sharing the responsibility of performing the adult male activities necessary to keeping the young ones alive, growing, and learning is universally recognized as of the utmost importance. In meeting the requirements of infant care and child development, sex differences are such that a cooperative division of labor makes for greater efficiency and skill. Childbearing can still be done only by women. Nursing ties women down, while men have greater freedom of movement. Mobility, combined with greater strength, inevitably allows men to become more efficient hunters. Many skills can be performed equally well by either sex, but each sex is more likely to develop high skills if it concentrates on certain tasks and relies on the opposite sex to do likewise with certain others.

At this juncture, the most relevant fact is that evidently no substitute can serve the functions of child development as well as an intimate kinship group, such as the family. Anthropologists who have paid especial attention to the relations of culture to personality formation by means of direct field observation agree that anthropological data give universal significance to the conclusions drawn from recent studies of children in institutions. Margaret Mead sums it up:

[2]M. J. Levy, Jr., "Notes on the Hsu Hypothesis," in F. L. K. Hsu (ed.), *Kinship and Culture*, p. 34.

(b)

(c)

FIGURE 22.2
The extended family is the basic social unit in the matrilineal kinship society of the Navajo. Daughters typically settle with their mothers. While the Navajo may work for wages, in recent tradition and culture, they are pastoralists. (a) In the Monument Valley part of the reservation (see facing page), sons and brothers tend the family flocks that are usually owned by the women. (Ray Manley.) (b) Shearing the sheep is the work of women who teach the task to the younger. (Josef Muench.) (c) Navajo women card the wool, spin and weave it into rugs, cook the food, and mind the baby. (Ray Manley.)

It has been . . . effectively demonstrated that children do not thrive, in spite of good physical care, if kept as young infants in impersonal institutions, and that separation from the mother—especially at certain periods—has serious deleterious effects on the child. Retardation, failure to learn to talk, apathy, regression, and death all appear as accompaniments to institutionalization when no mother surrogate is provided.[3]

Substitute, or surrogate, mothers may provide that direct emotional response which the human infant requires. Nursing involves more than the imbibing of mother's milk. The surrogates may in many instances be direct substitutes for the biological mother or father, as in the operation of the sororate and the levirate, or they may be collateral surrogates who play the parental roles on a less intensive level. A Navajo child may be cared for, and nursed by, a number of clan sisters of the mother, who are called "mother" and who call the child "son" or "daughter" from the beginning.

The family is not necessarily the small, nuclear family, isolated in its separate dwelling unit; it may also exist as a regular cell-like feature of a larger familial structure. The independent family of the Euro-American form is the sole familial unit in about half of all societies. In the other half of the world's societies, the nuclear family is encysted within some kind of extended family, a larger kinship group that includes more than a single set of spouses and their children.[4]

THE CONJUGAL-NATAL FAMILY

Every individual is a member of a primary and a secondary conjugal-natal family: that of the parents, into which the person is born, and that which is founded with a spouse in wedlock. These two families have also been called the family of *orientation* and of *procreation*, respectively (Figure 22.3). Viewed from the outside the two families are alike in terms of form and function. However, the statuses of an individual within the two families are very different.

The conjugal-natal family is limited both in scope of membership and in duration. It includes only persons the spouses produce or adopt, and it endures for no longer than two generations: the lifespan of the founding spouses, and the lifespan of the children who are born into their marriage.

The limited duration of the conjugal-natal family is a consequence of the universal incest taboo, for if parent could marry child and brother could marry sister, a conjugal-natal family could be continued indefinitely through internal replacement as the original members died. Perpetuity of the conjugal-natal family, however, must depend on outside recruitment of spouses.

Although the independent conjugal-natal family may be cherished as a social unit, it has certain functional disabilities. In the first place, the conjugal-natal family is very unstable. There is the possibility of divorce, and where divorce is not countenanced, emotional disturbances arising from the incompatibility of the father and mother can easily destroy the affective solidarity that is so important to good family functioning. True enough, the consequences of a conjugal-natal family breakup are not so serious in a preliterate society, where the mother is securely embedded in the protection of her extended family and where remarriage is easier than it is in urbanized Western civilization.

Also, the conjugal-natal family is a temporary association. It begins with the union of the married pair and ends with the dispersal of the children (Figure 22.4). Furthermore, upon marriage, a person enters a new conjugal-natal family, and loyalties are split. From our own experience, we know the tensions that can result from the pull of loyalty to our husbands or wives as against our fathers and mothers. The instability of the conjugal-natal family and its short lifespan also

[3]M. Mead, "Some Theoretical Considerations on the Problem of Mother-Child Separation" (*American Journal of Orthopsychiatry*, vol. 24, 1954), p. 474.

[4]E. Bourguignon and L. Greenbaum, *Diversity and Homogeneity*, p. 49.

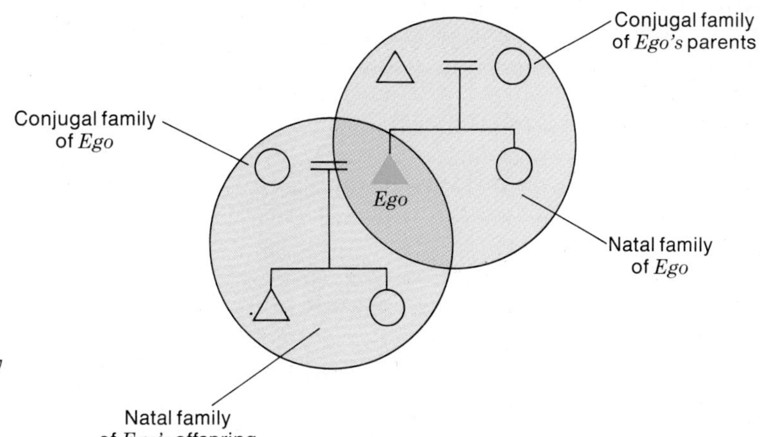

FIGURE 22.3
The dual nature of the conjugal-natal family. Each family is a conjugal family for the spouses who establish it and a natal family for the offspring who are born into it.

limit its usefulness as a means for the inheritance of property.

Nonetheless, sociologists maintain, and probably rightly, that

> *the family system of the urban United States is not a denuded form of a more "normal" or "natural" family system but is itself a highly specialized form that articulates most satisfactorily with a highly differentiated economic and political system and with institutionalized values that stress achievement rather than inheritance. It is argued that the smallness and relative isolation of the family from other kinship ties is an adaptation that makes possible the spatial and status mobility of its members.*[5]

Monogamy and Family Structure

The conjugal-natal family is possible only when marriage is monogamous (being married to only one person at a time), but monogamy is the sole permitted marital form in only one in six societies.[6]

The normal state of affairs is to allow polygamy, especially among men in positions of power and social leadership. Still, it is important to realize that what is *permitted* in a culture and what *prevails* in fact may be two different things. Thus, it is usual to refer to societies whose cultures permit multiple marriages as *polygamous;* yet it is unlikely that more than a few marriages in any society will actually be polygamous, since a number of factors limit multiple marriages.

First, there is the relative balance of the sex ratio. Approximately equal numbers of males and females are born. Unless some selective factor operates in favor of one sex and against the other, such as war or infanticide, there will be an approximate equality in the numbers of males and females available for marriage. If this is the case, whenever one man has two wives, some other man in the tribe has to do without. There is, of course, the possibility that the short-wived men may band together to share one wife among themselves, but such polyandrous (more than one husband at a time) arrangements are very rare.

If it is the current practice for a man to settle in the household of his wife, he obviously cannot live with all his wives simultaneously unless they are sisters. Uxorilocal residence[7] discourages the polygynous (more than one wife at a time) form of polygamy. Marriage is a kinship-group alliance, and a son-in-law whose affinal allegiances

[5] R. T. Smith, "Family: Comparative Structure" (*International Encyclopedia of the Social Sciences*, vol. 5, 1968), p. 311.
[6] Bourguignon and Greenbaum, op. cit., p. 49.

[7] The practice whereby a married couple settles in the locale of the wife's parents.

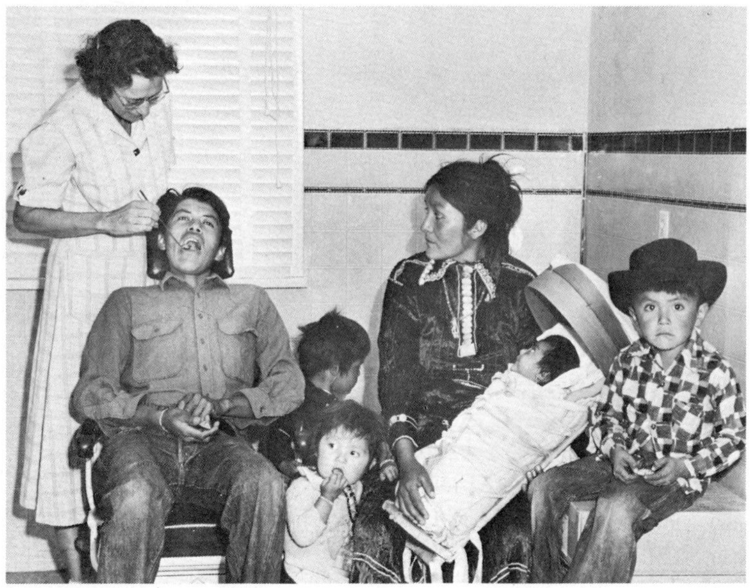

FIGURE 22.4
Navajo family togetherness. Wife and children back up their young father in his venture into the world of modern dentistry. (Joseph Muench.)

are multiple is apt to be less desirable than one whose affinity is to one group alone.

Few precise statistics are available, but all reports indicate that monogamous marriages actually predominate in most societies that permit polygamy. Contrary to the notions of nineteenth-century anthropologists, monogamy is not the end product of an evolutionary series of primitive promiscuity to civilized monogamy; monogamy is probably more the result of an adaptation to the economic situation. The Andaman Islanders and the Semangs of the Malay forests limit themselves to one wife apiece, but the Semangs marry again and again in serial monogamy, Hollywood style. Inca commoners were forbidden to marry more than one wife, but a man might receive a concubine as a gift in reward for faithful service to his overlord. The occurrence of prescribed monogamy among the matrilineal, uxorilocal Iroquois in New York and Canada and the equally matrilineal, uxorilocal Hopi and Zuñi suggests that in these instances, monogamy is correlated with female-dominated residence and economy.

Residence Patterns

Upon marriage, the first question to be settled is: "Where shall we live?" In most societies, this issue is established by custom and does not allow individual choice. The custom of the society may be *virilocal* (L. *vir*, "male," and *locus*, "place"), according to which the newlywed couple settles in the locality of the husband's primary conjugal-natal family. Or it may be *patrilocal* if most of the husband's paternal relatives customarily live in the same camp, neighborhood, village, or district.

On the other hand, the custom of the tribe may be for the couple to settle in the locality of the wife's parents, in which case it is called *uxorilocal* (L. *uxori*, "wife," and *locus*, "place"). We may call the practice *matrilocal* if the couple settle in the locality of the wife's matrilineal kinship groups.

A few societies with little fixed property give the couple free choice on whether to settle in the locality of the bride's or the groom's primary conjugal-natal family. This practice is known as

FIGURE 22.5
(a) A contemporary Eskimo family in its modern insulated cabin. Sleeping quarters for the entire family consist of the raised platform extending around the sides of the cabin, exactly as did the snow bench in the old-time igloo. (b) Andrew Oseavuk, an 80-year-old Eskimo craftsman and his elderly wife. In the primitive Eskimo culture of the nineteenth century, old people who could no longer contribute economically either committed suicide or were abandoned to die alone. Today, with welfare and family assistance, they can continue as useful adults. (Steve McCutcheon/Alaska Pictorial Service.)

(a)

bilocal or *ambilocal* (L. *ambi*, "both," and *locus*, "place") residence.

A small number of matrilineally oriented societies expect the couple to settle in the locality of the husband's mother's brother. In this situation, we have *avunculocal* (L. *avunculus*, "mother's brother," and *locus*, "place") residence.

Finally, some social systems, such as the Euro-American, provide for independent establishment of residence without too much reference to the prior location of the primary conjugal-natal families of the newly married pair. This condition is called *neolocal* (Gr. *neos*, "new," and L. *locus*, "place") residence, which is in effect an absence of restrictive rules of residence, leaving the options open for the newly founded, independent conjugal-natal family (Figure 22.5).

There are, then, five basic varieties of residence: (1) virilocal (with patrilocal), (2) uxorilocal (with matrilocal), (3) avunculocal, (4) bilocal (or ambilocal), and (5) neolocal. In most societies, one rule alone prevails for the married life of a couple, although some may use combinations of two or more. Thus, among the nomadic Plains Indians, a couple's first tepee was usually set up beside that of the bride's parents for a year or so. Then, when the new household was well established, the young couple was likely to camp beside the groom's family. Among the Dobuans, a couple alternated residence in each other's village every other year. And in some societies,

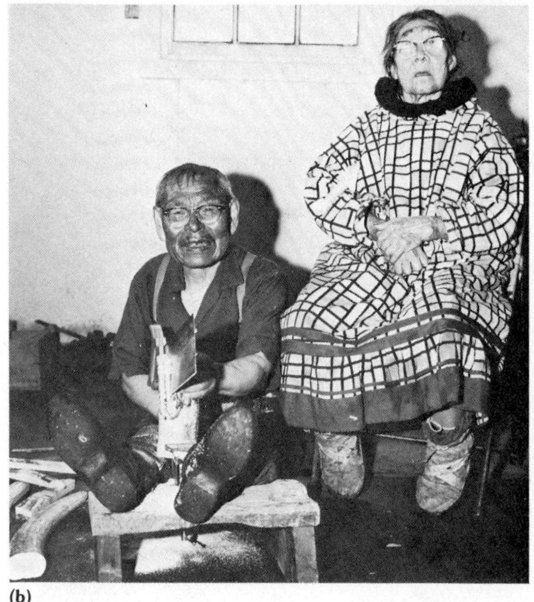

(b)

such as the Ashanti in Ghana, where the ideal rule is virilocal, there may actually be a good deal of informal variation from case to case.[8] Furthermore, it is not a simple open-and-closed matter as to whether a given household represents one kind of residence pattern or another, if it contains a mixture of several conjugal-natal families. It may also remain a moot matter as to how to classify a society as a whole, when two or more residential patterns are found to exist with equal frequency.[9]

A glance at Table 22.1 will quickly show that a great majority of human societies are male-oriented in residence patterns. The average for the world sample in the *Ethnographic Atlas* is 69 percent virilocal and patrilocal. But in the continental Old World the ratio rises to over 80 percent, while in North and South America the figures are 58 and 41 percent, respectively. Conversely, female-focused marital residence is almost nonexistent in the Mediterranean area and in Africa, thus reflecting the importance of intensive agriculture and pastoralism as subsistence bases in that part of the world. In the New World, women hold a better power position. Over a third (40 percent) of the South American societies in the sample are uxorilocal or matrilocal (Figure 22.6).

It should be immediately obvious that the nature of residence patterns strongly affects the internal quality of the family unit and its extensions. If residence is uxorilocal, the woman is in constant daily interaction with *her* parents and sisters. The children of sisters grow up together, and the children of brothers do not. Husbands are "aliens" in a new setting. Sisters are grouped in a continuing solidarity. The opportunity for women to exert a solid front is enhanced, and their position in the direction of social affairs is stronger. With virilocal residence, just the opposite occurs.

Another factor that affects the quality of the family is whether marriages are based on village exogamy or endogamy. If the marriages take place within the local group or village, the differentiating effects of residence rules are much reduced. In spite of virilocality, if the home of the bride's parents is only 100 yards away, the continuity of her tie to her primary conjugal-natal family is not so seriously strained as it is when she is transported to another village.

[8]M. Fortes, "Time and Social Structure: An Ashanti Case Study," in M. Fortes (ed.), *Social Structure*, pp. 54–84.

[9]Cf. W. H. Goodenough, "Residence Rules" (*Southwestern Journal of Anthropology*, vol. 12, 1956), pp. 22–37, for an examination of these problems in the study of Truk in the Micronesian Islands; also see P. Bohannon, *Social Anthropology*, pp. 86–99, for a comprehensive review of the problems found in using residence terminology.

TABLE 22.1
Relative Frequency of Dominant Patterns of Marital Residence, according to Geographic Areas

Dominant residence pattern	All societies n = 859	Sub-Saharan Africa n = 237	Mediterranean n = 96	East Eurasia n = 94	Oceania n = 126	North America n = 218	South America n = 88
Viri/patrilocal	69%	82%	80%	82%	62%	58%	41%
Uxori/matrilocal	13%	2%	0%	11%	14%	21%	38%
Avunculocal	4%	10%	2%	0%	3%	3%	2%
Neolocal	5%	5%	13%	2%	4%	5%	9%
Bi/ambilocal	8%	4%	4%	3%	14%	14%	10%
Husband/wife living separately	1%	0%	1%	1%	2%	0%	0%

SOURCE: Data adapted from E. Bourguignon and L. Greenbaum, *Diversity and Homogeneity*, table 28, p. 50.

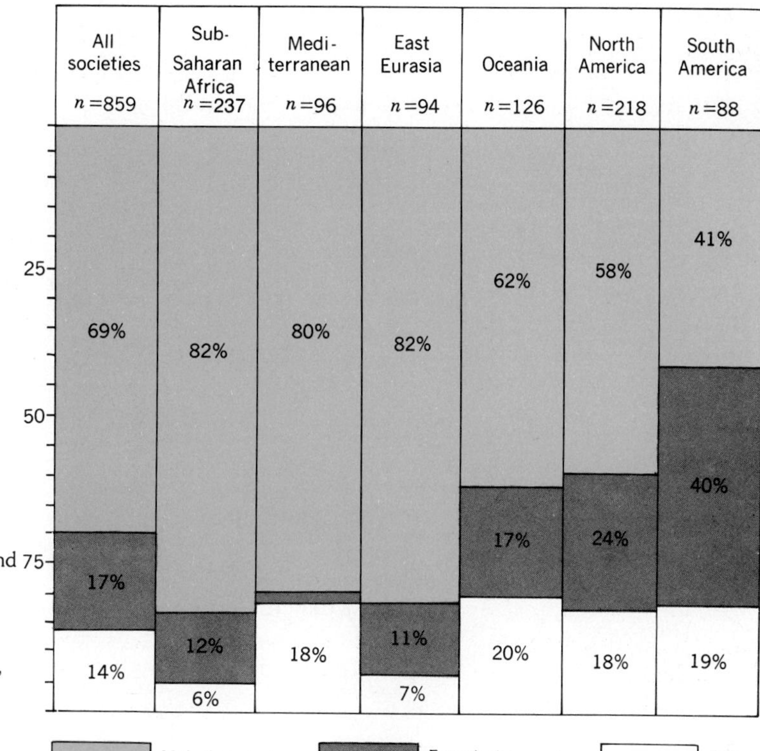

FIGURE 22.6
Relative frequency of male-focused and female-focused residence patterns, according to geographic areas. The male-focused pattern represents viri/patrilocal; the female-focused one, uxori/matrilocal, plus avunculocal. (Data from Table 22.1.)

THE COMPOSITE CONJUGAL-NATAL FAMILY

Within polygamous marriages, we have been drawing a distinction between polygyny and polyandry. In current usage *polygamy* means multiple spouses; *polygny* literally means multiple wives and *polyandry* means multiple husbands. If there is more than one husband or wife in a family at the same time, they constitute segments of a *composite conjugal-natal* family.

Polygyny

In spite of the Judeo-Christian insistence upon monogamy, this practice is shared by a small number of societies (16 percent of the sample in the *Ethnographic Atlas*). Nearly half (44 percent) of all societies hold the polygynous family to be the norm, while nearly as many permit polygyny but do not attempt to make it the regular thing. Almost all African societies are polygynous (see Figure 22.7).

There are a number of social motives underlying polygyny as an institution. If a man has the means to support several wives, he is able to present a richer and better-equipped household to the world. More women can prepare better clothes and food. If women's handicrafts are marketable or suitable for exchange, his household wealth will be increased. When the Blackfoot Indians found a lucrative outlet for tanned hides in the Canadian fur trade, women as tanners became an economic asset, and polygyny grew to an extent unprecedented in the Plains. Bride price went up, and the age of marriage for girls went down, while the age of marriage for men went up; well-established Blackfoot entrepreneurs cornered the available

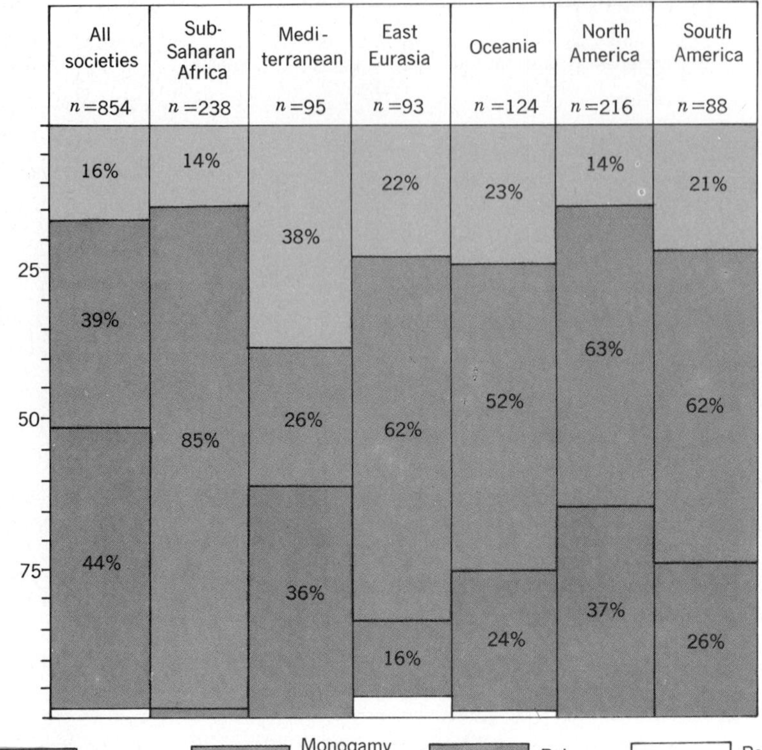

FIGURE 22.7
Relative frequency of monogamy, monogamy with polygyny, polygyny, and polyandry as expected marriage forms, according to geographic area. (Data adapted from E. Bourguignon and L. Greenbaum, *Diviersity and Homogeneity*, table 26, p. 48.)

women, and it took young men a longer time to acquire enough capital to marry.[10]

Strange as it may seem to some, it is repeatedly reported that in many tribes the women do not object to their husbands' taking on additional wives. This is more apt to be true when additional wives are co-workers, as among the Comanches of the Plains.

On the other hand, instances are on record of women in such tribes who have shown extreme jealousy when their husbands brought home a new wife. A Cheyenne woman hanged herself because her husband took a Pawnee captive to wife, but her own grandmother remarked, "She was foolish to hang herself over such a little thing."

Polygyny seems to work best when a man's several wives are sisters. This is psychologically reasonable, inasmuch as sisters are more used to one another's ways than are unrelated women; they are subject to the influence of emotional loyalty acquired in childhood as members of the same conjugal-natal family. *Sororal polygyny* (marriage to sisters) is in effect an anticipation of sororate privileges. A man does not wait for the death of his wife before he marries her younger sister. Instead, as among the Comanches, he expects that if he performs his son-in-law obligations, his wife's parents will reward him with his wife's younger sister when she becomes of age.

Where exchange marriage between two fami-

[10] O. Lewis, *The Effects of White Contact upon Blackfoot Culture, with Special Reference to the Role of the Fur Trade* (American Ethnological Society Monograph 6, 1942), pp. 38–40.

lies prevails, the levirate will also work to produce sororal polygyny, for example, when brothers have married sisters and a man inherits his deceased brother's wife.

Various household arrangements are made as adjustments to the requirements of the multiple-wife family (Figure 22.8). The Angola practice is probably typical of Sudanese African tribes. Hambly tells of an Angola headman with eleven wives, each with a separate hut in his compound. The husband customarily sleeps with each wife four or seven successive nights, as his personal habit may be.[11]

Within composite families, there is usually a firm hierarchical distinction between the wives. The first-married wife is given a number one position of authority, so that even though she may be displaced by a later wife as a sexual favorite, she still has the gratification of priority in privilege. The Comanches, again, made such distinctions, for secondary wives were "chore wives" who had to do household work under the direction of the first wife.

FIGURE 22.8

Among the Big Namba Islanders of the New Hebrides of the South Pacific, the polygynous compound family of a Big Man lives in a closely grouped household of several thatched houses—one for each wife and her children. (Kal Muller/Woodfin Camp.)

Polyandry

The marriage of several men to one woman is as rare (occurring in 4 of the 854 cultures in the *Ethnographic Atlas*) as the marriage of several women to one man is common. Tibetans and the Todas and other tribes of India are the most famous polyandrists.[12] The Toda polyandrous union is usually, but not necessarily, fraternal. Some polygynous marriages also occur, and quite a few monogamous ones. Children are ordinarily betrothed in infancy, and the boy makes progeny-price payments twice a year all through his childhood. He also has to provide a buffalo to help pay funeral expenses of members of his betrothed's family. Just before puberty, the girl is deflorated by a man from some clan other than her own. Then she is ready for marriage. Right after puberty, she is given a dowry and taken to the home of her husband. Although she may have been betrothed to just one man, it is understood that she is also the wife of all his brothers. Even a boy yet unborn may become her husband when he becomes of age.

All the brothers live together and share their wife without friction and supposedly without jealousy. When the wife becomes pregnant, one of the brothers goes through a ritual of "presenting the bow." This makes him the jural father of the ensuing child and the next couple of children to be born. There is no concern over whether he may be the progenitor or not. After he has sponsored his share of offspring, another brother "presents the bow," thus making himself the father of the next group of children, and so on.

Occasionally, a Toda woman may leave her legitimate husbands to live with another man without official approval, or she may take a lover, who pays her husbands for the privilege;

[11] W. D. Hambly, *Source Book for African Anthropology*, pp. 418–419.

[12] See G. D. Berreman, "Pahari Polyandry: A Comparison," in P. Bohannan and J. Middleton (eds.), *Marriage, Family, and Residence*, pp. 147–167.

in either case, her subsequent children still belong to the man who performed the bow ritual.[13]

Polyandry in the Darjeeling district of India is restricted to the younger brothers of the man who performs the wedding rite with the wife. If the elder brother dies and the wife has no children, she may break the polyandrous bond by first tying a string to a finger of her number one husband's corpse and binding it to one of her own fingers. Then by severing the string, she symbolically destroys the marriage tie.

Tibetan and Eskimo polyandry have been attributed to the practice of female infanticide. While it is quite true that both peoples practice infanticide, census figures do not indicate a surplus of adult men in Tibet, and reliable censuses of the Eskimo indicate that women outnumber men in almost all Eskimo communities, in spite of the common destruction of baby girls.

Although rare, polyandry is more common (at least in a modified form) than was thought to be the case a few decades ago. A form of polyandry has been reported from at least two East African tribes, leading us to suspect that there are probably several other unreported instances.[14]

Extensions of Brotherhood Both the Shoshones and the Eskimos formerly practiced polyandry. These are bilateral societies in which a man must depend on his brothers (and cousins) for security and survival.

The polyandry among the Comanches centered on the mutuality of the bond of brotherhood.

"A man loves his brother; he knows that if his brother dies, no one can replace him; he gives him everything he can," explained That's It. "A brother therefore sends his wife over to him occasionally as a gift. She cannot go of her own free will or meet him secretly, or her husband will be angry." It was also expected that when a man was on the warpath, his brother could sleep with his wife.[15]

Comanche young men frequently entered into a relation of institutionalized friendship with a chosen "chum." They usually married sisters, whom they freely lent to one another as wives. Shoshones and Comanches had to rely on "brothers," real or putative, in war, in love, and in play.[16] Their fraternal polyandry expressed the structural-functional significance of "brotherhood" as the keystone of their social life.

That such attitudes are not mere aberrations of the Comanches is fully attested by Murdock's findings that nearly two-thirds of the 250 societies in the Yale Cross Cultural Survey permit postmarital sexual intercourse between a man and his brother's wife (anticipatory levirate) or between a man and his wife's sister (anticipatory sororate).[17]

Eskimo polyandry is of the same order as that of the Shoshone. A traveling Eskimo needs a woman to dry his fur clothes and chew the hides to keep them soft. Most Eskimo men have at least one regular partner in each village, who will make his wife available on a basis of friendship. At the same time, he needs someone at home to look after his own wife when he goes off traveling. A good friend will normally agree to take on the task with all its responsibilities and sexual amenities.[18]

Wife Hospitality The practice of sharing wives with certain men on specific occasions is closely related to the institution of polyandry. Most commonly, a host deems that proper social form requires him to offer the hospitality of his wife to an overnight guest. The practice was

[13]W. H. R. Rivers, *The Todas*, pp. 477–480.

[14]J. Roscoe, *The Banyankole*, p. 123; "The Cow Tribe of Enkole in the Uganda Protectorate" (*Journal of the Royal Anthropological Institute of Great Britain and Ireland*, vol. 37, 1907), p. 105.

[15]E. Wallace and E. A. Hoebel, *The Comanches*, pp. 138–139.

[16]Ibid., p. 132.

[17]Murdock, *Social Structure*, p. 268.

[18]For more detail, see R. F. Spencer, "Spouse Exchange among the North Alaskan Eskimo," in P. Bohannan and J. Middleton (eds.), *Marriage, Family, and Residence*, pp. 131–144.

even extended to early white traders on the upper Missouri River. A man who accepted the woman for the duration of his stay in the village became a putative son-in-law or brother of his benefactor. Such arrangements helped to establish a network of trade in the eighteenth and early nineteenth centuries throughout the upper Plains. French, English, and American traders solidified their business interests with various Indian tribes by becoming "relatives" through sexual sharing.[19]

As an institutionalized practice, wife lending is functionally analogous to *blood brotherhood*, "a pact or alliance formed between two persons by a ritual act in which each swallows the blood of the other. The pact is one of mutual assistance and is backed by powerful sanctions."[20] At any rate, it should be clear that wife hospitality in societies that emphasize kinship obligations and privileges of brotherhood is not an act of immorality in the context of those societies. It serves as a means of broadening and strengthening social bonds.

THE JOINT FAMILY

Let us now return to an examination of some ways in which the concept of the family may be extended to incorporate a group of closely related conjugal-natal families into a single property-holding, residential group. Such a unit is usually called the *joint family*. Half the world's societies in the nineteenth century organized their family residential units in this way.[21]

The essential difference between the composite conjugal-natal family and the joint family is that the former involves only one spouse with several mates, while the latter involves married relatives living together in a single household, each with his or her spouse and offspring.

The Tanala Joint Family

Linton's description of the patrilineal joint family among the Tanala of Madagascar presents a good example of the smaller version of the composite unilineal family. A Tanala joint family begins with a single conjugal family. When the sons marry, they build new houses for themselves close to their parental home. The father, as head of the joint family, directs all activities concerning clearing and cultivating the fields for dry-rice culture, caring for the family cattle, and similar tasks. All earnings of the male members are placed in his hands for investment in cattle and for dispersal for progeny price and such little cash needs as the sons may have. As long as his father lives, a man has little chance to accumulate any personal wealth. The joint family is a cooperative work group and a corporate unit in dealing with other members of the society.

As long as the founder lives, his male lineal descendants are bound to the joint family, and it is not uncommon for a patriarch to have a dozen or more able-bodied sons and grandsons under his control. Upon his death, the process of fission starts. Although the family continues to live and work together under the leadership of the eldest son, his brothers do not have to put their earnings into the common holding unless they wish to. When he, in turn, is at last succeeded by his eldest son, the joint family begins to break up. The third-generation leader is younger than most of his uncles, who become restive under his leadership. Moreover, it is likely that the group will have grown too large for its land holdings. Then one or more men split off to found a new joint-family household elsewhere.[22]

The growth, development, and eventual demise of the Tanala joint family clearly exemplifies

[19]G. H. Smith, "J. B. Trudeau's Remarks on the Indians of the Upper Missouri, 1794–95" (*American Anthropologist*, vol. 38, 1936), p. 567.

[20]E. E. Evans-Pritchard, "Zande Blood-brotherhood," in *Essays in Social Anthropology*, p. 131.

[21]Bourguignon and Greenbaum, op. cit., p. 49.

[22]R. Linton, "The Tanala," in A. Kardiner (ed.), *The Individual and His Society*, pp. 251–290.

what has been said about the developmental cycles of domestic groups. Family groups of all kinds have forms which reflect a beginning, growth, and decline as members are added through birth and marriage and removed through marriage and death.[23]

Balkan and Asian Joint Families

Among gardening and pastoral peoples, the joint family appears as a corporate landowning entity, made up of the descendants of at least two siblings or cousins living in a single dwelling or in closely spaced houses that form a household. Archaic Indo-European peoples commonly favored this type of setup, which is known among the peoples of the Balkans as the *zadruga*. It has been described as follows:

> . . . [*W*]*e were guests in the home of a family counting sixty-eight members. It was one of the few remaining family* zadrugé, *or collectives, in Serbia. We met about forty of the members, including the* stareshina, *or head of the family, a patriarch of seventy and absolute ruler of the group. The enormous household, with a considerable tract of ground and a twenty-room house, was all but self-sufficient economically. Every member above ten had his or her special duty to attend to. Six women and girls, supervised by the* stareshina's *wife, did nothing but cook and bake. Eight other females only spun, weaved, sewed, and embroidered. Five men and boys attended to all the sheep, goats, buffaloes, cattle, and horses. One man was the family shoemaker. The husbands were all the* stareshina's *brothers, sons, and grandsons; their wives had married into the* zadruga *from near-by villages.*[24]

In India and Pakistan, the patrilineal joint family, called *kumbah* in Pakistan, is still a vital form even in the urban setting. In such large cities as Karachi, a joint family will occupy a single five- or six-story house, with the parents on the lower floor and each son establishing his secondary conjugal-natal family on succeeding floors in order of seniority—the youngest having the most flights to climb. Even fully trained professional men, if conservatively oriented, turn their salaries over to the household father and mother to administer on behalf of the group as a whole.

THE MATRILATERAL GROUP

Some societies utilize the brother-sister relationship to overcome some of the limitations of the conjugal-natal family. The result is a social unit that may be called the *matrilateral group*, which consists of a woman, her brother, and her offspring or a conjoint combination of lineal descendants of a female.[25]

The Dobu *Susu*

Thus, among the Dobu of Melanesia, the conjugal-natal family is the household unit; that is, its members live together. After a man marries, he never again enters his sister's house; consequently, the *susu*, as the matrilateral group is called in Dobu, has no household base. However, children cannot eat food grown in their father's fields; all fishing gear, including canoes, is used jointly and is inherited only by members of the *susu*. Consequently, the *susu* has an economic base, and the conjugal-natal family does not. Emotional security is found only in the *susu*, and not in the conjugal-natal family. All Dobuans believe that all other Dobuans except those of their own *susu* are their magical enemies. Husband and wife, coming as they do from different *susus*, are hostile at marriage and all their days thereafter. Each believes the other is trying to cause personal injury or death by foul magic. The *susu* inherits the corpses and skulls of its members. It bestows personal names and social status in relationship terms. Widows, widowers, and the children of a dead person may never enter the village of the deceased spouse or

[23] J. Goody (ed.), *The Developmental Cycle in Domestic Groups.*

[24] L. Adamic, *The Native's Return*, p. 215.

[25] It has also been called the *consanguineal family*.

parent, but *susu* relatives of a dead person may enter the village of the surviving spouse or children.[26]

The Zuni Household

The differentiation and interrelationship of conjugal-natal family and matrilateral group are also strikingly revealed by the Zunis of New Mexico, of whom Benedict wrote:

To the women of the household, the grandmother and her sisters, her daughters and their daughters, belong the house and the corn that is stored in it. No matter what may happen to marriages, the women of the household remain with the house for life. They present a solid front. They care for and feed the sacred objects that belong to them. They keep their secrets together. Their husbands are outsiders, and it is their brothers, married now into houses of other clans, who are united with the household in all affairs of moment. It is they who return for all the retreats when the sacred objects of the house are set out before the altar. It is they, not the women, who learn the word-perfect ritual of their sacred bundle and perpetuate it. A man goes always, for all important occasions, to his mother's house, which, when she dies, becomes his sister's house, and if his marriage breaks up, he returns to the same household.

This blood-relationship group, rooted in the ownership of the house, united in the care of sacred objects, is the important group in Zuni. It has permanence and important common concerns. But it is not the economically functioning group. Each married son, each married brother, spends his labour upon the corn which will fill his wife's storeroom. Only when his mother's or sister's house lacks male labour does he care for the cornfield of his blood-relationship group. The economic group is the household that lives together, the old grandmother and her husband, her daughters and their husbands.[27]

The Nayar *Taravad*

Of the matrilineal type of joint-family household, that of the famous Nayar caste of Kerala, on the Malabar coast of southern India, has long held the interest of anthropologists.

The Nayar are supposed to have been the ruling class of the aboriginal society predating the Hindu influx. Today they form the third-ranking caste of a complex caste society. Above them is the erstwhile royal house of great wealth and power, which may have emerged long ago from the Nayars themselves. Beneath the royal house (but far above the Nayars in sublimity) is the caste of Nambudiri Brahmans, whose sacred families are patrilineally organized on a strict basis of primogeniture. The Nayars are a closed caste of landowners and professional soldiers, who in contrast to the Brahmans are strictly matrilineal and matrilocal. The household, or *taravad*, is a joint organization housed under one roof. The eldest woman is the titular head of the household, but the house, lands, and joint property are administered by the eldest brother for the benefit of the group. All the males (brothers, sons, and grandsons) contribute to the maintenance of the *taravad* and draw their support from it. The offspring of the women belong to the *taravad* and are maintained within it. The men mate with women of other *taravad* without obligating themselves to any legal duties toward these "wives" or children, who live with their mothers.

Marriage by members of the *taravad* is often no more than a ritual bow to Hindu convention. If a ceremony is performed, it may soon be followed by legal divorce, even though the couple continues an enduring relation as mates. For unlike most joint-family practices elsewhere, the Nayar male may not live in the joint-family household of his mate. The couple merely visit together, and out of these visits come the children who people the *taravad* of the mother.

Both men and women may have several mates simultaneously, since mating involves no formal obligations. Younger sons of the Brahman class may enter into sexual alliances with Nayar women, but they still remain outside the *taravad*, and their children remain irrevocably fixed within it.

[26] R. F. Fortune, *Sorcerers of Dobu*, pp. 5–30.
[27] R. F. Benedict, *Patterns of Culture*, pp. 75–76.

Under changing economic and social conditions, the Nayar matrilineal joint family has been gradually dissolving, and patrilineal tendencies have become increasingly strong.[28]

What is defective or objectionable in the matrilateral group? The answer will be found in the incest taboo. The basis of the matrilateral group is the sibling bond of brotherhood and sisterhood. Yet all societies find it necessary to taboo sex relations between brother and sister. The matrilateral group encourages emotional and functional ties between a pair who must never become sexually involved with each other. This is dangerous business, so much so that many societies apparently prefer to make it impossible for such a situation to exist. In Dobu, for example, a married man may not enter his sister's house. Another disadvantage of the matrilateral group is that the splitting of loyalty between it and the conjugal-natal family may produce personal and cultural conflicts that are difficult to resolve.

The matrilateral group exists because it offers certain advantages in which the conjugal-natal family is weak. Yet the conjugal-natal family is definitely preferred over the matrilateral group. The conjugal-natal family is universal; the matrilateral group is not.

COMMUNES

We have seen that family and kinship have predominated as the almost universal means of internally organizing human societies and of allocating status and accessibility of privilege, power, and consumable resources. With advancing civilization, kinship recedes in relative importance, while more universalistic modes of social identity come to the fore. Still, down to the nineteenth century in the West, and to the twentieth century in China, the family and the extended kinship group remained the virtually unchallenged vehicle of living, reproducing, and inheriting.

Until the Russian revolution of 1917, challenges to conventional family organization came from small prototype movements of limited success and duration, engendered by intellectual idealists, both religious and sectarian. The Shakers of Mt. Lebanon, New York, founded in 1787, lived in "family" units of fifty or sixty "brothers" and "sisters," housed by sex in two separate buildings and maintaining themselves by gardening, fruit preserving, and craftwork. Shakers, however, did not allow mating among their members. New members were added through adult conversion and the adoption of children.[29]

Current communes are more in the stream of the socialistic utopias of the last century. They all represent withdrawal from urban industrialism to romanticism. The socialistic communes of the last century placed high value on work and common sharing. Contemporary communes seem more to emphasize common intimacy of feeling and being, with less value placed on work. It is too soon to tell whether they foreshadow a new trend in organization of family life or whether they will be no more than a marginal fad of passing historical interest.

SUMMARY

The universal functions of the family are: (1) the institutionalization of mating and the establishment of legal parents for children; (2) nurture and enculturation of the young; (3) organization of a complementary division of labor between spouses; and (4) the establishment of relationships of descent and affinity.

The conjugal-natal family has two overlapping forms from the point of view of an individual. The natal family is that into which one is

[28]K. Gough, in D. M. Schneider and K. Gough (eds.), *Matrilineal Kinship*, chaps. 6 and 7.

[29]See D. W. Douglas and K. du P. Lumpkin, "Communistic Settlements" (*Encylopaedia of the Social Sciences*, vol. 4, 1931), pp. 95–102.

born; it was founded by parents. The conjugal aspect is the family founded by the spouses at marriage.

The conjugal-natal family as an independent residential unit exists in about half the societies of the world.

Residence patterns greatly influence the character of the conjugal-natal family; they also reflect the dominant orientation of the kinship system in a society. In *virilocal* residence, a married couple lives in the locale of the husband's natal family; if this locale includes an aggregation of the husband's patrikin, marriage is recognized as *patrilocal*. When a couple settles in the locale of the wife's natal family, residence is *uxorilocal*; if the locale includes an aggregation of the wife's matrikin, marriage is recognized as *matrilocal*.

When kinship is matrilineally oriented, but power is focused in the men, residence may then be in the locale of the husband's mother's brother. In this case, it is called *avunculocal*.

Relatively few societies (16 percent) insist on monogamy. Half the known societies set up the polygynous (two or more wives) composite conjugal-natal family as the norm. The polyandrous composite conjugal-natal family of two or more husbands is interesting but very rare, centered mostly in northern India.

The joint family consists of joint households of kinfolk related through either their fathers or mothers. It is a corporate socioeconomic enterprise in which kinship overrides individualism.

To compensate for the relative fragility and lack of durability of the conjugal-natal family, some cultures use the matrilateral group to perform some functions which might otherwise be carried by the family. The matrilateral group consists of women and their children, plus the women's brothers. Examples are the Dobuan *susu*, the Zuni household, and the Nayar *taravad*. The major inhibiting factor for the matrilateral group is, of course, the universality of the brother-sister taboo. The matrilateral group may have potentially everything that marks the family, except for one thing. It cannot function as a unit of mating and reproduction.

Communes are efforts to found and maintain composite living groups devoid of kinship and private property. Thus far in human history such modes of organization have been rare and marginal to the societies in which they occur. They have interesting possibilities, however, which will be discussed in one of the closing chapters of this book (pages 640–642).

SELECTED READINGS

Bohannan, P., and J. Middleton (eds.), *Marriage, Family, and Residence* (1968). An excellently chosen collection of papers by leading contemporary anthropologists. The most useful single supplementary source for the subject of this chapter.

Goody, J. (ed.), *The Developmental Cycle in Domestic Groups* (1958). The product of joint examination by a group of anthropologists of what happens in families and other domestic groups during the natural history of the family group.

LaBarre, W., *The Human Animal* (1954). Brilliantly written, this book presents a biosocial theory of the development and essential nature of family relationships.

Mead, M., *Male and Female* (1949). A provocative and interesting synthesis of the author's field studies and views on family relationships in seven primitive cultures and in the United States.

23
Kinship Groups

CHAPTER OUTLINE

LEARNING GOALS

Explain the principles of extended kinship.

Discuss the bilateral form of kinship.

Define a ramage.

Explain the unilineal principle.

List the types of unilineal kinship groups.

Summarize the universal and secondary functions of unilineal groups.

Explain what is meant by double descent.

Describe the relationship between descent groups and adaptation.

One of anthropology's most fascinating discoveries is that the seemingly simple matter of descent and kinship can be so variously perceived, so intricately defined, and assigned so central a role in the ordering of many cultures. Yet, the contemporary Western cultural bias toward individuality produces a general impatience with the anthropological stress on the many forms and complexities of kinship relations. It is a hard fact, however, that it is simply impossible to understand the workings of most societies without grasping their approach to kinship—kinship systems, kinship functions, kinship terms.

The family tie nowhere ends with parents and children, for parents have their parents, grandparents, uncles, aunts, brothers, sisters, and cousins to whom the bond of kinship extends. In all societies, the cementing effect of these bonds is strong enough to produce a network of relations that makes the kinship group distinguishable within the larger society.

In most societies, the kinship bond is likely to override all others. Behavior toward relatives is not the same as behavior toward nonrelatives. As a striking manifestation of this fundamental fact, E. E. Evans-Pritchard observes:

If you wish to live among the Nuer you must do so on their terms, which means that you must treat them as a kind of kinsmen and they will treat you as a kind of kinsman. Rights, privileges, and obligations are determined by kinship. Either a man is a kinsman, actually or by fiction, or he is a person to whom you have no reciprocal obligations and whom you treat as a potential enemy.

Because we live in an industrialized society of great social mobility, in which we depend to a great degree upon our own efforts and those of mutual-aid associations (insurance and benevolent societies), unions, and philanthropic and governmental agencies to provide security, rather than depend on relatives, it is hard for most of us to comprehend the importance of kinfolk in other societies. In nonliterate society, most of these responsibilities rest with the kinship group.

[1]E. E. Evans-Pritchard, *The Nuer*, p. 183.

The contrast is philosophically stated by an old Pomo Indian of California, who soliloquized:

What is a man? A man is nothing. Without his family he is of less importance than that bug crossing the trail, of less importance than the sputum or exuviae. . . . A man must be with his family to amount to anything with us. If he had nobody else to help him, the first trouble he got into he would be killed by his enemies because there would be no relatives to help him fight the poison of the other group. No woman would marry him. . . . He would be poorer than a new-born child, he would be poorer than a worm. . . . If a man has a large family, . . . and upbringing by a family that is known to produce good children, then he is somebody and every family is willing to have him marry a woman of their group. In the White way of doing things the family is not so important. The police and soldiers take care of protecting you, the courts give you justice, the post office carries messages for you, the school teaches you. Everything is taken care of, even your children, if you die; but with us the family must do all of that. . . .

With us the family was everything. Now it is nothing. We are getting like the White people and it is bad for the old people. We had no old people's home like you. The old people were important. They were wise. Your old people must be fools.[2]

Among the Mossi, a proverb-loving tribe on the Upper Volta River in West Africa, the folk saying runs, "A chicken isn't very big without his feathers," meaning "Always have some relatives with you in court."

PRINCIPLES OF EXTENDED KINSHIP

The conjugal-natal family, although it is the seedbed of society, is itself always embedded within one or more of a series of kinship group-

[2]B. W. Aginsky, "An Indian's Soliloquy" (*American Journal of Sociology*, vol. 46, 1940), pp. 43–44.

FIGURE 23.1
Representatives of an Ifugao extended family at the ceremonial elevation of a young married boy and girl to the rank of *kadangyang*—the highest social class. The boy wears a headdress and has a white chicken hanging from his belt. His contracted wife stands next to him with a chicken in her hand. (Lowie Museum of Anthropology, University of California, Berkeley.)

ings (Figure 23.1). These are the *kindred*, the *ramage*, the *lineage*, the *clan*, the *phratry*, and the *moiety*.

What are these groups and how are they organized? The basic division rests on the distinction between the *bilateral* and *unilineal* principles. A *bilateral* kinship group is one in which members receive their identity through descent reckoned from both parents. A *unilineal kinship group* is one in which members receive their identity through descent reckoned from one parent. If the descent line is passed from father to sons to son's sons, the system is patrilineal. If the descent line is passed from mother to daughter to daughter's daughter, the system is matrilineal. A *unilineal kinship system* is one in which all the kinship groups are either matrilineal *or* patrilineal. *Ambilineal*, or *nonunilinear*, kinship organization exists when members of a society are allowed to trace descent *either* patrilineally or matrilineally. In a society in which individuals may affiliate with patrilineal kinship groups for some purposes, and with matrilineal kinship groups for other purposes, the system is one of *double descent*.

BILATERAL, OR COGNATIC, KINSHIP: THE KINDRED

The kindred expresses the bilateral principle in its most direct and undifferentiated form. In the largest sense, one's kindred includes every person to whom one can trace a genealogical bond. It includes all one's *cognates*, that is, everyone who can be traced as related through a common relative, whether ancestral or contemporary, whether male or female. It spreads in all directions, and in a small community constructing a complete bilateral genealogy could result in the inclusion of every member of the local group as a relative. Comanche Indians recognized this and gave it as a reason for not identifying as members of their kindred those cognates who lay beyond the degree of second cousin.

FIGURE 23.2
The formation of a Kwakiutl extended bilateral family early in the twentieth century. A bridal party returning to the groom's village in traditional war canoes. The bride and groom stand on a special platform near the stern of the boat. The crew, made up of the groom's relatives, sings and paddles in rhythm, while the groom's sister or other relative dances on the front platform. (Edward Curtis/Bayard Gallery.)

A kindred as a functioning unit never organizes all potential relatives. Because cognatic relationships extend in all directions and multiply geometrically, their boundaries are far too inclusive. The kindred is rather like a pool of personnel from which groups of individuals coalesce for specific cooperative activities, such as work parties, revenge groups, exchange groups, households, and transition rites (Figure 23.2). The composition of the actual kindred shifts and changes, dissolving and reappearing in altered form, depending on who among the kinfolk count themselves in for the occasion. Kindreds are flexible cells which are highly adaptable to fluid and relatively unstructured situations. They tend to be characteristic of hunting and gathering societies with limited resources, on the one hand, and of industrialized, free-market, urban civilizations, on the other.

Murdock describes the kindred for certain groups in the United States:

In our own society, where its members are collectively called "kinfolk" or "relatives," it includes that group of near kinsmen who may be expected to be present and participant on important ceremonial occasions, such as weddings, christenings, funerals, Thanksgiving and Christmas dinners, and "family reunions." Members of kindred visit and entertain one another freely, and between them marriage and pecuniary transactions for profit are ordinarily taboo. One turns first to them for aid when one finds oneself in difficulties. However much they may disagree or quarrel, they are expected to support one another against criticism or affronts from outsiders.[3]

While the bilateral kinship system appears to work satisfactorily in some societies, it does have inherent limitations and disadvantages, which have been summed up by Murdock as follows:

A particular disadvantage of the kindred appears in the instances in which an individual belongs to the kindreds of two other persons and thereby becomes involved in conflicting or incompatible obligations. If they get into serious difficulties with one another, for example, he may be required to avenge the one and yet to defend the other. If they become estranged, both are likely to turn to him for support and to subject him to emotional conflict and strain.[4]

The problem referred to by Murdock highlights a structural weakness in the kindred. Membership is always personal, or ego-oriented, with only siblings sharing the same kindred. In this way it would be possible to become involved in the conundrum of conflict cited above, for

[3]G. P. Murdock, *Social Structure*, pp. 56–57.
[4]Ibid., p. 61.

example, when ego is a member of the personal kindreds of two different first cousins.

The Occurrence of Bilateral Kinship

Because we are so accustomed in Western society to reckoning our kinfolk or relatives bilaterally (we are equally "related" to our paternal and maternal families), it is easy to assume that this type of family pattern is universal and best. On the contrary, only about one-third of all human societies build their social structures on this foundation.

In sub-Saharan Africa, where most tribes are gardeners or pastoralists, only one in twenty societies is based on the kindred. By contrast, two-thirds and three-fourths of the societies of North and South America, respectively, were (or are) bilaterally structured (see Figure 23.3).

AMBILINEAL KINSHIP: THE RAMAGE

The ramage is a blending of lineage organization in such a way that anthropologists call the result *nonunilinear* or *ambilineal organization.* A person claiming ramage membership must be able to trace unilineal descent from the putative founder of the ramage either patrilineally or matrilineally. Some persons acquire membership through their mothers, others through their fathers. Hence the paradoxical lineal nonunilineality of the system. Murdock calls *ramages* "ancestor oriented *ambilineal* kin-groups."[5]

Ramages have a stronger corporate quality than do most kindreds. Corporateness means they own land and other valued goods and can transmit them to descendent members. Hence, explicit ramage membership can have definite advantages for the individual. Conversely, the ramage is more demanding of its membership and, at the same time, is choosy about whom it acknowledges as rightful members.

To use the Samoan ramage as an example:

The Samoan 'aiga sa *is a descent group controlling garden land, house sites, and certain ceremonials. It is exogamous, since the incest taboo is extended to all known relatives. Associated with each 'aiga sa is one or more titles, from the senior of which the group takes its name. Title holders are selected from among the eligible males participating with the group. Affiliation with a descent group is through either father or mother, and a married couple may affiliate with the groups of either spouse. A person is mainly associated with one group—that with which he lives—but he may participate to some extent in several. Living with and using lands belonging to a particular 'aiga sa, as well as the right to speak at meetings of the group, are dependent upon the consent of its members, and this may be denied if there is doubt about a person's genealogical relationship to the group or if he has failed to fulfill his obligations to it. Here, too, indefinitely extended relationships through consanguinity become limited by the obligations of participation. Even though there is considerable overlapping membership, the number of potential affiliations is appreciably reduced by both remissness in obligations and failure to remember genealogical connections.*[6]

The Samoan example is particularly apt, for half the societies in which ramages have been recognized are Oceanic. It could be that island ecology imposes a limitation of available land for gardeners. Land is, therefore, highly valued. Thus, the exclusionary (yet flexible) membership qualifications, along with corporate landholding, make the ramage a useful social response to the situation.

In spite of the great interest in nonunilineal descent stirred up among anthropologists since the late 1950s, the ramage is actually very rare. Only 31 of the 310 cognatic societies in the *Ethnographic Atlas* have ramages. And this is but

[5]G. P. Murdock, *Ethnographic Atlas*, p. 49.

[6]W. Davenport, "Nonunilinear Descent and Descent Groups" (*American Anthropologist*, vol. 61, 1959), p. 561.

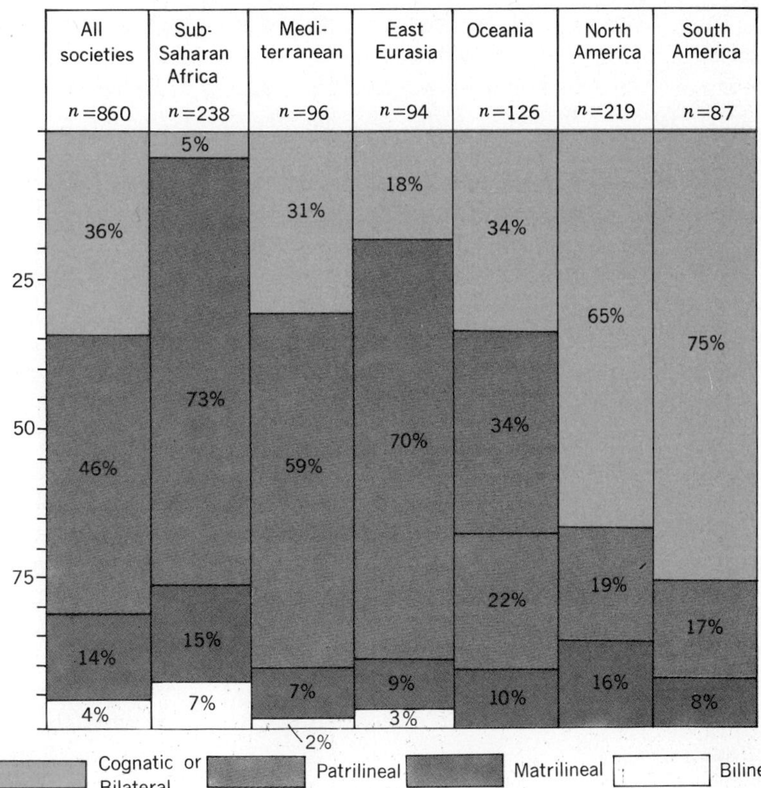

FIGURE 23.3
Relative frequency of forms of kinship organization, according to geographic area. (Data from L. Bourguignon and E. Greenbaum, *Diversity and Homogeneity*, table 29, p. 51.)

3.6 percent (31 in 860 societies) of all the societies in the sample.

THE UNILINEAL DESCENT PRINCIPLE

The majority of human societies—two-thirds of those represented in the *World Ethnographic Sample*—are organized around the principle of unilineal descent (see Figure 23.3). The popularity of the unilineal principle indicates that as an adaptive device, it overcomes some of the difficulties inherent in the kindred (vagueness of membership, unwieldy extension, and competing obligations at times of conflict). By tracing descent through one parental line, kinship becomes more clear-cut, and societies needing to rely on kinship groups to perform most of their basic functions are able to do so more predictably and reliably.

In a *patrilineal* system, all children belong to the group of their father, which is, in turn, the group of his father's father, his father's father's father, and so on, as far back as genealogies are kept. The children of the man's sons and of the sons' sons, and so on, belong to the same group, as long as the line does not die out or split off.

In a *matrilineal* system, all children belong to the group of their mother, which is, in turn, the group of her mother's mother, her mother's mother, and so on, as far back as genealogies are kept. The children of the woman's daughters and of the daughters' daughters, and so on, belong to the same group, as long as the line does not die out or break up.

This, of course, does not mean that the relatives in the group through which descent is *not* traced are meaningless people. They are recognized as relatives of some kind and they mean more than strangers or nonkin. They are simply not as important as lineal kin in the expectation of economic and political support.

Each unilineal kinship group is a collective body, a corporate entity, that endures through time. It has a beginning, and the potential of unending endurance—unlike the conjugal-natal family. Unilineal kinship membership is a matter of social heredity. One does not ordinarily join a unilineal group; one is born into it. Adoption makes it possible to change unilineal affiliation, however.

Unilineal group membership is discriminating and exclusive. It segments the population of a society; it separates kin from nonkin. In compensation, it cements the relatives who are included within the unilineal group into a firmer bond of kinship than is possible through bilateral extension. In a society with unilineal descent groups

> . . . *the individual knows exactly where he stands. . . . If both disputants are members of his own kin group, he is expected to remain neutral and to use his good offices to compose their differences. If neither is a member, the affair is none of his business. If one is a member but the other is not, he is expected to support his sibmate, regardless of the rights in the matter. In short, most conflict situations are simply and automatically resolved.*[7] Why?

Types of Unilineal Descent Groups

The simplest type of unilineal group is known as the *lineage.* A lineage is an extended unilineal kinship group descended from a known ancestor, or founder, who ordinarily lived not more than five or six generations back. He, in the case of the patrilineage, or she, in the case of the matrilineage, is a real person and not a mythological or legendary figure. On the next level, above the lineage, there is the *clan.* A clan is an enlarged unilineal kinship group that rests on the fiction of common descent from a founding ancestor who lived so far in the distant past as to be mythological. When a society is divided into two unilineal halves, each half is called a *moiety* (Fr. *moitié,* "half"). The groups are called *phratries (Gr. phratria,* "brother") if there are more than two such groups in the society.

The possible extended unilineal groups are therefore (1) the lineage, (2) the clan, (3) the moiety, and (4) the phratry.

The Lineage The lineage is a unilineal kinship group limited to closely related agnatic (male descent) or uterine (female descent) kin and is rarely more than six generations deep.

Lineages may be subdivided into smaller segments. In such cases, they are called *segmentary lineages.* In a common African form, such as described for the Nuer,[8] each lineage is divided into two secondary lineages, which divide into four tertiary lineages, then into eight quaternary (or minimal) lineages (see Figure 23.4). When a minimal lineage fights with its opposite lineage (for example, *a* versus *b*), no one else is directly involved except a local Priest of the Earth, who will evoke a settlement if anyone is killed. But if *a* becomes involved in a fight with lineages of *c* or *d*, then *a* and *b* join as segments of *1* to fight with *2*. If *1* gets into a dispute with *3* or *4*, *2* will join it as a segment of *A* against *B*. But all will join together as a maximal lineage, *I*, against all other maximal lineages. Such intensive lineage activity prevails in segmentary societies with weak central governments.

Lineages may or may not reside as territorially based units. Localized minimal lineages usually form joint-family households or compounds.

The Clan Apart from size, the only essential difference between a lineage and a clan is that

[7]G. P. Murdock, *Social Structure*, p. 61.

[8]E. E. Evans-Pritchard, op. cit.

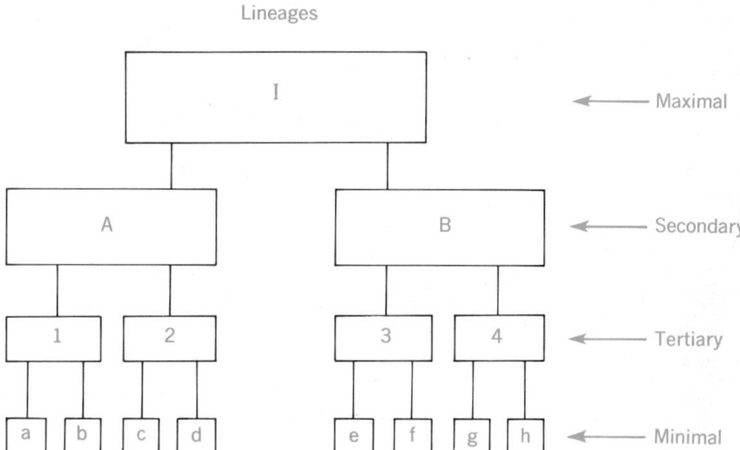

FIGURE 23.4
Segmentary lineage relations. A and B are secondary segments of the maximal lineage, I. These are in turn segmented into two tertiary lineages each, which in turn segment into two minimal lineages each.

the members of a lineage can actually trace common descent from a known ancestor, while clan members cannot. Nevertheless, members believe they have common descent from a mythical ancestor, and their behavior is regulated accordingly. Very often the folklore of the clan includes a myth, as part of its "charter," purporting to give a truthful account of how the clan came to be.

Dahomean Clans Among the patrilineal Dahomeans of West Africa, one clan was founded by the son of a horse "who, bounding from the water in a fury of passion, lay with a woman on the bank of the river." Another clan is said to have descended from the "offspring of a woman and a pig, another from that of a woman and a toad, one from that of a woman and a dog, and the royal family . . . originated from the mating of a female leopard with the King of Adja." Another clan is said to have been created when a peanut was magically transformed into a man, who then mated with a poor woman who lived on roots. Dahomeans believe that the members of the Peanut clan lack the fine, smooth skin of other Dahomeans: "It is rough like the shell of a peanut." Further, the members of the Peanut clan are said to be recognizable on sight.[9] How this can be genetically possible in view of clan exogamy is a little difficult to understand, but ideological stereotypes can color one's perception.

The members of a Dahomean clan have a rather special set of attitudes toward the animal or plant creature who begat their revered clan founder. All Dahomean clans except one abjure the flesh of the animal species associated with the founder, and many of them bear the name of the founder.

Crow Clans The Crow Indians have a different kind of clan-origin legend. The clan names are taken from certain alleged exploits of the founders, after the manner of a Plains Indian warrior who bestows names on children memorializing outstanding events in his life. It would be quite a mistake to jump to the conclusion that members of the Crow "Greasy-inside-of-their-mouths" clan are slippery-tongued, for the name is actually honorific. The clan founder was such a provi-

[9]M. J. Herskovits and F. S. Herskovits, *An Outline of Dahomean Religious Belief* (American Anthropological Association Memoir 41, 1933), pp. 24–27.

FIGURE 23.5
At the root of the Navajo matrilineal clan is the matrilocal residential group consisting of the senior woman (seated); daughter, standing in the doorway of the hogan; daughter's daughter; and unmarried sons. The daughter's husband resides in his wife's hogan, but belongs to another matrilineal clan. (The Bettman Archive, Inc.)

dent hunter that he was always surfeited with rich, fat meat. It is said that his mouth was so coated with fat that when he spat in the campfire, his saliva flared up in the flames.[10]

In all these instances, and in similar ones which could be drawn from a multitude of societies, the actual origin of the clan is lost in the hoary past; this is not the case with lineages. Lineages may exist without any relationship to clans. Clans may also exist with or without institutionalized lineages within them.

The Moiety When a society is divided into two halves or divisions, it is said to have moieties. In cases where there are only two clans in a tribe, such as the Water and Land groups of the Central Miwok in California, clan and moiety are automatically synonymous. Multiple clans are the more common order, however, and when clans are linked to moieties, the clans are subdivisions of the moieties. Among the Seneca, to take a typical example, the Bear, Wolf, Turtle, and Beaver clans constitute one moiety, and the Deer, Snipe, Heron, and Hawk constitute the other. Originally, the moieties were exogamous, but in recent centuries they have lost control over marriage, and only the clans have retained the exogamous rule. Each moiety performs the important mourning rituals on behalf of the other; the moieties compete against each other in the old Indian game of lacrosse, which is as much a ceremonial ritual as it is a sport.

Reciprocity is the basis of all social relationships. One of the most effective ways of institutionalizing reciprocity is to organize the society on a moiety basis. Moieties are exogamous with few exceptions; each moiety supplies the other with its marriage partners. Other reciprocal services are invariably linked to the moiety alignments. Moieties thus effectively control certain types of behavior.

The Phratry If clans are linked into more than two divisions, the divisions are referred to as phratries. The clans in a phratry system retain their separate identities, but each clan feels some sort of special affinity to the others within its phratry. Moreover, they may have special obligations to fulfill toward one another.

The Hopi Indians have a large number of matrilineal clans, which are loosely linked into twelve exogamous phratries. The Aztecs had four phratries embracing a number of clans among them. The Aztec phratries were important political and religious divisions in the structure of the empire.

Nevertheless, it may be said that in general, phratry organization is a relatively rare and functionally insignificant phenomenon. It does not usually control marriage, although Crow Indians think that it is better if members of the same phratry do not intermarry. Still, they have no prohibition against such action. For the most part, the phratry sentiment seems to rest either on a tradition of common origin or on common interests in ceremonial activity.

[10]R. H. Lowie, *The Crow Indians*, pp. 15–16.

The Universal Functions of Unilineal Groups

Unilineal groups, except for the phratry, have two universal functions: (1) to broaden the base of the kinship group by providing mutual aid and collective protection and liability in legal action and disputes, and (2) to regulate and control marriage.

Mutual Aid and Security The lineage, clan, or moiety provides a large mutual-aid organization rooted in kinship. There can be no doubt that the most generalized interest served by the clan is that of fulfilling the desire for security. The family, as we noted earlier, is the primary incubator of personal security. The clan expands this fundamental function while at the same time tightening up the structure by reducing the diffusive effects of bilateral extension.

To meet the needs of security, lineages usually present a solid front to the rest of the world. In personal interrelations with all persons outside the lineage, every lineage member must ideally be aided, abetted, and protected by all other members. This may lead to feuding in many societies.

As a complement of its unqualified protection of its members, the lineage or clan frequently becomes liable for the illegal acts of its own members. Thus, if a man commits murder, vengeance may commonly be taken on any member of the lineage, for even though a member is innocent in fact, his person is legally merged with the persons of all his fellow kinsmen.

The Regulation of Marriage The second universal function of the unilineal kinship group is to regulate marriage through the rule of exogamy. This, if we follow Malinowski's hypothesis, is a self-protective device that ensures solidarity by directing the sexual drive and marriage to persons outside the kinship group.

We must not, however, overlook the fact that an additional security device is to be found in clan exogamy. Marriage imposes affinal obligations on the spouse's kin and clan. It tends to reduce overt aggression between the maritally allied groups; it also extends the base of the economic and political support on which a person may depend (see Chapter 21, page 376).

Secondary Functions of Unilineal Groups

In addition to the broad and universal functions mentioned above, clans carry responsibilities in the maintenance of culture. Both the nature of these responsibilities and the means of carrying them out vary from culture to culture. However, in general, these secondary functions cover a broad range of legal, governmental, economic, religious, and symbolic purposes.

Legal Functions The lineage or clan commonly represents its individual members in lawsuits and legal matters and is, conversely, responsible for their illegal acts. This function is discussed in detail in Chapter 28.

Governmental Functions A function that the clan may take on is that of government. The Aztec clan heads, called *speakers*, made up the Aztec tribal council. This group controlled ordinary political decisions, made war and peace, and as a judicial body decided disputes between clans and members of different clans. These same clan speakers sat on the grand national council, whose jurisdiction covered the most important law cases and election of the king. Aztec clans were grouped in four phratries, each of which had a captain-general, who served as a high-ranking military officer and who, in addition to his military post, served on the grand national council.

Many societies have raised one clan to the position of royalty, and the hereditary chief must come from this clan. In Melanesia, this is true of the Trobriand Islanders; in Africa, the Dahomeans and the Ashanti are two examples among many.

Among the American Indians, the Winnebago of Wisconsin assigned political functions to seven of their twelve clans. The tribal chief was selected from the Thunderbird clan. In addition, this clan performed important functions connected with the preservation of peace (its governmental functions were mainly civil). The Warrior clan, as its name implies, provided war leadership; the village and hunt policemen came from the Bear clan; and the camp crier and aide-de-camp for the chief was always selected from the Buffalo clan. The Wolf, Water-spirit, and Elk clans had lesser political tasks.[11]

Economic Functions Among clan-organized peoples practicing hoe culture, the garden lands are almost inevitably owned or administered by the clans. Each Aztec clan owned its specific segment of land. Assignments for use were made by the clan headman, who kept a record of all holdings. Every family head had the right to a plot of land (unless he had forfeited his clan membership by refusing to marry or carry out his clan obligations, in which case he became a common laborer). As long as a clansman was in good standing, he could use his land or rent it to a fellow clansman. He could pass it on to a clan descendant, but he could not pass title to an outsider, for ownership of title was vested in the clan.

Clans may own other material goods in common, such as temples, meetinghouses, and sacred and ceremonial objects (see Chapter 26).

Religious and Ceremonial Functions Clans or lineages worship their own supernatural beings exclusively for their own benefit, or they may be expected to use them for the well-being of the whole society. The deceased ancestors of some African societies are elevated to the status of clan deities. The clan head is usually the chief priest of the clan and the intermediary between his relatives and the ancestral spirits. Among the Hopi and Zuni, the all-important ceremonial organization is inextricably intertwined with the clan system; each clan must perform its part of the ceremonial activities for the benefit of the whole pueblo.

Totemic Functions Finally, clans may have totemic associations involving a feeling of identity with a plant, animal, or other natural object. This bond of emotional identity may extend from a mere feeling of kinship to actual reverence and worship. It may also lead to symbolic representation of the totemic object in clan fetishes (Chapter 34, pages 596–598).

DOUBLE DESCENT[12]

Prior to 1927, anthropologists thought that a society could embrace only one clan system, which had to be either matrilineal or patrilineal. Evidence to the contrary was introduced by Rattray's studies of the Ashanti, who were shown to have matrilineal clans called *abusua* and patrilineal groups called *ntoro.* The ntoro principle of inheritance is associated with the semen, and although the ntoro group is not organized, it, like the abusua, regulates marriage and sets certain incest prohibitions. It is totemic and imposes certain food taboos on its members.[13]

A subsequent report by Forde on another African tribe, the Umor, analyzes an even more precise system of dual descent.[14] The Umoran

[11]P. Radin, *The Winnebago Tribe* (Bureau of American Ethnology, Annual Report 37, 1923).

[12]Also called dual, *duolineal,* and *double unilineal descent.*

[13]R. S. Rattray, *Ashanti; Ashanti Law and Constitution.* Dual descent as found in a neighboring people is explicitly examined in detail in a monograph by J. B. Christensen, *Double Descent among the Fanti.*

[14]C. D. Forde, "Kinship in Umor: Double Unilateral Organization in a Semi-Bantu Society" (*American Anthropologist*, vol. 41, 1939), pp. 523–553.

patrilineal, virilocal clan determines house and land affiliation and is called the *kepun*. There are twenty-two of these. At the same time, there are four *yajima* (plural form), which are matrilineal, nonlocalized clans through which movable property—principally livestock and currency—is inherited and marriage exchanges (progeny price and dowry) are made. "A man eats in his kepun and inherits in his lejima [singular form]," is the native adage. Murdock placed the phenomenon into focus by showing that double descent has a widely scattered distribution in Africa, India, Australia, Melanesia, and Polynesia.[15]

Ten percent of the Oceanic tribes use double-descent systems, as do 7 percent of the African societies; it is totally absent from the New World, giving a worldwide frequency of only 4 percent.[16]

DESCENT GROUPS AND SUBSISTENCE

Bilateral, patrilineal, matrilineal, and double-descent extensions of the kinship group appear on *all* levels of cultural development and in all the major geographic areas of the world.[17]

David Aberle has collated some relevant data in which the societies represented in the *World Ethnographic Survey* are cross-tabulated by type (or level) of subsistence techniques and type of descent system.[18] Table 23.1 shows the percentages of bilateral, matrilineal, patrilineal, and duolineal cultures that occur on each level of subsistence technology.

Hunters and Gatherers

If hunting and gathering are taken as the most primitive food-getting techniques, such as were characteristic of the cultures of the Paleolithic era, we see that a majority (60 percent) of such societies are bilateral and that there is no significant difference between the number that are patrilineal and the number that are matrilineal (19 and 13 percent, respectively). Altogether 39 percent of contemporary hunting and gathering cultures are unilineal or duolineal. Thus, it is not possible to say whether any specific prehistoric culture was organized bilaterally or unilineally.

[15]G. P. Murdock, "Double Descent" (*American Anthropologist*, vol. 42, 1940), pp. 555–561. See also J. Goody, "The Classification of Double Descent Systems" (*Current Anthropology*, vol. 2, 1961), pp. 3–26.

[16]E. Bourguignon and L. Greenbaum, *Diversity and Homogeneity*, table 29, p. 51.

[17]G. P. Murdock, *Social Structure*, p. 186.

[18]D. F. Aberle, "Matrilineal Descent in Cross-cultural Perspective," in D. M. Schneider and K. Gough (eds.), *Matrilineal Kinship*, table 17–4, p. 677.

TABLE 23.1
Percent of Occurrence of Types of Descent Groups in a Sample of 564 Societies, Classified by Dominant Type of Subsistence Base

Type of subsistence base	Bilateral N = 204	Patrilineal N = 248	Matrilineal N = 84	Duolineal N = 28	Number of societies in sample
Plow agriculture	(38) 32%	(69) 59%	(9) 8%	(1) 1%	117
Pastoralism	(19) 24%	(51) 65%	(5) 6%	(4) 5%	79
Horticulture	(71) 30%	(98) 42%	(52) 22%	(13) 6%	234
Intensive Foraging	(15) 45%	(11) 34%	(5) 15%	(2) 6%	33
Hunting and gathering	(61) 60%	(19) 19%	(13) 13%	(8) 8%	101

SOURCE: Data selected from D. Aberle, in D. M. Schneider and K. Gough (eds.), *Matrilineal Kinship*, table 17-4, p. 677.

Intensive Foragers

Among recent practitioners of hunting, fishing, and subsidiary gardening, there is a rise in the proportion of unilineal (including duolineal) systems to 55 percent. Patrilineality shows a marked increase. Thus, there is a slight trend toward lineages and clans.

Horticulturalists

On the level of developed agriculturalists, unilineality achieves a clear ascendancy: 64 percent of the societies in the sample are unilineal, with some difference between matrilineal and patrilineal frequencies (22 percent matrilineal, 42 percent patrilineal). Matrilineal descent as a principle of social organization reaches its highest frequency among horticulturalists, but even so, it is less common than either bilateralism or patrilineality. Gardening obviously encourages the formation of uxorilocal residence, for although women rarely hunt, they are the root and seed gatherers and, quite often, the gardeners. Mothers and daughters work together, and men come to live with their wives. Only in such situations are matrilineal and matrilateral socioeconomic interests sufficiently strong to coalesce into matrilineages and matriclans.[19]

Pastoralists

The intimate relationship between males and livestock is dramatically reflected in the overwhelming patrilineality of pastoralism. Almost two-thirds (65 percent) of all pastoral societies are patrilineal.[20] The cow "is the enemy of matriliny, and the friend of patriliny."[21] Pastoralism is characteristic of a relatively minor proportion (14 percent) of the societies covered in the *World Ethnographic Sample.*

Plow Agriculturalists

The hitching of the horse or oxen to the plow was the final step in the prehistoric evolution of subsistence techniques. It occurred in the Old World Late Neolithic Age. Plow agriculture subordinates the pastoralist's interest in animals to the horticulturalist's concern with farming. This is reflected in a reduction of the frequency of patrilineality: from 65 percent among pastoral societies down to 59 percent among plow agriculturalists. There is a rise in bilaterality (24 to 32 percent) as well as some increase in matrilineality and a decrease in duolineal organization.

In Western civilization, the shift to bilaterality is a reflection of the influence of urbanization and the invention of the legal instrument of contract, whereby a person is able to stand as a self-determining, individual legal entity rather than as a unit in the corporate kinship group (see pages 431–432 for further development of this point).

As Figure 23.6 graphically reveals, most hunters and gatherers are bilateral, and as one "moves up" the evolutionary scale to developed agriculture, bilaterality declines. The patrilineal curve is the obverse to the bilateral. Matrilineality realizes its highest potential among horticulturalists, but at no level does it ever exceed other forms of descent groups. On the most complex level of food production (plow agriculture), it is reduced to 8 percent.

Looking to the future, as the scientific, industrialized technology of Western civilization is introduced all around the world, it is improbable that any unilineal systems of kinship organization will survive into the twenty-first century, except perhaps in a few remote areas (see Chapter 36).

SUMMARY

The boundaries of kinship are never limited to the conjugal-natal family, for such a family is invariably embedded in a larger web of kinship.

---

[19]Aberle, op. cit., p. 659.

[20]This figure, as given in Figure 23.1 does not include Aberle's category of "New World pastoralists," which consists of societies that acquired domesticated livestock in post-Columbian times. There are 13 such tribes in the total sample of 565. Of the thirteen tribes, eleven (85 percent) are bilateral, and two (15 percent) are matrilineal.

[21]Aberle, op. cit., p. 680.

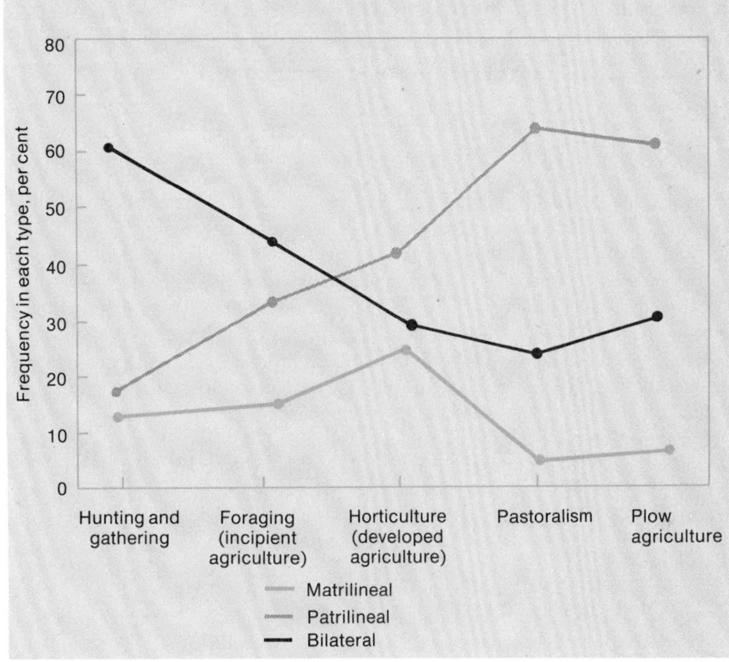

FIGURE 23.6
Inferred trends in the occurrence of types of descent groups as revealed by the percentage of frequencies of descent groups in societies classified according to subsistence. Pastoralism is not to be read as a higher evolutionary form than horticulture.

The major forms of kinship organization are bilateral, ambilineal (nonunilineal), unilineal (patrilineal or matrilineal), and double descent.

Bilateral extension of kinship produces the kindred. When extended beyond three generations, it embraces so many persons that it becomes unwieldy in size. But even more difficult is the fact that each person must belong to a number of such extended groups and is faced with the problem of conflicting loyalties.

A compromise form of the extended kinship group which partially overcomes these shortcomings is the ramage. The ramage allows choice in identifying membership through either one's paternal or maternal descent from a ramage ancestor. Ramages are usually landholding groups in which membership is necessary to have access to gardening land. Combining the possibility of two unilineal lines of descent within one structure makes the ramage ambilineal.

The majority of societies have found it expedient to utilize the unilineal principle for extended kinship reckoning. The unilineal principle has certain inherent advantages. It automatically reduces the number of potential members of the group by including only one-half of a person's relatives. Above all, it clearly establishes kinship identity and lessens the problem of conflicting loyalties.

Types of groups formed on the unilineal principle are the lineage, the clan, the moiety, and the phratry. Whether the matrilineal or patrilineal pattern prevails in a given culture is strongly influenced by residence customs. Residence, in turn, is strongly influenced by the type of dominant subsistence base in a culture. Although among simple hunters and gatherers the bilateral principle of organization is dominant, unilineal groups are found in one-third of human societies on this level. Bilaterality progressively gives way to lineage and clan organization as culture manifests foraging and intensive gardening. Its lowest frequency is found among the strongly patrilineal pastoralists. Patrilineality is relatively weak among hunters and gatherers; it becomes relatively stronger as cultures develop a horticultural base; it overwhelms all other forms among pastoralists; and it remains the dominant form among the practitioners of plow agriculture. Matrilineality exists as a relatively minor form of kinship organization in all types of cultural development.

SELECTED READINGS

Bohannan, P., and J. Middleton (eds.), *Kinship and Social Organization* (1968). Parts II, III, and IV contain basic articles on unilineal, nonunilineal, and bilateral systems.

Fortes, M., "Structure of Unilineal Descent Groups" (*American Anthropologist*, vol. 55, 1953), pp. 17–44. An excellent exposition of the application of the unilineal principle.

Fox, R., *Kinship and Marriage* (1967). Perhaps too advanced for the beginning student, but chapters 3, 4, and 5 will add much content to what has been outlined in the present book.

Goodenough, W. H., *Description and Comparison in Cultural Anthropology* (1970). Chapter 2, "Kindred and Clan," provides a clear discussion of some current problems and thoughts in kinship analysis.

Murdock, G. P., *Social Structure* (1949). Chapters 3 and 4, "Consanguineal Kin Groups" and "The Clan," are basic discussions.

Radcliffe-Brown, A. R., and M. Fortes (eds.), *African Systems of Kinship and Marriage* (1950). Descriptive analyses of a number of African examples of types of kinship organization.

Schneider, D. M., and K. Gough (eds.), *Matrilineal Kinship* (1961). An impressive work in which six anthropologists pool their efforts in an examination of a series of matrilineal societies.

24
Kinship Systems and Terms

CHAPTER OUTLINE

LEARNING GOALS

Explain the classificatory principle.

List the principles of kinship identification.

Discuss kinship systems based on classification of parental generation.

Discuss kinship systems based on classification of cousins.

List the different types of kin systems based on cousin classification.

Describe the Anglo-American kinship system.

Kinship behavior is not instinctive. The genetic code says little or nothing about how a person should behave toward any relatives.

Kinship, we have seen, is a matter of social organization, and social organization is an aspect of culture, reflecting ecology, subsistence, ideology, and a host of other things.

Kinship relations derive from the rules of behavior customarily ascribed by a people to different statuses. Every culture includes a set of words, or labels, symbolizing each of its kinship statuses. These labels are called *kinship terms*, and the whole is called the system of *kinship terminology*.

The terms used by people to classify those who are genealogically related have long been of primary interest to the anthropologist. Although there are many languages and societies in the world, systems of kinship and terminology can be reduced to a relatively few types. The student and the outsider, alike, wonder why anthropologists find this phenomenon so interesting.

The fact is that anthropologists have studied mostly isolated people with simple forms of technology, who live and interact intensively with persons who are closely related. In order to understand their behavior, the field worker has been forced to collect information on kinship and later to classify and explain it (Figure 24.1).

THE CLASSIFICATORY PRINCIPLE

The first important principle to grasp in the study of kinship systems is that *no system provides a separate and distinct term for every possible kind of genealogical relationship*. All systems equate, lump, or merge some relatives of different genealogical positions into one category, which is identified by a specific term. For example, the Comanche Indians merge father, father's brother, and mother's sister's husband all under one term, *ap'*.

Kinship terms that result from merging are called *classificatory terms*. The effect of classifi-

FIGURE 24.1
A pair of totemic house posts reflect the bilateral kinship system of the Kwakiutl Indians of British Columbia, Canada. The bear figure, with large canine teeth and long claws, represents the house owner's maternal ramage. The human figure between the bear's paws memorializes the time when a maternal ancestral chief "crushed" a rival. The top figures in the two poles are eagles, representing the paternal ramage to which the owner belongs. (Edward Curtis/Bayard Gallery.)

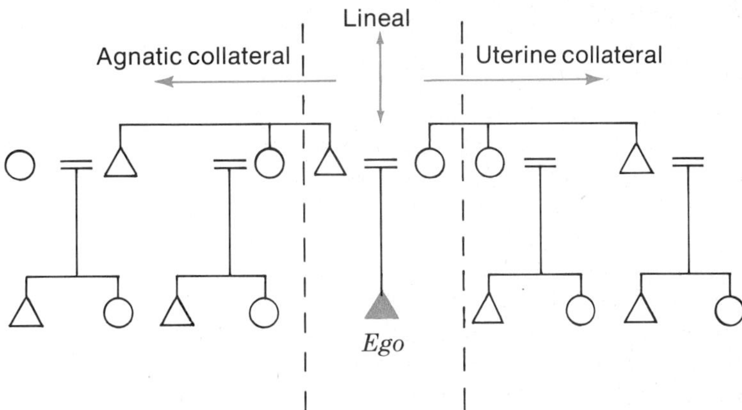

FIGURE 24.2
The distinction of collateral and lineal relatives.

catory terminology is to merge lineal relatives (as one's father) with collateral relatives (as one's father's brother). If some of one's collateral relatives are called by the same term as one's lineal relatives, we are dealing with a classificatory kinship system.

A kinship term that applies to a particular genealogical status and no other is called *particularizing* or *descriptive*. Anglo-Americans, for instance, tend to apply the kin terms "father" and "mother" only to actual progenitors. Our insistence on particularizing "father" and "mother" is sociologically significant. In addition, we use the words "son" and "daughter" to mean only our own children and not those of our brothers and sisters. Likewise, we use the terms "brother" and "sister" to refer exclusively to the siblings of our own primary conjugal-natal family. Other relatives of our own generation we call "cousins."

Our terminology thus places strong emphasis upon the exclusiveness of our primary conjugal-natal family; it rigidly distinguishes its members from more remote relatives. This reflects the great social significance of our close relatives in the conjugal-natal family as against the rest of our larger kindred. Lineal relatives are more important to us than collateral ones (see Figure 24.2).

Since kinship terms designate social statuses, what you must call a person ideally determines how you should behave toward that person. Further, all persons who are called by the same kinship term should, ideally, receive the same treatment.

Comanche Kinship Terminology

It will help to get the feel of kinship if we briefly explore how relatives are grouped and identified in a few systems other than our own.

Comanche social structure is bilateral and ambilocal. Polygynous marriages were permissible until forbidden by the federal law of the United States. The Comanche kindred is exogamous; no one may marry a relative within a specified relationship.

In analyzing any system of kinship terminology, it is necessary to have a reference point in a particular individual. This person is called *ego* (L. *ego*, "I"). In this example, we start with ego as a male, for it makes a difference whether a man or woman is speaking (Figure 24.3).

A Comanche male calls his mother *pia*. But there are also other female relatives called *pia*, namely, his mother's sisters, his mother's female cousins, and his father's brother's wife. *Pia* can thus be seen to mean not "mother" to a Comanche, but more exactly, "female relative of my mother's generation and of mother's and father's kindred."

His father he calls *ap'*. But there are also other male relatives called *ap'*, namely, his father's

ap' paha pia ap' ap' pia ap' pia ara pia

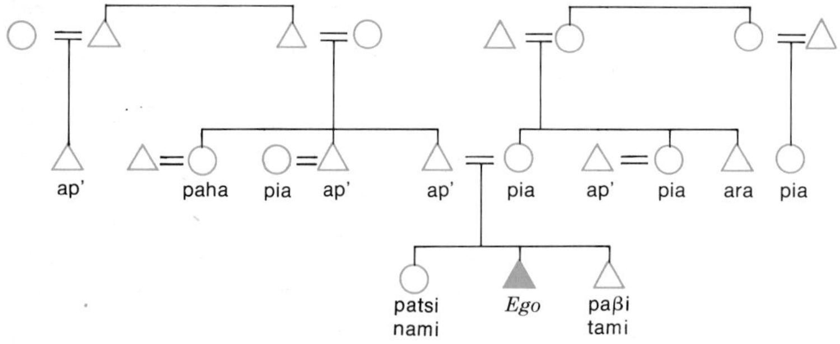

patsi nami Ego paβi tami

FIGURE 24.3
Comanche kinship terminology.

brothers, his father's male cousins, and his mother's sister's husband. *Ap'* thus does not mean "father" to a Comanche, but "male relative of my father's generation and of father's and mother's kindred."

The Comanche calls his mother's brother by a different term, *ara*. Thus, where we merge father's brother and mother's brother together as "uncle," the Comanche merges father and father's brother in one category, while distinguishing mother's brother in another.

The same thing is done with aunts. Mother's sister is classified with mother as *pia*, but father's sister is distinguished as *paha*. This practice is called *forked merging* or *bifurcate merging*.

Father's brother merged with father — Mother's brother kept distinct

Ego (speaker)

Members of the agnatic (father's) and uterine (mother's) kindreds are thus kept distinct.

Within his own generation, all relatives are "brother" and "sister" to a Comanche; cousins are not identified as such. But relative age is, so the Comanche distinguishes between *paβi* and *tami*, "older male relative of my own generation" and "younger male relative of my own generation." A *paβi* may be ego's elder brother, father's brother's son, father's sister's son, mother's brother's son, mother's sister's son, and wife's sister's husband (if ego is a male) or husband's sister's husband (if ego is a female). *Tami* applies to all these categories if the person referred to is younger than ego.

A "son" to ego includes not only his own boys but also the male offspring of all his *paβi* and *tami*, the sons of his wife's sisters, and his sister's daughter's husband. All these are called *tua*.

A "daughter" includes his own female offspring and the female offspring of his *patsi* (elder female relatives of his own generation) and *nami* (younger female relatives of his own generation), his wife's sister's daughters, and his sister's son's wife. All these are called *pedi*.[1]

By way of comparison: Anglo-Americans use exclusive, descriptive terms that isolate the two conjugal-natal families, whereas the Comanches merge such individuals within the larger kindred. For them, the kindred is the socially more important group.

All in all, the Comanches recognize thirty-six different kinship categories, each of which has a different kinship term. None of them is identical to the groupings or distinctions drawn by us in our kinship system.

PRINCIPLES OF KINSHIP IDENTIFICATION

In a classic paper, Kroeber identified the following eight principles that may be utilized in shaping a kinship system.[2]

---

[1] For a full presentation of the Comanche system, see E. A. Hoebel, "Comanche and H3kandika Shoshone Relationship Systems" (*American Anthropologist*, vol. 41, 1939), pp. 440–457.

[2] A. L. Kroeber, "Classificatory Systems of Relationship" (*Journal of the Royal Anthropological Institute of Great Britain and Ireland*, vol. 39, 1909), pp. 77–84.

1. Difference in generation levels (father, son; grandparent, grandchild; etc.)
2. Difference in age levels within the same generation (elder and younger brother; father's elder brother; etc.)
3. Difference between lineal and collateral relationships (father-uncle; brother-cousin; etc.)
4. Difference in sex of relatives (brother, sister; uncle, aunt, etc.)
5. Difference in sex of the speaker (males and females may have two separate systems of terms)
6. Difference of sex of the person through whom the relationship is established (*father's* brother, *mother's* brother; *father's* father, *mother's* father; etc.)
7. Difference between genetic relatives and those connected by marriage (mother; husband's mother; etc.)
8. Difference in status or life condition of the person *through whom* the relationship is established (living or dead, single or married, etc.)

Few systems make use of all eight distinctions, but many use the first seven.

With a careful examination of the Comanche terms that we have given, the reader will be able to identify each of the first seven principles. The Anglo-American system, on the other hand, utilizes only four of the eight (1, 3, 4, 7).

TYPES OF KIN TERM SYSTEMS

It is a remarkable fact that although a very large number of differing kin term systems are theoretically possible, society after society classifies its kinfolk in essentially similar ways, so that the types of kin term systems that actually come into existence are few in number.

The classification (or typing) of kin term systems presents all the usual problems of selection of criteria found in any ordering scheme. A system of classification is merely a tool of the mind created in order to organize knowledge. With kinship, as in any classification, fewer or more types result, according to the quality and number of criteria employed. The most significant criteria used by anthropologists for general classification of systems of kinship terminologies are of two orders: (1) the degree of merging and bifurcation of lineal and collateral kin in the parental generation, and (2) the degree of merging and bifurcation of collateral kin in ego's generation.[3]

Kin Term Systems Based on Classification of Parental Generation

Use of the criterion of classification of lineal and collateral kin on the parental level produces four types of kin term systems: (1) generational, (2) lineal, (3) bifurcate merging, and (4) bifurcate collateral (see Table 24.1).

Generational Systems The emphasis in this type of system is on merging of all relatives according to sex on a given generational level. Thus, mother, mother's sister, and father's sister are all lumped under a single kinship term. The same is true of father, father's brother, and mother's brother.

Lineal Systems A lineal system emphasizes the distinction between direct ascendant and descendant relatives as separate from collaterals. Therefore, mother is distinguished from mother's sister and father's sister, who are merged, as in English "aunt." The same holds for father, who is distinguished from his collaterals, who are merged, as in English "uncle." Lineal systems are generally associated with bilateral kinship groups.

Bifurcate-merging Systems Lineage systems tend to produce bifurcate-merging systems

[3]The first of these systems was formulated by R. H. Lowie "Relationship Terms," (*Encyclopaedia Britannica*, vol. 19, 1929), pp. 84–86. The second system was formalized by G. P. Murdock, *Social Structure*, pp. 223–259.

of terminology, as will be demonstrated in the analysis of Crow terminology given below. Father's brother is merged with father, while both are distinguished from mother's brother. Put in another way, father and paternal uncle are lumped, and maternal uncle is distinguished. Likewise, mother and maternal aunt are lumped, and paternal aunt is distinguished. Members of the two descent groups are rigorously kept separate from each other.

Bifurcate-collateral Systems In this type of system, all collaterals on the parental generation level are bifurcated, or distinguished. Father, father's brother, and mother's brother all are called by separate terms, as are mother, mother's sister, and father's sister. There is no significant correlation between bifurcate-collateral terminology and any particular descent system, nor is there an adequate theory to account for the prevalence of this highly particularizing method of classification.

Relative Frequency of Terminology Systems Based on Classification of Parental Generation Approximately 44 percent of the kinship systems in the *World Ethnographic Sample* are of the bifurcate-merging type. This happens because most descent systems are unilineal and automatically place mother's and father's brothers in different descent groups. Bifurcate-merging terminology reflects this simple fact.

Generational-type systems go with bilateral descent systems and occur in 30 percent of the cases. Bilateral systems do not separate mother's and father's kin, nor does generational terminology.

Lineal kinship systems, which occur in approximately one-eighth of the cases, are strongly associated with the occurrence of bilateral descent systems.

Bifurcate-collateral types are fairly rare and do not correlate with any particular type of descent; they have not been adequately explained.

Kin Term Systems Based on Classification of Cousins

Use of the criterion of merging and particularizing of siblings, cross-cousins, and parallel-cousins produces more refined results than analysis of the parental generation terminology alone.

TABLE 24.1
Types of Kin Term Systems according to Classification of Relatives in the Parental and in Ego's Own Generations

Type of descent group	Classification of parental generation		Classification of ego's own generation	
	Type	Merging and bifurcation	Type	Merging and bifurcation
Bilateral	Generational	[M = MZ = FZ] [F = FB = MB]	Hawaiian	[×Cos = ||Cos = Sib]
Bilateral	Lineal	M ≠ [MZ = FZ] F ≠ [FB = MB]	Eskimo	[×Cos = ||Cos] ≠ Sib
Matrilineal or patrilineal	Bifurcate merging	[M = MZ] ≠ FZ [F = FB] ≠ MB	Crow, Iroquois, Omaha	×Cos ≠ [||Cos = Sib]
No correlation	Bifurcate collateral	M ≠ MZ ≠ FZ F ≠ FB ≠ MB	Sudanese	×Cos ≠ ||Cos ≠ Sib

NOTE: The Hawaiian generational type merges all parents and all cousins; the Eskimo lineal type distinguishes parents and siblings from their collaterals; the three bifurcate-merging systems merge parents with collaterals of like sex and merge parallel-cousins with siblings, while distinguishing cross-cousins; the Sudanese bifurcate-collateral type distinguishes all parental kin and cousins.
KEY: [=] = merged categories; ≠ = distinguished or bifurcated categories; ×Cos = cross-cousins; ||Cos = parallel-cousins; Sib = siblings.

Murdock's classification sets up six types of kin term systems with respect to distinctions or lack of distinctions made in their terminologies for cousins. They are (1) the Hawaiian, (2) the Eskimo, (3) the Iroquois, (4) the Crow, (5) the Omaha, and (6) the Sudanese. These are actually the same as the generational categories, as can be seen from Table 24.1, except that the category of bifurcate merging is refined into the Crow, Iroquois, and Omaha types.

The Hawaiian System This is the same as the generational system. Because of its emphasis on generation equivalence, the Hawaiian system draws no distinction between cousins and siblings, all of whom belong to the same kindreds.

The Eskimo System The Eskimo system draws no distinctions between cross- and parallel-cousins but does distinguish cousins from siblings. Its emphasis is on the immediate chain of conjugal-natal families. The Eskimo system is familiar to all speakers of the English language, for this is the system used in Anglo-American culture.

The Iroquois System In the Iroquois system of terminology, siblings and parallel-cousins of the same sex are usually equated under one term, whereas cross-cousins are distinguished by different terms. Iroquois terminology is almost nonexistent among bilaterally organized societies. It is weakly correlated[4] with matrilineal and duolineal descent groups and appears to be the product of a weak matrilineal, uxorilocal system of social organization.

The Crow System The Crow system is based on a social structure that contains strongly developed matrilineal lineages and/or clans (Figure 24.4).

Cross-cousins are distinguished from each other (that is, there are separate terms for father's sister's son or daughter and mother's brother's son or daughter); these are also distinguished from parallel-cousins and from siblings. But paternal cross-cousins are merged with father and father's sister, according to sex.

It is in this last lumping of father's sister's daughter with her paternal aunt that the lineage emphasis is made clearest. Hocart has shown us how earlier anthropologists were trapped into false conceptions of kinship by thinking of such classificatory terms as "father" as meaning an extension of fatherhood.[5] Thus, Lowie translated the Crow Indian term *birupxe* as "father." *Birupxe* is the term applied to ego's father, father's brother, and father's sister's son (when ego is a male). Properly understood, it means not "father," but "male of my father's matrilineal lineage or clan." For the same reason, the term used in reference to ego's father's sister means "female of my father's matrilineal lineage or clan." The term for "mother" means "woman married to a male of my own matrilineal lineage or clan." Figure 24.4 diagrams this clearly.

Because father, father's brother, father's sister's son, and father's sister's daughter's son are all lumped together under one term as members of the same matrilineage, ego's mother is called "wife" by all of them. She may marry any one of them in secondary affinal marriage. The effect of all this on cousin terminology is that patrilateral cross-cousins are called by the same term as that used for father, and matrilateral cross-cousins, as children of the woman ego calls "wife," are designated by the same term as that used for son and daughter.

The Omaha System The Omaha system is the patrilineal obverse of the Crow system. Mother and female matrilateral cross-cousin

[4]A. D. Coult and R. W. Habenstein, *Cross Tabulations of Murdock's World Ethnographic Sample*, p. 512.

[5]A. M. Hocart, "Kinship Systems" (*Anthropos*, vol. 32, 1937), pp. 345–351.

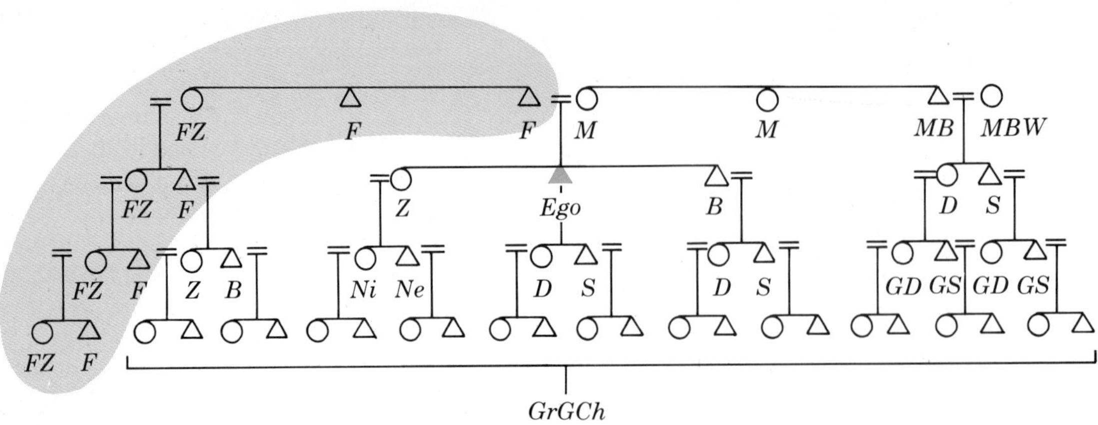

FIGURE 24.4
Crow-type identifications. Note that the male patrilateral cross-cousin may marry ego's mother and is called by the same term as father. The female patrilateral cross-cousin is merged with father's sister. Since ego may marry his maternal uncle's wife, matrilateral cross-cousins are thereby called by the same term as son and daughter.

(mother's brother's daughter) are merged under one term that means "female member of my mother's patrilineage or clan." Father's sister's daughter (patrilateral cross-cousin) is merged with sister's daughter under a term that means "daughter of a female in my father's patrilineage or clan" (see Figure 24.5).

The Sudanese System This type is at the opposite pole from the Hawaiian in that its terms are emphatically particularizing, or descriptive. Consequently, it has separate terms for each type of cousin, for siblings, and for aunts, nieces, uncles, and nephews.

THE ANGLO-AMERICAN KINSHIP SYSTEM

The Anglo-American kinship system is of the Eskimo type, as noted. It lumps all cousins, but distinguishes them from brothers and sisters. There are no lineages or clans, but a lineal emphasis occurs within the primary and secondary conjugal-natal families in that primacy is placed on parent-child relationships. These are sharply set off from the kindred by the exclusive limitation of terms like "father," "mother," "brother," "sister," "son," and "daughter" to those who actually belong to the two conjugal-natal families.[6]

Monogamy is reflected in the fact that the words "father," "mother," "husband," and "wife" can apply to only one person within the kinship system.

One thing that is distinctive about the Anglo-American kinship terminology is the abundance of alternative terms used in addition to "mother" and "father." For "father" these are "dad," "daddy," "pop," "pa," "old man," "boss," "pater," and "governor." None of these carries the respect connotations, however, of the word "father." Their use varies in accordance with the authority roles acknowledged to the father by his children within the particular family, and they reflect the flexible nature of American family patterns. The term "daddy," widely used by youngsters, is usually dropped by older boys. Father-son relations become more restrained and formal, whereas there is much evidence to

[6]T. C. Parsons, "The Kinship System of the Contemporary United States" (*American Anthropologist*, vol. 45, 1943), p. 24.

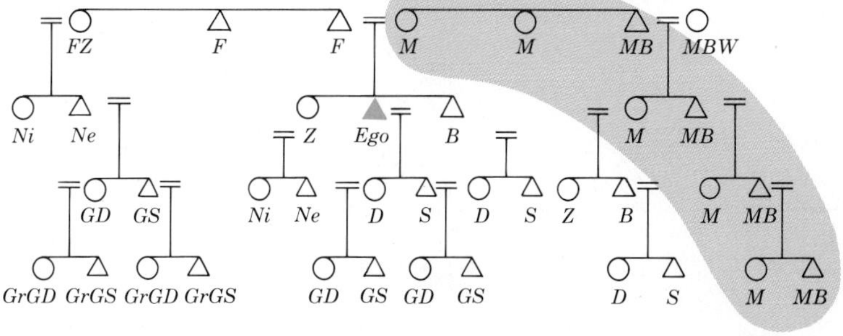

FIGURE 24.5
Omaha-type kinship identifications. The relatives within the shaded area are members of ego's mother's patrilineage. Females identified as "M" are all classified with "mother" under a term which means "female member of my mother's patrilineage." Note the differentiating terminologies on all generation levels.

support the inference that the persistence of the use of the word "daddy" by girls expresses a continuance of preadolescent affectivity between father and daughter.

A parallel series of terms exists for "mother": "mom," "mommy," "mummy," "ma," "mama," "mater," and "old woman." Very similar role qualities are ascribed to these terms as to the alternatives to "father." Both boys and girls tend to shift from use of informal mother terms to the more formal "mother" as they grow up.[7] Boys, in other words, do not keep the informal term for "mother," the way girls do for "daddy."

Affinal relatives are all distinguished by means of the "in-law" suffix. However, a device of *teknonymy*, the practice of calling an adult by the name used by the child, is often used to soften the stiffness of the "in-law" term. This is managed by identifying with the offspring and addressing spouses' parents as "grandmother" and "grandfather."

Except for a slight linguistic emphasis given to the patrilineal line through patronymy, the consequences of which are more attitudinal than structural or behavioral, the system is symmetrically multilateral. All ramifications extending out from the immediate lineal line are treated with equal weight (or lack of it). Such distinctions in emphasis as do occur are the result of personal preferences or aversions and proximity of residence.

Social Effects of the American Kinship System

The lack of structural cohesiveness outside the inner circle of lineal descent in the Anglo-American kinship system reflects the weak part kinship groups play in this society. This emphasizes the independence of separate nuclear family units. Many problems concerning marriage and the family rise directly or indirectly from this fact. Parent-child conflict is generated because children must develop independence to be able to found their own economically independent families with separate households.

Insecurity in old age is the lot of many parents whose family has been pared down until only they are left. When one of them dies, the survivor is at sea, with no comfortable harbor in which to dock. Old people's homes and old-age security legislation are palliative social consequences.

Marriage in the United States rests heavily on the bond of love and affection, for there are no preferential pairings, nor is there much family control of marriage. These are only some of the consequences of our open, weak kinship system.

The advantages of this system derive from

[7] D. M. Schneider and G. C. Homans, "Kinship Terminology and the American Kinship System" (*American Anthropologist*, vol. 57, 1955), pp. 1195–1199; also, R. M. Burling, "American Kinship Terms Once More" (*Southwestern Journal of Anthropology*, vol. 26, 1970), pp. 15–24.

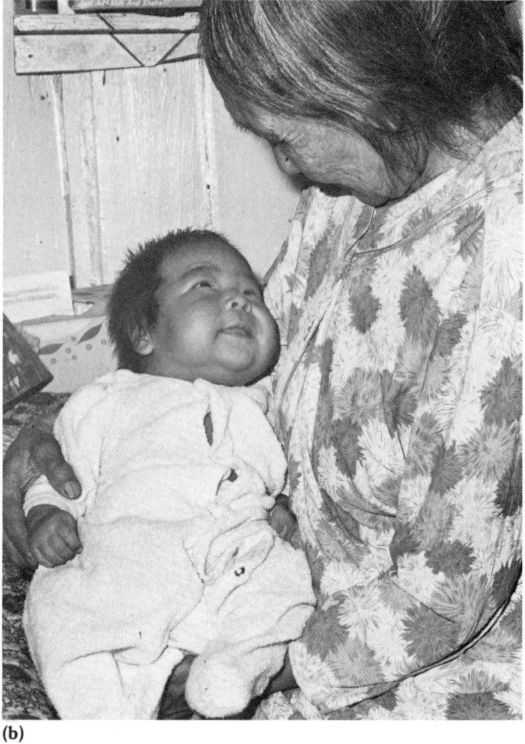

FIGURE 24.6
Kinship terminology reflects generation differences. (a) New Guinea father and son, Central Highlands near Garoka. (United Nations.) (b) Eskimo great-grandmother and great-grandchild. (Steve McCutcheon/Alaska Pictorial Service.)

individual freedom of action in social and economic relations: freedom to choose one's friends within or outside of the kinship group, freedom to choose one's mate, freedom to find an occupation fairly untrammeled by kinship status, and freedom to live where one wishes according to a self-determined life style.

In the United States today, the couple is largely on its own, to stand or fall according to its ability to surmount the hazards of the loose, and weak, kinship group, and to utilize the freedoms of a mobile and rapidly changing society. The divorce mills grind for those who fail, and many share "pads" and seek a substitute for the rejected extended family in experimental communes of peers—creating new, fictive kinship groups.

SUMMARY

Systems of kinship terminology reflect the kinship grouping in the social organization of any culture. The kinship terms of address or reference are tags or labels symbolic of each relative's status in relation to the speaker.

No kinship system distinguishes each separate genetic relationship. On the contrary, the tendency is to lump relatives into categories of the kinship status. Systems that merge lineal and collateral relatives in common categories are called *classificatory*; systems that emphasize genealogical distinctions are called *descriptive* or *particularizing*.

Kroeber's eight principles of kinship distinctions reveal the possible factors that may be used in developing kinship categories of terminological identification.

Lowie introduced a system for classifying kinship terminologies according to *merging* or *bifurcation* of the parental level of kinfolk. This results in a four-class system: *generational, lineal, bifurcate merging,* and *bifurcate collateral.*

Murdock's system classifies kinship terminologies according to merging or bifurcation of siblings and cousins. It produces a sixfold set of primary classes, which are identified with the names of the society or area in which the type was first described at length. They are the Hawaiian, Eskimo, Crow, Iroquois, Omaha, and Sudanese.

The American kinship system is bilateral, with an Eskimo, lineal type of terminology. Beyond the conjugal-natal family, there is only the kindred in weak form. Alternative kinship terms, used by Americans, reflect individual differences in degree of respect and familiarity between relatives, and in this there appear to be psychologically and socially significant differences on a sex basis.

SELECTED READINGS

Bohannan, P., and J. Middleton (eds.), *Kinship and Social Organization* (1968). Part I, pages 1–148, presents eight landmark papers in the development of kinship theory and method. These are not really for the introductory student, but they are worth knowing about.

Eggan, F., (ed.), *Social Anthropology of North American Tribes* (2d ed., 1955). Contains highly informative articles on the kinship systems of six American Indian tribes.

Graburn, N. (ed.), *Readings in Kinship and Social Structure* (1971). An excellent collection including many classic items not found in Bohannon and Middleton.

Murdock, G. P., *Social Structure* (1949), chaps. 6 and 7, "Analysis of Kinship" and "Determinants of Kinship Terminology." Requires hard thinking, but analysis of kinship systems is never easy.

Schusky, E. L., *Manual for Kinship Analysis* (2d ed., 1972). A helpful handbook for the identification and analysis of kinship systems.

25
Associations and Age Groups

CHAPTER OUTLINE

LEARNING GOALS

Describe the nature of associations.

Explain the functions of associations.

List the types of associations.

Describe tribal and nontribal secret fraternities.

Describe secular associations.

Explain age-classes or age-sets.

Investigate the relationship between associations and social dynamics.

Although kinship regulates and controls a large part of the lives of many peoples, it would be an error to assume that all areas of activity are confined to, or determined by, the kinship group, or by the class, caste, or geographical community. The urge to form voluntary associations, friendship groups, or clubs occurs in all contemporary societies. These associations and groups make life more intriguing, colorful, and meaningful, as well as carry out certain functions not handled by other segments of the social system.

Although many associations have a recreational factor, with feasting, drinking, dancing, and story telling incorporated into work or ceremonial activities, they usually also carry out activities necessary to the welfare of the society.

THE NATURE OF ASSOCIATIONS

An association is a group organized for the pursuit of one or more common interests. "Associations are usually contrasted with involuntary groupings . . . such as kin groups, castes, social classes and communities."[1]

However, membership in associations among some peoples, is not completely "voluntary." Some associations embrace all adults of a given sex in their membership; others include all males or females in a given age range; others invite only those with special characteristics, skills, or wealth. Kinship and locality may also play some part in determining these affiliations.

In general, associations, clubs, or *sodalities,* as some anthropologists call them, may be characterized as follows: They have an exclusive membership; they possess a formal institutional structure; they tend to cross kinship ties to form larger cohesive social units; and they promote congeniality and esprit de corps among members. Although many of these associations are traditionally known as "societies" (Plains Indian "military societies," Pueblo Indian "curing societies"), it may help to eliminate confusion if, in this chapter, we do not use the word "society" as a synonym for club or association, reserving it for its larger meaning. The term *fraternity* is traditional anthropological usage for a men's club in those instances where clubs promote the social fiction of brotherhood among their members. Those associations which include all the men or women of a given age range are known as *age-grades, age-classes,* or *age-sets.* Even where membership is not based on age per se, a certain amount of age grouping is found in most associations, including those in our own culture (Figure 25.1).

Functions of Associations

As an illustration of how associations enhance tribal life, Banton cites the Blackfoot Indians of the North American Plains, whose primary subsistence pattern was based on buffalo hunting. During the winters when pastures were meager and the buffalo roamed in small, dispersed herds, small bands of kinfolk were adequate for the task of hunting. Larger encampments could not be fed from such small herds. However, with the lush grasses of springtime, the buffalo gathered in enormous herds. At that time, the Blackfoot formed:

> *social and economic units that could most efficiently hunt the great herds. Most men were members of societies* [associations] *that included men of similar age. These societies organized the encampments, maintained order, and coordinated hunting operations during the summer migrations. The societies also performed dances and ceremonies. Quite apart from the explicit ends served by these associations, they brought men from different bands into relations of solidarity. Although a young man might choose which society he would join, it was hardly conceivable that he should belong to none.*[2]

[1]M. Banton, "Voluntary Associations: Anthropological Aspects" (*International Encyclopedia of the Social Sciences*, vol. 16, 1968), p. 357.

[2]Ibid., p. 358.

FIGURE 25.1
All the initiated males of an Australian tribal group form a secret society from which women are rigorously banned. The older keepers of rituals and mythological knowledge, however, form a special group within the tribal fraternity. (Bill Pedersen/Australian Information Service.)

Whereas the Blackfoot organized their associations around economic need, the Tswana of Bechuanaland utilize their highly structured associations to further the ends of political unity. Here, age is the sole basis of membership, and the groupings are called *age-regiments*. The regiments are formed every few years, and all the eligible boys and girls between about 16 and 20 years of age are initiated at the same time into separate regiments. Schapera notes:

Since every adult in the tribe must belong to one, a regiment consists of all tribesmen of the same sex and of about the same age. The initiation ceremonies they undergo simultaneously, the name given to their regiment and identifying it ever afterwards, their organization into a single body under the leadership of some member of the royal family, and the numerous activities they as a body are subsequently called upon to carry out, give them a strong feeling of group solidarity cutting across the parochial loyalties of family, ward, village, and tribal community. The regimental organization serves, therefore, as an effective means of binding together people on a tribal rather than a local basis. Next to the Chieftainship, it is perhaps the most conspicuous means of integrating the members of the tribe into a unified whole.[3]

[3]I. Schapera, *A Handbook of Tswana Law and Custom*, p. 104.

A regiment may be called on at any time to work for the chief or for the tribe. Any kind of public work may be required: building roads, making dams, searching for lost children, rounding up criminals, etc. Women's regiments may be called upon to thatch a roof, gather wood, or weed the fields for the chief's wife. The lengthy and torturous initiation ceremonies which formerly were an important function of the regiments have been replaced by simpler and more benign rites. However, the regiments still have responsibility for inculcating their members with appropriate values and suitable behavior, and it is the mates in a regiment who punish, by fines or thrashing, any member's transgressions in conduct or failure to work.

Explicitly or implicitly, many clubs and associations assume a variety of functions. "Bush schools," initiation ceremonies, and preparation for specialized leadership tasks are conducted by clubs or fraternities. These associations may also, either overtly or covertly, assume police, legal, or judicial functions. In recent years, as nonliterate societies have begun moving toward industrialization, associations have assumed increasing importance, taking on many of the roles carried in the United States by public welfare, labor unions, settlement houses, ethnic clubs, and credit unions. Opportunities for self-expression, fellowship, increased self-esteem, heightened status, and honor (frequently including elaborate ranking systems and honorific titles) often accrue from club membership, and these, too, serve a purpose—not only for the individual but also for society.

Club Life and Sex Roles

In the nonliterate world, men are the devotees of club life. The organizational woman of the modern world is one of the revolutionary developments of recent times. There was nothing like her in earlier human history.

The vast majority of all nonkinship-based social groups operate exclusively for men. Sometimes women enter into men's organizations as auxiliaries. When they do have clubs of their own, they are usually weak counterparts of the vigorous organizations of the men. There are rarely all-embracing tribal associations of women, as there are of men.

Indeed, club life among women in nonliterate societies is so underdeveloped that Schurtz, who at the turn of the century gave anthropology its classic study of men's societies and age grades, advanced the theory that females are innately unsociable. They are inhibited in the formation of clubs, wrote Schurtz, because by instinct their activities and interests concentrate on reproduction, hearth, and home.[4]

This, of course, must be dismissed as androcentric prejudice. In its stead, a cultural-functional explanation that is nearer the facts of human experience may be advanced. First, the demands of family nurture have tended to isolate women and leave them little time for club activities. American experience of the last few decades shows that given the opportunity, women readily participate in club and public life. Second, women in nonliterate societies, in addition to having little time for club activities, are, in most male-dominated societies, discouraged from entering into the club systems set up by men, and the men do not look with favor upon female imitations of their organizations. This is found to be true especially in tribes that link secret men's clubs with religious activities. Revelation of the secrets of ritual to women (and uninitiated boys) meant death in Australia and West Africa, and even among the matrilineal Pueblos of the American Southwest. A woman who accidentally witnessed the secret rites of Central Australian men's groups might possibly still be speared on the spot, as she would have been before the days of Australian governmental police and courts (Figure 25.2).

The demands of family and the discouragement of male attitudes notwithstanding, women have not been totally deprived of club affiliation. The Plains Indians often had women's clubs. Indeed, numerous societies included a few female functionaries within the men's clubs. There were craft guilds for Cheyenne women who had demonstrated special skills, such as the highly esteemed robe quillers club open to those who had quilled thirty buffalo robes with porcupine-quill embroidery.[5] Among the Crow Indians husband and wife were usually jointly initiated into the highly important and prestigious Tobacco organization.[6] The function of the Tobacco cult was the ceremonial planting of tobacco, believed necessary to the welfare of the tribe.

Similarly, in Africa, the subjugation and exclusion of women, so noticeable elsewhere, are much attenuated. Although the tribal associations may be for men, they often include women. And what is more notable, women frequently have powerful clubs of their own. In Sierra Leone and Liberia, although some men's associations admit females, no women's clubs admit men. In view of the greater social power and prestige of the men's organizations, when absolute exclusiveness breaks down, there is more

[4]H. Schurtz, *Altersklassen und Männerbünde* (*Age Classes and Men's Associations*).

[5]G. B. Grinnell, *The Cheyenne Indians*, vol. 1, pp. 159–169.

[6]R. H. Lowie, *The Crow Indians*, p. 14.

FIGURE 25.2
The privilege of seeing and learning about the *corroborees* marks membership in northern Australian men's tribal societies. A 1911 *corroboree* with painted symbolic ancestral poles is shown in the Northern Territories bush. (Australian Information Service.)

pressure from the women to penetrate the men's clubs than vice versa. An egalitarian attitude between the sexes is most evident when associations take over the functions of social service and economic aid as tribal members move into unfamiliar roles, becoming industrial workers in urban settings of developing countries.

TYPES OF ASSOCIATIONS

Everywhere club groups and associations are organized in a variety of ways. Here we can only review a few of the major types of associations found in nonliterate societies. These include secret fraternities, both tribal and nontribal in membership, secular associations, and age-classes.

Tribal Secret Fraternities

Secret associations that include all the adult men of a society are called *tribal fraternities.* The adjective "tribal" serves to distinguish them from the more limited type of associations that are open to only a privileged few. They are secret in that their meetings are not open to noninitiates and their lore and ritual may be revealed only to members.

Tribal fraternities are a direct outgrowth of adolescence transition rites. Those who successfully complete the demands imposed by the puberty rituals do not necessarily organize into an association because of this fact. But because passage through puberty gives an exalted status of maturity, all those men who have been made conscious of their newly achieved status by the rites are apt to crystalize their special status in an organized association.

Such rites emphasize the destruction of the preinitiation personality of the neophyte. As Webster long ago noted:

Almost universally initiation rites include a mimic representation of the death and resurrection of the novice. The new life to which he awakes after initiation is one utterly forgetful of the old; a new name, a new language, and new privileges are its natural accompaniments.[7]

A new name and a new language are not in fact always forthcoming, but seclusion from the women and children followed by "rebirth" is a regular feature of these initiatory rites.

The line to be drawn between puberty rites and tribal initiation ceremonies is not a sharp one. Whether we decide that a ritual falls into one class or the other depends on whether it leads merely to the status of adult or whether it brings adult status *plus* membership in a specific

[7]H. Webster, *Primitive Secret Societies*, p. 38.

association of adults. Sometimes there is an intermediary borderline condition on which it would be most arbitrary to make a classificatory judgment.

Thus, in the case of the Andaman Islanders' puberty rites, we contemplate solemn and elaborate but nonsecret rituals that effect status shifts for boys and girls. Full-fledged men are distinctly separated from fledgling boys, and they enjoy many perquisites of adult status. They seem to be bound together by the bonds of consciousness of their common privileges and interests. Yet they do not seem to form a men's fraternity.

On the other hand, in the case of the Central Australian tribes, the initiated married men form a domineering, tightly knit group, possessed of much secret lore and enjoying many special privileges, all of which indicates without doubt that here we have true tribal associations.

Aside from Central Australia and certain Melanesian areas (Figure 25.3), the great center for the development of tribal fraternities is Africa, particularly West Africa from Sierra Leone into Nigeria, Cameroon, and the jungle region of the Congo.[8]

Nontribal Secret Fraternities

Nontribal secret fraternities are secret in the same sense as the tribal ones. They differ in that their membership is more limited and selective. Not all the men or women in the tribe can belong—not even all those of a given age group.

By far the most notorious of the widespread African nontribal secret fraternities are the limited and exclusive secret orders of the Leopard, Crocodile, and Snake. Of these, the Leopards are the most feared. Human sacrifice and cannibalism give a terroristic aura to the Leopards. They strike in the dark against their victims, who are selected because they have evoked the ire of the membership or merely because sacrifices are needed for fertility rites. The Leopard men wear leopard-skin cloaks. With wooden dies they make false leopard imprints in the earth to leave the impression that real leopards have seized the victims. With clawlike knives they mutilate and lacerate the flesh of their victims.

Functions of Secret Fraternities

The functions of African secret orders are by no means wholly homicidal. Their bloody activities are only incidental to deeper-lying interests. The associations are mutual-aid organizations that have taken on important social control responsibilities in addition to their magical, religious, and purely sociable aspects.

They counterbalance the power of the tribal king and work to keep royal power in check. Unquestionably, they serve at times as the people's solution to the trying problems that result from the need to temper anarchy with monarchy, which in turn must be stopped short of despotism. Within the framework of the tribal constitution, the secret orders are often cited as assisting the king in the application of the sanctions that uphold the tribal laws.[9]

As mutual-aid protective associations, the secret orders of West Africa collect private debts from delinquent creditors on behalf of their members, and they punish other transgressions against the brotherhood. In some sections of Sierra Leone, the overextension of these practices into exploitative terrorism has caused violent public reactions, resulting in the outlawing of such clubs as the Leopard.

Experience proves that secret orders are dangerous devices for use as instruments of government and social control. With the best intentions they may serve the public weal, but since the members are not publicly accountable for their acts, there can be no safe check on the inevitable temptation to use their heady power in their own selfish interests. Exclusive secret orders are

[8]W. D. Hambly, *Source Book for African Anthropology* (Field Museum of Natural History, Anthropological Series, vol. 26, part 2, 1937), p. 498.

[9]See Webster, op. cit., p. 115–120; and R. H. Lowie, *The Origin of the State*, pp. 91–94.

(a)

FIGURE 25.3
In the New Hebrides Archipelago, as in much of Melanesia, the higher ranks within the tribal secret society of men must be purchased. (a) Two Mbotogote men ceremonially present fine taro plants to higher-grade older men from whom they are purchasing society rights and status. (b) A curved-tusk boar is led into the ceremonial plaza as a sacrificial purchase price of a higher ranking. Note the six curved tusks worn

(b)

(c)

on the breast of the old man in the center, who is a prestigious officer of the society rank which the purchasers wish to enter. (c) After prolonged singing and dancing, (d) the pig is gradually shot and killed, while the dogs wait their chance at the edible parts which will be left when the meat is butchered and distributed among the populace (1973). (Kal Muller/Woodfin Camp.)

(d)

inherently corruptible and corrupting in any society, be it the Leopard in Liberia or the Ku Klux Klan in the United States.

Secret clubs of a purely congenial, ceremonial, or magico-religious nature are generally exempt from such strictures. The various pueblos of the American Southwest each have several secret fraternities whose main functions are to perform masked *kachina* dances impersonating the gods and to carry out complex rituals according to calendric cycles. Most of the ritual and accompanying liturgy is secret among the initiated members, but public dances are also presented for the benefit of all people. Thus, the village *cacique* (sacred chief) of Sia Pueblo calls upon the Flint fraternity to perform the stick-swallowing dance on behalf of the whole pueblo. The dancers shove sticks down their throats, imitating the poking of planters' dibbles into the ground, and the dance works to ensure a good spring sowing. Among the Hopi, secret fraternities join in a dramatic rain-making dance. (See Figure 25.4.)

The functions of such fraternities in the pueblos are largely religious, magical, and ceremonial. The high-ranking leaders of the secret order form an ecclesiastical council which is even today the ultimate source of governing power in most pueblos.[10]

Secular Associations

Purely secular organizations, given to furthering nonmystic interests and not concerned with terrorizing, have no need for secrecy. The Dahomean *gbe* was (and is) organized by a group of young men, not necessarily of the same age group. They socialize together, but the basic function of their organization is to enable each member to make more impressive displays at weddings and funerals by calling upon the resources of all other members.[11] Women may belong to such clubs, or they may have separate clubs of their own. In effect, these secular nonsecret associations are exactly comparable to our own cooperative credit unions.

Plains Indian Military Associations

The military and dancing clubs of the Plains Indians were fellowships for conviviality among men, whose warlike flame was sustained and fanned by the stories, the rituals, and the songs and dances of their lodges. Their enjoyment was derived not from roistering but from the quieter glow that builds up in companionate smoking of a pipe, huddled singing about a thumping drum, parading two by two in all their finery upon their best horses, or dancing for all the tribe to see.

Although the Plains Indian men's clubs are commonly called "military societies," they were military only in the sense that the American Legion is military—their members all were, or had been, fighting men. Rarely did these clubs go to war as units. They did not form regular segments of an army, for Plains Indian fighting was too individualistic for that, but they idealized and glorified war and labored to sustain the war ideal among their members.

Their officers were "chosen to die." In battle, they planted their insignia—a crooked spear like a shepherd's crook or a trailing shoulder sash that could be pegged to the ground—in the face of the enemy. They could not retreat from that spot unless a fellow member dashed into the melee to pull up the peg or staff. Nominees for such offices were supposed to be bashful about accepting the honor. Witness what Lowie was told by a Crow Indian:

"All declined to smoke, then they came towards me . . . I was seated in the rear and tried to hide. They brought the pipe to me, but I refused to accept it. One of the pipe-carriers was my own older brother. He seized me by the hair, struck my chest, and said, 'You are brave, why don't you smoke the pipe?' He wished me to die, that is why he desired me to smoke the pipe. He said, 'You are of the right age to die, you are good-looking, and if you get killed your friends will

[10]See E. A. Hoebel, "Keresan Pueblo Law," in L. Nader (ed.), *Law in Culture and Society*, pp. 92–116.

[11]M. J. Herskovits, *Dahomey*, vol. 1, pp. 250–253.

FIGURE 25.4
Members of the Hopi Snake Fraternity gather snakes for their annual rainmaking ceremony. (Herti and Dorothy McLaughlin.)

cry. All your relatives will cut their hair, fast and mourn. Your bravery will be recognized; and your friends will feel gratified.' I took the pipe and began to smoke. They asked me whether I wished to have a straight or a hooked-staff. I chose the hooked-staff.'[12]

Age-Classes, or Age-Sets

Age-classes are associations which have as members all the men or women in a given age range. Usually, membership is determined when the individuals are at or near puberty. However, age-classes are sometimes established at younger and at older ages.

Plains Indian Age Clubs Among the Plains Indians, age-graded associations occurred only among the Mandan, Hidatsa, Arapaho, Gros Ventre, and Blackfoot. Each of these tribes had a system of associations that was graded in a prestige hierarchy from young to old. Normally, all members of a tribe, if they lived long enough, would pass through all grades. The higher grades naturally had progressively smaller membership, which, combined with the increasing age of the members, gave greater prestige.

Movement from one grade to another was by collective purchase of all the rights and paraphernalia of the club ranking just above. Among the Hidatsa, for example, all the adolescent boys banded together and, aided by their families, made a great collection of hides, arrows, parfleches, etc. After indicating to the Kit Foxes, the lowest club, that they wanted to buy, arrangements would be made for ceremonial payment and transfer of the club to the upstarts. In addition, each neophyte chose a ceremonial father, or sponsor, who had to be a member of the neophyte's father's clan, from among the members of the Kit Foxes. To this man he offered gifts and entertainment—including the temporary favors of his wife if he had one. The ethics of ceremonial wife lending were mixed, however. The gesture had to be made, but most ceremonial fathers were "afraid" to use the privilege.

[12]R. H. Lowie, *The Crow Indians*, pp. 177–178.

Thus, each candidate had to make individual payment to join an age society, but at the same time, it was absolutely necessary that his age group act collectively to acquire the rights to the club. Such clubs were therefore joint incorporeal property transferable only by sale (see pages 274–275). After an incumbent group of Hidatsa Kit Foxes sold their club to the next younger group, they were without any club organization until they succeeded in purchasing the Half-shaved Heads club from the group above them, who then had to purchase from the Dogs, who then had to purchase from the Lumpwoods. So it went up the line, until the oldest men entered the Bull club (see Figure 25.5).

African Age-Sets Age-grades, or age-sets (as they are called by British anthropologists), occur in their most highly developed form in Africa, and according to the *World Ethnographic Sample*, three-fourths of all societies containing age-classes are African.[13]

Nandi age-sets Keeping in mind what has already been said about the Tswana (see page 436), we may take the Nandi of Kenya as an additional example. There are a number of age grades of males in this tribe. The first grade is that of the uninitiated boys. For the scion of a wealthy family, initiation may occur as early as at 10 years of age, or a youth may be nearly 20 before he is put up by his family for initiation. Initiations, which occur every seven or eight years, are the highlights of tribal life and a rough time for the boys, who, as if circumcision were not enough, are beaten with stinging nettles and stung with hornets. The initiation at one time included military instruction, for, after initiation, the boys became warriors. The initiated group received name emblems and ornaments. War formerly was their chief concern; they could play at love and enjoy sex, but they were not to be fretted with the responsibilities of marriage and children. After four years of experience, they were ready to "receive the country" from the elder grades. The age-set above them, which was retiring from active warrior status, laid aside its warrior clothing, assumed the raiment of elders, and could then marry and settle down to connubial domesticity. This was not of an exclusive sort, however, since in formal custom each married man was expected to extend the hospitality of his home to any visiting classmate. Hospitality to a Nandi meant wife lending, a gratuity he would deny to all who were not members of his own age-set.[14]

Swazi age-sets To the south, the Swazi, a nation related to the better-known Zulus, reveal an age-set system remarkably similar to that just described. In the Swazi system, however, the whole organization was tightly controlled by the national king, who utilized the classes of fighting age as regiments in a standing army and as work corps in time of peace.

To this day, Swazi age-sets, although shorn of their military responsibilities, carry on important tasks. In 1963, Hilda Kuper reported:

> *When the regiments were not fighting they served as labor battalions, particularly for the aristocrats, and this remains one of their major duties. Their most intensive work depends on the agricultural routine of plowing, weeding, guarding the corn against the birds, reaping, and threshing; they may also be summoned to gather wood, cut leaves and poles for building, move huts, drive locusts off the fields, skin animals, run messages, fetch and carry. No matter how arduous a task may be, work begins and ends with . . . a dance song in the cattle pen. . . .*
>
> *The age classes are, however, still required for state ritual, and at the annual ceremony of kingship, designed to rejuvenate the king and strengthen the people, separate duties are allocated to the oldest*

[13]A. D. Coult and R. W. Habenstein, *Cross Tabulations of Murdock's Ethnographic Sample*, p. 27.

[14]A. C. Hollis, *The Nandi.* For an excellent detailed study of three variant systems of East African age-sets, see A. H. J. Prins, *East African Age Class Systems.*

(a)

(b)

FIGURE 25.5
The Horn Society of the Piegan (Blackfoot) Indians is the highest ranking of the graded-societies of that tribe. It is unique in that husbands and wives may join together. (a) Horn Society males, followed by their wives, display their society bundles and ritual paraphernalia at the transfer of the society to new purchasers (about 1913), Alberta, Canada. (b) Woman purchasers of Horn Society membership, segregated behind buffalo horn headdresses in the sundance lodge at which the transfer takes place. (Roland Reed/Kramer Gallery.)

regiments, to the regiment of men in full vigor of manhood, and to the youths who are considered sexually pure. Ritual is part of the educative process, a symbolic affirmation of certain social values, and in traditional Swazi society where specialized formal educational institutions are nonexistent, the age classes serve as the main channels for inculcating the values of loyalty and group morality. . . . In the past, special "old people" were appointed as instructors; teaching was not a separate career and learning was a gradual and continuous process of consolidation. The warriors are expected to master the main skills associated with adult life—in the barracks they even perform tasks normally left to women—and to develop the qualities of "manhood," specifically those related to the code of sexual morality. When a girl accepts a lover, she and her friends are expected to visit his barracks in special courting dress, which is brief but elaborately decorated with beads, and to sing and dance to make the relationship public. Should she on a subsequent visit find him absent, it is the duty of his agemates to try to see that she remains faithful to their friend. They find her accommodations and provide her with food. Lovers of other regiments are considered fair game, but the man who steals a girl of his own agemate is beaten and ostracized.[15]

Nuer age-sets Age-sets in Africa serve as devices of social integration and efficiency. They harness the energies of youth to the ends of the society and give to each age group a strong awareness of its status. In even so widely dispersed and

[15]H. Kuper, *The Swazi: A South African Kingdom*, pp. 55–56. (Quoted with permission of Holt, Rinehart and Winston, Inc.)

scattered a population as the Nuer in the Nilotic Sudan, who have only the weakest of tribal structures in spite of the fact that they number over 100,000 persons, the age-set system is one order of organization that runs through all divisions of the tribal society. As Evans-Pritchard reports:

> *The age sets have no corporate activities and cannot be said to have special political functions. There are no grades of "warriors" and "elders" concerned with the administration of the country, and the sets are not regiments, for a man fights with the members of his local community, irrespective of age. In the rites of initiation there is no educative or moral training. There is no leadership in the sets.*[16]

Nyakyusa age-sets In sharp contrast to the weakly developed Nuer age-sets are those of the Nyakyusa, who live on the northwest shores of Lake Nyasa. Boys of 6 to 11 years of age herd their father's cattle, and for several years, they spend their waking hours together on the range. When they reach 12 or so, they leave off herding to take up the hoe in the gardens of their fathers; they then move into a village of older boys. They return to the parental homestead for meals, but only when accompanied by a group of their age-mates. They live as members of a tightly knit juvenile gang, but without the element of gangsterism. They have no need to express hostility to the adult world. Their culture moves them steadily and early into shouldering the responsibilities of men through the concerted activities of youth.

When the young men approach the age of 25, one by one they marry. Each brings his wife into the age-village of his peers, and what was once Boys' Town is gradually transformed into a family village of husbands and wives and their children. It is unique in that all the men of the village are of an age. Now each youth receives fields from his father, and he ceases to return to his parents' house for meals, eating instead under his own roof, his food prepared by his wife rather than his mother.

In another ten years, when all the villages of a given age level within a district have matured, the formal government of the territory is ritually handed over to them, and they rule the land while their generation of sons begins anew the process, breaking off to start the formation of their own age-villages-to-be.[17]

Incidence of Age-Sets The use of age as a basis of status identification is, as was pointed out in Chapter 17, a universal cultural phenomenon. The institutionalization of age groups into definite age-sets is, on the contrary, exceedingly rare; it occurs in only 23 out of 547 cultures included in the *World Ethnographic Sample*, or 4 percent of the sample. Sixteen of the twenty-three are located in Africa,[18] where the frequency of age-grading (which even there equals only 15 percent of the tribes) is clearly a result of diffusion, as it is among the Plains tribes of North America. But the sporadic distribution of age-grades around the world is good evidence of its independent invention in the several continental areas.

Eisenstadt's Theory Eisenstadt developed the hypothesis that age groupings arise in those societies in which the allocation of roles, facilities, and rewards is not based on kinship ties.[19] Age groups would seem to be easily developed substitutes in view of the universality of age as a biological fact. However, the data of the *World Ethnographic Sample* raise serious doubts as to the significance of the hypothesis. There are too

[16] E. E. Evans-Pritchard, "The Nuer of the Southern Sudan," in E. E. Evans-Pritchard and M. Fortes (eds.), *African Political Systems*, p. 289.

[17] M. Wilson, *Good Company: A Study of Nyakyusa Age-Villages.*

[18] Coult and Habenstein, op. cit.

[19] S. N. Eisenstadt, *From Generation to Generation*, p. 54.

FIGURE 25.6
Masked spirit figures give oracular answers to questions in the initiation ceremonies of a men's secret fraternity on the Fly River, Papua, New Guinea. (American Museum of Natural History.)

many societies that allocate roles outside the kinship system and do not develop age-grades. Age-grades are, it is true, very interesting to contemplate in themselves, but they are not of as much significance in human affairs as anthropologists once thought.

ASSOCIATIONS AND SOCIAL DYNAMICS

Unlike age-grade societies, associations have taken an increasingly important place in the modernization of rural and peasant populations. No clear-cut relation of club occurrence and distribution shows up through such cross-cultural comparision as has been done to date. Obviously, however, one would expect these associations to occur more frequently in societies with larger, rather than smaller, populations, and with more complex cultures which provide for a greater differentiation of functions and interests. Urbanization and any other tendency which works to weaken the strength of the kinship bond will concomitantly contribute to a compensatory tendency to form clubs.

It is quite clear that associations flourish in rapidly changing, nontraditional social situations. Early in the nineteenth century de Tocqueville observed, "In no country of the world has the principle of association been more successfully used or applied to a greater number of objects than in America."[20] It will be remembered that Americans of that era, many of them migrants from either Europe or rural communities, were struggling to adjust to alien urban situations, separated from their kin, bewildered by new work and social roles, and frequently helpless in time of trouble. The multiplicity of voluntary associations of which de Tocqueville spoke was an adaptive response to new cultural circumstances. Just so, in a number of new African nations, voluntary credit unions among village and urban dwellers abound, and cooperative work groups and trade unions vie for members' loyalties, while helping to organize energy and resources for mutual improvement of their lot in life.

Professor A. L. Epstein, who pioneered the study of urbanization of mineworkers in Rhodesia, has penned an eloquently phrased summary of the process:

But as the urban communities themselves took root, new problems arose for which the traditional wisdom of the Elders provided no solution, and of which they were sometimes unaware. The need for new roads in the town, the need to seek avenues of employment for African women, the need in the towns for hostels for old people, the problem of discharged mine employees—these were some of the problems facing the new urban communities. . . .

The Africans who were led to join the Welfare Societies were of a younger generation, and were better educated. They were more conscious of the problems of urban life, and of the rapidly developing pattern of relations between the races. Significantly, the discussions of the Welfare Societies were conducted, and the minutes of their meetings recorded, in English. A District Commissioner had once sneered at the Welfare Societies as debating societies where the educated native had the opportunity to get up before his fellows and air his English. The District Commissioner did not appreciate that in using English at their meetings, the Africans were learning to handle one of the most important tools of the new culture. When Africans conversed together in English, they showed that they had interests in common which cut across tribal divisions. Furthermore, in the handling of novel concepts they were broadening their intellectual horizons, and making possible closer contact and acquaintance with the world outside. But more than this, in their professions of schoolteacher, of Christian minister of religion, and of clerk, they were actively engaged in pushing forward into a new form of society where clan affiliation or attachment to village headman and chief were no longer mechanisms of primary significance in ordering social relations. Through such organizations as the Welfare Societies, these people were beginning to stake out their claim to full membership in the new industrial society that was growing up around the mines.[21]

SUMMARY

Although kinship is the basis of social organization in all societies, groups whose membership cuts across kinship lines occur in numerous societies. These are *associations*, which are specifically organized to pursue special interests. Such associations are also called *clubs*, or *sodalities*, and *fraternities*. If such associations include all the men or women of a given age range, they are known as *age-grades, age-classes,* or *age-sets.*

Cross-culturally, the propensity to form and maintain clubs is predominantly a male activity. Many societies do contain women's clubs, sometimes organized around crafts or special skills, sometimes serving as auxiliaries to men's groups, often, but not always, established as age groupings. Both the Plains Indians and certain African societies provide for membership for both sexes in some associations. As associations assume mutual-help functions in the modern world, the participation of women on an equal basis increases.

Tribal secret fraternities include all men who,

[20]A. de Tocqueville, *Democracy in America* (1945), vol. 1, p. 198.

[21]Epstein, *Politics in the Urban African Community*, p. 84.

by virtue of passing through the tribally required puberty rites, achieve manhood; membership follows in the secret fraternity from whose esoteric knowledge and rituals women and uninitiated boys are barred—usually on pain of death. The possession of secret knowledge is used to keep women subordinate, while the acquisition of it in the initiation schools enculturates the youths to the tribal system.

Nontribal secret fraternities serve the vested interests of a more exclusive segment of the male population. Such fraternities may be largely secular and social, they may be primarily religious, or they may serve as units of military organization. In any event, they show a notable tendency to be involved in politics and government, often in terroristic ways, since they are not subject to open, public criticism and control.

Some Plains Indian societies are age-graded, as are a number of African systems. A group of boys enters the lowest grade as a body, progressing together to successively higher collective status as they move through life. Variations in the pattern are seen in the examples of Nandi, Swazi, Nuer, and Nyakyusa.

Voluntary associations provide a means of social organization which may complement, or even displace, the fundamental kinship groups. They tend to be associated with increasing heterogeneity and size of population—along with an increasing complexity of culture—which engenders greater division of labor and diversity of interests.

SELECTED READINGS

Anderson, R. T., "Voluntary Associations in History" (*American Anthropologist*, vol. 73, 1971), pp. 209–222. A review of the development and purpose of associations in modern society.

Banton, M., "Voluntary Associations: Anthropological Aspects" (*International Encyclopedia of the Social Sciences*, vol. 16, 1968), pp. 357–362. A helpful, brief summary of the subject.

Bradfield, R. M., *A Natural History of Associations: A Study in the Meaning of Community* (1973). This two-volume work carefully documents the function, content, meaning, and development of associations as a kind of social organization contrasted to kin-based organization. Detailed ethnographic analyses of several African, Melanesian, and North American Indian tribes illustrate the presentation.

Eisenstadt, S. N., *From Generation to Generation* (1956). Particularly interesting in its comparative analysis of youth movements in Germany and Israel in relation to age-grading.

Little, K. L., *West African Urbanization: A Study of Voluntary Associations in Social Change* (1965). An intensive study of associations in the shift from tribal to city life in new African nations.

Llewellyn, K. N., and E. A. Hoebel, *The Cheyenne Way: Conflict and Case Law in Primitive Jurisprudence* (1941), chap. 5, "The Military Societies." A case study of Cheyenne Indian men's clubs in operation.

Wilson, M., *Good Company: A Study of Nyakyusa Age-Villages* (1951). A truly fascinating account of a unique development of the age-grading principle.

PART SEVEN

Economics, Politics, and the Organization of Inequality

26
Economic Organization

CHAPTER OUTLINE

LEARNING GOALS

Explain primary and secondary consumption.

Describe the three modes of exchange.

Discuss reciprocity, using cross-cultural examples.

Describe redistributive exchange in complex states and tribal societies.

Understand trade and market exchange.

Summarize the different types of inheritance.

Economic organization involves the behaviors that center upon the production, the allocation and distribution, and the use and consumption of goods. Economic institutions include behavioral networks of food production and the manufacture of artifacts; gift exchange, trade, sale, and inheritance; utilization, hoarding, and consumption; and ownership, possession, and rights of use—everything which focuses upon production and utilization of goods and services.

Economic order, in one form or another, is a functional prerequisite to societal survival and continuity (see page 293). As such, it is a universal aspect of culture, for if there have been societies which have failed to motivate men and women to work and production, and which have failed to develop effective systems of distribution of the products of work input, such societies have failed in adaptation and no longer exist.

PRIMARY AND SECONDARY CONSUMPTION

A notable difference between simple and complex economic systems is that in the former a high proportion of food and goods is consumed by the producer and the members of the immediate family or household. The consumption is *primary* and no exchange outside the primary group is necessary. A man not only does his own hunting, his wife her own gathering, but he makes his own spear, his own bow and arrows, and they build their own house. But as soon as it becomes customary to share food with members of other primary groups, as soon as it is recognized that another man can make better arrows and specialized division of labor sets in—then a system of exchange is created. Exchange systems involve *secondary* consumption: food and goods are used by persons who are not members of the primary group of the original producer. Secondary consumption, as shall soon be demonstrated, occurs in nonliterate societies and sometimes to a high degree. However, in the complex society of urban dwellers, primary consumption is very low. Just consider what, if anything, of the food, clothing, shelter, and other goods which you are using this day, you have produced any part of!

THREE MODES OF EXCHANGE

The economist Karl Polanyi (1893–1964) brought into focus three contrasting modes of cultural access to valued goods in human societies. These are: (1) reciprocity, (2) redistribution, and (3) market exchange.[1]

Reciprocity consists of obligatory gift giving, receiving and repaying of goods and services between persons of specific statuses (see pages 297–301) within a social system. A Trobriand Islander, for example, raises yams on land which is assigned to him in his own village. All but the poorest of these he carries to another village where his married sister lives with her husband. There they are shown in ceremonial display and then carefully packed in thatched-roof storehouses made of horizontally laid logs through which the yams may be seen and continually admired until they are consumed. No man sells best-quality yams to another. Nor does he trade them to just anybody. Lesser-quality yams and melons he may trade for fish with an exchange partner, but he cannot walk up and down the beach looking for anyone with whom he may strike a good bargain. *This is not a market economy* (Figure 26.1).

From his sister's husband, a Trobriander receives return gifts, but most important, he gets his sister's sons, who leave home to live with him (a maternal uncle), well before the onset of puberty. They become the uncle's helpers, are trained and educated by him; they also become

[1] K. Polanyi, "The Economy as an Instituted Process," in K. Polanyi, C. M. Arensberg, and H. W. Pearson (eds.), *Trade and Market in the Early Empires*, pp. 243–270; for an expansion of the discussion of gift giving, see E. R. Service, *The Hunters*. Service posits end points in a continuum of reciprocity: generalized and negative reciprocity, with balanced reciprocity as a midpoint. Generalized reciprocity is altruistic, negative reciprocity is trying to get something for nothing, and balanced reciprocity is direct exchange.

FIGURE 26.1
Direct barter in Melanesia. Inland dwellers bring yams to exchange for fish with coastal dwellers. (United Nations.)

his heirs and successors to his rights of use in land, his magical formulas, his wealth and prerogatives—as well as membership in his matrilineal clan. The prime yams, which a man laboriously produces and ostentatiously gives to his sister's husband, are well repaid by services received from the latter and his sister's sons.[2]

Redistribution is exchange which occurs when a holder of economic or political office—a hereditary chief or monarch, or a priest, for instance—is vested with the power to exact goods or services as tribute. These goods or services are first funneled into the "royal" or cult centers. After the governing elite has creamed off what custom or its power enables it to use for its own consumption, a portion is redistributed to the populace. Redistribution may or may not be equitable. The basic handicraft producers are apt to get less in return than they put out. Yet, over all, the members of that society may collectively benefit from the higher levels of production which result from their combined, elite-directed efforts. Such systems are characteristic of a number of state-organized, nonliterate horticultural societies and early civilizations.

Market exchange is based on direct barter (Figure 26.2) or on sale and purchase through use of a medium of exchange such as money. Where markets exist within the economic systems of nonliterate societies, they are usually peripheral; that is, the goods available for exchange or sale through the market do not include "everything" available through the production system—especially land and labor. In other words, the bulk of exchange is reciprocal or redistributive, although markets do exist.

In societies in which *most* exchange of goods and services is effected through transfer of symbolic tokens of unitary value (money), *market exchange* dominates. In a market economy all money uses are related to "free exchange"—free of kinship requirements, fealty to overlords, personal friendship, and other status limitations. In the free market, there are but two questions: do you "own" what you have to offer? and do you have the money (or the credit) to make the purchase? The market is often impersonal. You can buy or sell to anyone. In reciprocal and redistributive exchange the relations are a matter of personal status and relationship.

---

[2]B. Malinowski, *Coral Gardens and Their Magic*, vol. 1, "The Customary Law of Harvest Gifts," pp. 188–217.

Authors' note: In 1967 when Hoebel visited the Trobriand Islands, he found the yam gardens, storage houses, and exchange system virtually unchanged from Malinowski's descriptions of 1914–1917.

Reciprocity

Within many nonliterate societies gift giving which builds into gift exchange marks every important crisis period in the life cycle or any other change of personal status. Birth, puberty, marriage, death, entrance into a club, or assumption of an office is called to public attention by the bestowal of gifts. The famous potlatches of the Northwest Coast Indians, with all their lavish expenditure of gifts, center around such occasions. Contractual arrangements such as marriage call for immediate two-way exchanges, often extending over months.

Gift exchange of economic significance may border on trade. Yet it may be merely symbolic in nature when the rule of equivalence is strong. The person who views our ceremonial gift exchanges on the occasion of the Christmas festival only in terms of the usableness of the gifts measured against cost and effort naturally thinks the whole business is silly. But such a person misses the point. Quite true, we all end up with a number of things we neither need nor want. Quite true, it would be more rational to offer gift certificates or even money to one's friends or family so that they could buy what they want and need. But how much less meaningful would be such gifts! Their donors confuse the social function of gift giving with utility. They forget that the gifts are symbolic of a social bond between giver and receiver. Gifts represent a state of social relations and a set of emotions, not just a business transaction.

FIGURE 26.2
A Bushman brings in bundles of redwood to trade with the Ovambos Negroes. (South African Information Service.)

Pig Exchange in Melanesia The elaborate extremes to which Melanesian "Big Men" go to operate exchange networks of pig growing and pig giving indicate clearly that there is more involved than just the utilitarian production and distribution of pork (Figure 28.2). Mead's account of the Arapesh of New Guinea will help give some feel for the meaning of pig exchange in Melanesia:

[*A*] *chain organization* [*is*] *grouped around a leader who is called the* trunk *or* base *of the enterprise. . . . In addition to organizing specific feasts centering about initiation, the exhumation of the bones of the dead, or the importation of some ceremonial dance complex from the Beach, the "big men" stand in a continuous exchange relationship with exchange partners, theoretically members of the opposite moiety, and always members of a different clan. These exchange partners call each other* buanyin, *are hereditary, usually in the male line, but not necessarily in the direct line. Old buanyin partnerships which have been unsatisfactory, that is, unequally matched, may be abandoned and new ones founded at any time. . . . The buanyin relationship is modeled upon the relationship of brothers-in-law and the relationship which continues from it in the next generation, the cross-cousin relationship. Buanyins are conceived as members of autonomous groups, and engage in exchanges one with the other. But whereas between relatives and between trade friends, cost accounting, dunning, reproaching in economic terms are regarded as disgraceful, between buanyins there is a frank accounting system. Each one is expected to initiate exchanges with the other, and they are expected to insult one another publicly and to goad one another on to economic activity. The major exchanges between buanyins are of meat, and an exchange is initiated usually by the present to one of the buanyins of big game—wild pig or cassowary—or a domestic pig which has been trussed to a pole ready to be killed. If the man who now has become the temporary owner of the meat does not wish to use it, he gives it to his buanyin. He cannot refuse it, and will owe a return of the same amount to his buanyin in the future. If he has no pig or game with which to repay, he will have to rear domestic pigs in order to return the gift. Giving meat to a buanyin is therefore a way of banking. When a man receives this large present of meat from his buanyin, he in turn distributes it to his relatives, who are thus obligated to help him make returns to his buanyin when necessary. Buanyins give each other feasts, at which neither buanyin eats, but each distributes food to his helping friends and relatives. . . . When the time for the final feast is set, each dog [cooperating pig partner] gives back a whole pig, representing the three-quarters of a pig which he has received, plus other food. The trunk thus has all his negotiable wealth in his hands at once, and exchanges it either for dance ceremonial or for other pigs, or arranges for a return feast in another community which has similarly been organized around a trunk.*[3]

Distribution of Marriage Cattle among the Nuer The joining of families by marriage affords a major means of reciprocal distribution. Since in much of Africa the cow is the principal unit of value—indeed, it has been written that the transfer of cows "has had the function of making concrete certain already existent social relationships"[4]—it is not surprising that weddings involve complicated transactions in cattle.

To illustrate the complex and highly ritualized socioeconomic aspects of progeny price, we may turn to the Nuer, a tribe of cattle raisers living on the upper reaches of the White Nile. Here, each marriage ideally calls for the transfer of forty head of cattle from the groom's to the bride's family. Of these, twenty go to members of the bride's primary joint family, ten to her father's primary joint family, and ten to that of her mother. The distribution is as follows (see Figure 26.3):

1. *Primary family of the bride:* To the bride's father (*a*), eight head, specified as three cows with their calves and two oxen; to her brother born of another mother (*b*), two cows; to her brother born of the same mother (*c*), two oxen, three cows, and a cow with its calf (seven head); to her mother (*d*), a cow with its calf and a heifer.
2. *Siblings of the bride's father:* To the bride's father's elder brother by the same mother (*e*), a cow with its calf, another calf, and an ox (four head); to the bride's father's younger brother by the same mother (*f*), a cow and an ox; to the bride's father's sister (*g*), one heifer; to the bride's father's brother by a different mother (*h*), a cow with its calf and an ox.
3. *Siblings of the bride's mother:* To the bride's mother's elder brother by the same mother (*i*), a cow with its calf, another cow, and an ox; to the bride's mother's younger brother by the same mother (*j*), a cow with its calf; to the bride's mother's sister (*k*), one heifer; to a brother of the bride's mother through a different mother (*l*), a cow with its calf and an ox.[5]

In addition to these specific rights to cattle, every patrilineal relative of the bride, even though the relationship be so remote as that of descent from a common ancestor six or seven generations back, may claim a small gift from the

[3]M. Mead (ed.), *Cooperation and Competition among Primitive Peoples*, pp. 32–34. (By permission of McGraw-Hill Book Company.)

[4]P. Gravel, "The Transfer of Cows in Gisaka (Rwanda): A Mechanism for Recording Social Relationships" (*American Anthropologist*, vol. 69, 1967), p. 322.

[5]These figures represent the ideal norm among the Eastern Nuer as reported by E. E. Evans-Pritchard, "Nuer Bridewealth" (*Africa*, vol. 16, 1946), p. 4. In the real situation, they vary by circumstance and district within the tribe. See P. P. Howell, *A Manual of Nuer Law*, pp. 101–124.

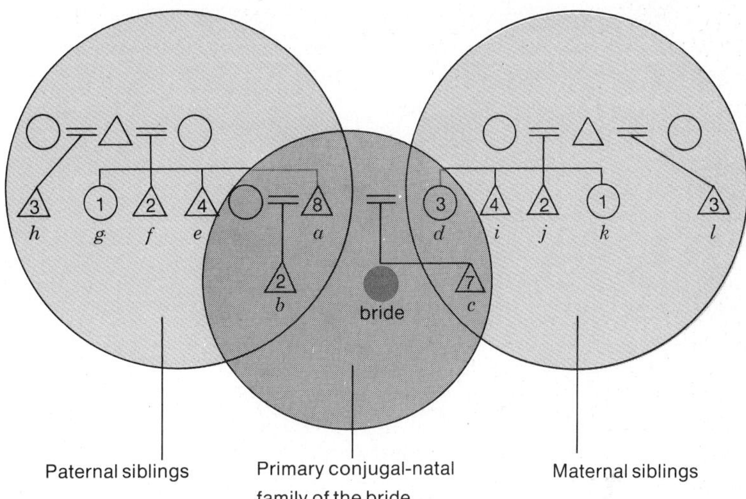

FIGURE 26.3
Identification of relatives in Nuer progeny price distribution with number of livestock received by each relative.

groom's kinfolk. Special symbolic gifts of cattle may be called for in the name of ancestral spirits of the bride, of her "father's best friend, of an age classmate of her father, of her father's fireplace, and to the priest who performs magic rituals for enhancement of the bride's fecundity."

All this should make it very clear how much more than just a commercial transaction is the transfer of progeny price.

The Kula Without doubt, the most elaborate and exciting system of reciprocal exchange yet noted for the nonliterate world is the *kula* of northwestern Melanesia. Malinowski's thorough description of the *kula* will continue to stand as a classic of anthropological economics for many years to come. The *kula* enterprise is a vast complex of trade, magic, ceremonial exchange, overseas travel, and pleasure seeking that involves the enterprisers of tribes many miles apart. The framework through which the whole organization is expressed is the exchange of white shell armbands, called *mwali*, and long necklaces of red shell, called *soulava*. Exchange is intertribal and interisland. *Soulava* are always traded in a clockwise direction. *Mwali* go counterclockwise (Figure 26.4). There is no exception to this rule.

Each of these articles . . . meets on its way articles of the other class, and is constantly being exchanged for them. Every movement of the Kula articles, every detail of the transactions is fixed and regulated by a set of traditional rules and conventions, and some acts of the Kula are accompanied by an elaborate magical ritual and public ceremonies.

On every island and in every village, a more or less limited number of men take part in the Kula—that is to say, receive the goods, hold them for a short time, and then pass them on. . . . Thus no man ever keeps any of the articles for any length of time. . . . One transaction does not finish the Kula relationship, the rule being "once in the Kula, always in the Kula," and a partnership between two men is a permanent and lifelong affair. . . .

The ceremonial exchange of the two articles is the main, the fundamental aspect of the Kula. But associated with it, and done under its cover, we find a great number of secondary activities and features. Thus, side by side with the ritual exchange of armshells and necklaces, the natives carry on ordinary trade, bartering from one island to another a great number of utilities, often unprocurable in the district to which they are imported, and indispensable there.[6]

This free barter for various goods includes coconuts, sago, vegetables, fish, mats, baskets, lashing materials, and mussel shells. Such activi-

[6]B. Malinowski, *Argonauts of the Western Pacific*, pp. 81–83.

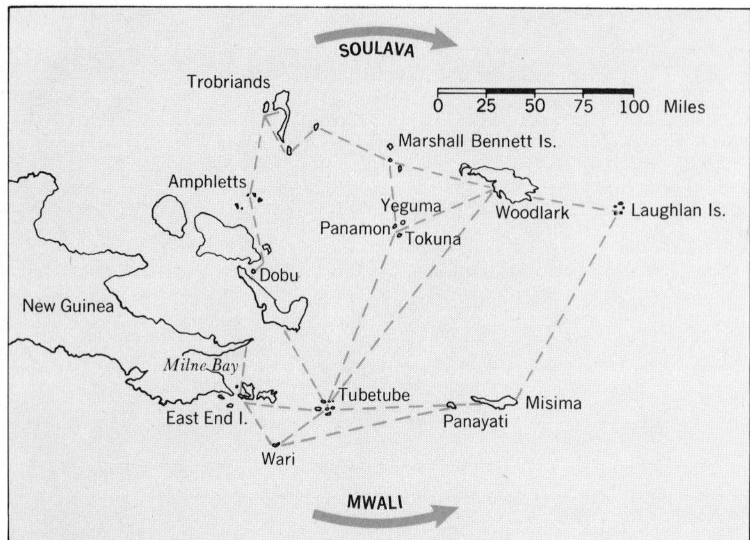

FIGURE 26.4
The *kula* ring of the southwest Pacific. Lines show overseas trade routes. Arrows indicate the directions in which necklaces (*soulava*) and armbands (*mwali*) are exchanged. (Adapted from Malinowski.)

ty, which takes on the character of market exchange, is recognized as being different in quality and function from the *kula*.

Redistributive Exchange

In redistributive exchange, "surplus" goods and labor are channeled as gifts, tribute, or corvée into the hands of a ruling or managerial class, which usually keeps some for its personal use but which also redirects a portion (often large) to "general" social goals.

Redistributive Exchange as the Foundation of Complex States We have already noted some aspects of redistributive exchange (Chapter 11). As agricultural efficiency increased so that not all working time went into food production, specialized labor developed, and assignments of both tasks and the necessities of life were directed by strong governmental leaders.

Sumerian civilization What we wrote in Chapter 11 of Sumer in its early dynastic period (3200 to 2800 B.C.) illustrates the significance of this mode of exchange.

> *Allotments of land, work assignments, and raw materials were designated by the head priest-administrator of the temple district. Each workman had to deliver a specified amount of produce; anything beyond this was his own. Some goods went to maintain the priests, and much was redistributed among the producing populace. Thus, the division of labor and the economic exchange necessary to effective civilization were achieved—in this case without an internal market system* [*page 203, above*].

Mayan civilization Far to the west, in Mesoamerica two thousand years after Sumer, the same type of redistributive exchange developed quite independently. Of the priests of the Maya civilization of 1000 B.C., Eric Wolf has written:

> *. . . [S]ociety had developed a body not only of full-time religious practitioners but also of specialists in organization, capable of exacting labor and tribute as well as worship from the mass of men. . . . As servitors of their gods they also administered the many goods made as offerings to the deities. The temple centers became veritable storehouses of the gods, where costly produce accumulated in the service of the supernatural.*[7]

[7] E. R. Wolf, *Sons of the Shaking Earth*, pp. 79, 81.

Redistributive Exchange in Nonliterate Societies: The Pueblos Lest one get the impression that redistributive exchange is characteristic only of civilizations and class-exploitative societies of more modern times, let us note that it is more pervasive.

Apart from the universal obligation to participate in ceremonial dances, every able-bodied man in the Rio Grande Pueblos of New Mexico and Arizona is required: (1) to help cultivate and harvest the field set aside for the head priest-chief, or cacique; (2) to join in the communal rabbit and deer hunts to fill the cacique's storeroom; (3) to join in the labor of cleaning and repairing the irrigation ditches; (4) to sweep the pueblo plaza in preparation for ceremonies; and (5) to help replaster the Catholic mission church once a year.

The cacique drains off very little of the economic goods for his own use. His house is as undistinguishably modest as any man's in appearance. He wears the same clothes as other men and eats no more than others. He is freed, however, from tilling the gardens, herding, and hunting. He concentrates all his efforts on "thinking good thoughts" and on ritual activity. He is freed to serve as the symbolic vessel of the pueblo's "collective soul," its full-time intercessor between his "children" and the manageable forces of the universe. In addition, he feeds ceremonial participants and redistributes meat and vegetables to widows, orphans, and the aged poor.

Trade and Market Exchange

The essential difference between trade and gift exchange is in their relative functions. In trade, the emphasis is on economic redistribution. In gift exchange, the emphasis is on social relationships. Trade rests on and fosters social interaction, but its main concern is with the distribution of goods. Gift exchange distributes goods, but its main concern is with personal relations.

Within small societies, there is little trade. Gift exchange suffices for the most part. It is primarily the complex cultures with large populations that have considerable specialization among their members. Services and products are then available for exchange and trade.

However, virtually all societies, large and small, engage in intergroup trade. Every society has its unique goods or possesses natural resources from which to supply materials not available elsewhere. Salt-water shells find their way hundreds of miles inland in New Guinea and North America. Melanesian inlanders trade vegetables for fish with the coastal dwellers.

Specialization based on custom rather than limitation of resources induces a good deal of trade. In New Mexico, Sia Indian women make excellent pottery. The pueblo of Jemez, less than ten miles away, made none for many centuries, although the same clays are available to both. Jemez exchanged corn for Sia pots in the old days. Hopis trade maize with the nearby Havasupai for buckskins and paint, and maize for wood and wool with the surrounding Navajo (Figure 26.5). But within the Hopi tribe, only the women of the pueblos on Second Mesa make coiled baskets; those who live on Third Mesa make them of wicker, and painted pottery is produced only on First Mesa.

Silent Trade It shocks many people to discover that trade is carried on between enemy nations. A high command will deliberately spare certain enemy industrial plants because, by means of trade through neutrals, it is possible to secure products of those plants. Enemies find it advantageous to let economic interests override their antagonisms.

This is the basis of the dumb barter, or silent trade. The pygmy Semang of Malaya, for example, exchange forest products for goods offered by their enemies, the Sakai. Neither group sees the other party during the transaction. The Semang set their goods in a customary place and retire. When the Sakai find the offering, they

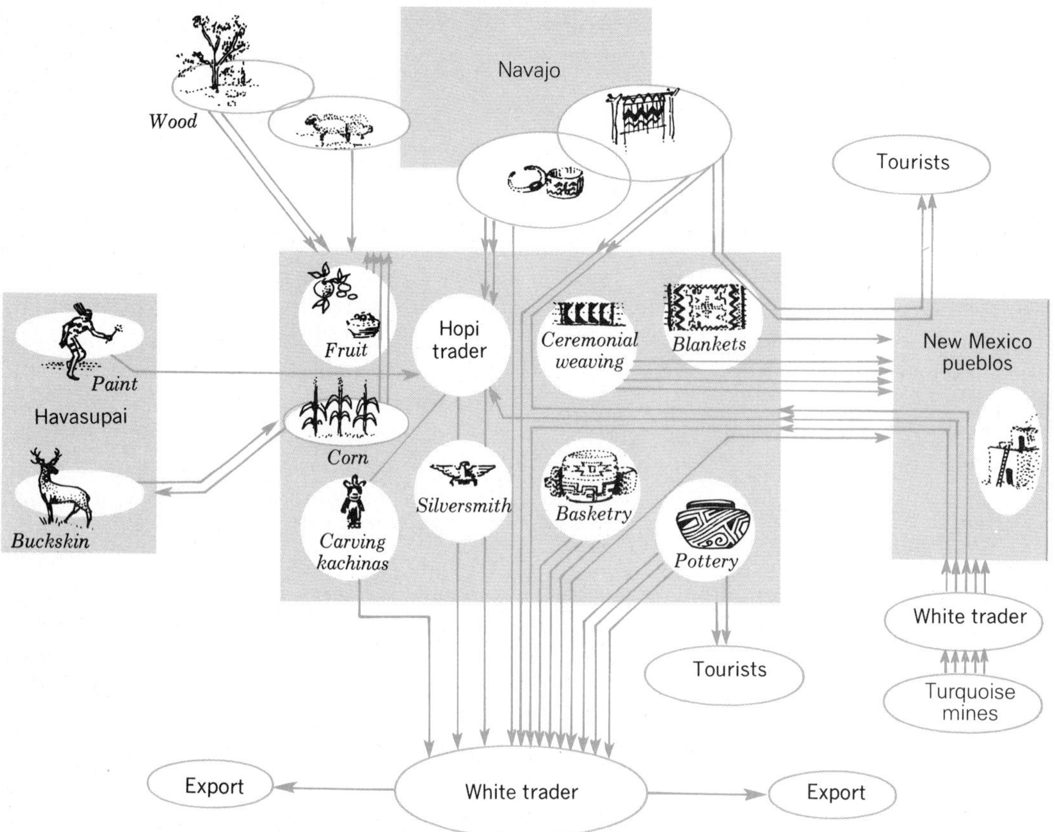

FIGURE 26.5
Hopi craftsmen trade agricultural and finished products to the Navajo and Havasupai in exchange for raw materials, paint, and blankets. From White traders and New Mexico pueblos they get raw and manufactured products. (From L. Thompson and A. Joseph, *The Hopi Way*, p. 23.)

replace it with whatever they wish to exchange. Later, the Semangs come back to pick up the goods before retiring to their jungle fastness.

Herodotus describes how Carthaginian merchants carried on silent trade with the natives of the northwest coast of Africa. The Carthaginians placed their goods on shore and retired to their ships, sending up a smoke signal. The natives replaced the goods with gold. They gave what they deemed necessary, for the natives knew that if the mariners were shortchanged they would not return.[8]

A modernized version of silent trade was practiced in the Ozark Mountain country of Arkansas into the 1930s, where "moonshine" corn whiskey could be bought as "stump liquor." As a means of avoiding revenue officers, it was the practice to leave one dollar on a known tree stump. During the night, a gallon of corn whiskey would replace it, to be picked up by the purchaser in the morning. The moonshiner did not have to expose himself to possible arrest.

[8]W. D. Hambly, *Source Book for African Anthropology* (Field Museum of Natural History, Anthropological Series, vol. 26, part 2, 1937), p. 650.

(a)

FIGURE 26.6
(a) An Indian trading post on the Navajo Reservation operates as a *market* type of exchange, but it also involves *barter* in that many Indians pawn their jewelry (seen hanging over the counter) for food and other supplies. (b) Some Navajo weavers use the direct open-market approach, displaying their blankets for sale along the highway in northern Arizona. (Joseph Muench.)

(b)

Markets Open trade is naturally much more convenient, and elaborate machinery has been developed for this purpose (Figure 26.6). In Nigeria, large market towns of great antiquity are in existence. Native artisans bring their brass-work, pottery, mats, baskets, leatherwork, and foodstuffs many miles to these trading centers. The Kede tribe of northern Nigeria act as river transporters of trade goods, for the Kede are the consummate voyagers of the Niger. They carry kola nuts and palm oil north from Nigeria, bringing back gowns, mats, fish, rice, horses, and potash from the Hausa and Nupe tribes.[9]

African markets In Africa, the marketplace is often under the magical protection of some great native chief, whose supernatural authority evokes the "peace of the market" so that enemy groups may trade in safety. Chiefs frequently

[9]S. F. Nadel, "The Kede," in E. E. Evans-Pritchard and M. Fortes (eds.), *African Political Systems*, p. 169.

provide police and courts for markets in their districts, as well.

Bohannan points out that African markets in subsistence economies are "peripheral"; that is, the markets are not essential to the economic livelihood of the societies because the number of people who actually derive their living from the markets is small. Markets are public meeting places and communication centers for dispersal of gossip, news, and official pronouncements. Entertainers use markets as fairs are used in the United States—as places where audiences are available. And markets, like fairs, are ready-made festivals. "The market day," observes Bohannan, "usually falls off into a beer drink."[10]

American Indian trade European traders found a strong trade network in existence among the Indians of the northern Plains of North America when they first arrived at the Mandan, Hidatsa, and Arikara villages on the Missouri River, in the middle of the eighteenth century. The village tribes grew surpluses of corn and squash which they traded to the nomadic tribes. They also tanned fur robes and painted hides and ornamental clothing. These they traded with the Assineboin, Cheyenne, and Crow for meat and skins. Spanish trade goods also found their way to the Middle Missouri along the intertribal trade routes from the Southwest by way of the Cheyenne, who in turn got them from the Kiowas, who got them from the Comanches and Spaniards.

When French and British traders introduced the gun and metal utensils, after 1738, and horses were acquired from the Southwest, the flow of new materials along the old trade networks drastically altered the cultures of the nomadic tribes. The great flowering of the buffalo-hunting cultures suddenly occurred. Within a hundred years, the same forces which had created them—European trade, the horse, and the gun—destroyed them in an epic tragedy.

[10]P. Bohannan, *Social Anthropology*, p. 242.

FIGURE 26.7
Shell money used for purchase of yams in market exchange at Rabaul, New Ireland, South Pacific. (United Nations.)

Primitive Money Not all trade among nonliterate peoples is by means of direct barter. Various media of exchange are known in several parts of the world. Shells serve most commonly as a kind of money: cowrie shells in the Pacific and in Africa, dentalium shells among the Indians of California (Figures 26.7, 26.8a). Wampum beads were used among the eastern Indians, and the early Dutch in New York treated wampum as good cash. Importation of poor counterfeits caused the city council of New Amsterdam in 1650 to pass an ordinance pegging the exchange value of good-quality beads at six white and three black per *stiver* (a Dutch coin). Poor wampum was pegged at eight and four, respectively.

Iron hoes have served as a medium of exchange in parts of Africa, but perhaps the strangest of all primitive moneys were the huge lime-

(a)

(b)

FIGURE 26.8
(a) "Big Men" may accumulate tremendous accretions of wealth in New Hebrides. Topoi, a Big Man whose hat also shows him to be an Australian-appointed district chief, shows off some of his treasure of many yards of shell money kept in large basket-covered rolls. (b) In Micronesia, wealth is symbolically represented by large limestone discs, called "wheel money."
(United Nations.)

stone wheels of the Island of Yap in Micronesia (Figure 26.8b).

INHERITANCE

The transfers of goods which have been discussed thus far consist of lateral exchanges between the living. The continuity of society, however, requires that there be an orderly flow of property from one generation to the next. This constitutes inheritance.

Inheritance, in the words of G. D. H. Cole, "is the entrance of living persons into the possession of dead persons' property."[11] This, however, leaves much unsaid. In a preceding chapter (see

[11]G. D. H. Cole, "Inheritance" (*Encyclopaedia of the Social Sciences*, vol. 20, 1935), p. 286.

page 262), property was identified as consisting of (1) an object (material or nonmaterial), and (2) a web of social relations that establishes and maintains a limiting and defined relationship between persons and that object. This web of relationships consists of the roles or patterns of behavior that are associated with certain statuses, which in turn allow certain persons the socially recognized right of limited control of the use or disposition of objects. Nonowners are under a duty to refrain from use of the object, or are subject to more restrictive access to its use.

Analyzed in terms of culture theory, inheritance is not transfer of possession; it is the transference of statuses, that is, the transfer of the rights to property inherent in the position or status of the previous owner. And although much inheritance involves transfer after death, many statuses may be transferred during life. Nyakyusa sons of chiefs "inherit the country," that is, they assume the chieftainship, while their fathers still live. Ifugao children inherit the parental rice fields on marriage.

Obviously not all transfers of status are what we recognize as inheritance. Cheyenne peace chiefs on the Council of Forty-four were replaced every ten years by selection, not inheritance. The Presidency of the United States involves a transfer of status, but the office is noninheritable. In these cases, we may speak of *succession*, that is, the transfer of the rank, rights, and responsibilities of a social position.

Effect of Unilineal Descent

Inheritance of rights of use in land follows fairly clear lines. Among matrilineal gardeners, where women till the soil, inheritance runs from mother to daughters. If the picture is complicated with matrilineal organization coupled with virilocal residence (see pages 396–398) and male gardening (as in the Trobriand Islands), inheritance runs from mother's brother to sister's son. In parts of Melanesia, although land is inherited matrilineally, fruit trees privately owned by males are inherited patrilineally.

Whether matrilineal or patrilineal organization prevails also strongly influences the lines of inheritance of movable and nonmaterial property. Patrilineal societies favor filial (father-son) inheritance. Matrilineal societies favor inheritance from maternal uncle to sister's son (avuncular). It is quite possible for a tribe to subject some forms of property to the avunculate and other forms to paternal inheritance. It is not necessary that the inheritance system be restricted to one principle or another.

The sexual equivalence of brothers in marriage arrangements is reflected in their equivalence in relation to property. Thus *collateral inheritance*, or inheritance by brothers or sisters from brother or sister in preference to inheritance by the children, indicates that the members of a siblingship have a solidarity that supersedes that of the conjugal-natal family. Plains Indians applied this rule to the inheritance of horses especially. The generation tie outweighed the filial or avuncular.

Incorporeal (nonmaterial) properties, especially magic formulas and medical powers, must be partially transferred before death if they involve secret knowledge. A man may transfer his charms or songs to son or nephew as a gift, before the man's death. Or it may be that the necessary knowledge is taught to the beneficiary without transfer of the right of use until after the death of the donor.

Distinctions by Sexes

In general, it may be said that husband and wife do not inherit from each other in the nonliterate world. This is an easily understood consequence to the nature of marriage as an alliance of two kinship groups. What is left by either spouse is more than likely to revert to the family or lineage from which he or she came. Two factors that are present may be responsible for these conditions. The first is the absence or undeveloped state of a free market and money economy. Goods cannot be divorced from use with any appreciable degree of ease. They are not readily convertible into fluid capital. Therefore, they must be possessed by a competent user; the sexual division of labor bars inheritance of sex-linked property across sex lines. Second, in all nonliterate societies a person is more closely tied to his or her kinship group than to the marriage partner. The claims of surviving relatives outweigh the claims of the surviving spouse.[12]

Testamentary Disposition

In instances in which an individual wishes to transfer property status to another person who is not specifically defined as an heir in custom or law, *testamentary disposition* may be allowed. This is what we know as "making a will." In those societies in which it exists, it does not apply evenly to all forms of property. The disposition of garden plots, for example, is usually governed by strict rules of inheritance not subject to individual meddling. At the same time, a man or woman may be quite free to alter the normal lines of inheritance of personal property by use of the will. In some instances, the spoken will is upheld; in others, it may be set aside as contrary to law and custom. What is proper and what is improper at this point may often be a troublesome question in all societies.

A case occurring among the Ashanti of Ghana in 1942 is a good example. Inheritance of land among the Ashanti runs down the maternal line; it should go from a man to his brother (who belongs to the same maternal clan) and then to a sister's son, but not to a son of either man, for this person belongs to a different clan (Figure 26.9).

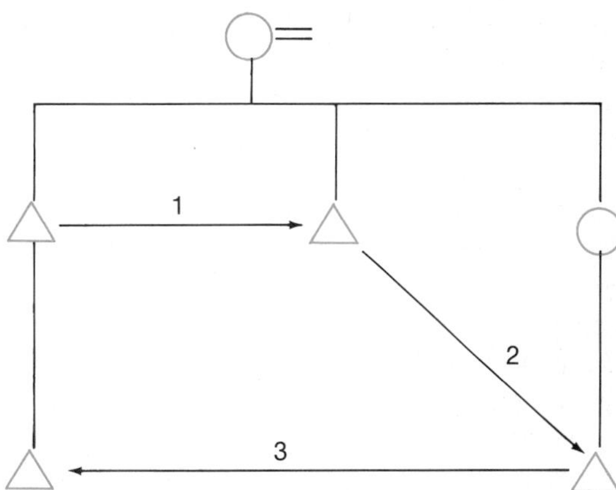

FIGURE 26.9
Ashanti inheritance in 1942 was still ideally from a man to (1) his brother and then to their sister's son (2)—all within the matriclan. In the case described on this page, the original owner orally willed the land to his own son. The brother, however, followed the traditional usage and passed the land on to the sister's son. When he died from a fatal accident, the sister's son transferred the land to his cousin (3) in accordance with his first uncle's wish.

A man when on his death-bed made a dying declaration giving one of his cocoa-farms to his son, and swore an oath enjoining his brother, who was his successor, to see that the gift was honoured. "If you do not give it to him," said the dying man, "I shall call you before the ancestors for our case to be judged."

. . . The man died and his brother succeeded to the property, but refused, with the concurrence of the other members of the family, to give the cocoa-farm to his deceased brother's son. Three months later a fire broke out in the village. The surviving brother fell from a roof while helping to put out one of the fires, and sustained an injury to his leg from which he subsequently died. Before he died, he told his family that he believed his deceased brother was summoning him to the spirit world to answer for his conduct in not honouring his brother's deathbed declaration. The general belief was that his death was due to his failure to carry out his deceased brother's instructions. The next successor to the property duly gave the cocoa-farm to the son to whom it had been left.[13]

Primogeniture

In societies of growing populations given to gardening or agriculture on limited land resources, there is always the problem of dispersal of the family holdings through inheritance by too many heirs. Primogeniture is the solution for some peoples. All property passes to the

[12]See R. F. Benedict, "Marital Property Rights in Bilateral Society" (*American Anthropologist*, vol. 38, 1936), pp. 368–374.

[13]K. A. Busia, *The Position of the Chief in the Modern Political System of Ashanti*, p. 43.

eldest son, who then has the duty to support the other members of the family in exchange for their labor. Primogeniture more often applies to succession to chiefship and office, however, than to inheritance of landed property. The mana of the Polynesian chief passes to the firstborn son in an unending line. So strong is the primogeniture rule among the Maoris of New Zealand that on occasion a firstborn woman may take a man's name and acquire the status of a firstborn son.

Primogeniture can be a force in an expansionistic movement. Power and glory are available to second-born sons who sally forth to gain new land, wealth, and rank and who found new lineages by leading a group of colonists to unsettled territory.

How much of the brunt of empire building was borne by the younger sons of Britain and Spain who were shut out at home by the laws of primogeniture? In the classical laissez faire economics of nineteenth-century England and fifteenth-century Spain, primogeniture was hailed as a double-acting social device: it avoided inefficient division of the family inheritance, and it forced the younger members to fend for themselves, thus enriching the society by their efforts.

Ultimogeniture

There are a few societies that turn the tables completely about. By means of *ultimogeniture*, the youngest son inherits the greater portion of the family estate. Among certain peoples of India, Asia, and Africa, the elder brothers are set up with herds or households in part by family resources used in progeny price. What is left over at the father's death tends in cases of ultimogeniture to go to the youngest son on the grounds that he is the least likely to be well set up in life.

In concluding a discussion of primogeniture and ultimogeniture, a note of caution should be sounded. A vast majority of societies adhere to neither of the rules.

Destruction of Property

In the instance of the Comanches:

> *In the disposal of a deceased's property there is but one rule which stood out with constancy:* upon the death of a person all effects of his (or her) personal usage were destroyed. *This included clothing, weapons, saddles, tools, paraphernalia, and horses customarily ridden by the deceased. . . . Further, even the tipi in which the dead person, man or woman, lived was totally destroyed; also for a child, but not for a baby. Articles of intimate personal usage were buried with the corpse. Other less important articles were burned. Possessions with medicine powers were either destroyed by throwing them into the river, or by placing them in an unfrequented tree where they could rot.*[14]

All Plains Indians had similar rules. Surpluses were variously handled. The Comanches passed the residual estate to the widow, who in turn was obliged to pass some of it on to her husband's friends and relatives, and especially to nonrelatives, who hung around as enthusiastic mourners; they mourned and mourned until they were given sufficient gifts.

On the economically simpler levels of culture, it is difficult to generalize inheritance rules with accuracy. Often there is no single rule of inheritance controlling all situations, or any single line of practice under any of the legal rules.

SUMMARY

As human society rests on reciprocity in social relations, the flow and exchange of goods among all peoples are important aspects of life. Gift exchange symbolizes the existence of mutual interdependence between individuals and groups. Its function is both utilitarian and social. Gift giving which is obligatory because of the status relationships between persons and groups characterizes most technologically simple socie-

[14]E. A. Hoebel, *The Political Organization and Law-ways of the Comanche Indians* (American Anthropological Association Memoir 54; Contributions from the Laboratory of Anthropology 4, 1940), pp. 120–121.

ties. Such a system is, following the economist Polanyi, called *reciprocal exchange*, or reciprocity. The bridewealth complex of cattle exchange in Africa is one highly institutionalized form of reciprocal exchange. Pig exchange in Melanesia is another.

Redistribution occurs when a managerial elite of chiefs (kings) or priests receives goods and services from farmers and artisans. From these donations the elite draw off some wealth for their own use and that of the community as a whole. The governing bureaucracy, temples, palaces, city walls, irrigation systems, armies, and ceremonies are all supported by "surpluses" of the workers.

Market exchange involves the free exchange of goods without the limitations of kinship or the exactions of rulers. In nonindustrial societies, market exchanges are usually managed through barter and trade rather than through a purchase-and-sale mechanism involving the use of money; they are also "peripheral" markets, since the marketeers do not usually derive their main living from buying and selling.

The devolution of statuses with respect to goods from deceased persons to living survivors is what constitutes the inheritance of property. In many cultures, however, some types of personal property are buried or destroyed at the death of the owner, for their spiritual essence remains tied to their owners. The most fundamental and general rule governing inheritance in nonliterate societies is that a person can inherit only those kinds of goods which he or she may customarily use. Thus, "men's goods" may not be inherited by women. The same rule holds in reverse for women's goods.

In matrilineally organized societies, because each man's kinship status is determined by his affiliation with his mother's kinship group, most of his inherited property status must come from male members of that group—his mother's brothers or his own brothers—rather than from his father as occurs in patrilineal societies.

Primogeniture gives precedence to the first-born as a means of preventing dispersal of basic property. Ultimogeniture gives precedence to the last born.

SELECTED READINGS

Bohannan, P., and G. Dalton (eds.), *Markets in Africa* (1962). An analysis based on good anthropological accounts of indigenous trading centers.

Codere, H., "Exchange and Display" (*International Encyclopedia of the Social Sciences*, vol. 5, 1968), pp. 239–245. A brief and concise discussion of exchange systems of nonliterate societies.

Dalton, G. (ed.), *Tribal and Peasant Economies: Readings in Economic Anthropology* (1967). A rich selection of materials.

Herskovits, M. J., *Economic Anthropology* (1952), part III, "Exchange and Distribution." Provides an extensive descriptive and theoretical analysis.

Sahlins, M. D., *Stone Age Economics* (1972). An analysis of economics of nonliterate societies, including detailed studies of various systems.

27
Class, Caste, and Slavery

CHAPTER OUTLINE

LEARNING GOALS

Define the concept of social class.
Define social class.
Summarize different types of class systems.
Describe the organization of three class systems.
Define caste.
Describe the different types of caste systems.
Explain the complex caste system of India.
Discuss the nature and distribution of slavery.

The notion is widely held that inequality is universal. If the meaning of inequality is taken in its most general sense, one cannot help but agree with this statement. Certainly, a biological inequality exists, in that some individuals have innate ability or intelligence which, when used appropriately, sets them apart from other persons who do not possess the same quality.

Social inequality is yet another thing. Inequality in its social meaning must be considered at the individual and at the societal level. Even in a kinship group, some persons, such as parents or lineage leaders, have more power, prestige, and material goods than do other persons, such as children or women. In associations, clubs, lineages, clans, factories, governments, institutions of all kinds, there exist some statuses (presidents, chairpersons, clan or lineage chiefs, elder statespersons, cabinet ministers, superintendents, principals, teachers) who have more power, prestige, privileges, and material goods than do others in the same group, institution, or society. Social inequality of different statuses with regard to each other within the same system, group, or institution can be called *ranked status*, or ranking. Social inequality used in this sense, however, is too narrow for our purposes in this chapter.

When used in a more general sense—that is, to apply at the level of society rather than the individual—we find that social inequality is less pervasive; although still existing in many societies, it is not universal. At the societal level, then, we shall consider social class, caste, and slavery. This type of inequality is sometimes referred to as *social stratification*, and it means that some categories of people are recognized and recognize themselves as having more or less of something than do other categories of people in the same society. This something, which is shared by some categories of persons and not by others, may be material goods, power, prestige, access to services or opportunities, offices, titles, leadership roles, or occupations.

To deal with the whole problem is more than we can manage in this introduction to anthropology. Nonetheless, we can bring the comparative findings of anthropology to bear on such questions as the following: Are there any societies that are classless? Is class differentiation the unique development of civilization? Is exploitation an inherent feature of class systems? Are classes in nonliterate society usually at war with one another? What purpose do castes serve? And how does slavery fit into the history of human societies?

THE CONCEPT OF SOCIAL CLASS

There are four major theorists on social class: Karl Marx, Max Weber, W. L. Warner, and Talcott Parsons.[1] We will have space only to briefly characterize each contribution. Other theories could be assumed as variants of the four we will discuss.

To begin with, these theories agree that social stratification has an intimate association with the core values of the society within which the stratified system lies.

One of the problems encountered in trying to understand Karl Marx (1818–1883) is that he was as much politician as social theorist, and activity in one arena colors our perception of his contributions in the other. Here we are concerned only with his social theory. The key phrase in Marxian theory is economic determinism. Marx believed that all societies were organized for biological survival and, as such, primary importance was placed on economic institutions as a means to achieve this end. Economics, thus, was designated as the determining cause of all social factors. A system of production was set up in each society to satisfy human needs, the necessary institutional procedures were devised, goals of production were set, and finally a set of

[1]For an expanded discussion of the overview presented here, see L. Reissman, "Social Stratification," in N. J. Smelser (ed.), *Sociology: An Introduction*, 2d ed., pp. 127–190.

interpersonal relationships was required to operate the system.

It was on this last requirement that his concept of class hinged, since classes were an inevitable result of the production system. He assigned a high priority to class as a determinant of behavior; a person was socialized into a class and derived views and values and consciousness from it. Ownership was one of the main aspects of class. Whoever owned the means of production controlled political power, and thus controlled society. In Marx's time, the bourgeoisie controlled the economy. This was a class of businesspersons, merchants, and capitalists who owned and controlled industry. Far below them were the masses, the proletariat, who had been convinced to help the bourgeoisie into power through the promotion of the ideology of political democracy. In between was a middle class, which included small entrepreneurs, independent farmers, and the professions. It was when Marx went on to forecast, and to try to manipulate the outcome, that he left the arena of social theoretician and became politician.

The German sociologist Max Weber (1864–1920) accepted Marx's economic criterion as a starting point for a system of stratified classes. Those persons with similar interests and economic power belonged to the same class. To this base Weber added two more factors:

1. Social factors, such as what Weber called *status*, by which he meant prestige provided by the community. All persons having the same honor or prestige belonged to the same *status group*. The community based the judgment of what prestige to accord on life styles, taste, patterns of consumption, levels of education, kinship, and occupation.
2. Political power, by which Weber meant the amount of power an individual could exert to influence a communal action. This was accomplished through some kind of organized political group.

W. L. Warner (1898–1970) used a concept of class different from that of either Marx or Weber. Where they were abstract, he was empirical. His theory, which was more of a method than a theory, was based on his study of "Yankee City," an American community. His method of study was eclectic, although heavily influenced by his anthropological training and previous field work in an Australian aboriginal community.

Warner emphasized the dimension of *status* (prestige) over the other two postulated by Weber. By "class," Warner referred to "two or more orders of people who are believed to be, and are accordingly ranked by the members of the community, in socially superior and inferior positions."[2] Members of each class were ranked according to their income, source of income, residence, education, occupation, and friends or associates. The residents of a community were able to place anyone in the class hierarchy of their community. Warner found that this hierarchy consisted of six classes, from the "upper-upper" to the "lower-lower" class. His work did much to stimulate the study of social stratification in the United States by sociologists.

Finally, there is the functional theory of Talcott Parsons, which has gone beyond the theories of Marx, Weber, and Warner in attempting to develop a series of concepts, categories, and definitions which would have universal application. Parsons is interested in a theory which will apply to nonliterate as well as to technologically advanced societies. As such, by necessity, the theory has had to be very abstract. Space does not permit a full rendition of Parsons' theory, and it would be out of place in a book such as this. Parsons has built on the work of his predecessors in the field, agreeing that stratification is widespread, if not ubiquitous. He reasons that if this is so, it must serve a function necessary to

[2]W. L. Warner and P. S. Lunt, *The Social Life of a Modern Community*, p. 82.

the survival of society. The basis for social stratification lies in the need for societies to develop a division of labor. In all societies there must be a means for allocating duties and responsibilities; otherwise people would be stumbling over each other. The allocation of duties and responsibilities, the system of stratification, and the evaluation of ranking in any society is done in accordance with the central or core values of that society. Parsons goes on to identify four categories of value patterns and to demonstrate how these work in different societies to produce class systems.

Social Class Defined

We may now specify a working definition of social class: *A social class is a category of persons within a society who hold a number of related statuses in common, who through the associated roles receive similar rewards and privileges, and who through a common life style develop an awareness of common interests in contrast to those of other such categories.*

In summary it can be said that by social inequality we mean social stratification, which includes class, caste, and slavery. Social class includes the following qualities or variables:

1. It includes a category of persons, and the views held about this category are patterned and accepted by most members of the society.
2. The class system reflects the dominant or core values of the society.
3. These values are ranked, that is, some are more important than others. Warfare may be more important in one society, the display of material goods in another, and each would establish a hierarchy of statuses which correspond to these values. To have a class system, stratification must exist; one group has some quality which the others do not.
4. Finally, a social class can exist only with reference to other social classes. If there is no consciousness of class, there can be no dynamics of class action. People must act in terms of class, if *class* is to be functionally significant.

Types of Class Systems

Inasmuch as social classes express themselves in attitudes associated with differences in status and role, which in turn mean differences in authority, power, and access to goods, the characteristics of class systems exhibit marked qualitative differences from one type of culture to another. Obviously, hunters and gatherers who have no food surpluses to manipulate and who allocate food and other goods through balanced reciprocal exchange are not likely to develop social classes.

On the other hand, post-Neolithic peoples who have a system of redistribution with ultimate title to the land vested in a paramount chief or a king, with royal lineage or clan, will almost certainly have a highly institutionalized class system.

Yet it does not necessarily follow that sedentary horticulturalists will develop social classes, either. Title to Pueblo Indian land, for example, is vested in the pueblo, in perpetuity, and plots are equably assigned to clans and households in universal succession (page 266) with enduring rights of use. Everyone has equal access to the available economic goods of the society. There is no possibility of differentiation based on wealth.

In the pueblos, power is very unequally distributed. The priests who head the religious secret fraternities form a totalitarian oligarchy with power of life and death over all members of the pueblo. Their prestige is often awesome; and a good part of their life style, devoted as it is to the management of the esoteric ritual through which the universe is kept operating (see Chapter 30, pages 528–530), is different from that of ordinary people. In terms of religion and politics, they certainly have more power and prestige; in terms of food, clothing, and shelter, they do not. The Pueblos have *ranked statuses,* but they do not have social classes.

Cross-cultural Categories Murdock's typology of societies in relation to social-class systems is as follows:

1. *Classless societies:* These are egalitarian, lacking social classes, castes, hereditary slavery, and important wealth distinctions.
2. *Societies with wealth distinctions:* Class distinctions are lacking, hereditary slavery prevails, and/or status differences exist based on the possession or distribution of wealth.
3. *Dual stratification:* Two social classes of free persons exist, but caste distinctions and hereditary slavery are lacking.
4. *Elite stratification:* An elite class derives and maintains its superior status by control over resources, especially land, in contrast to a propertyless proletariat or serf class; hereditary slavery and/or caste divisions exist.
5. *Complex stratification:* Three or more social classes or castes exist regardless of the presence or absence of slavery.

In sum, Murdock's classification presents two categories of classless societies (1 and 2, above) and three *types* of class systems (3, 4, and 5, above).[3]

Frequency of Social Classes

Taking the world at large, the majority (68 percent) of the societies in the *Ethnographic Atlas* are classless. A third of these recognize socially important wealth distinctions (prestige) but have no hereditary social classes (2, above). One-fourth (24 percent) of all societies have a ruling class which controls access to goods (types 3 and 4), and only one-twelfth (8 percent) have multiple class systems (type 5). As shown in Figure 27.1, complex class systems are limited almost exclusively to the civilizations of the Mediterranean area and Asia. In the New World, only such pre-Columbian societies as the Aztec, Maya, and Inca qualified as complex. Eighty-seven percent of all New World societies were classless! In sub-Saharan Africa and the Pacific, approximately two-thirds had no classes.[4]

The Organization of Class Systems

Having looked at the types of class systems and their relative frequency around the world, let us now examine examples of some class societies.

Plains Indians Among the nomadic Plains Indians, whose cultures encouraged competitive status achievement, a nascent sense of class was noticeable. Grinnell wrote:

> *Family rank, which existed among the Cheyennes as among other Indians, depended on the estimation in which the family was held by the best people. A good family was one that produced brave men and good sensible women, and that possessed more or less property. A brave and successful man has raised his family from low to very high rank; or a generation of inefficient men might cause a family to retrograde.*[5]

But there was no real social gap between good and not-so-good families, and the Cheyennes are considered classless. The poor, instead of being driven into servitude to the more prosperous by means of debt, wage dependence, or clientage, seem, rather, to have sponged upon the chief and the successful hunter.

Yet out of such elemental recognition of class differences, the Kiowa Indians of the Plains developed a strong sense of prestige ranking based on wealth and behavior.

Four classes were recognized by name: *onde, ondegupa, kɔɔn,* and *dapom.* The *onde,* who constituted about one-tenth of the population, were those whose family heads were "handsome on a horse," wealthy and generous, proud

---

[3]G. P. Murdock and C. Provost, "Measurement of Cultural Complexity" (*Ethnology,* vol. 12, 1973), pp. 382–383.

[4]Data from E. Bourguignon and L. Greenbaum, *Diversity and Homogeneity,* table 18, p. 40.

[5]G. B. Grinnell, *The Cheyenne Indians,* vol. 1, p. 129.

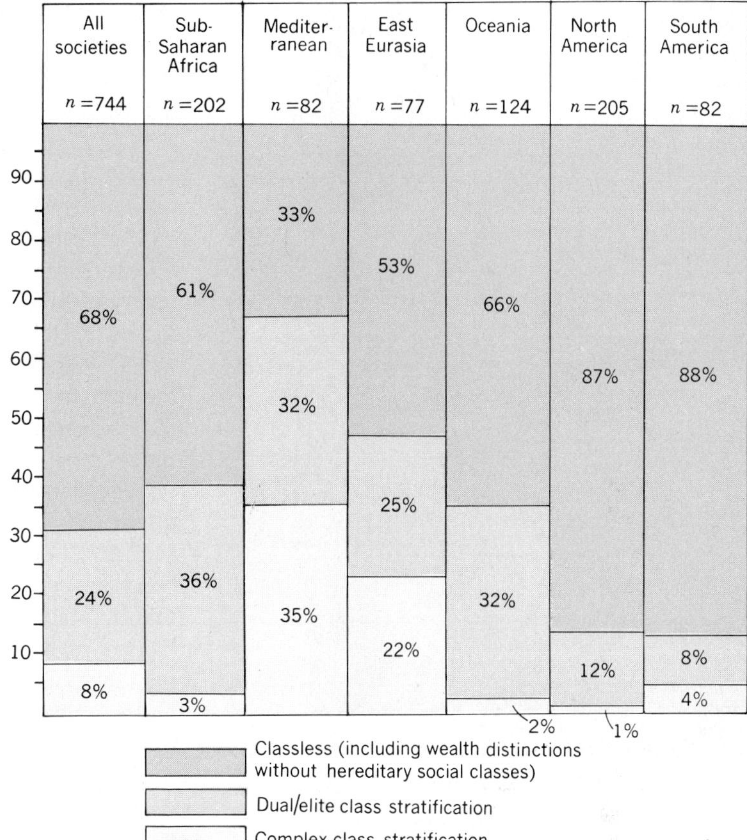

FIGURE 27.1
Relative frequency of social classes in percentages, according to major geographical areas. (Data from E. Bourguignon and L. Greenbaum, *Diversity and Homogeneity,* table 18, p. 40.)

in bearing, courteous in demeanor, and, above all, possessed of an outstanding war record. The *ondegupa* were the able artisans, hunters, herders, and medicine men, who had wealth, were generous, and were "noble" in character and behavior, but who lacked sufficient war credits. They made up one-third of the tribe. The *kɔɔn* were the common stuff, undistinguished in war or other accomplishments. They lived with their more illustrious kin as poor relatives. Half the tribe was of this lower class. The *dapom* were simply déclassé. Shiftless and lazy, they filched and stole within the camp. Practically disowned by their own relatives, they were virtual outcasts. They imposed upon the generosity of the good people; theft was not looked upon or treated as a legal infraction. The *dapom* were not punished or extruded from the group. They were merely scorned and tolerated.[6]

In general, all Plains Indian social systems were open and competitive, although there was a tendency, as in the Kiowa, toward wealth distinctions. Buffalo and antelope were there for all. In the nineteenth century, enemy horses were for the taking, and war was chronic. It was necessary only to have the "strong medicine" bestowed by "guardian spirits" (see pages 558–561) and the will, spirit, and skills—plus a little bit of luck—to move right up the social scale.

[6]J. Richardson, *Law and Status among the Kiowa Indians* (American Ethnological Society Monograph 1, 1940); and B. Mishkin, *Rank and Warfare among the Plains Indians* (American Ethnological Society Monograph 3, 1940).

FIGURE 27.2
A Kwakiutl titleholder wearing his crown of symbolic ancestral crests in London on the occasion of the coronation of Queen Elizabeth II, June 2, 1953. (United Press Photo.)

Northwest Coast Indians Class was more marked on the Northwest Coast of North America, where in every tribe a sharp division existed between free persons and slaves—unfortunates captured from other tribes. In the early nineteenth century, slaves constituted from 10 to 30 percent of the total populations of various Northwest Coast tribes. They were in effect a depressed social group whose functions were to produce food for their masters by hunting and fishing, to do the menial work around the village, and to paddle the seagoing canoes. Whatever their rank in their own tribe, all slaves were reduced to the level of productive capital in the tribe of their masters. Just as any valuable good, such as a canoe or copper, could be destroyed at a potlatch, slaves could be killed to show their master's unconcern for wealth.

Most authorities have described the body of free persons in Northwest Coast society as consisting of two classes (type 3): nobles and commoners. Nobles were those men (and their wives) who had attained the rank of chieftain through the inheritance of chiefly titles, which they had validated by potlatching (Figure 27.2). Since most tribes held to primogeniture, the nobility consisted of the firstborn, while subsequent offspring and nephews (in matrilineal societies) became commoners. Among the Tsimshian even finer distinctions were drawn. Intermarriage among the firstborn children of the highest-ranking families of the nobility was reputedly obligatory, so that there was even an endogamous "royalty" within the nobility (Figure 27.3).[7]

Drucker, who has studied Northwest Coast culture firsthand, takes issue with the orthodox view of Northwest Coast social classes. He maintains that there was no class of nobility set off from a class of commoners, with slaves standing outside the class order, much less a threefold or fourfold class system. What actually occurred, as he sees it, was "that each society consisted not of two or more social classes, but of a complete series of statuses graded relatively, one for each individual of the group."[8] He argues that between high and low there were differences in degree but not kind.

This particular conflict of interpretations is not resolvable; it merely points up the ambiguity of the concept of class in certain settings. It precisely parallels the situation that existed in the United

[7]D. Jenness, *The Indians of Canada* (National Museum of Canada Bulletin 68, Anthropological Series, no. 15, 2d ed., 1934), p. 337.
[8]P. Drucker, "Rank, Wealth, and Kinship in Northwest Coast Society" (*American Anthropologist*, vol. 41, 1939), p. 57.

States, when most Americans argued that we had no social classes at the same time that Warner and his co-workers were assiduously dividing us into upper-upper, lower-upper, upper-middle, lower-middle, upper-lower, and lower-lower classes.[9]

Murdock, however, classifies the Tsimshian, Haida, Bellacoola, and Kwakiutl tribes, all of the Northwest Coast, as having dual stratification (type 3) rather than as classless with wealth distinctions.[10]

The Aztecs Among the Aztecs of Central America, class differentiation was strongly fixed as a classical system of complex stratification (type 5).

The Aztecs, in their meteoric rise and fall, developed from an apparently classless, unsegmented society with a rude material culture, prior to A.D. 1300, to an organized, sophisticated protocivilization in the fourteenth century. At the time of the arrival of the Spaniards in 1518, they were rapidly evolving a feudal aristocracy at the expense of the earlier clan socialism. The society then consisted of royalty, nobility, common free persons, propertyless proletariat, and slaves.

The core and largest part of the Aztec population was the body of free commoners, members of one or another of twenty localized "clans" (*calpulli*). Every married man enjoyed the right to cultivate a plot of clan garden land and to have a flat-roofed, one-room hut of adobe or clay-plastered wattle. He might become a craftsman, specializing in one of the many productive arts and trades. He had security and continuous employment and an obligation to perform military service. But he was hedged in by a code of sumptuary laws that reserved to the rich and to distinguished warriors and officials the rights of wearing fine cotton, jewelry, and particular hairdos. Presumption above one's rank was summarily and severely punished.

FIGURE 27.3
At potlatches given by her noble father, the eldest daughter of the head chief of the Nakoaktok people of the Kwakiutl tribe sits on a platform supported on the heads of statues of slaves. Note the ropes around the slaves' necks. (Edward S. Curtis/Philadelphia Museum of Art.)

Class distinctions cut across kinship groups, for the class of honorary lords was recruited from all clans. They formed a nonhereditary order of merit with various grades conferred by the government as a lifetime reward for outstanding military accomplishment, service in civil office, service to the state as a traveling merchant-spy, or exceptional religiosity. They wore the beautiful and elaborate costumery depicted in Aztec art. They lived in the mansions of Tenochtitlan. They received homage and led a rich life apart from their common fellow clan members. In theory, the huge parcels of conquered lands that they received as rewards for their services could not be inherited as family estates. All such rewards were to be redistributed to a new worthy

[9] W. L. Warner and P. S. Lunt, op. cit.
[10] G. P. Murdock, op. cit., column 67, p. 105.

(a)

(b)

FIGURE 27.4
(a) A procession of Aztec nobility in their distinctive costumes. Carrying the standards of their respective orders, they are approaching the throne of the Supreme Aztec, Montezuma. (Painting by Keith Henderson, from W. H. Prescott, *The Conquest of Mexico*, T. A. Joyce, ed., Henry Holt & Company.) (b) A file of ordinary porters. (Paso y Troncoso, *Florentine Codex.*)

after the death of the holder. This was always done, but, by a process not difficult to understand, a system of preference was crystallizing whereby sons of nobles were appointed to their fathers' positions of nobility. Inheritance of rank and landed estates was thus leading rapidly to the formation of a hereditary aristocracy.

Above the nobles, in luxuriant splendor, stood the royal lineage, from among whose members the *tlacatecuhtli*, or king, was elected by the great council of lords (Figure 27.4).

Far below the royalty and nobles was the hapless proletariat. Aliens whose goods and lands had been expropriated by the state, and Aztecs who had lost their privileges for failure to fulfill clan obligations, eked out a meager and sweaty existence as burden-bearing laborers, or they grubbed for their livelihood upon the estates of the lords. Taxes and feudal services left little to them.

Slavery was the lot of impecunious Aztecs who could not meet their bills. In like manner, criminals who could not make restitution for their thefts became the slaves of the persons they had victimized. Children were sold into slavery by impoverished parents, and even adults among the proletariat might voluntarily sell themselves into servitude. Many slaves were alien boys and girls taken as tribute from conquered neighbors.

The society of the Aztec Indians was on the road to becoming the same type of pyramidal, exploitative society that existed in the flourishing days of the archaic Mediterranean civilizations. The Aztecs, however, had not hardened the inequalities of their society. Children of slaves were born free (into the proletariat). Slaves could not be killed or abused by their masters; they could even acquire property in their own right; they could not be sold to another master except by self-consent; and if married by master or mistress, they became free.[11]

CASTE

Caste represents a freezing of the principles upon which class is based: unequal distribution of goods and power; formation of social groups, each with its own life style; and differential patterns of relation between caste groups.

Castes are ranked in a hierarchical order. A person is born into a caste and can rarely escape from it; usually the person must marry within the caste, and the offspring will remain in it. Castes usually have traditionally prescribed occupations. Behavior toward members of other castes is rigidly prescribed. In India, for instance, each caste refuses to drink water or eat food handled by anyone belonging to a lower caste; to do so would be "polluting" and would acknowledge an equality for the handler. Although social intercourse between members of different castes may be highly circumscribed and severely limited, the intercaste relations form a functional social and economic network of interdependence in which even the lowliest and most economically deprived caste has its own autonomy and degree of independence. Caste members are not personal property; slaves are. Slavery and caste are separate social categories.

Types of Caste Systems

Caste systems tend to be *simple* or *complex*, without much gradation between the two types. A *simple* system has two or three castes. A *complex* system encompasses a multitude of castes.

Simple systems break down into two types, pariah and ethnic castes.

1. *Pariah* castes: One or more hereditary occupational groups, such as blacksmiths or leather workers, are treated as pariahs (low, despised, outcast) by the general population, and are strictly endogamous. The Japanese butchers (*Eta*), described on page 305, are a very good example of this type.
2. *Ethnic* castes: A socially superior endogamous caste (usually composed of conquerors) subordinates and creates a socially inferior caste of conquered people or of foreign immigrants of different culture, barring them from equal privileges. The white/Negro ethnic populations of the United States still show residues of ethnic caste distinctions in spite of great strides toward equalization of economic, political, and social opportunities in recent decades.

The Distribution of Caste Systems

Caste systems are relatively rare numerically. Of 819 societies in the *Ethnographic Atlas* on which there is sufficient information to make a judgment, only 103, or about 12.7 percent, have castes of any type. Of these, simple pariah caste systems are most common (65, or 8 percent of the whole), while simple ethnic caste systems are found in only 24 (less than 2 percent) of the whole. Complex caste systems occurred in 14 societies.[12]

[11]G. C. Vaillant, *Aztecs of Mexico*; but especially see *The Florentine Codex* (A. J. O. Anderson and C. E. Dibble, trans. and eds.), book 8, *Kings and Lords*, and book 10, *The People*.

[12]These data are compiled from column 67 of the *Ethnographic Atlas*.

The data on the comparative distribution of caste systems are summarized in Table 27.1.

The Complex Caste System of India

Identifiable castes in India number in the hundreds, and the web of caste forms a richly detailed tapestry. Caste is ubiquitous in daily life, and the system is so refined in its ramifications that some anthropologists propose that the term "caste" should be restricted solely to the Indian phenomenon. Most view the Indian system as the utmost, rather than the only, manifestation of complex caste organization. It is presented as such in this book.

The *Varna* Castes According to ancient Hindu belief, still very much alive, four so-called *varna* castes emerged from the body of primordial man. This was the beginning and the ideological justification of the whole Indian caste system for more than 2000 years.

From his mouth issued the Brahmins, who became priests and scholars. From his arms came the Kshatriyas, warriors and rulers; from his thighs came the Vaishyas, tradesmen, and from his feet rose the Shudras, cultivators.[13]

The four *varna* castes are all ritually clean and unpolluted, but the first three have superior purity and prestigious privileges because their male members are "twice-born." The "twice-born" go through a transition rite which symbolizes a second birth. Each "twice-born" wears a sacred thread over his left or right shoulder, depending on his caste's rank. Shudras, who are *varna*-caste farmers, are but once-born; their rank is middling.

Harijan Castes: The Untouchables The *harijan* castes are (were)[14] the untouchables. By the nature of their work, which puts them in close contact with "unclean" materials, they are considered polluted. As a result, great symbolic and actual social distance is maintained between the *varna* and *harijan* castes.

[13]D. G. Mandelbaum, *Society in India*, vol. 1, pp. 22–23.

[14]The constitution and law of India, since 1949, have abolished the social disabilities of the *harijans*, making their observance illegal. Old caste attitudes, though weakening, still persist, however.

TABLE 27.1
The Distribution of Caste Systems by Frequency and Percentage in Major Geographic Areas

Type of caste system	All societies $n = 819$	Sub-Saharan Africa $n = 216$	Mediterranean $n = 77$	East Eurasia $n = 81$	Oceania $n = 128$	North America $n = 219$	South America $n = 88$
Castes absent	86% (706)	82% (178)	48% (37)	73% (59)	98% (125)	100% (219)	100% (88)
Simple caste system: Pariah	8% (65)	12% (27)	48% (37)	— (0)	.08% (1)	— (0)	— (0)
Simple caste system: Ethnic	3% (24)	5% (11)	4% (3)	11% (9)	.08% (1)	— (0)	— (0)
Complex caste system	1.7% (14)	— (0)	— (0)	16% (13)	.08% (1)	— (0)	— (0)

SOURCE: Data compiled from G. P. Murdock, *Ethnographic Atlas*, column 69.
NOTE: Percentages above the figure have been rounded off; totals do not equal 100% in all cases.

Jatis Over all India the four *varna* castes and the *harijan* categories are divided into a thousand or more *jatis*, or specific castes. "A jati is an endogamous, hereditary social group that has a name and a combination of attributes."[15] The latter refers to the kinds of food which may be eaten or are prohibited, to the relative degree of pollution and purity, to sacred thread or no thread, and to learning and occupation, plus multitudes of lesser privileges and disabilities.

Yet, not every *jati*, nor even every *varna*, is present in every community. Thus, in Konduru, a South Indian village, thirty *varna* jatis are found—but none of them is *Kshatriya* (warrior). Among the thirty are clerk, priest, merchant and moneylender, temple lamplighter, goldsmith, blacksmith, carpenter, brassworker, farmer, braceletmaker, tailor, weaver, potter, bodyguard, fisherman, courtesan, herdsman, wine tapper, bodyservant, barber-surgeon, and washerman *jati.* Among the *harijans* are five *jatis* of priests, musicians, weavers, sweepers, and leatherworkers.[16] Special services are provided by itinerant members of other *jatis* who wander through the country as peddlers or entertainers.

The *Jajmani* System Each *jati* has traditional relations to various other *jatis* in the rendering of their special occupational services. At the center of a web of such relations stands a hereditary landlord. At harvest time the landlord, or *jajman*, used to pay grain to dependent field workers and "contracted" washerman, leather worker, carpenter, barber, etc. The share each took was fixed according to custom and service rendered. Each man came forward to claim his share in order of caste rank—Shudras first. When the barber's turn arrived, for example:

The Barber measures out a gift share, four to six fans of grain, for shaving the household males and a poli cherta *for ritual performances. He pulls aside his bonus . . . "for showing the mirror" to his prosperous masters so they can have the privilege of observing their tonsure while it is taking place. Since the poor do not give a bonus at harvesttime, they are shaved without the benefits of soap or a mirror. The Barber does more than shaving, however; his knife is used at births to sever the umbilical cord while his wife assists in the delivery of the child. After funerals he shaves his clients at the time of their purification. But it is at weddings that he is most needed. He prepares the groom and is given small gifts of grain, liquor, coins, and the clothes that the young man had been wearing. He pares the nails of the couple during the ceremonies and claims the unhusked rice used in making the ritual designs. He arranges for a Barber band to play for the ceremony and also for the many processions that welcome the bridal party, that fetch the ceremonial pots and sacred earth, that accompany the wedding party to the temple, and that parade the newlyweds through town. Finally, on an auspicious day fixed by the family* purohit, *the Barber performs the ritual tonsure and receives the groom's turban as a symbol of his assumption of the jajmani rights over the new home.*

*When the Shudras have taken their share, the Leatherworker approaches for his: a gift share of a half pot of grain for repairing shoes and harnesses and a share for repairing the irrigation bucket at the well. He also claims the meat and one-half of the skins of the jajman's cattle that die throughout the year. The other half of the skins he must tan and return for the jajman's use. After the grain is cleared from the threshing floor, the Leatherworker sweeps up the tailings as his bonus (*danda kattu*). The biggest reward of the harvest often goes to the Leatherworker who has been a faithful worker during the past year. Such a man helps in the field work by drawing water before dawn to irrigate the rice, by sleeping in the fields to protect the harvest from wild pigs from the surrounding forest, and by guarding the cut grain from thieves. He beats the large leather-covered drum in his master's processions and sleeps before his door at night. The jajman rewards such a servant with a generous portion which can amount to ten pots of grain.*[17]

A service caste worker might serve one or several *jajmans*, as the case may be.

[15]D. G. Mandelbaum, op. cit., p. 14.

[16]P. G. Hiebert, *Konduru*, pp. 17–28.

[17]Ibid., pp. 87–88.

In spite of the teeming millions of India's great cities, about 90 percent of India's half-billion population live in rural villages in *jajmani* caste ordering. It may be a unique social system, but it embraces about one-twelfth of all humanity!

SLAVERY

Slavery has entered several times into our discussion of class systems. Slavery has been one of the most important of human social institutions; it occurred in half the world's societies in the eighteenth and nineteenth centuries.

The Nature of Slavery

Slavery is not in itself an absolute concept. In operation, it ranges from the complete degradation of a whole class of people by means of dogmatic denial of their humanity (slaves as chattels) to the inclusion of slaves as adopted members of the master's family and kinship group. Slavery, we are safe in saying, is a condition rarely welcomed by the slaves. There are few social advantages in being a slave and usually a good many disadvantages. The lot of the slave depends to a large degree on whether the society customarily utilizes its slaves as household servants or as field workers. In the former case, the relation of slave to master is unavoidably intimate, and slaves reap the benefit. If slaves are used as field workers, the owner's chief interest becomes one of economic exploitation, and, especially where there are great numbers of slaves, relationships become impersonal and harsh.

Internal slavery occurs in connection with quasi-capitalistic practices of borrowing and lending. A borrower might pledge himself or a son or daughter as security on a loan. Default meant servitude. Or, as in the case of the Ashanti of Ghana, a man could pawn his brother's son to raise a sum. The boy then worked for the creditor until the loan was repaid; the labor he performed constituted the interest on the loan. Debt slavery did not ordinarily produce huge masses of slaves, nor were their positions inordinately harsh. A second internal source of slaves was the condemnation of criminals to servitude.

The great source of slaves, however, was war and exploitation of war captives, but war may or may not be waged specifically to take captives. Slaves are in the society, but not of it. Without citizenship, slaves are outside the realm of jural personality, and their debased status does not contradict the slaveholders' notions of social equality—for themselves, exclusive of the slaves.

The Distribution of Slavery

Table 27.2 shows the distribution of slavery according to the subsistence patterns of 565 cultures. Slightly more than one-fourth of the hunters and gatherers of recent times practiced slavery. The ratio drops to one-fifth among intensive foragers, rises to nearly half among horticulturalists, to one-third among pastoralists, and is more than half among societies based on plow agriculture. Slavery flourished in most preindustrial civilizations. After the industrial revolution, its economic usefulness disappeared, slavery was viewed as immoral, and it was legally rooted out as a social institution—but not until well into the nineteenth century.

TABLE 27.2
Frequency and Percentage Distributions of Slavery in 565 Societies, according to Subsistence Base

Subsistence base	Number of societies with slavery	Percent of societies with slavery
Plow agriculture	59 of 117	50
Pastoral	27 of 79	33
Horticulture	103 of 234	44
Foraging	6 of 33	20
Hunting and gathering	27 of 101	27

SOURCE: Data from A. D. Coult and R. W. Habenstein, *Cross Tabulations of Murdock's World Ethnographic Sample*, p. 522.

TABLE 27.3
Distribution of Societies with Slavery, by Major Geographic Areas

Geographic areas	Number of societies by area $n = 774$	Number of societies with slavery $n = 363$	Percentage of occurrence of slavery in each area
Africa	204	160	78
Circum-Mediterranean	82	50	61
Eurasia	77	43	56
Pacific Islands	124	26	21
North America	205	62	30
South America	82	22	27

SOURCE: Data from E. Bourguignon and L. Greenbaum, op. cit., table 19, p. 41.

Prior to the expansion of European cultures, slavery was unevenly distributed around the world (see Table 27.3). It was most rare in Oceania, where one-fifth of the societies practiced it. The Indians of North and South America had worked it into 30 and 27 percent of their societies, respectively. The Old World was by all odds the home of slavery. More than half the societies of Asia and two-thirds of those around the Mediterranean took slavery for granted. But sub-Saharan Africa was the true indigenous home of slavery. There, four-fifths of the societies included in the *Ethnographic Atlas* held slaves. The high incidence of pastoralism and developed agriculture might have contributed to the spread of slavery in Africa. Yet the presence of both these types of subsistence economies in high frequency in Eurasia and the Mediterranean regions did not produce nearly so much slavery in those parts of the world.

SUMMARY

Social classes are the product of unequal access to economic goods and differences in economic, religious, or political power and rewards. A social class is a category of persons within a society who hold a number of related statuses in common; who, through the associated roles receive differential rewards and privileges; and who, through a common life style, develop an awareness of common interests in contrast to those of other such categories.

Murdock classifies societies in five types: (1) classless; (2) classless with wealth distinctions; (3) dual stratification (with a hereditary aristocracy and a class of commoners); (4) elite stratification (in which an upper class controls land and other important productive resources, while a lower class is propertyless); and (5) complex stratification (with multiple classes linked to extensive occupational division of labor within the society).

More than two-thirds (68 percent) of all societies are classless, one-fourth have a dominant class controlling access to goods, and only 8 percent have complex class systems.

Classless societies were most frequent among the American Indian societies of both North and South America. Complex classes existed almost entirely in the Mediterranean and Asia, while dual stratification was highest in sub-Saharan Africa. Hunters and gatherers, such as the nomadic Plains Indians, tend to be classless, as do those horticultural societies which rely on reciprocal economic distribution. Class is related to redistributive economic systems in which the upper class has prestige resting on supernatural power and sanctity, or controls the use of land. The Aztecs manifested a complex class system.

Caste is class frozen by endogamy and hereditary ascription of membership. Simple caste systems are of two types: (1) *pariah*, in which one or more occupational groups is strictly endogamous and treated as low and despised; and (2) *ethnic*, in which a conquered people or foreign immigrants are forced into an inferior caste and held down by the indigenous upper caste. Complex caste systems encompass a great number of castes, graded and interwoven in a network of highly prescribed behavioral relations. Complex systems usually distinguish between higher, "clean" castes and degraded, polluted, and polluting castes. Within this dual division there will be many refinements of prestige and privilege relating to sanctity and caste separation. Not many societies (14 out of 819) have a complex caste system, but because of its presence in India, one-twelfth of all living human beings are locked into a caste order.

Until 100 years ago, slavery was one of mankind's most important social institutions. It occurred in half the world's societies in the eighteenth and nineteenth centuries! In nonliterate societies, slavery was generally not too harsh; slaves were frequently incorporated into the master's household and not seriously exploited as property. The development of intensive agriculture and the urban revolution made slavery economically profitable, however, and so it remained until the industrial revolution and the growth of a money economy made slavery less feasible.

In the absence of plow agriculture, pastoralism, and cities, only a few American Indian societies developed slavery, and Oceania was the least conducive to the institution. It flourished in the Mediterranean complex of civilizations and pastoralists, but still not to the degree that was manifest in sub-Saharan Africa, where slavery occurred in 78 percent of the indigenous societies.

SELECTED READINGS

Berreman, G. D., "Caste: The Concept of Caste" (*International Encylopedia of the Social Sciences*, vol. 2, 1968), pp. 333–338. A thorough discussion of ways of looking at caste.

Hiebert, P. G., *Konduru: Structure and Integration in a South Indian Village* (1971). Presents a clear and understandable description and analysis of the dynamics of caste in relation to other forms of social organization in a village community of India.

Mandelbaum, D. G., *Society in India*, vol. 1 (1970), parts 1, 3, and 4. A complete overview of the *jati* system in India set in the theory of modern social anthropology.

Polanyi, K., and A. Rotstein, *Dahomey and the Slave Trade* (1966). A historical, economic, and anthropological treatment of one of the great ports of trade in slaves.

Tuden, A., and L. Plotnicov (eds.), *Social Stratification in Africa* (1970). Contains eleven chapters on class, caste, and slavery in African societies.

28
Law and Social Control

CHAPTER OUTLINE

LEARNING GOALS

Discuss law and social control.

Identify the three basic features of law.

Define law.

Explain the function of law.

Examine case law and the settlement of disputes.

Provide examples of representative legal systems.

Summarize the trend of the law.

It was a common misconception until the beginning of the twentieth century to regard "law" in a rigidly limited manner: an invention of advanced civilizations, marked by written codes, legislation, and case decisions. Nonliterate peoples who lacked writing, formal legal codes, police officers, courts, and penal institutions were thus assumed to be without law. It is understandable, therefore, that "primitive law" was somewhat late in coming under investigation, and only since World War I has there developed a substantial body of literature on "legal anthropology," "anthropological jurisprudence," or the "ethnography of law"—some of the terms by which this specialization is called. Both lawyers with an interest in comparative legal systems and anthropologists concerned with systems of societal maintenance have contributed to the growing volume of work in this area.

There has been a radical shift of thinking about "the law." No longer is it conceived of in the static, formalistic "black-letter" law of written codes, statutes, and constitutions. Today law is seen through the behavioristic lens of legal realism, which holds that law consists of what people *do* in the realm of the legal—not what they say they do. The difference is that which we drew at the outset (pages 290–291) between ideal and real culture. Anthropologists today have learned to seek the norms of law in cases in action (the "trouble case" method), not in hypothetical rules.

Although the social ends sought and the outward legal appurtenances may differ markedly from society to society, certain basic principles and functions appear to have universal applicability. Some of these differences and, especially, the recurring similarities will be our concern in this chapter.

COURTS AND LEGISLATION

Most primitive law is not legislated, and modern sociological jurisprudence and legal realism have made it clear that much of modern law is not legislated either.[1] English jurisprudence has long since given assent to this point of view.[2]

This behavioristic concept of law gives the anthropologist a handle that can be grasped, but still it is not enough. For if we think of courts as a formal sitting of professional judges, with bailiffs, clerks, and advocates, we must conclude: no courts, no law. This is what bothered Max Radin, who well understood the anthropologist's problem:

> *But there is an infallible test for recognizing whether an imagined course of conduct is lawful or unlawful. This infallible test, in our system, is to submit the question to the judgment of a court. In other systems exactly the same test will be used, but it is often difficult to recognize the court. None the less, although difficult, it can be done in almost every system at any time.*[3]

Max Radin is right. But what sorts of courts did he have in mind? Some courts are difficult to identify. Anthropologically, they may be regularly constituted tribal courts, such as the tribal council of an American Indian tribal sitting in judicial capacity[4] (Figure 28.1) or a court of the West African Ashanti, constituted of the chief, his council of elders, and his henchmen (see pages 497–498).

That type of primitive court is not hard to recognize. Any member of the American Bar Association would readily see it for what it is. But a more obscure type of court may be found in the old Cheyenne military fraternity. Consider the case of Wolf Lies Down, whose horse was "borrowed" by a friend in the absence of the owner. When the friend did not return from the warpath with the horse, Wolf Lies Down put the matter before his fraternity, the Elk Soldiers. "Now I want to know what to do," he said. "I

[1]O. W. Holmes, Jr., "The Path of the Law" (*Harvard Law Review*, vol. 10, 1897), p. 457.

[2]J. W. Salmond, *Jurisprudence*, p. 49.

[3]M. Radin, "A Restatement of Hohfeld" (Harvard Law Review, vol. 51, 1938), p. 1145.

[4]E. A. Hoebel, "Keresan Pueblo Law," in L. Nader (ed.), *Law in Culture and Society*, pp. 92–116.

FIGURE 28.1
Indian tribes possessing a constitution have wide legal authority over their resident tribal members. Judge William Roy Rhodes presiding over the tribal court of the Gila River Indian Community, located in Arizona (1972). (Arizona State Museum.)

want you to tell me the right thing." The fraternity chiefs sent a messenger to bring the friend in from the camp of a remote band. The friend gave an adequate and acceptable explanation of his conduct and offered handsome restitution to the complainant in addition to making him his blood brother. Then said the chiefs: "Now we have settled this thing." But they went on, half as a legislature: "Now we shall make a new rule. There shall be no more borrowing of horses without asking. If any man takes another's goods without asking, we will go over and get them back for him. More than that, if the taker tries to keep them, we will give him a whipping."

Can anyone deny that the Elk Soldiers were in effect sitting as a court for the entire tribe? The test is, first, one of responsibility. That they knew. Second, it is one of effective authority. That they achieved. Third, it is one of method. Unhampered by a system of formal precedent that required them to judge according to the past, they recognized that the rule according to which they were settling the case was new, and so they announced it.[5]

Among the Yurok Indians of California, as typical of a less specifically organized people, the court was less definite, but it was nevertheless there. An aggrieved Yurok who felt he had a legitimate claim engaged the services of two nonrelatives from a community other than his own. The defendant did likewise. These persons were called *crossers* because they crossed back and forth between the litigants. The litigants did not face each other in the dispute. After hearing all that each side offered in evidence and argument, the crossers rendered a judgment on the facts. If the judgment was for the plaintiff, they rendered a decision for damages according to a well-established scale that was known to all. For their footwork and efforts, each received a piece of shell currency called a *moccasin*. Here again we have a court.[6]

Consider the Eskimo dealing with repeated homicide. Killing on a single occasion leads merely to feud, inasmuch as the avenger enjoys no recognized privilege of imposing the death penalty on the murderer of a relative with immunity against a counterkilling. A feud, of course, represents an absence of law, since blood revenge is more a social matter than a legal one. But to kill again makes the culprit a public enemy in the Eskimo view. It then becomes incumbent upon some public-spirited man of initiative to interview all the adult males of the community to determine whether they agree

[5]For a full account of this case, see K. N. Llewellyn and E. A. Hoebel, *The Cheyenne Way: Conflict and Case Law in Primitive Jurisprudence*, p. 127.

[6]See A. L. Kroeber, "Yurok Law" (*Proceedings of the Twenty-second International Congress of Americanists*, 1926), pp. 511ff. A dramatic presentation of a Yurok case-in-action is given in *The Ways of Mankind*, Series 1, Record 5, "The Sea Lion Flippers: A Study in Ethics."

that the murderer should be executed. If unanimous consent is given, the leader then undertakes to execute the criminal, and no revenge is taken on him by the murderer's relatives.[7] A community court has spoken. Such are the kinds of courts Max Radin had in mind.

THE NATURE OF LAW

We have seen in the above that lawmaking and a system of courts exist in many nonliterate societies. Yet neither of these features defines law, or what is actually fundamental to law. Law is obviously a complex of human behavior. The problem is: What kinds of behavior? What sets off legal behavior from that which is not legal? What is it that makes law, law?

Law, Custom, and Social Control

It has been stressed that, in every society, human behavior must be narrowed down from its full range of potential variety to a moderately limited body of norms, so that people can manage their lives with a reasonable degree of certainty that their own activities will evoke anticipated responses and results from their fellows. Social control is exerted to guide the learning process of all members of the society in the development of the appropriate behavioral customs. Law is one aspect of social control.

Custom consists of social norms (Chapter 16, pages 289–290), and all social norms are sanctioned. Behavior in accord with norms is usually rewarded. Behavior which departs too far from the norms is penalized. Social control consists of the entire gamut of rewards and dissuasions. All child training, all education, all the unending responses of peers and associates throughout life are involved. Their positive responses range from the smile, the giving of food, the friendly pat, through consent to do something strongly desired, to bestowal of privileges, honors, and wealth. These are the positive sanctions that are constantly at work. On the other hand, there are negative sanctions which punish with a frown, a hateful word, a scornful curl of the lip, or a slap in the face (or elsewhere); by ostracism (social isolation); by deprivation of food, of clothing, or of other wanted things; by humiliation—all of these in everyday intercourse. They may be very effective, indeed. Yet their simple effectiveness does not make law of them.

FIGURE 28.2
Legal disputes may be settled by negotiation and payment of damages, without the intervention of police or judges. In this New Guinea example, a Chimbu "Big Man" presides at the distribution of sixty-seven slaughtered and roasted pigs given to members of a neighboring village in settlement of a land dispute (1967). (E. A. Hoebel.)

So, too, the supernatural enters into social control. Ghosts, spirits, and gods may be believed to reward the moral and the just and punish the wrongdoer. Sin is the violation of a social norm which is negatively sanctioned by the supernatural.

Law consists of social norms, *plus*. Not all enculturation is effective for all individuals. Some ignore the norms now and then, or go beyond permissible limits. Ordinary day-to-day social control has not worked in their cases. Then it is that law may be invoked. The pressure of the sanctions is stepped up and the penalties are no longer only psychological. The wrongdoer's

[7] For a report of such a case, see F. Boas, *The Central Eskimo* (Bureau of American Ethnology, Annual Report 6, 1888), p. 668.

goods may be confiscated: damages are assessed or a fine must be paid (Figure 28.2). Or the offender may be physically injured or constrained: whipped, mutilated, incarcerated (a form of ostracism), exiled, or killed (the absolute form of ostracism, an irrevocable removal from the social scene).

Three Basic Features of Law

Within the broad area of social control, law is set off from the general social norms by three characteristics:

1. The legitimate use of economic deprivation or physical coercion
2. The allocation of official authority
3. The presence of regularity (consistency)

The Legitimate Use of Physical Coercion The essential element of law in any society is the legitimate use, or threat, of physical coercion. The law has teeth, and teeth that can bite, although they need not be bared, for, as Holmes put it: "The foundation of jurisdiction is physical power, although in civilized times it is not necessary to maintain that power throughout proceedings properly begun."[8] We would merely add to that declaration that nonliterate people often found that it was not necessary to display the power behind the law when the defendant acceded to proceedings carried through properly. Jhering has emphasized the factor of force in law: "Law without force is an empty name." Again, more poetically, we find: "A legal rule without coercion is a fire that does not burn, a light that does not shine."[9]

However, it is true that not all writers on law, especially primitive law, accept the criterion of force as an essential attribute of law. Professor Leo Pospisil, for example, holds that *how* a social obligation is enforced is less important than that it *is* enforced. "Is not the effect (social control, conformity) of a sanction more important than its form?" he asks. "Some psychological sanctions, although of nonphysical nature, perform as strong a control as do physical sanctions."[10] In this age of familiarity with brainwashing, no one will deny that. Nor will we deny the effective importance of "ostracism, ridicule, avoidance, or a denial of favors—sanctions that are sometimes very subtle and informal."[11] These, however, are (we believe) better viewed as other-than-legal forms of control.

The threat of the law is more often than not a sufficient deterrent; people wish to avoid the public exposure, the embarrassment, inconvenience, and ultimate risk of economic loss or physical coercion. Law has an effect of psychological deterrence. For law exists primarily not to punish but to channel behavior toward socially acceptable goals, thus preventing the breach of social norms.

The Official Element in Law Force means coercion, which in its absolute form is physical compulsion. There are, of course, as many forms of coercion as there are forms of power, and only certain methods and forms are legal. Coercion by gangsters is not legal. Even physical coercion by a parent is not legal if it is extreme in form. The essentials of legal coercion are general acceptance of the application of physical power, in threat or in fact, by a privileged party, for a legitimate cause, in a legitimate way, and at a legitimate time. This distinguishes the sanction of law from other social rules.

Private law The privilege of applying force constitutes the official element in law. In most nonliterate societies, this privilege is vested in the wronged individual or kinship group (Figure 28.3). They must prosecute on their own behalf

[8] O. W. Holmes, Jr., *McDonald v. Maybee* (*Supreme Court Reporter*, vol. 37, 1917), p. 343.

[9] R. von Jhering, *Law as Means to an End*, p. 190.

[10] L. Pospisil, *Kapauku Papuans and Their Law* (Yale University Publications in Anthropology, no. 54, 1958), p. 267.

[11] Ibid., p. 267.

FIGURE 28.3
Physical mutilation as legal punishment (sanction). Plains Indian husbands were permitted to cut off the nose of a wife found guilty of adultery, as in the case of this unfortunate Apache woman. (Arizona Historical Society.)

and exact the proper legal penalty. This is known as *private law*. If a public official is responsible for penalizing a breach of law, it is *public*, or *criminal law*. The person who is generally or specifically recognized as rightly exerting the element of physical coercion is an instrument of social authority. It is not necessary that it be an official with legal office or a constable's badge. In any nonliterate society, the so-called private prosecutor of a private injury is implicitly a public official for the moment and for that particular incident, and cannot be acting solely for personal reasons or on behalf of family or clan and still enjoy the approval or tacit support of the disinterested remainder of the society. If the rest of the population supports the action in opinion, even though not overtly, it can mean only that the society feels that the behavior of the defendant was wrong. Thus the behavior is in itself an injury to the society, although the group feeling may not be strong enough to generate overt and specific action by the group as a group and on its own initiative.

However, the private prosecutor remains the representative of the general social interest as well as of that which is specifically personal. This fundamental fact is ordinarily ignored in discussions of primitive law, and it is in this sense that we may say that the difference between criminal law and private law is a difference in degree rather than in kind.

Public law When responsibility for initiating legal action against a wrongdoer rests not with the person wronged or a relative, but rather in the hands of a public officer—a headman, a chief, a bailiff, or a member of the chief's staff or royal household, or perhaps a shaman or a priest—then the offense is a *public wrong* (Figure 28.4). Public wrongs are traditionally called *crimes* in Anglo-American usage. Public law is the concern of government; private law operates apart from government. But it must be reemphasized that the actions of the private prosecutor have legitimacy (when in accordance with the provisions of the system of private law) because the public at large supports the rightfulness of the action against the socially defined wrongness of the transgressor.

Regularity in Law Regularity is what law shares at the core with social norms. Regularity is what law in the legal sense has in common with law in the scientific sense. Regularity means predictability. Yet, regularity, it must be warned, does not mean absolute certainty. There can be no true certainty where human beings are involved, and yet there is much regularity. In law, the doctrine of precedent (*L. stare decisis*, "to adhere to decisions") is not the unique possession of the Anglo-American common-law jurist. Primitive law also builds on precedents, for new

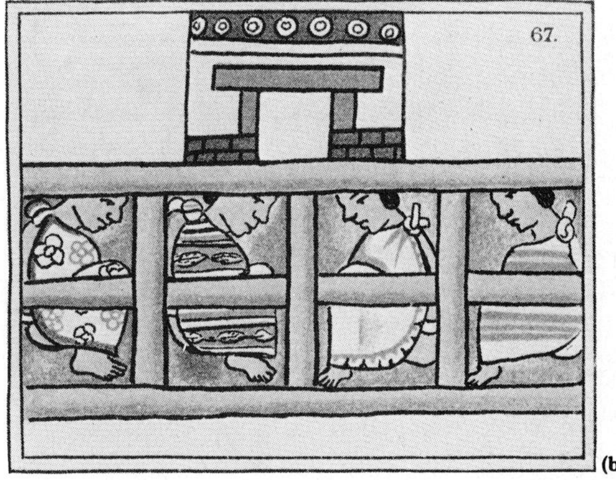

FIGURE 28.4
Aztec paintings represent the legal authority of the state in portraying (a) bound prisoners being tried by judges seated on official chairs, with words emanating from their mouths, and (b) caged criminals in cramped confinement. (F. del Paso y Troncoso.)

decisions rest on old rules of law or norms of custom. Regularity removes the threat of personal whim and caprice from law. Regularity lends to law its attribute of certainty. The norms of law make prediction of legal outcomes reasonably certain.

The characteristics of law are therefore *the right to apply economic sanctions or force (legitimate coercion), official authority,* and *regularity.* It is these qualities taken together which distinguish law from custom in any culture.

LAW DEFINED

Thus we may form a working definition of law that fits primitive as well as civilized law in the following terms:

A law is a social norm which, if violated beyond permissible limits, usually will evoke a formal procedural response initiated by an individual or a group possessing the socially recognized privilege-right of determining guilt and of imposing economic or physical sanctions upon the wrongdoer.

We may further define *civilized law* as the law of societies whose cultures include writing; *archaic law* as the law of early civilizations; and *primitive law* as the law of nonliterate peoples.

Two other kinds of distinctions in law should be mentioned. These are the distinctions between *substantive* and *procedural*, or *adjective*, law, and between *organic* and *tyrannic* law.

Substantive Law and Adjective Law

Legal norms are social norms that are reinforced by legal sanctions, as identified above. They are selected in accordance with their consistency in relation to the cultural assumptions that undergird the legal system.

Substantive law identifies the norms that are to be sanctioned by legal action. In most instances, substantive law translates basic cultural postulates into social action by deciding what particular behavior in a given instance conforms best to the basic assumptions underlying the culture. Law implements selection by saying implicitly: "In this society, this is permitted and that is not."

Procedural or *adjective law* designates the person, or persons, who may rightly punish a breach of substantive law; it also lays down the rules for prosecuting a case and fixes the customary penalties to be applied to each type of offense. In one form or another, the idea of due process of law exists in every society. Due process consists of the socially approved ways of carrying through a legal action once a plaintiff moves to act against an infringement of the substantive law. The "approved ways" limit and channel the time and place of prosecution; the finding of evidence; the relevance of evidence; and the kinds and degree of coercion that may be used: what goods may be confiscated, or what physical sanctions are appropriate and allowable.

Organic versus Tyrannic Law

Because of its coercive powers, law has its peculiar dangers. Out of control or in the hands of a vested minority, it can become a tyranny of terror directed not to the realization of the basic values of the society at large but to the subjugation of those who are not a part of the ruling clique, class, or caste.

When a law system is imposed on a people through conquest, or by a minority which dominates through raw power not consensually allocated by society, that law system is *tyrannic*.

When a law system is self-developed by a people, when its rules and practices are generally accepted as being in accord with commonly held ideas as to the nature of their society, its goals, and the legitimacy of its leaders and rulers, we can call it *organic law*. Most, but not all, law systems in nonliterate societies have been of this order. And in the ensuing discussion, it will be of organic law that we speak, unless otherwise noted.

THE FUNCTIONS OF LAW

Law performs four fundamental functions essential to the maintenance of societies and their cultures. They are substantive, adjective, mediative, and readaptive in quality. These functions are:

1. The definition of the obligatory relationships between the members of a society, so as to assert which activities are permitted and which are ruled out and to maintain at least minimal integration between the activities of individuals and groups within the society (substantive).
2. The allocation of authority and the designation of the person who has the socially recognized privilege-right to initiate and carry through legitimate corrective actions leading to economic or physical sanctions when substantive norms are violated, so that force is controlled and directed toward social goals (adjective).
3. The disposition of trouble cases as they arise; to clean up social messes (tangled claims, squabbles and fights, killings and woundings) so that people may get on with everyday living with reasonable certainty and security (mediative).
4. The continuing redefinition of relations between individuals and groups as the conditions of life change, to maintain adaptability and flexibility in both substantive and procedural law in response to shifting values and new technologies (readaptive).

A society may manage these functions with more or less skill; its legal system may function with sure effectiveness, achieving justice and order with a minimum of bungling and harshness; or it may be rigid and brutal, with order imposed by tyranny, and justice a fugitive in the land.

CASE LAW AND THE SETTLEMENT OF DISPUTES

In the search for understanding of legal systems and how they came into being, the anthropologist has benefited greatly from modern jurisprudence, which points up the fact that breach and disputes in conflicts of claims are the most constant source of the law. In this vein, Pound has written: "The law is an attempt to reconcile, to harmonize, to compromise . . . overlapping or conflicting interests."[12] Law exists to channel behavior so that conflicts of interest do not result in an overt clash. New decisions are ideally so shaped as to determine which interests best accord with the accepted standards of what is good for the society. Of course, it is unfortunately true that tyrants, usurpers, and pettifoggers can and do pervert the ends of law to their own designs without regard to social interests or prevailing standards of what is right.

Realistically, we may say that regardless of the law that exists concerning a particular situation, an actual dispute must arise before the principles of the law can be tested; a law that is never broken may exist as nothing more than a custom, for one will never know the full implications of it until it is tested in a legal action.

But no society is wholly static. New exigencies always arise. One permanent thing about human society is its impermanence. Especially when unlike cultures come into contact, new materials, new ways of behaving, and new ideas enter into the cultural picture.

These new elements are not usually adopted simultaneously by all members of the society. The consequence is that when some members get new goods and new ideas, they have new interests for which the old lines of the culture have made no provision. Their use of these new acquisitions comes into conflict with the old standards held by others. New custom and new law must then be generated.

However or by whomever the judgment may be rendered in any dispute, it is the claimant and the defendant who lay the grounds of the claim and counterclaim or denial. If one or the other does it skillfully, soundly, and wisely, the basis of decision is likely to be found in the statement of the claim. No matter how selfish the motivation of a disputant may be, unless it is a fool indeed, a claim is posed against the background of social principles and the well-being of the entire social group. How else can enduring social acceptance be gained for a position? Naturally, also, the more skillfully the case is argued in terms of the consonance of the claim with the well-established principles of social order, the greater the probability that the disputant will shape the law.[13]

Evidence

Any lawsuit or criminal trial involves at least two questions: "Is the alleged offense an illegal act?" "If so, is the defendant guilty of the offense?" The first is a question of law. The second is a question of fact. If the first can be brought to a negative answer, then there is no need to seek an answer to the second. The case must be dropped.

Assuming that there is a legal rule covering the alleged act, how are the facts then determined? In less complexly developed legal systems, the question of evidence is not of great importance. In a small community, not much behavior is secret. As a Shoshone once commented to Hoebel: "They just wait around. Sooner or later the facts will come out." In Comanche trials, the question of guilt or innocence was rarely raised. The usual point of argument was only the extent of damages.

Judicial Hearings

In systems in which the administration of law is centralized in the hands of regular judges, the eliciting of evidence may be skillfully conducted. As an example, Gluckman's penetrating analysis of the judicial process among the Barotse of Rhodesia, in Africa, reveals in rich detail the institutional structure of the Lozi courts (*kuta*), made up of three sets of councilors: headmen or

[12] R. Pound, "A Theory of Legal Interests" (*American Sociological Society Publications*, vol. 16, 1920), p. 44.

[13] Many examples of this process may be found in Llewellyn and Hoebel, op. cit., or in J. Richardson, *Law and Status among the Kiowa Indians* (American Ethnological Society Monograph 1, 1940). Because Cheyenne and Kiowa societies were undergoing rapid change during the period covered by these studies, the process of lawmaking was more intensified than is the case in more stable cultures.

nonroyal chiefs, royal officers or stewards, and princes and prince consorts. Because the Lozi have no lawyers, "the whole onus of eliciting and analyzing the evidence falls on the judges." Standards of judicial impartiality are explicitly strong: "A marked feature in all the judgments is the emphasis that the kuta decides by evidence and reasoning, and without favour."[14] Kinship allegiance should not enter.

*The key concept here . . . is trial by due process of law (*tatubo kamulao*). The process is based on hearing evidence (*bupaki*) which establishes proof (also* bupaki*) on the facts. . . . Evidence itself is reduced by concepts of relevance (*bupaki bobuswanela, *appropriate or right evidence;* bupaki bobukena, *evidence which enters); of cogency (*bupaki bobutiile, *strong evidence); of credibility (*bupaki bobusepehala*); and of corroboration (*bupaki bobuyemela*). These types of evidence are tested as direct, circumstantial, or hearsay.*[15]

When, through direct examination, the judges have elicited evidence sufficient to their needs, they enter a process of explicit formulation of a judgment. One after another, from the most junior judge up, in reverse order of seniority, the members of the *kuta* render individual opinions, until the holding of the case is stated in the opinion of the senior chief:

Large parts of the judgments read like sermons, for they are all lectures on the theme "your station and its duties." The standards publicly stated for the parties are the norms involved in their social positions and relationships. . . . The essence of the judicial process is to state these norms to the world and to assess against them the behaviour of the parties in a specific series of situations.[16]

Lozi judges are shrewdly appraised by the people, who express the reputations of individual judges in special terms.

Supernatural Legal Devices

Generally speaking, however, the role of judges is much less significant in primitive legal systems than it is in the more developed legal orders of civilizations. Other devices used by nonliterate societies include resort to supernatural devices such as *divination, conditional curse,* and *ordeal.*

Extortion of confessions by third-degree methods occurs in a few societies; for example, a Comanche husband could choke his wife or hold her over a fire until she named her lover. But more commonly, when the facts could not be gotten by direct means, there was recourse to the supernatural.

Divination The most common device is divination. It is the process of evoking knowledge of some secret or hidden thing by mechanical or manipulative techniques. Thus an Eskimo shaman searches out answers by tying a thong to some reclining object such as a person, a bundle, or even his own foot. After inducing a spirit into the object, he asks it questions to which "yes" or "no" answers may be given. Then he tries to lift the object with the thong. If it is hard to lift, the answer is "no." If it raises easily, the answer is "yes."

Among many North American Indians, the still surface of water that has been put into the abdominal cavity of an animal reveals the image of the culprit. "Just as easy as reading a newspaper," said Post Oak Jim, the Comanche informant.

The Azande of Africa fed poison to a chicken, declaring repeatedly: "If this charge be true, let the chicken die. If this charge be false, spare its life." After the test of the first chicken had provided an answer, a second was given the test, but with the invocation reversed ("If the charge be true, let the chicken live; if it be false, let it die"). Thus, if the first chicken died and the second lived, the allegation was confirmed.[17]

[14]M. Gluckman, *The Judicial Process among the Barotse of Northern Rhodesia*, pp. 82 and 61.

[15]Ibid., p. 316.

[16]Ibid., p. 49.

[17]E. E. Evans-Pritchard, *Witchcraft, Oracles and Magic among the Azande*, pp. 258–351.

FIGURE 28.5
Ifugaos of Northern Luzon using the ordeal by boiling water to settle a question of evidence. If the litigant's hand is scalded, he has been lying. (Lowie Museum of Anthropology, University of California, Berkeley.)

Conditional Curse The conditional curse enters into trial procedure among almost all peoples. It is the assertion that always includes or implies the sentence: "If what I say is not true, *then* may the supernatural destroy me."

Even our own courts do not rely wholly upon our laws against perjury, since every witness must first swear a conditional curse: "So help me God." ("May God smite me if I lie.") Or is it, since the laws of criminal perjury are more recent than the conditional curse, that the courts do not have faith in the efficacy of the laws?

Ordeal Ordeal is peculiarly rare in the New World, which was to the good fortune of the Indians, to say the least. But most of the hideous forms known to medieval Europe were also known with variations throughout Asia, Indonesia, and Africa (Figure 28.5). Various Philippine tribes used the old technique of tying up the two litigants and throwing them in a river. The one who rose to the surface first was guilty. Ordeal by poison was popular in Africa. In Ashanti, the defendant in a trial could drink a poison brew. If he vomited, he was innocent; if he did not vomit, he died. And that is proof enough for anyone!

Oath An oath is merely a formal declaration that the testimony given is true. It may or may not imply the sanction of a supernatural power against falsehood. Often it is accompanied by a ritual act, such as touching the pipe to the lips among Indians, touching an arrow laid across the horns of a buffalo skull, or—as in American courts—placing one's hand upon the Bible.

Cultural Correlates of Conditional Curse and Ordeal A cross-cultural statistical survey undertaken by Professor John M. Roberts indicates that the use of conditional curse and/or ordeal for settling issues of fact and simultaneously invoking supernatural punishment is rare among hunters and gatherers, important among pastoralists, but most frequent among peoples who rely on agriculture for subsistence. Also, the more stratified the society, the more likely the use of conditional curse and ordeals. Finally, the same holds with respect to political systems: the more centralized the government and the larger the community governed, the more likely the appeal to the supernatural in the legal settlement of disputes.[18]

What this means is this: In small nonliterate communities in which there is little differentiation in access to goods and resources, there tend to be fewer conflicts of property interests to generate disputes, and when disputes do occur, it is harder to hide the facts. Contrariwise, as populations become larger and more heterogeneous, as there are more goods to quarrel about, the task of the law becomes greater and more difficult. Direct and rational juridical devices fall short of meeting the demands of the law in societal maintenance. Recourse is then had to the convenience of the supernatural, until in modern, rationalistic, and secularized societies the ritual oath loses its efficacy.

REPRESENTATIVE LEGAL SYSTEMS

In order better to understand the nature of primitive law systems, it will be useful to sketch several examples, ranging from very simple and poorly developed types to highly developed ones that employ centralized governmental control. For this purpose we shall use the Eskimo, Ifugao, Nuer, and Ashanti.

[18]J. M. Roberts, "Oaths, Autonomic Ordeals, and Power," in L. Nader (ed.), *The Ethnography of Law* (*American Anthropologist*, vol. 67, no. 6, part 2, Special Publication, 1965), pp. 186–212.

Eskimo Law

The Eskimos provide a good example of law on the simplest levels of social organization. The small Eskimo local group rarely numbers more than 100 members. Its organization is based on the bilateral family, beyond which there is nothing. There are no lineage, no clan, no clubs of either men or women, and no government. Each group has its headman, but no Eskimo will give an order to another; therefore, the headman exercises no legal or judicial authority.

Prior to the imposition of Danish law in Greenland, of Canadian law in Canada, and of United States law in Alaska, many acts prohibited under these legal systems were accepted as necessary by the Eskimos. Thus, certain forms of homicide were socially justified and legally permitted. Infanticide, invalidicide, suicide, and senilicide fell in this category. They are all responses to the basic Eskimo postulate that only those may survive who contribute to the subsistence economy of the community.

There were few legal offenses against property among the Eskimos because there was no property in land and free borrowing of goods made stealing pointless.

Eskimo law grew out of the aggressive status struggle that bedeviled the men. The society was wholly democratic, but prestige rivalry among the men was strong. Prestige could be gained through superior hunting skill and by stealing the wives of other men. The better the reputation of the man, the more likely he was to have his wife stolen. Wife stealing was not done primarily for sexual reasons. An Eskimo could enjoy sex without running the risks involved in home breaking. The motive lay in an attempt to outrank the man whose wife he took, if he could get away with it.

Wife stealing was not a crime, but most litigation arose from it. The challenge resulted either in murder or in wager of song, wrestling, or buffeting. Rasmussen found in the 1920s that all the adult males in a Musk Ox Eskimo group had been involved in murder, either as principals or as accessories, and "the motive was invariably some quarrel about a woman."[19] The fact that Eskimo husbands would lend their wives did not mean that they were free of jealousy. If a man lent his wife, he enjoyed the prestige of a giver of gifts. But if another man assumed sexual rights without permission, that was adultery and an assault on the husband's ego that could not go unchallenged. He would try to kill the wife stealer. But if he himself were killed, his murder had to be avenged, sooner or later. Since it was the usual Eskimo custom for the killer to marry his victim's widow and to adopt his children, a man might raise the boy whom, when coming of age, would slay him in revenge for the murder of his father.

The alternative to killing an aggressor (and thus becoming involved in feud) was to challenge him to a juridical song contest. The two litigants scurrilously abused each other with songs composed for the occasion:

Now I shall split off words—little sharp words
Like the splinters which I hack off with my ax.
A song from ancient times—a breath of the ancestors
A song of longing—for my wife.
An impudent, black-skinned oaf has stolen her,
Has tried to belittle her.
A miserable wretch who loves human flesh.
A cannibal from famine days.[20]

He who received the most applause won. Thus was the issue settled without reference to the right or wrong of the case. But what was more important, the dispute was laid to rest.[21]

Ifugao Law

The Ifugaos, mountain-dwelling headhunters of Luzon, possessed no government worthy of the name. Over 100,000 people live scattered throughout the deep valleys that crease their rugged homeland. Although there are clusters of houses in the more favorable spots, the Ifugaos have no true villages, nor do they have a clan organization. The bilateral group of kinfolk is tightly knit, however. In the course of centuries, the Ifugaos have carved the steep walls of their mountains into stupendous rice terraces fed by intricate irrigation systems. Their paddies are privately owned and protected by a complex body of substantive law. Ifugaos are capitalists who have many legal rules controlling credit and debt. In addition, they are litigious in the extreme, for each man is sensitive about his "face" and quick to take offense. Their list of possible legal wrongs is long indeed.

How did they handle a legal case prior to the establishment of American legal control around 1905, and, subsequently, of Philippine national law? A man with a grievance or a claim tried first to exact a satisfactory settlement from the opposite party. Failing this, he went to a *monkalun*, or "go-between," who was a member of the highest social class and who had a reputation as a man of affairs and a number of enemy heads to his credit. The *monkalun* heard his story and accosted the defendant with the charges. The defendant in turn pleaded his cause. Meanwhile, both plaintiff and defendant marshaled their fighting relatives—just in case. The *monkalun* shuttled back and forth between the two parties, wheedling, arguing, threatening, cajoling—attempting to induce them to give ground so that they might meet on terms acceptable to each. Customary law made the penalties and obligations of both parties quite explicit for every conceivable offense, but first there had to be agreement on the exact nature and degree of the offense. Claim was balanced against counterclaim. Each side weighed the fighting strength and inclination of the other. But at long last, if the patience of the *monkalun* and the litigants endured, a settlement was reached and damages were paid (if it was an assault case) or the debt

---

[19]K. Rasmussen, *Across Arctic America*, p. 250.

[20]K. Rasmussen, *Grønlandsagen*, p. 235.

[21]E. A. Hoebel, "Law-ways of the Primitive Eskimos" (*Journal of Criminal Law and Criminology*, vol. 13, 1941), pp. 663–683, or *The Law of Primitive Man*, chap. 5.

was satisfied (if it was an economic dispute). But if no settlement satisfactory to each disputant could be reached, the *monkalun* finally withdrew from the case. Then the plaintiff or his kin undertook to kill the defendant—or any of his relatives. Feud was forthcoming. The legal machinery had broken down.[22]

The *monkalun* represented the public interest by his intervention. Yet he was only incipiently a public officer. He made no decision and enforced no judgment, but he provided the means, through his good offices, of bringing disputants to a resolution of their conflict. All Ifugao legal offenses were wrongs to be prosecuted by the aggrieved individual. There were no recognized crimes against society at large and, therefore, no public law.[23]

Nuer Law

The legal system of the Nuer of the African Sudan was similar to that of the Ifugaos in many respects. The Nuer, like the Ifugaos, had no state. Unlike the Ifugaos, they were organized into segmented lineages (see page 414). The lineages represented the legal units that stood in opposition to one another.

According to Evans-Pritchard's analysis, feud and the threat of feud were the legal mechanisms by means of which adherence to norms was maintained. Violation of a norm could set off a feud between lineages. But among the Nuer, "A feud cannot be tolerated within a village and it is impossible to maintain one for a long period between nearby villages."[24]

We have already indicated that formal judges are not a necessary attribute of law. The Nuer, like the Ifugaos, employed the services of a mediator, the Priest of the Earth, to settle serious

FIGURE 28.6
The Nuer Priest of the Earth, also known as a Leopard Skin Chief, exercises legal authority in cases of homicide, and wears a leopard skin cape as a symbol of his position and power. (Pitt Rivers Museum, Oxford University.)

disputes (Figure 28.6). Most Nuer offenses were legally settled by direct negotiation between the lineages without intervention of the Priest of the Earth. Bodily injuries gave rise to damages paid in cattle according to a definite and detailed scale commensurate with the degree of injury to the victim. Adultery and seduction of unmarried

[22]Ifugao procedure is dramatized in "The Case of the Bamboo-sized Pigs: Ifugao," in *The Ways of Mankind*, Series II.

[23]R. F. Barton, *Ifugao Law*; also Hoebel, *The Law of Primitive Man*, chap. 6.

[24]E. E. Evans-Pritchard, "The Nuer of the Southern Sudan," in E. E. Evans-Pritchard and M. Fortes (eds.), *African Political Systems*, p. 159.

girls were also private wrongs for which compensation in cattle could be demanded and received. There were also suits over the return of progeny price after a divorce had taken place.

Failure to pay the customary damages in cattle might bring deadly resort to the spear; then a feud could be launched and the equilibrium of the society seriously disturbed. But in spite of their truculence, the Nuer valued good relations among neighbors and within the society.

The killing of a Nuer by a Nuer resulted in the spiritual contamination of the murderer and all the murderer's household. The contamination, called *nueer*, was believed to bring disease and death unless it was ritually removed by the Priest of the Earth.

A killing could entail the inconvenience of a feud, and it certainly entails (even today) the dangers and costs of *nueer*. A murderer would therefore seek asylum in the homestead of the Priest of the Earth. There the murderer was secure against revenge while the priest arranged the payment of blood money by the killer's lineage to the lineage of the victim. If one or the other lineage held out unreasonably in agreeing to an acceptable settlement, the priest could threaten to curse them. If the curse were uttered, their cattle would sicken, their crops wither, and their people die—not a happy prospect! The ultimate sanction in Nuer law, therefore, was physical, albeit by supernatural means. When the blood money had finally been paid, the homestead, cattle, and body of the murderer were ritually purified in elaborate ceremony. Social relations between the two kinship groups were thus restored, and life could resume its course.

Ashanti Law

Finally, the Ashanti of West Africa may be cited as a people who were well on the road toward civilized law by the middle of the last century. Today they are part of the nation of Ghana.

The Ashanti were a powerful nation who developed a constitutional monarchy. Clan feuding was checked, and all private law was brought within the potential jurisdiction of the royal criminal courts. Any private dispute ordinarily settled between the household heads of the two disputants could be thrown into royal hands by the simple device of one of the quarreling persons swearing an oath on the Great Forbidden Name of a god that the other was guilty of an offense. In rebuttal, his adversary would swear on the same forbidden name that he did not commit the wrong. One or the other was then guilty of a false oath, perjury, which was a capital crime for which the liar lost his head.

Whoever heard the swearing had to arrest the two, for every citizen was the king's agent in such an event. He led them to a log kept for the purpose and chained them to it, after which he trotted off to the king's bailiff with the news. A day was then set for the trial. When hauled before the king and his council of elders, each litigant was called upon to tell his story. The stories were then repeated verbatim by the king's speaker, and each affirmed the accuracy of the repetition. Next, one of the prisoners named a witness, who was brought forth to swear a deadly conditional curse that what he was about to say was the truth. In this the Ashanti placed implicit faith, for the whole trial hinged on what was now said. On the testimony of the single witness, one party was freed and the other condemned to be beheaded—unless the king in deference to the needs of his treasury allowed the luckless one "to buy his head," that is, to pay a fine.[25]

Aside from this crude but remarkable device for extending the king's peace, there was also a great body of criminal regulations; the violation of any one of these would be punished by death. These ranged from homicide—"only the king

[25]Ashanti procedure and the techniques of shifting a quarrel from the area of private law to that of criminal law are dramatized in "The Forbidden Name of Wednesday: Ashanti," *The Ways of Mankind*, Series II.

may wield the knife"—to carrying a chicken on top of a load. Even suicide was a capital offense, for it constituted a usurpation of the king's exclusive right to kill. The corpse of the suicide was hauled into court, tried, and ostentatiously decapitated. As a more practical gesture, the suicide's properties were also confiscated on behalf of the king's treasury.

Ashanti criminal law overreached the mark in much the same way as did the law of eighteenth-century England, with its 200 capital crimes. It is significant as an example of the way in which monarchy becomes the means of expressing the social interest in the maintenance of order by replacing private law by criminal law. This is a genuine social advance over the chaos of societies that allow feuding.[26]

THE TREND OF THE LAW

It is a seeming paradox, on first thought, that the more complex a society becomes, the greater is the need for law, and the wider the reach of law becomes. But it is no paradox if the functions of law are kept in mind. Simple societies have little need of law, and in the simplest societies there were probably no legal institutions. In such groups as the Shoshones, Eskimos, Andaman Islanders, and African Bushmen, there is only a little of what we would call law. Almost all relations are face to face and intimate. The demands imposed by culture are relatively few; child training is direct and comprehensive. Ridicule is keenly felt, for there is no escape in anonymity. Taboo and the fear of supernatural sanctions cover a large area of behavior. Special interests are few, for there is little accumulated wealth. Conflict arises mostly in interpersonal relations. Hence, homicide and adultery are the most common legal focuses. Sorcery as a form of homicide always looms large as an illegal possibility, but in the nonliterate societies, sorcery, which uses supernatural techniques, is usually met with supernatural countermeasures rather than with legal action.

Among the hunters, the pastoralists, and the gardening peoples, the size of the group and the increased complexity of the culture make possible greater divergence of interests between the members of the tribe. Conflict of interests grows, and the need for legal devices for settlement and control of the internal clash of interests is felt. Private law emerges and spreads. It exerts a restraining influence, but it has inherent limitations that prevent it from completely satisfying the need it must meet. As no one is competent to judge a personal cause, procedure under private law leads too often not to a just settlement but to internecine fighting—to feud.

Feud and Law

Feud is a state of conflict between two kinship groups within a society, manifest by a series of killings and counterkillings, usually initiated in response to an original homicide or other grievous injury. Legal historians traditionally have seen nonliterate society as marked by a horrid and constant state of feud, rent by violent retaliation and blood revenge, and, in general, an arena of violence, ruled by the law of the jungle and retaliation—"an eye for an eye, a tooth for a tooth." The fact is that there is very limited evidence for the actual occurrence of feud in nonliterate societies. Legal procedures or ritual devices such as regulated combat as a means of avoiding or terminating feud are universal in such cultures. People in these societies actually prefer to accept damages rather than take blood revenge.

An example would be the case of the Trobriand Islanders for whom Malinowski reported that although honor makes "vendetta" obligatory in cases of homicide, it was evaded by the substitution of blood money (compensation). There was much Trobriand talk of feud, but Malinowski found not one specific case. In all

[26]This description applied a century ago. R. S. Rattray, *Ashanti Law and Constitution*; K. A. Busia, *The Position of the Chief in the Modern Political System of Ashanti*; and E. A. Hoebel, *The Law of Primitive Man*, chap. 9

anthropological reports, this is the rule rather than the exception.

There is no question but that the folk belief in feud as a cultural expectancy, as both ideal and presumed behavior, is widespread. It is a folk phenomenon in its own right. The idea of feud, if not its reality, assumes importance.

Real feud is socially destructive and dangerous, but law exists everywhere to preclude the recourse to bloody battles within societies. Folk belief in the expected requirements of honor to engage in feud is customarily blown up to feed the fear of the effects of feud. It seems quite likely that this very fear of feud is one of the factors that nourishes and sustains primitive legal systems.

World Law

The next development in law that may be foreseen on the basis of past trends and growing need is the freeing of the individual from the limitations of nationality and, concomitantly, the expansion of the scope of law to embrace a worldwide system framed and administered by a world commonwealth. Today, primitive law prevails between nations. What passes as international law consists of no more than normative rules for the conduct of affairs between nations as they have been agreed upon from time to time through treaties, pacts, and covenants. In addition, a body of prevailing custom in international intercourse, recognized by tacit consensus or verbalized in arbitration, World Court awards, and United Nations decisions, provides the other main source of its substance. But this body of social norms for international intercourse is no more than the bylaws of the subgroups we call nations. International law now consists of substantive rules without imperative legal sanctions.

The United Nations today, like the League of Nations of yesterday, because the power of universal, coercive, absolute force is withheld from it, cannot make law of the international norms upon which it determines. Whatever the idealist may desire or the nationalist fear, force and the threat of force remain the ultimate powers in the implementation of law between nations, as they do in law within the nation or tribe. But until the use of force and the threat of force as now exercised by nation against nation are brought under the socialized control of a world community, by and for world society, they remain not the sanctions of world law but the instruments of social anarchy and the constant threat to the survival of present societies.

The metamorphosis from primitive law to modern law on the international plane awaits the emergence of the consciousness of world community.

SUMMARY

Law is one aspect of the system of social control which is an implicit part of every culture. Social control consists of all those practices engaged in by the members of a society to reward and encourage approved behavior and to penalize and discourage disapproved behavior. Law is a part of the system of the selection and maintenance of norms relied upon by each society in its organization.

Law, like custom, consists of social norms. Law shares with custom the element of regularity: that which is normally done (the *is*) and that which is expected to be done (the *ought*). Law sustains predictability in behavior.

Law, like custom, is sanctioned. Some deviation from social norms is usually allowed. Yet in many societies, deviation beyond permissible limits in certain spheres is negatively sanctioned by confiscation of economic goods or by the application of physical coercion. Economic sanctions are classed as *damages* or *fines*, depending upon who has legal authority and to whom the penalty is paid. In *private law* they are damages; in *public law* they are fines.

The difference between public and private law depends upon who has the authority to initiate legal proceedings and impose the sanctions. The legal official is a person or group of persons who has the socially recognized privilege-right of acting against another person in accordance with the rules of due process of law. In most systems of primitive law, the wronged party, or the party's kinship group, is vested with the privilege-right of initiating a legal action and carrying it to completion by punishing the wrongdoer. This is called *private law*, but it has the backing of general social approval. On the other hand, if the legal action must be initiated by a headman, a chief, or a chief's representative, the offense is called a *crime*, and the whole process is in the area of *public law*.

A law is, therefore, defined as *a social norm which, if violated beyond permissible limits, will usually evoke a formal procedural response initiated by an individual or a group possessing the socially recognized privilege-right of determining guilt and of imposing economic or physical sanctions upon the wrongdoer.*

Substantive law consists of the norms to be enforced (the *what*). Procedural, or adjective, law consists of the norms which determine due process of law (the *how*). Law has four major functions: (1) to identify acceptable lines of behavior for inclusion in the culture and to penalize contradictory behavior, so as to maintain at least minimal integration of individuals within the society; (2) to allocate authority and to determine who may legitimately apply force to maintain the legal norms; (3) to settle trouble cases as they arise; and (4) to redefine relationships as the conditions of life change, so as to help keep the culture adaptable.

The modern study of primitive legal systems is based upon the analysis of actual cases of dispute and conflict. Law is what people do, not what they say they do.

Cases may be settled through direct negotiation between the disputants. This process may involve the use of a go-between or mediator; it may call for an arbitrator; or it may be put in the hands of a judge or judges.

In very small societies, where most relations are face to face, the problem of evidence does not raise many difficulties. When the facts are not known, however, or the claims of the aggrieved party are denied by the defendant, recourse is usually to the supernatural powers by means of divination, conditional curse, or ordeal. In some rare cultures or situations, a simple oath suffices.

In the evolution of law, public law tends to gain in importance as societies become more complex. The trend of the law has been one of an increasing shift of responsibility for the maintenance of legal norms away from the individual and kinship group to the agents of the society as a whole. In like manner, the individual tends to be allowed greater freedom in contractual determination of social responsibilities.

Feud has been viewed as an absence of law and as a breakdown of the legal machinery. The "law of blood revenge" was believed to be a common feature of many nonliterate societies. More recent studies indicate that although the idea of feuding is quite widespread, the more regular and frequent practice is to accept damages rather than seek blood revenge. Fear of feud may promote primitive legal systems.

As society expands, so does the scope of the law, for unless the functions of law are adequately fulfilled, the existence of the society is endangered. The great modern problem of survival and cultural adaptation is the creation of an effective system of world law to meet the functional prerequisites of world society.

SELECTED READINGS

Barton, R. F., *Ifugao Law* (1969). This classic monograph on the Ifugao is highly recommended.

Gluckman, M., *The Judicial Process among the Barotse of Northern Rhodesia* (1955). How trouble cases are settled in an African tribe. Also, *The Ideas in Barotse Jurisprudence* (1965). A brilliant comparative analysis of Barotse legal concepts.

Hoebel, E. A., *The Law of Primitive Man* (1954). Presents a theory of law and society and analyzes the legal culture of seven societies.

Llewellyn, K. N., and E. A. Hoebel, *The Cheyenne Way: Conflict and Case Law in Primitive Jurisprudence* (1941). Contains case records of legal disputes and a systematic analysis of the law-ways of the Cheyenne.

Nader, L. (ed.), *Law in Culture and Society* (1969). A comprehensive collection of case studies of law in non-Western and Western societies.

Pospisil, L., *Anthropology of Law: A Comparative Theory* (1971). A theoretical and empirical treatment of law and society from an anthropological point of view which is both sound and informative.

29
Political Organization and Process

LEARNING GOALS

Discuss political organization and the concept of the state.

Identify three principles of organization.

Describe stateless systems.

Specify how age-sets are a type of political organization.

Summarize state systems of government.

List the functions of the council.

Indicate the attributes of politics.

Describe the Cheyenne and Tswana political organizations.

Law can exist without government in the form of private law as explained in the previous chapter. Much political activity does not express itself as law. Yet the very existence of law is itself an expression of political organization, for the legal acts of a private prosecutor are an expression of public interest and public consensus.

The political process performs much the same functions as have been specified for law: (1) the definition of behavioral norms for acceptable conduct, (2) the allocation of force and authority, (3) the settlement of disputes, and (4) the redefinition of norms for conduct.

Political organization, and especially government, may well go beyond this, however. In addition, (1) it may organize group efforts for public works, such as communal hunts, tending the chief's gardens, digging and repairing irrigation ditches, and building roads, temples, and pyramids; (2) it may carry ritual and ceremonial responsibility for religious control of the supernatural world and human conduct (see Priests and kings, pages 508–509); (3) it may organize and maintain markets and trading networks; and (4) it usually carries responsibility for defense of the home territory and the waging of war against enemy societies.

GOVERNMENT: LAW, POLITICAL ORGANIZATION, AND POLITICS

It will be clear by now that there is a good deal of overlapping in the attributes of law, political structures, and political processes, and also in the manner in which each relates to government. Implied in all these concepts are the organization of activities for the general welfare, the establishment of norms, the use of coercion and the assignment of authority for the maintenance of these norms, and the legitimation of all these ends.

For our purposes, it is sufficient to say that the political sphere of social organization here means "everything that is at once public, goal-oriented, and that involves a differential of power (in the sense of control) among the individuals of the group in question."[1]

Political organization is more than government as such, and it is not synonymous with the state, for the state is a specialized social phenomenon, while political organization is generalized.

Government is the executive instrument of political organization, and consists of the men and women who hold designated statuses as decision makers and exercisers of power in the public sphere. It is expressed in the way they exercise power and in the way the governed respond to (and sometimes limit) their power (Figure 29.1).

The study of the ongoing maneuvering—pushing, wheedling, cajoling, arguing, threatening, punishing, and rewarding—by which the goals are agreed upon or set, and by which the people are led or shoved in the desired direction (or by which they resist and obstruct the "official" intent) is the study of *political processes*, or *politics.*

Modern (since World War II) anthropology, like modern political science, has become much more interested in the study of political *processes* than of political *structure.* And well it might, for this tells us much more of what is going on than does a formal comparison of the organization of different kinds of "chiefdoms" and "states."[2]

Political Organization

The only kind of society that could be said to be without political organization would be one consisting of a single bilateral extended family within which there were no organized subdivisions. Sex and age differences would be present, to be sure, and there could be one or two religious specialists. But the society would be organized as

[1]M. J. Swartz, V. W. Turner, and A. Tuden (eds.), *Political Anthropology*, p. 7.

[2]For an excellent exemplification of this trend, see H. A. Powell, "Competitive Leadership in Trobriand Political Organization" (*Journal of the Royal Anthropological Institute*, vol. 90, 1960), pp. 118–45; reprinted in R. Cohen and J. Middleton (eds.), *Comparative Political Systems*, pp. 155–192.

FIGURE 29.1
The popularly elected Tribal Council of the Papago Indians in Arizona electing its officers at a meeting held in a school gymnasium. (Arizona State Museum.)

a single large family operating under familial controls. All problems would be settled as family problems, and there would be no other divisive groupings within the community. Family and community would be one. This kind of society was approximated among some of the simpler societies, such as the Shoshones, but it exists nowhere today.

Political organization comes into being wherever societies are segmented on the basis of kinship, economics, religion, sex, fraternities, or community. Where there are subgroups that are discrete entities within the entire society, there political organization exists—a system of regulation of relations between groups or members of different groups within the society at large and between one society and another.

Because the members of a community live together with a common culture, they share patterns of living and ideas. Community means that the feeling of oneness—a sense of entity, an esprit de corps—extends to the whole territorial society. It means that the culture sets values that orient behavior in the direction of common as well as individual or subgroup interests. The common interests are what constitute political interests. The community is the polity. Political organization, therefore, is *that part of the culture which functions explicitly to direct the activities of the members of the society toward community goals.*

The State

It is quite possible to analyze political organization without referring to the concept of the state. Indeed, the failure of political scientists to realize this until quite recently seriously handicapped the development of viable political theory beyond the realm of European types of government.[3] For a long time, thinking in terms of the state did more harm than good because it diverted attention from the broader, institutional aspects of political processes as they are woven through the entire weft of social life. This kept both political scientists and anthropologists from paying attention to the political process in simply organized societies. Yet the state is so overpoweringly important in modern civilization, and is growing steadily more so, that it cannot be

[3]G. A. Almond and J. S. Coleman (eds.), *The Politics of Developing Areas.*

ignored. Anthropologists now distinguish between stateless and state-organized societies.

The idea of a state embodies three elements: (1) a territory, (2) a population with a common culture, and (3) a centrally organized government with strong coercive powers.

The state is an institution among other institutions within a given culture. It is not the society or the community; it is a complex of behaviors characteristic of the members of the community in one part of their lives—the political.

Three Principles of Organization

A political system may use one or more of three major units of social structure as the basis for its organization: (1) kinship units; (2) geographical, or territorial, units; or (3) associational units.

Kinship Nonliterate societies generally rest most heavily on the kinship principle. Lineages, clans, phratries, and moieties may each have their leaders who not only are responsible for the regulation and guidance of affairs within their respective kinship groups but who also formally represent their groups vis-à-vis other kinship groups. Collectively, they may form the several levels of councils that act within or for the group in public affairs. But note, on the other hand, that so far has the kinship principle fallen into disuse in modern times, and especially in the United States, that favoritism on behalf of relatives, called *nepotism*, is often forbidden by law.

Territorialism On the other hand, since every community is a distinguishable territorial entity, every political system uses the geographical unit as a basis of organization as well. The smallest such unit is the *household.* The next largest is the *camp* (among nomadic hunters and gatherers) or the *village* (among sedentary peoples). The next largest is the *band*, comprising a number of camps (among the nomads) or the *district*, comprising several villages (among sedentary people). Then there is the *tribe* or *nation*, the largest group with a common language and culture. (Actually, a tribe may incorporate alien groups.)

Tribes may ally on a more or less permanent basis with other tribes to form a *confederacy.* This is usually done on a voluntary basis for mutual defense or aggression, but in the confederacy each tribe remains self-determining in political matters to a great extent. The only real difference between an alliance and a confederacy is in the development of more enduring and explicit institutions for determination of questions of mutual concern between the societies.

Associations The use of special associations as a principle of political organization is, on the whole, relatively weak in nonliterate cultures, but nevertheless quite widespread. The heads of the secret religious fraternities form the tribal council in a number of pueblos. The military fraternities of the Plains Indians performed major governmental functions, as do many of the secret societies of Africa and Melanesia. The age-sets of other parts of Africa do likewise. In India, castes still operate as political units, although the modern constitution of India proscribes them.

TYPES OF POLITICAL ORGANIZATION

As a society emphasizes one or another principle of organization, or a combination of principles, it produces political organizations of different types. Some of these are identifiable among nonliterate cultures as follows.

Stateless Systems

Stateless systems have no formal government embracing the entire society. Political functions are performed by subgroups and by functionaries whose political jobs are secondary to other interests and responsibilities. There is no person or group of persons with authority applicable to the society as a whole.

Undifferentiated In such cultures as those of the South African Bushmen, the Eskimos, and the Shoshones, kinship and political relations are one and the same. Small, local groups live as isolated, self-governing units, subject to no higher political power. Tensions between members of individual families are settled directly without intervention of a group leader.

Segmentary Lineage This is the uncentralized political system in which lineages rather than villages or bands form the significant units of organization. There is little or no common decision making for the tribe, nor is there much in the way of broadly integrative ceremony or ritual. The segmentary lineage organization provides the structural framework. The Nuer of the African Sudan are the classic example.

Age-Set Under this system, political matters are largely in the hands of age-sets and their officers. The age-sets cut across village and district boundaries and form the framework of political integration, as among the Nyakyusa. By virtue of the relatively limited distribution of age-sets, this system is quite rare.

Village Council and Associations In this type, there is no tribal government as such, nor do corporate lineages function in government, but authority is vested in village councils (Figure 29.2) and men's fraternities. The Pueblos of the southwestern United States and such tribes as the Ibo of West Africa are representative.

Village or Band with Headman Here, the tribe lacks overall government; each band or village, as the case may be, has a headman or chief endowed with weak political authority. Kinship may be important in other aspects of life, but it is not a major factor in political organization. Territorial identity and personal qualities of leadership on the part of a headman are the determining factors.

The leader is expected to speak on all important occasions. Among the Yavapai of Arizona, the headman was moderate in speech, stopped quarrels, and knew the best campsites. People followed him because his personality won their confidence. Of the Comanche headmen, That's It sagely observed: "I hardly know how to tell about them; they never had much to do except to hold the band together."[4] That's It put his finger on it. The headman rarely has explicit authority; his functions are so subtle that they defy easy description. Yet he is the focal point of the local group.

State Systems

State systems have chiefs, kings, or councils with authority over certain spheres of social activity covering the entire society.

Chiefdoms Complexity of social life increases the need for leadership and the delegation of responsibility. Societies that are sufficiently complex to have a state always possess chiefs. A chief is differentiated from the headman by an increased degree of authority and prestige. The position may be inherited. The chief's functions and powers are variable among different peoples.

In North America, it was unusual for a chief to have strong power. Great care was taken in many tribes to separate the offices of peace chiefs and war chiefs. Peace chiefs were the civil governors. Usually they were band or clan headmen elevated to the status of membership in the tribal council. They supervised internal tribal relations and had judicial powers over a few classes of crime. Most legal offenses, however, remained in the area of private wrongs to be settled by the parties concerned. Sometimes, as in the case of the Cheyennes (see pages 512–514), Omahas, and Iroquois, the civil chiefs were

[4]E. A. Hoebel, *The Political Organization and Law-ways of the Comanche Indians* (American Anthropological Association Memoir 54; Contributions from the Laboratory of Anthropology 4, 1940), p. 18.

FIGURE 29.2
Modern Eskimo self-government. Mayor Dan Lisbourne with members of the Point Hope, Alaska, council and other officers. (Steve McCutcheon.)

explicitly chosen for limited tenure. War chiefs were the heads of military fraternities, or a war chief could be any man who had an outstanding war record. Naturally, war chiefs could make their opinions felt in the tribe, but they had very limited constitutional powers in the operation of the camp in peacetime.

The functional significance of chiefs in the Bantu tribes of South Africa may be sensed from Schapera's listing of their activities:

1. *He attends habitually at his council-place where he listens to news, petitions, and complaints, from all over the tribe, and gives orders for whatever action is required.*
2. *Legislation has always been a recognized function of the chief.*
3. *He periodically creates a new age-regiment, and thus formally admits youths into the social category of adults.*
4. *He controls the distribution and use of land.*
5. *He also regulates the calendar of agricultural and certain other activities.*
6. *He organizes large collective hunts.*
7. *He mobilizes his people for defense and aggression.*
8. *He organizes religious ceremonies upon the due performance of which his tribe's security and prosperity are held to depend and which ensure that the rainfall is adequate.*[5]

Small wonder that Tsonga proverbs say: "A tribe without a chief has lost its reason; it is dead." And, "In a country without chiefs, the people devour one another."[6]

[5] I. Schapera, *Government and Politics in Tribal Societies*, pp. 68–75.
[6] Ibid., p. 105.

Kingdoms Kingship results from the development of the hereditary principle. Its main function is to introduce stability into the administration of government. Strong clans make for intra-tribal strife. Lineages and central government are inherently incompatible. Lineage autonomy must be superseded by a stronger law of the whole society. This can conveniently be the king's law and the king's peace. But the power of paramount leaders is in itself a luscious prize for power-hungry people. With bloody intrigue and with turmoil in their struggles to project themselves into chieftainship, they can rend the peace of the society. Clearly defined hereditary succession puts a check on such social abscesses. Yet the oftentimes fatal defect of the hereditary principle is that the heir to succession may have no aptitude for the job. The king may be an indecisive weakling or, worse still, a dangerous egomaniac. In the one event, the state may fail to function effectively in times of crisis. In the other, tyranny supplants social justice, and people suffer under corruption.

The hereditary principle develops quite naturally and without conscious awareness. We can see this among those American Indian societies which explicitly deny hereditary succession to chieftainship. In spite of the fact that any good man may become a chief, records show again and again that a chief is succeeded by one of his sons or maternal nephews. Chieftainship runs in family or lineage lines. This arises from the fact that the training and high example set by the senior relatives engender chiefly qualities in the boys. People come to expect leadership from such lines. The boys assume that people will respond to their superior leadership—and they do. Eventually, the tendency may become a prescription.

Priests and kings The skeins of religion and politics are composed of separate threads. Yet they are woven into the tapestry that is society, sometimes carefully separated, each forming its own design, and sometimes intertwined, joining church and state in one pattern. The warrior's sword and the magician's wand are different artifacts. A man may wield one or the other, but if he is skilled enough and if his culture permits, he may seize the sword in his right hand and the wand in his left. Then, indeed, he becomes an awesome power. The essential doctrine of separation of church and state in American democratic tradition is a needful defensive reaction to that power.

Shamans and priests are specialists in controlling the action of the supernatural; headmen, chiefs, and kings are specialists in controlling the actions of people. But the actions of people must be controlled in their relations to the supernatural as well as to their fellow citizens; the priest always has temporal influence (Figure 29.3). The politician uses religious means for political purposes when the control of religious power is possible; the priest in turn is apt to use political means to attain religious ends when the techniques are available. In many societies, however, a working agreement between the two often exists; for example, the Trobriand chief employs his hereditary sorcerer to destroy upstarts,[7] and the Yokuts-Mono chiefs in California connived with medicine men to mulct the guileless public.[8] On the other hand, use of supernatural power for self-advantage through black magic is almost universally treated as a deadly crime if carried too far.

In general, supernaturalism is so ubiquitous in the nonliterate world that it colors all government to some degree. Political officers almost invariably possess some magic power or religious sanctity. War making, legislation, and judicial procedure inevitably involve religious ritual.

In highly organized gardening societies of sedentary peoples dependent on fixed crops, the

---

[7]B. Malinowski, *Crime and Custom in Savage Society*, pp. 85–86 and 92–93.

[8]A. H. Gayton, *Yokuts-Mono Chiefs and Shamans* (University of California Publications in American Archaeology and Ethnology, vol. 24, 1930), pp. 361–420.

FIGURE 29.3 (a) (b)

(a) Among the Ashanti of Ghana, the priest of the god Bonsam is a farmer like everyone else. Ordinary men wear their hair cut short, however, while his is plaited in long strands. (b) Every nine days, the priest becomes ritually possessed by the spirit of the god, who speaks through him in response to petitions and complaints of the people of his district. (From *The Ashanti: A Proud People* by Robert A. Lystad. Published by Rutgers University Press, New Brunswick, N.J.)

chief is usually the high priest of the rain, fertility, and garden cults. As the supervisor of politico-legal relations, the chief is also responsible for the economic well-being and religious security of the people. In Africa, again and again, the chief symbolizes the tribal soul: a soul that must be hale and vigorous, or else the tribe wanes and dies. Hence, it was the fate of the king who became feeble or sickly to be poisoned or strangled by his chief councilors.[9] It is no unalloyed privilege for one to be a ruler. Eminence always entails responsibility.

The chief's speaker "A White House spokesman announced today. . . ." The device of presidents is a possession of chiefs and kings the world over. The Ashanti king or the paramount chief of a district rarely speaks in public. To do so is bad etiquette and bad policy. He has his *okeyame* to serve as his mouthpiece (Figure 29.4). In Samoa, each chief has his Talking Chief, who recites his chief's genealogy before every meeting of the native council. He speaks his chief's mind in debate. Kwakiutl and other Northwest Coast chieftains have their speakers at potlatches to extol the ancestry and virtues of their masters.

The reason for these speakers is subtle but sound. When chieftains rise above the level of headmen, their power increases. Those who

[9]See J. G. Frazer, *The Golden Bough*, chap. 24, "The Killing of the Divine King."

FIGURE 29.4
The spokesman of an Ashanti chief holds his symbol of office, an intricately carved wood staff sheathed with gold leaf. He talks on behalf of the chief, even though the chief is present. An ordinary person who wishes to speak to the chief must do so through the spokesman. (From *The Ashanti: A Proud People* by Robert A. Lystad. Published by Rutgers University Press, New Brunswick, N.J.)

wield powers of decision and enforcement must not be too familiar to the multitude. Some good leaders can maintain influence and fraternity simultaneously, but they are rare. It is a safer and surer technique to let a minion undertake the vulgar task of shouting to the masses.

The Council The one universal instrument of government is the council. No tribe or nation does without it. No man or woman can govern alone, nor is one permitted to do so. Monarchy, if taken literally, is a misnomer. Every king or chief operates within a network of advisers. Some are helplessly enmeshed in it.

In small, simple societies, the council is a democratic gathering of adult males. In gerontocratic Australia, participation was limited to the elders. Among American Indians, tribal councils commonly consisted of all the band headmen. The decision of the council had to be unanimous; one stubborn holdout could effectively block action. Still there were neat devices for attaining unanimity.

Among the great African monarchies, the king had the superficial appearance of an absolute autocrat. Yet he could rarely act without full approval of the council, and this was not forthcoming until the royal elders had sounded out public opinion. Kings who abused their power could generally be deposed; in the old days, they could be destroyed.

The conduct of a monarchy, like every other social relation, rests on reciprocity. If the exalted ruler receives great social privilege, that ruler must give service to the people in return. Some kings and dictators may ignore this precept, but it is difficult for them successfully to ignore for long the principle voiced in the Balinese proverb: "The ruler owes his might to the people."

Nonpolitical Associations in Government It is an error to think of government solely in terms of the organs explicitly designed for governmental purposes. All government is pluralistic, and various outside organizations play their parts in determining and executing political policy.

Take, for example, a small-town volunteer fire company in New York State. It is a closed fraternity, which elects its members by secret vote. It has all the trappings of a lodge: sworn secrecy, uniforms with gold buttons, rituals, dances, and ceremonial feasting. It also puts out fires as the occasion demands. This firemen's fraternity is a private association, a true men's club. Yet it is an official branch of government under the laws of the State of New York. The costs of its fire-fighting equipment and meeting rooms are met by public taxation. It is regulated by public law and is controlled by publicly elected fire commissioners. It remains a club and yet is an organ of government, just as the Plains Indian military fraternities were, the social aspects of which have already been discussed in Chapter 25. Fraternity, feasting, dancing, and social enjoyment were the primary activities of such men's clubs, but they also took on police, judicial, and legislative powers when the need arose.[10] The councils constitutionally possessed all judicial and legislative powers covering criminal activity. However, the council chiefs were peace chiefs not given to coercive action. When coercive restraint or punishment was needed, they were not suited to the task. They were "fathers" to the people, and Indian fathers do not punish their children. What was more natural than that the extragovernmental societies of warriors should take over policing the hunt, the rice harvest, and the great tribal ceremonials of the sun dance? This they did with vigor and dispatch. In later years, as the Plains tribes began to crumble before the onslaught of the white people, the Cheyenne military societies assumed more and more governmental power as crisis piled on crisis. But to no avail; they were overwhelmed.

THE POLITICAL PROCESS, OR POLITICS

Having briefly examined how societies are politically organized, let us turn to the more intricate matter of how these structures work.

All role definition, which runs through every aspect of culture, defines activities and duties, expectancies and obligations. All norms of social organization spell out who does what, who gets what—when, where, and how. Politics is but one aspect of the cultural patterning and behavioral processes which are involved.

As we examine political processes in the anthropological context, it is important to keep in mind what has already been said on social structure in the preceding chapters, especially those on economic organization, kinship, associations, social classes and castes, and law. Every one of these facets of society has implications for politics, and politics sinks its roots into each.

Politics, it must always be remembered, is not something discrete, an arena of life absolute unto itself. Politics is social behavior with an orientation, a slant, that gives it a coloring sufficiently different to warrant its own identity. But it is many-hued, and its colors, taken separately, are shared with other fields.

The Attributes of Politics

Swartz, Turner, and Tuden,[11] specify several qualities which identify the political process:

1. It is public rather than private: it is not an individual matter, nor familial. "An activity that affects a neighborhood, a whole community, a whole society, or a group of societies is unquestionably a public activity; whether it is *also* a political activity depends upon other characteristics—in addition to its being public" (Figure 29.5).

2. Politics is goal-oriented; it is concerned with ends and means—"What is it we want?" and "How do we go about getting it?" The political process always involves decision making—the selection of specified aims from among possible alternatives and the choice of administrative procedures.

Politics involves public goals. However much a vested group within the society may strive and quarrel in pressing its own interests over those of others, the political decision relates to what goal shall be sought by the action of the community *as* community on the question at issue.

3. A third feature of the political process is that it allocates and focuses power. It assigns authority, either in decision making (as in the case of law

[10]R. H. Lowie, *Primitive Society*, p. 415; *The Origin of the State*, pp. 94–107; "Property Rights and Coercive Powers of the Plains Indian Military Societies" (*Journal of Legal and Political Sociology*, vol. 1, 1943), pp. 59–71.

[11]M. J. Swartz, V. W. Turner, and A. Tuden (eds.), op. cit., p. 4.

FIGURE 29.5
The Navajo Tribal Council hall is a modern structure built in the shape of a hogan and decorated with murals depicting Navajo life. (Josef Muench.)

enforcers) or in directing activities (as in the case of task-force leaders in hunting, war, temple building, ritual, or whatever).

In small face-to-face hunting and gathering societies power allocation poses few problems. With his usual astuteness, That's It (the Comanche informant previously quoted) stated the reason for this: "We were not like you white men. We didn't have to have an election every four years to see who would sit in the White House. A *paraivo* [band headman] just got that way. Everybody knew who he was." So clear and consensual were cultural goals and leadership requirements that leaders "emerged."

On the other hand, in larger, more complex societies in which the decision-making powers of a chief, king, or president are far-reaching, control of the office is of utmost importance; legitimation of the political administration is a matter of critical concern if tyranny is to be avoided.

To demonstrate the operation of the political processes in their varied manifestations, let us look first at the Cheyennes, who represent the chiefdom type of political organization as integrated with both a tribal council and politically active military associations. Then, we shall summarize the structure and functioning of a monarchistic state, the Tswana of Bechuanaland in southern Africa.

Cheyenne Government and Politics

Professor John Roberts has extolled the old Cheyenne system for its outstanding self-management. Specifically, he comments on its excellence in respect to (1) "the storage and retrieval" of traditional knowledge and information, (2) the Cheyennes' skill at problem solving on the societal level, and (3) their effective implementation of decisions through "staff work" and "command responsibility."[12]

Tribal Organization The Cheyennes had a bilateral family system with no lineages or clans. Beyond the family, there were uxorilocal kindreds, each headed by an active senior male. Related kindreds tended to camp together, thus forming the band, of which there were ten major ones. During the fall and winter months, when the buffalo herds were dispersed, the Cheyennes adjusted by scattering the band camps miles

[12]J. M. Roberts, "The Self-management of Cultures," in W. H. Goodenough (ed.), *Explorations in Cultural Anthropology*, p. 452.

apart in protected river bottoms. Bands were then politically autonomous. In late spring, when the grasses were green, the Cheyenne kindreds all drew together for one of the great tribal ceremonies—the Sacred Arrow Renewal, the Sun Dance, or the Animal Dance. Throughout the summer the Council of Forty-four Tribal Peace Chiefs ruled supreme, assisted by the military associations.

Allocation of Leadership Membership in the Council of Forty-four was for a term of ten years. Nominally, each band had four representatives on the council—and these chiefs were headmen in their own bands. They were chosen for their even tempers, energy, wisdom, courage, kindliness, generosity, and altruism. They were the "fathers" of everyone in the tribe and addressed as such. Although on page 472 we indicated that the Cheyennes recognized wealth distinctions, there was no class exploitation in the distribution of power.

By combining the dual roles of band headman and tribal chieftain in the same person, the Cheyennes effected an efficient link between the kinship and local interests of the band and the tribal entirety. This is an absolute essential for maintenance of the tribe as an integrated whole.

Within the Council of Forty-four there were five sacred chiefs who represented the great spirits of the five directions. One of them held a supreme ritual position as the Sweet Medicine Chief—the personification of the culture hero who gave the Cheyennes their way of life. The legitimacy of the chief was chartered by the deepest of Cheyenne beliefs.

Alongside of, but subordinate to, the supreme and sacred Council of Forty-four, stood the ungraded military associations. They enforced the Cheyenne law against intratribal killing and violation of the rules of the communal buffalo hunt. They sometimes made new law for the entire tribe. They also interacted with the Council when important tribal decisions had to be faced.

Tribal Decision Making The customary way of making tribal decisions, before the breakdown of tribal unity which began in 1850, followed the pattern indicated in the following example.

A war party of eight Cheyennes, on its way south to take horses from the Kiowas, Comanches, or Apaches, was stopping at a large [friendly] Arapaho camp. At the same time some Apaches came to visit Bull, an Arapaho leader. The Apaches told their host that the Kiowas and Comanches were seeking peace with the Arapahoes and Cheyennes. Bull took the opportunity to bring the eight Cheyennes together with the Apaches in his tipi; he filled his pipe and offered the smoke. The Cheyennes declined, Seven Bulls, the leader of the war party saying, "Friend, you know that we are not chiefs. We cannot smoke with these men, nor make peace with them. We have no authority; . . . I have listened to what you say and tomorrow with my party I will start back [he has authority to call off his own raid] to our Cheyenne village. . . . It is for them to decide what must be done. We are young men and cannot say anything, but we will take your message back to the chiefs."

When Seven Bulls reached the Cheyenne camp with his companions, he told of the Kiowa-Comanche proposition. That night a crier went about the camp calling for the chiefs to convene the next day. The big double-sized chiefs' lodge was pitched and early the next morning the chiefs all gathered there. Seven Bulls and his companions were sent for to deliver their message officially. The proposal was then on the floor.

After the first speakers had sat down, it was evident that there was no ready agreement at hand within the Council, so the proposition was made and accepted that the Dog Soldier Society should be asked to render a decision to the Council on the question.

High Backed Wolf, who was the directing head chief of the Council, sent one of the door-servants to bring in White Antelope and Little Old Man, the bravest chiefs of the Dog Soldier Society. When these two had been greeted in the chiefs' lodge, High Backed Wolf told them . . . the state of opinion in the Council. "Now, my friends," he concluded, "you go and assemble your Dog Soldiers. Tell them about this matter and talk it over among them . . . Tell us what you think is best to be done."

When the Dog Soldiers had assembled, White

Antelope laid the problem before them. "The chiefs are leaving this matter to us," . . . "because we are the strongest of the military groups. It is my own thought that our chiefs are in favor of making peace. What do you all think about it?"

Said another of the Dog Soldier chiefs, "I think it best to leave the decision to you two, White Antelope and Little Old Man. Whatever you say will please us all." All the Dogs agreed to this. . . .

The two men accepted it and declared for peace. Leaving their troop, they went back . . . to tell the Council that they would make peace with the enemies. The chiefs all stood up at this and gladly said, "Thank you, thank you, Dog Soldiers."[13]

The political process, we have said, is public, goal-oriented, and allocates and focuses power. There can be no question of the public nature of this case. It concerned the well-being of the entire Cheyenne society. It was also clearly goal-oriented: peace with the Comanches from whom the Cheyennes could obtain horses and a useful ally. Allocation of authority? Authority was designated clearly. The war-party leader said he could not speak for his people. He conveyed the message to a proper authority who convened the Council of Forty-four. The tribal chiefs knew they had the formal power to make a decision. But they also knew that without public support they could not make it stick. Opinion was divided. So the Dog Soldier Society—the most powerful and prestigious of all the fighting associations—was delegated to "decide" the issue. The Dogs, in turn, knew that unending filibuster could prevent achievement of unanimous consent which was always required for action on a proposal. So they put it to their two bravest chiefs. The decision was for peace. Back up the line it went, as the military fraternity's recommendation to the Council of Forty-four who accepted the "decision" with thanks—and relief. Finally, the Sweet Medicine Chief announced it to the entire tribe *as the decision of the Tribal Council,* so giving the decision the seal of the highest authority possible. The soldiers had been coopted, and no Cheyenne hothead would dare to lift a hand against the Comanche again. None ever did—from that day to this.

Political Organization among the Tswana

The Cheyenne represented a simple form of state organization in a small society. The Tswana of Bechuanaland in southern Africa represent state organization on the level of monarchy in a larger society.

The Tswana, or Bechuana, constitute a distinct group of tribes. Each tribe is a politically independent unit, although the more newly formed tribes recognize the seniority of the tribes from which they broke off. The population of the Tswana exceeds 100,000.[14]

Tribal Organization The integrating focus of the tribe is in the person and office of the chief, who is not only the supreme ruler but also "the visible symbol of its cohesion and solidarity." Each Tswana tribe has a capital town (ranging in population from 600 to 25,000) and a number of smaller outlying villages.

Within the village or town, the households (which consist of one or more conjugal-natal families) are clustered to form the spatially distinguished family group. Closely related family groups live in a well-defined administrative unit, called a *ward.* All the wards together make up the tribe, except that in two of the larger tribes, the wards are grouped in sections.

A small hamlet may contain no more than one household. A small village may consist of a single family group. A larger village may have only one ward. A village, if large enough, may, however, embrace several wards.

Local Leaders The leader of the household

[13] K. N. Llewellyn and E. A. Hoebel, *The Cheyenne Way,* pp. 91–93.

[14] I. Schapera, *A Handbook of Tswana Law and Custom,* pp. 1–34 and 53–124.

FIGURE 29.6
Village voters arrive as a group to cast their ballots in a district election held at Waga-Waga, New Guinea. (United Nations.)

is the husband and father; for the family group, the leader is the senior male descendant of the paternal grandfather whose name the group bears. His position is hereditary and ascribed. He directs the group's activities and keeps the peace. In important matters, he acts in consultation with a family-group council of all adult males.

The headman of a ward holds his position by right of hereditary descent as the senior son of the preceding headman. He is his ward's representative to the chief and is responsible for the orderly conduct of his people and the execution of the chief's commands. He collects tribute for the chief and holds judicial authority in minor cases involving two family groups within his jurisdiction. He is also the age-set leader of the men of his ward.

The Council A headman must act in consultation with a ward council made up of the senior members of his own family group and the leaders of the other family groups in his ward. If guilty of malfeasance in office, his own council will reprimand him or complain to the chief, who may then try to punish him through the Royal Court. Occasionally, the ward headman convenes all the adult males of the ward for a review of problems of wide concern. The headman carries many burdens of responsibility for which he receives little material compensation but great prestige and respect—providing he does his job well.

Each village, in turn, has its headman. If the village and ward are one, the ward headman and village headman are one and the same. Should there be two or more wards, the headman of the senior ward is the village head. His duties are similar to those of the ward headman, except that they are townwide in scope.

In those tribes which have districts, village

organization remains the same as that described above, but the district will have, as a special representative to the capital, the headman of one of its more important indigenous villages (some outlying villages will consist of immigrant aliens).

Age-Sets All Tswana men and women are initiated into sex-segregated age-sets at puberty. These have important congeniality functions to perform, but they are equally important as units of political organization. An age-set cuts across the local segments of the tribe and counteracts the parochialism that inherently exerts a neutralizing effect on national integration. Each age-set (which numbers from fifty to several hundred boys or men, depending on the size of the tribe) is headed by a commander, who is always a member of the royal family. In war, the age-sets constitute regiments in the tribal army. The men of a given ward form "companies" within the regiment under the leadership of a son or close relative of their ward headman. In times of peace, the age-sets serve as work brigades to perform any public service or job of construction that the king deems necessary.

Women's age-sets are organized along the same lines as the men's. In the sphere of women's work, they also perform public services, though of a lighter nature.

The King (chief) This brings us to the central tribal government organized around the hereditary chief, or monarch. He is chief of state (king) through primogeniture. In succession, the direct line precedes all collateral lines; that is, the sons of the king succeed, but his brothers and their sons cannot, although a brother of a dead king may serve as regent during the minority of the heir. If a monarch dies with no male issue, the chieftainship passes to his next senior brother.

Functionally, the Tswana chief "is at once ruler, judge, maker and guardian of the law, repository of wealth, dispenser of gifts, leader in war, priest and magician of the people."[15] He and his family take precedence in all things and receive high honors. Failure to obey his orders or to show him respect is a criminal offense. He is sustained by a royal coterie and with tribute.

In return, much is expected of him. His time is his people's. "Every man thinks he is the king's only subject" is a common folk saying. He must keep himself well informed of tribal affairs, be accessible to all who have complaints, organize and direct the army, sit as chief justice, preside over the tribal council, perform the major religious rituals, and above all be generous, redistributing most of the tribute that comes to him.

Other Functionaries The male relatives of the chief form a nobility, a kind of privy council, with whom he must remain in close consultation. To maintain effective democratic control, the chief has an informally constituted body of confidential advisers (a "cabinet") drawn from among the important men of the tribe; they are usually, but by no means always, paternal relatives.

The government also includes a formal tribal council of all the ward headmen, who meet in secret executive session whenever convened by the chief.

Schapera has published a translation of the condensed record of a Tswana enactment of partial prohibition in 1924. After discussing the problem of rowdy nighttime beer drinking with his council of senior uncles and getting their approval, Isang, king of the Kagatla tribe of the Tswana, convened the council of headmen. The record reads as follows:

Chief Isang: "I do not say that beer should be prohibited, but that a law should be made about it."

[15]Ibid., p. 62.

Segale Pilane (chief's uncle and principal adviser): "We seek a plan for dealing with beer-drinking. Beer has ruined us; we have no children; we tried to educate them, but beer has spoiled them."

Komane Pilane (another senior uncle): "Let there be a law about beer-drinking, and let whoever violates it be punished."

Abel Madisa: "Let the sale of beer be prohibited." (Supported by Nasone Pilane, Montswe Rapalai, Mokalane Makgale, Pilane B. Pilane, Ramodisa, Klaas Segogwane, Antipas Sello, Masilo Ntsole.)

Chief Isang: "I endorse the suggestion that beer should no longer be sold. But now I ask, is there not some one who can suggest a law whereby beer may continue to be sold, but in such a way as not to cause trouble among the people?"

Maretele Mangole: "Let beer be sold, but the purchaser should go home to drink it."

Pule Mogomotsi: "Let it be sold, but on condition that it is no longer drunk at night."

Motshwane Pilane: "Let beer-drinking at night be prohibited, and also let beer be sold only for consumption at home."

Kgari Pilane: "Beer-drinking goes together with sexual immorality. You should not find fault with the boys alone, and ignore the girls. As long as beer continues to be brewed, immorality will be associated with it."

Mabuse Letsebe: "I say, let beer continue to be sold."

Segale Pilane: "Headmen, you have helped us; it is you who are the chief's policemen, and whoever breaks the law must be dealt with by you."

Chief Isang: "Let those who say that beer should not be sold raise their hands."

(85 men raised their hands; only two said that beer should still be sold.)

Chief Isang: "You are not of two opinions, you are unanimous. And what I say to you is that when you go astray and are turned back you should listen. To err is human, but to find fault with oneself is often lacking. Therefore I say: Beer must no longer be drunk at night. See to it that beer is brewed not by the girls but by their mothers. I shall allow the brewing and sale of beer from the beginning of June until December, and if there is no improvement I shall call you together again to kill the sale of beer. Women of the Maatlametlo age-regiment and downwards must not any one of them drink beer. Headmen, help to support the law."[16]

In this situation, the chief and his principal adviser put their problem to the headmen. Some of the latter advance a suggestion that does not immediately satisfy the chief, and he asks them to consider a more specific issue. After further discussion, during which several different views are expressed, a vote is taken on the original and more drastic suggestion. Despite almost unanimous agreement, the chief finally decides to try out a compromise for an experimental period. The two points that seem most important in the whole procedure are the method of consultation and the fact that the chief is guided but not bound by the views of the headmen.

Affairs of great tribal import, although they are first taken up by the two preceding groups of advisers, cannot become official policy until they have been discussed and approved in open tribal assembly. To this all the headmen come and all adult men who are interested.

A System of Checks and Balances

The Tswana system exemplifies how the state, as a political system, weaves and balances kinship, territorial, and associational groupings into a harmonious whole. It shows how the functional prerequisite of allocation of authority to responsible leaders is checked and balanced with concomitant reliance on organized group consultation, through the provision of councils on each level of administrative structure, with a final check imposed through general assemblies at each level for consideration of all major or crucial decisions. Tswana political organization has the essential elements of monarchy, democracy, oli-

[16] I. Schapera, *Tribal Legislation among the Tswana of the Bechuanaland Protectorate*, pp. 14–15.

garchy, theocracy, and gerontocracy. It is each of these and all. It has no need for elective procedures and spares itself a good deal of trouble and uncertainty thereby, for internal social mobility is limited and in this type of society the hereditary principle works well enough.

SUMMARY

Politics consists of those activities which (1) are concerned with public or community decision making; (2) are goal-oriented; and (3) distribute and allocate decision-making authority and the power to carry out the policies decided upon.

Political organization consists of the network of institutions that regulate relations between groups within a society and between one society and another. The units of political organization may be based on kinship, territorial, or associational principles.

The functions of political organization include definition of norms, allocation of force and authority, settlement of disputes (all shared with law), plus public works, ceremony and ritual control of the supernatural (shared with religion), economic activities (redistribution of goods and control of markets), and war.

Political organization may be stateless, but where government is added in the form of centralized authority for the whole society and endowed with specific (if even only part-time) functionaries, it becomes a state.

All governments include the council in one form or another. Very simple societies vest leadership in headmen rather than chiefs. All adult males participate directly in decision making. Small societies are essentially democracies. Chieftainship is characteristic of the more developed simple societies. Kingship exists in those societies in which chieftainship has become hereditary.

The state is always multidimensional; it is made up of diverse elements. Governments can also consist of a variety of agencies that have nongovernmental aspects. Thus kinship groups and associations that exist primarily for other purposes may perform governmental functions and so exist as an integral part of the state system.

SELECTED READINGS

Balandier, G., *Political Anthropology* (1970). Translation of a book originally published in France in 1967. Excellent overview and history of the field.

Banton, M. (ed.), *Political Systems and the Distribution of Power* (1965). Especially good for the article by Ralph Nicholas on factions in the political process and for the analysis of differing types of African kingdoms by Peter Lloyd.

Cohen, R., and J. Middleton (eds.), *Comparative Political Systems* (1967). A reader with selections on political organization and process in a wide range of societies.

Evans-Pritchard, E. E., and M. Fortes (eds.), *African Political Systems* (1940). A symposium of excellent studies of political structure in a number of African societies.

Gluckman, M., *Politics, Law, and Ritual in Tribal Society* (1965). Especially read chapters 3 and 4, on stateless societies and on the state and civil strife.

Mair, L., *Primitive Government* (1964). A general, nontheoretical description of the major types of government in African societies. Contains an informative final chapter entitled "Primitive Government and Modern Times."

Schapera I., *Government and Politics in Tribal Societies* (1956). A comparative study of three South African systems.

PART EIGHT

Symbolic Expression

30
Culture and World View

CHAPTER OUTLINE

LEARNING GOALS

Explain what is meant by world view.

Define etic, emic, and ethos.

Discuss the Navajo world view.

Describe the Hopi way and the Pueblo world view.

Explain the Cheyenne world view.

Describe the American world view.

From the moment of birth, a child is bombarded by preformed ideas, values, norms, material goods, a social structure, and all those things which make up the culture of the child's native society. This bombardment, or *enculturation* as the anthropologist calls it, is most intense during the early formative years, but actually never stops. Adults continue to learn new statuses and roles throughout life as new situations engender new opportunities for learning.

All this creates a particular outlook which is shared by the group. This *world view*, as it is called, is a shared perspective on, and philosophy or ideology about, the natural world, including such things as humanity, gods and religion, animals and spirits, and other aspects perceived by the individual.

THE NATURE OF WORLD VIEW

The cognitive view of life and the total environment which an individual holds or which is characteristic of the members of a society is frequently referred to as *Weltanschauung*, or world view. World view carries the suggestion "of the structure of things as man is aware of them,"[1] and it is thus the life scene as people look out upon it. It is the human being's inside view of the way things are colored, shaped, and arranged according to cultural preconceptions. The planet we live on, a world of physical objects and living things, is by no means the same world to all peoples. Indeed, a simple description of the most basic observable components of this world (the sky, the land, water, trees) by a member of one culture might prove totally unintelligible to a member of another. This was well understood by a good friend of Hoebel's, a Sia Pueblo Indian, who stood beside him at the ruin of Pueblo Bonito. "You see this bush," he said, pointing to a desert plant called *chamiso*. "You may not understand this, but that plant is I. I am it, and it is me and all my ancestors. We call it '*wawshap*.' "

Juan was a member of the *Wawshap* clan. He was telling Hoebel that in his eyes and in his deepest feelings, as he looked on that bush, he was embodied in it—he and all his clan ancestors. As an anthropologist Hoebel had an intellectual understanding of what he was saying, but his own world view would forever prevent him from feeling the same kind of emotional identification with that plant. Hoebel could see the chamiso in botanical terms. He could think of its functions as a symbolic representation of *Wawshap* clan unity in the maintenance of Durkheimiam organic solidarity of the social group (see pages 35–36). He could analyze Juan's perception of the plant in terms of its moral effect in maintaining a vital sense of "the meaning of life." But he could not *be wawshap* as his friend is. Juan's world view is that of a Sian.

Institutions, relationships, arts, and technology vary throughout the world in manifestly observable forms, but underlying them are the existential postulates that orient a people's particular slant on life and the ways in which they organize their culture.

Etic, Emic, and Ethos

When seen from the outside and reported by an observer who is not, by training and living, thoroughly enculturated in the culture observed and being written about, the view is called *etic*. The inside view is labeled *emic*. Regarding the chamiso, Juan's view was emic; Hoebel's could be only etic.

World view as a concept focuses on the ways of knowing and identifying the component elements of the world—the existential and cognitive. *Ethos* expresses a people's qualitative feeling, their emotional and moral sensing of the way things are and ought to be—their ethical system.

Not all peoples or persons can by any means articulate systematically what their world view is. It is improbable that any Comanche could. At

[1] R. Redfield, *The Primitive World and Its Transformations*, p. 86.

(a)

(b)

FIGURE 30.1
Preparations for a Navajo curing chant, Monument Valley, Arizona. (a) A curer, or chant singer, sits with his medicine bundle spread out before him while his assistant pulverizes sands of different colors. (b) The humanlike figures of two gods are drawn by pouring polychrome sands on a smooth-surfaced base. (c) The family of

(c)

(d)

the patient gathers to watch the finishing stages of the sand painting. (d) The little girl who is to be cured is blessed before she takes her place on the painting. Here she will be sung and prayed over, while the power symbolized by the myth represented in the painting enters into her. Important chants usually last nine days and draw many visitors. Most chants and prayers are actually performed inside a hogan. (Josef Muench.)

the same time, it is quite probable that many of the more reflective Hopi priests could have spelled out a Hopi world view quite clearly and consistently. Usually it is up to the anthropologist or philosopher to analyze and formulate a people's world view from what is learned of their thinking, feelings, and actions. World view and ethos are expressed in technology, personal relations, myth, song, dance, art, and religious and magical ritual in a multitude of gross and subtle ways. They are the reflected essence of a people's inner feelings and their ways of knowing "the way things are."

No world view is a given, in spite of the numerous peoples who believe that their way of life was bestowed upon them by culture heroes (such as Sweet Medicine and Erect Horns of the Cheyennes) or tribal ancestors (such as those of the Ashanti) or the divine revelation of prophets (such as the early Hebrews, Christians, and Muslims). World views grow with cultures. Generations of anonymous human beings contribute to the unending quest to make the unknown knowable, to transform meaningless bafflement into meaningful understanding.

To exemplify the nature of world view, let us explore the phenomenon more deeply by considering the Navajo, Hopi, Cheyenne, and United States versions.

THE NAVAJO WORLD VIEW

The Navajos, it will be remembered from the discussion of housing (Chapter 13), are an Athabascan-speaking people who migrated from the north into the high, arid lands of the southwestern part of the United States some five hundred or more years ago. Originally hunters and foragers, they became gardeners in their new environment. After the Spanish brought horses, sheep, and goats, they also became pastoralists, but remained basically gardeners. The cultivation of corn, beans, and squash was learned from the Pueblo Indians, as was much of their mythology and the visual imagery and technique of sand painting. In like manner, the Navajo system of matrilineal clans appears to have been copied from that of the Western Pueblos. But it has already been noted how the Navajos did not imitate the settled, compact villages of pueblo structure, preferring to live in scattered hogan camps. Their social organization is decentralized and quite amorphous. Clan exogamy is rigidly adhered to, and the sanction for incest is an obsessive urge to burn oneself to death—a fate that relatives try to forestall. The punishment is self-imposed. The Navajos hold elaborate ceremonies, known as *chants*, which become occasions for social get-togethers (Figure 30.1). But chants are performed at the request of individuals or families to cure illness; they are not part of a cult cycle. Singers are individual practitioners, not members of religious fraternities.

An Orderly But Dangerous Universe

The basic orientation of the Navajos is individualistic-familistic rather than collectivistic. They view the universe as an orderly but extremely dangerous place that must be treated with the utmost circumspection and caution.

The basis for this view is in the Navajo origin myth, which accounts for the history and character of the Holy People—the supernatural beings who belong to the sacred part of the world, as opposed to the Earth Surface People, who are ordinary human beings, living and dead. The origin myth tells "The People that, from time immemorial, the universe has been a very dangerous place, inhabited by people who were untrustworthy, if not completely evil . . . [who] are forever present . . . as threats to prosperity."[2]

Earth Surface People, except for living relatives, are all potentially dangerous, and even slight contact with nonrelatives may cause serious illness. Anyone may be a witch, but especially anyone who becomes too prosperous. Witch-

[2] C. Kluckhohn and D. Leighton, *The Navaho*, p. 125.

es are werewolves and ghouls who practice incest and who are the source of the greatest anxiety. But death, too, is horrible in the Navajo view, for ghosts are the witches of the world of the dead; they harass and plague the living with dire portents and unnerving teasing. Even the most forgiving friend may become a malignantly vengeful ghost bent on punishing some slight or neglect. Fear of ghosts makes even adult Navajos loath to face the dark alone.

Eight Fundamental Navajo Postulates

Against this background, Kluckhohn formulated eight "keystones on which the Navaho view of the world appears to rest":

1. *The universe is orderly: all events are caused and interrelated.*
   a. *Knowledge is power.*
   b. *The basic quest is for harmony.*
   c. *Harmony can be restored by orderly procedures.*
   d. *One price of disorder, in human terms, is illness.*
2. *The universe tends to be personalized.*
   a. *Causation is identifiable in personalized terms.*
3. *The universe is full of dangers.*
4. *Evil and good are complementary, and both are ever present.*
5. *Experience is conceived as a continuum differentiated only by sense data.*
6. *Morality is conceived in traditionalistic and situational terms rather than in terms of abstract absolutes.*
7. *Human relations are premised upon familistic individualism.*
8. *Events, not actors or qualities, are primary.*[3]

These foregoing precepts expand into a world view with the two major focuses being on the compulsive effect of prayer and ritual and the presence of disharmonic forces.

[3]C. Kluckhohn, "Philosophy of the Navaho Indians," in F.S.C. Northrop (ed.), *Ideological Differences and World Order*, pp. 359–360.

The Compulsive Effect of Prayer and Ritual

The universe is mechanistically viewed as an interrelated system of cause and effect. The Holy People may indeed be spirit beings, but they are not free to act capriciously, for they are controlled by laws of their own making. Chant and ceremony are compulsive acts that are meant to control results rather than petition for gifts from the gods.

So it is that mastery of an esoteric terminology, along with pragmatically tested, immediately apprehended sense data, gives one power. It is not mystic experience—neither visions nor ascetic self-torture—but *knowledge* (in Navajo terms) that gives power. Power, however, does not mean mastery over nature as the Western person seeks it. Rather, the Navajo's basic quest is for harmony. "Individually acquired knowledge can assist in the restoration of harmony in one person's life, in that of the community, in that of the universe."[4] Everything in Navajo symbolism, verbal and visual, is in balanced pairs or quadruplets.

Disharmonic Forces

Disharmony, which is an imbalance, is manifested in flood, catastrophe, and above all, personal illness. Every Navajo ceremony is a "cure" sung over a patient, even though some cures may also improve the state of the world. Witches are forever bent upon disturbing the harmony of things. The Holy People, and all people and things, witches excepted, are neither inherently good nor inherently evil. Good and evil are complementary and ever-present. If things stay in balance, people will do all right, but the universe is full of dangers.

The compensatory mechanism of compulsive orderliness in behavior, art, ritual, and religion is their positive response. Complementary to formalism is the felt need to avoid risks. Excess of any sort is dangerous. Most acts are not immoral

[4]Ibid., p. 362.

in themselves, but cause trouble if performed too intensively. "Stay within safe limits! Likewise," say the Navajos, "be wary of nonrelatives." Merely to touch a stranger can make one sick. The Enemy Way nine-day chant may be necessary to restore the order upset by the presence of a stranger.

In their response to the world as seen, Navajos are industrious individualists who work hard within the framework of the known. Much time and effort are devoted to combating the disruptive forces that imbalance the world. Navajos strive to be courteous, polite, and nonaggressive, avoiding trouble and witches; they seek above all to have health and strength, to work and to acquire knowledge, to present a good figure with clothes and jewelry, and to provide for the family—but not to acquire glory or the power to rule or govern people. There is no place for dominance over one's fellows in the Navajo world view.

THE HOPI WAY AND THE PUEBLO WORLD VIEW

The Hopis are the nearest neighbors of the Navajos, and they are also the westernmost of the living Pueblos of the United States today. A brief examination of the Hopi world view will be useful because of the common historico-cultural base from which both Hopi and Navajo have drawn much of their ideology and because of the different orientation and greater conceptual complexity of the Hopi system.

The Hopis are intensive gardeners living in compact, permanently settled villages built of plastered stone houses set wall to wall around a central ceremonial plaza. Fields and houses are owned by women; the matrilineage is the bridge between household and strong matriclans. Kinship and economic life are female-centered, although men may own sheep. Ceremonial life and political life are male-centered and are organized around a complex system of secret religious fraternities (Figure 30.2).[5]

An Intricate Balance of Parts

Laura Thompson summarizes the Hopi world view in these words:

Here we recognize an organic view of the universe. The cosmos is formulated as a living whole in which the subtly balanced relationships of the various parts to one another and to the multidimensional totality are similar to those which characterize living organisms. The parts and the whole are believed to transact for the good of all, according to a single, harmonious, immanent law. Man is a psychophysiological whole, differentiated from the rest of nature by his power of volition, which is an integral part of the scheme and is to be used for the commonweal. He cooperates with other men and with his nonhuman partners in fulfilling the law, through kinship and ceremonial groups. And the main mechanisms through which he expresses symbolically the cosmic process are ritual and art, reinforced by concentrated will-prayer.[6]

Expressing it more simply, a Sia Indian put it this way, "Yes, it's like the Hopi. If I would refuse the request to drum in the Fiesta, it would delay the answers to the people's prayers. There would be no rain. Or else too much rain would come and flood everything. It wouldn't come just right."

Among all the Pueblos, as a matter of fact, this orientation is general. The late Professor Edward Dozier, born and raised in Santa Clara Pueblo, said:

The dominant integrating factor of Rio Grande Pueblo culture is the view of the universe as an orderly phenomenon. People or things are not merely "good" or "bad." "Evil" is a disturbance in the equilibrium that exists between man and the universe,

---

[5]The best general summary of the Hopi social system is found in F. Eggan, *Social Organization of the Western Pueblos*, chap. 2, pp. 17-138.

[6]L. Thompson, *Toward a Science of Mankind*, p. 189.

FIGURE 30.2
Priests of the Flute Society of the Hopi pueblo of Mishongnovi, Arizona, in a ceremonial taking place at the sacred spring in 1902. (A. C. Vroman.)

while "good" is a positive frame of mind or action that maintains harmonious balance.

To keep man and the universe in harmonious balance, all must work together and with "good" thoughts. Unanimous effort of body and mind is not only a key value, but it is also enforced. . . . Any action, whether physical or verbal, which is construed by Pueblo authorities to be contrary to group concerns and unanimous will of the village is promptly and severely punished.

Rio Grande Pueblo culture thus makes rigorous demands on the individual and fills him with deep anxiety and suspicion toward his fellow men. Not only is his personal behavior and social interaction strictly circumscribed, but his thoughts as well are rigidly harnessed. He is constantly plagued by an apprehension that he or his fellow man may break the harmonious balance of the universe and bring illness, famine, or some other form of dreaded disaster.[7]

Thus, for the Hopis and other Puebloans, the most fundamental postulate premises the world as a complex, ordered system in which all parts are intimately interdependent on an essentially equivalent footing, each with its part to play in the maintenance of the harmonious working of the whole.

The Human Role in the Universe

Unlike the Navajos, who view the world as dangerous, the Hopis see it as beneficent and predictable—except where human irresponsibility disrupts it. The nonhuman part of the universe is automatically controlled by what people do.

[7] E. P. Dozier, "Rio Grande Pueblos," in E. H. Spicer (ed.), *Perspectives in American Indian Culture Change,* p. 122.

But humans have a measure of willful self-determinism. They have a margin of choice. They may or may not carry out their functions according to the Great Scheme. If they do, the universe continues its orderly unfolding of events—healthily, happily, productively, satisfyingly. If they do not, crops fail, babies die, and famine, pestilence, and disaster sweep over the community. Chaos and disorder reign.

Hopis, in the Hopi view, must *want* things to go right. They must want this with all their might, which means that they must work industriously in the fields, at weaving, and at pottery or basketmaking, and that they must participate faithfully in all the ceremonies in which a part is assigned. In addition, they must concentrate all psychic energy on "willing" or "praying for" (synonymous terms in Hopi) the result. They must think "happy" thoughts.

There is no room for the indifferent or uncommitted person in the Hopi scheme of things, nor is there room for individualistic innovators who think they can improve on the Great Scheme. Such a person is a dangerous deviationist, even more immediately dangerous than the slovenly slacker. Both are potential saboteurs of the order, one because the effort to will is not enough, the other because the wrong things are willed. Each of these two deviations is *ka-hopi*, un-Hopi; each runs a great risk not only of being called a "two-heart" (a witch who stays alive by taking the lives of relatives), but also of being condemned and killed as a witch by the Kwan secret society. Hopi society is theocratic, collectivistic, and totalitarian.

Hopis fear witches, but in a way different from the way Navajos fear them. Navajo anxiety is diffuse, and witchcraft is directed toward individuals, as is ghost malice. Pueblo witchcraft is directed against the whole system. That Hopi witches kill individuals is incidental, for their major motive is to prolong their own lives by killing others, especially relatives.

To the Navajo, knowledge is power. To the Hopi, knowledge is not only power but also an obligation. Knowledge is a requisite to maintaining the balance of the universe; one must strain to know what is expected and needed, and one must will to make it work. But what one is privileged to know is ordained in the pattern. Statuses for all persons and things are ideologically blueprinted, and to presume to statuses that have not been assigned to one is *ka-hopi*. To know a ceremony for which one is not properly a priest means only that one will misuse it. Possession of unauthorized knowledge is feared by men and women throughout the pueblos, for to say of a man, "He knows something," is to mean that he is a witch.

As an ideological adaptation to a harsh environment in which the Hopis have achieved a highly effective survival capacity, their world view unquestionably represents a high level of consistent integration that permeates their social structure, their art and ritual, and their personalities. Its demands upon the individual are severe, for each person is an Atlas, supporting the weight of the world.

The Mechanistic-Vitalistic Character of Navajo and Hopi World Views

Although the Hopis and the Navajos posit the existence of spirit beings, and in this sense their world views are colored with animism, both are fundamentally mechanistic in their outlook. The Navajos assume that the acts of Big Holy People, Earth Surface People, and witches may be counteracted by compulsively effective ritual knowledge. The Hopis are even more mechanistic in their view of the universe as an intricately meshed set of systems, delicately interrelated in a total order that each person must help to maintain by positive willing and correct role performance.

THE CHEYENNE WAY AS WORLD VIEW

Among yet another American Indian tribe a mechanistic view of the universe predominated, but in essentially different ways from those of the

Navajo and Hopi. Cheyennes believed in Heammawihio, the all-knowing High God who lives above. He knows more about how to do things than all other creatures. Heammawihio once lived on earth as a being, but ages ago retired to the sky where, symbolically represented by the sun, he lives remote from all things. All first offerings of the pipe or smoked cigarette were made to him. There were other big spirits such as Aktunowihio, the Wise One Below (in the earth), and the Thunder, Heammawihio's great bird who brings the summer rains. There were the innumerable animal and bird spirits who were sought on the vision quest, who appeared in visions and bestowed medicine power for curing, divination, or war on lucky women. All these were animistic beings, not in themselves mechanical forces. Yet they behaved mechanically. One offered them food, cloth, an enemy scalp, a piece of one's flesh, perhaps a chopped-off joint of a finger. Anderson observes that "the goal or response was a concrete return—health for oneself or kin, a wealth of horses, many coups on a raid, success in the hunt, or a shaman's powers."[8] The spirits, great and small, were like puppets who responded to the strings that were manipulated by compulsive ceremony and ritual.

The Theory of Limited Energy

Cheyenne wise men did not speak of an energy theory of the universe. Nonetheless, they subscribed to one; it was implicit rather than explicit in the tribal world view.

All Cheyennes knew that if a man wanted his son to mature as an outstanding person, he, the father, had to vow not to have sexual relations for seven, or fourteen, years after the boy's birth. All the father's "growth energy" had to be concentrated in that one child until he was mature.

FIGURE 30.3
Cheyenne Sun Dance pledger and instructor wearing yellow paint of the first day. Body paint changes with each day of the ceremony, as the symbolic focus progresses. (American Museum of Natural History.)

If he had a colt which he wanted to become a fast, long-winded war pony, he asked a shaman with "horse medicine" to bless it with symbols of male sexual energy, while he himself vowed not to ride it at all for a given number of months. Then he rode it only in battle. Its energy had to be generated and stored for the special occasion.

[8]R. Anderson, "The Buffalo Men: A Cheyenne Ceremony of Petition Deriving from the Sutaio" (*Southwestern Journal of Anthropology*, vol. 12, 1956), p. 102.

Every year, the world has to be regenerated through the tribal Sun Dance or the Sacred Arrow Renewal ceremony, for each year the world runs down (Figure 30.3). But in the ceremonies, replete with imagery and symbolism of rebirth and growth of human, animal, and plant life, the energy quotient of the universe was renewed.

The Cheyenne myths tell that eons ago there was famine. "Vegetation withered, the animals starved, the land became barren and dry, and the ancient Cheyenne were on the verge of starvation, for they had no food but dried vegetation and their dogs of burden."[9] One of the two Cheyenne culture heroes, Erect Horns, went into the Sacred Mountain, where the spirits taught him the Sun Dance, which he in turn taught to the Cheyennes.[10]

By not wasting energy and by ritual knowledge of how to recharge it, the Cheyenne, in their view, could keep things going. The power of mechanical manipulation was learned from an instructor who was a priest, who had learned from a priest, who had learned from a priest, in an unbroken chain back to Sweet Medicine and Erect Horns, the mythical heroes who had been given the secrets of the universe by the Big Spirits themselves.

The Cheyennes believed that they bore a special burden of maintaining the universe for all humanity.[11]

Cheyenne Personality

Not all Cheyennes incorporated the Cheyenne world view with equal intensity. The many who did, acted in accordance with moral and personal norms of behavior which clearly distinguished the Cheyenne from other tribes.

Reserved and dignified, the adult Cheyenne male moves with a quiet sense of self-assurance. He speaks fluently, but never carelessly. He is careful of the sensibilities of others and is kindly and generous. He is slow to anger and strives to suppress his feelings, if aggravated. Vigorous on the hunt and in war, he prizes the active life. Towards enemies he feels no merciful compunctions. . . . He is well versed in ritual knowledge. . . . Usually quiet, he has a lightly displayed sense of humor. He is sexually repressed and masochistic but that masochism is expressed in culturally approved rites. He does not show much creative imagination in artistic expression, but he has a firm grip on reality. He deals with the problems of life in set ways while at the same time showing a notable capacity to readjust to new circumstances. His thinking is rationalistic to a high degree and yet colored with mysticism. His ego is strong and not easily threatened. His superego, as manifest in his strong social conscience and mastery of his basic impulses, is powerful and dominating. He is . . . secure in his social position, capable of warm social relations. He has powerful anxieties, but these are channeled into institutionalized modes of collective expression with satisfactory results. He exhibits few neurotic tendencies.[12]

THE UNITED STATES WORLD VIEW

It may seem that the formulation of a descriptive analysis of *a* world view for the people of the United States is too great an undertaking. There are so many, and such diverse, cultural backgrounds represented in their recent immigrant origins; there is such a wide range in manifest belief, from atheism to devout religiosity; there is such a broad spectrum of interests in terms of occupation, recreation, and learning; and there are such vast differences between life in a tiny crossroads hamlet and life in New York's megalopolis, between the black separatist and white segregationist, between the middle-aged Kiwanian and the countercultural revolutionist, that one

---

[9]G. A. Dorsey, *The Cheyenne*: I, *Ceremonial Organization*, p. 46.
[10]Ibid., II, *The Sun Dance*, p. 57.
[11]This is still true; the Sun Dance is performed every year, culminating on the Fourth of July.

[12]E. A. Hoebel, *The Cheyennes*, p. 90.

may well wonder where lies the common denominator, or if one exists at all.

Yet outsiders generally agree that Americans are, by and large, highly standardized in outlook and manner. Relatively speaking, this is true. A distinctive world view for the people of the United States does exist and may be stated in its bolder outlines. Subgroup and individual variations are screened out in order that the major themes can be brought into clearer focus.

Rationalism and the Mechanistic View

Historically, the world view of the people of the United States is a derivative of the Judeo-Christian-Hellenistic traditions as they were blended and modified through the Renaissance, the Reformation, and the industrial revolution in Europe.

However much the Judeo-Christian traditions may survive, American thought patterns are rational rather than mystic; the operative conception of the universe is mechanistic. The bedrock proposition upon which the whole world view stands is that the universe is a physical system operating in a determinate manner according to discoverable scientific laws. Thus, these people use religion for purposes of social organization, but they rely relatively little upon prayer or ritual to achieve their ends. Instead, they depend primarily upon basic scientific research and its technical application. Because they view the universe as a mechanism, Americans implicitly believe that they can manipulate it. They need not accept it as it is; they may work on it, and as they gain in knowledge and improve their techniques, they may even redesign it so that it is more to their liking.

From this springs the conviction that the conditions of living are improvable: materially, biologically, and socially. Improvement means betterment; betterment means progress. People can, in this world view, eliminate hunger and poverty, disease, and social injustice—if they set the task for themselves. This fundamental motivating postulate of contemporary American culture expresses itself in a focal value orientation of "effort-optimism." Because the world view is rational-mechanistic rather than mystic-vitalistic, it leads to action rather than contemplation, to aggressive engagement rather than passive renunciation. Americans "make war" on poverty, "stamp out" disease, "wipe out" illiteracy, and embark on the "conquest" of space, as their forebears "conquered" the wilderness. Such an action orientation leads to an emphasis upon technology and science rather than upon philosophy and the arts. It has produced a mechanized agricultural-, industrial-, business-centered civilization rather than an ecclesiastical, scholarly, militaristic, or feudalistic one.

Pragmatic Empiricism

Concomitantly, the American cultural emphasis is pragmatic-empirical rather than theoretical-dogmatic. Americans are concerned more with "know-how" and "can-do" than with abstract wisdom or ancient knowledge. In universities and colleges, and in government grants-in-aid for research, this emphasis may be seen in the lopsided support for medicine, technology, and agriculture as against the humanities and social sciences.

The test of the validity of the American premise is the continued expansion of the gross national product, ever-new medical breakthroughs, and continuous expansion of social well-being and opportunity. When the system temporarily collapsed in the Great Depression of the 1930s, Americans panicked and had to be reassured. What unnerved them, however, was an anxiety that the basic premise of the American world view was an unworkable illusion.

Individual-centeredness

When the American looks away from the universe and turns inward, the focus of view is individual-centered rather than kinship-centered, class-centered, or collectivistically oriented, even through Americans are widely given to group organization. In the religious belief that has permeated much of the morality of the culture, it is premised that a person's moral responsibility rests in a private conscience. In the view of human nature held by Christianity, which is the dominant religion, people are inherently corrupt and sin-ridden by nature, and personal salvation (that is, purification from the moral stain of sin) is possible only in an emotional act of identification with God through Jesus (or his mother, Mary). Americans are therefore generally internally plagued with inner conflict and anxiety. Believing in the improvability of the self as an individual responsibility, and yet also holding (to a certain extent) that humans are sorry beings, they accept the proposition that inner psychic conflict is the very essence of human existence. Pastors are expected to be half counselor and half priest. To control the extreme consequences of inner conflict, there is less reliance upon religious or philosophic solutions than upon psychiatry and mental hygiene programs.

Two-thirds of the American population are nominally religious in that they belong to some church. One-third are sufficiently uninterested in religion as to identify with no church. In contrast to the primitive world view, gods, spirits, ghosts, witches, and ancestors in the American world view are more residual than dominant.

Achievement and Social Mobility

The individual-centeredness of the world view of the citizens of the United States, combined with its pragmatic action orientation, gives emphasis to achievement and social mobility. Achievement-in-being is what counts, not an illustrious background. American egalitarianism and its proposition that all people are created equal derive from this combination of qualities. Every American has to demonstrate self-confidence first and ability second. This necessitates fluid status symbols whereby achievement can be tangibly expressed. In a business-based culture, money serves this function. Money is the measure of success; it validates one's efforts, and therefore oneself, by providing the means to purchase such external symbols of success as a college education, a discreetly selected foreign car, or a large house at a good address.

The world view of older, but contemporary, stratified societies in Europe deprecates the materialism of Americans. At the same time, a major feature of the revolutionary innovations of the postcolonial world since World War II has been the avid desire of the so-called developing nations to learn the mechanical-material techniques that have followed from the kind of world view that has had its most intensive development in the United States.

SUMMARY

World view, as stated by Redfield, is the "insider's total vision and conception of everything," the person's outlook on life.[13] As a science, anthropology might be content to work with reports on what the anthropologist as an objective observer sees and notes of behavior. Such observations must be so phrased that they are comparable within a scientific frame of analytical reference. Most of the chapters of this book have been presented from this point of view.

But as a humanity, anthropology must strive to tell us what the world looks like to a Navajo, a Hopi, an Ashanti, a Trobriand Islander, a Nuer, or an Ifugao. Such a task calls for the treatment of whole cultures and lifeways as viewed from the inside. The aim is to feel and understand the universe not in scientific terms but in the terms, cognitions, and affects of the people concerned. A complete anthropology requires both approaches.

A few world views have been sketched in this chapter. Obviously, the sketches are much too thin to convey how it feels to see the universe as a Navajo does, or as a Hopi does. It is important, though, to sense the basic fact that cultures are not simply ways of doing, or of organizing

[13]R. Redfield, *The Little Community*, p. 95.

societies. They also define the nature of the world, of people (existential postulates), and of what is to be sought after and what is to be avoided (normative postulates or values).

The Navajo world view builds on the assumption that spirit beings established the world as it is and endowed it with order; it is, however, a very dangerous and threatening world, but it may be controlled by compulsive symbolic acts. Individualism is important, and social structure and material culture both reflect this basic fact. Disharmony and imbalance produce personal illness.

The Hopis intensify the concept of an orderly universe, and although they populate it with spirit beings, they tend to depersonalize it. All elements of the universe interrelate in an intricately delicate balance that is designed to operate beneficently for the well-being of all. People, however, are endowed with will and they are required to will the patterned maintenance of the system while fulfilling ordained roles. Failure on either count disrupts the system and brings on social disaster as well as possible personal sickness. Individuals are consequently under extreme social pressure to conform meticulously to traditional patterns.

The Cheyennes viewed the universe as a spirit-peopled mechanical system charged with a limited quotient of energy. They believed that it was their responsibility to keep the energy quotient at full charge. They did not see this as feeding the forces of good to aid them in their struggle against the forces of evil. Rather, their basic theory was much more morally neutral. The world-maintenance energy runs down as it is used up. Therefore, it must be used carefully and annually recharged through ritual action.

The world view of the people of the United States is predominantly rational-mechanistic in its conception of an orderly universe operating according to discoverable scientific laws. The American approach to life is marked by effort-optimism, an activist conviction that the material, biological, and social state of the world is improvable through human efforts. The social system emphasizes achievement and individual self-validation through the winning of material tokens of success in which know-how is more important than contemplative wisdom. Individual responsibility, combined with a religious tradition of human sinfulness, contributes to internal anxiety and self-censure. At the same time, an egalitarianism fits into the notion that every one should have an equal chance to show what he or she can do. It is a world view which looks forward to an always-changing future and which is concerned with the past largely as a key to what may be.

SELECTED READINGS

Forde, C. D. (ed.), *African Worlds: Studies in the Cosmological Ideas and Social Values of African Peoples* (1954). Nine studies of the world views of a selected group of African societies. Includes a very remarkable formulation of world view by a native informant from the Dogon of the French Sudan (pp. 83–110).

Hoebel, E. A., *The Cheyennes* (2d ed., 1978). Part II, A, "Ritual and Tribal Integration," and Part II, D, "World View and the Cheyenne Personality," show how the Cheyenne need to husband and renew the limited energy quotient of the universe is culturally expressed.

Hsu, F. L. K., *Americans and Chinese: Purpose and Fulfillment in Great Civilizations* (1970). A presentation of comparative contrasts of American and Chinese cultural orientations and their related behaviors. The account presents rich data and penetrating insights.

Leslie, C. M., *Now We Are Civilized: A Study of the World View of the Zapotec Indians of Mitla, Oaxaca* (1960). A penetrating and gracefully written expression of the world view of a Mexican people in transition from the old to the new.

Redfield, R., *The Primitive World and Its Transformations* (1953). Chapter 4, "Primitive World View and Civilization," explores some implications of the concept of world view for modern life.

———, *The Little Community* (1955). Chapter 6, "The Little Community as an Outlook on Life," emphasizes the differences between the outside and inside views of cultures and the problems of investigation of the latter, plus the theoretical significance of world view.

31
Religion, Myth, and Ritual

CHAPTER OUTLINE

LEARNING GOALS

Discuss anthropological theories of religion.

Define animism.

Explain Tylor's theory of religion.

Define mana.

Explain how religion is a mixture of the sacred and the profane.

Summarize Geertz's definition of religion.

Discuss some theories of mythology.

Describe religion in Mandan culture.

Describe the Okipa myth.

Throughout history, world view and religion have been intimately intertwined, for both are expressions of human intelligence and emotional concern.

World view, as we have just explored it, provides each people with its "set" toward the universe. Religion defines a part of that experience through the spirits and gods it creates; it clothes them with their own peculiar attributes of behavior and provides people with some guidelines for action in response to the presence and demands of the spirit beings. Religion does more than this, however. Through ritual and myth, religion provides symbolic expression which subtly and pervasively impresses on participants and observers an emotional and intellectual commitment to the ordered belief system on which their lives rest.

ANTHROPOLOGICAL THEORIES OF RELIGION

Over a period of a hundred years, anthropology has worked to develop an objective understanding of religion, an understanding that is free of dogma and separate from the value judgments that the religions of the East and West may have imposed on the intellectual climate of our times.

The earliest theories, those of the late nineteenth century, such as Sir Edward Tylor's, were primarily psychological; they undertook to explain the origins of religion in terms of mental responses to the puzzling aspects of life—dreams and death in particular. They were directly and simply concerned with overt belief in spirit beings. The theory of animism, as it was called, dominated anthropological thought until challenged by the sociological theory of Émile Durkheim.

Today, anthropologists combine both the sociological and psychological approaches to religion in a kind of master theory which, while it embraces Tylor's simple animism, goes far beyond it in sophistication. In this and the following chapter, we shall present the essence of the modern view.

Animism

Although the overall purpose of religion is the symbolic transformation of the human being's perception of the universe, thus creating a conviction of order and purpose for society and individual alike, all religions encompass manifestations of *animism* and *mana*.

Animism (L. *anima*, "soul," "spirit"), as defined by Tylor, is the belief in spirit beings.[1] They are known by many names: plant and animal spirits, souls, ghosts, goblins, genies, elves, pixies, leprechauns, fairies, witches, demons, devils, angels, and gods. They are beings without real flesh and blood—nonmaterial, but real enough for those who believe in them (Figure 31.1).

Tylor's Theory In his remarkable study (1871), Tylor examined many manifestations of animism among nonliterate peoples, but he was interested in more than just describing its forms. Tylor was essentially an evolutionist. For him the ultimate question was: "How and why did human beings create the notion of spirit beings?"

Tylor saw the origin of animism in the phenomena of dreams and death. Dreams are a form of hallucination, an illusory experience. But a person's dream is an empirical fact. In dreams we transcend reality. We soar to great heights of attainment and pleasure; we experience horrible happenings; we relive the past and anticipate the future; we visit places once visited and those where our feet have never touched; we commune with the dead or with the living who are far away. Limitations of time, space, and the body do not hinder us—in our dreams.

Yet, in sleep or in coma, the body does not leave its resting place. We wake where we lie down to rest. The body has not performed the miracles dreamed, but it is hard, even for the sophisticate, not to take dream experiences as real.

[1] E.B. Tylor, *Primitive Culture*, vol. 1, p. 424.

FIGURE 31.1
A ritual performance of the Mud Head kachinas (masked dancers representing ancestral supernaturals) in the plaza of Zuni Pueblo 100 years ago (1879). (J. K. Hillers/The Bettmann Archive, Inc.)

The Soul Concept Nonliterate peoples concluded that there were two parts to the individual—the bodily self of mortal flesh and the spiritual self, the soul. The soul concept is the universal root of animism.

In the language of many peoples, the word "soul" is synonymous with "shadow" or "shade." The soul is the vital force. Its presence animates the body; its departure stills it. It is in the stillness of sleep that the soul goes wandering.

The long sleep that is death comes when the sojourning soul does not return. The body that is the vessel for the soul has no further function once its soul has abandoned it. Disintegration follows. Illness is due to intrusive corruption of the soul or to soul loss.

This, according to Tylor, is the logic of the soul concept—in part.

People do not live alone. The beasts of wood and field, the fowl of the air, and the fishes of the waters are also endowed with vitality. So too are the plants. By means of analogical reasoning, nonliterate peoples attributed souls to them also, as the cause of their vitality.

Souls after death may become ghosts or free spirits. They live on in the world within the human community or in a special realm, which the spirits of living persons may on occasion visit or from which souls may come to visit the living.

Nature Worship The attribution of spirit qualities to plants and objects produced, according to Tylor, what we call *nature worship*. From this came totemism and the creation of species deities, that is, the deification not of persons (ancestor worship) but of animals and plants (Figure 31.2). From these practices, Tylor derived the higher polytheism of the later barbarians, with its sky, earth, rain, thunder, lightning, fire, wind, water, sun, and moon gods, as well as gods of agriculture, hunting, birth, war, and death.

Tylor's theory of religion suffers some inadequacies, but in the main we concur with Lowie's judgment:

His theory is avowedly a psychological interpretation pure and simple, but inasmuch as it not only explains the empirical observations, but operates exclusively with facts like death, dreams and visions, all of which demonstrably exercise a strong influence on the minds of primitive men, it must be conceded to have a high degree of probability. I, for one, certainly have never encountered any rival hypothesis that could be considered a serious competitor.[2]

Like all evolutionary theories that try to formulate the details of nonmaterial culture in prehistoric times, Tylor's theory is speculative and unverifiable. But, stripped of its evolutionary ordering of the data, it constitutes a valuable general analysis of a large part of religious attitudes and behavior. Animism, however, is not the whole story. There is also *mana*, which calls for theoretical explanation.

Mana

Supernaturalism does not find its only expression in beliefs in spirit beings; there are also beliefs in the existence of supernatural forces that do not emanate from any being. Such forces are expressed as special attributes of things, much as the force of gravity is related to objects that have mass. Following the suggestion of another early student of primitive religion, R. R. Marett (1866–1943), anthropologists call it *mana*, a word derived from the languages of Melanesia where the concept of mana is strong and clear in native life.

Mana is a force, but not a vitalistic force. It exists as a supernatural attribute of persons and things. Above all, it is the exceptional power to do unusual things.

Extraordinary aptitudes of people are explained in terms of mana. The master artisans in Polynesia excel in their skill because they possess mana. The learned pundits excel in lore and knowledge because they possess mana. The mighty warrior excels in killing because he possesses mana. The outstanding healer, the expert sailor, and any others who stand above their fellows do so because of personal possession or control of mana. Mana, though it is an impersonal force, can be manifest in and through persons, as well as in stock and stone. The queerly shaped or unusually marked stone may be believed to possess miracle-working power. This is its mana. The canoe that can outdistance all others, the song that heals, the war club that smashes more than a normal quota of skulls, the talisman that brings good luck—all these have mana.

[2]R. H. Lowie, *Primitive Religion*, p. 108.

FIGURE 31.2
San Ildefonso Pueblo (New Mexico) Corn Dance. The clown figure at the left is a member of a special medicine society called *Koshare.* The dancers perform secret rituals and act as messengers between the living members of the pueblo and their ancestors. (John Running.)

The Sacred and the Profane

Much religion is, indeed, a matter of individual

(a)

(b)

FIGURE 31.3
The sacred and the profane. The ritual sweat bath is widely used by Indians of the western parts of the United States as purification from profane contamination.

(c)

(d)

(a) Two Navajo men set up the frame for a bathhouse. (b) Hot stones are placed in the house. (c) After prayer and sweating, the medicine men emerge. (d) They complete their purification by rubbing themselves with the sand. (Josef Muench.)

experience, such as that of the North American Indian who must seek a vision in which a spirit bestows the supernatural power upon him. Yet all religions build on public participation, if only as spectators, in acts that not only affect the workings of extrahuman forces but also express the solidarity of the group and at the same time internalize group loyalty and commitment to unified social purposes. This was the thesis of Émile Durkheim, to whom society was the supreme reality. According to Durkheim, to explain religion on the basis of dreams, as did Tylor, was to explain a reality by recourse to a fantasy.

Durkheim saw ritual participation as the true essence of religion. All people rise above the humdrum monotony of eking out a living and share in the ecstasy of sacred experience obtainable only through periodic group dances and ceremonies. Religion, for Durkheim, is an expression of social solidarity and collective beliefs. Human beings alone are nothing. They realize their significance and worth only as members of a social group. Sacred rituals and beliefs symbolize society. Out of the ritual experience arises the difference between the sacred and the profane.

Religious belief is essentially mystical and subjective, whereas naturalistic belief emphasizes objective and rational determination of the facts. This becomes clearer when put in terms of *profane* and *sacred,* as suggested by Durkheim.

The Profane

The sphere of the routine, mundane, taken-for-granted, workaday world.

Attitudes: blasé acceptance on a basis of common familiarity.

The Sacred

The sphere of the unusual, extraordinary, not-to-be-taken-casually, "out-of-this-world."

Attitudes: awe, sense of mystery, circumspection in dealing with something special.

The terms "profane" and "sacred" have meanings somewhat broader than ordinarily accorded them in common English usage, and care should be taken to keep this constantly in mind. The profane, then, is that which is viewed as natural, as secular; the sacred, that which is viewed as supernatural. The natural works in ways that are accepted as ordinary, as in accord with daily experience. The supernatural works in ways that are looked upon as unusual and special. The emotional connotations are consequently different (Figure 31.3).

Religion and magic therefore rest upon a belief in the supernatural, and they are basically matters of ideology and the feelings that accompany them. They are in the "sacred" sphere, in Durkheimian terms.

A Comprehensive Definition of Religion

The anthropologist Geertz, defines religion as:

1. *A system of symbols which acts to*
2. *establish powerful, persuasive and long-lasting moods and motivations in men by*
3. *formulating conceptions of a general order of existence and*
4. *clothing these conceptions with such an aura of factuality that*
5. *the moods and motivations seem uniquely realistic.*[3]

What Geertz is saying is that religion is a body of things (ideas, objects, norms, myths, rituals) which signify or stand for something with deep meaning (symbols) for the people involved (Figure 31.4). This body constitutes an ordered system of knowledge about the nature of the world and includes rules telling people how to behave in different circumstances. It also presents this body of knowledge in such a context of reality, reverence, and mystery that people want to believe it, to use it as a guide for behavior, and actually do.

[3]C. Geertz, "Religion as a Cultural System," in W. A. Lessa and E. Z. Vogt (eds.), *Reader in Comparative Religion* (2d ed.), p. 206.

FIGURE 31.4
Hopi clowns performing at a *kachina* ceremony. Painting by Fred Kabotie, about 1930. (Museum of the American Indian, Heye Foundation.)

Theories of Mythology

The searching human mind has always asked the eternal "Why?" The creative mind has always spun a web of answers in words and ideas. One form these answers have taken in many societies has been myths.

Myths, as distinct from folklore and legends, deal with sacred and semidivine beings in a time when the world was different and they tell how, through the activity of such beings, things came to be as they are. They teach people what must be done to avoid chaos.

In Malinowski's functional theory, myth is more than idle speculation about the origins of things: "It justifies by precedent the existing order and it supplies a retrospective pattern of moral values, of sociological discriminations and burdens and of magical belief."[4] Myth believing is more than infantile self-deception; it is social reassurance—a device of education and learning, of culture maintenance.

Today, however, anthropological interests, while not ignoring function, relate myths more to symbolic transformations in which change and establishment of a new order of things is of more interest than origins. Turner writes:

Myths relate how one state of affairs became another: how an unpeopled world became populated; how chaos became cosmos; how immortals became mortal; how the seasons came to replace a climate without seasons; how the original unity of mankind became a plurality of tribes or nations; how androgynous beings became men and women; and so on.[5]

Myths are an important component of transition rites (see Chapter 20). They restate the first principles upon which a people's belief system and social structure rest. Myths define the nature

[4] B. Malinowski, "Culture" (*Encyclopaedia of the Social Sciences*, vol. 4, 1931), p. 640.

[5] V. W. Turner, "Myth and Symbol" (*International Encyclopedia of the Social Sciences*, vol. 10, 1968), p. 576.

of the personality each individual must translate into behavior. Because they are told in a sacred context and deal with sacred beings, myths are the timeless handmaidens of religion. They are the fertile seedbeds from which grew the sacred books of the great religions of later civilizations.[6]

We shall now try to make this clearer with a single interpretive example: the Okipa ceremony of the Mandan Indians of the Plains region in what is now South Dakota. Although the Okipa ceremony and its myths made up but one part of a fabulously rich myth-ceremonial system, we believe it will serve to exemplify myth and ritual as religious expression.

MANDAN CULTURE

One may think of the Mandans as the Parisians of the Plains. Their villages were centers of sophistication and intertribal trade for the northern Plains area. Their archaeological tradition goes back a thousand years.[7]

The subsistence base of Mandan culture was, equally, intensive horticulture (maize, squash, and tobacco growing in the bottoms of the Missouri River and its tributaries) and buffalo hunting. The Mandans were prosperous producers and traders, exchanging surplus corn and beautifully dressed and ornamented hide robes for meat and furs from farther south and west.

Nonetheless, theirs was a precarious existence. Fixed villages of large earth lodges were well fortified against marauding attackers. Equally important, corn raising in the area has always been unpredictable. The Mandan had much to cope with, and in the course of a thousand years of experience developed an ideology and ritual to manage it.

Finally, we should note that Mandan social organization was based on matrilocal households, matrilineal clans, and a dual organization of a Sky and an Earth moiety, symbolizing the twofold nature of the subsistence base upon which their survival depended.

The Moiety Symbolism

The Earth People, also called Those-Below and Corn People, were believed to have once lived under the ground, later emerging from a hole in the earth, bringing the corn plant with them. Whenever an Okipa ceremonial lodge was built, the Earth People placed yellow corn under the postholes on their side of the Okipa lodge. They owned all the corn medicine bundles, which had power over growing plants, and also the priesthoods which carried secret knowledge of the origin myths and how to perform the elaborate corn ceremonies. The corn bundles and their accompanying priesthoods were *inherited* from priest to sister's son (matrilaterally) within the clans which were within the Corn, or Earth People, moiety.

The Sky People (Those-Above) belonged to six clans named after birds and animals. They were symbolically related to the creatures of the animal world, and they planted mats of buffalo hair under the posts on their side of the Okipa lodge. They owned all the animal medicine bundles, which had power over buffaloes, antelope, birds, etc. They owned the priesthoods which carried secret knowledge of the origin myths and how to perform the ceremonies which controlled the animal world.

Thus the dual nature (above/below and animal/plant) of their mythically based concept of the universe and of their livelihood was fundamentally built into the social structure which controlled tribal well-being.

The Mandan Theory of Power

The Mandan image of humanity was one of inherent lack of personal aptitudes. "I claim no power for myself," a Mandan would say, "I have no power except what my sacred objects have promised me."[8]

[6]For example, see J. G. Frazer, *Folklore in the Old Testament.*
[7]See D. J. Lehmer, *Introduction to Middle Missouri Archeology.*
[8]A. W. Bowers, *Mandan Social and Ceremonial Organization*, p. 336.

Power could primarily be acquired from three sources: (1) inheritance and purchase of clan-owned medicine bundles and the priestly knowledge which went with them—this was the main road to prestige; (2) the personal vision quest in which one fasted, chopped off segments of fingers, and cut out strips of one's own flesh as offerings to the spirit beings; and (3) "walking with the buffalo," an act in which a young man asked an older power holder to have ritual sex relations with the young man's wife. The woman, wearing a buffalo shirt, played the role of a female bison: the vessel of power from which a man could draw strength, ability, and success.

Like the Cheyennes (who surely got the idea from the Mandans), the Mandans believed that the energy available to any individual was limited and was steadily used up. A man went on only four war parties and went "walking" no more than four times—his powers were then exhausted.

Psychological Factors A few fortunate individuals received power through adoption by a supernatural being without being aware of it. This accounted for the rare achievers who had no important medicine bundles.

Generally, however, a Mandan was born empty. He had to strive and struggle hard to establish himself. His need for achievement exceeded that of *all* other nonliterate populations rated by McClelland in his comparative analysis of achievement motivation.[9] For the Mandan male, the absolute test of his worthiness to succeed came in his performance in the torture rites of the Okipa.

The male personality The Mandan was born into a mother-dominated, semisubterranean earth lodge in which his father was an outsider. His inherited bundles came from his mother's brother and were paid for by his wife's brothers and sisters. He, in turn, had to pay them for his rights to the bundles. For everything he learned, every song, every technique, every ritual act, he had to pay in goods. With no striving to win the help of relatives and friends, with no uncanny trading and skillful hunting on his part to get the goods to buy power, a Mandan remained—nothing.

Only by surrendering his wife to a ceremonial "father" could he help his wife maintain a good home, keep his family in good health, and be successful in war and hunt. "The sexual act was tantamount to intercourse with the buffaloes. . . ."[10] So even when acting as a ceremonial father, the sexually giving male was nothing in his own right.

In psychodynamic terms, the Mandan male had to deal with a culturally engendered sense of worthlessness and self-hatred. Hostility to the father, who possessed his mother, is indicated. The ceremonial "fathers" who substituted for him as potent buffaloes with his wives (polygamy was practiced), would be included; so also, his mother's brother, who had sexual rights in a maternal nephew's wife and from whom the younger man had to buy the hereditary medicine bundles on which his ultimate standing would depend. Internalization of tribal values led to repression of sexual and aggressive aims in favor of manipulatory striving for externals—goods, medicine bundles, and priestly office. Repressed hostility and sense of self-worth found orgiastic outlet in the extreme sadism and masochism of the Okipa rite.

For the male there were delayed rewards in fraternity membership in the graded societies, but not in war. Remember, after being used on four war parties his fighting power was normally depleted. He could become a village chief, but in this there was little political authority. The greatest ultimate rewards were in the ritual and ceremonial roles that would come with bundle priesthoods, but these rewards were long deferred.

[9]D. C. McClelland, *The Achieving Society*, p. 66.

[10]Bowers, op. cit, p. 336.

The female personality Woman's personal position in Mandan society was clear. She was the generator of life and the transmitter of vital power upon whom her husband had to depend. A woman's kin bought bundles for her husband. Women were the owners of the houses in which men lived all their lives. The psychosymbolic implications of the lodge as earth-womb are very clear. Women were not only the corn growers; they were also the symbolic bison from whom men drew their war and hunting powers. Mandan women had little cause for self-doubt.

How, then, were these deep-seated factors reflected in world view and religion? How did the myth and ritual, the religious system, provide the support needed for making a livable world?[11]

THE OKIPA MYTH

The essence of the sacred Okipa myth is as follows:

Lone Man wandered for a long time. Later he came upon Coyote, the First Creator, who had made the world. They argued over their relative ages (Coyote won) and then they decided to fix up the earth, which was too sandy and wet. They made it as it is today and went their separate ways.

Lone Man met the first buffalo, from whom he received tobacco (the sacred herb).

After he had traveled all over the land, he decided it should have people on it. He created a man and a woman from the ends of his own ribs. In time their number increased to form a large village, of which Lone Man was the protector-adviser. However, the people kept calling him back from his wanderings so much for advice that he said he would only send the South Wind to them instead of appearing himself.

Next, the Sky People arrived—and the Corn People (each event accounted for in separate myths)—until there were five separate villages.

Lone Man returned and liked what he saw, so he decided he should be reborn as one of the people. He picked a virgin to be his mother but failed to get into her womb as a seed of corn. Later, he made himself into the kidney fat of a buffalo, which she ate and so conceived. Lone Man grew up to be the Buffalo Spirit.

Another spirit man was born of a virgin in another village. This was Hoita, the Spotted Eagle. He grew up to be the Eagle Spirit and a rival of Lone Man. In anger at Lone Man, Hoita enclosed all the living animals and birds inside Dog Den Butte, which lies east of the Missouri River and north of Bismarck, North Dakota. The Mandans starved.

Lone Man got into the cave by various stratagems and learned the Animal (Buffalo) Dance, or Okipa, by means of which Hoita had called all the animals into the cave. He had a young Mandan, acting as his son, impersonate Hoita in the dance. Hoita released the buffalo and said that thereafter he would work with Lone Man for the good of the people.

Later, Lone Man got three turtle-effigy drums for the Okipa ceremony from the Great Turtle Spirit. To save the Mandan from the flood that would be sent by Maniga, a mythological chief of another tribe, Lone Man put a cedar post, symbolizing himself, in the center of the village with a cedar plank palisade around it. The planks were tied with willow withes above which water could never rise. The post and palisade protected the village from floods.

Origin Myth of Oxinhede, the Foolish (Evil) One

A virgin Mandan girl was impregnated by a shadow (the Sun). She gave birth to a hyperactive black baby, called Oxinhede (see Figure 31.5). Nobody could do anything with him. He was always jumping and running about. When he got to be a little older, he was given a bow and arrows. With these he killed the sacred snakes and many other holy things. He would

[11]For the theoretical basis for this analysis, see C. Geertz, "Ethos, World View and the Analysis of Social Symbols," in A. Dundes (ed.), *Every Man His Way*, p. 309.

not stay away from sacred things, always molesting them. He was known as the Foolish, or Evil, One. Although the people liked him, the Spirits of Sacred Things decided he had to be killed. And this was done.

THE OKIPA: A RITUAL DRAMA IN THREE ACTS AND AN EPILOGUE

The Okipa took five days and nights to perform.[12] It was put on every summer in each of the villages, if possible. The producer of each Okipa performance was a man of a wealthy family who had managed to accumulate large amounts of food and fine goods to be given away in connection with the rite. He was called the Okipa Maker. Primary roles were played by chosen impersonators of Lone Man, Hoita, and the Foolish One. Owners of appropriate bundles performed as Buffalo Bulls, Beavers, Wolves, Bears, etc. (all the creatures who controlled the animal powers on which the Mandan depended). Other officiants beat the three turtle drums. Two masked priests performed as surgeons. A number of young men played the roles of sacrificial initiates. Major bundle holders painted the actors.

Act I. The Father Figure: First Day

At dawn of the first day, the chiefs and medicine priests were called to the Okipa ceremonial lodge. At sunrise, the figure of Lone Man approached from the south. A fraternity met him at the village gate and reverentially led him to the lodge where he was solemnly received by the chiefs and priests. In an archaic tongue Lone Man retold all the myths of his life when he was alive among the Mandan. That done, he walked about the village throughout the day, collecting bone knives with which the skin of the initiates would be pierced and their finger joints severed. In return he would give them buffalo meat. Women, children, and dogs were confined in their lodges, for this was the time of the male, the father figure. At various places around the village, Lone Man gave orations on the origins of the people, their struggles against floods and starvation, reminding them of how he had given them all the things to make life better.

At dusk, he retired to the Okipa lodge. Soon after, the sacrificial initiates (boys from 8 years of age to men of 35) entered to begin their fasting, while Lone Man ate buffalo meat.

The meal ended, Lone Man transferred his pipe, the symbol of his power, to the Okipa Maker. Hoita was next called forward by Lone Man, who exhorted him to supervise the Animal Dance and see that it was performed exactly as it had been when Hoita kept the animals captive in Dog Den Butte. Lone Man's work was done; he quietly left to return to his home in the south. Immediately, the dancing began—in the lodge as it had in the cave in Dog Den Butte.

Interpretive Comment Lone Man returned to the Mandan as an asexual, benign father figure, the designer of the Mandan lifestyle, the bestower of buffalo, the bringer of all animal spirits from whom vital medicine power was derived. He brought the turtle drums on which the world rests. He reasserted the authenticity of all the symbolic acts which legitimated the Mandan view and way of life. With the transfer of his pipe, he bestowed his active power on the Okipa Maker, called upon Hoita to do his part, and so retired from the immediate affairs of men. He became a remote deity who might be appealed to from afar, but who left the management of the affairs of the universe to lesser executive gods (Hoita and the Okipa Maker) and to human beings who were now on their own.

---

[12]The 1867 account, George Catlin's *O-kee-pa: A Religious Ceremony and Other Customs of the Mandans*, is now available in a 1967 reprint by Yale University Press. In this summary description, we rely mostly on Catlin and A. W. Bowers, *Mandan Social and Ceremonial Organization.*

Act II. The Male Principle Conquered: Second, Third, and Fourth Days

During the second day, the eight Buffalo Bull dancers emerged eight times from the lodge to dance in the plaza. The Okipa Maker took a position at the plank wall around the Lone Man cedar post in the center of the plaza. There he wept and beseeched Lone Man to help the people. The presence of Lone Man was now an ungraven image—a faceless idol.

Throughout the morning the animal impersonators and sacrificers were being painted. Each was first prepared by an old man who tightly tied the prepuce over the head of each initiate's penis with sinew. Then he obliterated the whole genital area with clay plaster. The impersonators were then meticulously painted with symbolic designs over their entire bodies.

The third day was called "Everything Comes Back Day." All the creatures who inhabited the earth with Lone Man and Hoita emerged from the lodge to do their mimetic dances along with the Bull dancers and to chant appropriate songs.[13]

In the meantime, in the lodge, the preparation of the initiates continued. Each one had selected a man from his father's clan to perform the operation. With a serrated knife to make a jagged wound, the clan father cut four holes over the shoulder blades or breasts and pushed two wooden skewers through the flesh for the thongs by which the initiate would be suspended. More skewers were put into the legs from which buffalo skulls would be attached.

On the fourth day, the Bulls and other animal dancers "came out" to dance twelve times. The Okipa Maker was again at the Lone Man post, crying and praying to Lone Man.

In the course of one dance, a crazy figure appeared, leaping and running zigzag across the prairie from the west. He rushed in among the spectators as women and children scattered in shrieking alarm. It was the Foolish (Evil) One (Figure 31.5). His body was painted black with white circles. He had a grotesque phallus. He jumped over sacred paraphernalia. He burlesqued a buffalo bull in intercourse with a man masquerading as a woman. He advanced threateningly toward the women. They screamed in terror. The Okipa Maker left the Lone Man post, advancing deliberately, Lone Man's pipe in hand. Thrusting it in the Foolish One's face, he paralyzed him, while the crowd of spectators hissed and groaned at the sacrilegious one as the Animal Dance proceeded unheedingly. The Foolish One controlled, the Okipa Maker returned to his prayers and supplications at the cedar post.

FIGURE 31.5
The Foolish One of the Mandan Okipa ceremony as painted by George Catlin in 1832. (G. Catlin/Yale University Press.)

Three times the Foolish One recovered and assaulted the women. Three more times he was

[13]Catlin, op. cit., p. 57.

subdued by the Okipa Maker. Each time the women became less terrified and began closing in on the Foolish One. After the fourth time, he turned his attention to the Buffalo dancers, simulating mating with four of them. His energy expended, one woman threw yellow ocher in his face. Others smothered him from all sides. The leader of the women took his mock phallus from him. He collapsed within himself, whimpered, and bolted for the prairie, pursued by hissing, screaming women, who pelted him with filth.

In triumph the women returned, escorting the woman who had deprived the Foolish One of his power. She mounted the entrance to the Okipa lodge and took command. In a long declamation she let it be known that *she* held the power of creation, the power of life and death over the people, and all control over the buffalo. They would come or stay away at *her* command.

She ordered the animal dancers to stop dancing. She directed the chiefs to go back in the lodge and witness the sacrifices of the young men which should now begin. She also demanded the most beautiful dress in the village, and this was dutifully given to her by the Okipa Maker.

Interpretive Comment The turtle drums symbolized the eternal and deathless continuity of life. The dancing animals reaffirmed the constructive power of Lone Man and all associated with him. The lamentations of the Okipa Maker in his prayers to Lone Man reiterated the theme of dependency on the far-removed father figure.

Into this scene of variegated order came Chaos—the Male Principle Uncontrolled. It was Foolish One, the sacrilegious scoffer at Mandan ethos. In his phallic grotesqueries, the unbridled male id, he terrified both women and children. Only the calm, controlled male power of Lone Man could master him.

Finally, the Female Principle boldly took over. With yellow clay signifying corn pollen and the People Below, women subdued Chaos and mocked him. In smashing the symbol of his exaggerated sexuality, they destroyed all his power and banished him from Mandan life, even as the spirit beings had killed him in the long ago.

The Female Principle was now dominant; even Lone Man (in the form of the Okipa Maker) was subordinate to the imperious control of the symbolic Mother of All.

Act III. In and Out of Limbo: Fifth Day

With all the initiates painted and ready, two of them were led to a position beneath the smokehole of the Okipa lodge. A war shield and four buffalo skulls were tied to the skewers in the skin of each one. By means of rawhide ropes fastened to the skewers in his chest or back, each man was drawn upward three or four feet off the floor, while his body was spun crazily around until he fainted (Figure 31.6). Onlookers cried out, "Dead! Dead!" Lowered to the floor, the two initiates lay lifeless. On recovering consciousness, each made his way to a buffalo skull to offer his little finger in thanks. Others then went through the same process.

Thereafter, in groups of six, the revived initiates came out to run around the Lone Man post until the buffalo skulls, skewered to their legs and dragging on the ground, tore loose. Then, and only then, could they make their ways unassisted to their homes.

Interpretive Comment The initiates had been in limbo since first they entered the lodge. Their sex had been neutralized with sinew and clay. They neither ate nor drank. They had retired from normalcy. Suspension betwixt heaven and earth is limbo. The rites of torture were clear in their intent—the ultimate test of worth and self-esteem. For the sacrificer, the masochism meant, "I surmount everything and achieve pleasure [goals]." For the priests and onlookers, the sadism of the act meant, "I triumph." With symbolic death the initiate's suffering was ended. He returned from limbo to creep back to the symbolic womb of his maternal

FIGURE 31.6
In the Okipa lodge. Suspended initiates are whirled with sticks while the turtle drums are beaten in the right foreground. At the left, an initiate is offering his finger to be chopped off on the buffalo skull. Painting by George Catlin, 1832. (G. Catlin/Yale University Press.)

earth lodge for recovery and reconstitution as a matured male, ready for marriage and the bundles he might now acquire.

Epilogue. Woman Triumphant: Fifth Night

The O-kee-pa having ended, and night having approached, several old men . . . perambulated the village . . . announcing that "the whole government of the Mandans was in the hands of one woman—she who had disarmed the Evil Spirit, and to whom they were to look during the coming year for buffaloes to supply them with food; . . . that the chiefs on that night were old women; that they had nothing to say. . . ."[14]

The Bull dancers and the priests of the Okipa were invited by the Chieftess to a Feast of the Buffalo before the Lone Man pole. Ten young women came with her. All other people had to remain secluded in their lodges. One by one, the women led the men onto the prairie to mate as buffaloes, until each man bought his release with a small payment.

Interpretive Comment It was driven home to all Mandans that this was indeed a matrilocal, matrilineal, matrifocal society. Men were an integral but subordinate part, while the Female Principle was the locus of power. Buffalo hunting was important to Mandan survival, but it was the female bison who was acknowledged as the major factor in the reproduction of the herds. Nonetheless, for the Mandans it was horticulture which most uniquely marked their character in the northern Plains. Anybody could hunt buffalo but only very special people could grow corn. And horticulture was associated with women. This, all Mandans had to learn and accept. This was the central focus of Mandan religion. This was the message of the Okipa.

SUMMARY

Animism, which is the belief in spirit beings, is the most basic and universal component of religious ideology. Tylor explained the origin of animistic thought as derived from early attempts to account for dream experience and death, separating the body from its spirit, or soul. After death, the disembodied soul was thought to live on as a ghost. Once the soul concept was

[14]Ibid., p. 69.

developed, human beings attributed spirits to natural phenomena and so developed *nature worship*.

Mana is a belief in supernatural attributes of persons and things which are not ascribed to the presence of spirit beings. Unusual talents and extraordinary prowess, if not the gift of spirits, may be accounted for in this way.

Religion is viewed by anthropologists as a system of symbolic transformations of chaotic reality through which human beings provide themselves with conceptions of a general order of existence which they accept as true and real. The moods and convictions which are generated by the symbolic experiences of religion reinforce the general world views of each society and contribute to the motivation of its people. Religion and its associated myths are directed toward stating the meaning of life and why and on what terms human beings should seek fulfillment.

Mythology is an intrinsic part of religion. It deals with the character and activities of sacred beings and tells how things were transformed from their primordial to their present state of being. Myth justifies the existing order of the universe and of society.

Myths are also important components of transition rites; they restate the basic postulates of the society and they tell what must be done, in limbo and in the new personality achieved after an act of transition.

The annual Okipa ceremony of the Mandan Indian religion is used to exemplify myth and ritual as religious expression.

The Mandan had a subsistence base of buffalo hunting and intensive horticulture. Their social structure included matrilocal residence and matrilineal descent, with clans and moieties.

The Mandan believed that men were born without any personal aptitudes. Capabilities were derived only from sacred objects contained in medicine bundles. Major bundles were inherited within the matriclan but had to be purchased with the aid of the wife's clanmates. Special powers could be obtained on the vision quest and through lending one's wife to a power holder. Woman was viewed as the generator of life and as the symbolic source through which a man drew his power.

In the religious mythology of the Okipa, Lone Man created the first couple from whom the Mandan are descended. When Hoita locked up all the animals in Dog Den Butte, Lone Man obtained their release, and with it the Animal Dance of the Okipa. Lone Man obtained the three turtle drums. When Lone Man left the people, he placed a cedar pole representing himself in the center of each village plaza. It had a plank wall which kept back the floods.

The Foolish One was born a sacrilegious prankster, for which he was killed by the Sacred Beings.

The Okipa reenacts all these mythic happenings, except that the Foolish One is destroyed by women in the Okipa. Lone Man is a remote, benevolent father figure. The Okipa Maker becomes his symbolic substitute for the duration of the ceremony. Hoita becomes Lone Man's "executive counterpart." The Foolish One symbolizes the male id running wild.

The initiates, who are symbolically desexed and hung in limbo, submit to torture and "death." They are killed as immature males, and return to their mothers' or wives' earth lodges to emerge, on recovery from their ordeal, as reconstituted adult males who understand and acknowledge things as they are.

The Okipa ends with the symbolic triumph of the woman who destroyed the Foolish One, followed by the Feast of the Buffalo in which the chiefs and medicine men of the tribe must "give" some of their power to the females, who will pass it on to their husbands.

The Okipa ceremony established Mandan dependence on animals, while asserting the superiority of horticulture and of women, who were the gardeners and the mistresses of life.

SUGGESTED READINGS

Evans-Pritchard, E. E., *Theories of Primitive Religion* (1965). A readable summary of the major theories of religion.

Geertz, C., "Religion: Anthropological Study" (*International Encyclopedia of the Social Sciences*, vol. 13, 1968), pp. 398–406. A brief summary.

Lessa, W. A., and E. Z. Vogt, *Reader in Comparative Religion* (3d ed., 1971). Contains very valuable papers by Geertz, Kluckhohn, Levi-Strauss, and others.

Turner, V. W., "Myth and Symbol" (*International Encyclopedia of the Social Sciences*, vol. 10, 1968), pp. 576–582. Offers a lucid analysis of myths and structural transformations.

32
Religion, Magic, and Sorcery

CHAPTER OUTLINE

LEARNING GOALS

Discuss the religious and magical attitude.

Explain the practice of sorcery.

Explain the functions of taboo.

List the roles and functions of shamans and priests.

Describe ancestor worship and cults of the dead.

Describe nature worship.

Identify the High God concept and Radin's theory.

Religion is manifest not only through myth and ritual. It also permeates the thought and feeling of individuals; it expresses itself through spells and incantations; it blends into magic and sorcery; it is managed by specialists—the shaman and the priest; and it may be organized into cults. Each of these manifestations will now be treated in turn.

RELIGION AND MAGIC

Human beings act on the basis of their beliefs. Animism and mana are the subjective aspects of supernaturalism. Religion and magic are concepts based upon the ways in which an individual behaves in relation to the supernatural forces in which he or she believes. They constitute two forms of the external objectification of beliefs. The distinction rests on an assessment of the motivating forces behind the supernatural. Is the individual subordinate to the caprice and will of the supernatural beings? If the answer is "yes," the individual's dealing with these beings, and vice versa, will be religious in nature. Can the individual under certain conditions dominate and control the supernatural forces, be they animistic or manaistic? If the answer is "yes," the individual's dealings with the supernatural will be magical in nature.

Prayer and magic are the two basic techniques of dealing with the supernatural. The first is a means of seeking spiritual rapport on a basis of subordination to animistic beings. The second is a technique of gaining external control over supernatural powers. Between these poles every possible form of interpersonal behavior may find its religious counterpart.

The Religious Attitude

What distinguishes religion from magic is neither the goodness of one nor the evil of the other, but the consequent modes of behavior and state of mind of the believer. This is the distinction made originally by Sir James Frazer.[1] In the religious state of mind, the individual acknowledges the superiority of the supernatural powers upon whose action well-being depends. The believer's attitudes are preponderantly those of submission and reverence. The behavior exhibited is beseeching, petition, and appeasement in prayer, offerings, and sacrifice.

Father have pity on me,
Father have pity on me,
I am crying for thirst,
I am crying for thirst,
All is gone—I have nothing to eat,
All is gone—I have nothing to eat.

Such is the tenor of an Arapaho ghost-dance song, "sung to a plaintive tune, sometimes with tears rolling down the cheeks of the dancers."[2] It epitomizes the religious attitude, as does the Lord's Prayer, with its "Hallowed be thy name" (reverence); "Give us this day our daily bread" (petition); "Thine is the Kingdom, the Power and the Glory, forever" (subordination and awe).

The Magical Attitude

The magician, on the other hand, believes that supernatural power is controlled under certain conditions. The magician feels sure that if a tested formula is possessed and executed perfectly, barring outside interference, it will provide the results which that formula is specified to give. The supernatural power has no volition or choice of its own. It must respond. The magician works with a confidence similar to that of the student in the laboratory who knows that if the manual instructions are followed correctly, a predictable result will be obtained.

---

[1]See J. G. Frazer, *The Golden Bough*, chap. 4.

[2]J. Mooney, *The Ghost Dance Religion and the Sioux Outbreak of 1890* (Bureau of American Ethnology, Annual Report 14, 1896), p. 977.

Magic often appears to produce the expected results. It seems to meet the pragmatic test. At least, it must work in its initial applications, or the magical formula is usually rejected as false or worthless. When magic works, it does so for two reasons: (1) coincidence—if sufficient time is allowed, the desired event may well come to pass—and (2) psychological suggestion—when magic is directed against persons who suspect or fear that they are its objects, hysteria or compulsion grips them; they sicken and often die. Psychologists call this *somatic compliance* and *thanatomania* (the depression of the will to live to the point of extinction). The records of travelers and anthropologists abound with cases from the nonliterate world. Clinical records reveal many authentic cases among civilized people. Doctors well know the importance of the psychological state of the patient in crucial illness or injury.

Magic also serves its ends by giving the magician and the client a needed psychological boost. As Malinowski reiterated, magic begins where mechanical technology ends. A Melanesian knows that magic cannot dig the soil in which he must plant yams, so he does his own digging. He knows that he must hoe to keep down weeds, so he hoes. But he also knows that, no matter how great his skill, pests, foraging animals, and climate are beyond his technological ability to control. He desperately needs a good crop. So he endeavors to control the unknown element by magic or religion, and the confidence they give him helps him make greater efforts toward the wished-for goal.

The warrior who believes he has magical invulnerability can surmount fear and leap to heroism far more easily than the man who confronts danger without such support.

Not only does magic actually help the magician to attain an end in reality, but it also fosters the illusion of attainment. When the dogma of magic is strong, the practitioner often thinks the magical result has come to pass when nothing has occurred. Magic has much in common with daydreaming as a form of wish fulfillment.

Thus, magic, in some of its aspects, is similar to science. When the magician proceeds on the mechanistic assumption that the magical formula is a cause that must produce a given effect, then thinking parallels that of the scientist. This method, however, rests on fantasies. But it may be well to remind ourselves that much scientific belief, formerly useful but now discarded, also rested on similar unrealistic belief. It would, perhaps, be more accurate to call magic a technique based upon different premises.

Finally, it should be noted that magic often appears to work because the magician is a canny prestidigitator, deceiving the credulous with skilled stage settings and sleight-of-hand artistry.

It is thus possible analytically to distinguish magic from religion. The difference between the two approaches to the supernatural has tremendous social consequences. Religious emphasis on supernaturalism leads to subordination of people to gods and to the power of cult functionaries—the shaman and the priest. Religion is much more readily centralized and organized than magic, which is inherently more individualistic. Although organized religions always use a certain amount of magic in their rituals, churches are implicitly antagonistic to magic, since the magical attitude is incompatible with the religious attitude of submission.

Because of its elemental kinship to science, magic is more susceptible to displacement by technological advances than is religion. Modern scientists may still hold to their religious faiths, but all renounce magic.

Sorcery

Sorcery is magic used for antisocial purposes. Magic is in itself amoral, neither good nor bad. It is the uses to which magical technique is put that determine its moral qualities. Thus, a medicine man, or "witch doctor," as one who has control over magic, may be thoroughly good in the eyes of his people, or he may be evil, or both.

Sorcery is a form of aggression against fellow beings or their possessions that is not socially approved. Magic may also be used aggressively, but it is not sorcery unless it is used in a socially disapproved manner (Figure 32.1). This is clearly shown in the attitudes of the Azande of Africa.

Among the Azande, good magic is *wene ngua* and bad magic is *gbigbita*. Vengeance magic (*bagbuduma*) may be legitimately used to kill a person if the poison oracles used by the sorcerer's kinfolk and those used by their chief both say the alleged sorcerer is guilty. *Pe zunga* magic, which may be used when the perpetrator of homicidal sorcery is not known, is also good. "It is regarded as a judge which seeks out the person who is responsible for the death, and as an executioner which slays him." In the words of the Azande, "it decides cases" and "settles cases as judiciously as princes." Even though its effect is to kill, it is socially approved because it will work only on behalf of a just cause. If there is no just cause, it will return to kill the person who evoked it. The Zande who wants to kill another without just cause can use a number of forms of *gbigbita* magic, but if discovered, he will be executed.[3]

TABOO

Taboo is the inevitable negative element in religion. Supernatural power is implicitly dangerous. It is like fire or a heavy charge of electricity. When under control and directed toward desirable ends, it is beneficent. When out of control, it may well be disastrous. Human beings cannot get along without fire, and yet they must fight a constant battle against it. Modern civilization cannot function without electricity, but electricity must be handled with insulated tools and gloves.

Spirits and mana are deemed by most people

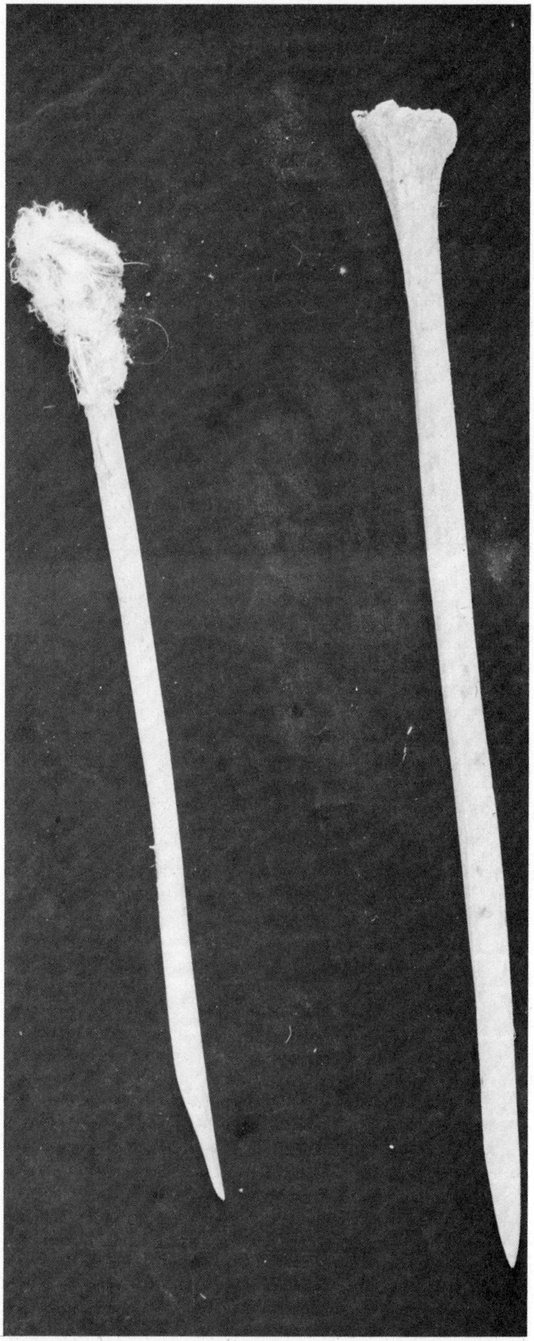

FIGURE 32.1
Australian pointing bones, which are used in a magical ritual to kill personal enemies. (Australian Official Photo.)

[3]E. E. Evans-Pritchard, *Witchcraft, Oracles and Magic among the Azande*, pp. 388–389.

to be absolutely essential forces in the human conception of the universe. They must be manipulated for human ends, but if improperly approached or used, they can react most dangerously.

Supernatural power, it must be remembered, is above the realm of the ordinary. Because of this, it may not be approached or dealt with casually. It, too, must be handled with rubber gloves. Figuratively, taboos are great "Caution! Handle with Care!" signs. Taboo does not mean *verboten*, in the German sense. Rather, it carries the overtones of the French *défense de toucher.*

In content, taboo consists of a series of negative rules, each of which states a form of behavior that will cause a supernatural power to backfire and injure the user. In reality, very few tabooed acts are physically or socially dangerous in themselves. This is why rationalistic attempts to explain the Hebraic or Islamic taboos on the eating of pork in terms of hygiene are really beside the point.

Typical of most taboos was the injuction that went with the war bonnet of the famous Cheyenne chieftain, Roman Nose. His bonnet had the power to give invulnerability in battle. With it Roman Nose rose, unscathed, to fame on the western Plains. One of the rules of the bonnet was that its wearer must not eat any food taken from a dish with an iron utensil. If he did, a bullet or iron-tipped arrow could pierce him, just as the sharp metal pierced the meat, and the protective power of the hat would be nullified until restored through a long and elaborate ceremony of purification and atonement.

Just before the famous Beecher's Island fight with Colonel Forsyth's men on the Republican River of western Nebraska, in 1868, Roman Nose ate as a guest in the camp of the Sioux Indians. When it was pointed out to him that the wife of his host was using a fork in her cooking, he said, "That breaks my medicine." The battle began before Roman Nose could make atonement, so, like Achilles, he sulked in his tent. But under pressure, like Achilles, he donned his war gear, saying, "My food was lifted with an iron tool. I know that I shall be killed today." Roman Nose was killed by a bullet before he had a chance to strike a single blow in the battle.[4]

The Functions of Taboo

The first function of taboo, as just indicated, is to sustain the awesomeness of the supernatural by reinforcing attitudes of care and mystery and by punishing attitudes of carelessness and profanity in dealing with the supernatural. It helps keep the sacred, sacred.

The second function of taboo is to set off the members of one social group from those of another and to strengthen their sense of solidarity. Just as a traditional hairdo may indicate that the social status of a married woman is different from that of an unmarried girl who has only reached puberty, or as men's hairdos used to set them apart from women, so adherence to special taboos may help set off the medicine man from the ordinary laypersons. Thus the Hebraic and Islamic taboos on pork help to identify membership in these religious groups, as did abstinence from meat on Friday by Catholics and as does the Mormon taboo on the use of tobacco and the drinking of coffee, tea, or alcoholic beverages.

Third, taboo is an essential ingredient of social control. In Polynesia, where the word "taboo" originated, high-ranking nobles possess mana because of their direct descent from the gods. So potent is their charge of mana that their very persons are surrounded with taboos, as is everything they touch. Sin, in Polynesia as elsewhere, is the violation of a taboo—an act punishable by supernatural sanction.

RELIGIOUS SPECIALISTS

All people participate in some aspect of religious observances. Yet, because every society is internally segmented by sex, age, kinship, and mari-

[4]A full account of the episode is given in G. B. Grinnell, *The Fighting Cheyennes,* pp. 267–282.

tal groupings, access to religious power and the privileges of religious participation are not equally distributed. In the first place, years of experience and learning are necessary before an individual can know enough about basic religious beliefs to master religious activities. Children always participate on a lower level.

Religion and magic are sources of power; they are means of influencing or controlling supernatural power, the greatest of all powers. Authority vested in adults is implicitly necessary to the perpetuation of culture. This is a special reason for keeping the heart of religious power in the hands of grownups.

Although women are shamans and priestesses, the centers of religious power are usually vested in men. Dominance tendencies lead men to keep access to the supernatural as a vested interest. The matrifocal emphasis of Mandan religion was, as we saw, an expression of their matrilineal system and as such represents a minority of human societies.[5] In more complex class-stratified societies, official religious power is almost inevitably an upper-class monopoly, while folk practitioners operate on a lower-class level.

Within the group of those who qualify for religious power, there are those who achieve an even more intimate access to the supernatural. They become religious specialists. Religion and magic are always so complex and, by their very nature, so extraordinary that the layperson who is wrapped up in the day-to-day acitvities of making a living cannot penetrate very far into the realm of the sacred. To do this, a person must spend time away from the basic tasks of food production and must have an unusual personality and special aptitudes and skills. Those who have the time and the skills may become religious functionaries: shamans or priests.

Shamans

The shaman is the more elementary type of specialist, and exists in systems in which religion has not developed a church. *The shaman derives power directly from a supernatural source*, either through mystic experience or through an ability to perform rites and the possession of paraphernalia (Figure 32.2).

Siberian Shamanism A center of the most intensive development of shamanism is aboriginal Siberia. The very word "shaman" comes from a Siberian language. Synonyms also meaning "shaman" are "medicine man" (usually applied to American Indians), "witch doctor" (usually applied to shamans of Africa and Melanesia), and *angakok*, in Eskimo.

The Siberian shaman is more clearly set off from his fellow men than his North American counterpart. For one thing, his personality is more clearly marked. For another, his "call" and training are more definite. Bogoras wrote of the Chukchi:

> *For men, the preparatory stage of shamanistic inspiration is in most cases very painful, and extends over a long time. The call comes in an abrupt and obscure manner, leaving the young novice in much uncertainty. . . . He feels "bashful" and frightened. . . . The young novice, the "newly inspired," loses all interest in the ordinary affairs of life. He ceases to work, takes little food and without relishing it, ceases to talk to people, does not even answer their questions. The greater part of his time he spends in sleep.*[6]

Bogoras observed that shamans were as a rule excitable and hysterical. He even opined that not a few of them were "half crazy." Psychiatry was not the vogue in Bogoras' day or he might have labeled the personality of the Siberian shaman "schizophrenic."

Becoming a Shaman The experience of a Northern Paiute Indian, who lived in western Nevada, is more or less typical of the way in

[5]See page 413.

[6]W. Bogoras, "The Chukchee: I Religion" (*Jesup North Pacific Expedition*, vol. 7), p. 420.

FIGURE 32.2
All members of a Bushman camp participate in helping the shaman go into a trance in which he becomes possessed of one of his helping spirits. (L. K. Marshall/Harvard Peabody-Smithsonian Expedition.)

which an American medicine man received power. As recorded by Willard Park, it runs as follows:

When I was a young man I had dreams in which I doctored people. I did not take those dreams seriously. My uncle was an Indian doctor. He knew what was coming to me. He told me to be careful in talking, not to speak harshly [in order not to offend the supernatural spirits]. I did not become a doctor from these dreams. Finally, I decided to go to the cave near Dayton. I was about fifty then. . . .

I went into the cave in the evening. As soon as I got inside, I prayed and asked for power to doctor sickness. I said, "My people are sick. I want to save them. I want to keep them well. You can help me make them well. I want you to help me save them. When they have died give me power to bring them back [return the lost soul]." I said this to the spirit in the cave. It is not a person. It comes along with the darkness. This is a prayer to the night.

Then I tried to go to sleep. It was hard to sleep there. I heard all kinds of noises. . . . There were bears, mountain lions, deer, and other animals. They were all in caves in the mountain. After I went to sleep I could hear people at a doctoring . . .at the foot of the mountain. I could hear their voices and the songs. Then I heard the patient groan. A doctor was singing and doctoring for him. A woman with a sage-brush shoot in her hand danced. She moved around the fire jumping at every step. Each time she jumped she said, "hə,' hə,' hə'." Then the shaman sprinkled water on the patient with sage-brush. The singing and dancing went on for a long time. Then the singing stopped. The patient had died and the people began to cry.

After a while the rock where I was sleeping began to crack like breaking ice. A man appeared in the crack. He was tall and thin. He had the tail-feather of an eagle in his hand. He said to me, "You are here. You have said the right words. You must do as I tell you. Do that or you will have a hard time. When you doctor, you must follow the instructions that the animals give you. They will tell you how to cure the sickness. I have this feather in my hand. You must get feathers like it. You are also to find the things that go with it. Get dark beads. Put them on the quills of the feathers and tie a strip of buckskin to the quills. Also get a hoof of a deer, and down from the eagle. With these you can go to people to cure them. These are your weapons against sickness. You must get three rolls of tobacco. You can use them to tell your patients what made them sick and then you can cure them. The tobacco will also help you if you are choked with clots of saliva when you suck out the disease. With this you are beginning to be a doctor. You will get your songs when you doctor. The songs are now in a straight line [ready for use]. Bathe in the water at the foot of the cliff and paint yourself with . . . [white paint]."

Then I woke up. It was daylight. I looked around but I could not see anyone. The man was gone and there was no sign of the animals or the people who had been singing and doctoring. Then I did as the spirit had ordered and waited to become a doctor. In about six years I had received enough instructions to begin to cure.[7]

FIGURE 32.3
A Bushman in a state of spirit possession cures a patient by drawing out the source of his illness. (DeVore/Anthro-Photo.)

Suggestibility and a degree of emotional instability are essential traits of the shaman. The person who can not respond with visions and hallucinations to the pervading cultural suggestion that these form the road to power cannot become a shaman (Figure 32.3). Crashing Thunder, a Winnebago Indian, was one of these. Even when he faked a vision and luck seemed to confirm his power, he knew that his power was false. An extrovert whose aggressive personality demanded social prestige and the opportunity to amount to something, he was frustrated by intellectual hardheadedness. Not finding the social means (supernatural power) to greatness open to him, he took the antisocial road—drunkenness, rowdyism, debauchery, murder, and fraud. Then when peyote at last reached the Winnebagos, the vision-stimulating drug brought visions and power to the tortured man. With power came the reorientation of his personality. He became a pillar of society, a moral leader, and a decent citizen—much to the relief of his fellows.[8]

The evidence is clear that as far as becoming a spirit-endowed shaman is concerned, the odds favor those who belong to what might unkindly be called the "lunatic fringe." But the cultures of these people turn their peculiarities to good and

[7]W. Z. Park, *Shamanism in Western North America*, pp. 27–28.

[8]P. Radin (ed.), *Crashing Thunder.* This book should not be missed by any student of anthropology.

make honored medicine men and women of them.

Shamanistic Magic Magicians are dupes of their own beliefs, but it is possible for them to work with cold calculation. Highly developed magic often involves sheer fraud, skill in prestidigitation, and the creation of optical illusions. Siberian and Eskimo shamans are skilled ventriloquists, using their tambourines so to deflect their voices that the listeners "after a few minutes . . . begin to lose the power to locate the source of the sound. . . . The song and drum seem to shift from corner to corner, or even to move about without having any definite place at all."[9]

Pueblo Indian priests put on miracle dramas in which corn grows and ripens overnight and deer and bears materialize before the astounded eyes of uninitiated spectators. Some *kivas* are equipped with secret tunnels through which the props and actors are brought upon the scene.[10]

However, the deceit practiced by shamans may not always be the crass charlatanism it at first appears. Eskimo shamans often disclaim their own skill. But the effect of their performances on the people is ecstasy. People are not averse to being fooled if it gives pleasure. Beyond that, of course, credulous ones are duped without their being the wiser.

It is difficult to draw an accurate balance between the exploitative and the social-service activities of shamans. It is a false gesture to dismiss them solely as a class of exploiters. Yet it is true that they often turn their position and power to self-advantage. Eskimo shamans can impose almost any taboos they wish on individuals. They can sexually exploit women, married and unmarried, to gratify themselves in the name of spirits. Shamans can use their power particularly to consolidate the position of the elders as against the younger generation. But for this they must pay a price in self-denial of many things, for their work is dangerous in its own terms, and the burden of shamanism is often hard.

Priests

Priesthood is a manifestation of developed religion. It occurs in societies whose cultures are rich and complex. On the whole, it calls for an economic base of sufficient richness to support fairly large populations, plus food and wealth surpluses. It is necessary to be able to organize and sustain permanent cults. The priest may have mana, but personal power is less important than the power resident in the office held (Figure 32.4). Unlike the shaman who acquires sacredness personally, the priest is vested by succession to the *office*.

There are basically three kinds of priests: (1) those who serve inherited or enduring medicine bundles; (2) the family heads in ancestor-worshiping religions who serve as priestly intermediaries between the kinship group and the deceased ancestors; and (3) the priests who serve cult groups whose interests are directed toward special spirits or deities.

Although in many simple societies there is a recognized division of function between priests and shamans, in the more complex societies in which cults have become strongly organized churches, the priesthood fights an unrelenting war against shamans. Priests work in a rigorously structured hierarchy fixed in a firm set of traditions. Their power comes from, and is vested in, the organization itself. They constitute a religious bureaucracy. Shamans, on the other hand, are arrant individualists. They are on their own, undisciplined by bureaucratic control; hence, a shaman is always a threat to the order of the organized church.

---

[9]Bogoras, op, cit., p. 430.

[10]E. A. Hoebel, "Underground Kiva Passages" (*American Antiquity*, vol. 19, 1953), p. 76; and F. M. Hawley, "Jemez Kiva Magic and its Relation to Features of Prehistoric Kivas" (*Southwestern Journal of Anthropology*, vol. 8, 1952), pp. 147–163.

FIGURE 32.4
A Tana Island, Melanesia, priest concludes his prayer by blowing chewed kava from his mouth. (Kal Muller/Woodfin Camp Associates.)

Priestesses are much less common than female shamans, probably because the organization of associations tends to be correlated almost exclusively with the male in most societies.

ANCESTOR WORSHIP AND CULTS OF THE DEAD

All cultures acknowledge ghosts, and all provide some means of dealing with them. The intensity of ghost awareness, however, and the amount of concern over the activity and feelings of ghosts are variable. In North America, the Pueblo Indians pay little attention to ghosts; the Plains Indians fear them, but their ghosts are not too prevalent; and the Navajos and Eskimos are bedeviled by ghost anxiety. They possess definite ghost cults, a body of practices and ritual observances associated with the propitiation or avoidance of ghosts.

Most traditional Plains Indians and the Navajos abandon any house in which a person has died. The ghost haunts the house and disturbs the inhabitants. Navajos, therefore, take a seriously ill patient who is about to die outdoors in order to save the house, or they rush the patient to the Indian Health Service hospital, which is already heavily inhabited by ghosts: a house of the dead, not of healing. The Navajo reservation is dotted with hogans abandoned because a death has occurred within. One of Hoebel's Shoshone friends dismantled a log house that he had inherited from his brother, moved it a few hundred feet, and then reassembled it, after mixing up the logs to fool the ghost of his brother, who was then unable to recognize the new house. Ghost fear has been a hindrance to the Bureau of Indian Affairs' efforts to provide modern housing on some reservations. In the northern Plains, a workable expedient acceptable to the Indians in some places has been the fumigation of the house as an effective antidote to ghosts.

Eskimos believe that ghosts are harmful and relentlessly malicious as long as they remain in the memory of the living. On death, the corpse is not removed from the igloo by way of the door; this would make it too easy for the lingering ghost to reenter. Rather, a hole is chopped in the back, later to be refilled after removal of the body. This baffles the ghost. Then, in case the ghost does find the entrance, knives are set in the snow floor of the doorway for three nights after burial. Such booby traps discourage ghosts.

Comanches taboo names of the dead, but when they want to mention a defunct friend named Pork, for example, they call him Bacon. Ghosts are literal-minded, but people can get the idea.

Eskimos, like many other people, bury the dead with grave offerings—the personal equipment and gifts of friends and relatives to serve the ghost in the other world. These are "killed." They are broken to release the animate soul of the object. It is the spiritual counterpart of the goods that obviously is used in the spirit world.

Grave sacrifices were stepped up to extravagant heights for the royalty of Africa and India. Into the nineteenth century, Hindu wives were immolated on the funeral pyres of their princely husbands. In Dahomey in West Africa, whole corps of wives and retainers were slain to provide an adequate retinue for the deceased king. Shoshone and Comanche tradition has it that in ancient times, wives were killed to accompany their husbands' spirits, but in more recent days, the wives followed the general Plains Indian practice of self-mutilation and abnegation.

Ghost cults usually emphasize the malevolence of ghosts. The people of Manus in Melanesia are an exception. The ghost of the last deceased household head is the preceptor and protector of his family. He is addressed as "Sir." He punishes their moral derelictions, but above all he is busy thwarting the malignant efforts of other ghosts. All ghosts are malicious toward people not of their own kinship group. The social and economic rivalry that is characteristic of everyday Manus life continues in the afterworld through the jealousy and rivalry of the ghosts. Each ghost enjoys a brief span of immortal existence while his skull adorns the doorway of his family hut. But the death of an adult male in the household is an indication that the family ghost has not been on the job. He has been negligent enough to permit a rival ghost to kill his descendant. Therefore his skull is thrown out and replaced by that of his successor, who then rules as the Honored Ghost of the household. [11]

Ancestor Cults

Ancestor worship is both an elaboration and an abstraction of the ghost cult. As an elaboration, it is best seen among the Bantu tribes of Africa. Every lineage and clan has its distinct ancestral deities, who are gods to their descendants but who are ignored by the members of other kinship groups. The gods of royal clans, because the heads of such clans must be honored by all the kingdom, are worshiped not only by the royal clan itself but also by all the subjects of the king. In ancestor-worshiping cults of this order, the eldest ranking member of the kinship group is not only its headman but also its priest. On the gods' behalf, he is the intermediary who is responsible for controlling the acts of his family or clan members. As in modern Japan, he has to keep the ancestral gods informed of the state of affairs within his domain. The Mikado had merely to make a ceremonial report at the ancestral shrine, but in Dahomey in West Africa, it was customary to execute a couple of victims to carry the royal message to the ancestors whenever the king had anything of moment to report.

Periodic elaborate feasts and sacrifices on behalf of the ancestral gods are characteristic of the western Sudan. In Dahomey, such ceremonies are held by each clan every year, with litanies, dancing, offerings of food and libations of liquors, and sacrifice of animals. In the annual ceremonies of the royal clan, human victims used to be offered.

---

[11] R. F. Fortune, *Manus Religion* (Proceedings of the American Philosophical Society, 1935); and M. Mead, "The Manus of the Admirality Islands," in M. Mead (ed.), *Cooperation and Competition among Primitive Peoples,* pp. 210–239. But see M. Mead, *New Lives for Old,* for post- World War II changes in Manus religion.

Vodun,[12] among West Indies Negroes, is a syncretism of Dahomean ancestral rites and Catholicism.[13] The clan founders of Dahomey are known as *tovodun*, from whom the *vodun* cult is named. Vodun rites are fundamentally family rituals with offerings and sacrifices accompanied by chants and dances, in which various gods are impersonated and called upon to visit the ceremony. Dancers representative of specific gods are possessed in turn as each god is called with his drum *salute* (greeting). The trance behavior of the votaries and the ecstasy of the worshipers lend the eerie wildness to the performance that has given *vodun* its exotic reputation.

Social conservatism is a characteristic feature of ancestor-worshiping religions. The ancestors as moral preceptors do not favor change from the social practices they knew as human beings. Since they punish moral lapses with death and illness and their standards are the old ones, the religious sanctions toward conformity are powerful.

FIGURE 32.5
Aztec sacrifice of a human heart to the sun. (From Bernardo de Sahagun, *General History of the Things of New Spain: The Florentine Codex.* Translated by Arthur J. O. Anderson and Charles E. Dibble. Published by The School of American Research and The University of Utah. Illustration from Book II. Copyright 1957 by The University of Utah.)

NATURE WORSHIP

Cults deifying various features of nature abound in the nonliterate world. Among agricultural and gardening peoples, sun, rain, and fertility deities are outstanding. Solstitial rites marked the annual crisis of the sun in the religion of the megalith builders of Neolithic Europe. Mysterious Stonehenge and Avebury in England and the cromlechs of Carnac in Brittany are aligned to the rising sun at the time of the spring solstice, as is the sun stone in the famous Sun Temple of Mesa Verde National Park, built by prehistoric Pueblo Indians 700 years ago. In ancient Rome, the solstice rites of the Mithraic cult gave way to the Christian Christmas celebration of the birth of Christ as the new light of the world. Each pueblo in the Southwest today has its priestly sunwatcher, who controls the ceremonial cycle with the movements of the sun.

All the religions in the great Central American culture complex made much of the sun. The Pyramid of the Sun near Mexico City is one of the truly great monuments of all the world (Figure 32.5). The Incas of Peru built theocratic states around the principle of sun divinity. The Inca was the personification of the divine sun. And until the disaster of 1945 induced the

[12]*Vodun* is the phonetically correct name for the cult complex popularly called *voodoo*.

[13]See M. J. Herskovits, "African Gods and Catholic Saints in New World Negro Belief" (*American Anthropologist*, vol. 39, 1937), pp. 635–643; and G. E. Simpson, "The Vodun Service in Northern Haiti" (*American Anthropologist*, vol. 42, 1940), pp. 236–254.

Emperor of Japan to deny it by imperial edict, he was supposed to be a divinity directly descended from the mythical sun goddess.

The sun figured greatly in Plains Indian religion. All tepees opened east, and tribal camp circles likewise. By the nineteenth century, the midsummer Sun Dance had come to be one of the most spectacular of Plains ceremonials.[14]

In Africa and Polynesia, although the sun is not glorified, nature worship is not neglected. The entire universe is departmentalized among gods of the skies, earth, waters, trees, and thunder, with myriads of subdivisions among the specialized deities. On the less-than-god levels, all primitive religions include multitudes of nature spirits associated with particular spots, trees, volcanoes, mountains, rivers, lakes, and rocks.

To nonliterate peoples, the whole world lives. Souls, animate things, and whatsoever embodies the soul are spirit beings to be treated with religion or magic—or both.

THE HIGH GOD CONCEPT

The time has passed when informed contemporary people can think the nonliterate mind incapable of conceiving of a Supreme Being or High God. Tylor's greatest error was to infer that the High God concept could be only the end product of a long intellectual evolution, beginning with the soul concept and leading through ghost and ancestor worship to polytheistic nature worship and monotheism[15]

The actual occurrence and distribution of the High God concept is now clearly delineated. It is rarest in Pacific Island religious systems, where only one-fourth manifest it. In East Eurasia and North and South America, somewhat less than half the cultures include the idea of a High God.

Among the Oceanic and American Indian tribes which did have the High God concept, he was usually unapproachable and disinterested.

Clearly, however, the center of the idea is the Mediterranean area, where 97 percent of all cultures center around it. Judaism, Christianity, and Islam are its most evident manifestations, but the idea goes much deeper than that. In sub-Saharan Africa 86 percent of the tribal religions include the High God. There is a marked difference in the relation of the High God to societal ethos in the Mediterranean and sub-Saharan areas, however. In black Africa the High God figures in the cosmology but is not involved with human affairs or morality. What human beings do is their concern and that of their ancestral gods, but none of his. In Mediterranean religions, on the other hand, the High God is very much concerned with human affairs and morality (in 86 percent of the societies). He is a moral censor, rewarding and punishing according to strict behavioral codes. He is the apex of the system of social control.[16]

Outside of the strongly monotheistic Mediterranean religions, the acts of creation by the High God are only vaguely conceived in cosmological lore. Myths tell how he created departmental, executive subdeities charged with the responsibility for filling in the details of creation and running the universe. These are the gods who must be appeased and prayed to. They are the ones who deliver or withhold the goods. Evil in life is due to their perversity or maliciousness. A common counterpart of the High God is a Trickster or Transformer, like Coyote among the western American Indians, who spoils or modifies the good work of the creator to burden people with death, sin, and travail. The Trickster is the equivalent of the serpent in the Garden of Eden.

[14]See G. A. Dorsey, *The Cheyenne: II, The Sun Dance* (Field Columbian Museum, Publication 103, Anthropological Series, vol. 9, no. 2, 1905) for a good description of a typical sun dance with many illustrations. Volume 16 of the Anthropological Papers of the American Museum of Natural History contains descriptions of other tribal sun dances.

[15]E.B. Tylor, *Primitive Culture.*

[16]Data from E. Bourguignon and L. Greenbaum, *Diversity and Homogeneity*, table 23, p. 45.

Radin's Theory

Paul Radin (1885–1963) posited two contrasting types of human mentality, idealist and realist.[17] Idealists are persons of intellectual and reflective temperament, persons whom anthropological experience has shown to be present in small numbers among all peoples. They philosophize on the conundrum of life and the universe. Their thought seeks a direct, unified, orderly cause in explaining the universe. The product of their thought is the Supreme Being. As idealists, they are little concerned with crass, material desires. Their god is free from the petty demands of ordinary mortals.

Pospisil's description of Kapauku religious ideology exemplifies Radin's theory exactly:

> *Most of the Kapauku people do not ponder the nature of life and the universe around them. They are empiricists who are not inclined to speculate and philosophize. The topics that interest them do not concern the supernatural or metaphysics; indeed, they usually talk about such unphilosophical subjects as contemporary power relations, concrete monetary transactions, love affairs, or news concerning pig feasts and dancing. Philosophizing they leave to the few especially gifted individuals who make it their hobby to try to penetrate the nature of things beyond the barrier imposed by the human senses. Accordingly, the systematic and logically consistent philosophy that is described next is by no means the property of the Kapauku tribe as a whole; it belongs to a few very intelligent individuals from the southern part of the Kamu Valley who have elaborated their views of the universe into a logical systematic whole.*[18]

Most people, indeed, are materialists. Their bellies, their health, wealth, and social power mean much to them. They develop religion in terms of gods and spirits who control the means to satisfy these needs. When prayer, appeasement, and magic suffice to win the desired results, all goes well. But hunger, illness, failure, and death stalk the earth, for which the lesser gods and the forces of evil are responsible. Toward them people's emotions are ambivalent. The gods and spirits are both loved and feared. The emotional overtones of religion are mixed indeed. But taken in the main, the anthropologist cannot, on the basis of the facts, concur in the idealistic belief that religion in all its history represents solely a human striving for the highest values of life. Nor is it possible to derive religion from any single mainspring of motivation. Belief in souls, fear of ghosts, fear of fear, worship of ancestors, traffic with hosts of spirits, nature worship, and philosophical reflection all play their parts. Emphasis shifts from culture to culture, but religion is a growth with many roots and many fruits.

SUMMARY

Religion and magic are both aspects of supernaturalism. Their difference lies in the attitudes of the religious and magical practitioners. The religious person acknowledges an inferiority to spirit beings; the magician is believed to have mastered a supernatural force through the possession of a compulsive formula.

Prayer is a supplication expressing dependence; an act of magic is an act of mechanical compulsion. Magic is basically amoral and usually socially accepted. Magic used for antisocial ends becomes sorcery, socially feared and frequently punished by society.

All religions involve *taboo*. Taboo is an expression of constraints designed to protect the sacred. It consists of prohibitions: "Thou shalt not's." Violation of taboos is *sin*; and the sanctions for sin are various forms of supernatural punishment.

Religious specialists are found in all societies. They are either *shamans* or *priests*. Shamans receive their supernatural power directly from spirit beings, usually in a vision experience or through possession. Priests receive their power

[17]P. Radin, *Monotheism in Primitive Religion*; see also *Primitive Man as Philosopher*.

[18]L. Pospisil, *The Kapauku Papuans of West New Guinea*, p. 83.

through the authority of their position in a cult or church. They are officers; shamans are not.

Ancestor worship as a special cult form represents an intensification of the ghost cult. The High God concept expresses belief in a creator deity who is a supreme being. Although this concept occurred in religions in all parts of the world, the idea of a Supreme Deity was lacking in most of the religions of Oceania and the New World. The High God who is concerned with human affairs and morality is primarily a feature of the Mediterranean complex of civilizations where Judaism, Christianity, and Islam flourished, as well as being found extensively in sub-Saharan Africa.

SELECTED READINGS

Evans-Pritchard, E. E., *Nuer Religion* (1956). A penetrating field study of the concept and role of supernatural forces in a culture that lacks dogma, liturgy, sacraments (in a strict sense), and a developed religious cult and mythology.

Goode, W. J., *Religion among the Primitives* (1951). This book scrutinizes the interrelations of religion with other aspects of culture.

Hsu, F. L. K., *Religion, Science and Human Crisis* (1952). A case study of the uses of magic, religion, and scientific medicine in the folk response to a cholera epidemic in a Chinese village.

LaBarre, W., *The Ghost Dance* (1970). The origins of religions brilliantly analyzed and presented as a crisis phenomenon. The approach combines anthropology, psychoanalysis, and classical scholarship with great erudition, insight, and readability.

Lessa, W.A., and E. Z. Vogt, *Reader in Comparative Religion* (3d ed., 1971). Contains a wealth of original articles and selections on the subjects of the present chapter.

Norbeck, E., *Religion in Primitive Society* (1961). A concise and well-balanced general introduction to the subject of religion as a social phenomenon.

33
Language

CHAPTER OUTLINE

LEARNING GOALS

Discuss anthropological linguistics.

Indicate what is meant by the structure of language.

Explain synchronic, or structural, linguistics.

Describe structural linguistics.

Explain the relationship between language and culture.

Review the Sapir-Whorf hypothesis.

Define cognitive anthropology.

Summarize the growth and divergence of languages.

Without language, human culture would be wholly impossible. All sentient animals communicate, and some, like bees and porpoises, apparently can do so extremely well. But only human beings are able to generalize, to create explanations, and thus to build up the body of traditions identified as human culture. What is not clear about nonhuman animals is the extent to which communication is learned. The human being learns language just as culture is learned. Thus language is "a distinctly human system of behavior based on oral symbols" which is "used to describe, classify and catalogue experiences, concepts, and objects."[1]

ANTHROPOLOGICAL LINGUISTICS

Ideally, to comprehend the ways of life of a people requires more than the use of an interpreter. The conscientious field worker will try to learn and use the language of the group being worked with. But quite apart from the need to communicate in an alien speech, to learn it and achieve some degree of mastery over it, an anthropologist quickly becomes aware that through a study of language new perspectives on human behavior are opened.

Linguistics is a field of study in its own right. The specialists are not necessarily anthropologists, although they may be. The linguists' interests lie in the many and varied forms of expression through language of which human beings are capable. Linguists may be concerned, for example, with differing grammatical structures or in the fact that one language may have very different modes of expression from another. They may be interested in the history of language, in learning how one language is related to another, or they may analyze and compare languages as structured systems.

To the conventional linguist, the study of languages is often an end in itself. Anthropological linguists, however, while sharing these linguistic concerns, add a somewhat different dimension. They are more interested in the ways in which language and culture relate to each other.

Out of necessity, anthropological linguists like Franz Boas, Edward Sapir, and Leonard Bloomfield were in the forefront in development of ways of learning strange languages quickly and of reducing unwritten languages to writing by means of phonetic alphabets. In recent years, the techniques and problems associated with language have been so refined that a virtually new discipline of vast proportions begins to emerge. Anthropological linguists are engaged in opening some suggestive and sometimes startling frontiers (see page 581).

The Origins of Language

Prehistoric archaeology, as we now know well, provides some evidence on the origins of culture, but we can find no artifacts that suggest when or how language might have come into being. Does the making of fire or a stone ax require language? Who knows? But the development of technological traditions over time implies that some sophisticated means of communication beyond mere imitation or emotive expression proved necessary. Around the turn of this century, scholars devoted considerable time to speculation about the origins of language. Then the question was abandoned as a fruitless pursuit, only to be revived as better knowledge of the ecological, social, and physiological preconditions of language has grown.[2]

It is an interesting fact that the human being has no organs which have evolved especially to produce speech. Most mammals can make sounds, and they have tongues, lips, teeth, larynx, and lungs, none of which has sound

This chapter was written with the collaboration of Robert F. Spencer.

[1] R. F. Spencer, "Language," in J. Gould and W. L. Kolb (eds.), *Dictionary of the Social Sciences*, p. 377.

[2] For a full and well-informed discussion of this matter, see C. D. Hockett and R. Ascher, "The Human Revolution" (*Current Anthropology*, vol. 5, 1964), pp. 135–168.

FIGURE 33.1
Washoe, a young chimpanzee trained by psychologists, responds to a lollipop with the American Sign Language symbol for *sweet.* (Courtesy of Drs. R. Allen and Beatrice T. Gardner, Department of Psychology, University of Nevada at Reno.)

making as a primary function. Yet human beings have these body parts so combined that they can produce the sounds of language. Apes, which are like humans in their general facial and mouth structure, are capable of producing most sounds that human beings make. Yet none of our closest primate relatives has developed speech. How is it then that people can talk? The answer is that rather than any special adaptiveness to speech as such, the human being possesses a brain which makes speech possible.

Perhaps it is here where language bridges the gap between the biological and the cultural. Any language is a learned system, it is true; but there is every indication that the human capacity for language is genetic, related to the growth of the forebrain and reflecting a neurophysiological breakthrough toward speech. It is known that mammals and primates other than human beings make calls in which meaning may be present. But sounds or even meaning alone is not language. What humankind has achieved is to structure utterances, giving them significant form and clothing them with an "aura of displacement," that is, a quality of metaphorical allusion and abstraction. To some extent, animals other than human beings can do this, and there is laboratory evidence in the recent studies of the chimpanzee Washoe (Figure 33.1), who achieved mastery of eight signs from the American Sign Language used by deaf people.[3] Yet Washoe cannot do what a human infant does; she cannot accord meaning to verbal cues and signs, form them by analogy, and so develop a series of speech patterns reflecting a true mastery of language.

The ability to achieve this sense of *grammar*, or patterned structure, must have been slow in coming. A human being gets it early in life, and relatively quickly, receiving a neural "imprint." The human brain, like the computer, has developed to the point where information can be stored and retrieved, patterned and reproduced at will.

Assuming that a genetic breakthrough for true language as a result of biological evolution took place in Lower or Middle Pleistocene times, it no longer becomes necessary to ask why human languages are so diverse. The preconditions of human behavior which evoked language, social life, and the use of tools appeared at various places wherever clusters of human populations arose. By the same token, wherever human beings appeared they quickly produced languages as finished systems. This is why there is no such thing as a "primitive" language today. All languages (however much they differ) are matured speech systems.

Cues, Kinesics, and Proxemics

Many ways of communicating exist that do not utilize language. Cries of warning and aggression and "purrs" of contentment and affection are forms of communication not limited to human beings. Much progress has been made since the early 1960s by ethologists, the students of the comparative behavior of all living beings, toward

[3]J. Bronowski and U. Bellugi, "Language, Name, and Concept" (*Science*, vol. 168, 1970), pp. 669–673; R. A. Gardner and B. T. Gardner, "Early Signs of Language in Child and Chimpanzee" (*Science*, vol. 187, 1975), p. 752.

FIGURE 33.2
A San Bushman illustrates the hunter's sign with which he silently signals to a hunting companion that he has sighted a secretary bird. The secretary bird has a conspicuous feathered crest on the back of its head. (Anthro-Photo.)

the understanding of communication of various living species. The mating dances of various birds, the grooming and licking in which some species engage, and the establishment and defense of space by other species are aspects of communication. Nor can people be excluded from ethological studies. Human beings use their bodies to communicate as much as they employ formal language. What indeed can be more universal than the friendly expression of a smile? And yet such facial expressions, in themselves modes of communication, are also learned. There are happy smiles and sad smiles, smiles accompanying appropriate occasions. Even the smiling baby can become aware that this expression may carry with it an element of reward.[4]

We know that languages may call for the use of the hands or the body as a means of conveying what the verbal sentence does not say (Figure 33.2). Gestures, in short, may become an adjunct of language and a vital factor in various kinds of social communication. The study of body language (*kinesics*) is still in its infancy. By examining the nature of the message expressed through the use of gestures, one can perceive a good deal of the emotive, the psychological, direction of communication. Such gestures may be seen to relate to culturally defined habits. To an American, the nod of the head means "yes," but in the Near East, a single nod of the head is a clear "no."

Some students have been concerned with *proxemics,* an area which may be defined as reflecting nearness or distance in human communication. The use of space in communication is also culturally learned. North American business people in a conference may choose to sit or stand at a prescribed distance from each other, usually keeping a table between them; they may well be taken aback by a Latin American colleague who inclines to move in much closer in a conversation. To a Westerner, it is sometimes surprising to see two Arab boys walking hand in hand. Yet this is expected behavior in the Arab world and carries with it no sexual implication. American men usually walk closely side by side, while they permit women to precede them as a form of politeness. But among Shoshone Indians

[4]R. L. Birdwhistell, *Kinesics and Context*, pp. 29–39.

it is different; the clincher in an argument over the senior author's presence at a sun dance was, "He is one of us. He is not like those whites who hold hands with their wives. Haven't you seen how he always walks in front of his wife?" (An anthropological adage: When in Shoshone, do as the Shoshones do.)

These are only some of a vast range of cues which people may use. It is clear, however, that all social behavior depends on the understanding of cues: events or things that have a conventional meaning. The responder who "reads" a cue is in a position to act in a predictable manner within a given situation. The understanding of cues is absolutely essential to effective participation in any social setting, be it animal or human. In order to have the inside view of a culture, one must know its cues like a native.

Parallels and Process in Language and Culture

Culture and language, both learned, are the distinctive attributes of human beings. But language and culture do not necessarily go together. There are peoples who speak mutually unintelligible languages who share in the same cultural traditions. In the American Southwest, for example, the town-dwelling Pueblo Indians, basically much alike in culture, speak languages related to four quite separate groupings. Unless a man from Zuñi learns Hopi, he cannot communicate with a Hopi, unless they both speak Spanish or English! On the other side, peoples with very different cultures may be able to communicate through language across the barriers of cultural difference. Again, in the American Southwest, the Navajo can converse quite readily with an Apache neighbor, even though the two have essentially different cultures.

Culture and language may relate in special and subtle ways. The reason people speak the language that they do depends largely on such factors as isolation, contact, migration, or conquest. It does not follow that because people have a certain culture, they will speak a certain language. It is, in fact, easier to delimit linguistic boundaries than it is to draw cultural ones. Where one language leaves off to be replaced by another, even though there may be bilingualism at the borders, is still easily seen. Great Russian, for example, a dominant language of the U.S.S.R., shades off in the western part of the country and is displaced by Ukrainian and Polish. Closely related to Russian though these languages may be, they are still quite distinct; there is no doubt in the mind of anyone familiar with them that a linguistic boundary has been crossed.

Language Borrows Words and Grammar A culture, as we know, may incorporate borrowed elements; it may have inventions added; it changes gradually and organically through time. Language operates in the same way. Speakers of one language may borrow and incorporate words from other languages. In English, for example, there is a vast number of *lexemes* (words, dictionary entries) drawn from languages all across the world. From Japanese come "typhoon" and "kimono," and from Carib, an American Indian language of the West Indies, there are "cigar," "hammock," and "hurricane." English can invent as well, admitting new concepts to both the language and the culture. "Hi-fi," "generation gap," or "pot" would be pure nonsense words to Shakespeare. But just as some cultures accept change readily, others may resist change. The same is true of language, where there can be striking conservatism. Unlike English, there are languages whose very structure is incapable of accommodating new terms or words. Chinese, to name one such, with its basic vocabulary made up of words of essentially a single syllable, cannot adapt to polysyllables. As a result, the Chinese translate a new item of technology into its nearest cognate; for example, the telephone is called "lightning speak." Yet the Chinese clearly understand this to mean "telephone." Chinese evolves a whole series of single-syllable combinations which handle adequately the complexities not only of technology from the West, but philosophical ideology as well. The Navajo in the American Southwest, to cite another example, becomes quite anatomical in referring to the parts of an automobile; an engine is the car's "stomach," the fenders its "wings."

Some languages borrow not only words from others, but elements of grammar as well. In the Far East, there are the many languages classed with Chinese. To be sure, there are the different languages, sometimes erroneously called "dialects," of Chinese. But there are also Burmese, Thai, Vietnamese, Laotian, and many others that seem to share with Chinese the tonalities, the pitch of the voice. Although there may be a genetic relationship between these languages, it appears that they resemble each other primarily in the tonal pitch.

Language Fits Cultural Needs What becomes clear from the foregoing is that each language represents a finished product, a perfect system in the sense that each tongue is wholly adequate to all human situations. The ideas that a language can express are in some measure dependent on the interests of the society which develops them. It would be surprising to hear a discussion of logical positivism or cultural anthropology in Eskimo, but this does not mean that ideas of this kind cannot be expressed in Eskimo. English, similarly, must resort to circumlocutions to convey with exactness the subtleties of which Eskimo is eminently capable. Neither of these languages, nor any of the other 6000 languages of the world, can thus be regarded as more archaic or primitive than another.

Anthropologists are fond of pointing out that Eskimos have a large number of words for "snow," each denoting snow of a particular state of being, such as softly-falling-snow, dry-wind-driven-snow, drifting-snow, powder-snow, wet-packed-snow, dry-packed-snow-suitable-for-cutting-into-blocks (for igloo building), ice-crust-surface-snow, and so on. It is perfectly true that we can linguistically express different conditions of snow through the use of modifiers, but the point is that Eskimos, whose very survival depends upon snow conditions, do not view snow as "crystallized water vapor" or "that beautiful white fluffy stuff that falls from the sky," but rather as a series of *different* substances.

The American city dweller does recognize snow, sleet, and slush as three distinct linguistic categories for crystallized water in different states of being—because this much, and no more, is culturally significant to comfort and well-being. Since the birth of wide popular enthusiasm for skiing in the United States, however, a skier's vocabulary for snow, similar in its distinctions to that of the Eskimo, has been borrowed from the Austrian Tyrol because the state of snow is important to ski culture. Hence we hear the terms *Pappschnee* (wet, heavy snow), *Kornschnee* (barley snow that has melted under spring sunshine and frozen at night), *Pulverschnee* (powder snow), *Fernschnee* (broad expanse of breakable crust), and so forth.

The basic principle illustrated by these examples is that every language is adequate to express the needs of its culture. As the culture expands, the language expands (Figure 33.3). If the belief or knowledge system embodied in the culture requires the expression of abstract ideas, the language will provide the means of getting those ideas across. If a culture stresses rhetorical style, oratory, folktale, or poetry, these cultural interests will find their linguistic expression. No existing language is so primary as to contain half-formulated grunted thoughts or so limited in expressions as to suggest that it exemplifies the dawn of human speech. English, it is true, like other European languages, accompanies a culture in which there is great diversity of occupation and activity. Since each specialty has its specialized vocabulary, no one person can command the whole lexicon of the language. But every culture has its specialties, occupational or otherwise. If anyone still has the notion, which was so common in the nineteenth century, that the languages of nonliterate peoples are childlike

FIGURE 33.3
In 1972, audio recordings and the *National Geographic* were new means of communication to Big Nambas Islanders. (Kal Muller/Woodfin Camp.)

and inherently incapable of expressing complex thoughts and ideas, this error should be dispelled.

Writing and Language

When anthropological linguists study language, they are concerned only with the oral-aural system, the spoken and the heard. Writing is not a part of language in any vital sense. English could be written equally well with Chinese characters. As it happens, it uses a Latin alphabet. Systems of writing are inventions going back to relatively recent times, to the Bronze and Iron Ages (Figure 33.4). Language had been in existence long before. Nor should we think that because a language lacks writing it is slovenly or debased. On the contrary, it is more frequently the unwritten language which preserves oral tradition with fidelity, which stresses correctness and precision of speech.

Some languages, such as Latin (in the past) and English, French, German, Chinese, and Russian, by virtue of writing and the accompanying transmission of elaborated traditions, have assumed greater importance in world affairs. There are also the "great" languages, whose traditions and associations have taken on enlarged significance. Such languages are usually found in association with one of the great religious systems. There is Latin, for example, which, although "dead" in the sense that it has no living native speakers, still retains importance

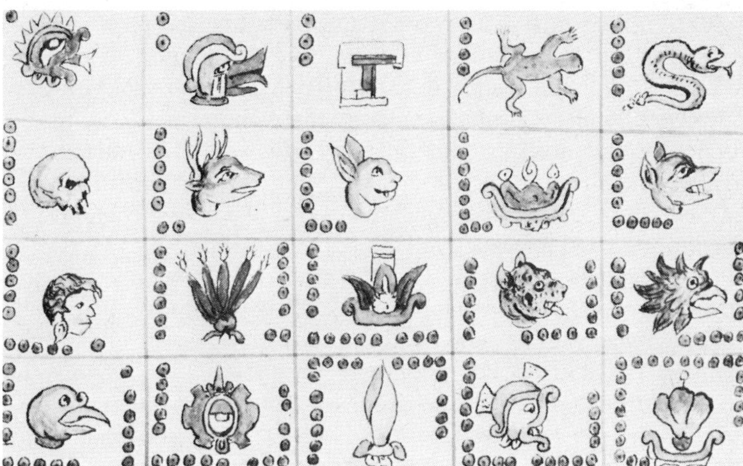

FIGURE 33.4
Aztec pictorial and numerical writing. The twenty days of the Aztec month are shown: Alligator, Wind, House, Lizard, Serpent, Death, Deer, Rabbit, Water, Dog, Monkey, Grass, Reed, Jaguar, Eagle, Buzzard, Motion, Flint Knife, Rain, and Flower. (After Duran/University of Oklahoma Press.)

in the total world of Roman Catholicism. Similarly, Hebrew, with its link to Judaism and its modern renaissance in Israel, and Arabic in the world of Islam, and Sanskrit in the religious traditions of India, and Chinese and its tie with Confucianism and Taoism, are all examples of the cultural effects of the written tradition in the functioning of "universalistic" religious ideology and practice.

When a language is not written, there is an unfortunate tendency on the part of literate people to think of it as possessing limited worth. From the broad perspective of human history, this may be in a sense true, but from another standpoint, considering that any language serves the needs of the culture which speaks it, all languages have equal value and function.

THE STRUCTURE OF LANGUAGE

Whether English is spoken by an American in the Midwest or in the Deep South, by an Englishman at Oxford, or by a cockney cab driver in London, English still remains English. There are dialects, to be sure, local turns of expression and sound variations which sometimes make it difficult for the speaker of one dialect to understand another, but the *structure of the language* remains consistent. The speaker has learned the basic structure of the language and knows how to generate new utterances to suit the occasion and to transform mere words into *sentences* and *phrases of meaning* framed according to strict, "unconscious" rules.

The Time Element in Linguistic Analysis

In thinking about language, as in thinking about culture, one may ask initially how the system works. In doing so, we place language at a point in time with no concern for the origin of the finished product or for its relationships. The structure of English today is different from what it was in Chaucer's time, but the speaker of English need not know the history of the language. To see language (or culture) as a temporal end product and to ask how the system operates at a given time is to look at structure, at the parts which interrelate to make up the whole. This approach is structural, or *synchronic.* In synchronic studies, languages are analyzed as each exists at a given moment in history.

The historical, or *diachronic,* approach poses a very different kind of question. Rather than "How does it work?" we ask, "How did it get that way?" If the history of English as a language is the issue, then clearly, Chaucer's English and Shakespeare's English must be taken into account. Further, one wishes to see the parts of English which relate to the Germanic ancestor, to Latin, to Norman French, or to the great Indo-European family of which English, German, French, Latin, Russian, and the languages of modern India are also descendants.

Both approaches, the synchronic and the diachronic, have relevance for the understanding of language processes. The historical relationships of language may provide a clue to cultural relations. Similarly, to comprehend a language as it is spoken—not only to speak and understand it but also to see it as a structured entity—may provide some leads to a greater awareness of how cultures, too, are organized.

Synchronic, or Structural, Linguistics

Although any language contains a distinctive series of patterns, because language is oral and aural, the initial approach to a language is through its sound system by means of phonology (Gr. *phono,* "sound").

Phonology Every language has a distinctive and characteristic total series of sounds. A single sound in one language, or even a series of them, can appear in another. Taken as a total system, however, the sounds of a language offer a remarkable uniqueness. Linguistic science employs the term *phoneme* (Gr. *phonema,* "a sound") to refer to these characteristic sound units in a given language. Some languages, such as Hawaiian, possess only a few basic sounds; others, such as Kwakiutl, may have considerably more. Rarely are there more than 45 to 50 basic sounds in any language.

A phoneme is thus the smallest sound unit of a language. But the sound alone, in isolation, is only a starting point. In human speech, sounds, usually conventionally divided into vowels and consonants, appear in combination with each other, but in a given language, a sound is articulated or pronounced in a way peculiar to that language. The sound usually designated /t/ is pronounced by most speakers of English by placing the tip of the tongue on the gum just back of the front teeth (postdental). The sound is *stopped,* meaning that /t/, unlike /s/, cannot be continued, even though /s/ is pronounced in much the same position as /t/ in English.

There are thus classes of sounds—those that are *stopped, continued, nasalized,* or *trilled,* along with possible combinations of these—as well as points of articulation—the use of the tongue, lips, teeth, vibration and resonance, and the various hard and soft parts of the oral chamber—to produce particular types of sounds. /t/ in English is not the same as /t/ in some other languages. In Tagalog, a Philippine language, for example, /t/ is pronounced with the tongue directly against the teeth. As between English and Tagalog this makes little immediate difference. But it could happen, and often does, that a language differentiates between a postdental and a dental /t/, /s/, or /n/, and the result can be most confusing, at least to an English-speaker. Being accustomed to a single postdental /t/, the English-speaker actually fails to hear the difference in the points of articulation and is not receptive to two, three, or four different tongue locations of /t/.

Sounds in a language also follow a pattern of arrangement. English /sk/ is wholly compatible with the sound structure of the language. But the same sound is impossible to pronounce in Spanish, where an initial vowel must enter before /s/ followed by any consonant, as Spanish *escuela* (eskwela). Bantu languages in Africa build many words beginning with /ng/ (for instance, *ngbatu*). Not a single word in English starts so; it is against the English rule which requires that /ng/ may be used only at the end of a phonemic series. Strongly fixed motor habits in forming one's own speech make it extremely difficult to pronounce a foreign language like a native when it involves different habits. The difference between the English /z/ and /th/ is only a matter of a few millimeters in the placement of the tongue. In /z/, the tip of the tongue

"When the Myth people went to make war against Southeast-Wind, | then Great-Inventor questioned his younger brothers, and | said: 'Who among you controls the weather?' Thus he said. ‖ Immediately a short man spoke, | and said, 'O Myth people! whenever you wish | for a northwest wind in our world,'—thus said the short | man, the Crab—'then take four of my | fellow-crabs and hang them up over the fire of ‖ your house; and as soon as our backs begin to be red, | take us down and put us into four | large clam-shells, and hide us in | holes of trees,' thus he said—'and if I do not make the | northwest wind in our world, then take one ‖ of the crabs again out of the hole of the tree and pray to it; | and as soon as you finish praying to it, put it into the | place where you took it from.' Thus said the Crab. |

"As soon as the Crab had finished speaking, one (person) who had | hair over his face and red ochre on his face also spoke. He had two ‖ dentalia on each side in his ears, and he had one dentalium shell in his nose. | He said: 'O chief, Great-Inventor! | I am the fern, and I control the weather. If | we go to make war on Southeast-Wind, take me | just as I am dressed now, and three of my ‖ tribe here;

Wä, hë'ᵋmaālaxs la'ē wī'nēda nū'x̣ᵘnēᵋmisē lāx MEłā'lanukwē. Wä, lā'ᵋlaē K!wēk!waxā'waᵋyē ŵŭLā'xēs ts!ā'ts!aᵋya. Wä, lā'ᵋlaē ᵋnē'k·a: 'ᵋya, ts!ā'ts!āᵋyē, ă'ngwadzēs ᵋnēᵋnā'lanukwaq!ōs?' ᵋnē'x·ᵋlaē. Wä, hë'x·ᵋidaEmᵋlā'wisē ts!E'k!ŭxsdē' bEgwā'nEm yā'q!Eg·aᵋła. Wä, lā'ᵋlaē ᵋnē'k·a: 'ᵋya, nū'xᵘnēᵋmis, hë'ᵋmaāxs ᵋnē'k·ēlā'xaqōs qa dzā'q!wax·ᵋīdēlaxsEns ᵋnā'lax,' ᵋnē'x·ᵋlaēda ts!E'k!ŭxsdē' bEgwā'nEma, yîx q!ō'mäsē. 'Wä, lā'laxs ăxᵋē'dlax mō'sgEma lā'xEn q!ō'swutēx, wä, lā'laxs tē'x̣ᵘstōdlax g·āxEnuᵋx̣ᵘ lā'xa lEgwī'łaxsōs g·ō'kwaq!ōs; wä, g·î'lᵋmēsEk· L!ā'xᵋwīdg·anuᵋx̣ᵘ ăwī'g·ik·, wä, las ăxā'xōd g·ā'xEnuᵋx̣ᵘ qas ăxts!ō'daōs g·a'xEnuᵋx̣ᵘ lā'xa mō'sgEmē ăwō' xā'laētsa g·ā'wēq!ānEmē. Wä, las q!ŭᵋlā'łᵋīd g·āxEnuᵋx̣ᵘ lā'xa kwā'wagaᵋyasa Ḷax̣ᵘḶō'sē,' ᵋnē'x·ᵋlaē. Wä, g·îlᵋmēsEn wē'ᵋstamās qa dzā'q!ŭx̣ᵘᵋīdēsEns ᵋnā'lax, wä, las ē't!ēd la ăxᵋē'dxa ᵋnE'msgEmē q!ō'mäs lā'xa kwā'wagaᵋyasa Ḷax̣ᵘḶō'ᵋsē. Wä, las ts!E'lwaqa. Wä, g·î'lᵋmēts gwāł ts!E'lwaqaq, wä, las ē't!ēd ăxbEtE'ndEq lā'xēs g·ā'yanEᵋmasōsaq," ᵋnē'x·ᵋlaē q!ōmä'sē.

Wä, lā'ᵋlaē gwāł q!ayō'łe q!ōmä'sē, la'ē ō'gwaqa yā'q!Eg·aᵋłēda sEᵋyā'ts!â mEgwôgE'mxa gwôgŭ'myîmē. Wä, lā'ᵋlaē maē'małēda ăLE'la lāx ᵋwa'x·sōdatâ'ᵋyē p!Esp!Eyō's; wä, lā'ᵋlaē k·ī'dzēłbā'lāxa ᵋnE'mts!aqē ăLE'la. Wä, lā'ᵋlaē ᵋnē'k·a: ᵋya, g·ī'gămēᵋ, K!wēk!waxā'wē, nō'gwaEm sā'laēdāna. Wä, lEn ᵋnēᵋnā'lanu'kwa. Wä, hë'ᵋmaa qE'nsō lāł wīnaLēx MEłā'lanukwē. Wä, lā'LEs â'Em ăxᵋē'dEL g·ā'xEn lā'xg·în lāk· gwä'łaā'sa. Wä, hë'ᵋmisē yū'dukwa gā'yuL lā'xEn g·ō'kŭlōtēx. Wä, las q!wā'nōlīsEn lāx ᵋnā'laqEnwaᵋlisasēs lEgwī'łōs.

FIGURE 33.5
Phonetic transcription of an oral Kwakiutl Indian myth, recorded and translated by Franz Boas. In the absence of American Indian systems of writing, Boas and other anthropological linguists invented a phonetic system of symbols applicable to any spoken language. (Boas, *Ethnology of the Kwakiutl*, p. 625.)

rests against the lower edge of the gums of the upper dental arch. In /th/, it is between the teeth. But how many English-speaking French people and Germans never succeed in mastering that little shift!

It should be clear that even so apparently simple a system as the sounds of language is fraught with difficulties. True, the number of sounds a human being can make is limited, and a person learns to follow native linguistic patterns. But when secondary phonemes, such as stress or accent, tone or pitch, length of vowel, presence or absence of resonance, throating, nasalizing, and many other possible factors, are added to the basic patterns, we can readily see that no language is a simple, phonetic system.

Languages are culturally determined systems not only in their sounds but in the ways in which they put these basic elements together in structured order.

Phonemic analysis How is a phoneme recognized? The trained linguist brings a judgment to bear, which is based on a knowledge of *phonetics,* the general science of sounds (Figure 33.5). Blessed with a good ear and through training and practice, the linguist has acquired a sense of the general range of sounds which human speech has produced. In respect to a single language, the linguist looks for contrasts, for the differentiation of minimal pairs, /t/, for example, as against /d/. Both, as in English, may be aspirated; one is unvoiced, the other voiced. Both sounds thus stand out in English as distinctive phonemic elements. But in another language, even the trained linguist, unless an exceptional mimic, may do something wrong, failing to get the hang of a particular unit of articulation and making an utterance—often to the amusement of native speakers—with an atrocious accent. The linguist can generally locate the uttered sound in its proper place and can describe it scientifically. But neither with mouth nor mind can the linguist replicate the action of the native speaker.

But a kind of impasse is reached. There is nothing abstruse about a phonetic-phonemic distinction. One returns again in fact to the problem of the universal as against the specific. Yet it is this issue which has come to have some implications for the study of culture and which again suggests some analogies in process between language and culture.

Etics and emics Some years ago, the well-known descriptive linguist Kenneth Pike, in working with the problem of the objective description of cultural perception by an outside student as against the awareness of the world held by a native, sought a resolution by coining the terms *etic* and *emic,* drawn obviously from the linguistic terminology *phonetic* and *phonemic.*[5] Some anthropologists, examining both language and culture, have found the terms suggestive of modes of analysis. *Etic* analysis brings the judgment of the observer to bear in making a statement about a people's behavior based on a broad comparative knowledge and in not emphasizing what the people themselves think or say. A formal analysis of kinship (Chapter 24) may provide a sense of the structure of social units; when a paternal uncle, the father's brother, is called by the same term as the progenitor, a specific structure comes to light. But of itself this does not tell what the user of this "father" term thinks or feels in regard to the persons so designated. The *emic* element takes this into account. How, in fact, does the native participant in a cultural system think and feel? With culture as with language, one knows the "correct" grammar from linguistic experience or the correct mode of action from the experience of the culture. A person may not be able to explain an act. The meanings and associations of symbols, whether verbal or behavioral, may go deeper than conscious awareness. In language, phonetics and phonemics are two sides of the same coin; the crucial issue is the reference point of observation. And the same is true of cultural behavior viewed in terms of an etic-emic distinction.

Morphology and Syntax A language is a whole system with a structure, or morphology. The parts of language may be assembled in a particular way and reflect a special kind of adaptation. Some languages build meaningful

[5]K. L. Pike, *Language in Relation to a Unified Theory of the Structure of Human Behavior*, parts 1–3.

concepts out of verbs, forming names for things and concepts, that is, nouns, from stems that reflect action. In English, any verb may be made into a noun. In fact, the tendency in English is to teach children the names of things first—"mouth," "kitty," "doggie," and so on—and to introduce the child to verbs only later. Conversely, in Navajo, the child first becomes familiar with actions—"sitting," "running," "moving," and so forth. Whether the concept expressed refers to a thing or an action (a noun or a verb) depends on its relations to other conceptual units expressed in an utterance.

Morphemes The basic element in any language is the phoneme, but phonemic units are put together in various ways to form the elements of *structure,* or the *morphology.* If phonemes are basic units of sound, *morphemes* (Gr. *morphe,* "form") are basic, meaningful units of structure. Synchronic linguists interested in determining the structure of a language, reduce the language first to its bedrock of sounds. Then they note that sound arrangements follow a pattern, that a clustering of certain kinds of discernible elements occurs. These may be actual words, although again, the problem of what constitutes a word in a given language poses some difficulties. More often, these clusters are parts that form units which are set off by the secondary phonemic element of *juncture.* Junctures are simply the breaks between words. The sentence *The man is eating* suggests these junctures. Almost no break occurs between /the/and/man/, indicating that when the definite article is used in English, it is almost a prefix, that is, something bound to the element following. Between /man/and/is/ and between /is/ and /eating/ there is a slight rest, a tiny hesitation that sets each element off. In French, for instance, the junctures are less apparent; words flow together. The point here is that any language may have "free" morphemes (in this instance they equal words) or "bound" morphemes, that is, those which are in some way modified.

To illustrate further what a morpheme is, let us take a closer look at the sentence given: *The man is eating.* /man/ is a primary morpheme with the bound /the/; /is/ refers to the state occupied by some singular person or object; /eating/ consists of two morphemes—the root form /eat/ and a suffixed bound form /-ing/ which in English refers to an action going on, continuing, proceeding. Again, a sentence such as *Birds fly* consists of several morphemes. /bird/ is made plural by a bound suffixed /z/.[6] /fly/ is a single morpheme, but since it is preceded by the plural noun /birds/ it is not the same as /fly/ in /to fly/; a third-person plural, present tense is understood. The linguist can treat this as a "zero" morpheme, one in which there is no inflection but in which a distinct environment, in this instance, agreement between noun and verb, is held to prevail.

By listing and categorizing the morphemes of a language, one obtains a total perspective on the potential range of variations in the whole system. It is here that the understanding of language cues begins. Since languages differ, it is also necessary to obtain some sense of the meaning of the morphemes and the contexts in which they are used. Can one get all of the nuances, can one understand all that is conveyed in the oral-aural situation in a language that is not one's own? Morphemic analysis, which takes account of the language in its structural totality, offers a lead.

Morphemes and meaning So far, little has been said about meaning in language. A morpheme, however, is a meaningful unit, not only in the

[6]This also illustrates the problem of the change of a sound because of morphological factors. The rule in English is that if a noun ends in a vowel or a voiced consonant, i.e., a consonant which is accompanied with resonance, the suffixed /-s/ becomes itself voiced, i.e., /z/. A word such as *bee* /bij:/ takes its plural as /bijz/; *dog* /dawg/ becomes /dawgz/; but *cat* /kaet/ becomes /kaets/. This is true of any suffixed /-s/ in English, however variable the function of /-s/ may be. Its functions include: inflection of the third-person singular verb, present tense; possession; and designation of number, i.e., the plural.

sense that it may be a word with the psychological and emotive reactions that words evoke, but because it appears in environments with other morphemes to create meaningful forms.

A few examples chosen from selected languages may illustrate the point.

To an English-speaker, the sentence *When I was going to the store, I saw a dog* seems infinitely logical and simple. In Turkish, the same thought possesses a rather different structuring. The Turkish sentence is: *Magasine gittiğim zaman bir köpek gördüm.*

English uses eleven word units, with several more morphemes, while Turkish employs only five. The Turkish morphemes are: /magasin/ which means "store," with a suffixed /e/ "place to which action is directed"; /gittiğim/ consisting of a root morpheme /git/ "go," with a suffixed /*d(t)ik/ which is marked with an asterisk because it can never appear without some pronoun modification, but which refers to a continuous action in the past, and /-im/ referring to action by a first person "I," "my"; /zaman/ "time";/bir/ "one," an indefinite single something; /köpek/ "dog," an indefinite noun (if the noun were definite, that is, "the dog," the Turkish would be köpeği/, the /-i/ morpheme being used only where there is a definite direct object of a verb); /gördüm/ from a root morpheme /gör/ "see," plus /d(t)/ indicator of any part action, plus /-um/ action by a first person, again "I," "my."

In this case, what is the literal meaning of the Turkish sentence? One might render it into English, although meaninglessly: *To* (definite) *store my wenting time* (indefinite) *dog I saw.* Such a contrived rendition is scarcely necessary, since the Turkish sentence has much the same meaning as the English. We are simply attempting to convey the difference in the way in which concepts are put together.

Syntax A language, however, is much more than a series of morphemes clustered haphazardly. Generally, morphemes, bound or free, follow some kind of ordered pattern. The pattern may be quite strict or fairly free. *Syntax* refers to *the arrangement of elements in phrases and sentences.* English, which has shed many of its inflections, or morphemic modifications, depends on a fairly rigid syntax. In the sentence *John and Mary to the movies went,* the hearer is at once aware of something wrong. But *John went the movies to Mary and* violates the rules of all English syntax and meaning.

When a language is more dependent on morphology, syntax may relax. In Latin, for example, the sentences *Canis ursum videt, Videt ursum canis, Videt canis ursum,* and so on through any other possible variations, all make good sense: *"The dog sees the bear."* The morphemic arrangement of /canis/ and /ursum/ make it completely clear that it is the dog which is doing the seeing and the bear which is being seen. Mandarin Chinese, and the Chinese languages generally, even more than English, have shed their morphology almost completely. For them, syntax has become a wholly necessary feature.

Every language is bound by its own firm rules of grammar, and each speaker who wants to be understood must master the rules and abide by them. Language is a tyrant that does not permit much individual liberty, although there will always be great differences in individual skill in the use of a language.

One really intriguing point, however, is that although firm grammatical, that is, morphological and syntactic, rules control the use of language, the rules are not made by grammarians. They have been arrived at by generations of speakers who had no consciousness of what they were doing. Once certain elemental ways of shaping and combining morphemes were established, the mold for the future growth of the language was pretty well set. Rules of grammar give consistency to the tongue; they integrate the use of vocal symbols. Yet, the tyranny of grammatical rules notwithstanding, no ordinary speaker can state the rules of grammar. The native speaker can only tell you that a certain thing must be said this way and not that way. It is only the linguist who can analyze a language into expressly stated rules.

A bright informant working with a field worker may discover some elemental rules, however. This happened when a Shoshone Indian was asked how to say: *my house, his house, her house, our house, their house.* /gani/ is the morpheme for "house." In the informant's responses each word contained *ngani* preceded by a different personal pronoun prefix. As Hoebel wrote down the words, a great light dawned upon the Shoshone and he excitedly exclaimed, "Say! That /n/ in there must mean that something belongs to someone." On being assured that this was so (he had discovered the possessive infix), he marveled, "Well, what do you think of that? Here I've been talking Shoshone all my life and I never knew that /n/ in the middle of a word means it belongs to someone."

The rules of a language are unconsciously obeyed by its speakers. The normal way to learn any language is to become habituated to its unformulated rules through using the language, not by learning the rules. It has taken American language teachers a long time to learn this simple fact.

Transformational Grammars Grammatical transformations are the ways in which speakers combine and recombine strings of morphemes to form phrases and sentences.

There is considerably more to the concept of language as a total system than the mere rules of sound and structure. There is, in addition, an ordering that description alone cannot cope with. In English, for example, one can say, "three big round red balloons," and there is no quarrel with the ordering of the adjectives. However, suppose you modify this to, "three red big round balloons." The sense is changed, the adjectives are given a slightly different emphasis and the listener is clearly bothered. Go a step further and say, "red big three round balloons," and the listener will think you are nutty. On the other hand, the famous illustrative sentence coined by the linguist Chomsky, "colorless green ideas sleep furiously," makes perfect structural sense, even though it lacks meaning; it "feels" all right—even good. But what gibberish to utter, "furiously sleep ideas green colorless!" This transformation of the word order is chaotic. It was awareness of problems of this kind that led Chomsky to a reformulation of some of the concepts of linguistics.[7]

The "transformational" model conceived by Chomsky stresses the element of syntactic structure. The model seeks to account for all the potential variations in a language system. These include not only the patterning of sound, but also the element of meaning. As a speaker, one generates concepts in language by putting elements together in structured ways. Transformationalists are concerned with the "deep structures" of a language—not only with the surface structures of sound and morpheme, but with the phrase and the ways in which a speaker of a language rearranges the parts to form sets of meanings. The semantic quality relates to the deeper structure of the language. The result is that in transformational grammars the way is opened for a much fuller understanding of language as a total structure. More than this, however, the transformational approach strives for a uniform theory of language in terms of description and as a communicative device.

The theories of syntactic structure as put forth by Chomsky have drawn increasing attention from both anthropologists and linguists and may well be a highway to a broader and more comprehensive theory of the components of language.

SEMANTICS: THE MEANING OF MEANING

Because the primary function of language is communication, the question of meaning is cen-

[7] N. Chomsky, *Language and Mind.*

tral. A linguist can, to be sure, look only at the structure of a language, noting the variety of verb forms or what constitutes a noun under varying circumstances. But this would be linguistics without meaning, an approach to language aimed solely at an analysis of the interaction of parts. It is not a treatment of the whole language. It is precisely this sense of the whole which the transformationalists are seeking, and they suggest that meaning lies in the "deep structure," vitally related to all other facets. The study of semantics is to some extent still in its infancy.

Between languages, meaning is constantly a problem. This is true not only on the level of words alone but in terms of the basic definitions that are resident in the structure of language. It has been contended that because Russian and English employ different built-in concepts of time—that is, time is differently expressed in the structure of the two languages—there is a basis for much misunderstanding on the international level. Whether or not this is so in this particular case, it is probable that the varying structures of languages do inhibit cross-cultural understanding. A case in point is provided by the Keresan-speaking Pueblo Indians of New Mexico. Suppose a missionary were to bring to these peoples his particular brand of religion. In Keresan, no idea can be expressed without containing the morphemes indicating whether the action described depends on direct experience by the speaker or whether the speaker has the information from hearsay. If listeners are told in Keresan that in the beginning God created heaven and earth, the missionary cannot use the experienced mode because the speaker was not there. The remarks can only imply, "So I've been told."

Does one really need "meaning" in a study of language? If one is considering structured units only, the concern may be solely with phonology, morphology, and syntax. No one who takes the study of language seriously, however, will wish to ignore the semantic issues. It is this point which the transformationalists stress. A perspective on a whole language seeks to answer both the question of structure and of meaning.

Emotional Quality in Meaning

But what of meaning within a language? Every person has an *ideolect,* a particular style of speech, consisting of favorite words and expressions, a particular set of images and thoughts which are evoked by words. Everyone can agree on the definition of "table"; what each hearer visualizes may reflect a host of differing images, all of which, however, are acceptable tables. The field of psycholinguistics, which relates to the psychology of language, is as yet only in its infancy. However, some breakthroughs have been made in the area of language learning. A speaker encodes an utterance, delivers it, and the hearer decodes it and responds. The linguistic system is internalized; the cues relate intimately to individual personality. It is clear from the experience of our own culture that some words are holy, some are obscene, some are proper for certain social occasions and improper for others. These distinctions indicate the continuing presence of the emotive quality of language. An expressed thought may be purely neutral, but it serves to relate the speaker to the cultural environment.

Meaning in a language poses some further problems. Just what does an utterance mean? The answer to this question depends in part on the social setting of the conversation, who is present, whether those present are men or women of superior or inferior statuses.

Getting away from the emotive element in meaning, we should mention the purely academic issue of just what words do mean. Does one really express primary thoughts with any exactness? Actually not, since the word is accompanied by a host of other culturally determined nonlinguistic cues. I do not have to say precisely what I think. Indeed, in our own culture and in most others, care is necessary to avoid creating problems in social interaction. In dealing with relatives or close friends, some Americans prefer to say that a person has "passed away" rather than that the person is "dead." Clearly, to say that the person has "kicked the bucket" is in very bad taste. Meanings thus have social as well as psychological dimensions.

CULTURE AND LANGUAGE

Language has absolutely nothing to do with biological inheritance. If, as is sometimes the case, a certain language is spoken solely by the members of a given population, it is only because isolated populations developed their own mode of speech. Once the isolation breaks down, this need no longer be so. Twenty million Afro-Americans speak only English, but their ancestors of one and two centuries ago spoke African languages.

The fact that it is extremely difficult for English-speakers to master some of the phonemes of other languages—ones that are used with ease by native speakers—does not mean that the native speakers have a natural proclivity to produce such sounds. Once vocal habits are set, they become so firm that to break them is quite a task. There is nothing in the physical structure of any people, however, that makes certain populations genetically suited to the pronunciation of some phonemes and not others.

Subgroup Dialects

Most languages, although they are internally consistent, include subgroup variations. When such subgroup languages are localized, they are recognized as dialects or subdialects. Such groups may be status groups within a society. Men employ certain speech usages that differ from those of women. In the same way, usages of adults differ from those of infants; those of professors from those of laborers; those of politicians from those of preachers. In Javanese, for example, socially inferior people address their superiors with one form of speech and are answered in another. Superiors use yet a third speech among themselves, while inferiors have still another.

The Sapir-Whorf Hypothesis: Language and Thought

Every language is adequate to the needs of its culture insofar as the speakers of the language can communicate to each other the ideas and feelings present in their culture. But the very structure of a language subtly molds the way in which people conceive of the world in which they find themselves. Philosophically, we know that a people's idea systems are the screens through which reality is perceived. We saw in Chapter 16 how the basic postulates of each culture provide the assumptions about the general nature of things with which the members of every society view the environment and themselves. Taken together, culture at large and language in particular grind the multiple lenses through which human beings view the world that surrounds them. Indeed, Edward Sapir (1884–1939) was one of the first to perceive that "language and our thought-grooves are inextricably interwoven, [and] are, in a sense, one and the same."[8]

We say we have mastered a language, but only in the present generation have we begun to perceive that the language we learn to speak in turn masters us.

How does this identity of language and thought-grooves become manifest? Perhaps two illustrations will suffice.

English- and Indo-European-language speakers confront time as a divisible entity that falls "naturally" into a past, the present, and a future. Until Einstein pushed the special language of mathematics and physics into a new sphere that could not be described by any of these conventional Indo-European distinctions, time could not be thought of by any of us in other terms.

Benjamin Lee Whorf (1897–1941), a chemical engineer and fire insurance executive, be-

---

[8]E. Sapir, *Language*, p. 232.

came concerned with the problem of how English words betray people into burning down buildings. One example from Whorf's argument will do:

In a wood distillation plant the metal stills were insulated with a composition prepared from limestone and called at the plant "spun limestone.". . . After a period of use, the fire below one of the stills spread to the "limestone," which to everyone's great surprise burned vigorously. Exposure to acetic acid fumes from the stills had converted part of the limestone (calcium carbonate) to calcium acetate. This, when heated in a fire, decomposes, forming inflammable acetone. Behavior that tolerated fire close to the covering was induced by use of the name "limestone," which because it ends in "-stone" implies noncombustibility.[9]

Shawnee Syntax and Conceptualization An example of the principles put forth by Whorf can readily be demonstrated by Shawnee, a language spoken by American Indians in what is now the southeastern United States.

Whorf presents two English sentences:

1. I push his head back.
2. I drop it in the water and it floats.

The acts performed according to these two statements are quite unlike. In (1), the physical act is presented as the exertion of a force: subject→force→object. In (2), the emphasis is on an attribute of the object (it floats).

Shawnee language is so structured that in describing these same two events the Shawnee Indian sees and thinks of them in terms of similarity. How? To tell what happens in the first situation the Shawnee says:

1. *ni kwaskwi*	*tepē*	*n*	*a*
I push back	on the head	by action of the hand	cause to a person

To tell what happens in the second situation, the Shawnee says:

2. *ni kwask*	*ho*	*to*
I push back	at the surface of water	cause to an inanimate thing

Literally translated, (1) means, "I cause the head of a human being to be pushed back by action of my hand." Similarly translated, (2) means, "I cause an inanimate thing to be pushed back at the surface of water." Pushing against, a reverse force, is what Shawnee grammar induces the Shawnee-speaker to see in *both* situations; not pushing and floating as separate phenomena.

It is not always the case that "sentences are unlike because they tell about unlike facts" (although, of course, in some situations other than those just mentioned, they may be unlike in fact). In some cases, it may be that: "Facts are unlike to speakers whose language background provides for unlike formulation of them."[10]

Cognitive Anthropology: Emic Classification and Folk Categories

More than four decades have passed since Sapir and Whorf formulated their views of language structure and cultural perception. In recent years anthropologists have become increasingly interested in the problem of how a given folk perceives and classifies its world.

The emic approach, noted previously suggests that it is possible to free data from the categories which objectivity might seem to impose. The question is: "Can anthropologists shed biases derived from their own culture and see the world through the eyes of the people with whom they are concerned?" Perhaps they can; then the question is: "How?"

Ethnosemantics An initial answer lies in the

[9]B. L. Whorf, *Language, Thought, and Reality*, pp. 135–136.

[10]Ibid., p. 235.

development of an *ethnosemantics,* a study of meanings resident in the system being analyzed. What, for example, does the speaker of a language perceive about the surrounding world? The speaker possesses a *cognitive system,* that is, a built-in system of classification. An example of such a human tendency to classify can be seen in the use of color words in various languages. There are about 3000 words in English dealing with the possible shades of color—"red," "crimson," "scarlet," "cerise," "rust," etc. Another language, however, may not express such subtle differences in color tones. A recent study has shown that all languages have terms for black and white. If there is a further distinction, it will predictably be red. Does this mean that the native speaker of a language fails to perceive the variations in color? Hardly; it is simply that the language limits the kind of classifications available.[11]

Any culture has different domains which reflect the native taxonomy of things. When the Navajo says "green," the word also means "blue" and "purple." The Zuñi language embraces both "yellow" and "orange" in a single term. In English, for example, a "chair" describes a vast array of things on which people sit, from camp stools to reclining armchairs. Yet hassocks and sofas are not chairs, even if made to be sat on, while the difference between "chair" and "table" is certainly taxonomically distinct.

Componential Analysis Componential analysis is a conceptual tool for the ordering of taxonomy and classificatory principles within a culture; it elicits the cognitive realms of the bearers of the culture in question.[12] These are often difficult to get at, especially if the ordering and classification employed by the group are on an unconscious level.

One important focus of componential analysis and ethnosemantics is in studies of kinship and kinship terminologies. These are related not so much to the actual behavioral or structural implications of such a system as they are to the domains of semantic contrast in a kinship pattern. Floyd G. Lounsbury, for example, by applying principles of category and meaning to the sets of kinship terms in both the Crow and Omaha systems, is able to demonstrate the inherent relatedness of terms for relatives, suggesting that one system is a mirror image of the other and that there are semantic issues in generational designation which relate to the bases of kinship classification.[13] The effect is to avoid the errors in categorization which arise when an outsider imposes culturally biased categories. In other words, the meaning of a structured system of kinship is the one generated by the group employing it.

Ethnoscience The upshot of these concerns with meaning lies in the development of the special focus of *ethnoscience.* In ethnoscience the purpose is to lay bare the semantic element, the kinds of taxonomies with which various linguistic and cultural systems are concerned. Just as in a grammar there is an elicitation of a series of paradigms and the formulation of a series of rules applicable to the specific language, so also in an ethnoscientific approach there is the concern with the paradigms and rules of cultural behavior. A grammar allows for a tightly focused prediction of form and structure. An ethnoscience allows the same for a statement about culture. And by the same token, just as an anthropological linguist does not impose categories on a grammar, the ethnoscientist does not impose categories on the cultural situation, but

[11] B. Berlin, "A Universalist-Evolutionary Approach in Ethnographic Semantics," in A. Fischer (ed.), *Current Directions in Anthropology,* vol. 3, no. 3, part 2, p. 8.

[12] See W. C. Sturtevant, "Studies in Ethnoscience," in A.K. Romney and R. G. d'Andrade (eds.), "Transcultural Studies in Cognition" (*American Antrhopologist,* vol. 66, no. 3, part 2, Special Publication, 1964), pp. 99–131.

[13] F. G. Lounsbury, "A Formal Account of the Crow and Omaha-type Kinship Terminologies," in W. H. Goodenough (ed.), *Explorations in Cultural Anthropology,* pp. 351–387.

allows the cultural system to generate its own. The anthropologist as ethnoscientist is a neutral vehicle for the expression of the system.

THE GROWTH AND DIVERGENCE OF LANGUAGES

The origins of languages are lost in the distant past. The spoken word does not turn to stone—it leaves no remains for the archaeologist to unearth.

Because all the people we study have a developed language, there is no way to reconstruct the processes by which their languages began or how they changed.

Diachronic (Historical) Linguistics

The scientific study of the patterns of change in given languages may be done in two ways. Once a language is written, the changes may be followed through a sequence of documents. The other approach is to postulate a historical relationship between languages through the internal analysis of homologous languages. The major principle underlying this second method is similar to that used in the reconstruction of organic phylogenies; namely, that forms are genetically related which have in common a number of functionally similar qualities greater than expected by chance occurrence.

The Comparative Method The criteria used in historical linguistics are morphemic and syntactic identities. The quickest way to get an indication as to whether two languages are related is to compare their vocabularies, or word forms. By sheer chance under the law of limited possibilities, they may have some words in common.

Two languages that are clearly unrelated and phonemically unlike in structure will ordinarily share only 4 percent of their total terms in like form and meaning. If it happens that the phonemic structure of morphemes in the two languages is similar, then the concurrences may be double. It is therefore safe to hold that vocabulary identities of less than these percentages are the products of chance, and the two languages do not have a historical relationship. Conversely,

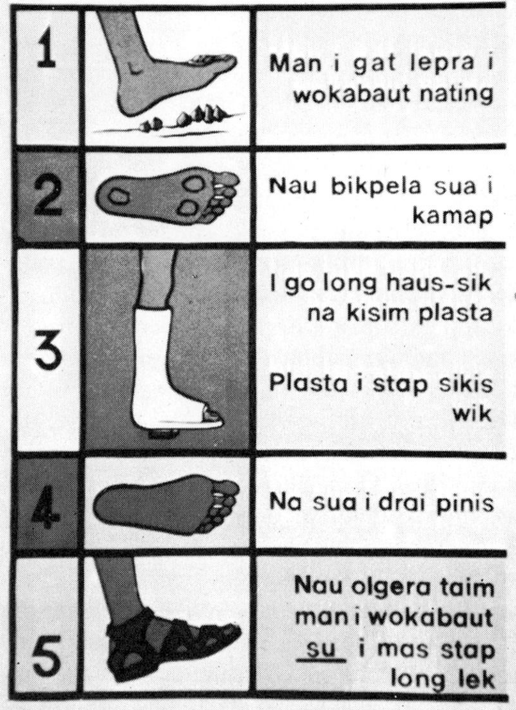

FIGURE 33.6
Language adaptation. Nineteenth-century Melanesians developed their own simplified version of spoken English, called "Pidgin." Today, in the form of "Neo-Melanesian" it has become the common language of the area. This anti-leprosy sign tells New Guinea highlanders: (1) Man he got leprosy, he walks about barefoot; (2) now a big sore comes up; (3) he goes along to a hospital and gets plaster (cast); plaster stops the sickness; (4) sore it dries up (finish); (5) now whenever (altogether time) he walks about, he puts a shoe on his leg. (E. A. Hoebel.)

It can be safely asserted that a resemblance of 20 per cent in vocabulary always requires a historical explanation and that, unless similarity of phonetic structure leads to the expectation of a high degree of chance

similarity, even 8 per cent is well beyond what can be expected without the intervention of historical factors.[14]

Languages are apt to include a large number of words borrowed from other languages (for example, in English, *totem, canoe, tobacco, taboo, automobile,* and so forth) (Figure 33.6). Fundamental words such as pronouns and those representing parts of the body are most likely to retain their original form. Free borrowing from unrelated languages occurs more commonly in nonpersonal material items. Therefore, when linguists find a group of languages with similarities which are greater than chance probability would account for in their fundamental vocabularies, while at the same time lacking similarities in their nonpersonal material vocabularies, they can be certain that these languages have a remote common ancestor. If they had only recently come into contact, one would have borrowed words from the cultural vocabulary of the other without displacing its fundamental words. Thus another device for establishing historical relations between languages is available.

Sounds change over time. This means that the phonemic system of any language does not remain constant. In seeking relationships among languages, the linguist with historical interests may study phonology. In comparing sounds between languages assumed to be related the linguist may observe a systematic change in the phonology of both.

This principle, called Grimm's *law of phonetic change*, set forth in 1822, made possible the designation of the great Indo-European speech family. Taking Sanskrit, the language of ancient India, as a kind of prototype of Indo-European, the brothers Grimm observed that systematic changes took place from one language to another through time. For example, the Sanskrit word *pitar* became *pater* in Greek, *patér* in Latin, *vater* in Germanic (*v* is pronounced *f*), and *father* in English. Similarly, Sanskrit *bhrata* becomes Latin *frater*, Germanic *bruder*, English *brother*, and Russian *brat.* These, of course, are only some obvious examples of what emerges as a complex and predictable series of patterns of sound changes. It can be seen that earlier Indo-European *p* may become *f*, that a weak *b* (bh) may also move to *f*, and the *f* may move back to *b*. Other regular modifications are demonstrable among the numerous Indo-European tongues, and similar relationships have been established for many other language groups.

This means that in comparing vocabularies, exact phonemic similarity is not to be expected. The linguist, however, recognizes phonemic correlates that should be treated as identical.

Languages may also be related by comparison of their morphological and syntactic features. Thus an isolating language, such as Chinese, which sets up its words as simple monosyllables, is not likely to be related to such an extremely polysynthetic language as Eskimo, which builds up single words with as many as a dozen or more morphemes.

Looking thus at Indo-European, it becomes possible to suggest some ultimate relationships. The speech phylum (family) has grown over a period of thousands of years, presumably from a single geographic center. Dialect changed to language as mutual intelligibility ceased; groups moved, forming their own variations on the original language. Once a parent language broke off from the main stem, it, too, was subject to further changes, giving rise to a kind of family language tree, with lesser branches off the main branches of the trunk. The process is analogous to genetic speciation and the radiating evolution of organisms, described in Chapter 3, except that language phyla cannot be traced back to one single original form, as is theoretically true of organic evolution. This comparative method has been applied to all the world's languages so that, in a general way, it is possible to see wide relationships.

[14]J. H. Greenberg, "Historical Linguistics and Unwritten Languages," in A. L. Kroeber (ed.), *Anthropology Today*, p. 270.

Thus, although the Cheyenne Indians live far out on the western Plains, we know that they are an offshoot of the great Algonkian group of tribes that dominated the northeastern part of North America. The linguistic fact confirms Cheyenne legend that they came from the vicinity of a great body of water in a wooded land to the east.

Glottochronology The use of radioactive carbon counting as a means for the dating of archaeological sites is one of the really exciting techniques developed since 1947. Equally exciting is glottochronology, the method for calculating the approximate time of the divergence of two dialects or languages from a common mother tongue.

The fundamental premise of the method is that the basic vocabularies of a language change at a given rate. A basic vocabulary is one which consists of words referring to universal "culture-free" phenomena, such as air, cloud, sun, rain, hand, foot, and so forth. Standard word lists of 100, 200, or more terms are used for comparison and analysis. Judgments are made according to established principles of linguistic analysis as to whether the two forms of a given word are cognate (that is, of the same stock or origin) or noncognate. The relative number of noncognates to cognates is calculated. This provides a statement of the relative amount of change that has occurred since the two languages were separated from the original parent stock.

The rate of language change was first calculated on the basis of documented changes in a number of historic (written) languages. The replacement of terms in the fundamental vocabulary was measured. The residue of cognates represents the rate of retention. The rate of retention actually varies among Indo-European languages from 86.4 percent to 74.4 percent per thousand years. This means that fundamental vocabularies may in fact change at rates of from 13.6 percent to 25.6 percent per thousand years. The average figure is 19.5 percent, but, for convenience, 19 percent is used.

By use of a standard algebraic formula for computation of time depth, the number of years which have elapsed since the languages became separated can be calculated.[15]

In a number of applications of the principle, the dates derived through glottochronology coincide nicely with known dates from the archaeological sites of the presumed ancestral populations. Glottochronology is not reliable where no other supporting evidence is at hand, however. Its validity decreases outside the range of 500 to 2000 years.

While glottochronology has been much criticized, it appears that where data can be carefully controlled, as when there are closely related languages or dialects, it has some validity. The studies of Shoshone dialects in the Great Basin of the United States, for example, show fairly conclusively a series of changes occurring within a time span of roughly a millennium.[16]

Lexicostatistics The statistical summations that reside in the glottochronological word lists may have yet another utility. Lexicostatistics suggests previously unsuspected relationships between languages. The problem of whether or not one language relates to another, easily resolved for Indo-European and other languages with a long written history, is less easily resolved for unwritten languages where historical depth must be inferred. Lexicostatistic similarities (cognate words) shed some light on the matter.

We said that a treelike scheme can be used for depicting linguistic relationships. However, in the light of lexicostatistical formulations, such a

[15]See S. C. Gudschinsky, "The ABC's of Lexicostatistics (Glottochronology)," in D. Hymes (ed.), *Language in Culture and Society,* pp. 612–623, for a succinct discussion of the assumptions and procedures to be followed.

[16]W. R. Miller, J. L. Tanner, and L. P. Foley, "A Lexicostatistic Study of Shoshoni Dialects" (*Anthropological Linguistics,* vol. 13, 1971), pp. 142–164.

pattern needs to be reconsidered. Morphological features, syntactic elements, as well as cultural items of the lexicon, may spread by a process of diffusion. The suggestion that there is a parallel between diffusion of language and diffusion of culture has some further application. A language can assimilate new elements from without, whether these are in lexicon, element of sound, or element of structure. This happens to such an extent that some languages appear to take on the structure of neighboring but unrelated languages. The linguist Morris Swadesh formulated the concept of a "mesh principle," showing that diffused or convergent patterns may be operative among unrelated languages over wide areas. When languages are compared lexicostatistically, using the basic word lists, relationships are found between languages where previously none were thought to exist.

SUMMARY

Language is a distinctly human system of communication that is symbolic and oral. It must be learned and is an aspect of culture. Other animals can communicate, and some, in controlled laboratory situations, appear to be capable of limited symbolic associations. But only human beings are able to abstract and form complex symbolic vocal combinations in the highly structured way that we identify as language. This human achievement apparently came about as a result of a fairly sudden genetic breakthrough in Lower or Middle Pleistocene times.

Every language is a complete system, wholly adequate to all human situations. Thus, although there are thousands of languages spoken by nonliterate peoples, we cannot say that one language is more or less developed than another. Vocabularies vary in richness by stylistic and pragmatic criteria—not by primitiveness.

Although so-called primitive languages are unwritten, writing is not in itself an intrinsic part of language.

As a total, self-contained system, every language has a structure that can be analyzed. The analysis of structure is the concern of *synchronic linguistics*. Structure begins with *phonemes,* the smallest units of sound on which a language builds. The way phonemic units are combined constitutes the *morphology* or structure of a language, and *morphemes* are the basic units of structure. The patterned arrangement of morphemes in phrases and sentences makes up the *syntax* of a language. For the anthropologist as anthropologist, the main language problem is one of *semantics,* or the meaning of meaning. What are the denotive and connotive intentions of speakers and informants?

The discovery of transformational grammars is one of the potentially great developments of contemporary linguistics. Transformational grammar is concerned with meaning and structure as governed by the "deep" rules which determine syntactic ordering of word units and phrases.

The extent to which the syntax of a language preconditions, limits, and directs the thought patterns of the carriers of a given culture is the subject of the Sapir-Whorf hypothesis. We now realize that we think and perceive in the thought-grooves that the patterns of our own peculiar grammar set for us. This interest in how people categorize their universe linguistically has led to *ethnosemantics*, a study of the meanings found in each society, to *componential analysis*, which is a conceptual tool for classificatory purposes, and to the development of *ethnoscience*, a branch of linguistics concerned with the subjects mentioned above.

Diachronic linguistics is concerned with the historic processes of growth and change in languages. The comparative method involves the compilation of vocabulary lists to establish genetic identities in languages and also traces patterns of phonetic shifts as dialects diverge and become new languages. On the assumption that basic vocabularies change at a fixed, determinable rate, *glottochronology* provides a method of determining the time elapsed since the speakers of two related tongues separated. *Lexicostatistics* is a later development of glottochronology. In this technique, interest is shifted from time determinations to identification of statistical concordances which suggest historical affinities among languages which do not appear to be related.

SELECTED READINGS

Birdwhistell, R. L., *Kinesics and Context: Essays on Body Motion Communication* (1970). Body signals as language adjuncts.

Bloomfield, L.,in H. Hoijer (ed.), *Language History* (1965). The modern classic, first published in 1933 as a part of Bloomfield's *Language*, now reprinted. Covers the basic principles underlying the historical derivation of languages.

Burling, R. M., *Man's Many Voices: Language in Its Cultural Context* (1970). The effect of the cultural setting on the whole process of communication. The emphasis is on the nonlinguistic factors which affect the use of language; linguistics with a strong cultural anthropological slant.

Carroll, J. B. (ed.), *Language, Thought, and Reality: Selected Writings of Benjamin Lee Whorf* (1956). Whorf's original essays in metalinguistics.

Chomsky, N., *Language and Mind* (1968). By the formulator of modern transformational grammatic methods.

Gumperz, J., and D. Hymes (eds.), *Directions in Sociolinguistics: The Ethnography of Communication* (1972). An excellent collection of articles in the field of the social context and social meaning of language.

Hall, E. T., *The Silent Language* (1959). A popular and intriguing account of extralinguistic cues as they operate in cultural communications. Particularly helpful in its analysis of failure in cross-cultural communication because of unsophisticated awareness of meaning of cues on the part of business and public officials.

Hall, R. A., Jr., *Linguistics and Your Language* (2d rev. ed. of *Leave Your Language Alone!* 1960). A penetrating, easily understandable exploration of process and function in languages.

Hymes, D. (ed.), *Language in Culture and Society* (1964). A comprehensive reader which includes many classic articles representing the whole field of linguistics and anthropology.

Tyler, S. A. (ed.), *Cognitive Anthropology* (1969). Essays on method and results in the study of how different people define and classify their world and experience.

34
Art and Culture

CHAPTER OUTLINE

LEARNING GOALS

Define art.

Explain what is meant by primitive art.

Discuss the functions of art.

Explain the forms of graphic art.

Explain the relationship between religion and art.

Discuss art as semantics.

It must be obvious by now, from what has been discussed so far in this book, that art forms are intricately meshed with all other aspects of life, although the manifestations vary from one society to another. We have observed weapons and tools, housing and temples, clothing and jewelry, cooking utensils and containers adorned far beyond the requirements of utility. Naming ceremonies, initiation rites, funerals, hunting and war parties, medicine and healing, government, religion, magic—all, we have seen, are conducted or presented in a rich mixture of ritual and pageantry which includes drama, dance, music, and, frequently, tangible art objects as well.

WHAT IS PRIMITIVE ART?

Before defining primitive art, one must, of course, ask first, "What is art?" Definitions proffered by artists, art historians, aestheticians, philosophers, politicians, semanticists, and others "vary with the purposes of the definers,"[1] the artist stressing the creative impulse, the art lover emphasizing the emotional response, and the Marxist official stressing the opinion-molding purpose of the art. All definitions, by whomever given, cast valuable illumination on the fascinating, complicated behaviors involved in the creation of, and response to, the artistic process. For these reasons art must be perceived in the total cultural context.

Art Defined

One definition of art for anthropological purposes is given by Herskovits:

In the widest sense . . . art is to be thought of as any embellishment of ordinary living that is achieved with competence and has describable form. . . . [T]he student of culture must regard as art whatever a people recognizes as manifestations of the impulse to make more beautiful and thus to heighten the pleasure of any phase of living.[2]

Sieber feels that it is necessary to add that "there are two basic aspects of art: its esthetic or presentational context comprised of form and skill and embodying style, and its meaning context comprised of subject and symbolic associations."[3]

Certain basic elements are stated or implied in most definitions of art: there is a creator(s), a process, a medium, a product presented for public (sometimes limited) view, a content and meaning, and a response on the part of the beholder(s).

Art and Handicrafts

Many handicraft works may be viewed as art. Jacques Maquet, in a penetrating analysis of problems in the anthropology of art, spells out the distinction between *instrumental form* and *noninstrumental* features. He suggests:

Let us take an example: a wooden bowl with some engraved marks. Its context is everyday life; it is used to serve food. Its shape is circular, its rim rounded, its bottom flat. These formal characteristics are instrumental; circular shape and rounded edge make cleaning easier; flat bottom prevents the vessel from being overturned. Some of the engraved marks are magical signs that keep the evil spirits away and prevent them from spoiling the food; they are instrumental too. But we notice also that the rim of the bowl is a perfect circle, which is not easy for a carver working with only adze and knife to achieve. The magical symbols are well balanced and elegant; and beside them there is an engraved pattern, which is just ornamental. These noninstrumental characteristics pertain also to the form. By revealing noninstrumental features, the bowl's form discloses its aesthetic quality.[4]

---

[1]G. Mills, "Art: An Introduction to Qualitative Anthropology," in C. M. Otten (ed.), *Anthropology and Art*, p. 77.

[2]M. J. Herskovits, *Cultural Anthropology*, p. 235.

[3]R. Sieber, "The Arts and Their Changing Social Function" (*Annals of the New York Academy of Sciences*, vol. 96, 1962), p. 653.

[4]J. Maquet, "Introduction to Aesthetic Anthropology" (*McCaleb Module in Anthropology*, 1971), p. 8. Quoted with permission of Addison-Wesley Publishing Company, Inc.

Noninstrumental expression is the embellishment of an artifact. Plains Indian moccasins were embroidered with dyed porcupine quills. Basket makers found that variations in twilling produced interesting and pleasing designs within the structure of the basket and that the use of varicolored fibers further enhanced the beauty of the work. Potters discovered that slips, painting, and sculptural detail made infinite variety a possiblity in ceramic production. Rawhide boxes could have been left as crude and undecorated as our corrugated shipping cartons. But Plains Indians preferred to decorate them with geometric designs in color. A lime spatula could be a simple stick, but the natives of eastern New Guinea prefer to carve out a handle with painstaking skill.

These are all examples of noninstrumental embellishment—modification in line, form, or color of useful articles—which is superfluous in the sense that such modifications do not contribute to the utilitarian effectiveness of the article. But they please their owner, impress guests, and whet the acquisitive appetities of museum collectors.

A valid principle seems to be that as soon as a people solves the fundamental technical problems in the production of an artifact or tool, the artistic impulse begins to assert itself. The more aesthetically endowed individuals begin to play with the surface in an effort to increase the interest potential of the object.

As a rule, technique must be mastered before art develops. Beyond this, the more leisure the subsistence techniques and resources of a culture allow, the greater the likelihood of decorative embellishment. This must not, however, be taken as a bald assertion that leisure produces art. It may, or may not. Surplus energies and time may be directed into other channels to satisfy other interests, such as war, trading, or games.

To take one more step with Maquet, the quality that makes the noninstrumental significant rather than just "useless" is *aesthetic contemplation*. If one sets aside other concerns for the sake of beholding the object for the interest evoked by its form (not its symbolic content), then that is aesthetic experience.

Primitive Art

Primitive art is simply the art of so-called primitive peoples. It includes music, dance, myths and oral literature, religious ceremonies such as the sun dance (pages 315–317) and the Okipa (pages 544–550), decorative arts and crafts, religious icons, weaving, pottery, statuary, carvings, and painting. Ideally, our discussion of art should perhaps give equal attention to all these media, but because of both the superabundance of graphic and plastic art objects and the greater ease of reproducing them on the printed page, we shall deal primarily with these permanent and visible products.

An unfortunate semantic confusion arises over the term"primitive" in art discussions. The so-called primitivists in recent Occidental art stripped down their art forms to an essential simplicity but were not necessarily emulating primitive art, even though they may have been consciously influenced by the art of certain nonliterate peoples, especially African sculpture. On the other hand, the "American Primitive" school of art consisted of the untutored representatives of an American offshoot of the European cultural tradition. These painters, working in the early nineteenth century (and some, like Grandma Moses, more recently), had access to only a very limited history and knowledge of technique.

The inclination in art criticism to equate "primitive" with "crude" or "childish" is in part due to the fact that, when nonliterate people's art objects were first presented to European artists and connoisseurs (a presentation beginning several centuries ago, but accelerating rapidly in the nineteenth century), these objects were evaluated in terms of classical and traditional standards. "Everything was reckoned according to the degree it approached Judeo-Christian and

Classical-Western concepts. Thus, art (meaning idealized nature) was beyond the achievements of primitive man. . . ."[5]

The art of nonliterate peoples runs a wide gamut from technical clumsiness to high skill, from simplicity to complexity, from naturalism and realism to abstraction. Even when we eliminate the more florid forms of art from our consideration and concentrate on the arts of the technologically most simple peoples, this is still true. Bushman art is naturalistic and full of vitality (Figure 34.1). Australian art is highly stylized and in certain forms is abstract and symbolic (Figure 34.2). Eskimo art is naturalistic and technically quite sophisticated.

No qualities that universally characterize primitive art forms can be adduced, unless it is that nonliterate people never solved the problem of perspective, that is, nonliterate artists have not depicted depth relationships or three-dimensional objects on a two-dimensional surface.

FIGURE 34.1
Bushman rock painting. The dancers.

THE FUNCTIONS OF ART

The universality of art indicates a significant role and several potential functions in human life. Exactly what these functions may be is more difficult to state.

Psychological Functions

It has been commonly assumed that one function of art is to release tensions by enabling the artist to externalize emotions and ideas in an objective way. In the classical and Western view, the artist experiences "divine discontent" or "creative tension," which is expended or "sublimated" in a specialized "artistic process," culminating in the production of a "work of art"—be it drama, music, dance, or a graphic art form. The release of tensions brings satisfaction and pleasure to the artist. In their turn, the viewers of the art object are stimulated to responses of pleasurable feelings of euphoria. This is not to deny, however, that the artistic experience may be highly disturbing and may even cause both the artist and audience great discomfiture while it runs its course. The expression of art begins in a state of tension, and the process of translating these feelings of tension into high artistic form is not easy.

Thus, even from the individualistic point of view, art never exists literally for art's sake alone. It exists for psychophysiologic reasons—at least in Western cultures. And because our scientific knowledge of the physiology of emotion is still crude, we understand little of the workings of the artistic impulses. Aesthetics, the study of beauty, remains almost entirely a branch of philosophy, for beauty is still subjective, as far as our understanding of it goes.

Societal Functions

But art may not be seen in its entirety if analyzed only from the individualistic point of view. Art is also a social expression and, therefore, exists as a part of culture.

Art is inextricably tied to religion and magic—and to politics. It cannot help expressing and reflecting social relations and systems. It can serve to sustain them, as Renaissance art so notably served medieval Christianity. It can also aim at the destruction of society, as has protest art at various times in recent history, and as does the contemporary anarchist art of those who hold modern civilization to be so false and

[5] D. Fraser, "The Discovery of Primitive Art," in C.M. Otten (ed.), op. cit., p. 26.

FIGURE 34.2
Australian aboriginal bark painting. The kangaroo hunt. The style combines naturalism with a special interest in the vital interior organs, which produces the stylistic so-called x-ray effect. (UNESCO.)

meaningless that the artist can only ridicule it in the hope of bringing about its downfall.

The Functions of Art in Nonliterate Society

Whereas the modern artist consciously creates or invents a personal style in defiance of convention, "the primitive artist is . . . making works of art within a highly formalized, intensely local and very long established style, . . . [and] probably largely unaware of the qualities of the style he follows; he uses it as he does his language, rightly, and without self-consciousness."[6]

In nonliterate societies the artist-creator, therefore, works from a clear set of social expectations, with traditional media, from agreed-upon values toward known and approved social ends. Personal satisfactions and achievements are incidental. What is important is that the product must satisfy the social needs of the occasion, must evoke the appropriate response, must fulfill the given social function. These social functions may be specific, as with the Navajo artist who makes sand paintings (see Figure 30.1, pages 524–525) for both religious and medical functions "because art for the Navajos is intimately bound up with the maintenance of health and cosmic organization."[7] Or they may be generalized. The Okipa maker must plan, cast, choreograph, rehearse, and present, with each part being played out correctly, the great Mandan myth in such a way as to reaffirm societal goals and reinspire moral and proper behavior.

The function, then, of primitive art is to communicate symbolically the value scheme of the culture.

> *[T]he arts . . . are for the most part oriented positively, that is, toward man's search for a secure and ordered existence. . . . [T]hey can be considered positive, integrated cultural manifestations, reflecting and reinforcing the basic values of the cultures that gave rise to them. . . . The arts at any time or place . . . evolve what might be called the "value image" that culture has of itself.*[8]

In this regard, art is inextricably intertwined with politics, religion, world view—the entire complex of social institutions which seeks to bind each community.

The vital importance of art as social communication in nonliterate societies cannot be emphasized too strongly. The heterogeneous populations of complex societies, with their plurality of backgrounds, values, and identifications, their geographic and social mobility, and their multiplicity of communications media (books, news-

[6] R. Redfield, "Art and Icon" in C. M. Otten (ed.), op, cit., p. 48.
[7] G. Mills, op. cit., p. 68.

[8] R. Sieber, op. cit. p. 655.

papers, periodicals, radio and television, movies, tapes, satellites) are dramatically different from the small, isolated, homogeneous, closely knit, stable (slow-changing) nonliterate societies. The function of art in the two types of societies, while sharing certain attributes, thus assumes an important difference. In nonliterate societies, art must carry a far greater burden in maintaining the society's cohesiveness than does modern art. Indeed, according to Charlotte Otten,

> *Here . . . lies the heart of the matter, and a crucial reason why we cannot validly equate the arts of nonliterate peoples with those of late civilizations in which writing has permeated the culture as the ordinary medium of communication and information storage. . . . In pre-literate or proto-literate culture, the art symbol becomes the fact; that is it simultaneously represents, defines, and manifests its referent. In such cultures, art objects and events serve as media for information storage. . . .* [9]

For the very same reasons, when a nonliterate society comes into contact with a civilization and starts to change, one of the first things to go is its traditional art. It is not production for the tourist trade that destroys primitive art. It is the disintegration of the value system which the art had been originally produced to sustain.

FORMS OF GRAPHIC ART: STYLE

Art forms may be *naturalistic* or *abstract*, with all degrees of transition between the extremes. A form is naturalistic if the transformation of the object is a faithful representation of the original model (Figure 34.3). The form is abstract if the identifying attributes of the original object have been transformed by means of a symbolic identity which does not closely resemble the original form. The face and body of the ancestral figure painted on the facade of a Sepik River men's spirit house in New Guinea, as shown in Figure 34.4, is more abstract than naturalistic. The ideographic wall paintings from prehistoric Portugal, shown in Figure 34.9 (page 603), are wholly abstract.

FIGURE 34.3
Crow Indian symbolism in tepee painting. A naturalistic representation of a wounded eagle. (Museum of the American Indian.)

The term "style" means a departure from absolute naturalism. Artists always compose their creations to some degree. Documentary photography, as well as the snapshots of most amateurs, is not art. But by selective lighting, screening, and retouching, photography can be made into art. Style denotes a standardized selective modification of the image in a way that produces an aesthetically effective and distinctive representation.

Style in Northwest Coast Art

One of the most distinctive of all primitive art styles is that of the Northwest Coast of North America, exemplified in the carving and painting

[9] C. M. Otten (ed.), op. cit., pp. xiv–xv.

FIGURE 34.4
Abstract of a human face and body, painted on the facade of a man's spirit house (Haus Tambaran), Maprik District, Sepik River, New Guinea. (E. A. Hoebel.)

of masks, totem poles, boxes, rattles, dishes, spoons, canoes, houses, and other objects. Exaggerations in representative art have led not to geometric design but to a unique stylization in which a body form can still be distinguished, in spite of the fact that it is greatly distorted in size and arrangement. All Northwest Coast art objects are utilitarian in intent, and therefore the decorative element is more or less subordinated to the object. This is definitely not free art.

The effects of this subordination of the art to the object are most interesting. The artist is given, so to speak, a decorative field that must be covered. The artist abhors blank spaces, and also wants all decorative elements to represent some aspect of animal life. Hence, the artist is impelled to dissect, dismember, distort, and remold creatures to fill the space, whether it is the surface of a box, bowl, wooden hat, or rattle. Distortion becomes such that the representation is in the end a caricature.

Design does not annihilate representation wholly, however, because the impulses of the Northwest Coast artist are not unalloyedly aesthetic. Totemic heraldry, with its rich mythology of clan and lineage origins from heroic animal ancestors, pervades most Northwest Coast art. The representative art portrays not just an animal, but an animal that symbolizes some mythical or historic event in the social background of the artist. This interest in the art counterbalances the tendency for caricature to get out of hand. The device to make this purpose effective is the standardization of certain immutable symbols based on one or a few outstanding anatomical traits of the natural creature portrayed.

The marks of the beaver in Northwest Coast art are the most readily recognizable—the flat, scaly, mud-slapper tail and efficient cutting teeth. These are always present in any artistic representation of the beaver (Figure 34.5).

The bear in Figure 34.5 fills in a square design area. Again the ears prove it to be an animal. The teeth are bear teeth, but the most important mark is found in the long claws. Notice, too, that the bear looks as though it had been split down the back and then opened to fill out the flat space.

The best example of the use of this tricky device is in the treatment of the shark. The distinguishing shark features (Figure 34.5), which are all on the face, are (1) a large mouth, drawn down at the corners, (2) many sharp teeth, (3) gill slits on the cheeks, (4) large round eyes, and (5) a high, tapering forehead on which are drawn two circles like eyes and gill slits to form a pseudo subface. Since these features are all best seen from the front, the shark head is never shown in profile. In order that symmetry may be attained, the artist has split the fish down

FIGURE 34.5
Northwest Coast Indian art, Haida tribe. Top left, carved totem-pole beaver; top right, painted bear on a flat surface; bottom, painted shark or dogfish. (After Boas.)

the back and folded the two sides out to the right and left of the head. What looks to us at first glance like wings are the outspread right and left sides of the shark's body. So that a large void is not left beneath the body, the pectoral fins are much enlarged; and then to keep the whole within the rectangular decorative area, the split tail is turned down and inward at both ends of the body.

Thus we see how the Northwest Coast artist, with great skill and ingenuity, compromised and balanced in a sophisticated art style the hunter's interest in animal anatomy, an interest in design, an abhorrence of blank spaces, and the totemic mythology which explained and reinforced the social system.

RELIGION AND ART

Religion and art are not inseparable, but for deep-rooted reasons they have a strong affinity. In essence, religion is subjective—a matter of belief. Yet the covert concepts of religious belief need objectifying, and art is an outstandingly effective medium. By artistic embellishment, the paraphernalia of religion and magic may be lifted out of the realm of ordinary artifacts or activities to become endowed with the qualities that should be associated with the supernatural—the sacred.

Yet even more important than the elaboration of religious paraphernalia is the representation of the spirits and gods. Gods are imaginative conceptions who exist in belief. If the belief can be translated into concrete form, it becomes more real and convincing. Paintings and statues objectify the subjective concepts of the divinities (Figure 34.6). The presence of a god at a ceremony is more directly felt if it is there in solid stone or wood looking out on the believers. Edmund Leach has stated it well:

> *It is intended to be understood. And in the ordinary way it will be understood by the audience for whom it is designed. For the audience for which a primitive artist works is composed of members of his own community steeped in the same mythological tradition as himself and familiar with the same environment of material fact and ritual activity; the primitive artist can therefore afford to communicate in shorthand; symbols have the same basic significance and the same range of ambiguity for artist and audience alike.*[10]

Leach goes on to observe that the European art critic who tries to understand primitive art is forced to concentrate on its form alone, without reference to its meaning; the critic is ignorant of the religious and mythic context of the object being analyzed.

Masks and Rituals

The use of masks to portray supernatural beings is prevalent among nonliterate peoples in many parts of the world. Only Polynesia and Micronesia, in the Pacific, and the Plains and Basin areas,

[10]E. R. Leach, "Aesthetics," in E. E. Evans-Pritchard, *The Institutions of Primitive Society*, p. 32.

FIGURE 34.6
Ambrym artists in the New Hebrides at work painting the carved head on a large slit-gong or wooden drum, 1972. (Kal Muller/Woodfin Camp Associates.)

in the United States, are conspicuous in that masking is absent, or nearly so. In the religion of the Plains Indians, deities are of little importance; there is nothing much to mask. In Polynesia, although the pantheon is elaborate and deities are portrayed as statues, masking is abjured for reasons that are obscure.

In North America, the masks of the Northwest Coast attain a richness of variety and form that is rivaled only in parts of Melanesia (Figure 34.7). Many Northwest Coast masks, by means of hinges and strings, have movable parts that may be manipulated by the actor to heighten the dramatic effect. Some have an inner and an outer face to portray the dual character (animal and human) of the early mythological progenitors. The most important of the factors that have combined to produce the exotic elaborateness of Northwest Coast masks are (1) a social organization emphasizing hereditary status based in part on descent from mythological ancestral lineage founders, (2) elaboration of dance drama depicting the deeds of the mythical heroes, (3) technical mastery of the skills of carving, and (4) a vigorous creative drive.

At the eastern end of North America, Iroquois masks as made and used by the False Face Society of curers are not so rich in variety or so elaborate as those of the Northwest Coast, but they bear the stamp of a grotesquely humorous realism designed to frighten away evil spirits. While the intent of the masks is serious, one cannot help feeling that the artist carves with tongue in cheek.

The Malanggan of New Ireland The *malanggan* ceremonies of New Ireland, which lies northeast of New Guinea in the Southwest Pacific, celebrate the memory of the recently deceased, plus the initiation of adolescent boys.[11] This system of festivals involves the production and use of intricately carved plaques and masks colored in red, yellow, blue, and white.

Each clan has a sacred spot in the bush where its guardian spirit dwells. When the time for the *malanggan* cycle was at hand, the men prepared a walled enclosure and planted special gardens in the vicinity. These provided dedicated foodstuffs. Shell money and currency were accumulated for gifts and exchange and the rites, which

[11]P. H. Lewis, *The Social Context of Art in Northern New Ireland* (Fieldiana: Anthropology, vol. 58, 1969), p. 45.

FIGURE 34.7
The cast of masked dancers participating in a Kwakiutl ceremonial which dramatizes the mythical origins of the kinship group and household in which the ritual takes place. Photographed about 1912. (E. Curtis.)

covered the better part of a year, were under way.

The carving of masks, some of which were to be worn, others of which would crown the bodies of manufactured dummies, took weeks of secret activities, from which women and noninitiates were barred. Much planning and discussion went into the selection of mask forms and their execution by the carvers. It was in itself a highly social, albeit exculsive, undertaking.

When all was ready, the circumcision rites of the boys were carried out—in the seclusion of the *malanggan* enclosure.

Then it was time for the memorial services for the recent dead. Display halls for the masks and plaques had been built within the compound. Guests arrived from miles around.

The initiates were brought out of the compound and returned to their families. Then a great, masked ancestral figure came forth to dance. "The crowd watched silently with great consternation."[12]

When the dance was over,

> [*T*]*he entire crowd, men, women, and children, filed in through the gateway. The malanggans were at the peak of their effectiveness. . . .* [*T*]*his viewing time was a tense and dramatic episode. The people would come forward to the display houses exclaiming in wonder and sometimes with tears in their eyes.*[13]

Subsequently, the great pig distribution ceremonies and the final removal of the carved spirit figures from the compounds closed the ritual.

The point to be made here is a reiteration of the theme that such art is *socially* meaningful and devoid of the individual self-centeredness which marks so much of contemporary Western art. Its import is to emotionalize the fact of social (in the case of the *malanggan* clan) identity.

African Sculpture

Statuary as a medium of primitive religious art is common in Africa and Melanesia, and also in Polynesia and Central America. African statuary has had considerable influence upon modern European artists, beginning with Picasso. It possesses a living quality eagerly sought after by modernists. It embodies the people's hopes and fears; it terrorizes or delights them as it portrays the nature of the gods on whom they lean or before whom they prostrate themselves, not only in African sculpture, but also in Polynesian and Melanesian. The artist is close to the art, and the art is close to the interests and well-being of the people.

[12] Ibid., p. 62.

[13] Ibid., pp. 62–63.

Mass, solidity, and plainness of surface are the impressive features of African sculpture, even though the figures are not usually very large. These qualities are induced partly by the nature of the material in which the artist works and partly by an inimitable style. The material is hardwood—mahogany, the aristocrat of timbers, and ironwood—tough, challenging material. No light-minded whittler can work the sculptor's transformation on such a block. The wood is close-grained and invites a high polish with dark lustrous tones. The glistening highlights of the smooth African skin are beautifully reflected in the finished statues. The wedding of subject matter and materials is perfect.

African sculpture is characteristically disproportionate. The head is always large in relation to the torso; the legs are squat and sturdy. All the work is subject to the limitations of the mass of the block with which the artist works. Since projecting pieces cannot be attached to the mass, the arms must be formed close to the body and the legs confined within the area of the original block (Figure 34.8). Concentration of attention on the head of the statue, lineal elongation of the body, and dwarfing of the lower limbs are matters of stylistic choice in the African tradition.

Most African statues represent dead ancestors; they are created to house their spirits. The statue, when the spirit has taken up its abode, is in the true sense a fetish, an object possessing a supernatural quality. It is not just a work of art to be viewed objectively in a museum. It is a personage, alive with all the pulsating powers of the personality it represents—powers that are superhumanly potent because the personality it represents is no longer that of mere human but is godlike. As Maquet notes, contemporary Africans often protest with vehemence against the inclusion of their religious and political symbolic objects in European and American art museums.[14]

[14]J. Maquet, op. cit., p. 13.

FIGURE 34.8
Bakonga wood statue of mother and child. The large head and small legs, along with cicatrization on the upper torso, reveal common stylistic features of West African sculpture. (Museum of Primitive Art.)

ART AS SEMANTICS

Throughout this book, but particularly in this section, we have emphasized the symbolic attributes of culture. Art, too, speaks a symbolic message. The message may be clear and explicit, as when a Tlingit totem pole presents the actors in a household mythic "history." Or it may be diffuse and ambiguous but nonetheless sensed, as it is in contemporary junk art and the works of the modern abstractionists, which give vent to the emotional instability, anxieties, irritation, free-floating anger, and frustrations so widely experienced throughout the modern world. What art communicates is not explicit but, rather, implicit.

The messages in Northwest Coast totemic art, for example, are clear and explicit only to the members of the tribe and clan who know the meanings of the "signs" in the art through knowing the myths, the specific forms (like the beaver's tail), and the symbolic referents of the different colors. Art as language speaks only to those who understand the language. It is particularistic and ethnocentric. Symbolic content is more important than the form. The form is conventionalized. The more the art is intended to convey a narrow and specific message rather than to evoke a generalized social effect, the greater will be the tendency toward economy of effort in the production of visible artistic signs and symbols. The movement in the development of visual language may be expected to be from naturalistic representation to simplified abstract representation. From such a process writing has developed. Hence, writing will be treated here as the most specialized outgrowth of art.

Capsian and Azilian Picture Writing

In the cavern of Cogul, in Portugal, is a painted wall upon which prehistoric peoples of the Capsian culture left many paintings (Figure 34.9a). One shows a man confronting a stag, possibly as a shaman getting special curing power from it. On another part of the wall is a crudely conventionalized picture of a hunter who has just shot a large arrow at a stag. In yet another spot is a very queer figure, which by itself would be unintelligible. We know, however, that the Capsian hunters were very much interested in dead deer, and with the more naturalistic examples before us, we can compare the number of prongs in the forklike projections on this figure with the prongs of the antlers in the naturalistic pictures. That a deer is meant is certain. Furthermore, since the four feet of the object are sticking straight up in the air, we may feel reasonably sure that this is the symbol for a dead deer, presumably a magic hunting symbol to help the deerslayer.

What took place at Cogul occurred elsewhere on the Iberian peninsula. Obermaier, in arguing for a genetic relationship between the Azilian painted pebbles and the painted petroglyphs of the Spanish caves and rock shelters, prepared the compartive chart shown in Figure 34.9b. Clearly, the Azilian ∧ symbolizes a squatting female, and the m is a male. The Azilians had apparently progressed from picture writing to the use of ideographs—symbols that stand directly for things or notions instead of the sounds of words in the language of the users. Such is the first step in the evolution and origin of all systems of writing. The scribe is the intellectual offspring of the artist.

Chinese Ideographs

On a much more elaborate level, the Chinese system of characters is fundamentally an ideographic picture writing which has become reduced to a set of timesaving brushstrokes and which is in some aspects also phonetic. Its ideographic quality may be readily discerned in the manner of writing such words as "prisoner," and "happiness." In the character for "prisoner," we see a man, 人, in an enclosure, 囚. "Happiness" is a woman (wife), 女, with a son, 女子. The earlier pictographic derivation of a number of Chinese characters may be seen in Figure 34.10.

The occurrence in all languages of words that

(a)

(b)

FIGURE 34.9
(a) Three degrees of conventionalization in the representation of the stag in Capsian art from Cogul, Portugal. (b) Probable male and female symbols on painted pebbles from Le Maz d'Azil (right) compared with female and male pictographs from the Late Upper Paleolithic cave art in eastern Spain (left). (After Obermaier.)

are identically pronounced but have different meanings (*homophones*)[15] makes possible a ready extention of ideographic writing as soon as people are able to make the mental leap of partially disassociating the picture from the idea and linking it to sounds as such. Thus the Chinese word for "horse," which is "mar," is represented by 馬. The Chinese term for "mother" used within the intimate confines of the family is sometimes "mama." Phonetically, then, it would be possible for the Chinese to write "mama" as 馬馬. This, however, would be ambiguous, for unless the context made it clear, the reader would not be certain whether the symbol represented two horses or one mother. The Chinese get around this difficulty by first writing the symbol for woman, 女, followed by the homophone symbol for "mar." Thus they have produced a way of writing "mama" that is half ideogram and half phonogram. Because of its way of mixing ideograms and phonograms, Chinese writing is classed as a *transitional system*, a means of written communication which has gone beyond the earlier forms of pictography but which still falls short of pure phonetic representation.

The ancient Egyptian, Hittite, Cretan, and cuneiform (Sumerian, Babylonian, Assyrian) script systems also developed out of picture writing by use of similar basic principles, although each evolved its own special forms. These and the Chinese, plus the Indic and Mayan-Aztec systems (see Figure 33.4, page 575), are the only definitely known independent basic scripts. The transformation of art to writing is a supreme human achievement, so difficult that few peoples have accomplished the feat. Most human beings have achieved literacy through borrowing.

Alphabetic Origins

Our own alphabet had its beginnings in Egyptian pictography. Its development from early Greek inscriptions is well known and, indeed, testified

[15]For example, *saw*: (1) past tense of *to see*; (2) a cutting tool with a serrated edge; (3) to cut with a sawlike tool; (4) to cut as if with a sawlike tool; (5) a sententious saying or proverb.

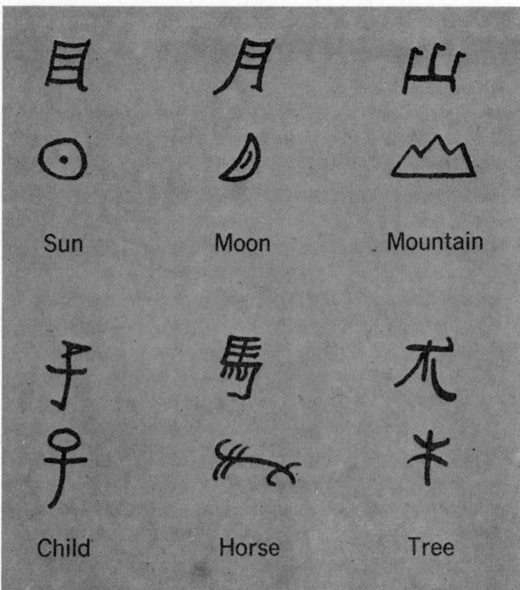

FIGURE 34.10
Pictographic derivation of some seventeenth-century Chinese characters. (After Brouner and Fang.)

to by the very word by which we identify it: a compound of the first two words of the Grecian system, the *alpha* and *beta*. Beyond the Grecian alphabet, however, lies the Semitic from which it in turn is clearly derived: Hebrew, *aleph*, *beth*, *gimel*. Some Semitic symbols have clear derivation from Egyptian hieroglyphs; many do not. Known archaic Semitic inscriptions are few, far too few to enable paleographers to advance well-founded reconstructions of the full history of the emergence of the alphabet. Although there are indications that parallel attempts at developing alphabetic systems were more or less simultaneously under way among several different Semitic peoples around the second millennium B.C., only one system (that of the Phoenicians) was finally perfected. From this, and this alone, all the extant alphabets of the world have descended. Here was a cultural triumph so difficult to conceive, and so perfect in form and function, that with minor modifications it could be adapted to any and all languages. It has susperseded all other alphabetic systems; there has never again been the need to evolve a new system.

Of the Semitic symbols derived from Egyptian hieroglyphic ideograms, the first letter of the alphabet will suffice for illustrative purposes. *Aleph*, in Semitic, means "ox." The Egyptian hieroglyph is . In a Semitic inscription in the ninth century B.C., the symbol is formed with three straight lines, . In later Greek it was inverted on its horns, and became A. Similar transitions may be seen for other letters. The Egyptian word sounds for "ox," "house," and so on were ignored by the Semitic scribes; what they succeeded in doing was to make pictorially derived symbols from Egyptian prototypes, which were subsequently associated with the separate consonants that went to make up their speech. The Semites never included vowels in their script, but wrote each word with only its consonantal sounds. The *aleph* symbol stood for the glottal stop, which is exceedingly important in Semitic speech. The Greeks had no use for the glottal stop, but they were able to represent the vowels of their speech in a way the Semites could not, and they completed the basic modern alphabet with the invention of vowel symbols. They converted the A to represent the first vowel and made other adjustments to take care of the rest.

The capstone was thus put on the transition from art to writing. The communication of generalized states of emotion and ideas through the aesthetic medium had at long last been transmuted to the communication of precise linguistic expression through phonetically representative symbols.

SUMMARY

The concept of art involves the transformation of an object or an idea into an objective form which has a noninstrumental attribute. Thus instrumental artifacts, or dance forms, or stories which are sufficient for practical uses will not ordinarily qualify as art. But if noninstrumental embellishment is added, such extra creative effort is in the direction of art. If the object, because of its effect on the senses, stimulates a contemplative pause, an arresting, thoughtful, or feeling-laden consideration of it for its own sake, then it has evoked an aesthetic response. All art, it is held with Jacques Maquet, has this aesthetic attribute, and the aesthetic response is a universal feature of humankind.

Most definitions of art imply or state a creator (art is a human product), a process of transforming a medium to a patterned form, a product which is publicly viewed, a content which is usually symbolic, and a response on the part of the beholder (the aesthetic experience).

Primitive art is simply the art of nonliterate peoples. It is not implicitly naïve or technically deficient—except for the lack of perspective in graphic art.

The nonliterate artist works in close communication with an audience. The primary function of so-called primitive art is to communicate the value scheme of the culture.

In form, art may be naturalistic or abstract, with intermediate mixtures of the two. Style denotes a recurrent or standardized way of structuring the image in the transformation that is effected.

Because religions are symbolic systems, religion finds a ready expression in the objective forms provided by art. Masks are linked to religious expressionism in many parts of the world. Statues find their widest use in societies in Africa and Melanesia, and also in Polynesia and Central America.

As systems of communication, art has much in common with language. When graphic art is developed to communicate particular, rather than general, messages, it tends to move toward simplicity of form and abstraction. Out of it comes ideographic representation and, finally, writing.

SELECTED READINGS

Breuil, H., *Four Hundred Centuries of Cave Art* (1950). The most comprehensive summary of Paleolithic art.

Buehler, A., T. Barrow, and C. P. Mountford, *The Art of the South Seas, Including Australia and New Zealand* (1962). Many beautiful color plates and numerous line drawings together with a very competent ethnography of Oceanic art.

d'Azevedo, W. L. (ed.), *The Traditional Artist in African Societies* (1972). Deals with the role of the artist in society, the definition of art, and its place in nine societies.

Gunther, E., "Art in the Life of Primitive Peoples," in J. A. Clifton (ed.), *Introduction to Cultural Antrhopology* (1968), pp. 77–114. The best short overview of primitive art by one of its real experts. Covers Northwest Coast and African art, sculpture, weaving, basketry, and cave art.

Hatcher, E. P., *Visual Metaphors: A Formal Analysis of Navajo Art* (1974). Offers a method for analysis of art form and meaning, exemplified by Navajo art.

Holm, B., *Northwest Coast Indian Art: An Analysis of Form* (1965). A study of the basic principles underlying the decorative art of the Northwest Coast.

Inverarity, R. B., *Art of the Northwest Coast Indians* (1950). A profusely and beautifully illustrated book on the distinctive aboriginal art of the Northwest Coast of North America.

Maquet, J., "Introduction to Aesthetic Anthropology" (*McCaleb Module in Anthropology,* 1971). A penetrating and beautifully reasoned formulation of a general anthropological theory of art.

Otten, C. M., *Anthropology and Art: Readings in Cross-Cultural Aesthetics* (1971). Contains twenty-four well-chosen articles on theory and method in the study of art, artists, and art forms in relation to culture areas.

Tanner, C. L., *Southwestern Indian Painting: A Changing Art* (2d ed., 1973). The development of modern Indian painting—a wedding of contemporary techniques and Indian cultural interests.

Taylor, D., "Anthropologists on Art," in M. H. Fried (ed.), *Readings in Anthropology*, vol. 2 (1959), pp. 478–490. On the history of the interest in art by anthropologists.

PART NINE

Anthropology and the Future

35
Applications of Anthropology

CHAPTER OUTLINE

LEARNING GOALS

- Explain how to apply anthropological principles in solving human problems
- Understand the theoretical basis of applied anthropology
- Identify the value of culture as an adaptive mechanism for the applied field
- Discuss the steps in an application project
- Explain why the Vicos Project is so important in the field
- Describe the relevance of the Gila River Project to the applied field

Applied anthropology uses all the knowledge gained about the processes of change and stability in societies to help introduce new changes so that those societies can utilize programs to better their health, economy, government, education, or other aspects of their culture.

THE VALUE OF APPLIED ANTHROPOLOGY

One of the ways in which anthropology helps others, or is applied, is by the examples it provides about how others do similar things. In this way it holds up a mirror so that people can see themselves. By recognizing humanity in others, by taking their places for a moment, and in so doing thinking about our own practices, we come to understand how much our own behavior is embedded in our culture.

But one can well ask: "What good is this? It is interesting and quaint, but how can it help me run a psychiatric ward, or deal with a farm worker's strike? How can it put food on my table, or money in the bank?"

Similar questions thus posed tell much about the materialistic basis of United States society. This, too, must be considered in showing how applied anthropology can help. Then, how do anthropologists answer the questions regarding the utility of the case studies they provide? Citizens of this country are always looking for the key to the solution to a problem. The problem can be how to improve the taste of breakfast cereal, how to land a person on the moon, or how to create a synthetic material which is comfortable to the touch *and* at the same time is easy to care for and fire resistant. Usually the solutions to these and similar problems involve a technological improvement—a better tool, a better alignment of a cutting machine in the assembly line, a new source of raw materials, or a new synthetic fiber. The human aspect of the problem is often ignored. How the assembly line worker feels about the job or what the effect of synthetic fiber will be or what living adjustments are required are not generally considered.

How can we translate into application such practices as how African nonliterate people teach their young mostly in bush schools? Or closer to home, how do we apply the analyses of laughter in medical staff meetings, or research into the social uses of space on a psychiatric ward? These are difficult to grasp as mechanisms which will oil the machinery of progress and provide greater material benefits.

The truth is that people—supervisors, superintendents, managers, teachers, hospital ward attendants—are not automatons. If each can develop an insight as to how the system really works, how the symbols of authority work and why, and how to evaluate all these things and to learn how to make the system work better for the humans who spend most of their working hours behind machines or in assembly lines of various sorts (including mental hospitals, classrooms, and offices), then applied anthropology will have accomplished one goal. If a worker approaches the solution of a technical problem with insight into the human elements involved, the job should be better done at the end. If teachers understand the values inculcated in the social backgrounds of their ethnic students, and at the same time understand the structural problems in the educational system the teachers, themselves, are embedded in, the final product should be better for society, and they will take greater pleasure in their jobs.

The dozen or more books and the hundreds of articles and reports which have been produced in applied anthropology all point to an increasing awareness by administrators and technicians that national boundaries may temporarily obliterate the differences which are found between peoples, but that in the long run, cultural and class distinctions will prevail and continue to affect the conduct of everyday life. Another factor that administrators and technicians have reluctantly recognized is that dominated peoples appear to acculturate as often as they actually acculturate. They acculturate in only some obvious aspects of the new culture, and only some members of the society participate fully and completely in the assimilative process. Many members of a group retain views, values, and actions which preclude full participation in the dominant society. The leaders of industry, business, and government are also finally beginning to realize and accept that the differences which exist between groups will not be obliterated in the direction of making all peoples more like themselves. There is an increasing acceptance of cultural pluralism in the world, and a recognition that cultural pluralism does not diminish technological efficiency, standard of living, or intellectual ability.

Demonstrating the commonality of one's problems with those found in other societies or how one is embedded in one's own culture or how to improve job satisfaction or how to help accept cultural pluralism are not the only tasks in which applied anthropologists are involved. Many anthropologists, if not most, are employed in universities and colleges where they teach and do research. The applied aspect of their employment is in the anthropology courses they teach, in the applied anthropologists they train, and in their parttime consulting or summer research endeavor. Their main work, however, is as teachers and consultants in medical, dental, and nursing schools, and in colleges of education and law, where they help students and professionals understand the special problems of ethnic, minority, and regional populations. Because most of this work takes place in academic settings, it is referred to as academic anthropology.

The main thrust of what we want to say in this chapter is in nonacademic anthropology, that is to say, that most of the work which is generally referred to as applied anthropology occurs outside of academia on a full-time basis. Although we will focus on the applied aspects of social and cultural anthropology, it is worthwhile to note that there are applied anthropologists in the other subfields of anthropology.

In physical anthropology, for example, there are those people who help design seats to fit the average airline passenger, those who work in genetic research, nutrition, medicine, biology, population, epidemiology, and in helping police departments to identify human remains and solve crimes.

In linguistics there are psycholinguists who are interested in the relation between psychology and language and between language and mental illness. There are sociolinguists, who are interested in language learning and culture, in dialects and ethnic groups, in the so-called street talk of urban blacks, in how language affects or limits one's perception of the world, and in how all these factors are related to helping educate the lower classes and ethnic groups of the United States.

A revolution has occurred in archaeology in the past five to ten years which will have long-range repercussions for anthropology. As a result of federal legislation in what is called cultural resource management, archaeologists work to help preserve natural, historical, and prehistorical treasures which are in the path of the construction of telephone lines, utilities, highways, roads, bridges, dams, housing developments, public buildings, or other construction which threatens the destruction of historic, prehistoric, or social resources. In the past these resources would have been ignored or destroyed. Today, by law, the archaeologist must be called to survey and recover any remains which may be endangered by construction activity.

As far as sociocultural anthropology is concerned, all anthropologists have at some time in their careers been concerned with the application of anthropology. Today, cultural anthropologists are called upon by government, industry, or education as consultants to help solve problems dealing with ethnic groups, for example. They may be asked to do a special report or study under the same environmental impact statement requirement as does the archaeologist. In contrast, however, they are concerned with the impact of public or private works on the social and cultural "environment" of living peoples.

Anthropologists are employed regularly as researchers, advisors, consultants, administrators, and staff members in a variety of different fields such as: (1) in ethnohistory to help establish the boundaries of the previous lands of Indian groups, or to assist Indian tribal councils in such activities as preparing tribal membership rolls; in understanding health practices of ethnic groups and as cultural interpreters between ethnic patients and private health practitioners, psychiatric hospitals, and social welfare departments; (2) administrators, supervisors, staff members, or consultants in state Indian commissions, county health planning, mental health programs, and urban planning; and in special programs in such foundations as the Ford and Rockefeller, and at all levels of city, county, state, and federal governments; (3) research background and expert witnesses for private attorneys and for public interest law firms; and (4) researchers, investigators, or consultants for private consulting firms which specialize in evaluating government social programs, such as job training, model cities, education, welfare, and others.

It would be out of place to continue this list. The reader can see that the areas of involvement are many; this list is intended only to give a flavoring of some of the activity of applied anthropology.

Although not new, there has been a recent increase in the number of training programs developed in applied anthropology. Prominent have been efforts at the University of California at Berkeley and at the Universities of South Florida, Kentucky, and Arizona. These programs have focused on medical anthropology, general applied programs, education, and cultural resource management. It is significant to point out that practically every department of anthropology in the country has a research, if not also a training, program in cultural resource management.[1]

The *Guide to Departments of Anthropology* published annually by the American Anthropological Association reveals an increasing number of higher degrees which focus on applied anthropology. In 1976-77, for example, about 20 percent of over 400 Ph.D. dissertations were concerned with subjects related to applied anthropology. Societies have been organized to deal with the major subfields of applied anthropology: medical, educational, and general applied, the latter society having been organized in 1941. In addition to *Human Organization*, which has been published since 1941 as the official organ of the Society for Applied Anthropology, other journals are the *Anthropology and Education Quarterly* and the *Medical Anthropology Newsletter*. Many other journals regularly publish materials in the field. Additionally, each of the applied societies holds annual meetings for hearing reports of recent advances in the field.

It is easy to see from what has been mentioned so far that applied anthropology is not a new field. An interest in using and applying anthropological knowledge to help humanity goes back to the early 1930s with the efforts of anthropologists in Mexico to help indigenous populations, to the British social anthropologists' attempt to assist administrators understand the problems of peoples in the British empire, to the

[1]E. Leacock, N. L. Gonzalez, and G. Kushner (eds.), *Training Programs for New Opportunities in Applied Anthropology*; M. G. Trend, "Government and Industry," (*Human Organization*, vol. 36, no. 1, 1977), pp. 87–89; B.C. Maday, "Anthropologists in the U.S. Government," (*Human Organization*, vol. 36, no. 1, 1977), pp. 89–97; for the history of the field see E. H. Spicer, "Beyond Analysis and Explanation? The Life and Times of the Society for Applied Anthropology," (*Human Organization*, vol. 35, no. 4, 1976), pp. 335–343; E. H. Spicer, "Early Applications of Anthropology in North America," (*American Anthropologist*, Special Publication, no. 10, 1977), pp. 116–141.

efforts of anthropologists to understand and assist the Indian groups in the United States, as well as providing knowledge to help industry, government, and rural communities.

THE BASES OF APPLIED ANTHROPOLOGY

The practice of applied anthropology strikes at the very heart of the general field of anthropology in that it calls upon and tests the major principles and concepts of the field. This occurs because applied anthropology involves the *application* of the principles of anthropology. It is not passive and analytic. Rather, practitioners in this field often promote change for some given end.

Culture Change

When anthropologists speak of cultural change, they refer to an event that has occurred, how a cargo cult operates in a tribe in New Guinea, for example, or how a lineage has segmented among the Nuer in Africa. It would be a different matter if the anthropologist were concerned with introducing a cargo cult or with causing a lineage to segment. At a theoretical or structural level, this is comparable to what applied anthropologists try to do, except that they are concerned with calling public attention to poor economic conditions in a California Indian rancheria, or trying to improve health conditions in Appalachia, or making suggestions for the improvement of management techniques on an Indian reservation.

In order to introduce change, applied anthropologists must understand under what conditions a culture is stable, under what conditions it changes, how it changes, and what the consequences are of those changes. Ideas on how this occurs have been gained from years of studying isolated small communities around the world (see Chapter 18, on culture change).

Cultural Relativity

The reader will recall that cultural relativity was defined as the position taken by anthropologists that what is done in one society must be considered according to the standards, norms, and values in that society, what the action does for that society, rather than in terms of how favorably the action compares with behavior in some other society such as our own (see Chapter 16).

If people behave in a particular manner, and have adapted that behavior to their society and environment, how can the anthropologist play God by seeking to change the practice? Take, for example, the female infanticide or senilicide practiced among the Eskimo at one time. Anthropologists tell us that they had the function of population control, so that there would be sufficient food for the able-bodied hunters to continue to go out to get more food. If we follow the dictum of cultural relativity, we would support this practice.

However, with the advances made by Western civilization in modern medicine, in population control techniques, and especially under the influence of the uniquely Western notion of the worth of the individual, applied anthropologists feel that cultural relativity does not apply in certain areas, and that every individual has the right to life, to good health care, to comfort, security, and education.

To be an applied anthropologist means a willingness to state that some values are better than others, that the right to life is ubiquitous, that people have a right to the natural resources which are extracted from their native soils, and that all people have an equal ability to learn and a right to do so.

Culture as an Adaptive Mechanism

Anthropologists believe that people, if left alone, will adapt their ways to a given environment and successfully exploit it to achieve a fulfilling life. However, in most of the world today where people are found in poverty, malnourishment, and poor health, some outside agent caused the problem by intervening and in some way upsetting the intricate balance which the original, untouched society had developed over many years of intimate contact with its environment.

The situation exists in which a people have been disturbed and they cannot now solve their own problems. This is usually because they have been moved from their native habitat, or because their native habitat has been disturbed or changed. In some instances a forest has been cleared that once formed the basis of a group's culture, or a mineral resource is being exploited which has a high value to the outsider but which breaks the holistic cycle of adjustment that prevailed. Perhaps old foods have been replaced by foods with higher prestige value but less nutritional value. Or the old hierarchy of religious and political leadership has been replaced by one which has not been thoroughly integrated into the old culture. It could be that some more highly acculturated natives have taken control and reserve the benefits of such a position for themselves or for their immediate relatives only, at the expense of the society as a whole.

In any event, the outside culture or newly imposed social organization, be it military, religious, or economic, has broken the tight adaptive network which existed in previous times, with the result that the old culture and the old traditions are no longer adequate for coping with a rapidly changing environment. The ill effects of this maladjustment are manifested in higher rates of infant mortality, of malnourishment, of crime, alcoholism, disease, unhappiness, and so on.

The goal of the applied anthropologist in such an event is to suggest adjustments in the social organization of the present society which will compensate for the maladjustments which have developed in the group. Sometimes this involves supporting the social organization which existed before the changes occurred. This can be done by creating prestige and support for the old leadership structure in the eyes of members of society, or in the view of the administering governmental agency, by showing them how it can work better and how it had been integrated and successful in the old culture before the unplanned intervention changed the old ways. At other times it may be more expedient or more salubrious for the native society if the anthropologist supports the new social organization. The old religious or political organization may not work in the face of the broad-scale changes which have been introduced and which cannot now be reversed without causing greater damage to the society than now exists. For example, although the Navajo were well adapted to an environment which included horticulture, hunting, and raiding as a means of making a living, it would be impossible for the applied anthropologist to encourage the resumption of raiding the Hopis, Pimas, Apaches, and white Americans around them today. The old way of life might be more entertaining and interesting for the Navajo than tending small gardens or working on highway repair crews, at electronic factories, and in governmental offices, and living at a substandard level as many Navajos do today. It might also be exciting to the surrounding society. But it would require military adjustments in the lives of the Navajos and their neighbors which would have unacceptable consequences in today's world.

Holism and Functionalism

Two other concepts which are helpful to the applied anthropologist are holism and functionalism. The reader will recall that holism refers to the notion that a society has a culture which has parts, and that these parts must be considered as coexisting and interrelated into a whole unitary system. It is impossible to consider a part of a society, say its religion, without also considering another part, such as its economic structure (see Chapter 16).

Functionalism, of course, is a related concept which refers to the part that an action, belief, or other aspect of a culture plays in the survival and ongoing efficient operation of the culture as a whole. The anthropologist has found that changes in one part of the culture usually will have effects on other parts of that culture. For example, the loss of the *taboo* concept among the native Hawaiians was one of the factors which led to the disorganization of that society because of the intimate relationship the notion of *taboo* had with the religious and political leadership roles of the group.

Intervention to Change

The first problem in approaching a situation in which applied anthropology may be needed is to consider whether or not to intervene. Why should these people change? Did they ask for help? Are they in some life-threatening situation? Do they have a high infant mortality rate? A particular health problem? Poor nutrition? A high rate of unemployment? Poor housing? Who wants to change them? Why?

What would happen if you left them alone? Would they eventually solve their own problems? Do they now have governmental agencies that can help them? In other words, what would happen if one did not intervene?

It is entirely possible that the situation which appears to call for intervention is a temporary one which can be handled by the normal adaptive measures of the local group or by the normal administrative or other actions of the governmental agency responsible for the group.

Are there some negative consequences of the plannned intervention that are immediately apparent which would preclude involvement? If the answer is yes, the applied anthropologist should not become involved.

Here we refer to such long-range negative effects as undermining local leadership. The anthropologist will be present only for a relatively brief period of time, and someone will have to assume a leadership or promotional role when the anthropologist leaves. If this warning is not heeded, the situation may become worse than it was before the anthropologist intervened. The experiences of Peace Corps volunteers in various countries around the world certainly bear out this cautionary statement.

Ethics and the Responsibility of the Anthropologist

The question of intervening in the culture of a society to bring about change has long perplexed anthropology.[2] In facing the question, anthropologists have taken three positions: no intervention, research intervention, and action intervention.

(1) *No intervention.* Those who hold the view of no intervention are of two minds: (a) those who feel that it is wrong to interfere with the natural adaptive processes of a society because the society will develop its own solutions given sufficient time and (b) those who feel that it is not the anthropologist's duty to change a culture; societies are made up of people who are subjects of a scientific endeavor; they are not to be influenced by the scientist because it would ruin the scientific observation. In short, they view other societies as research laboratories.

(2) *Research intervention.* For too long, the anthropologist has taken the view that societies were there to be studied, that the relation of the anthropologist to the field station was one of scientist and subject. It was difficult, however, to watch the "subjects" die of starvation, suffer malnutrition, disease, and the calumny of oppressive overlords. But how could the anthropologist at the same time wear the hats of scientist and humanitarian? Perhaps part of the answer might lie in the fact that science is often

[2]The whole issue of ethics and the responsibility of anthropologists to their various clients and cohorts, and the problems of anthropology and the third world, racism, poverty, education, pollution, violence, and intervention are discussed in T. Weaver (ed.), *To See Ourselves: Anthropology and Modern Social Issues.*

advanced by studying the process of problem situations as well as by studying static ones. Another part of the answer was that the anthropologist, in reality, could not stand aside while societies perished when help was within the grasp and knowledge of the anthropologist. Many of the older anthropologists had intervened to help in small, singular ways, without fanfare and without recording it in their notes.

The anthropologists who hold the research intervention point of view believe that research should be conducted on a social problem affecting the indigenous group, but that the group should be allowed to do the manipulation of its own society, to be instrumental in conducting the change, both as a learning experience and as a prior right and responsibility. Those holding this position also know that the anthropologist will leave the group sooner or later and it is better to leave knowledge for the local group to do the changing than for the anthropologist to leave the image of being a powerful, godlike figure who alone possesses the knowledge and ability to change a cultural system.

(3) *Action intervention.* The third position held by some anthropologists on the subject of intervention to change a society was one which championed direct and active intervention. This could mean purposefully introducing new ideas, acting as advocate or spokesperson for the group, acquiring legal counsel or direct help from some agency for them, directing discussions and meetings, wording proclamations or writing letters, operating equipment, retraining them in values selected by the intervenor, and similar direct action activities, all meant to take a positive, pro-local group stance. In many instances, this position meant abandoning the scientific aspects of the anthropologist's interest in favor of the humanitarian ones. It also meant, many times, that the result was little or poor data collection because the action situation did not allow sufficient time for observation and recording notes. Such a strong advocacy position also meant that it placed the anthropologist in a different psychological frame of reference with regard to the people *being helped* (rather than the people *being studied*) and this state of mind often precluded productive science.

The problem of intervention in a society's culture has plagued applied anthropology from the beginning. It has brought into the foreground questions of what is right and wrong, of ultimate purposes for the anthropologist's work, of who is paying for the work and why, of looking at one's own society and asking what we are doing to all those people out there.

Early in its infancy the Society for Applied Anthropology had faced this problem squarely and had devised a code of ethics. In the late 1960s the American Anthropological Association faced a crisis in its ranks over this issue and developed a code entitled "AAA: Principles of Professional Responsibility," which delineated responsibilities to those studied, to the public, to the discipline, to students, to sponsors, and to one's own and other governments. The Society for Applied Anthropology revised its own code and it merits close examination and study (see Table 35.1).

The remaining part of this chapter outlines the steps taken in research and development (research intervention) projects, and provides two case studies of this type of work.

STEPS IN PLANNED INTERVENTION

Although unanimity is lacking among applied anthropologists, one can generalize from what has been written about the steps which are necessary in projects and programs involving planned changes. These steps or phases are: (1) preliminary tasks, (2) gathering and analyzing relevant facts, (3) planning and making recommendations, (4) acting or monitoring, and (5) evaluating.

Preliminary Tasks

Preliminary tasks include (1) negotiating the goals and terms of the project and signing a contract with the responsible agency, or otherwise agreeing on terms and conditions of work with the sponsoring community, (2) presenting a

TABLE 35.1
Statement on Professional and Ethical Responsibilities*

Recognizing that any ethical stance derives from or is intimately related to one's political convictions, we are not offering any absolute set of rules or code of ethics. Ultimately we must define and accept our own responsibilities in each category discussed below. However, in the hope of stimulating greater awareness of the issues involved, we offer the following as general guidelines to assist individuals in their actions.

As Fellows and Members of the Society for Applied Anthropology, we should not undertake to act with or without remuneration in any situation where we cannot honor all of the following responsibilities within the limits of the foreseeable effects of our actions. When these responsibilities are in conflict, we should insist on a redefinition of the terms of our employment or other involvement. If the conflict cannot be resolved, or if we have good reason to suspect that the results of our work will be used in a manner harmful to the interests of any segment of the concerned population, we should decline to make our services available.

(1) *To the community being served* we owe respect for its dignity, integrity, and internal variability. We should be constantly aware that it may not be possible to serve the interests of all segments of the community at the same time that we serve the interests of the contracting agency. Therefore, we should not recommend any course of action on behalf of our employers' interests when the lives, well-being, dignity, and self-respect of any portion of the community are likely to be adversely affected, without adequate provision being made to insure that there will be a minimum of such effect and that the net effect will in the long run be more beneficial than if no action were taken at all. We should take the greater care to protect our respondents, especially in the area of confidentiality which they may not be able to stipulate for themselves.

We should publicly declare the position from which we are operating, or at least make clear with what interest group or issues we are primarily concerned in order that all groups in the community may be informed about how our findings may be biased and may possibly affect them. We should endeavor to include the fullest possible participation by the community itself in the formulation of policy recommendations which may be expected by the client agency as part of its contract with us.

(2) *To our colleagues* we have the responsibility of avoiding any action or recommendation that would impede the continued advancement of knowledge. With due regard to our other responsibilities as set forth here, we should undertake to make data and findings available for scientific purposes. It is recognized that sometimes a delay in publication is necessary in order to protect persons or segments of populations. Confidentiality of our work as applied social scientists should be determined by our clients in consultation with us and in terms that do not violate or contradict other stipulations of this statement on responsibilities. We should not consent to employment in which our activities and/or scientific data remain permanently secret and inaccessible. We should not represent hypotheses or personal opinions as scientifically validated principles.

Furthermore, to our colleagues, whether acting in applied or research capacities, we owe professional respect. We should not malign individuals or categories of persons so as to impede future projects in the area, even though the latter may rest upon philosophical positions different from our own.

(3) *To society as a whole* we owe the benefit of our special information and skills in interpreting socio-cultural structures and processes. We should undertake to translate into general terms and to bring to society at large, both through formal educational opportunities and in general publications, the results of our research and our recommended actions.

(4) *To our employers or other sponsors* we should make no promises nor should we encourage any expectations that we cannot reasonably hope to fulfill. Yet, we should give them the best of our scientific knowledge and skill. We should always consider the sponsor's specific goals in light of the general interests and welfare of the community in which we are to act. We should establish a clear understanding with each employer as to the nature of our responsibilities to that employer in relation to our other responsibilities as outlined above. In particular, the client agency should be made aware of the intentions we may have to take the community into our confidence on the review of research data and formulation of policy recommendations.

*Approved by mail ballot validated March 13, 1974. *Human Organization,* vol. 35, no. 4, 1976, p. 344

preliminary research design, work flow charts, and time schedule to the target community and sponsoring or funding agency for their input and approval or dissent, and finally, (3) hiring and training the research team, if there is to be one.

Gathering and Analyzing Facts

There are two kinds of data the anthropologist must gather and analyze to fulfill the applied mission: (1) cultural background information, which does not differ from the usual data gathered by the ethnographer, and (2) cultural information which is related directly to the problem being investigated. This means, for example, if the problem is to improve tribal governmental procedures, that the anthropologist will first gather data which set political, governmental, and management procedures in the widest possible cultural framework by identifying customary practices, attributes, and values in other institutions to find how they are related to the particular topic in the society being studied. Second, the anthropologist focuses exclusively in the data collection activity on those political, management, and governmental practices, attitudes, and values which relate to the problem at hand. The particular problem may include poor records management, inefficient election procedures, poor communications with community members, and ineffective decision-making procedures in council meetings. This is only a brief list intended to exemplify the general point rather than an attempt to provide an exhaustive list of the possible gamut of problems.

Planning and Making Recommendations

Once the research has been conducted and the data analyzed, an effort is set afoot which relates the general information collected to the specific problem which needs correcting. The work which is part of this phase of an applied project consists of devising recommendations to correct the problem within the cultural context and capabilities of the society being studied. For instance, it would be inappropriate to recommend a computerized payroll or indexing system for an American Indian reservation which does not have access to computer facilities. Hiring a part-time bookkeeper to come to the reservation once or twice a week to teach and supervise a tribal employee, or having a business management expert develop and supervise a color-coded filing system, would be more practical solutions for an isolated Indian reservation.

Acting and Monitoring

The only action required of the research and application project may be writing the final report and recommendations and their presentation to the client and sponsoring agencies. This may require writing a preliminary draft and its discussion with key persons in the client populations, with experts, and with fellow team members. The submission of the final report may be a formal presentation at a special meeting, in which case it may be accompanied by audiovisual aids. Informal presentation may involve simply delivering sufficient copies of the report.

Acting on the report may include implementing and supervising some or all of the recommendations by assisting in hiring experts for the client population, such as a business manager, or such other activities as helping to set up a filing system and training personnel in how to maintain the files. Usually it is best to train members of the community in self-help measures, but all these matters would have been negotiated and agreed upon during the first phase of the project.

Supervision of some tasks may be called for, or monitoring of activities may be required, either because the client group requested it or because the applied anthropologist wants to know how effectively the recommendations are being implemented or how effective the project has been.

Evaluating

The evaluation of a project in applied anthropology is a difficult but necessary activity. It is difficult because it requires some honest and straightforward review of what was intended, compared to what actually occurred. It is a necessary activity because only through evaluation and correction can we continue to advance the discipline of applied anthropology.

Some of the difficult questions which must be raised include: "What recommendations should have been made that were not? Have the recommendations been effective? What was the quality and effectiveness of the communication between applied anthropologist and client group? How could it have been improved? What were some of the major problems in running the project? How could they have been avoided? What would you do if you were doing it again? How would you avoid the mistake made?"

The phases in an applied project discussed above are not meant to be followed rigidly and blindly. They merely constitute a summary of ideas gained through experience by applied anthropologists. The case studies which follow are meant to place the generalizations presented above into the context of actual projects.

THE VICOS PROJECT

The Vicos Project was a program of research and development carried out in Peru under the direction of anthropologists from Cornell University for five years beginning in 1952. In subsequent years, the anthropologists continued as advisors.[3]

The Cultural Setting

Until 1952 Vicos was a hacienda, or large estate located in a small valley in Peru, 250 miles north of Lima, the capital city. The hacienda included about 40,000 acres, with a population of less than 2000 monolingual Quechua-speaking Indians, situated at an altitude ranging from 9000 to 20,000 feet above sea level.

Vicos was a feudal manor with the Indians bound to the land as serfs, or laborers. Title to the property was held by a Public Benefit Society and operated by renters who acquired rights to the use of the land and its resident workers through a public bidding. The renter had the right to exploit the rich bottomlands for commercial purposes, with the local labor force providing, free of charge for several days each week, the means for cultivating the crops which were sold for a profit by the renter. The profits were supposed to be used for constructing hospitals or for other public welfare purposes, but this was not always the case.

The hacienda was organized with a *patrón* (renter), most frequently not living locally, at the top of the hierarchy. He had the ultimate power over the entire system to do much as he pleased with land and person alike. Under the patrón was an administrator, like the patrón usually was also a mestizo (mixed Indian and Spanish) and also probably an absentee manager. He was assisted by several mestizo foremen, who were responsible for the supervision of the cultivation, irrigation, fertilization, and harvesting of crops. Below this non-Indian elite stood the local field supervisors, with a number of *peones*, or workers, under their direction. In 1952 there were 8 field supervisors in Vicos who supervised a labor force of 380 men. The workers, in addition to the free labor required, also provided free services as cooks, servants, herders, and watchmen. People were kept in their respective social positions through force or expropriation of property.

The Indian community was organized tradi-

[3]Material on the Vicos project is summarized from A. R. Holmberg, "The Research and Development Approach to the Study of Change" (*Human Organization*, vol. 17, 1958), pp. 12–16; A. R. Holmberg, "The Changing Values and Institutions of Vicos in the Context of National Development" (*American Behavioral Scientist*, vol. 3, no. 7, March 1965), pp. 3–8; J. Lear, "Reaching the Heart of South America" (*Saturday Review*, Nov. 3, 1962), pp. 55–58; H. F. Dobyns, C. Monge Medrano, and M. C. Vasquez, "A Contagious Experiment" (*Saturday Review*, Nov. 3, 1962), pp. 59–62. This was a famous experiment and it has been reported on extensively elsewhere, but the four citations above contain the major findings and results of the project.

(a)

(b)

Figure 35.1

Agriculture on the Vicos Project. (a) Corn is cultivated with short-handled hoes by Vicos workers. The growing of crops in the Peruvian highlands is labor-intensive. (b) Sheep are pastured on open mountain rangeland. (From Vicos Collection, Cornell University Libraries.)

tionally under a religious hierarchy of seventeen officials known as *varas*, who were responsible for settling local disputes over land and animals, repairing bridges and the church, regulating marriages, celebrating religious ceremonies, and representing the community to outsiders. At the head of this Indian group was the *alcalde*, an official elected for one year.

In 1952 everyone was a subsistence farmer in a poor unproductive system, long depleted of natural resources and with an unmotivated, depressed population. The chief crops were maize, potatoes, wheat, barley, rye, and beans. Most families also raised cattle, sheep, goats, swine, guinea pigs, and chickens to supplement a meager diet (see Figure 35.1). The land had lost its fertility, crops and animals were stunted and diseased, and income was low. The population was demoralized, and 80 percent were infected with parasites and subject to epidemic diseases such as whooping cough and measles. Native curers used magico-religious techniques and herbs to try to stem the tide of disease and misfortune.

Preliminary Tasks

The Carnegie Corporation had funded Lauriston Sharp, a professor of anthropology from Cornell University, to direct a worldwide study of the effects of industrialism on agrarian peoples. The sites chosen for this research were in New Mexico, Canada, India, Thailand, and Peru. Allan Holmberg was selected to direct the Peru project because of his previous experience as an anthropologist in Peru and Bolivia. One of the first persons to join Holmberg's staff was Mario Vasquez, a Peruvian anthropologist who had lived in and studied Vicos for two years prior to the project's commencement.

Originally the Vicos site was selected because a steel mill and a hydroelectric plant were planned in its vicinity. An avalanche forced the abandonment of the technological aspect of the project, but by this time Holmberg had recognized the opportunity for a rare experiment of intervened change on the Vicos hacienda.

Holmberg approached the problem of development from the point of view of a psychoanalyst, trying to portray how such a person would conceptualize the project:

He starts with a patient who desires but is unable to function in the fullest capacity in the world in which he interacts. The fact that he cannot do so may be the fault of the society in which he lives, but if the patient is to make a satisfactory and desirable adjustment to life, he must change his behavior in various ways. The analyst cannot change his behavior for him; the patient must do it for himself. Ideally, what happens is this: through a process of self-enlightenment, with occasional strategic intervention by the analyst, the patient cures himself so that he can face up to his anxieties and shoulder his responsibilities to the best of his native abilities.

It seems to me that the role of the participant interventionist in the process of community development is much the same. His job is to assist the community to develop itself, and to study this process while it is taking place. He cannot 'cure' the community as a surgeon cures a patient; the community must perform the operation on itself.[4]

Before Holmberg could proceed with his plans he had to acquire control of the Vicos hacienda. The hacienda had been in a generally run-down condition and the current lessor was involved in a bankrupt operation, so acquiring the lease was not a major problem. Holmberg succeeded in renting the estate in the name of Cornell University for five years. This was accomplished with the cooperation of the National Institute of Indigenous Affairs, the Ministry of Labor, and other official departments.

Gathering and Analyzing Facts

The first entry into the community coincided with a potato crop failure, with a resultant general community crisis involving starvation, theft of food and animals, and complaints against the traditional system. The major complaint was having to supply free services to the manor. Since Holmberg was now the patrón, he paid volunteers for performing these services and reimbursed laborers for other work performed for previous administrations for which they had not been paid for as long as three years.

Holmberg and his staff had access to previously collected background information for the development problems at Vicos. Mentioned earlier was Holmberg's experience in Peru and Bolivia, and that of Vasquez, who had lived with an Indian family for two years while conducting an extensive study of the Vicos community. In the process Vasquez had gained the respect of the community and made many friends.

Since the emphasis of the Vicos project was more on development than on research, and because the research had been previously accomplished, the gathering of additional data proceeded along with the application phase.

Planning and Making Recommendations

Several months before the assumption of control over Vicos, Holmberg developed a general plan of operations. The principal goals of the plan were to turn the reins of power over to the community, to produce and share economic wealth, to train the Vicos people in new skills, to promote better health, to increase the prestige of local inhabitants, and to promote better education. It was hoped that these changes could be brought about by utilizing traditional values and institutions, but new values would be generated if necessary.[5]

In collaboration with several colleagues Holmberg laid out 130 potential lines of research and development, each related to a specific goal such as the diversification of agriculture, the

[4] J. Lear, op. cit., pp. 55–56.

[5] A. R. Holmberg, "The Changing Values and Institutions of Vicos in the Context of National Development."

development of leadership, the reduction of social distance between mestizo and Indian, and the increase of educational opportunities. Precise statements were made about each goal where possible. The various possibilities thus identified were subject to revision once the research and development strategy unfolded.[6]

Acting and Monitoring

In 1952, when the Cornell team first resided in Vicos they found a demoralized, poorly organized community. Public services were lacking, alliances were restricted to immediate kinship groups, the religious fiesta offered the only relief to frustration and despair, and there existed a great feeling of hostility toward the patron and the old system. In addition, health and nutritional standards were extremely low, educational facilities were poorly developed, cooperation within the community was almost totally lacking, and contacts with the outside world were minimal and based on distrust and suspicion.

Holmberg set to work to improve the situation. He began by retaining the old foreman and allowing him six assistants. The weekly meetings of the Indians, at which they had received instructions for work, were changed from passive to active discussion periods. Personal services for the patrón were abolished. The crops from the patrón's land were declared community property and sold to accumulate cash reserves for the ultimate purchase of the estate for the Indians. A better potato was introduced on the old patrón lands, along with modern planting, fertilizing, spraying, and harvesting methods. The profits from this endeavor were invested in building a new school and health clinic.

Evaluating

A partial indication of the success of the Vicos project can be gained from the evaluation made by Holmberg in 1958 in the following list:

[6]A. R. Holmberg. "The Research and Development Approach to the Study of Change."

(1) Organization

1952. *Vicos had an* hacienda*-type organization. Outside renters not only had free use of* hacienda peones *for labor and personal services, but also of their animals and tools. Power was concentrated in the hands of the* patrón.

1957. Hacienda *system and free services have been abolished; new system of community organization now in march is based on shared interests and local control.*

(2) Land Ownership

1952. *No title to land, although Vicosinos had tried on numerous occasions to purchase the land on which they had been living as* peones *for 400 years.*

1957. *Based on reports of development by the Cornell-Peru Project, the Institute of Indigenous Affairs asked the Peruvian Government to expropriate Vicos in favor of its indigenous population. This expropriation has now taken place.*

(3) Local Authority

1952. *Under the* hacienda*-type organization there were no responsible secular authorities within the community.*

1957. *The Vicosinos have organized a board of their own delegates elected from each of 6 zones of the* hacienda. *They have the legal responsibility for the direction of community affairs.*

(4) Income.

1952. *The indigenous community of Vicos had no source of income of its own.*

1957. *Former* hacienda *lands are now farmed for the public good, providing a steady income for the payment of lands and the development of public service.*

(5) Education.

1952. *In the aspect of education Vicos had a very small school, with one teacher, 10–15 students.*

1957. *Vicos now possesses the most modern school in the whole region, recently made a* nucleo escolar, *with a capacity of 400 students. There are now 9 teachers and about 200 students, many of whom have had five years of continuity in school* [see Figure 35.2].

(6) Production.

1952. *Low economic production—each* hectare *of potato land produced a value of only $100.*

1957. *Each* hectare *of potato land is now producing a value of $400–$600.*

(7) Health Facilities.

FIGURE 35.2
(a) The children of Vicos now learn to read at an early age. (b) Within five years' time, a new school had been built and school attendance was increased fifteen-fold. (From Vicos Collection, Cornell University Libraries.)

1952. *There were no modern health facilities.*
1957. *A modern health center has been built by the Vicosinos and a neighboring community; a clinic is held twice a week and a public health program is underway*[7] [see Figure 35.3].

The obvious success of the Vicos project spread beyond the limits of the local community, but it also met with opposition in some quarters. The most outstanding negative example was the violent resistance to change by some traditionally oriented neighbors. One of these actions involved the use of police force to suppress peasants and resulted in the death of three of them and the serious wounding of five others. One can well imagine that there would also exist opposition from local and national politicians, many of whom were involved in the system which owned and perpetuated the hacienda pattern.

The measurements of success, however, far outweighed those of opposition. One of these was the return of migrants to Vicos with new ideas gained away from home. The Indians living around Vicos reacted favorably, asking for assistance from Vicos when they could not get help from the local or national governments. This included assistance in crop management and, surprisingly, in asking Vicos for loans to purchase their own lands in the same manner as had the people of Vicos. The national community development and education program has been extended to many of the surrounding communities, and the local example set has influenced national indigenous policy in Peru. The added prestige to the once downtrodden Indians has improved their image and relationships with their mestizo neighbors. Newspaper accounts in the country have generally been favorable.

Not the least impact of all has been on the academic and applied anthropological sectors. It

[7]Ibid.

FIGURE 35.3
Vicos men and women work together to produce adobe bricks from local clay and straw and roughhew their own lumber with which they then construct improved housing and community facilities. (From Vicos Collection, Cornell University Libraries.)

is, undoubtedly, the most discussed and emulated project.[8] Many articles, papers, and books have resulted from the Vicos experiment and its influence will continue for a long time.

THE GILA RIVER INDIAN COMMUNITY PROJECT

The project at the Gila River Indian Community was an interdisciplinary study of political organization and business management conducted by the University of Arizona in 1970–1971.[9]

The Cultural Setting

Indians from two linguistic groups inhabit the 372,000 acre reservation in southeastern Arizona. The Pima, Uto-Aztecan speakers, at one time inhabited an area which extended from their present location south to include much of northwestern Mexico. Another smaller group, the Maricopa, a Yuman speaking group originally from the lower Colorado River, came to live with the Pima Indians some two hundred years ago. Together the Pimas and Maricopas number slightly more than 7,000 persons, of whom about 5,000 permanently live on the reservation in seven political districts and fourteen villages or on small farms.

Archaeologists theorize that the Pimas are descendants of the Hohokam people who have lived in the area since about 300 B.C. When Spanish missionaries first contacted the Pimas in 1694 they found peaceful farmers irrigating fields of maize, beans, pumpkins, and cotton. Cotton was woven into fine fabrics. Agriculture, which provided 60 percent of their sustenance, was supplemented by hunting rabbit and deer,

[8]H. F. Dobyns et al, op. cit.

[9]T. Weaver (ed.), *Political Organization and Business Management in the Gila River Indian Community*; T. Weaver, "Social and Economic Change in the Context of Pima-Maricopa History" (*Atti Del XL Congresso Internazionale Degli Americanisti*, vol. 2, 1974), pp. 579–592.

gathering wild desert plants, and fishing from the constantly running Gila River.

The residents were organized politically into a loose confederation of small villages, each composed of ten to twenty patrilineally related families. There may have been a ceremonial leader, but probably no political official.

Spanish influence lasted for about 150 years. Although missionizing efforts were unsuccessful, other Hispanic cultural influences included the introduction of horses, cattle, sheep, metal knives, wooden plows, and wheat. Spanish contact was not disruptive to the Pima way of life.

Interaction with early nineteenth-century frontiersmen from the United States was also amicable at the beginning, and Pima culture continued as a viable entity, often providing surplus food and clothing as trade or gifts. Soon, however, the upstream settlement by non-Indian farmers led to overgrazing, erosion, and loss of water by its diversion and overuse.

Helped along by successive years of drought, the result was a slow erosion of Pima and Maricopa culture. No longer were the tribes able to support themselves. A reservation had been established in 1859, and before the end of the century the Indians were totally dependent on government rations and secondhand clothing doled out by Indian agents and missionaries.

Matters did not improve during the first sixty years of the twentieth century despite numerous governmental programs designed for that purpose. The Allotment Act led only to residential dispersal from villages to small family farms and to land fragmentation and loss, but not to the creation of farmers assimilated to the American way of life as intended by the law. The creation of an irrigation district to include Indians and non-Indians and the construction of an upriver dam only provided more water for non-Indian neighbors. Most able-bodied and better trained people left the reservation temporarily or permanently during these years to work in nearby towns. An Act of 1924 gave Indians the right of citizenship and voting, but it did not diminish the prejudice of the surrounding white communities. Likewise, another law passed in 1934, intended to provide a council form of self-government, was prevented from functioning by a paternalistic government agent until 1951.

The seventy years of dependency and the erosion of a once viable way of life were reflected in vital and social statistics. In 1952, for example, 40 percent of the population was receiving an average welfare assistance income of $490 per year. Conditions did not improve even after 1963, when the tribal council and Gila River community citizens began a grand plan of self-help and rehabilitation. The following social and economic conditions were depicted in a planning grant written in 1968: an average adult education of eight years, an unemployment rate of 32 percent, 27 percent seasonal employment, 80 percent substandard housing with only 20 percent of the homes having water and sewerage and only 60 percent having electricity, an infant mortality rate of 35.9 per 1000 births, a rate of tuberculosis amounting to 5.5 per 1000 persons, 10 to 15 times the national average for diabetes, and a birth rate equal to the most underdeveloped of underdeveloped countries (42 per 1000).

The Problem

The Gila River Indian Community had been trying to stem the tide of poverty since 1963. A second grand plan formulated in 1966 outlined projects designed to solve problems in recreation, education and training, housing, sanitation, community development, industrial development, tribal government, and business management. This plan included fifty-one different projects, including three industrial parks, a marina, cattle feed lots, and factories—all involving complex decisions and actions. For this reason the tribal council had decided it needed assistance in reorganizing its governmental and business management procedures.

The many committees which had been initiated in the past fifteen years, although serving the intended function at first, never seemed to disband. The consequence was the presence of dozens of committees that never met or presented reports. The authority between the tribal council and the chief executive, the tribal Governor, was never clear-cut. The Governor could not dismiss his own staff without approval from the council. Agendas were not prepared ahead of time, and the council did not have access to committee reports before they heard them in the council meeting. Resolutions were passed without anyone realizing that similar or contradictory resolutions had been passed several years before. Business records and resolutions were found in boxes stacked in the reception room which also served as a room for the secretaries. The tribe was paying several hundred dollars each month for checks drawn on insufficient funds, while at the same time an official had uncashed checks in his desk which could have covered the deficiency. Payrolls were late. Minutes of the council meeting were not available for months, if at all. These were but a few of the problems which prompted the tribe to decide it needed a study of its governmental and business procedures.

Preliminary Tasks

The Government Management Committee of the Gila River tribal council invited to a meeting representatives of three relevant University of Arizona research institutes: the Institute of Government Research, the Division of Business and Economic Research, and the Bureau of Ethnic Research. After this initial meeting the invited representatives agreed to present a proposal to include team members from each of the relevant disciplines and to place the project administratively under the Bureau of Ethnic Research.

The proposal was satisfactory to the Government Management Committee. It called for a broad review of business and government procedures in the context of current and planned tribal activities. A timetable and schedule for the completion of each research task and report was presented in the form of a large flow diagram.

The Government Management Committee had authority delegated from the tribal council to negotiate a contract with the invited representatives, and constant contact between the two groups appeared to indicate that all was in order. As it turned out, the tribal council was providing 20 percent of the funding, with the remainder coming from the Model Cities Program, a U.S. Housing and Urban Development Grant, which was under semiautonomous direction. The new Model Cities Program director questioned the value of an anthropological approach to a political organization and business management study, and so the whole project seemed doomed because the contract required his signature. After three hours of intensive discussion the director became convinced and the contract was signed.

Gathering and Analyzing Facts

The day the contract was signed two members of the research team were asked to serve on a Financial Advisory Committee because of the serious financial problems that the tribe faced. Members of the Committee included an anthropologist, an economist, a retired director of one of the largest banks in Arizona, and a financial specialist from the area office of the Bureau of Indian Affairs. All business and finance records were opened to the committee, and within two weeks a series of recommendations were made which helped the tribe solve its immediate problems and created much good will and prestige for the research team.

Each member of the research team was assigned a different task. The project director, an anthropologist, was responsible for research and administrative coordination. The political scientist was responsible for the study of political organization; but because of the nature of the tribal political system, the research required close cooperation and coordination with the work of the anthropologists. One research assistant, a political scientist, studied the tribal constitution and bylaws; another political science graduate student used a public opinion survey to find out about political opinion on the reservation. The political scientist also administered brief structured questionnaires to selected government officials and committee members. The economist reviewed organizational linkages and communication between the tribal government and various tribal business activities, including the Arts and Crafts Center, the industrial parks, the Skills Training Center, the Model Cities Program, and other tribal enterprises such as the tribal farms, a tent manufacturing plant, and a construction company. The economist was assisted by an anthropology graduate student. A fourth co-investigator, an anthropologist, reviewed cultural and historical background material relevant to improving reservation political and economic programs. Four other anthropology graduate students were assigned independent research tasks: decision making and communication in tribal council meetings, committee organization and operation, the tribal court and tribal police, and the relationships of the Bureau of Indian Affairs to the tribe. Finally, four consultants provided assistance, advice, or research in the following areas: tribal laws and constitutions, programs in the Bureau of Indian Affairs, computer programming, and Indian education. Each of the chief researchers and consultants and most of the research assistants had prior experience in applied work and on Indian reservations.

In addition to the two questionnaires mentioned, other research techniques included participant observation which involved attending all tribal council meetings for one year, observing government and industry in operation, interviewing key personnel in tribal government and the Bureau of Indian Affairs, observing committee and community meetings. Also involved were weekly team discussions, and careful review of all tribal records. Information and data were available from the taped weekly staff meetings and from field notes which were typed and distributed to chief co-investigators, and available for staff use in the research office.

Planning and Making Recommendations

Once observations and interviews were typed as field reports, and copies of relevant documents were collected, there was another series of research team meetings in which recommendations were discussed. Consultations were held with experts in economics, business, law and government, and Indian affairs. Discussions were also held again with tribal and Bureau of Indian Affairs officials at this stage. Several guiding principles directed the construction of the recommendations: (1) to present alternate recommendations together with the reasoning which led to them and the potential consequences of each action, (2) to use ordinary language, devoid of theoretical or conceptual terms, so that the recommendations could be understood by ordinary citizens, and (3) to construct recommendations which could be implemented either immediately or later as the tribe acquired the monetary resources and experience necessary.

Acting or Monitoring

Once the collected data had been analyzed and evaluated, and the recommendations were drafted, the next step was to write a preliminary report. This report was presented to members of the tribal council, the Model Cities Program staff, Bureau of Indian Affairs officials, government leaders, and members of the Government Management Committee. The report was presented verbally, together with charts and diagrams, and criticisms were tape-recorded for later review. There were opportunities to present additional oral and written responses over the next two months, and some were received from the superintendent of the Indian agency, the business manager, the tribal judge, the Model Cities director, and some consultants. These comments helped to clarify the final report and recommendations.

Although final action required only the presentation of the report in sufficient copies to the client population, actions taken during the project also involved acting and monitoring. As mentioned earlier, two of the team members served on a Financial Advisory Committee. One duty of this committee was to assist a hiring committee to find a tribal business manager. Consultations were held throughout the duration of the project with the business manager who was hired. The director of the project also served as an advisor on the Government Management Committee and provided assistance in planning for a tribal membership roll. An anthropologist, another team member, advised community members on audiovisual education and communications programs and the tribal museum on the construction of exhibits. All advice and consultation was on a self-help basis, that is, community members were given the information but were encouraged to perform the necessary action themselves.

Evaluating

Feedback on the project report was immediate. The Indians and the Bureau of Indian Affairs liked the report. Many of the recommendations were implemented at once; others had to wait for monetary resources or proper timing. Altogether the report included some eighty-eight recommendations. Some of the first to be implemented were disbanding superfluous committees, placing tribal council members on salary, adopting a standing committee system for the council, and initiating a departmental organization for the executive branch. The business manager had already done much to streamline the bookkeeping and filing systems and had begun changing office procedures by the time the project was completed. Other recommendations implemented within three years after the project was completed included a new council chamber that eliminated the metal desks which although they allowed council members to face the front of the chamber, required persons making reports to talk to the backs of the council members.

This is only a partial list of the changes brought about by the study of government and business procedures on the Gila River Indian Community. Of course, not all changes can be attributed to the efforts of the applied behavioral scientists. The tribe had recognized many of its problems and had initiated the study. The Bureau of Indian Affairs had been helping the Indians to recognize their problems and to do something about them. The new business manager was very successful in training Indians in modern business procedures. The study conducted by the University of Arizona seemed to serve as a catalyst for the ongoing activity and to help the Indians achieve some of the goals for which they had been striving for many years.

The local people, whether administrators or community members, often have insights into the nature of local problems and their solution which can accomplish the ends desired. Highlighting these ideas and suggestions in a formal report by an outside group often lends them the prestige and visibility needed so that they will be followed, whereas they may have been ignored previously. One tribal leader commented in this vein about the content of the report: "There is nothing new in that report. We know about those problems you write about, and some of us know how to solve them. The value of your report is that it pulls it all together in a book that we can keep going back to. The problems and solutions are written there. We only have to wait for the money and time to correct them."

SUMMARY

Applied anthropology uses all the knowledge gained about the processes of change and stability in societies to help introduce changes so that those societies can utilize programs to better their health, economy, or education. The application of anthropology calls upon and tests the major principles and concepts of the field. One of these concepts, cultural relativity, is challenged in certain areas by applied anthropologists, since they maintain that every individual has the right to life, to good health care, to comfort, security, and education.

In introducing change in a society, applied anthropologists are not contradicting the anthropological principle of culture as an adaptive mechanism. Poverty, malnourishment, and poor health in a society are caused by the intervention of some outside agent which upsets the balance between culture and environment. In such an event, the goal of the applied anthropologist is to suggest social or technological adjustments to compensate for the maladjustments which have developed in a society.

The concepts of holism and functionalism are also important to applied anthropologists, since in introducing change they must consider the interrelated parts of the cultural system and the function each part plays in the survival and ongoing efficient operation of the culture as a whole. Changes in one part of a culture usually have effects on other parts of the culture, and the anthropologist must be able to predict, as far as possible, the consequences of intervention.

The steps or phases necessary in projects and programs involving planned changes include (1) preliminary tasks, (2) gathering and analyzing facts, (3) planning and making recommendations, (4) acting or monitoring, and (5) evaluating.

Applied research differs very little from research which has as its goal the solution of a scientific problem. The concepts, theories, and research techniques are the same. Applied anthropologists, however, must negotiate the goals and conditions of work with their client communities, and recommendation for change is the goal of their work.

The potential application of the findings and theories of anthropology has become more apparent recently. Current conditions point to a fuller development of applied anthropology in the future.

SELECTED READINGS

Arensberg, C., and A. H. Niehoff, *Introducing Social Change: A Manual for Americans Overseas* (1964). An anthropologically oriented book for technical assistance specialists, governmental and private, who are undertaking tasks of induced cultural and social change in other countries. Good reading and full of useful leads.

Clifton, J. (ed.), *Applied Anthropology: Readings in the Uses of the Science of Man* (1970). Probably the most representative collection of readings available with items on different aspects of the subject.

Foster, G. M., *Applied Anthropology* (1969). A very good textbook detailing the theoretical background to the field with examples and consequences of the applied anthropologist in the field.

Spicer, E. H. (ed.), *Human Problems in Technological Change* (1952). A casebook of introduced change in various societies involving fifteen case studies reporting successes and failures.

Weaver, T. (ed.), *To See Ourselves: Anthropology and Modern Social Issues* (1973). Readings on the major problems facing the application of anthropology. Topics discussed include the social responsibility of the anthropologist, the third world, racism, poverty, education, violence, the environment and intervention.

36
The Future Society

CHAPTER OUTLINE

LEARNING GOALS

Describe how the nonliterate world has been transformed.

Identify the special qualities of peasant society.

Discuss the changes in peasant society.

Discuss the changes brought about by surbanization.

Using functional prerequisites as a theoretical framework, explain how society may change in the future.

The study of human experience as presented so far has focused on the ways of life which have dominated the scene for several million years. A life centered on small bandlike groups characterized the entire Pleistocene period. It evolved slowly and steadily into ever larger units of social organization with small variations on the common themes of obtaining a living, distributing goods, adapting to the surrounding environment, and giving symbolic expression to all these factors in language, art, myth, and ritual.

Then came the domestication of plants and animals followed by civilization. Civilization means "the culture of cities," the urban way of life. Like tribal culture before it, civilization manifests a number of variations in subsistence, kinship, government, and world view. Perhaps the most radical changes it produced, however, were a quantum leap in the usable energy made possible by the domestication of plants and animals; the addition of writing, monumental architecture, and public buildings to art, myth, and religion as forms of symbolic expression; the decline of the kinship group in social importance; and the increasing dominance of controlling elites over the economic and political orders.

Anthropologists have been much concerned with what has happened to humanity in the transformation from nonliterate to civilized life. Civilization has been the great triumph of human achievement during the past six millennia. Now it is giving way to a new level of culture. The task for anthropology is not only to complete the story of the prehistoric past and to reveal the nature of all known and knowable social systems, but also to clarify the transformations that so confuse our times and to help build a decent and rational lifeway for the future.

THE TRANSFORMATION OF THE NONLITERATE WORLD

The process of revolutionary culture change that is now overtaking civilization has occurred repeatedly in the world of nonliterate peoples as civilization overtook them. It involves accepting technological innovations, followed by far-reaching changes in ideology and social structure. The effects are manifest in a crises in the "moral order."[1]

The Moral Order

The moral order is what generates the sense of social commitment in a people—the emotional sense of being a significant part of a community of human beings to whom one has obligations and duties and from whom one receives support, emotionally and socially. *The moral order consists of shared understandings about individual and collective goals.* It is manifest as patterns of kinship, neighborhood, club, and work groups, and of recreational, artistic, religious, and community roles performed with an accompanying sentiment of "rightness" and gratification.

The cultures of most nonliterate societies have been governed through the values and sentiments implicit in their moral order. Few nonliterate individuals have doubted the validity of the social systems which sustain them from their early period of enculturation until death.

Redfield characterized nonliterate societies as possessing certain general characteristics: (1) the community is usually small; (2) kinship relations and close, personal bonds extend throughout the community; (3) economic and social interests are homogeneous, and there are few specialists; (4) attitudes and behavior are dominated by religious-mystical assumptions about the nature of humanity and the outer world; and (5) suspicion of outsiders (nonrelatives) commonly leads to a chronic state of warfare with some other groups.

As we know full well by now, the expression, or cultural form, of these traits varies among nonliterate groups, but as general characteristics,

[1]R. Redfield, *The Primitive World and Its Transformations*, pp. 20–25.

they describe behavior in all small, nonliterate societies held together by the moral bond.

The Technical Order

A complement to the moral order within cultures is what Redfield called the *technical order:*

The bonds that co-ordinate the activities of men in the technical order do not rest on convictions as to the good life; they are not characterized by a foundation in human sentiments; they can exist even without the knowledge of those bound together that they are bound together. The technical order . . . results from mutual usefulness, from deliberate coercion, or from the mere utilization of the same means. In the technical order men are bound by things, or are themselves things.[2]

A city is rarely, if ever, the product of a local population that has simply increased without outside input or influence. As far back as the time of Çatal Hüyük, trade was the lifeblood of the city, although it relied, too, on the food products of the immediately surrounding country. All cities incorporate strangers, and in the initial phases of a city's life, the separate little moral orders, according to which the strangers have previously been organized in tribal lifeways, dissolve. New urban civilizations are held together mainly by reliance on the technical order. Regulations, prescripts, and edicts set the formal patterns to be observed. Magisterial and priestly exactments drive or exhort men to obey. Religious spectaculars and civil celebrations are designed by the priests and rulers to substitute as symbolic integrators for the old tribal rituals. Soldiers, jailers, and executioners coerce the recalcitrants into behavior which they feel insufficiently committed to adopt.

Civilization, the city way of life, is always marked by a new kind of social bonding. At the outset, the moral order of each urban culture is *managed* in contrast to the *self-maintaining* moral order of nonliterate societies. For the great civilizations of the past, such orders sufficed for long periods of time. Eventually, they declined in effectiveness as disintegrating forces dissolved their influence.

Anomie and Civilization

Anomie occurs when drastic change causes moral orders to lose their bonding and motivating effect, or when segments of the population are left behind—alienated because no satisfying place exists for them in the changing social structure. The resulting anomie is marked by

. . . the retreat of the individual into his own ego, the skeptical rejection of all social bonds. . . . It signifies the state of mind of one who has been pulled up from his moral roots, who no longer has any standards but only disconnected urges, who no longer has any sense of continuity, of folk, of obligations.[3]

Anomie is the disease of the disintegrating or reconstituting civilization—or of the shattered nonliterate society. Apathy and demoralization characterize many American Indian populations that have not become extinct or been absorbed into the civilization that has engulfed them. A contemporary journalist's description of anomie embraces much of Western society:

The sense of belonging, of place, of a shared heritage of memories, has disappeared in an anonymous urban sprawl, and each of us forages orphan-like in alien streets where all the dreams have died, armed with plastic credit cards that vainly protest our identity.[4]

A major task of applied anthropology is to assist national planners and international development agencies in finding ways to promote modernization without causing the paralyzing disruption of ongoing moral orders before new and effective orders can replace them. This requires, in the first place, a genuine understand-

[2]Ibid., p. 21.

[3]R. I. MacIver, *The Ramparts We Guard*, p. 77.

[4]S. Hempstone, "Leaving Grandpa to Die by a Dry Waterhole" (*Minneapolis Tribune*, Dec. 5, 1971), p. 37A.

ing of the moral orders by which people who are to be "modernized" now live. Even in city slums, the anthropological approach provides the understanding, in ways that otherwise seem to be overlooked. The work of Oscar Lewis in Mexico City, San Juan, Puerto Rico, and New York City is the prototype of what the new anthropology can offer to this end.

In Lewis's words:

We know a great deal about the statistics and economics of poverty, but we are only beginning to understand the psychology and inner life of some of the very poor. In the case of the Puerto Ricans, many of whom have come from rural areas or urban slums, the obstacles to understanding are even greater because of the barrier of language and the differences between cultures. And while Puerto Ricans have been one of the most surveyed and studied groups, most of the studies have been of a questionnaire type and have told us too little about the intimate details of their lives and the conditions which have formed their character.[5]

PEASANT SOCIETY

Before we look to the next stage of cultural evolution, an overview of the place of peasant society in the scheme of things is in order.

Peasant societies are the communities of the nonliterate world transformed into a special and long-enduring type of little community within the structure of civilizations.

[A] peasant society *may be defined as a subsociety of a large stratified society which is either preindustrial or only partly industrialized. It is further characterized by most or all of the following traits: rural residence; familial agriculture on self-owned small land holdings or other simple rural occupations providing a modest or subsistence livelihood; the family as the centrally important social unit; low social status; economic interdependence in varying degree with urban centers; simple culture; and attachment to the soil, the local community and tradition.*[6]

The peasant community is like the nonliterate society in certain aspects of the quality of its moral order; it differs in its lack of autonomy and independence and in other respects mentioned below. It is part of a larger social system in which it is related to and dominated by the cities of the civilization of which it is a part. "It required the city to bring it into existence. There were no peasants before the first cities. And those surviving primitive peoples who do not live in terms of the city are not peasants."[7]

Historically, the original peasants were Neolithic agriculturalists who did not migrate to the cities and who retained a subcultural identity of their own. They lived in marginal and partial isolation upon the land they tilled. Their food and craft surpluses were taken through taxation, or traded or bartered in open markets located in the towns and cities, and fed into the exchange and consumption systems of the local states and empires of which they were part. Usually illiterate, they could not master the arts and learning essential to knowing the mysteries of civilized life. Or, as individuals, they entered at first into the lower bureaucracy of the state and church systems, cutting off their peasant ties. Or they disappeared in time into the urban proletariat. Cities have always replenished themselves and nourished their own growth with migrants from nonliterate and peasant populations. The reservoir of peasants has been vast, for it "has constituted the most numerous social group in all organized states, from ancient to modern times."[8]

During the eighteenth and nineteenth centuries, extinction was the fate of many nonliterate

[5]O. Lewis, "Mother and Son in a Puerto Rican Slum; Part 1: Felicita" (*Harper's Magazine*, December 1965), p. 72.

[6]E. Norbeck, "Peasant Society," in J. Gould and W. L. Kolb (eds.), *A Dictionary of the Social Sciences*, p. 490.

[7]Redfield, op. cit., p. 31.

[8]D. Thorner, "Peasantry" (*International Encylcopedia of the Social Sciences*, vol. 11, 1968), p. 504.

communities. In the twentieth and twenty-first centuries, except in the case of such marginal peoples as the African Bushmen, incorporation, rather than extinction, will undoubtedly be achieved by most such groups. As populations, either they will be pulled into the industrial–urban complex, or they may retain a measure of group identity for a while through a transformation into a peasant existence.

Qualities of Peasant Culture

The peasant has an integrity and a clear sense of identity, but is usually backward, unsophisticated, and underprivileged relative to the city dweller—and knows it. The peasant may resent this lowly and powerless position but has rarely revolted. Peasants must pay tribute or taxes to landlords, intermediaries, and the state; they go to market and touch the life of the city, but they are not in it.

The home village is the peasant's base of security; yet it is not a whole society, because of the presence of the city. The peasant community has its own cycle of folk rituals and festivals, usually marking the high points of the annual cycle of crops and movements of the sun. Folk beliefs are thinly watered versions of the great religions which characterize each major civilization. The peasants' folk ceremonies may be colorful and boisterous enough, but they rarely seem to exhibit the rich symbolic tapestry of many of the great rituals of nonliterate (tribal) peoples. For the peasant, world view expresses a limited segment of culture and society—and therefore a limited conception of the universe.

The Image of the Limited Good In a limited and constricted corner of the great world upon which experience impinges but rarely penetrates, the peasant adjusts to a marginal status with an "image of the limited good," as George M. Foster has labeled it.[9] The peasant sees not an expandable universe but a fixed and immutably limited, closely bounded source of many available resources. It is a "zero-sum" situation in which it is believed that if one gets more, another must get less. As expressed by Foster:

> [*B*]*road areas of peasant behavior are patterned in such a fashion as to suggest that peasants view their social, economic, and natural universes—their total environment—as one in which all of the desired things in life such as land, wealth, health, friendship and love, manliness and honor, respect and status, power and influence, security and safety,* exist in finite quantity *and* are always in short supply, *as far as the peasant is concerned* . . . [*I*]n addition there is no way directly within peasant power to increase the available quantities.[10]

The result, according to the reports of many anthropological field workers, is that peasants struggle desperately for survival with sweat, hard work, and resignation. A stroke of good luck may bring a windfall to a villager, but in the tight little village community this commonly brings with it "envy, gossip, criticism, and calumny."[11] Such cutting down of the fellow villager is a functionally effective way of choking off competition for closely limited goods and minimizes the possibilities of disruption of the conservative, face-to-face social order.

Kinship Structure An interesting feature of peasant social structure is that although peasant societies are strongly male-centered, they do not develop patrilineages or patriclans. The most common residential unit of peasant societies is the patrilineal joint family. Of forty-six peasant societies analyzed by Goldschmidt and Kunkel, ten have virilocal "stem" families and eighteen are organized around virilocal joint families. In

[9] G. M. Foster, "Peasant Society and the Image of the Limited Good" (*American Anthropologist*, vol. 67, 1965), pp. 293–315.

[10] Ibid., p. 304; also see G. M. Foster, "A Second Look at Limited Good" (*Anthropological Quarterly*, vol. 45, 1972), pp. 57–64.

[11] G. M. Foster, "Peasant Character and Personality," in J. M. Potter, M. N. Diaz, and G. M. Foster (eds.), *Peasant Society: A Reader*, p. 297.

the stem families, one son continues to reside in his parents' household after marriage. Others move out when they marry. The stay-at-home son inherits the family farm as a unit, since the estate is indivisible.

In peasant societies which are built around virilocal joint families, all (or most) sons stay on in the homestead when they marry, working the land jointly for a time but eventually each taking his separate share of the land. The estate in these instances is partible (divisible).

The stem family and indivisible estate exist where land is scarce, while the joint family and divisible estate occur where new farmland is, or has recently been, available.

In thirteen of the forty-six peasant societies studied, newly married couples establish independent households of their own with neolocal residence, and all sons and daughters inherit equally from their parents.

Finally, "peasant societies never show a preference for matrilineal land inheritance, and none consistently forms joint households on the basis of matrilocal residence."[12]

One may ask: "Why the male-centeredness of peasant society? And why have lineage and clan, which are so important to nonliterate social systems, disappeared so completely in the peasant complex?" The answers seem to lie in the facts that peasant subsistence is agricultural, not horticultural (and agriculture is a predominantly male activity); that war is no longer an activity for kinship groups among peasants (it is the prerogative of the national state); that hunting lands are not open to exploitation by peasants; and that major legal crises with respect to land and homicide must be settled within the legal framework of the larger civilization in which the peasant segment is embedded.

The Passing of Peasant Society

The advent of industrialization first sounded the death knell of the peasant way of life. The swelling factories of Europe and North America in the nineteenth and twentieth centuries were urban generators of a new form of life into which millions of European peasants were fed. The same flight to the cities is occurring all around the world as industrial development takes root in South America, Asia, and Africa, while simultaneously peasant society dissolves. For:

> *In the modern world peasant societies are anachronisms, and it is inevitable that they disappear. Peasants themselves have demonstrated time and time again that they prefer a different, and what they believe to be a better life. Poverty, illiteracy, oppression, disease and early death, and a backbreaking life of sweating over a piece of land, have little nostalgic value to peasants, a great many of whom will take every reasonable opportunity to escape to the new life of the city. Modern technology as well as human desires have conspired to hasten the end of traditional peasantry.*[13]

Peasant societies are the little communities of the world transformed into culturally marginal units of civilizations. They occupy a developmental position between nonliterate society and industrial urban society.

But urban society itself is now in the process of a great transformation. For today we are witnessing not only the passing of the nonliterate world and the demise of peasant society, but also the transformation of civilization itself.

THE ATOMIC SPACE AGE AND SURBANIZATION

Professor Leslie White has emphasized the close correlation between technology, the amount of controlled energy at the disposal of a society,

[12] W. Goldschmidt and E. J. Kunkel, "The Structure of the Peasant Family" (*American Anthropologist*, vol. 73, 1971), p. 1061.

[13] J. M. Potter, "Peasants in the Modern World," in Potter, Diaz, and Foster (eds.), op. cit., p. 378. (Quoted with permission of Little, Brown and Company.)

and the evolutionary development of the nontechnological aspects of culture.[14]

Energy and Culture

The difference between the simple hunting society at the beginning of human social evolution and the vastly complex technological society of the twentieth century is a good deal more than the difference between a population of 100 persons and one of over 200 million for the United States or over 700 million for China.

We have already touched on the qualitative differences in the moral and technical orders which characterize the two extremes in size and social structure. But underlying it all is the great difference in the amounts of energy utilized.

At the Stone Age end of the continuum the daily average energy output of a healthy person is estimated to have equaled approximately 50 pounds lifted 1 foot in 1 second, or roughly 1/600 horsepower-hour. Taking into account infants, the sick, and aged or feeble adults who could do little or no work, the daily amount of energy available in the earliest societies was approximately 1/1200 horsepower-hour per person. As long as human beings were restricted to such a level, the development of culture was limited.

The first great revolution was the domestication of plants and animals. Domestication of plants increased the control over solar energy, which is stored in plants. Domestication of animals allowed for the exploitation of animal energy. More efficient tools reduced energy waste and made possible new applications of energy. All culture expanded rapidly; the mode of life changed from hunting to gardening and pastoralism.

The Bronze and Iron Ages are but extensions of the Neolithic Age, which fulfilled its potential in the urban revolution. Metal was substituted for stone. Increased efficiency of tools, leading to stepped-up productiveness in handicraft industries and gardening, gradually expanded the cultures of the Old World.

The next cultural revolution awaited the harnessing of steam, the invention of the internal combustion engine, and the artificial production of electricity. With the industrial revolution, feudalism gave way to modern capitalism.

To sense the significance of the energy increase brought about by the industrial revolution, consider that the total horsepower capacity of all prime movers (work animals, automobiles, factories, mines, railroads, ships, aircraft, windmills, electric power generators, and farms exclusive of work animals) in the United States was 8495 in 1850. At the beginning of the second half of the twentieth century (in 1955), it was 7,143,723.[15] Yet in 1955, the horsepower capacity of animals in use had dropped for the first time to a level below that of 1850.

In 1965, the actual electrical energy output and consumption of the United States was 1.5 billion horsepower-hours.[16] This is nearly 10 billion times the total from all sources which is estimated for the typical Stone Age society—and the figure does not include automotive energy or fossil fuel energy used in steam and internal combustion engines in factories, ships, or airplanes.

Thermonuclear Energy

In 1945, the most stupendous energy conquest of all time was accomplished. Einstein's theory of the equivalence of mass and energy ($E = mc^2$) indicates that 1 kilogram (2.2 pounds) of matter, if it could be converted entirely into energy, would release 25 billion kilowatt-hours of energy, or approximately 33 billion horsepower-hours. Splitting the uranium atom in 1945 converted 0.1 of 1 percent of the uranium mass into energy, thereby demonstrating Einstein's the-

[14] L. A. White, "Energy and the Evolution of Culture" (*American Anthropologist*, vol. 45, 1943), pp. 335–356. See also W. F. Cottrell, *Energy and Society*.

[15] U. S. Bureau of the Census, *Historical Statistics of the United States, Colonial Terms to 1957*, p. 506.

[16] *Britannica Book of the Year: 1968*, p. 364.

ory.[17] This was but the beginning, for not only have the techniques for splitting the atom been improved, but also we have learned how to release energy through fusion of the hydrogen atom.

By 1971 the efficiency of energy conversion by fission had been increased tenfold. In November 1971, the U.S. Atomic Energy Commission tested a nuclear warhead deep in an underground shaft in Amchitka Island in the Aleutian Island chain off the coast of Alaska. It was described as a 5-megaton bomb, meaning that it had an explosive power equal to that of 5000 tons of TNT. But what does this mean in terms of energy conversion? One way to illustrate the meaning is this: *that* single instantaneous conversion released 10^{10} (10 billion) horsepower-hours of energy, or nearly 500 million times as much as an entire Paleolithic society could put to work in one day. Nuclear bombs capable of releasing 2000 × 10 billion horsepower-hours of energy stood ready for war use by Russia and the United States at the beginning of 1972.

In 1957, there were no atomic-powered electric plants at work in the United States. In 1970, thermonuclear electricity was just becoming a significant factor in the productive energy output, but still accounted for less than 1 percent of the total productive energy used in the United States. What fabulous amounts of energy will be harnessed for human use in the future is only beginning to be realized.

Yet one may ask, "How, in the face of the current energy crisis, can anyone talk about a new cultural revolution arising from an expanding energy base?" It is true that the world is exhausting its supplies of fossil (coal, oil, and gas) fuels at a rapid rate. It is true that we shall all be in a tight energy bind for several decades to come. Although in the late 1970s environmental concerns slowed down the development of nuclear energy generating systems, there can be no serious doubt that the United States will be forced to turn to increased nuclear energy production, with all its attendant risks. However, the earth's potential supply of uranium is, like coal and oil, limited. Long-range use of nuclear power depends on the development of new means of fusion of hydrogen atoms—particularly from seawater, which is an all but inexhaustible resource. This feat is now recognized as theoretically feasible and perhaps technically achievable by the year 2000.

Solar energy conversion also holds great, and less risky, potential. It will not be through the use of mirror collectors placed on the earth, except in a minor way, however. The solar energy collectors may be carried by satellites orbiting in the natural vacuum just outside the earth's atmospheric layer. The converted solar energy could be beamed as microwaves (although other possibilities exist) to power stations on the earth. Distribution of power will occur through grids of superefficient microfiber glass conductors, which were developed in the mid-1970s.

Of course, if these and other alternative possibilities fail, or if all-out atomic warfare takes place, then there will be neither civilization nor the realization of the cultural revolution which is opening before us.[18]

However, let us assume that technical success and world stability are both achieved. What then?

Surbanization

By the end of this century, it is possible that we will have witnessed the passing of the last nonliterate society, the disappearance of most peasant societies, and the dissolution of cities into residual nuclei within vast settlement sprawls covering hundreds of square miles (Figure 36.1). The Atlantic seaboard of the United States has already become one continuous residential, factory, and commercial complex from Virginia to

[17]H. D. Smyth, *Atomic Energy for Military Purposes*, pp. 2 and 224.

[18]A somewhat speculative view of the possibility of diversifying future world energy sources has been explored in A. Lovins, "Energy Strategy: The Road Not Taken?" (*Foreign Affairs*, October 1976).

FIGURE 36.1
Surbanization. Continuous settlement sprawl marks the pattern of the near future. (Wide World Photos.)

Maine. From eastern Wisconsin, across southern Michigan and northern Ohio, and into western Pennsylvania, more than a quarter of what was farmland in 1900 has already been converted into "urban" land. The same process is well-advanced in England and other countries. Indeed, the great planner Constantinos Doxiadis finds it impossible to form any idea of the sizes of cities of the future, because "all cities will be interconnected in major urban complexes where no distinction between large and small will be possible; they will all have become one"[19] (Figure 36.2).

Kenneth Boulding was one of the first writers to coin a new term for the social system ahead, offering "post-civilization" as the appellation of the future.[20] Sociologist Daniel Bell suggested "post-industrial,"[21] while Doxiadis refers to the huge urban complex of tomorrow as "ecumenopolis."[22] Toffler's choice is "super-industrial," a term "intended to mean a complex, fast-paced society dependent upon extremely advanced technology and a post-materialist value system."[23]

Toffler comments, "There is, as yet, no widely accepted or wholly satisfactory term to describe the new stage of social development toward which we seem to be racing."[24] It is interesting to note, however, the frequency of the prefixes "post-," "beyond-," and "super-" in the various tentative labels. Interesting, also, is the common agreement that "civilization" (with its implication of "cities" surrounded by settled

[19]C. A. Doxiadis, "Ecumenopolis: Tomorrow's City," in *Britannica Book of the Year: 1968,* p. 26.
[20]K. E. Boulding, "The Death of the City: A Frightened Look at Post-Civilization" (1961, mimeographed); also, *The Meaning of the 20th Century: The Great Transition.*
[21]D. Bell (ed.), *Toward the Year 2000.*

[22]C. A. Doxiadis, op. cit.
[23]A. Toffler, *Future Shock*, p. 491. See his discussion, pp. 490–491, of other terminology to describe the social system of the future.
[24]Ibid., p. 490.

Figure 36.2
Surbanization. Superhighways provide mobile arteries through the industrial and settlement sprawl.

communities, whether "suburban" or "rural," and "wilderness") will no longer be a satisfactory rubric. The sheer mass and concentration of people in the noncity, noncountry, nonanything-ever-before-known, plus the immediacy of the electronic-connectedness of all populations, makes the era ahead different not only in quantity, but in kind. Our term to describe the new social setting of mankind is *surbanization.* "Post-civilization," "post-industrial," "super-industrial," etc., attempt to define the future in terms of the admittedly outmoded past. The social setting that is to come (and that is already well on its way) must be recognized as that which has evolved *above and beyond the cities.* Why not, then, call it *surbanization,"* a convenient contraction of "sur-urbanization," and meaning "above and beyond the culture of cities?"[25]

The Transformation of Society

Surbanization, the society of the future, is not yet a historical fact. Nonetheless, without even suggesting that *futurology* is a discipline, to say nothing of its being an empirical science, let us read the outlines of future society insofar as past experience and current trends tell us what we may expect.

How long will it take to work the great transformation? How long before surbanization will be a reality? Whether it will be achieved in 100 or 500 years, no one can predict. A Third World War, with hydrogen bombs directed from outer space, could initiate a new Dark Age of retrogression around the globe from which recovery could take several centuries. Even without global war, there is serious danger that if the values and societal structures of civilization progressively lose their hold, more and more human beings may lapse into apathy or rage in violent social destructiveness. If human beings lapse into apathy, the human energy to carry on the transformation will be lacking. If rage takes hold, the problem will be to survive in a world of anarchy.

However it goes, the immediate future is bound to be beset with dissension, uncertainty, and swirling tides of controversy and disorder as new life-styles vie for acceptance. The scientific postulates which engendered the Atomic Space Age are not compatible with many of the assumptions of traditional world views. Religion, government, and science will be under continuous pressure to redefine, reformulate, and reshape new and viable postulates, values, and institutions. One can not expect such a gigantic task to be easily or smoothly accomplished. Yet if several million years of human endeavor mean anything, we are probably safe in prophesying that most human populations will retain their integrity and maintain an adaptive stance. Realistic innovators and enough creators of culture will continue to work to achieve the breakthrough into the next order of human experience.

In the future, as in the past, human beings will require a social system. Early in this book (page 293) six functional prerequisites for societal survival were introduced into our discussion. Let us restate them here and see how they relate to future adaptive possibilities. Each society must (1) maintain the biologic functioning of the group members; (2) reproduce new members; (3) socialize new members into functioning adults; (4) produce and distribute goods and services necessary to life; (5) maintain order within the group, and between the group and outsiders; and (6) define the "meaning of life" and maintain the motivation to survive and engage in the activities necessary for survival.

Maintenance of Biological Functioning Despite the great scientific advances of recent times, this will be a more complex problem than ever before. While technology has made possible humanity's adaptation to an

[25] "Sur-urbanization" was first proposed in the third edition of this book, but the word proved to be phonetically too clumsy.

ever-widening range of habitats, it has also brought grave problems of pollution and population growth beyond that which can be fed even by advanced scientific agricultural and food production techniques. The population explosion of the twentieth century could have serious carry-over effects for a long time to come. The year 2000 will see 6 billion people crowding the earth, and demographers do not expect to see the total stabilize there. They project a probable maximum global population of 20 billion and a possible saturation of the earth's surface with 50 billion people. How well such numbers may be fed remains a dubious question. Certainly they are not likely to be meat eaters, for animal raising will probably be too inefficient a method of energy conversion. Fish, synthetic foodstuffs, and distilled seawater will be the primary human-energy-producing inputs.

Another significant threat to the biological functioning of future groups is pollution. Each development that seems to make better or more pleasant our relationship with the environment also apparently changes the environment, thus presenting new problems to solve and new restrictions on old, often habitual and preferred forms of behavior. It appears that given the pressure of incremental world population growth, the earth does not have the capacity to absorb unlimited amounts of waste. Solutions to problems of pollution require the analysis not only of technological changes but also of the basic sociocultural motivations and needs for these developments so that the social value of innovations can be weighed against their environmental costs before they are widely adopted.

The future of the biological functioning of humanity is not all dim though, especially in the area of health. Health, a basic concern of all peoples, will no longer be a source of serious worry. Debilitating and death-producing diseases as we now know them will have been conquered, as have polio, tuberculosis, smallpox, and others in the present era. Hereditary defects in biological constitution will have been wholly eradicated through genetic engineering. Prenatal diagnosis of such serious genetic defects as may occur will almost certainly lead to selective abortion. Far more likely will be the restructuring of the genetic codes of individual gametes to tailor living human beings for healthy functioning in the kinds of environments—physical and social—which will then exist. With tissue and organ transplants, it is predicted that life expectancy will rise to 100 or more years and that adults will look and feel young and vital for most of that long lifespan. The age curve will be changed from a predominance of young to a predominance of old people.

Reproduction of New Members This, we may be sure, will be the least serious of all the societal maintenance problems for the future. In the first place, when once the global population has been stabilized, the need for reproductive replacements will be minimal. A newborn replacement for each living person will be needed only at the rate of one a century or thereabouts. Babies will be relatively rare; children and young people will be minorities.

Sexual activity will be wholly obsolete—imagine that! Will it be retained for erotic amusement and as an antidote to boredom? This much is certain, the actual sexual relation of male and female will be biologically unnecessary.

Bisexual reproduction, wholly or partly accomplished in population-replenishment laboratories—with or without a female host—could well continue for purposes of experimental development of new variations of human types designed for new functions (such as life in space) or for specific characteristics (reduced sexuality, increased range of visual or auditory acuity) or for particular social niches (managerial, artistic, physical sports, or drone). But if the reproduction of new individuals directly from single body cells is accomplished, as biologists soberly predict, then previously existing individuals could be reproduced over and over in genetically exact replications. Cloning would take care of most of the reproductive needs. Would functional "specialist populations," differing from others in intelligence, physical skills, and emotional affect, be produced according to plan? Who is to decide who gets to be reproduced, when, in what type, in what numbers, for what purposes? This could be the major issue in political contests in the future.

Socialization of New Members With the population replacement input at a low level, infant care and child training will be easily handled. Even though socialization will continue to be extremely important, it will be a relatively simple task which will take but a small part of the time of grownups. The specific techniques which may be utilized cannot be foreseen, but they may be akin to the operant psychology advocated by B. F. Skinner.[26]

The tantalizing question is: "What will happen to the family and kinship?" As anthropological evidence has so overwhelmingly demonstrated, the family has been the seedbed of socialization in all previous cultures (except Nayar). The extended kinship group has been the supportive socializer of the young, the vehicle of physical and economic security, and the means of inheritance of property and the transmission of statuses. Through marriage and the family, sex has been regulated to establish jural parents who are socially responsible for the nurture and enculturation of the young. The family has provided for the division of labor by sex.

The signs are now clear that the family is atrophying. Hair and clothing styles, women's liberation, equality in jobs and pay, plus the growing social acceptance of homosexuality, all point to the shrinking significance of the conjugal base of family structure. A continuing spread of governmental underwriting of economic needs (aid to dependent children, free and universal education, guaranteed basic income, Medicare, and old-age security) with little private wealth left over for inheritance presages the disappearance of the economic functions of family and kinship. As for legal protection, kinship has long since been stripped of this important function.

But what of the intimacy and emotional support of close personal ties? Is interpersonal dependency a universal human requirement that will persist into the next stage of human living? Surely it is at the present time. The countercultural experiments of the 1960s and 1970s all prove it. Communes extoll love and sharing, calling themselves "families"; they speak the kinship ideology without the fact of kinship. Yet they may well be one variant of the residential groups of the future. Group life in innumerable variations will abound. Clubs, associations, and other interest groups, including a revival of ethnocentric movements, will be the antidote to individual separateness, providing rich variety to the social fabric in co-residential "cells" of fictive brotherhood and enduring comradeship.

Production of Goods and Services Subsistence needs will be no less important in the future than they have been in the past. Whether food production can be expanded to meet the survival needs of expanding populations is a moot issue. Whether the balance between world population and world subsistence resources is achieved at a level which provides enriched living for all or marginal subsistence for most will depend on the degree of success in population control and management.

The need for a greatly expanded production of food is not the only significant problem of overpopulation. The 1974 World Food Conference in Rome held that the *distribution* of food from "have" to "have not" nations may be an even more difficult problem. Here the knowledge of social scientists, in the past not often sought by politicians, will be needed to assist in making the social structural and ideological changes necessary to establish a balance in the access to food around the world. The "have" countries, beginning to feel population pressures

[26] B. F. Skinner, *Beyond Freedom and Dignity.*

themselves and having already expended much of their former food reserves, are understandably reluctant to commit their food production to the "have-nots" when their own futures are uncertain. The complexities of international and national economies and problems of supply and demand force politicians and business people to make decisions about food distribution not only on the basis of need or the market but also with a consideration of how such transfers will affect the national economic situation.

It is not unreasonable to expect that the great free market economies of the world today will be displaced by managed systems of rationed distribution according to controlled allocation plans.

Power-generating, construction, communication, transportation, entertainment, health, and other personal service activities may be the central productive concerns of surbanization. Of these, only construction (for there may be much building and rebuilding), entertainment, health, and personal services may give occupation to many people.

One thing is clear: very few workers will be engaged in basic food production. In precivilized societies, all able-bodied adults were engaged in food production. In early civilizations, probably not more than 10, or at most 20, percent of a population could be freed from food production to serve as administrators, artisans, and soldiers. In the United States today, not more than 10 percent of the population is directly engaged in agriculture. At the end of this century, it will be 3 percent or less. In surbanization the family farm will be only a historical memory, and farming will be a large-scale industry. Most food production, however, will be synthetic.

Certainly not the least challenge to future society is the problem of the rapidly disappearing supplies of nonrenewable resources. The energy specialists seem most concerned about the scarcity of oil, which is basic not only to the generation of electricity and heat, and to fuel motor vehicles, but also to the production of plastics, some fertilizers, and other products. The oil supply crisis has suddenly made many small and politically weak nations of the world (especially in the Near East) political giants, as they control significant deposits of oil, one of the life-giving fluids desperately needed by industrialized nations. To maintain life, future peoples will require the discovery of more efficient ways to use present resources and the development of wholly new energy sources.

The production of food for the world, its allocation and distribution, the useful employment of people, and the allocation of power and recreational time may be reflected in the development of corresponding basic personality types. In the view of G. S. Stent:

The will to power will not have vanished entirely, but the distribution of its intensity . . . will have been drastically altered. At one end of this distribution will be a minority of the people whose work will keep intact the technology that sustains the multitude at a high standard of living. In the middle of the distribution will be found a type, largely unemployed, for whom the distinction between the real and the illusory will still be meaningful and whose prototype is the beatnik. He will retain an interest in the world and seek satisfaction from sensual pleasures. At the other end of the spectrum will be a type largely unemployable for whom the boundary of the real and the imagined will have been largely dissolved, at least to the extent compatible with his physical survival. His prototype is the hippie. His interest in the world will be rather small, and he will derive his satisfaction mainly from drugs or, once this has become technologically practicable, from direct electrical inputs into his nervous system. This spectral distribution, it will be noted, bears some considerable resemblance to the Alphas, Betas, and Gammas in Aldous Huxley's Brave New World.[27]

Stent's view of the nonproducing, sensate, consuming majority in the image of the hippie must not be narrowly construed. What he means to say is that the bulk of humanity in surbanization will be consumers with lots of time and little

[27] G. S. Stent, *The Coming of the Golden Age*, pp. 137–138.

work. And what will they do for fun, for satisfaction, for fulfillment?

Maintenance of Order Law, as we have found, has been a nearly universal feature of human societies. Will it so continue in the new social order of surbanization? Presumably. The functions of law in society, as they were stated on page 490, are:

1. The definition of obligatory relationships between the members of a society, so as to assert which activities are permitted and which are ruled out and to maintain at least minimal integration between the activities of individuals and groups within the society.
2. The allocation of authority and the designation of the person who has the socially recognized privilege-right to initiate and enforce legitimate corrective sanctions when substantive norms are violated.
3. The disposition of trouble cases as they arise; that is, to clean up social messes (tangled claims, squabbles and fights, killings and woundings) so that people may continue everyday living with reasonable certainty and security.
4. The continuing redefinition of relations between individuals and groups as the conditions of life change, to maintain adaptability and flexibility in the law in response to shifting values and new technologies.

Crowding and the heterogeneity of humanity will require insistence on standard and predictable behavior in crucial areas of public interaction. A great increase in the intensity and scope of communications will increase the frequency of personal and intergroup contacts. They will require increased regulation.

The instruments of power and social control will be so sophisticated in their effects that the allocation of legitimate power (the second function of law) will be of critical importance. Will this be determined through mass public participation (democracy) or by a self-perpetuating managerial elite? There is no answer at the present time. One thing is certain, however: throughout the transition decades (or centuries) which lie ahead, the power struggles for control of the reshaping of social machinery will be waged with the greatest intensity.

Dispute settlement may shift from person against person, business against business, to the hearing and disposition of grievances against the great bureaucracy itself. This would certainly be the case if there were no longer much in the way of private property or free economic enterprise.

Once surbanization is achieved, society will be stabilized for a long future, as discussed below. The fourth function of law will then become less weighty. But between now and then, law will be put to such strains as it has rarely experienced in the past. Can legal systems adapt rapidly and skillfully enough to contain criminal disorder, preventing destructive anarchy, and at the same time respond to shifting values and new technologies?

The legal order of surbanization must solve the major, basic issues for all humanity. This means at least a minimal world law and a multiplex global government. Failure in achieving these goals will mean that there will be no surbanization. If they are achieved, then it is not too much to expect that the central concerns and creative energies of humanity will no longer focus on technology but will shift to developing a justice directed toward a fuller, richer life for all.

Definition of the Meaning of Life Just as the breakdown of the moral order in the rise of early civilizations was ultimately met by the emergence of universalistic religions—Zoroastrianism, Buddhism, Christianity, Islam—expressing enlarged views of human nature and the universe, new philosophies of life will certainly emerge.

What will be the world view of surbanized society? No one can yet tell. It may be quite matter of fact. Almost certainly this may be expected to be true of the managers and technocrats who will organize, maintain, and operate the automated production and computerized memory and problem-solving systems. Their world will of necessity be ordered and mechanistic. And since it will be central to the very lives and livelihood of the leisured masses, their outlook will most likely be dominant, if not universal.

The concern of the vast majority will not be with the mechanics of subsistence and the ordering of society, however. It will be with the finding of meaning in life in a system in which there is little biological turnover (death will rarely occur), little child raising, and no work for the vast majority. Will people develop masochism in order to sustain a contrast to endless horizons of hedonism? What prophets will speak? In what words? What symbolic drama, what forms of ritual, will vitalize a mechanical existence? Philosophers, artists, and playwrights will have their work cut out for them.

Social Equilibrium or Endless Innovation?

The final question to be considered is "Will evolution go on forever?" Many alarms have been raised over the potential unmanageability of rapidly increasing new knowledge. How can knowledge and technology—which together mean culture—keep on expanding indefinitely? Many scientists now hold that an inevitable slowdown in the expansion of science is near at hand. The era of exciting discovery is drawing to a close with the climax of civilization.

Bentley Glass has observed:

The great conceptions, the fundamental mechanisms, and the basic laws are now known. For all time to come, these have been discovered, here and now, in our lifetime. They can never be discovered again unless man loses his scientific heritage. . . .

The uniformity of nature and the general applicability of natural laws set limits to knowledge. If there are just 100, or 105, or 110 ways in which atoms may form, then when one has identified the full range of properties of these, singly and in combination, chemical knowledge will be complete. There is a finite number of species of plants and of animals—even of insects—upon the earth. We are as yet far from knowing all about the genetics, structure and physiology, or behavior of even a single one of them. Nevertheless, a total knowledge of all life forms is only about 2 $\times$ 10^6 times the potential knowledge about any one of them. Moreover, the universality of the genetic code, the common character of proteins in different species, the generality of cellular structure and cellular reproduction, the basic similarity of energy metabolism in all species and of photosynthesis in green plants and bacteria, and the universal evolution of living forms through mutation and natural selection all lead inescapably to a conclusion that, although diversity may be great, the laws of life, based on similarities, are finite in number and comprehensible to us in the main even now. We are like the explorers of a great continent who have penetrated to its margins in most points of the compass and have mapped the major mountain chains and rivers. There are still innumerable details to fill in, but the endless horizons no longer exist.[28]

Whether the mineral resources of the earth and other planets will be adequate to meet the material needs of surbanized society indefinitely, only the future can tell. If they are inadequate, then there will be no ultimate stability. If they are adequate, however, then a state of homeostasis in environment and technology may be realized. And if technical evolution slows to a halt, so too will social and biological evolution. Equilibrium theory will be the order of the day; progress will be a historical memory, rather than an expression of human aspiration. Humanity could live long generation after long generation on a "golden plateau," working toward an ultimate refinement of social life.

SUMMARY

A first widespread crisis was produced in the moral orders of human societies with the rise of

[28]B. Glass, "Science: Endless Horizon or Golden Age?" (*Science*, vol. 171, no. 3966, 1971), p. 24.

civilization. The moral orders of nonliterate societies bind the individual in personal relationships which extend from family and kin to the whole community. People are bound in a network of society-wide reciprocity of obligations and expectancies. They share a common understanding of the nature of things and of the ends and purposes of life.

With the advent of civilization a new type of social ordering—called the *technical order*—displaced the old moral order for those who moved to the cities. Social convenience, rather than moral commitment, became the order of the day. Anomie is its complement.

Civilization transformed rural populations from independent communities into dependent peasant communities. The peasant society has its own moral order, but its relation to the city is ephemeral in that while peasants adapted to the existence of the city, they steadfastly remained apart and marginal to it. Peasants have always outnumbered urbanites in preindustrial civilizations; they have fed the cities but have been but little nourished by civilized beliefs and arts.

In the final, industrialized phases of civilization, with mechanization of agriculture, the need for great numbers of factory workers, and the spread of universal education, the breakup of the peasant way of life is inevitable.

The increasing complexity of culture through time has been positively related to a progressive increase in the amount of controlled energy utilized by societies. The first great energy-controlling revolution came with the domestication of plants and animals. It laid the technological foundation for civilization, transforming human beings from hunters and gatherers to urbanites and peasants. The second great energy-controlling revolution began with the invention of the steam engine but moved rapidly into the generation of electricity and on to the production of thermonuclear energy. Humanity has just entered the Atomic Space Age in which surbanization will replace civilization.

People in the future society will be distributed over vast areas in unbroken settlement sprawls. Society will be made up of 10, 20, or 50 billion human beings packed around the earth's surface.

The six functional prerequisites of societal maintenance may be met through far-reaching transformations of culture. Human beings will be long-lived, infants and the young few in number. Sexual relations will probably be treated as biologically obsolete, with reproduction selectively controlled and genetically managed. Socialization of the young will be simple. Mutual-interest groups may replace the family in providing social intimacy.

The production of goods and services will be largely automated and allocated by a controlled distributive economy functioning without money. Few will work, and most of the population will be leisured consumers.

The great concentrations of people will certainly increase the need for social regulation and control, unless socialization produces passive conformers. During the transition to surbanization, however, the outlook is for an increase in conflict and crime, as old values lose their bonding effect and as civil and regional groups vie for dominance in the system. With a world ordering achieved, law can move from emphasis on technical order to the search for refined justice.

The ultimate problem is sure to be the most difficult: "How can life be made meaningful?"

SELECTED READINGS

Boulding, K. E., *The Meaning of the 20th Century: The Great Transition* (1965). One of the most imaginative contemporary social thinkers examines the barriers that are to be surmounted in reaching the new society of the era that is just opening.

Potter, J. M., M. N. Diaz, and G. M. Foster (eds.), *Peasant Society: A Reader* (1967). A compendium of articles presenting anthropological thought and studies concerning peasant society.

Redfield, R., *The Primitive World and Its Transformations* (1953). Nonliterate, peasant, and urban lifeways are reviewed to provide an overview of how urbanization has transformed humanity from the nonliterate to the civilized state.

Rosenfeld, A., *The Second Genesis: The Coming Control of Life* (1969). The potential of biological engineering presented and rationally explained.

Scientific American, "Energy and Power" (*Scientific American*, vol. 224, 1971). The entire issue is devoted to well-illustrated articles on all aspects of the physical, industrial, and social components of energy, earth, and human beings.

Toffler, A., *Future Shock* (1970). Discusses the social and individual disorientations of today which are the consequences of too much change coming too rapidly; this best seller also suggests strategies for surviving into the future.

Glossary

Ab″be·vil′li·an A transitional phase of the Lower Pleistocene in Europe which is characterized by the use of stone axes. The comparable phase in Africa is the Chellean.

ac·cul″tur·a′tion The process of interaction between two societies in which the culture of the society in the subordinate position is modified in various degrees to conform to the culture of the dominant society.

A·cheu′le·an A culture of the Lower Pleistocene.

ad·ap·ta′tion The adjustment made by an organism, whether human or nonhuman, in order to survive in a specific social, physical, or biological environment.

a·do′be An unfired, sun-dried clay brick.

af·fi′nal Related by marriage.

age-class, age-grade, age-set An organized association that includes all the members of a tribe who are of a given age and sex.

ag′nate A relative in the male line of descent, i.e., patrilineally.

al·lele′ One of a pair of genes which give rise to contrasting Mendelian characters and which have identical loci on homologous chromosomes.

Al′len's rule The tendency for species living in colder climates to have shorter appendages than closely related species in warmer places.

al·li′ance theory The study of descent which gives priority to the reciprocal exchanges between descent groups as the basic mechanisms for analyzing social integration.

al·ter′na·tive A behavior pattern in which two or more permissible response norms occur for a given situation.

al′ve·o·lar arch The part of the jawbone in which the teeth are set.

am·bi·lin′eal Affiliation with either the father's or the mother's descent group, at the option of the individual.

am·bi·lo′cal *See* bilocal.

am′i·tate The complex of special behavior patterns governing relations between a child and its father's sister.

a·mok′ (to run amok) A form of psychotic behavior prevalent among Malayan peoples. It is characterized by inattention followed by a violent outbreak, often directed toward homicidal assault.

An″a·sa′zi The prehistoric and contemporary culture of the Pueblo Indians of the Southwest.

an′i·mat·ism The attribution of life to inanimate objects.

an′i·mism The belief in the existence of influencing or controlling spiritual beings, such as spirits, ghosts, or witches.

an″thro·po·ge·og′ra·phy The study of the effect of geographical factors upon human society.

an′thro·poid Having the characteristics of the higher suborder (Anthropoidea) within the Primate order including Old and New World monkeys, apes, and humans.

an″thro·po·morph′ism The attribution of human form to any object.

an″thro·poph′a·gy Cannibalism.

apes A common term applied to certain members of the Anthropoidea, namely the great apes, consisting of the gorilla, chimpanzee, and orangutan, and the other apes, the gibbon and siamang.

Ap°ol·lo′ni·an A configuration of culture that emphasizes restraint, moderation, and "middle-of-the-road" behavior in human conduct.

ap·plied′ an″thro·pol′o·gy The use of anthropological concepts or knowledge to influence behavior between peoples, or to change or maintain any social institution, for the betterment of the lives of the target population.

ar″chae·ol′o·gy The subfield of anthropology which studies the cultures of prehistoric and historic peoples by analyzing material remains.

ar′ti·fact Any material object that has been manufactured or used as a tool.

as·so″ci·a′tion A social group specifically organized for the pursuit of special interests.

at′latl The Aztec name for a dart or spear thrower.

Au″rig·na′cian The second culture of the Upper Paleolithic Age in Europe; 28,000 to 22,000 B.C.

aus·tra″lo·pith′e·cine Any of the varieties of fossil hominoids closely related to *Australopithecus* and found in Early to Middle Pleistocene deposits in central and southern Africa. Included are *Australopithecus africanus* and *Australopithecus robustus,* as well as *Australopithecus boisei,* a more heavy-bodied genus of fossil hominoid.

a·void′ance The inhibition of social interaction, especially between affinal relatives.

a·vun′cu·late The complex of special relations between a mother's brother and his sister's child.

A·zil′i·an A culture that is transitional between the Upper Paleolithic and Neolithic Ages in Western Europe; usually associated with the Tardenoisian.

bal′anced pol″y·mor′phism The equilibrium which exists between contrasting alleles where a heterozygote advantage exists or where each of the alleles has an equal possibility of selection.

band A territorially based social group, with little political organization and consisting of small groups of related families.

Ban′tu A group of related languages found over large parts of central, eastern, and southern Africa.

bar′ba·rism An evolutionist's classification of cultures possessing gardening, agriculture, or domesticated herds but devoid of written language.

bar′ri·o A Spanish word referring to a neighborhood consisting of a single ethnic group and having clearly recognized boundaries. The barrio is believed to be a survival of the localized descent group of the Aztecs (calpulli) and the Incas (ayllu).

bar′ter, silent Exchange of goods between hostile people without face-to-face contact or the use of intermediaries.

ba′sic per″son·al′i·ty The central core of adaptive psychological characteristics shared by all or most members of a society.

Bas′ket Mak′er A prehistoric culture (or the people who produced it) widely spread throughout the southwestern parts of the United States and antecedent to the Pueblo cultures.

ber·dache′(ber·dash′) An American Plains Indian transvestite who assumes the roles ascribed to women.

Berg′man's rule The tendency for animals living in colder climates to have greater body bulk than closely related species who live in warmer places.

Be′ring land bridge A land area which connected Alaska and Siberia during various periods in the Late Pleistocene, and which enabled people to cross into the New World from the Old.

bi″fur·cate col·lat′er·al A system of kinship terminology which employs separate terms for each member of the parental generation (M, F, MB, MZ, FB, and FZ).

bifurcate merg′ing A system of kinship terminology on the parental level so that M and MZ are called by the same term, F and FB are called by the same term, but MB and FZ are called by different terms.

bi·lat′er·al kin′ship The system of kinship structure in which an individual belongs equally to the kindred of both parents.

bi·loc′al The practice in which a newly married pair establishes residence with or near the parents of either spouse. (*See also* ambilocal.)

B.P. This means that the date cited is in years "before the present."

brach″i·a′tion Use of the arms for movement through the trees by swinging from the branches.

brach″y·ce·phal′ic Roundheaded; having a cephalic index of 81 or more.

broad spec′trum rev″o·lu′tion A gradual evolutionary shift from foraging activities which centered on big-game hunting to a more generalized foraging that included many different plants and animals. It began in Europe around 15,000 B.C., in the Near East around 18,000 B.C., eventually leading to the production of agricultural foods around 10,000 B.C. in the latter region.

bull′-roar″er A flat board that, when whirled at the end of a string, makes a whirring noise.

bu′rin An Upper Paleolithic flint blade, one end of which has a sharp-pointed, chisel edge.

ca·cique′ The Carib word for "chief"; often used for the sacerdotal head of a Pueblo Indian tribe or any Central or South American tribe.

cal·var′i·um The skullcap, or upper portion of the cranium.

ca′nines Projecting eye teeth which are used as attack and defensive mechanisms by apes and terrestrial monkeys.

Cap′sian An Upper Paleolithic culture in North Africa and Spain.

car′bon 14 A radioactive isotope that provides the basis for a method of archaeological dating. It is found in organic materials and the measurement of its rate of disintegration allows for dating estimates accurate to about 50,000 years ago.

car′go cult A revitalization movement whose name comes from the Melanesian area; characterized by the belief that a new era will be signaled by the arrival of ships and planes bringing European goods (cargo).

caste A stratified, endogamous group of people with a common name and, usually, a traditional occupation; each caste has differential access to prestige and economic resources and membership is ascribed by birth.

Cat′ar·rhi″ni One of the two infraorders of the Primate suborder Anthropoidea, consisting of humans, Old World monkeys, and apes.

Ce·boi′de·a The superfamily of the infraorder Platyrrhini which includes the New World monkeys.

Ce″no·zo′ic The geological era in which we are living; it began about 70 million years ago.

ce·phal′ic in′dex A metric expression of the ratio between head breadth and head length:

$$C.I. = \frac{HB}{HL} \times 100$$

Cer″co·pi·the·coi′de·a One of the two superfamilies of the infraorder Catarrhini which includes Old World monkeys.

Cha″tel·per·ro′ni·an blade An Upper Paleolithic flint blade with a curved cutting edge. Characteristic of the Chatelperronian culture, 32,000 to 28,000 B.C.

Chel′le·an The Lower Paleolithic "hand ax" culture.

chief′dom A type of political organization based on agriculture or horticulture, with kinship still important, a centralized political authority, a redistributive economy, and viewed as a transitional form between tribal society and the state.

chro′mo·some″ A threadlike structure within the cell nucleus containing the DNA responsible for inheritance.

cic″a·tri·za′tion Scar tissue produced by making incisions in the skin. Often done in patterns for ornamentation.

civ″i·li·za′tion A level of cultural development characterized by large urban centers, monumental public works, writing, science, formalized organizations based on division of labor, classes, and position based on economic standing rather than on kinship and heredity.

Clac·to′ni·an flake A large Lower Paleolithic chopping flake.

A unilineal kinship group that claims common descent from a remote ancestor, usually legendary or mythological.

class A social stratum composed of persons sharing similar wealth, power, prestige, and other cultural characteristics such as occupations and education. The system is ranked and not necessarily hereditary.

clas′si·fi·ca″to·ry kin′ship A kinship terminology which merges lineal relatives (as one's father) with collateral relatives (as one's father's brother).

cline A smoothed, curving line drawn on a map connecting geographic points having like numerical values for a given variable.

clon′ing The reproduction of plants or animals by propagation of individual body cells.

Clo′vis point A flint blade which is the basis of a stone tool tradition depending on hunting in the plains of North America around 9500 B.C.

cog·na′tic de·scent′ A form of kinship reckoning in which an individual affiliates with either the mother's or father's kinship group; also called *ambilineal descent.*

cog·na′tic kin Relatives on both sides of the family (mother's and father's) of all generations to some culturally defined limits.

col·lat″er·al′i·ty The separation of the kin types related lineally (through an ancestor) from those related through siblings of father or mother, or through siblings of other lineals.

com″po·nen′tial a·nal′y·sis One of the methodologies known as formal semantic analysis, in which students analyze their data through the identification of contrastive features of categories of folk taxonomies or ideological systems.

con·di′tion·al curse A ritual declaration that if the facts are not as stated, or if certain conditions come to pass, ill fortune may strike the person cursed.

con·fig″u·ra′tion of cul′ture The distinctive quality of a culture that derives from the special relationship of its parts to one another.

con·san′guine Kinfolk related by descent or filiation rather than through marriage; "blood relatives."

cop′ro·lite Preserved or petrified animal feces.

coup An attested deed of valor among the Plains Indians.

coup counting The practice of publicly reciting coups.

coup de poing A flint hand ax characteristic of the Chellean, Acheulean, and Mousterian cultures.

cou·vade′ The practice whereby a husband retires to bed upon the birth of his offspring and acts as though he had just gone through childbirth.

cow′rie shell A small glossy marine shell of the genus *Cypraea*, highly valued for decoration and used as a medium of exchange in the Pacific area and Africa.

cra′ni·al ca·pac′i·ty The interior volume of the cranium measured in cubic centimeters; approximates the volume of the brain.

cra′ni·um That portion of the skull which encloses the brain.

Cro-Mag′non A variety of *Homo sapiens* found in Western Europe during the last half of the fourth glaciation.

cross-cous′ins Cousins whose related parents are siblings of opposite sex. Offspring of a person's mother's brother or father's sister.

Crow kin′ship ter·min·ol′ogy Found in matrilineal societies. Cross-cousins are distinguished from each other and from parallel-cousins and siblings, but terms for paternal cross-cousins are merged with father and father's sister according to sex.

cult An organized system or group characterized by performance of supernatural rituals and ceremonies and possessing an underlying body of dogmatic belief.

cul′tur·al an″thro·pol′o·gy The study of human behavior and its social and cultural products in all times and all places.

cultural rel′a·tiv·ity The notion that a people's values are the product of a particular social, cultural, and physical environment, and that the behavior in that society should be judged in terms of the society's own values rather than by some external standard.

culture The integrated sum total of learned behavior characteristic of the members of a society.

culture area A geographical territory within which the cultures tend to be similar in some significant aspects.

culture, ideal A formulation of normative patterns for behavior as stated by the members of a given society.

culture of poverty A concept proposed by Oscar Lewis, more properly called a *subculture of poverty*, which refers to a way of life of the lowest socioeconomic classes of many parts of the world that allows them to cope with the hopelessness and despair which derives from the realization that they will not be able to achieve the statuses and acquire the material goods of the dominant society.

culture shock The reaction experienced by a person when confronted by strange values, rules, and practices of a different culture than the one learned as a child. The feeling is one of helplessness, frustration, ineptness, and loneliness.

culture trait or element A reputedly irreducible unit of learned behavior or a material product thereof.

deep struc′ture A set of very abstract, implicit rules about the ways in which a speaker of a language rearranges the parts to form sets of meanings. Transformational linguistics, according to Chomsky, is concerned not only with the surface structure of sound and meaning, but also with deep structure.

deme An endogamous community consisting of a single kindred.

den″dro·chro·nol′o·gy The dating of wood or charcoal fragments from prehistoric sites by matching the patterns of tree ring width found in the specimen to those in a master chart which has been constructed for the region using certain tree species which are sensitive to fluctuations in climatic conditions.

de·scent′group A corporate group whose membership is made up of persons who share a genealogical connection to a single ancestor.

descent rule The principle which is used to trace lineal kinship relationships between generations; a person is filiated (related) to both parents, but this rule stresses one parent's line over the other.

de·scrip′tive kin′ship A system of kinship terminology in which there is a separate form of address for each kin type.

descriptive lin·guis′tics The recording, description, and structural analysis of languages.

di″a·chron′ic In anthropology, the comparative study of cultures as they change through time.

di″a·ste′ma A gap between two teeth.

dib′ble A pointed digging stick.

dif·fu′sion A process in cultural dynamics wherein culture elements or complexes spread from one society to another.

dif·fu′sion·ism The empirically unverified notion held by some European anthropologists of the late nineteenth and early twentieth centuries that culture began in one or two areas of the world and spread to other areas.

di·mor′phism, sexual A difference in bodily characteristics between the two sexes.

Di″o·nys′i·an A categorical label attached to cultures that emphasize sensate experience.

DNA Deoxyribonucleic acid; its molecular structure constitutes the hereditary determinants in that instructions are coded in the arrangement of the nucleotide bases along the strands of the DNA molecule(s).

dol″i·cho·ce·phal′ic Long- or narrow-headed; having a cephalic index of less than 75.9.

dom′i·nance hi′er·ar″chy The whole gamut of behavior which exists among adult male baboons, and macaques, involving subordinate-superordinate relationships.

dou′ble de·scent′ The coexistence of matrilineal and patrilineal descent systems within the same society.

drift In genetic theory, a change in allele frequencies which is attributed to chance rather than selection and is more likely to be effective in very small breeding populations.

drive, basic A need that is innate in the organism, the satisfaction of which is ultimately necessary to survival of the organism or the species.

Dry″o·pi·the′cus A genus of Miocene fossil ape from which humans and the great anthropoids evolved.

e·col′o·gy The study of the relationships between organisms and their total environments.

ec″o·nom′ic an″thro·pol′o·gy The anthropological study of the way in which different societies produce, distribute, allocate, and use the economic resources found in their environment.

ec′o·sys″tem A system which includes the physical environment and the organisms that inhabit it.

e′go (1) In kinship analysis, the person who is used as the reference point for identification of kinship relations and terms. (2) In psychoanalysis, one of the three structural aspects of personality, called the *control center* because it mediates between the demands of the id and the reality of the outside world.

em″bry·ol′o·gy The study of an organism from the time it is a fertilized egg until it is born.

em′ic The perception of a phenomenon as seen and felt by a participant inside the system.

en·cul·tu·ra′tion The process by which the individual learns the patterns of the culture of which that person is a member.

en·dog′a·my The rule that requires a person to marry exclusively within a group.

E′o·cene The second period of the Cenozoic era.

ep″i·can′thic fold A fold of the upper eyelid.

Es′ki·mo″ kin′ship ter″mi·nol′o·gy A kin system that draws no distinction between cross- and parallel-cousins but distinguishes cousins from siblings; it is the system of Anglo-American and other cultures.

eth′nic group A group of people within a larger society, members of which identify themselves and are identified as members, and who share a distinctive subculture because of historical, linguistic, religious, or other traditions.

eth·no·cen′trism The view that the values and ways of one's own group are superior; all others are judged with reference to this view.

eth″no·graph′ic pres′ent The description of a culture as though it were existing at the present time without consideration of the changes which have taken place since it was originally described.

eth·nog′ra·phy The division of anthropology devoted to the description of cultures.

ethno·his′to·ry The recovery of ethnographic data from the study of written records.

eth·nol′o·gy The division of anthropology devoted to the analysis, systematic interpretation, and comparison of cultures and societies.

eth·no·sci′ence The systematic study of the cognitive systems, or ways of classifying the experienced world, found in different societies.

eth″no·se·man′tics The study of meaning from the point of view of speakers in societies with different languages.

eth·ol′ogy The scientific study of animal behavior.

et′ic The perception of a phenomenon by an outside observer.

ev″o·lu′tion, biological or organic The continuous adaptive modification of Mendelian populations through change in genetic composition.

evolution, cultural Modification of culture patterns in a given direction through persistent social adaptation. *General evolution* purports to express modifications characteristic of all cultures at specific stages in their development. *Multilineal evolution* purports to express modifications characteristic only of like cultures. *Specific evolution* purports to express changes characteristic of specific cultures.

evolution, divergent or radiating The process of biological evolutionary development that results in several lines of progressive change from an original common form.

evolution, unilinear The evolution of social forms in a universal and ordered sequence; a theoretical process.

ex·og′a·my Marriage outside a specific social group, as required by custom or law.

fam′i·ly (1) In biological terms, a subdivision of an order or suborder. (2) In cultural terms, a group made up of one or more adults of each sex, together with their offspring; also called a *conjugal-natal family.*

family, conjugal-natal The kinship group to which an individual belongs. Every individual is a member of a primary and a secondary conjugal-natal family: that of the parents, into which the person is born, and that which is founded with a spouse in wedlock. These two families (or two aspects of the same group) have been called the family of *orientation* and of *procreation*, respectively.

family, extended A larger kinship group that includes more than one set of spouses and their children, and possibly other near relatives.

family, joint A group of closely related conjugal-natal families which is a property-holding, residential group; it includes a number of married relatives living together in a single household, each with spouse and offspring.

fa′ther·hood, sociological The practice whereby the adult male who is the husband of a child's mother is functionally the father tó the child, regardless of his biological relationship.

fe′mur The thighbone.

fet′ish An object that is revered because it is believed to house a supernatural power.

fib′u·la The long bone that, with the tibia (shinbone), makes up the lower part of the leg.

fil·i·a′tion The condition or fact of being the child of a particular parent; a child is filiated to both parents, but is descended from only one in a unilineal system.

flu′o·rine dat′ing A dating technique which tests for the amount of fluorine absorbed from the ground water to ascertain whether the fossil has been in the ground as long as other fossils found in the same stratum or plane.

for′ag·ing An economy based on the intensive use of available resources such as collecting wild plants, hunting, and fishing, usually depending on the time of the year.

fo·ra′·men mag′num The hole in the base of the skull through which the spinal cord leaves the cranium.

for′mal·ism The adoption by some economic anthropologists of the principles of economics as being general enough to be applied to all societies. (Also see substantivism.)

fos′sil An organic object that has

been mineralized or has left an imprint in stone.

foun′der ef·fect′ In genetics, the observation that since the founding population in a new area does not represent the total range of genetic variation of the parent population, its descendants will differ from the ancestral population and from other descendant populations in different areas.

fra·ter′ni·ty An association of men. A men's society.

func′tion·al·ism A theoretical and methodological approach to society that emphasizes concern with the part each unit plays in the maintenance and survival of the culture.

ga′mete A sex cell; sperm in males, egg in females.

gene The minimum part of a chromosome that functions to control a single chemical synthesis in a cell; the unit of inheritance.

gene flow The spread of genes to a neighboring population through mating along the boundaries rather than through permanent migration of individuals.

gene pool The total sum of genetic characteristics available to a breeding population.

gen′er·al·ized″ ex·change′ The giving of gifts without the expectation of an immediate and direct reciprocity; also, in alliance theory, the prescriptive marriage system in which women of group A marry men of group B, whose women marry men of group C, whose women marry men of group A.

gen′er·a″tive gram′mar The system of rules which allows the speaker to make sound-meaning correlations and which generates the structural descriptions which make up the language in question. According to Chomsky, it is the speaker-hearer's knowledge of language.

gen′o·type The genetic component received by each person from parents.

gens A patrilineal clan.

ger″on·toc′ra·cy A society dominated by the old (usually men in nonliterate societies).

Ghost′ Dance A nativistic reactive movement among western American Indians in 1890. The dance was intended to revive the dead and restore the old way of life.

gift ex·change As a socioeconomic system, a culturally controlled giving activity in which the reciprocities involved fulfill contracts and act as a means of establishing prestige.

Glo′ger's rule The tendency for animals living in hot damp places to have darker skins than those living in hot dry places.

glot″to·chro·nol′o·gy A method of calculating the time elapsed since the speakers of two related languages separated from each other.

gra·vette′ blade An Upper Paleolithic straightedged, pointed flint blade, the back edge of which has been blunted by the removal of small flakes. Characteristic of the Gravettian culture, 26,000 to 20,000 B.C.

half-life The amount of time required for a radioactive substance to lose one-half of its radioactivity.

Har′dy-Wein′berg law In genetics, the principle that, given random mating in a population, an equilibrium in the proportion of genotypes is established and maintained from generation to generation.

Ha·wai′ian ter″mi·nol′o·gy A kinship terminology system that has two terms for each generation, one for males and one for females.

Hei′del·berg jaw A fossil mandible found in first interglacial deposits at Mauer, near Heidelberg, Germany; *Homo erectus heidelbergensis.*

het″er·o·zy′gous Having dominant and recessive alleles at a chromosome locus.

hi′er·o·glyph″ A highly conventionalized symbol developed from pictorial representation and used as an element in certain archaic writing systems.

ho′gan The Navajo dwelling.

Ho′ho·kam A prehistoric culture localized in the desert areas of southeastern and central Arizona.

ho′lism The view that all parts of a culture are interrelated; leads to the study of all aspects of a culture and how they are interrelated.

hom′i·nid (1) A primate who belongs to the order of Hominidae; a human being. (2) Having the characteristics of a human being.

hom′i·noid Belonging to the superfamily Hominoidea, which includes fossil and contemporary apes and humans.

Ho′mo e·rec′tus e·rec′tus A Lower Pleistocene fossil species of human found in Java and Africa. Formerly called *Pithecanthropus erectus.*

Ho′mo e·rec′tus mau″ri·tan′i·cus A Middle Pleistocene fossil species of human found in North Africa.

Ho′mo e·rec′tus pe″ki·nen′sis A Middle Pleistocene fossil species of human found in China. Formerly called *Sinanthropus pekinensis.*

Ho′mo e·rec′tus rho·de″si·a·nen′sis An Upper Pleistocene fossil variety of human found in Rhodesia.

Ho′mo e·rec′tus so″lo·en′sis An Upper Pleistocene fossil variety of human found in Java.

"Ho′mo ha·bi′lis" A fossil hominid found in Bed 1 at Olduvai Gorge. It may be either an advanced form of australopithecine or one of the earliest known members of the genus *Homo.*

Ho′mo sa′pi·ens sa′pi·ens Modern humans. The sole existing species of the genus *Homo.*

Ho′mo sa′pi·ens stein″heim·en′sis The Middle Pleistocene fossil precursor of modern humans (*Homo sapiens sapiens*), found in Europe and represented by the Steinheim, Swanscombe, and Fontechevade fossils.

ho″mo·zy′gous Having two identical

alleles at the same locus on a chromosome.

hor'ti·cul''ture Plant cultivation which involves the use of a digging stick or hoe and in which small plots of land are fallowed for varying periods of time.

hu'mer·us The upper longbone of the arm.

hy·per'ga·my Marriage upward from a lower social class or caste into a higher one.

id The Freudian term for the innate biological impulses of the human being.

id'e·o·graph'' A drawn, carved, or painted symbol which stands directly for an object or idea and which is nonphonetic in the language of its user.

il'i·um The broad, flaring bone which forms the upper side of the pelvis.

in'cest ta·boo' The prohibition of sexual intercourse between closely related persons as defined by the culture in question.

in'dus·try In archaeology, all the known objects, artificially produced or not, used by a group of prehistoric people in one area over a span of time.

in·fan'ti·cide The killing of infants.

in·her'i·tance The procedure in each culture for the transmission of property, rights, or status after the death of its owner.

in''sti·tu'tion, social A complex of behavior patterns organized around some dominant central interest.

in·ven'tion, independent *See* parallelism.

is'chi·um The lower posterior bone in the pelvis.

jaj·ma'ni The system of customary services between the members of a Hindu *jati* and a landlord

ja'ti A localized subcaste in India which is endogamous, named, and possesses a distinctive combination of culture traits.

jok'ing re·la'tion·ship'' An institutionalized pattern of privileged familiarity or joking between persons of specific social statuses.

jur'al par'ent The culturally defined adult from, or through, whom a child receives its kinship identity. The jural parent may or may not be its genitor.

ka·chi'na The gods in Pueblo society who are represented in ceremonials by masked dancers.

K-A dat'ing The long-range method of archaeological dating by measuring the degree of disintegration of potassium 40 into argon 40 that has occurred in geological materials.

kin'dred An ego-centered kinship group, including bilateral relatives and shared with siblings. The members may come together for occasional purposes, such as funerals.

ki·nes'ics The study of gestures as communication.

kin'ship sys'tem The classification of statuses and roles of relatives.

kinship ter''mi·nol'o·gy The set of names applied to the various statuses in a kinship system.

kitch'en mid'den A refuse heap.

ki'va A semisubterranean ceremonial chamber, usually round, in the Southwest Indian pueblos.

ku'la ring The trading system involving ceremonial exchange of shell armbands and necklaces in southwestern Melanesia.

Kul·tur'kreis Large culture complexes that, in the theory of the culture historical school (*Kulturkreislehre*) of ethnology, diffuse en bloc over large areas of the globe.

la'bret A plug worn through an incision in the lip.

lau'rel-leaf point A flint blade shaped like a laurel leaf and characteristic of the Solutrean culture.

law A social norm whose violation beyond permissible limits evokes a formal procedural response initiated by an individual or group that possesses the socially recognized privilege-right of determining guilt and of imposing sanctions upon the wrongdoer.

law, adjective The part of the law that governs legal procedure and the application of legal sanctions.

law, private Law that is normally enforced by the wronged party rather than by a public officer.

law, public Criminal law; that which is enforced by a public officer.

law, substantive The norms that define illegal activity.

le'mur A primitive type of primate that first emerged in the Eocene period.

Le·val·loi'si·an A Lower Paleolithic culture characterized by a flint flake tool with a prepared striking platform.

lev'i·rate Brother-in-law marriage. The marriage of a woman to her deceased husband's brother.

levirate, anticipatory The practice in which a husband extends limited sexual privileges with his wife to his younger brother.

lex''i·co·sta·tis'tics A method of counting the frequency of cognate (related) words in basic vocabulary lists for languages in order to suggest historical affinities not previously suspected. (*See also* glottochronology.)

li·bi'do The Freudian term for the id's sexual energies.

lin'e·age A unilineal kinship group that traces descent from a known common ancestor, who lived not more than five or six generations back.

lin·guis'tics The study of language with a historical branch interested in the evolution of languages and their origins, and a descriptive branch which records, analyzes, and transcribes the structures of languages.

loess A deposit of rock dust carried by wind from glacial moraines and outwash deposits.

lost-wax meth'od A process of casting metal objects in molds shaped about a wax form, which is then melted out.

Mag″da·le′ni·an The final culture of the Upper Paleolithic Age in Europe.

mag′ic The control of supernatural forces by means of compulsive formulas.

magic, contagious A form of sympathetic magic. It operates on the principle that things once in contact with each other can exert a continuing influence upon each other.

magic, imitative A form of sympathetic magic. It operates on the principle that like influences like.

magic, sympathetic Magic that operates on the principle of homeopathic association, i.e., that one object can exert an influence upon others that have an identity with it.

Mag″le·mo′si·an A local manifestation of the Mesolithic Age in the Great Swamp of the Baltic Coast.

ma′na A diffuse force or energy, magical in character, which is believed to reside in various objects, places, and persons. This belief occurs in Melanesia, Polynesia, and other places.

man′i·oc A tropical plant whose roots yield a nutritious starch; also called *cassava*.

ma′no A grinding stone that is held in the hand.

mar′ket e·con′o·my A system in which goods and services are exchanged and their relative values established by supply and demand.

mar′riage The social institution that regulates the special relations of a mated pair to each other, their offspring, their kinfolk, and to their society.

marriage, cross-cousin, asymmetrical A preferred marriage form that is restricted to one type of cross-cousin only. Marriage of a man to his mother's brother's daughter is permitted, while marriage to his father's sister's daughter is prohibited, or vice versa.

marriage, cross-cousin, symmetrical Marriage in which either type of cross-cousin is permissible or preferred as a spouse.

mas′toid pro′cess The bony downward projection of the skull located immediately behind the ear.

mat′ing The pairing of individuals for sexual intercourse.

ma′tri·arch″ate A society distinguished by uxorilocal residence and matrilineal descent.

mat″tri·lat′er·al Pertaining to some matter, such as descent, marriage, or other relationship, with the mother's side or kinship group.

ma″tri·lin′eal Of or pertaining to descent through the mother; descended through the mother.

ma″tri·lo′cal *See* uxorilocal.

mean, arithmetical The average. That point in the range of variability of a phenomenon at which exactly equal quantities fall on either side.

me·chan′i·cal sol″i·dar′i·ty Durkheim's phrase to refer to the binding together of human groups by consensus, with the division of labor being minimal and all members of the group sharing similar activities, interests, and values, (*Also see* organic solidarity.)

me′di·an The midpoint. That point in the range of variability of a phenomenon which falls exactly at the middle of the two extremes.

meg′a·lith A large stone used as a marker, altar, or monument.

mei·o′sis The process of cell division whereby the number of chromosomes is halved (reduction division), with the second division the same as mitotic division in which daughter cells are produced which duplicate parental chromosomal patterns. The end result is the formation of sex cells (gametes).

Mel″a·ne′si·a The island area of the Southwest Pacific inhabited by dark-skinned peoples.

Men·de′li·an pop·u·la′tion A localized group of members of a species who breed mostly among themselves but occasionally with members of other populations.

merg′ing (in kinship systems) *See* classificatory kinship.

mes″o·ce·phal′ic Medium-headed; having a cephalic index of 76 to 80.9.

Mes″o·lith′ic (Middle Stone Age) The period characterized by intensive seed gathering and foraging.

mes·ti′zo A term applied in Latin America to persons of mixed Spanish and Indian ancestry.

me·ta′te A flat, grooved grinding stone that functions as a mortar.

mi′cro·liths Fine flint flakes placed in rows to form a tool or weapon.

Mi″cro·ne′si·a Small islands. The island area of the West Central Pacific.

mil·le′nar·ism A reactive social movement based on the belief that the gap between cultural ideal and social reality will be closed (and will last for a thousand years).

mil′pa The Maya Indian method of gardening, involving the slash-and-burn technique of clearing garden plots in the forest; also the name of such a field.

mi·nor′i·ty A group that is distinguished from the larger society by some characteristics, such as those of an ethnic group (*for which see* ethnic group), or by a characteristic such as sex, as with women. Although the group may actually be a majority in numbers, it is the object of discrimination in social, political, or economic sectors of the society.

Mi′o·cene The fourth epoch (period) of the Cenozoic era.

mi·to′sis A form of cell division that results in daughter cells having chromosomes identical to the parent cell.

mo′dal per″son·al′i·ty A combination of those personality characteristics that are present most frequently among individuals in a society.

mode The high point. That point in the range of variability of a phenomenon which occurs with the greatest frequency.

Mo″gol·lon′, or Mim′bres A prehistoric Pueblo culture localized in the mountainous area of southeastern Arizona and southwestern New Mexico.

moi′e·ty Half. The social unit based upon kinship that occurs when the tribe is divided into two units.

mo·nog′a·my Marriage of one man to one woman.

mon′o·the·ism The worship of one god.

mo·raine′ The debris of earth and rocks deposited along the edges of a glacier.

mor′pheme A minimal unit of language that has meaning.

mor·phol′o·gy The study of the form and structure of an organism or social manifestation.

Mous·te′ri·an The culture associated with Neandertal populations during the third interglacial and fourth glacial epochs in Europe.

mu·ta′tion A physical or chemical change of a gene or chromosome which results in a change in the phenotype which is new and different from antecedent forms.

myths Tales or narratives which explain orgins and meanings of various beliefs or customs.

na′tion·al char′ac·ter The personality characteristics shared by the residents of a nation.

na·tiv·ist′ic move′ment A reactive movement to remove foreign persons or cultural elements so as to restore a by-gone culture.

nat′u·ral se·lec′tion The principle that those forms better adapted to their environment live to produce more offspring than those which are not as well adapted.

Ne·an′der·tal A human fossil variety found in Europe from the second interglacial epoch to the climax of the fourth glacial; *Homo sapiens neandertalensis.*

Ne″o·lith′ic (New Stone Age) The period during which plants were domesticated and people lived in farming villages and used ground stone tools.

neo·lo′cal The practice in which a newly married pair establish a new household in a locality other than that of either of their parents.

net′work a·nal′y·sis A study of the social relations of a single person (egocentric), in which interactions are plotted in an ever-extending network and compared for linkages and overlappings.

Ni·lot′ic Pertaining to or designating a people who live in the Nile Basin.

no·bil′i·ty A class or caste with hereditary status of high prestige and ceremonial or political power.

nor′ma·tive Relating to or inducing conformity to a norm.

oc·cip′i·tal torus The horizontal bony ridge across the rear portion of the skull to which the back muscles of the neck are anchored.

oc′ci·put The bone that forms the rear and lower segment of the cranium.

Oed′i·pus com′plex A psychological state of a child characterized by sexual desire for the mother and antagonism toward the father.

Old′o·wan cul′ture A Villefranchian and Early Pleistocene pebble-tool culture.

ol′i·gar″chy A state whose government is controlled by a small group within the larger society.

O′ma·ha″ kin′ship sys′tem The patrilineal obverse of the Crow kinship system, with mother and female matrilateral cross-cousins merged under one term that means "female member of mother's patrilineage or clan," and with father's sister's daughter merged with sister's daughter under a term that means "daughter of a female of my father's patrilineage or clan."

or·deal′ A ritual method of verification of testimony in which the litigants are subjected to a physical test designed to injure or kill the falsifier.

or′der A taxonomic label which is more inclusive than a family but less than a class.

or·gan′ic sol″i·dar′i·ty Durkheim's phrase for reference to human groups which are bound together through a sense of common purpose based on complementary and interdependent relationships and with an elaborate system of division of labor. (*Compare with* mechanical solidarity.)

os·te·o·don″to·ker·a′tic An assemblage of bone, tooth, and horn artifacts; allegedly the culture of the australopithecines.

Pa″le·o·lith′ic (Old Stone Age) The period lasting from about 2.5 million to about 10,000 years ago, characterized by the use of chipped stone tools.

pal″y·nol′o·gy The study of pollen and spores. Prehistoric climatic conditions can be determined by counting the different kinds of pollen in soil samples.

par′a·digm″ According to Kuhn, a shared body of theories, generalizations, methodology, and methods of observation and evaluation which define the problems, appropriate research techniques, the data to be gathered, and the explanations which are produced by a community of scholars or scientists at a point in time, or until the paradigm is replaced by a competing model.

par′al·lel-cous′ins Cousins whose related parents are of like sex. The offspring of a person's mother's sister or father's brother.

par′al·lel·ism The development of similar cultural forms through identical steps without historical interaction or contact.

Par'a·pi·the'cus A genus of fossil primate found in Oligocene deposits and believed to be ancestral to Old World monkeys.

par'fleche An oblong rawhide box made by Plains Indians.

participant observation A field research technique by which the ethnologist participates in community activities to the extent possible and, doing so, learns about the culture of the group being studied.

pas'to·ral·ism A subsistence technique centered about the herding and husbandry of domesticated animals.

pa''ter·fa·mil'i·as The authoritarian father in the Roman family.

pa'tri·arch''ate A society dominated by the father as head of the kinship group, characterized by patrilineal descent and virilocal residence.

pat''ri·lin'e·al Pertaining to descent through the father. Children belong to the kinship group of their father.

pat''ri·lo'cal *See* virilocal.

pa·tron'y·my The custom of giving children the last name of a paternal ancestor.

peas'ant A member of a subsociety of a large stratified society, who lives in a rural area, is family oriented, depends primarily on subsistence agriculture, and has a social and economic interdependence with an urban center.

Pe'king fossil A Middle Pleistocene fossil human; *Homo erectus pekinensis* (formerly called *Sinanthropus pekinensis*).

pem'mi·can A preserved cake of shredded dried meat and berry pulp.

per·cus'sion flak'ing The technique of shaping flint artifacts by removing flakes with blows of a hammerstone.

pet'ro·glyph A symbol incised in rock.

pe·yo'te A variety of cactus (*Lophophora williamsii*) ingested by North American and Mexican Indians to stimulate visions as a form of religious experience.

phe'no·type The physically apparent expression of heredity.

phen'·yl·thi'o·car'bam·ide (PTC) A bitter synthetic chemical. The ability to taste it is transmitted genetically; some people cannot taste it.

pho'neme The smallest sound unit used in a language.

pho·net'ics The general study of spoken sounds.

phra'try A division of a society into subunits by linking clans for some purpose, such as exogamy. Two such units are called *moieties*; more than two are called *phratries*.

phy·log'e·ny The natural history of a species or variety.

phys'i·cal an''thro·pol'o·gy The branch of anthropology concerned with the study of human beings as biological organisms.

pic'to·graph A simple picture, or series of pictures, intended to describe a situation or record an event.

pile dwell'ing A house raised from the ground or built over water on pilings.

pit dwelling An earth lodge built over an excavated pit.

plan'ti·grade'' Standing or walking on the soles of the feet.

Plat''yr·rhi'ni One of the two infraorders of the primate suborder Anthropoidea, consisting of New World monkeys, which are characterized by vertical nostrils and, often, prehensile tails.

Pleis'to·cene The sixth epoch (period) of the Cenozoic era during which humans rose to dominance among life forms.

Pli'o·cene The fifth epoch (period) of the Cenozoic era; a warm period during which early human types became differentiated from early apes.

Pli''o·pi·the'cus A genus of Pliocene fossil ape that is directly ancestral to the gibbon.

plu'ral·ism The condition of complex society in which several subgroups with separate subcultures exist and share a common economic and political structure.

plu'vi·al A rainy period which may have occurred in tropical areas contemporaneously with glacial periods in colder areas.

po·lit'i·cal an''thro·pol'o·gy The focus of study within cultural anthropology which is concerned with the organization and conduct of behavior relating to the uses of power in a society.

pol'y·an''dry The marriage of a woman to two or more men simultaneously.

polyandry, attenuated The marriage relationship in which a married brother extends limited sexual privileges with his wife to his unmarried younger brothers. Also called *anticipatory levirate.*

polyandry, fraternal A polyandrous marriage in which the husbands are brothers.

po·lyg'a·my Any marriage involving multiple spouses.

pol''y·gen'e·sis The evolutionary hypothesis which assumes that the several genera of prehistoric humans evolved from different species of Pliocene anthropoids.

po·lyg'y·ny The marriage of a man to two or more women simultaneously.

pol''y·mor'phism The occurrence of two or more alleles at one or more loci so that variability results within a Mendelian population.

Pol''y·ne'si·a Many islands. The area of the Central Pacific that falls within a triangle formed with Hawaii, Easter Island, and New Zealand as the apexes.

pol'y·the·ism Worship of many gods. A system of religion recognizing multiple gods.

pon'gid Of or relating to the three great apes: orangutan, gorilla, and chimpanzee.

pop''u·la'tion ge·net'ics The study of gene frequencies and changes in Mendelian populations.

pos'tu·late, cultural A basic proposition as to the nature of things (existential) or the desirability or undesirability of things (normative) which underlies a cultural system.

po·tas'si·um ar'gon dat'ing *See* K-A dating.

pot'latch The Northwest Coast Indian institution of ceremonial feasting accompanied by lavish distribution of gifts.

pot'sherds Fragments of pottery used by archaeologists to reconstruct aspects of, and date, prehistoric cultures.

pref''er·en'tial mar'riage A form of marriage that is enjoined or preferred between two persons of specifically defined statuses or groups.

pre·hen'sile Adapted for grasping objects with hands, feet, or tail.

pres'sure flak'ing The technique of shaping flint artifacts by removing fine flakes by means of steady pressure applied with a stick or bone.

priest A religious functionary who receives supernatural authority from a cult or organized church, in contrast to the shaman, who derives power directly from supernatural sources.

Pri'mate An order within the mammalian class which includes humans, apes, Old and New World monkeys, and prosimians.

pri''ma·tol'o·gy The study of primates, especially of nonhuman primates.

prim'i·tive Pertaining to a culture or an aspect of a culture that does not include a written language; also pertaining to an individual whose culture includes no written language. Therefore, nonliterate or preliterate.

pri''mo·gen'i·ture Inheritance by the firstborn child.

pri'vi·lege-right The legal relation in which a person is free to behave in a certain way to another without legal prohibition or consequence.

Pro·con'sul An East African Miocene hominoid. (See Dryopithecus).

pro·fane' In an anthropological and sociological sense, all that is ordinary—that is, not sacred.

prog'e·ny price The wealth transferred by the relatives of a groom to the kinfolk of his bride in compensation for their release of claim to the children that are produced in the marriage; also known as *bride price* and *bridewealth.*

prog'na·thous Having a projecting jaw.

pro''le·tar'i·at The class of industrial workers without access to capital and the means of production, who must earn a living through their own labor.

prom''is·cu'i·ty The absence of any social restraints limiting or regulating sexual behavior.

pro'no·grade Walking on four legs.

prop'er·ty The special and socially sanctioned relation of a person or group to the utilization of some object.

property, communal Property that is owned by the entire community.

property, incorporeal Property that involves a nonmaterial object.

property, joint Property that is owned by a group smaller than the entire community.

Pro''pli·o·pi·the'cus A genus of fossil ape found in Oligocene deposits of Egypt. It is ancestral to the gibbon.

Pro·sim'·ii· A suborder of the order Primates, which includes lemurs, lorises, tarsiers, and similar forms.

prox·e'mics The study of the use of space (nearness and distance) in communication and social relations.

psy''cho·log'i·cal an''thro·pol'o·gy The name applied to that aspect of cultural anthropology which is concerned with the psychological aspects of personality and how they interrelate with different aspects of culture.

pueb'lo A village constructed of clay bricks (adobe) or stones, characteristic of the Indians of the southwestern United States and northern Mexico.

race A term of questionable scientific value which refers to a group of people arbitrarily identified by what some believe are distinctive physical traits. (*See* ethnic group.)

rac'ism A doctrine that assumes the inherent superiority of one group of people over others.

ra'di·o·car'bon dat'ing *See* Carbon 14.

ram'age A nonexogamous, extended corporate kinship group in which members get their identity by descent from a common ancestor traced either patrilineally or matrilineally, according to individual preference and convenience. It is thus ambilineal.

Ra''ma·pi·the'cus A Late Miocene hominoid which lived from Africa to India, and believed by many to be one of the earliest hominoids.

ran'dom sam'ple A probabilistic sample chosen so that each item has an equal chance of being represented.

re·ces'sive In genetics, an allele which is not expressed in the phenotype unless it is homozygous.

rec''i·proc'i·ty The giving and receiving of gifts or services so that a gift is given for one received.

rel'a·tive dat'ing A dating technique used by archaeologists to determine the relative sequence of the deposition of cultural remains.

rel'a·tives, affinal Persons related through marriage.

relatives, consanguineal Genetically related persons.

re·li'gion A belief in supernatural beings and the attendant ways of behaving in consequence of such a belief.

Rho·de'si·an fossil An Upper Pleistocene human fossil found at Broken Hill in Rhodesia, South Africa; *Homo erectus rhodesianensis.*

rite de pas·sage' *See* transition rites.

rite, fertility A ritual complex designed to promote genetic reproduction.

role The customary complex of behavior associated with a particular status.

sa'cred Pertaining to objects, rites, positions, or ceremonies which relate to religion; opposite of profane.

sa'crum The wedge-shaped bone formed by the joining of the vertebrae that form the posterior segment of the pelvis.

sag′it·tal crest A ridge running longitudinally along the roof of the skull.

sanc′tion Any social reaction operating to induce conformity to a normative standard of behavior.

sanction, legal A coercive penalty involving the use of physical force or economic deprivation, attached to the violation of a social norm, when the application of the sanction is considered legitimate according to the prevailing standards of the culture.

sav′age·ry A state of cultural development identified by evolutionists, which is marked by the absence of gardening or agriculture and written language.

scap′u·la The shoulder blade.

scar″i·fi·ca′tion The process of mutilation of the body through the artificial raising of scar tissue. *See also* cicatrization.

schiz″o·phre′ni·a A behavior disorder marked by a replacement of the learned behavior systems with desocialized behavior dominated by hallucinations.

seg′men·ta·ry lin′e·a·ges A hierarchy of inclusive lineages, which form alliances in opposition to other similar units.

se·nil′i·cide The killing of the aged.

se″ri·a′tion In archaeology, a method of dating artifacts based on the principle that the popularity and prevalence of a type of artifact or style increases after its initial introduction to reach a point of maximum use, then declines.

se·rol′o·gy The study of the chemical and physical properties of blood.

sex-linked Located on either the X or Y chromosomes, which determine sex. An inherited characteristic is said to be sex-linked if it is determined by a sex-linked gene, for example, color blindness.

sha′man A religious curing specialist who has received power directly from supernatural sources; synonymous with *medicine man, witch doctor, angakok* (Eskimo).

sib A unilineal kinship group; synonymous with *clan.*

sib′ling Brother or sister.

sick′le-cell a·ne′mi·a, or **sick·le′mi·a** A genetically inherited disease found in people whose ancestors lived in a region of the world with malaria. When the allele is heterozygous it tends to provide the carrier with some resistance to malaria, but when it prevails in a homozygous state, the individual may die young of anemia. The red blood cells are sickle-shaped.

sim′i·an Apelike.

Sin·an′thro·pus pe″ki·nen′sis See *Homo erectus pekinensis.*

Skhūl fossils The remains of a highly variable human population found in Palestine. The fossils reveal both Neandertaloid and *Homo sapiens sapiens* characteristics.

slash-and-burn ag′ri·cul″ture *See* swidden farming.

slav′er·y The institution whereby persons are subjected to involuntary servitude, are denied the right of freedom of movement or action, and must place their productive efforts at the disposal of a master.

so′cial class A category of persons within a society who (1) hold a number of distinctive statuses in common, (2) receive differential rewards and privileges, and (3) have an awareness of their similar interests and lifestyle in contradiction to other social classes.

so′cial dis′tance A term covering the relative "spatial positions" of two statuses; generally used to emphasize limitations on social intercourse.

so′cial struc′ture The ways in which groups and individuals are organized and relate to one another.

so·ci′e·ty A spatially identifiable human population, self-consciously oriented, acting in accordance with a distinctive culture, and emotionally bound through common language and symbolic experiences.

society, military An association of warriors.

society, secret An association whose membership and activities are shrouded in secrecy. A tribal secret society embraces all adults of one sex in its membership.

so′ci·o·lin·guis′tics The study of how people use language in different social situations and contexts.

So′lo hominid An Upper Paleolithic human fossil type found on the Solo River, Java; *Homo erectus soloensis.*

So·lu′tre·an A culture of the Upper Paleolithic Age in Europe; characterized by the laurel-leaf point.

sor′cer·y The use of supernatural power as an aggressive instrument to further the interests of the sorcerer. *Magic* is a more neutral term.

so·ro′ral po·lyg′y·ny The simultaneous marriage of two or more sisters to one husband.

so·ro′rate The practice whereby a sister marries the husband of her deceased sister.

spe″ci·a′tion The genetic divergence of a species to produce two new populations that are no longer capable of gene exchange (interbreeding).

spe′cies A population of organisms, members of which are genetically related and cannot breed with other species. Subspecies share genetically controlled characteristics, but do not breed frequently with other subspecies for geographic or other reasons, even though they are capable of doing so. From a genetic point of view, a human race is a subspecies, or localized population. *See* race.

sta′di·a The minor advances of ice sheets interspersed with interstadia within a glacial epoch.

stan′dard de″vi·a′tion A statistical measure of the variation within a group of data.

standard er′ror A measurement of the degree of error in a statistical calculation which is dependent on the size of the sample and its variability.

state The association within a society that undertakes to direct and organize social policy on behalf of and in the name of the entire society.

sta′tus The social position of an individual with reference to the other members of the society. (*See* role.)

Stein′heim hominid A type of fossil human found in Middle Pleistocene deposits at Steinheim, Germany; *Homo sapiens steinheimensis.*

stim′u·lus dif·fu′sion The process of cultural dynamics in which one people receive the idea of a cultural invention from another but give a new and unique form to the idea.

stra·tig′ra·phy Analysis of geological deposits in terms of discernible layers. Derivative time sequences are inferred from the relative positions of the strata or layers.

struc′tur·al·ism The analytical approach of Lévi-Strauss and his followers based on the idea that observed phenomena are the results of underlying structural principles or relationships.

struc′tur·al lin·guis′·tics The study of the basic elements (phonemes, morphemes, syntax, semantics) of and the rules which make up language.

sub′cul·ture The culture of a subgroup of a society which is distinctive, yet shares many characteristics, such as political structure, with the larger society.

sub″in·ci′sion A surgical operation in which the urethra of the male sex organ is slit open; a mutilation performed as a part of the male puberty rites in certain Australian tribes.

sub·stan′tiv·ism A school in economics, primarily represented by economic anthropologists, which claims that the formal models developed by economics cannot be applied on a cross-cultural basis to all societies. (*See* formalism.)

suit′or ser′vice A substitute for, or equivalent of, progeny price, in which the potential groom works for his intended bride's relatives.

su″per·or·gan′ic Pertaining to the phenomena, known as *cultural,* that occur on a level over and above the organic; i.e., they are not preset in the organic structure.

su″pra·or′bit·al ridge A bone ridge above the orbits, or eye sockets.

sur·ban·i·za′tion The culture of the future. That which is beyond civilization. The mode of the life-to-be in the Atomic Space Age (authors' term).

Swans′combe hominid A fossil hominid found in Middle Pleistocene deposits in southern England; classified as *Homo sapiens steinheimensis.*

swid′den ag′ri·cul″ture A form of horticulture in which the fields are cleared by burning and cultivation for a varying number of years, after which the land is allowed to lie fallow and regenerate by returning to natural vegetation. Also called *slash-and-burn agriculture* and *shifting agriculture.*

sym·bi·o′sis The living together of two or more species or societies in which the relationship is economically interdependent and mutually beneficial or necessary.

sym′bol The culturally assigned meaning which resides in an object or event in a human society.

sym·pat′ric Pertaining to living forms that inhabit a common territory.

syn·chron′ic Existing at the same time.

syn′cre·tism The fusion of two distinct systems of belief and practice.

ta·boo′ Prohibition of an act, violation of which is punishable by supernatural sanctions.

tar′a·vad The joint-family household consisting of the members of a matrilineage among the Nayar caste in Kerala on the Malabar Coast of India.

Tar″de·nois′·i·an A prehistoric culture of France representing the Mesolithic Age and characterized by microlithic flints.

ta′ro A staple food plant of the Pacific area.

Taung fossil An *Australopithecus africanus* fossil found in South Africa. *See* australopithecine.

tau″ro·dont′ism An enlargement of the pulp cavity and fusion of the roots in molar and premolar teeth.

tax·on′o·my The systematic classification of things according to scientific principles which indicate their relationship.

tech·nol′o·gy The part of a society's culture which refers to the knowledge available to manufacture tools and use them to exploit the natural resources available and to produce goods and services.

tek·non′y·my The practice of addressing an adult after the name of its child, and vice versa.

tell In the Near East, a mound built up by prolonged human occupation of a site.

te′pee A conical skin tent.

ter″ri·to·ri·al′i·ty The notion that a group of hominoids or other species occupies and defends a designated or otherwise bounded territory; the idea behind this is that territoriality serves to space out individuals and to maximize the use of resources.

than″a·to·ma′ni·a The depression of the will to exist to the point of death.

the·oc′ra·cy A social order controlled by religious specialists.

to′tem An object, often an animal or plant, held in special regard by an individual or social group.

trans″for·ma′tion·al gram′mar *See* deep structure *and* generative grammar.

trans·hu′mance The seasonal movement of herders and their livestock from winter to summer pastures and back.

tran·si′tion rites Ritual complexes associated with important changes in personal status, such as birth, adolescence, marriage, and death.

trans·ves′tite An individual who effects a transfer of sex roles, such as occurs when a male takes on the dress and roles of a female, or vice versa.

tra·vois′ A carrying device that has two poles, like the tongues of a buggy, hitched to a draft animal. The free ends of the travois drag along the ground.

tribe A social group speaking a distinctive language or dialect and possessing a distinctive culture that marks it off from other tribes. It is not necessarily organized politically.

Trick′ster A character in mythology who alters the order of things by tricking humans or animals into choices or circumstances that they do not expect or desire.

ul″ti·mo·gen′i·ture Inheritance by the youngest son or daughter.

u″ni·lin′e·al Pertaining to descent through one parent only.

ur′ban an″thro·pol′o·gy The application of anthropological research techniques, concepts, and methodology to the study of people in cities.

ur′ban·ism Refers in general to the qualities of an individual or individuals which are characteristic of an urban way of life.

ur″ban·i·za′tion The process of urban growth, especially as it refers to the movement of rural peoples to the city.

u′su·fruct The right to use an object of property without possessing title of ownership.

ux·or″i·lo′cal The practice whereby a married couple settles in the domicile of the wife's family; synonymous with *matrilocal residence.*

var′na The four mythically founded castes of India which emerged from the body of primordial man.

varve A band of clay deposited annually in a glacial outwash.

ves·tig′i·al re·mains′ Organs whose physiological functions have been lost (as far as can be determined).

Vil·la·fran′chi·an The early part of the Pleistocene, prior to the first glaciation, in which modern genera of animals appear for the first time.

vir″i·lo′cal The practice whereby a married couple settles in the domicile of the husband's family; synonymous with *patrilocal residence.*

vo·dun′ A system of religious belief and practice developed by Caribbean Negroes and combining elements of Catholicism and African, particularly Dahomean, religions. Magic is only a minor element in the entire complex. It is called *voodoo* in the American vernacular.

wam′pum Elongated beads drilled out of clamshells and strung in beltlike forms, used by Indians of the northeast woodlands.

warp The parallel-lying foundation threads of a fabric.

weft The threads woven at right angles through the parallel-lying foundation threads, or warp; also called the *woof,* or *filler.*

wer′gild The money payment made by the kin of a murderer to the kin of a murdered man.

wick′i·up″ A beehive-shaped grass hut.

wife lend′ing The custom whereby a husband extends to a household guest the sexual favors of his wife as a symbolic gesture of brotherhood.

wig′wam A domed bark hut of the Algonkian Indians of the northeast woodlands.

wil′low-leaf point A long, slender flint blade characteristic of the Solutrean culture.

win·di′go A type of homicidal psychosis involving cannibalism in Ojibwa and other Algonkian Indian cultures.

woof *See* weft.

world view The system of beliefs, values, philosophy, and ideology which characterize the outlook of the members of a society regarding nature and the world.

wrong, private An offense against an individual that is customarily punished by legal action instituted by the injured person or kinfolk of the injured person. Private wrongs make up the body of private law.

wrong, public An offense against the social entity punished by the legal action of the group at large or by its official representatives.

yuc′ca A plant belonging to the lily family and possessing long fibrous leaves. The sap of its roots produces suds in water.

Zin·jan′·thro·pus boi′sie A form of *Australopithecus* found in Bed 1 at Olduvai Gorge (See Australopithecines).

zy′gote A cell formed by the fertilization of an ovum by a sperm.

Bibliography

Aarne, A., *Die Tiere auf der Wandershaft* (Folklore Fellows Communications, no. 11, 1913).

Aberle, D. F., *The Psychosocial Analysis of a Hopi Life History* (*Comparative Psychology Monographs,* serial no. 107, vol. 21, 1951).

———, "Matrilineal Descent in Cross-Cultural Perspective," in D.M. Schneider and K. Gough (eds.), *Matrilineal Kinship* (Berkeley, Calif., 1961).

Adamic, L., *The Native's Return: An American Immigrant Visits Jugoslavia and Discovers His Old Country* (New York, 1934).

Adams, R. M., *The Evolution of Urban Society: Early Mesopotamia and Prehispanic Mexico* (Chicago, 1966).

Aginsky, B. W., "An Indian's Soliloquy" (*American Journal of Sociology,* vol. 46, 1940), pp. 43-44.

Alland, A., *Evolution and Human Behavior* (Garden City, N. Y., 1967).

Allison, A. C., "Aspects of Polymorphism in Man" (*Cold Spring Harbor Symposium on Quantitative Biology,* vol. 20, 1955), pp. 239-255.

Almond, G. A., and J. S. Coleman (eds.), *The Politics of Developing Areas* (Princeton, N.J., 1960).

Amsden, C., "The Loom and Its Prototypes" (*American Anthropologist,* vol. 34, 1932), pp. 216-235.

———, *Navaho Weaving* (Albuquerque, N. Mex., 1949).

Anderson, A. J. O., and C. E. Dibble (trans. and eds.), Fray B. de Sahagun, *Florentine Codex: General History of the Things of New Spain* (10 vols., Santa Fe, N. Mex., 1950–1966).

Anderson, R., "The Buffalo Men: A Cheyenne Ceremony of Petition Deriving from the Sutaio" (*Southwestern Journal of Anthropology,* vol. 12, 1956), pp. 92-104.

Anderson, R. T., "Voluntary Associations in History" (*American Anthropologist,* vol. 73, 1971), pp. 209–222.

Ardrey, R., *African Genesis* (New York, 1961).

Arellano, A. R. V., "Some New Aspects of the Tepexpan Case" (*Bulletin of the Texas Archaeological and Paleontological Society,* vol. 22, 1951), pp. 217–225.

Arensberg, C. M., and A. H. Niehoff, *Introducing Social Change* (Chicago, 1964).

Bada, J. L., R. A. Schroeder, and G. F. Carter, "New Evidence for the Antiquity of Man in North America Deduced from Aspartic Acid Racemization" (*Science,* vol. 184, 1974), pp. 791–793.

Baker, P. T., "The Biological Adaptation of Man to Hot Deserts," in T. W. McKern (ed.), *Readings in Physical Anthropology* (Englewood Cliffs, N.J., 1966), pp. 174–185.

Balandier, G., *Political Anthropology* (New York, 1970).

Banton, M. (ed.), *Political Systems and the Distribution of Power* (London, 1965).

———, *Roles: An Introduction to the Study of Social Relations* (London, 1965).

———,"Voluntary Associations: Anthropological Aspects" (*International Encyclopedia of the Social Sciences,* vol. 16, 1968), pp. 357–362.

Baratz, S. S., and J. C. Baratz, "Early Childhood Intervention: The Social Science Base of Institutional Racism" (*Harvard Educational Review,* vol. 40, no. 1), reprinted in T. Weaver (ed.), *To See Ourselves: Anthropology and Modern Social Issues* (Glenview, Ill., 1973), pp. 299–309.

Barnett, H. G., "The Nature of the Potlach" (*American Anthropologist,* vol 40, 1938), pp. 349–358.

———, "Culture Processes" (*American Anthropologist,* vol. 42, 1940), pp. 21–48.

———, "Applied Anthropology in 1860" (*Applied Anthropology,* vol. 1, 1942), pp. 19–32.

———, *Innovation: The Basis of Cultural Change* (New York, 1953).

———, *Anthropology in Administration* (Evanston, Ill., 1956).

———, "The Innovative Process" (*Kroeber Anthropological Society Papers,* no. 25, 1961), pp. 28-41.

Barnouw, V., *Culture and Personality* (Homewood, Ill., 1973).

Barth, F., "Father's Brother's Daughter Marriage in Kurdistan" (*Southwestern Journal of Anthropology*, vol. 10, 1954), pp. 164–171.

———, *Nomads of South Persia* (New York, 1961).

Barton, R. F., *Ifugao Law* (University of California Publications in American Archaeology and Ethnology, vol. 15, 1919); also (Berkeley, 1969).

———, *The Kalinga: Their Institutions and Custom Law* (Chicago, 1949).

Bascom, W., "Urbanism as a Traditional African Pattern" (*Sociological Review*, vol. 7, 1959), pp. 29–43.

Beals, R. L., "Urbanism, Urbanization and Acculturation" (*American Anthropologist*, vol. 53, 1951), pp. 1–10.

———, P. Carrasco, and T. McCorkle, *Houses and House Use of the Sierra Tarascans* (Washington, D.C., 1944).

Beardsley, R. K., P. Holder, A. D. Krieger, B. J. Meggers, J. B. Rinaldo, and P. Kutsche, "Functional and Evolutionary Implications of Community Patterning," in *Seminars in Archaeology: 1955* (Memoirs of the Society for American Archaeology, no. 11, 1956).

Beattie, J., *Understanding an African Kingdom: Bunyoro* (New York, 1965).

Bee, R. L., *Patterns and Processes: An Introduction to Anthropological Strategies for the Study of Sociological Change* (New York, 1974).

Bell, D. (ed.), *Toward the Year 2000* (Boston, 1968).

Belo, J., "A Study of a Balinese Family" (*American Anthropologist*, vol. 38, 1936), pp. 12–31.

Bender, M. A., and E. H. Y. Chen, "The Chromosomes of Primates," in J. Buettner-Janusch (ed.), *Evolutionary and Genetic Biology of Primates* (2 vols., New York, 1963), chap. 7.

Benedict, R. F., *Patterns of Culture* (New York, 1934).

———, "Marital Property Rights in Bilateral Society" (*American Anthropologist*, vol. 38, 1936), pp. 368–374.

———, *The Chrysanthemum and the Sword: Patterns of Japanese Culture* (Boston, 1946).

Bennett, J. W., "The Development of Ethnological Theories as Illustrated by Studies of the Plains Sun Dance" (*American Anthropologist*, vol. 46, 1944), pp. 162-181.

——— and M. M. Tumin, *Social Life, Structure and Function: An Introductory General Sociology* (New York, 1948), pp. 45–59.

Berlin, B., "A Universalist-Evolutionary Approach in Ethnographic Semantics," in A. Fischer (ed.), *Current Directions in Anthropology* (*Bulletin of American Anthropological Association*, vol. 3, no. 3, part 2, 1970).

Berreman, G. D., "Caste: The Concept of Caste" (*International Encyclopedia of the Social Sciences*, vol. 2, 1968), pp. 333–338.

———, "Pahari Polyandry: A Comparison," in P. Bohannan and J. Middleton (eds.), *Marriage, Family, and Residence* (Garden City, N. Y., 1968), pp. 147–167.

Birdwhistell, R. L., *Kinesics and Context: Essays on Body Motion Communication* (Philadelphia, 1970).

Bloomfield, L., in H. Hoijer (ed.), *Language History* (New York and others, 1965).

Boas, F., *The Central Eskimo* (Bureau of American Ethnology, Annual Report 6, 1888), pp. 399–669.

———, *Social Organization and Secret Societies of the Kwakiutl Indians* (United States National Museum, Annual Report, 1895).

———, *Tsimshian Mythology* (Bureau of American Ethnology, Annual Report 31, 1916), pp. 393–558.

———, "The Methods of Ethnology" (*American Anthropologist*, vol. 22, 1920), pp. 316–323.

———, *Primitive Art* (Oslo, 1929).

——— (ed.) *General Anthropology* (New York, 1938).

Bodmer, W. F., and L. L. Cavalli-Sforza, "Intelligence and Race" (*Scientific American*, vol. 223, 1970), pp. 19–29.

Bogoras, W., "The Chukchee: 1, Religion" (*Jesup North Pacific Expedition*, vol 7, 1904–1909).

Bohannan, P., *Social Anthropology* (New York, 1963).

——— and G. Dalton (eds.), *Markets in Africa* (Evanston, Ill., 1962).

——— and J. Middleton (eds.), *Kinship and Social Organization* (Garden City, N. Y., 1968).

——— and——— (eds.), *Marriage, Family, and Residence* (Garden City, N. Y., 1968).

Bordes, F., *The Old Stone Age* (New York, 1968).

Boulding, K. E., "The Death of the City: A Frightened Look at Postcivilization" (1961, mimeographed).

———, *The Meaning of the 20th Century: The Great Transition* (New York, 1965).

Bourguignon, E., and L. Greenbaum, *Diversity and Homogeneity: A Comparative Analysis of Societal Characteristics Based on Data from the Ethnographic Atlas* (Columbus, Ohio, 1968).

Bowers, A. W., *Mandan Social and Ceremonial Organization* (Chicago, 1950).

Boyd, W. C., *Genetics and the Races of Man: An Introduction to Modern Physical Anthropology* (Boston, 1950).

Brace, C. L., "Review of Evolution und Hominisation" (*American Journal of Physical Anthropology*, vol. 21, 1963), pp. 87–91.

———, "The Fate of the 'Classic' Neanderthals: A Consideration of Hominid Catastrophism" (*Current Anthropology*, vol. 5, no. 1, 1964), pp. 3–46.

———, "On the Race Concept" (*Current Anthropology*, vol. 5, 1964), pp. 313–314.

———, *The Stages of Human Evolution* (Englewood Cliffs, N. J., 1967).

———and M. F. A. Montagu, *Man's Evolution: An Introduction to Physical Anthropology* (New York, 1965).

Bradfield, R. M., *A Natural History of Associations: A Study in the Meaning of Community* (London, 1973).

Braidwood, R. J., "Jericho and Its Setting in Near Eastern Prehistory" (*Antiquity*, vol. 31, 1957), pp. 73–80.

———, *Prehistoric Men* (8th ed., Chicago, 1975).

———and B. Howe, "Southwestern Area beyond the Lands of the Littoral," in R. J. Braidwood and G. Willey (eds.), *Courses toward Urban Life* (Viking Fund Publications in Anthropology, no. 32, 1962), pp. 132–146.

———and G. R. Willey (eds.), *Courses toward Urban Life: Archeological Considerations of Some Cultural Alternatives* (Viking Fund Publications in Anthropology, no. 32, 1962).

Breuil, H., *Four Hundred Centuries of Cave Art* (New York, 1950).

Brew, J. O. (ed.), *One Hundred Years of Anthropology* (Cambridge, Mass., 1968).

Britannica Book of the Year: 1968 (Chicago, 1968).

Bronowski, J., and U. Bellugi, "Language, Name, and Concept" (*Science*, vol. 168, 1970), pp. 669–673.

Brose, D. S., and M. H. Wolpoff, "Early Upper Paleolithic Man and Late Middle Paleolithic Tools" (*American Anthropologist*, vol. 73, no. 5, 1971), pp. 1156–1194.

Brown, H., "The Age of the Solar System" (*Scientific American*, 1957, S. A. Reprint 102).

Brown, J., "A Cross-Cultural Study of Female Initiation Rites" (*American Anthropologist*, vol. 65, 1963), pp. 837–853.

Buehler, A., T. Barrow, and C. P. Mountford, *The Art of the South Seas, Including Australia and New Zealand* (New York, 1962).

Buettner-Janusch, J., *Origins of Man: Physical Anthropology* (New York, 1966).

———, *Physical Anthropology: A Perspective* (New York, 1973).

Bunzel, R., *The Pueblo Potter* (Columbia University Contributions to Anthropology, vol. 8, 1929).

———, *Introduction to Zuni Ceremonialism* (Bureau of American Ethnology, Annual Report 47, 1932).

Burling, R. M., "American Kinship Terms Once More" (*Southwestern Journal of Anthropology*, vol. 26, 1970), pp. 15–24.

———, *Man's Many Voices: Language in Its Cultural Context* (New York and others, 1970).

Busia, K. A., *The Position of the Chief in the Modern Political System of Ashanti: A Study of the Influence of Contemporary Social Changes on Ashanti Political Institutions* (Oxford, 1951).

———, "The Ashanti of the Gold Coast," in D. Forde (ed.), *African Worlds: Studies in the Cosmological Ideas and Social Values of African Peoples* (London, 1954), pp. 190–209.

Campbell, B., "Quantitative Taxonomy and Human Evolution," in S. L. Washburn (ed.), *Classification and Human Evolution* (Viking Fund Publications in Anthropology, no. 37, 1963), pp. 50–70.

———, "Conceptual Progress in Physical Anthropology: Fossil Man" (*Annual Review of Anthropology*, vol. 1, 1972), pp. 27–54.

———, "A New Taxonomy of Fossil Man" (*Yearbook of Physical Anthropology*, vol. 17, 1973), pp. 194–201.

Campbell, D. T., and R. Naroll, "The Mutual Methodological Relevance of Anthropology and Psychology," in F. L. K. Hsu (ed.), *Psychological Anthropology* (new ed., Cambridge, Mass., 1972), pp. 435–463.

Caneiro, R. L., "Slash and Burn Cultivation among the Kiukuru and Its Implications for Cultural Development in the Amazon Basin," in *The Evolution of Horticultural Systems in Native South America, Causes and Consequences—A Symposium* (Anthropologica Supplement No. 2, Caracas, 1961), pp. 47–67.

Carney, J., A. Hill, J. A. Miller, and A. Walker, "Late Australopithecine from Baringo District, Kenya" (*Nature*, vol. 230, 1971), pp. 509–514.

Carrol, J. B. (ed.), *Language, Thought, and Reality: Selected Writings of Benjamin Lee Whorf* (New York, 1956).

Carter, G. F., "Origins of American Indian Agriculture" (*American Anthropologist*, vol. 48, 1946), pp. 1–21.

Cartmill, M., "Rethinking Primate Origins" (*Science*, vol. 184, no. 4135, 1974), pp. 436–443.

Casagrande, J. B. (ed.), *In the Company of Man* (New York, 1960).

Caso, A., *The Aztecs: People of the Sun* (Norman, Okla., 1958).

Catlin, G., (J. C. Ewers, ed.), *O-kee-pa: A Religious Ceremony and Other Customs of the Mandans* (New Haven, Conn., 1967).

Cavalli-Sforza, L. L., "The Genetics of Human Populations" (*Scientific American*, vol. 231, 1974), pp. 81–89.

Chang, K.-c., "New Evidence on Fossil Man in China" (*Science*, vol. 136, 1962), pp. 749–760.

———, "The Beginnings of Agriculture in the Far East" (*Antiquity*, vol. 44, 1970), pp. 175–185.

Chase, S., *Mexico: A Study of Two Americas* (New York, 1931).

Childe, V. G., *What Happened in History* (London, 1942).

———, "The Urban Revolution" (*Town Planning Review*, vol. 21, no. 1, 1950), pp. 3–17.

———, *Man Makes Himself* (rev. ed., New York, 1951).

Chomsky, N., *Language and Mind* (New York, 1968).

Christensen, J. B., *Double Descent among the Fanti* (Behavior Science Monographs, New Haven, Conn., 1954).

Clark. G., *The Stone Age Hunters* (New York, 1967).

———and S. Piggott, *Prehistoric Societies* (New York, 1965).

Clark, J.D., *The Prehistory of Africa* (New York, 1970).

———, "African Origins of Man the Toolmaker," in G. L. Isaac and E. R.

McCown (eds.), *Human Origins: Louis Leakey and the East African Evidence* (Menlo Park, Calif., 1976), pp. 1–53.

Clark, J. G. D., *Prehistoric Europe: The Economic Base* (New York, 1952).

———, *World Prehistory: An Outline* (Cambridge, England, 1961).

Clifton, J. (ed.), *Applied Anthropology: Readings in the Uses of the Science of Man* (Boston, 1970).

Codere, H., *Fighting with Property: A Study of Kwakiutl Potlatching and Warfare* (Seattle, 1950).

———, "Exchange and Display" (*International Encyclopedia of the Social Sciences*, vol. 5, 1968), pp. 239–245.

Cohen, R., and J. Middleton (eds.), *Comparative Political Systems* (Garden City, N. Y., 1967).

Cohen, Y. A., *The Transition from Childhood to Adolescence: Cross-Cultural Studies of Initiation Ceremonies, Legal Systems and Incest Tabus* (Chicago, 1964).

———, "The Conceptualization of Culture," in Y. A. Cohen (ed.), *Man in Adaptation: The Cultural Present* (Chicago, 1968), pp. 7–12.

——— (ed.), *Man in Adaptation: The Cultural Present* (2d ed., Chicago, 1974).

Cole, G. D. H., "Inheritance" (*Encyclopaedia of the Social Sciences*, vol. 8, 1932), pp. 35–43.

Cole, S., *The Prehistory of East Africa* (New York, 1963).

Coon, C. S., "Climate and Race," in H. Shapley (ed.), *Climatic Change* (Cambridge, Mass., 1953), pp. 14–29.

———, S. M. Garn, and J. B. Birdsell, *Races: A Study of Race Formation in Man* (Springfield, Ill., 1950).

Cooper, J. M., "Is the Algonquian Family Hunting Ground System Pre-Columbian?" (*American Anthropologist*, vol. 41, 1939), pp. 66–90.

———, "The Yahgan," in J. H. Steward (ed.), *Handbook of South American Indians* (6 vols., Washington, D.C., 1946–1950), vol. 1, pp.81–107.

Cottrell, W. F., *Energy and Society: The Relation between Energy, Social Change, and Economic Development* (New York, 1955).

Coult, A. D., and R. W. Habenstein, *Cross Tabulations of Murdock's Ethnographic Sample* (Columbia, Mo., 1965).

Curtis, E. S., *The Kwakiutl* (New York, 1919).

Curtis, G., T. Drake, R. Cerling, and T. Hampel, "Age of KBS/Tuff in Koobi Fora Formation, East Rudolf, Kenya" (*Nature*, vol. 258, 1975), p. 395.

Dalton, G., "Traditional Production in Primitive African Economies" (*Quarterly Journal of Economics*, August 1962), pp. 360–378.

——— (ed.), *Tribal and Peasant Economies: Readings in Economic Anthropology* (Garden City, N. Y., 1967).

Daniel, G., *The Origins and Growth of Archaeology* (New York, 1967).

Dart, R. A., "The Predatory Implemental Technique of Australopithecus" (*American Journal of Physical Anthropology*, vol. 7, 1949), pp. 1–16.

———, "The Predatory Transition from Ape to Man" (*International Anthropological and Linguistic Review*, vol. 1, 1953), pp. 14–29.

———, *The Osteodontokeratic Culture of Australopithecus prometheus* (Transvaal Museum Memoir 10, 1957).

Davenport, W., "Nonunilinear Descent and Descent Groups" (*American Anthropologist*, vol. 61, 1959), pp. 557–572.

———, "The 'Hawaiian Cultural Revolution': Some Political and Economic Considerations" (*American Anthropologist*, vol. 71, 1969), pp. 1–20.

Davidson, D. S., "Knotless Netting in America and Oceania" (*American Anthropologist*, vol. 37, 1935), pp. 117–134.

Day, M. H., *Guide to Fossil Man: A Handbook of Human Paleontology* (Cleveland and New York, 1965).

D'Azevedo, W. L. (ed.), *The Traditional Artist in African Societies* (Bloomington, Ind., 1972).

de Jong, Josselin, *Lévi-Strauss's Theory on Kinship and Marriage* (Mededelingen van het Rijksmuseum voor Volkenkunde, Leiden, no. 10, 1952).

de Lumley, H., "A Paleolithic Camp at Nice" (*Scientific American*, vol. 220, 1969), pp. 42–50.

de Schlippe, P., *Shifting Cultivation in Africa: The Zande System of Agriculture* (London, 1956).

de Terra, H., J. Romero, and T. D. Stewart, *Early Man in Mexico* (Viking Fund Publications in Anthropology, no. 11, 1949).

De Vore, I. (ed.), *Primate Behavior: Field Studies of Monkeys and Apes* (New York, 1965).

Dobyns, H. F., C. M. Medrano, and M. C. Vasquez, "A Contagious Experiment" (*Saturday Review*, Nov. 3, 1962), pp. 59–62.

Dobzhansky, T., *Mankind Evolving: The Evolution of the Human Species* (New Haven, Conn., 1962).

———, "Evolution: Organic and Superorganic" (*The Rockefeller Institute Review*, vol. 1, no. 2, 1963), pp. 1–9.

———, "Race Equality," in R. H. Osborne, *The Biological and Social Meaning of Race* (San Francisco, 1971), pp. 13–24.

Dorsey, G. A., *The Cheyenne: I, Ceremonial Organization* (Field Columbian Museum, Publication 103, Anthropological Series, vol. 9, no. 1, 1905).

———, *The Cheyenne: II, The Sun Dance* (Field Columbian Museum, Publication 103, Anthropological Series, vol. 9, no. 2, 1905).

Douglas, D. W., and K. du P. Lumpkin, "Communistic Settlements" (*Encyclopaedia of the Social Sciences*, vol. 4, 1931), pp. 95–102.

Downing, T. E., and M. Gibson (eds.), *Irrigation's Impact on Society* (Anthropological Papers of the University of Arizona, no. 25, 1974).

Downs, J. F., and H. K. Bleibtreu (eds.), *Human Variation: Readings in Physical Anthropology* (Beverly Hills, Calif., 1971).

Doxiadis, C. A., "Ecumenopolis: Tomorrow's City," in *Britannica Book of the Year: 1968* (Chicago, 1968), pp. 16–38.

Dozier, E. P., "Rio Grande Pueblos," in E. H. Spicer (ed.), *Perspectives in American Indian Culture Change* (Chicago, 1961), pp. 94–186.

Draper, P., "Comparative Studies of Socialization" (*Annual Review of Anthropology*, vol. 3, 1974), pp. 272–293.

Drucker, P., "Rank, Wealth, and Kinship in Northwest Coast Society" (*American Anthropologist*, vol. 41, 1939), pp. 55–65.

———, *Cultures of the North Pacific Coast* (San Francisco, 1965).

———, *Indians of the Northwest Coast* (New York, 1967).

——— and R. F. Heizer, *To Make My Name Good: A Reexamination of the Southern Kwakiutl Potlatch* (Berkeley and Los Angeles, 1967).

DuBois, C., *The People of Alor* (Minneapolis, 1944).

———, "The Alorese," in A. Kardiner (ed.), *The Psychological Frontiers of Society* (New York, 1945), pp. 101–145.

Dunn, L. C., *Heredity and Evolution in Human Populations* (Cambridge, Mass., 1960).

——— and T. Dobzhansky, *Heredity, Race, and Society* (rev. ed., New York, 1951).

Durkheim, E., *Elementary Forms of the Religious Life* (London, 1914).

Dyson-Hudson, R., and N. Dyson-Hudson, "Subsistence Herding in Uganda" (*Scientific American*, vol. 220, 1969), pp. 76–89.

Eames, E., and J. Goode, *Anthropology of the City* (Englewood Cliffs, N. J., 1977).

Eddy, E. M. (ed.), "Urban Anthropology: Research Perspectives and Strategies" (*Proceedings of the Southern Anthropological Society*, no. 2, 1968).

Edgerton, R. B., "Method in Psychological Anthropology," in R. Naroll and R. Cohen (eds.), *A Handbook of Method in Cultural Anthropology* (Garden City, N. Y., 1970), pp. 341–42.

Eggan, F., *Social Organization of the Western Pueblos* (Chicago, 1950).

———, "Social Anthropology and the Method of Controlled Comparison" (*American Anthropologist*, vol. 56, 1954), pp. 743–763.

———(ed.), *Social Anthropology of North American Tribes* (2d ed., Chicago, 1955).

Eiseley, L. C., "In the Beginning Was the Artifact" (*Saturday Review*, Dec. 7, 1963).

Eisenstadt, S. N., *From Generation to Generation* (Glencoe, Ill., 1956).

Ekvall, R. B., *Fields on the Hoof: Nexus of Tibetan Nomadic Pastoralism* (New York, 1968).

Embree, J. F., *The Japanese Nation* (New York, 1945).

Epstein, A. L., *Politics in an Urban African Community* (Manchester, 1958).

Erasmus, C. J., "Patolli, Pachisi, and the Limitation of Possibilities" (*Southwestern Journal of Anthropology*, vol. 6, 1950), pp. 369–388.

———, *Man Takes Control: Cultural Development and American Aid* (Minneapolis, 1961).

Erikson, E. H., "Life Cycle" (*International Encyclopedia of the Social Sciences*, vol. 9, 1968), pp. 286–292.

Evans-Pritchard, E. E., *Witchcraft, Oracles and Magic among the Azande* (Oxford, 1937).

———, *The Nuer: A Description of the Modes of Livelihood and Political Institutions of a Nilotic People* (Oxford, 1940).

———, "The Nuer of the Southern Sudan," in E. E. Evans-Pritchard and M. Fortes (eds.), *African Political Systems* (Oxford, 1940).

———, "Nuer Bridewealth" (*Africa*, vol. 16, 1946), pp. 1ff.

———, *Kinship and Marriage among the Nuer* (Oxford, 1951).

———, *Nuer Religion* (Oxford, 1956).

———, *Essays in Social Anthropology* (Glencoe, Ill., 1963).

———, *Theories of Primitive Religion* (Oxford, 1965).

———and M. Fortes (eds.), *African Political Systems* (Oxforu, 1940).

Ewers, J. C., *The Horse in Blackfoot Indian Culture: With Comparative Material from Other Western Tribes* (Bureau of American Ethnology Bulletin 159, 1955).

Fagan, B. M., *Introductory Readings in Archaeology* (Boston, 1970).

Fallers, L. A., *Bantu Bureaucracy: A Study of Integration and Conflict in the Political Institutions of an East African People* (London, 1956).

Fenton, W. N., "Locality as a Basic Factor in the Development of Iroquois Social Structure," in *Symposium on Local Diversity in Iroquois Culture* (Bureau of American Ethnology Bulletin 149, 1951).

———, "J.-F. Lafitau (1681–1746), Precursor of Scientific Anthropology" (*Southwestern Journal of Anthropology*, vol. 25, 1969), pp. 173–187.

Firth, R., *We the Tikopia, A Sociological Study of Kinship in Primitive Polynesia* (London, 1936).

———(ed.), *Man and Culture: An Evaluation of the Work of Bronislaw Malinowski* (London, 1957).

Fitch, J. M., and D. P. Branch, "Primitive Architecture and Climate" (*Scientific American*, vol. 207, 1960), pp. 134–144.

Flannery, K. V., "The Ecology of Early Food Production in Mesopotamia" (*Science*, vol. 147, no. 3663, 1965), pp. 1247–1256.

———, "Origins and Ecological Effects of Early Domestication in Iran and the Near East," in P. J. Ucko and G. W. Dimbleby (eds.), *The Domestication and Exploitation of Plants and Animals* (London, 1969), pp. 73–100.

Fletcher, A. C., and F. LaFlesche, *The Omaha Tribe* (Bureau of American Ethnology, Annual Report 27, 1911), pp. 115–198.

Flint, R. F., *Glacial Geology and the Pleistocene Epoch* (New York, 1947).

Ford, C. S., *A Comparative Study of Human Reproduction* (Yale University Publications in Anthropology, no. 32, 1945).

Forde, C. D., *Habitat, Economy, and Society: A Geographical Introduction to Ethnology* (2d ed., New York, 1937).

———, "Kinship in Umor: Double Unilateral Organization in a Semi-Bantu Society" (*American Anthropologist*, vol. 41, 1939), pp. 523–553.

———, "Applied Anthropology in Government: British Africa," in A. L. Kroeber (ed.), *Anthropology Today: An Encyclopedic Inventory* (Chicago, 1953), pp. 841–865.

———(ed.), *African Worlds: Studies in the Cosmological Ideas and Social Values of African Peoples* (London, 1954).

Fortes, M., *The Dynamics of Clanship among the Tallensi* (Oxford, 1945).

——— (ed.), *Social Structure: Studies Presented to A. R. Radcliffe-Brown* (Oxford, 1949).

———, *The Web of Kinship among the Tallensi* (Cambridge, England, 1949).

———, "Structure of Unilineal Descent Groups" (*American Anthropologist*, vol. 55, 1953), pp. 17–34.

Fortune, R. F., *Sorcerers of Dobu: The Social Anthropology of the Dobu Islanders of the Western Pacific* (New York, 1932).

———, "Manus Religion" (*Proceedings of the American Philosophical Society*, 1935).

Foster, G. M., "What Is Folk Culture?" (*American Anthropologist*, vol. 55, 1953), pp. 159–173.

———, "Peasant Society and the Image of the Limited Good" (*American Anthropologist*, vol. 67, 1965), pp. 293–315.

———, "Peasant Character and Personality," in J. M. Potter, M. N. Diaz, and G. M. Foster (eds.), *Peasant Society: A Reader* (Boston, 1967), pp. 296–299.

———, *Applied Anthropology* (Boston, 1969).

———, "A Second Look at Limited Good" (*Anthropological Quarterly*, vol. 45, 1972), pp. 57–64.

———and R. Kemper (eds.), *Anthropologists in Cities* (Boston, 1974).

Fox, R., *Kinship and Marriage* (Baltimore, 1967).

Frankfort, H., *The Birth of Civilization in the Near East* (Bloomington, Ind., 1951).

Fraser, D., "The Discovery of Primitive Art," in C. M. Otten (ed.), *Anthropology and Art* (Garden City, N. Y., 1971), pp. 20–36.

Frazer, J. G., *Folklore in the Old Testament: Studies in Comparative Religion Legend and Law* (abridged ed., New York, 1923).

———, *The Golden Bough: A Study in Magic and Religion* (abridged ed., New York, 1941).

Friedl, J., and N. Chrisman (eds.), *City Ways: A Selective Reader in Urban Anthropology* (New York, 1975).

Gallanter, M., "Law and Caste in Modern India" (*Asian Survey*, 1963), pp. 544–559.

Gardner, R. A., and B. T. Gardner, "Early Signs of Language in Child and Chimpanzee" (*Science*, vol. 187, 1975), pp. 752–753.

Garfield, V. E., *Tsimshian Clan and Society* (University of Washington Publications in Anthropology, vol. 7, no. 3, 1939).

Garn, S. M., *Human Races* (Springfield, Ill., 1961).

———and C. S. Coon, "On the Number of Races of Mankind" (*American Anthropologist*, vol. 57, 1955), pp. 996–1001.

Gayton, A. H., *Yokuts-Mono Chiefs and Shamans* (University of California Publications in American Archaeology and Ethnology, vol. 24, 1930).

Geertz, C., *The Religion of Java* (Glencoe, Ill., 1959).

———, "Religion as a Cultural System," in W. A. Lessa and E. Z. Vogt (eds.), *Reader in Comparative Religion* (2d ed., New York, 1965), pp. 204–215.

———, "Ethos, World View and the Analysis of Social Symbols," in A. Dundes (ed.), *Every Man His Way* (Englewood Cliffs, N. J., 1968).

———, "Religion: Anthropological Study" (*International Encyclopedia of the Social Sciences*, vol. 13, 1968), pp. 398–406.

Gerlach, L. P., and V. H. Hine, *People, Power, Change: Movements of Social Transformation* (Indianapolis, 1970).

Gibbs, J. L., Jr. (ed.), *Peoples of Africa* (New York, 1965).

Gifford, E. W., *Tongan Society* (Bernice P. Bishop Museum Bulletin 61, 1929).

Giles, E., *Culture and Genetics* (Bulletins of the American Anthropological Association, vol. 3, no. 3, 1970), pp. 87–98.

Glass, B., "Science: Endless Horizon or Golden Age?" (*Science*, vol. 171, no. 3966, 1971), pp. 23–29.

Gluckman, M., *Custom and Conflict in Africa* (Oxford, 1955).

———, *The Judicial Process among the Barotse of Northern Rhodesia* (Manchester and Glencoe, Ill., 1954 and 1955).

———, *The Ideas in Barotse Jurisprudence* (New Haven, Conn., 1965).

———, *Politics, Law, and Ritual in Tribal Society* (Chicago, 1965).

Goldfrank, E. S., "Socialization, Personality, and the Structure of Pueblo Society (with Particular Reference to Hopi and Zuñi)" (*American Anthropologist*, vol. 47, 1945), pp. 516–539.

Goldschmidt, W., and E. J. Kunkel, "The Structure of the Peasant Family" (*American Anthropologist*, vol. 73, 1971), pp. 1058–1076.

Goode, W. J., *Religion among the Primitives* (Glencoe, Ill., 1951).

Goodenough, W. H., "A Problem in Malayo-Polynesian Social Organization" (*American Anthropologist*, vol. 57, 1955), pp. 71–83.

———, "Residence Rules" (*Southwestern Journal of Anthropology*, vol. 12, 1956), pp. 22–37.

———, *Cooperation in Change: An Anthropological Approach to Community Development* (New York, 1963).

———, "Rethinking 'Status' and 'Role': Toward a General Model of the Cultural Organization of Social Relationships," in M. Banton (ed.),

The Relevance of Models for Social Anthropology (New York, 1965), pp. 1–22.

———, *Description and Comparison in Cultural Anthropology* (Chicago, 1970).

———, *Culture, Language and Society* (Reading, Mass., 1971).

Goodman, M., "Man's Place in the Phylogeny of Primates as Reflected in Serum Proteins," in S. L. Washburn (ed.), *Classification and Human Evolution* (Chicago, 1963), pp. 204–234.

Goody, J. (ed.), *The Developmental Cycle in Domestic Groups* (Cambridge, England, 1958).

———, "The Classification of Double Descent Systems" (*Current Anthropology*, vol. 2, 1961), pp. 3–26.

———, *Death, Property and the Ancestors: A Study of the Mortuary Customs of the Lodagaa of West Africa* (Stanford, Calif., 1962).

Gould, J. L., "Honey Bee Recruitment: The Dance-Language Controversy" (*Science*, August 29, 1975), pp. 685–693.

Graburn, N. (ed.), *Readings in Kinship and Social Structure* (New York, 1971).

Gravel, P., "The Transfer of Cows in Gisaka (Rwanda): A Mechanism for Recording Social Relationships" (*American Anthropologist*, vol. 69, 1967), pp. 322–331.

Greenberg, J. H., "Historical Linguistics and Unwritten Languages," in A. L. Kroeber (ed.), *Anthropology Today: An Encyclopedic Inventory* (New York, 1953), pp. 265–286.

———, *Anthropological Linguistics: An Introduction* (New York, 1968).

Greenman, E. F., "Material Culture and the Organism" (*American Anthropologist*, vol. 47, 1945), pp. 211–231.

Grinnell, G. B., *The Fighting Cheyennes* (New York, 1915).

———, *The Cheyenne Indians: Their History and Ways of Life* (2 vols., New Haven, Conn., 1923).

Gross, N., W. S. Mason, and A. W. McEachern, *Explorations in Role Analysis* (New York, 1958).

Gudschinsky, S. C., "The ABC's of Lexicostatistics (Glottochronology)," in D. Hymes (ed.), *Language in Culture and Society: A Reader in Linguistics and Anthropology* (New York; Evanston, Ill.; and London, 1964), pp. 612–623.

Gulick, J., "Urban Anthropology: Its Present and Future" (*New York Academy of Sciences*, ser. 2, vol. 25, 1963), pp. 445–458.

Gulliver, P. H., *The Family Herds: A Study of Two Pastoral People of East Aftica, the Jie and Turkana* (London, 1955).

———, "The Jie of Uganda," in J. L. Gibbs, Jr. (ed.), *Peoples of Africa* (New York, 1965), pp. 159–196.

Gumperz, J., and D. Hymes (eds.), *Directions in Sociolinguistics: The Ethnography of Communication* (New York, 1972).

Gunther, E., "Art in the Life of Primitive Peoples," in J. A. Clifton (ed.), *Introduction to Cultural Anthropology* (Boston, 1968), pp. 77–114.

Gutkind, P. C. W., *Urban Anthropology: Perspectives on Third World Urbanization and Urbanism* (Assen, Netherlands, 1974).

Haines, F., "The Northward Spread of Horses among the Plains Indians" (*American Anthropologist*, vol. 40, 1938), pp. 429–437.

———, "Where Did the Plains Indians Get Their Horses?"(*American Anthropologist*, vol. 40, 1938), pp. 112–117.

Hall, E. T., *The Silent Language* (New York, 1959).

Hall, G. S., *Adolescence: Its Psychology and Its Relations to Physiology, Anthropology, Sociology, Sex, Crime, Religion and Education* (2 vols., New York, 1904).

Hall, R. A., Jr., *Linguistics and Your Language* (2d rev. ed. of *Leave Your Language Alone!* Garden City, N. Y., 1960).

Halloway, R. L., "The Casts of Fossil Hominid Brains" (*Scientific American*, vol. 231, 1974), pp. 111–114.

Hallowell, A. I., "Bear Ceremonialism in the Northern Hemisphere" (*American Anthropologist*, vol. 28, 1926), pp. 1–175.

———, "Culture and Mental Disorders" (*Journal of Abnormal and Social Psychology*, vol. 29, 1934), pp. 1–9.

———, "The Nature and Function of Property as a Social Institution" (*Journal of Legal and Political Sociology*, vol. 1, 1943), pp. 115–138.

———, "The Beginnings of Anthropology in America," in F. De Laguna (ed.), *Selected Papers from the American Anthropologist: 1888–1920* (Evanston, Ill., 1960), pp. 1–90.

Hamblin, D. J., *The First Cities* (New York, 1973).

Hambly, W. D., *Source Book for African Anthropology* (Field Museum of Natural History, Anthropological Series, vol. 26, part 2, 1937).

Hamilton, W. H., and I. Till, "Property" (*Encyclopaedia of the Social Sciences*, vol. 12, 1934), pp. 528–538.

Hammel, E. A., "A Transformational Analysis of Comanche Kinship Terminology" (*American Anthropologist*, vol. 67, part 2, no. 5, 1965), pp. 65–105.

——— and W. A. Simmons (eds.), *Man Makes Sense* (Boston, 1970).

Haring, D. G. (ed.), *Personal Character and Cultural Milieu* (3d rev. ed., Syracuse, N. Y., 1956).

Harrington, M., *The Other America* (New York, 1962).

Harris, M., *The Rise of Anthropological Theory: A History of Theories of Culture* (New York, 1968).

Harrison, G. A., et al., *Human Biology* (New York, 1964).

Harrison, G. G., "Primary Adult Lactase Deficiency: A Problem in Anthropological Genetics" (*American Anthropologist*, vol. 77, no. 4, 1975), pp. 812–835.

Hart, C. W. M., "Contrasts between Prepubertal and Postpubertal Education," in G. D. Spindler (ed.), *Education and Anthropology* (Stanford,

Calif., 1956), pp. 127–145.
Hatcher, E. P., *Visual Metaphors: A Formal Analysis of Navajo Art* (American Ethnological Society Monograph, 1974).
Haury, E. H., "The Greater American Southwest," in R. J. Braidwood and G. R. Willey (eds.), *Courses toward Urban Life: Archeological Consideration of Some Cultural Alternatives* (Viking Fund Publications in Anthropology, no. 32, 1962), pp. 106–131.
Hawley, F. M., "Jemez Kiva Magic and Its Relation to Features of Prehistoric Kivas" (*Southwestern Journal of Anthropology*, vol. 8, 1952), pp. 147–163.
Hays, H. R., *From Ape to Angel: An Informal History of Social Anthropology* (New York, 1958).
Heine-Geldern, R., "One Hundred Years of Ethnological Theory in the German-speaking Countries: Some Milestones" (*Current Anthropology*, vol. 5, 1964), pp. 407–429.
Heizer, R. F., and L. K. Napton, "Biological and Cultural Evidence from Human Coprolites" (*Science*, vol. 165, 1969), pp. 563–568.
Helm, J., *Pioneers of American Anthropology: The Uses of Biography* (American Ethnological Society Monograph 43, 1966).
Hempstone, S., "Leaving Grandpa to Die by a Dry Waterhole" (*Minneapolis Tribune*, Dec. 5, 1971), p. 37A.
Henry, J., *Culture against Man* (New York, 1963).
Herskovits, M. J., "African Gods and Catholic Saints in New World Negro Belief" (*American Anthropologist*, vol. 39, 1937), pp. 635–643.
———, "A Note on 'Woman Marriage' in Dahomey" (*Africa*, vol. 10, 1937), pp. 335--341.
———, *Acculturation: The Study of Culture Contacts* (New York, 1938).
———, *Dahomey: An Ancient West African Kingdom* (2 vols., New York, 1938).
———, *Cultural Anthropology: A Study in Comparative Economics* (New York, 1952).
———, *Economic Anthropology* (New York, 1952).
———and F. S. Herskovits, *An Outline of Dahomean Religious Belief* (American Anthropological Association Memoir 41, 1933).
Hiebert, P. G., *Konduru: Structure and Integration in a South Indian Village* (Minneapolis, 1971).
Hobhouse, L. T., G. C. Wheeler, and M. Ginsberg, *The Material Culture and Social Institutions of the Simpler Peoples* (London, 1930).
Hocart, A. M., "Kinship Systems" (*Anthropos*, vol. 32, 1937), pp. 345–351.
Hockett, C. F., and R. Ascher, "The Human Revolution" (*Current Anthropology*, vol. 5, 1964), pp. 135–168.
Hoebel, E. A., *Shoshone Field Notes* (unpublished, 1934).
———, "The Sun Dance of the H3kandika Shoshone" (*American Anthropologist*, vol. 37, 1935), pp. 570–581.
———, "Comanche and H3kandika Shoshone Relationship Systems" (*American Anthropologist*, vol. 41, 1939), pp. 440–457.
———, *The Political Organization and Law-Ways of the Comanche Indians* (American Anthropological Association Memoir 54; Contributions from the Laboratory of Anthropology 4, 1940).
———, "The Asiatic Origin of a Myth of the Northwest Coast" (*Journal of American Folklore*, vol. 54, 1941), pp. 1–12.
———, "The Comanche Sun Dance and Messianic Outbreak of 1873" (*American Anthropologist*, vol. 43, 1941), pp. 301–303.
———, "Law-Ways of the Primitive Eskimos" (*Journal of Criminal Law and Criminology*, vol. 13, 1941), pp. 663–683.
———, "Fundamental Legal Concepts as Applied in the Study of Primitive Law" (*Yale Law Journal*, vol. 51, 1942), pp. 951–963.
———, "Law and Anthropology" (*Virginia Law Review*, vol. 32, 1946), pp. 836–854.
———, "Eskimo Infanticide and Polyandry" (*Scientific Monthly*, vol. 64, 1947), p. 535.
———, "Underground Kiva Passages" (*American Antiquity*, vol. 19, 1953), p. 76.
———, *The Law of Primitive Man: A Study in Comparative Legal Dynamics* (Cambridge, Mass., 1954).
———, *The Cheyennes: Indians of the Great Plains* (2d ed., New York, 1960; rev. ed., 1978).
———, "William Robertson: An Eighteenth Century Anthropologist-Historian" (*American Anthropologist*, vol. 62, 1960), pp. 648–655.
———, "Keresan Pueblo Law," in L. Nader (ed.), *Law in Culture and Society* (Chicago, 1969), pp. 92–116.
Hoffman, H., "Money, Ecology, and Acculturation among the Shipibo of Peru," in W. H. Goodenough (ed.), *Explorations in Cultural Anthropology* (New York, 1964).
Hogbin, H. I., *Social Change* (London, 1958).
Hole, F., and R. F. Heizer, *An Introduction to Prehistoric Archaeology* (New York, 1973).
Hollis, A. C., *The Nandi* (Oxford, 1909).
Holm, B., *Northwest Coast Indian Art: An Analysis of Form* (Seattle, 1950).
Holmberg, A. R., "The Research and Development Approach to the Study of Change" (*Human Organization*, vol. 17, 1958), pp. 12–16.
———, "The Changing Values and Institutions of Vicos in the Context of National Development" (*American Behavioral Scientist*, vol. 3, no. 7, March 1965), pp. 3–8.
Holmes, O. W., Jr., "The Path of the Law" (*Harvard Law Review*, vol. 10, 1897).
———, *McDonald v. Maybee* (*Supreme Court Reporter*, vol. 37, 1917), p. 343.
Homans, G. C., and D. M. Schneider, *Marriage, Authority, and Final Causes: A Study of Unilateral Cross-Cousin Marriage* (Glencoe, Ill., 1955).
Hooton, E. A., *Up from the Ape* (rev. ed., New York, 1947).

Hostetler, J. A., *The Amish* (Baltimore, Md., 1964).

Howe, J. W., and W. E. Knowland, "Letters to the Editor" (*Science,* vol. 179, Sept. 9, 1977), p. 1034.

Howell, F. C., "The Place of Neandertal Man in Human Evolution" (*American Journal of Physical Anthropology,* vol. 9, 1951), pp. 379ff.

———, "The Evolutionary Significance of Variation and Varieties of 'Neanderthal' Man" (*Quarterly Review of Biology,* vol. 32, no. 4, 1957), pp. 330–347.

———and the Editors of Time-Life Books, *Early Man* (New York, 1968).

Howell, P. P., *A Manual of Nuer Law: Being an Account of Customary Law, Its Evolution and Development in the Courts Established by the Sudan Government* (London, 1954).

Howells, W. W., *Back of History* (Garden City, N. Y., 1954).

———, *Mankind in the Making* (New York, 1959).

Howitt, A. W., *The Native Tribes of South-east Australia* (New York, 1904).

Hsu, F. L. K., *Religion, Science and Human Crisis* (London, 1952).

———, *The Study of Literate Civilizations* (New York, 1969).

———, *Americans and Chinese: Purpose and Fulfillment in Great Civilizations* (Garden City, N. Y., 1970).

———, *Psychological Anthropology* (Cambridge, Mass., 1972).

Huang, S.-S., and T. M. Bayless, "Milk and Lactose Intolerance in Healthy Orientals" (*Science,* vol. 160, 1966), pp. 83–84.

Hulse, F. S., *The Human Species* (rev. ed., New York, 1971).

Hymes, D. (ed.), *Language in Culture and Society* (New York, 1964).

Inverarity, R. B., *Art of the Northwest Coast Indians* (Berkeley, Calif., 1950).

Isaac, G. L., and E. R. McCown (eds.), *Human Origins: Louis Leakey and the East African Evidence* (Menlo Park, Calif., 1976).

Jay, P. C. (ed.), *Primates: Studies in Adaptation and Variability* (New York, 1968).

Jeffreys, M. D. W., "Lobola Is Child-Price" (*African Studies,* vol. 10, 1951), pp. 145–184.

Jelínek, J., "Neanderthal Man and *Homo Sapiens* in Central and Eastern Europe" (*Current Anthropology,* vol. 10, no. 5, 1969), pp. 475–503.

Jenness, D., *The Indians of Canada* (National Museum of Canada Bulletin 68, Anthropological Series, no. 15, 2d ed., 1934).

Jennings, J. D., "The Desert West," in J. D. Jennings and E. Norbeck (eds.), *Prehistoric Man in the New World* (Chicago, 1964), pp. 149–174.

———, *Prehistory of North America* (2d ed., New York, 1974).

———and E. Norbeck (eds.), *Prehistoric Man in the New World* (Chicago, 1964).

Jerison, H. J., "Interpreting the Evolution of the Brain" (*Human Biology,* vol. 35, 1963), pp. 263–291.

———, "Fossil Evidence of the Evolution of the Human Brain" (*Annual Review of Anthropology,* vol. 4, 1975), pp. 27–58.

Jhering, R. von, *Law as Means to an End* (translated from the German, New York, 1924).

Jochelson, W., "Past and Present Subterranean Dwellings of the Tribes of North Eastern Asia and North Western America" (*Proçeedings of the Fifteenth International Congress of Americanists,* Quebec, 1907).

Johnston, F. E., *Microevolution of Human Populations* (Englewood Cliffs, N. J., 1973).

Jolly, A., *The Evolution of Primate Behavior* (New York, 1972).

Jolly, C. J., "The Seed-Eaters: A New Model of Hominoid Differentiation Based on a Baboon Analogy" (*Man,* vol. 5, 1970), pp. 5–26.

Kardiner, A. (ed.), *The Individual and His Society* (New York, 1939).

———, "The Concept of Basic Personality Structure as an Operational Tool in the Social Sciences," in R. Linton (ed.), *The Science of Man in the World Crisis* (New York, 1945), pp. 107–122.

———(ed.), *The Psychological Frontiers of Society* (New York, 1945).

———and E. Preble, *They Studied Man* (New York, 1961).

Kawamura, S., "The Process of Subculture Propagation among Japanese Macaques," in C. H. Southwick (ed.), *Primate Social Behavior* (Princeton, N. J., 1963), pp. 82–90.

Keesing, R. M., "Theories of Culture" (*Annual Review of Anthropology,* vol. 3, 1974). pp. 73–97.

Kennedy, J., "Cultural Psychiatry," in J. J. Honigmann (ed.), *Handbook of Social and Cultural Anthropology* (Chicago, 1973), pp. 1119–1198.

Kenyon, K., *Digging up Jericho* (London and New York, 1957).

King, M. C., and A. C. Wilson, "Evolution at Two Levels in Humans and Chimpanzees" (*Science,* vol. 188, 1975), pp. 107–116.

King, R. C., *Genetics* (New York, 1976).

Kitching, J. W., *Bone, Tooth and Horn Tools of "Paleolithic Man"* (Manchester, 1963).

Klein, R. G., *Ice-Age Hunters of the Ukraine* (New York, 1973).

Klima, G. J., *The Barabaig: East African Cattle Herders* (New York, 1970).

Kluckhohn, C., "Some Reflections on the Method and Theory of the Kulturkreislehre" (*American Anthropologist,* vol. 38, 1936), pp. 157–196.

———, "The Place of Theory in Anthropological Science" (*Philosophy of Science,* vol. 6, 1939).

———, "The Influence of Psychiatry on Anthropology in America during the Past One Hundred Years," in J. K. Hall et al. (eds.), *One Hundred Years of American Psychiatry* (New York, 1944).

———, *Mirror for Man: The Relation of Anthropology to Modern Life* (New York, 1949).

———, "Philosophy of the Navaho Indians," in F. S. C. Northrop (ed.), *Ideological Differences and World Order* (New Haven, Conn., 1949), chap. 17.

———and D. Leighton, *The Navaho* (Cambridge, Mass., 1946).

Knopf, A., "Measuring Geologic Time" (*Scientific Monthly*, November 1957), pp. 225–236.

Köhler, W., *The Mentality of Apes* (New York, 1925).

Kortland, A., "Chimpanzees in the Wild" (*Scientific American*, vol. 206, 1962), pp. 128–134.

Krieger, A. D., "Early Man in the New World," in J. D. Jennings and E. Norbeck (eds.), *Prehistoric Man in the New World* (Chicago, 1964), pp. 23–84.

Kroeber, A. L., "Classificatory Systems of Relationship" (*Journal of the Royal Anthropological Institute of Great Britain and Ireland*, vol. 39, 1909), pp. 77–84.

———, "The Superorganic" (*American Anthropologist*, vol. 19, 1917), pp. 168–213.

———, "Yurok Law" (*Proceedings of the Twenty-second International Congress of Americanists*, 1926), pp. 511–516.

———, "Caste" (*Encyclopaedia of the Social Sciences*, vol. 3, 1930), pp. 254–256.

———, *Cultural and Natural Areas of Native North America* (University of California Publications in American Archaeology and Ethnology, vol. 39, 1939).

———, "Seminar in Psychological Approaches to Culture" (lecture, University of California, 1941).

———, *Configurations of Culture Growth* (Berkeley, 1944).

———, *Anthropology* (rev. ed., New York, 1948).

———, "Art," in J. H. Steward (ed.), *Handbook of South American Indians* (6 vols., Washington, D.C., 1946–1950), vol. 5, pp. 411–492.

———(ed.), *Anthropology Today: An Encyclopedic Inventory* (Chicago, 1953).

———, *Style and Civilizations* (2d ed., Ithaca, N. Y., 1963).

———, *An Anthropologist Looks at History* (Berkeley, 1966).

———and C. Kluckhohn, *Culture: A Critical Review of Concepts and Definitions* (Anthropological Papers, Peabody Museum, no. 47, 1952).

Kuhn, T. S., "The Structure of Scientific Revolutions" (*International Encyclopedia of Unified Science*, 2d ed., vol. 2, no. 2, 1970).

Kummer, H., *Primate Societies: Group Techniques of Ecological Adaptations* (Chicago, 1971).

Kuper, H., *An African Aristocracy: Rank among the Swazi* (New York, 1947).

———, *The Swazi: A South African Kingdom* (New York, 1963).

Kurth, G. (ed.), *Evolution und Hominisation* (Stuttgart, 1962).

LaBarre, W., *The Human Animal* (Chicago, 1954).

———, *The Ghost Dance: Origins of Religion* (Garden City, N. Y., 1970).

Lamberg-Karlovsky, C. C. and J. A. Sabloff, *The Rise and Fall of Civilizations* (Menlo Park, Calif., 1974).

Lancaster, J. B., *Primate Behavior and the Emergence of Human Culture* (New York, 1975).

Landes, R., "The Ojibwa of Canada," in M. Mead (ed.), *Cooperation and Competition among Primitive Peoples* (New York, 1937), pp. 87–126.

Langness, L. L., *The Study of Culture* (San Francisco, 1974).

Lantis, M., "The Alaskan Whale Cult and Its Affinities" (*American Anthropologist*, vol. 40, 1938), pp. 438–464.

Laqueur, W., "Revolution" (*International Encyclopedia of the Social Sciences*, vol. 13, 1968), pp. 501–507.

Lasker, G. W., *Physical Anthropology* (New York, 1973).

Leach. E. R., "Aesthetics," in E. E. Evans-Pritchard, *The Institutions of Primitive Society* (Glencoe, Ill, 1954), pp. 32–47.

———(ed.), *Aspects of Caste in South India, Ceylon and North-West Pakistan* (Cambridge, Mass., 1960).

———, *Rethinking Anthropology* (London School of Economics, Monographs on Social Anthropology, no. 22, 1961).

———, *Claude Lévi-Strauss* (rev. ed., New York, 1974).

Leacock, E., N. L. Gonzalez, G. Kushner (eds.), *Training Programs for New Opportunities in Applied Anthropology* (Special Publication, American Anthropological Association, 1974).

Leakey, L. S. B., *Olduvai Gorge: A Report on the Evolution of the Hand-axe Culture in Beds I-IV, with Chapters on the Geology and Fauna by the Late Prof. Hans Reck and Dr. A. T. Hopwood* (Cambridge, England, 1951).

———, "A New Lower Pliocene Fossil Primate from Kenya" (*Annals and Magazine of Natural History*, vol. 14, 1961), pp. 689–696.

———, "East African Hominoidea and the Classification within this Superfamily," in S. L. Washburn (ed.), *Classification and Human Evolution* (Chicago, 1963), pp. 32–49.

Leakey, M. D., "Preliminary Survey of the Cultural Material from Beds I and II, Olduvai Gorge, Tanzania," in W. W. Bishop and J. D. Clark (eds.), *Background to Evolution in Africa* (Chicago, 1967), pp. 409–419.

Leakey, R. E. F., "Early *Homo sapiens* Remains from the Omo River Region of Southwest Ethiopia" (*Nature,* vol. 222, 1969), pp. 1132–1138.

———, "Fauna and Artifacts from a New Plio-Pleistocene Locality near Lake Rudolf in Kenya" (*Nature,* vol. 226, 1970), pp. 222–226.

Lear, J., "Reaching the Heart of South America" (*Saturday Review*, Nov. 3, 1962), pp. 55–58.

Lechtman, H., and R. Merrill (eds.), *Material Culture: Styles, Organization, and Dynamics of Technology* (Proceedings of The American Ethnological Society, 1975).

Lee, R. B., and I. DeVore (eds.), *Man the Hunter* (Chicago, 1968).

Le Gros Clark, W. E., *The Fossil Evidence for Human Evolution: An Introduction to the Study of Paleoanthropology* (Chicago, 1955).

———, *History of the Primates: An*

Introduction to the Study of Fossil Man (5th ed., Chicago, 1966).

———and L. S. B. Leakey, *The Miocene Hominidae of East Africa* (British Museum Fossil Mammals of Africa, no. 1, 1951).

Lehmer, D. J., *Introduction to Middle Missouri Archeology* (Washington, 1971).

Leonard, J. N., *The First Farmers* (New York, 1973).

Leone, M. P. (ed.), *Contemporary Archaeology: A Guide to Theory and Contributions* (Carbondale, Ill., 1972).

Lerner, J. M., and W. J. Libby, *Heredity, Evolution, and Society* (2d ed., San Francisco, 1976).

Leslie, C. M., *Now We Are Civilized: A Study of the World View of the Zapotec Indians of Mitla, Oaxaca* (Detroit, 1960).

Lessa, W. A., and E. Z. Vogt, *Reader in Comparative Religion: An Anthropological Approach* (3d ed., New York, 1971).

Lévi-Strauss, C., *Tristes Tropique* (J. Russell, trans., New York, 1964).

———, *Structural Anthropology* (C. Jacobson and B. G. Schoepf, trans., Garden City, N. Y., 1967).

———, *Les Structures Élémentaries de la Parenté (The Elementary Structures of Kinship)* (rev. ed., J. H. Bell, J. R. von Sturmer, and R. Needham, trans., Boston, 1969).

Levy, M. J., Jr., "Notes on the Hsu Hypothesis," in F. L. K. Hsu (ed.), *Kinship and Culture* (Chicago, 1971), pp. 33–41.

———and L. A. Fallers, "The Family: Some Comparative Considerations" (*American Anthropologist*, vol. 61, 1959), pp. 647–651.

Lewis. O., *The Effects of White Contact upon Blackfoot Culture, with Special Reference to the Role of the Fur Trade* (American Ethnological Society Monograph 6, 1942).

———, "An Anthropological Approach to Family Studies" (*The American Journal of Sociology,* vol. 55, 1950), pp. 468–475.

———, *Life in a Mexican Village: Tepoztlán Restudied* (Urbana, 1951).

———, "Urbanization without Breakdown: A Case Study in the Culture of Poverty" (*Scientific Monthly,* vol. 75, 1952), pp. 31–41.

———, *Five Families: Mexican Case Studies in the Culture of Poverty* (New York, 1959).

———, *The Children of Sanchez* (New York, 1961).

———, *Pedro Martinez: A Mexican Peasant and His Family* (New York, 1964).

———, *La Vida* (New York, 1965).

———, "Mother and Son in a Puerto Rican Slum; Part 1: Felicita" (*Harper's Magazine*, December 1965).

———, *A Death in the Sanchez Family* (New York, 1969).

Lewis, P. H., *The Social Context of Art in Northern New Ireland* (Fieldiana: Anthropology, vol. 58, 1969).

Lewontin, R. C., "The Apportionment of Human Diversity," in T. Dobzhansky, M. K. Hecht, and W. C. Steere (eds.), *Evolutionary Biology* (New York, 1972), vol. 6, pp. 381–398.

Lindzey, G., *Projective Techniques and Cross-Cultural Research* (New York, 1961).

Linton, R., *The Study of Man* (New York, 1936).

———, "The Marquesas," in A. Kardiner (ed.), *The Individual and His Society* (New York, 1939), pp. 197–250.

———, "The Tanala," in A. Kardiner (ed.), *The Individual and His Society* (New York, 1939), pp. 251–290.

———(ed.), *Acculturation in Seven American Indian Tribes* (New York, 1940).

———, *The Cultural Background of Personality* (New York, 1945).

Little, K. L., *West African Urbanization: A Study of Voluntary Associations in Social Change* (Cambridge, England, 1965).

Little, M. A., and G. E. B. Morren, *Ecology, Energetics and Human Variability* (Dubuque, Iowa, 1976).

Livingstone, F. B., "On the Non-existence of Human Races" (*Current Anthropology,* vol. 3, 1962), p. 297.

Llewellyn, K. N., and E. A. Hoebel, *The Cheyenne Way: Conflict and Case Law in Primitive Jurisprudence* (Norman, Okla., 1941).

Loeb, E. M., and J. O. M. Broek, "Social Organization and the Long House in Southeast Asia" (*American Anthropologist*, vol. 49, 1947), pp. 414–425.

Loehlin, J. C., G. Lindzey, and J. N. Spuhler, *Race Differences in Intelligence* (San Francisco, 1975).

Lounsbury, F. G., "A Formal Account of the Crow and Omaha-Type Kinship Terminologies," in W. H. Goodenough (ed.), *Explorations in Cultural Anthropology: Essays in Honor of George Peter Murdock* (New York, 1964), pp. 351–393.

Lovins, A., "Energy Strategy: The Road Not Taken?" (*Foreign Affairs,* October, 1976).

Lowie, R. H., *The Northern Shoshone* (American Museum of Natural History, Anthropological Papers, vol. 2, 1909).

———, *Plains Indian Age Societies: Historical Summary* (American Museum of Natural History, Anthropological Papers, vol. 11, 1916), pp. 877–984.

———, *Primitive Society* (New York, 1920).

———, *Notes on Shoshonean Ethnography* (American Museum of Natural History, Anthropological Papers, vol. 20, part 3, 1924).

———, *Primitive Religion* (New York, 1924).

———, *The Origin of the State* (New York, 1927).

———, "Incorporeal Property in Primitive Society" (*Yale Law Journal*, vol. 37, 1928), pp. 551–563.

———, "Relationship Terms" (*Encyclopaedia Britannica*, vol. 19, 1929), pp. 84–86.

———, "Kinship" (*Encyclopaedia of the Social Sciences*, vol. 3, 1931), pp. 568–572.

———, *The Crow Indians* (New York, 1935).

———, "Lewis Henry Morgan in Historical Perspective," in *Essays in Anthropology in Honor of Alfred Louis Kroeber* (Berkeley, Calif., 1936), pp. 169–181.

———, *The History of Ethnological Theory* (New York, 1937).

———, "Property Rights and Coercive Powers of the Plains Indian Military Societies" (*Journal of Legal and Political Sociology*, vol. 1, 1943), pp. 59–71.

Lurie, N. O., "Culture Change," in J. A. Clifton (ed.), *Introduction to Cultural Anthropology* (Boston, 1968), pp. 275–303.

McClelland, D. C., *The Achieving Society* (Princeton, N.J., 1961).

McCown, T. D., and A. Keith, *The Stone Age of Mt. Carmel*, vol. II, *The Fossil Human Remains from the Levalloiso-Mousterian* (Oxford, 1939).

MacIver, R. M., *Society: Its Structure and Changes* (New York, 1931).

———, "Government and Property" (*Journal of Legal and Political Sociology*, vol. 4, 1946), pp. 5–18.

———, *The Ramparts We Guard* (New York, 1950).

McKern, S. S., and T. W. McKern, *Living Prehistory: An Introduction to Physical Anthropology and Archaeology* (Menlo Park, Calif., 1974).

Mackey, W. C., "The Adult Male-Child Bond: An Example of Convergent Evolution" (*Journal of Anthropological Research*, vol. 32, 1976), pp. 58–69.

McLennan, J. F., *Primitive Marriage* (Edinburgh, 1865).

MacNeish, R. S., "The Origin of New World Civilization" (*Scientific American*, vol. 211, 1964), pp. 29–37.

McNickle, D., *Native American Tribalism: Indian Survivals and Renewals* (New York, 1973).

Maday, B. C., "Anthropologists in the U.S. Government" (*Human Organization*, vol. 36, no. 1, 1977), pp. 89–97.

Maier, H. W., *Three Theories of Child Development* (New York, 1965).

Maine, H. S., *Ancient Law: Its Connection with the Early History of Society, and Its Relation to Modern Ideas* (3d American ed., New York, 1879).

Mair, L., *Primitive Government* (Baltimore, 1964).

Malinowski, B., *Argonauts of the Western Pacific: An Account of Native Enterprise and Adventure in the Archipelagoes of Melanesian New Guinea* (London, 1922).

———, *Crime and Custom in Savage Society* (New York, 1926).

———, *The Father in Primitive Psychology* (New York, 1927).

———, *Sex and Repression in Savage Society* (New York, 1927).

———, "Culture" (*Encyclopaedia of the Social Sciences*, vol. 4, 1931), pp. 621–646.

———, *Coral Gardens and Their Magic: A Study of the Methods of Tilling the Soil and of Agricultural Rites in the Trobriand Islands* (2 vols., New York, 1935).

———, *Magic, Science and Religion and Other Essays* (Glencoe, Ill., 1948).

Mallowan, M. E. L., *Early Mesopotamia and Iran* (New York, 1965).

Mandelbaum, D. G., *Society in India* (2 vols., Berkeley, Calif., 1970).

———, G. W. Lasker, and E. M. Albert, *The Teaching of Anthropology* (Berkeley and Los Angeles, Calif., 1963).

Mangin, W., "Urbanization Case History in Peru" (*Architectural Design*, vol. 8, 1963), pp. 366–370.

——— (ed.), *Peasants in Cities: Readings in the Anthropology of Urbanization* (Boston, 1970).

Maquet, J., "Introduction to Aesthetic Anthropology" (*McCaleb Module in Anthropology*, Reading, Mass., 1971).

Mason, O. T., *Aboriginal American Basketry* (United States National Museum, Annual Report, 1904), pp. 171–548.

Masserman, J. H., *Principles of Dynamic Psychiatry* (2d ed., Philadelphia, 1961).

Mauss, M., *The Gift: Forms and Functions of Exchange in Archaic Societies* (I. Cunnison, trans., London, 1954).

Mead, M., *Coming of Age in Samoa: A Psychological Study of Primitive Youth for Western Civilization* (New York, 1928).

———, *Growing up in New Guinea: A Comparative Study of Primitive Education* (New York, 1930).

———, *Sex and Temperament in Three Primitive Societies* (New York, 1935).

———(ed)., *Cooperation and Competition among Primitive Peoples* (New York, 1937).

———, "The Manus of the Admiralty Islands," in M. Mead (ed.), *Cooperation and Competition among Primitive Peoples* (New York, 1937), pp. 210–239.

———, *Male and Female: A Study of the Sexes in the Changing World* (New York, 1949).

———, *New Lives for Old: Cultural Transformation—Manus, 1928–1953* (New York, 1953).

———, "Some Theoretical Considerations on the Problem of Mother-Child Separation" (*American Journal of Orthopsychiatry*, vol. 24, 1954), pp. 471–483.

———and M. Wolfenstein (eds.), *Childhood in Contemporary Cultures* (Chicago, 1955).

Meggitt, J. M., "Male-Female Relations in the Highlands of Australian New Guinea" (*American Anthropologist*, vol. 66, no. 4, part 2, Special Publication, 1964), pp. 204–224.

Mellaart, J., "A Neolithic City in Turkey" (*Scientific American*, vol. 210, no. 4, 1964), pp. 94–105.

———, *The Neolithic of the Near East* (London, 1975).

Middleton, J. (ed.), *From Child to Adult: Studies in the Anthropology of Education* (Garden City, N.Y., 1970).

Middleton, R., "Brother-Sister and Father-Daughter Marriage in Ancient Greece" (*American Sociological Review*, vol. 27, 1962), pp. 603–611.

Miller, W. R., J. L. Tanner, and L. P. Foley, "A Lexicostatistic Study of Shoshoni Dialects" (*Anthropological Linguistics*, vol. 13, 1971), pp. 142–164.

Mills, G., "Art: An Introduction to Qualitative Anthropology," in C. M. Otten (ed.), *Anthropology and Art,* (Garden City, N.Y., 1971), pp. 66–92.

Miner, H., "The Folk—Urban Continuum" (*American Sociological Review*, vol. 17, 1952), pp. 529–537.

———, *The Primitive City of Timbuctoo* (Princeton, 1953).

Mishkin, B., *Rank and Warfare among the Plains Indians* (American Ethnological Society Monograph 3, 1940).

Mitchell, J. C., "A Note on the Urbanization of Africans on the Copperbelt" (*Rhodes–Livingstone Journal*, vol. 12, 1951), pp. 20–27.

———, *African Urbanization in Ndola and Kuanshya (Rhodes–Livingstone Communication,* no. 6, 1954).

——— (ed.), *Social Networks in Urban Situations: Analyses of Personal Relationships in Central African Towns* (Manchester, 1969).

Montagu, M. F. A., *Coming into Being among the Australian Aborigines* (New York, 1938).

———, "On the Origin of the Domestication of the Dog" (*Science,* vol. 96, 1942), pp. 111–112.

———*Man's Most Dangerous Myth: The Fallacy of Race* (2d ed., New York, 1945).

——— *(ed.), Culture; Man's Adaptive Mechanism* (London and New York, 1968).

Mooney, J., *The Ghost Dance Religion and the Sioux Outbreak of 1890* (Bureau of American Ethnology, Annual Report 14, 1896).

Morant, G. M., "The Form of the Swanscombe Skull" (*Journal of the Royal Anthropological Institute of Great Britain and Ireland*, vol. 68, 1938), pp. 67–97.

Morgan, L. H., *Ancient Society, or Researches in the Lines of Human Progress from Savagery, through Barbarism to Civilization* (New York, 1877).

———, *The League of the Ho-dé-no-sau-nee or Iroquois* (2 vols., New Haven, Conn., 1954, originally published in 1851).

Morley, S. G., *The Ancient Maya* (Standord, Calif., 1946).

Morris, D., *The Naked Ape: A Zoologist's Study of the Human Animal* (New York, 1967).

Murdock, G. P., *Our Primitive Contemporaries* (New York, 1934).

———, "Double Descent" (*American Anthropologist*, vol. 42, 1940), pp. 555–561.

———, "Bifurcate Merging: A Test of Five Theories" (*American Anthropologist*, vol. 49, 1947), pp. 56–68.

———, *Social Structure* (New York, 1949).

———, "Family Stability in Non-European Cultures" (*Annals of the American Academy of Political and Social Sciences*, vol. 272, 1950), pp. 195–201.

———, "World Ethnographic Sample" (*American Anthropologist*, vol. 59, 1957), pp. 664–687.

———(ed.) *Social Structure in Southeast Asia* (Viking Fund Publications in Anthropology, no. 29, 1960).

———, *Ethnographic Atlas* (Pittsburgh, 1967).

———, "The Current Status of the World's Hunting and Gathering Peoples," in R. B. Lee and I. DeVore (eds.), *Man the Hunter* (Chicago, 1968), pp. 13–20.

———, and C. Provost,"Measurement of Cultural Complexity" (*Ethnology,* vol. 12, 1973), pp. 382–383.

Murphy, R. F., and L. Kasdan, "The Structure of Parallel Cousin Marriage" (*American Anthropologist*, vol. 61, 1959), pp. 17–29.

Murra, J. V. (ed.), *American Anthropology: The Early Years* (St. Paul, 1976).

Nadel, S. F., "The Kede: A Riverian State in Northern Nigeria," in E. E. Evans-Pritchard and M. Fortes (eds.), *African Political Systems* (Oxford, 1940), pp. 165–195.

Nader, L. (ed.), *Law in Culture and Society* (Chicago, 1969).

Naroll, R., and R. Cohen, *A Handbook of Method in Cultural Anthropology* (Garden City, N.Y., 1970).

Nelson, R. K., *Hunters of the Northern Ice* (Chicago, 1969).

Netting, R. M., *Hill Farmers of Nigeria: Cultural Ecology of the Kofyar of the Jos Plateau* (American Ethnological Society Monograph 46, 1968).

Newman, R. W., "Human Adaptation to Heat," in A. Damon (ed.), *Physiological Anthropology* (New York, 1975), pp. 80–92.

Niehoff, A. H. (ed.), *A Casebook of Social Change* (Chicago, 1966).

Nisbet, R. (ed.), *Social Change and History* (New York, 1972).

Norbeck, E., *Takashima: A Japanese Fishing Community* (Salt Lake City, 1954).

———, *Religion in Primitive Society* (New York, 1961).

———, "Peasant Society," in J. Gould and W. L. Kolb (eds.), *A Dictionary of the Social Sciences* (Glencoe, Ill., 1964), pp. 490–491.

Oakley, K. P., *Man, the Tool-Maker* (Chicago, 1957).

Oliver, D. L., *A Solomon Island Society: Kinship and Leadership among the Siuai of Bougainville* (Cambridge, Mass., 1953).

O'Neale, L. M., "Weaving," in J. H. Steward (ed.), *Handbook of South American Indians* (6 vols., Washington, D.C., 1946–1950), vol. 5, pp. 97–138.

Opler, M. E., *An Apache Life-Way: The Economic, Social, and Religious Institutions of the Chiricahua* (Chicago, 1942).

———, "Themes as Dynamic Forces in Culture" (*American Journal of Sociology*, vol. 51, 1945), pp. 198–206.

Opler, M. K., "The Integration of the Sun Dance in Ute Religion" (*American Anthropologist*, vol. 43, 1941), pp. 550–572.

Otten, C. M. (ed.), *Anthropology and*

Art: Readings in Cross-Cultural Aesthetics (Garden City, N.Y., 1971).

Park, R. E., "The City: Suggestions for the Investigation of Human Behavior in the Urban Environment" (*American Journal of Sociology,* vol. 20, 1916), pp. 577–612.

——— and E. W. Burgess (eds.), *The City* (Chicago, 1925).

Park, W. Z., *Shamanism in Western North America: A Study in Cultural Relationships* (Evanston and Chicago, Ill., 1938).

Parmenter, R., "Glimpses of a Friendship," in J. Helm MacNeish (ed.), *Pioneers of American Anthropology* (Seattle, 1966), pp. 83–148.

Parsons, T. C., "The Kinship System of the Contemporary United States" (*American Anthropologist,* vol. 45, 1943), pp. 22–38.

Patterson, T. C., *America's Past: A New World Archaeology* (Glenview, Ill., 1973).

Perkins, D. Jr., and P. Daly, "The Beginning of Food Production in the Near East," in R. Stigler (ed.), *The Old World: Early Man to the Development of Agriculture* (New York, 1974), pp. 71–97.

Pike, K. L., *Language in Relation to a Unified Theory of the Structure of Human Behavior* (Glendale, Calif., 1950).

Pilbeam, D., *The Ascent of Man* (New York, 1972).

———and S. J. Gould, "Size and Scaling in Human Evolution" (*Science,* vol. 186, 1974), pp. 892–901.

Poirier, F. E., *Fossil Evidence: The Human Evolutionary Journey* (New York, 1977).

Polanyi, K., "The Economy as an Instituted Process," in K. Polanyi, C. M. Arensberg, and H. W. Pearson (eds.), *Trade and Market in the Early Empires* (New York, 1957), pp. 243–270.

———and A. Rotstein, *Dahomey and the Slave Trade: An Analysis of an Archaic Economy* (Seattle and London, 1966).

Pospisil, L., *Kapauku Papuans and Their Law* (Yale University Publications in Anthropology, no. 54, 1958).

———, *The Kapauku Papuans of West New Guinea* (New York, 1963).

———, "Structural Change and Primitive Law: Consequences of a Papuan Legal Case," in L. Nader (ed.), *Law in Culture and Society* (Chicago, 1969), pp. 208–229.

———, *Anthropology of Law: A Comparative Theory* (New York, 1971).

Potter, J. M., "Peasants in the Modern World," in J. M. Potter, M. N. Diaz, and G. M. Foster (eds.), *Peasant Society: A Reader* (Boston, 1967), pp. 378–383.

———, M. N. Diaz, and G. M. Foster (eds.), *Peasant Society: A Reader* (Boston, 1967).

Pound, R., *A Theory of Legal Interests* (American Sociological Society Publications, vol. 16, 1920).

Powell, H. A., "Competitive Leadership in Trobriand Political Organization," in R. Cohen and J. Middleton (eds.), *Comparative Political Systems: Studies in the Politics of Pre-industrial Societies* (Garden City, N.Y., 1967), pp. 155–192.

Prins, A. H. J., *East African Age Class Systems: An Inquiry into the Social Order of Galla, Kipsigis and Kikuyu* (Groningen and Djakarta, 1953).

Protsch, R., and R. Berger, "Earliest Radiocarbon Dates for Domesticated Animals" (*Science,* vol. 179, no. 4070, 1973), pp. 235–239.

Provinse, J. H., "Cooperative Ricefield Cultivation among the Siang Dyaks of Central Borneo" (*American Anthropologist,* vol. 39, 1937), pp. 77–102.

Radcliffe-Brown, A. R., *The Andaman Islanders* (Cambridge, England, 1922).

———, "On the Concept of Function in Social Science" (*American Anthropologist,* vol. 37, 1935), pp. 394-402.

———, "Patrilineal and Matrilineal Succession" (*Iowa Law Review,* vol. 20, 1935), pp. 286–298.

———, *Structure and Function in Primitive Society: Essays and Addresses* (Glencoe, Ill., 1952).

——— and M. Fortes (eds.) *African Systems of Kinship and Marriage* (Oxford, 1950).

Radin, M., "A Restatement of Hohfeld" (Harvard Law Review, vol. 51, 1938), pp. 1141ff.

Radin, P., *The Winnebago Tribe* (Bureau of American Ethnology, Annual Report 37, 1923).

——— (ed.), *Crashing Thunder: The Autobiography of an American Indian* (New York, 1926).

———, *Monotheism in Primitive Religion* (New York, 1927).

———, *Primitive Man as Philosopher* (New York, 1927).

Rapoport, A., *House Form and Culture* (Englewood Cliffs, N.J., 1969).

Rasmussen, K., *Grønlandsagen* (Berlin, 1922).

———, *Across Arctic America* (New York, 1927).

Rattray, R. S., *Ashanti* (Oxford, 1923).

———, *Ashanti Law and Constitution* (Oxford, 1927).

Ray, V. F., *The Sanpoil and Nespelem: Salishan Peoples of Northeastern Washington* (University of Washington Publications in Anthropology, vol. 5, 1932).

Redfield, R., *Tepoztlán: A Mexican Village* (Chicago, 1930).

———, *The Folk Culture of Yucatan* (Chicago, 1941).

———, "Maine's Ancient Law in the Light of Primitive Societies" (*Western Political Quarterly,* vol. 3, 1950), pp. 574–589.

———, *The Primitive World and Its Transformations* (Ithaca, N.Y., 1953).

———, *The Little Community, and Peasant Society and Culture* (Chicago, 1960).

———, *The Social Uses of Social Science: The Papers of Robert Redfield* (2 vols., edited by M. P. Redfield, Chicago, 1963).

———, "Art and Icon," in C. M. Otten (ed.), *Anthropology and Art: Readings in Cross-Cultural Aesthetics* (Garden City, N.Y., 1971), pp. 39–65.

———, R. Linton, and M. J. Herskovits, "Memorandum for the Study of

Acculturation" (*American Anthropologist*, vol. 38, 1936), pp. 149–152.
———and M. B. Singer, "The Cultural Role of Cities" (*Economic Development and Cultural Change*, vol. 3, 1954), pp. 53–73.
Reissman, L., "Social Stratification," in N. J. Smelser (ed.), *Sociology: An Introduction* (2d ed., New York, 1967), pp. 127–190.
Richardson, J., *Law and Status among the Kiowa Indians* (American Ethnological Society Monograph 1, 1940).
Richerson, P. J., "Ecology and Human Ecology: A Comparison of Theories in the Biological and Social Sciences" (*American Ethnologist*, vol. 4, no. 1, 1977), pp. 1–26.
Riley, J. W., Jr., "Death and Bereavement" (*International Encyclopedia of the Social Sciences*, vol. 4, 1968), p. 19.
Rivers, W. H. R., *The Todas* (London, 1906).
———, *Kinship and Social Organization* (London, 1914).
Roach, M. E., And J. B. Eicher, *Dress Adornment, and the Social Order* (New York, 1965).
Roberts, J. M., "The Self-Management of Cultures," in W. H. Goodenough (ed.), *Explorations in Cultural Anthropology: Essays in Honor of George Peter Murdock* (New York, 1964), pp. 433–454.
———, "Oaths, Autonomic Ordeals, and Power," in L. Nader (ed.), *The Ethnography of Law (American Anthropologist*, vol. 67, no. 6, part 2, Special Publication, 1965), pp. 186–212.
——— and B. Sutton-Smith, "Child Training and Game Involvement" (*Ethnology*, vol. 1, 1962), pp. 166–185.
Robertson, W., *The History of America* (2 vols., 1st American ed., Philadelphia, 1812).
Robinson, J. T., *The Dentition of the Australopithecinae* (Transvaal Museum Memoirs no. 9, 1956).
———, "The Origins and Adaptive Radiation of the Australopithecines," in G. Kurth (ed.), *Evolution und Hominisation* (Stuttgart, 1962), pp. 120–140.
———, "Adaptive Radiation in the Australopithecines and the Origin of Man," in F. C. Howell and F. Bourlière (eds.), *African Ecology and Human Evolution* (Chicago, 1963), pp. 385–416.
———, *Early Hominid Posture and Locomotion* (Chicago, 1972).
——— and R. J. Mason, "Occurrence of Stone Artifacts with *Australopithecus* at Sterkfontein" (*Nature*, vol. 180, 1957), pp. 521–524.
Rohner, R. P., "Parental Rejection, Food Deprivation, and Personality Development: Tests of Alternative Hypotheses" (*Ethnology*, vol. 9, 1970), pp. 414–427.
Roscoe, J., "The Cow Tribe of Enkole in the Uganda Protectorate" (*Journal of the Royal Anthropological Institute of Great Britain and Ireland*, vol. 37, 1907), pp. 93–118.
———, *The Banyankole* (London, 1923).
Rosenfeld, A., *The Second Genesis: The Coming Control of Life* (Englewood Cliffs, N.J., 1969).
Rowe, J. H., "Inca Culture at the Time of the Spanish Conquest," in J. H. Steward (ed.), *Handbook of South American Indians* (6 vols., Washington, D.C., 1946–1950), vol. 2, pp. 183–330.
———, "The Renaissance Foundations of Anthropology" (*American Anthropologist*, vol. 67, 1965), pp. 1–20.
Rowell, T., *The Social Behavior of Monkeys* (Harmondswork, 1972).
Sahlins, M. D., *Stone Age Economics* (Chicago, 1972).
——— and E. R. Service (eds.), *Evolution and Culture* (Ann Arbor, Mich., 1960).
Salmond, J. W., *Jurisprudence* (7th ed., New York, 1924).
Sapir, E., *Language* (New York, 1949).
Sauer, C., "American Agricultural Origins: A Consideration of Nature and Culture," in *Essays in Anthropology in Honor of Alfred Louis Kroeber* (Berkeley, Calif., 1936), pp. 279–297.
Schaller, G. B., *The Mountain Gorilla: Ecology and Behavior* (Chicago, 1963).
———, *The Year of the Gorilla* (Chicago, 1964).
Schapera, I., *A Handbook of Tswana Law and Custom: Compiled for the Bechuanaland Protectorate Administration* (Oxford, 1938).
———, *Tribal Legislation among the Tswana of the Bechuanaland Protectorate: A Study in the Mechanism of Change* (Monographs on Social Anthropology, London School of Economics and Political Science, no. 9, 1943).
———, *Government and Politics in Tribal Societies* (London, 1956).
Schneider, D. M., and K. Gough (eds.), *Matrilineal Kinship* (Berkeley and Los Angeles, 1961).
———and G. C. Homans, "Kinship Terminology and the American Kinship System" (*American Anthropologist*, vol. 57, 1955), pp. 1194–1208.
Schurtz, H., *Altersklassen und Männerbunde* (Berlin, 1902).
Schusky, E. L., *Manual for Kinship Analysis* (2d. ed., New York, 1972).
Scientific American, "Energy and Power" (*Scientific American*, vol. 224, 1971).
Scribner, S., and M. Cole, "Cognitive Consequences of Formal and Informal Education" (*Science*, vol. 182, 1973), pp. 553–559.
Segall, M. H., D. T. Campbell, and M. J. Herskovits, *The Influence of Culture on Visual Perception* (New York, 1966).
Service, E. R., *Primitive Social Organization: An Evolutionary Perspective* (New York, 1962).
———, *The Hunters* (Englewood Cliffs, N.J., 1966).
Shapiro, H. L., "Revised Version of UNESCO Statement on Race" (*American Journal of Physical Anthropology*, vol. 10, 1952), pp. 363–368.

Shapley, H. (ed.), *Climatic Change: Evidence, Causes, Effects* (Cambridge, Mass., 1953).

Sharrock, F. W., *Prehistoric Occupation Patterns in Southwestern Wyoming and Cultural Relationships with the Great Basin and Plains Cultural Areas* (University of Utah Anthropological Papers, no. 77, 1966).

Sieber, R., "The Arts and Their Changing Social Function" (*Annals of the New York Academy of Sciences*, vol. 96, 1962), pp. 653–658.

Simmel, G., "The Metropolis and Mental Life" in R. Sennett (ed.), *Classic Essays on the Culture of Cities* (New York, 1969).

Simmons, L. (ed.), *Sun Chief: The Autobiography of a Hopi Indian* (New Haven, Conn., 1942.)-

———, *The Role of the Aged in Primitive Society* (New Haven, Conn., 1945).

Simons, E. L., "The Earliest Apes" (*Scientific American*, vol. 217, 1967), pp. 28–35.

———, *Primate Evolution* (New York, 1972).

Simpson, G. E., "The Vodun Service in Northern Haiti" (*American Anthropologist*, vol. 42, 1940), pp. 236–254.

Simpson, G. G., *The Meaning of Evolution* (Oxford, 1950).

———, *Principles of Animal Taxonomy* (New York, 1961).

———, "The Meaning of Taxonomic Statements," in S. L. Washburn (ed.), *Classification and Human Evolution* (Chicago, 1963), pp. 1–31.

Singer, M. B., "Culture: The Concept of Culture" (*International Encyclopedia of the Social Sciences*, vol. 3, 1968), pp. 527–543.

———, "Robert Redfield's Development of a Social Anthropology of Civilizations" (*Proceedings of the American Ethnological Society*, 1974).

Skinner, B. F., *Beyond Freedom and Dignity* (New York, 1971).

Slater, M. K., "Ecological Factors in the Origin of Incest" (*American Anthropologist*, vol. 61, 1959), pp. 1042–1059.

Smith, G. H., "J. B. Trudeau's Remarks on the Indians of the Upper Missouri, 1794–95" (*American Anthropologist*, vol. 38, 1936), pp. 565–568.

Smith, M. G., "Secondary Marriage among Kadara and Kagoro," in P. Bohannan and J. Middleton (eds.), *Marriage, Family, and Residence* (Garden City, N.Y., 1968), pp. 109–130.

Smith, M. W., "The War Complex of the Plains Indians" (*American Philosophical Society Proceedings*, vol. 28, 1938), pp. 425–464.

Smith, R. T., "Family: Comparative Structure" (*International Encyclopedia of the Social Sciences*, vol. 5, 1968), pp. 301–312.

Smyth, H. D., *Atomic Energy for Military Purposes: The Official Report on the Development of the Atomic Bomb under the Auspices of the United States Government, 1940–1945* (Princeton, N.J., 1946).

Solecki, R. S., *Shanidar: The First Flower People* (New York, 1971).

Solheim, W. G., II, "Reworking Southeast Asian Prehistory" (*Paideuma*, vol. 15, 1969), pp. 125–139.

Southall, A. W., "Stateless Society" (*International Encyclopedia of the Social Sciences*, vol. 15, 1968), pp. 157–168.

——— (ed.), *Urban Anthropology: Cross-Cultural Studies of Urbanization* (New York, 1973).

Southwick, C. H. (ed.), *Primate Social Behavior: An Enduring Problem—Selected Readings* (Princeton, N.J., 1963).

Spencer, R. F., "The Arabian Matriarchate: An Old Controversy" (*Southwestern Journal of Anthropology*, vol. 8, 1952), pp. 478–502.

———, "Language," in J. Gould and W. L. Kolb (eds.), *Dictionary of the Social Sciences* (Glencoe, Ill., 1964), p. 377.

———, "Spouse Exchange among the North Alaskan Eskimo," in P. Bohannan and J. Middleton (eds.), *Marriage, Family, and Residence* (Garden City, N.Y., 1968), pp. 131–144.

Spengler, O., *The Decline of the West* (C. E. Atkinson, trans., New York, 1970, originally published in 1926–1928).

Spicer, E. H. (ed.), *Human Problems in Technological Change* (New York, 1952).

———, "Beyond Analysis and Explanation? The Life and Times of the Society for Applied Anthropology" (*Human Organization*, vol. 35, no. 4, 1976), pp. 335–343.

———, "Early Applications of Anthropology in North America," in A. F. C. Wallace, et al. (eds.), *Perspectives on Anthropology, 1976* (Special Publication no. 10, American Anthropological Association, 1977), pp. 116–141.

Spielman, R. S., E. C. Migliazza, and J. V. Neel, "Regional Linguistic and Genetic Differences among Yanomamö Indians" (*Science*, vol. 184, no. 4137, 1974), pp. 637–644.

Spier, L., *The Sun Dance of the Plains Indian* (American Museum of Natural History, Anthropological Papers, vol. 16, part 7, 1921).

———, *Havasupai Ethnology* (American Museum of Natural History, Anthropological Papers, vol. 29, 1928).

———, *Yuman Tribes of the Gila River* (Chicago, 1933).

———, "Inventions and Human Society," in H. L. Shapiro (ed.), *Man, Culture, and Society* (rev. ed., New York, 1971), pp. 224–246.

Spier, R. F. G., *From the Hand of Man: Primitive and Preindustrial Technologies* (New York, 1970).

Spindler, G. D., *Sociocultural and Psychological Processes in Menomini Acculturation* (University of California Publications in Culture and Society, vol. 5, 1955).

———, "Psychocultural Adaptation," in E. Norbeck, D. Price-Williams, and W. M. McCord (eds.), *The Study of Personality: An Interdisciplinary Appraisal* (New York, 1968), pp. 326–347.

Spindler, L., and G. D. Spindler, "Male and Female Adaptations in Culture Change" (*American Anthropologist*, vol. 60, 1958), pp. 217–233.

Spuhler, J. N. (ed.), *The Evolution of Man's Capacity for Culture* (Detroit, 1959).

Stent, G. S., *The Coming of the Golden Age* (Garden City, N.Y., 1969).

Stern, B. J., *Lewis Henry Morgan: Social Evolutionist* (Chicago, 1931).

Stern, C., *Principles of Human Genetics* (San Francisco, 1973).

Steward, J. H., "A Uintah Ute Bear Dance, March, 1931" (*American Anthropologist*, vol. 34, 1932), pp. 263–273.

———, "The Economic and Social Basis of Primitive Bands," in *Essays in Anthropology in Honor of Alfred Louis Kroeber* (Berkeley, Calif., 1936), pp. 331–350.

———, "Ecological Aspects of Southwestern Society" (*Anthropos*, vol. 32, 1937), pp. 82–104.

———, *Basin-Plateau Aboriginal Socio-Political Groups* (Bureau of American Ethnology Bulletin 120, 1938).

———(ed.), *Handbook of South American Indians* (6 vols., Washington, D.C., 1946–1950).

———, "Evolution and Process," in A. L. Kroeber (ed.), *Anthropology Today: An Encyclopedic Inventory* (Chicago, 1953), pp. 313–326.

———, *Theory of Culture Change: The Methodology of Multilineal Evolution* (Urbana, Ill., 1955).

Stewart, G. R., *Ordeal by Hunger* (Boston, 1960).

Stewart, O. C., "Fire as the First Great Force Employed by Man," in W. L. Thomas (ed.), *Man's Role in Changing the Face of the Earth* (Chicago, 1956), pp. 115–133.

Stewart, T. D., "A Physical Anthropologist's View of the Peopling of the New World" (*Southwestern Journal of Anthropology*, vol. 16, 1960), pp. 259–273.

Stigler, R. (ed.), *The Old World: Early Man to the Development of Agriculture* (New York, 1974).

Stirling, M. W., *Historical and Ethnographical Materials on the Jivaro Indians* (Bureau of American Ethnology Bulletin 117, 1938).

Stocking, G. W., Jr., *Race, Culture, and Evolution: Essays in the History of Anthropology* (New York, 1968).

———, "Tylor, Edward Burnett" (*International Encyclopedia of the Social Sciences*, vol. 16, 1968), pp. 170–177.

Stoll, N. R., et al., *International Code of Zoological Nomenclature* (London, 1961).

Stow, G. W., *The Native Races of South Africa: A History of the Intrusion of the Hottentots and Bantu into the Hunting Grounds of the Bushman* (London, 1905).

Strum, S. C., "Primate Predation: Interim Report on the Development of a Tradition in a Troop of Olive Baboons" (*Science*, vol. 187, 1975), pp. 755–757.

Sturtevant, W. C., "Studies in Ethnoscience," in A. K. Romney and R. G. d'Andrade (eds.), "Transcultural Studies in Cognition" (*American Anthropologist*, vol. 66, no. 3, part 2, Special Publication, 1964), pp. 99–131.

Swartz, M. J., V. W. Turner, and A. Tuden (eds.), *Political Anthropology* (Chicago, 1966).

Symposium: "Recent Developments in Hominoid Evolution, 1973" (*Yearbook of Physical Anthropology*, vol. 17, 1974).

Talmon, Y., "Millenarism" (*International Encyclopedia of the Social Sciences*, vol. 10, 1968), pp. 349–362.

Tanner, C. L., *Southwestern Indian Painting: A Changing Art* (2d ed., Tucson, 1973).

Tax, S., "The Origins of Man" (*Current Anthropology*, vol. 6, no. 4, 1965), pp. 342–438.

Taylor, D., "Anthropologists on Art," in M. H. Fried (ed.), *Readings in Anthropology*, vol. 2 (New York, 1959), pp. 478–490.

Taylor, G. R., *The Biological Time Bomb* (New York, 1968).

Teleki, G., "The Omnivorous Chimpanzee" (*Scientific American*, vol. 228, 1973), pp. 32–42.

ter Haar, B., *Adat Law in Indonesia* (translated from the Dutch and edited with an introduction by E. A. Hoebel and A. A. Schiller, New York, 1948).

Thomas, E. M., "The Herdsmen" (*The New Yorker*, May 1, 8, 15, and 22, 1965).

Thompson, J. E. S., *The Civilization of the Mayas* (Field Museum of Natural History, Anthropology Leaflet 25, 4th ed., 1942).

———, "A Survey of the Northern Maya Area" (*American Antiquity*, vol. 2, 1945), pp. 2–24.

Thompson, L., *Toward a Science of Mankind* (New York, 1961).

Thompson, R. A., *Psychology and Culture* (Dubuque, Iowa, 1975).

Thorne, A. G., and P. G. Macumber, "Discoveries of Late Pleistocene Man at Kow Swamp, Australia" (*Nature*, vol. 238, 1972), pp. 316–319.

Thorner, D., "Peasantry" (*International Encyclopedia of the Social Sciences*, vol. 11, 1968), pp. 503–511.

Titiev, M., *Old Oraibi: A Study of the Hopi Indians of the Third Mesa* (Peabody Museum of American Archaeology and Ethnology, Harvard University, vol. 22, no. 1, 1944).

Tobias, P. V., "The Kanam Jaw" (*Nature*, vol. 184, no. 4714, 1960), pp. 946–947.

———, "Early Man in East Africa" (*Science*, vol. 149, 1965), p. 27.

———, *Olduvai Gorge*, (vol. 2, Cambridge, 1967).

———, "New Developments in Hominid Paleontology in South and East Africa" (*Annual Review of Anthropology*, vol. 2, 1973), pp. 311–334.

Tocqueville, A. de, *Democracy in America* (New York, 1945; translated from the French, first published in 1835).

Toffler, A., *Future Shock* (New York, 1970).

Tönnies, F., *Community and Society* (C. P. Loomis, trans. and ed., New York, 1963, originally published in 1887).

Treistman, J. M., *The Prehistory of China: An Archaeological Exploration* (Garden City, N.Y., 1972).

Trend, M. G., "Government and Industry" (*Human Organization,* vol. 36, no. 1, 1977), pp. 87–89.

Tuden, A., and L. Plotnicov (eds.), *Social Stratification in Africa* (New York and London, 1970).

Turner, V. W., "Myth and Symbol" (*International Encyclopedia of the Social Sciences,* vol. 10, 1968), pp. 576–582.

Tyler, S. A. (ed.), *Cognitive Anthropology* (New York, 1969).

Tylor, E. B., *Primitive Culture: Researches into the Development of Mythology, Philosophy, Religion, Language, Art and Custom* (2 vols., New York, 1874).

———, "On the Game of Patolli in Ancient America and Its Probable Asiatic Origin" (*Journal of the Royal Anthropological Institute of Great Britain and Ireland,* vol. 8, 1879), pp. 116–129.

———, "American Lot Games as Evidence of Asiatic Intercourse before the Time of Columbus" (*Internationales Archiv fur Ethnographie,* vol. 9, supplement, 1896), pp. 55–67.

Underhill, R., *Ceremonial Patterns in the Greater Southwest* (American Ethnological Society Monograph 13, 1948).

Underwood, J., *Biocultural Interactions and Human Variation* (Dubuque, Iowa, 1975).

UNESCO, *The Race Concept* (Paris, 1952).

———, *African Worlds: Studies in the Cosmological Ideas and Social Values of African Peoples* (Oxford, 1954).

U.S. Bureau of the Census, *Historical Statistics of the United States: Colonial Times to 1957* (Washington, D.C., 1970).

Vaillant, G. C., *Aztecs of Mexico: Origin, Rise and Fall of the Aztec Nation* (New York, 1941).

van Gennep, A., *The Rites of Passage* (M. B. Vizedom and G. L. Caffee, trans., Chicago, 1960).

van Lawick-Goodall, J., "A Preliminary Report on Expressive Movements and Communication in the Gombe Stream Chimpanzees," in P. C. Jay (ed.), *Primates* (New York, 1968), pp. 313–374.

Vayda, A. P. (ed.), *Environment and Cultural Behavior* (Garden City, N.Y., 1969).

von Frisch, K., "Dialects in the Language of the Bees" (*Scientific American,* August 1962), pp. 3–7.

———, "Decoding the Language of the Bees" (*Science,* August 23, 1974), pp. 663–668.

Waddell, J. O., and O. M. Watson (eds.), *The American Indian in Urban Society* (Boston, 1971).

Walker, D. E. (ed.), *The Emergent Native Americans: A Reader in Culture Contact* (Boston, 1972).

Wallace, E., and E. A. Hoebel, *The Comanches: Lords of the South Plains* (Norman, Okla., 1952).

Warner, W. L., *A Black Civilization* (New York, 1937).

———, *The Living and the Dead* (New Haven, 1959).

——— and P. S. Lunt, *The Social Life of a Modern Community* (New Haven, 1941).

——— and ———, *The Status System of a Modern Community* (New Haven, 1947).

——— and L. Srole, *The Social Systems of American Ethnic Groups* (New Haven, 1945).

——— and J. O. Low, *The Social System of the Modern Factory* (New Haven, 1947).

Washburn, S. L., "The New Physical Anthropology" (*Transactions of the New York Academy of Sciences,* series II, vol. 13, 1951), pp. 298–304.

———, "Australopithecines: The Hunters or the Hunted?" (*American Anthropologist,* vol. 59, 1957), pp. 612–614.

———, "Tools and Human Evolution" (*Scientific American,* vol. 203, 1960), pp. 62–75.

———(ed), *Social Life of Early Man* (Viking Fund Publications in Anthropology, no. 31, 1961).

———(ed.), *Classification and Human Evolution* (Viking Fund Publications in Anthropology, no. 37, 1963).

——— and R. Moore, *Ape into Man: A Study of Human Evolution* (Boston, 1974).

Waterbolk, H. T., "The Lower Rhine," in R. J. Braidwood and G. R. Willey (eds.), *Courses toward Urban Life: Archaeological Consideration of Some Cultural Alternatives* (Viking Fund Publications in Anthropology, no. 32, 1962), pp. 227–253.

Wax, M. L., S. Diamond, and F. Gearing, *Anthropological Perspectives on Education* (New York, 1971).

Weaver, T., *Indians in Rural and Reservation Areas: Report for the California State Advisory Commission on Indian Affairs* (Sacramento, 1966).

——— (ed.), "Essays on Medical Anthropology" (*Proceedings of the Southern Anthropological Society,* no. 1, 1968).

———, "Sampling and Generalization in Anthropological Research on Spanish-speaking Groups" (*Proceedings of the American Ethnological Society,* 1968), pp. 1–19.

———, "Use of Hypothetical Situations in a Study of Spanish American Illness Referral Systems" (*Human Organization,* vol. 29, 1970), pp. 140–154.

———(ed.), *Political Organization and Business Management in the Gila River Indian Community* (Bureau of Ethnic Research, University of Arizona, 1971).

———(ed.), *To See Ourselves: Anthropology and Modern Social Issues* (Glenview, Ill., 1973).

——— (ed.), *Indians of Arizona* (Tucson, Ariz., 1974).

———, "Social and Economic Change in the Context of Pima-Maricopa History" (*Atti Del XL Congresso Internazionale Degli Americanist,* Casa Editrice Tilgher, Genova, Italy, vol. 2, 1974), pp. 579–592.

———(ed.), *Tribal Management Procedures Study of Seven Reservations (Ak Chin, Camp Verde, Cocopah, Ft.*

McDowell, Havasupai, Hualapai, and Payson) (Bureau of Ethnic Research, University of Arizona, 1974).

———and T. E. Downing (eds.), *The Douglas Report: The Community Context of Housing and Social Problems* (Bureau of Ethnic Research, University of Arizona, 1975).

———and R. H. Gartell, "The Urban Indian: Man of Two Worlds," in T. Weaver (ed.), *Indians of Arizona* (Tucson, Ariz., 1974), pp. 72–96.

——— and A. Magid (eds.), *Poverty: New Interdisciplinary Perspectives* (San Francisco, 1969).

——— and D. White (eds.), *The Anthropology of Urban Environments* (Society for Applied Anthropology Monograph, no. 11, 1972).

Weber, M., *The City* (D. Martindale and G. Neuwirth, trans., New York, 1958, originally published in 1921).

Webster, H., *Primitive Secret Societies: A Study in Early Politics and Religion* (New York, 1908).

Weiner, J. S., *The Piltdown Forgery* (Oxford, 1955).

——— and B. G. Campbell, "The Taxonomic Status of the Swanscombe Skull," in C. D. Ovey (ed.), *The Swanscombe Skull—A Survey of Research on a Pleistocene Site* (London, 1965).

Weisz, P. B., *The Science of Biology* (2d ed., New York, 1963).

Weltfish, G., "Prehistoric North American Basketry Techniques and Modern Distributions" (*American Anthropologist*, vol. 32, 1930), pp. 454–495.

Westermarck, E., *The History of Human Marriage* (3 vols., London, 1925).

White, J. P., "New Guinea: The First Phase in Oceanic Settlement," in R. C. Green and M. Kelly (eds.), *Studies in Oceanic Culture History*, vol. 2 (Pacific Anthropological Records, no. 12, Bishop Museum, Honolulu, 1971), pp. 45–52.

White, L. A., "A Problem in Kinship Terminology" (*American Anthropologist*, vol. 41, 1939), pp. 566–573.

———, "Energy and the Evolution of Culture" (*American Anthropologist*, vol. 45, 1943), pp. 335–356.

Whiting, B. B., *Paiute Sorcery* (Viking Fund Publications in Anthropology, no. 15, 1950).

———(ed.), *Six Cultures: Studies of Child Rearing* (New York and London, 1963).

Whiting, J. W. M., and I. L. Child, *Child Training and Personality: A Cross-Cultural Study* (New Haven, Conn., 1953).

———, R. Kluckhohn, and A. S. Anthony, "The Function of Male Initiation Ceremonies at Puberty," in E. E. Maccoby, T. M. Newcomb, and E. L. Hartley (eds.), *Readings in Social Psychology* (New York, 1958), pp. 359–370.

Whitman, W., *The Pueblo Indians of San Ildefonso* (New York, 1947).

Whitten, N., and J. Szwed (eds.), *Afro-American Anthropology: Contemporary Perspectives* (Glencoe, Ill., 1970).

Whorf, B. L., *Language, Thought, and Reality* (Cambridge, Mass., 1956).

Willey, G. R., *An Introduction to American Archaeology:* vol. 1, *North and Middle America* (Englewood Cliffs, N.J., 1966).

———and J. A. Sabloff, *A History of American Archaeology* (San Francisco, 1974).

Wilson, M., *Good Company: A Study of Nyakyusa Age-Villages* (London, 1951).

Wirth, L., "Urbanism as a Way of Life," in A. J. Reiss, Jr. (ed.), *On Cities and Social Life* (Chicago, 1938).

Wissler, C., "The Influence of the Horse in the Development of Plains Culture" (*American Anthropologist*, vol. 17, 1914), pp. 1–25.

———, *The American Indian* (3d ed., New York, 1938).

Wolberg, D. L., "The Hypothesized Osteodontokeratic Culture of the Australopithecinae: A Look at the Evidence and the Opinions" (*Current Anthropology*, vol. 11, 1970), pp. 23–28.

Wolf, A. P., "Adopt a Daughter-in-Law, Marry a Sister: A Chinese Solution to the Problem of the Incest Taboo" (*American Anthropologist*, vol. 70, 1968), pp. 864–874.

———, "Childhood Association and Sexual Attraction: A Further Test of the Westermarck Hypothesis" (*American Anthropologist*, vol. 72, 1970), pp. 503–515.

Wolf, E. R., "Closed Corporate Peasant Communities in Mesoamerica and Central Java" (*Southwestern Journal of Anthropology*, vol. 13, 1957), pp. 1–18.

———, *Sons of the Shaking Earth* (Chicago, 1959).

Wood, C. S., "Preferential Feeding of *Anopheles gambiae* Mosquitoes on Human Subjects of Blood Group O: A Relationship between the ABO Polymorphism and Malaria Vectors" (*Human Biology*, vol. 46, 1974), pp. 385–404.

Woodall, J. N., *An Introduction to Modern Archeology* (Cambridge, 1972).

Worsley, P., *The Trumpet Shall Sound: A Study of "Cargo" Cults in Melanesia* (London, 1957).

Index

CULTURE AREAS:

I. **North Africa**
  A. Mediterranean Coast
  B. Egypt
II. **Sahara**
III. **Sudan**
  A. Western Sudan
  B. Eastern Sudan
IV. **Guinea Coast**
V. **East Horn**
VI. **Cattle Area**
  A. Eastern Cattle Area
  B. Western Cattle Area
VII. **Congo**
VIII. **Khoisan**
  A. Bushman
  B. Hottentot
IX. **Madagascar**

TRIBAL GROUPS:

1. Dogon
2. Wolof
3. Mano
4. Hausa
5. Kpelle
6. Tallensi
7. Nupe
8. Ashanti
9. Dahomeans (Fon)
10. Yoruba
11. Ibo (incl. Ibibio)
12. Tiv
13. Azande (Zande)
14. Pygmy Tribes—Twa (Batwa)
15. Herero
16. Bushman
17. Hottentot (incl. Nama, Bergdama)
18. Lozi (Barotse)
19. Ba-Ila (Ila)
20. Zulu
21. Tswana
22. Swazi
23. Bemba (Babemba)
24. Nyakyusa
25. Chaga (Tschagga)
26. Ankole (Banyankole, incl. Bahima and Bairu)
27. Sukuma
28. Watussi (Tussi)
29. Nyoro (Banyoro or Bakitara)
30. Alur
31. Masai
32. Nuer
33. Dinka
34. Tanala-Betsileo
35. Sakalava

Scale at equator
500 0 500
Miles

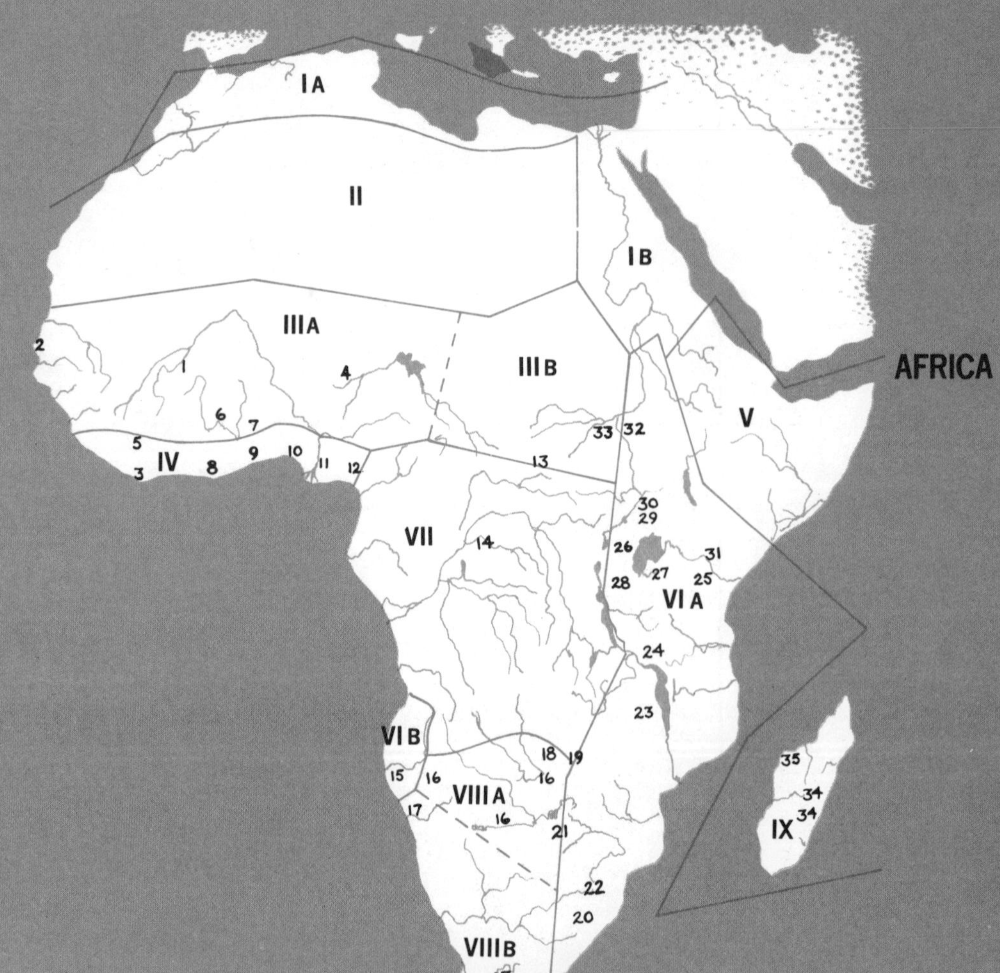